CHILD AND ADOLESCENT DEVELOPMENT

CHILD AND ADOLESCENT DEVELOPMENT

F. PHILIP RICE

University of Maine

Prentice Hall, Upper Saddle River, New Jersey 07458

Library of Congress Cataloging-in-Publication Data

Rice, F. Philip.
Child and adolescent development / F. Philip Rice.
p. cm.
Includes bibliographical references and indexes.
ISBN 0-13-566019-X
1. Child psychology. 2. Adolescent psychology. 3. Child development. 4. Adolescence. I. Title.
BF721.R498 1996
305.23'1—dc20 96-12716
CIP

EDITOR IN CHIEF: Peter Janzow
ASSISTANT EDITOR: Nicole Signoretti
EDITORIAL ASSISTANTS: Marilyn Coco and Ilene Kalish
PRODUCTION EDITOR: Bruce Hobart (Pine Tree Composition)
DIRECTOR OF PRODUCTION AND MANUFACTURING: Barbara Kittle
SENIOR MANAGING EDITOR: Bonnie Biller
MANUFACTURING MANAGER: Nick Sklitsis
PREPRESS AND MANUFACTURING BUYER: Tricia Kenny
PRODUCTION ASSISTANT: Yvonne Thrower
CREATIVE DESIGN DIRECTOR: Leslie Osher
INTERIOR DESIGNER: Anne Bonanno Nieglos and Hothouse Designs, Inc.
COVER DESIGNER: Anne Bonanno Nieglos
COVER ART: © Barnaby Hall/Photonica
PHOTO RESEARCHER: Kathy Ringrose
LINE ART COORDINATOR: Michele Giusti
ILLUSTRATOR: Accurate Art, Inc.

This book was set in 10/12 Palatino by Pine Tree Composition, Inc. and was printed and bound by Von Hoffman. The cover was printed by The Lehigh Press. Film supplied by York Graphics. Color separations by York Graphics.

For permission to use copyrighted material, grateful acknowledgment is made to the copyright holders on page 552, which is hereby made part of this copyright page.

Printed in the United States of America

10 9 8 7 6 5 4 3 2 1

ISBN 0-13-566019-X

Prentice-Hall International (UK) Limited, *London*
Prentice-Hall of Australia Pty. Limited, *Sydney*
Prentice-Hall Canada Inc., *Toronto*
Prentice-Hall Hispanoamericana, S.A., *Mexico*
Prentice-Hall of India Private Limited, *New Delhi*
Prentice-Hall of Japan, Inc., *Tokyo*
Simon & Schuster Asia Pte. Ltd., *Singapore*
Editora Prentice-Hall do Brasil, Ltda., *Rio de Janeiro*

To

Irma Ann Rice

with Deepest Love

Brief Contents

Contents

Preface

The story of child and adolescent development is an exciting portrayal of life in the process of becoming. From conception to puberty, the drama unfolds, revealing an ever more complex being in the making. This story is about our own youth and children as well as those of others: how they began, how they grew, and how they changed before they were born and during their infancy, childhood, and adolescence. As you read this story you will be asked to examine the lives of your own children and adolescents and those with whom you work or will be working. You may be encouraged not only to think about the roles you play now, but to set new sights for the future, to adjust your behavior and relationships so those who depend upon you, or who will depend upon you, for love and guidance may grow to successful maturity.

Organization and Approach

DIVISIONS

This child and adolescent development text is divided into four major parts as follows.

PART I introduces a developmental perspective, the periods of development, research methods in the study of development, and theories of development.

PART II discusses hereditary and environmental influences on development, prenatal development, childbirth, and the characteristics of the neonate.

PART III examines child development and includes perspectives on child development, and two chapters each on physical, cognitive, emotional, and social development from infancy to puberty.

PART IV covers adolescent development and includes perspectives on adolescent development, and physical, cognitive, emotional, and social development from puberty through age 19.

Some courses on child development include just the years of childhood. The first thirteen chapters of this text provide comprehensive coverage of child development, more than enough material for a one-semester course. Other courses include adolescent development along with the child development material. This text includes five full chapters on adolescence, more than most texts cover. So the text is suitable for either type of course.

CHRONOLOGICAL AND TOPICAL APPROACH

There are two basic ways to write about and to teach the subject of child and adolescent development. One is the *chronological approach*: to present all aspects of development under each and every minute age division. The other is the *topical approach*: to discuss each aspect of development under broader age spans. This text combines the best features of both approaches. The life span is divided into two chronological age divisions: childhood and adolescence. Under each major age division, five topics are discussed: perspectives, and physical, cognitive, emotional, and social development. The topical presentation within each age division allows the text to be used in courses emphasizing either a topical or a chronological format.

SOLID RESEARCH BASE

The text uses the findings of over 2,000 references, which are incorporated into the body of the narrative and provide a solid factual basis for the discussion. Of these, approximately one-third are new research references from the years 1991 to 1993 that have been incorporated into this text. Another 133 references are from 1993 to 1995.

CROSS-CULTURAL EMPHASIS

Individual differences and cultural influences in physical, cognitive, emotional, and social development are emphasized.

ECLECTIC APPROACH

The discussion emphasizes not just one but many developmental theories, reflecting an eclectic approach. The emphasis here is on presenting the most important and various approaches to human development.

PRACTICAL AND PERSONAL DIMENSIONS

The teaching and counseling experiences of the author as well as those of other teachers and therapists are used as real-life examples to illustrate situations and relationships under discussion. Case studies, anecdotal material, and quotations from students and clients are intended to add human interest. Personalized discussion questions help students to apply the principles examined to their own lives, which can result in individual growth and change.

COMPREHENSIVENESS

This book encompasses a very broad range of subject matter, as much as is feasible within the confines of one text. The approach enables the student to be exposed to a wide range of topics, emphases, and issues.

Topical Highlights

EMOTIONAL DEVELOPMENT

A special feature of this text is the inclusion under each age division of separate chapters on emotional development.

MORAL DEVELOPMENT

The text includes detailed discussions of moral development, especially the development of conscience and the internalization of values.

THE FAMILY AND SOCIALIZATION

This edition emphasizes the family's changing role in the socialization of children, and it highlights such topics as the father's role, effects of maternal employment on children, the grandparents' role, sibling relationships and rivalry, and effects of divorce on children.

REPRODUCTIVE TECHNOLOGY

The text explores the latest developments in alternative means of conception in the treatment of infertility, along with advances in neonatal care for small or preterm infants.

CHILD CARE ISSUES

Women and employment and the influences of various types of substitute child care on children are discussed.

WOMEN'S ISSUES

A number of important women's issues are presented: empowerment of adolescent girls, together with the development of identity and self-esteem.

CONTEMPORARY ISSUES DURING ADOLESCENCE

Sex education of adolescents, including a new emphasis on education for abstinence, is discussed, along with the increasing problem of the use of handguns by teens who kill.

LANGUAGE DEVELOPMENT

Learning to read is discussed, in addition to learning to speak.

CHILDREN WITH DISABILITIES

Important sections include the development of both physically handicapped children and those with learning disabilities.

HUMAN SEXUALITY

Sexual relationships and sexual behavior of adolescents are discussed, with an emphasis on AIDS prevention and on sexually responsible and responsive behavior. Special guidance is offered on the sex education of children.

RELATIONSHIPS

Since development is so influenced by relationships, they are emphasized throughout the discussion. Parent–child, sibling, peer, family, and other social relationships are highlighted.

For Teachers and Students

SPECIAL BOXED SECTIONS

Parenting Issues are discussed in boxed sections and present practical problems in raising children and adolescents. **Living Issues** highlight everyday problems and issues faced by adolescents and enable students to see the relevance of the discussion to their own lives. **Focus** sections include research findings, opinions, and viewpoints about specific subjects and issues that need to be clarified.

LEARNING AIDS

Each chapter contains a detailed outline at its beginning. At the end of each chapter are a summary, a list of key terms, questions for discussion, and suggested readings. Within each chapter, the key terms are printed in boldfaced type; they are frequently defined next to the text as well as in the glossary at the end of the book. Key thoughts and phrases in selected paragraphs are italicized throughout. The text includes a full bibliography of references as well as author and subject indexes.

VISUAL AIDS

The textbook includes over forty photographs, seventy diagrams and graphs, and thirty-eight tables. These facilitate the learning process and greatly add to visual appeal.

Teaching Aids and Instructor Supplements

INSTRUCTOR'S MANUAL

The Instructor's Manual accompanying *Child and Adolescent Development* includes learning objectives, extended lecture outlines, teaching strategies, individual and classroom demonstrations and activities, and suggested videos and films for each chapter.

ABC NEWS/PRENTICE HALL VIDEO LIBRARIES

ABCNEWS

Lifespan Development, 1996
Child Development, 1995
Human Development, 1993
Two video sets consisting of feature segments from award-winning programs such as *Nightline, 20/20, PrimeTime Live*, and *The Health Show* are available to qualified adopters of this text.

TEST ITEM FILE

A comprehensive and extensive Test Item File with more than 2,000 questions is also available. A variety of questions are provided, including multiple choice, true-false, short answer, and essay. Questions cover a balance of conceptual, applied, and factual material from the text.

TEACHING TRANSPARENCIES FOR CHILD DEVELOPMENT

A full set of color transparencies add visual impact to the study of child development. Designed in large format for use in lecture hall settings, many of these high-quality images are not found in the text.

PRENTICE HALL CUSTOM TEST FOR WINDOWS, MACINTOSH, AND DOS

Prentice Hall's exclusive computerized testing software supports a full range of editing and graphics options, network test administration capabilities, and greater ease-of-use than ever before.

"800-NUMBER" TELEPHONE TEST PREPARATION SERVICE

A toll-free test preparation service is also available. Instructors may call an 800-number and select up to 200 questions from the Test Item File available with the text. Prentice Hall will format the test and provide an alternate version (if requested) and answer key(s), then mail it back within 48 hours, ready for duplication.

Student Supplements

STUDY GUIDE

The comprehensive Study Guide for *Child and Adolescent Development* features chapter outlines, learning objectives, and self-test questions to facilitate student review.

THE NEW YORK TIMES SUPPLEMENT FOR HUMAN DEVELOPMENT

The core subject matter in the text is supplemented by a collection of time-sensitive articles from one of the world's most distinguished newspapers, *The New York Times*. Also included are discussion and critical thinking questions that relate developmental perspectives and topics in the text to issues in the articles.

Acknowledgments

I would particularly like to thank the following people who helped me on this project: Peter Janzow, Editor in Chief; Nicole Signoretti, Assistant Editor; Ilene Kalish and Marilyn Coco, Editorial Assistants; and Bruce Hobart, Production Editor. I would also like to offer my appreciation to all those professors who read the manuscript and offered valued advice, particularly: Mark Alcorn, University of Northern Colorado; James L. Dannemiller, University of Wisconsin—Madison; Vernon Hall, Syracuse University; and Elizabeth Lemerise, Western Kentucky University.

F. Philip Rice

Part One

THE STUDY OF CHILD AND ADOLESCENT DEVELOPMENT

A Developmental Perspective

Chapter 1

Introduction to the Study of Child and Adolescent Development

SCOPE

Congratulations on enrolling in this course in child and adolescent development! You should find it a fascinating and intriguing subject, primarily because it is about our children and our adolescents and those of others. *This course is about the changes that take place in their lives:* in their bodies, their personalities, their ways of thinking, their feelings, their behavior, their relationships, and in the roles that we as adult leaders, teachers, and parents play during different periods of their lives.

In this course, we seek to *describe* the changes that take place from conception through adolescence. Information about these changes comes primarily from scientific research that accurately observes, measures, records, and interprets so that objective data are obtained. For example, one researcher may want to understand better the changes that take place in sexual behavior during childhood and adolescence. Another researcher may want to trace physical growth and development; another may want to measure changes in cognitive thinking.

In addition to describing the changes, we will seek to *explain* the changes insofar as possible. Why have they occurred? What roles do heredity and environment play in causing these changes?

Explaining the reasons for changes is vitally important. A parent may ask: "Why has my preschool child developed so many fears?" An adolescent may wonder: "Why have I become so self-conscious?" The mother of an adolescent may complain:

> I don't understand what's happening to my son. He used to be so dependable and conservative. He'd come straight home from school every afternoon. We spent most evenings together at home. Now, he dresses in horrible clothes, and he never does his homework or helps around the house without nagging. He stops off at a youth hangout after school, and sometimes doesn't get home until 8:00 or 9:00. He never spends any time with the family, says he would like to spend most of the time with his friends. (Author's counseling notes)

This mother needs some explanation of her son's changed behavior.

Human developmental psychology also seeks to *predict* changes that may occur. What types of parent–child relationships are most conducive to the development of emotional security or positive self-esteem in children? What nutritional habits are most conducive to maximizing the health of our children? If an adolescent achieves a particular score on an SAT, what is the statistical probability of academic success in college?

Each of these questions seeks to predict future behavior. We need to remember, however, that general research evaluates statistical probability of something happening under a given set of conditions. The findings do not suggest that every individual is affected in the same way or to the same extent. No research predicts with 100 percent accuracy what happens to every individual in a group.

Once we are able to describe, explain, and predict changes, the last step is to be able to *influence* changes. If we know, for

The goal of life-span developmental psychology is to help people live meaningful, productive lives.

LIVING ISSUES

Changing Ourselves

One of the ways that people develop understanding of the changes needed in their lives, and are able to make these changes, is through psychotherapy. Psychotherapy can facilitate growth.

When people go to therapists, several questions are usually uppermost in their minds: "Will therapy do any good?" "Can the situation be changed?" Or parents ask: "Do you think my child will ever change?" These questions reflect the fact that a favorable outcome of therapy depends partially on change. Either the situation has to be changed or the people in it need to change.

One of the purposes of therapy is to help people make changes in themselves.

As a therapist, I cannot predict ahead of time whether the situation can be changed or whether the people will change. Much depends upon the insight they are able to achieve, their own flexibility and adaptability, their motivation to succeed, and their willingness to assume personal responsibility. I can counsel some people for months, and they don't make any changes. Other people institute significant changes in a relatively short time.

Some people want their children to change, but don't want to change themselves. A mother will say: "You have to get my adolescent straightened out and everything will be all right." A father will complain: "If my wife would only stop getting so upset, our child could get along a lot better." These fathers and mothers feel that the fault lies with their children, not themselves, and that the way to make the situation better is for the child to stop the offensive behavior. As a consequence, they consistently pressure the child to change and may use every power tactic they can think of to make this happen.

Realistically, we really can't change another person's behavior unless that person wants to change. In many cases, we probably shouldn't try. This is really saying: "I can like you only if you change." But what is most helpful and possible is to gain some control over ourselves. *We can change ourselves, if we want to and need to, although sometimes it may take therapeutic help to make these changes.* By changing ourselves, we may find that our whole situation and our relationships with our children have changed as well. (Composite of the author's counseling experiences)

example, that we have been raised in an abusive family, what can we do to overcome possible negative effects so we don't become abusive parents to our own children? We may decide to go for therapy or join a support group for adults who were abused as children.

The goal of child and adolescent developmental psychology is to help children and adolescents live meaningful, productive lives. The more ways we can learn about how children grow and change, the more positive relationships we can develop with them. Thus, the personal goal of the study of child and adolescent development is to become better leaders, teachers, and parents of children and youth (Heckhausen and Krueger, 1993).

Periods of Development

For ease of discussion, the life span is usually divided into three major developmental periods: child development, adolescent development, and adult development. Child development encompasses the prenatal period, infancy and toddlerhood, early childhood or preschool period, and middle childhood or school-age period. Adolescent development covers early adolescence and late adolescence. The developmental framework comprises the following periods and age divisions:

Early childhood—the preschool period of development from 3 to 5 years

Child development
- Prenatal development: conception through birth
- Infancy and toddlerhood: first 2 years
- Early childhood or preschool period: 3 to 5 years
- Middle childhood or school-age period: 6 to 11 years

Adolescent development
- Early adolescence: 12 to 14 years
- Late adolescence: 15 to 19 years

Middle childhood—the elementary school years, from 6 to 11 years

The age ranges within specific periods differ slightly, particularly during adolescence, depending on the preferences of the individual psychologist.

PRENATAL PERIOD (CONCEPTION THROUGH BIRTH)

Prenatal period—the period from conception to birth

The **prenatal period** includes the developmental process from conception through birth, during which time the human organism grows from a fertilized cell to billions of cells. During this period, the basic body structure and organs are formed. Both heredity and environment influence development. During the early months, the organism is more vulnerable to negative environmental influences than during any other period of growth.

Adolescence—the period of transition from childhood to young adulthood, from about 12 to 19 years of age

INFANCY AND TODDLERHOOD (FIRST 2 YEARS)

Infancy—the first two years of life

Infancy, which extends from childbirth through toddlerhood—usually the second year of life—is a period of tremendous changes. Infants grow in motor ability and coordination, and develop sensory skills and an ability to use language. They form attachments to family members and other caregivers, learn to trust or distrust, and to express or withhold love and affection. They learn to express basic feelings and emotions and develop some sense of self and independence. Already, they evidence considerable differences in personality and temperament.

EARLY CHILDHOOD OR PRESCHOOL PERIOD (3 TO 5 YEARS)

During the **early childhood** preschool years (from ages 3 to 5), children continue their rapid physical, cognitive, and linguistic growth. They are better able to care for themselves, begin to develop a concept of self and of gender identities and roles, and become very interested in play with other children. The quality of parent–child relationships is important in the socialization process that is taking place.

MIDDLE CHILDHOOD OR SCHOOL-AGE PERIOD (6 TO 11 YEARS)

During **middle childhood,** children make significant advances in their ability to read, write, and do arithmetic; to understand their world; and to think logically. Achievement becomes vitally important, as does successful adjustment with parents. Both psychosocial and moral development proceed at a rapid rate. The quality of family relationships continues to exert a major influence on emotional and social adjustments.

EARLY ADOLESCENCE (12 TO 14 YEARS)

Adolescence is the period of transition between childhood and adulthood. During early adolescence, sexual maturation takes place, and formal operational thinking begins. As adolescents seek greater independence from parents, they also want increased contact and a closer sense of belonging and companionship with peers.

LATE ADOLESCENCE (15 TO 19 YEARS)

The formation of a positive identity is an important psychosocial task. The late adolescent begins to make career choices, to seek to complete his or her education, and to enter the world of work. Heterosexual relationships are developed along with the ability to relate in friendly and intimate ways to others.

LIVING ISSUES

Rethinking Our Timetables

Our biological and social clocks have changed, so we need to change our timetables for living. For one thing, puberty comes much earlier than it used to. The average age of menarche (onset of menstruation) for American girls is about 12 years of age, a decline of about two years since the beginning of this century. This change, known as the secular growth trend, is probably due to more sedentary lifestyles and higher fat consumption than in years past. Puberty brings with it earlier sexual maturation, an increase in interest in matters related to sex and to boy–girl relationships, and younger ages in beginning dating. While adolescents are physically mature, they are not mature financially, emotionally and socially. Government statistics indicate that 53 percent of young adults 18 to 24 years of age are still living with parents. The time required to get an education to prepare for a vocation has increased drastically. In nineteenth-century industrial America, the student body at Harvard University consisted mostly of boys 14 to 17 years of age. They graduated with their degrees at age 17. Marriage by age 18 was considered appropriate for women. Today, if students go to graduate school, they may not complete their education until their late twenties. This has resulted in prolonged adolescence and dependency. The median age of marriage today has also increased. Boys, on the average, marry at a median age of 26, girls at 24. This means that there is a period of about 12 years between the onset of puberty and marriage. No wonder there has been an increase in premarital sex.

Life expectancy continues to increase. Since 1920, the average life expectancy from birth has increased from 54 to 76 years of age (U.S. Bureau of the Census, 1995). As a consequence, the proportion of older people in the United States continues to increase. By the year 2020, approximately 22 percent of the country's population will be age 60 and older. This means we need to begin to rethink the ideal age for retirement. With people living longer, can they really afford to retire at age 65? Today, many people start new jobs and families at age 50 or 60. It is a mistake, therefore, to categorize people by age brackets. Grandparents may be 35; students may be 70. The 35-year-old grandparent is certainly not old, but the 70-year-old student—by tomorrow's standards—may not be old either (Neugarten & Neugarten, 1987).

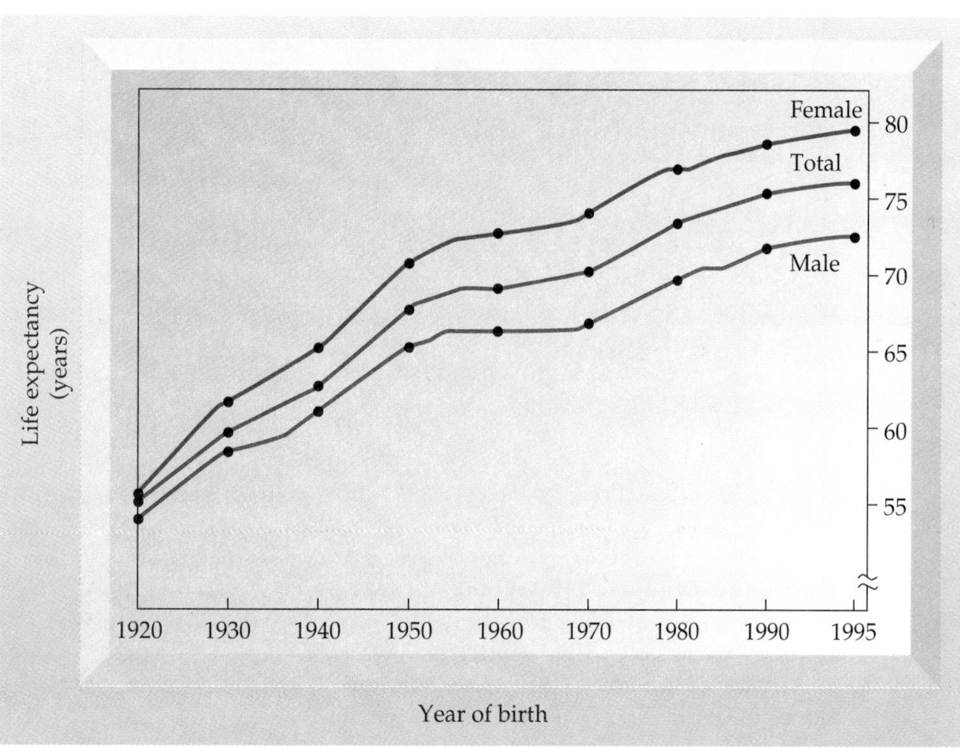

FIGURE 1.1 Expectation of life at birth, United States: 1920–1995.

From *Statistical Abstract of the United States, 1995* (p. 86), U.S. Bureau of the Census, 1995, Washington, DC: U.S. Government Printing Office.

During early childhood children begin to develop a concept of self.

A Philosophy of Human Development

The science of human development has slowly evolved over the years and a large body of research has also emerged that sheds increasing light on the developmental process. Gradually, there has emerged a philosophy of human development that reflects this increasing knowledge (Baltes, 1987). The most important elements of this philosophy are discussed here.

DEVELOPMENT IS MULTIDIMENSIONAL AND INTERDISCIPLINARY

Physical development

Cognitive development

Emotional development

Social development

Human development is a complex process that may be divided into four basic dimensions: **physical, cognitive, emotional,** and **social development.** These four dimensions are discussed in this book under each of the major age periods. Though each dimension emphasizes a particular aspect of development, there is considerable interdependency among the areas. Cognitive skills, for example, may depend on physical and emotional health and social experience. Social development is influenced by biological maturation, cognitive understanding, and emotional reactions. In effect, each dimension reflects the others. Figure 1.2 outlines the four dimensions.

In describing all four of these areas, human development has become a multidisciplinary science, borrowing from biology, physiology, medicine, education, psychology, sociology, and anthropology (Baltes, 1987). The most up-to-date knowledge available is taken from each of these disciplines and used in the study of human development (Hinde, 1992).

BOTH HEREDITY AND ENVIRONMENT INFLUENCE DEVELOPMENT

For years, psychologists have tried to sort out the influences of heredity and environment on development (Himelstein, Graham, & Weinter, 1991). If heredity plays the

Late adulthood requires increasing attention to health care to maintain vigor and well-being.

primary role, the human race would be improved through genetic counseling to eliminate genetic faults. If environment plays the primary role, the task would be to determine what positive influences enhance development, and to control these influences toward the desired results. Actually, both **nature** (heredity) and **nurture** (environment) exert important influences. Some aspects of development seem to be influenced more by heredity, others by environment (Coll, 1990). Most are influenced by both. Children inherit their physical constitutions that enable them to stand, walk, and play as maturation proceeds. Poor diet, illness, drugs, and physical restriction can retard the process. Because some children are not very strong or well coordinated, they have poor athletic ability, but practice may overcome these deficiencies. Children are born with the capacity to love, but must learn how to express it.

The critical question is not *which* factor—heredity or environment—is responsible for our behavior, but how these two factors interact and how they may be controlled so that optimum development takes place. *Both nature and nurture are essential to development.*

DEVELOPMENT REFLECTS BOTH CONTINUITY AND DISCONTINUITY

Some developmental psychologists emphasize that development is a gradual, continuous process of growth and change. Physical growth and language development, or other aspects of development, show smooth, incremental changes. Other developmental psychologists describe development as a series of distinct stages, each preceded by abrupt changes that occur from one phase to another.

Continuous development can be compared to the growth of an acorn. After planting, it sprouts and gradually grows as an oak tree. Growth is quantitative. Discon-

Nature—biological and genetic factors that influence development

Nurture—the influence of environment and experience on development

Human Development

Physical Development	Cognitive Development	Emotional Development	Social Development
Physical development includes genetic foundations for development; the physical growth of all the components of the body; changes in motor development, the senses, and in bodily systems; plus related subjects such as health care, nutrition, sleep, drug abuse, and sexual functioning.	Cognitive development includes all changes in the intellectual processes of thinking, learning, remembering, judging, problem solving, and communicating. It includes both heredity and environmental influences in the developmental process.	Emotional development refers to the development of attachment, trust, security, love, and affection; and a variety of emotions, feelings, and temperaments. It includes development of concepts of self and autonomy, and a discussion of stress, emotional disturbances, and acting-out behavior.	Social development emphasizes the socialization process, moral development, and relationships with peers and family members. It discusses marriage, parenthood, work, and vocational roles and employment.

FIGURE 1.2 The dimensions of human development.

tinuous development is illustrated by the life cycle of a frog. It begins as an egg, which then hatches into a tadpole, and then fairly abruptly changes into an amphibious frog. Growth takes place as a sequence of stages, each qualitatively different from the others. Psychologists who emphasize continuous development tend to emphasize the importance of environmental influences and social learning in the growth process. Psychologists who emphasize discontinuous development or stage theories of development tend to stress the role of heredity (nature) and maturation in the growth sequence.

Today, many psychologists do not ally themselves with either extreme point of view. They recognize that some aspects of development are continuous, whereas others show stagelike characteristics (Fischer & Silvern, 1985). Environment continuously affects people, but because people grow and develop from within, in stages, they can in turn influence their environment. (The nurture–nature issue is discussed later.) Several psychologists have combined the two points of view by emphasizing the way individuals experience and negotiate the various stages (Neugarten & Neugarten, 1987; Rosenfeld & Stark, 1987).

DEVELOPMENT IS CUMULATIVE

We all recognize that our lives today are affected by what has happened before. Psychoanalysts especially emphasize the influence of early childhood experiences on later adjustment. Block, Block, and Keyes (1988) were able to show that girls who were undercontrolled by parents during their nursery school years—that is, raised in unstructured, laissez-faire homes—were more likely to use drugs during adolescence than those whose parents exerted more control. In a study of 206 females and 192 males, ages 30–31, Dubow, Huesmann, and Eron (1987) showed that children of parents who were accepting, used nonauthoritarian approaches to punishment, and were closely identified with their children, showed higher levels of adult ego development 22 years later. Both studies emphasized the influence of early childhood experiences on later life.

Some psychologists emphasize that development is a continuous process of growth and change.

Other studies propose a link between early family experiences and depression or other psychological problems in adulthood (Amato, 1991). Depressed individuals typically recall more rejecting and coercive behavior on the part of parents than do nondepressed individuals. Those who recall their parents' marriage as unhappy report lower life satisfaction and more psychological distress than those who remember their parents' marriage as happy. One interview survey conducted with a representative sample of 367 elderly community residents, ages 65–74, showed that early experiences with parents had an impact on the well-being of these elderly persons (Andersson and Stevens, 1993).

One longitudinal study (a study of the same group over a period of years) of 75 white, middle-class children from infancy to adolescence revealed that children who were excessively aggressive and hostile and who showed negative emotional states (anxiety, depression, or rejection) in early childhood showed poorer emotional and social adjustment as adolescents (Lerner, Hertzog, Hooker, Hassibi, & Thomas, 1988). The researchers were able to predict adolescent adjustment through emotional behavior in early childhood. They also suggested that early intervention might ameliorate later behavior and adjustment problems. This study is consistent with others that show that early temperamental patterns are predictive of later social behavior (Calkins & Fox, 1992).

Does this mean that if we have an unhappy childhood, we are condemned to maladjustment and unhappiness as adults? A traumatic incident or abusive childhood may have serious consequences, but neither is 100 percent predictive of later adjustment. Countless people have emerged from dysfunctional family backgrounds and found nurturing environments that enable them to lead productive, meaningful lives.

DEVELOPMENT REFLECTS BOTH STABILITY AND CHANGE

We have already suggested that the study of human development investigates the changes that occur over the life span (Sroufe, Egeland, & Kruetzer, 1990). The question arises: "Are there elements of personality that remain stable? If a person manifests certain personality characteristics during childhood, will these persist into adolescence or adulthood?"

Psychologists are not in agreement as to how much personality change can take place and how much remains stable. Will the child who is shy and quiet ever become an outgoing, extroverted adult? Sometimes this happens. Will the child who is a mediocre student become a brilliant scholar in college? Sometimes this happens. The adolescent who earns a reputation for being wild and irresponsible can sometimes settle down to become a responsible, productive adult. Not all students who are voted "most likely to succeed" make it. Some who are overlooked capture top honors later in life. All we can say for certain is that there is evidence for personality stability in some people, and change of personal-

FOCUS

Childhood Environment and Adult Outcomes

George Vaillant (1977a, 1977b), a psychiatrist teaching at Harvard Medical School, made a longitudinal study of 94 males who were among 268 college sophomores carefully selected for the Grant Study begun in 1938. The average age in 1969 was 47. Childhood histories were obtained from parental interviews. Physical, physiological, and psychological examinations were conducted each year until 1955, and every two years after that. A social anthropologist conducted in-depth home interviews with each subject between 1950 and 1952. Vaillant interviewed each man in 1967, usually at home, using identical interview questionnaires.

One of the study's most interesting aspects was the comparison of the childhoods, family backgrounds, and earlier years of the men who, in their 50s, were labeled *Best Outcomes* and *Worst Outcomes*. One-half of the men who had experienced unsatisfactory (poor) childhood environments were among the 30 *Worst Outcomes*. Twenty-three of these men whose childhoods had been bleak and loveless showed four characteristics: (1) they were unable to have fun, (2) they were dependent and lacking in trust, (3) they were more likely to have become mentally ill, and (4) they were lacking in friends. However, 17 percent with poor childhood environments were among the 30 *Best Outcomes*, indicating that childhood environment was not the sole determinant of adult success.

ity in others. Sometimes external events of a traumatic nature completely change the course of a person's life. For this reason, developmental trajectories are not always predictable.

One longitudinal study of IQ scores of children from 4 to 13 years of age showed that high-risk factors such as stressful life events, disadvantaged minority status, mother's poor mental health, low educational attainment, or little family support in the lives of some children explained one-third to one-half of the variance in IQ at 4 and 13 years of age (Sameroff, Seifer, Baldwin, & Baldwin, 1993). It appears that the stability versus change controversy is far from settled. There are many variables affecting both.

DEVELOPMENT IS VARIABLE

Growth is uneven. Not all dimensions of the personality grow at the same rate. A child may be exceptionally bright, but lag in physical growth and development. Most adolescents become physically mature before they are emotionally mature or socially responsible. An adolescent boy who is physically mature, with the body of a man, may be childish and immature in behavior and actions, leading his parents to ask: "When is he going to grow up?" Similarly, an adolescent girl who develops early may have the body of a woman and the social interests of an adult, but the emotions of a child. Her parents may feel very confused about her behavior because she acts childish in some ways and adultlike in other ways.

DEVELOPMENT IS SOMETIMES CYCLICAL AND REPETITIVE

There may be some repetition of adjustment phases during anyone's life. Both the toddler and the adolescent rebel in an effort to establish autonomy. School-age children go through a period of value conflict, and adolescents may face similar conflicts years later.

In addition to repetition in an individual life, there may be a repetition of similar phases occurring at different times in the life cycle of other individuals. Different persons may experience similar stages of life, but with individual and cultural differences. Different influences shape each life, producing alternate routes (one may marry and another may remain single). A variety of factors speed up and slow down the timetable, or even stop the development process altogether. But where similarities in developmental phases do exist, we can learn from the experiences of others. This fact makes a human development approach meaningful.

DEVELOPMENT REFLECTS INDIVIDUAL DIFFERENCES

Whereas there is some repetition of developmental sequences from one person to another, *there is also a wide range of individual differences.* Individuals differ in timing and rates of development; in such factors as height, weight, body build, physical abilities, and health; and in cognitive characteristics, emotional reactions, and personality characteristics. They differ in social abilities, leisure-time preferences, and relationships with friends. When discussing development, one must refer to averages: average height or weight, or average vocabulary at a certain age. However, these averages do not reflect the wide range of individual differences. We must be careful not to assume that every child must conform to these averages.

DEVELOPMENT REFLECTS CULTURAL DIFFERENCES

Cultural differences also exert a profound influence on human development (Julian, McKenry, & McKelvey, 1994). A study of variation in the sleeping arrangements of Mayan infants and toddlers revealed that all Mayan children sleep in their mothers' beds through toddlerhood. A comparison with U.S. infants revealed that none slept in their mothers' beds. The Mayan parents emphasized the value of closeness with infants; the U.S. parents emphasized the value of independence for infants (Morelli, Oppenheim, Rogoff, & Goldsmith, 1992). A comparison of variations in maternal responsiveness among the Gusii of Kenya, with mothers from Boston, Massachusetts, and those from the Mexican city of Cuernavaca revealed significant differences, dependent mostly upon the mother's school attendance and educational level. Gusii

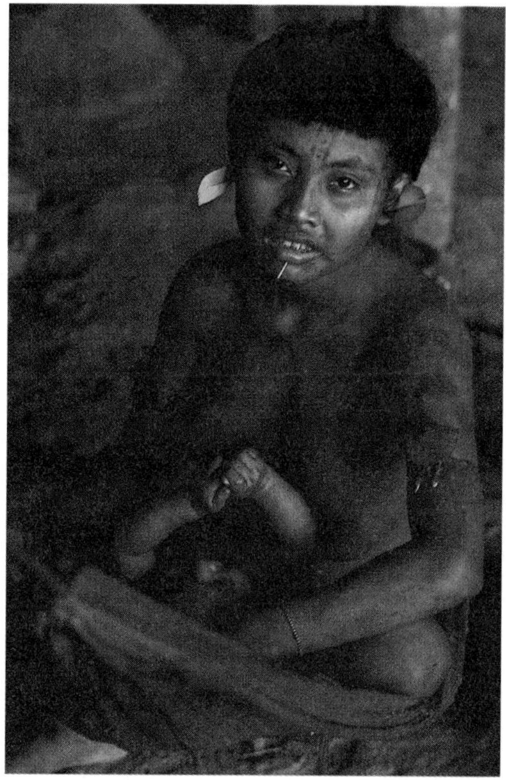

Cultural differences exert a profound influence on how parents relate to their children.

mothers averaged two to three years of schooling and were physically responsive to their infants, particularly to their crying, and sought to maintain calm and reduce distress. The Boston mothers responded visually and vocally to their infants to offer positive stimulation and emotional arousal. The Mexican mothers varied in educational attainment and showed maternal responsiveness similar to that of Boston mothers of similar educational background (Richman, Miller, & Levine, 1992). Just how the psychological development of these infants is affected by the differences in maternal responsiveness is a challenge for future research.

Cross-cultural differences exist also in social time clocks. A girl may be betrothed at age 13 in a primitive society, a mother at 14, and a widow at 30 or 35, whereas these events usually come at later ages in industrial societies. Each society prescribes an ideal time for assuming various responsibilities and for the bestowal of privileges, but these ages differ from one culture to another.

DEVELOPMENTAL INFLUENCES ARE RECIPROCAL

Psychologists used to emphasize the influence of adults and environment on children. Now the emphasis is also on how the difference in children can influence caregivers (Scarr, 1992). Rather than being passive recipients of care, infants and children are active, influential partners in their interactions with the people around them.

PARENTING ISSUES

Korean-American and Anglo-American Preschoolers' Social Interaction

One study analyzed cultural differences in Korean-American and Anglo-American preschoolers' social interaction and play behaviors. The analysis of the activity-setting teachers shows that there were two culturally defined social environments. Consistent with their scripts for adult–child interaction and developmental beliefs, values, and goals, the Anglo-American teachers provided an environment that was conducive to problem solving, independent thinking, and active involvement in learning. Children had many opportunities for play and social interaction and were also involved in play activities with teachers.

In the Korean-American preschool, teachers organized their classrooms and lessons to encourage the development of task perseverance, academic skills, and passive involvement in learning. Children's social interaction and play were limited to periods of outdoor activity. The environmental differences in these two preschool settings may partially explain the differences found in children's social behaviors, social competence, pretend play, and cognitive functioning. The Korean-American preschool showed a highly structured daily schedule centered primarily on academic-related activities, providing few opportunities for children to interact socially with peers. In contrast, the Anglo-American children had a wide variety of play materials and self-select activity centers, which provided more opportunities for social interaction and play. As a consequence, the Anglo-American children and their teachers engaged in more social interaction. Korean-American children viewed teachers as authority figures who were to be respected and to be shown deference. This attitude is fostered early in young Korean children, and they are taught to listen to their teachers' instructions without question. One consequence is that the Asian children outperformed American children in academic skills. The Anglo-American children's higher social functioning was related to the frequent opportunities to learn social skills by interacting and playing with peers that were provided in their preschool program.

Thus, cultural differences and the nature of the activities being performed in the two settings resulted in different developmental outcomes for children (Farver, Kim, & Lee, 1995).

A placid, pleasant, easy-to-care-for child may have a very positive influence on parents, encouraging them to act in a friendly, warm, and loving manner, but an overactive, temperamental, hard-to-care-for child who is easily upset may stimulate parents to be hostile, short-tempered, and rejecting. From this point of view, children—however involuntarily—are partly responsible for creating their own environments. And because of individual differences, different people, at different developmental stages, interpret and act upon their environments in differing ways that create different experiences for each person.

Scientific method—a series of steps used to obtain accurate data; these include formulating the problem, developing a hypothesis, testing the hypothesis, and drawing conclusions that are stated in the form of a theory

Research in Human Development: The Scientific Method

Psychologists use scientific methods to obtain information on human development. The **scientific method** involves four major steps:

1. Formulate the problem to be solved or the question to be answered.
2. Develop a hypothesis in the form of a proposition to be tested.
3. Test the hypothesis through research to determine the truth or fallacy of the proposition.
4. Draw conclusions and state them in the form of a theory that explains the data or facts observed.

The conclusions of the study are usually published in scientific journals. Other scientists may seek to replicate the findings of the study, or to clarify the conclusions to further increase their knowledge about the subject.

Data Collection Methods

Before a hypothesis can be tested, the researcher must gather as much data about it as possible. The primary data-gathering techniques are naturalistic observation, interviews, questionnaires and checklists, case studies, and standardized testing.

NATURALISTIC OBSERVATION

Naturalistic observation involves watching children in natural environments (such as at home, in school, in a neighborhood, in a park, in a shopping center, or at a party), and then recording their behavior without making any effort to manipulate the situation. This approach provides information about what is happening, but not why or how it is happening, or how the behavior might change under a different set of circumstances. Because observers make no effort to influence what is happening, they are limited to recording what they see.

Naturalistic observation—research conducted in a natural setting by watching and recording behavior

INTERVIEWS

Interviews are appropriate in studying only those children who are old enough to be verbal. Because **interviews** are conducted face to face, much detailed and personal information can be obtained with probing follow-up questions to clarify responses. Interviews review feelings, emotions, and attitudes, which are sometimes more important than factual information. Another advantage is that it is a flexible method so that a broad range of subjects may be explored, depending on the needs of the interviewer. Questions may be predetermined and the same ones asked of everyone to be certain to obtain information on the same topic from each person.

This technique has some disadvantages. Interviews are time-consuming, expensive, and usually involve only a limited number of subjects. The success of the interview depends on the ability of the interviewer to establish a rapport with the subject and encourage self-disclosure.

Establishing rapport with children may take considerable time before information is forthcoming. Some subjects are less verbal than others, making it difficult for the interviewer to obtain information. Sometimes subjects give false data, simply because they don't remember accurately. Interviewers need training in how to be both objective and professional. Because of biases, an interviewer might distort or misunderstand a subject's responses. In spite of this disadvantage, the technique continues to be a rich source of information for researchers.

QUESTIONNAIRES AND CHECKLISTS

One frequently used method in human development research is the survey method, by which one gathers information through **questionnaires.** Questionnaires may be used to obtain relevant information from older children and adolescents. Subjects may be asked to fill out a written questionnaire. At other times, an interviewer asks questions orally and then records the responses. One advantage of questionnaires is that large numbers of people may be surveyed fairly easily through the mail or in

Interviews—a research method conducted face to face between an interviewer and subject where information is obtained through recorded responses to questions

Questionnaires—a research method whereby the subject answers written questions

FOCUS

The Use of Puppets

Young children, especially those of school age and younger grade school age, have trouble verbalizing feelings in the therapeutic situation. One of the ways of helping them to overcome their self-consciousness and to become more verbal is to let them use puppets in acting out situations that have occurred. For example, suppose the interviewer or therapist wants to try to get some insight into parent–child relationships in the family. Imagine that there is a mother and a father and an older brother and a younger sister in the family. If the therapist is working with the older son, for example, he might ask him to assume his own role and to choose the puppet that represents himself. The interviewer may then select a puppet that might represent either the mother or the father. The interviewer can ask the son what the son has to say, what the mother does or what the father does. The boy will express his feelings and his ideas through the talking of the puppet. Many times, by observing what the child acts out when playing the part of a puppet, the interviewer will discover what kind of relationships exist between the child and the parents.

The author found in interviewing one son that the father and the son always seemed to be in conflict with the mother and the daughter. In this case, the son was extremely jealous of the daughter, so when the interviewer played the part of the daughter puppet, the son expressed his anger and hostility by hitting and otherwise pummeling the puppet representing his sister. He couldn't express his anger toward his sister without speaking through the figure of the puppet. Children who cannot express their feelings verbally can act out these feelings in the play situation. Thus, using puppets is a helpful way of enabling them to express themselves more freely.

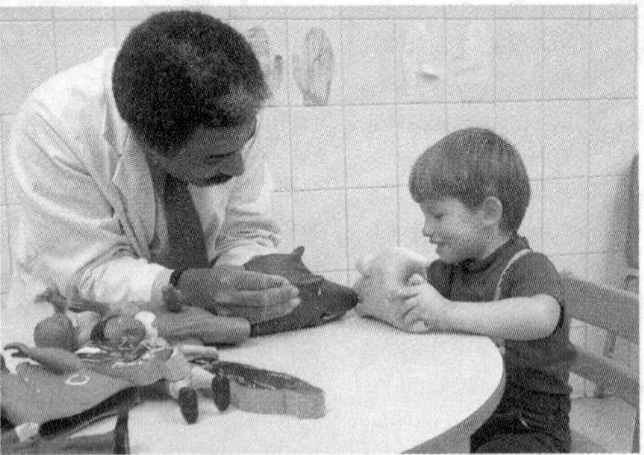

Puppets are sometimes used in therapy with children.

large groups with a minimum of expense, and data are standardized and easy to summarize. Because questionnaires are given anonymously, people usually respond honestly.

However, questions can be misunderstood and wrong answers can be obtained. If the researchers omit significant questions, they may not receive some important information.

Checklists provide a short form of questionnaires by which to obtain data easily and quickly.

CASE STUDIES

Case studies involve longitudinal investigations of individuals rather than groups of subjects. Clinical psychologists use case studies extensively in gathering data as a foundation for the treatment of emotionally disturbed individuals. However, the method is also used to do in-depth studies of normal individuals. The primary drawback of this approach is that data obtained about individuals may not be applicable to other persons. Conclusions about groups of people cannot be made from a sample size of one person.

STANDARDIZED TESTING

Psychologists have developed a wide variety of **tests** to measure specific characteristics. Tests include those for intelligence, aptitude, achievement, vocational interests, and personality; there are also diagnostic tests and a wide variety of other types. Tests have a high **validity** if they measure what they claim to measure. If a test is supposed to measure intelligence, it has a high validity if it predicts performance on tasks that most people agree require intelligence. A test has high **reliability** if the same scores are obtained when the test is administered on two or more occasions, or by two or more examiners. If the scores change from one testing to the next, the test may not be a reliable means of evaluation. For example, the younger children are when given intelligence tests, the less valid the tests are in predicting IQ later in life.

Validity

Case studies—a research method involving in-depth, longitudinal investigations and records of individuals

Reliability

Tests are usually used in addition to other means of obtaining data. Tests can be a valuable source of information, but are most helpful when supplemented by data from other sources. Many colleges require scores on SATs as a basis for admission, but they also evaluate high school grades, class standings, letters of recommendation, interviews, and essays.

Tests—research instruments used to measure specific characteristics such as intelligence, aptitude, achievement, vocational interests, personality traits, and so forth

Sampling

The **sample** (the group of subjects chosen) is an important consideration in research. **Random samples** are often taken from groups enlisted for study. A truly **representative sample** of a population includes the same percentages of children from the different cultural, ethnic, socioeconomic, and educational backgrounds as contained in the population. In addition, sufficient numbers are necessary to be representative of a much larger group. Practical considerations often prohibit such a sampling. However, researchers have to be careful not to generalize to apply their findings to groups that are different from those studied.

Sample

Random sample

Representative sample

Experimental Methods

PROCEDURE

Experimental methods are closely controlled procedures whereby the experimenter manipulates variables to determine how they affect one another. Changes are compared with those in control groups that have not been exposed to the variables. Because the experimenter changes the variables, a link between cause and effect is more easily established than by other methods. Experiments can be conducted in a laboratory, in the field, or as part of a subject's everyday experience. Laboratory experiments are usually easiest to conduct because they permit a high degree of control over the situation.

Experimental methods—methods of gathering scientific data, in which procedures are closely controlled and the experimenter manipulates variables to determine how one affects the other

Suppose, for example, we wanted to observe attachment behavior and separation anxiety in three different ages of children attending nursery school for the first time. The population of fifteen children is divided into three age groups—2-year-olds, 3-year-olds, and 4-year-olds—and each separate group of five children is brought into the nursery room along with their parents. We might want to keep changing the situation, or altering the variables, as follows:

Observe the children with both parents present.
Observe the children when the mother leaves the room.
Observe the children when the father leaves the room.
Observe the children when both parents leave the room, but with a teacher present.

We might compare the behavior of these children with a control group that had attended the nursery school continuously for one month. We might want to compare the behavior of the boys and girls. And we certainly would want to compare the behavior of the children of different age groups. A number of variables might be introduced. For example, would there be any difference in the reaction of the children whose parents sneaked out without telling them, compared with children whose parents explained that they were going to leave?

Correlation—the extent to which two factors are associated or related to one another

INDEPENDENT AND DEPENDENT VARIABLES

Note that in the previous example, both independent and dependent variables are used. The **independent variable** is the variable over which the experimenter has direct control. The **dependent variable** is so named because it changes as a result of changes in the independent variable. In this case, the independent variable is the changing situation under which the children are observed—both parents present, only the mother present, and so forth. The dependent variable in the example is the behavior and separation anxiety experienced by the children. The purpose of the experiment is to change the independent variable to determine how that change affects the dependent variable (the behavior and separation anxiety of the children).

Independent variable—a factor that is manipulated or controlled by the experimenter to determine its effect on the subjects' behavior.

Dependent variable—in an experiment, a factor that is influenced by the independent or manipulated variable

In another example, suppose that an experimenter wants to sort out social and demographic factors that influence the effect of divorce on children (Breault and Kposowa, 1987). The experimenter decides to test a selected number of independent variables: age of child, age of mother at the time of divorce, race of the child, socioeconomic status of the family, and whether the mother remarries or not. By looking at one independent variable at a time, and establishing correlations with the dependent variable, the researcher is able to show the relationship of each independent variable to the dependent variable (the probability of divorce). By changing one variable at a time while holding the others constant, the researcher can sort out the variables that exert the most influence.

ESTABLISHING RELATIONSHIPS: CORRELATIONAL STUDIES

One way of evaluating data, once obtained, is to establish the degree of **correlation** between variables (Green, 1992). When a correlation exists, there is a relationship, or association, between the variables. Correlation is indicated statistically from –1.0 to +1.0. Minus 1 indicates a completely negative association: When one variable increases, the other decreases. Plus 1 indicates a completely positive association: When one variable increases, the other also increases. Zero means there is no correlation or relationship at all. Correlation coefficients are expressed in *r* values from –1 to +1. A correlation of +.8 is not twice the correlation of +.4 (because the relationships are not linear), but it would indicate a high degree of positive association.

Researchers have established a great number of correlations relating to human development. There is a positive correlation between children's exposure to violence on television and showing aggression themselves (Tooth, 1985). There is a negative correlation between the degree of religiousness of adolescents and premarital sexual permissiveness (Fisher & Hall, 1988). There is a positive correlation between educational achievement and adolescent income after school is completed (U.S. Bureau of the Census, 1992). If we measured the emotional security of an older group of children during an economic recession, and later measured the security of a younger group of children during an economic boom, and we found that the younger reported greater security than the older group, would this finding be the result of a younger age or the differences in time of testing? Researchers seek to sort out exact causes.

Correlation is an important concept, but it does not indicate causation. A relationship between A and B does not mean that A causes B, or B causes A. Both A and B may be caused by other factors. For years, for example, psychologists showed a relationship between broken homes and delinquency. But does this mean that divorce causes delinquency? Not necessarily. There may be other variables that need to be taken into consideration. For example, divorce may follow family conflict. And there has been research indicating that family conflict contributes to delinquency, whether or not divorce has occurred (Demo & Acock, 1988). In addition, there are many other factors that may accompany divorce. After divorce, some mothers with custody of their children may be forced to live in poverty, in poor sections of town with high crime rates. The mothers have to go out to work and leave their children unsupervised. Their children are not as likely to complete their education as they would be in intact families. Any one of these factors, and not the divorce alone, may have some relationship to delinquency. We need to be careful, therefore, not to assume that because there are correlations, causes are also established (Scarr, 1984).

Research Designs

AGE, COHORT, AND TIME OF TESTING

Researchers often want to sort out the effects of age, cohort, and time of testing on findings. If changes are noted as people age, is age responsible or are there other causes? One cause may relate to a cohort. A **cohort** consists of a group of people born during the same time period, for example, during 1960–1965. There may be significant differences among children born at different time periods, not because of differences in their ages, but because of the different economic and social conditions under which they grew up.

Cohort—a group of subjects born during the same time period

The three basic research designs are (1) cross-sectional studies, (2) longitudinal studies, and (3) sequential studies. Each design has its own characteristics.

CROSS-SECTIONAL STUDIES

A **cross-sectional study** compares one age group or cohort, with another age group at the time of testing. For example, a cross-sectional study conducted in the year 2000 might compare four groups of cohorts: those born in 1980 with those born in 1985, 1990, and 1995. As illustrated in Figure 1.3, group D (5-year-olds born in 1995) would be compared to group G (10-year-olds born in 1990 with group I (15-year-olds born in 1985) with group J (20-year-olds born in 1980). This method measures the different age groups during one testing period and compares these groups to determine differences. As shown, comparisons of groups C, F, and H during 1995 or groups B and E during 1990 would also represent cross-sectional studies.

Cross-sectional study—comparing one age group with others at one time of testing

LONGITUDINAL STUDIES

Longitudinal research studies one group of people repeatedly over a period of years. For example, a select group might be studied at ages 5, 10, 15, and 20. Referring to Figure 1.3, if a group of children born in 1980 were studied during 1985, 1990, 1995, and 2000 (those groups, labeled A, E, H, J), the study would be longitudinal. Similarly, a study of the 1985 cohort during 1990, 1995, and 2000 (groups B, F, I) at ages 5, 10, and 15, or of the 1990 cohort during 1995

Longitudinal research—the repeated measurement of a group of subjects over a period of years

Year of Birth (cohort)	Age 5	Age 10	Age 15	Age 20
1980	1985 data A	1990 data E	1995 data H	2000 data J
1985	1990 data B	1995 data F	2000 data I	
1990	1995 data C	2000 data G		
1995	2000 data D			

Cross-Sectional Studies
2000 Study: DGIJ
1995 Study: CFH
1990 Study: BE

Longitudinal Studies
Groups AEHJ in 1985, 1990, 1995, and 2000
Groups BFI in 1990, 1995, and 2000
Groups CG in 1995 and 2000

FIGURE 1.3 Research designs.

and 2000 (groups C, G), would be longitudinal as well.

Cross-sectional studies confound age and cohort effects; that is, they fail to differentiate whether differences in age or differences due to time of birth are responsible for change. *Longitudinal studies confound age and time of testing;* that is, they fail to differentiate whether age differences or differences that relate to time of testing are responsible for change.

SEQUENTIAL STUDIES

Sequential study

Cohort-sequential study

A third pattern of research is the **sequential study.** The **cohort-sequential study** is probably the best sequential design for separating the effects of different ages and cohorts. The simplest cohort-sequential study is illustrated by Figure 1.4. Two age groups (10 and 15) representing two cohort groups (born in 1985 and 1980) are measured three different times (1990, 1995, and 2000). By comparing A + B with C + D, age and time measurements are confounded (that is, the effects of each are not sorted out), but cohort effect is eliminated.

By comparing A + C with B + D, cohort and time measurements are confounded (the effect of each is not determined), but age effect is eliminated. *Of all the assumptions that can be made in developmental research, the assumption that time of testing is unimportant may be the most tenable.* If the effect of time of the study is discounted, the effects of age and cohort are sorted out, and they can be meaningfully compared in research design. Of course, the longer the total time span of the study, the greater will be the effect of time of measurement.

ADVANTAGES AND DISADVANTAGES OF RESEARCH DESIGNS

Each type of study design has advantages and disadvantages. The primary purpose of a cross-sectional study is to compare age groups, for example, the social behavior of children at ages 9, 12, and 15 as studied. But this method makes it difficult to determine the exact cause of any detected age differences. For example, if dif-

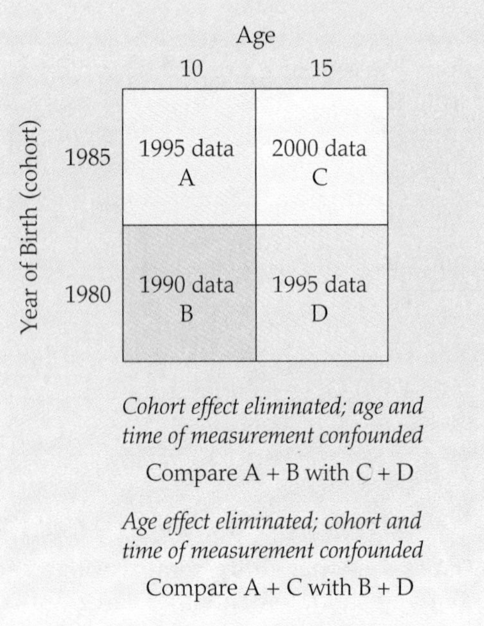

FIGURE 1.4 Cohort-sequential design.

ferences in social behavior are found, are they due to physical maturation, intellectual changes, or learned social differences, with age? Are these same differences present in children of other cultures? What effect does age have on these differences? What cross-sectional studies often attribute to age, may, in fact, be due to cohort or cultural effects.

The chief advantage of the cross-sectional approach is that data for different age groups can be obtained over the same time period, usually a brief one. Therefore, it is easier to obtain information and conclude the study fairly quickly.

A *longitudinal study* periodically compares the same group of people over the years. Obvious difficulties are the amount of time and money necessary to complete the study. In addition, researchers might die or lose interest. And subjects might move, leaving no address, or otherwise become unavailable. Some parents become uninterested in their children's participation over a period of time. There is therefore a selective subject dropout and availability factor: Subjects who tend to perform poorly become less available over time than those who perform well. As time passes, the most confident subjects remain, tending to distort findings. Thus, the combination of random and selective availability factors can easily lead to invalid conclusions (Tennstedt, Dettling, & McKinley, 1992).

The primary advantage of a longitudinal study is that it eliminates cohort effects. Because the same people are studied, change with age or time really is due to these factors.

Cohort-sequential studies come closest to separating differences due to age from those related to cohort effects, but only if you assume that the time of testing has no effect.

CROSS-CULTURAL RESEARCH

In recent years, interest in cross-cultural research has continued to grow. There are many benefits to this growing interest. One important contribution is the documentation of the diverse culturally structured environments in which people develop. Such documentation gives us insight into larger patterns of cultural organization and captures the diversity of human experience. Knowledge of the spectrum of environments for healthy development provides reconsideration of developmental theories

Cross-cultural research gives us knowledge of the diverse environments in which people develop.

FOCUS

Research with Children

The *Society for Research in Child Development* has issued a set of guidelines for research with children (Cooke, 1982). Research on children raises sensitive issues since minor children have a limited ability to give informed consent. *The Belmont Report* of the Department of Health and Human Services identifies three elements of adequate informed consent: *information, comprehension,* and *voluntariness.* Children of very young ages cannot meet the criteria of informed consent. One ethics panel has stated that children age 7 or over should be asked for their consent and should be overruled only if the research promises direct benefit to the child (National Commission for the Protection of Human Biomedical and Behavioral Research, 1978). One research study found that, in general, children of ages 5 to 12 have the capacity to assent meaningfully to participation in research, but that there are substantial problems in guaranteeing that they are able to make this decision freely (Abramovitch, Freedman, Thoden, & Nikolich, 1991). When parents and guardians are empowered to decide whether minors will be used as research subjects, they must decide what is in the best interests of the children. Researchers, too, have a responsibility to proceed objectively and as humanely as possible. They have a responsibility for the welfare of the children (Heatherington, Friedlander, & Johnson, 1989).

that reflect only a middle-class Western way of life (Harkness, 1992).

ETHICAL ISSUES IN RESEARCH

A number of ethical issues are important in human development research. The ethical standards of the *American Psychological Association (APA)* and the *American Sociological Association (ASA)* insist upon two fundamental principles: *informed consent* and *protection from harm* (APA, 1982). Informed consent of adolescents entitles subjects to a complete explanation of the nature, purpose, and methods of the research before the study begins. Subjects also must be told exactly what will happen and what they agree to do if they participate. They must be informed of their right to choose not to participate and of their freedom to withdraw from the research at any time.

Researchers must be careful to minimize physical and psychological stress during the procedures in order to protect their subjects from harm. If subjects are to suffer electrical shock, for example, it should be moderate and necessary. If subjects are to be asked certain questions that will cause emotional stress, questions must be carefully selected and worded, and must be asked in ways to minimize the upset. If abused adolescents are being interviewed, for instance, this may be an extremely stressful experience for them. In any case, interviewers need to take the subjects' stress into account, to ask questions tactfully, and to provide therapeutic help if required.

Protection from harm includes keeping the confidentiality of subjects. Exposure might result in embarrassment, ridicule, or conflict within relationships. Thus, data on individuals may be assigned code numbers and may also be restricted and kept in locked places. All possible means of identifying individuals with the findings of a study should be eliminated.

Universities have special committees to review planned research projects before they are begun. If particular ethical questions arise, the committee may ask the researchers to withdraw their proposal or to modify it to meet required standards.

Summary

1. Child and adolescent development seeks to describe, explain, predict, and influence the changes that take place from conception through adolescence. The ultimate goal of child and adolescent developmental psychology is to help children and adolescents live meaningful, productive lives.
2. Child development may be subdivided into the prenatal period (from conception to birth), infancy and toddlerhood (the first two years), early childhood or preschool period (3 to 5 years), and middle childhood or school-age period (6 to 11 years).
3. Adolescent development extends from approximately 12 to 19 years of age. Early adolescence is from 12 to 14, late adolescence from 15 to 19 years of age.
4. A philosophy of childhood and adolescent development includes the following important elements:

   Development is multidimensional and interdisciplinary and includes four dimensions: physical, cognitive, emotional, and social development.

   Both heredity and environment influence development.

   Development reflects both continuity and discontinuity.

   Development is cumulative, although what happens early is not 100 percent predictive of what happens later.

   Development reflects both stability and change.

   Development is variable, so that not all dimensions of the personality grow at the same rate.

   Development is sometimes cyclical and repetitive.

   Development reflects individual differences.

   Development reflects cultural differences.

   Developmental influences are reciprocal. Children influence caregivers and their environment as well as being influenced by them.
5. Research in human development utilizes scientific methods to obtain information. Both nonexperimental and experimental research methods are used.
6. Data collection methods include naturalistic observation, interviews, questionnaires and checklists, case studies, and standardized testing. The selection of a subject sample representative of the group studied is important in obtaining accurate results.
7. Experimental methods manipulate variables to see how one affects the others. By changing variables, a link between cause and effect is more easily established than in nonexperimental methods. An independent variable is one over which the experimenter has control. A dependent variable is dependent on the independent variable. Correlational studies show the relationship between the independent variables and the dependent variables.
8. In developmental research, experimenters seek to sort out the relative influences of age, cohorts, and time of testing.
9. Research designs are of three basic types: cross-sectional studies, longitudinal studies, and cohort-sequential studies. Each has advantages and disadvantages.
10. Ethical standards governing research insist upon two fundamental principles: informed consent and protection from harm.
11. Research with children raises sensitive issues. For example, to what extent can minor children give informed consent? If they cannot, parents, guardians, and researchers must decide issues according to what is in the best interests of children.

Key Terms

Adolescence *p. 6*
Case studies *p. 17*
Cognitive development *p. 8*
Cohort *p. 19*
Cohort-sequential study *p. 20*
Correlation *p. 18*
Cross-sectional study *p. 19*
Dependent variable *p. 18*
Early childhood *p. 6*
Emotional development *p. 8*
Experimental methods *p. 17*
Independent variable *p. 18*
Infancy *p. 6*
Interviews *p. 15*
Longitudinal research *p. 19*
Middle childhood *p. 6*
Naturalistic observation *p. 15*
Nature *p. 9*
Nurture *p. 9*
Physical development *p. 8*
Prenatal period *p. 6*
Questionnaires *p. 15*
Random sample *p. 17*
Reliability *p. 17*
Representative sample *p. 17*
Sample *p. 17*
Scientific method *p. 14*
Sequential study *p. 20*
Social development *p. 8*
Tests *p. 17*
Validity *p. 17*

Discussion Questions

1. Have you ever known anyone who changed a lot during his or her lifetime? How did the person change? What was the cause of the changes?
2. Can people continue to develop physically, cognitively, emotionally, and socially during their entire lifetime? Why? Why not? What factors may prevent continued development in any of these areas?
3. Do you believe that development is continuous or that it occurs in stages? Give examples.
4. To what extent is your life now partially a product of what has happened to you before? Explain. Have you faced any traumatic or unusual incidents that have changed the course of your life? Describe.
5. In what ways are you the same person today that you were five years ago? Explain with examples. How are you different, and why? Explain.
6. The text says that development is variable, that not all aspects of our lives develop at the same rate. Can you describe a person you know whose personality structure shows uneven development?
7. What aspects of development do you believe are more controlled by heredity, and which are more controlled by environment?
8. If you had to select a subject for a research study, what would it be? What method or methods would you use to obtain information? Who would your subjects be, and how would you select them? Would you prefer a cross-sectional or longitudinal study? Why?

Suggested Readings

Ambert, A. (1992). *The effect of children on parents.* New York: Haworth Press. Children have significant positive and negative effects on parents.

American Psychological Association. (1982). *Ethical principles in the conduct of research with human participants.* Washington, DC: American Psychological Association. A basic guidebook.

Brim, O. G., & Kagan, U. (Eds.). (1980).

Constancy and change in human development. Cambridge, MA: Harvard University Press. A book of readings by experts on how stable or changeable are our lives throughout the life span.

Cohen, D. H., & Stern, V. (1983). *Observing and recording the behavior of young children* (3rd ed.). New York: Teachers College Press.

Eckardt, G., Bringman, W. G., & Sprung, L. (Eds.). (1985). *Contributions to a history of developmental psychology.* Berlin: Morton. A series of articles by experts.

Garbarino, J. (1992). *Children and families in the social environment.* New York: Aldine deGruyter. Emphasizes the development of healthy, normal children and families in social context, utilizing Bronfenbrenner's ecological model.

Irwin, D. M., & Bushnell, M. M. (1980). *Observational strategies of child study.* New York: Holt, Rinehart and Winston. Observational techniques for studying children along with applications in the class situation.

Kagan, J. (1984). *The nature of the child.* New York: Basic Books. Argues against the irreversibility of early experience and emphasizes the capacity to change throughout life.

Kegan, R. (1982). *The evolving self: Problems and process in human development.* Cambridge, MA: Harvard University Press. Humans organize their world in meaningful ways so that their lives make sense to themselves and others.

McClusky, K. A., & Reese, H. W. (Eds.). (1985). *Life-span developmental psychology: Historical and cohort effects.* New York: Academic Press. How historical events and year of birth affect life-span development.

Ray, W. J., & Ravizza, R. (1988). *Methods toward a science of behavior and experience* (3rd ed.). Belmont, CA: Wadsworth. Scientific methods in conducting experimental research and in writing research articles.

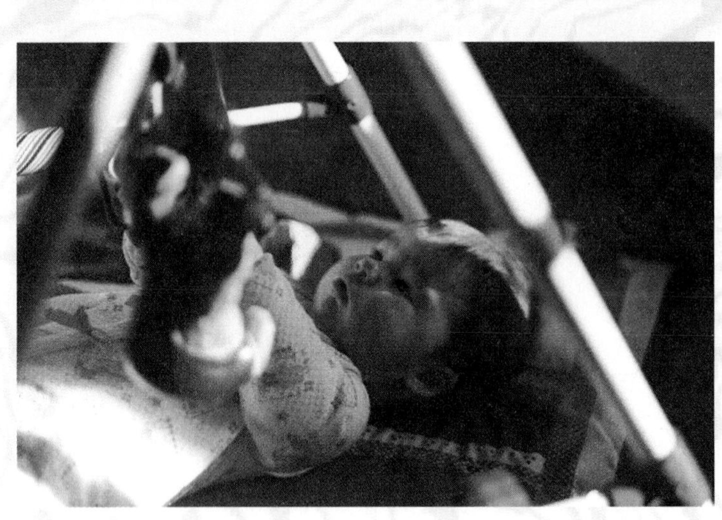

Theories of Development

Chapter 2

The Roles of Theories

One of our human characteristics is that we seek logical explanations of things that happen. We ask "What happened?" or "How did it happen?" or "Why did it happen?" Last summer a house in our neighborhood caught fire. The owner, an elderly gentleman who lived alone, was found dead in his chair in the living room. Apparently he had been asleep and had been overcome by smoke inhalation before he could wake up and get out of the house. Everyone in our neighborhood sought an explanation of what, how, and why it happened. Investigators were called in to make an official report.

We all seem to have been born with a natural curiosity and with logical minds that seek to make sense out of events. Most of us have said at one time or another, "I have a theory about that"—meaning, "I think I have a logical explanation." Human development theories are really one expression of the human tendency to want to explain things. As we've seen, the scientific method involves formulating a problem, developing a hypothesis, testing it, and then drawing conclusions that are stated in the form of a **theory.** *A theory organizes the data, ideas, and hypotheses and states them in coherent, interrelated, general propositions, principles, or laws.* These propositions, principles, or laws are useful in explaining and predicting phenomena, now and in the future. Theories are particularly useful because they look beyond detailed data and give broad, comprehensive views of things.

Theory—a tentative explanation of facts and data that have been observed

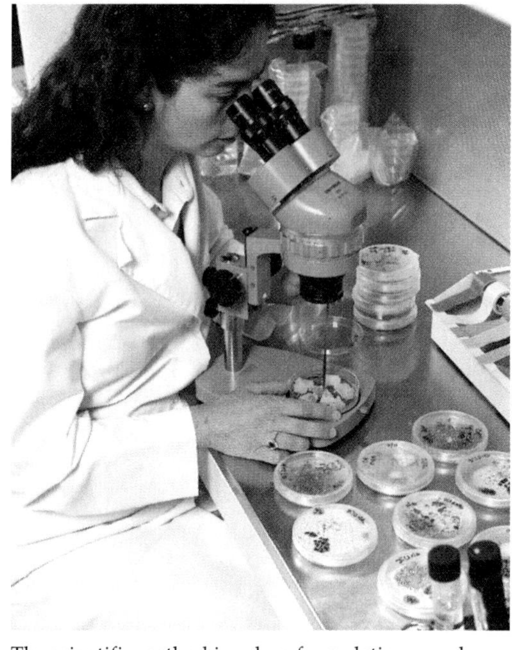

The scientific method involves formulating a problem, developing a hypothesis, testing it, and then drawing conclusions in the form of a theory.

A human development theory may focus on only one aspect of development, such as cognitive development, or may emphasize development of the total self. A theory may focus on only one time period: adolescence, for example, or it may cover the entire life span.

In this chapter, we will examine some of the major theories that researchers have developed to explain human development. The theories may be arranged into five categories: *psychoanalytic theories, learning theories, humanistic theories, cognitive theories,* and *ethological theories.*

Psychoanalytic Theories

Psychoanalytical theory—Freud's theory that the structure of personality is composed of the id, ego, and superego, and that mental health depends on keeping the balance among them

FREUD: PSYCHOANALYTICAL THEORY

Sigmund Freud (1856–1939) was the originator of **psychoanalytical theory** (Freud, 1917). *This theory emphasizes the importance of early childhood experiences and unconscious motivations in influencing behavior.* Many instinctual urges and memories of traumatic experiences are repressed early in life. They are driven out of conscious awareness into the unconscious mind, where they continue to cause anxiety and conflict and to influence behavior.

Freud was a Viennese physician in the Victorian era. He became interested in neu-

Sigmund Freud was the originator of psychoanalytical theory.

rology, the study of the brain, and in nervous disorders. At first, he used *hypnosis* in treating these nervous disorders, but became interested in delving further into his patients' thoughts to uncover the causes of emotional disturbances. In a method he called **free association,** he asked patients to lie down on a couch and to talk about anything that came to mind. Freud sat behind his patients so they couldn't see his facial reactions. His patients would gradually reveal repressed thoughts and urges that were the causes of their conflicts. Freud also used *dream interpretation* to delve into the unconscious.

Freud felt that sexual urges and aggressive instincts and drives were the primary determinants of behavior. The individual was motivated by the **pleasure principle,** the desire to achieve maximum pleasure and to avoid pain. However, sexual and aggressive instincts put people in direct conflict with social mores, especially during the Victorian era, when prudishness and social convention were emphasized. The conflict within the individual between these instinctual urges and societal expectations was the primary cause of emotional disturbances and illnesses.

In outlining his theory, Freud developed an explanation of the basic structure of personality (Singer, 1984). His theory states that *personality is composed of three components: the id, ego, and superego.* The **id** is present from birth and consists of the basic instincts and urges that seek immediate gratification, regardless of the consequences. Left unchecked, the id places the individual in deep conflict with other people and society.

The second element of personality structure is the **ego,** which begins to develop during the first year of life. The ego consists of mental processes, the powers of reasoning and common sense, that seek to help the id find expression without getting into trouble. The ego operates according to a *reality principal.*

The third element of personality structure is the **superego,** which develops as a result of parental and societal teaching. It represents those social values that are incorporated into the personality structure of the child. It becomes the conscience that seeks to influence behavior to conform to social expectations. The id and superego are often in conflict, causing guilt, anxiety, and disturbances. The ego strives to minimize the conflict by keeping the instinctual urges and societal prohibitions in balance.

According to Freud, one of the ways people relieve anxiety and conflict is by employing **defense mechanisms,** which are mental devices that distort reality to minimize psychic pain. Defense mechanisms are employed unconsciously and become pathological only when used in excess to impair effective functioning. The defense mechanisms include the following (Clark, 1991):

Repression—dealing with unacceptable impulses by pushing them down into the unconscious mind, where they continue to cause conflict and exert powerful influences over our behavior.

Regression—reverting to earlier, childish forms of behavior when confronted with anxiety. For example, an older child reverts to bed wetting or to thumb sucking.

Sublimation—replacing distasteful, unacceptable behavior with behavior that is socially acceptable. For example, a man filled with anger and hostility and aggression participates in competitive sports, lest he explode into violence (Kohn, 1988).

Displacement—transferring strong emotions from a source of frustration and venting them on another object or person

Ego—the rational part of the mind, which uses the reality principle to satisfy the id

Superego—the socially induced moral restrictions that strive to keep the id in check and help the individual attain perfection

Free association—a method of treatment in which the patient is encouraged to say anything that comes to mind, allowing unconscious thoughts to slip out

Defense mechanisms—according to Freud, unconscious strategies used by the ego to protect itself from disturbance and to discharge tension

Pleasure principle—the motivation of the id to seek pleasure and avoid pain, regardless of the consequences

Id—the inborn instinctual urges that a person seeks to satisfy

who becomes the scapegoat. An example would be a child who becomes angry at her parents and takes out her hostile feelings on a pet dog.

Reaction formation—acting completely opposite of the way one feels to hide unacceptable feelings or tendencies. A person might crusade against child sexual abuse (pedophilia) because he or she has such tendencies.

Denial—protecting oneself from anxiety by refusing to acknowledge that a situation exists. One example might be to refuse to acknowledge that a child is mentally retarded.

Rationalization—making up excuses for behavior that would otherwise be unacceptable.

Electra complex—according to Freud, the unconscious love and sexual desire of female children for their fathers

Freud not only developed a theory of personality structure, but he outlined a **psychosexual theory** of development as well. According to Freud, the center of sensual sensitivity, or *erogenous zones*, shifts from one body zone to another as children mature. The stages of psychosexual development according to Freud are as follows:

Psychosexual theory—Freud's theory in which the center of sensual sensitivity shifts from one body zone to another in stages as children mature

Oral stage—first year of life, during which the child's chief source of sensual gratification centers around the mouth. The infant's chief source of pleasure and gratification is through sucking, chewing, and biting. Such activity increases security and relieves tension.

Anal stage—ages 2 and 3, during which the child's principal source of greatest pleasure is through anal activity. This is the age when the child becomes very interested in eliminative functions, toileting activities, and training.

Phallic stage—ages 4 and 5. The center of pleasure shifts to the genitals as children explore their bodies through self-manipulation.

Fixated—according to Freud, remaining at a particular psychosexual stage because of too much or too little gratification

Freud also taught that boys experience *castration anxiety* and that girls develop *penis envy* because of a lack of phallus. Freud said that penis envy in girls becomes a major source of what he termed women's sense of inferiority (Simon, 1988). Also, during this period boys develop an **Oedipal complex** and fall in love with their mothers, becoming jealous of their fathers as they compete for their mother's love and affection (Thomas, 1991). Gradually, they repress their incestuous feelings and begin to identify with their father during the next stage of development. Meanwhile, during this period, girls develop an **Electra complex** and fall in love with their fathers, becoming jealous of their mother as they compete for their father's love and affection. They also blame their mother for the fact that they have no penis. They are ready for the next stage when they are able to repress their incestuous feelings for their father and identify with their mother.

Oedipal complex—according to Freud, the unconscious love and sexual desire of male children for their mothers

Latency stage—age 6 to puberty, during which time the child represses sexual urges and devotes time and energy to learning and physical and social activities. The source of pleasure shifts from self to other persons as the child becomes interested in cultivating the friendship of others.

Genital stage—begins with sexual maturation, after which the young person seeks sexual stimulation and satisfaction from a member of the opposite sex. This stage continues through adulthood.

Freud said that if children receive too much or too little gratification at any given stage, they become **fixated** at that stage, so their psychosexual development is incomplete. Thus, if children receive too little oral gratification during that stage, they may continue to try to find oral gratification later in life through smoking, eating, kissing, drinking, or chewing. Children who become fixated at the latency stage seek to repress sexual feelings and continue to identify with the same-sex parent, never moving on to make mature heterosexual adjustments (Emde, 1992).

ERIKSON: PSYCHOSOCIAL THEORY

Psychosocial theory—the term used to describe Erikson's stage theory of development in which there are psychosocial tasks to master at each level of development

Erik Erikson (b. 1902) studied under a Freudian group in Germany before coming to the United States in 1933. He became a U.S. citizen and taught at Harvard University. Erikson disagreed with Freud on several points. For example, he felt that Freud placed too much emphasis on the sexual basis for behavior. In contrast to Freud, Erikson concluded in his **psychosocial theory** that there are other psychosocial moti-

PARENTING ISSUES

The Overly Developed Superego

Five-year-old Stephen was a very quiet, shy, inhibited child. In kindergarten he usually sat in a chair, watching the other children play. When given finger paint, the typical 5-year-old will put the fingers in, then the whole hand, then the other hand, then smear it all over the paper, and if not supervised, may smear it over the table, wipe it on the clothes, or on the clothes of another child nearby.

In one-half hour, Stephen had barely put the end of one finger in the paint and had quickly withdrawn it. Stephen was obviously a very inhibited child.

The teacher discussed the situation with the parents. The parents were very strict and were pleased that Stephen was such a "good boy," but they were willing to admit that perhaps they had been too strict in disciplining him. At the teacher's suggestion, both the parents and teacher agreed to encourage more initiative and spontaneity.

A year later Stephen was more relaxed and far happier, willing to try new things and to enter into all activities along with the other children.

Keeping the id and superego in balance is not always easy. Some children are undercontrolled; others, like Stephen, overcontrolled with a too highly developed superego. Either extreme can cause problems for individuals who need to learn to consider both their own desires and needs and those of other individuals as well. (Author's counseling notes)

vations and needs that become the driving forces in human development and behavior. Erikson accepted Freud's emphasis on early experiences but rejected Freud's neglect of the adult years (Erikson, 1982). Also, Erikson rejected Freud's cynical view of human nature and his belief that humans are unable to deal with their problems. Erikson said that humans can resolve their difficulties and conflicts as they arise.

Erik Erikson developed a psychosocial theory that divided the developmental process into eight stages.

Erikson divided human development into eight stages and said that the individual has a psychosocial task to master during each stage. The confrontation with each task produces conflict with two possible outcomes. If the task during each stage is mastered, a positive quality is built into the personality and further development takes place. If the task is not mastered, and the conflict is unsatisfactorily resolved, the ego is damaged because a negative quality is incorporated in it. The overall task of the individual is to acquire a positive identity as he or she moves from one stage to the next.

The positive solution of each task and its negative counterpart are shown in Figure 2.1 for each period (Erikson, 1950, 1959). The stages are as follows:

Trust vs. distrust (0 to 1 year). Infants learn that they can trust caregivers for sustenance, protection, comfort, and affection, or they develop a distrust because their needs are not met.

Autonomy vs. shame and doubt (1 to 2 years). Children gain control over eliminative functions, learn to feed themselves, are allowed to play alone and to explore the world (within safe limits), and develop some degree of independence, or if too restricted by caregivers, develop a sense of shame and doubt about their own abilities.

Initiative vs. guilt (3 to 5 years). Children's motor and intellectual abilities continue to increase; they continue to explore the

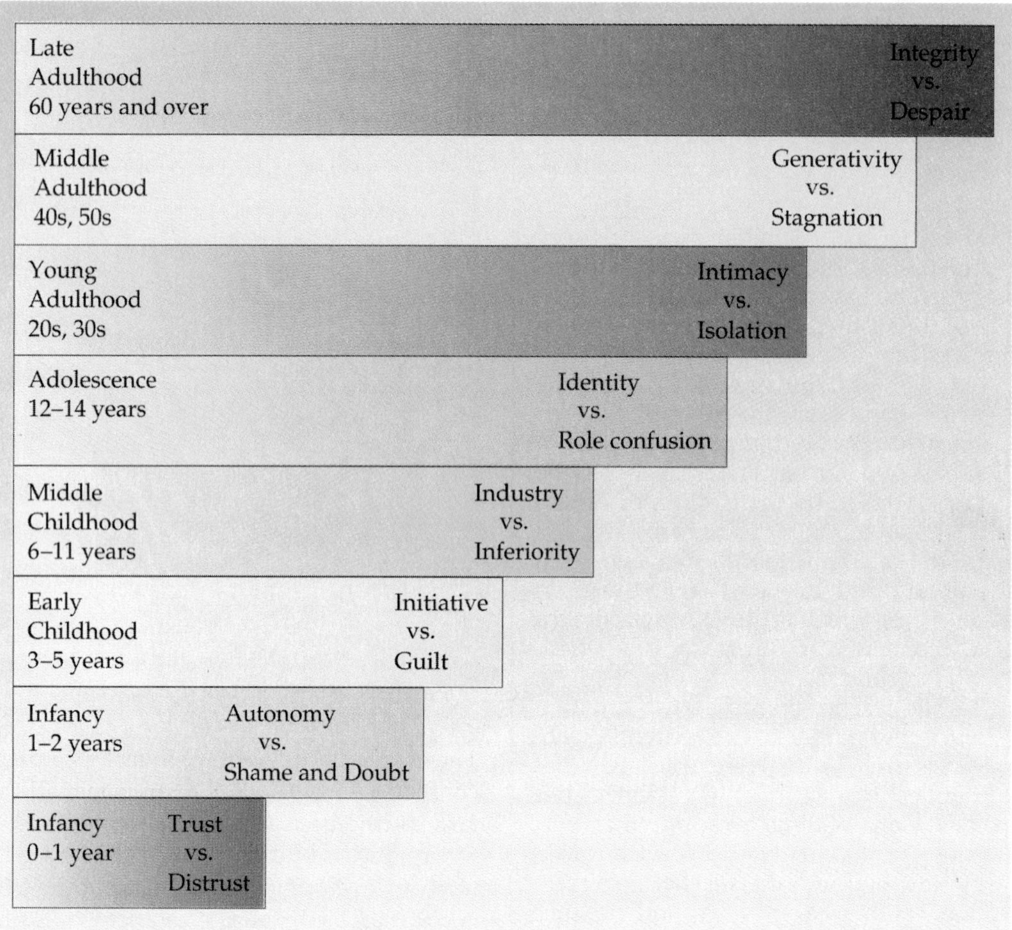

FIGURE 2.1 Erikson's eight developmental stages.

environment and to experience many new things, assuming more responsibility for initiating and carrying out plans. Caregivers who cannot accept children's developing initiative instill a feeling of guilt over misbehavior.

Industry vs. inferiority (6 to 11 years). Children learn to meet the demands of home and school, and develop a feeling of self-worth through accomplishment and interaction with others, or they come to feel inferior in relation to others.

Identity vs. role confusion (12 years to 19 years). Adolescents develop a strong sense of self, or become confused about their identity and their roles in life.

Intimacy vs. isolation (young adulthood: 20s and 30s). Young adults develop close relationships with others or remain isolated from meaningful relationships with others.

Generativity vs. stagnation (middle adulthood: 40s and 50s). Middle adults assume responsible, adult roles in the community, at work, and in teaching and guiding the next generation, or they become personally impoverished, self-centered, and stagnant (McAdams & de St. Aubin, 1992).

Integrity vs. despair (late adulthood: 60 and over). Late adults evaluate their lives, and accept them for what they are, or they despair because they cannot find meaning in their lives.

Table 2.1 shows a comparison between Freud's and Erikson's stages of development.

EVALUATION OF PSYCHOANALYTICAL THEORIES

Freud's psychoanalytical theory is an influential one (Hofer, 1981). His emphasis on unconscious motivations and ego defense mechanisms has been particularly valuable for psychotherapists in gaining insight into the mental health or illnesses of their

TABLE 2.1
COMPARISON OF FREUD'S AND ERIKSON'S STAGES OF DEVELOPMENT

Approximate Age	*Freud*	*Erikson*
Birth–1 year	Oral Stage	Trust vs. Distrust
1–2 years	Anal Stage	Autonomy vs. Shame and Doubt
3–5 years	Phallic Stage	Initiative vs. Guilt
6–11 years	Latency Stage	Industry vs. Inferiority
12–Young Adulthood	Genital Stage	Identity vs. Role Confusion
Early Adulthood	Genital Stage	Intimacy vs. Isolation
Middle Adulthood	Genital Stage	Generativity vs. Stagnation
Late Adulthood	Genital Stage	Integrity vs. Despair

clients. Freud's method of treatment was unique, and became the foundation for subsequent development of a variety of treatment techniques. Freud also made parents and professionals realize how important the experiences of the early years can be. His emphasis on environmental influences placed the responsibility for development directly into the hands of all caregivers of children.

Freud's psychosexual theory of development is limited in scope, with an overemphasis (according to some) on sexual motivations as the basis of behavior, and the resolution of psychosexual conflict as the key to healthy behavior. Freud developed his theory on the basis of treatment of adult patients, so the theory was not tested on children. In fact, much of Freud's ideas are not easily tested by research. Freud also had a very cynical view of human nature that certainly does not explain the motivations of countless millions who act out of genuine care and concern.

Freud has been criticized recently because he suppressed his original belief that his patients' parents had maltreated and sexually abused them (Masson, 1984; Tribich & Klein, 1981). He claimed instead that children are naturally seductive, that as victims they are to blame, a point of view that has encouraged society to overlook the extent of child abuse.

Erikson's theory is much broader than Freud's, focusing on the importance of both maturational and environmental factors in development and on the importance of a variety of psychological motivations for behavior. In addition, Erikson's theory encompasses the entire life span, outlining the stages that occur. Erikson also emphasized individual responsibility during each stage of development and the opportunity to achieve a positive and healthy resolution of the identity crisis. In Erikson's view, it is the ego and not the id that is the life force of human development (Hamachek, 1988). Erikson has also been criticized for his antifemale bias and his failure to take into account different social and cultural influences in the lives of men and women. Erikson's descriptions of development are validated by a considerable body of research findings.

Learning Theories

BEHAVIORISM

The theory of development known as **behaviorism** emphasizes the role of environmental influences in molding behavior. For the behaviorist, *behavior becomes the sum total of learned or conditioned responses to stimuli.* Such a view is labeled **mechanistic** or **deterministic.**

Behaviorists are not interested in unconscious motives for behavior. Furthermore, they see learning as progressing in

Behaviorism—the school of psychology that emphasizes that behavior is modified through conditioning

Mechanistic or deterministic—as applied to behaviorism, a criticism that behavior is a result of mindless reactions to stimuli

Pavlov discovered how learning takes place through classical conditioning.

Classical conditioning—a form of learning through association, in which a previously neutral stimulus is paired with an unconditioned stimulus to stimulate a conditioned response that is similar to the unconditioned response

Conditioning—a simple process of learning

a continuous manner, rather than in a sequence of stages, as in psychoanalytical theory.

The process of learning, according to behaviorist theory, is called **conditioning.** There are two types of conditioning: classical conditioning and operant conditioning.

PAVLOV: CLASSICAL CONDITIONING

The Russian physiologist Ivan Pavlov (1849–1936) first discovered the link between stimulus and response. He was doing research on salivation in dogs and noticed that a dog would begin to salivate not only at the sight of food, but also at the sound of the approaching attendant. The dog began to associate the sound of the approaching attendant with being fed.

Pavlov then began a series of experiments to test what was happening. He presented a clicking metronome to the dog, then blew a small amount of meat powder into the dog's mouth to elicit salivation. Eventually, after some repetition, he found that the sound of the metronome alone elicited salivation. The dog began to associate the sound of the metronome with the subsequent presentation of food. The best results were obtained when the metronome preceded the food powder by about half a second. This type of learning through association has been called **classical conditioning.** Figure 2.2 shows the apparatus used by Pavlov.

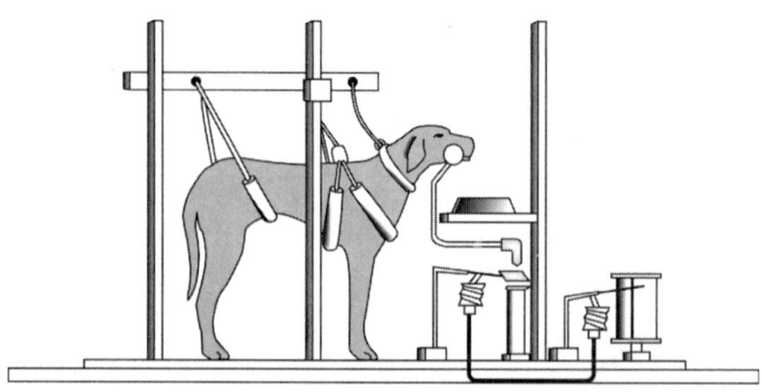

FIGURE 2.2 Apparatus used by Pavlov in his studies of conditioning.

Learning through classical conditioning always involves a series of stimuli and responses: an unconditioned stimulus (UCS), an unconditioned response (UCR), a conditioned stimulus (CS), and a conditioned response (CR). In the case of Pavlov and his dogs, the stimuli and responses were as follows:

Unconditioned stimulus (UCS)—was the meat powder in the dog's mouth that elicited the response of salivation without any learning.

Unconditioned response (UCR)—was salivation in response to meat powder in the mouth, an inborn reaction

Conditioned stimulus (CS)—was the metronome, which, when associated with the meat powder, acquired the ability to elicit a response

Conditioned response (CR)—was salivation in response to the metronome alone.

Classical conditioning is a form of learning because an old behavior can be elicited by a new stimulus.

Some years later in the United States, John Watson (1878–1958) and his associate Rosalie Rayner tested this idea by teaching fear to a young child named Albert. Albert was first allowed to play with a white laboratory rat and was not in the least afraid of it. Then Watson began striking a steel bar with a hammer just behind Albert's head as he played with the rat. The loud noise made Albert cry. After seven such pairings, Albert showed fear of the rat when it was placed near him. He had been conditioned to fear it. Furthermore, his fear responses became generalized; that is, Albert became afraid of other white, furry objects as well. The conduct of this experiment raises some serious ethical issues about research with children and would not be permitted today

(Watson & Rayner, 1920). Watson made no effort to extinguish Albert's fears after the experiment was over. Nevertheless, this example illustrates how a series of responses may be conditioned in children.

As a result of his experiments, Watson came to feel that conditioning was the sole process responsible for development. He felt that experience and the environment were the factors that shaped the human behavioral repertoire (F. D. Horowitz, 1992). Human behavior was a result of learning.

SKINNER: OPERANT CONDITIONING

The second type of conditioning is **operant conditioning,** which is learning from the consequences of behavior. According to B. F. Skinner (1904–1990), who originated the term, our behavior operates on the environment to produce consequences: either rewards or punishments. The nature of the consequences determines the probability of the behavior's reoccurrence. Put very simply, if our behavior results in a reward (a **positive reinforcement**), the probability that the behavior will reoccur is increased. If our behavior results in punishment, the consequence decreases the probability that the behavior will reoccur. In summary, *operant conditioning is learning in which the consequences of behavior lead to changes in the probability of that behavior's occurrence.* This principle has numerous applications in child rearing and in adult learning (Skinner, 1953).

B. F. Skinner originated the concept of operant conditioning.

In a classic study in the 1960s, a group of preschool teachers decided to help a young girl overcome her shyness with other children (Allen, Hart, Buell, Harris, & Wolf, 1964). The teachers were concerned that the girl spent too little time playing with other children and too much time with adults, so they decided to give her praise only when she was playing with another child. When she was doing anything else, they paid very little attention to her. As a result of the positive reinforcement of the praise and attention, the little girl's frequency of playing with other children increased considerably.

Many kinds of behavior can be encouraged with positive reinforcement. Even

Operant conditioning—learning from the consequences of behavior so that the consequences change the probability of the behavior's reoccurrence

Positive reinforcement—a consequence of behavior that leads to an increase in the probability of its occurrence

PARENTING ISSUES

Learned Helplessness in Children

Unfortunately, undesirable behavior can also be learned by reinforcement. One of the things that can be learned is helplessness. If, for example, children who do poorly in school learn to attribute their failure to external factors rather than to lack of effort, they have learned helplessness and tend to show even more decrements in performance (Licht & Dweck, 1984). Fincham, Hokoda, and Sanders (1989) found a relationship between learned helplessness in third grade (as measured by lack of effort) and achievement test scores in the fifth grade. Once students begin to get an idea that they can't do anything about their poor academic performance, they quit trying, and of course, this lowers their test scores even more. Their concept of being unable to do the work encourages their lack of motivation, which further lowers their performance scores, thus reinforcing their poor self-concept.

pain can be a learned response. After minor surgery at the Johns Hopkins Children's Center, 2-year-old Adam was woozy but ready to go home. The surgeon told his mother: "Be cheerful and optimistic, compliment him when he moves around without whimpering or crying. Don't ask him if it hurts. Give him a baby aspirin only if he really complains about pain. But he won't."

After a full night's sleep Adam toddled downstairs for breakfast—slowly, but without complaints of pain (Rodgers, 1988, p. 26).

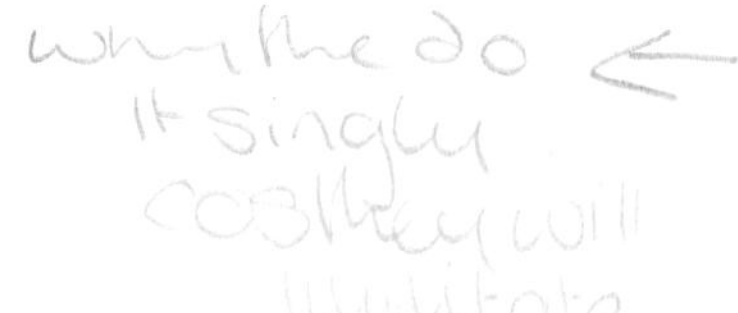

BANDURA: SOCIAL LEARNING THEORY

Social learning theory—a view of learning that emphasizes that behavior is learned through social interaction with other persons

Social learning theorists accept the view of behaviorists that behavior is learned and that development is influenced by the environment, but they reject the mechanistic view that altered behavior is a mindless response to stimuli. **Social learning theory** emphasizes the role of both cognition and environmental influences in development. We are all thinking creatures with some powers of self determination, not just robots that show B response when A stimulus is introduced. We can think about what is happening, evaluate it, and alter our responses accordingly.

Vicarious reinforcement—observing the positive consequences of another's behavior increases the probability of the behavior in the observer

Vicarious punishment—Observing the punishment of another's behavior decreases the probability of the same behavior in the observer

Modeling—learning through observing and imitating the behavior of others

Albert Bandura (1977, 1986), Stanford University psychologist, is one of the most important contemporary exponents of social learning theory. Bandura says that children learn by observing the behavior of others and imitating and **modeling** their behavior (Grusec, 1992). Thus, a child may watch another play baseball: how to hold the bat and swing it, how to run the bases, how to catch and throw a ball. The child learns the fundamentals of the game through watching others. When given the opportunity, he or she then tries to imitate, or model, what was seen. Children are great imitators: They imitate parents caring for the baby; imitate them mowing the lawn; or imitate them in learning how to eat, talk, walk, or dress.

Albert Bandura developed social learning theory.

In his classic study, Bandura let children observe a film in which an adult kicked, hit, and sat on a blow-up Bobo doll (Bandura, Ross, & Ross, 1963). When the children were placed in a playroom with a Bobo doll, they were significantly more aggressive toward the Bobo doll than a group of children who had not seen the film. They learned to act more aggressively through modeling.

Once modeled, behavior can be strengthened or weakened, through rewards or punishments. Behavior can also be influenced by seeing others rewarded or punished. Suppose, for example, the children had seen the adult rewarded for hitting the Bobo doll. Their own aggressive behavior would be increased through **vicarious reinforcement.** If the adult's aggressive behavior had been punished, the children's similar behavior would decrease because of **vicarious punishment.** So children learn to behave both by modeling and by observing the consequences of their own behavior and the behavior of others.

EVALUATION OF LEARNING THEORIES

Learning theorists have contributed much to the understanding of human development. Their emphasis on the role of environmental influences in shaping behavior patterns has put the responsibility for creating positive environments for child development directly in the hands of parents, teachers, and other care givers. The principles of social learning through modeling and reinforcement have also made adults very aware of the example they set in teaching children and youth. When psychologists concluded that much behavior is caused and learned, they began to develop many *behavioral modification* programs to

LIVING ISSUES

Racial Prejudice

One good example of social learning through observation, imitation, and modeling is the development of racial prejudice. Children are not born prejudiced against those of other races. They do begin to be aware of racial differences at a young age. Some 3-year-olds and the majority of 5-year-olds can identify racial differences between blacks and whites (Branch & Newcombe, 1986). By 8 years of age, they can label themselves as a member of a particular ethnic group (Spencer & Markstrom-Adams, 1990). But becoming aware of one's ethnic identity and that of others doesn't lead to racial prejudice and discrimination unless the child is exposed to prejudice as modeled by other people. If a young boy hears his father ridicule blacks, his exposure to his father's attitude is likely to affect his attitude toward blacks. If the boy then goes to school and hears disparaging remarks about blacks made by his peers, prejudicial attitudes will be strengthened. This creates problems for minority children who must reconcile their own self-image with the unpleasant stereotypes and prejudices that they encounter. They learn that their differences make them unwelcome and are held against them.

Because racial prejudices permeate our whole society, children gradually absorb the cultural attitudes of those around them as the children get older. One study in California found that children in older grades were less likely to have a friend of a different race than were younger children. The reason is that children exert pressure upon one another to avoid friendships with those of other groups (Hallinan & Teixeira, 1987). Prejudices can be partly minimized by promoting positive interracial contacts and by desegregation in schools at early ages and in neighborhoods (Howes & Wu, 1990).

eliminate problem behaviors such as phobias, explosive tempers, compulsions, or drug addiction. Behaviorist approaches to treating problem behaviors are among the most successful of the treatment approaches. They are based on a very optimistic view of the ability to control and change behavior.

Social learning theories have been criticized for leaving out the role of unconscious, psychodynamic factors and of underlying feelings in influencing behavior. As a result, social learning theorists tend to focus on surface behavior and to deemphasize the search for causes. They also neglect the role of biology and maturation in development. In spite of these criticisms, learning theories have contributed much to the overall understanding of human development.

Humanistic Theories

Humanistic theory—psychological theory that emphasizes the ability of individuals to make the right choices and to reach their full potential

Holistic view—emphasizes the functioning of the total individual to try to grow, improve, and reach his or her full potential

Humanistic theory has been described as the third force in modern psychology. It rejects both the Freudian determinism of instincts and the environmental determinism of learning theory. Humanists have a very positive, optimistic view of human nature. The humanistic view states that *humans are free agents with superior ability to use symbols and to think in abstract terms.* Thus, people are able to make intelligent choices, to be responsible for their actions, and to realize their full potential as self-actualized persons. Humanists hold a **holistic view** of human development, which sees each person as a whole and unique being of independent worth. In the holistic view, a person is more than a collection of drives, instincts, and learned experiences. Three of the most famous leaders of humanistic psychology were Charlotte Buhler (1893–1974), Abraham Maslow (1908–1970), and Carl Rogers (1902–1987).

BUHLER: DEVELOPMENTAL PHASE THEORY

Charlotte Buhler, a Viennese psychologist, was the first president of the Association of Humanistic Psychology. Buhler rejected the contention of psychoanalysts that restoring psychological *homeostasis* (equilibrium) through release of tensions is the goal of human beings. According to Buhler's theory, *the real goal of human beings is the fulfillment they can attain by accomplishment in themselves and in the world* (Buhler, 1935). The basic human tendency is **self-actualization,** or self-realization, so that the peak experiences of life come through creativity. Buhler emphasized the active role that humans play through their own initiative in fulfilling goals.

Self-actualization—according to Buhler, the drive of individuals to try to grow, improve, and reach their full potential

Buhler (1935) analyzed 400 biographies of individuals from various nations, classes, and vocations, plus additional data from clinical interviews. Three types of data were collected: the external events surrounding a person's life, the internal reactions to these events, and the accomplishments and production of each person. From these data, Buhler outlined five phases of the life span and showed the parallels between biological and psychological development during each phase (Buhler & Massarik, 1968). Table 2.2 illustrates the phases outlined by Buhler (1935). In the last phase of life, most human beings evaluate their total existence in terms of fulfillment or failure.

MASLOW: HIERARCHY OF NEEDS THEORY

Abraham Maslow was one of the most influential leaders in humanistic psychology. He was born into an Orthodox Jewish family in New York, and earned his Ph.D. in psychology from Columbia University in 1934. According to him, human behavior can be explained as motivation to satisfy needs. Maslow arranged human needs into five categories: *physiological needs, safety needs, love and belongingness needs, esteem needs,* and *self-actualization needs* (Maslow, 1970). Figure 2.3 shows the hierarchy of needs as arranged by Maslow.

TABLE 2.2
BUHLER'S DEVELOPMENTAL PHASES OF LIFE

Phase	*Development*
Phase One: 0 to 15 Years	Progressive biological growth; child at home; life centers around narrow interest, school, family
Phase Two: 16 to 27 Years	Continued biological growth, sexual maturity; expansion of activities, self-determination; leaves family, enters into independent activities and personal relations
Phase Three: 28 to 47 Years	Biological stability; culmination period; most fruitful period of professional and creative work; most personal and social relationships
Phase Four: 48 to 62 Years	Loss of reproductive functions, decline in abilities; decrease in activities; personal, family, economic losses; transition to this phase marked by psychological crises; period of introspection
Phase Five: 63 Years and over	Biological decline, increased sickness; retirement from profession; decrease in socialization, but increase in hobbies, individual pursuits; period of retrospection; feeling of fulfillment or failure

Adapted from "The Curve of Life as Studied in Biographies" by C. Buhler, 1935, *Journal of Applied Psychology, 19,* pp. 405–409.

Abraham Maslow said that human behavior can be explained as motivation to satisfy needs.

In Maslow's view, our first concern as human beings is to satisfy basic needs for survival: food, water, protection from harm. Only when these needs are satisfied can we direct our energy to more exclusively human needs: for love, acceptance, and belonging. The satisfaction of these needs makes possible our concern about self-esteem: We need to gain recognition, approval, and competence. And finally, if we grow up well-fed, safe, loved, and respected, we are more likely to become self-actualized persons who have fulfilled our potential. According to Maslow, *self-actualization is the highest need, and the culmination of life.*

Like other humanists, Maslow was very optimistic about human potential: "Healthy children enjoy growing up and moving forward, gaining new skills, capacities, and powers. . . . In the normal development of the healthy child . . . if he is given a full choice, he will choose what is good for his growth" (Maslow, 1968).

ROGERS: PERSONAL GROWTH THEORY

Carl Rogers was raised in a very religious family in the midwest and became a Protestant minister, graduating from Union Theological Seminary in New York (Rogers, 1961). During his career as a minister, Rogers became more and more interested in counseling and therapy as a means of ministering to people with problems, for whom he developed a specialized form of therapy

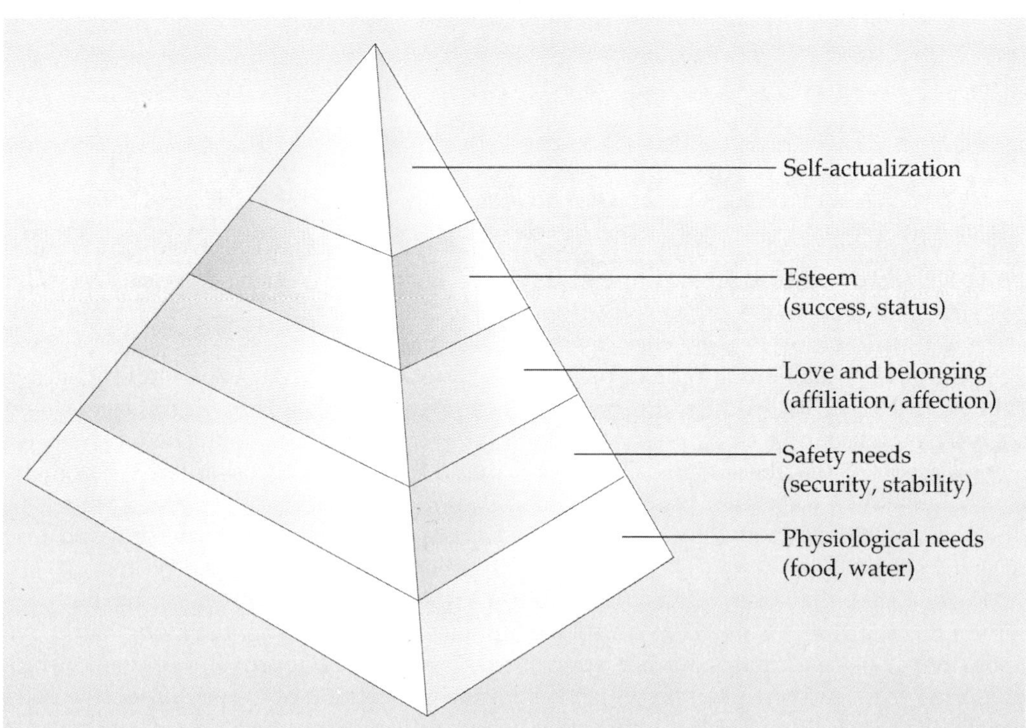

FIGURE 2.3 Maslow's hierarchy of needs.

FOCUS

The Self-Actualized Person

There are a number of characteristics of a self-actualized person as described by Maslow (1971). They include the following:

- Realistic orientation
- Self-acceptance and acceptance of others and the natural world as they are
- Spontaneity
- Problem-centered rather than self-centered
- Air of detachment and need for privacy
- Autonomous and independent
- Fresh rather than stereotyped appreciation of people and things
- Generally has had profound mystical or spiritual, though not necessarily religious, experiences
- Identification with humankind and a strong social interest
- Tendency to have strong, intimate relationships with a few special, loved people rather than superficial relationships with many people
- Democratic values and attitudes
- No confusion of means with ends
- Philosophical rather than hostile sense of humor
- High degree of creativity
- Resistance to cultural conformity
- Transcendence of environment rather than always coping with it

From: A. Maslow (1971). *The Farther Reaches of Human Nature.* © 1971 by Bertha G. Maslow.

Client-centered therapy—Rogers's approach to humanistic therapy, in which the discussion focuses on the client's thoughts and feelings and the therapist creates an atmosphere of acceptance

Conditional positive regard—giving love, praise, and acceptance only if the individual conforms to parental or social standards

Unconditional positive regard—giving acceptance and appreciation of the individual regardless of socially unacceptable behavior

called **client-centered therapy** (Rogers, 1951). His theory is based on the humanistic principle that if people are given freedom and emotional support to grow, they can develop into fully functioning human beings. Without criticism or direction, but encouraged by the accepting and understanding environment of the therapeutic situation, people will solve their own problems and develop into the kind of individuals they wish to become.

Rogers said that each of us has two selves: the self that we perceive ourselves to be (the "I" or "me" that is our perception of our *real self*), and our *ideal self* (which we would like to be). Rogers (1961) taught that each of us is a victim of **conditional positive regard** that others show us. We can't have the love and approval of parents or others unless we conform to rigid parental and social standards. We are told what we must do and think. We are criticized, called names, rejected, or punished when we don't live up to the standards of others. Too often we fail, so we develop low self-esteem, we devalue our true self, and lose sight of who we really are.

Rogers said that when we have a very poor self-image, or are behaving badly, we need the love, approval, companionship, and support of others even more. We need **unconditional positive regard,** not because

The humanist Carl Rogers developed client-centered therapy.

we deserve it, but because we are human beings of worth and dignity. With it, we can find self-worth and the ability to achieve our ideal self. Without unconditional positive regard we cannot overcome our faults and become fully functioning persons (Rogers, 1980).

Rogers taught that the healthy individual, the fully functioning person, is one who has achieved a congruence between the real self and ideal self, a situation that results in freedom from internal conflict and anxiety. When there is a merger between what people perceive themselves to be and what they want to be, they are able to accept themselves, be themselves, and live as themselves without conflict.

EVALUATION OF HUMANISTIC THEORIES

Humanists teach people to believe in themselves and to assume responsibility for developing their full potential. They also emphasize that people have very real human needs that must be met for growth and development. Adults are also taught to respect the uniqueness of each child. This places an obligation to meet these needs on those who are responsible for directing the development of growing children.

Humanists are sometimes criticized for having a view of human nature that is too optimistic. Children don't always choose what is best for them. They need some direction and guidance. Nevertheless,

LIVING ISSUES

Female Empowerment

The feminist movement has been concerned with the struggle of women to free themselves from male domination, to win equal rights and recognition as persons in their own right (McWhirter, 1991). The traditional concept of power describes the effort to gain control over others, so that the increase in power for one leads to a decrease in power for the other. This usually leads to inequality, in dominance and submission, in the stronger prevailing over the weaker. The newest concept of female empowerment involves the process of gaining control over one's own life, not by seeking to dominate males, but through the development of one's capacities, skills, and abilities (Lips, 1991). Through such development, women use professional training to free themselves of any feelings of inferiority or submissive behavior. Along with assertiveness training, they develop concrete skills to use in the work force.

Just as important, this newer concept means recognizing that the feminine qualities of sensitivity and understanding that caused women to be labeled as the weaker sex are really strengths that enable them to relate to others and to solve problems in relationships. Women's power rests partly in their ability to be nurturers, to support the growth of others by promoting family cohesion and stability. Women's care of children and the elderly and their emotional support of the entire family is being increasingly recognized as the cement that holds the fabric of our society together.

humanism has exerted a very positive influence on the whole mental health movement, especially in relation to counseling and therapy.

Cognitive Theories

Cognition—the act of knowing

Adaptation—adjustment to new conditions or situations

Assimilation

Accommodation

Cognition is the act or process of knowing. There are three basic approaches to understanding cognition. One is the *psychometric approach,* which measures quantitative changes in intelligence as people mature. The second approach is the *Piagetian approach,* which emphasizes the qualitative changes in the way people think as they develop. The third approach is the *information-processing view,* which examines the progressive steps, actions, and operations that take place when people receive, perceive, remember, think about, and use information. The Piagetian and information-processing approaches are discussed here in relation to developmental theory. The psychometric approach is discussed in Chapters 7, 12, and 17.

PIAGET: COGNITIVE DEVELOPMENT

Jean Piaget (1896–1980) was a Swiss developmental psychologist who became interested in the growth of human cognitive capacities. He began working in Alfred Binet's Paris laboratory, where modern intelligence testing originated. Piaget began to explore how children grow and develop in their thinking abilities. He became more interested in how children reach conclusions than in whether their answers were correct. Instead of asking questions and scoring them right or wrong, Piaget questioned children to find the logic behind their answers. Through painstaking observation of his own and other children, he constructed his theory of cognitive development (Piaget, 1950; Piaget & Inhelder, 1969).

Schema—original patterns of thinking for dealing with specific situations in the environment

Piaget taught that cognitive development is the combined result of maturation of the brain and nervous system and adaptation to our environment. He used five terms to describe the dynamics of development. A **schema** represents a mental structure, the pattern of thinking that a person uses for dealing with a specific situation in the environment. For example, infants see an object they want, so they learn to grasp what they see. They form a schema that is appropriate to the situation. **Adaptation** is the process by which children adjust their thinking to include new information that furthers their understanding. Piaget (1954) said that children adapt in two ways: assimilation and accommodation. **Assimilation** means acquiring new information and incorporating it into current schemas in response to new environmental stimuli. **Accommodation** involves adjusting to new information by creating new schemas when the old ones won't do. Children may see dogs for the first time (assimilation),

Jean Piaget studied how children's thinking changes as they develop.

but learn that some dogs are safe to pet and others aren't (accommodation). As children acquire more and more information, they construct their understanding of the world differently.

Equilibriation

Equilibriation means achieving a balance—an equilibrium—between schemas and accommodation. Disequilibrium arises when there is conflict between children's reality and their comprehension of it, when assimilation won't work and accommodation is necessary. Children resolve the conflict by acquiring new ways of thinking, to make what they observe agree with their understanding of it. The desire for equilibrium becomes a motivating factor that pushes children upward through the stages of cognitive development.

Piaget outlined four stages of cognitive development (Beilin, 1992).

Sensorimotor stage

During the **sensorimotor stage** (birth to 2 years), children learn to coordinate sensory experiences with physical, motor actions. Infants' senses of vision, touch, taste, hearing, and smell bring them into contact with things with various properties. They learn how far to reach to touch a ball, to move their eyes and head to follow a moving object, to move their hand and arm to pick up an object. Elkind (1970) labels the principal cognitive task during this period the *conquest of the object.*

Preoperational stage

Through the **preoperational stage** (2 to 7 years), children acquire language, and learn that they can manipulate these symbols that represent the environment. Preoperational children can deal with the world symbolically, but still cannot perform mental operations that are reversible. That is why Piaget (1967) called this stage the preoperational stage of thought. Elkind (1970) labels the principal cognitive task during this period the *conquest of the symbol.*

Concrete operational stage

Children in the **concrete operational stage** (7 to 11 years) show a greater capacity for logical reasoning, though this is limited to things actually experienced. They can perform a number of mental operations. They can arrange objects into *hierarchical classifications;* they can understand *class inclusion relationships, serialization* (grouping objects by size or alphabetical order), and the principles of *symmetry* and *reciprocity* (two brothers are brothers to each other). They understand the principle of *conservation,* that you can pour a liquid from a tall to a flat dish without altering the total quantity of the liquid. Elkind (1970) calls the major cognitive task of this period *mastering classes, relations, and quantities.*

Formal operational stage

In the **formal operational stage** (11 years and up), adolescents move beyond concrete, actual experiences to think in more abstract, logical terms. They are able to use systematic, *propositional logic* in solving hypothetical problems and drawing conclusions. They are able to use *inductive reasoning* to systemize their ideas and to construct theories about them. They are able to use *deductive reasoning* to play the role of scientist in constructing and testing theories. They can use *metaphorical speech* and *algebraic symbols* as symbols for symbols. They can move from what is real to what is possible, and they can think about

LIVING ISSUES

Cognitive Development and the Use of Birth Control

Large numbers of adolescents are becoming sexually involved at young ages (Hofferth, Kahn, & Baldwin, 1987). Unfortunately, about a third of sexually active 15- to 19-year-old, unmarried females or males never used contraceptives when they had intercourse, according to one study. Another third only sometimes used some method of contraception (Zelnick & Kantner, 1980). There are many reasons why some adolescents are not regular contraceptive users. Effective contraceptive use requires (1) acceptance of one's sexuality, (2) acknowledgment that one is sexually active, (3) anticipation in the present, and (4) the ability to view future sexual encounters realistically, so they can be prepared for. This requires the ability to do formal operational thinking. Adolescents who are functioning only at a concrete operational stage of cognitive development are not able to project themselves into the future and to prepare themselves for sexual encounters (Pestrak & Martin, 1985).

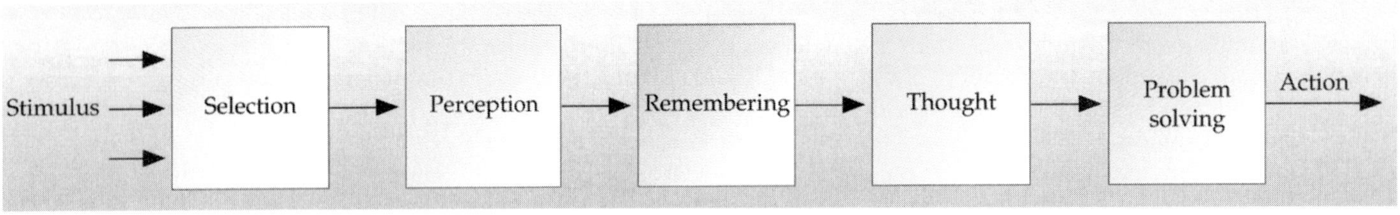

FIGURE 2.4 Steps in information processing.

what might be, projecting themselves into the future and planning for it.

INFORMATION PROCESSING

Information-processing approach—an approach to cognition that emphasizes the steps, actions, and operations by which persons receive, perceive, remember, think about, and utilize information

The **information-processing** approach to cognition emphasizes the progressive steps, actions, and operations that take place when the person receives, perceives, remembers, thinks about, and uses information. The steps in information processing are illustrated in Figure 2.4. The diagram shows the information flowing in one direction, but there may be some flow backward also. A person may take information in and out of memory to think about it for a time before making a decision. Nevertheless, the steps shown help us to understand the total process.

The process begins with our being bombarded with stimuli that are received through our senses. Because we are interested in some happenings more than others, we select that which is of value to us. However, the information is not just photocopied by our mind; it is interpreted and evaluated according to our perception of it, which, in turn, depends partly on our past experience. If information seems of value, it is then stored in our memory for future use. When needed, the information is retrieved from memory stores. We think about it, seek to relate it to our own present situation, and use it as a basis for solving our problems. In subsequent discussions in this book, we talk about the development of information-processing skills during various phases of the life span (Rice, 1993).

EVALUATION OF COGNITIVE THEORIES

Piaget has exerted more influence on cognitive theory and applications than any other person. He has revolutionized developmental psychology by focusing attention on mental processes and their role in behavior. He has made us aware that children think differently than adults, and that children can only do what they can understand at different stages. Piaget has helped educators, parents, and researchers understand the capabilities of children at different stages. Many school curricula have been redesigned based on Piagetian findings.

Piaget has been criticized for several points. He underestimated the role of the school and home in fostering cognitive development, because he stressed biological maturation rather than environmental influences. However, he did teach that children influence the course of their development through their exploratory activities and that they should be given learning materials appropriate to each stage of growth. A major criticism of Piaget is the lack of evidence for comprehensive stages across domains. Piaget's depiction of stages as universal is not always true. Many persons never reach the higher stages of development. In fact, formal operational thinking may have limited usefulness in adult life. For example, a carpenter needs the ability to do concrete operational thinking, whereas an architect needs formal operational abilities. Furthermore, people may advance to a certain cognitive level in one aspect of their lives, but not in others. The separation of stages is not always distinct. Growth then is uneven.

The information-processing approach has stimulated much research on learning, memory, and problem solving. It is a useful concept in describing mental processes. However, both the Piagetian and information-processing approaches ignore the role of unconscious emotions and emotional conflict as causes of behavior.

Ethological Theories

LORENZ: IMPRINTING

Ethology emphasizes that behavior is a product of evolution and is biologically determined. Each species learns what adaptations are necessary for survival, and through the process of natural selection, the fittest live to pass on their traits to their offspring.

Konrad Lorenz (1965), a Nobel Prize–winning ethologist, studied the behavior patterns of graylag geese and found that goslings were born with an instinct to follow their mothers. This behavior was present from birth and was part of their instinct for survival. Lorenz also found that if goslings were hatched in an incubator, they would follow the first moving object that they saw, believing that object to be their mother. Lorenz stood by when the lid of one incubator was lifted. He was the first being the goslings saw, so from that point on they followed Lorenz as they would their mother. The goslings would even follow him when he went swimming.

Konrad Lorenz's goslings developed an attachment to him, a process he called imprinting.

Lorenz called this process **imprinting,** which involved rapidly developing an attachment for the first object seen. Lorenz found that there was a critical period, shortly after hatching, during which imprinting would take place.

Ethology—the view that behavior is a product of evolution and biology

Imprinting—a biological ability to establish an attachment on first exposure to an object or person

BONDING AND ATTACHMENT THEORIES

Efforts have been made to apply the principles of ethology to human beings. While there is no human equivalent to imprinting, bonding shows some similarities. There is some evidence to show that parent–infant contacts during the early hours and days of life are important to later parent–child relationships (Klaus & Kennel, 1982). Studies at Case-Western Reserve University in Cleveland confirmed the maternal feeling that the emotional bonds between mother and infant are strengthened by intimate contact during the first hours of life (Klaus & Kennel, 1982). One group of mothers was allowed sixteen extra hours of intimacy during the first three days of life—an hour after birth and five hours each afternoon. When the babies were one month of age and a year old, these mothers were compared with a control group that had gone through the usual hospital routine. The mothers who had had more time with their babies fondled them more, sought close eye contact, and responded to their cries. The researchers concluded that keeping the mother and baby together during the first hours after birth strengthened a mother's "maternal sensitivities" and that prolonged infant–mother separation during the first few days would have negative effects.

Although early parent–infant contact is important, other studies fail to confirm Klaus and Kennel's finding that there is a critical period during which **bonding** must take place, and that if it does not, harmful effects will be felt and lasting (Goldberg, 1983). In contrast, Egeland and

Bonding—the formation of a close relationship between a person and a child through early and frequent association

FOCUS

King, the Guard Duck

A number of years ago I raised Labrador retrievers for hunting and field trial work. Part of the training procedure was to teach the dogs to retrieve live birds. I was able to find two white ducks, newly hatched, at a nearby farm. Apparently, the ducks thought I was their mother because they developed a very special attachment to me. The male, whom we named King, would follow me around the yard of our camp. He became very protective of me and would attack any person who tried to come into the yard. If someone tried to come too close to me when I was swimming, King would dive underwater, swim to the outsider, and bite the person's legs and toes. King became the terror of the neighborhood. Even the Labrador retrievers were afraid of him. So King lived in style, king of our castle, until he died. (From the author's experience)

Vaughn (1981) found no greater incidence of neglect, abuse, illness, or adjustment problems among infants who had been separated from their mothers for a time after birth. The point is that the importance of a few crucial hours immediately after birth has not yet been conclusively established.

It is evident, however, that there must be a powerful genetic predisposition in the child that encourages the formation of a relationship. But no emotional bond ties the infant to its mother immediately at birth. Infants taken from their mother can form a bond with another person. However, Schaffer (1984) pointed out that the infant has certain biological biases and tendencies that facilitate the development of a bond with someone.

Sensitive period—a period during which a given effect can be produced more readily than at other times

John Bowlby (1969) shed a great deal of light on the subject in his discussion of **attachment theory** (Bretherton, 1992). Infants are not born with attachment to anyone: mother, father, or others. However, since the infant's survival depends upon a loving caregiver, the infant needs to develop attachments. Bowlby suggested that during the first six months, infants' attachments are quite broad. Infants become attached to people in general, so they seem to have no particular preference who cares for them. However, from six months on, attachments become more specific. The child may develop multiple attachments, but these are with individuals—the mother, father, a baby-sitter—so that the child is upset when left with an unfamiliar caregiver.

Attachment theory—the description of the process by which infants develop close emotional dependence on one or more adult caregivers

HINDE: SENSITIVE PERIODS OF DEVELOPMENT

Ethologist Robert Hinde (1983), professor of psychology at Cambridge University, England, prefers the term **sensitive period** to "critical period" in reference to certain times of life when the organism is more affected by particular kinds of experiences. The term *sensitive period*, originally used by Maria Montessori, seems broader and is a more flexible concept than the narrow concept of critical period. With human children, there seem to be particularly sensitive periods for development of language, emotional attachments, or social relationships (Bornstein, 1987). When deficits occur during these sensitive periods, the question remains whether they can be made up during subsequent periods of development. Much depends on the extent of the early deprivation and the degree to which later environmental influences meet important needs (Werner & Smith, 1982).

FOCUS

Mother's Recognition of Newborn

The mother's recognition of her newborn is a milestone in the unique relationship between the mother and her infant. An integral component of attachment, it promotes and fosters care. During their earliest contacts, a mother is exposed to her infant's visual and olfactory characteristics. She is able to recognize her infant by odor and sight after an exposure of less than one hour. Even more amazing, 36 percent of nursing mothers were able to recognize their newborns by stroking their hand after an average exposure of less than one hour, 65 percent after a mean exposure of 6.7 hours (Kaitz, Lapidot, Bronner, & Eidelman, 1992).

EVALUATION OF ETHOLOGICAL THEORIES

Ethological theories have emphasized the role of evolution and biology in human development and behavior, an emphasis that deserves serious attention. Although ethological emphasis on critical periods of development is too rigid and narrow, the principle of sensitive periods of development is a helpful one. Even then, the theories overlook the importance of positive environmental influences in overcoming the deficits of early deprivation. Biology has a marked influence on behavior, but it is not destiny. People are more than a combination of genes and chromosomes; they are developing human beings, influenced by a wide variety of environmental experiences over many years.

An Eclectic Theoretical Orientation

The point of view of this book is that no one theory completely explains human developmental processes or behavior. The theories represent different and enlightened perceptions, all of which are worthy of consideration. For this reason, the book presents an *eclectic* theoretical orientation. This means that no one point of view has a monopoly on the truth, and that each theory has contributed an element of understanding to the total, complex process of human development over the life span.

Summary

1. The scientific method involves formulating a problem, developing a hypothesis, testing it, and drawing conclusions that are stated in the form of a theory. A theory organizes the data, ideas, and hypotheses and states them in coherent, interrelated, general propositions, principles, or laws.

2. Freud's psychoanalytical theory emphasizes the importance of early childhood experiences and unconscious motivations in influencing behavior. Freud thought that sexual urges and aggressive instincts and drives were the primary determinants of behavior, or that people operated according to the pleasure principle.
3. Freud said that the basic structure of the personality consists of the id, ego, and superego, and that the ego strives to minimize the conflict within by keeping the instinctual urges (the id) and societal prohibitions (the superego) in balance.
4. According to Freud, one of the ways people relieve anxiety and conflict is by employing defense mechanisms: repression, regression, sublimation, displacement, reaction formation, denial, and rationalization.
5. According to Freud's psychosexual theory, the center of sensual sensitivity shifts from one part of the body to another as development proceeds through the following series of stages: oral stage (to age 1); anal stage (ages 2, 3); phallic stage (ages 4, 5); latency stage (age 6 to puberty); and genital stage (puberty on).
6. Erikson thought that Freud placed too much emphasis on the sexual basis for behavior and that his view of human nature was too cynical. Erikson divided human development into eight stages and said that the individual has a psychosocial task to master during each stage.
7. The eight stages, according to Erikson, are trust vs. distrust (0–1 year); autonomy vs. shame and doubt (1–2 years); initiative vs. guilt (3–5 years); industry vs. inferiority (6–11 years); identity vs. role confusion (12–19 years); intimacy vs. isolation (young adulthood: 20s and 30s); generativity vs. stagnation (middle adulthood: 40s and 50s); and integrity vs. despair (late adulthood: 60 and over).
8. Freud's psychoanalytical theory is an influential one. His emphases on unconscious motivations and defense mechanisms, as well as on environmental influences, and his treatment methods have made a real contribution to psychological theory and practice. Some feel his psychosexual theory of development is limited in scope, with overemphasis on sexual motivations and aggressive instincts as the basis of behavior. He has also done a disservice to women by blaming the survivors—the female victims themselves—for incest.
9. Erikson's theory is much broader than Freud's and encompasses the entire life span, with emphasis on a greater variety of motivational and environmental factors.
10. Behaviorism emphasizes the role of environmental influences in molding behavior. Behavior becomes the sum total of learned or conditioned responses to stimuli, a view that is somewhat mechanistic.
11. According to behaviorists, learning takes place through conditioning. There are two types of conditioning: classical conditioning, which is learning through association, and operant conditioning, which is learning from the consequences of behavior.
12. Social learning theory says that children learn by observing the behavior of others and by modeling their behavior after them.
13. Learning theorists have contributed much to the understanding of human development by emphasizing the role of environmental influences in shaping behavior. However, learning theories have been criticized for being too mechanistic, and for neglecting the role of biology and maturation in development.
14. Humanism takes a very positive view of human nature and says that people are free to use their superior abilities to make intelligent choices and to realize their full potential as self-actualized persons.
15. Buhler said that the real goal of humans is fulfillment through accomplishment.
16. Maslow said that human behavior can be explained as motivation to satisfy needs, which can be classified into five categories: physiological needs, safety needs, love and belongingness needs, esteem needs, and self-actualization needs. Self-actualization is the highest need and the culmination of life.

17. Carl Rogers reflected the humanistic philosophy that if people are given freedom to grow and emotional support (which he called unconditional positive regard), they can develop into fully functioning human beings.
18. Humanists have taught people to believe in themselves and in human nature, but are sometimes criticized for having a too optimistic view of human nature.
19. Cognition is the act or process of knowing. The Piagetian approach to cognitive development emphasizes the qualitative changes in the way people think as they develop.
20. Piaget divided the process of cognitive development into four stages: sensorimotor stage (birth to 2 years), preoperational stage (2 to 7 years), concrete operational stage (7 to 11 years), and formal operational stage (11 years and up).
21. The information-processing approach to cognition emphasizes the progressive steps, actions, and operations that take place when a person receives, perceives, remembers, thinks about, and utilizes information.
22. The cognitive theorists have made a real contribution by focusing attention on mental processes and their role in behavior. Piaget has been criticized for stressing biological maturation and minimizing the importance of environmental influences. Both Piagetian and information-processing approaches emphasize mental processes at a conscious level, ignoring any unconscious, psychodynamic causes of behavior.
23. Ethology emphasizes that behavior is a product of evolution and is biologically determined. Imprinting, bonding, and attachment theory are examples of this emphasis. Ethologist Robert Hinde prefers the term *sensitive period,* referring to certain times of life when the organism is more affected by particular kinds of experiences.
24. This book presents an eclectic theoretical orientation.

Key Terms

Accommodation *p. 42*
Adaptation *p. 42*
Anal stage *p. 30*
Assimilation *p. 42*
Attachment theory *p. 46*
Autonomy vs. shame and doubt *p. 31*
Behaviorism *p. 33*
Bonding *p. 45*
Classical conditioning *p. 34*
Client-centered therapy *p. 40*
Cognition *p. 42*
Concrete operational stage *p. 43*
Conditional positive regard *p. 40*
Conditioning *p. 34*
Defense mechanisms *p. 29*
Denial *p. 30*
Displacement *p. 29*
Ego *p. 29*
Electra complex *p. 30*
Equilibriation *p.* 43
Ethology *p. 45*
Fixated *p. 30*
Formal operational stage *p. 43*
Free association *p. 29*
Generativity vs. stagnation *p. 32*
Genital stage *p. 30*
Holistic view *p. 37*
Humanistic theory *p. 37*
Id *p. 29*
Identity vs. role confusion *p. 32*
Imprinting *p. 45*
Industry vs. inferiority *p. 32*
Information-processing approach *p. 44*
Initiative vs. guilt *p. 31*
Integrity vs. despair *p. 32*
Intimacy vs. isolation *p. 32*
Latency stage *p. 30*
Mechanistic or deterministic *p. 33*
Modeling *p. 36*
Oedipal complex *p. 30*
Operant conditioning *p. 35*
Oral stage *p. 30*
Phallic stage *p. 30*
Pleasure principle *p. 29*
Positive reinforcement *p. 35*
Preoperational stage *p. 43*

Discussion Questions

1. Give examples of human behavior that support Freud's view of human nature and motivations. Give examples that do not support Freud's view of human nature and motivations.
2. What do you think of Freud's theory of psychosexual development? Which points do you agree with? Which do you disagree with? Give examples.
3. If you have children of your own, or if you teach children or care for them, give examples of their behavior that support Erikson's descriptions of one or more stages of psychosocial development.
4. Describe and give examples of learning through:
   a. Classical conditioning
   b. Operant conditioning
   c. Modeling
   d. Vicarious reinforcement
5. Do you agree or disagree with Buhler that the real goal of humans is fulfillment that is attained through accomplishment? Explain your views.
6. Is it possible to find self-actualization without first having the needs for love and belonging and esteem met? Explain.
7. According to humanistic theory, if children are given freedom and emotional support, they will make right choices and develop into fully functioning people. According to this view, do children need parental guidance? Why or why not? What are your views?
8. Compare formal operational thinking with the scientific methods of discovering truth.
9. Do you believe that bonding between a mother and her baby shortly after birth is a prerequisite for a satisfying parent–child relationship later in life? Explain.
10. Give examples of sensitive periods for optimum development of particular characteristics, skills, habits, or relationships in the lives of children. Describe.

Suggested Readings

Bandura, A. (1986). *Social foundations of thought and action.* Englewood Cliffs, NJ: Prentice-Hall. Bandura's social learning view of development.

Eibl-Eibesfeldt, I. (1989). *Human ethology.* New York: Aldine DeGruyter. An ethological interpretation of human behavior.

Erikson, E. H. (1980). *Identity and the life cycle.* New York: W. W. Norton. Erikson's basic views on identity development.

Flavell, J. H. (1985). *Cognitive development* (2nd ed.). Englewood Cliffs, NJ: Prentice-Hall. A helpful summary.

Ginsburg, H., & Opper, S. (1979). *Piaget's theory of intellectual development* (2nd ed.). Englewood Cliffs, NJ: Prentice-Hall. Outline of Piaget's research on infancy through adolescence.

Kegan, O. (1982). *The evolving self: Problem and process in human development.* Cambridge, MA: Harvard University Press. An integration of a number of theories to explain personality during adolescence and adulthood.

Loevinger, J. (1987). *Paradigms of personality.* New York: W. H. Freeman. General summary and comparison of major theories.

Miller, P. (1989). *Theories of developmental psychology.* 2nd ed. New York: W. H. Freeman. An overview of the major developmental theories.

Rogoff, B. (1990). *Apprenticeship in thinking: Cognitive development in social context.* New York: Oxford University Press. Cross-cultural theory and research on children's thinking.

Salkind, N. J. (1985). *Theories of human development* (2nd ed.). New York: Wiley. General discussion of theories.

Schwartz, B., & Lacey, H. (1982). *Behaviorism, science, and human nature.* New York: Norton. Conditioning theories.

Thomas, R. M. (1985). *Comparing theories of child development* (2nd ed.). Belmont, CA: Wadsworth.

Part Two

THE BEGINNINGS OF HUMAN LIFE

Heredity, Environmental Influences, and Prenatal Development

Chapter 3

The development of a human being from a fertilized egg cell to full-term baby is a fascinating process. This chapter covers the periods of prenatal development, with an emphasis on the kind of environment and prenatal care essential to the birth of a healthy baby. The roles of heredity and environmental influences in development are highlighted. Some hereditary defects and environmentally caused disorders are discussed, together with ways and means to avoid them.

Reproduction

Gametes—Sex cells

Zygote—A fertilized ovum

Two kinds of sex cells, or **gametes**, are involved in human reproduction: the male gamete, or sperm cell, and the female gamete, or ovum. Reproduction begins when a sperm cell fuses with an ovum to form a single new cell called a **zygote**. But let's begin at the beginning.

SPERMATOGENESIS

Spermatogenesis—Process by which sperm are produced

Meiosis—Process of cell division by which gametes reproduce

Spermatogenesis refers to the process of sperm production that takes place in the *testes* of the male after he reaches puberty. Through a repeated cell division called **meiosis**, about 300 million sperm are produced daily and then stored in the *epididymis*, a system of ducts located at the back of the *testis*. Ordinarily, 200 million to 500 million sperm are released at each ejaculation. Some of these sperm are abnormal or dead, but for the sperm count to be normal, a minimum of 20 million healthy sperm per milliliter of *semen* need to be present (Jones, 1984). Sperm are microscopic in size—only about 1/500 of an inch long. About ten to twenty ejaculations contain as many sperm as there are people on the planet. The sperm has a *head*, containing the cell nucleus that houses the chromosomes; a *midpiece*; and a *tail*. The midpiece produces chemical reactions that provide energy for the tail to lash back and forth, to propel the sperm along.

During intercourse, millions of sperm are ejaculated into the *vagina* during male orgasm, and begin a fantastic journey up the *vagina*, into the *uterus*, and up the *fallopian tubes*. When fertilization occurs, only a single sperm gains entrance to each available ovum.

OOGENESIS

Oogenesis—Process by which ova mature

Ova—Female egg cells

Oogenesis is the process by which female gametes, or egg cells called **ova**, are ripened in the *ovaries*. All of the egg cells that will ever be in the ovaries are present at birth, though undeveloped. Beginning at puberty, ordinarily only one ovum ripens

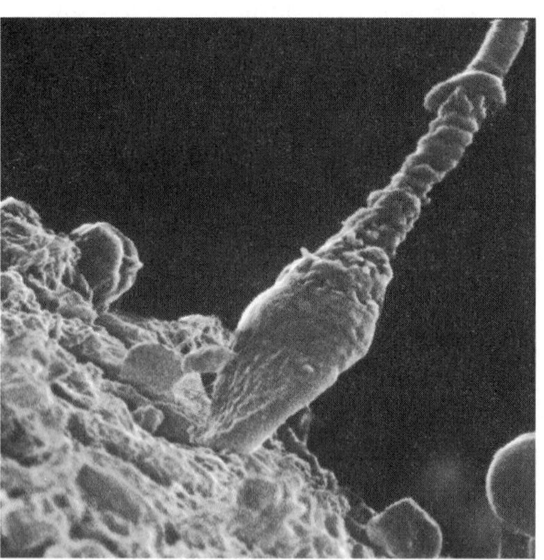

Two hundred million to 500 million sperm are released at each ejaculation.

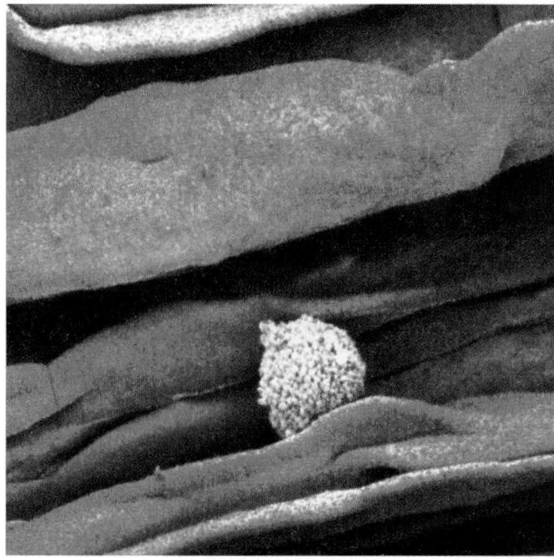

Ordinarily, at the time of ovulation, only one ovum ripens and is released during each menstrual cycle.

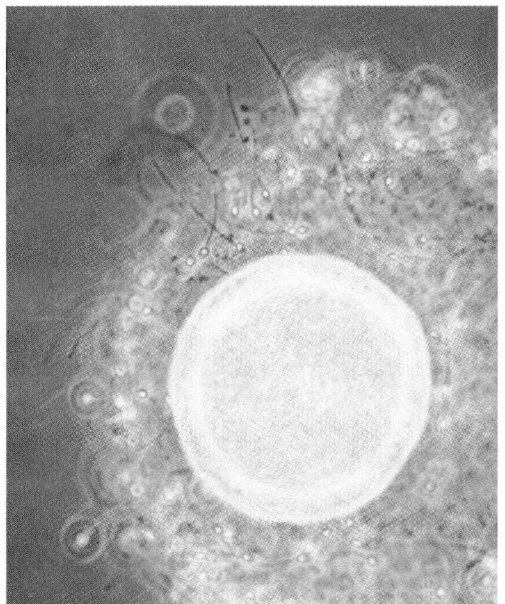

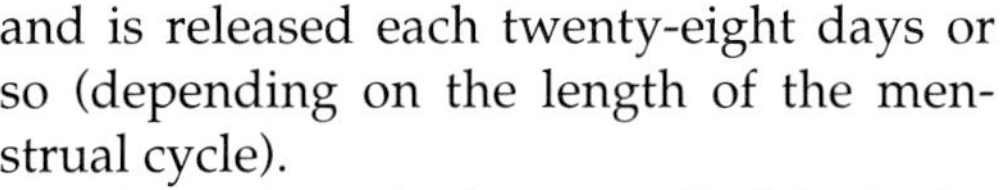

Millions of sperm attempt to fertilize the ovum, but only one will be able to penetrate the wall.

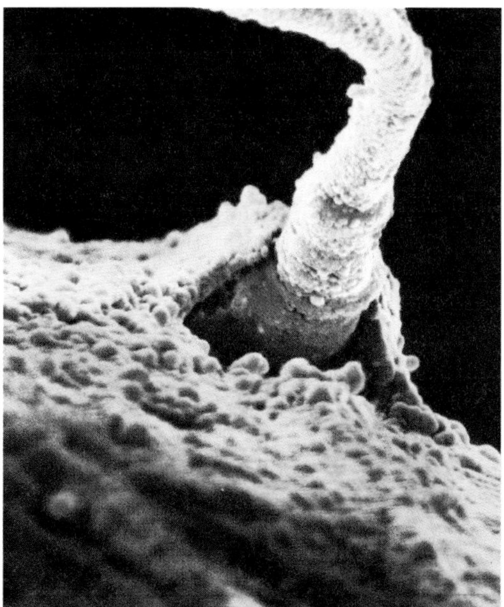

This sperm is penetrating the ovum.

and is released each twenty-eight days or so (depending on the length of the menstrual cycle).

The ovum is the largest cell of the body, about $1/200$ of an inch in diameter, large enough to be visible. In this cell, a clear thin shell encloses a liquid composed of hundreds of fat droplets and proteins in which a nucleus containing the chromosomes is found.

CONCEPTION

After the ovum is released (a process called **ovulation**), fingerlike projections of the fallopian tube sweep the egg into it. Inside the tube, hairlike projections called *cilia* propel the ovum toward the uterus. The journey from the ovary to the uterus usually takes about three to four days, but fertilization must take place within forty-eight hours after ovulation. **Fertilization**, or **conception**, normally takes place in the third of the fallopian tube nearest the ovary. Eventually, a few sperm reach the egg, but a sperm cannot penetrate the egg's outer wall without the help of chemical *enzymes* released from the head of the sperm. The enzymes dissolve the wall of the ovum, allowing one sperm to penetrate. Immediately, the outer layer of the egg hardens so the other sperm cannot enter (Schatten & Schatten, 1983). The tail of the sperm drops off and its nucleus unites with the nucleus of the ovum so that the first single new cell is formed (Grobstein, 1989; Silber, 1980).

Fertilization or conception—Union of sperm and ovum

Ovulation—Process by which the mature ovum separates from the ovarian wall and is released from the ovary

Family Planning

Family planning means having children by choice and not by chance. Its goal is to enable people to have the number of children they want, when they want to have them. This objective covers prevention of unintended pregnancy as well as pursuit of infertility treatment by couples having difficulty conceiving. Another important goal of certain family planning methods is to prevent the spread of sexually transmitted disease (Cates & Stone, 1992b; Williams, 1991).

BENEFITS

There are many benefits of family planning. The most urgent need is to protect the health of the mother and her children. Births spaced too close together pose an added health risk for both the mother and the baby. A study in Hungary, Sweden, and the United States found that birth intervals of less than two years posed a 5–10 percent increased risk of low birth weight, preterm birth, and neonatal death (J. E. Miller, 1991). The mother who bears one child this soon after the other is also at risk.

The timing of childbirth is a crucial factor. The psychological impact of parenthood is lessened if the parents are ready for parenthood and the birth is welcomed. Unfortunately, unintended pregnancy rates are high, among both married and unmarried women. It is estimated that, in 1990, 44 percent of married women living with their husbands were at risk for unintended pregnancy. The rate was 54 percent for unmarried women or those not living with their husbands (Klitsch, 1993).

Unplanned parenthood is a major factor in child neglect and abuse. A child from a family with two unplanned births is almost three times more likely to have been abused than is a child from a family with no unplanned births. One from a family with three unplanned births is 4.6 times more likely to have been abused (Zuravin, 1991).

Family planning is also necessary for the good of marriage. Adolescents who marry because of pregnancy have the poorest prognosis of marital success. Since both premarital pregnancy and early postmarital pregnancy are followed by higher-than-average divorce rates, large numbers of children grow up without a secure, stable family life (Gershenson, 1983). Adolescent mothers are more likely to be unemployed, out of school, and on welfare. Many live with their parents after the baby is born (Nathanson, Baird, & Jemail, 1986). Older couples with large families also experience financial and management problems that often put a great strain on their relationship. Parents who have small families are able to offer their children intellectual and educational advantages (Blake, 1991).

CONTRACEPTIVE FAILURE

Data from the 1988 National Survey of Family Growth (NSFG) reveal that contraceptive failure remains a serious problem in the United States, contributing substantially to unintended pregnancy (Jones & Forrest, 1992). The birth control pill continues to be the most effective reversible method for which data were available (8 percent of users accidentally became pregnant during the first year of use), followed by the condom (15 percent). Periodic abstinence is the method most likely to fail (26 percent), but accidental pregnant is also relatively common among women using spermicides (25 percent). Table 3.1 shows the failure rates by method, uncorrected and corrected for the underreporting of abortion. Failure rates vary more by user characteristics such as marital status, poverty status, and age than by method, suggesting that failure results from improper and irregular use rather than from the inherent limitations of the method. The category "Other" in the "Method" column of the table includes withdrawal and douche. As can be seen, the table does not include sterilization, yet it is the single most common contraceptive method used by married or formerly married people (U.S. Bureau of the Census, 1992).

TABLE 3.1
PERCENTAGES OF WOMEN EXPERIENCING CONTRACEPTIVE FAILURE DURING THE FIRST 12 MONTHS OF USE

Method	*Uncorrected*	*Corrected*
Pill	5.1	8.3
Condom	7.2	14.8
Diaphragm	10.4	15.9
Periodic abstinence	20.9	25.6
Sponge	14.5	—
Spermicides	13.4	25.2
Other	13.3	27.8

Reproduced with the permission of the Alan Guttmacher Institute from Elise F. Jones and Jacqueline Darroch Forrest, "Contraceptive Failure Rates Based on the 1988 NSFG," *Family Planning Perspectives*, Vol. 24, No. 1, Jan./Feb. 1992, pp. 12–19.

LIVING ISSUES

AIDS and the Use of Condoms

Since the advent of AIDS, the use of condoms has increased significantly (Sonenstein, Pleck, & Ku, 1989). The reason is that, except for abstinence, condoms are the best method of preventing the spread of sexually transmitted diseases. When used in addition to spermicides, which are detrimental to the HIV virus, they provide even better protection.

Condom failure is due to one or more reasons. Natural lambskin condoms are permeable to the AIDS, herpes, and hepatitis B viruses. Intact latex condoms do not allow the viruses to pass through, but some latex condoms leak. One government study found that 11 of 106 batches of American-made condoms and 30 of 98 imported condoms flunked a leak test (Parachini, 1987). These figures indicate that condoms should be blown up and submerged in water to test for leaks before usage.

The most common reasons for condom failure are breakage or slipping off (Trussell, Warner, & Hatcher, 1992). The end of the condom should protrude over the end of the penis to minimize strain on the material during intercourse. Slippage can occur during intercourse or withdrawal, even if the penis remains erect. Holding onto the condom during withdrawal minimizes slippage during that time (Cates & Stone, 1992a).

Certainly condoms provide *safer*, but not completely safe, sex.

Prenatal Development

PERIODS OF DEVELOPMENT

Prenatal development takes place during three periods (Rice, 1989b):

1. The **germinal period**—from conception to implantation (attachment to the uterine wall)—about 14 days
2. The **embryonic period**—from 2 weeks to 8 weeks after conception
3. The **fetal period**—from 8 weeks through the remainder of the pregnancy

Figure 3.1 shows the early stages of the germinal period.

GERMINAL PERIOD

The fertilized ovum is called a **zygote** (see Figure 3.2), which continues to be propelled through the fallopian tube by the cilia. About thirty hours after fertilization, the process of cell division begins. One cell divides into two, two into four, four into eight, and so on, the collection forming a **morula** (from the Latin word meaning "mulberry"). Every time the cells divide they become smaller, allowing the total mass, called the **blastula**, to pass through the fallopian tube. The result of the repeated cell dividing is the formation of a hollow inner portion containing fluid.

Morula

Germinal period

Blastula

Embryonic period

Fetal period

Three to four days after fertilization, the newly formed blastula enters the uterus and floats around for another three to four days before the inner layer, called the **blastocyst**, begins to attach itself to the inner lining of the uterus (the *endometrium*) in a process called **implantation**. The implanting blastocyst releases an enzyme that literally eats a hole in the soft, spongy tissue of the endometrium until it completely buries itself in the uterine wall. By about ten days after the blastula enters the uterus, implantation of the blastocyst is complete.

Blastocyst

Implantation

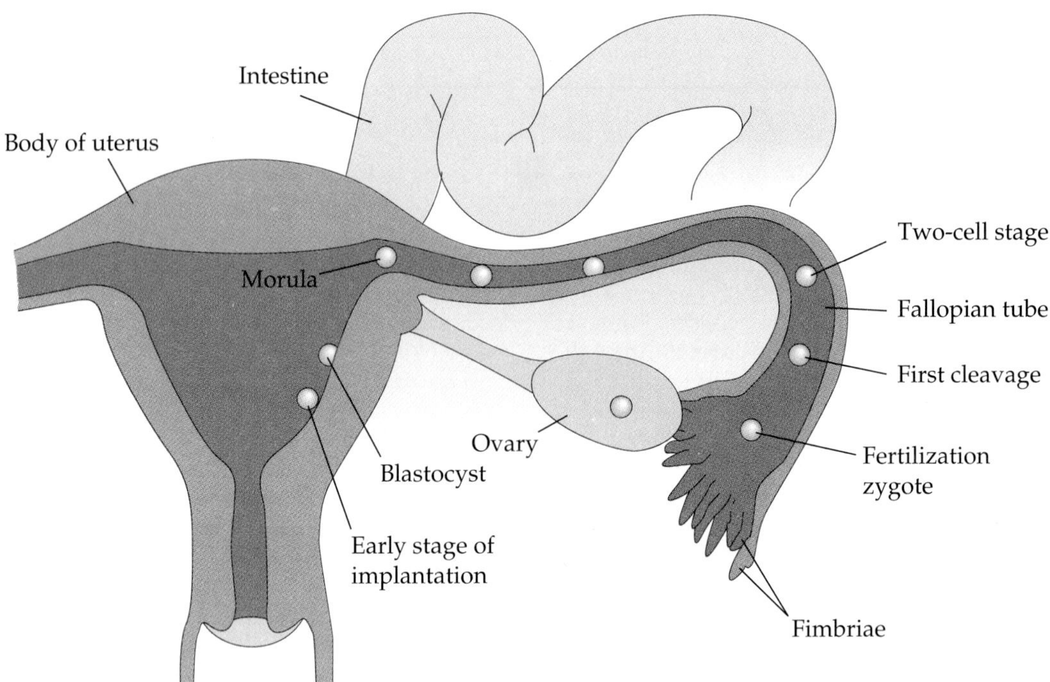

FIGURE 3.1 From zygote to implanted blastocyst. From the time of ovulation, it takes about two weeks before the fertilized egg is completely implanted in the wall of the uterus. In the meantime, the ovum divides and subdivides, forming the *morula* and then the *blastocyst*.

Ectopic pregnancy—Attachment and growth of the embryo in any location other than inside the uterus

Sometimes the blastocyst implants itself in the fallopian tube or elsewhere in the body cavity. Such a condition is called an **ectopic pregnancy**. An embryo that begins forming in this way, outside the uterus, usually dies or has to be removed surgically.

EMBRYONIC PERIOD

As stated previously, *about fourteen days after conception, the blastocyst implants itself in the uterine wall.* The embryonic period begins at the end of the second week. The

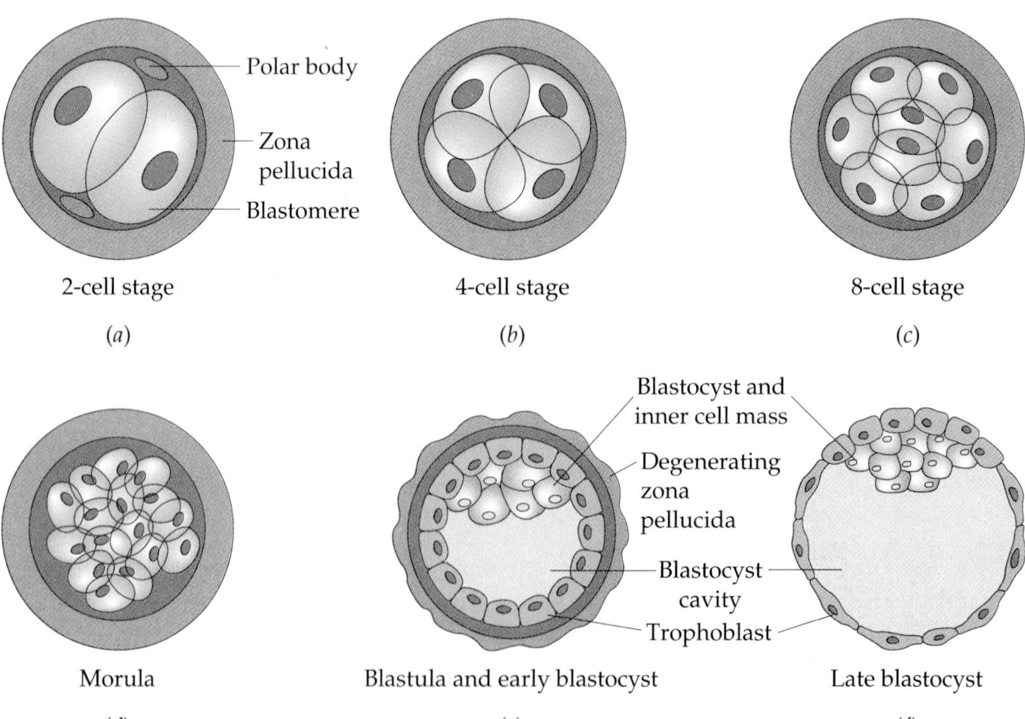

FIGURE 3.2 Early development from zygote to blastocyst.

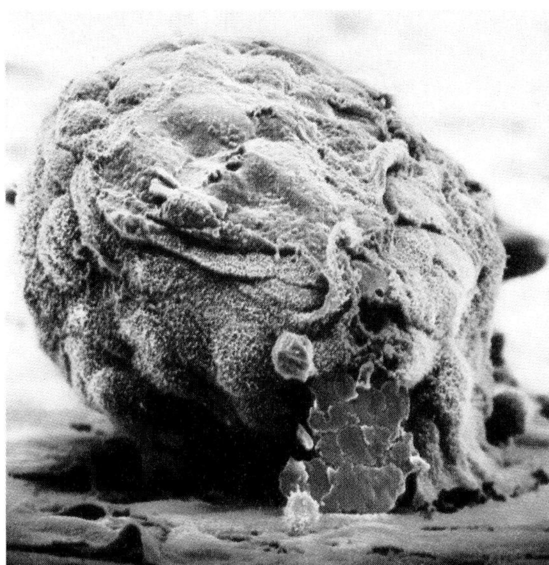

The blastocyst facilitates its landing on the uterine wall with leglike structures composed of sugar molecules.

embryo develops from a round layer of cells across the center of the blastocyst. At eighteen days, the **embryo** is about 0.0625 (1/16) of an inch long. During its early weeks, human embryos closely resemble those of other vertebrate animals, as Figure 3.3 illustrates. The embryo has a tail and traces of gills, both of which soon disappear. The head develops before the rest of the body. Eyes, nose, and ears are not yet visible at one month, but a backbone and vertebral canal have formed. Small buds that will develop into arms and legs ap-

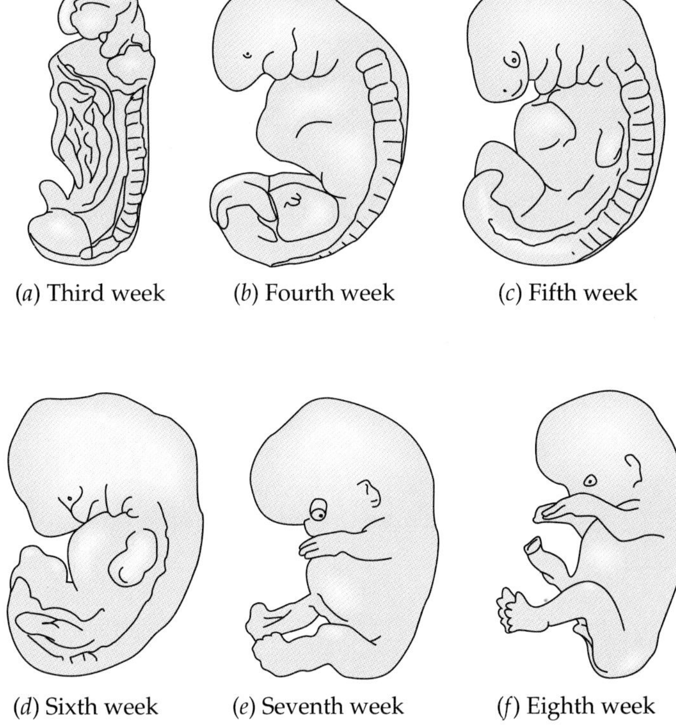

FIGURE 3.3 Development of human embryo from the third week to the eighth week after conception. The embryo grows from about 1 inch in length after the third week to 1 1/4 inches at the end of the eighth week.

Adapted from "The Thalidomide Syndrome," by Helen B. Taussig, *Scientific American*, August 1962. Copyright © 1962 by Scientific American, Inc. All rights reserved.

pear. The heart forms and starts beating; other body systems begin to take shape.

Embryo—Growing baby from the end of the second week to the end of the eighth week after conception

FETAL PERIOD

By the end of the embryonic period (two months), the **fetus** has developed the first bone structure and distinct limbs and digits that take on human form. Major blood vessels form, and internal organs continue to develop. By the end of the first **trimester** (one-third the length of pregnancy, or 12.7 weeks), the fetus is about three inches long; most major organs are present, a large head and face are well formed, and a heartbeat can be detected with a stethoscope. Figure 3.4 shows embryonic and fetal sizes from two to fifteen weeks following conception.

Fetus—Growing baby from the beginning of the third month of development to birth

Trimester—One-third of the gestation period, or about 12.7 weeks

By the end of the fourth or fifth month, the mother can usually feel fetal movement. The skin of the fetus is covered with a fine hair, usually shed before birth. At the

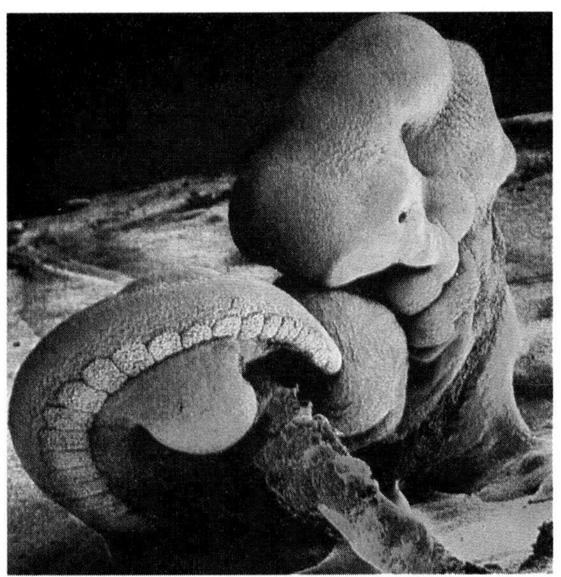

By 4 1/2 weeks a rudimentary heart and an early eye have formed. The tail will disappear, leaving behind shrunk vertebrae which remain.

end of the fifth month, the fetus weighs about one pound and is about twelve inches long. It sleeps and wakes, sucks, and moves its position. At the end of the sixth month, eyes, eyelids, and eyelashes form. The fetus's eyes are light sensitive, and he or she can hear uterine sounds and respond to vibrations and acoustical stimulation (Kisilevsky, Muir, & Low, 1992).

The head and body of the fetus become more proportionate during the third trimester. Fat layers form under the skin. By the end of the eighth month, the fetus weighs about five pounds and is about eighteen inches long. By the end of the ninth month, the nails have grown to the ends of the fingers and toes. The skin becomes smoother and is covered with a protective waxy substance called *vernix caseosa*. The baby is ready for delivery.

Prenatal Care

MEDICAL AND HEALTH CARE

Ordinarily the fetus is well protected in its uterine environment, but as soon as a woman suspects she is pregnant, she needs to receive good prenatal care. Time is of the essence because the first three months of fetal development are crucial to the optimum health of the child. Initial prenatal visits include a complete physical examination. Because the prospective father is involved and concerned as well, it is helpful for him to accompany his partner on prenatal visits. The examiner will take a complete medical history of the mother, and the father if necessary, and perform various tests and make recommendations regarding health care during pregnancy. Sexual relations, minor complications of pregnancy, and danger signs to watch for

LIVING ISSUES

Ethnicity, Race, and Infant Mortality

Infant mortality refers to the number of infants dying per 1,000 population during the first year of life. Overall, the rate among whites was 8.2 in 1989 (U.S. Bureau of the Census, 1992). This is in sharp contrast to the rates among minority races or ethnic groups. The rate of infant mortality is highest among Native Americans. One study of infant mortality on an Oregon Indian reservation showed a rate almost three times higher than the overall U.S. rate (Remez, 1992). The rate among blacks is about two times greater than for whites (U.S. Bureau of the Census, 1992). Infants born to poor, young, undereducated, or unmarried black women are at special risk (Jamieson & Buescher, 1992). However, the rates among poor women of all races, including whites, are high, although not as high as among blacks (R. Turner, 1992). Infant mortality among Hispanics is lower than among blacks, but still higher than among whites (Klitsch, 1991). The rate is especially high among Puerto Ricans as compared to Mexican Americans and Cuban Americans.

The most significant factor in relation to these figures is the lack of proper prenatal care from the beginning of pregnancy. Nationally, 16 percent of all pregnant women receive inadequate prenatal care. Either they don't go to the doctor at all, go late in pregnancy, or make fewer visits than recommended (Harvey & Faber, 1993). Yet early and regular prenatal care is associated with reduced infant mortality and favorable outcomes on key measures of child health, such as birth weight. The primary reason for lack of care is financial. Medicaid coverage for pregnant women with family incomes below 133 percent of the poverty level has been expanded. This increase has helped considerably. Nonetheless, there are still many women not eligible for Medicaid who lack the resources to get insurance coverage and, as a result, go without care (Althaus, 1991a). Only some of these women are able to obtain help through local public health departments, community hospitals, or other maternity care providers. Providing adequate prenatal care is actually cost-effective. Every dollar spent on prenatal care for high-risk women saves an average of over $3 in the care of low-birth-weight infants (Harvey & Faber, 1993).

in avoiding major complications will be discussed to allay the couple's fear and anxieties (Rice, 1989b).

MINOR SIDE EFFECTS

No pregnancy is without some discomfort. Expectant mothers may experience one or several of the following to varying degrees: *nausea (morning sickness), heartburn, flatus (gas), hemorrhoids, constipation, shortness of breath, backache, leg cramps, uterine contractions, insomnia, minor vaginal discharge,* and *varicose veins.* The caregiver, or examiner, will suggest the best ways in which each woman can minimize her discomforts (Rice, 1989b).

MAJOR COMPLICATIONS OF PREGNANCY

Major complications of pregnancy arise infrequently; however, when they do, they threaten the health and life of the woman and the developing embryo or fetus more seriously than do the usual minor discomforts of pregnancy.

Pernicious Vomiting

This is prolonged and persistent vomiting, which may dehydrate the woman and rob her of adequate nutrients for proper fetal growth. One woman in several hundred suffers from vomiting to the extent that she requires hospitalization.

Toxemia

This is characterized by high blood pressure; waterlogging of the tissues (edema), indicated by swollen face and limbs or rapid weight gain; albumin in the urine; headaches; blurring of vision; and eclampsia (convulsions). If not treated, toxemia can be fatal to mother and embryo or fetus. Most commonly it is a disease of neglect because proper prenatal care is lacking. Toxemia during pregnancy ranks as one of three chief causes of maternal mortality (Guttmacher, 1983).

Threatened Abortion

The first symptoms are usually vaginal bleeding. Studies reveal that about one in six pregnancies is spontaneously aborted before the fetus is of sufficient size to survive. Most spontaneous abortions occur early in pregnancy. Three out of four happen before the twelfth week, and only one in four occurs between twelve and twenty-eight weeks (Guttmacher, 1983).

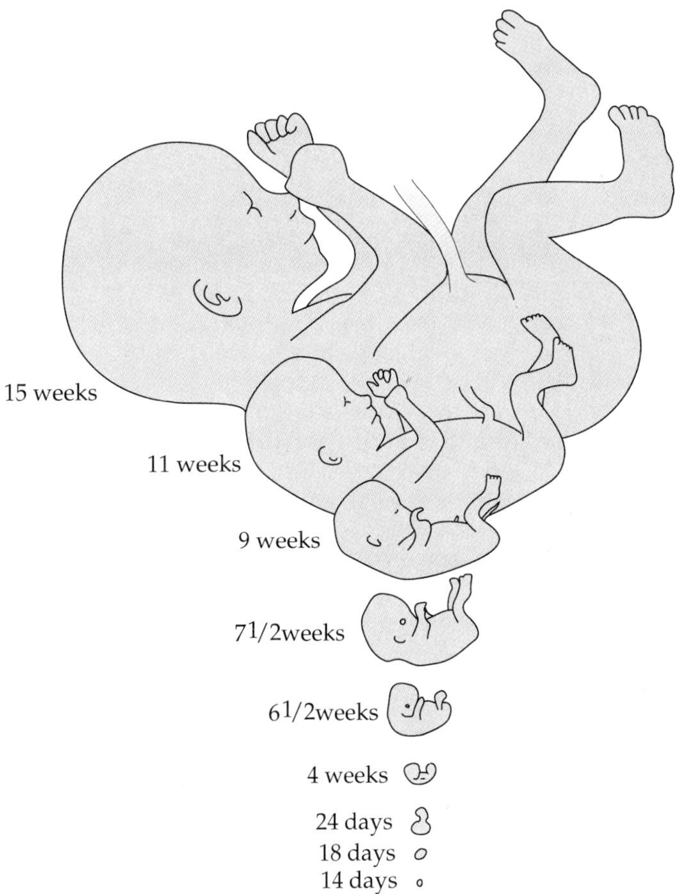

FIGURE 3.4 Embryonic and fetal development from two to fifteen weeks following conception.

Placenta Praevia

Placenta praevia refers to the premature separation of the placenta from the uterine wall, usually because the placenta grows partially or entirely over the cervical opening. One in two hundred pregnant women suffers from this problem, which usually occurs in the third trimester. If they are given proper treatment, 80 percent to 85 percent of the babies will survive. About 60 percent are delivered by cesarean section.

Tubal Pregnancy

Tubal pregnancy occurs when the fertilized ovum attaches itself to the wall of the fallopian tube and grows there rather than

LIVING ISSUES

Abortion and the Question of Viability

On January 22, 1973, the United States Supreme Court ruled that a state could not inhibit or restrict a woman's right to obtain an abortion during the first trimester of pregnancy (12.7 weeks) and that the decision to have an abortion was the woman's own in consultation with her doctor (*Roe* v. *Wade*, 1973). In a 5–4 decision announced on July 3, 1989, the court overthrew the trimester provisions of *Roe* v. *Wade*, and said that a doctor, before aborting a fetus believed to be at least twenty weeks gestation, will determine if the fetus is **viable** and perform tests that establish the fetus's gestational age, weight, and lung maturity. The court reaffirmed that states may pass laws regulating abortion after viability "except where it is necessary . . . for the preservation of the life or health of the mother" (*Webster* v. *Reproductive Health Services*, 1988). The majority opinion in this decision said the statement was interpreted to mean that only those tests that are necessary to determine viability be performed. If viability is determined, the mother and doctor are subject to any special laws passed by the particular state.

Several comments need to be made.

1. Tests to determine viability are expensive and, because of their costs, prevent women who cannot afford them from having an abortion.
2. The tests sometimes impose health risks for both the pregnant woman and the fetus.
3. The tests are sometimes unreliable and inaccurate.
4. At twenty weeks of age, no fetus is viable or can be made viable by any foreseeable new scientific techniques (Rosoff, 1989).
5. Tests of lung maturity cannot provide the necessary information until the fetus is at least twenty-eight to thirty weeks gestation. Any tests before these ages are imprecise ("The court edges," 1989).
6. Using viability tests as a basis for decision eliminates the woman's right to choose whether she will have an abortion.
7. There is confusion over calculating the weeks of gestation. Physicians and a number of health agencies calculate the period of gestation from the first day of the woman's last menstrual period instead of from the day of fertilization, which comes two weeks later (DiPetro & Allen, 1991). Because the law does not specify how the period of gestation should be calculated, there is confusion as to when a viability test is necessary (Santee & Henshaw, 1992). For these reasons, many thoughtful persons are opposed to viability tests as one determinant of whether a woman can have an abortion.

within the uterus. Sometimes the pregnancy, termed *ectopic*, is situated in the ovary, abdomen, or cervix. Such pregnancies have to be terminated by surgery. Surveys indicate that the number of ectopic pregnancies has been climbing steadily. Possible causes may be the postponement of childbearing, during which time the fallopian tubes age; previous abortion; pelvic inflammatory disease (PID); sexually transmitted diseases (STDs); frequent douching with commercial preparations; and previous surgery (Althaus, 1991b). Any condition that affects the fallopian tubes can impede transport of the fertilized ovum, thus contributing to an ectopic pregnancy. ("Increasing rates of ectopic pregnancies," 1984, p. 14). Despite the increase in ectopic pregnancies, which must always be terminated, fetal mortality rates have fallen because women are getting prompter and better treatment (Rice, 1989b).

RH Incompatibility

This involves an expectant mother with Rh negative blood who carries a fetus with Rh positive blood (Rice, 1989b).

Infertility

CAUSES

Infertile—Unable to conceive or to effect pregnancy

About 17 percent of all couples are **infertile** and would not be able to have children without medical help (Porter & Christopher, 1984). About half of those with problems are able to conceive with medical help (Collins, Wrixon, Janes, & Wilson, 1983).

About 20 percent of infertility cases involve both partners. Both are "subfertile": they have too frequent or too infrequent intercourse; they have intercourse only during those times of the month when the woman is least likely to get pregnant; they use Vaseline or some other vaginal lubricant that injures sperm cells or acts as a barrier preventing the sperm from entering the *cervix;* or they are too old or in poor health.

About 40 percent of infertility cases involve the man. To impregnate a woman a man must meet four biological requirements. He must

1. Produce healthy live sperm in sufficient numbers
2. Secrete seminal fluid in proper amounts and with the right composition to transport sperm
3. Have an unobstructed throughway from the testicle to the end of the penis, allowing the sperm to pass
4. Be able to achieve and sustain an erection in order to ejaculate sperm within the vagina

A number of physical and psychological factors may cause male infertility.

About 40 percent of infertility cases involve the woman. To be capable of pregnancy, a woman also must meet several basic biological requirements. She needs to be ovulating, the passage through the fallopian tubes needs to be clear, and the cervical mucus must allow passage of the sperm (Ansbacher & Adler, 1988). Several additional factors may affect female fertility: Abnormalities of the uterus sometimes prevent conception or full-term pregnancy (Malinak & Wheeler, 1985); the climate of the vagina may be too acid, thus immobilizing the sperm; and the age of the mother may also be a factor. Fertility decreases gradually after age 35 and ceases completely after menopause.

IMPACT

Involuntary childlessness due to infertility can cause significant emotional and psychological distress for some persons (Daniluk, 1991). A lack of self-esteem, a sense of loss of internal control of one's life, and depression may result from infertility (Abbey, Andrews, & Halman, 1992). Grief, anger, and guilt reactions are common (Higgins, 1990). Stress is often higher among wives than among husbands, if the women are less willing than their husbands to forgo parenthood, or if they see infertility as role failure on their part (Benazon, Wright, & Sabourin, 1992; Ulbrich, Coyle, & Llabre, 1990). Also, if a couple seeks treatment, the majority of tests and treatments focus on the woman's body, regardless of whether it is the man or the woman whose physical problems are causing the infertility. Other people may assume that infertility is the wife's fault and treat her as a second-class citizen. She may feel out of place around other women who are mothers.

Continued infertility may have an effect on marital and sexual satisfaction (Pepe & Byrne, 1991). If treatment does not seem to be working, couples show greater dissatisfaction with their sexual relationship as time goes on (Benazon, Wright, & Sabourin, 1992). Social changes may also occur, as infertile couples alter their network interactions in an attempt to avoid painful reminders of their childlessness (Higgins, 1990).

In contrast to these unhappy couples, some couples report that their problems brought them closer together, that they were more affectionate and had higher levels of communication. They became even more committed to their marriage and to sharing their lives together (Ulbrich, Coyle, & Llabre, 1990). Much depends on the attitudes of the couple. The longer they are married and childless, the less trouble they have adjusting to involuntary childlessness as a permanent state. Two-career couples usually have less trouble adjusting to the situation than those in which the wife does not work. Some research suggests that couples usually divorce if the husband wants a child and the wife does not, but they tend to stay together if the wife wants a child and the husband does not. The couples' attitude toward a childless lifestyle has a significant attitude on their marital adjustment (Ulbrich, Coyle, & Llabre, 1990).

ALTERNATE MEANS OF CONCEPTION

Artificial Insemination

If other medical treatments for infertility don't succeed, several techniques may permit couples to have children (Cushner, 1986). One technique is **artificial insemination**. In this procedure, the sperm are injected into the woman's vagina or uterus for

Artificial insemination—Injection of sperm cells into the vagina or uterus for the purpose of inducing pregnancy

FOCUS

Treatments for Infertility

Generally speaking, if couples are younger than 35 years of age, they should wait for a full year of attempting pregnancy before consulting a physician. This gives enough time for conception to take place if the couple are fertile. If they are older than 35, they should see a doctor after six months of unsuccessful attempts. Older couples should get help sooner because psychological and physical factors that work against conception grow stronger with time. For the younger couple, waiting for a reasonable period of time (one year) improves the chances of fertility (Rice, 1990b).

Homologous insemination (AIH)—Artificial insemination with the husband's sperm

In vitro fertilization—Removal of the ovum from the mother and fertilizing it in the laboratory, then implanting the zygote within the uterine wall

Heterologous insemination (AID)—Artificial insemination using the sperm from a donor

Surrogate mother

Gamete intrafallopian transfer (GIFT)—Inserting sperm cells and an egg cell directly into the fallopian tube, where fertilization is expected to occur

Embryo transplant—Insemination of a female with the sperm of an infertile woman's partner; the resulting zygote is transferred, about five days later, into the uterus of the mother-to-be

the purpose of inducing pregnancy. If the husband's sperm are used, the process is called **homologous insemination**, or **AIH** (artificial insemination husband). If the husband's sperm count is low, the sperm may be collected, frozen, and stored until a sufficient quantity is available, then thawed and injected. Generally, AIH is effective in only 5 percent of the cases, because the sperm was incapable of effecting pregnancy in the first place (Pierson & D'Antonio, 1974). Using sperm from a donor is called **heterologous insemination**, or **AID** (artificial insemination donor).

Surrogate Mother

Sometimes a woman not able to bear a child still wants to have one by her partner, so together they find a consenting woman who acts as a **surrogate mother**. The surrogate mother agrees to be inseminated with the semen of the male member of the couple, to carry the fetus to term, and then to give the child (and all rights to it) to the couple. When seventy women were questioned regarding their motives for serving as surrogate mothers, they gave the following reasons: money, compassion for the childless couple and desire to help them, or enjoyment of pregnancy (Sobel, 1981). Half the surrogate mothers were married and already had children of their own. There are many unsettled legal questions relating to the rights to the child and to the legitimacy of surrogate agreements.

In Vitro Fertilization

This is the procedure whereby a "test tube baby" is conceived. It is used when the fallopian tubes are blocked so that the sperm never reaches the ovum. The egg is removed from the mother, fertilized in the laboratory with the partner's sperm, grown for several days until the uterus is hormonally ready, then implanted in the uterine wall (Zimmerman, 1982). The procedure is opposed by those who feel it is immoral and consider it tampering with nature.

Since the success rate of IVF is low, some couples simultaneously apply for adoption (Williams, 1992).

Gamete Intrafallopian Transfer (GIFT)

This involves inserting a thin plastic tube carrying the sperm and egg directly into the fallopian tube, where the gametes unite just as they would in normal conception. "GIFT is what nature really does, with a little help from us," says Dr. Ricardo Asch, professor of obstetrics and gynecology at the University of California at Irwin (Ubell, 1990). The success rate is 40 percent—double that of in vitro fertilization.

Embryo Transplant

This procedure is even more controversial (Dunn, Ryan, & O'Brien, 1988). In this procedure, a volunteer female donor is artificially inseminated with the sperm of the in-

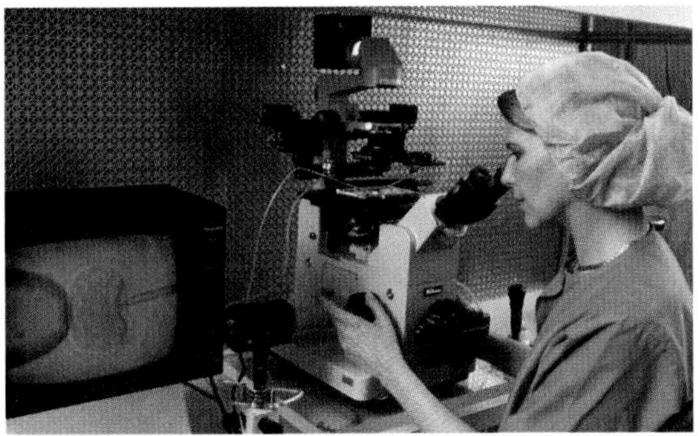
In in vitro fertilization, scratching the surface of the ovum allows the sperm to penetrate more easily.

fertile woman's partner. After about five days, the zygote is removed from the donor and transferred into the uterus of the mother-to-be, who carries the child during pregnancy. Embryos may even be frozen and stored prior to implantation in a uterus. At present, the procedure is experimental and costly, and has a low success rate.

Heredity

CHROMOSOMES, GENES, AND DNA

Chromosomes are rodlike structures in the nucleus of each cell. The chromosomes carry the hereditary material, called **genes**, which control physical characteristics that are inherited. The genes do this by directing the physical changes in the body throughout its development. Each body cell, except the sex cells, or gametes, contains twenty-three pairs of chromosomes, and each chromosome has between twenty thousand and a hundred thousand genes. The gametes contain only half the number of chromosomes present in other body cells. Instead of twenty-three pairs, each sperm or ovum has twenty-three single chromosomes. *When the sperm and ovum unite, the twenty-three single chromosomes within the nucleus of each gamete combine in pairs with those in the other gamete to produce forty-six chromosomes in the resulting zygote.* Figure 3.5 shows the process. After fertilization takes place and the one-celled zygote begins to divide and subdivide, the forty-six chromosomes each split in half with each cell division, so that each daughter cell contains the same twenty-three pairs of chromosomes. This means that each new cell produced contains the same twenty-three pairs of chromosomes with their genes.

Genes are made up of numerous molecules called deoxyribonucleic acid or **DNA**. The DNA molecule looks like a double helix, or a spiral staircase, with a phosphate–sugar structure on the outside framework and with four *base* molecules (*adenine, thymine, guanine,* and *cystosine*) occurring in pairs that form the steps of the staircase on the inside. The bases are labeled A, T, G, and C, as shown in Figure 3.6. One strand of DNA may continue for thousands of base pairs, and the number of different strands that can be made is almost infinite. Each section of DNA is a separate

Chromosomes—Rodlike structures in each cell, occurring in pairs, that carry the hereditary material

Genes—The hereditary material of the chromosomes

DNA—Complex molecules in genes that form the basis for the genetic structure, deoxyribonucleic acid

Body cells of men and women contain 23 pairs of chromosomes.

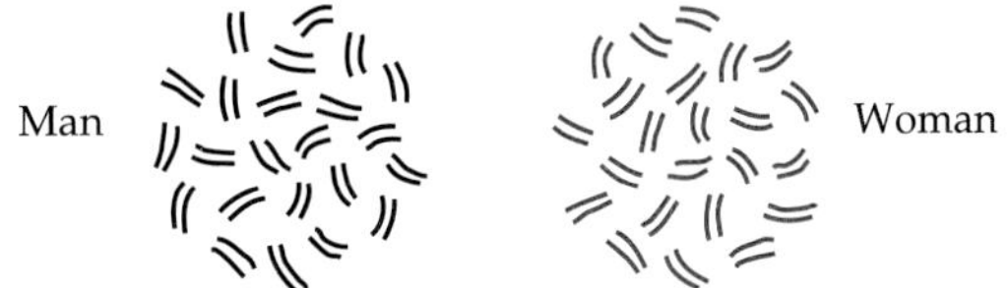

At maturity, each sex cell has only 23 single chromosomes. Through meiosis, a member is taken randomly from each original pair of chromosomes.

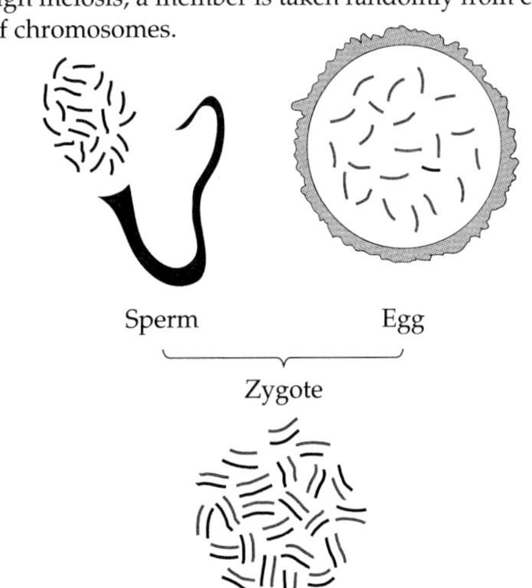

At fertilization, the chromosomes from each parent pair up so that the zygote contains 23 pairs of chromosomes—half from the mother and half from the father.

FIGURE 3.5 Hereditary composition of the zygote.

Autosomes—Twenty-two pairs of chromosomes that are responsible for most aspects of the individual's development

Sex chromosomes—Twenty-third pair of chromosomes that determine the gender of the offspring

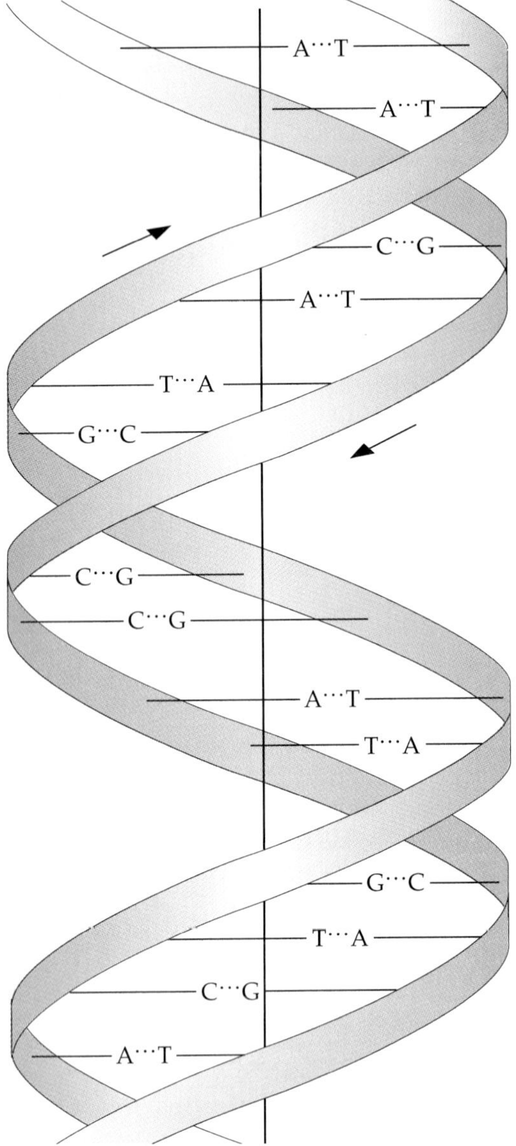

FIGURE 3.6 DNA molecule.

gene, and the vertical sequence of the base pairs acts as a code to direct the cells as they reproduce and manufacture proteins that maintain life. Each cell of the body has the same DNA code and the same genes that direct growth. The particular code that we inherit from our parents directs our growth as humans rather than other creatures, and is responsible for all the physical characteristics we develop.

THE TWENTY-THIRD PAIR AND SEX DETERMINATION

Each sperm cell and each ovum contains twenty-three chromosomes. Twenty-two of these are labeled **autosomes** and are responsible for most aspects of the individual's development. Figure 3.7 illustrates the twenty-third pair, the **sex chromosomes**, which determine whether the offspring will be male or female. As shown in Figure 3.8, the man produces two types of sperm: one type with an X chromosome, having a larger head and shorter tail; another type with a Y chromosome, having a smaller head and longer tail. The woman produces ova with only X chromosomes. If a sperm containing an X chromosome unites with the ovum (producing an XX combination), a girl is conceived. If a sperm containing a Y chromosome unites with the ovum (producing an XY combination), a boy is conceived. Because the Y-carrying sperm have a longer tail and a lighter head, they swim faster and may reach the egg cell sooner. For this reason, there is a conception ratio of 160 males to 100 females. However, the male zygote is more vulnerable, so the ratio is reduced to 120 males to 100 females by the time of implantation; to 110 males to 100 females by full term; and to 105 males to 100 females born live (Rice, 1989).

MULTIPLE BIRTHS

Monozygotic (identical) twins—One-egg, or identical, twins

Twins may be of the same sex or of both sexes, depending on whether they start from one egg, as **monozygotic (identical)**

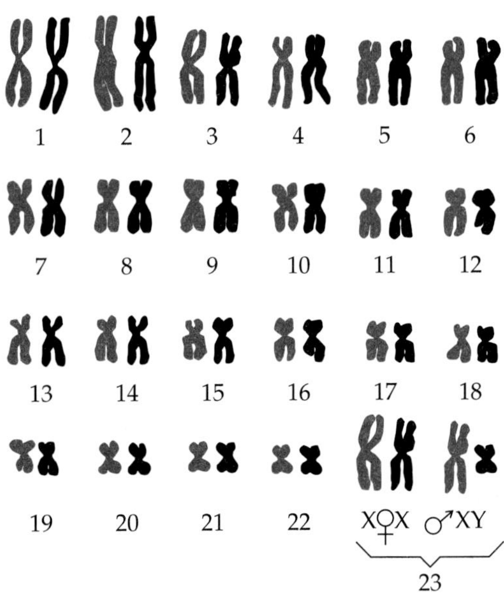

FIGURE 3.7 The twenty-third pair of chromosomes.

PARENTING ISSUES

Selecting the Sex of Your Child

Various techniques have been used to try to control the sex of the child that is conceived. Sperm carrying Y chromosomes are more fragile than X-carrying sperm, and all sperm are more viable in an alkaline environment. So if a male baby is desired, one theory suggests that everything possible be done to keep the Y-carrying sperm alive and healthy: use an alkaline douche; have intercourse two days or so after ovulation (so the sperm can reach the egg easily); use deep penetration during intercourse; and have the female orgasm precede male ejaculation (so the sperm are not squirted out during female orgasm). The opposite measures would be taken if a female baby is desired. Some researchers have found this total approach to sex selection reliable (Simcock, 1985).

A more promising technique is to separate the Y and X sperm and through artificial insemination to inject the type needed, depending on the sex desired (Glass & Ericsson, 1982).

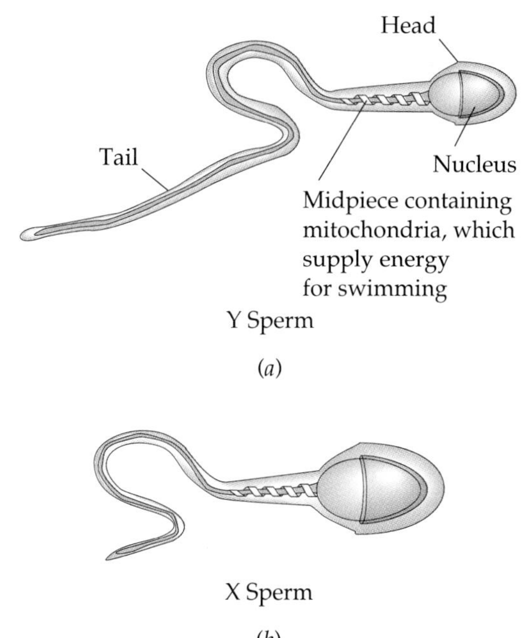

FIGURE 3.8 The two types of sperm.

twins, or from two eggs, as **dizygotic (fraternal) twins**. *Identical twins result when an ovum fertilized by one sperm divides during development to produce two embryos* (see photo on p. 70). The embryos have the same heredity, are always of the same sex, and usually share a common *placenta*. If the two developing embryos do not completely separate, **Siamese twins** result. *Fraternal twins result when two ova are fertilized by two separate sperm*. They may be of the same sex or different sexes and will be as different in heredity as are any other siblings. They develop with separate placentas. Triplets, quadruplets, and so forth may be all identical (from one ova), all fraternal (from separately fertilized ova), or a combination. Two of three triplets may be identical, for example, with the third fraternal. In this case, two ova are fertilized by two sperm, and one of the resulting zygotes divides after fertilization to produce two embryos.

Dizygotic (fraternal) twins—Two-egg, or fraternal, twins

Siamese twins—Monozygotic twins where complete separation did not occur during development

LIVING ISSUES

Infanticide in Other Cultures

Unfortunately, one method of sex selection in many parts of the world is female infanticide. When the Chinese government decided to limit the number of children per family to one, and the first child born was a girl, the infant was often abandoned or killed in hopes the next baby born would be a boy. Today, abortion of female fetuses is widely practiced in modern-day China, India, and other countries where girls are considered a burden on the family.

SIMPLE INHERITANCE AND DOMINANT–RECESSIVE INHERITANCE

An Austrian monk named Gregor Mendel (1822–1884) first discovered the laws that govern inheritance. He experimented by crossing garden pea plants with one another, and noticed that various traits such

Identical twins are called monozygotic twins because they develop from one egg.

Law of dominant inheritance

Dominant gene

Recessive gene

Alleles

Homozygous

Heterozygous

as yellow or green color, wrinkled or smooth seeds, tall or short height appeared or disappeared from one generation to the next.

The peas that Mendel used for his experiments came in two colors: yellow or green. When Mendel crossed purebred plants producing yellow peas with other purebreds containing yellow peas, he noticed that all the resulting offspring plants produced yellow peas. When he crossed two purebred plants producing green peas, the result was always plants with green peas. However, when he crossed purebred plants producing yellow peas with those producing purebred green peas, all the offspring plants produced yellow peas. If he then bred these hybrids, 75 percent of the offspring had yellow peas and the remaining 25 percent had green peas. Mendel explained this result by formulating the **law of dominant inheritance**. The law says that when an organism inherits competing traits (such as green and yellow colors), only one trait will be expressed. The trait that is expressed is *dominant* over the other, which is recessive. The dominant trait is written with a capital letter, the *recessive* with a lowercase letter. The diagrams in Figure 3.9 illustrate possible results when peas are crossed.

Let's see how **dominant genes** and **recessive genes** work. Genes that govern alternate expressions of a particular characteristic (such as skin color) are called **alleles**. An organism receives a pair of alleles for a given characteristic, one from each parent. When both alleles are the same, the organism is **homozygous** for the trait; when the alleles are different, the organism is **heterozygous** for the characteristic. When the alleles are heterozygous, the dominant allele is expressed. Thus, in Figure 3.9, YY or gg alleles are *homozygous*, and gY or Yg are *heterozygous*. Only when there is a pairing of recessive alleles (gg) can the recessive trait be expressed.

Phenotype

Genotype

Gregor Mendel discovered the laws that govern inheritance by crossing garden pea plants with one another.

An observable trait (like seed color) is called a **phenotype**, while the underlying genetic pattern is called a **genotype**. Organisms may have identical phenotypes but different genotypes. For example, the plants that produce yellow peas (the phenotype) may have different genotypes (YY, Yg, or gY).

The same principle holds true in humans. Brown eyes, for example, are dominant over blue eyes. If we let B = brown eyes, and b = blue eyes, and pair a brown-eyed man with heterozygous alleles with a blue-eyed woman with homozygous alleles, we get the possible results shown in Figure 3.10. In this case, half the offspring would have brown eyes (bB and bB) and half would have blue eyes (bb and bb) because two recessive genes would have to be paired to produce blue eyes.

Table 3.2 shows a variety of dominant and recessive human characteristics.

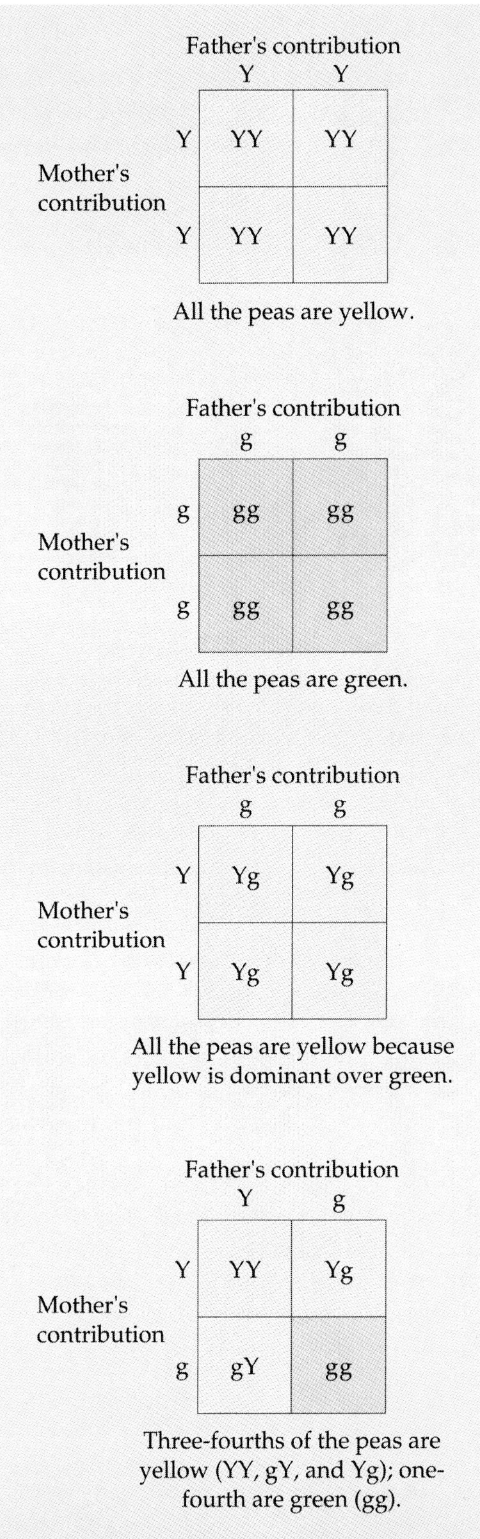

FIGURE 3.9 Mendelian inheritance in peas.

TABLE 3.2
DOMINANT AND RECESSIVE TRAITS IN HUMANS

Dominant	*Recessive*
Brown eyes	Blue or hazel eyes
Long eyelashes	Short eyelashes
Near- or farsightedness	Normal vision
Dark hair	Light or red hair
Curly hair	Straight hair
Cataract	Normal vision
Skin pigmentation	Albinism
Glaucoma	Normal eyes
Color vision	Color blindness
Free earlobes	Attached earlobes
Normal metabolism	Phenylketonuria
Broad lips	Thin lips
Scaly skin (Ichthyosis)	Normal skin
Polydactylism (extra fingers & toes)	Normal
Dwarfism (Achondroplasia)	Normal
Huntington's disease	Normal
Normal hearing	Deafness

An example is *sickle-cell anemia*, a condition common among blacks. In this condition, the red blood cells of a person are sickle- or crescent-shaped instead of circular, and they tend to clog the blood vessels, restricting blood circulation, causing tissue damage and even death. Also, the spleen tries

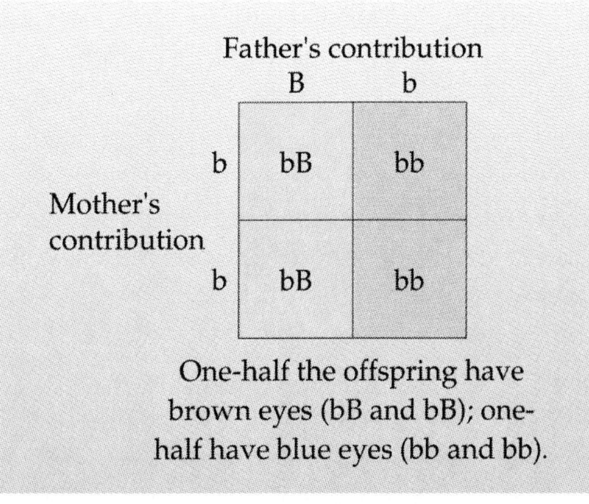

FIGURE 3.10 Inheritance for eye color.

INCOMPLETE DOMINANCE

Sometimes one allele is not completely dominant over the other. This phenomenon is known as **incomplete dominance**.

Incomplete dominance—When one paired allele is not completely dominant over the other

Skin color is an example of polygenetic inheritance since it is controlled by a number of genes.

to destroy the blood cells, causing anemia. Sickle-cell anemia occurs only in persons who carry homozygous genes for that trait. The result for these people is that both sickle-cell genes direct the body to manufacture the abnormal blood cells. Other people are heterozygous with respect to the sickle-cell trait, having one sickle-cell gene and one normal one. The result is that neither gene is dominant or recessive, so the person has a mixture of two types of blood cells: part normal and part sickle-cell. Such a person functions all right except at high altitudes, where oxygen is scarce. Interestingly, people with sickle-cells are protected against malaria because the malaria parasite apparently doesn't thrive in blood containing these cells.

POLYGENIC INHERITANCE

In many instances, traits do not result from a single gene pair, but from a combination of many gene pairs. For example, numerous genes or gene pairs are involved in body height, weight, and shape. When gene pairs interact, one gene pair may inhibit or allow the expression of the other gene pair. A system of interacting gene pairs is called a **polygenic system of inheritance**. Such systems produce a wide variety of phenotypes that may differ from those of either parent.

One example is skin color, which is the result of the action of a number of genes. A light-skinned person and a dark-skinned person usually have children with skin tone between their own because half the genes come from each parent. However, the child may also have a lighter or darker skin than either parent, with the child inheriting only the light- or dark-skin genes from the parents.

Many other characteristics, including personality traits such as intelligence, sociability, and temperament, are a result of polygenic inheritance. Even then, inheritance only predisposes us toward certain traits. We inherit a range of possibilities called the **reaction range**, which is the range of phenotypes for each genotype (Scarr, 1984). Environmental influences may enhance or detract from the inherited possibilities.

Reaction range—Range of possible phenotypes given a particular genotype and environmental influences

Some genotypes seem to produce characteristics that persist regardless of environmental influences. A child who seems to have a predisposition toward superior intelligence, for example, may evidence this characteristic in spite of adverse environmental circumstances (Kagan, 1984). This tendency for a trait to persist is called **canalization**.

Canalization—Tendency for inherited characteristics to persist along a certain path regardless of environmental conditions

Polygenic system of inheritance—A number of interacting genes that produce a phenotype

SEX-LINKED TRAITS

Some defective, recessive genes are carried on only the twenty-third pair of chromosomes, the sex chromosomes, and produce what are called **sex-linked disorders**. One example is *hemophilia*, a disorder characterized by inability of the blood to clot. If a woman inherits a defective, recessive, he-

Sex-linked disorders—Disorders carried only by the mother, through defective, recessive genes on the X chromosome

mophilic gene on the X chromosome she receives from her mother, and a second, normal, dominant gene on the X chromosome she receives from her father, she will not be a hemophiliac but will be a carrier (because she has one defective gene). However, if she has a son, and passes the defective, recessive gene on the X chromosome to him, there is no corresponding dominant, healthy X chromosome to counterbalance the defective gene, so the son inherits hemophilia. Figure 3.11 shows the possible combinations and results when a woman who is a carrier has children. *Color blindness, baldness,* some *allergies, Duchenne's muscular dystrophy,* and other diseases are examples of sex-linked traits that are inherited. A woman cannot inherit such a trait unless she received two defective genes, one from her mother who is a carrier, and one from her father who manifests the defect.

Mother's contribution	Father's contribution X	Father's contribution Y
X.	X.X Girl (carrier)	X.Y Boy (hemophiliac)
X	XX Girl (normal)	XY Boy (normal)

The odds for a male child being a hemophiliac are 50%;
the odds for a female child being a carrier are 50%.
The odds for having a male child who is also a hemophiliac are 25%;
the odds for having a female child who is also a carrier are 25%.
X. = defective chromosome.

FIGURE 3.11 Sex-linked inheritance.

Hereditary Defects

CAUSES OF BIRTH DEFECTS

The majority of babies coming into the world are healthy and normal. Occasionally, however, a child is born with a **congenital deformity**: a defect that is present at the time of birth. Currently, one in sixteen infants is born with some sort of serious defect (National Foundation for the March of Dimes, 1977).

Congenital deformity—Defect present at birth, which may be the result of hereditary factors, conditions during pregnancy, or damage occurring at the time of birth

Birth defects result from three causes: (1) hereditary factors, (2) faulty environments that prevent the child from developing normally, and (3) birth injuries. Only 20 percent of birth defects are inherited. The other 80 percent are caused by a faulty environment, birth injuries, or a combination of causes. Let's concentrate here on defects that are inherited due to faulty genes.

GENETIC DEFECTS

Some defects are inherited via a single, dominant, defective gene. Scientists are in the process of identifying which gene is responsible for each inherited disorder. McKusick's catalog of genetic diseases lists 1,172 dominant gene disorders, 618 recessive gene disorders, and 124 sex-linked disorders (McKusick, 1986). *Huntington's disease* is a common example of a dominant gene disorder. The disease causes a gradual deterioration of the nervous system, physical weakness, emotional disturbance, mental retardation, and eventually death. The symptoms do not appear until after 30 years of age (Pines, 1984).

Large numbers of diseases are caused by pairs of recessive genes. These include *cystic fibrosis, phenylketonuria (PKU), Tay-Sachs disease,* and many others (Welsh, Pennington, Ozonoff, Rouse, & McCabe, 1990). Babies born with cystic fibrosis lack an enzyme. This lack causes mucous obstructions in the body, especially in the lungs and digestive organs. Treatments have improved, but death is still inevitable. PKU is caused by an excess of *phenylalanine,* an amino acid, which causes mental retardation and neurological disturbances. The disease is treatable with diet regulation. Tay-Sach's disease is caused by an enzyme deficiency. It is characterized by progressive retardation of development, paralysis, dementia, blindness, and death by age 3 or 4. It is most common in families of Eastern European Jewish origin (Berkow, 1987). Carriers of both cystic fibrosis and Tay-Sachs disease can be detected through genetic counseling. All three diseases can usually be detected through prenatal examinations.

A large number of defects have multiple factors as causes. The defects do not become apparent until a faulty prenatal or postnatal environment triggers their onset. *Cleft palate* or *cleft lip* is one example. It may be related to hereditary factors, to the position of the embryo in the uterus, to the blood supply, or to some drugs taken during pregnancy. *Spina bifida* is another example, characterized by incomplete closure of the lower spine. Both hereditary defects and environmental factors play a causative role. Recent data points to a vitamin deficiency as a contributing factor (Berkow, 1987).

CHROMOSOMAL ABNORMALITIES

Chromosomal abnormalities are of two types: sex chromosomal abnormalities and autosomal chromosomal abnormalities. Five of the most common sex-linked chromosomal abnormalities are summarized in Table 3.3 (Berch & Bender, 1987). These abnormalities arise during meiosis. When an ova or sperm are formed, the forty-six chromosomes divide unevenly, producing a gamete that has too few or too many chromosomes (Moore, Nielsen, & Mistretta, 1982).

TABLE 3.3
COMMON SEX-LINKED CHROMOSOMAL ABNORMALITIES

Name	*Chromosome Combination*	*Characteristics*	*Incidence*
None	XYY	Tall stature, subnormal intelligence; severe acne; impulsive and aggressive behavior, which may stem from psychosocial problems	1 in 1,000 males
Kleinfelter's Syndrome	XXY	Feminine appearance; small penis and testicles; infertile; low sexual drive; decreased body hair; prominent breasts; tendency toward mental impairment	1 in 1,000 males
Fragile X	Usually XY	X chromosome is not influential. Some persons normal, others are retarded. Males may have enlarged testicles.	1 in 1,000 males; 1 in 5,000 females
Turner's Syndrome	XO	Lack of functioning ovaries; incompletely developed internal and external sex organs; loose skin; webbed neck; widely spaced nipples; short stature; deafness and mental deficiency are common (McCauley, Kay, Ito, & Treder, 1987).	1 in 10,000 females
None	XXX	Characteristics vary; some women are normal, fertile; others are sterile, suffer mental retardation	1 in 1,000 females

Down's syndrome is the most common chromosomal disorder resulting in physical and mental retardation.

Sometimes problems result from abnormalities in the autosomes rather than the sex chromosomes. One of the most common of these is *Down's syndrome.* Down's children have an extra chromosome: forty-seven instead of forty-six. The overall incidence is about one in seven hundred live births, but the rate rises to about one in forty live births in mothers over age 40 (Adams, Oakley, & Marks, 1982). There is also a greater risk when the father is over age 45. Characteristics include a flattened skull; folds of skin over the eyes; a flattened bridge of the nose; protruding tongue; short, broad hands and fingers; and short stature. Congenital heart disease is common. Both physical and mental development are retarded; mean IQ is about 50. Most individuals without a major heart disease survive to adulthood.

GENETIC COUNSELING

Couples who have inherited disabilities themselves, or who have a family history of some types of disability, should get genetic counseling to discover the possibility of passing on the defect to a child yet to be conceived. Once the couple know the odds of passing on a defect, they are faced with making a decision regarding whether or not to risk having children. After pregnancy occurs, there are various procedures for discovering defects.

Amniocentesis

Amniocentesis can be performed between the fifteenth and sixteenth weeks of gestation. It involves inserting a hollow needle into the abdomen to obtain a sample of *amniotic fluid* containing fetal cells. The cells are cultured for genetic and chemical studies. One disadvantage of this procedure is that it can be performed only in the second trimester of pregnancy, after the fetus is fairly well developed. Another disadvantage is that it results in fetal loss in one in two hundred amniocenteses. Some of these fetuses are normal and would have survived if the test had not been done. The risk of amniocentesis is that it may cause spontaneous abortion or limb abnormality (Turner, 1992a).

Amniocentesis—Removal of cells from the amniotic fluid to test for abnormalities

Sonogram

A **sonogram** uses high-frequency sound waves to obtain a visual image of the fetus's body structure, to see if growth is normal or if there are any malformations (Hill, Breckle, & Gehrking, 1983). It is often used to confirm or deny the presence of fetal defects indicated by an elevation of a-Feto-protein in the amniotic fluid (Berkow, 1987).

Sonogram—Visual image of the fetus, produced from sound waves, used to detect fetal abnormalities

Fetoscope

A **fetoscope** is passed through a narrow tube that is inserted through the abdomen into the uterus to observe the fetus and placenta directly.

Fetoscope

Chorionic Villi Sampling (CVS)

The **chorionic villi** are threadlike protrusions from the membrane enclosing the fetus. The test involves inserting a thin catheter through the vagina and cervix into the uterus, from which a small sample of the chorionic villi is removed for analysis (Cadkin, Ginsberg, Pergament, & Verlinski, 1984). The real advantage of the procedure is that it can be performed in the eighth week of pregnancy.

Chorionic villi sampling (CVS)

PARENTING ISSUES

The Process of Decision Making in Cases of Possible Defects

Genetic counseling provides information with which couples can make informed decisions in cases of possible defects. Couples can find out before pregnancy the risk of having a baby with a genetic defect, so they can decide whether to take the risk of having a child at all. After pregnancy has occurred, couples can find out if a defect is present, and—if it is—make a decision regarding the course of action to take. The flow chart shown in Figure 3.12 traces the decision-making process involved.

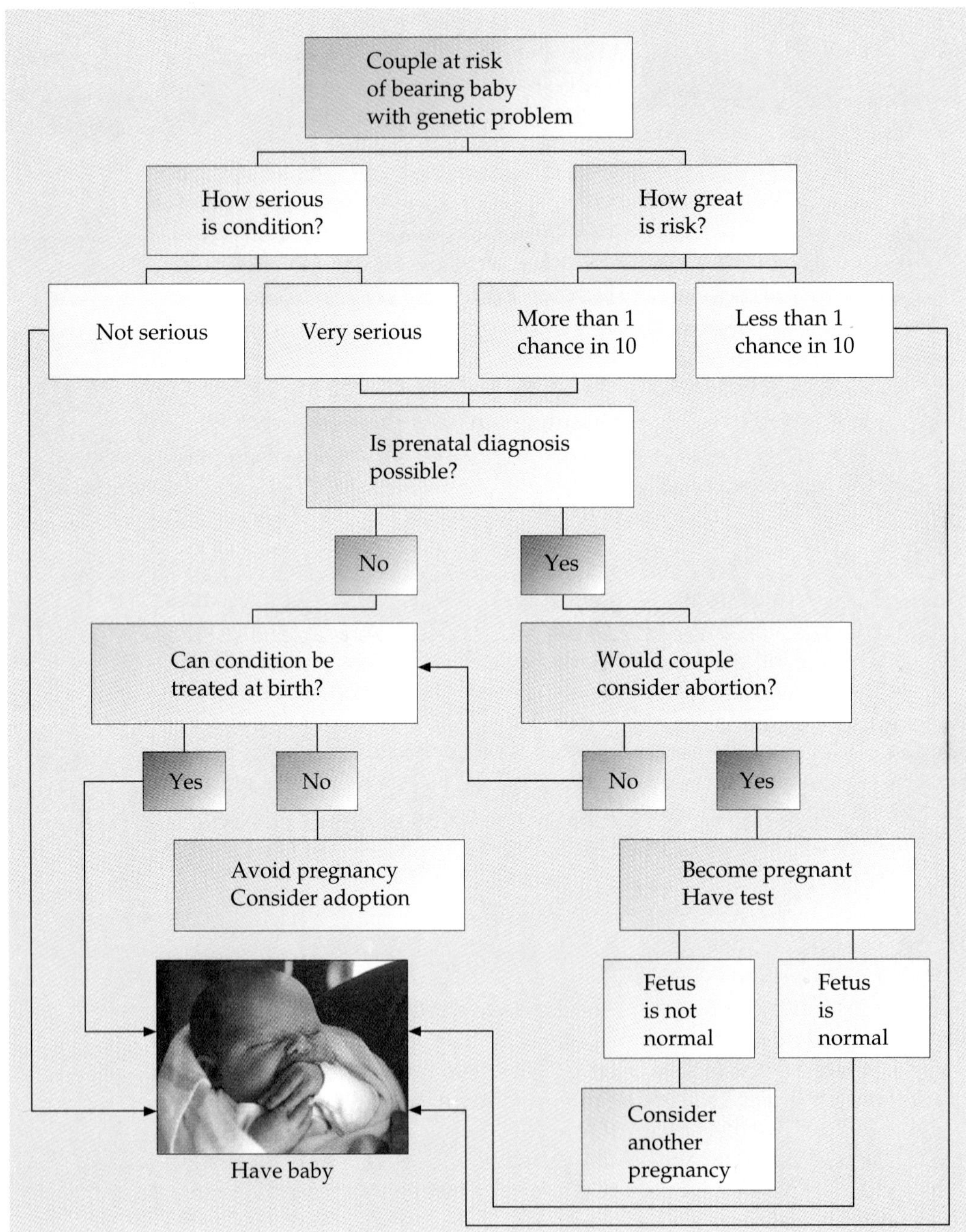

FIGURE 3.12 The process of decision making in case of possible defect.

From *The Developing Person Through the Life Span,* 2nd ed. (p. 74) by K. S. Berger, 1988. New York: Worth Publishers. Reprinted by permission.

Prenatal Environment and Influences

Following conception, the environment in which the fetus grows is crucial to healthy development. Let's focus now on the environment to which the pregnant mother is exposed.

TERATOGENS

Teratogens are any substances that cross the placental barrier, harm the embryo or fetus, and cause birth defects. The timing of exposure to teratogens is particularly important because there is a critical period during which organs and body parts develop, and during which exposure to teratogens is most damaging. Figure 3.13 shows the most sensitive periods. As can be seen, the first eight weeks of development are most critical, but damage to the central nervous system (including the brain), the eyes, and the genitals may occur during the last weeks of pregnancy as well.

Teratogen—Harmful substance that crosses the placenta barrier and harms the embryo or fetus and causes birth defects

Drugs

Doctors now recommend that the pregnant mother not take any medication, even aspirin, without medical approval. The list of harmful drugs continues to grow. The list includes drugs that are commonly used and abused. This section contains a brief discussion of the effects on offspring associated with some of the most used drugs.

Narcotics, sedatives, and *analgesics* are all central nervous system depressants. These include heroin and other forms of narcotics, barbiturates, aspirin, and other substances. If a mother is a heroin addict, the baby will be born an addict also. Large doses of aspirin may cause prepartal and postpartal bleeding.

Alcohol is a particular cause for concern. *Fetal alcohol syndrome* is seen in babies born to mothers who are heavy drinkers (National Institute on Alcohol Abuse and Alcoholism, NIAAA, 1986). Consuming one or two drinks a day substantially heightens the risk of growth malformation, as well as physical and mental retardation (Mills, Graubard, Harley, Rhoades, & Berendes, 1984).

Tranquilizers and *antidepressants* have been associated with congenital malformation.

Nicotine is clearly a factor in low birth weight. The mean birth weight of infants of mothers who smoke during pregnancy is six ounces less than that of infants born to nonsmoking mothers. Growth retardation occurs when mothers smoke five or more cigarettes a day (Nieburg, Marks, McLaren, & Remington, 1985). The incidence of spontaneous abortion, premature birth, stillbirth, and neonatal death is increased, as is the risk of placenta praevia (Edwards, 1992; Rind, 1992b). Also, children of mothers who smoke ten or more cigarettes per day run 50 percent greater risk of developing cancer during childhood (Stjernfeldt, Berglund, Lindsten, & Ludvigsson, 1986).

Cocaine use may produce spontaneous abortion, stillbirth, a malformed baby, or sudden infant death syndrome (Bingol, Fuchs, Diaz, Stone, & Gromisch, 1987; Chasnoff, Burns, Schnoll, & Burns, 1985). See "Living Issues" on p. 80.

Marijuana use has been associated with premature birth and low birth weight (Fried, Watkinson, & Willan, 1984). Lester and Dreher (1989) have labeled marijuana as a behavioral teratogen because it affects the functioning of infants after birth. They found that marijuana smoking during pregnancy affected a newborn infant's cry, suggesting respiratory involvement. Other studies have shown a relationship between prenatal risk factors and various developmental outcomes (Lester, 1987).

Chemicals, Heavy Metals, Environmental Pollutants

In recent years, authorities have become concerned about chemicals, heavy metals, and environmental pollutants as a source of birth defects (Stokols, 1992). Herbicides containing *dioxin*, called Agent Orange in Vietnam and labeled 2,4,5-T in this country, have been associated with an alarming rate of miscarriages, malformed infants, and cancer. The herbicide has now been banned in this country. However, health authorities in Maine recently found unsafe

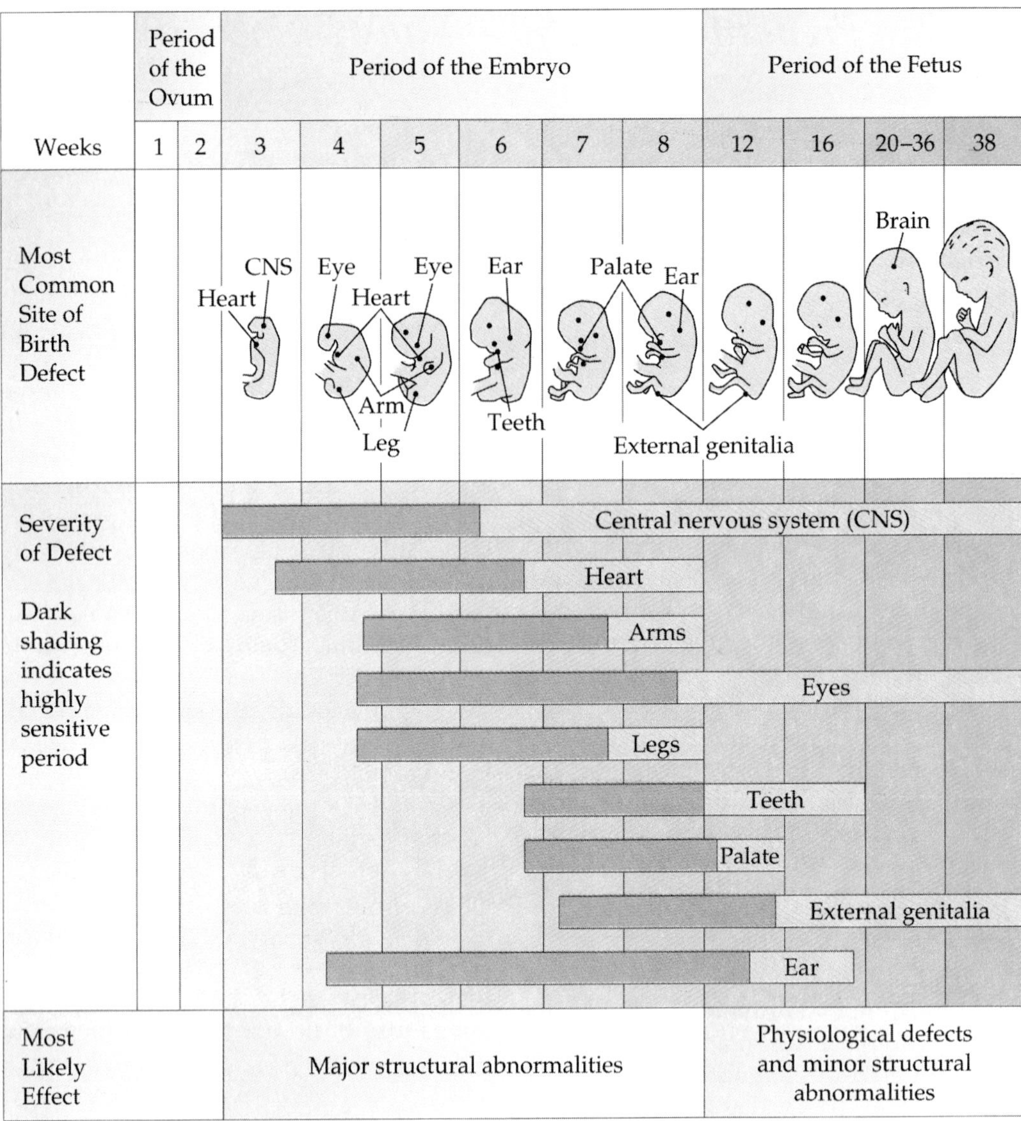

FIGURE 3.13 Sensitive periods of development.

levels of dioxin in the flesh of fish found in several major Maine rivers. These are rivers into which paper companies discharge their wastes.

Industry is still a major source of pollution in many states (M. W. Miller, 1985). *PCB* (an industrial chemical, now banned) was found in Lake Michigan fish. Infants of mothers who ate the fish showed developmental deficits at birth and after (Jacobson, Jacobson, Fein, Schwartz, & Dowler, 1984; Raloff, 1986). *Lead* is a particularly toxic metal, and mothers who are exposed to it may bear infants with low birth weight, slow neurological development, and reduced intelligence (Bellinger, Leviton, Watermaux, Needleman, & Rabinowitz, 1987; Raloff, 1986). This is one reason why tetraethyl lead has been removed from gasoline for automobiles. Women workers who are exposed to *gaseous anesthetics* in hospitals have an increased number of spontaneous abortions and congenital malformations (Bronson, 1977).

RADIATION

Exposure to *radiation* may also endanger the fetus. Survivors of the atomic bombing of Hiroshima and Nagasaki in Japan showed great increases in stillbirths, miscarriages, and birth of babies with congenital malformations. Researchers found prenatal chromosome malformations in children in West Germany, which they be-

PARENTING ISSUES

Prenatal Exposure to Drugs in California Newborns

A recent survey found that more than one in ten pregnant women in California use drugs, smoke cigarettes, or drink alcohol shortly before giving birth (Klitsch, 1994). Using the results of this survey, the researchers estimated that in California in 1992, more than 67,000 newborns had been exposed to one or more drugs in utero, including nearly 40,000 exposed to alcohol and more than 30,000 exposed to licit or illicit drugs. More than 52,000 had been exposed to tobacco. Overall, levels of substance use were generally lowest among women who began prenatal care in the first trimester, and the highest among those who received late or no prenatal care. Public care officials recommended that extensive clinical and educational interventions be introduced. This should include prenatal counseling and residential treatment programs especially designed for pregnant women.

LIVING ISSUES

Reproductive Results Associated with Smoking Cigarettes During Pregnancy

Preconception
- Infertility
- Cardiovascular disease associated with oral contraceptive use

Pregnancy
- Abruptio placentae—premature detachment of the placenta from the wall of the uterus
- Vaginal bleeding
- Premature rupture of membranes
- Fetal death
- Birth weight deficits

Lactation
- Higher levels of pesticide residues in breast milk

Infants
- Neonatal death
- Sudden infant death syndrome
- Linear growth deficit
- Possible emotional/intellectual deficits

From "Fetal Tobacco Syndrome and Other Problems Caused by Smoking During Pregnancy" by N. M. McLaren and P. Nieburg, August 1988, *Medical Aspects of Human Sexuality, 22,* 70.

lieved were associated with the nuclear power plant disaster at Chernobyl in Russia (West Berlin Human Genetic Institute, 1987). The whole area around Chernobyl is now deserted because of the continued hazard of radiation. Prenatal exposure to *X rays*, especially in the first three months of pregnancy, has the potential of harming the fetus if the level of radiation is too high (Kleinman, Cooke, Machlin, & Kessel, 1983). Even radiation from video display terminals (VDTs) used in industry may be a factor in high miscarriage rates of pregnant women working on them (Meier, 1987).

MATERNAL DISEASES

Many bacteria and viruses cross the placental barrier, so if a pregnant woman is infected, her baby becomes infected also. A variety of maternal illnesses during pregnancy cause birth defects. The extent of the damage depends on the nature and timing of the illness.

Rubella

In the case of rubella, or German measles, if the mother is infected with the virus before the eleventh week of pregnancy, the baby is almost certain to be deaf and to have heart defects and visual and intellectual deficiencies. The chance of defects is one in three for cases occurring between thirteen and sixteen weeks, and almost none after sixteen weeks (Miller, Cradock-Watson, & Pollock, 1982). For these reasons, immunization against rubella is recommended for all children (age 15 months and older) and for adults who show no evidence of

LIVING ISSUES

Cocaine Babies

The alarming rise in the use of cocaine by pregnant women has led to increased concern about the potential deleterious effects of in utero cocaine exposure on the infant. If the mother ingests cocaine, the drug is transmitted to the infant through the placenta. The drug causes vasoconstriction of the mother's blood vessels—including constriction of the uterine arteries, which impairs the blood supply and oxygen delivery to the fetus. This results in reduction in infant birthweight, length, and head circumference (Lester et al., 1991). Together with an increase in heart rate and blood pressure, vasoconstriction often stimulates preterm labor, the separation of the placenta from the uterine wall, followed by hemorrhage, shock, and anemia in the mother. Furthermore, the mother who ingests cocaine usually provides poor postnatal care of the infant.

Cocaine exposure also has a direct effect on the neonates. Some are born very excitable. Neurological findings include tremors, irritability, high-pitched and excessive crying, jitteriness, hyperactivity, rigidity, hypertension, vigorous sucking, and abnormal neuromuscular signs. The infant may have feeding difficulties and poor sleep–wake schedules. Other infants are born depressed or underaroused, have fleeting attention, and are difficult to wake (Lester et al., 1991). Early intervention after birth may reduce some of the harmful effects of prenatal exposure.

Delivery and neonatal hospital costs are much greater when a cocaine baby is delivered. According to one Oregon study, costs for neonatal care averaged about $12,000 more (Klitsch, 1992). It is estimated that at least 5 percent of babies born in the United States are exposed to cocaine use during gestation, adding about $500 million to the cost of neonatal medical services each year (Klitsch, 1992).

rubella immunity. Pregnant women should not receive the vaccine; adult women should not become pregnant for three months after immunization (Berkow, 1987).

Toxoplasmosis

Toxoplasmosis is a parasite found in uncooked meat and in fecal matter of cats and other animals. The pregnant mother should not change the cat's litter if blood tests reveal that she is not immune. The parasite affects the nervous system of the fetus, resulting in retardation, deafness, and blindness (Larsen, 1986).

Sexually Transmitted Diseases

These are a major cause of birth defects. *Congenital syphilis* is contracted by the fetus of the pregnant woman when the spirochete crosses the placental barrier. If the disease is diagnosed and treated before the fourth month of pregnancy, the fetus will not develop syphilis. Later in pregnancy the fetus may suffer bone, liver, or brain damage (Grossman, 1986). If a woman is not treated in the primary or secondary stage of the disease, her child is likely to die before or shortly after birth.

Genital herpes, gonorrhea, and *chlamydial infections* are STDs transmitted to infants when they pass through the birth canal, so doctors recommend a cesarean section if the woman has an infection. Between 50 percent and 60 percent of newborns who contract *herpes* die, and half of the survivors suffer brain damage or blindness (Subak-Sharpe, 1984). Infants of infected mothers may get *gonorrhea* of the eyes when passing through the birth canal and, if not treated with silver nitrate or antibiotics, can become blind. Some babies born to infected mothers contract the *chlamydia bacterium* when passing through the birth canal and become subject to eye infections, pneumonia, and sudden infant death syndrome (Faro, 1985). Chlamydia is the greatest single cause of preventable blindness (Crum & Ellner, 1985). The best precaution against birth defects caused by STDs is to make sure the woman is not exposed before or during pregnancy.

Other Diseases

Large numbers of other diseases may cause birth defects. *Poliomyelitis, diabetes, tuberculosis,* and *thyroid disease* have all been implicated in problems of fetal development.

OTHER MATERNAL FACTORS

Maternal Age

At first glance, maternal age seems to be associated with the well-being of the fetus. *Younger teenage mothers are more likely to have miscarriages, premature birth, and stillbirths than are mothers in their twenties.* The infants are more likely to be of low birth weight, to have physical and neurological defects, and to be retarded than are babies born to women over 20 (Smith, Weinman, & Malinak, 1984). However, it is not necessarily the mother's age that is the problem, but the fact that many of these babies are born out of wedlock to low-socioeconomic-status mothers who do not receive adequate nutrition and prenatal health care ("Social factors," 1984). Black children born to very young adolescent mothers are more likely to be born prematurely and to have low birthweights than are white children, primarily because of poor postnatal care of black children (Ketterlinus, Henderson, & Lamb, 1991).

The most recent findings indicate that births to women in their middle and late thirties have risen among both the black and the white population since 1980 (Turner, 1992b). *The statistics indicate that women over 35 run progressively greater risks during pregnancy.* These include greater

PARENTING ISSUES

Pregnancy and Hot Tubs

Too much heat can also harm a fetus. If a pregnant woman immerses herself in very hot water, the temperature of the fetus may be raised enough to damage its central nervous system. As little as fifteen minutes in a hot tub at 102°F or ten minutes at 106°F may cause fetal damage. Studies have shown that some women gave birth to malformed babies after spending forty-five minutes to one hour in hot tubs (Harvey, McRorie, & Smith, 1981).

PARENTING ISSUES

Maternal Stress and Infant Hyperactivity

Most expectant mothers experience some stress during pregnancy. A moderate amount of stress probably has no harmful effects on the fetus, but persistent, excessive stress does. When the mother is anxious, afraid, or upset, adrenaline is pumped into the blood stream, which increases heart rate, blood pressure, respiration, and levels of blood sugar, and diverts blood away from digestion to the skeletal muscles to prepare the body for emergency action. The emergency mobilization leaves the body exhausted afterward, severely disrupting bodily functioning.

The physical changes that occur in the mother's body take place in the fetus as well, since *adrenaline* passes through the placenta and enters the blood of the fetus. The fetus becomes hyperactive for as long as the mother is stressed. Furthermore, the stress is associated with low birth weight, infant hyperactivity, feeding problems, irritability, and digestive disturbances. Furthermore, the overly stressed mother is more likely to have complications during pregnancy and labor (Istvan, 1986).

FOCUS

AIDS and Fetal Development

One of the most serious of the sexually transmitted diseases is *acquired immunodeficiency syndrome (AIDS)*. A person who has been exposed to the virus may become a carrier prior to actually having the disease. The AIDS virus can cross the placental barrier, so if the mother is a carrier, there is a substantial risk she will give birth to children with the disease. Infected infants have head and face abnormalities; small heads, boxlike foreheads, short, flattened noses, slanting eyes, "scooped out" profiles, fat lips, and growth retardation (Iosub, Bamji, Stone, Gromisch, & Waserman, 1987; Marion, Wiznia, Hutcheon, & Rubinstein, 1986). The virus is present in mother's breast milk, and, although rare, transmission through this means has been implicated (Rogers, 1985). Approximately one-third of babies born to AIDS-infected mothers will also become infected (Koop, 1986). Most of the infected babies will eventually develop the disease and die (Cowan, Hellman, Chudwin, Wara, Chang, & Ammann, 1984).

More and more women in their late thirties and early forties are having babies.

risks of miscarriages, of complications during pregnancy and delivery, a greater chance of having twins and of developmental abnormalities than for women under 35. Here again, however, age may not be the causative factor but the fact that the older mother may not be in as good health as the younger. She is more likely to be obese, have high blood pressure, or have diabetes than is the younger woman. *Modern health care has made it possible for older women to deliver healthy full-term babies.* The risks of pregnancy for women over 40 have not been found to be greater than those for women 20 to 30, particularly when such factors as maternal weight, health condition, and cigarette smoking are taken into account (Kopp & Kaler, 1989). However, if any woman has health problems, she is certainly at greater risk.

Nutrition

Lack of vitamins, minerals, and protein in the diet of the expectant mother may affect the embryo adversely. Nutritional deficiencies have been associated with stillbirths, miscarriages, and major deformities. The extent of damage depends on the time during the pregnancy, and on the duration and severity of the deficiencies. A lack of vitamin A or calcium in the mother may result in improperly developed teeth in the infant. A serious protein deficiency may cause mental retardation, premature birth, low resistance to infections, or low fetal birth weight (Guttmacher, 1983).

Heredity-Environment Interaction

STUDYING HEREDITY AND ENVIRONMENT

For years, psychologists have been trying to sort out the relative influences of heredity and environment on development and behavior. There are two principal methods for sorting out these influences: the study of twins and the study of adopted children.

Twin Studies

Identical twins share the same heredity, but if they are reared apart they would be subject to different environmental influences. Any shared traits that are still similar, therefore, would be caused by heredity and not environment. Fraternal twins are as different in heredity as are any other brothers or sisters. Comparisons are sometimes made between fraternal twins and identical twins, or between fraternal twins or other siblings and adopted children raised in the same family. Such comparisons help to sort out environmental versus hereditary influences. Table 3.4 gives a summary of the degree of similarity (concordance) between monozygotic twins, dizygotic twins, and siblings on measures of intelligence (comparisons of twins and of siblings are of children raised in the same home). The findings are summaries of a number of studies (Bouchard & McGue, 1981).

Twin studies help psychologists examine the influences of heredity and environment.

Adoption Studies

Studies of adopted children enable researchers to try to disentangle the relative contributions of heredity and environment. In the Texas Adoption Project, researchers have found that the influence of heredity on intelligence is a strong one (Horn, 1983; Loehlin, 1985). *Children reared away from their biological parents are still more similar in IQ to their biological mother than to their adoptive parents.* As seen in Table 3.5, the

TABLE 3.4
Concordance Between Monozygotic Twins, Dizygotic Twins, Siblings, and Unrelated Children on Measures of Intelligence

Relationship	*Concordance Rate (%)*
Monozygotic twins	74
Same-sex dizygotic twins	36
Siblings	22
Unrelated children (raised in different homes)	00

Abstracted with permission from "Family Studies of Intelligence: A Review" by T. J. Bouchard and M. McGue, 1981, *Science, 212,* 1055–1059.

TABLE 3.5
IQ CORRELATIONS IN THE TEXAS ADOPTION PROJECT

Pairing	*Number of Pairs*	*Observed Correlations*
SHARE GENES ONLY		
Adopted child and biological mother	297	0.28
SHARE ENVIRONMENT ONLY		
Adopted child and adoptive mother	401	0.15
Adopted child and adoptive father	405	0.12
All unrelated children	266	0.18
SHARE GENES AND ENVIRONMENT		
Natural child and mother	143	0.21
Natural child and father	144	0.29
Natural child and natural child	40	0.33

From "The Texas Adoption Project" by J. M. Horn, 1983, *Child Development, 54,* 268–275. © 1983 The Society for Research in Child Development.

strongest correlations of intelligence were between natural children and their father or between natural siblings. The weakest correlations were between adopted children and their adopted parents, indicating that the influence of environment alone was not high.

In one longitudinal Minnesota adoption study, black children adopted into white homes were still more closely related in intelligence to their biological parents than to their adoptive parents, indicating that genetics had more influence than environment (Scarr & Weinberg, 1983). However, these adopted black children had higher average intelligence test scores than their biological parents, indicating that performance had been improved by environmental influences. Other studies show a striking diversity of genetic and environmental influences that determine continuity and change in individual differences in general cognitive ability during the period of development from infancy to middle

FOCUS

Twins Reared Apart

Jack Yufe and Oskar Stohr are identical twins. They were separated at 6 months of age from their parents and reared apart. Jack was raised in Israel as a Jew, and he spent time in an Israeli kibbutz and in the navy. Oskar was brought up in Germany as a Catholic and was involved in Hitler's youth movement. When they were brought together at age 47 by University of Minnesota researchers, they had similar personality profiles, and they both did well in sports, had trouble with math, had mustaches, wore wire-rimmed glasses, and read magazines from back to front (Bouchard, 1984). The researchers concluded that at least half the similarities in a wide range of personality characteristics were caused by heredity.

adulthood (Cardon, Fulker, DeFries, & Plomin, 1992).

INFLUENCES ON PERSONALITY AND TEMPERAMENT

Heredity not only has an important influence on intelligence, but it also exerts a strong influence on personality and temperament (Chipuer, Plomin, Persensen, McClearn, & Nesselroade, 1993; Emde et al., 1992; Heath, Kessler, Neale, Eaves, & Kendler, 1992). Intensive studies of 348 pairs of identical twins at the University of Minnesota, including 44 pairs who were reared apart, revealed that heredity was a stronger influence than environment on a number of key personality traits (Goleman, 1986; Leo, 1987). Figure 3.14 shows the extent to which selected personality traits were found to be inherited. A 60 percent figure would mean that 60 percent of the trait is due to heredity, and 40 percent to environmental influences.

The influence of heredity can be seen in identifiable characteristics that seem to be present in very young infants (Braungart, Plomin, DeFries, & Fulker, 1992). One study showed some heritability of empathy in both monozygotic and dizygotic twin pairs between fourteen and twenty months of age (Zahn-Waxler, Robinson, & Emde, 1992). These twins showed emotional concern, reaction to the distress of others, and some ability to engage in prosocial acts. Infants' temperament is also strongly influenced by genetics, as indicated by their level of activity, irritability, sociability, and sleep patterns (Wilson & Matheny, 1983). Goldsmith (1983) found that identical twins were more similar than fraternal twins in personality traits such as emotionality: in the expression of anger and aggressive feelings, in activity level and sociability, and in work habits in school such as task persistence. In the New York Longitudinal Study, 133 children were followed from infancy into early adulthood (Thomas & Chess, 1984). The researchers investigated various characteristics: activity level, regularity of biological functioning, sensory sensitivity, intensity of responses, readiness to accept new people and situations, adaptability, distractibility, persistence, and cheerfulness or unhappiness.

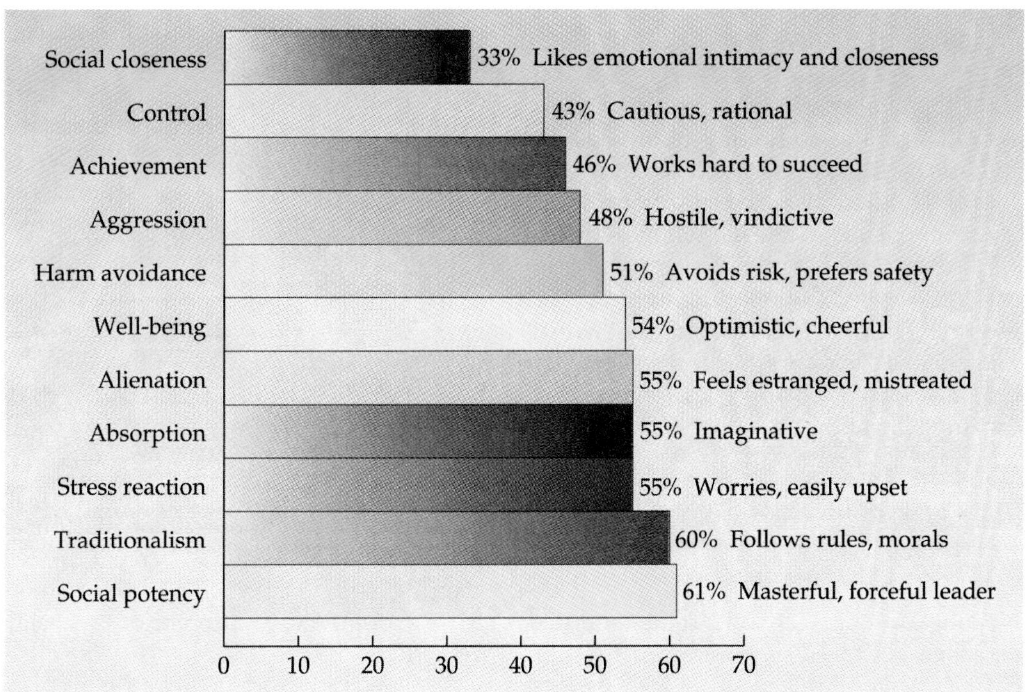

FIGURE 3.14 The extent to which different personality traits are inherited.

From "Major Personality Study Finds That Traits Are Mostly Inherited" by D. Goleman. December 2, 1986. *New York Times*, pp. 17, 18.

Individuals varied greatly in these characteristics, and differences remained into early adulthood. However, differences in parental handling and in other experiences did modify these behavioral characteristics somewhat.

Goldsmith and Gottesman (1981) found that, as infants got older, the relative influence of heredity on temperament usually declined, whereas environmental influences became more important (Riese, 1990). Kagan and his associates studied the development of inhibited and uninhibited 2- to 3-year-old children for 6 years to discover the relative stability of the tendency to be shy or not shy (Kagan, Reznick, Clarke, Snidman, & Garcia-Cole, 1984; Reznick, Kagan, Snidman, Gersten, Baak, & Rosenberg, 1986; Robinson, Reznick, Kagan, & Corley, 1992). About 5 percent to 10 percent of the children seemed to be born with a biological predisposition to be fearful of unfamiliar people, events, or objects. After 5 1/2 years, 40 percent of the originally inhibited children—usually boys—had become much less inhibited. However, 10 percent had become more timid. Some parents had helped their shy children overcome timidity by bringing playmates into the home, offering encouragement and support, and through other means. Other parents made matters worse by undermining their children's confidence. Certainly then, the quality of nurturing experiences exerted strong modifying influences on children's temperament and behavior. Of course, children also exerted strong influences on parents. Children who are different tax the patience of parents, but if parents start to become rejecting, critical, and punishing, they may make matters worse. The children who are hardest to love are the ones who need love, acceptance, and encouragement the most.

SOME DISORDERS INFLUENCED BY HEREDITY AND ENVIRONMENT

Not only are some superior traits inherited and then enhanced or minimized through environmental influences, but also various disorders with genetic origins can either be promoted or counteracted to some degree by environment. Several of these disorders are the focus in this section.

Alcoholism

Alcoholism runs in families and develops because of a combination of genetic and environmental factors. The evidence for genetic factors in alcoholism is convincing: (1) the concordance rate for alcoholism between identical twins is twice that between fraternal twins; (2) sons of alcoholics are four times as likely as sons of nonalcoholics to become alcoholics themselves, even if they are adopted at birth, and regardless of whether the adoptive parents are alcoholics; and, (3) children whose natural parents are nonalcoholics, but whose adoptive parents are, do not appear to have an unusually high risk themselves (Schuckit, 1985, 1987). Alcoholics tend to inherit an ability to metabolize alcohol differently, and thus to find drinking more pleasurable, than nonalcoholics do. In contrast to alcoholics, some people can't drink because their bodies can't tolerate alcohol (Zucker & Gomberg, 1986). There is some evidence, also, that male alcoholics exhibit different brain wave patterns than nonalcoholics prior to exposure to alcohol (Porjesz & Begleitner, 1985).

Environmental influences are also a factor in alcoholism. In families where there is a lack of closeness, love, and recognition or trust; where there is parental rejection, hostility, conflict, inadequate role models or discipline; or where children do not learn coping skills from parents, the children are more prone to become alcoholics or abusers of other drugs than are those brought up in a more positive home environment (Jurich, Polson, Jurich, & Bates, 1985).

Schizophrenia

Schizophrenia is another disorder that has both hereditary and environmental causes. The incidence of schizophrenia in the general population is about 1 percent, but if one parent has it, about 12 percent of their offspring will be affected. If both parents are schizophrenic, 39 percent of their children will be afflicted (Kinney & Matthysse, 1978). One study found that 48 percent of the monozygotic twins of schizophrenic individuals also had schizophrenia, whereas only 10 percent of the dizygotic twins of a schizophrenic parent had the disease

FOCUS

The Nobel Prize Winners' Sperm Bank

Robert Graham of Escondido, California, has founded a sperm bank with the intent of producing geniuses. He accepts only the sperm of Nobel Prize–winning scientists and then offers it free of charge to healthy and intelligent women of good breeding whose husbands are infertile. The second child born through the sperm bank, a boy named Doran, had a mental age of 4 when he was only 1 year old. His genetic father had a math score of 800 on the SATs. However, the father also passed on to Doran a 30 percent chance of inheriting hemorrhoids. It's too early to say how many of the children sired through the sperm bank become creative geniuses. Certainly, a genius has other attributes besides a high IQ.

The bank offers a life-giving service to couples where the husband is unable to conceive a child. The bank is severely criticized, however, by those who are set against scientific breeding of any kind. Others emphasize that brighter is not necessarily better. One of the donors, Burton Richter, a Nobel Prize winner in physics from Stanford University, reports that his students ask him if he supplements his salary with stud fees. He is not amused (Garelik, 1985).

(Farmer, McGuffin, & Gottesman, 1987). However, the fact that the majority of children were not affected indicates that children do not inherit the disease, per se. Rather, some inherit a predisposition toward it. Schizophrenia seems to be particularly sensitive to the action of *dopamine,* which is a neurochemical transmitter that speeds nerve transmission. In schizophrenia, the rapid speed of transmission between neurons or nerve cells causes incoherent, bizarre behavior. Administering the drugs called *phenothiazines* inhibits the effect of dopamine on nerve transmission and is an effective treatment (Uhr, Stahl, & Berger, 1984). Environmental influences, such as coming from a dysfunctional family situation, tend to increase the chances of developing the illness.

Depression

Depression is another disorder that may be caused by biological factors including a genetic predisposition. Identical twins have a 70 percent concordance rate; fraternal twins, other siblings, and parents and their children have about a 15 percent concordance rate, indicating a genetic influence (U.S. Department of Health and Human Services, 1981). Depression seems to be accompanied by an excess of *acetycholine,* a chemical that inhibits the transmission of messages between nerve cells (Nadi, Nurnberger, & Gershon, 1984). Here again, depression may be triggered by stressful life events, such as the sudden loss of love. However, some people apparently have a predisposition to the illness.

Infantile Autism

Infantile autism is first noticed in early infancy, with a diagnosis confirmed by age 2 or 3 (Rutter & Schopher, 1987). The word *autism* comes from *auto,* meaning "self." Autistic children are self-involved, oblivious to other people; they don't cuddle, smile, or make eye contact when greeted (Kasari, Sigman, Mundy, & Yirmiya, 1988). Autistic children may spend hours performing repetitive motions such as clap-

FOCUS

Treatment of Depression

The most common medical treatment for depression is the administration of *antidepressant drugs* that elevate mood and reduce self-blame and suicidal thoughts. *Psychotherapy* is also helpful and effective, especially when used in combination with the drugs. *Electroconvulsive therapy (ECT)* is now employed as a treatment of last resort with severely depressed patients for whom drug treatment and psychotherapy have failed. It is believed that ECT affects the metabolism and storage of neurotransmitters implicated in depressive disorders. *Exposing patients to large amounts of sunlight or to intense light from banks of light panels* has been found to be a very effective treatment of depression. No wonder people like to go to sunny climates for the winter!

ping their hands or turning a ball over and over. They may scream in terror when something in the environment is changed. They are often mute, but may echo, word for word, things that they hear, such as a television ad (Wetherby & Prutting, 1984). About one-third have IQs of 70 or more. One in six makes fair adjustment and is able to work as an adult.

Autism is very rare (about three cases per ten thousand people). One study found a concordance of 96 percent among identical twins and 23 percent among fraternal twins; the evidence suggested that autism is an inherited neurobiological disorder passed on through recessive genes, and that environmental influences as causes are minimal (Ritvo, Freeman, Mason-Brothers, Mo, & Ritvo, 1985).

PATERNAL FACTORS IN DEFECTS

Advanced *paternal age* is also associated with reduced fertility and several hereditary defects. Negative environmental influences in the life of the father also contribute to birth defects. *Chronic marijuana use* suppresses the production of the male hormone testosterone, reduces sexual desire, interferes with erectile responses, and inhibits sperm production and motility (Relman, 1982; U.S. Department of Health and Human Services, June 1980). Sperm from *alcoholic men* have been found to be highly abnormal. Exposure to *radiation, lead, tobacco, arsenic, mercury, some solvents,* and *various pesticides* may contribute to male infertility, to lower sperm count, or to genetic abnormalities in sperm cells (Meier, 1987; Brody, 1981). Wives of oral surgeons and dentists exposed to *anesthetic gas* for three hours or more a week were found to have a 78 percent higher incidence of spontaneous abortions than did other wives (Bronson, 1977). Even passive exposure of the fetus to *smoking* by the father reduces fetal birth weight and interferes with lung development of the fetus (Rubin, Craskilnikoff, Leventhal, Weile, & Berget, 1986). Another study at a University of North Carolina hospital revealed a twofold increase in risk for developing cancer during their lifetime among children of men who smoked (Sandler, Everson, Wilcox, & Browder, 1985). This may have been due to prenatal or postnatal exposure or both.

We do know that excessive heat is detrimental to sperm production and viability. Sperm are most effectively produced and most healthy when the temperature in the testes is 5.6°F below body temperature. This lower temperature is achieved because the testes hang outside the body cavity in the scrotum. But when sperm are exposed to

FOCUS

Does Marijuana Smoking by Men Cause Birth Defects?

We know that marijuana smoking by men interferes with male potency and fertility, but does it contribute to birth defects? The answer is not conclusive.

Dr. Susan L. Dalterio, assistant professor of pharmacological research at the University of Texas Health Science Center at San Antonio, has been giving oral dosages of THC (the active ingredient in marijuana) to mice. Giving THC to pregnant female mice has resulted in increased fetal losses, and has reduced testosterone in male fetuses, which has interfered with their sexual development.

When adult male mice were given THC, they had more difficulty impregnating the females. If pregnancy occurred, many male fetuses died before full term and before weaning. An examination of the testes of fathers and sons revealed abnormal sex chromosomes that were transmitted from one generation to the next.

Confirmation or rejection of these findings in humans can be obtained only when third-generation offspring of marijuana users can be tested (Dalterio, 1984). To date, there is no proof of chromosomal damage in humans.

sources of artificial heat, their temperature rises, which is very detrimental.

As can be seen, the great majority of birth defects are preventable. Every effort needs to be made to keep them from happening.

Summary

1. Reproduction begins when the male gamete, or sperm cell, fuses with the female gamete, or ovum.
2. Spermatogenesis refers to the process of sperm production; oogenesis is the process by which ova are ripened in the ovary.
3. Conception, or fertilization, normally takes place in the upper third of the fallopian tube.
4. Family planning means having children by choice and not by chance. It is necessary to protect the health of the mother and baby, to reduce the psychological impact of unintended pregnancy, and to promote the good of the marriage.
5. Contraceptive failure is a serious problem, resulting in a high rate of unintended pregnancy. Since the advent of AIDS, condom use has increased. Unfortunately, some condoms are defective and leak, or tear and come off.
6. Prenatal development may be divided into three periods: (1) the germinal period—from conception to completion of implantation, about fourteen days; (2) the embryonic period—from two

weeks to eight weeks after conception; and (3) the fetal period—from eight weeks through the remainder of pregnancy.

7. The expectant mother ought to get prenatal medical care as early in her pregnancy as possible.
8. Infant mortality in the United States is high among minority groups, primarily because of a lack of proper prenatal care from the beginning of pregnancy.
9. Minor side effects may cause varying degrees of discomfort during pregnancy. Major complications of pregnancy include pernicious vomiting, toxemia, threatened abortion, placenta praevia, tubal pregnancy, and Rh incompatibility.
10. Many thoughtful people object to viability tests as determinants of whether a woman can have an abortion, because the tests are expensive, impose health risks for the mother and fetus, and are sometimes unreliable and inaccurate, especially if performed between twenty and thirty weeks.
11. About 20 percent of infertility cases involve the couple, about 40 percent the man, and about 40 percent the woman.
12. Involuntary childlessness can cause significant emotional and psychological distress for some persons.
13. Alternate means of conception include artificial insemination (both homologous insemination and heterologous insemination), use of a surrogate mother, in vitro fertilization, gamete intrafallopian transfer (GIFT), and embryo transplant.
14. Couples younger than 35 years of age should wait a full year to see if conception takes place before seeking medical treatment. Older couples should get help after six months of unsuccessful attempts.
15. Chromosomes carry the hereditary material called genes that direct the physical changes in the body throughout development. When the sperm and ovum unite, the twenty-three single chromosomes within the nucleus of each gamete combine in pairs with those in the other gamete to produce forty-six chromosomes in the resulting zygote.
16. Genes are made up of molecules called DNA. Each cell of the body has the same DNA code and the same genes that direct growth.
17. In the zygote, twenty-two of the chromosomes from each gamete are labeled autosomes; the twenty-third pair are sex chromosomes, which determine whether the offspring will be male or female. An XY chromosome pairing produces a male; an XX combination produces a female.
18. Various techniques are employed to control the sex of the child conceived. In some countries, such as China and India, female infanticide is practiced because of the social and economic premium placed on having boy babies.
19. Twins may be identical (monozygotic, or one-egg) twins, or fraternal (dizygotic, or two-egg) twins.
20. Mendel formulated the law of dominant inheritance, which says that when an organism inherits competing traits, the trait that is expressed is dominant over the other, which is recessive. An organism may be homozygous or heterozygous for a trait.
21. A trait that is observable in an organism is called a phenotype, while the underlying genetic pattern is called a genotype.
22. When one allele is not completely dominant over the other, the phenomenon is known as incomplete dominance. Polygenic inheritance is when numerous interacting genes produce a trait.
23. We inherit a range of possibilities for many traits. This is known as the reaction range. Canalization is the tendency for a trait to persist regardless of environment.
24. Sex-linked disorders are inherited by being passed on through defective recessive genes on the X chromosome.
25. Birth defects result from three causes: (1) hereditary factors, (2) faulty environments, and (3) birth injuries. Some genetic diseases are inherited through dominant genes, others through recessive genes.
26. Chromosomal abnormalities are of two types: sex chromosomal abnormalities and autosomal chromosomal abnormalities.
27. Couples who have inherited disabilities themselves, or who have a family

history of such disabilities, should get genetic counseling to discover the possibility of passing on a defect.

28. Procedures for discovering defects include amniocentesis, sonogram, fetoscope, or chorionic villus sampling (CVS).
29. Adverse prenatal environmental influences include various teratogens, drugs, chemicals, heavy metals, environmental pollutants, radiation, and excessive heat. The earlier in development the embryo or fetus is exposed, the greater the possibility of harm. Thus, there are sensitive periods when exposure is most harmful.
30. There are also many maternal diseases that can affect the development of the unborn child.
31. Other maternal factors that need to be taken into account are maternal age, nutrition, and stress.
32. There are two principal methods for sorting out the relative influence of heredity versus environment: twin studies and adoption studies. Heredity seems to have a greater influence on intelligence than do environmental influences. Heredity exerts a strong influence on personality and temperament also.
33. Some disorders are influenced by both heredity and environment. These include alcoholism, schizophrenia, depression, and infantile autism.
34. Paternal factors important in defects include paternal age; use of some drugs; and exposure to radiation, lead, arsenic, mercury, some solvents, and various pesticides or gases.

Key Terms

Alleles *p. 70*
Amniocentesis *p. 75*
Artificial insemination *p. 65*
Autosomes *p. 68*
Blastocyst *p. 59*
Blastula *p. 59*
Canalization *p. 72*
Chorionic villi sampling (CVS) *p. 75*
Chromosomes *p. 67*
Congenital deformity *p. 73*
Dizygotic (fraternal) twins *p. 69*
DNA *p. 67*
Dominant gene *p. 70*
Ectopic pregnancy *p. 60*
Embryo *p. 61*
Embryonic period *p. 59*
Embryo transplant *p. 66*
Fertilization or conception *p. 57*
Fetal period *p. 59*
Fetoscope *p. 75*
Fetus *p. 61*
Gamete intrafallopian transfer (GIFT) *p. 66*
Gametes *p. 56*
Genes *p. 67*
Genotype *p. 70*
Germinal period *p. 59*
Heterologous insemination (AID) *p. 66*
Heterozygous *p. 70*
Homologous insemination (AIH) *p. 66*
Homozygous *p. 70*
Implantation *p. 59*
Incomplete dominance *p. 71*
Infertile *p. 64*
In vitro fertilization *p. 66*
Law of dominant inheritance *p. 70*
Meiosis *p. 56*
Monozygotic (identical) twins *p. 68*
Morula *p. 59*
Oogenesis *p. 56*
Ova *p. 56*
Ovulation *p. 57*
Phenotype *p. 70*
Polygenic system of inheritance *p. 72*
Reaction range *p. 72*
Recessive gene *p. 70*
Sex chromosomes *p. 68*
Sex-linked disorders *p. 72*
Siamese twins *p. 69*
Sonogram *p. 75*
Spermatogenesis *p. 56*
Surrogate mother *p. 66*
Teratogen *p. 77*
Trimester *p. 61*
Viable *p. 64*
Zygote *p. 56*

Discussion Questions

1. What do you think about each of the following alternate means of conception?

   Artificial insemination: AIH, AID
   Using a surrogate mother
   Gamete intrafallopian transfer (GIFT)
   In vitro fertilization
   Embryo transplant

2. If you wanted a child of a particular sex, would you try to employ means to determine your child's sex? Explain.
3. Do any members of either side of your family have inherited defects, or might they be carriers of defects? Has any member of your family received genetic counseling? With what results?
4. What do you think of the Nobel Prize Winner's Sperm Bank? Explain your feelings about it.
5. Do you know of anyone who has borne defective children because of exposure to teratogens, radiation, heat, or maternal diseases?
6. Regardless of whether you are now a parent, would you want to consider having children when you are over 35 years of age? Why or why not?
7. Do you know any mothers who are nervous, hyperactive people? Were they that way during pregnancy? Compare their children with children of mothers who are calm, easygoing persons who do not get upset easily. Do you notice any difference in the temperament of the children? Is a nervous temperament inherited or due to environmental influence?
8. To women who are mothers: Did you have any minor discomforts during your pregnancy? What bothered you the most? What did you do about it? Did you have any of the major complications of pregnancy that are mentioned in the text? Explain.
9. To men who are fathers: How did you feel about your wife becoming pregnant? In what ways were you able to assist her? What bothered you the most during her pregnancy?
10. Do you know anyone who tests HIV positive for AIDS? How was the virus contracted? Do you know anyone who is sexually active with different persons who is not using protection against AIDS? Describe.
11. Do you know anyone who has a problem with infertility? Are they seeking treatment? What has been their reaction to unwanted childlessness?
12. Do you know a woman who took drugs during her pregnancy? With what result?

Suggested Readings

Abel, E. L. (1984). *Fetal alcohol syndrome and fetal alcohol effects.* New York: Plenum. An enlightening book on this subject.

Anderson, G. R. (1986). *Children and AIDS: The challenge for child welfare.* Washington, DC: Child Welfare League of America. Implications of AIDS for social workers.

Anthony, E. J., & Cohler, B. J. (Eds.). (1987). *The invulnerable child.* New York: Guilford Press. A book of readings on how children are resistant to unfortunate environments.

Baker, R., & Mednick, B. R. (1984). *Influences on human development.* Boston: Kluwer-Nijhoff.

Corea, G. (1986). *The mother machine.* New York: Harper & Row. Ethics of new reproductive technologies.

Farber, S. (1981). *Identical twins reared apart: A reanalysis.* New York: Basic Books. Summary of findings of studies.

Glass, R., & Ericsson, R. J. (1982). *Getting pregnant in the 1980s.* Berkeley: University of California Press. A nontechnical presentation of pregnancy and birth control.

Kelly, T. E. (1986). *Clinical genetics and genetic counseling* (2nd ed.). Chicago and London: Yearbook Medical Publishers. A textbook on genetics and its clinical applications.

Kevles, D. J. (1985). *In the name of eugenics.* New York: Knopf. A thought-provoking discussion.

Nilsson, L. (1990). *A child is born.* New York: Delacorte Press. Full-color photos and helpful text on the psychological and medical facts of prenatal development.

Norwood, C. (1980). *At highest risk: Environmental hazards to young and unborn children.* New York: McGraw-Hill.

Plomin, R. (1990). *Nature and nurture: An introduction to human behavioral genetics.* Pacific Grove, CA: Brooks/Cole. For the lay reader.

Rubin, S. (1980). *It's not too late for a baby.* Englewood Cliffs, NJ: Prentice-Hall. Pregnancy and child-rearing concerns for the parent over 35.

Schwarz, R. H., & Yaffe, S. J. (Eds.). (1980). *Drug and chamical risks to the fetus and newborn.* New York: Alan R. Liss.

Shapiro, H. J. (1983). *The pregnancy book for today's woman.* New York: Harper & Row. Issues during pregnancy.

Synder, L. A., Freifelder, D., & Hartl, D. L. (1985). *General genetics.* Boston: Jones and Bartlett. A textbook.

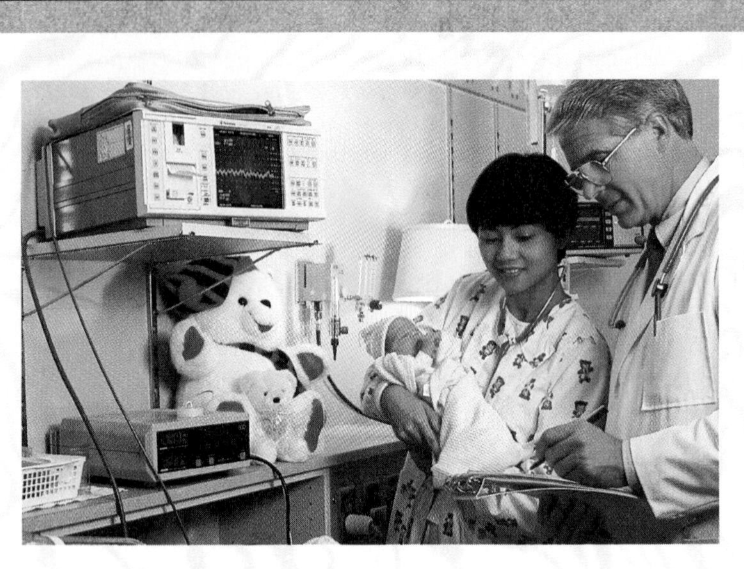

Childbirth and the Neonate

Chapter 4

CHILDBIRTH

Prepared Childbirth • Methods of Natural Childbirth • Birthing Rooms and Family-Centered Care • **PARENTING ISSUES:** ***Home Versus Hospital Delivery***

LABOR

Beginning • **FOCUS:** ***Induced or Accelerated Labor?*** • Duration • Stages • Use of Anesthesia • Fetal Monitoring

DELIVERY

Normal Delivery • Stress on the Infant • **FOCUS:** ***Too Many Cesareans?*** • Delivery Complications • Anoxia and Brain Injury

POSTPARTUM

Leboyer Method • Evaluating Neonatal Health and Behavior • Postpartum Blues • **PARENTING ISSUES:** ***Circumcision Pros and Cons*** • **PARENTING ISSUES:** ***Returning Home*** • Returning to Work

PREMATURE AND SMALL-FOR-GESTATIONAL-AGE (SGA) INFANTS

Classifications • Premature Infants • **FOCUS:** ***Kilogram Kids and Intensive Neonatal Care*** • Small-for-Gestational-Age (SGA) Infants • Parental Roles and Reactions • Prevention

THE NEONATE

Physical Appearance and Characteristics • Physiogical Functioning • The Senses and Perception • Reflexes • Motor Activity • Brain and Nervous System • **FOCUS:** ***Sudden Infant Death Syndrome (SIDS)*** • Stress Reactions • Individual Differences

Having a baby is a normal occurrence, happening millions of times every year. But it is an experience that requires considerable knowledge and preparation if the maximum health of baby and mother is to be assured. This chapter describes the process of childbirth from the beginning of labor to postpartum care, emphasizing the importance of preparation ahead of time.

Some babies are born prematurely or are small for their gestational age. These require special care and modifications of the parental roles.

Once born, the neonate is a miraculous creature. This chapter describes the physical appearance and characteristics, the physiological functioning, the senses and perception, reflexes, brain and nervous system, and individual differences in neonates that enable them to survive and to adjust to the new world into which they are born.

Childbirth

PREPARED CHILDBIRTH

Prepared childbirth—the physical, social, intellectual, and emotional preparation for the birth of a baby

The term **prepared childbirth** here refers to the physical, social, intellectual, and emotional preparation for the birth of a baby. Good physical care of the body provides a favorable environment for the growing fetus, and physical conditioning readies the body for labor and childbirth. Social preparation of the home and family provides a secure environment in which the child can grow. Intellectual preparation ensures adequate instruction in and understanding of the birth process, prenatal and postnatal hospitalization, and infant and child care (Hicks & Williams, 1981). Emotional preparation minimizes fear and tension so that childbirth can be as pleasant and painless as possible.

Prepared childbirth, as used in this context, does not necessarily mean labor and delivery without medication, although these may be drug free if the mother so desires. Emphasis is not just on natural childbirth (in a sense all childbirth is natural), but on the overall preparations a woman and her partner can make for the experience of becoming parents.

METHODS OF NATURAL CHILDBIRTH

Dick-Read Method

Dick-Read method—a natural childbirth method emphasizing childbirth without fear

Dr. Grantley Dick-Read (1953), an English obstetrician, pioneered the concept of prepared childbirth with an article published in 1933, then later with his book, *Childbirth Without Fear*. He believed that fear causes tension that inhibits the process of childbirth. According to him, if women could be educated to understand what was happening to their bodies, they could eliminate their tension and fear. If they could also be conditioned for the experience, pain during childbirth could be eliminated without medication in all but a minority of cases. Women who took no drugs during labor and delivery had perfectly healthy babies and were able to resume their duties sooner after delivery than those who had anesthesia (Bean, 1974).

These are three important elements of the **Dick-Read method**:

1. Education about birth, including deconditioning from earlier fears, myths, and misconceptions
2. Physical conditioning and exercises, including voluntary muscle relaxation and proper breathing
3. Emotional support from the partner, family, nurses, and physician during pregnancy, labor, and delivery

The Dick-Read approach is a fairly passive method, emphasizing relaxation and proper breathing as each contraction comes.

Lamaze Method

Lamaze method—a natural childbirth method emphasizing education, physical conditioning, controlled breathing, and emotional support

The **Lamaze method** originated in Russia and was introduced to the Western world in 1951 by Dr. Fernand Lamaze (1970), a French obstetrician. The following are important elements of the Lamaze method:

Couples need to be prepared for childbirth and the experience of becoming parents.

1. Education about birth, including the ability to relax muscles not involved in the labor and delivery process
2. Physical conditioning through exercises
3. Controlled breathing, providing the psychological technique for pain prevention and the ability to release muscular tension by "letting go"
4. Emotional support during labor and delivery, primarily through instruction of the partner in coaching and supportive techniques

The Lamaze method emphasizes the man–woman relationship and communication. In this method, as well as in the Dick-Read method, attendance of the partner or another support person in childbirth education classes is essential (Bean, 1974). The underlying feature of the Lamaze method is its focus on teaching the woman that she can be in control during the experience.

Critique

Prepared childbirth, by whatever method, is not without its critics, especially if a particular advocate emphasizes a drug-free labor and delivery. Medical opinion is changing gradually in relation to the role of the father. Because fathers are encouraged to attend classes with their partners and to act as coaches during labor and delivery, many couples are insisting that the father be present during the entire process, even during the delivery. Certainly, a partner's willingness to participate in childbirth can be critical to the physical comfort and satisfaction of his mate's experience (Block, Norr, Meyering, Norr, & Charles, 1981). One study revealed that fathers who were present at delivery showed more interest in looking at and talking to their infants than fathers who did not attend the birth (Miller & Bowen, 1982). To avoid misunderstanding, the issue of the father's presence during delivery needs to be worked out between the couple and physician beforehand. In some cultures, fathers are not allowed to attend the birth of their child. Other fathers just don't want to be present.

A majority of obstetricians accept most concepts of prepared childbirth and think they are advantageous. The combined benefits of psychological suggestion and physical conditioning can enhance the woman's comfort and happiness throughout the labor and delivery process.

BIRTHING ROOMS AND FAMILY-CENTERED CARE

Birthing rooms are lounge-type, informal, pleasantly decorated rooms with homelike settings within the hospital itself. Medical

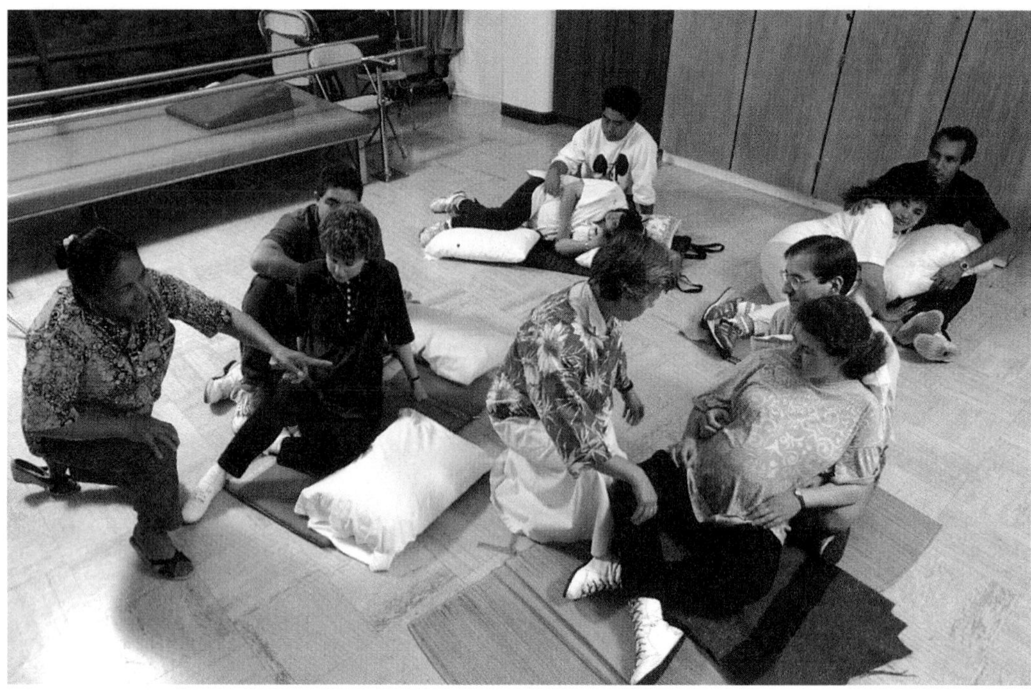

Both prospective fathers and mothers attend childbirth education classes.

equipment is present but unobtrusive. Both labor and delivery take place in the birthing room, attended by the father and a nurse-midwife or obstetrician. The woman can be moved into another room if complications arise. The mother is encouraged to keep her baby with her after delivery to encourage bonding.

Birthing centers are another alternative to the standard hospital setting. They are separated from, but near, a hospital. They seek to combine the advantages of delivery in a homelike environment with the medical backup of a hospital. Birthing centers provide complete prenatal and delivery services to families. They emphasize childbirth as a family-centered event, giving both parents maximum involvement (Eakins, 1986). One big advantage of birthing centers is that new parents learn about infant care while still at the center.

Labor

BEGINNING

Labor—rhythmic contractions of the uterus that expel the baby through the birth canal

Show—blood-tinged mucus expelled from the cervix

Amniotic sac (bag of waters)—sac containing the liquid in which the fetus is suspended during pregnancy

Real **labor** is rhythmic in nature, recurring at fixed intervals, with uterine contractions usually beginning about fifteen to twenty minutes apart and then decreasing to three- to four-minute intervals when labor is well under way. In addition, the total length of each contraction increases from less than half a minute to more than one minute. The **show**, or discharge of the blood-tinged mucus plug sealing the neck of the uterus, may precede the onset of labor by as much as seventy-two hours. At other times, it is an indication that labor has begun (Berkow, 1987).

Sometimes the first sign of impending labor is rupture of the **amniotic sac** (bag of waters), followed by a gush or leakage of watery fluid from the vagina. In one-eighth of all pregnancies, especially in first pregnancies, the amniotic membranes rupture *before* labor begins. When this happens, labor will commence six to twenty-four hours later if the woman is within a few days of term. If she is not near term, doctors try to delay labor until the fetal lungs are mature. Bed rest in the hospital is usually prescribed, or medication is necessary. The real problem is the risk of infection. If infection is suspected or fetal maturity is reached, delivery is accomplished (Berkow,

PARENTING ISSUES

Home Versus Hospital Delivery

Around 1900, about 95 percent of all babies were born at home. Birthing was a family event. Today, that ratio has been reversed: 95 percent are born in the hospital and only 5 percent at home (Gordon & Haire, 1981). The switch has been at the urging of physicians who prefer delivery in sterile, well-equipped, more convenient hospital settings.

Some expectant parents are concerned about hospital practices being too rigid, impersonal, and expensive. They object to the separation of family members and want more control over the childbirth process. Some parents seek midwives to perform home deliveries. Midwives should be certified nurse-midwives (CNMs) who practice in conjunction with physicians, referring problem pregnancies to them and calling upon them as needed. The American College of Nurse-Midwives certifies members who have completed a one-year course at such places as the University of Miami or Georgetown University. Two organizations, the Association for Childbirth at Home (ACAH) and the Home Oriented Maternity Experience (HOME), offer classes to prepare couples for home birth (Parfitt, 1977).

Studies of nurse-midwifery practice, past and present, consistently show delivery outcomes as good as or better than those with physicians. Births through nurse-midwives result in fewer forceps deliveries, cesarean sections, episiotomies, stillbirths, and low-birth-weight babies (Boston Women's Health Book Collective, 1984). Similarly, a study of paired samples of 1,146 home and hospital births revealed no differences in infant mortality rates, but lower rates of infant and maternal disease and birth injuries in home births (Mehl & Peterson, 1981).

One reason for the high success rate of home births is that a prospective candidate for home delivery must be screened carefully. The National Association of Parents and Professionals for Safe Alternatives in Childbirth (NAPSAC) recommends certain standards to ensure maternal and infant health. The woman must live less than ten miles from the hospital and be willing to go there in case of complications. She must be educated about birth, learn to identify birth and labor complications, and agree to prepare her home for delivery. She also must locate a pediatrician who will see the infant soon after birth.

The NAPSAC advises against home birth if the woman

1. Is not in good health
2. Has a history of previous birth complications
3. Has chances of a premature, breech transverse, or multiple birth
4. Has a blood incompatibility with the baby
5. Has a pelvic size insufficient for normal passage of the baby's head

Many physicians will not deliver babies at home. Even those who approve may lose hospital privileges or insurance coverage. Many couples also find that their health insurance policies will not cover home deliveries.

Even with careful screening, there are risks and disadvantages to home births. The couple must weigh the benefits against the risks.

1987). About half the time, however, the bag of waters does not rupture until the last hours of labor.

DURATION

Bean (1974) studied 10,000 patients who delivered at Johns Hopkins Hospital. The study encompassed length of labor and delivery of each patient from onset of the first contraction until extrusion of the afterbirth. The median length of labor for *pripara* (first labor) women was 10.6 hours; for *multipara* (refers to all labor subsequent to the first) women, 6.2 hours. One woman in a hundred may anticipate that her first child will be born in less than 3 hours. One woman in nine requires more than 24 hours.

FOCUS

Induced or Accelerated Labor?

There are various reasons why physicians sometimes induce labor: Rh incompatibility problems, diabetes, toxemia, rupture of the bag of waters, cessation of labor, overdue baby, or unavailability of trained personnel located near the mother's home. In 1978 the Federal Drug Administration took a stand against elective induction (that which is solely for the woman's or physician's convenience). Elective induction is rare and is usually used when patients live long distances from the hospital and when weather would make transportation difficult. Risks of induced labor include internal hemorrhaging, uterine rupture, hypertension, oxygen deprivation to the fetus, premature birth, or excessive labor pain.

The most successful and safest method for induction is giving dilute intravenous oxytocin, using an infusion pump for precise control. External fetal monitoring is essential. Internal monitoring is performed as soon as the membranes can be safely ruptured (Berkow, 1987).

STAGES

The actual process of labor can be divided into three stages. The first and longest is the *dilation stage,* during which the force of the uterine muscles pushing on the baby gradually opens the mouth of the cervix. The cervix increases from less than 0.8 (4/5) inch in diameter to 4 inches. The woman can do nothing to help except relax as completely as possible, allowing the involuntary muscles to do their work. Dilation progresses faster if the mother is not tense. Dilation is complete when the baby's head can start to pass through the cervix.

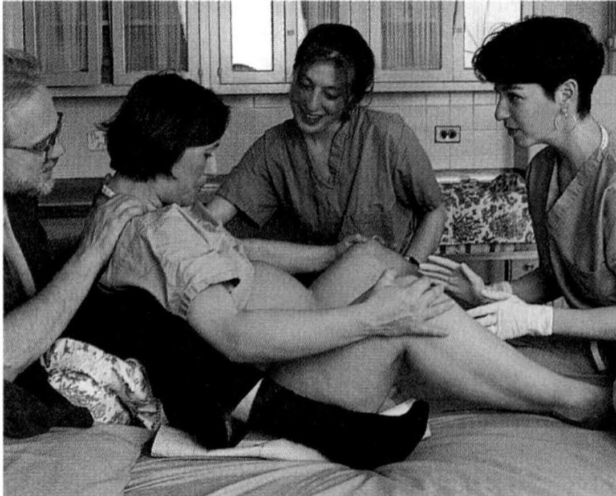

Birthing centers are an alternative to the standard hospital setting.

Upon complete dilation of the cervix, the second stage of labor begins, during which *the baby passes through the birth canal.* When hard contractions come, the woman alternatively pushes and relaxes to help force the baby through the vagina. After the baby is born and tended to, the obstetrician again turns his or her attention to the mother to assist in the third stage of labor.

Passage of the placenta, or afterbirth, occurs during the third stage.

USE OF ANESTHESIA

General anesthesia

Local or regional anesthesia

To alleviate pain in childbirth, **general anesthesia** or **local or regional anesthesia** may be used. General anesthesia affects the body by acting on the whole nervous system; it can slow or stop labor and lower the mother's blood pressure (Wilson, Carrington, & Ledger, 1983). It crosses the placental barrier and affects the fetus as well, decreasing the responses of the newborn infant. Local or regional anesthesia blocks pain in specific areas; some types have a minimal effect on the baby. Table 4.1 describes various types of anesthesia under each category.

FETAL MONITORING

Electronic fetal monitoring, with external devices applied to the woman's abdomen, detects and records fetal heart tones and uterine contractions. Internal leads may also be used, with an electrode attached to the fetal

TABLE 4.1
TYPES OF ANESTHESIA USED IN CHILDBIRTH

General Anesthesia	*Effects*
Inhalation anesthesia nitrous oxide ether halothane thiopental	In sufficient quantities, renders women unconscious. Used only in advanced stage of labor. May cause vomiting and other complications; leading cause of maternal death. Depresses infant's nervous system and respiration. Nitrous oxide may delay infant motor skill development.
Barbiturates Nembutal Seconal Amytal Sodium Pentothal	Usually taken orally, except for Sodium Pentothal. Reduce anxiety and cause drowsiness. Pentothal is injected intravenously to induce sleep. All types may slow labor and depress infant's nervous system and respiration.
Narcotics Demerol Dolophine Nisentil	Reduce pain, elevate mood; may inhibit uterine contractions; may cause nausea and vomiting; depress infant's nervous system and respiration.
Tranquilizers Valium Vistaril Sparine promethazine	Induce physical relaxation, relieve anxiety, may reduce pain. Have minimal effect on infant.
Amnesics scopolamine atropine	Do not reduce pain, but induce "twilight sleep" or forgetfulness. May cause physical excitation. Have minimal effect on infant.
Local or Regional Anesthesia	*Effects*
Pudendal: local injection of novocaine in vulval-perineal area	Blocks pain in vulva and perineum in 50 percent of cases. Has minimal effect on infant.
Paracervical: local injection of novocaine into cervix and uterus	Blocks pain in cervix and uterus for short duration; not effective late in labor. Can lower mother's blood pressure, cause complications, slow fetal heartbeat, precipitate fetal death.
Spinal: regional injection into space around spinal column	Used during delivery to anesthetize entire birth area from abdomen to toes. Stops labor, motor functions. Requires forceps delivery. Generally does not affect infant unless misadministered; then can cause heart and respiratory failure and death.
Epidural: regional injection administered continuously through a tiny catheter and a needle in the back	Effectively numbs area around perineum, lower uterus, and belly to knees. Can cause serious drop in mother's blood pressure and seizures. May require forceps delivery. Used frequently for cesarean sections.
Caudal: regional injection administered continuously through a catheter and needle in the back	Requires larger doses than epidural. Carries greater risk to infant and mother. May cause sudden drop in mother's blood pressure and lack of oxygen to infant.

Coaching the mother during labor helps her to relax and speeds the birth process.

scalp and a catheter through the cervix into the uterus to measure amniotic fluid pressure. The external devices are generally employed for normal pregnancies, and the internal methods for high-risk or problem pregnancies. External fetal monitoring is routinely used in all labors by many obstetricians. Other obstetricians feel it is not always necessary and restricts the mother's movement. If a problem occurs or has been previously identified, internal monitoring is used to provide more reliable information about fetal heart patterns and uterine contraction patterns (Berkow, 1987). There is some disagreement among physicians over when to use fetal monitoring.

Delivery

NORMAL DELIVERY

In normal delivery, the baby's head is delivered first, the baby's body then rotates so that one shoulder then the other is delivered, and then the rest of the baby's body is delivered without difficulty. The baby's nose, mouth, and pharynx are aspirated with a bulb syringe to remove mucus and fluid and help establish breathing. The umbilical cord is double clamped, cut between the clamps, and tied. Normally, obstetricians recommend that an **episiotomy** be performed on almost all patients having their first baby, or on those who have had a previous episiotomy (Berkow, 1987). An episiotomy involves a surgical incision to prevent excessive stretching or tearing of the tissues of the **perineum**. It is easily stitched up after birth and heals more easily than a tear.

Episiotomy—a surgical incision of the perineum to allow for passage of the baby from the birth canal without tearing the mother's tissue

Perineum—area of skin between the vagina and anus

STRESS ON THE INFANT

Giving birth produces stress on the baby as well as on the mother. The powerful muscles of the uterus squeeze the baby, usually head first, through the birth canal. Contractions may compress the *placenta* and *umbilical cord* periodically, causing some oxygen deprivation during those times. Furthermore, the infant passes from its dark, warm, secure environment into the outside world with bright lights, cool temperatures, and noises.

Research has revealed that the stress of birth produces large amounts of *adrenaline* and *noradrenaline* in the baby's blood. These are the same hormones that prepare the adult to flee or fight in situations of danger or emergency. The hormones in the infant have a stimulating affect on breathing, heart action, and all organs and cells of the body. As a consequence, the baby is usually born

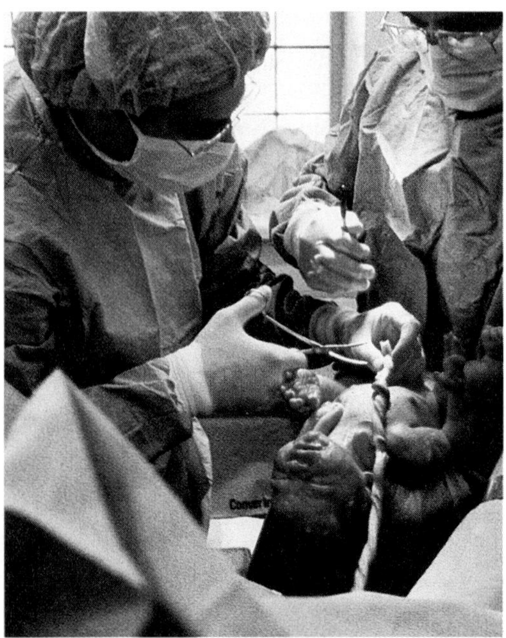

A normal delivery of a healthy baby boy.

FOCUS

Too Many Cesareans?

As discussed, cesareans can be a life-saving procedure in many emergency situations. Cesarean sections now account for up to 18 percent of all births (Pritchard, MacDonald, & Grant, 1985). The rapid increase in their use has led some to cry out that too many cesareans are being performed without sufficient cause, although numerous reasons account for the increase.

1. Obstetrician anxiety, the doctor's fear of being sued if a baby is born less than perfect. Physicians think that cesarean procedures cover them legally.
2. Once a cesarean, always a cesarean. However, in 1982 the American College of Obstetricians and Gynecologists reversed its seventy-five-year-old policy and said that some women who had previously had a cesarean could have a vaginal delivery (Gellman et al., 1983; Lavin, Stephens, Miodovnik, & Barden, 1982; Porreco & Meier, 1983).
3. Obstetrician unwillingness or inability to perform difficult deliveries.
4. Improved obstetrical technology, which detects fetal distress that requires cesarean intervention.
5. Improved training, which reduces the surgical risks.
6. Obstetrical practices making cesarean intervention more necessary; for example, in the case of complications arising from labor induction.
7. Belief that cesareans mean better babies.
8. Patient pressure: Some women want to avoid labor.
9. Medical enthusiasm for cesareans: "What's so great about delivery from below? . . . You don't want the baby squeezed out like toothpaste in a tube. . . . You might say we're helping women to do what nature hasn't evolved to do for herself" (Boston Women's Health Book Collective, 1984, p. 386).
10. Financial incentives: Physicians and hospitals make more money, and many insurance companies reimburse most of the cost of cesareans, though they cover only a small portion of the cost of vaginal delivery (Remez, 1991).

alert. Babies delivered by **cesarean section** before labor has begun lack these high levels of hormones, which is one reason why these babies may have problems breathing right after birth (Lagercrantz & Slotkin, 1968).

Cesarean section—removal of the fetus through a surgical incision of the abdominal and uterine walls

DELIVERY COMPLICATIONS

Complications during delivery may include vaginal bleeding during the first stage of labor, abnormal fetal heart rate, a disproportion in size between the fetus and the pelvic opening, or abnormal fetal presentations and positions. Abnormal presentations include a *face presentation, brow presentation, shoulder presentation,* or *breech presentation* (when the buttocks present rather than the head). Sometimes feet are presented before the buttocks. All of these abnormal presentations require expert attention. Sometimes delivery by cesarean section is essential to protect the infant.

ANOXIA AND BRAIN INJURY

Anoxia—oxygen deprivation to the brain

Prolapsed umbilical cord—squeezing of the umbilical cord between the baby's body and the wall of the birth canal during childbirth, causing oxygen deprivation to the fetus

Two of the most serious delivery complications are **anoxia** (oxygen deprivation to the brain) and *brain injury*. Anoxia may result from a **prolapsed umbilical cord** (the cord is squeezed between the baby's body and the birth canal). It also may result from placental insufficiency, premature labor, severe maternal bleeding, maternal hypotension, toxemia, neonatal pulmonary dysfunction, placental passage of maternal analgesics or anesthetics, or because of malformations (Berkow, 1987). The result of anoxia may be permanent damage to the infant's brain cells or even death. The brain can also be injured during difficult deliveries, especially when forceps are used improperly during the procedure.

Postpartum

LEBOYER METHOD

Leboyer method—ideas for gentle birth procedure

In his book *Birth Without Violence*, the French obstetrician Dr. Frederick Leboyer (1975) emphasized gentle, loving treatment of the newborn. His ideas, combined in **Leboyer method**, include the use of dim lights, gentle voices, and delay in cutting the cord until the naked newborn is soothed, massaged, and stroked while resting on the mother's abdomen. After the cord is cut, the baby is bathed in water of similar temperature to the amniotic fluid in which he or she lived for nine months. American obstetricians do not accept all of Dr. Leboyer's ideas.

Apgar score—method of evaluating the physical condition of the neonate

The theory behind the Leboyer method is that bringing a newborn into a world of blinding lights and loud voices, where it is jerked upside down, spanked, treated roughly, and immediately separated from its other, is a terrifying, traumatic experience after the secure, warm world of the womb. Leboyer explained why we do this: "Because we never really thought of the infant as a person. The newborn is a sensitive, feeling human being, and in the first few moments after birth, he should be treated that way. We must introduce him to the world gradually" (Braun, 1975, p. 17). Advocates of the Leboyer method are highly enthusiastic.

Brazelton Neonatal Behavior Assessment Scale—method of evaluating the neurological condition of the neonate

Results of research to date do not offer substantial proof that the benefits are as great as claimed. One research study found that infants delivered by the Leboyer method were only slightly more contented and easier to care for then those delivered by other methods (Maziade, Boudréault, Cote, & Thivierge, 1986). However, the emphasis on gentle treatment is a positive one, and the mother is happier that her baby has received special care.

EVALUATING NEONATAL HEALTH AND BEHAVIOR

Apgar Score

After delivery, the physician will evaluate the health status of the neonate. The most common method is a widely used system developed by Virginia Apgar in 1952 called the **Apgar Score**. The system has designated values for various neonatal signs and permits a tentative and rapid diagnosis of major problems (Apgar, 1953). The neonate is evaluated at one minute and again at five minutes after birth.

There are five signs of the baby's physical condition that compose the Apgar Score: *heart rate, respiratory effort, muscle tone, reflex response* (response to breath test and to skin stimulation of the feet), and *color*. Each sign is given a value of 0, 1, or 2, as shown in Table 4.2 (Greenberg, Bruess, & Sands, 1986). The maximum score on all five scales is 10, and is rare.

Brazelton Assessment

Dr. T. Berry Brazelton (1984) developed the **Brazelton Neonatal Behavior Assessment Scale**, which is used to evaluate both the neurological condition and the behavior of the neonate (Brazelton, 1990). The scale is a useful indicator of central nervous system maturity and of social behavior and is helpful in predicting subsequent developmental

TABLE 4.2
APGAR SCORE

The Apgar scoring, developed in 1952 by Dr. Virginia Apgar, is an index to the health status of the newborn infant. The scoring system was developed to predict survival, to compare various methods of resuscitation, to evaluate certain obstetrical practices (such as inducing labor, maternal anesthesia, cesarean section), and to ensure closer observation of the infant during the first minutes of life.

Five signs of a baby's physical condition at birth were chosen for measurement: heart rate, respiratory effort, muscle tone, reflex response (response to breath test and to skin stimulation of the feet), and color. Each sign is given a score of 0, 1, or 2, as shown in the table.

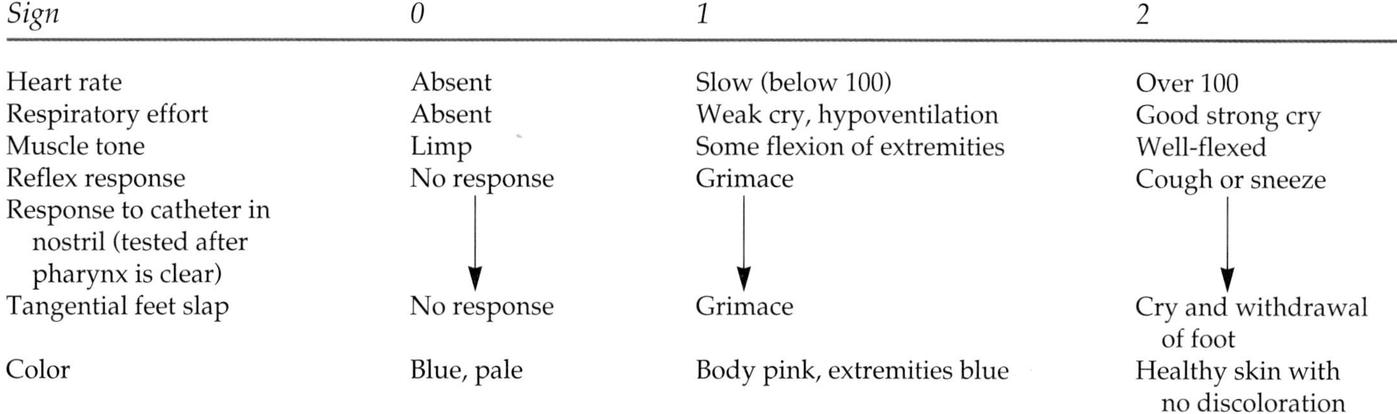

Sign	*0*	*1*	*2*
Heart rate	Absent	Slow (below 100)	Over 100
Respiratory effort	Absent	Weak cry, hypoventilation	Good strong cry
Muscle tone	Limp	Some flexion of extremities	Well-flexed
Reflex response	No response	Grimace	Cough or sneeze
Response to catheter in nostril (tested after pharynx is clear)	↓	↓	↓
Tangential feet slap	No response	Grimace	Cry and withdrawal of foot
Color	Blue, pale	Body pink, extremities blue	Healthy skin with no discoloration

The Apgar Score is the sum of the five values and ranges from 0 to 10, with 10 being the optimum. A score of 0 may indicate neonatal death; a score of 1–3 indicates that the infant is very weak; 4–6, moderately weak; and 7–10, in good to excellent condition. One-minute and five-minute scoring are done. The one-minute score indicates the condition at birth; the five-minute score combines the condition at birth and the results of care given during the first five minutes.

problems (Behrman & Vaughan, 1983). The scale assesses four areas of infant behavior:

- Motor behaviors (reflexes, hand-to-mouth coordination, and muscle tone)
- Interactive, adaptive behavior (alertness, cuddliness)
- Response to stress (startle reaction)
- Physiological control (ability to calm down after being upset)

Altogether, the scale looks at 26 specific behaviors as well as the strength of various reflexes (Brazelton, 1984).

POSTPARTUM BLUES

The period following childbirth is one in which conflicting feelings may surface (Leifer, 1980). The long pregnancy is over, which brings a feeling of relief. If the baby is wanted and healthy, the family experiences considerable happiness and elation. Within several days after delivery, however, the woman may suffer varying degrees of "baby blues," or **postpartal depression**, characterized by feelings of sadness, periods of crying, depressed mood, insomnia, irritability, and fatigue (Hopkins, Marcues, & Campbell, 1984).

Postpartal depression—feelings of sadness, crying, depression, insomnia, irritability, and fatigue commonly experienced by the mother several days after her baby is born

Numerous causes precipitate postpartal depression. The mother may have been under emotional strain while she anxiously awaited her baby. Once the baby comes, feelings of exhaustion and depression may result from a letdown of tension. Childbirth itself may impose considerable physical strain on a woman's body, which requires a period of rest and recovery. Estrogen and progesterone levels decline rapidly following delivery, which may have an upsetting, depressive effect on her (Waletzky, 1981). Other reports have suggested that diminished thyroid activity following delivery is associated with postpartum depression (Albright, 1993).

Upon returning home, the mother may feel the strain of "trying to do everything right" in caring for the baby. One young mother remarked: "I never imagined that one small baby would require so much extra work. I'm exhausted." (Author's counseling notes). If the baby is colicky and fussy, even the most patient and experienced mother can become tense and exhausted.

If the woman does not have much help from her partner, or if the baby or other children in the household continue to make personal demands upon her, she may become exhausted from the lack of sleep, and from the physical and emotional strain. Some women even return to their jobs outside the home very soon after having a baby. Clearly, the mother needs help and understanding. A conscientious partner will do everything he can to be a full part-

PARENTING ISSUES

Circumcision Pros and Cons

Although many people regard and practice **circumcision** as a mark of entrance into manhood, the question arises as to whether or not circumcision is necessary other than for cultural or religious reasons. Because of the way in which many societies performed circumcisions, young boys were subjected to extreme pain, infection, and hemorrhage. In our culture, male infants are usually circumcised without anesthetic almost immediately following birth. This has been found to produce severe physiological responses (Porter, Porges, & Marshall, 1988).

From a health standpoint, medical professionals are divided concerning the necessity of circumcision. Those in favor contend that it reduces the incidence of *carcinoma* (cancer) of the penis, as well as urinary tract infections and *cervical cancer* in women sex-partners. Proponents also contend that a circumcised penis is easier to keep clean and improves sexual sensation and fulfillment. When the foreskin is too tight and cannot be retracted, circumcision is necessary.

The latest research is inconsistent in relation to these arguments. Wallerstein (1980) compiled and analyzed the data available and found no causal relationship between circumcision or lack of it and any kind of cancer. But carcinoma of the penis is more likely to occur in men who do not thoroughly and regularly cleanse themselves. If the glans is kept clean, whether the foreskin has to be retracted or not, cancer is less likely to occur. Similarly, the presence or absence of a foreskin does not cause urinary tract infections or cervical cancer in men's sexual partners; however, the lack of penile cleanliness does.

Opponents of the procedure contend that circumcision does not increase sexual satisfaction. During erection, the foreskin retracts from the glans so sensation is not affected. Some authorities even feel that circumcision reduces sexual sensitivity because the penis constantly rubs on clothing. However, there is really no evidence to substantiate whether circumcision affects sexual function one way or the other (Masters & Johnson, 1966).

Because routine circumcision has been practiced for so many years, the custom is hard to break. A national survey of several hundred pediatricians and obstetricians revealed that 38 percent of the pediatricians and 60 percent of the obstetricians supported routine circumcision for sound medical reasons (Herrera & Macaraeg, 1984). However, in strong opposition to the view of most obstetricians, the American Academy of Pediatrics concluded in 1975 that if there was no medical need for circumcision of the newborn, the procedure should not be performed routinely (Kirkendall, 1981). Canadian researchers recommended that government medical plans not pay for the procedure because no significant benefits could be demonstrated from routine circumcision (Cadman, Gafni, & McNamee, 1984).

ner in the process and to assume maximum responsibility in caring for her. He will share the responsibility of caring for the baby, and take full or increased responsibility in the care of other children and in managing the household during at least the first several months with a new baby. The father is more likely to do this if he is included in prebirth planning and the total procreative experience is shared with him from the beginning of the pregnancy. Marsiglio (1991) suggests that the male's procreative consciousness and responsibility must be encouraged.

Cultural Factors in Postpartum Care

Cultural factors influence the postpartum care the new mother receives. That care is often very different in the United States from that in other countries. In the United States, women without physical complications may be sent home from the hospital within twenty-four to seventy-two hours after giving birth. Once out of the hospital, the focus of care shifts from the mother to the baby. The mother often feels inadequate, with lowered self-esteem. This is in sharp contrast to the expectations of the mother in China or Japan. The behavioral restrictions on the Chinese mother promote rest and award her special attention during the first postnatal month. The traditional Japanese mother is expected to go to her parents' home for a month to be cared for with her baby and to have generally more support from multigenerational living arrangements (Albright, 1993).

RETURNING TO WORK

One of the considerations following childbirth is whether or not a mother returns to work and the timing of such return. One study of 597 women was used to analyze when women start paid work following a birth (Joesch, 1994). This study investigated which month after the birth of the child women started to work outside the home, as well as the factors related to timing of reentering the work force. Timing of paid work was hypothesized to depend upon a woman's opportunity cost to working for pay relative to her opportunity cost of staying home. Findings showed that close to one in five women interrupted paid work for one month or less after giving birth, 53 percent had begun to work by month six, and 61 percent by the beginning of month twelve.

The question arises as to what entices women to stay home longer. According to the opportunity cost argument, the more a woman gives up by staying at home, the more likely she is to work for pay. Thus, financial considerations seem to play an important role in the timing of women's employment after childbirth. In particular, women from families that own a home and therefore have to make mortgage payments, those with higher income tax rates, and those working during pregnancy were all found to start to work sooner. Higher family income from sources other than women's earnings had the opposite effect: women were more likely to stay home longer.

Could maternity leave entice women to stay home longer? In 1993, the *Family and Medical Leave Act* enabled women to take time off from work without pay without being penalized by losing their job. They are entitled to return to work without penalty. The opportunity cost argument would predict that this act will lengthen the time out of employment to some degree since health benefits are covered by the employer during the leave. More importantly, the law guarantees the same or a comparable position upon the woman's return from leave, reducing the cost associated with finding a new job, which lowers the opportunity cost of staying at home. However, relinquished earnings during the absence and consequences for future earnings, child security, and promotions are likely to be more important considerations than the relatively minor aspect of health insurance. These findings underlie the importance of access to quality nonparental child care, if children's welfare is not to be compromised. Apparently, the desire for paid work is stronger than the desire to stay home with one's children while the children are young, but such a decision requires adequate care of the children while the mother is at work. Surprisingly, additional child-care costs are not substantial enough to influence the timing of the mother's return (Joesch, 1994).

PARENTING ISSUES

Returning Home

In an effort to save on medical expenses, more and more mothers are being discharged within twenty-four hours of birth. Some medical insurance companies insist upon early discharge following childbirth. Many family-centered obstetrical units discharge as early as six hours postpartum if the patient does not have major complications. For most mothers, early discharge may be unwise because of medical complications or for personal and family reasons. There is always a possibility of maternal infection, hemorrhage, and pain. Pain from an uncomfortable or painful episiotomy needs to be relieved with hot sitzbaths several times daily as long as necessary. Pain medication often needs to be prescribed. Bladder care is important. Urine retention and bladder overdistention should be avoided if possible. Constipation needs attention if it exists. Regular diet should be offered as soon as the patient requests food. Full ambulation is encouraged as rapidly as possible as are exercises to strengthen abdominal muscles while lying in bed. Some of these medical administrations require hospitalization, while all require careful instruction to the new mother and her partner. If the mother is rushed out of the hospital before instruction and care can be given, she may face some of the problems at home where it is not easy to take care of them. If labor has been long and difficult, the mother may be completely exhausted, and completely unready to care for herself, a newborn infant, and perhaps other children and family upon returning home. Every effort should be made to help the new mother regain her health and strength as soon as possible. This requires help at home and somebody to perform most of the family duties, while the other turns her attention to the baby, and regains her health.

Most authorities indicate that sexual intercourse may be resumed as soon as desired and comfortable; contraceptive measures are required, however, since pregnancy is possible. Contraceptive pills may be started after the first menstrual period but only in women who are not breast feeding. Some authorities advocate starting birth control pills within the first postpartum week in nonnursing mothers. A diaphragm may be fitted only after complete involution of the uterus at six to eight weeks. In the meantime, foams, jellies, or condoms may be used. Conception has been reported as early as two weeks postpartum so caution must be exercised to prevent pregnancy. Nursing mothers tend to ovulate usually at ten to twelve weeks postpartum but an occasional nursing mother will ovulate and menstruate as quickly as a nonlactating woman (Berkow, 1987).

Premature and Small-for-Gestational-Age (SGA) Infants

CLASSIFICATIONS

Postmature infant

Full-term infant

Premature infant

Each newborn may be classified as full-term, premature, or postmature. A **full-term infant** is one whose gestational age is 37 to 42 weeks. A **premature infant** is one whose gestational age is less than 37 weeks. (Duffy, Als, & McAnulty, 1990). A **postmature infant** has a gestational age of over 42 weeks. The neonate may also be classified as of appropriate size and weight for gestational age, small for gestational age, or large for gestational age. Figure 4.1 represents intrauterine growth based on birth weight and gestational age of liveborn, single, white infants (Sweet, 1979).

PREMATURE INFANTS

A premature infant is one who is born before 37 weeks gestation. Previously, any infant weighing less than 2.5 kg (5.5 lb) was termed premature, but this definition was inappropriate because many newborns weighing less than 2.5 kg are actually mature or postmature but small for gestational age (SGA) and have different appearance and problems than premature infants (Berkow, 1987). However, most premature infants are also small, weighing less than 2.5 kg, and have thin, shiny, pink skin with underlying veins that are easily seen. They have little fat, hair, or external ear cartilage. Spontaneous activity and tone are at a minimum, and their extremities are not held in a fixed position. The testes are undescended in males; the labia majora do not cover the labia minora in females.

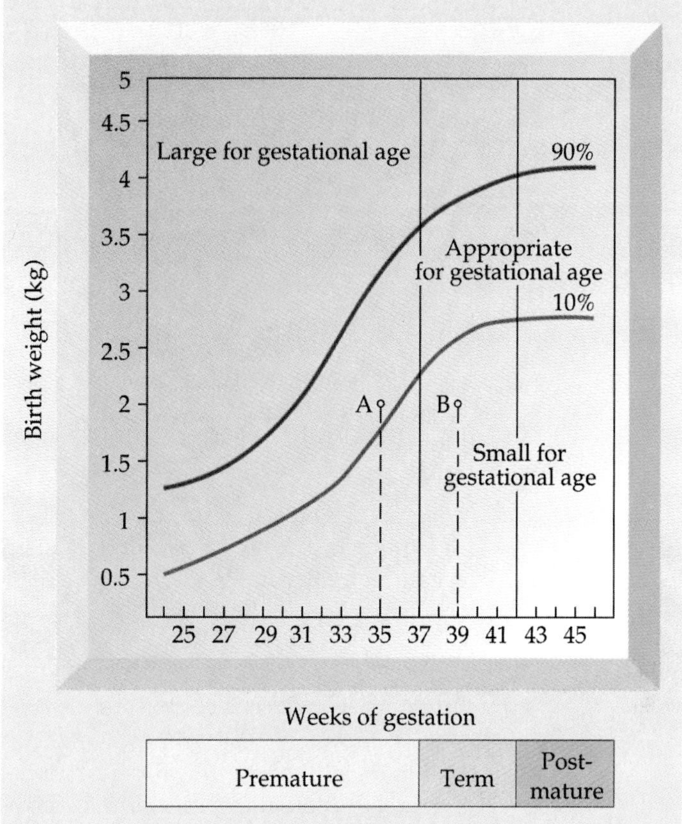

FIGURE 4.1 Intrauterine growth of liveborn, white infants. Baby A is premature, whereas baby B is mature but small for gestational age. Curves show growth of infants for tenth and ninetieth percentiles.

Adapted from A. Y. Sweet, "Classification of the Low-Birth-Weight Infant," in *Care of the High-Risk Neonate*, 2nd ed., by M. H. Klaus and A. A. Fanaroff (1979). Copyright 1979 by W. B. Saunders Co.

Problems with premature infants relate to immaturity of the organs. Premature infants have various kinds of respiratory difficulties. They may have inadequate sucking and swallowing reflexes; they may have a small stomach capacity and may have to be tube fed or fed intravenously. They often suffer from colitis and other gastrointestinal problems. They have lower immunity and are more subject to various infections than full-term infants. They exhibit various signs of metabolic difficulties: hypothermia (below normal body temperature); hypoglycemia (low blood glucose levels); hypocalcemia (low calcium levels); and hypernatremia (high sodium concentrations) are common. Renal function is immature, so the kidneys are less able to excrete fluids. Premature infants are also more prone to cerebral hemorrhage and injury (Ross, Tesman, Auld, & Nass, 1992; Sostek, Smith, Katz, & Grant, 1987).

Assuming there have been no significant abnormalities, and assuming proper medical, emotional, and social care and attention, preterm infants can often make up deficits in cognitive, language, and social development during the first three years of life (Greenberg & Crnic, 1988). When there are developmental deficits, it is usually because of significant medical complications. Altogether only 10 percent to 15 percent of all preterm infants have major intellectual impairment or neurological problems (Kopp, 1983), but as many as 100 percent of survivors in the lowest birth weight categories (less than 800 g, or 1.8 lbs) may be neurologically impaired (Britton, Chir, Fitzhardinge, & Ashby, 1981; Murray, 1988). Infants with birth weights less than 1.5 kilograms (3.3 lb) are at special risk (Rose, Feldman, McCarton, & Wolfson, 1988). The *Neurobehavioral Assessment of the Preterm Infant (NAPI)* scale was developed to assess neurological development (Korner, Constantinou, Dimiceli, & Brown, 1991). Behavioral problems of both preterm and small-for-gestational-age (SGA) infants are assessed

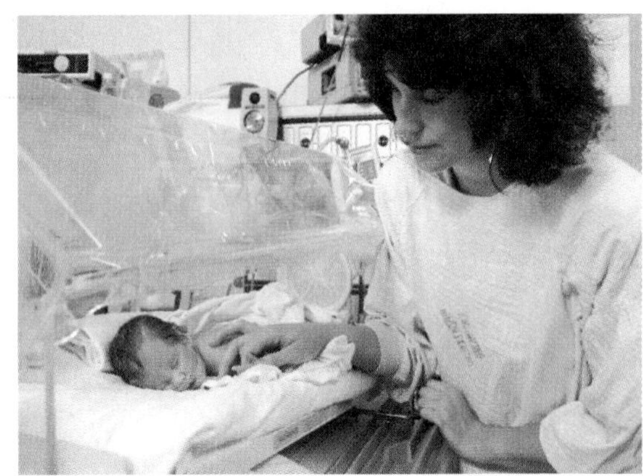

A premature infant is one whose gestational age is less than 37 weeks.

with various instruments (Spiker, Kraemer, Constantine, & Bryant, 1992).

SMALL-FOR-GESTATIONAL-AGE (SGA) INFANTS

An *SGA infant* is one whose weight is below the tenth percentile for gestational age, whether premature, full-term, or postmature (Achenbach, Phares, & Howell, 1990). Despite their small size, SGA infants have physical characteristics and behavior similar to normal-size infants of the same gestational age. An infant weighing less than 2.5 kilograms, but born between thirty-seven and forty-two weeks gestation, may have the same skin, ear, genital, and neurologic development as any other full-term infant. If low birth weight is due to prenatal malnutrition, such infants catch up quickly when given an adequate caloric intake (Berkow, 1987).

Perinatal (near the time of birth) *asphyxia* (lack of oxygen) is the greatest problem of these infants. If intrauterine growth retardation is due to placental insufficiency, asphyxia during labor is common, so a rapid delivery, sometimes by cesarean section, is needed. An infant who does not breathe spontaneously requires immediate resuscitation to sustain life and avoid brain damage. If asphyxia can be avoided, the neurologic prognosis is good. *Hypoglycemia* (low blood sugar) is also common due to inadequate glycogen storage (Berkow, 1987).

Assuming there have been no serious complications, the question still arises regarding the effects of low birth weight on health during subsequent childhood. In 1981, 15,400 interviews were carried out among the parents of children age 17 or younger that year. This study, known as the Child Health Supplement (CHS), was part of the National Interview Survey (Overpeck et al., 1989). About 8 percent of the children in the CHS sample were of low birth weight. (No distinction was made between prematurity and low birth weight.) Overall, 7 percent of the white children and 15 percent of the black children were of low birth weight. (When both the white and black mothers are poor, the percentages having low-birth-weight infants are more similar [R. Turner, 1992c].) The study found that throughout childhood, but especially during the first six years, children who had been of low birth weight had a greater number of chronic conditions, were hospitalized more often, and generally exhibited a pattern of poorer health than did children who were of normal birth weight. The most common chronic condition was *respiratory illness* (Overpeck et al., 1989). Other studies show that the lower the birth weight the greater likelihood a

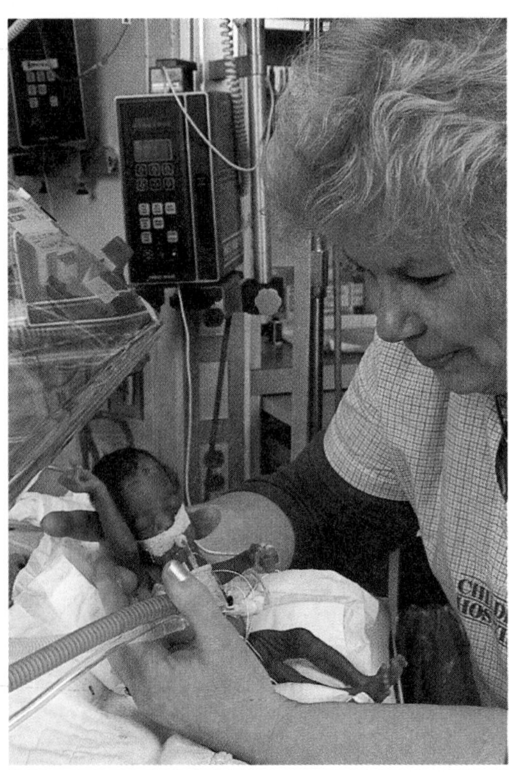

Only 10 percent to 15 percent of all preterm infants have major intellectual impairment or neurological problems.

FOCUS

Kilogram Kids and Intensive Neonatal Care

Remarkable advances have been made in caring for preterm infants. Highly specialized neonatal intensive-care units (NICUs) have been developed to take over various functions of organ systems of the body that are not sufficiently mature to sustain life on their own. The NICU is a series of blinking lights, numbers, monitors, and alarms, all of which are connected by tubes, catheters, and electrodes to the tiny infant. The NICU monitors brain waves, heartbeat, respiration, and other vital signs, and provides food, oxygen, and medicines. The infant lies on an undulating water bed in an incubator that carefully controls temperature and humidity.

Researchers have found that, even when confined to incubators, these tiny infants need formal skin contacts, handling, cuddling, talking, singing, and rocking from caregivers and parents. Such contacts facilitate development (Scafidi, 1986; Zeskind & Iacino, 1984).

The survival rate of premature infants closely correlates with their birth weight. Kilogram infants weigh 1,000 grams (2.2 lb). In the best hospitals, 80 percent to 85 percent of infants 2.2 to 3.2 pounds (1 kg to 1.5 kg) survive. Remarkably, about a fourth of those weighing 1.6 pounds (750 g) survive (Davis, 1986; Fincher, 1982). Intensive care of these smallest infants poses a real dilemma, however. They may survive, but up to 100 percent of 750-gram babies are neurologically impaired. Costs for intensive care in the hospital may run from $100,000 to $200,000, leaving a family poverty-stricken. The question remains: How much care is too much? At what point should infants be allowed to die, rather than be saved to live with such severe impairments that they can never have a chance for a normal life?

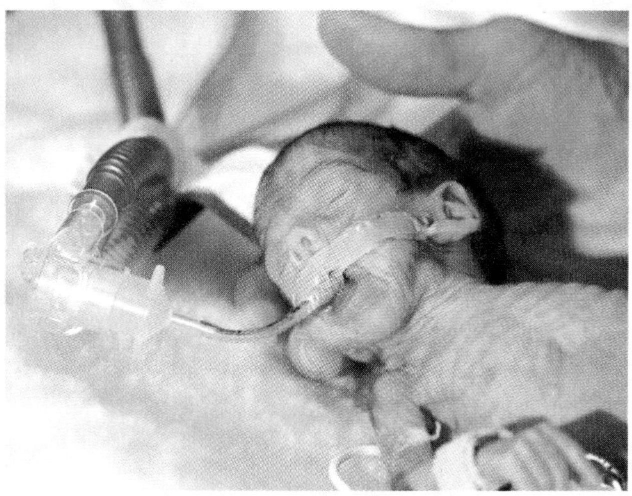

Intensive care of kilogram infants (2.2 lbs) poses a real dilemma: The majority survive but are neurologically impaired.

child will have physical, health, intellectual, and behavioral problems at school age (R. Turner, 1992d).

PARENTAL ROLES AND REACTIONS

Ordinarily, the birth of a full-term infant is a positive event bringing happiness and closeness to family members. The birth of a preterm infant is a stressful event, leaving family members unsure of their roles and how to respond. Grandparents, for example, may need to grieve over the loss of their idealized grandchild. Rituals such as showers and birth announcements may be eliminated or postponed, leaving other family members in the dark. The anxiety and stress of the parents is increased when they don't find positive social supports (Coffman, Levitt, Deets, & Quigley, 1991). Furthermore, parents often find preterm infants less attractive, more irritating, and less likable (Easterbrooks, 1989). Mothers of preterm infants have been found to have lower maternal sensitivity to their infants than do mothers of full-term babies (Zarling, Hirsch, & Landry, 1988). The mother's reduced sensitivity interferes

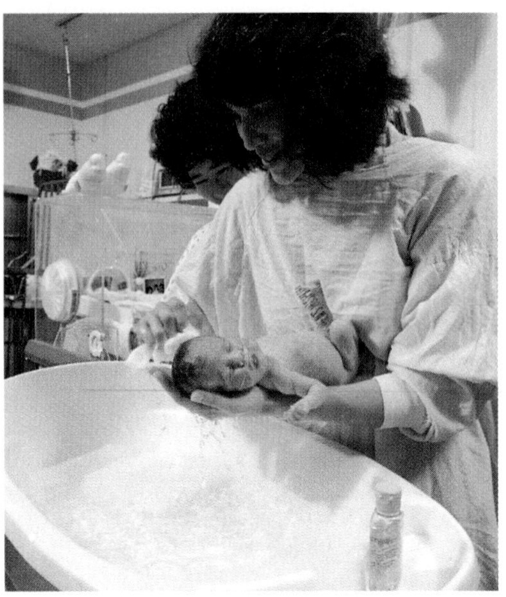

Preterm infants are critically dependent on parents to provide an adequate care-giving environment.

with the infant's total development because preterm infants are critically dependent on parents to provide an adequate care-giving environment, social enrichment, and encouragement (Levy-Shiff, Sharir, & Mogelner, 1989).

Intervention programs for parents of low-birth-weight, preterm infants are needed to help parents gain more self-confidence and satisfaction with parenting and to develop more positive perceptions of their infants (Affleck, Tennen, Rowe, Roscher, & Walker, 1989). Such programs usually consist of a series of teaching sessions in the hospital and follow-ups in the parents' home after the infant is discharged (Rauh, Achenbach, Nurcombe, Howell, & Teti, 1988).

PREVENTION

The risk of low birth weight is reduced when pregnant women receive more complete prenatal care. Care that is recommended includes such components as conducting appropriate physical examinations, appropriate laboratory tests for high risk patients, taking a health history, and advising women on behavior such as drug or alcohol use (R. Turner, 1994). In one experimental prenatal care program conducted in Los Angeles, preterm deliveries were reduced by 20 percent. The prenatal care program included increased prenatal visits combined with instruction on how to prevent a preterm birth (Donovan, 1994).

The Neonate

PHYSICAL APPEARANCE AND CHARACTERISTICS

Vernix caseosa—waxy substance covering the skin of the neonate

At birth, the average full-term baby in the United States is about twenty inches long (50.8 cm) and weighs about seven pounds (3.2 kg). Males tend to be larger and heavier than females, and size at birth bears a relationship to size during childhood. Most newborns lose 5 percent to 10 percent of their birth weight in the first few days of life because of fluid loss, until they take in and digest enough food to begin gaining weight (Berkow, 1987).

Some newborns are not very attractive (Ritter, Casey, & Longlois, 1991). The *head* may be long, pointed, or misshapen from being squeezed through the birth canal. The ears and nose may be flattened for the same reason. The head is disproportionately large in relation to the rest of the body, and too heavy for the neck muscles to support it. The *legs and buttocks* are small in proportion to the rest of the body. The face, especially the flesh around the eyes, is usually puffy; the brow is wrinkled. The skin of the baby is covered with a protective cheeselike substance: **vernix caseosa**. Some babies have fuzzy body hair that drops off in a short time. Underweight babies look like wrinkled old people.

PHYSIOLOGICAL FUNCTIONING

Although most neonates will not win any beauty contests, they are remarkable creatures with their own independently functioning systems. They must *breathe* on their own as soon as they emerge into the air. In the beginning, breathing may be rapid, shallow, and irregular, but it gradually settles into a more regular rhythm. The infant can cough and sneeze to clear mucus from air passages.

The baby has had an *independent circulatory system*, with a heart pumping blood to the embryo, since the end of the sixth week of gestation (Witters & Jones-Witters, 1980). At birth, the heartbeat is still accelerated at about 120 to 150 beats per minute. Blood pressure begins to stabilize in about ten days.

The baby has a strong *sucking reflex* to be able to take in milk. However, the mother's breasts don't begin secreting milk for two to three days after birth. In the meantime, a thin, watery, high-protein liquid called **colostrum** is produced, which is nutritionally rich and contains antibodies that enable the baby to fight infections. Some babies develop *physiological jaundice* for a while because of the immaturity of the liver. The condition is characterized by a yellowish tinge to the skin and eyeballs. The condition is not serious and is treated by exposure to fluorescent light, which helps the action of the liver.

Because newborns lack fat layers under their skin, they lose heat very quickly, so they have difficulty maintaining stable body temperature. Crying and physical activity help them control the temperature.

THE SENSES AND PERCEPTION

Infants cannot gain information, learn about the world, or interact socially unless they actively attend to relevant features of their environment (Gardner, Zarmel, & Magnano, 1992). At one time it was thought that newborns' senses were not very well developed. Now it is recognized that *neonates are seeing, hearing, feeling, smelling, touching, tasting creatures who respond to a variety of stimuli, including pain.* There are, however, wide individual differences in infants' reactivity to environmental stimuli (DiPetro, Porges, & Uhly, 1992).

Vision

Vision is the least developed of the senses. Newborns can see clearly objects between seven and fifteen inches away. Their eyes cannot focus properly at closer or farther distances. They have poor *visual acuity*: the ability to distinguish details of objects. Their visual acuity at distances has been estimated to be between 20/150 and 20/800. (Normal vision is 20/20). This means the neonate can see details of objects at twenty feet no more clearly than adults with normal vision would see them at 150 to 800 feet. However, at close distances, newborns can discriminate among circles, crosses, squares, and rectangles (Bronson, 1991; Slater, Morison, & Rose, 1983). They prefer looking at faces to looking at objects, and by 1 month of age can distinguish their mother's face from those of others (Ludemann, 1991). They can tell the difference between different facial expressions and even imitate some of them (Field, Woodson, Greenberg, & Cohen, 1982).

Colostrum—high-protein liquid secreted by the mother's breasts prior to her milk coming in; contains antibodies to protect the nursing infant from diseases

By 6 months of age, visual acuity is about normal (Banks & Salapatek, 1983). The irises of babies' eyes open and close as lights go from dim to bright. Some infants have *binocular vision* at birth; that is, they use both eyes to focus on an object. It is not known whether they can see colors immediately, although this ability can be demonstrated by a few months of age (Bornstein, 1985b).

Hearing

Infants can hear sounds while still in the uterus. They respond to various loud noises such as cars honking (Birnholz & Benecerraf, 1983). In fact, they can probably distinguish between their mother's voice and the voices of others (Aslin, Pisoni, Jusczyk, 1983). After birth, their hearing is only slightly less sensitive than that of adults (Acredolo & Hake, 1982). They seem to be able to discriminate among sounds of different intensity, pitch, and duration; are more sensitive to higher-pitched than lower-pitched sounds; and are most sensitive to human voices (Aslin, Pisoni, & Jusczyk, 1983; Spetner & Olsho, 1990). They can also detect the direction from which sound comes and turn their head toward it (Brody, Zelazo, & Chaike, 1984). Like adults, neonates can get bored with the continuous presentation of a sound, but when presented with a new sound, such as a bell ringing, will pay attention or even show a startle response to it (Madison,

Madison, & Adubato, 1986; Weiss, Zelazo, & Swain, 1988). They apparently are able to retain memory for a specific sound over a twenty-four-hour period when presented with the same sound over both days (Swain, Zelazo, & Clifton, 1993).

Smell

Human neonates are responsive to various odors, including odors from their mother's breast. Within several days after birth, breast-feeding infants respond preferentially either to breast or axillary odors from their own mother when paired with comparable stimuli from an unfamiliar lactating female (Cernoch & Porter, 1985). In another experiment, 2-week-old bottle-feeding girls with no prior breast-feeding experience found the breast odors of lactating females especially attractive (Makin & Porter, 1989).

Taste

Newborns can also discriminate among various taste stimuli. Rosenstein and Oster (1988) demonstrated that within two hours of birth, infants with no prior taste experience differentiated sour and bitter stimuli as well as sweet versus nonsweet taste stimuli. The responses to the sour, salty, and bitter stimuli were all characterized by negative facial actions in the brow and midface regions. This study and others showed clearly that newborns also have an innate preference for sweet solutions (Beauchamp & Cowart, 1985), and that sucrose can have a calming effect and relieve pain in the newborn infant (Blass & Smith, 1992; Smith, Stevens, Torgerson, & Kim, 1992).

Human neonates are responsive to various odors, including odors from the mother's breast.

Touch and Pain

There is strong evidence of touch sensitivity in neonates, with no discernable differences between the sexes. If you stroke the cheeks of newborns, they will turn their head in that direction. Stimulate the soles of infants' feet, and they flex their toes. Every parent knows that one way to soothe infants is to hold and stroke them. Recent studies indicate that infants are also sensitive to pain and that this sensitivity increases during the first five days of life (Haith, 1986).

REFLEXES

Reflexes—unlearned behavioral responses to particular stimuli in the environment

Reflexes are unlearned behavioral responses to particular stimuli in the environment. Table 4.3 describes some of the reflexes of the neonate. Some of these reflexes, such as the *rooting and sucking reflex*, are critical to the infants' survival. Others evolved during evolutionary development. For example, *Palmar's grasp* was necessary to keep babies from falling when their mothers carried them around all the time. The *Moro reflex* could help infants to grasp something when in danger of falling. Other reflexes, such as blinking or the rage reflex, help protect the baby from physical discomfort. Only the *blinking, knee jerk,* and *sneezing reflexes* are permanent for a lifetime. The rest of the reflexes gradually disappear and are replaced by more deliberate, voluntary movements, as development proceeds. The majority of newborn infants show stronger and more coordinated movements on the right side of the body than on the left, which forms the basis for right-handedness and right-biased movements in adulthood (Grattan, DeVos, Levy, & McClintock, 1992).

TABLE 4.3
REFLEXES OF THE NEONATE

Reflex	*Stimulus and Response*
Babinski	Stimulate the sole of the foot; the infant's toes fan out and upward.
Babkin	Apply pressure to both palms of the infant's hands; the infant's eyes close, mouth opens, and the infant turns its head.
Blinking	Flash on a light, or move an object toward the infant's eyes; they blink.
Knee jerk	Tap on the kneecap; the foot kicks upward.
Moro	Make a sudden loud noise or suddenly remove body support; the infant's arms and legs fling outward and toward the body as if to hold onto something.
Palmar grasp	Place an object or finger in the infant's palm; the infant grasps tightly and may even be lifted to a standing position.
Rooting	Touch the infant's cheek; the baby turns toward the touch and attempts to suck.
Rage	Restrain the infant's movements or put a cloth over its mouth; the baby cries and struggles.
Sneezing	Stimulate or tickle the nasal passages; the infant sneezes to clear the passages.
Stepping	Hold the infant upright with feet on the ground; the baby attempts to step as in walking.
Sucking	Put object in infant's mouth; infant begins rhythmic sucking.
Swallowing	Put food in mouth; the neonate swallows it.
Swimming	Place infant on its stomach; its arms and legs fan out and move as in swimming.

MOTOR ACTIVITY

Although newborns have a variety of reflexes, they don't have much control over voluntary movements. Their arms and legs jerk and flail and they have trouble getting their fingers or hands to their mouths. When awake and in a supine position, neonates makes general movements such as whole-body flexes or more localized movements of the limbs. As they gain control over their muscle activity, they become more successful at accomplishing their goals with less excess motion. Studies of the development of hand-mouth coordination in newborn infants suggest that the relationship between the hand and mouth is not random, but it is far from skilled. However, considerable development does occur in hand-mouth coordination after the newborn period (Lew & Butterworth, 1995). Training can influence early motor development. One research study shows that practice facilitated stepping in eight-week-old infants and led to an earlier onset of unaided walking. Similarly, infants who received sitting exercises were able to sit upright longer than infants who received no exercise (Zelazo, Zelazo, Cohen, & Zelazo, 1993).

BRAIN AND NERVOUS SYSTEM

Neurons—nerve cells

The nervous systems are composed of **neurons**, or nerve cells, which transmit messages. A neuron contains a *cell body; dendrites*, which receive neural messages; and an *axon*, which passes along the neural messages, in the form of electrical impulses, to the dendrites of the next neuron. The axon is insulated with a *myelin sheath*, which prevents the electrical impulses from leaking out. Figure 4.2 shows a typical neuron.

There are several differences between the brain and neurons of a neonate and those of a mature adult. (1) The neonate continues to form new nerve cells, a process that continues until about the second month after birth (Lipsitt, 1986). (2) The billions of nerve cells that are present continue to mature. Especially the dendrites grow and develop, increasing

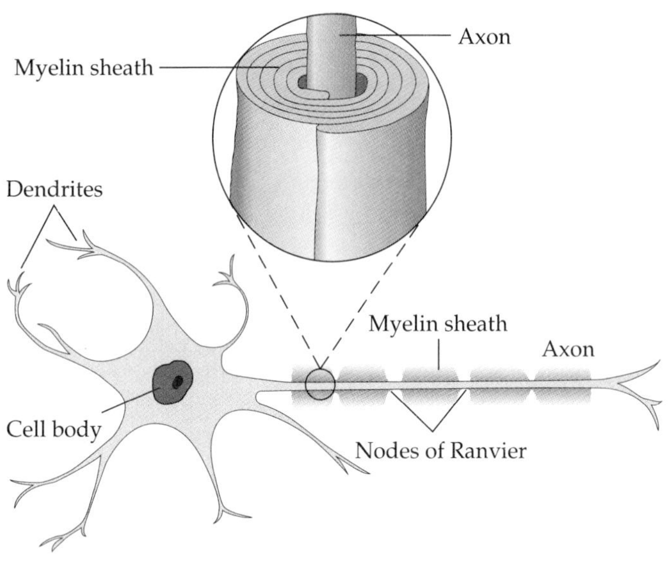

FIGURE 4.2 Neuron. The neurons are wrapped in an insulation substance called myelin. The myelin sheath also speeds transmission through the neuron by preventing the electrical charge from escaping.

their efficiency in receiving messages. (3) Many of the neurons in the newborn are not yet *myelinated*, or enclosed in a sheath, which allows electrical impulses to escape and results in inefficient nerve transmission, jerky responses, and lack of coordination (Morell & Norton, 1980). Myelination continues until adolescence (Guthrie, 1980). (4) The brain of the newborn is noticeably immature, with large areas dysfunctional. Brain activity is concentrated in the *brain stem*, which controls automatic physiological functions such as breathing, digestion, and a variety of reflexes. The *cerebral cortex*, or upper levels of the brain that control more complex functions, is quite immature in newborns. Growth of the cortex as the infant matures allows more flexible, complex motor and intellectual functioning as time goes by (Bell & Fox, 1992; Chugani & Phelps, 1986).

STRESS REACTIONS

Infants show physiological reactions to stress. Stress produces an elevation of cortisol from the adrenal cortex. Epinephrine is secreted and travels in the bloodstream to every cell of the body. Cardiovascular function increases, including an increase of heart rate and blood pressure, and a constriction of blood vessels. Respiration increases, as does muscular tension and strength. Infants show differences in stress reactions during labor itself. These reactions reflect differences in temperament. Uterine contractions are an example of intermittent stress, and suggests that stress responses may be individually specific at births and influence behaviorial style throughout infancy. In one study, 40 percent of infants whose heart rates during labor were characterized by either acceleration or deceleration were rated by their mothers as being temperamentally difficult at 4 months and 1 year of age. Infants who showed variable and mixed heart rate reactions to labor were always rated as easy or agreeable.

Literature indicates that responsiveness to stress, particularly intermediate stress early in life, can have a permanent physiological effect on brain tissues. The effect on brain tissue produces adaptive and maladaptive temperamental characteristics. This mechanism implies the existence of physiological basis of stress responses that may predispose individuals to unique behavioral characteristics. Thus, some forms of stress reactivity have biological underpinnings, and the data supports the hypothesis that stress reactivity is a characteristic of temperament (Davis & Emory, 1995).

INDIVIDUAL DIFFERENCES

It must be emphasized that babies show distinct individuality in temperament from the first weeks of life. There are differences in activity level as well. Some babies are very alert, responsive, and active; others are lethargic and quiet. Some are very happy and cheerful, always smiling and pleasant. Others are irritable, cry a lot, or express frequent frustration and anger. Some babies are very sociable and outgoing; others are shy and withdrawn. Some show regular patterns of eating and sleeping and are easy to care for on a routine basis. Others do not show regular cycles. Some babies want to be held and cuddled; others seldom do. These differences in temperament mean that parents have to be flexible in the care they give. Not all babies can be cared for alike, since all infants are not the same (Thomas & Chess, 1987).

FOCUS

Sudden Infant Death Syndrome (SIDS)

SIDS is the sudden death of any infant or young child that is unexpected according to the health history and for which an adequate cause of death cannot be demonstrated. It is the most common cause of death between 2 weeks and 1 year of age, amounting to 30 percent of all deaths in this age group. Peak incidence is between the second and fourth month of life. The incidence is greater among lower socioeconomic groups, in premature infants, during the cold months, in siblings of SIDS victims, and in infants born to mothers who smoke during pregnancy or who are narcotic addicts.

Almost all the deaths occur while the infant is sleeping: He or she just stops breathing. Parents are usually grief-stricken, and because no definite cause of the death can be found, usually have excessive guilt feelings. These feelings are increased if social workers or the police become involved in investigating the death. To deal with the grief and guilt, family members will need a great deal of support for several months (Berkow, 1987).

Summary

1. Prepared childbirth refers to the physical, social, intellectual, and emotional preparation for the birth of a baby. In this context, it does not necessarily refer to labor and delivery without medication.
2. Methods of natural childbirth include the Dick-Read method and the Lamaze method.
3. Birthing rooms and centers provide homelike settings where birth takes place and where the mother, and sometimes the whole family, may take care of the infant afterward. These settings seek to combine the advantages of delivery in a homelike environment with the medical backup of a hospital.
4. About 95 percent of babies are delivered in the hospital. If couples consider a home delivery, they ought to follow certain standards as outlined by the NAPSAC. Even with careful screening, home delivery has risks and disadvantages.
5. Real labor is rhythmic in nature and may be divided into three phases: the dilation phase; the childbirth phase; and passage of the placenta, or afterbirth, during the third phase.
6. General anesthesia or local or regional anesthesia may be used to alleviate pain during childbirth. General anesthesia affects the body by acting on the whole nervous system. It crosses the placental barrier and affects the fetus as well. Local anesthesia blocks pain in specific areas; some types have minimal effect on the baby.
7. Electronic fetal monitoring is used to provide information about fetal heartbeat and condition during labor and delivery.
8. There are various reasons why physicians sometimes induce labor, but elective induction solely for the woman's or the physician's convenience is restricted by the Federal Drug Administration.

9. In normal delivery the baby's head is delivered first. Complications during delivery may include vaginal bleeding, abnormal fetal heart rate, a disproportion in size between the fetus and pelvic opening, or abnormal fetal presentations and positions.
10. Birth is a stress on the baby, but the infant produces large amounts of adrenaline and noradrenaline, which have a stimulating affect on the infant and help it to breathe immediately after birth.
11. One of the most serious delivery complications is anoxia (oxygen deprivation to the brain) from a prolapsed umbilical cord or other causes. The result may be permanent damage to the infant's brain cells or even death. Brain injury can also occur during difficult deliveries, especially when forceps are used improperly.
12. A cesarean section can be a life-saving procedure when rapid delivery is needed, but some authorities complain that cesareans are being performed unnecessarily.
13. The Leboyer method of childbirth emphasizes gentle, loving treatment of the newborn, including the use of dim lights and gentle voices as well as soothing, massaging, and stroking the baby while it rests on the mother's abdomen. American obstetricians as well as research do not always support the validity of Leboyer's claims, but the emphasis on gentle treatment is a positive one.
14. After delivery, the physician evaluates the health status of the neonate and gives it an Apgar Score. The Brazelton Neonatal Behavior Assessment Scale is also used to evaluate both the neurological condition and the behavior of the neonate.
15. Postpartal depression is common following childbirth. The mother needs help and understanding. Cultural factors influence the care the new mother receives.
16. There are pros and cons regarding circumcision, but the American Academy of Pediatrics indicates there is no medical need for routine circumcision of the newborn.
17. To save on medical expenses more and more mothers are being discharged from the hospital within twenty-four hours or less after delivery, in some cases to the detriment of the mother and family.
18. One of the considerations following childbirth is whether the mother returns to work and the timing of such return. Financial considerations play a big part in that decision.
19. Newborns may be classified as full-term (37 to 42 weeks gestation), premature (less than 37 weeks gestation), and postmature (over 42 weeks gestation). Premature infants may have problems because of the immaturity of their organs.
20. Small-for-gestational-age (SGA) infants weigh below the tenth percentile for gestational age, whether premature, full-term, or postmature. They have physical characteristics and behavior similar to normal-size infants of the same gestational age. Perinatal asphyxia (lack of oxygen) is the greatest problem of these infants. However, throughout childhood, especially the first six years, they have poorer health than normal-size infants.
21. Remarkable advances have been made in intensive neonatal care for preterm infants. However, intensive care of the very smallest infants, especially those less than 1.6 pounds (750 grams), poses a special dilemma. These infants may survive, but up to 100 percent are neurologically impaired. How much intensive care is too much? Costs may run from $100,000 to $200,000.
22. The birth of a preterm infant is stressful to the parents, who may be less sensitive to an infant who is less attractive, more irritating, and less likeable.
23. The risk of low birth weight is reduced when pregnant women receive more complete prenatal care.
24. The average full-term neonate is about twenty inches long and weighs about seven pounds. Some are not very attractive.
25. The neonate is a remarkable creature. It must breathe on its own; it has had an independent circulatory system operating since the sixth week of gestation. It has a strong sucking reflex to take in milk. It may have problems for a few days with physiological jaundice and may have some trouble regulating body temperature.

26. Neonates possess all the senses, though not all of these are well developed. Vision is the least developed. Newborns can see clearly objects between seven and fifteen inches away, but have difficulty at closer or farther distances. By 6 months of age, visual acuity is about normal.
27. Infants can hear sounds while still in the uterus. After birth, their hearing is only slightly less sensitive than that of adults.
28. Human neonates are responsive to various odors, including odors from their mother's breast. They can also discriminate among various taste stimuli. There is strong evidence of touch sensitivity.
29. Reflexes are unlearned behavioral responses to particular stimuli in the environment. Reflexes help the infant to survive, to protect itself from harm and from physical discomfort. Only the blinking, knee jerk, and sneezing reflexes are permanent. The rest of the reflexes gradually disappear and are replaced by more deliberate, voluntary movements.
30. Newborns don't have much control over voluntary movements, but coordination is developed through practice and training.
31. The nervous systems are composed of neurons, or nerve cells. The cells in neonates continue to multiply for about the first two months. The existing cells become more mature and more capable of transmitting messages. The brain also continues to develop, especially in the cerebral cortex, or higher levels. Growth of the cortex allows more flexible, complex motor and intellectual functioning as time goes by.
32. Sudden Infant Death Syndrome (SIDS) is a frequent cause of death between 2 weeks and 1 year of age, amounting to 30 percent of all deaths in this age group. The incidence is greater among some groups of mothers than others. Parents are usually grief-stricken and often feel guilty.
33. Infants show physiological reactions to stress.
34. Babies show distinct individuality of temperament from the first weeks of life.

Key Terms

Amniotic sac (bag of waters) *p. 98*
Anoxia *p. 104*
Apgar score *p. 104*
Brazelton Neonatal Behavior Assessment Scale *p. 104*
Cesarean section *p. 103*
Circumcision *p. 106*
Colostrum *p. 113*
Dick-Read method *p. 96*
Episiotomy *p. 102*
Full-term infant *p. 108*
General anesthesia *p. 100*
Labor *p. 98*
Lamaze method *p. 96*
Leboyer method *p. 104*
Local or regional anesthesia *p. 100*
Neurons *p. 115*
Perineum *p. 102*
Postmature infant *p. 108*
Postpartal depression *p. 105*
Premature infant *p. 108*
Prepared childbirth *p. 96*
Prolapsed umbilical cord *p. 104*
Reflexes *p. 114*
Show *p. 98*
Vernix caseosa *p. 112*

Discussion Questions

1. What do you think of the Lamaze method of natural childbirth? What are some advantages and disadvantages? Have you known any parent who used the Lamaze method or a similar method for having their baby? How did it work out?
2. For yourself, what do you think about

having both parents participate actively in the labor and delivery process? About both parents being present in the delivery room when the baby is born? Explain your answers.

3. Do you know anyone who had induced labor? Delivery by cesarean section? With what results?
4. Do you know any couple who had a premature baby? What were some of their reactions? What problems did they encounter?
5. Assume you had a 750-gram baby that was premature. Would you want the doctor to try to save the life of your baby if it would be severely mentally retarded afterward?
6. To you who have had a child: What was your first feeling and reaction when you saw your baby? What pleased you the most? What troubled you the most? Explain.

Suggested Readings

Bean, C. A. (1990). *Methods of Childbirth.* New York: William Morrow. All aspects of childbirth from late pregnancy to postpartum considerations.

Brazelton, T. B., & Lester, B. M. (1982). *New approaches to developmental screenings of infants.* New York: Elsevier. Brazelton method of neonatal evaluation and other new approaches.

Goldberg, S., & Divitto, B. A. (1983). *Born too soon: Preterm and early development.* San Francisco: Freeman. Focus on the first three years of life of preterm infants.

Henig, R. M., with Fletcher, A. B. (1983). *Your premature baby.* New York: Rawson. Guide for parents.

Klaus, M. H., & Klaus, P. H. (1985). *The amazing newborn: Making the most of the first weeks of life.* Reading, MA: Addison-Wesley. Latest scientific findings; profusely illustrated.

Korte, D., & Scaer, R. (1984). *A good birth, a safe birth.* New York: Bantam. Options for delivery, including natural childbirth.

Lamaze, F. (1981). *Painless childbirth: The Lamaze method.* New York: Pocket. Full explanation.

Leach, P. (1983). *Babyhood* (2nd ed.). New York: Knopf. Covers infancy.

Restak, R. M. (1986). *The infant mind.* Garden City, NY: Doubleday. Early brain development.

Sargov, S. E., Feinbloom, R. I., Spindel, P., & Brodsky, A. (1984). *Home birth: A practitioner's guide to birth outside the hospital.* Rockville, MD: Aspen Systems Corporation.

Sumner, P., & Phillips, C. (1981). *Birthing rooms: Concept and reality.* St. Louis: C. V. Mosby. Experiences of thirteen couples.

Part Three

CHILD DEVELOPMENT

Perspectives on Child Development

Chapter 5

CHILD DEVELOPMENT AS A SUBJECT OF STUDY

Child Development as a Subject of Study

Child development—all aspects of human growth from birth to adolescence; the study of this growth

Child development is a specialized discipline devoted to the understanding of all aspects of human development from birth to adolescence. It is a relatively new field of study. Sara Wiltse (1894), the first secretary to the child study section of the National Education Association, remarked that child study really began in America and that "previous to 1888, practically no scientific observations of child life had been done. . . . One searched libraries in vain to find what the average child could either know or do at a given age" (p. 191). Child development leader Margaret Schallenberger (1894) of Stanford University wrote that children were "among the last of nature's productions to become the privileged subjects of scientific study" (p. 87).

Historical Perspectives

CHILDREN AS MINIATURE ADULTS

One reason that interest in child development was so long in happening is that, *during the Middle Ages and until several hundred years later, childhood was not considered a separate stage of life.* Children were permitted a few short years of dependence, then expected to be little adults. Aries (1962) reported that as soon as children outgrew their swaddling clothes (which were wrapped around their bodies), they were dressed like adult men and women. They played adult games, drank with adults, and worked beside them in fields and shops. Children could be married, crowned as monarchs, or hanged as criminals. Medieval law made no distinction between childhood and adult crimes (Borstelmann, 1983). No effort was made to protect their innocence in sexual matters. For example, Louis XIV of France became king at age 5 and played sexual games with his nursemaids. Because childhood was not considered a special stage, and because children were treated as little adults, no effort was made to consider them special in any way.

CHILDREN AS BURDENS

Before modern birth control was available, many of the children brought into the world were really not wanted. Children were con-

Child development is a specialized discipline devoted to understanding all aspects of human development from birth to adolescence.

FOCUS

Paintings of Children

Art before recent times portrayed children as little adults. Their bodily proportions and appearances were shown to resemble those of grown-ups, and certainly the clothing they wore would not permit them to run and play like today's children.

Paintings during the Middle Ages portrayed children as miniature adults.

sidered a burden rather than a blessing. Each child born meant one more body to clothe and look after, and one more mouth to feed. While infanticide was a crime during the Middle Ages and after, it was probably the most frequent crime in all of Europe until 1800 (Piers, 1978). Unwanted babies were sometimes abandoned or drowned. In the 1300s, Pope Innocent III established the first foundling home in Italy when he became upset at the sight of so many infants' bodies floating down the Tiber River. Some parents, not wanting to kill their infants, sent them to the country to be wet-nursed, or they put them in foundling homes or orphanages where they most likely died. As late as the nineteenth century, one Irish orphanage had admitted 10,272 children, of which only 45 survived (Thompson & Grusec, 1970, p. 603). Conditions were not any better in the United States. One 1915 study in Baltimore, Maryland, revealed that 90 percent of children admitted to foundling homes and orphanages in the city died within one year of admission (Gardner, 1972).

UTILITARIAN VALUE OF CHILDREN

Until the twentieth century, child labor was an accepted practice. Like animals and slaves, children were forced to work at a variety of arduous tasks for the economic benefit of the family. During the Middle Ages, children were sent out as apprentices to tradespeople and farmers. With the beginning of the industrial revolution in the eighteenth century, children were employed in textile mills, mines, and other industries for twelve hours a day, six days a week. The work was dangerous, dirty, exhausting, and unhealthy. Children as young as 5 or 6 crawled into the narrow, dark passages of mines to sit alone for twelve hours a day while they tended the doors that sealed off the shafts. Older children were "hurriers," whose job was to haul coal out of the narrow tunnels. They were harnessed to sleds that they pulled like draft animals. One child recalls:

In the early 1900s, most children admitted to orphanages died within a year after admission.

> I went into a pit at seven years of age. When I drew with the girdle and chain the skin was broken and blood ran down. . . . If we said anything, they would beat us. I have seen many draw at six [years]. They must do it or be beat. They cannot straighten their backs during the day. I have sometimes pulled till my hips have hurt me so that I have not known what to do with myself (Bready, 1926, p. 273).

Children working in textile mills fared only a little better. Small children 5 years old had to crawl into the looms to retie threads. Older children were loom operators, exposed to turning spindles and

During the Industrial Revolution in the eighteenth century, children as young as 5 to 6 years of age were employed to work in mines for twelve hours a day.

These spindle boys in a Georgia cotton mill were exposed to the dangers of turning spindles and whirling machinery.

whirling machinery. The photo on p. 126 gives some idea of the dangers involved.

England passed the first child labor laws in 1832. Ten years later laws to regulate the use of children in mines were passed. Girls were not allowed to work underground and boys had to be at least 10 years of age. However, the widespread use of child labor continued abroad and in the United States. Not until the twentieth century were laws passed really to regulate child labor, require children to get an education, and prosecute parents for child abuse. Gradually, societies for prevention of cruelty to children, children's aid societies, and various social programs were established to further the welfare of children (Siegel & White, 1982). In addition, machines were used increasingly to replace people, and the first to be freed were the children who worked in factories and mills.

Early Philosophies Regarding the Moral Nature of Children

ORIGINAL SIN

Historically, there were three major philosophies regarding the moral nature and development of children. One view was the Christian doctrine of **original sin**. According to this view, children were born sinful and rebellious, depraved in nature and spirit, and were in desperate need of redemption. They were unable to save themselves; their only hope lay in conversion and surrender to God, who would save them from eternal damnation. In the meantime, the role of parents and teachers was to break the rebellious spirit of children, to employ strict punishment and discipline, and to guide them toward virtue and salvation. *The New England Primer*, originally published in puritan America in 1687, began: "A—In Adam's fall we sinned all." This was the child's first reader. In school, the three Rs—reading, 'riting, and 'rithmetic—were taught to the tune of the hickory stick, which was routinely used to beat disobedient pupils.

Not all adults agreed with this philosophy. Many were reluctant to use harsh measures and sought to achieve a balance between discipline and kindness (Moran & Vinovskis, 1986). Horace Bushnell (1888) in his book *Christian Nurture*, first published in 1861, objected to raising children in an atmosphere of unchristian love, in which parents did nothing positive while they prayed for their children's salvation. *Bushnell said that the family as a social group influences the life and character of children, and that God's love and grace are mediated through caring parents.* "The child must not only be touched with some gentle emotions toward what is right, but he must love it [what is good] with a fixed love, love it for the sake of its principle, receive it as a vital and formative power" (Bushnell, 1888). Bushnell further observed that "infancy and childhood are the ages most pliant to good" (p. 14). Bushnell's view was certainly the forerunner of modern concepts of child development and of the family's role in the socialization of children.

Original sin—the Christian doctrine that, because of Adam's sin, a sinful nature has been passed on to succeeding generations

TABULA RASA: JOHN LOCKE

Regarding the moral nature and development of children, *the second major philosophy was that of John Locke (1632–1704), who said that children are morally neutral.* Locke said

Schoolmasters often employed strict punishment and discipline to break the rebellious spirit of children.

foster self-control and only teaches fear and anger. Locke was a forerunner of modern behaviorism and encouraged treating children with kindness and love.

In the late 1800s, Horace Bushnell said that God's love and grace are mediated through caring parents.

Noble savages—beings endowed with a sense of right and wrong; a term used by Jean-Jacques Rousseau to describe his view of children

Tabula rasa—literally, a blank slate; refers to John Locke's view that children are born morally neutral

Maturation—the unfolding of the genetically determined patterns of growth and development

that children are a **tabula rasa**, a "blank slate" in the literal translation. According to this view, children have no inborn tendencies. They are neither good nor bad, and how they turn out depends on what they experience while growing up. Locke said that parents could mold their children in any way they wished through the use of associations, repetitions, imitations, rewards, and punishments (Locke, 1892). Locke suggested parents reward their children with praise and approval. He objected to physical punishment because he said it does not

NOBLE SAVAGES: JEAN-JACQUES ROUSSEAU

The third major philosophy reflecting the moral nature and development of children was espoused by Jean-Jacques Rousseau (1712–1778). *Rousseau (1762/1955) said that children are* **noble savages,** *endowed with a sense of right and wrong.* They will develop positively according to nature's plan because they have an innate moral sense. Rousseau felt that any attempt by adults to provide indoctrination and training would only interfere with children's development and corrupt them. Rousseau outlined four stages of development: *infancy, childhood, late childhood,* and *adolescence,* and said that adults should be responsive to the child's needs at each stage of development. Rousseau was the first to emphasize **maturation—**the unfolding of the genetically determined patterns of growth and development, which reflect unique patterns of thought and behavior at each stage of growth.

Evolutionary Biology

ORIGIN OF THE SPECIES: CHARLES DARWIN

Natural selection

Survival of the fittest

Charles Darwin (1809–1882) published *On the Origin of Species* in 1859 (Darwin, 1936). He emphasized that the human species had evolved over millions of years through the process of **natural selection** and the **survival of the fittest.** Natural selection means that certain species were selected to survive because they had characteristics that helped them adapt to their environment (implying that the human species has evolved from lower life forms). Survival of the fittest means that only the fittest live to pass on their superior traits to future generations. Gradually, higher and more adaptable forms of life evolved. Darwin also observed that the embryos of many species were very much alike during certain stages of their development, indicating that they had evolved from common ancestors (see Figure 5.1).

Modern theorists emphasize that human behavior is still adaptive (Hinde, 1991). For example, children develop different personality characteristics in an insecure family environment than in a secure one. Fears of falling, darkness, or being left alone were formerly called irrational fears of childhood, but make good sense in an environment where proximity to the mother is essential to survival. Many aspects of infant behavior such as the rooting reflex and bonding are also necessary for the infant's survival. Anthropologists suggest that society-specific cultural practices produce personalities conducive to the maintenance of the society.

There are at least four major contributions that Darwin made to developmental psychology. One, humans are kin to all living things by virtue of sharing a common origin. There is a recognition that there is a substantial continuity in mental functioning between animals and humans. Two, Darwin emphasized individual differences. Third, Darwin focused on human behavior as an adaptation to the environment. Four, Darwin emphasized the importance of scientific observation in gathering data. Thus, he broadened psychological methodology and extended it beyond the introspection of the day (Charlesworth, 1992).

RECAPITULATION THEORY: G. STANLEY HALL

Darwin's idea concerning natural evolvement and maturation clearly influenced the subsequent work of G. Stanley Hall (1846–1924), who was the first Ph.D. in psychology in the United States and the founder of the child study movement in North America. *Hall said that the development of the growing child parallels the evolution of the human species* (Hall, 1904). He outlined four major stages:

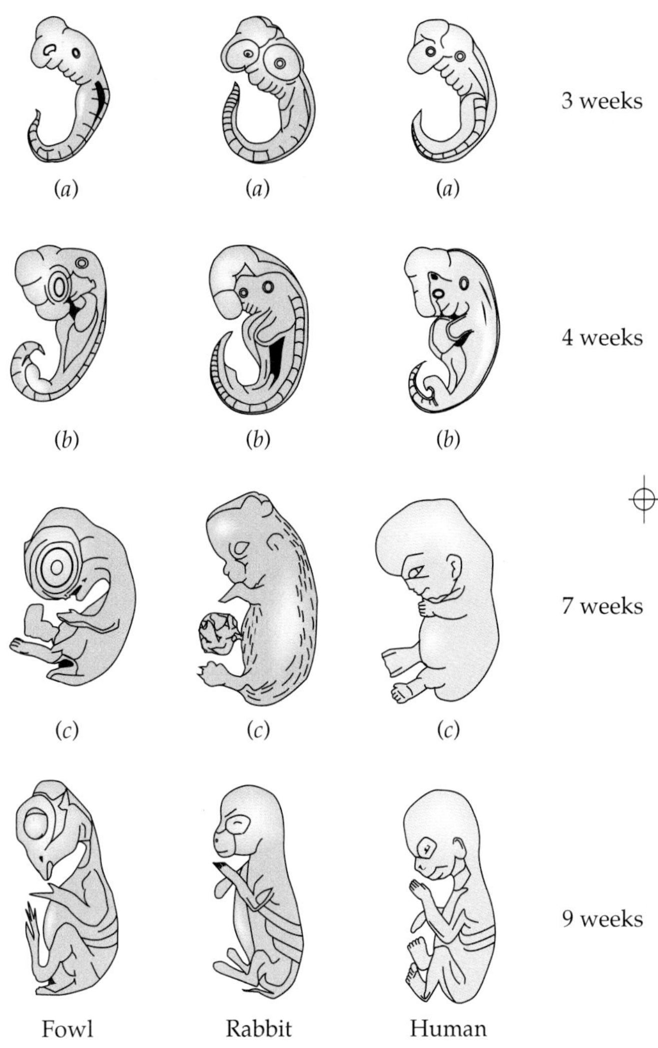

FIGURE 5.1 Embryonic development of a fowl, rabbit, and human shown in four parallel stages.

Charles Darwin emphasized natural selection and the survival of the fittest.

1. Infancy (to age 4), during which the child reenacts the animal stage of development
2. Childhood (age 5 to 7), which corresponds to the cave-dwelling, hunting-fishing epoch of human history (children play survival games and use toy weapons)
3. Youth (age 8 to 12), the preadolescent stage of development during which the child recapitulates the life of savagery but begins to be civilized by learning to

read, write, draw, calculate, and learn language, music, and so on
4. Puberty (age 13 to 24), the period of adolescence, during which the child grows into adulthood

Today, Hall's recapitulation theory is outdated. It is mentioned here for its historical interest only.

Elements of Darwin's theory are also evident in Piaget's ideas. Piaget said that children's development is an effort to adjust their behavior to societal demands. Ethologists also compare animal and human behavior. For example, they compare imprinting and bonding behavior to better understand how human children develop.

Baby Biographies

During the late nineteenth and early twentieth centuries attempts were made to study children by keeping biographical records of their behavior. Darwin (1877) himself kept an account of the development of his young son. Milicent Shinn (1900) published *The Biography of a Baby,* which recorded the growth of her young niece during her first year of life. The baby biographies did not yield very much objective, scientific information about child development, but they were the forerunners of later observations that tried to describe normal growth patterns during various stages of development.

Normative Studies

THE CONTENTS OF CHILDREN'S MINDS: G. STANLEY HALL

G. Stanley Hall attempted to record facts concerning children's development during different stages. His approach launched the movement to make normative studies of children, to find out what to expect during each age regarding their growth and behavior. Hall made up elaborate questionnaires that were distributed to schoolchildren. The questionnaires asked the children to describe almost everything in their lives: their interests, play, friendships, fears, and so forth. Hall's stated purpose was to "discover the contents of childrens' minds" (Hall, 1891). The casual data-collecting procedures left sample characteristics undetermined. The results were difficult to summarize and the usefulness of the data was doubtful, but this approach spawned several decades of more sophisticated normative research.

GROWTH PATTERNS: ARNOLD GESELL

Arnold Gesell (1880–1961) was one of Hall's pupils. He devoted a major part of his career to observing infants and children and to collecting normative information on them. He wrote volumes describing typical motor skills, social behavior, and personality traits to help parents and professionals know what to expect at each stage (Gesell & Ilg, 1943; Gesell & Ilg, 1946; Gesell & Ames, 1956). Gesell's books became the bibles of child development during the 1940s and 1950s. Actually, Gesell drew his conclusions from samples of boys and girls of favorable socioeconomic status in school populations in New Haven, Connecticut, where the Gesell Institute of Child Development is located. Gesell contended that such a homogeneous sample would not lead to false generalizations. However, to try to correct the deficiencies of the earlier studies, the Gesell Institute has since con-

G. Stanley Hall made the first normative study of children's development during different stages.

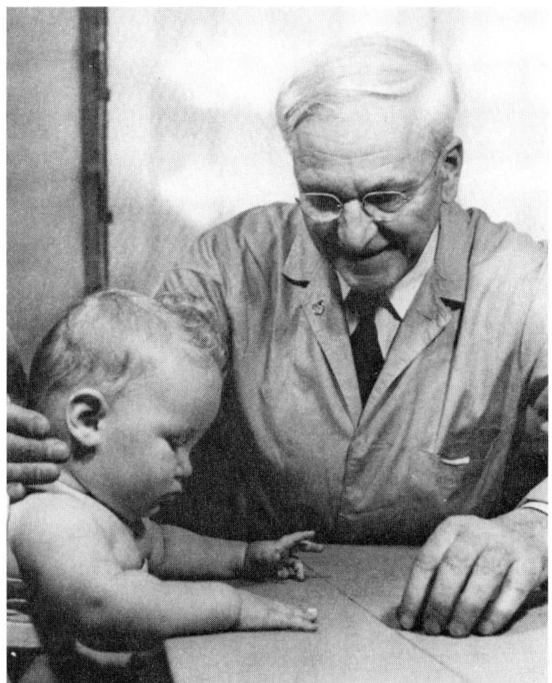

Arnold Gesell, founder of the Gesell Institute of Child Development in New Haven, Connecticut.

ducted new normative studies of diverse samples of preschool children from different socioeconomic groups (Ames, Gillespie, Haines, & Ilg, 1978).

Gesell's theory is a biologically oriented one, in which maturation is mediated by genes and biology that determine behavioral traits and developmental trends. Since development is biologically determined, there is very little that parents and teachers can do to alter its progress. Gesell felt that acculturation can never transcend the primary importance of maturation. In spite of genetically determined individual differences, Gesell considered many of the principles, trends, and sequences to be universal among humans.

Although it is interesting, Gesell's normative theory has generally been discounted today by behaviorists and social learning theorists, who tend to emphasize the importance of experience and environmental influences on children's development. (See "Focus" box on pp. 132–133.)

INTELLIGENCE TESTING: LEWIS TERMAN

Lewis Terman (1877–1956) was another student of Hall. A professor at Stanford University, he published in 1916 the first widely used intelligence test for children in the United States. He called it the *Stanford-Binet Intelligence Scale,* which was a revision of Binet's test that had been developed earlier in Paris. Binet's test had been used to identify retarded children in the Paris school system and to sort out children of varying scholastic abilities. Terman also conducted the first longitudinal study of children of superior intelligence. Terman followed more than 1,500 children with IQs

Lewis Terman published the first widely used intelligence test for children in the United States.

FOCUS

Gesell's Behavior Profile of the 2-Year-Old

At 2 years the child cuts his last milk teeth. He is no longer an infant though compared with a 3-year-old child he is still very immature. There is danger of overestimating his capacities, simply because he is sturdy on his feet and is beginning to put words together. . . .

He does not yet walk erect. There remains a little of the angularity of the ancient man in his posture. . . . When he picks up something from the floor, he half bends at the waist as well as at the knees; whereas at 18 months he squatted. Stooping is more advanced behavior than squatting. But the 2-year-old still leans forward as he runs. . . .

To get up from a sitting position on the floor, he leans forward, pushes up buttocks first, and head second, instead of raising an erect trunk as he will later. He goes up and down stairs mark-time fashion, without alternating his feet. . . .

He is still geared to gross motor activity, and likes to run and romp, lug, push and pull, but with better coordination than at 18 months. His fine motor control also has advanced. . . . He also likes to take things apart and fit them together again.

The muscles of eyes and face are more adept. He moves his eyes more freely and is sensitive to marginal fields, whereas at 18 months he ran headlong as though he had blinders on. He stops and engages in long periods of looking. . . .

The whole linguistic apparatus, mouth, lips, tongue, larynx and thorax is undergoing rapid organization. Jargon is dropping out, sentences are coming in. Soliloquy is taking the place of the babbling of the 6-month-old child, as though on an advanced level the

averaging 150 and above from 1921 into mature adulthood to determine the relationship between intelligence and social adjustment, emotional stability, professional and marital success, health, and other characteristics. Generally, *he found intellectually gifted children to be superior in other ways as well* (Terman, 1925; Terman & Oden, 1959). Daniel Goleman (1980) has since reported on follow-up studies of Terman's subjects, now in their 60s and 70s. Terman's work produced a useful instrument for measuring intelligence and launched the whole intelligence test movement. Contemporary studies focus on the relative roles of genetics versus environmental influences on intellectual abilities, as was discussed in Chapter 3.

Modern Contributions to Child Development

RESEARCH CENTERS

By the beginning of the twentieth century, thousands of adults working with children began to demand public and government intervention to help protect children who were under their care. The first White House Conference on Child Health and Protection was held in 1909. The conferences became yearly events and led to the

2-year-old is under a similar compulsion to exercise his vocal abilities, to repeat words, to name things, to suit words to action and action to words. Vocabularies vary enormously in size from a half dozen to a thousand words. . . .

The third year is also the year when the sphincter muscles of bladder and bowel are coming under voluntary control. . . .

The action system of the 2-year-old is not yet sufficiently advanced to effect delicate and long sustained interpersonal relations. He still prefers solitary play to parallel play and seldom plays cooperatively. He is in the pre-cooperative stage; watching what others are doing rather than participating. He cannot share; he cannot as a rule let someone else play with what is his own. He must learn "It's mine" first. He does so by holding on and by hoarding. . . . The hitting, patting, poking, biting, hairpulling, and tug of war over materials so characteristic of Two need to be handled with understanding and sensible techniques on the part of parent and guidance teacher. . . .

So to sum him up, what are his dominating interests? He loves to romp, flee, and pursue. He likes to fill and empty, to put and to pull out, to tear apart, and to fit together, to taste (even clay and wood), to touch and rub. He prefers action toys such as trains, cars, telephones. He is intrigued by water and washing. Although he is not yet an humanitarian, he likes to watch the human scene. He imitates the domesticities of feminine laundry work and doll play. He has a genuine interest in the mother–baby relationship. (Excerpts from pages 159–161 from Infant and Child in the Culture of Today by Arnold Gesell and Frances L. Ilg. Copyright 1943 by Arnold Gesell and Frances L. Ilg. Renewed 1971 by Frances L. Ilg, Gerhard Gesell and Katherine Gesell Walden. Reprinted by permission of HarperCollins Publishers, Inc.).

establishment of the U.S. Children's Bureau in 1912 (McCullers & Love, 1976).

Interest in research in child development blossomed during the years following World War I. In 1917, the Iowa legislature allocated $50,000 for an Iowa Child Welfare Research Station. This effort was the first of its kind and was followed by the establishment of the Teachers College Child Development Institute (at Columbia University), the Yale University Psycho-Clinic (later called the Yale Clinic of Child Development and still later the Gesell Institute of Child Development), the University of Minnesota Institute of Child Welfare, and the University of California Institute of Child Welfare (at Berkeley). In the early period, most of the money for the child-research institutes was provided by the

Today, there are child-development research centers scattered throughout the United States.

FOCUS

John Dewey

John Dewey (1859–1952) was an American psychologist-philosopher-educator of international acclaim. In Dewey's day, psychology was becoming a laboratory-based enterprise devoted to the search for empirical knowledge. Dewey warned of the limits to the knowledge that could be gathered in those laboratories and established a small primary school at the University of Colorado. He called his school a "laboratory school" and used it for his scientific experimentation in education. He felt that by controlling the school environment, he could foster the natural growth of children. The school was an experiment in the possibilities of human development in arranged environments. By varying the school's social environment, child development could be directed toward desired ends. The classroom became the context in which Dewey's ideals for society were expressed as desirable norms of growth for the individual child.

Dewey felt that education should be in accordance with nature, that educational procedures should encourage the unfolding of the physical, mental, and moral nature of children. The immediate goals and objectives of education are set by the interests and capabilities of the child and are not imposed by adults as fixed ends. Dewey placed a great deal of emphasis on learning through experiences and on self-directed activities. The school was a laboratory of life and not just a preparation for life. The school reproduces within itself the typical conditions of social life. *The school is structured as a small society unto itself.* Direct experience enables the child to develop intellectual and moral virtues that enable him or her to develop a better society (Cahan, 1992).

Laura Spellman Rockefeller Memorial Fund. Federal funds became available after World War II. Today, there are hundreds of universities and organizations involved in child development research. One of the most prestigious organizations is the *Society for Research in Child Development* located in Chicago.

MEDICAL AND MENTAL HEALTH PRACTITIONERS

Substantial information on child development has also been provided by medical and child guidance practitioners. *Pediatrics* was developed as a medical specialty, and pediatricians have made tremendous strides in treating acute illnesses and diseases of children. Pediatricians have also been called upon by concerned parents to answer their questions about normal development as well as about behavior problems. Benjamin Spock's *Commonsense Book of Baby and Child Care,* first published in 1946, has sold millions of copies and has become many modern parents' bible of child rearing (Spock, 1946; Spock & Rothenberg, 1985). Dr. T. Berry Brazelton's (1974, 1983) books for parents of infants and toddlers are also popular. Numerous child psychologists, one of whom is Dr. Lee Salk (1974), have published popular guidebooks for parents.

Recently, child development specialists and pediatricians have collaborated to

John Dewey said that the school classroom ought to be a laboratory for living.

share their knowledge, which has resulted in the emergence of a new field, **developmental pediatrics**, which integrates medical and psychological understanding, health care, and parental guidance.

Child guidance professionals who are psychiatrists, social workers, clinical and/or child psychologists, or child development specialists have always been concerned especially with the mental health and the intellectual, emotional, and social development of children. Behavioral misconduct, school failure, social maladjustments, or problems in parent or peer relationships are better understood than ever before. Hundreds of child guidance clinics now provide assessment of children's problems and guidance for parents, teachers, and other concerned adults.

CHILD DEVELOPMENT ISSUES TODAY

Interest in child development continues. Research studies by the thousands pour out of universities and child development centers. These studies provide a wealth of information on all aspects of child care, growth, and development. Countless organizations seek to apply this knowledge in ways that will benefit the children they serve. Medical and psychological help for children with problems is more accurate than ever before, but is often unavailable to those who need it the most. Conscientious parents seek to improve their parenting skills whenever possible.

Numerous problems remain. There is still tremendous need for adequate child care for working parents. Public attention continues to be focused on physical and sexual abuse of children. All too many children, born in and out of wedlock, do not receive the necessary physical and emotional care to grow into healthy, happy individuals. Infant mortality in the United States of one of the highest in the Western world, reflecting the lack of prenatal and postnatal care of mothers and their infants. Too many children suffer the consequences of their parents' drug abuse, or of the growing incidence of AIDS and other sexually transmitted diseases. Thousands of children are born unplanned and unwanted—and thus suffer the lack of proper care. It is vital that all caring people join in the effort to provide the kind of environment in which children can be cared for and loved, and to deliver necessary services to those needing extra care.

Developmental pediatrics—a new field of study that integrates medical knowledge, psychological understanding, health care, and parental guidance in relation to children

Dr. Spock's book has been a best-seller for fifty years.

PARENTING ISSUES

Changing Child-Rearing Philosophies in the Government's Bulletin on Infant Care

One thing that has been evident throughout the study of child development is how much the philosophies and emphases in child rearing have changed over the years (Young, 1990). This is especially evident in the government's bulletin on *Infant Care* (Arkin, 1989). This booklet, first published in 1914, has gone through many editions and has been completely rewritten numerous times. Between 1914 and 1921, the dangers of thumb sucking and masturbation were emphasized: Parents were advised to bind their children to the bed, hand and foot, so they would not suck their thumbs, touch their genitals, or rub their thighs together. Between 1929 and 1938, autoerotic impulses were not considered dangerous, but lack of proper bowel training and improper feeding habits were. The emphasis was on rigid schedules, strictly according to the clock. Bowel training was to be pursued with great determination. Weaning and the introduction of solid foods were to be accomplished with firmness, never yielding to the baby's protests for one instant, for fear the infant would dominate the parents.

Between 1942 and 1945, the views expressed in the bulletin changed drastically. The child was then thought to be devoid of dominating impulses. Mildness was advocated in all areas. Thumb sucking and masturbation were not to be discouraged. Weaning and toilet training were to be put off until later and to be accomplished more gently.

At the present time, *Infant Care* has a fairly permissive attitude toward thumb sucking, weaning, discipline, and bowel and bladder training. It is evident that child-rearing philosophies change from one generation to the next, so that parents often have to sort out conflicting advice.

Summary

1. Child development is a specialized discipline devoted to the understanding of all aspects of human development from birth to adolescence. It is a relatively new field of study.
2. One reason that interest in studying child development was so long in happening is that, during the Middle Ages and until several hundred years later, childhood was not regarded as a separate stage of life. Children were expected to be little adults.
3. Before modern birth control, many children were unwanted and were considered a burden rather than a blessing. Unwanted children were killed, abandoned, or put in foundling homes or orphanages, where most of them died.
4. Until the twentieth century, the use of child labor was an accepted practice. Children had to work in shops, fields, mines, and mills for twelve hours a day, six days a week.
5. Historically, there were three major philosophies regarding the moral nature and development of children. The first of these, the Christian doctrine of original sin, held that children were born sinful and rebellious. The role of parents was to break the rebellious spirit of children and to pray for their

salvation. Opposing this philosophy, Horace Bushnell held that God's love and grace are mediated through caring parents who should raise their children in an atmosphere of Christian love.

6. Representing the second major philosophy of child development, John Locke said that children are a tabula rasa, a blank slate; that they are morally neutral, and how they turn out depends on how they are raised. In effect, that parents can mold their children in any way they wish.
7. In the third major philosophy concerning children, Jean-Jacques Rousseau said that they are noble savages, endowed with a sense of right and wrong, and that they will develop positively according to nature's plan if parents don't interfere with their development and corrupt them.
8. Charles Darwin was the first of the evolutionary biologists. He taught that the human species evolved over millions of years through the process of natural selection and the survival of the fittest.
9. Modern theorists emphasize that humans are still adapting to their environment.
10. G. Stanley Hall said that the development of the growing child parallels the evolution of the human species.
11. During the late nineteenth and early twentieth centuries, attempts were made to study children by keeping biographical records of their behavior.
12. G. Stanley Hall made the first attempt to study children's behavior during different stages. His effort launched the movement to make normative studies of children.
13. Arnold Gesell of Yale University devoted a major part of his career to observing infants and children and collecting normative information on them. Gesell's theory is biologically oriented and states that maturation is mediated by genes and biology, which determine behavioral traits and developmental trends. Gesell felt that acculturation can never transcend maturation.
14. Lewis Terman of Stanford University published the Stanford-Binet Intelligence Scale, the first widely used intelligence test for children in the United States. He also conducted the first longitudinal studies of intellectually gifted individuals.
15. Early in the twentieth century, numerous organizations and research centers were established to study child development and to discover how best to protect and guide children.
16. John Dewey said the school classroom should be a laboratory of life and offer children the kinds of experiences that enable them to grow physically, mentally, and morally so that they can develop a better society.
17. Substantial contributions to understanding child development have also been made by pediatric and child guidance practitioners. Developmental pediatrics integrates medical and psychological understanding, health care, and parental guidance. Hundreds of child guidance clinics now provide assessment of children's problems and guidance for parents, teachers, and other concerned adults.

Key Terms

Child development *p. 124*
Developmental pediatrics *p. 135*
Maturation *p. 128*
Natural selection *p. 128*
Noble savages *p. 128*
Original sin *p. 127*
Survival of the fittest *p. 128*
Tabula rasa *p. 128*

Discussion Questions

1. Historically, children were considered miniature adults. Can you give any evidence or examples of this view still being held today? Explain.
2. Unwanted children were considered burdens and were killed, abandoned, or given to orphanages. What do you think should be done about the problem of unwanted children today?
3. It is hard for us to imagine the extent to which child labor was exploited before laws were passed outlawing it. Do you think that children today are exploited, *or* not given enough work to do? Explain your views.
4. Of the three philosophies—that children are born sinful and rebellious, that they are born neutral, that they are born with an innate sense of right and wrong—with which do you most agree? Why? Are there elements of truth in all three views? Explain.
5. What might be some of the values of Gesell's normative studies? What might be some disadvantages? Why are his findings discounted by behaviorists and social learning theorists? From a cognitive point of view, how would you evaluate Gesell's findings?
6. According to Terman, is intelligence innate? What are some advantages and disadvantages of IQ tests? Would you want your children to know their IQ scores? Explain.
7. Have you had any contacts with child guidance clinics, child development specialists, or child psychologists? Under what circumstances? With what results?
8. In what ways do modern schools resemble John Dewey's concept of laboratories of living? What type of teaching methods reflect John Dewey's philosophy?
9. To parents: What do you like about your child's pediatrician, and what don't you like? Should pediatricians give advice to parents about child rearing?
10. In what ways are your views of child rearing similar to and different from those of your parents? What do you like about your parents' views, and what do you disagree with?

Suggested Readings

Aries, P. (1962). *Centuries of adulthood: A social history of family life* (R. Baldick, Trans.). New York: Knopf (original work published 1960). The status of children throughout history.

Borstelmann, L. J. (1983). Children before psychology: Ideas about children from antiquity to the late 1800s. In P. H. Mussen (Ed.), *Handbook of child psychology* (4th ed., Vol. 1). New York: Wiley. Historical views of children from ancient times.

Bowlby, J. (1990). *Charles Darwin: A new life.* New York: Norton. Darwin's internal struggles, family life, and achievements.

Coles, R. (1990). *The spiritual life of children.* Boston: Houghton Mifflin. Children's understandings of the meaning of life.

Eckardt, G., Bringman, W. G., & Spring, L. (Eds.). (1985). *Contributions to a history of development psychology.* Berlin: Morton. The status of children throughout history.

Grant, J. P. (1986). *The status of the world's children.* New York: Oxford University Press. Written by the executive director of the United Nation's Children's Fund, it summarizes the often horrible plight of children around the world.

Hewett, S. (1991). *When the bough breaks: The cost of neglecting our children.* New York: Basic Books. The plight of children in our society.

Kessen, W. (1965). *The child.* New York: Wiley. The child is viewed by Rousseau, Darwin, Baldwin, Freud, Piaget, and others.

Sommerville, J. (1982). *The rise and fall of childhood.* Beverly Hills, CA: Sage. The status of children at different times in history.

Physical Development: Growth, Motor Skills, and Disabilities

Chapter 6

PHYSICAL GROWTH

MOTOR DEVELOPMENT

CHILDREN WITH DISABILITIES

In this chapter we are concerned with the physical development of children: with growth in height, weight, body proportion, and organ systems including the brain and nervous system. We are concerned with the development of fine-motor and gross-motor skills, with handedness, physical fitness, and disabilities.

Physical Growth

BODY HEIGHT AND WEIGHT

Growth from birth to adolescence occurs in two different patterns. The first pattern (from birth to age 1) is one of very rapid but decelerating growth; the second (from age 1 to before the onset of puberty) shows a steadier and more linear annual increment. Typically, the infant's increase in length is approximately 30 percent up to 5 months of age and greater than 50 percent by 1 year of age. Height doubles by age 5. Figure 6.1 shows median heights by age of boys and girls. Boys and girls have little difference in size and growth rates during infancy and childhood. Note the very rapid increase in height from birth to age 1, followed by a gradual slowing of increase until about age 10 for girls and age 12 for boys.

Figure 6.2 shows the rates of increase in height in boys and girls. Ages 10 to 12 represent the onset of puberty in girls; ages 12 to 14, the onset of puberty in boys. The growth spurts are evident during these periods. If puberty is delayed, growth in height may virtually cease.

Infants' increases in weight are even more dramatic than their early growth in length. The infant doubles in weight by 5 months of age, triples in 1 year, and almost quadruples by age 2. Annual increases are fairly constant from ages 2 to 6, and then are slower until the onset of puberty. (See Figure 6.3.)

FIGURE 6.1 Median heights (by age) of boys and girls.

Adapted from *The Merck Manual of Diagnosis and Therapy*, 16th ed. (p. 1941) by R. Berkow, Ed., 1992. Copyright 1992 by Merck & Co., Inc., Rahway, NJ. Used with permission.

INDIVIDUAL DIFFERENCES

There are wide individual differences in growth patterns. At 36 months, boys in the 5th to the 95th percentiles may be 36 to 41 inches in length and weigh between 27 and 38

Physical growth after the first year shows a fairly linear and steady annual increment.

pounds. At the same age, girls in the 5th to the 95th percentiles may be 35½ to 40 inches in length and weigh between 25½ and 36½ pounds. Growth differentials depend upon heredity (tall parents bear tall children), nutrition and eating habits, and total health care. Children from upper-class, better-educated families are taller than lower-class children, primarily because of superior nutrition and health care that allows them to grow as tall as their genes permit (Vaughn, 1983).

Cultural and ethnic differences also influence growth (Widmayer et al., 1990). In the United States, black children tend to have longer legs and be taller than white children, who, in turn, are taller than Asian-American children. In Canada, English-speaking children tend to be taller than French-speaking children.

Children with slower physical maturation suffer social disadvantages. They may be the last ones selected on teams for games and sports, may have some difficulty in establishing friendships, and may be lonely and unhappy because they are "different" (Hartup, 1983).

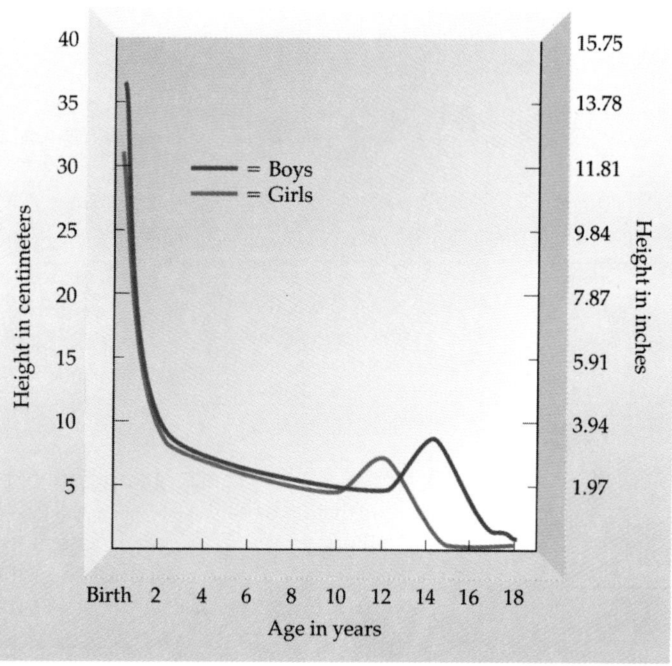

FIGURE 6.2 Rates of increase in height in boys and girls.

Adapted from *The Merck Manual of Diagnosis and Therapy*, 16th ed. (p. 1941) by R. Berkow, Ed., 1992. Copyright 1992 by Merck & Co., Inc., Rahway, NJ. Used with permission.

BODY PROPORTIONS

Not all parts of the body grow at the same rate. Development follows the **cephalocaudal principle;** that is, it proceeds downward from the head to the feet. Growth comes first in the head region, then in the trunk, and finally in the leg region. From birth to adulthood, the head doubles in size, the

Cephalocaudal principle—downward distribution of physical growth, starting in the head and proceeding, by stages, down the body to the feet

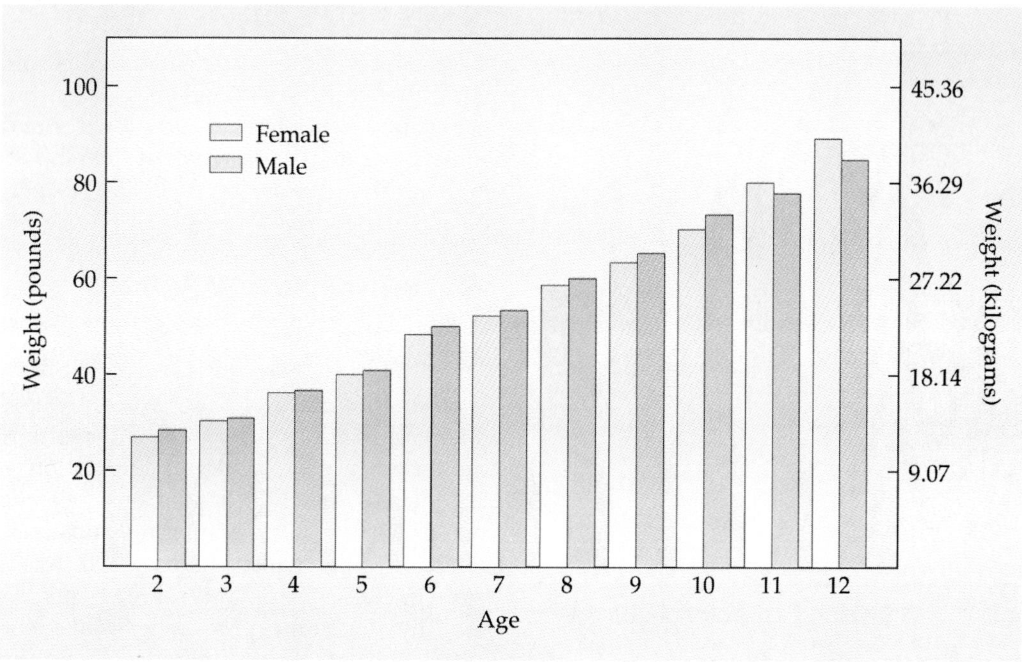

FIGURE 6.3 Weight at 50th percentile for U.S. children, by age.

Proximodistal principle—outward distribution of physical growth, starting in the center of the body and proceeding out to the extremities

There are wide individual differences in growth patterns.

Myelinization—the process by which neurons become coated with an insulating, fatty substance called myelin

trunk trebles, the arms and hands quadruple in length, and the legs and feet grow fivefold (Bayley, 1956). At birth, the newborn's head is about one-fourth of the total body length, compared to one-eighth of the body length in adults. The legs of the newborn are one-quarter of the total body length, but about one-half of the body length in adults. (See Figure 6.4.)

Development also follows the **proximodistal principle;** that is, it proceeds from the center of the body outward to the extremities. This is why large-muscle development in the trunk, arms, and legs precedes small-muscle development in the hands and fingers. Infants are able to run and jump before they can perform detailed manual and grasping movements.

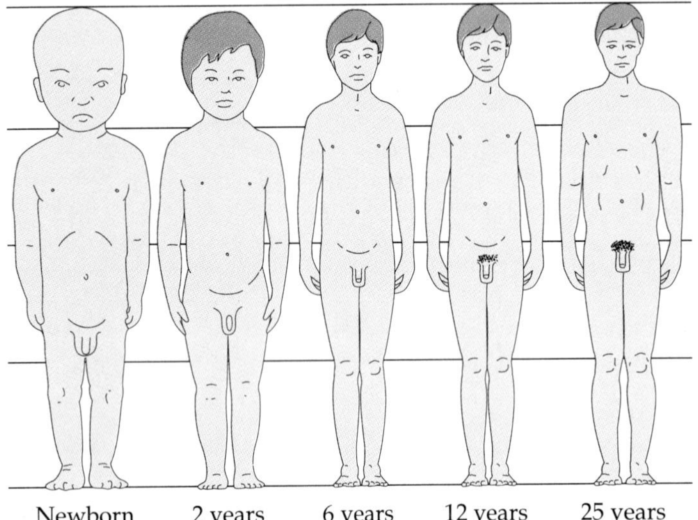

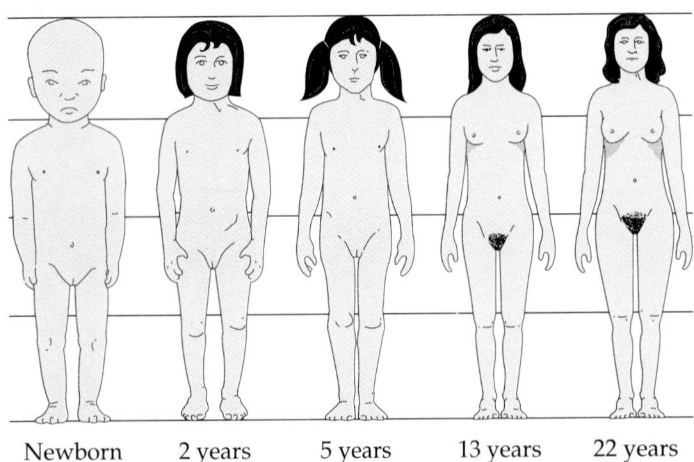

FIGURE 6.4 Bodily proportions at different ages.

ORGAN SYSTEMS

Three organ systems do not follow the general pattern of growth of the rest of the body and organs. The *lymphoid system* grows fairly constantly and rapidly during childhood, so that at puberty the adolescent has almost twice the lymphoid tissue of the adult. After puberty, the lymphoid size recedes. The *reproductive system* shows little growth until puberty. Most of the growth of the *central nervous system* occurs during the early years of life. At birth, the brain is 25 percent of adult size; at 1 year it is 75 percent of adult size. Growth gradually slows down, but the brain has reached 80 percent of adult size by 3 years, and 90 percent by age 7 (Berkow, 1987). Figure 6.5 shows the growth patterns of the different systems.

BRAIN GROWTH AND NERVE MATURATION

Not only does the brain grow in size, but increasingly complex nerve pathways and connections among nerve cells develop so the central nervous system is able to perform more complex functions. Figure 6.6 shows the development of nerve-cell connections from birth to 15 months.

Myelinization

Another important change is the increase in **myelinization** of individual neurons (discussed in Chapter 4). Myelinization is the process by which neurons become coated with a fatty insulating substance called myelin, which helps to transmit nerve impulses faster and more efficiently. The myelinization process parallels the maturation of the nervous system. The

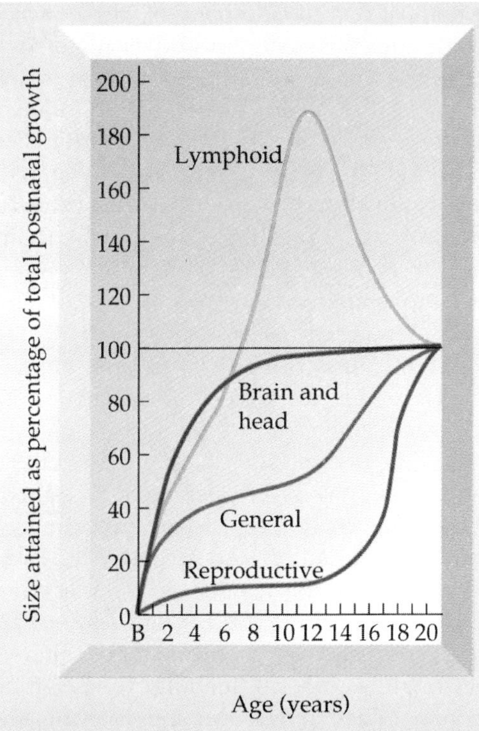

FIGURE 6.5 Growth patterns of different organ systems. These curves are based on the percentage of a person's total growth attained by age 20. Thus, size at age 20 is 100 on the vertical scale. The lymphoid system includes the thymus and lymph nodes. The curve labeled "Brain and head" includes the brain, the skull, and the spinal cord. The curve labeled "General" covers the skeletal system, lungs, kidneys, and digestive organs. The reproductive system covers testes, ovaries, prostate, seminal vesicles, and Fallopian tubes.

From "The Measurement of the Body in Childhood" by Richard E. Scammon, 1930, in *The Measurement of Man* (Figure 73, p. 193) by J. A. Harris, C. M. Jackson, D. G. Paterson, and R. E. Scammon, Eds. Minneapolis: University of Minnesota Press. Reprinted by permission.

pathways between the brain and sense organs are partly myelinated at birth, so the neonate's senses are in fairly good working order. As neural pathways between the brain and skeletal muscles myelinate, the child becomes capable of more complex motor activities. Though myelinization proceeds rapidly for the first few years of life, some areas of the brain are not completely myelinated until the late teens or early adulthood (Guthrie, 1980).

Multiple sclerosis results when the myelin sheaths begin to disintegrate. As the condition worsens, the person loses muscular control and may become paralyzed or die. Myelinization is very important, therefore, in the development of the total nervous system.

Cerebral Cortex

The **cerebral cortex** is the largest structure of the forebrain and contains the higher brain centers controlling intellectual, sensory, and motor functions. The cerebral cortex is larger in proportion to total body weight and is more highly developed in humans than in any other animals. In humans, the cerebral cortex accounts for 70 percent of the neurons in the central nervous system. It is divided into two hemispheres, with the left side of the brain mainly controlling the right side of the body and the right side of the brain controlling the left side of the body. The two hemispheres are connected by a band of fibers called the corpus callosum.

Cerebral cortex—two large hemispheres of the forebrain, which control intellectual, motor, and sensory functions

The two sides of the brain each perform specialized functions. The *right hemisphere* is superior in music, drama, fantasy, intuition, and art. It is superior in recognizing patterns, faces, and melodies, and in visualizing spatial relationships. Thus, it is better in arranging blocks in a pattern, completing a puzzle, or drawing a picture. The *left hemisphere* is superior in logic, mathematics, language, writing, and judging time. About 95 percent of all adults use the left hemisphere in speaking, writing, and understanding language (Levy, 1985). In addition, 97 percent of right-handed peo-

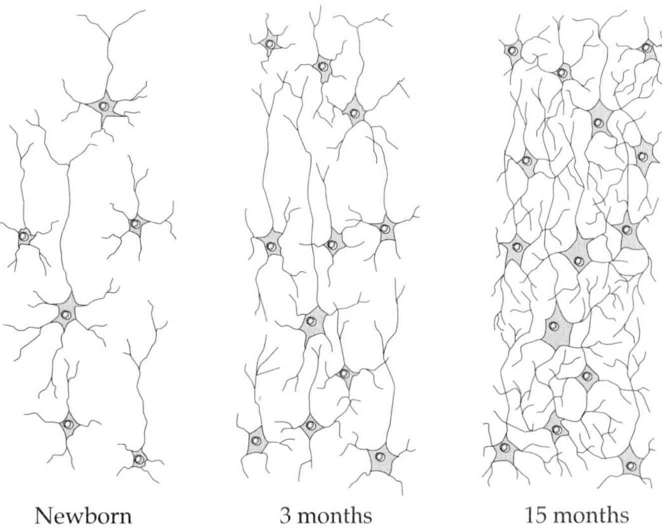

FIGURE 6.6 The development of nerve cell connections.

ple use the left hemisphere more than the right. They are said to be left-hemisphere dominant. About 60 percent of left-handed people are right-hemisphere dominant. Dyslexic children have difficulty learning to read and show a type of abnormal lateralization, with spatial functions being directed from both hemispheres (Tan, 1985).

Lateralization—the preference for using one side of the body more than the other in performing special tasks, depending on which hemisphere is dominant for the task

Lateralization is the preference for using one side of the body more than the other in performing special tasks. Lateralization may be biologically programmed from the day a baby is born. It is a tendency that occurs throughout childhood, becoming stronger over time, and is not complete until puberty. Recognizing shapes by touch is a spatial ability controlled by the right hemisphere, and is most easily accomplished with the left hand. Rose (1984) found that 1-year-olds are not especially proficient at recognizing shapes with either hand, but 3-year-olds are already better at recognizing shapes with their left than with their right hand.

Cortical Functions

The control of particular functions is located in various areas of the cerebral cortex. Figure 6.7 shows the location of several major functions in the left cerebral hemisphere. The development of these functions results from brain and nervous system maturation combined with experience and practice. Neurons that are stimulated continue to grow new dendrite branches and myelin sheaths, increasing synaptic connections and the efficiency of nerve transmission. Thus, the growth of the brain and nervous system is influenced by both heredity and environment.

Different regions of the cortex mature at different rates. The first area to mature is the *motor area,* followed by the *sensory area.* The *association areas* are the last to mature, continuing their growth into the twenties or thirties (Spreen, Tupper, Risser, Tuokko, & Edgell, 1984). The higher functions of thinking, planning, and problem solving, performed by the frontal lobes, take years to develop. Adults with frontal lobe damage show decreased emotionality, altered personalities, and an inability to reason or to plan. They repeat the same wrong answers over and over (Springer & Deutsch, 1985). Injury to the left hemisphere of the frontal lobe of adults may produce either depression or increased aggression (L. Miller, 1988). When brain damage occurs during childhood, lost abilities are sometimes regained, depending on the extent of the damage.

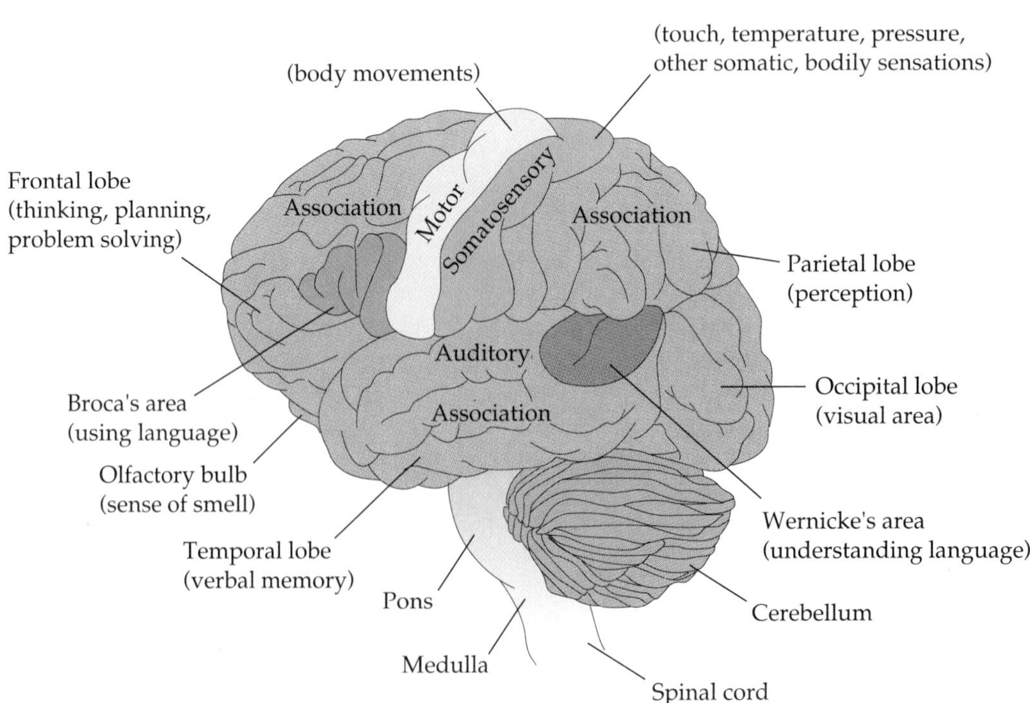

FIGURE 6.7 Location of major functions in the left cerebral hemisphere.

Two areas of the cortex are related to language. The *Broca's area* is involved in using language, the *Wernicke's area* in understanding it. Injury to either area can cause *aphasia,* an impaired ability to use language.

Growth of cortical structures depends partly upon environmental influences (Greenough, Black, & Wallace, 1987). Particularly during the third trimester of pregnancy, during which development of the central nervous system is proceeding at an astounding pace, malnutrition can lead to a permanent loss in brain weight, a reduction in the number of brain cells, and serious mental retardation. Sensory deprivation in the early years of life can lead to degenerative changes in the cortex. Light deprivation for a brief period of three or four days can cause degenerative changes in the visual cortex of a 4-week-old kitten.

TEETH ERUPTION TIMES

The timing of teeth eruption is somewhat variable, depending on family factors (both heredity and nutrition). Occasionally, teeth

PARENTING ISSUES

Maturation and Toilet Training

The importance of both maturation and learning in development can be illustrated by discussing the task of toilet training. Experience plays an important role in toilet training—children must be taught to use the toilet. However, maturation also plays an important part. In a classic study, McGraw (1940) began training one identical twin, Hugh, when he was only 50 days old. No progress was achieved until Hugh was about 650 days (21 months) of age. Training of the other twin, Hilton, began at 700 days (23 months) of age. Hilton's progress was rapid from the beginning. Both children learned, but only when they reached a particular level of maturation. Figure 6.8 illustrates the progress of the twins.

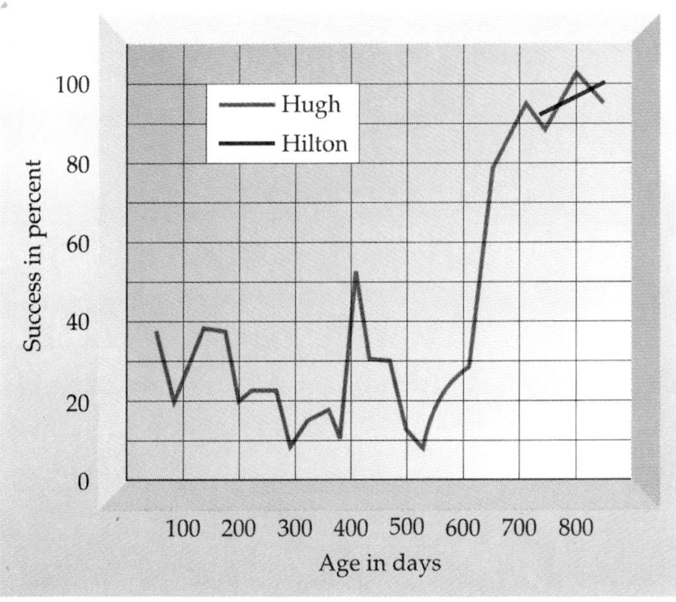

FIGURE 6.8 Maturation and achievement of bladder control.

Adapted from "Neural Maturation as Exemplified in Achievement of Bladder Control" by M. B. McGraw, 1940, *Journal of Pediatrics, 16,* 580–590.

PARENTING ISSUES

Dental Care for Children

Parents sometimes think they don't have to take a small child to a dentist because all the baby teeth are going to fall out anyway. This is unwise thinking. Decayed teeth may cause pain to the child, or lead to a jaw infection. If a baby tooth is so painful it has to be pulled, nearby teeth tend to grow into the space and out of position, so there isn't enough room for the permanent tooth when it's ready to come through. The last baby teeth are not lost until around 12 years of age. This is a long time to go without dental care.

Children should be given a toothbrush and be taught to brush their teeth beginning at about age 2. They aren't very efficient brushers at first, but they enjoy imitating parents, and early training in dental hygiene is important. Ordinarily, regular trips to the dentist—every 6 months to a year—may begin at about age 3. Tooth decay may start early, and the time to fill cavities is when they are small. Even if the child has no cavities, getting used to going to the dentist without fear is important. Dentists need to be consulted about jaw malformations or misaligned teeth. However, teeth that come through crooked or out of place often straighten out later. Permanent teeth often erupt behind baby teeth and later move forward. A dentist will help to determine whether any special treatments are needed for these conditions.

eruption is significantly delayed because of *hypothyroidism. Deciduous teeth* (baby teeth) eruption is similar in both sexes; *permanent teeth* tend to appear earlier in girls. Deciduous teeth are smaller than their permanent counterparts. Table 6.1 shows average teeth eruption times.

The first permanent molars (so-called 6-year molars, which erupt between the ages of 5 and 7 years) come in farther back than the baby molars. The first baby teeth to be lost are the *incisors,* followed by the *molars,* and *canines (cuspids).* The permanent teeth that take the place of the baby molars are called *bicuspids.* The second molars (or 12-year molars, which erupt between the ages of 11 and 13 years) come in behind the 6-year molars, with the third

TABLE 6.1
TEETH ERUPTION TIMES

Deciduous Teeth[1] *(20 in number)*	*Number*	*Time of Eruption*[2] *(in months)*	*Permanent Teeth 32 in number)*	*Number*	*Time of Eruption*[2] *(in years)*
Lower central incisors	2	5–9	First molars[3]	4	5–7
Upper central incisors	2	8–12	Incisors	8	6–8
Upper lateral incisors	2	10–12	Bicuspids	8	9–12
Lower lateral incisors	2	12–15	Canines (cuspids)	4	10–13
First molars[3]	4	10–16	Second molars[3]	4	11–13
Canines (cuspids)	4	16–20	Third molars[3]	4	17–25
Second molars[3]	4	20–30			

[1]The average child should have 6 teeth at age 1 year, 12 teeth at 1½ years, 16 teeth at 2 years, 20 teeth at 2½ years.
[2]Varies greatly.
[3]Molars are numbered from the front to the back of the mouth.
From *The Merck Manual of Diagnosis and Therapy,* 16th ed. (p. 1942) by R. Berkow (Ed.), 1992. Copyright 1992 by Merck & Co., Inc., Rahway, NJ. Used with permission.

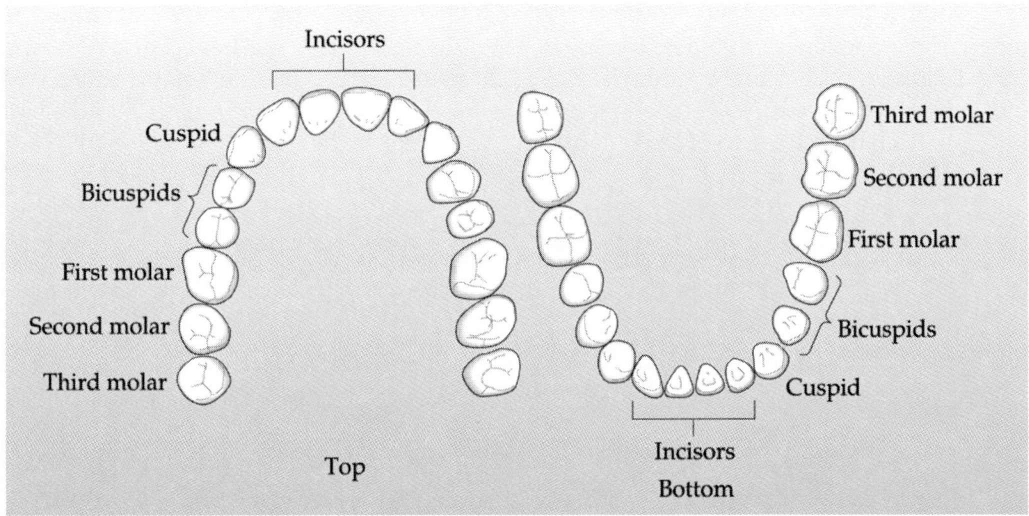

FIGURE 6.9 Permanent teeth.

molars (18-year molars, also called wisdom teeth) coming behind the 12-year molars. Figure 6.9 identifies the location of different teeth.

Motor Development

A major function of human nervous systems is the coordinated control of limb and body movements. Coordinated motor activities enable children to explore their environment and to sample and attend to sensory stimuli, which is essential for their survival. Initially, motor capabilities of newborns are generally inadequate to accomplish any vital task, but these capabilities undergo profound changes over an extended period of postnatal development. This period is of particular interest in human infants, many of whose motor abilities at birth appear to be among the least developed compared to those of other vertebrate species. A child's continued progress in achieving precise control of motor functions is an obvious prerequisite for his or her further cognitive, behavioral, and social development (Sporns & Edelman, 1993).

GROSS-MOTOR SKILLS AND LOCOMOTION DURING INFANCY

Children's motor development is dependent primarily on overall physical maturation, especially on skeletal and neuromuscular development. To a lesser extent, motor development is also influenced by the opportunities children have for exercise and practice. Infants spend a great deal of time in *rhythmic motor activity*—kicking, waving, bouncing, rocking, banging, rubbing, swinging, twisting, thrusting, and scratching. These rhythmic activities are an important transition between uncoordinated activity and more coordinated, complex motor behavior (Thelen, 1981).

Gross motor development is dependent primarily on overall physical maturation.

Figure 6.10 shows the sequence of motor development in average infants as they finally develop the ability to walk alone. Note that they can raise their chin up by 1 month, sit with support at 3 months, sit alone at 6 months, creep at 8 months, pull to a standing position holding onto furniture by 10 months, climb stairs at 11 months, and walk alone at 13 months. However, there are variations in abilities with different individuals. Table 6.2 shows age norms for motor skills according to the Denver Developmental Screening Test (Frankenburg, Frandal, Sciarillo, & Burgess, 1981). According to the table, by 20 months of age half the infants could kick a ball forward, but not until 24 months had 90 percent of them mastered this skill.

FINE-MOTOR SKILLS DURING INFANCY

Fine-motor skills involve the smaller muscles of the body used in reaching, grasping, manipulating, pincering, clapping, turning,

FIGURE 6.10 Sequences of motor development in average infants.

TABLE 6.2
AGE NORMS FOR MOTOR SKILLS (IN MONTHS)

Skill	*When 50% Master the Skill*	*When 90% Master the Skill*
Lifts head 90% when lying on stomach	2.2	3.2
Rolls over	2.8	4.7
Sits propped up (head steady)	2.9	4.2
Sits without support	5.5	7.8
Stands holding on	5.8	10.0
Walks holding on	9.2	12.7
Stands momentarily	9.8	13.0
Stands alone well	11.5	13.9
Walks well	12.1	14.3
Walks backward	14.3	21.5
Walks up steps	17.0	22.0
Kicks ball forward	20.0	24.0

From "The Newly Abbreviated and Revised Denver Developmental Screening Test" by W. K. Frankenburg, A. Frandal, W. Sciarillo, and D. Burgess, 1981, *Journal of Pediatrics, 99,* 995–999.

opening, twisting, pulling, or scribbling (Mathew & Cook 1990). Table 6.3 shows the age in months at which 90 percent of a normal sample of infants could accomplish each of the designated tasks according to the Denver Developmental Screening Test (Frankenburg, Frandal, Sciarillo, & Burgess, 1981). Note that 90 percent of the infants were 4 months old before they could grasp a rattle, 15 months before they could grasp a raisin with a neat pincer grasp, and 25 months before they could scribble spontaneously.

GROSS-MOTOR SKILLS OF PRESCHOOL CHILDREN

Preschool children between 2 and 5 years of age make important advances in motor development. With stronger bones, muscles, lung power, and neuromuscular coordination between the arms, legs, senses, and central nervous system, these children show increased skill and mastery of their bodies in performing physical feats that would have been impossible before. Table 6.4 shows some gross-motor skills of preschool children of different ages. Notice the skills of 5-year-olds. They can skip smoothly; broad jump up to three feet; jump one foot high; hop on one foot a distance of sixteen feet; start, turn, and stop effectively in playing games; descend a long stairway unaided, alternating the feet; walk a balance beam; throw a ball with one leg stepping forward on the same side as the throwing arm; and catch a ball using their hands only.

FINE-MOTOR SKILLS OF PRESCHOOL CHILDREN

Fine-motor skills involve a high degree of small-muscle and eye–hand coordination. With small muscles under control, children gain a sense of competence and independence because they can do a lot of things, such as eating or dressing, for themselves. Table 6.5 shows some small-muscle motor skills of average preschool children of different ages. For eating, note that 2-year-olds can hold a glass with one hand, and 3-year-olds can eat with a spoon and pour from a pitcher. For dressing, 2-year-olds can put on simple clothing, 4-year-olds can dress themselves, and 5-year-olds may be able to manage a zipper, fasten buttons, or even tie shoelaces. For other small-muscle activities, 2-year-olds will scribble; 3-year-olds can copy a circle or draw a straight

TABLE 6.3
AGE NORMS FOR FINE-MOTOR SKILLS WHEN 90 PERCENT OF INFANTS COULD ACCOMPLISH A TASK

Fine-Motor Task	*Months*
Hands together	3.7
Grasps rattle	4.2
Reaches for objects	5.0
Sits, takes 2 cubes	7.5
Transfers cube hand to hand	7.5
Thumb–finger grasp	10.6
Neat pincer grasp of raisin	14.7
Scribbles spontaneously	25.0

From "The Newly Abbreviated and Revised Denver Developmental Screening Test" by W. K. Frankenburg, A. Frandal, W. Sciarillo, and D. Burgess, 1981, *Journal of Pediatrics, 99,* 995–999.

FOCUS

The Onset of Walking and Mother–Infant Relationships

The infant's achievement of upright mobility is a dramatic developmental event in the life of the infant and the family, one that may lead to dramatic changes in the emotional communication in the mother–infant relationship. With walking, infants begin to show an intense engagement with their environment, including greater interest in exploration as well as an emotionally expressive interaction with their caregivers. Infants usually become more emotionally positive during this time. The improvement in infant emotionality with transition to upright locomotion usually engenders a positive reaction of mothers. Mothers are excited and pleased that their infant has started to walk. At the same time, however, it is possible that infant autonomy may create a context for negative perceptions of feelings in the mother. As infants take the initiative in moving away from mother, they are likely to experiment also with their sense of control and power in the mother–child relationship. It is interesting that maternal concerns show a dramatic shift toward the end of the first year from nurturing to nurturing and discipline. As an infant is able to explore with greater ease, the mother is likely to issue more prohibitions, but the infant may also retaliate willfully, having his or her own agendas in mind. Earlier and later walkers differ somewhat in maternal relationships. As compared with the later walking group, earlier walkers and their mothers engage in fewer positive interactions at first observation. Gradually positive encounters increase but these encounters are accompanied by a rise in testing of wills between mother and child in the context of prohibition. Infants increase their exploratory activity and are more likely to get into trouble, requiring more guidance on the part of the mother (Biringen, Emde, Campos, & Applebaum, 1995).

line; 4-year-olds can draw simple figures, cut on a line with scissors, and make crude letters; and 5-year-olds can copy squares, which takes considerably more manipulative skill and eye–hand coordination than drawing a circle.

HANDEDNESS

Handedness—preference for using one hand rather than the other

Handedness is the preference for using one hand rather than the other in the performance of a variety of motor functions. Approximately 90 to 93 percent of the population eventually develop a preference for use of the right hand as the left hemisphere of the brain assumes dominance and control over motor functions (Searleman, Porac, & Coran, 1989). The remainder of the population either develop left-handedness, become hand-specific, in which they prefer one hand for one activity and another hand for another, or ambidextrous, possessing equal skill with both hands.

Handedness develops slowly in children and is not always consistent in the early years (Ramsey, 1985; Ramsey & Weber, 1986). One study found that 7- to 9-month-olds used their right hands to reach for a toy, but often used either hand when manipulating an object (Michel, Harkins, and Ovrut, 1986). Before 2 years of age, most

TABLE 6.4
LARGE-MUSCLE MOTOR SKILLS OF AVERAGE PRESCHOOL CHILDREN

2-Year-Olds	*3-Year-Olds*	*4-Year-Olds*	*5-Year-Olds*
Jump 12 inches	Broad jump 15 to 24 inches	Broad jump 24 to 34 inches	Broad jump 28 to 36 inches
Throw ball overhand, body stationary	Balance on 1 foot, 1 second	Gallop	Skip smoothly
Cannot turn or stop smoothly or quickly	Hop up to three times	Hop up to 6 steps on one foot	Hop a distance of 16 feet on one foot
Kick a large ball forward	Propel a wagon with one foot	Catch a bounced ball	Catch small ball using hands only
	Ascend a stairway unaided, alternating the feet		Descend a long stairway unaided, alternating feet
	Pedal a tricycle		Jump 1 foot high
	Basket catch of ball using body		Start, turn, and stop effectively in games
			Walk a balance beam

children show considerable flexibility in shifting from one hand to another (McCormick and Maurer, 1988). By age 4, most children show a preference for use of the right hand. By first grade, shifts from one hand to the other become relatively infrequent. Some specialists feel that forcing a left-handed child to become right-handed may cause stuttering, reading problems, or emotional problems, so parents and teachers would be wise not to confuse a possible left-hander (Spock & Rothenberg, 1985).

There are both advantages and disadvantages to being left-handed. Southpaws

TABLE 6.5
SMALL-MUSCLE MOTOR SKILLS OF AVERAGE PRESCHOOL CHILDREN

2-Year-Olds	*3-Year-Olds*	*4-Year-Olds*	*5-Year-Olds*
Scribble spontaneously	Copy a circle	Draw shapes, simple figures	Copy squares
Imitate vertical line within 30%	Draw a straight line	Draw man, 3 parts	String beads
Put on simple clothing	Eat with a spoon	Dress self	Fasten buttons that are visible to the eye
Construct tower of 6 to 8 blocks	Smear and daub paint	Make crude letters	
Hold a glass with one hand	Pour from a pitcher	Use blocks to build buildings	Manage zipper
Turn pages of a book singly		Cut on a line with scissors	May tie shoelaces

Fine-motor skills involve a high degree of small-muscle and eye-hand coordination.

have some advantages in sports. The left-handed batter is harder to pitch to. The curve ball of the left-handed pitcher swerves the opposite way from expectation. The serve of the left-handed tennis player spins in the opposite direction. Left-handed people are right-hemisphere dominant: the side of the brain that controls such skills as art, drama, sculpture, and spatial relations. Michelangelo, Leonardo

Handedness develops slowly in children, but, by first grade, shifts from one hand to the other are fairly infrequent.

da Vinci, and Pablo Picasso were all left-handed. However, left-handed people suffer more from environmental risk so that their accident-related injuries are five times those of right-handed persons (Coran & Halpern, 1991). They are twelve times more likely than right-handers to have learning and reading disabilities. It is most likely that handedness is caused by a combination of genetic, prenatal, and learning factors.

CHANGES DURING THE SCHOOL YEARS

Elementary-school-age children gradually increase in motor ability as their bodies continue to grow. Muscles increase in size and coordination continues to improve, so that most children can run, hop, skip, and jump with agility. Most 6-year-olds can ride a bicycle, jump rope, skate, climb trees, and scale fences if given the opportunity to learn.

Fine-motor skills also increase. Most 8- or 9-year-olds can learn to hammer, saw, use garden tools, sew, knit, draw in proportion, write, print, and cut fingernails.

There are inconsistent gender differences in motor development between boys and girls during middle childhood. Girls are more physically mature than same-age boys; that is, girls have reached a greater percentage of their adult height than same-age boys (Eaton & Yu, 1989). This means that in comparing boys and girls of the same chronological age, developmental studies often compare developmentally more mature girls to less mature boys. This ignores substantial sex differences in maturational tempo.

In general, older children are less active than younger ones, with activity level decreasing with maturational age (Kendall & Brophy, 1981). Boys are thought to be superior in physical skills requiring strength and gross-motor performance, such as football. Girls are considered superior in physical skills requiring grace, flexibility, and agility, such as gymnastics. However, prior to puberty, many of these differences are due to differential expectations and experiences of boys and girls. A group of third-, fourth-, and fifth-grade boys and girls who had been in coeducational physical education classes for at least a year were compared on scores on sit-ups, shuttle run, 50-yard dash, broad jump, and 600-yard walk-run. The girls scored as well as the boys on most measures. In the third year of the program, the girls performed better than the boys on a number of tests (Hall & Lee, 1984). *The American Academy of Pediatrics has said that there is no reason to separate prepubertal boys and girls for physical activities.* After puberty, girls are lighter than boys, and their smaller frames make them more subject to injury in heavy collision sports (American Academy of Pediatrics Committee on Pediatric Aspects, 1981).

One important factor in motor skills is reaction time, which depends partly on brain maturation. One study of reaction time of children aged 5 through 14 found that older children were almost twice as fast as younger ones (Southard, 1985). In another study, none of the children 7, 9, or 11 years old did as well as any adults, even 75-year-olds, in pressing a button in response to a flash of light (Stern, Oster, & Newport, 1980). Seven-year-olds took twice as long as the typical adult to react to the flash of light. Nine-year-olds were better than 7-year-olds, and 11-year-olds were even better. Thus, *older children have a decided advantage over younger children in sports that require quick reactions. Adults are better still.* This is one reason why so many children have trouble in catching balls. By the time they close arms, hands, or mitts, the ball has fallen through or bounced out. Also, throwing or batting balls efficiently requires distance judgment, eye-hand coordination, and quick reaction times—all skills that young elementary school children may not possess. Many sports that adults play are not ideal for children.

PARENTING ISSUES

Rough-and-Tumble Play

Rough-and-tumble play is a part of the motor activities of many preschool children, especially after they have been sitting for a period of time. It's a way of releasing excess energy, of enjoying social contact, and of having fun (DiPetro, 1981). All children need frequent periods of physical activity.

Rough-and-tumble play is not the same as aggression, but it sometimes gets out of hand, especially among children who are used to roughhousing at home. Hank, a big 5-year-old in our preschool class, was used to roughhousing with his dad. He and his father generally interacted with playful but vigorous physical contact. As a result, Hank was usually too rough when he played with smaller children in his class. He was not a bully, but he often hurt other children only because he had learned to be so rough (Author's teaching experience).

PHYSICAL FITNESS

Today's schoolchildren are less physically fit than were children in the 1960s (National Children and Youth Fitness Study, 1984). They have more body fat. They are less fit in terms of heart rate, muscle strength, lung capacity, and physical endurance. Many have high levels of cholesterol, or high blood pressure.

The reason is they are not active enough. Only about half of all children are involved in physical education classes twice a week. Generally, children spend too much time watching television. One survey indicated that the average American child aged 2 to 11 views television 27.5 hours per week (Tooth, 1985). Sometimes physical activities in or out of school emphasize competitive sports or games rather than teaching lifetime fitness activities such as walking, running, bicycling, skating, swimming, golf, tennis, or bowling, which they can continue to enjoy in the adult years.

One health education and fitness program involving 24,000 children in Michigan schools taught children what foods to eat; how to measure their own blood pressure, heart rate, and body fat; and how to resist unhealthy foods and drugs. It also encouraged them to participate in activities and games that build fitness. An analysis of the effects of the program on 360 second-, fifth-, and seventh-graders revealed that the children had lowered their cholesterol levels, blood pressure, and body fat, and had improved their time for running a mile (Fitness Finders, 1984). Children's fitness can be improved through carefully designed programs.

PARENTING ISSUES

Organized Sports

In the past, both the National Education Association and the American Medical Association have opposed organized sports activities for children under the age of 14 because of the chances of physical injury or psychological stress (Seefeldt, 1982). In spite of these objections, organized sports for children are growing, and physical injuries are increasing (Micheli, 1988). The most common injuries are fractures, sprains, and twisted ligaments. Head and neck injuries are common in football, wrestling, and gymnastics. Even in such safe sports as swimming or tennis, overuse injuries involving swelling, inflammation, and pain can have long-term consequences that can be debilitating. Coaches need to be careful not to overtrain children and cause overuse injuries.

The possibility of psychological stress is even greater if the emphasis is on winning rather than just having fun (Martens, 1988). Little League coaches, or parents who pressure their children to win, cause considerable stress. Sports are supposed to build character and improve self-esteem. But how can the child who consistently does poorly, or whose team is at the bottom of the Little League standing, have a positive self-image if the measure of success is competence and victory?

Benjamin Spock (1990) told Yale University graduates that one of the worst ailments of American society is excessive competitiveness. One of his recommendations was to abolish Little League baseball because "it takes the fun out of athletics at an early age—we ought to raise our children with quite a different spirit." Not all adults would agree with Spock, but most would agree that children ought to come first and winning second.

Adults have a decided advantage over younger children in sports that require quick reactions.

Children with Disabilities

Physical disabilities in children may be divided into at least four basic categories: *Speech disorders, hearing impairments, visual impairments,* and various types of *skeletal, orthopedic, or motor skills disabilities.* Mental retardation and learning disabilities will be discussed in Chapter 7 on cognitive development of children.

CHILDREN WITH SPEECH DISORDERS

Speech disorders are among the most common of all physical disabilities in children. They may be due to congenital malformations, such as cleft palate, or arise as a consequence of hearing, neurological, or developmental problems. *Infantile autism* appears in the first two years of life and is characterized by language disorder with impaired understanding as well as abnormal social relationships, rituals and compulsive activities, and uneven intellectual development. Other children with *developmental expressive language disorder* have trouble expressing themselves. Other children with *developmental articulation disorder* have trouble making themselves understood. The basic task is to get a correct diagnosis to discover the cause of the difficulty to see what can be done (Berkow, 1987).

CHILDREN WITH HEARING IMPAIRMENTS

Hearing problems in children may not be discovered until the child is 1 or 2 years old. Young infants are visually responsive, but after 6 months or so the parent–child communication starts to break down. The child seems to ignore what the parents say and is not responsive enough for their satisfaction. The child seems to be disobedient and is startled by persons approaching whom he or she does not hear. Two-year olds may either withdraw or manifest behavioral problems with frequent anger and temper tantrums. If hearing deficits are suspected, the child is given a complete examination, including various types of hearing tests. Children from birth to 6 months of age are exposed to relatively intense levels of sound and their reflexes recorded. In the child from 6 months to 2 years of age, localized responses to tones and speech are evaluated. If a child is 12 months of age or more, the *speech reception threshold (SRT)* is determined by having the child point to body parts or identify common objects in response to speech of controlled intensity. In the child above 3 years of age, play audiometry is used by conditioning the child to perform a task in response to a tone. Once the level of hearing is established, the next task is to diagnose the cause and establish treatment if possible. *Hearing aids* can be given to children as young as 6 months of age if sound amplification will correct the problem. *Surgical remedies* are sometimes possible. If the child suffers chronic and irremedial loss of hearing, special education is needed and should be started as soon as possible since there is an optimum time for the acquisition of language. Children are able to learn American Sign Language (ASL) readily if given an opportunity.

Congenital hearing loss (present from birth) is commonly caused by *rubella* during the first trimester of pregnancy. Other causes are *anoxia* (lack of oxygen) during birth, *bleeding* into the inner ear because of birth trauma, *ototoxic drugs* (for ear infections) given to the mother, or *hereditary conditions* (Berkow, 1987).

CHILDREN WITH VISUAL IMPAIRMENTS

Blindness in children may be congenital or may develop gradually or suddenly from a wide variety of causes. Ordinarily, visual communication between caregivers and children is basic to the establishment of an attachment relationship. Babies look at and follow everything new going on around them. They follow movements and especially like to look at human faces. In turn, caregivers rely heavily on subtle responses of the infant—smiling, babbling, moving, laughing—to maintain and support their own behavior. However, infants with visual impairments may not develop their signals for "I want you to do something" or "pick me up" until near the end of the first year. This lack of communication can be very frustrating to both the caregiver and the infant. *The baby's lack of responsiveness* can be emotionally upsetting to the caregiver, who cherishes some response. Visually impaired babies may not develop smile language as do sighted children and may have very few facial expressions. However, they rapidly develop a wide variety of hand signals and body language to direct and relate these signals to their caregivers. Parents and caregivers need training to learn how to interpret signals and to react to the visually impaired child so that attachment and socialization can take place.

Infants with visual impairments usually lag behind infants with normal sight in mobility and locomotion, usually taking longer to crawl and to walk. They lag behind in fine-motor coordination and in developing basic manual skills. Postural motor skills such as sitting and standing become more difficult without the ability to see. In general, lack of sight contributes to developmental delays (Troster and Brambring, 1993).

If the child is not totally blind and corrective lenses will help, glasses should be prescribed and worn as soon as feasible, which for some children is by 3 years of age. *Cross-eyes* (eyes turned in), *walleyes* (eyes turned out), or *near-sightedness* are common difficulties in children. Nearsightedness commonly develops in children between 6 and 10 years of age. It can come on quite rapidly (Spock & Rothenberg, 1985).

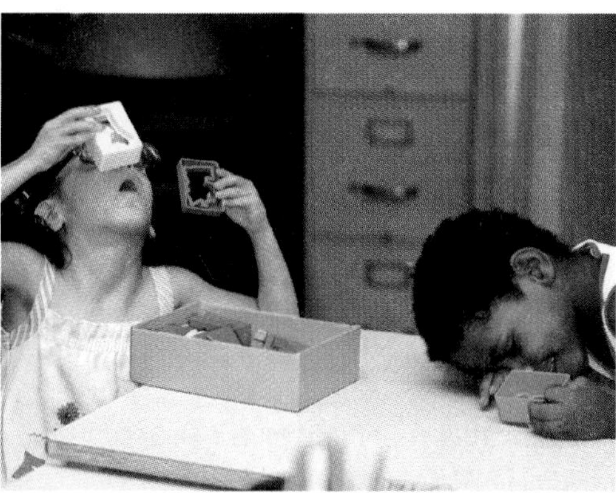

Visual impairments in children may be congenital or develop gradually from a wide variety of causes.

FOCUS

Otitis Media

Otitis media (middle ear disease) is the most frequently diagnosed childhood disease except for upper respiratory infections. Although the disease may be mild, it is usually associated with a mild to moderate hearing loss that may affect the short-term language and speech of young children and has been associated with long-term effects on language, with behavioral problems, and with school achievement difficulties in older children. Some infants and children develop symptoms associated with otitis media, including fussiness, pulling of the ear, and fever. However, many children do not have any symptoms at all, which makes it difficult to diagnose. Children in the first few years of life are most likely to have otitis media but certain groups are more at risk than others. These groups include those who are in day care, or children who live in large families or in crowded conditions. Children who are in close contact with many other children and adults have more otitis media. Some treatments, like antibiotics and tube placement, can be effective in reducing the accompanying fluid in the middle ear. Up to one-third of young children have chronic middle ear disease (Feagans, Kipp, & Blood, 1994).

CHILDREN WITH SKELETAL, ORTHOPEDIC, OR MOTOR-SKILLS DISABILITIES

These types of disabilities range all the way from almost complete disability, such as the *quadraplegic* with paralysis of all four limbs, to minor orthopedic or motor skills dysfunctions. Some disabilities, such as those from *spina bifida,* are congenital. Others, such as *Duchenne muscular dystrophy,* are also hereditary but not evident in children until later in childhood. In the case of MD, the disease typically appears in boys from 3 to 7 years old. Most are confined to a wheelchair by age 10 or 12, with most dying by age 20. Some less serious disabilities, such as *clubfoot,* are caused by a combination of hereditary and prenatal environmental factors and are amenable to treatment. Other disabilities are caused by injuries during childhood.

ADJUSTMENTS

Children with disabilities may be subject to cruel remarks and teasing by other children. They may feel stigmatized and rejected, and denied opportunities and activities open to those without disabilities. Physical appearance has been found to be important in influencing children's desire to interact socially with others (Zebrowitz & Montepare, 1992). Life is not always fair for those with disabilities, but many children are able to overcome discrimination and to make very happy social adjustments. In fact, some able children compete to be their friends, and become very protective of those less fortunate.

This child is sponsored by The National Foundation for Wheelchair Tennis.

PARENTING ISSUES

Rearing a Child with Disabilities

Rearing a child with a physical disability is particularly stressful. Such children require extra physical care at home and more visits to doctors and other professionals. Parents must make decisions about a child's school, medical treatment, and other aspects of care. They must also cope with the stigma of having a child with a disability and with the long-term uncertainty regarding the child's future functioning.

More important, parents must come to terms with the loss of the "perfect" child. Many parents initially experience a sense of guilt or failure at having a child with a disability. Parents may develop depression and anxiety over the long term. In addition to a child's special needs, the parents must meet the child's normal developmental needs, including the need for independence. Elevated stress may be one reason that mothers of children with disabilities report more doubts about their abilities as parents and less enjoyment of their children.

Paradoxically, the demands of rearing a child with physical disabilities make it more difficult for social networks to be established. Parents of children with disabilities have less energy and less time available for network associations. Indeed, mothers of children with disabilities report smaller and less satisfying social networks compared to mothers of children without disabilities. They also report that they feel isolated. Mothers with satisfying networks have been found to have more positive relationships with their children during infancy and early childhood. Mothers who have satisfying social networks are able to depend upon other people and to have more of their own emotional needs met and, consequently, are better able to meet the needs of their children (Jennings, Stagg, Connors, & Ross, 1995).

Just as important, large numbers of the physically disabled lead productive lives, accomplishing amazing things. Some of the blind and physically disabled students in the author's classes have done superior work in relation to other students.

EDUCATION

In 1975, federal law in the United States mandated that all children, regardless of their disability, receive public education in the least restrictive environment that is educationally sound. This means that disabled children should be mainstreamed (put in schools with able children) unless mainstreaming is deleterious to them. The purpose of mainstreaming is to try to avoid stigmatizing disabled children as being different and to give them the same educational and social advantages as others.

Some schools adopted the idea of resource rooms where specially trained people could assist disabled pupils for part of the day. In spite of some advantages, mainstreaming has not always met the needs of disabled children. When school budgets are cut, it is frequently the special educational programs that suffer. Moreover, children with disabilities are different to some extent. Putting them in regular classrooms to be taught by an already overworked teacher who may not have special training is not necessarily the wisest decision. The children may be left on their own to sink or swim. Certainly blind children, deaf children, and children who are severely disabled in other ways can profit more by being sent to special schools just for them where they receive total assistance, training, and education to develop their capacities to the fullest.

Summary

1. Physical growth from birth to adolescence manifests two different patterns: (1) very rapid but decelerating growth from birth to age 1, and (2) linear and steady annual increments after age 1. Increases both in height and weight are dramatic during the first year of life.

2. There are wide individual, cultural, ethnic, and socioeconomic class differences in growth patterns.
3. Body parts grow at different rates. They grow according to the cephalocaudal principle, from the head to the feet, and according to the proximodistal principle, from the center of the body outward.
4. Three organ systems—the lymphoid system, the reproductive system, and the central nervous system—do not follow the general patterns of growth of the rest of the body and organs.
5. Brain growth and nerve maturation include increased myelinization and the development of increasingly complex nerve pathways.
6. The cerebral cortex is the largest structure of the forebrain and contains the higher brain centers controlling intellectual, sensory, and motor functions.
7. The cerebral cortex is larger in proportion to total body weight and is more highly developed in humans than in any other animals.
8. The cerebral cortex is divided into two hemispheres; the left side of the brain controls mainly the right side of the body and the right side of the brain controls mainly the left side of the body.
9. Right- or left-handedness is reasonably well established by age 2. Lateralization is the preference for using one side of the body more than the other in performing specific tasks.
10. The right hemisphere specializes in music, drama, fantasy, intuition, and art; in recognizing patterns, faces, and melodies; and in visualizing spatial relationships. The left hemisphere specializes in logic, mathematics, language, writing, and judging time.
11. The motor, sensory, and association areas of the cortex each control particular functions.
12. The Broca's area of the cortex is involved in using language, the Wernicke's area in understanding language.
13. Both maturation and learning are important in the development of cortical structures and in learning such functions as toilet training.
14. The eruption of deciduous teeth (baby teeth) begins at about 5 months and is completed by 30 months of age. The eruption of permanent teeth begins at 5 years of age and is completed by age 25. Children need dental care of baby teeth as well as permanent teeth.
15. Gross-motor skills develop in infancy before fine-motor skills. The average infant can walk alone by 15 months of age, and can scribble spontaneously by 25 months.
16. As infants begin to walk they increase their exploratory activity and are more likely to get into trouble, requiring more guidance on the part of the mother.
17. Five-year-olds can perform a variety of physical feats, involving both gross-motor skills and fine-motor skills, that would have been impossible several years earlier.
18. Handedness develops slowly in young children and is not always consistent in the early years. There are advantages and disadvantages to being left-handed.
19. Most differences between elementary school boys and girls in motor abilities are due to differential expectations and experiences. Children exposed to the same physical education classes show few gender differences in abilities.
20. Reaction time of children decreases with age. This is an important factor in many games children play.
21. Many authorities disapprove of organized sports for children under the age of 14 because of the chances of physical injury and psychological stress.
22. Today's children are less physically fit than were children in the 1960s.
23. Physical disabilities discussed here include speech disorders, hearing and visual impairments, and skeletal, orthopedic, and motor skills disabilities.
24. Otitis media (middle ear disease) is frequently diagnosed in childhood and may result in some temporary hearing loss.
25. Children with disabilities may be subject to cruel remarks and teasing by other children, but many are able to overcome these things and live happy, productive lives.
26. Rearing a child with a physical disability may be particularly stressful.
27. Federal law mandates that all children, regardless of their disability, receive public education in the least restrictive environment that is educationally sound.

Key Terms

Cephalocaudal principle *p. 143*
Cerebral cortex *p. 145*
Handedness *p. 152*
Lateralization *p. 146*
Myelinization *p. 144*
Proximodistal principle *p. 144*

Discussion Questions

1. Do you know any children who are smaller or larger than average for their age group? Describe them. What are some of the social and psychological consequences for them?
2. Should parents play an active role in helping children develop gross-motor skills and fine-motor skills? Explain. Does it help? What might be some of the possible negative results? Should parents help children to learn sports?
3. What do you think of having boys and girls in the same physical education classes at school? Explain.
4. Are any of you left-handed? Do you experience any particular difficulty as a result? Explain.
5. Do you know anyone personally who has a physical disability? Tell about that person.

Suggested Readings

Batshaw, M. L., & Pettet, Y. M. (1986). *Children with handicaps.* Baltimore: Paul H. Brooks. Dental care, vision, hearing, attention-deficit disorder, and cerebral palsy.

Brown, E. W., & Franta, C. F. (Eds.). (1988). *Competitive sports for children and youth.* Champaign, IL: Human Kinetics. A series of articles summarizing research and issues.

Caplan, F. (1981). *The first twelve months of life.* New York: Bantam. A summary, easily read.

Caplan, J., & Caplan, F. (1983). *The early childhood years: The 2- to 6-year-old.* New York: Putnam. Physical, cognitive, social, and emotional growth during the years 2 to 6.

Collins, A. (Ed.). (1984). *Development during middle childhood: The years from 6 to 12.* Washington, DC: National Academy Press. All aspects of development during these years.

Dodson, F., & Alexander, A. (1986). *Your child: Birth to age 6.* New York: Fireside. Summary.

Field, T. (1990). *Infancy.* Cambridge, MA: Harvard University Press. The latest on infant research, plus current practical concerns.

Haywood, K. M. (1986). *Life span motor development.* Champaign, IL: Human Kinetics. Summary of development over the life span.

Lamb, M. E., & Bornstein, M. C. (1987). *Development in infancy.* New York: Random House. Description by two leading researchers.

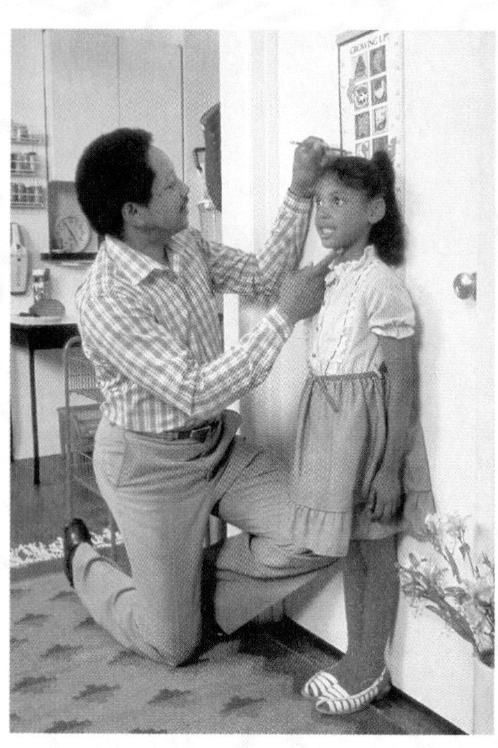

Physical Development: Nutrition, Sleep, Health Care, Sexual Development, and Sex Education

Chapter 7

NUTRITION

Breast-Feeding Versus Bottle-Feeding • Dietary Requirements • **PARENTING ISSUES:** ***When Are Solid Foods Introduced?*** • Obesity • **PARENTING ISSUES:** ***How Not to Create Eating Problems*** • **FOCUS:** ***Sugar Consumption and Children's Behavior*** • Malnutrition • What Is Safe to Eat?

SLEEP

Needs, Habits, and Disturbances • Sleeping with Parents

HEALTH CARE

Health Supervision of the Well Child • **FOCUS:** ***Immunization Schedule*** • Health Education

SEXUAL DEVELOPMENT

Infancy • Early Childhood • Middle Childhood

SEX EDUCATION OF CHILDREN

Parents as Sex Educators • Goals • Methods • **PARENTING ISSUES:** ***Questions about Sexual Relations***

SEXUAL ABUSE OF CHILDREN

Patterns of Activity • **PARENTING ISSUES:** ***Easy Victims and Bad Witnesses***

In this second chapter on the physical development of children we are concerned about their health: nutrition, sleep, and health care. We want to discuss the pros and cons of breast-feeding versus bottle-feeding, the dietary requirements of children, when to introduce solid foods, how not to create eating problems, and the problems of obesity and malnutrition. We want to discuss sleeping habits, and especially health care, including health supervision, immunization, and health education. We are also concerned about the sexual development of children, sexual abuse, and sex education.

Nutrition

BREAST-FEEDING VERSUS BOTTLE-FEEDING

Another way to improve physical health is through good nutrition. The question arises whether children are healthier being breast- or bottle-fed. Breast-feeding declined rapidly in popularity during the early years of this century and up until about 1970. This decline occurred not only in the United States but in countries all over the world. By the early 1970s, fewer than one in four mothers in North America breast-fed their babies (Eiger & Olds, 1987). Latham (1977) reports that breast-feeding of infants in Chile declined from 90 percent in 1960 to less than 10 percent in 1968; the breast-feeding of infants in Mexico declined from 95 percent in 1960 to 40 percent in 1966; the breast-feeding of infants in Singapore declined from 80 percent in 1951 to 5 percent in 1971. Whenever this occurred in developing countries, infant mortality rates increased because commercial formula was diluted with contaminated water that transmitted intestinal diseases to infants (Hinds, 1982). As a consequence, the World Health Organization is urging women in these countries to return to breast-feeding and is discouraging the distribution of formula.

The downward trend in the popularity of breast-feeding has been reversed, especially among middle- and upper-class mothers, so that today between 55 percent and 60 percent of new mothers breast-feed their babies and they are more likely to nurse their babies until at least the fifth or sixth month (Eiger & Olds, 1987; Martinez, Dodd, & Samaltgedes, 1981). Breast-feeding continues to be less common among black women, women with less than a high school education, economically poor women, and women who have never

The overall health and energy of children depends on their receiving good nutrition.

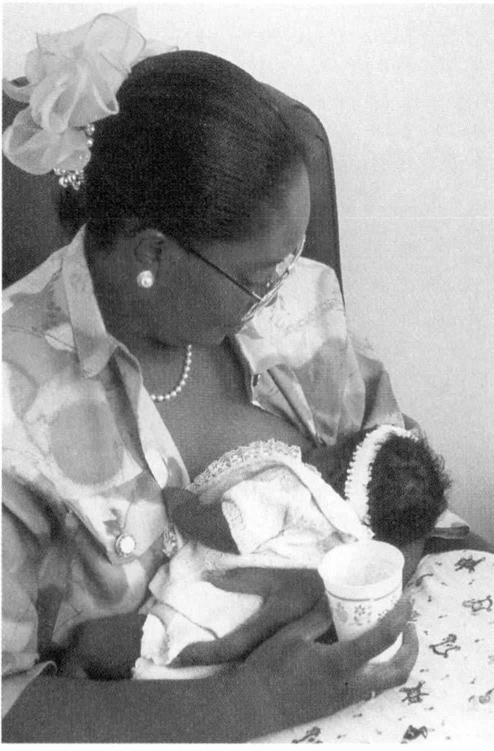

Breast milk is the best food available for infants.

worked outside the home (U.S. Bureau of the Census, 1988, p. 64).

Advantages

Breast-feeding has some distinct advantages. It is the *best food* available for infants and is nutritionally superior to formulas and to cow's milk (Eiger, 1987). It contains the right proportion of fats, calories, proteins, vitamins, and minerals. In relation to cow's milk, it contains several additional amino acids necessary for neural development. It also contains more iron and vitamins A and C. It is more digestible than cow's milk. Breast-fed babies have fewer cases of digestive upsets, allergies, coughs, respiratory difficulties, gastrointestinal infections, and diarrhea (Short, 1984). Breast milk is clean and always at body temperature. Breast-fed babies gain weight more rapidly than bottle-fed babies, yet Kramer (1981) suggests that breast-fed babies are less prone to subsequent obesity. One big advantage is that breast milk *contains antibodies* derived from the mother's body that immunize the infant from disease and infection. Another advantage is that nursing *helps shrink the uterus* back to normal size more quickly.

In some respects, breast-feeding is also *convenient and practical.* There are no bottles to sterilize, no formulas to mix, no refrigeration required, no bottles to warm. In those ways, it saves time and money. And parents don't have to bring along as much equipment when they go on a trip.

There are also some *psychological advantages.* Many nursing mothers gain a great deal of satisfaction from breast-feeding: from giving good nutrition to their baby, from seeing their devotion, and from the feeling of closeness.

Infants also gain emotional satisfaction and security from the closeness of breast-feeding, from feeling the mother's warmth, and from the experience of sucking. All infants need to suck. Usually, they have to suck harder and longer during breast-feeding than during bottle-feeding to get enough milk. This fulfills their psychological needs and provides nutrition. Parents need to recognize, however, that babies can achieve the same emotional security from bottle-feeding as from breast-feeding, provided they are held and cuddled during feeding. All infants need physical contact and warmth, the sound of a pleasant voice, and the sight of a happy face. A warm, accepting parent who is bottle-feeding the baby can help the infant feel more secure and loved. The important consideration is the total parent-infant relationship, not just the method of feeding.

Disadvantages

There are also some disadvantages to breast-feeding and some advantages to bottle-feeding. One of the most frequent criticisms of breast-feeding is that *it is too confining, that it limits the mother's physical freedom, and that it is inconvenient,* especially for the mother who works outside the home. Few working mothers can take time off during the day to nurse the baby, unless the infant is being cared for nearby or in a child-care center at the place of business and the business allows time during the day for the mother to nurse. Even mothers who do not work must sometimes leave the home, at which time they have to either find a time and place to nurse their babies, or hurry home in time for feeding. Before bottle-feeding was widespread, nursing mothers used to feel free to nurse in public—while shopping, on buses, even in church—but as nursing became less acceptable, the practice gradually declined.

Nursing a baby also means that baby-sitters cannot be employed during feeding times. One answer, of course, is to use a breast pump and keep the milk in a relief bottle for the caregiver to feed the baby when the mother is out of the house. Formula may also be used in a relief bottle. Spock and Rothenberg (1985) suggest that the baby be introduced to the bottle at about 6 weeks of age, only after the flow of milk has become well established.

Some fathers object to breast-feeding because they are excluded from feeding the baby themselves. Insecure fathers may be jealous of the time and attention given the baby. Of course, the father can hold the baby as well as the mother can, apart from feeding times.

One disadvantage of breast-feeding is that *some drugs and chemicals are passed to the baby through the breast milk.* Some drugs are not passed in large enough quantities to affect the baby. Other drugs, such as alcohol and narcotics, come through in sufficient amounts to cause addiction. The mother needs to check with her doctor to determine what medication she is allowed to take. Some diseases, such as AIDS, may also be transmitted through the mother's milk (Rogers, 1985).

Some mothers do not produce enough milk to satisfy the baby. There are various possible reasons for this. At the outset, it may take extra time for the milk to begin flowing. The colorless liquid called colostrum, produced by the breasts the first couple of days after birth, supplies liquid and antibodies to the baby; and nervous upset may curtail the milk's "coming in" for a longer time. The mother may need to consume more liquids to increase the supply. Breast size is not a factor because the number of mammary glands, which produce the milk, is usually about the same in all women.

For some, breast-feeding becomes a painful experience. The nipples get dry and cracked. The baby bites the nipple and makes it sore. Spock and Rothenberg (1985) suggest putting the entire areola in the baby's mouth so their gums squeeze the areola rather than the nipple. The baby gets more milk this way also. Other mothers complain that nursing is *too fatiguing* and that it takes too much out of them. They certainly do need proper diet and rest.

Personal Choice

One of the most important considerations is the mother's attitude toward nursing itself. Breast-feeding requires a personal choice. Some women find breast-feeding to be a challenge, and they become very upset if they can't manage it. Others really want to breast-feed but let other people dissuade them. In these cases, the father's support can be a crucial positive contribution. Individual mothers can follow their best instincts and do what they really want to do and what seems to be best for the baby. If needed, they can receive support and consultation from La Leche League, an organization that promotes breast-feeding and offers help to nursing mothers; the league has chapters all over the world.

DIETARY REQUIREMENTS

As children get older, a balanced diet is vitally important for their good health and vigor. Their bodies need protein, minerals, vitamins, carbohydrates, fats, roughage, and water. These nutrients are derived from four basic food groups: *milk and dairy products, meat, fruits and vegetables,* and *breads and cereals.* Children can be taught to eat foods from the four basic food groups every day as the best way of assuring good nutrition.

OBESITY

Body weight 20 percent over that in standard height-weight tables is considered obesity. Obesity may be a health problem as children get older and it is a distinct disadvantage to children in a society that places a social stigma on being fat (Kolata, 1986). Even young children have negative attitudes toward obesity (Reaves & Roberts, 1983). Because fat children tend to become fat adults, obesity presents a future health hazard to them (Brownell, 1982).

Several factors influence obesity. One is *heredity.* If parents are obese, children tend to be obese also, and not just because the parents teach their children to overeat (Stunkard, Foch, & Hrubec, 1986). Obese children tend to be born with more and larger fat cells than slim children, and the number of fat cells increases even more if there is excess weight gain before the age of 12 (Krieshok & Karpowitz, 1988). Another finding is that obese people have longer intestines than slim people, allowing more calories to be absorbed (Powers, 1980). Of course, appetite is partly inherited. From birth, some children seem to have voracious appetites. Others appear less interested in food.

Another factor in obesity is *eating habits* (Olvera-Ezzell, Power, & Cousins, 1990). Obese children do not necessarily eat more food, but they prefer calorific foods high in fats, starches, and sugars (Keesey & Pawley, 1986). When they eat such foods, their level of insulin increases, which, in turn, further increases hunger and food consumption. It's a vicious circle (Rodin, 1982).

One major problem that contributes to obesity is the habit of eating junk food—potato chips, sweets, and sodas—which are high in calories from fats and sugars, but low in nutritional value. The fat content and calorie ratings of foods from various fast-food restaurants is shown in Table 7.1 (Center for Science in the Public Interest, 1990). The American Heart Association recommends that the percentage of calories

PARENTING ISSUES

When Are Solid Foods Introduced?

Sometimes conflict develops between the mother and the pediatrician over the age at which solid foods are to be introduced to the child. Some pediatricians insist that infants do not need solid foods before 6 months of age. Some mothers prefer to give solid foods after several months of age because they say "it helps the baby sleep through the night."

There are several important considerations. Infants must develop a new movement of the tongue and mouth to swallow solid foods. Neurologic development has progressed sufficiently for this to happen at about 3 to 4 months of age. Infants can swallow foods at a younger age only if the food is placed on the back of the tongue, but this represents a kind of force-feeding. Some infants rebel and develop feeding problems later.

The time to start solid foods depends partially on the infant's needs and readiness. An infant who has loose bowels may not tolerate solid foods as easily. Certainly, babies do best with breast milk or formula, rather than cow's milk, until at least 6 months of age (American Academy of Pediatrics, Committee on Nutrition, 1986). If there are not other problems, infants can benefit from beginning to eat cereal at about 4 months of age. Cereal has a high iron content that babies need. Fruit is usually started after babies have become used to cereal, followed by vegetables, then strained meat at about 6 months of age. Parents need to avoid too many "dinners" (combination foods) with large amounts of starch, cellulose, and sodium. Puddings and other desserts contain large quantities of cornstarch and sugar that are not advisable for children, especially for obese children or for those not getting enough other nutrients. By 6 months of age most babies are eating cereal and a variety of fruits, vegetables, and meats (Spock & Rothenberg, 1985). Wheat, eggs, and chocolate should be avoided until the child is 1 year of age to prevent unnecessary food sensitivities (Berkow, 1987).

Infants must develop a new movement of the tongue and mouth to swallow solid foods.

from fat should be no more than one-third. This means no more than fifteen teaspoons of fat per day for women and twenty teaspoons of fat per day for men. As seen in Table 7.1, most of the foods from fast-food restaurants are high in fat.

Activity level also affects obesity. Obese children tend to be less active, which reduces metabolism and the amount of food burned up, thus increasing fat accumulation. There is a similar link between television watching and obesity. A study of 7,000 children between the ages of 6 and 11 and of 6,500 adolescents found that every hour per day spent watching television increases the prevalence of obesity by 2 percent (Dietz & Gortmacher, 1985). The reason is that television watching reduces physical activity and increases snack consumption. *Psychological factors* may also be a cause of obesity. Children may eat as a means of relieving tension or gaining security when they are tense, unhappy, or lonely.

One major problem that contributes to becoming overweight is the habit of eating junk food.

Inanition—starvation

Marasmus—starvation in young children

The important question is what to do about obesity. Parents must try to prevent it in the first place by regulating the diet and eating habits of children while they are young. They should serve nutritious foods, low in calories from fat, starches, and sugars. As infants, fat children may look cute, but they will feel bad about themselves when they are older.

Parents should not put their obese children on crash diets. Children may lose weight, but not permanently. *There are two principal ways to help children reduce their weight.* The first way is to gradually help them change their eating habits. Avoid keeping junk foods in the house, for example, and serve only healthy foods. The second way is to increase children's physical activity so they will use up more calories—for example, enroll children in groups emphasizing physical activities. Parents also can exercise with their children, acting as good role models and having fun as well. And they can encourage their children to cut down on TV.

MALNUTRITION

Inanition, or starvation, also called **marasmus** in young children, results from the inadequate intake of all nutrients: proteins, calories, vitamins, and minerals. Marasmus is common in developing countries: in countries like Somalia, where warfare among competing factions has destroyed the government and agricultural production of the land. It is also common in coun-

TABLE 7.1
FAT, CALORIE, AND SODIUM CONTENT OF SELECTED FAST-FOOD MEALS

Selected Meal	*Calories*	*Fat (tsp.)*	*Sodium Content*
Burger King Whopper, medium fries, chocolate shake	1,312	15	1,301
McDonalds Big Mac, medium fries, iced cheese danish	1,070	16	1,520
Kentucky Fried Chicken, original recipe, two-piece dinner	1,002	12	2,362
Arby's regular roast beef sandwich, two potato cakes, side salad with light Italian dressing	607	6	1,270
Wendy's bacon swiss burger, small fries, medium Frosty	1,470	17	1,771
Dairy Queen double hamburger, onion rings, chocolate-dipped large cone	1,320	15	1,045
Hardee's big country breakfast with sausage, juice, milk	1,050	14	2,110
Burger King croissan'wich (sausage, egg, cheese), milk	665	10	1,107

Adapted from *CSPI's Fast Food Eating Guide.* Copyright © 1995, Center for Science in the Public Interest. Reprinted/Adapted from Nutrition Action Healthletter (1875 Connecticut Ave., N.W., Suite 300, Washington, D.C. 20009-5728. $24.00 fopr 10 issues). Used by permission of the publisher.

PARENTING ISSUES

How Not to Create Eating Problems

Feeding problems most often develop because overly zealous parents try to make their children eat well, because careless parents don't feed them properly, or because overindulgent parents give children anything they want, including too many sweets. The following suggestions will help to avoid eating problems:

1. Avoid force-feeding children, or use of excessive urging to get them to eat. And avoid fighting with them over food. When pushed too hard, children will rebel and refuse to eat.
2. Recognize that children's appetites vary. Sometimes they eat a lot, sometimes a little. The amount usually evens out over time. Serve small portions—less than they will eat, not more—giving seconds as needed. This way, you can avoid hostility about their finishing their meals.
3. Use a gradual introduction to new foods, giving only small amounts at first and allowing the child time to learn to like them. Sometimes children will never accept a particular food, but as long as other foods provide the basic nutrients, there is no problem. Most adults admit there are foods they now eat that they didn't like as children.
4. Keep mealtimes happy and pleasant, avoiding arguments, controversy, and threats.
5. Serve balanced meals, avoiding excess sweets and fats. Some parents complain that their children will not eat vegetables. These parents may dislike vegetables and seldom serve them.
6. When children are old enough to eat adult table food, serve the same food to the whole family; don't cook separately for the children. It's certainly all right to serve children's favorites now and then, but not in addition to or as a substitute for food eaten by the rest of the family.
7. Generally avoid asking children what they want to eat. It may be all right occasionally or for special occasions, but if you do it on a regular basis, you'll be forever catering to their whims. Some children ask for one food, then when given it, don't want it and prefer something else. Letting children dictate their diets is really asking for trouble.
8. Don't bribe children to eat by promising a reward of any kind, whether it is a piece of candy, a gold star, or any other prize. The less fuss about eating, the better.

tries without famine where it is associated with the early abandonment or failure of breast-feeding, with consequent *gastroenteritis infections.* In marasmus, the energy intake is insufficient to match requirements and the body draws on its own stores. Marasmic infants show gross *weight loss, growth retardation,* and *wasting of subcutaneous fat and muscle. Vital organs* lose weight and function. The *heart, liver, kidney,* and *intestines* are affected. *Heart* and *lung capacity* and output are reduced. *Blood pressure* drops. The *endocrine system* is disturbed. Energy capacity is diminished due to *muscle destruction* and *anemia. Hypothermia* may contribute to death (Berkow, 1987).

Emaciation is obvious. The *bones* protrude; the *skin* becomes thin, dry, inelastic, and cold. A patchy, brown pigmentation may occur. The *hair* is sparse and falls out easily.

Research reveals that an inadequate diet prenatally and after birth may result in retarded brain development and mental retardation. Malnourished children do not perform well on intelligence and cognitive tasks. The degree of mental impairment is related to the duration of malnutrition and

FOCUS

Sugar Consumption and Children's Behavior

Not only is excessive sugar consumption unhealthy, but it also may be associated with behavior problems. Many parents feel that candy, cookies, and other sweets transform children into overactive and irrational hellions, furniture-destroying versions of their former selves (Chollar, 1988a). There is evidence to show that high sugar consumption increases aggression, hyperactivity, and inattentiveness, especially in unstructured situations when children are bored (Goldman, Lerman, Contois, & Udall, 1986). One of the problems is that many processed foods have large amounts of sugar, so there is much hidden sugar in children's diets. The negative effects can be greater when snacks or meals already consumed have been very high in carbohydrates. When the child's basic diet contains high amounts of carbohydrates, sugar consumption increases inappropriate behavior; but if balanced with necessary proteins, the added sugar has less effect. If a child's blood sugar is low, as when he or she has not had breakfast, additional carbohydrates may have a calming effect (Chollar, 1988a).

to the age of onset. The infant with marasmus is more severely affected than the older child.

An investigation of the relation between physical growth and cognitive development of infants growing up in India showed that underweight infants performed relatively poorly on cognitive measures and failed to show the clear age-related improvements and speedier processing found among the heavier infants. Although birth weight, previous illness, and parental education are also related to development, the relation to infant growth and cognition remains significant even after these variables are statistically controlled (Rose, 1994).

Kwashiorkor—protein deficiency

Kwashiorkor results when children have a protein deficiency even though the calorie intake is sufficient. Kwashiorkor is characterized by generalized edema, flaky dermatosis, thinning and decoloration of the hair, enlarged fatty liver, a protruding belly due to the liver enlargement and water retention, and to general apathy and retarded growth. In addition to famine-stricken countries, kwashiorkor is found in parts of the world, such as the Caribbean and the Pacific islands, where staples and weaning foods, such as yams, cassava, or green bananas are protein-deficient (Berkow, 1987).

WHAT IS SAFE TO EAT?

Health and injury statistics indicate that children, especially preschool children, do not always understand what objects are appropriate to eat. Poisoning and choking accidents are most commonly treated injuries for children in emergency rooms. But at what ages do children develop understanding of what is appropriate to eat? What factors enter into their ingestion of inappropriate objects?

Krause and Saarnio (1993) presented 3- to 5-year-olds with nondeceptive common food and nonfood objects and with deceptive objects (e.g., a magnet that looks like a piece of candy). For each of eighteen objects, children were asked what the object looks like, what the object really is, and whether it is okay to eat. The researchers found that 3-year-olds did not understand the edibleness of nondeceptive objects although 4- and 5-year-olds clearly did. Examples of nondeceptive food objects included a cookie, a peanut, a carrot, a lollypop, and an apple. Nondeceptive nonfood items included a key chain, a magnet, an eraser, a rock, a pen, and a candle. The children of all ages had trouble distinguishing the edibleness of deceptive objects, that is, clearly distinguishing between the appearance and reality of objects. Deceptive nonfood items included a key chain that looks like a cookie, an eraser that looks like a peanut, a pencil sharpener that looks like an ice cream cone, a pen that looks like a lollypop, and a candle that looks like an apple. These objects were chosen to reflect the types of items that are readily available in stores. Apparently, children were not able to use sensory clues to determine whether objects were what they appeared to be. For example, the pencil sharpener that looked like an ice cream cone did not melt, was not cold, and felt like rubber, and the cone housed the pencil sharpener. It appears that young children are not always able to pick up the clues or to integrate the clues they do notice when making decisions about edibleness of objects. This means that young children's safety may be at risk when they encounter deceptive objects, such as play foods made of plastic, which may be mistaken as edible, as may objects such as wax food. Similarly, various poisons, such as rodenticides, may mislead or confuse children because of their similarity in appearance to common foods (Krause & Saarnio, 1993).

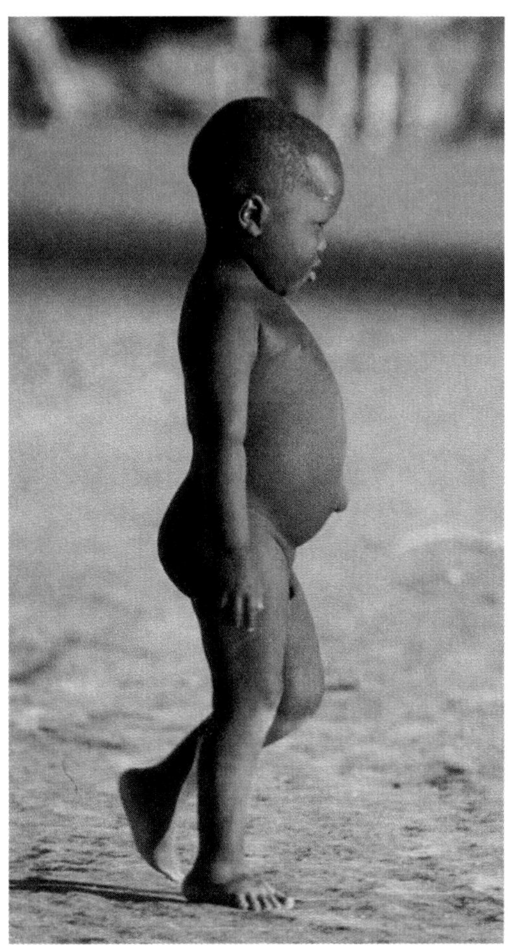

Kwashiorkor, characterized by a protruding belly, results from a protein deficiency even though the calorie intake is sufficient.

Sleep

NEEDS, HABITS, AND DISTURBANCES

If they are made comfortable, get enough food to eat, and have plenty of fresh, cool air, most infants will get the amount of sleep they need. In the early months, most infants sleep from feeding to feeding, although, from the beginning, some are wakeful during certain times of the day. By the end of the first year, most infants take only two naps a day, after the breakfast and lunch feedings. Between 1 and 1½ years they usually give up one of these (Spock & Rothenberg, 1985). If naps are too long in the afternoon, children don't want to go to bed at night.

Infants will take the sleep they need. Two-year-olds won't. They may be kept awake by overexcitement, conflicts, tenseness, or fears of various kinds. Resistance to going to bed generally peaks between 1 and 2 years of age. Children cry when left alone in the crib, or climb out and seek their par-

Separation anxiety—anxiety experienced by children when they are separated from care givers to whom they are emotionally attached

ents. The cause is usually **separation anxiety,** or an effort to control their environment. When children get out of bed, the best way for parents to handle the situation is to put them back in the crib, and then wait in the hallway to make sure the children stay in bed. Parents need to avoid: (1) letting the children stay up; (2) lying down in bed with them; (3) reading more stories and allowing more play; or (4) taking children into bed with them. Once children learn that they will not be allowed out of their own bed and cannot entice parents for some stories or play, they will usually settle down and go to sleep (Berkow, 1987).

It is up to parents to see that children get the sleep they need. The average 2-year-old child needs twelve hours of sleep at night plus one to two hours of nap. Naps are gradually discontinued over several years. From age 6 to 9, children need about eleven hours sleep; 10- to 12-year-olds need about ten hours. Some children need more or less than these averages.

There are several things that parents can do to develop regular sleeping habits for their children.

1. Put children to bed at the same time every night.
2. Develop a relaxed bedtime routine: Get washed and undressed, put pajamas on, have a snack, put the doll to bed, read a story, get tucked in, give a good-night kiss. Children thrive on routine and are upset by variations. Routines help to give them security and condition them to settle down to sleep. Also, it's easier to put them to sleep in their own bed than in strange places, which requires extra effort and attention.

It is easier to put children to bed if a routine is established.

3. Avoid excessive stimulation before bedtime. Rough play, disturbances in the parent–child relationship, or tension in the home cause wakefulness. Parents can't let children roughhouse and then expect them to settle down and go to sleep immediately.
4. Keep bedtime relaxed and happy. It's far more pleasant to carry children to bed lovingly than to order them angrily to bed, or to spank them for not obeying instantly.
5. Avoid sending children to bed as a means of discipline. They will come to associated going to bed with punishment, which makes it harder to get them to bed at other times.
6. Avoid frightening stories or television programs, which may precipitate **nightmares,** especially in 3- to 4-year-olds, who cannot distinguish fantasy from reality. **Night terrors** are characterized by sudden awakening, panic, and screaming. They are most common between ages 3 to 8 years. **Sleepwalking** is estimated to occur in 15 percent of children between 5 and 12 years of age. Stressful events may trigger an episode of sleepwalking. If these difficulties persist, psychological help may be necessary.

Nightmares

Night terrors

Sleepwalking

SLEEPING WITH PARENTS

At some time or another, most children want to sleep with their parents, either in the same room, or actually in bed with them. The question arises whether this is a good idea. Many parents want their newborn in a crib, but in the same room with them so they can hear the baby cry. This may be a good idea up until about 6 months of age. If the practice continues too long, however, it can be hard to get children to sleep anywhere else. Also, even infants may be upset by the sounds of parents having intercourse, which they don't understand. An alternative arrangement is to put an electronic monitor (a microphone) in the baby's room, with the speaker in the parents' room so they can hear the infant at all times and be alerted if there is trouble.

Some parents feel that it's better not to take children into bed with them, even if the child wakes up frightened at night. Once established, the habit is hard to break. Children need to be taken back to their own bed and comforted. However, letting children come into bed for a cuddle in the morning is a different situation. It's a loving, reassuring thing to do.

Health Care

HEALTH SUPERVISION OF THE WELL CHILD

Proper health supervision of the well child will help to promote optimum development of infants and children. Such supervision by medical personnel ought to include: (1) instruction of parents in child rearing, health maintenance, accident prevention, and nutrition; (2) routine immunizations for the prevention of disease; (3) early detection of disease through interview and examination; and (4) early treatment of disease. To meet these objectives, parents and children should be seen by their doctor at regular intervals throughout the early years of life. The frequency of subsequent visits will vary, depending upon children's age and condition and the population served (Bowker, 1987).

The American Academy of Pediatrics has recommended the preventive health-care schedule, which is found in Table 7.2. This schedule is for children who have not manifested any important health problems and who are growing and developing satisfactorily. More frequent and sophisticated visits are necessary for children with special problems. (See "Focus" box and Table 7.3 for an immunization schedule for infants and children.)

HEALTH EDUCATION

Beginning at an early age, children ought to be taught responsibility for their own health. This means instruction in good health habits, proper nutrition, and daily hygiene, as well as the importance of adequate sleep and exercise (Blecke, 1990). Children's health attitudes and behavior are influenced by the family, peers, the school, and the media (Tinsley, 1992). Free or reduced-price lunches at school can help make up for nutritional deficiencies (Glovinsky-Fahsholtz, 1992).

Sexual Development

INFANCY

The infant's capacity for sexual response begins early. Ultrasound pictures reveal that erections occur in developing male fetuses several months before birth (Calderone, 1983). Many male babies have erections even before the umbilical cord is cut or in the first few months after birth. Erections can occur with or without penile stimulation, and they often occur during feeding and sleep. Apparently, the warmth and softness of the mother's body, along with the stimulation of sucking, are pleasurable sensations that stimulate sexual reflexes.

Female infants also exhibit sexual response, evidenced by the presence of vaginal lubrication and clitoral erection during the first 24 hours of life (Langfeldt, 1981). Vaginal lubrication can also occur during nursing. Although their sexual reflexes respond to emotional and physical stimuli, both male and female infants are too young to consciously be aware of the

TABLE 7.2

Recommendations for Preventive Pediatric Health Care

Committee on Practice and Ambulatory Medicine

Each child and family is unique; therefore, these **Recommendations for Preventive Pediatric Health Care** are designed for the care of children who are receiving competent parenting, have no manifestations of any important health problems, and are growing and developing in satisfactory fashion. Additional visits may become necessary if circumstances suggest variations from normal. These guidelines represent a consensus by the Committee on Practice and Ambulatory Medicine in consultation with the membership of the American Academy of Pediatrics through the chapter presidents. The committee emphasizes the great importance of continuity of care in comprehensive health supervision and the need to avoid fragmentation of care.

A prenatal visit by first-time parents and/or those who are at high risk is recommended and should include anticipatory guidance and pertinent medical history.

	Infancy							*Early Childhood*					*Late Childhood*					*Adolescence*[2]			
Age[3]	*2–3 d*[1]	*By 1 mo*	*2 mo*	*4 mo*	*6 mo*	*9 mo*	*12 mo*	*15 mo*	*18 mo*	*24 mo*	*3 y*	*4 y*	*5 y*	*6 y*	*8 y*	*10 y*	*12 y*	*14 y*	*16 y*	*18 y*	*20 y+*
History																					
Initial/Interval	•	•	•	•	•	•	•	•	•	•	•	•	•	•	•	•	•	•	•	•	•
Measurements																					
Height and weight	•	•	•	•	•	•	•	•	•	•	•	•	•	•	•	•	•	•	•	•	•
Head circumference	•	•	•	•	•	•	•	•	•	•											
Blood pressure											•	•	•	•	•	•	•	•	•	•	•
Sensory Screening																					
Vision	S	S	S	S	S	S	S	S	S	S	S	O	O	O	O	S	O	O	S	O	O
Hearing	S	S	S	S	S	S	S	S	S	S	S	O	O	S[4]	S[4]	S[4]	O	S	S	O	S
Developmental/ Behavioral Assessment[5]	•	•	•	•	•	•	•	•	•	•	•	•	•	•	•	•	•	•	•	•	•
Physical Examination[6]	•	•	•	•	•	•	•	•	•	•	•	•	•	•	•	•	•	•	•	•	•
Procedures[7]																					
Hereditary/ Metabolic screening[8]	—	•																			
Immunization[9]			•	•	•		—	—•	•			—	•—				—	•—			
Tuberculin test[10]							•—	—				•—	—					•—			
Hematocrit or Hemoglobin[11]		—	—	—	—•	—	—	—	—	•	—	—	—	—	•	—	—	—	—	•	—
Urinalysis[12]		—	—	—	•	—	—	—	—	•	—	—	—	—	•	—	—	—	—	•	—
Anticipatory Guidance[13]	•	•	•	•	•	•	•	•	•	•	•	•	•	•	•	•	•	•	•	•	•
Initial Dental Referral[14]											•										

Key: • = to be performed, **S** = subjective, by history, **O** = objective, by a standard testing method

[1]For newborns discharged twenty-four hours or less after delivery.

[2]Adolescent-related issues (e.g., psychosocial, emotional, substance usage, and reproductive health) may necessitate more frequent health supervision.

[3]If a child comes under care for the first time at any point on the schedule, or if any items are not accomplished at the suggested age, the schedule should be brought up to date at the earliest possible time.

[4]At these points, history may suffice; if problem suggested, a standard testing method should be employed.

[5]By history and appropriate physical examination; if suspicious, by specific objective developmental testing.

[6]At each visit, a complete physical examination is essential, with infant totally unclothed, older child undressed and suitably draped.

[7]These may be modified, depending upon entry point into schedule and individual need.

[8]Metabolic screening (e.g., thyroid, PKU, galactosemia) should be done according to state law.

[9]Schedule(s) per *Report of Committee on Infectious Diseases,* 1991 Red Book, and current AAP Committee statements.

[10]For high-risk groups, the Committee on Infectious Diseases recommends annual TB skin testing.

[11]Present medical evidence suggests the need for reevaluation of the frequency and timing of hemoglobin or hematocrit tests. One determination is therefore suggested during each time period. Performance of additional tests is left to the individual practice experience.

[12]Present medical evidence suggests the need for reevaluation of the frequency and timing of urinalyses. One determination is therefore suggested during each time period. Performance of additional tests is left to the individual practice experience.

[13]Appropriate discussion and counseling should be an integral part of each visit for care.

[14]Subsequent examinations as prescribed by dentist.

NOTE: **Special chemical, immunologic, and endocrine testing** is usually carried out upon specific indications. Testing other than newborn (e.g., inborn errors of metabolism, sickle disease, lead) is discretionary with the physician.

The recommendations in this publication do not indicate an exclusive course of treatment or serve as a standard of medical care. Variations, taking into account individual circumstances, may be appropriate. Used with permission of the American Academy of Pediatrics, *AAP News,* January 17, 1996.

FOCUS

Immunization Schedule

During the first 6 months of life, infants are given diphtheria, tetanus, pertussis (whooping cough), and polio vaccines. Vaccinations against measles, mumps, and rubella viruses are given at 15 months. Booster shots for diphtheria, tetanus, pertussis, and polio vaccines are repeated at various intervals, but ought to occur at or before school entry. *Hemophilus influenzae* b (flu) vaccine is given at 24 months. Adult tetanus and diphtheria toxoid are given between 14 and 16 years of age and repeated every ten years throughout life. Table 7.3 shows the recommended schedule for normal infants and children.

TABLE 7.3
Recommended Schedule for Active Immunization of Normal Infants and Children

Age[1]	*Vaccine(s)*[2]	*Comments*
2 months	DTP-1[3]; OPV-1[4]	Can be given earlier in areas of high endemicity
4 months	DTP-2; OPV-2	Interval of six weeks to two months desired between OPV doses to avoid interference
6 months	DTP-3	An additional dose of OPV at this time is optional for use in areas with a high risk of polio exposure
15 months[5]	MMR[6]	
18 months[5]	DPT-4; OPV-3	Completion of primary series
24 months	Hib	*Hemophilus influenzae* b vaccine
4–6 years[7]	DTP-5; OPV-4	Preferably at or before school entry
14–16 years	Td[8]	Repeat every ten years throughout life

[1]These recommended ages should not be construed as absolute; e.g., 2 months can be 6 to 10 weeks.

[2]For all products used, consult manufacturer's package enclosure for instructions for storage, handling, and administration. Immunobiologics prepared by different manufacturers may vary, and those of the same manufacturer may change from time to time. The package insert should be followed for a specific product.

[3]DTP, diphtheria and tetanus toxoids and pertussis vaccine.

[4]OPV, oral, attenuated poliovirus vaccine contains poliovirus types 1, 2, and 3.

[5]Simultaneous administration of MMR, DTP, and OPV is appropriate for patients whose compliance with medical care recommendations cannot be assured.

[6]MMR, live measles, mumps, and rubella viruses in a combined vaccine.

[7]Up to 7th birthday.

[8]Td, adult tetanus toxoid and diphtheria toxoid in combination, contains the same dose of tetanus toxoid as DTP or pediatric diphtheria and tetanus toxoid (DT) and a reduced dose of diphtheria toxoid.

Modified from *Morbidity and Mortality Weekly Report,* January 14, 1983, vol. 32, no. 1, Centers for Disease Control, Atlanta, Georgia.

encounters; therefore, they cannot be considered sexually awakened.

Infants begin to discover their bodies during the first year of life. During their exploration, they randomly touch their genitals. Later, as their motor abilities develop, children deliberately touch and rub their genitals. In the process, they discover that such touching brings pleasant sensations.

EARLY CHILDHOOD

Preschool children are curious about everything. This curiosity extends to their own bodies, which they continue to explore. Most masturbate at some time or another. Both boys and girls are fascinated with toileting procedures. They also develop curiosity about other children's bodies and about boy–girl differences. As a result, they peek at one another's bodies to see what they look like. "Doctor" games are one method of body exploration.

Parents need to recognize that some exploration, peeking, and touching is fairly common behavior that results from children's curiosity. If sexual exploration during play becomes too frequent, however, children may require greater supervision. In addition, parents need to be concerned about protecting younger children from advances of those who are older. They should teach children to report sexual requests from older children or adults, such as solicitations to take off their clothes or to touch their genitals.

MIDDLE CHILDHOOD

Society becomes less accepting of children's sexual interests during middle childhood, so sexual activities take place more covertly than during the preschool years. Sexual experimentation does not cease or decrease. In fact, it may become more frequent. In one survey, parents of 6- and 7-year-old children reported that 83 percent of their sons and 76 percent of their daughters had participated in sexual play with siblings or friends of the same sex (Kolodny, 1980). Hunt (1974a) found that one-third of females and two-thirds of males who responded to a questionnaire reported that they masturbated by age 13.

Children remain fascinated with sex and with facts concerning sexual development, human reproduction, and sexual intercourse. The delightful thing about children of school age is that they are not embarrassed to ask detailed questions, given the opportunity. An ideal time to teach children all the basic facts about sex is before they reach puberty and become self-conscious about discussing the subject openly.

Sex Education of Children

PARENTS AS SEX EDUCATORS

Transmission of values and attitudes about sexuality from parents to children is inevitable; values and attitudes are transmitted whether parents choose to participate actively in the sex education of their children or to neglect it completely. Empirical evidence indicates that adolescents whose parents communicate openly with them about sexuality when they are young feel much more comfortable discussing sexual topics with their parents and are more likely to make personal decisions about sexual behavior that reflects parental values and morals.

Parents who successfully communicate with their children about sex seem to be the exception rather than the rule. Research indicates that parents have the desire and willingness to teach the children about sexuality, but both children and parents believe that parents have not functioned adequately in their role as sex educators. It appears that many parents are conducting sex education in much the same way their parents did, in spite of their stated desire to do better. There is some evidence that parents feel one conversation about sexuality during a child's development is sufficient (Geasler, Dannison, & Edlund, 1995).

Good books can help parents answer children's questions about physical development.

GOALS

Since sex education is such an important subject, it might be well to look at some important goals and what they attempt to accomplish.

Attitudes

One of the important purposes of sex education is to help children to develop healthy attitudes about the body and its functions. All children are curious about their own bodies. Infants will spend long hours looking at their own hands. They will learn that they can move their hands as well as open and close them. They try to put their hands into their mouths and suck on them. They also discover other body parts. Babies may spend long hours of time examining their navels or playing with their toes.

In the process of exploration, children discover their genitals. They touch them and are curious about them and play with them but no more so than in relation to other body parts. However, if a parent says, "That's nasty, don't do that" and spanks the daughter's hand when she scratches her itchy vagina, or if a parent reprimands a son for playing with his penis, children begin to learn some parts of the body are not to be examined, that they are somehow different than other parts, that they are dirty and nasty, and that "nice boys and girls" shouldn't be interested in these body parts. Consequently, children grow up learning that having anything to do with their organs of reproduction is somehow "evil" and "bad." They learn to repress sexual interest, and they grow up with the attitude that anything having to do with human reproduction is a forbidden subject.

Most girls and boys are interested in each other's bodies. But their interest is in naive innocence. Little girls look with intense interest, certainly not with lust, at baby brother's penis, or they are amazed to discover that daddy can urinate standing up. They may even try to imitate him when they go to the bathroom. The parents' goal is to accept children's curiosity as quite normal and to be matter of fact about the body, nudity, and bodily functions. There is certainly no harm in preschoolers seeing one another or their parents nude. If parents find their children touching themselves, the best thing to do is nothing. It should be of no concern at all. It's quite normal and harmless.

As children grow older and want privacy, they should have it. Reasonable modesty is a good thing. But excessive modesty can be quite harmful. There are adult women who won't go to a physician until the final stages of pregnancy because of their excessive modesty. Yet adequate prenatal care is vital to the health of the baby and the mother during the early stages of pregnancy. Excessive modesty, then, can be quite harmful. How many women and men never make a happy sexual adjustment in marriage because of negative conditioning about sexual matters?

Physical Development

Sex education can help children to understand the process of physical development of their own bodies and to prepare for the bodily changes at puberty. Parents need to explain such things as nocturnal emissions or menstruation. A girl who has not been prepared for menstruation ahead of time may become very frightened or embarrassed. She may be afraid that she has been injured or is bleeding to death. She will feel embarrassed that she has stained her clothes and may be too fearful to tell the teacher. One teenage boy thought he had wet the bed when he had a nocturnal emission. His father scolded him severely and told him not to let that happen again.

Parents should try to explain bodily changes before such changes take place. Children need the information and need to have fears and anxieties minimized.

Sex Roles

Sex education also seeks to help children accept their own sexuality: their femaleness or maleness and their appropriate sex roles in the society in which they are growing up. These roles are changing so rapidly that the old standards of what is a woman or a man and what each should be and do in life are no longer valid. Parents teach their children these things primarily by the example they set, by the roles they themselves play. Parents who believe in equality between the sexes and equal opportunities regardless of gender, and in flexible sex roles in the family, can best teach their children by becoming living examples of these ideas themselves. Sex education does include teaching boys that it is not unmanly to babysit or to change a diaper, and teaching girls that it is all right to prepare for a career in a traditionally masculine profession.

Reproduction

One more usual purpose of sex education is to help children understand the great miracle of life, where babies come from; how they are conceived, grow, and are born; and how life is passed on from generation to generation. Children are interested in all kinds of babies, both human and animal—chickens, dogs, birds, people. Children need to know that all babies grow from tiny eggs but some creatures (turtles, birds, and others) lay their eggs outside of the body where the babies hatch out. Other creatures (whales, cats, people, and others) keep their eggs inside their bodies where their babies grow until they are born. There is a great need for truthful answers about all phases of human reproduction. If parents are honest and truthful, they can maintain the confidence and trust of their children and build better relationships with them as they grow up.

Behavior

Another major role of sex education is to encourage mature, responsible, knowledgeable sexual conduct. Parents need to discuss morals and behavior along with the facts of life. The day has passed when parental silence, which tries to keep children ignorant, is the way to keep children from sexual experimentation. Children are taught from movies, magazines, television, books, street corners, and in public rest rooms. Not all such information is factual, and much is associated with negative feelings and attitudes and with an irresponsible use of sex. The mass media seldom portrays sex within the context of marriage, as an intimate expression of two people who love each other. It often portrays nonmarital (either extramarital or premarital) sex, sadistic sex, perverted sex, or meaningless, physical sex without emotional involvement. There is need, therefore, for parents to present a more mature point of view to help their children not only to grow to be sexually responsive but to be sexually responsible. Such things as sexually transmitted disease and premarital pregnancies are preventable—with the right sex education and with parental and medical help.

METHODS

The key question is: How is the best way to go about sex education? What can parents do and say? What methods or techniques work best at home?

Begin Early

The first step is to begin early. Sex education begins almost from the time a child is born. When a father says to his young daughter, "Come sit on my knee and give daddy a big hug," he's helping his daughter to learn the meaning and expression of love. Learning to express feelings physically begins with physical demonstrations of affection between family members. Attitudinal development takes place gradually, from birth on as babies are bathed, dressed, diapered, and toilet trained, and as they absorb the feelings and attitudes of their parents.

The first question usually arrives at around three years of age. It is probably best to use correct words for the various parts of the body. It's just as easy to use the words "vagina," "penis," "testicles," "breasts," and "urine" as it is to use their slang counterparts.

Generally speaking, parents should answer all questions as they arise, as honestly and simply as they know how. If children are old enough to ask, they are old enough

The birth of puppies is a good opportunity to teach children where babies come from.

to get an answer. Parents can take advantage of natural opportunities to initiate discussion and impart information: a neighbor's pregnancy, the mother's pregnancy, the birth of animals or human babies, or bathing a baby. It's all right to use the birds-and-bees approach if it tells children how bees are born, but parents eventually need to get around to talking about human babies. Children can learn all about the birth of kittens but still not realize where human beings come from.

One of the chief obstacles to discussions about sex between parents and children is the parents' own embarrassment. There are several things parents can do. (1) They should read all the good books and literature they can that will help them to understand the subject of human sexuality. (2) Parents should discuss the subject between themselves, because the more they talk about sex and use the words that they will employ in teaching their children, the easier it will be to talk to the children. They can ask each other sample questions and practice answering them. (3) If the discussions begin when children are young, parents will become more experienced as children grow and as the questions become more difficult to answer.

Most parents worry about sex play. Some amount of peeking or sex play, such as playing doctor, should be considered quite normal. However, it's best not to leave young children unsupervised, especially with older children who are known to initiate sex play. If such children are discovered in the neighborhood, one solution is simply to keep one's own children away from them. Teaching children not to take their clothes off if other children or adults ask them to, instructing them to tell parents if such requests are made, and telling them not to accept favors or rides with strangers are all basic in preventing molestation.

Grade-School Children

School-age children are filled with questions, and they are quite uninhibited about asking them and discussing them unless parents have reprimanded or punished them for doing so. Generally speaking, children should have all of the basic facts about conception, fertilization, the growth and birth of babies, physical maturation at puberty, the names and functions of the male and female reproductive organs, and sex as a means of expressing love in marriage before they reach puberty. In fact, the younger children are told, within the level of their understanding, the less embarrassed they are and the easier it is to discuss such matters with them. Unless parents have laid a good foundation of years of honesty and matter-of-factness, adolescents will be too embarrassed to ask their parents the things they most want to know. One teenage boy complained: "For years, every time I asked my parents a question, they replied: 'Wait until you are older.' Now that I am 18, they say to me: 'What, you're 18 and you don't know that!' They still won't tell me."

Sexual Abuse of Children

PATTERNS OF ACTIVITY

Sexual abuse may include a variety of activities. Exhibitionism, suggestive language or looks, and passive and active petting and fondling are the most common abusive activities. Sexual encounters are usually quite brief, involving fondling of nongenital and genital areas. The offender may achieve orgasm during the episode,

PARENTING ISSUES

Questions about Sexual Relations

The hardest questions for parents to deal with are those concerning fertilization and sexual relations. Here are some sample questions and answers.

Q: What starts the egg growing into a baby?
A: Before it can start to grow, it has to be fertilized, or joined, by a sperm from the father. (It's helpful to show diagrams of a sperm, an ovum, and a sperm entering the egg.)
Q: Where did this sperm come from?
A: They grow in the father's testicles. (A diagram helps here, too.)
Q: How does the sperm get out of the father and into the mother?
A: When a mother and father make love, or have sexual intercourse as it's called, they hug and kiss each other and lie next to each other. The father puts his penis in the mother's vagina and releases millions of sperm inside her.
Q: How does the sperm find the egg?
A: They have long tails and swim up the vagina, through the opening in the womb, or uterus, through the uterus and into the fallopian tubes, where the egg is. There, one sperm joins with the egg, or fertilizes it, to start the egg growing into the baby. (Show diagram.)
Q: Why do people want to make love even though they already have all the children they want?
A: Because they love each other and that is one way they show their love. Besides, they like to have sexual intercourse because it feels good and it gives them a lot of satisfaction and pleasure.

Such answers are honest, are factual, and are explained simply without overburdening children with too much information until they are interested. When they are, then more details can be given.

or through fantasy about the incident, accompanied by masturbation, at a later time. Anal and/or vaginal intercourse is infrequent. The older the child, the more likely coitus will occur.

Molestation is most likely to take place in the child's own home or in that of the molester. Only a small percent of molesters are complete strangers to the child. Usually the molester is a family member or a friend of the family. A stranger may have to spend days or hours winning the child's trust. The molester may seduce by offering candy, toys, trips to parks or movies, but first must find situations in which children are available. Volunteering for service in organizations, schools, sports groups, boys' or girls' clubs, nursery schools, church choirs, or children's theater groups is a way of establishing contact with children.

As the child begins to feel comfortable, "Mr. Nice Guy" tries some wrestling, tickling, or fondling. The child may be shown some pornography with children in the nude, touching, and playing. The seducer convinces the children that these are ways to have a good time, and may ask the child to disrobe.

Abused children may get involved in frequent sexual activity such as oral sex. The more involved the children become, the more they feel trapped. They are threatened with blackmail or with the murder of parents if they tell anyone. One question frequently asked is: "How come they never said anything?" The reason is that the children believe that threats against them or their parents will be carried out if they reveal the sexual abuse. Plus, they feel guilty and are afraid they will get into trouble, so they keep quiet (Pienciak, 1984).

PARENTING ISSUES

Easy Victims and Bad Witnesses

Two sets of parents—of a 3-year-old boy and a 4-year-old girl—believed that their children were among several toddlers who were forced into sexual acts by three counselors at a summer day camp.

Authorities investigated the incident, but warned parents of a frequently insurmountable problem involving such cases: small children make easy victims and bad witnesses. The parents, in separate interviews, told similar stories about what had happened involving three unnamed counselors. The 3-year-old described bizarre games involving anal and oral sex. The 4-year-old described a lot of sex play in the camp, initiated by the counselors.

All four parents felt their children would be able to testify. The 3-year-old told his mother the perpetrators had threatened to kill his mother if he told, and that he would go to jail and be molested there also. He first spoke of the incidents to his grandmother, since he was fearful for his mother's life. The toddler was put under a therapist's care. He said he thought that people who did this should get a spanking. Every day he asked if the counselors were in jail. He felt he'd like to testify to help put them in jail. However, the boy became suicidal and deliberately ran out into a busy street to try to get run over. "I should be dead now," he said.

The mother of the 4-year-old girl felt she would be a good witness. The case worker was surprised at how astute she was. However, the girl was very troubled. She became convinced that she would have to go to jail because she had done the same thing the counselors had done. She had also been warned that if she told anyone her parents would die. She began bedwetting and passing stools in inappropriate places. She received therapy but told her therapist that she would go to jail for what was done to her (Lovell, 1984).*

*Subsequent investigation revealed that this case was dropped for lack of evidence.

Summary

1. Breast-feeding and bottle-feeding both have advantages and disadvantages, but most authorities would say that breast-feeding is superior from a health standpoint alone. The chief disadvantage of breast-feeding is that it is hard to manage for mothers who work.
2. It is vitally important for children to eat a balanced diet derived from four basic food groups daily: milk and dairy products, meat and other protein, fruits and vegetables, and breads and cereals.
3. Generally speaking, solid foods are introduced about 4 months of age so that by 6 months babies are eating cereal, fruits, vegetables, and meat.
4. Obesity is a distinct disadvantage to children and has multiple causes: heredity; eating habits that involve eating a lot of high-calorie food; low activity level; and using eating to ease tension or gain security.
5. Excessive sugar consumption makes children hyperactive if the basic diet is unbalanced or if the sugar is not combined with sufficient protein.
6. Inanition, or starvation, also called marasmus in young children, is all too common in many parts of the world. Kwashiorkor results from a deficiency of protein even though calorie intake is sufficient.
7. Most infants will take the amount of

sleep they need; 2-year-olds won't. It is up to parents to see that children get the required sleep.

8. Some authorities discourage having children sleep with parents on a regular basis.
9. Health supervision of the well child ought to include: (1) instruction of parents in child rearing, health maintenance, accident prevention, and nutrition; (2) routine immunizations; (3) early detection of disease through interview and examination; and (4) early treatment of disease.
10. The American Academy of Pediatrics has a recommended schedule for child health supervision and a recommended schedule for immunizations.
11. Health education of children ought to begin at an early age to teach children to be responsible for their own health.
12. Children's capacity for sexual responses begins in infancy.
13. Both preschool and grade-school children engage in body exploration and masturbation, and are interested in matters pertaining to sex.
14. Parents transmit their attitudes and values about sex whether they choose to or not.
15. Parents should begin early, be honest and frank, take advantage of natural opportunities such as birth, supervise children to prevent abuse, and explain fertilization and sexual relations simply.
16. Sexual abuse of children is most commonly perpetrated by members of the child's own family or by a family friend. Sexual abuse can have a devastating effect, depending on the nature and extent of the abuse, and the age of the child. Children usually make easy victims and bad witnesses so it is difficult to convict offenders.

Key Terms

Inanition *p. 168*
Kwashiorkor *p. 170*
Marasmus *p. 168*
Nightmares *p. 172*
Night terrors *p. 172*
Separation anxiety *p. 172*
Sleepwalking *p. 172*

Discussion Questions

1. Have you breast-fed or have you been the father of a breast-fed baby? How did you get along? What do you think of it? What are your attitudes toward breast-feeding versus bottle-feeding?
2. Have you bottle-fed a baby, or do you know someone who has? What were the results?
3. What should parents do about children who are obese? Were you obese as a child? If so, how did it affect you and your relationships with others? If not, what were your experiences or friendships with children who were obese? How did obesity affect their behavior and attitudes as you saw them?
4. Do you know any children who have a very inadequate diet? Why is their diet inadequate? What is the effect?
5. What do you or would you do about children who won't go to bed at night? Explain your choices.
6. Did you sleep with your parents while you were growing up? How do you feel about it now? How did it affect you? Do you think it encourages sexual stimulation, guilt, and anxiety? Why or why not?

7. What do you think of the recommended health-care schedule for well children that is found in the book? Are there any aspects you object to? What do you think of taking a child who is not sick to the doctor? Why do some people never want to take their children to the doctor, while others run at every little illness?
8. Evaluate the sex education you received while growing up.
9. Are you able to talk frankly about sex, with your children, spouse, fiancé(e), parents, friends? Why or why not?
10. Do you know anyone who was sexually abused as a child? Describe. What has been the effect on that person?

Suggested Readings

Osofsky, J. D. (1987). *Handbook of infant development* (2nd ed.). New York: Wiley. Numerous topics about infants.

Spock, B., & Rothenberg, M. B. (1985). *Dr. Spock's baby and child care.* New York: Pocket Books. Updated revision of this best-seller.

Cognitive Development: Perception, Language, Reading, and a Piagetian Perspective

Chapter 8

The word *cognition* means, literally, "the act of knowing or perceiving." So in discussing the cognitive development of children we seek to inquire into the process by which children grow in knowledge and in the ability to perceive, think, and understand, and then utilize these abilities to solve the practical problems of everyday living.

We begin this chapter with a discussion of perception, and continue with a discussion of the development of language, which is so important to all communication, learning, and problem solving. We then discuss the three basic approaches to the study of cognition. The first is the Piagetian approach, which emphasizes the qualitative changes in the way children think. The second is the information-processing approach, which examines the progressive steps, actions, and operations that take place when the child receives, perceives, remembers, thinks about, and utilizes information. The third approach is the psychometric approach, which measures quantitative changes in children's intelligence.

The chapter ends with a discussion of school, education, and achievement.

Perceptual Development

Perception

Perception means the act of apprehending or understanding by means of the senses.

DEPTH PERCEPTION

The ability to see things in three dimensions—to distinguish things that are closer from those that are farther away—is an ability that develops very early in infancy. Infants as young as 6 weeks of age will blink or show other avoidance reactions when objects approach their faces (Dodwell, Humphrey, & Muir, 1987). However, it takes about 4 months for full binocular vision to develop (Aslin & Smith, 1988). Five-month-old infants will try to grasp a closer object rather than a more distant one.

One well-known test of depth perception involves a special box on legs, two to three feet long (see Figure 8.1). One-half of the box has a shallow side, with a heavy piece of glass over a checkered floor which is about ten inches below the sides. The other half of the box provides an illusion of a cliff by the placement of the checkered material on the floor of the room several feet below the glass. The infant's mother stands first on the shallow side and then on the deep side, coaxing her infant to crawl toward her. Most of the infants 6 to 14 months of age who were old enough to crawl would not crawl to the deep side, indicating that they perceived depth. Those not old enough to crawl showed heart-rate changes when they were placed on the cliff side. Some cried, others crawled away from their mothers when coaxed to crawl over the cliff (Reed, 1988).

Not only do children develop the perception of depth, but they also develop the ability to portray depth and distance in the drawings they make. Preschool children represent front or behind by placing objects side by side. As they get older, children draw diagonal alignments to represent depth. Still older children use vertical arrangements more frequently, with the objects at the top of a picture being smaller and looking farther away (Braine, Schauble, Kugelmass, & Winter, 1993).

PERCEPTION OF FORM AND MOTION

During the first two years of life, the way that infants perceive the form of objects changes. Two-month-old infants notice patterns that have a high degree of contrast and that move (Bertenthal & Bradbury, 1992). Before 4 months of age, infants will notice the corners of black triangles that are mounted on white paper. They perceive parts of figures, rather than whole representations. Thus, infants see a square and a circle, rather than a square within a circle. By 4 or 5 months of age, and as they mature, they increasingly see a whole figure rather than just its parts. By 3 to 12 months

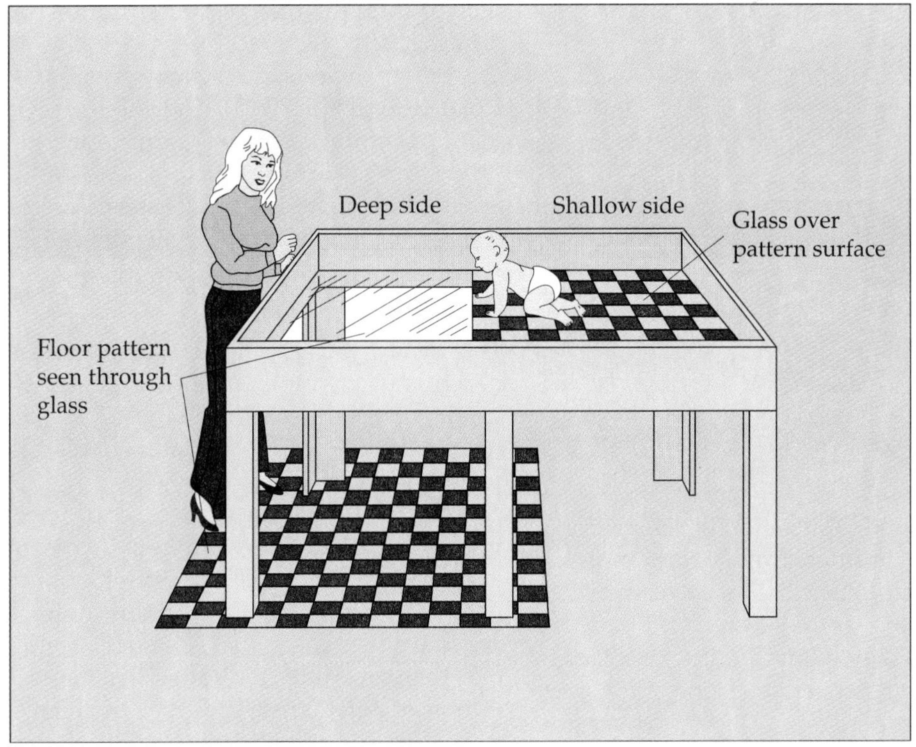

FIGURE 8.1 The mother calls her infant to the deep side to determine if the child perceives depth.

of age, children notice figures that are familiar enough to be recognized, but different enough to be novel. Figures that are too novel do not receive as much attention.

In one study, 12-month-olds were tested for object recognition through touch and through visual familiarization. The infants took longer to become familiar with objects through touch than through visual means. The researchers also found that the infants could recognize objects by touch that they had become familiar with visually and vice versa. This ability, called **cross-modal perception,** shows that infants have the ability to recognize the visual equivalent of objects that previously have only been touched (Rose & Orlian, 1991). They have somewhat less ability to recognize tactically objects that previously have only been seen.

Cross-modal perception—the ability to perceive objects with more than one sense

Research has also shown that there are wide individual differences in the speed at which infants process visual information. When presented with visual stimuli, some infants, called *long-lookers,* focus on the stimuli for relatively long periods of time, while others, called *short-lookers,* focus their attention for short intervals. Short-lookers are superior at perceptual-cognitive tasks because they are speedier and more efficient at stimulus-interpretation processing. In one study, these differences were found in infants who were only 4 months of age (Colombo, Mitchell, Coldren, & Freesemen, 1991).

PERCEPTION OF THE HUMAN FACE

Infants prefer to look at human faces rather than inert objects. This preference is characteristic of infants only 5 days old. By 1 month of age, babies can discriminate the faces of their mothers from the faces of strangers. By 3 months of age, they can recognize their mothers' faces in photographs and can recognize and discriminate faces of strangers. By 7 months of age, they can discriminate between fearful and happy facial expressions. It is evident that by 7 months of age their perceptual abilities are quite sophisticated (Nelson & Dolgin, 1985; Younger, 1992).

AUDITORY PERCEPTION

Auditory perception depends upon four factors: (1) auditory acuity or the ability to detect sound of minimum loudness, (2) the ability to detect sound of different frequen-

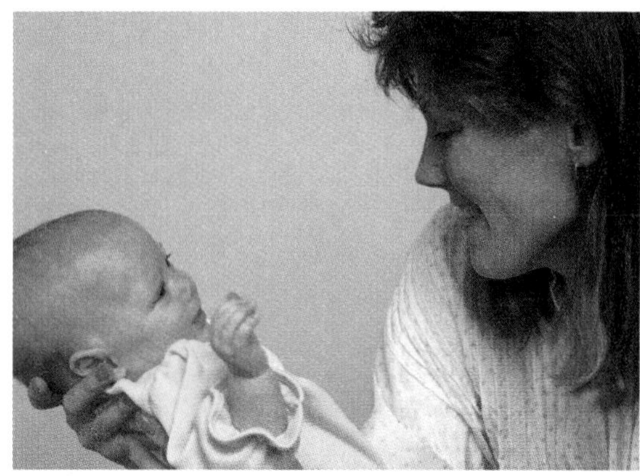

By one month of age babies can distinguish the face of their mothers from the faces of strangers.

cies, (3) sound localization or the ability to detect the direction from which sound is coming, and (4) the ability to detect silent gaps between words—also called auditory temporal acuity. Only the last two factors will be discussed in this section.

Gap threshold—the minimum detectable gap between sounds

Sound Localization

Sound localization is possible because the ears are placed on opposite sides of the head. This means the sound from one side arrives sooner and with a higher sound level than from the other side. These interaural time and level differences enable the listener to detect the direction from which the sound is coming. Research has shown that sound localization improves substantially during the first year after birth, with an especially high rate of change during the first half-year (Ashmead, Davis, Whalen, & Odom, 1991). The auditory system apparently has a very precise mechanism for registering interaural time differences and that this mechanism is in operation from the first few months of life.

Gap Detection

The ability to understand human speech depends partly on the ability to detect the spaces or gaps between words. If we did not detect these gaps or silent intervals, the words would seem to run together, so that speech would sound garbled. Gap detection, in turn, depends on a high degree of auditory temporal acuity. The minimum detectable gap, called the **gap threshold,** is considerably worse for 3- and 6-month-olds than for adults, indicating that gap-detection abilities are quite poor in infants. Gap detection is better for low-frequency sounds than for those of higher pitch. Tests of 12-month-olds indicate a wide variation in gap detection. Some perform no better than 3- to 6-month olds, while others attain thresholds close to those of adults (Werner, Marean, Halpin, Spetner, & Gillenwater, 1992). This means that adults need to speak more slowly to young children than to adults in order to make themselves understood.

Language

LANGUAGE AND COMMUNICATION

Long before they can use spoken words, human infants can communicate. The *rooting reflex* indicates an ability to suck and to eat. Various types of cries indicate upset, pain, or tiredness. *Nonverbal body language* includes such things as posture, facial expressions, still or tense muscles, movement, tears, sweating, shivering, or quivering. Alert parents learn to interpret these body signs and to give correct meaning to their expression.

Research indicates that gestural symbols or sign language may begin to appear earlier than vocal symbols; that is, gestural symbols can be easily acquired if parents encourage their development and read well their children's efforts. Verbal symbols follow rapidly as well. Around the first year of life, children may begin to acquire gestural symbols and use them in communication (Goodwyn & Acredolo, 1993).

Language, therefore, represents only one method of communication. It is certainly the most important, however. With it humans are able to transmit information, ideas, attitudes, and emotions to one another. With-

Infants communicate with body language long before they can speak.

out it, what we think of as meaningful human relationships would be impossible. Language enables humans to transcend space or time, to pass on the knowledge of millions of years gone by to future generations. Words and phrases convey information and share knowledge about things in general (Baldwin, 1993).

Language has a *generative function* also. It can be used to originate new ideas and thoughts by reordering words and phrases in combinations that have not been expressed before. Language goes beyond concrete experiences by using symbols to represent reality, yet in such a way that reality is understood. Above all, through thousands of words, language is an efficient way of communicating unlimited pieces of information, thoughts, ideas, and feelings from one person to others.

One study investigated the role of verbalization as children worked with partners on a scientific reasoning task (Teasley, 1995). When partners talk to one another during performance of the task, learning was affected very positively. The benefits of talk were more pronounced when children talked with a partner than when they talked to themselves. Fewer of the talk-alones were able to refine their scientific hypothesis. In addition, the talk dyad (that is, the pairs of children), developed their general hypothesis much more quickly than did the talk-alones. It is evident that verbalization supported reasoning about theories and evidence, and the presence of a partner made it more likely that this kind of reasoning would occur.

ELEMENTS AND RULES OF LANGUAGE

In accurately fulfilling its functions, language contains a finite set of elements that are used according to set rules. The basic elements of language include *phonemes, morphemes, syntax and grammar, semantics,* and *pragmatics* (Bialystok, 1992).

Phonemes

A **phoneme,** derived from the Greek word meaning "sound," is the smallest unit of sound in a language. There may be twenty to sixty phonemes, depending on the language. In English, everything we say is made up of only forty-four phonemes; that is, our language is generated from only forty-four basic sound distinctions. There are more phonemes than letters of the alphabet, because some letter combinations, such as *ch* and *th,* stand for different phonemes.

Phoneme—the smallest unit of sound in a language

Morphemes

Morphemes are the smallest units of meaning in a language. They may be single words, such as *word* or *help,* or they may exist in combination with other morphemes, such as *anti-biotic* or *push-ed.* Combinations of morphemes always occur in particular sequences according to set rules. We wouldn't say *biotic-anti,* for example. We know too that the article "the" occurs at the beginning of noun phrases and that the auxiliary verb "was" occurs at the beginning of verb phrases (Gerken and McIntosh, 1993). In developing language, children come to know thousands of morphemes.

Morpheme—the smallest unit of meaning in a language

Syntax

Syntax is the system of rules by which phonemes are combined in morphemes and morphemes are combined in words

Syntax—the grammatical rules of a language

Nativist view—says that children have a predisposition to learn language at a certain age

Language acquisition device—the inherited characteristics that enable children to listen to and imitate speech sounds and patterns

Semantics—the meaning of words and sentences

Pragmatics—the practical use of language to communicate with others in a variety of social contexts

and words are combined in phrases and sentences to form acceptable utterances. In English, we would say, "Mr. Jones went to town." We would not say, "Mr. Jones gone to town" or "Mr. Jones to town went." The formal description of syntactical rules comprises the grammar of the language.

Semantics

Semantics deals with the meanings of words and sentences. It assures proper word usage. Thus, a child learns that a pair of puppies is "two puppies," not "too puppies," or that *mother* is not synonymous with *woman*.

Pragmatics

Pragmatics refers to the practical use of language to communicate with others in a variety of social contexts (Capelli, Nakagawa, & Madden, 1990). Children learn appropriate choices of words and intensity of tone of voice when talking with their parents. They may use other words or vocal expressions when talking to their peers. These are practical applications of language. Pragmatics also refers to the ability to engage in meaningful conversation, to describe an event, or to explain something to a teacher. It's not enough to be able to know the correct usage of words and sentences. Children must be able to apply this knowledge in specific situations. This is the science of pragmatics.

THEORIES OF LANGUAGE DEVELOPMENT

One of the most amazing aspects of human development is how quickly children learn language. Infants progress from simple cooing and babbling of sounds to the acquisition of a vocabulary of thousands of words, plus an understanding of the basic rules of syntax and grammar. How can we explain this very rapid development of language? Basically there are four different theories of language development: *biological theory, learning theory, cognitive theory,* and *interactionist theory.*

Biological Theory

Biological theory (called the **nativist view**) says that children inherit a predisposition to learn language at a certain age (Chomsky, 1968). Chomsky (1980) and McNeill (1970) maintained that infants are born into the world with a **language acquisition device** (LAD) that enables them to listen to speech and to imitate sounds and sound patterns. The LAD enables them to produce phonemes at about 6 months, the first word at about 1 year, and the first sentences at about 2 years, regardless of the child's language, race, ethnic origin, or nationality. The development of language parallels neurological changes that occur as a result of maturation. In a sense, this biological view does not explain the origins of language. All it says is that children learn language because they have the neurological structure and biological equipment to learn it. If children are not exposed to a particular language, they don't learn it.

Learning Theory

Learning theory suggests that language is learned like other behavior is learned: through *imitation, conditioning, association,* and *reinforcement* (Skinner, 1957; 1983). Children hear others talk, they imitate the sounds. Parents point to objects, name them, and children repeat the words. Examples would be naming articles of clothing: "shoes," "shirts," "pants," and "socks" as each is put on. At other times when children repeat words, their behavior is rein-

Cultural influences shape speech habits and patterns.

PARENTING ISSUES

Maternal Speech in Four Cultures

Verbal interactions between mothers and children establish ties of closeness and warmth. Maternal speech also plays a substantial role in the child's early language learning. Bornstein and colleagues (1992) analyzed the contents of maternal speech to infants 5 and 13 months old in four cultures: Argentina, France, Japan, and the United States. Speech content was classified into whether it was predominantly affect (that is, with emotional content), or for purposes of giving information. Substantial differences were found in the speech content of mothers from the four different cultures in spite of the fact that mothers everywhere express feelings and supply information.

Mothers from all four cultures speak more to older infants than to younger ones, and the proportion of affect becomes a smaller proportion of maternal speech, while the proportion of information-giving increases. Apparently, over the second half of the first year of life, mothers expect that their infants need to be directed more.

Japanese mothers were highest in the use of speech with affect content reflecting an early child-rearing goal of empathizing with their infant's needs. Mothers from the three Western cultures more often favored information-giving speech and grammatically complete utterances in speaking to babies, indicating a desire to impart information to children at an early age. Argentine mothers more frequently made direct statements than mothers from the other three cultures, reflecting an authoritative, traditional child-rearing orientation. U.S. mothers tended to question their infants the most, emphasizing the child's participation in his or her own language development. "What does the toy do?" was a typical question. French mothers placed less emphasis on achievement-stimulation and more emphasis on using language to establish closeness and to provide emotional support.

The study reveals how cultural forces shape maternal speech to infants, which in turn reflects child-rearing emphasis and goals.

forced with a positive response. If they say "mama" or "dada" and are greeted with smiles, appreciation, and laughter, they are encouraged to repeat the word again. Not only do they learn to associate "mama" or "dada" with their parent, but calling mama or dada may bring food, a clean diaper, or cuddling. Their use of the word is *positively reinforced* because the repetition of it attracts their parents' attention and care. Similarly, they learn to say "bottle" when they want their milk, or they learn that saying "cookie" may bring a sweet.

Learning theory goes a long way in explaining the acquisition of language, but it does not explain everything. Children create sounds, words, phrases: "Mr. Fester, Dester, Mester, Pester." Children seem to like the sounds they create. Or they make up words for things if they don't know the correct names. A pacifier becomes a "gully." They can compose sentences that they have never heard before: "Daddy, bye bye, big truck."

Cognitive Theory

Cognitive theory emphasizes that language develops out of mental images, that it is a direct result of cognitive development. (Another theory, the Whorfian hypothesis, says that language influences thought rather than the other way around. This hypothesis has not been validated with research.) Piaget (1926) said that children form a mental scheme and then apply linguistic labels to it. For example, Eskimos have several different words for snow. It seems plausible that they first learned to perceive different consistencies among types of snow, and then invented a vocabulary for talking about them to others. Chil-

The biological theory of language development says that children inherit a predisposition to learn language at a certain age.

dren do the same thing. They begin to form concepts of things and actively construct their own grammar to express their thoughts. Children begin to master language near the end of the sensorimotor stage and near the beginning of the preoperational stage of cognitive development, when they use symbols to represent the environment.

Interactionist Theory

Interactionist theory emphasizes the equal importance of both biological maturation and the role of environmental influences and experiences in language development. Clearly the role of biology is important, but developing structures must have an environment in which they can be expressed.

INFLUENCES ON LANGUAGE DEVELOPMENT

It seems clear that no one theory alone explains language development. As a result, this book tends to reflect an interactionist perspective in which both biological maturation and environmental influences play important roles. A large body of research supports this point of view. It has been found, for example, that differences in children's temperament (which is partly inherited) exerts a major influence on language development from toddlerhood to middle childhood (Slomkowski, Nelson, Dunn, & Plomin, 1992). Extraversion or sociability increases language susceptibility and thus may be important for the development of language abilities. Phonological memory skills are also partly inherited and appear to exert a direct causal influence on lan-

Reading to children is one of the best ways to accelerate language development.

guage acquisition (Gathercole, Willis, Emslie, & Baddelep, 1992).

Environmental influences on language development are well known. Parental influences are especially important (Peterson & McCabe, 1994). Frequent dyadic interactions between infants and responsive adults are conducive to early language learning, as are mother-infant-sibling interactions (Barton & Tomasello, 1991). One study found that the time mothers spent interacting with 18- to 29-month-old children in different settings was an important influence on children's linguistic experience (Hoff-Ginsberg, 1991). The quality of parental speech also affects the quality of infants' vocalizations (Masataka, 1992). Hart and Risley (1992) divide group parenting variables that influence language development into three major categories: (1) the absolute amount of parenting per hour, (2) parents' social interaction with their children, and (3) the content quality of what parents say to their children. These factors were found to be related to the social and economic status of the family, and the subsequent IQ of the child (Hart & Risley, 1992). Another important factor is the interest parents show in their children's language development. One study showed that when parents correct the morpheme usage of their children, the children were two to three times more likely to use correct grammar (Farrar, 1992).

SEQUENCE OF LANGUAGE DEVELOPMENT

Prelinguistic Period

Children the world over seem to follow the same timetable and sequence of language development. Table 8.1 shows the sequence through 48 months of age. During the prelinguistic period, before children actually verbalize, they seem to understand far more than they can express (Kuczaj, 1986). Even newborns come to recognize their mother's voice. Even very young infants can perceive the sounds of human speech phonetically. They demonstrate categorical perception of consonants and can perceive different vowels (Marean, Werner, & Kuhl, 1992). Crying is the first

FOCUS

Accelerating Language Development of Mexican Day-Care Children Through Picture Book Reading

A research study was carried out with twenty Mexican 2-year-olds (from low-income backgrounds, who were attending day care) to determine the effect that reading children's books had on their language development. The children were monolingual (Spanish-speaking) from Tepic, Mexico. They were read to (in Spanish), one-on-one, for ten to twelve minutes on thirty consecutive school days, becoming very involved in discussing the stories with their teacher. The children were asked many questions and encouraged to help the teacher tell the story. Subsequent evaluations of the children's language development revealed large and enduring improvement, indicating that a dialogue-reading program is an important intervention technique in improving the language abilities of culturally deprived children (Valdez-Menchaca & Whitehurst, 1992).

Cooing—the initial vowel-like utterances by young infants

Babbling—one-syllable utterances containing vowels and consonants in combination

Holophrases—single words that infants use to convey different meanings

major sound uttered by the newborn. **Cooing** begins at about 2 months of age. It consists of squeals, gurgles, or vowel-like sounds of short duration such as "ahhh." Babbling begins at about 6 months of age. **Babbling** is one-syllable utterances, usually containing vowels and consonants in combinations, for example, "ma-ma-ma-ma." Most babbling is of sounds without meaning. Even deaf infants babble, so they are not imitating sounds they hear.

First Spoken Words

At about 10 months of age, infants use **holophrases,** which are single words that convey different meanings, depending on the context in which they are used. Only the parents may understand what the child is saying. By 12 months of age most infants are speaking one to three words that are recognizable language. "Mama" or "dada" may be the first words spoken. By 18 months, the average toddler knows three to ninety words, usually naming objects ("car"); animals ("doggie"); items of clothing ("shoes"); a part of the body ("eye"); or an important person ("mama") (Clark, 1983; Waxman & Hall, 1993).

Young children readily learn the meaning of words through definition, that is, through hearing the word used when things are pointed out ("This is an X") (Hall & Waxman, 1993). Action words such as "bye-bye," adjectives such as "hot," or adverbs such as "no" may also be included (Barrett, 1986; Nelson, 1981). The number of new words that children learn depends a lot on the extent of parent–child interaction. Some parents talk to their infants all the time. They name objects (Baldwin, 1991), repeat single words and phrases, ask questions, speak in short sentences, and converse with them whenever they are together. Word production and comprehension increase dramatically during the second year of life (Reznick and Goldfield, 1992). Children as young as two years of age may be able to identify proper names (e.g., "Tom," "Janet") (Hall, 1994).

An analysis of the speech of American and Japanese mothers to discover the differences in the ways mothers talk to their infants revealed that the American mothers emphasize the names of objects, providing labels frequently and consistently as they

TABLE 8.1
SEQUENCE OF LANGUAGE DEVELOPMENT

Age in months	*Language*
2	Begins making vowellike cooing sounds
4	Smiles, coos pitch-modulated, makes vowellike sounds interspersed with consonant sounds
6	Begins babbling (one-syllable utterances), vowels interspersed with consonants
8	Often uses two-syllable utterances such as "mama" or "baba," imitates sounds
10	Understands some words, gestures (may say "no" and shake head); uses holophrases (single words with different meanings)
12	Understands some simple commands; uses more holophrases such as "baby," "bye-bye," and "hi"; may imitate sounds of dog: "bow-wow"; some control over intonation
18	Vocabulary of 3 to 50 words; may use 2-word utterances; still babbles; uses words with several syllables with intricate intonation pattern
24	Vocabulary over 50 words; 2-word phrases; interested in verbal communication
30	Rapid increase in vocabulary; uses 3- to 5-word phrases; many grammatical errors; some children hard to understand; excellent comprehension
36	Vocabulary of 1,000 words, of which 80 percent intelligible; colloquial grammar; fewer syntactic errors
48	Well-established language; style may differ some from adult speech

Adapted from F. Caplan, *The First Twelve Months of Life* New York: Grosset and Dunlap, 1973, and E. H. Lenneberg, *Biological Foundations of Language,* pp. 128–130, New York: Wiley, 1973.

played with their infants. Japanese mothers label their toys less often than did American mothers, but used them more often in rituals of social exchange, for example, in verbal politeness routines (Fernald & Morikawa, 1993).

This tendency of adults to adjust their speech when talking to children is called **motherese**, though it could also be called fatherese. (D'Odorico & Franco, 1985; Lederberg, 1982). When speaking to young children, adults usually use a slower rate of speech, try to speak correct grammar, usually use a higher and more varied pitch, and use more present-tense words (Cooper & Aslin, 1990). When parents say "tum-tum" for stomach, or "choo-choo" for train, they are speaking motherese. Children pay more attention to speech that is directed specifically to them than they do to adult directed speech (Cooper & Aslin, 1994). Such interaction facilitates the development of understanding and the ability to communicate. It encourages children to talk about things they are experiencing.

Motherese—baby talk that adults use in speaking to infants

Two-Word Utterances

Two-word utterances **(duos)** usually begin when children are from 18 to 24 months of age. Children begin to combine words to express ideas that they want to communicate with others: "Amanda cry," "milk gone," "mama bye-bye." These expressions indicate knowledge of subject–predicate order. Other constructions are not acceptable English sentences: "More-water," "noup," "mamahat," "allgone soup." Two-word utterances represent attempts of children to express themselves through their own unique language (Clark, Gelman, & Lane, 1985).

Adults tend to speak at a slower rate, with correct grammar, when talking to young children.

TABLE 8.2
MEANINGS CONVEYED IN TWO-WORD UTTERANCES

Meaning	*Utterances*
Identification	"See kittie"
Location	"Table there"
Repetition	"More juice"
Nonexistence	"Allgone milk"
Negation	"Not doggie"
Possession	"Katy dress"
Attibution	"Big house"
Agent action	"Baby eat"
Action object	"Hurt daddy"
Action location	"Sit potty"
Question	"Where car?"

Children begin to use literally hundreds of two-word utterances, expressing many different meanings. Table 8.2 shows some of the meanings possible with two-word utterances.

Duos—two-word utterances

Telegraphic Speech

Telegraphic speech consists of two-, three-, or several-word utterances that convey meaning but exclude any unnecessary words such as articles, auxiliary verbs, conjunctions, prepositions, or other connectives. The speech is telegraphic, like a telegram that omits any unnecessary words, but still conveys meaning. "Daddy give Billy money" is an example of telegraphic speech. By 30 months of age, children are using three- to five-word phrases. Vocabulary may have grown to 1,000 words by age 3 (R. Brown, 1975).

Telegraphic speech—several-word utterances that convey meaning

Sentences

From $2^1/_2$ to 4 years of age, children are using multiple-word sentences (three to five words are common), each with a subject and predicate and with fewer grammatical errors. The syntax may still differ from adult speech, but improvement continues. The following are examples (Wood, 1981).

FOCUS

Is There a Critical Period for Learning Language?

One major question in language development research is whether there is a critical period during which human beings are especially receptive to acquiring language. As we have seen in Chapter 6, brain lateralization (or localization) of language functions takes place in the left hemisphere of the brain (Kee, Gottfried, Bathurst, & Brown, 1987). One point of view is that because language lateralization in the left hemisphere begins during the early years of life, language itself must also be acquired early or it becomes impossible or difficult to learn (Witelson, 1987).

Studies of severely abused and neglected children who are not exposed to language early in childhood lend some support for this hypothesis. Historically, there have been about sixty recorded cases of children who are abandoned in the wild at an early age, but who survived and were eventually returned to human society. Among the sixty cases, eleven children (ranging in age between 4 and 18) acquired some but very immature language ability. The rest of the children never learned any language (Reich, 1986).

The most famous modern case was *Genie,* who was a normal, alert, responsive baby until 20 months of age. At that time she was isolated naked in the back room of her parents' home, harnessed to a potty-chair, and only able to move her hands and feet. At night,

"She's a pretty baby."
"Read it, my book."
"Where is daddy?"
"I can't play."
"I would like some milk."
"Take me to the store."
"Ask what time it is."

Between the ages of 4 and 5, children's sentences average four to five words. They can use locative words like *over, under, in, on, up, down, here,* and *behind,* and they use more verbs than nouns (Stockman & Cooke-Vaughn, 1992). Between ages 5 and 6, sentences consist of six to eight words, including some conjunctions, prepositions, and articles. The first interrogatives are usually "where?" and "what?", followed by "who?", "how?", and "why?" (Bloom, Merkin, & Wooten, 1982). By ages 6 and 7, children's speech resembles that of adults. They can use correct grammar, all parts of speech, and can construct compound and complex sentences.

VOCABULARY AND SEMANTICS

Preschool and early school-age children seem to soak up new words like a sponge. Children typically produce about 320 words at 24 months of age and about 570 words at 30 months (Mervis & Bertrand, 1994). Their vocabulary continues to grow to between 8,000 and 14,000 words at age 6 (Carey, 1977; Smith, Jones, & Landau, 1992). Estimates of the size of children's vocabulary vary widely (Nagy & Anderson, 1984). We do know that vocabulary growth continues at a high rate well through adolescence and adulthood. Children learn nouns before verbs, followed by adjectives, adverbs, conjunctions, and interrogatives (Waxman &

she was laced in a kind of straight jacket and enclosed in a wire cage. She was fed sparingly by her brother, who was not permitted to talk to her. She only heard her father's doglike barking when he beat her for crying or making noise.

When she was discovered at age 13 in 1970, she had no bowel or bladder control, could not stand erect, could not chew solid food, and could neither speak nor understand language. After her release, doctors at Los Angeles Children's Hospital took care of her bodily needs and nursed her back to health. Psychologists were called in to evaluate her mental and emotional state and begin socialization, including teaching language.

Genie made some limited progress in language development. After seven years, she learned as much language as a normal child learns in two to three years. By age 24, she lacked some of the language skills of 5-year-olds. She developed a fairly large vocabulary, could comprehend everyday conversation, but had limited knowledge of grammar, could not use some syntactic forms such as pronouns, showed poor pitch control, and was not able to use intonation to express meaning. Neurolinguistic assessments revealed that Genie used the right hemisphere of her brain to process linguistic information. Apparently, the developmental period had passed during which specialized language areas in the left hemisphere could facilitate language learning (Curtis, 1977). Nonlanguage areas in the right hemisphere were forced to take over language functioning, but never efficiently, particularly with grammar. The case of Genie gives some support to the critical period hypothesis, although it is impossible to determine the extent to which malnutrition, physical and mental abuse, and social isolation affected her language retardation (Pines, 1981).

Kosowski, 1990). Basic nouns such as *cars* are learned before specific nouns such as *Porsches* or more inclusive nouns such as *vehicles* (Matlin, 1983; Waxman & Senghas, 1992). Upon hearing a new word for an object, children have to learn whether it is a proper noun that refers to an individual (e.g., "Garfield") or a regular noun that refers to a kind of object of which the individual is a member (e.g., "cat") (Hall, 1991). By about 1 year of age, children begin to group objects from a single category: for example, they place all balls in a single pile. By 18 months of age, children begin to form multicategory groupings of all objects in an array. For example, they will place all boxes in one pile and all balls in another. This ability to categorize objects bears a close relation to naming in young children (Gopnik & Meltzoff, 1992).

Children learn new words through conversation and reading.

One of the difficulties in obtaining an accurate assessment of the size of vocabulary is in finding an acceptable definition of what it means to "know a word." Does it mean being able to comprehend the word, to define it, or to use it in a sentence? Usually children comprehend a word before they can define it or speak it. However, their knowledge may be only partial or incorrect. Because some words have several meanings, comprehension of meanings is built slowly, usually through repeated exposure (Mezynski, 1983). Children learn new words by noticing how they are used, the context in which they are found, and their relationships to other words (Golinkoff, Hirsh-Pasek, Bailey, & Wenger, 1992; Nagy, Herman, & Anderson, 1985). A single exposure teaches little about a word's many meanings and the subtleties of its use. Children learn new words through conversation and through reading. The more others talk and read to children, and the more children read themselves, the more opportunities they have of learning new vocabulary (Wilson, 1985). Children who are early talkers do not necessarily become early readers, but parents' reading to children contributes to the development of their reading skills (Crain-Thoreson & Dale, 1992). Children who have superior phonological skills do have an advantage in learning about spelling sequences in reading (Goswami, 1991b).

GRAMMAR

Grammar—the formal description of structure and rules that a language uses to communicate meaning

Grammar is the formal description of structure and rules that a language uses to communicate meaning. Grammar defines word from (such as singular or plural of nouns or verbs); word order in sentences; the relationship of words to one another; the use of modifiers; the use of clauses and phrases; tenses of verbs; the use of suffixes and prefixes; the subjective, objective, and possessive forms of pronouns; and the use of interrogatives and negatives. Grammar includes the correct pronunciation of words and proper intonations. Grammar is all-important in understanding language. It makes a difference whether we are told "Billy hit Johnny" or "Johnny hit Billy." Our knowledge of grammar enables us to understand who hit whom.

Children do not use adult syntactic structures immediately, but they do start showing some knowledge from the time they begin to combine words into sentences (MacWhinney, 1982). They learn to put the subject before the verb and the verb before the object. They learn singular and plural forms, verb tenses, and interrogatives such as "Where are you going?" Their understanding of negatives progresses from "no nap" to "I don't want to go to sleep because I am not tired." They learn which words can modify nouns and in what order. They will make increasing use of adjectives to describe nouns, and adverbs to modify verbs, adjectives, or other adverbs. They will say: "That's a very beautiful bicycle," for example. School-age children continue to learn increasingly complex structures, such as those with conjunctions and difficult clauses: "Although Wednesday was a school day, George did not go because he was sick." They learn to sort out ideas in clauses that are embedded in sentences: "The man who is 75 years old finished painting the house."

Children as young as five years of age can identify and repeat the subjects of a sentence (Ferreira & Morrison, 1994). Children younger than school age have difficulty in understanding the use of verbs in the passive voice. Children are used to the subject of the sentence acting upon an object, and not the subject being acted upon. During the elementary school years, they learn the difference between saying "The ball was hit by the boy" and "The boy hit the ball." They learn that the ball didn't do the hitting. Romaine (1984) found that compared with 6-year-olds, 8-year-olds used the passive voice two and a half times more frequently, and 10-year-olds three and a half times more frequently.

PRAGMATICS

Pragmatics, the practical ability to use language to communicate with others in a variety of social contexts, is an aspect of language use that develops during the

Children often use bad language to get attention.

PARENTING ISSUES

When Your Child Uses Bad Language

By the age of 2 to 4, most children have picked up a number of words their parents prefer they not use in polite company. Children seem to delight in bathroom language: "poo-poo," "ca-ca," and "wee-wee" (and large numbers of other words). They enjoy repeating them at the most inappropriate times, and soon learn that such words bring giggles from other children and that they can be used to shock parents and get their immediate attention. If parents swear, children pick up this language also.

With young children (preschool age), the less fuss made about such words, the better. If parents pay too much attention, and act shocked, the attention children receive acts as positive reinforcement and only encourages their using the language even more.

As children get older, they will hear a variety of sexual words and swear words from other children and adults. Four-letter slang words for sexual parts or functions sound indecent when repeated by 10-year-olds.

There are several things parents can do.

1. They need to avoid using the language themselves. If parents say it, children will say it.
2. They need to avoid being shocked. If children can shock parents, they may try to do it even more.
3. They can use correct language for sexual parts and functions. Certainly, *penis, vagina, anus,* or *urinate* don't have the negative connotations of their slang counterparts.
4. Parents need to let children know that they and other parents disapprove of the language. Parents don't need to accept "dirty talk" from children. Sometimes children use words but don't know the real meaning. Parents need to explain the meaning and why they disapprove. Usually, by discussing the issues of language with their children, and setting up a few guidelines, the cooperation of children can be obtained.

elementary school years. Preschool and young school-age children may talk a lot, but they sometimes have difficulty in making themselves understood. They often begin by getting attention: "Guess what?" They may stop to see if others are listening or if they are understood. "Are you listening?" They may pause, start again, repeat themselves, correct themselves, or change subjects. However, they do learn to take turns in talking and to show by various means that they are listening. Parents try hard to teach them to say "please" and "thank you," not to interrupt others, and to speak respectfully to adults. The following is a conversation among second-graders (Dorval & Eckerman, 1984):

1. Well, we . . . uh . . . have paper plates . . . with turkey on it and lots of (unintelligible). You know.
2. Doo-doo-doo-doo-doo (singing)
3. I don't know what you're talking about.
4. You know what? My uncle killed a turkey.
5. Not frying pan?
6. No.
7. I seen a frying pan at Hulen's store!

Children's conversation can be quite disjointed, shifting off topic and often containing many false starts ("The car . . . it was . . . uh . . . the door . . . the kid he pushed on the door . . . he closed it hard.")

Contrast this conversation with that of fifth-graders (Dorval & Eckerman, 1984, p. 22):

1. Be quiet! Start off, Billy, what if you was the teacher?
2. OK. If I was the teacher, I'd give us less work and more time to play . . . and I'd be mean to y'all, too.

FOCUS

The Importance of Context

Ebeling & Gelman (1994) told a story of conducting a study that involved showing children a series of pictures that were each stored in a separate envelope. Hoping to sustain the children's interest, the researchers sometimes gave subjects the opportunity to help out by removing pictures from the envelopes. One day, the researcher held out an envelope containing a card, and asked the 4-year-old she was testing, "Would you like to take this one out?" The boy gave the researcher a surprised look and then, without saying a word, took the envelope, opened the door of the testing room, and carried it outside the building. The child's misinterpretation shows how important it can be to make appropriate use of context.

3. OK. Ann (meaning that it is her turn).
4. If I was the teacher, I'd do work . . . um. I'd sit around and watch TV. I wouldn't assign no papers . . . umm . . .
5. I'd let y'all watch TV stories.
6. I'd turn the TV on Channel 4 at 9:30 to watch "Popeye"!

One characteristic of children's conversation at this age is that it stays with a topic.

GENDER AND COMMUNICATION PATTERNS

Peer interactions are influential contexts for modeling and enforcing gender norms for social relationships and roles. Boys' interactions are often oriented around independence, competition, and dominance. In contrast, girls' interactions are generally based on cooperation, closeness, and interpersonal harmony. Girls are more likely than boys to deploy language strategies that demonstrate support, responsivity, and attentiveness. In contrast, boys use more strategies that establish dominance, give orders, and demand attention.

Gender differences in interpersonal style have been observed in children as young as 3 years of age. Preschool boys tend to use more demanding and more direct communicative strategies with their peers; preschool girls typically use more cooperative and polite strategies.

These trends continue in children between the ages of 3 and 7 years. By age 7, children have acquired gender constancy (knowledge that one will remain a particular gender) and learned gender stereotypes. During the shift to middle childhood, interaction strategies become even more gender-differentiated. Girls become

There are some gender differences in communication style.

PARENTING ISSUES

Talking about Feelings

The ability to talk about feelings—to communicate when distressed or happy—has major implications for children's social relationships. Language studies have revealed substantial increases in the frequency of children's references to feelings in the third and fourth years. During this period, children develop increasing ability to use their knowledge of others' thoughts, desires, and intentions to explain observed behavior and to infer how others feel in emotion-provoking situations.

In the emotionally charged atmosphere of daily family life, talk about feelings is important in children's efforts to influence their own and others' emotions. Studies of family conversations about feelings offer a unique opportunity to examine quantitative and qualitative developments in children's social interactions in the preschool period. To whom does the child relate and talk as he or she grows up and becomes a more capable participant in family conversations?

One longitudinal study examined the developmental changes in early conversations about feelings. Some fifty families with second-born children were observed at home when the younger siblings were 33 months old and again at 47 months of age. The mean age gap between the siblings was 43 months (range 16–73 months) (Brown & Dunn, 1992). The patterns of interactions between preschool children and their parents changed a great deal over the fourteen months. As the siblings aged, they directed more conversation to each other and discussed feelings more often. However, when talking about feelings, each sibling usually tried to draw the other's attention to his or her own feelings. The conversation tended to be self-centered. In contrast, mother–child talk was "care-taking" in which the mother tried to comfort, acknowledging the child's hurts or fears, and referring to the child's reactions in an effort to influence the child's behavior.

Some children are taught to suppress their emotions and feelings.

more competent in their collaborative strategies; boys remain relatively unchanged in their domineering influence patterns. Girls' use of language that emphasizes mutual cooperation and boys' use of language that emphasizes dominance reflect these learned gender stereotypes (Leaper, 1991).

BILINGUALISM

One half of the world's population is *bilingual.* In North America, millions of children grow up in bilingual families or in families where English is not the dominant or preferred language. Many questions arise regarding bilingualism. What effect does a second language have on the first? When should a second language be taught?

From some children in groups where their first language is a minority language, a second language may be a subtractive influence. That is, the minority children become less fluent in their first language as their language skills improve in the second. Because the second language is the dominant language, the one others speak and the one used in the community and the media, the

PARENTING ISSUES

Stuttering

In the past, shuttering was considered a symptom of disturbed interpersonal relationships and emotional maladjustment. As a consequence, parents bore a burden of guilt for their child's problem. Currently, except in cases of a traumatic event or illness, stuttering appears to have a genetic base with environmental factors either aggravating the predisposition to stutter or helping children to overcome it. If one identical twin stutters, there is a 77 percent chance the other will too. Only one out of three fraternal twins of stutterers also stutters. Stuttering seems to result from difficulty in coordinating respiration, larynx functioning, and articulation.

There are several ways parents can help.

1. Speak slowly and simply, giving children the feeling that they have more time to talk.
2. Before responding to the child's speech, allow more time after he or she talks, so children feel more relaxed and less hurried.
3. Minimize stress in the home because anxiety and stress can trigger stuttering.
4. Find a quiet time during the day to talk with the children.
5. Don't overreact to early speech problems or temporary lapses in fluency. Many young children stutter over words or repeat phrases, particularly when tired or excited.
6. If the problem persists, seek professional help during the period of most rapid speech development, between ages 2 and 7. It's better to correct the problem before children become neurotic about their speech (Chollar, 1988b).

children come to prefer it. The first language receives little support and attention outside the home; it is not taught in school, so the children have little opportunity to read or write it (Landry, 1987). As a result, competence in the minority language suffers.

For children whose first language is the majority language, learning a second language is largely an additive experience (Cummins & Swain, 1986). Thus, English-speaking children enrolled in French- or Spanish-language programs can develop linguistic skills in the second language without interfering with their competence in English (Genesee, 1985). Good bilingual programs not only develop proficiency in a second language, but also can strengthen the first language (Umbel, Pearson, Fernandes, & Oiles, 1992).

Research indicates, however, that *instruction for minority group children should be primarily in the minority language,* with English learned as the second language. One study showed that when French minority group children were taught in French, with English taught as the second language, their French not only became better than that of French children who were taught primarily in English, but their English became better as well (Cummins, 1986). When a person learns two languages, the process does not involve competition for mental resources (Hakuta & Garcia, 1989). Research has also shown that formal instruction in the second language can be introduced in early elementary grades, provided the children are already proficient in their majority language, that the teachers are bilingual and trained and skilled in language teaching, that the language to be learned and the native language are both of relatively high status in the culture, and that parents and the community are supportive of the program (McLaughlin, 1985).

Learning to Read

Learning to read is an important milestone in the total development of children. Educators are not in complete agreement as to the best ways to teach children to read. In this section, we are concerned with the total process, with various methods that are used, and with those factors that contribute to the development of this skill.

FAMILY BACKGROUND INFLUENCES

Early experiences at home have an influence on children's literacy development. One of those experiences is reading stories. Children who are read to during early years typically enjoy higher levels of success in learning to read than their peers who have not been read to. When stories are read to children, children learn that words have meanings and that words can be used to tell stories. They begin to associate the content of the story with what is written on the pages of the book. Most children's stories have pictures that add meaning to the words themselves. The more that children are read to, the more they want the experience because they want to know what the words and the story are about. The evidence suggests that hearing and responding to stories read from books is probably the most important literacy experience a preschooler can have. Parents also provide other literacy experiences. One of these is talking and conversing with children. Parents who are quite verbal expose their children to numerous words, and help the children to learn that the words are associated with certain meanings. Many parents teach children letters of the alphabet. Other parents point to words and to the letters in these words so children learn to recognize what some words say. Parents may give children a piece of paper and a pencil to write a letter to grandma or for the child to learn to write his or her name. Some parents even sound out letters phonetically so children learn what different letters say. In summary, experiences in the family help children develop an understanding that reading involves deriving meaning from print and the knowledge that letters of the alphabet represent phonemes (speech sounds). Children bring these understandings to their first-grade reading instruction. High levels of language development in preschoolers are associated with easy and frequent access to literacy activities in the home.

APPROACHES TO TEACHING READING

Skills approach

Whole-language approach

Phonics approach

Word recognition approach

There are essentially two different approaches to teaching reading, the **skills approach** and the **whole-language approach.** The skills approach may include either the **phonics approach** or the **word recognition approach.** As explained earlier in this chapter, a phoneme is the smallest unit of sound in the language. In English, everything we say is made up of forty-four phonemes; that is, our language is generated from only forty-four basic sound distinctions. There are more phonemes than letters of the alphabet because some letter combinations, such as *ch* and *th* stand for different phonemes. The phonics approach to teaching reading involves learning what sounds different letters make. Children learn that letters of the alphabet represent phonemes and that each phoneme has a particular sound. By sounding out the phonemes in a word, and then combining these, the words are distinguished. The child has learned to read a word when he or she has correctly sounded out all the let-

One approach to teaching reading is the word recognition approach.

ters of that word. There is now a massive body of evidence to link the development of reading skills in children to their underlying phonological skills. (Hatcher, Hulme, & Ellis, 1994). Children who are good at phonological analysis have early reading success. Thus the ability to learn to read suggests ability to detect phonemes. (Hansen & Bowey, 1994). Phonological awareness tasks are among the best predictors of reading skill and, typically, these relationships can be shown to account for significant amounts of variance in reading skill, even after the effects of intelligence have been sorted out. The relation between phonological skill and reading skill is reciprocal. Phonological sensitivity facilitates early reading acquisition, and learning to read facilitates subsequent psychological awareness (Wagner, Torgesen, & Rashotte, 1994).

Another skill approach in teaching reading is to teach word recognition. In this approach, which is sometimes called the "look-say" approach, the child starts with whole words and eventually begins to think about them in terms of their parts—letters and sounds. By looking at the word while it is repeated, the child learns to make the same sound when he or she is looking at the word. Or sometimes a word is a description of a picture so the teacher can point to the picture and say, "What picture is this?" and the child repeats the whole word. To be able to recognize words, children have attained some word-decoding skills. In recognizing the word *house,* they perhaps have used the "ou," as well as the "h" and the "se," in order to not be able to confuse *house* with similarly spelled words. Word recognition sets the stage for increasing reading comprehension because children can now devote their mental resources to understanding the meaning of the text rather than recognizing words.

Children who are good at phonics have early reading success.

There is no question about it—the more capable children become in phonologically processing, the better they are able to read. In turn, early reading experiences teaches phonological analysis. Here again, the relationships are reciprocal. Phonological sensitivity facilitates early reading acquisition, and learning to read facilitates subsequent phonological awareness. For this reason, many teachers teach phonics as well as word recognition because each skill enhances abilities of the other (Wagner, Torgesen, & Rashotte, 1994).

The second major approach to teaching reading is the whole language approach, which stresses that reading instruction should parallel children's natural language learning. Reading materials are presented as a whole and are meaningful. That is, in early reading instruction, children are presented with materials in their complete form, such as in stories and poems. The whole-language approach helps children appreciate language's communicative function. Thus children learn the meaning of a text and they then begin to abstract and arrive at word attack skills.

From one point of view, this approach is very natural to children. They learn a story before they learn the words that comprise that story and before they learn the phonetic pronunciation of those words. This is like learning to play music by ear before one learns to read the notes. Proponents of the whole-language approach emphasize that it engages children in actual reading while they are acquiring basic decoding skills, and not after a long initial period of skills instruction. Critics of the whole-language approach say that teachers sometimes underplay the need for some explicit skills instruction, certainly some instruction in phonics.

It must be emphasized that the whole-language approach does not emphasize memorizing complete sentences or whole utterances. The number of permissible English sentences of twenty words or less is on the order of 10^{20}. It would take about one hundred billion centuries simply to utter these, let alone learn them by rote. What is stored there, therefore, cannot be

FOCUS

Functional Illiteracy

Literacy is essential for functioning in industrial societies. Reading and writing skills are keys to a lifetime learning process in our society where job requirements change continuously. Moreover, literacy enables active participation in society, because many of political and economic transactions are based on written documents. However, there are significant literacy problems in the United States. The United States ranks 49 among 159 members of the United Nations in its average level of literacy. The number of adults who are not functionally literate in the United States is estimated to be between 54 and 64 million. About one-fifth of all young adults and about one-half to one-third of minority young adults in the United States read under the eighth-grade level. The number of individuals who have levels of literacy that are not adequate for active participation in advanced society is a real problem.

There are all degrees of functional illiteracy. Some individuals may have the ability to sign documents even though they cannot read them very well. They may be able to recognize traffic signs or extract information from television program listings. Others have skills that are insufficient for daily tasks, such as making out a check, locating dosage information on a medicine label, filling in a school registration form, or using classified advertisements. Because of the historical trend in the job market that requires increasing proportions of jobs with higher levels of skill and literacy, functionally illiterate adults or semi-illiterate adults are ill equipped to enter today's work force (Baydar, Brooks-Gunn, & Furstenberg, 1993).

whole sentences; instead, it must be the discreet units—words—of which utterances are composed (Jusezyk, Cutler, Redanz, 1993). Most experts agree that a balance between explicit skills instruction and experience in authentic reading offers the best approach to beginning, reading.

Approaches to the Study of Cognition

There are three basic approaches to the study of cognition during childhood. One is the **Piagetian approach,** which emphasizes the qualitative changes in the ways children think. A second is the **information-processing approach,** which examines the progressive steps, actions, and operations that take place when the child receives, perceives, remembers, thinks about, and utilizes information. The third approach is the **psychometric approach,** which measures quantitative changes in children's intelligence. Each of these approaches is discussed in this chapter.

Piagetian approach

Information-processing approach

Psychometric approach

A Piagetian Perspective

As discussed in Chapter 2, the Swiss developmental psychologist Jean Piaget outlined four stages of cognitive development: the *sensorimotor stage* (birth to 2 years), the *preoperational stage* (2 to 7 years), the *concrete operational stage* (7 to 11 years), and the *formal operational stage* (11 years and up). The formal operational stage is discussed in the sections of this book on adolescence.

SENSORIMOTOR STAGE (BIRTH TO 2 YEARS)

Piaget (1954, 1963) labeled the first stage of cognitive development the sensorimotor period because it involves learning to respond through motor activity to the various stimuli that are presented to the senses. The child not only hears and sees a rattle, but learns how to grasp it, shake it, or suck on it (Ruff, Saltarelli, Capozzoli, & Dubines, 1992). *The task is learning to coordinate sensorimotor sequences to solve simple problems.* Piaget has subdivided the sensorimotor period into six substages.

1. *Stage one (0 to 1 month)—exercising reflexes.* Infants use their inborn reflexes and gain some control over them. For example, they suck whatever is near their mouth or grasp whatever touches their palm. They practice these and other reflexes repeatedly and become more proficient, but they can't reach out to deliberately suck or grasp the object.

The sensorimotor period of cognitive development involves learning to respond to various stimuli through motor activity.

2. *Stage two (1 to 4 months)—primary circular reactions.* Infants repeat pleasurable behavior that occurs by chance (such as thumb sucking). By chance, a child's thumb touches the mouth, which triggers the sucking reflex, which results in a pleasurable sensation, which leads to a repetition of the response. This circular reaction is called *primary* because it involves the child's own body.

3. *Stage three (4 to 8 months)—secondary circular reactions.* The child accidentally does something interesting or pleasing, like moving an overhead mobile. The action is then deliberately repeated to obtain the same result. (The action-reaction is circular.) It is called *secondary* because it happens outside the child's own body.

4. *Stage four (8 to 12 months)—purposeful coordination of secondary schemes.* Behavior is more deliberate and purposeful as infants coordinate motor activities with sensory input. Thus, infants will look at and grasp a rattle, or see a toy across the room and crawl to it. They begin to anticipate events and to try out previous schemes to solve problems in present situations. They will, for example, lean toward an object when trying to grasp it when their arm is too short (McKenzie, Skouteris, Day, Hartman, & Yonas, 1993). If they feel the distance is too great to reach across even when leaning, some children by 5 months of age will not attempt the reach (Yonas & Hartman, 1992).

5. *Stage five (12 to 18 months)—tertiary circular reactions.* In this stage, babies begin to experiment with novel actions to see what will happen rather than merely repeating behavior patterns they have already learned. They use trial and error to find the most efficient way of reaching new goals. The stage is called *tertiary reactions* because their purpose is to explore. For example, a child will crawl into a box, then lie down in the box, then put it on his or her head, or try to put the cat into the box.

6. *Stage six (18 to 24 months)—mental solutions.* Children begin to think about problems to find mental solutions; that is, they begin to internalize actions and their consequences, no longer relying exclusively on trial and error. Thus, they begin to develop insight into how to solve simple problems. This development is accompanied by a growing ability to use word symbols (language) in dealing with people and situations.

Object Permanence

One of the accomplishments during the sensorimotor stage is the development of a concept of **object permanence—**the knowledge that an object continues to exist independent of our seeing, hearing, touching, tasting, or smelling it (Piaget, 1954). According to Piaget, during stage three (4 to 8 months), infants will search for a partially hidden object that is already present (Baillargeon & DeVos, 1991). During stage four (8 to 12 months), infants will search for objects that have disappeared, but only in the place previously found, even if they saw it moved to a new place. During stage five (12 to 18 months), toddlers will follow a series of object displacements and will search for the object, but only where they have observed it being hidden. They can't imagine it being moved without their seeing it. And finally, during stage six, object permanence is fully developed. Toddlers can figure where an object might be, and will look for it, though they didn't see it placed there (Bai & Bertenthal, 1992).

According to some modern researchers using different and more refined techniques, the acquisition of object permanence comes at younger ages than Piaget claimed (Harris, 1983). Baillargeon (1987) found that infants as young as $3^1/2$ months seemed to hold some primitive and short-lived memories of absent objects. But this does not mean that the infants would search for objects that had not been present recently. So there was no real sense of object permanence.

One study of infants under 1 year of age tested their ability to group animals into two basic categories—cats and horses. The infants excluded cats, zebras, and giraffes under the horse category. Lions were excluded from the category of cats. It is only gradually that young infants are able to arrange animals into categories based upon perceptual knowledge. Acquiring an understanding of the perceptual basis of categorization, even a partial understanding, is always relevant in as much as the appearance of things informs children and adults, at least in part, about the functions of objects (Eimas & Quinn, 1994; Thomas, 1995).

Imitation

Another characteristic of the sensorimotor stage is **imitation,** or copying the behavior of another. Meltzoff and Moore (1977, 1979) found that 2-week-old infants will imitate adults sticking out their tongue or opening their mouth wide. In more recent studies, Reissland (1988) in an experiment with twelve neonates in the first hour after birth found that when adults bent over the infants and either widened their lips or pursed them, the neonates moved their lips in a similar manner. Kaitz, Meschulach-Sarfaty, Auerbach, and Eidelman (1988) found that infants 10 to 51 hours old demonstrated modeling of tongue protrusion but not of facial expressions.

Imitation—copying the behavior of another

Object permanence—the concept that an object continues to exist independent of our perceiving it

Piaget (1962) maintained that imitation is not likely to occur before 9 to 12 months of age, but he was talking about **deferred imitation—**imitating someone or something no longer present. A 2-year-old who diapers her dolly in the absence of her mother is exhibiting deferred imitation. Meltzoff (1988) had a model perform six different actions with six different objects in the presence of a group of 14-month-old infants. The infants were not allowed to interact with the model and objects. One full week later, when showed the same objects, the infants showed a tendency to imitate the behavior of the model. This means the infants had the ability to make mental images of the behavior, to remember it, and to do it one week later. This ability is important to language development and to many aspects of learned behavior.

Deferred imitation—imitating someone or something no longer present.

PREOPERATIONAL STAGE (2 TO 7 YEARS)

Piaget called the second stage preoperational thinking because a mental operation involves logical thought, and children at this stage do not yet have this ability to

PARENTING ISSUES

Offering Environmental Stimulation

One important requirement for mental growth is that children be reared in an intellectually stimulating environment (Pellegrini, Perlmutter, Galda, & Brody, 1990). Infants begin to get acquainted with their world from the moment of birth. If they have a variety of objects to see, touch, or taste; different sounds to hear; or different odors to smell; they learn more than if their exposure is quite limited. Sensory stimulation encourages motor learning and coordination as infants reach out to grasp or as they toddle forward. Auditory stimulation, especially exposure to words, encourages language development and speech.

But what children learn, and how much, depends not only on the amount of stimulation but also on its type, variety, intensity, regularity, duration, and timing. Children who are regularly given appropriate materials are going to learn more from their play activities over periods of time than children whose exposure is more limited. Children who are encouraged to explore the environment around them will learn faster than those who are not given much opportunity to move about. Children whose parents handle them, talk to them, and play with them will learn more than children who are left alone for long periods of time without social contacts. Parents who take their children out with them are going to increase their knowledge and understanding of the world to a greater extent than parents who never permit their children out of their own yard.

Maximum mental growth takes place when children are stimulated mentally from infancy on, year after year. No one year, experience, or situation is as important as what happens over several years of growth. Mental growth may accelerate when children are exposed to an enriching environment, such as that provided by a superior teacher, but growth then stops or even reverses when children are economically and intellectually deprived for a period of time.

Of course, it is entirely possible to expose children to excessive stimulation or to experiences inappropriate to their age level. In face-to-face interactions with their infants, some parents try too hard to get their attention, resulting in an information overload that causes infants to avert their gaze and turn away. Children can tolerate only a certain amount of stimulation, after which they want to escape and not respond. The same principle holds true in the classroom. The teacher who tries to expose the students to too much material in too short a time causes them to become uninterested in further learning. The maximum learning takes place when teachers or parents take their cues from their children and expose them to as much as they can assimilate at a time and no more.

think logically. Instead, children develop the ability to deal with the word *symbolically,* or *representationally.* That is, they develop the ability to imagine doing something, rather than actually doing it. For example, a child in the sensorimotor stage of development learns how to pull a toy along the floor. A child reaching the preoperational stage of development develops a mental representation of the toy and a mental picture of pulling the toy. If the child can use words to describe the action, it is accomplished mentally and symbolically through the use of words. One of the major accomplishments during this period is the development of language, the ability to think and communicate by using words that represent objects and events.

Symbolic play—using one object to represent another in play

Symbolic Play

Symbolic, or pretend, **play** also becomes more frequent each year of the preoperational period (Rubin, Fein, & Vandenberg, 1983). A 2-year-old child may use one object (such as a teddy bear) to symbolize an-

Pretend play becomes frequent during the preoperational period.

other (such as a mommy). As children get older, they will pretend a series of events: going shopping, cooking dinner, playing house; or they will play doctor and have mommy or daddy go off to the hospital.

Much of the symbolic play of 5- or 6-year-olds involves other children: playing store or army, for example (Corrigan, 1983; Harris, Kadanaugh, & Meredith, 1994).

Magic and the Supernatural

Parents tend to view their 4- and 5-year-old children as having some trouble distinguishing fantasy from reality. In one survey, parents reported that their children believed that Santa Claus, the Easter Bunny, and the Tooth Fairy were real figures. Parents who encouraged belief in fantasy figures found that their children were more likely to believe in the reality of these figures.

Four- and 5-year-old children do not rule out the existence of extraordinary, even supernatural events. They tend to label magic tricks and extraordinary events as magic. For young children, magic is not something that is learned, but something that involves special powers that an individual is either born with or that is bestowed upon him or her by someone vested with these powers. By age 5, however, children begin to view magic as involving tricks and deception. These children see magic as a skill that can be learned through reading, from other magicians, or at a special "magic" school.

Many parents feel that children should come to learn the distinction between fantasy and reality by age 5 or 6. This implies that parents may shift from actively encouraging belief in certain supernatural figures to allowing children to figure things out on their own. As children come into greater contact with peers with different beliefs, as well as an educational system that actively discourages magical beliefs, they may replace the magical explanations with more natural ones, and begin to think that tricks of deception underlie the occurrence of seemingly impossible events (Rosengren & Hickling, 1994).

Four- and five-year-olds believe that Santa Claus is a real figure.

Transductive Reasoning

Transductive reasoning occurs when the child proceeds from particular to particular, without generalization, rather than from the particular to the general **(inductive reasoning)** or from the particular **(deductive reasoning).** For example, the dog Sport jumps on you because he has before, and Blackie will jump on you because he is frisky like Sport, but Rex will not jump on you because he is too big (when in fact he may). An error in judgment is made because the general concept that dogs jump on you is never developed (Rice, 1990a).

Transductive reasoning—proceeding from particular to particular in thought, without making generalizations

Inductive reasoning—gathering individual items of information and putting them together to form a hypothesis or conclusions

Deductive reasoning—beginning with a hypothesis or premise and breaking it down to see if it is true

Syncretism

Syncretism involves making errors of reasoning by trying to link ideas that are not always related. Mother had a baby last time she went to the hospital, so the next

Syncretism—trying to link ideas together that are not always related time she goes to the hospital, she is mistakenly expected to bring home another baby (Rice, 1990a).

Egocentrism

Egocentrism—the inability to take the perspective of another, to imagine the other person's point of view

Egocentrism is the inability to take the perspective of another, to imagine the other person's point of view. Children get upset, for example, when they cannot convince their mother not to wash their dirty rag doll. They gain security from it, and that is the important thing to them, whereas to their mother the important thing is that the doll is dirty. Children are also egocentric in their attitudes about other things. Space and time are focused on them: When they walk, the moon follows them. Gradually, however, children lean to conceive of a world in time and space existing independently of themselves and, through social interaction, they learn to take into account the viewpoints of others (Rice, 1990a).

Animism

Animism—ascribing lifelike qualities to inanimate objects

Animism is ascribing lifelike qualities to inanimate objects. Children will usually ascribe life to objects that represent figures that are alive in real life: stuffed animals, toy people, and so on. They may be confused about things in nature—flowers, trees, the wind, or the moon—and talk to them or about them as though they could hear. Animism probably reveals incomplete knowledge and understanding of the world, but it is also a reflection of children's vivid imagination (Bullock, 1985; Dolgin & Behrend, 1984).

Living Kinds

Early research has shown that children under 10 may not understand what it means to be a living thing. Piaget claims that young children do not understand the word *alive;* instead, children progress from having no concept of what it means to be alive to using movement as a criterion. Thus, he found that young children do not believe that plants are alive, but they do believe that the sun is alive. Preschool children draw the living kind boundary either too widely or too narrowly. Some children say plants are alive but those who attribute life to plants may also attribute life to inanimate objects. It seems that young children may have only rote knowledge of which objects are, or are not, alive.

Nevertheless, other research suggests that children have knowledge about some of the properties that separate living things from nonliving things. First, children know something about animal growth and something about plant growth. Children realize that living things grow because they take in food, not because they simply want to grow, and they realize animals' change in weight is affected by food intake, not by intention and desire.

Finally, preschoolers know that both plants and animals grow, and they also know the different factors affect growth. Overall, preschoolers realize that plants and animals heal through regrowth and that this ability separates artifacts from both plants and animals. Overall, children show some biological knowledge by implicitly grouping plants and animals together and differentiating them from artifacts. Thus, children know something about growth, an important biological property, and something about biological cause (Backscheider, Shatz, & Gelman, 1993). Other research confirms that preschoolers have an accurate concept of seeds and their place in the plant growth cycle (Hickling & Gelman, 1995).

One of the characteristics of children's increasing biological knowledge is the development of an understanding that biological processes are autonomous; that is, that they take place whether we want them to or not. That is, children recognize that the growth of living things is beyond intentional control. Along with this, children recognize that illness is caused not by moral but by medical factors. They develop substantial knowledge of contagion and contamination as causes of illness (Inagaki & Hatano, 1993; Blewitt, 1994).

Centration

Centration—focusing attention on only one aspect, or detail, of a situation

Part of the reason that preoperational children can't think logically is that they focus attention on one aspect of a situation, or on one detail, and are unable to take into account other details. This tendency is called **centration—**meaning to center on only one idea at a time. For example, our 6-year-old grandson knew his mother was coming home this morning, so he woke us up an

Planting seeds helps children understand that living things grow.

hour earlier than usual. When told it was too early to get up, he replied, "But mommy is coming home." Or, the other day he wanted to go to the beach. When told it was cloudy, wet, and misty, he insisted it was not and that we should go to the beach. Children of this age will get an idea in their head and completely ignore other thoughts. They fail to understand that beliefs sometimes do not match reality (Lillard & Flavell, 1992).

Conservation

The tendency to practice centration is revealed in tasks of **conservation.** For example, children may conclude there is more water in a shallow dish than in a glass because the dish is wider, even though they have already seen all the water poured from the glass into the dish. Figure 8.2 shows that the child has ignored the greater height of the glass and the demonstration of pouring. As a result of their inability to maintain more than one relationship in their thinking at a time, children make errors of judgment, give inadequate or inconsistent explanations, show a lack of logical sequence in their arguments, and a lack of comprehension of constants. Similarly, other tests of conversation of numbers, volume, length, or area are beyond the cognitive ability of preschoolers (Rice, 1990a).

However, by the age of 3, children can understand that matter can be decomposed into tiny pieces by being dissolved in liquid, and that this matter still exists even though it cannot be seen with the naked eye. This concept is important in understanding things like germs that are too small to be seen (Kit-Fong Au, Sidle & Rollins, 1993; Rosen & Rozin, 1993).

Classification

Classification means that objects can be thought of in terms of categories or classes (Jones, Smith, & Landau, 1991). Preoperational children are somewhat limited in their ability to classify objects according to categories (Waxman, Shipley, & Shepperson, 1991). Suppose children are shown 7 cats of different breeds: 4 Siamese, 1 Persian, 1 tiger, and 1 coon. The examiner makes certain and the children know they are all cats, and that the children can name each breed. The children are then asked: "Are there more Siamese or more cats?" Until about 7 or 8 years of age, most children will reply: "More Siamese." They cannot segregate the concept of cats from the subclassification "Siamese." They do, however, have some ability to categorize ac-

Classification—arranging objects into categories or classes

Conservation—the idea that properties of objects such as weight and mass stay the same regardless of how the shape or arrangement changes

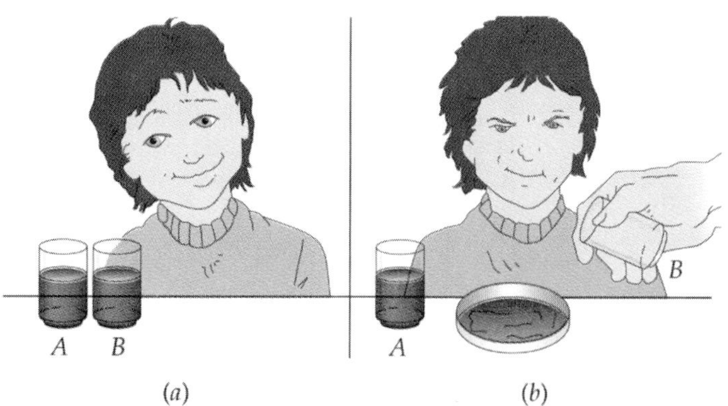

FIGURE 8.2 Understanding the principle of conservation of liquid. (a) The child agrees that glasses A and B have the same amount of water. (b) The water from B is poured into the dish. The child is unable to understand that glass A and the dish still have the same amount of water, because the dish appears broader even though it is shallower. The child is unable to retain one aspect (the amount) when another aspect changes (the height of the water column and the width of the column).

FOCUS

Concept of Color

Many children experience great difficulty in learning their first color word. This phenomenon is supported by parental reports and by empirical research. To learn a color word, children must make a mapping between a word and a color. That is, they must represent the word, they must represent the color, and then make an association between the two. In one experimental setting, children who knew no color words were taught the words "red," "green," and "yellow." Initially, they were taught "red" by showing each child a series of red objects and asking the child to name the color of each. Whenever a child failed, the correct color word was provided. It took an average of eighty-five trials to reach success (Rice, 1980). However, once children have learned one color word, they learn additional color words more easily (Soja, 1994).

cording to different properties (Kalish and Gelman, 1992). Even 3-year-olds will categorize a given object, depending on the property in question.

Irreversibility

Irreversibility—failure to recognize that an operation can go both ways

Preoperational children also make errors in their thinking because of **irreversibility,** that is, their inability to recognize that an operation can go both ways. For example, they do not understand that if water is poured from a tall container into a flat container, it can also be poured back again, keeping the same amount of water. Preoperational children cannot mentally accept that the original state can be regained (Rice, 1990).

CONCRETE OPERATIONAL STAGE (7 TO 11 YEARS)

In scientific practice as well as everyday life, children are called upon to evaluate some hypothesis or theory in light of evidence. Science involves the creation of hypotheses or theories to describe and explain the observed facts. Furthermore, a full understanding of science requires that children recognize that the hypotheses they encounter are formed on the basis of evidence, which is plausible though not necessarily a correct way of explaining data. Clearly, the ability to evaluate claims or theories in their relation to evidence is an important skill. Early research suggested that before the age of about 11 to 12 years, children have little insight into how hypotheses are supported or contradicted by evidence, and that even at this age and into adulthood, understanding is quite shaky. However, one study showed that by 6 years of age, most children can understand how simple evidence influences a story character to form a particular hypothesis. In this study, most children showed a clear understanding of how exposure to different evidence leads the informed and uninformed story characters to different predictions of behavior and how exposure to the same evidence leads them to the same predictions. The study showed that understanding a hypothesis was formed on the basis of patterns of evidence. Thus, by 6 years of age, children's cognitive abilities are sufficiently developed to allow them some form of insight into hypotheses and how they are constructed in patterns of evidence. In some, results showed that children possess understanding of a very basic prerequisite that is needed to understand properly much of science education. The researchers did note that children cannot understand more complicated forms of evidence as studied by Inhelder and Piaget (Ruffman, Perner, Olson, & Doherty, 1993).

During the concrete operational stage, children show a greater capacity for logical reasoning, though still at a very concrete level (Jacobs & Potenza, 1991). The child's thinking is still linked to empirical reality (Piaget, 1967a). Inhelder and Piaget (1958) wrote: "Concrete thought remains essentially attached to empirical reality.... Therefore, it attains no more than a concept of 'what is possible,' which is a simple (and not very great) extension of the empirical situation" (p. 250). Children have made some progress toward extending their thoughts from the actual toward the potential (Elkind, 1970), but the starting point must still be what is real because concrete operational children can reason only about those things with which they have had direct, personal experience. When children have to start with any hypothetical or contrary-to-fact proposition, they have difficulty. They can distinguish between hypothetical belief and evidence, but they fail to test hypotheses in a systematic, scientific way (Sodian, Zaitchik, & Carey, 1991).

Elkind (1967) also pointed out that one of the difficulties at this stage is that the child can deal with only two classes, relations, or quantitative dimensions at the same time. When more variables are present, the child flounders.

However, concrete operational children are able to arrange objects into **hierarchical classifications** and comprehend **class inclusion relationships** (the inclusion of objects in different levels of the hierarchy at the same time). This gives children the ability to understand the relations of the parts to the whole, the whole to the parts, and the parts to the parts. Suppose children are given a randomly organized array of yellow and red squares and black and white circles. If they understand inclusion relationships, they discover there are two major collections (squares and circles) and two subtypes of each (yellow versus red squares and black versus white circles). There is a hierarchy whose higher level is defined by shape and whose lower level is defined by color. This enables the children to say that all squares are either yellow or red, that there are more squares than yellow squares, that there are more squares than red squares, that if you take away the red squares, the yellow ones are left, and so on.

The ability to group things into categories enables children to expand their scope of knowledge through category-based inductions. They are able to conclude that a property that is true of some category members may also be true of other category members. For example, humans have tonsils, therefore gorillas probably have tonsils. Without categories, children would have to learn about each instance anew, being unable to benefit from past instances. Inductive inferences allow them to set forth assumptions, make predictions, and generalize from the known to the unknown, extending knowledge beyond the range of direct experience (Farrar, Raney, & Boyer, 1992; Lopez, Gelman, Gutheil, & Smith, 1992).

Concrete operational children are capable also of **serialization,** or serial ordering. They learn that different objects may be grouped by size, or by alphabetical order.

Conservation refers to the recognition that properties of things such as weight or volume are not altered by changing their container or shape. Conservation tasks involve some manipulation of the shape of matter without altering its mass or volume (Piaget & Inhelder, 1969). A typical conservation problem is represented by the ball of clay in Figure 8.3.

Muuss (1988b) summarizes four concrete operations the child is able to perform:

1. **Combinativity.** This represents the ability to combine two or more classes into one larger, more comprehensive class. For example, all men and all women equals all adults; A is larger than B and B is larger than C can be combined into a new statement that A is larger than C.
2. **Reversibility.** This is the concept that every operation has an opposite operation that reverses it. Supraclasses can be taken apart, reversing the effect of combining subclasses. All adults except all women equals all men.
3. **Associativity.** The child whose operations have become associative can reach a goal in various ways ... but the results obtained ... remain the same. For

Serialization—arranging objects into hierarchy of classes

Hierarchical classification—arranging objects into categories according to level

Class inclusion relationships—the inclusion of objects in different levels of hierarchy at the same time

Combinativity—ability to combine two or more classes into one larger class

Reversibility—the concept that every operation has an opposite operation that reverses it

Associativity—the understanding that operations can reach a goal in various ways

FOCUS

Research on Abilities During the Preoperational Stage

A vast amount of research has been conducted to determine children's cognitive abilities during the preoperational stage. Some of these findings are summarized here.

Two-and-one-half-year-old children have difficulty appreciating the relation between a scale model and the larger figure it represents although they understand the relation between a picture and its referent (DeLoache, 1991).

Knowing the location of things, such as the location of food, shelter, or danger, is necessary for survival. Children ages 3, 4, and 5 can code spatial locations in terms of a frame of spatial reference and can use these codings to answer questions about occupied points and locations stored in memory. They can clearly indicate locations relative to another position (Newcombe & Huttenlocher, 1992).

The concept of the distance between two points is fundamental to mature notions of space. Only about 40 percent of 4-year-olds are able to say that a direct route between two points is shorter than an indirect route because it is straight and the indirect route is not (Fabricius & Wellman, 1993).

Children as young as 4 years old have some conception of density that allows them to make accurate predictions about the buoyancy of objects in water. The difficulty children have in making buoyancy judgments is similar to the difficulty that adults have: weight and volume sometimes cause confusion. Heavy objects of an intermedi-

example, (3 plus 6) plus 4 equals 13, and 6 plus (3 plus 4) equals 13.

Identity or nullifiability—the understanding that an operation that is combined with its opposite becomes nullified

4. **Identity or nullifiability.** This is the understanding that an operation that is combined with its opposite becomes nullified, resulting in no change. An example is that to give 3 and take away 3 results in null (p. 185).

VYGOTSKY'S THEORY OF COGNITIVE AND LANGUAGE DEVELOPMENT

Over the past decade there has been a major upsurge of interest in the ideas of the Russian psychologist L. S. Vygotsky (1896–1934). Perhaps the major reason for Vygotsky's current appeal in the West is his analysis of the social origins of mental processes (Wertsch and Tulviste, 1992). *In Vygotsky's views, mental functioning primarily is derived, not from maturation, but from social and cultural influences.* To Vygotsky, the social dimensions of consciousness are primary; the individual dimensions are derivative and secondary. Instead of beginning with the assumption that mental functioning occurs first and foremost within the individual (intramentally), Vygotsky emphasizes that mental processes occur between people on an intermental plane. Intramental functioning is a derivative, emerging through the mastery and interate buoyant density are mistakenly thought to sink, and lightweight objects of an intermediate nonbuoyant density are mistakenly thought to float (Kohn, 1993).

Children as young as age 6 can make some proportional judgments. They can discriminate between less than half and more than half. Their recognition of "half" may eventually lead them to the understanding of part–whole relations (Spinillo & Bryant, 1991).

From ages 3 and older, children understand that animals grow larger over time. They are able to think beyond present appearances and make judgments about transformations caused by growth (Rosengren, Gelman, Kalish, McCormick, 1991).

What a person believes has a causal impact on his or her actions, statements, and emotions. The ability to recognize false beliefs, to recognize those perspectives that run counter to reality, is important in avoiding unreasonable actions. Children's understanding of false beliefs and deceptive ploys emerges at about 4 years of age. Two- and 3-year olds will participate in removing true trails and laying false one to mislead someone about the location of a hidden object, but they show no clear understanding of the effect of their deception on others (Sodian, Taylor, Harris, Perner, 1991).

Adults recognize that other people can have beliefs different from their own and that these mental representations of things can be different from the things themselves. Not so with 3-year-olds. When children of ages 3, 4, and 5 were told or shown that characters in children's stories held different beliefs from their own or from one another, the 3-year-olds had difficulty in attributing to others deviant beliefs of all types (Flavell, Mumme, Green, Flavell, 1992). Beginning about age 6, children understand that even though different people all hear the same message, individuals may perceive it differently (Montgomery, 1993).

By 4 or 5 years of age, children begin to understand the biological implications of kinship, that family members share more biological properties than unrelated members of the same species, even though the latter may look alike or have social ties (Springer, 1992).

nalization of social processes. Due to Vygotsky's influence, psychologists now speak of *socially shared cognition* (Resnick, Levine, & Behrend, 1991), *socially distributed cognition* (Hutchins, 1991), and *collective memory* (Middleton, 1987). Mental functioning is viewed as a kind of action carried out by dyads or larger groups.

This concept is basic to Vygotsky's idea of the **"zone of proximal development" (ZPD).** The ZPD is Vygotsky's term for tasks too difficult for children to master alone that need to be mastered with the guidance and assistance of others. The zone is the distance between the child's actual development level reached through individual problem solving, and the higher level of potential development as determined through problem-solving under adult guidance or in collaboration with more capable peers (Vygotsky, 1978). Vygotsky argued that measuring the child's potential level of development is just as important as measuring the actual level, since instruction needs to be tied closely to the level of potential development. To Vygotsky, the actual level of functioning corresponds to intramental processes; the potential level of functioning derives from intermental processes. The goal is to improve and change intramental functioning through reciprocal teaching.

Vygotsky also had important things to say about language development. Vygot-

Zone of proximal development—the distance between a child's actual development level reached through individual problem solving, and a higher level of potential development

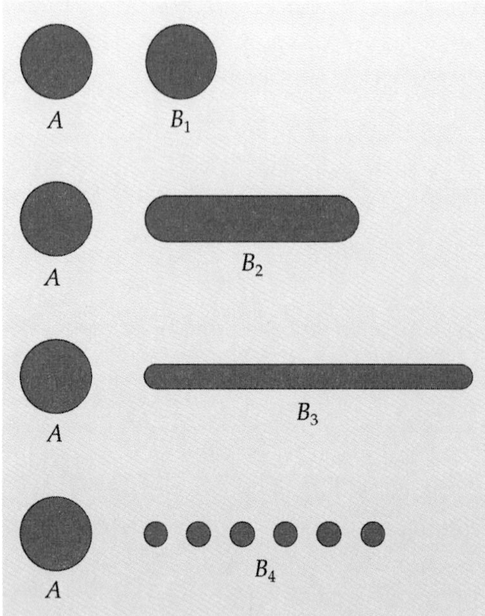

FIGURE 8.3 Conservation of mass. In this example, the child is asked to confirm that A and B_1 are the same size. Then B_1 is changed to B_2, then to B_3, then to B_4. The child is asked to compare A with B_2, then with B_3, and with B_4, each time stating whether A and B are still the same. Children in the preoperational stage are guided by the shapes they see. Children in the concrete operational stage preserve recognition of the equal quantity between A and B that transcends their physical shape.

sky said that *language and thought initially develop independently of each other, but eventually merge.* Children learn to talk because they must communicate with others, make social contact, and influence surrounding individuals. Gradually, beginning at about 3 years of age, children make a transition from *external speech* to *inner speech.* Inner speech is the child talking to himself or herself and becomes the child's thoughts. Speech during the transitional period is referred to as *egocentric speech.* Its purpose is partly to make social contact and partly to express inner thoughts. The more the child engages in self-talk, the more the ideas become a part of himself or herself that can be acted upon without further verbalizing. Eventually, egocentric speech is internalized and becomes the inner speech or the thoughts of the child. Vygotsky claimed that inner speech enables humans to plan and regulate their action and derives from previous participation in verbal social interaction (Wertsch and Tulviste, 1922).

Summary

1. Perceptual developments discussed in this chapter include depth perception, perception of form and motion, perception of the human face, and auditory perception.
2. Language is only one of many methods of communication.
3. Research on verbal interactions between mothers and children revealed that Japanese mothers were highest in the use of speech with affect content; mothers from Argentina, France, and the United States favored information-giving.
4. The basic elements of language include phonemes, morphemes, syntax and grammar, semantics, and pragmatics.
5. Theories of language development include biological theory, learning theory, cognitive theory, and interactionist theory.
6. Parental influences on language development are especially important.
7. Reading stories from picture books and discussing them were found to be effective ways of accelerating language development of Mexican children in a day-care center.
8. The sequences of language development are: prelinguistic period, first spoken words, two-word utterances, telegraphic speech, and sentences.
9. There is considerable support for the theory that there is a critical period for language development.
10. The vocabulary of preschool and early school-age children grows from over

50 words at age 2 to 8,000 to 14,000 words at age 6.
11. Grammar is the formal description of structure and rules that a language uses in order to communicate meaning.
12. Pragmatics is the practical ability to use language to communicate with others in a variety of social contexts.
13. Studies of gender differences in communication patterns in children reveal that boys use more demanding, domineering patterns; girls use cooperative, polite, and collaborative strategies.
14. Studies of communication in families reveal that children express more feelings to one another as they age, but the conversation tends to be self-centered, whereas mother–child talk is caretaking and comforting.
15. Stuttering appears to have both a genetic base and to be influenced by environment.
16. For children in groups where their first language is a minority language, a second language may be a subtractive influence. For children whose first language is the majority language, learning a second language is largely an additive experience.
17. Early experiences at home have an influence on children's literacy development.
18. There are two approaches to teaching reading: the skills approach, including the phonics approach and word recognition, and the whole-language approach. Combining both approaches works best.
19. There are three approaches to the study of cognition: the Piagetian approach, the information-processing approach, and the psychometric approach.
20. Piaget divided the stages of cognitive development into four stages: the sensorimotor stage (birth to 2 years), the preoperational stage (2 to 7 years), the concrete operational stage (7 to 11 years), and the formal operational stage (11 years and up).
21. During the sensorimotor stage children learn to respond through motor activity to stimuli.
22. During the sensorimotor stage children develop the concept of object permanence. They also develop the ability to imitate.
23. The parental role is to offer a stimulating intellectual environment so children can grow cognitively.
24. During the preoperational stage, children develop the ability to deal with the world symbolically and representationally. They acquire language, reason transductively, make errors of reasoning because of syncretism, and may be characterized as exhibiting egocentrism, animism, centration, and lack of comprehension of conservation. They are limited in their classification ability and make errors because their thinking is irreversible.
25. Research on cognitive abilities during the preoperational stage indicates that children understand the relation between a picture and its referent, remember the location of things in rooms, can make proportional judgments in relation to half, understand that animals grow larger, can recognize false beliefs, and begin to understand kinship. They have trouble understanding the relation between a scale model and the larger figure it represents, that a straight line is the shortest distance between points, and that other beliefs may be different from their own.
26. During the concrete operational stage, children show some ability to do logical thinking, but only at a concrete level. They are capable of classification and serialization, understand conservation, and can perform tasks involving combinativity, reversibility, associativity, and identity or nullifiability.
27. Vygotsky's theory of cognitive and language development emphasizes that both are derived from social and cultural influences. He introduced the concepts of zone of proximal development, inner speech, egocentric speech, and external speech.

Key Terms

Animism *p. 210*
Associativity *p. 213*
Babbling *p. 194*
Centration *p. 210*
Classification *p. 211*
Class inclusion relationships *p. 213*
Combinativity *p. 213*
Conservation *p. 211*
Cooing *p. 194*
Cross-modal perception *p. 187*
Deductive reasoning *p. 209*
Deferred imitation *p. 207*
Duos *p. 195*
Egocentrism *p. 210*
Gap threshold *p. 188*
Grammar *p. 198*
Hierarchical classification *p. 213*
Holophrases *p. 194*
Identity or nullifiability *p. 214*
Imitation *p. 207*
Inductive reasoning *p. 209*
Information-processing approach *p. 205*
Irreversibility *p. 212*
Language acquisition device *p. 190*
Morpheme *p. 189*
Motherese *p. 195*
Nativist view *p. 190*
Object permanence *p. 207*
Perception *p. 186*
Phoneme *p. 189*
Phonics approach *p. 203*
Piagetian approach *p. 205*
Pragmatics *p. 190*
Psychometric approach *p. 205*
Reversibility *p. 213*
Semantics *p. 190*
Serialization *p. 213*
Skills approach *p. 203*
Symbolic play *p. 208*
Syncretism *p. 209*
Syntax *p. 189*
Telegraphic speech *p. 195*
Transductive reasoning *p. 209*
Whole-language approach *p. 203*
Word recognition approach *p. 203*
Zone of proximal development *p. 215*

Discussion Questions

1. Have you ever known a young preschool child who did not talk? What were the reasons?
2. Have you ever known an infant who seemed to be advanced in language development? Describe. What were the reasons for this advanced development?
3. When you were growing up were family members encouraged or discouraged from talking about feelings? With what result?
4. What can parents do to stimulate the cognitive development of their children?
5. Why has the influence of Piaget been so felt in the psychological world? What are some of the characteristics of his theories that you like? What are some of your major criticisms of his viewpoints?
6. In what ways is the distractibility of young children a handicap to parents? In what ways is it a help?

Suggested Readings

Anisfield, M. (1984). *Language development from birth to three.* Hillsdale, NJ: Erlbaum.

Bruner, J. (1983). *Child talk.* New York: Norton. Language development of children.

Carroll, D. W. (1986). *Psychology of lan-*

guage (2nd ed.). Pacific Grove, CA: Brooks/Cole. Language development.

Case, R. (1985). *Cognitive development: A systematic reinterpretation.* New York: Academic Press. Research.

Cummins, J., & Swain, M. (1986). *Bilingualism in education: Aspects of theory, research, and practice.* London: Taylor and Fry. Current discussion.

Daehler, M. W., & Bukatko, D. (1985). *Cognitive development.* NY: Random House. Theory, attention, memory, and reasoning.

Flavell, J. H. (1985). *Cognitive development* (2nd ed.). Englewood Cliffs, NJ: Prentice-Hall. Piaget's theories.

Forman, G. E. (Ed.). (1982). *Action and thought: From sensorimotor schemes to symbolic operations.* New York: Academic Press. Research-based articles.

Furth, H. G. (1981). *Piaget and knowledge* (2nd ed.). Englewood Cliffs, NJ: Prentice-Hall. Simplified discussion of Piaget.

Kessel, F. (Ed.). (1988). *The development of language and language researchers.* Hillsdale, NJ: Erlbaum. Chapters by experts.

McLane, J. B., & McNamee, G. D. (1990). *Early literacy.* Cambridge, MA: Harvard University Press. Pros and cons of early reading for young children.

Porter, R. P. (1990). *Forked tongue: The politics of bilingual education.* New York: Basic Books. Successes and failures of bilingual education in the United States.

Siegler, R. (1991). *Children's thinking* (2nd ed.). Englewood Cliffs, NJ: Prentice-Hall. Cognitive development from infancy to adolescence.

Sternberg, R. J. (1984). *Mechanisms of cognitive development.* New York: W. H. Freeman.

Sternberg, R. J. (1985). *Beyond IQ: A triarchic theory of human intelligence.* New York: Cambridge University Press. Sternberg's theory.

Cognitive Development: Information Processing, Intelligence, and School

Chapter 9

INFORMATION PROCESSING

Stimuli • Habituation • Selective Attention • Memory • FOCUS: *Distractibility* • PARENTING ISSUES: *Children's Memory for Spatial Locations in Organized and Unorganized Rooms*

INTELLIGENCE

Views of Intelligence • Intelligence Tests • Critique of IQ and IQ Tests • FOCUS: *Terman's Study of Gifted Men* • IQ and Race • Infant Intelligence and Measurement • FOCUS: *The Kaufman Assessment Battery for Children (K-ABC)* • FOCUS: *The Fagan Test of Infant Intelligence* • Early Intervention • PARENTING ISSUES: *Pushing Preschoolers* • Mental Retardation

SCHOOL

Early Childhood Education • FOCUS: *The Importance of the Teacher* • American Education • Successful Schools • Achievement • FOCUS: *How American Children Compare with Asian Children* • FOCUS: *Helpless and Mastery-Oriented Children* • PARENTING ISSUES: *Report Cards*

So far we have discussed only the Piagetian approach to cognitive development. In this chapter, we will discuss two additional approaches: the information-processing approach and the psychometric approach. We are also concerned here with school and the education of the child.

Information Processing

The *Piagetian approach* to cognition describes the stages involved in the development of logical thinking. The *information-processing approach* describes the way children obtain information, remember it, retrieve it, and use it in solving problems. These abilities during the first year of life have been found to be predictive of both specific cognitive abilities and IQ at 6 years of age (Rose, Feldman, & Wallace, 1992).

Information processing has often been compared to the actions of a computer. Information is coded and fed into a computer in an organized way, and then it is stored in the memory banks. When any of that information is required, the computer is asked to produce it. The machine searches for the relevant information and reproduces or prints out the items requested.

Information processing by children is basically similar but far more sophisticated. The child receives information, organizes it, stores it, retrieves it, thinks about it, and combines it to answer questions, solve problems, and make decisions. The most elaborate computer used in creating *artificial intelligence* cannot match the capacity of the human mind and nervous system in the input and output of information. Each new generation of computers is more advanced than the last. Similarly, as each year passes, the child's ability to process information increases, partly because of the continued development of the brain and nervous system, and partly because of the learning experience and practice that improve mental abilities and strategies (Teyler & Fountain, 1987; Goodman & Haith, 1987).

Habituation—the tendency to adapt to a repeated stimulus and to lose interest in it

Information processing has been likened to the actions of a computer.

STIMULI

Before information can be processed it must be received. Children are constantly bombarded with stimuli. Their senses are their receptors, their contacts between themselves and the world outside, and the method by which they learn. *Research has shown the importance of stimulation in the learning process.* Maternal stimulation during the first year has been associated with infants' 1-year vocabulary size (Bornstein, 1985a), 2-year cognitive/language competence (Olson, Bates, & Bayles, 1984), 3-year language performance (Bee et al., 1982), 4-year intelligence test performance (Bornstein, 1985a), and 6-year school performance (Coates & Lewis, 1984).

HABITUATION

Stimulation is important to cognitive development, but researchers also have found that when infants get used to a sound or sight, it loses its novelty, and the infants do not pay as much attention to it, a process called **habituation.** Infants can become habituated to every type of sensory stimulation (Rovee-Collier, 1987b). Furthermore, this tendency becomes increasingly developed during the first 3 months of life (Lipsitt, 1986). It is important in parent–infant interaction that parents repeat stimuli to facilitate learning, but once children stop responding, the parents need to stop or change the type of stimulation (Rosenblith & Sims-Knight, 1985).

Habituation is important because it has been used to measure infants' sensory perception, memory, and neurologic health. It can have important implications for a child's present and future cognitive, emotional, and social development (Dunham, Dunham, Hurshman, & Alexander, 1989). Habituation assessments during the first year are predictive of later IQ (McCall & Carriger, 1993). For example, habituation in the first 6 months of life has been reported to explain 59 percent of the variance in indexes of childhood intelligence between 2 and 8 years (Bornstein & Sigman, 1986; Tamis-LeMonda & Bornstein, 1989). Babies with low Apgar scores, brain damage, or Down's syndrome show impaired habituation.

SELECTIVE ATTENTION

Another important factor in learning is that children don't pay equal amounts of attention to everything. *They attend selectively to stimuli, with dramatic increases in selectivity with age.* One study showed that when 5- to 6-year-old children were shown a video tape of a routine medical exam, they showed reduced memory for events witnessed in the tape when it showed children in distress. The children witnessing the distress became upset themselves and did not pay attention to other events that were happening (Bugental et al., 1992). The older the children, the more they develop a selective strategy, that is, they are better able to sort out relevant from nonrelevant information, and to learn more efficiently (DeMarie-Dreblow & Miller, 1988; Woody-Ramsey & Miller, 1988).

MEMORY

The ability to remember is basic to all learning. Without memory, we would never be able to recall or recognize what we have already experienced. We would not be able to accumulate a body of useful knowledge, to learn from past mistakes, or to think and reason intelligently. Memory is a central part of information processing. While memory depends partly upon knowledge (something can't really be remembered unless it is first known), the process is more complicated, because it also involves the capacity to recall (DeMarie-Dreblow, 1991). Memory ability also is related to IQ (Schneider & Bjorklund, 1992).

Infant Memory

Studies of infants reveal some memory ability from the early weeks of life (Borovsky & Rovee-Collier, 1990; Perris, Myers, & Clifton, 1990). Newborns can distinguish different speech sounds and odors, and by one month of age can distinguish their mother's face from others. These abilities are evidence of memory (Cernoch & Porter, 1985; Rovee-Collier, 1987a). Rovee-Collier (1987a) hung a mobile over an infant's crib and attached a ribbon from the mobile to one of the baby's legs. The 6-week-old infant quickly learned which leg would move the mobile. Two weeks later the child was put into the crib and, as a "reminder," was allowed to look at the mobile without having the ribbon attached. The next day, with the ribbon reconnected, the infant kicked to move the mobile as it had learned to do two weeks before. Obviously, it had remembered the behavior previously taught (Hayne & Rovee-Collier, 1995; Linde, Morrongiello, & Rovee-Collier, 1985).

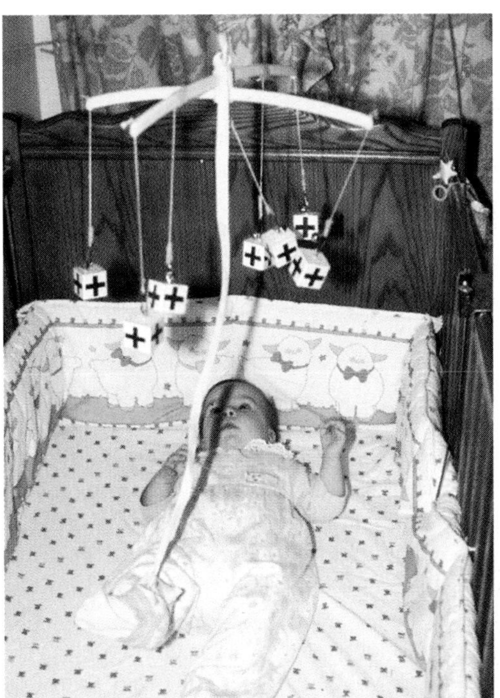

The infant quickly learned which leg kicked the mobile and two weeks later remembered how to make the mobile move.

The ability to remember is facilitated if infants are tested in the same context in which they first learned. For example, the same context might mean the same room or same crib (Amabile & Rovee-Collier, 1991), or use of the same test equipment (Rovee-Collier, Schecter, Shyi, & Shields, 1992; Shields & Rovee-Collier, 1992; Singer & Fagen, 1993). Other research has shown that by late in the first year of life children are able to remember the sequence of specific events (Bauer & Mandler, 1992).

Infantile amnesia—the lack of memory of events experienced before age 3

Haptic processing

Infants are also able to remember objects that they have seen and touched previously. **Haptic processing** involves the use of touch to convey information about the features and identity of objects and relies principally on input from kinesthetic receptors in the hands and fingers. In one experiment, forty-eight infants (mean age 8 months) were familiarized haptically with a small cube or sphere with rough or smooth surface texture and subsequently tested for recognition of the shape and texture of this stimuli. The test stimuli were presented (a) immediately, (b) after a five-minute delay, (c) after a second interference phase in which they were presented with different shapes and textures than the first. The infants demonstrated recognition of shape and texture in the no-delay condition of shape and marginally of texture in the delayed condition but only of texture in the interference condition. The results for the delayed group confirmed that infants can retain haptic information at least for a brief interval beyond initial exposure. This outcome aligns infant haptic memory with infant visual memory in that it demonstrates that infants are capable of delayed recognition in both modalities (Catherwood, 1993).

The memory of infants is fairly short-lived, however. Without a repetition of the stimuli, the memory trace fades fairly quickly (Hayne, Rovee-Collier, & Perris, 1987). Infants have to be over 7 months of age before they will search for objects that have disappeared. One mother reported that her 9-month-old daughter was looking for ribbons. She looked first in the old drawer from which they had been removed. She then looked in other drawers until she found them. The next day she went directly to the new drawer to find the ribbons (Ashmead & Perlmutter, 1979).

These early memories are not permanent, however. *Only a few people can recall events that happened prior to 3 years of age.* We don't remember being born; we don't remember nursing, crawling, starting to walk, or the birth of a sibling 2 or 3 years younger than us. I have a sister who is 4 years younger than I am. I can remember my mother nursing her. I can remember my first day in kindergarten at age 5, but very little before that. This phenomenon is known as **infantile amnesia,** the essential lack of memory of events experienced before 3 years of age (Sheingold & Tenney, 1982).

One study of 9- and 10-year-old children measured their ability to remember the faces of former preschool classmates. Recognition of faces was at a low level but significantly above chance. This study shows that infantile amnesia may not always involve complete loss of encoded information (Newcombe & Fox, 1994).

Memory Capacity and Storage

Sensory storage—the process by which information is received and transduced by the senses, usually in a fraction of a second

Short-term storage—the process by which information is still in the conscious mind and being rehearsed and focused on

Long-term storage—the process by which information is perceived and processed deeply so it passes into the layers of memory below the conscious level

Recall—remembering without cues

Recognition—remembering after cues have been given

The process of remembering involves a series of steps. The most widely accepted model is a three-stage one: **sensory storage, short-term storage,** and **long-term storage.** Information is seen as passing from one compartment to another, with decreasing amounts passed on at any one time to the next stage (Rice, 1990a). Figure 9.1 illustrates the three-stage model of memory. Information is held only briefly (as little as a fraction of a second) in sensory storage before the image begins to decay or is blocked out by other incoming sensory information. Information that has not already faded from the sensory storage is read out to the short-term storage, where it may be held for up to thirty seconds. Because of the limited capacity of the short-term storage, information to be held longer must be rehearsed and transferred to the relatively permanent long-term storage. For all practical purposes, long-term storage capacity is infinite. In the process of retrieval, stored information is obtained by searching, finding, and remembering, either through **recall** (remembering without cues) or **recognition** (remembering with cues). Memory efficiency depends on all three of these processes.

Sensory Storage

In sensory storage, no cognitive processing takes place. Our senses of vision, hearing, taste, smell, or touch are momentarily stimulated. We pay attention to some of the stimuli, then the sensation fades. Some significant information is passed on to the short-term storage.

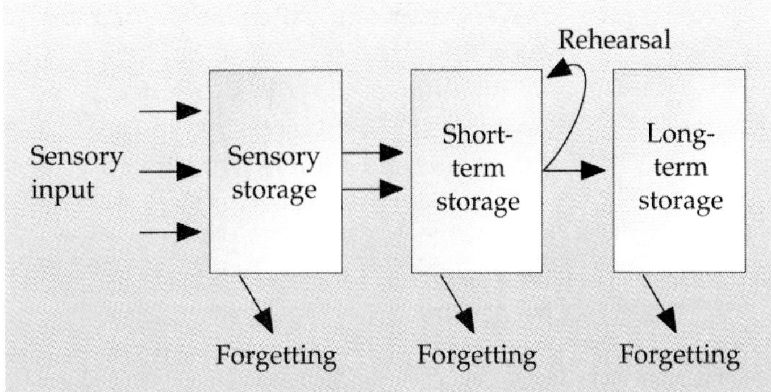

FIGURE 9.1 Three-stage model of memory.

Short-Term Storage

Short-term storage involves very little processing of information. As a result, it is not remembered for longer than about thirty seconds. Furthermore, it involves the equivalent of only about seven digits—the same amount of data as in a local telephone number. Siegler (1989) suggests that children are often unable to solve certain problems because they can't keep all the relevant information in mind long enough. Obviously, they have not rehearsed it long enough to put it in long-term storage.

Short-term memory ability increases during childhood (Raine, Hulme, Chadderton, & Bailey, 1991). One way to measure short-term memory is to ask subjects to repeat a series of digits that they have heard repeated at a fairly rapid rate. In one study, 2- to 3-year-old children were able to remember two digits. By 9 years of age, the children were able to repeat six digits. After that, the number remembered continued to increase, but at a much slower rate, so that 12-year-olds could repeat six and a half digits and adults could repeat about seven (Dempster, 1981). As mentioned, short-term memory capacity is usually about seven digits. *The short-term memory span is fairly constant throughout adolescence and adulthood* (Kail, 1979).

Long-Term Storage

Long-term memory contains information that is processed deeply (for example, it is rehearsed and repeated until it is thoroughly familiar) and stored on a fairly permanent basis. Unlike short-term memory, *long-term memory increases fairly rapidly with age during middle and late childhood; it continues to increase until young adulthood* (Price & Goodman, 1990).

Research has shown that children as young as 3 years of age have well-organized representations of events, and that they remember those events over long periods of time. Repeated experience is not necessary for recall to be possible. Three- to 7-year-olds provide well-organized accounts of events after only a single experience of them (Bauer & Hertsgaard, 1993).

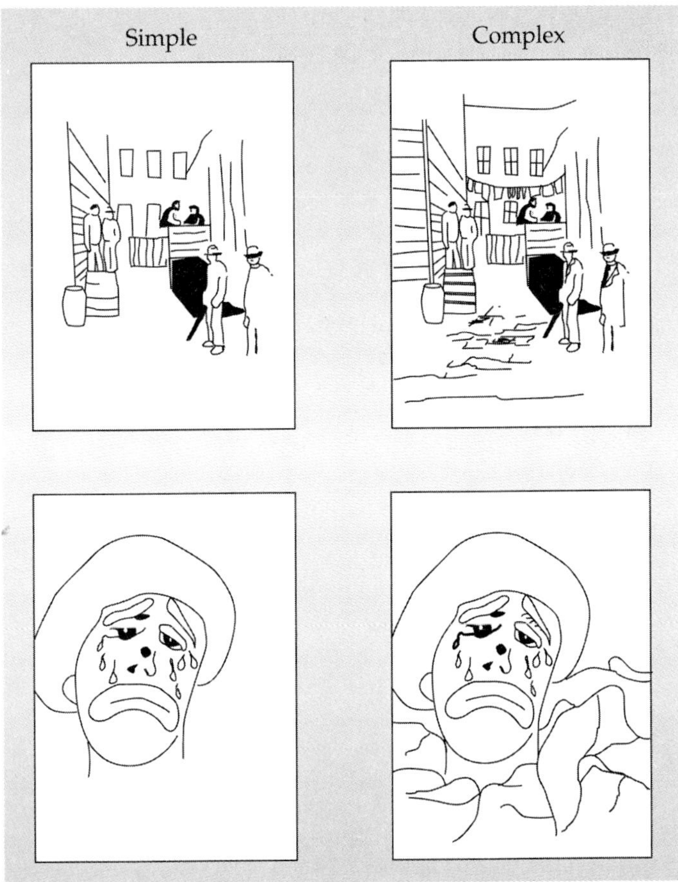

FIGURE 9.2 Examples of pictures in both simple and complex forms.

From: "Memory for Pictures: A Life-Span Study of the Role of Visual Detail" by K. Pezdek, 1987, *Child Development, 58*, pp. 807–815.

A life-span study of memory for pictures was conducted for 7-year-olds, 9-year-olds, young adults, and older adults over 68 (Pezdek, 1987). Subjects were presented with simple and complex line drawings and then tested with the same and changed forms of these pictures, at both five-second and fifteen-second presentation rates. For each test picture the experimenter asked: "Is this picture the same as a picture you saw before, or are there some changes in the picture?" The questions were asked long enough after the picture was presented (three minutes) to ensure that the test measured long-term memory. Figure 9.2 shows examples of pictures in both simple and complex forms. Figure 9.3 shows the percentage correct, by age group, when the test pictures presented were complex forms of simple pictures. The graph shows the results of both five-second and fifteen-second presentation rates. As can be seen, the ability of subjects to remember the pictures increased from age 7 to college age, then declined in older adults over 68 years of age. For all age groups, pictures presented in their simple form were recognized more accurately than pictures presented in their complex form. Also, memory for pictures increased as the exposure duration per picture increased. Longer study intervals allowed for greater efficiency in encoding and storing the information on picture details. Other research shows that with increasing age, up to young adulthood, individuals execute cognitive processes more rapidly (Kail, 1992). In other words, memory ability increases from early childhood to young adulthood (Brainerd & Reyna, 1995).

Metamemory—knowledge of memory strategies people employ to learn and remember information

Mnemonic—memory-aiding

Chunking—dividing material into meaningful parts to remember it

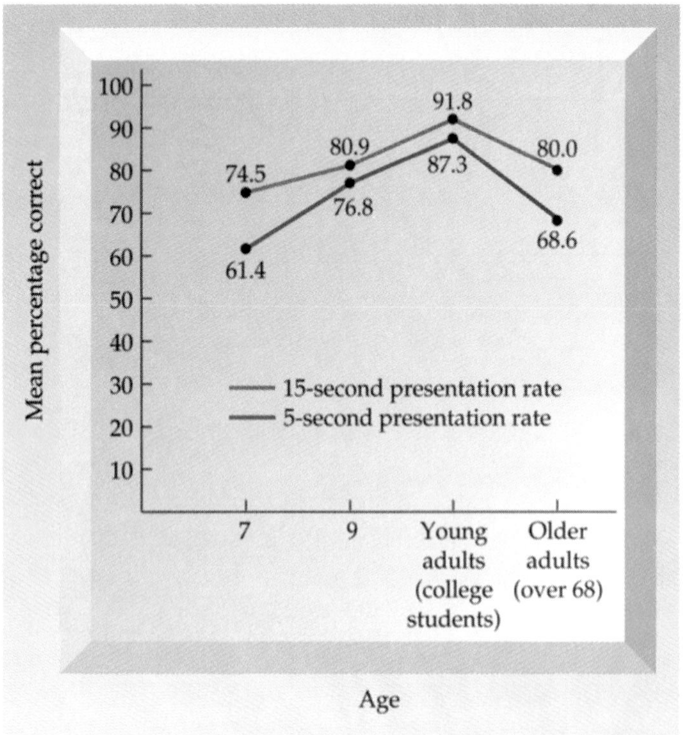

FIGURE 9.3 Memory for pictures by age of subject.

Data from "Memory for Pictures: A Life-Span Study of the Role of Visual Detail" by K. Pezdek, 1987, *Child Development, 58*, pp. 807–815.

Other research shows that levels of memory performance are overall greater for high-IQ than for low-IQ children, but that the levels of performance can be enhanced as a result of training. Individual differences in knowledge base can compensate for some differences in memory ability. For example, third-grade soccer experts had higher levels of recall from a soccer story than did fifth- and seventh-grade soccer novices (Bjorklund, Schneider, Cassel, & Ashley, 1994).

Metamemory

Metamemory consists of knowledge of memory strategies people employ to learn and remember information. There are a number of **mnemonic**, or memory-aiding, strategies that are useful (Best, 1993). One is *rehearsal*, the repetition of information to be remembered. This helps to process information deeply and to store it in long-term memory. Another way to aid memory is through *organization*. Material can be arranged by categories (for example, animals), alphabetically, or in some other logical order. **Chunking** consists of dividing material into meaningful parts. Thus, it is easier to remember the telephone number 1-516-799-4362 than it is to remember 15167994362. Material can also be *coded:* for example, by color. A map with its symbols is a good illustration of visual representation of roads, cities, railroads, rivers, highways, and so forth. Children often use codes to make maps or posters. A code may also be audible, such as the ringing of a timer bell to remind a child it's bedtime.

Another mnemonic device is to provide children with *memory cues:* for example, the letters representing notes on a music staff, shown in Figure 9.4. The letters F A C E

FIGURE 9.4 Cues to remember notes on a music staff.

refer to the notes between the lines. The letters E G B D F are the first letters of the words in the phrase "Every Good Boy Does Fine." These letters represent the notes on the lines.

Another way to remember material is by *visualizing position or place:* the so-called **method of loci.** Children often remember material they have read by visualizing its position on a page of their textbook. Children are also better able to remember material or events that are *meaningful and familiar* (Farrar & Goodman; Fivush, Kuebli, & Clubb, 1992). They would have more trouble remembering the letters NOTGNISHAW than they would the letters WASHINGTON, unless they were able to recognize that NOTGNIHSAW is WASHINGTON backward. If children are motivated to learn material because it is *interesting,* or if it is *important,* it's surprising how much they can learn and remember (Lorch, Bellack, & Augsbach, 1987). They may never learn material that they are not interested in. In support of this assertion, it has been found that preschool children have extremely good memories for stories or for social or family events (Mandler, 1983). In one study, children were told a detailed story about two boys who had lunch at McDonald's. The children were later asked to identify which words from a list were in the story. The memory of these children was extremely accurate (Mistry & Lange, 1985). Researchers have found that the use of *mnemonic devices* increases from preschool years through adolescence (Brown, Bransford, Ferrara, & Champione, 1983). Teachers can play an important role in teaching memory strategies to children in their classrooms (Lange & Pierce, 1992; Moely et al., 1992).

Method of loci—remembering by visualizing the position of something

F O C U S

Distractibility

Every parent knows that young children are easily distracted by competing stimuli (Pillow, 1988). Toddlers may start to do one thing, be attracted to something else, and turn their attention to the second thing. As a result, it is hard to get them to focus their attention on any one activity for very long (Ruff, Lawson, Parrinello, & Weissberg, 1990). In contrast, preschool children may be able to focus their attention for much longer periods. In one experiment, 3- and 5-year-old children were observed as they watched a fifty-eight-minute "Sesame Street" program on television. They were distracted during the program by the presentation of attractive pictures projected through colored slides. Altogether, the children watched the television during 43 percent of the program, with older children paying more visual attention (47 percent) than younger children (35 percent) (Anderson, Choi, & Lorch, 1987). The attention span of children increases even more dramatically with age between early preschool and early elementary school age (Kail & Bisanz, 1982).

PARENTING ISSUES

Children's Memory for Spatial Locations in Organized and Unorganized Rooms

Locating objects in places is a practical task that occupies a great deal of everyday human and animal behavior. Adults spend a considerable amount of time searching for valued items such as car keys, checkbook, and papers containing important pieces of information. Likewise, children and adults are frequently confronted with requests for information on the whereabouts of missing objects. The daily routine in many households, for example, is getting children to describe where they put their shoes or the last place they remember seeing their homework. Clearly, children's skill in searching for missing objects and describing their whereabouts has important practical consequences (Plumert et al., 1994).

Every parent is faced with the task of teaching children orderliness by putting things back where they belong and then remembering where they are. One study of children from 3 years of age through the second grade showed that children remembered the spatial location of an object if they had seen the item in a logically organized room, as opposed to an unorganized one (Golbeck, 1992). Logical organization meant clustering together in space those objects sharing functional or abstract properties. Even 3- and 4-year-olds remembered where an object could be found if they had previously seen that object in an organized arrangement. *Moral:* If parents want to teach children to put things away and to remember where to put them, they first need to organize those things in the room.

In another study, 1-year-old infants were able to remember the location of a toy hidden in one of many possible locations within a circular bounded space. Search performance was highly successful when a landmark was placed in the location of the toy (Bushnell, McKenzie, Lawrence, & Connell, 1995). An example of a landmark might be a basket on the table (Plumert, Ewert, & Spear, 1995).

When rooms are well organized, children are better able to remember where things go and to put them away.

Intelligence

So far we have discussed two approaches to the study of cognition: the *Piagetian approach* and the *information-processing approach.* The third approach, discussed here, is the *psychometric approach.* This is a quantitative approach, concerned with the level of intelligence as measured by test scores.

VIEWS OF INTELLIGENCE

To measure successfully the quantity or level of intelligence, it is necessary to know what intelligence is. Unfortunately, psychologists are not in complete agreement as to what constitutes intelligence.

Binet

One of the first persons to address the problem was *Alfred Binet* (1857–1911), a professor of psychology at the Sorbonne, the University of Paris. In the 1890s, he was asked by the Paris Ministry of Education to develop a test to sort out those children who were slow learners and who could not benefit from regular classroom instruction. The result was the creation of an intelligence test that was later revised and translated in America to become the current, widely used *Stanford-Binet Intelligence Scale.* To Binet, intelligence was a general capacity for comprehension, reasoning, judgment, and memory (Binet & Simon, 1916). Binet described this capacity as **mental age (MA):** the level of development in relation to **chronological age (CA).** The higher MA is in relation to CA, the brighter the child. The German psychologist *William Stern* originated the term **IQ, intelligence quotient,** which is calculated as follows:

$$IQ = \frac{MA}{CA} \times 100$$

If MA is equal to CA, IQ is 100. If MA is greater than CA, then IQ is over 100. If MA is less than CA, the IQ is under 100.

Spearman

In England, *Charles Spearman* (1863–1945) advanced a **two-factor theory of intelligence** (Spearman, 1927). He concluded that there is a *general intellectual factor* that he labeled *g*, and a number of *specific abilities*—*s* factors—that are useful for different tasks: for example, arithmetic or spatial relations.

Binet developed a test to sort out learning ability.

Thurstone

This concept of many kinds of intelligence was expanded by *Louis Thurstone,* a mathematician who worked in Thomas Edison's laboratory. Thurstone believed that if persons were intelligent in one area, they were not necessarily intelligent in other areas (Thurstone, 1938). Thurstone's research enabled him to identify seven distinct **primary mental abilities:**

1. verbal meaning
2. perceptual speed
3. logical reasoning
4. number
5. rote memory
6. word fluency
7. a spatial or visualization factor

These factors were tested separately in the *Primary Mental Abilities Test.* A version was eventually developed for young schoolchildren (Thurstone & Thurstone, 1953). After additional research, Thurstone found that his primary mental abilities correlated moderately with one another, so he eventually acknowledged a *g* factor as well as the individual primary factors.

Guilford

More recently, *J. P. Guilford* (1967) expanded the idea of specific abilities by identifying 120 factors in intelligence. Other psychologists agree that there are different kinds of intelligence, but disagree as to the number.

Gardner

Howard Gardner (1983) divides intelligence into seven dimensions:

1. Linguistic intelligence—verbal abilities
2. Logical mathematical intelligence—ability to reason logically and to use mathematical symbols
3. Spatial intelligence—ability to form spatial images and to find one's way around in an environment. The sailors in the Caroline Islands of Micronesia navigate among hundreds of islands using only the stars and their bodily feelings.
4. Musical intelligence—ability to perceive and create pitch and rhythmic patterns. There are individuals who are otherwise mentally retarded who can

Primary mental abilities—seven basic abilities described by Thurstone

Mental age (MA)—describes the intellectual level of a person

Chronological age (CA)—age in years

Intelligence quotient (IQ)—MA divided by CA × 100

Two-factor theory of intelligence—concept that intelligence consists of a general factor—"g"—and a number of specific abilities—"s" factors

play a song on the piano after hearing it once.

5. Body-kinesthetic intelligence—the gift of graceful motor movement as seen in a surgeon or dancer
6. Interpersonal intelligence—understanding of others, how they feel, what motivates them, and how they interact
7. Intrapersonal intelligence—individual's ability to know himself or herself and to develop a sense of identity

Crystallized intelligence—Cattell's concept that knowledge and skills arise out of acculturation and education

Fluid intelligence—Cattell's concept of inherited ability to think and reason abstractly

Gardner's concept is unique because he claims independent existences for different intelligences in the human neural system. He would like to stop measuring people according to some unitary dimension called intelligence. Instead he would like to think in terms of different intellectual strengths.

Sternberg

Triarchic theory of intelligence—three components of intelligence described by Sternberg

Robert Sternberg (1985) and his colleagues at Yale University arranged abilities into the following three major groupings in describing intelligence. His theory is called the **triarchic theory of intelligence.**

Componential intelligence includes the ability to acquire and store information; general learning and comprehension abilities such as good vocabulary and high reading comprehension; ability to do test items such as analogies, syllogisms, and series; and ability to think critically. This is the traditional concept of intelligence as measured on tests.

Experiential intelligence (intelligence based on experience), includes ability to select, encode, compare, and combine information in meaningful ways to create new insights, theories, and ideas.

Contextual intelligence includes adaptive behavior in the real world, such as the ability to get along with other people, size up situations, achieve goals, and solve practical problems (Sternberg & Wagner, 1986).

Sternberg developed the triarchic theory of intelligence.

Cattell

In an effort to include the influence of both heredity and environment in the development of intelligence, *Raymond Cattell* (1963) described two dimensions of intelligence: *crystallized* and *fluid.* **Crystallized intelligence** includes knowledge and skills measured by tests of vocabulary, general information, and reading comprehension. It arises out of experience and represents the extent of acculturation and education. **Fluid intelligence** is a person's ability to think and reason abstractly as measured by reasoning tests, such as figural analogies and figural classifications. It involves the processes of receiving relationships, deducing correlates, reasoning inductively, abstracting, forming concepts, and solving problems as measured by tasks with figural, symbolic, and semantic content. Fluid intelligence has a hereditary base in neurophysiological structures; therefore it is not influenced as much as crystallized intelligence by intensive education and acculturation.

INTELLIGENCE TESTS

Stanford-Binet

Revisions of Binet's tests were made by *Lewis Terman* of Stanford University and became the Stanford-Binet test. It is used with individuals from age 2 through adulthood. The fourth edition of the Stanford-Binet was published in 1985 (Thorndike, Hagan, & Sattler, 1985) and yields scores in four areas: *verbal reasoning, quantitative reasoning, abstract/visual reasoning,* and *short-term memory.* It also provides a composite score that can be interpreted as an *Intelligence Quotient (IQ)* that reflects overall intelligence. Figure 9.5 shows a normal distribution of intelligence test scores on the Stanford-Binet. Note that 68.26 percent of individuals have scores between 85 and 115. Only 2.28 percent score above 130 and below 70.

The Wechsler Scales

The Wechsler Scales, developed by *David Wechsler*, are also widely used. There are three scales: the *Wechsler Adult Intelligence Scale—Revised (WAIS-R)*, the *Wechsler Intelligence Scale for Children—Revised (WISC-R)* for use with children ages 6 to 16, and the *Wechsler Preschool and Primary Scale of Intelligence—Revised (WPPSI-R)* for use with children ages 4 to 6½ (Wechsler, 1967, 1974, 1981, 1989). The Wechsler Scales yield a composite IQ score, plus a verbal IQ from the six verbal subscales, and a performance IQ from the six performance subscales. Table 9.1 describes the various subtests in the WISC-R.

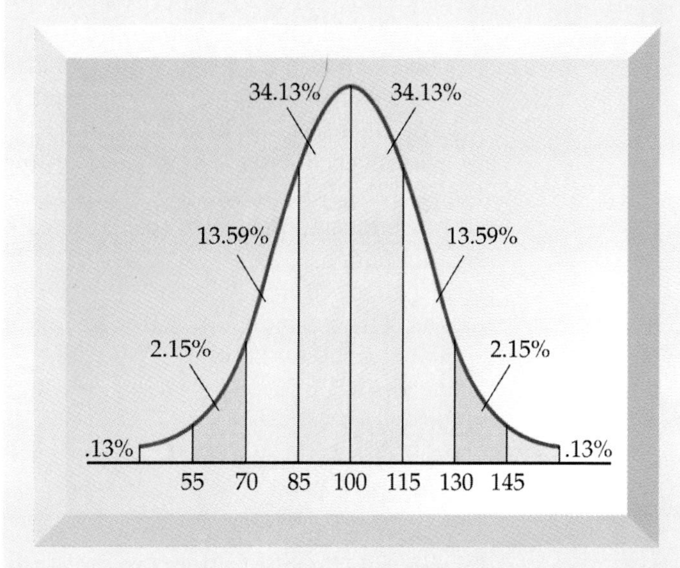

FIGURE 9.5 Normal distribution of IQ scores.

CRITIQUE OF IQ AND IQ TESTS

IQ School Performance, Job and Personal Success

IQ tests were designed initially to predict school performance. They do a pretty good job of this. Correlations between measured IQ and grades in school usually average about +.65 (Stevenson, Hale, Klein, & Miller, 1968). This accounts for about 45 percent of the variance in school grades. Still, over one-half of the variance in school grades is not predicted by IQ. Future school success is better predicted by past and present school success than by IQ. IQ tests are more predic-

TABLE 9.1
THE WECHSLER INTELLIGENCE SCALE FOR CHILDREN REVISED (WISC-R)

Verbal Scale	*Performance Scale*
1. *General information.* Questions relating to information most children in our society have the opportunity to acquire.	1. *Picture completion.* Child indicates what is missing in pictures; measures visual alertness and ability to organize visually.
2. *General comprehension.* Questions designed to assess child's judgment and common sense.	2. *Picture arrangement.* Series of pictures must be arranged to tell a story; ability to think logically and meaningfully.
3. *Arithmetic.* Oral arithmetic problems: addition, subtraction, multiplication, division.	3. *Block design.* Child is required to copy exactly a design with colored blocks; visual-motor coordination, perceptual organization, spatial visualization.
4. *Similarities.* Child thinks logically and abstractly to determine how certain things are alike.	4. *Object assembly.* Puzzles to be assembled by the child; visual-motor coordination and spatial visualization.
5. *Vocabulary.* Child gives meanings of words of increasing difficulty.	5. *Coding.* Child pairs symbols with digits following a key; visual-motor coordination and speed of thought.
6. *Digit span.* Child repeats orally presented sequence of numbers forward and backward; measures short-term memory.	6. *Mazes.* Child traces way out of mazes with pencil; an optional scale.

tive of job success in some occupations (for example, stockbroker) than they are in others, such as police officer. If a job requires academic skills, an IQ test will be a fairly good predictor of success on that kind of job. However, IQ scores tell us nothing about the ability to get along with other people; flexibility and the ability to adapt to different situations; work habits, motivation, interest, and effort; or emotional factors such as self-esteem, emotional security, or emotional stability. Yet these are all important factors in job success or in interpersonal relationships.

Stability of IQ

As is covered in a subsequent discussion of infant intelligence testing, tests given in infancy (at about age 2) are almost worthless in predicting later IQ scores. By age 5, future IQ scores are more predictable. By age 10, scores are even more stable. However, there are wide individual variations in patterns even after this age. For some children, IQ may remain fairly constant. Correlations between tests in middle childhood and later scores are generally quite high (about + .7 or more). In other children, IQ scores may increase, decrease, or go up and down like a bouncing ball (François, 1990). Pinneau (1961) reanalyzed the data from the *Berkeley Growth Study* and converted all the scores to deviation IQs. He found that children tested at 5 years and at subsequent ages up to 17 years showed median changes from 6 to 12 points, with the range of individual changes from 0 to 40 points. Eichorn, Hunt, and Honzik (1981) found a correlation of + .80 between IQ in adolescence and IQ in middle age. However, 11 percent of the persons showed IQ gains of 13 points or more between adolescence and middle age. Another 11% showed IQ drops of 6 points or more. Overall, there was a 4-point gain in IQ between adolescence and middle age. IQ scores, therefore, are not fixed norms. They can vary, depending on many factors. Even Binet emphasized frequent retesting. He explained that intellectual development is uneven, reflecting both different rates of maturation and different educational experiences (Siegler, 1992).

Personal Factors Influencing Test Results

Test results may be influenced by such personal factors as *test anxiety, motivation* and *interest* in the tasks, or *rapport* with the *test giver*. A prime example is that of a 10-year-old in the Boston school system who would not answer test questions and whose record subsequently contained this entry: "The child's IQ is so low, she is not testable." After a young psychologist talked with the child and established rapport with her, he tested her and found she achieved an IQ score of 115 ("Aptitude Test Scores," 1979).

Cultural Bias

The chief criticism of intelligence tests is that they are biased in favor of white, middle-class children. Tests to measure IQ were originally designed to measure "innate" general intelligence apart from environment influences. But research over a long period has shown that sociocultural factors play a significant role in the outcome of the tests (Carmines & Baxter, 1986). Children reared in stimulus-rich environments may show superiority in intelligence, whereas those reared under intellectually sterile conditions may not reach their full intelligence capacities. Further-

Intelligence tests may discriminate against culturally deprived children reared in the ghetto.

FOCUS

Terman's Study of Gifted Men *

A follow-up of fifty-two superintelligent men from a study begun in 1921 at Stanford University by Lewis Terman revealed some interesting results (Hagan, 1983). Sixty years after the initial study began, the men with the highest IQs could scarcely be distinguished from the general population in relation to marriage, family, and domestic relations. However, the majority had received advanced degrees and were successful and superior achievers in their professions, though those with IQs of 150 were as successful as those with IQs of 180. IQ at best taps only a few facets of intelligence and prerequisites for success in life (Trotter, 1986).

*One of the criticisms of Terman's research is that it did not include women.

more, the test language, illustrations, examples, and abstractions are middle-class, and thus are designed to measure intelligence according to middle-class standards. Many children from low socioeconomic backgrounds grow up in a nonverbal world or a world where words used are so different, that to understand middle-class expressions on an intelligence test is difficult. These children do poorly not because they are less intelligent but because they do not comprehend language foreign to their backgrounds and experiences. Children from minority groups who are also from lower socioeconomic families experience greater difficulties (Roberts & DeBlossie, 1983). Native American children and others from rural areas who have been raised in an environment free from considerations of time do poorly on tests with a time limit. When allowed to do the test at their own rate, they score much higher.

Efforts to develop culturally unbiased tests have been very frustrating. The general approach has been to use language familiar to the particular minorities for which the test is designed. But the major problem is how to evaluate their accuracy. Most have been measured against IQ scores, which continue to reflect a cultural bias (Rice, 1979).

A more promising approach is known as *SOMPA (System of Multicultural Pluralistic Assessment),* which consists of the Wechsler IQ test; an interview in which the examiner learns the child's health history; a "sociocultural inventory" of the family's background; and an "adaptive-behavior inventory" of the child, which evaluates the child's nonacademic performance in school, at home, and in the neighborhood. A complete medical exam evaluates the child's physical condition, manual dexterity, motor skills, and visual and auditory ability. The final score on the SOMPA is obtained from not only the IQ test but also from the other inventories. A child who receives 68 on the Wechsler, for example, may earn an *adjusted IQ* of 89 when scores on the sociocultural and the adaptive-behavior inventories are taken into account (Rice, 1979). Thus, SOMPA tries to measure potential rather than current ability.

IQ AND RACE

Although the full range of IQ scores is found in all ethnic groups, the average IQ difference for blacks is about 15 points lower than for whites. The question is: "Why the difference?"

In 1969, Arthur Jensen sparked a heated debate by claiming that IQ differences were hereditary. He said that because intelligence is 80 percent genetic in origin, differences between blacks and whites are largely due to inheritance.

There are several weaknesses in this argument. Jensen's estimate of the percent by which intelligence is inherited is too high. A maximum figure is closer to 60 percent due to heredity and the rest due to environmental influences. The same differences in IQ scores exist among those of all races if scores of those from lower classes are compared with those of higher classes. Ethnic differences in intelligence are really social class differences in disguise. When blacks from poor socioeconomic backgrounds are adopted into more well-to-do white families, the blacks score as high or higher than the whites, indicating that social environment plays an important role in determining the average IQ level of black children. Furthermore, IQ tests are culturally biased, so that the scores of blacks are lower, not because of lower intelligence, but because the tests are not valid when used with blacks; the tests measure the mastery of white middle-class values and language skills rather than innate intelligence. The gap in IQ scores is gradually closing, however, as educational opportunities for blacks improve (MacKenzie, 1984).

Developmental quotient (DQ)—score developed by Gesell to evaluate an infant's behavioral level in four categories: motor, language, adaptive, and personal-social

INFANT INTELLIGENCE AND MEASUREMENT

For a number of years, psychologists have been interested in testing the intelligence of infants. If measurements could be made accurately, this would be of considerable help in matching adoptive parents and children, or in planning educational activities. The problem is that infants are less verbal than older children, so they are tested on the basis of what they do, not what they say. However, infants are distractible; it's hard to get their attention to test them. If they don't do something, is it because they don't know how to do it, don't feel like doing it, or because they don't know what is expected?

Intelligence tests may discriminate against minorities.

Developmental Quotient (DQ)

Arnold Gesell (1934) developed a measure that was used to sort out babies for adoption. The Gesell test divided behavior into four categories: *motor, language, adaptive,* and *personal-social.* The scores in these four areas could be combined into a **developmental quotient (DQ).** The problem is that DQs during infancy do not correlate highly with IQs in later childhood, so any efforts to predict IQs of normal children before age 2 are practically worthless.

Bayley's Scales of Infant Development

The *Bayley Scales of Infant Development* were developed by Nancy Bayley (1969). The three scales assess the developmental status of children from 2 months to 2½ years of age in three areas: *mental abilities* such as memory, learning, perception, and verbal communication (for example, infants are asked to imitate simple actions or words); *motor abilities,* including both gross- and fine-motor skills; and *infant behavior record* (during mental and motor assessments). Separate scores are given for each scale. Unfortunately, the scores for infants are highly unreliable in predicting later IQ in

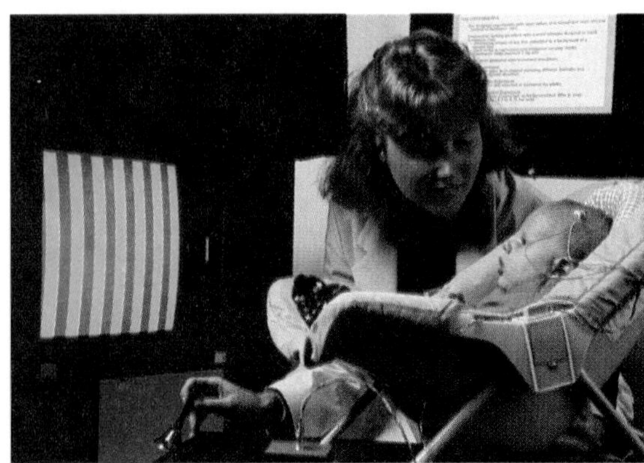

It is difficult to test the intelligence of infants because they are easily distracted.

childhood and adolescence. However, the closer children are to their 5th birthday when tested, the higher the correlation between their intelligence scores and those in later childhood (Bornstein & Sigman, 1986). It's easier to predict the future IQ of a handicapped infant than of one with normal intelligence, but some of those who are handicapped as infants improve greatly as they get older (Kopp & McCall, 1982).

Parental IQ and educational level is a much more reliable predictor of childhood IQ (Kopp & McCall, 1982). Also, measures of *habituation or dishabituation* in infancy have been found to be a much better predictor of intelligence in childhood than the developmental scales (Bornstein & Sigman, 1986), as was discussed previously in this chapter in the section on habituation.

Recent Studies

The classical longitudinal studies of mental development found little stability in performance from infancy to later childhood. Subsequent research confirmed these early results, repeatedly finding standardized infant tests to be disappointing as predictors of later intelligence. However, the most recent studies indicate that there is more stability in early intelligence than previously thought. Using newly developed indexes of infant mental functioning, researchers have found significant relations between infant cognition and later intelligence. The new infant measures include visual recognition memory, habituation, cross-modal transfer (both visual and tactual recognition memory), object permanence, and various qualitative and quantitative aspects of attention. These measures appear to involve some of the same basic cognitive abilities that characterize later intelligence. In one study, two infancy measures (a 7-month visual recognition memory test, and a 1-year cross-modal transfer test) predicted IQ at 11 years of age. These infancy measures were related to perceptual speeds, even with IQ controlled, and were selectively related to other 11-year abilities, independent of both speed and IQ. These findings suggest that perceptual speed in infancy predicts IQ at 11 years. These findings support the speculation that speed of processing is an important factor underlying individual and developmental differences in many aspects of cognition, both in infancy and older children (Rose & Feldman, 1995).

EARLY INTERVENTION

Can early intervention through remedial programs increase the intelligence of young children (Wasik, Ramey, Bryant, &

FOCUS

The Kaufman Assessment Battery for Children (K-ABC)

This test was developed by Alan and Nadeen Kaufman in the early 1980s, in part to reduce racial differences. The test cuts the IQ differences between blacks and whites by 50 percent (to about 7 points) and eliminates the differences between Hispanic and white children, thus reducing cultural bias.

The K-ABC has been found to correlate well with achievement tests (Childers, Durham, Bolen, & Taylor, 1985; Valencia, 1985). This means that the K-ABC distinguishes between those who have acquired knowledge and those who haven't, without reflecting as much racial or ethnic bias.

FOCUS

The Fagan Test of Infant Intelligence

Visual recognition memory (VRM) is a potential index of cognitive functioning. *The Fagan Test of Infant Intelligence* (FTII) is the first screening measure that has been commercially marketed to identify those infants at high risk for later cognitive delays. The test is given to infants 6.5 to 12 months of age and is based on the tendency of infants to fixate on novel—as compared to previously seen—visual stimuli. Novelty preference is tested by presenting the infant with one (or two identical) pictures to study for a preset accumulated looking time and then pairing the now familiar picture with a new or novel picture. A novelty preference score is computed by calculating the percentage of time the infant looks at the novel picture relative to time spent looking at both stimuli. These scores in relation to age are used to estimate the level of cognitive functioning. The test is well thought out and systematized, but still has some major deficiencies: an inadequate standardization sample and insufficient reliability and validity information. It shows promise, but needs additional statistical documentation (Benasich & Bejar, 1992).

Sparling, 1990)? The general consensus seems to be that *high-quality programs for economically deprived children can have lasting and valuable effects* (Casto & Mastropieri, 1986). The best example comes from research on *Head Start* programs, which were designed to help disadvantaged preschool children do better in school as they grow older (Lee, Brooks-Gunn, Schnur, & Liaw, 1990). An eighteen-year study of the progress of 123 children, beginning when they were 3- and 4-year-olds, at Perry Elementary School in Ypsilanti, Michigan, showed that those who had been in the Head Start program scored higher on reading, math, and language achievement tests than children in a control group. The Head Start children also showed fewer antisocial and delinquent tendencies as they grew up.

If programs are well funded and teachers are competent, Head Start children show "improved intellectual performance during early childhood, better scholastic placement and improved scholastic achievement during elementary school years, and, during adolescence, a lower rate of delinquency and higher rates of both graduation from high school and employment at age 19" (Schweinhart & Weikert, 1985, p. 547). These are significant findings.

An important part of Head Start is the involvement of parents: giving them information and training in child development and care, home management, family relationships, nutrition, health, and other topics. Parents are involved in planning their own programs. In one study, trained mothers gave their children more instruction, information, and praise; more encouragement to think and talk; were more emotionally responsive, sensitive, and accepting of their children; and were less critical than mothers in a control group (Andrews et al., 1982). Overall, parent–child relationships are important factors in cognitive development.

This is why intervention programs for parents can also be effective. One study of a family support program sponsored by the *Yale Child Welfare Project* resulted in better school adjustment for first-borns. Information was also obtained for older chil-

Early intervention programs stimulate intellectual achievement.

dren. Intervention group siblings had better school attendance than did control group siblings and were less likely to need supportive or remedial services and were more likely to be making normal school progress. The results suggested that changes in the caregiving environment resulting from early family support led to benefits for all the family's children. Parent-focused programs thus appear to provide a particularly efficient strategy for intervention efforts (Seitz & Apfel, 1994).

Research indicates that intervention should begin early in the preschool period and continue intensively for as long a period as needed. One study measured the effects of early intervention on intellectual and academic achievement of children from low-income families. The follow-up data was obtained four to seven years after intervention ended. The subjects were randomly assigned to one of four intervention conditions: educational treatment from infancy through three years in public school (up to age 8); preschool treatment only (infancy to age 5); primary school treatment only (age 5 to 8 years), or an untreated control group. Positive effects of preschool treatment on intellectual development and academic achievement were maintained through age 12. School-age treatment alone was less effective. Results generally supported an intensity hypothesis in that scores on cognitive and academic achievement measures increased as duration of treatment in-

PARENTING ISSUES

Pushing Preschoolers

Programs like Head Start have been found to help children from economically disadvantaged homes overcome disparity in their backgrounds. But what is the effect of providing accelerated, academically enriched programs for preschool children from middle-class families? Two psychologists, Dr. Marion Hyson at the University of Delaware and Dr. Leslie Rescoria at Bryn Mawr College, compared eighty-five children who had gone to academically enriched preschools with those who went to preschools where they simply played. Accelerated activities included learning numbers, letters, computer instruction, social studies, and foreign languages. When tested at age 4, in comparison to those in other preschools, those in the accelerated program tended to share the following characteristics:

1. They showed a slight advantage on ability tests, but the advantage disappeared a year later when the children went on to kindergarten.
2. They knew their numbers and letters better, but there was no difference in other cognitive skills that contributed to academic success.
3. Their parents tended to push them and to have higher academic expectations. These parents tended to be more controlling, critical, and emotionally negative.
4. The net result emotionally was that the children tended to be more anxious, less critical, and less positive toward school (Goleman, 1989).

creased. It is interesting that when treatment began early in the preschool years, the intellectual and academic gains from the program persisted through seven years of school (Campbell & Ramey, 1994).

MENTAL RETARDATION

Mental retardation—below normal intelligence

Mental retardation may be genetically or environmentally determined. The incidence of familial retardation in the offspring of two retarded persons is 40 percent; of one, 20 percent. About 1.5 percent of the total U.S. population has been identified as mentally retarded. The total group may be classified into categories as follows (Berkow, 1987).

Borderline. This includes slow learners with IQs of about 84 to 71. They are rarely identified before they begin school, at which time educational and behavioral problems become evident. When they leave school they generally blend in with the rest of the population. They usually can support themselves as long as they can find employment.

Mild Retardation. These are educable children with IQs of 70 to 50 and various degrees of educational achievement, and educational skills. They usually require some supervision and support, special education or training, and sheltered living. They have trouble reading but learn enough for everyday functioning. Their thinking is concrete and shows poor judgment and gullibility. Adjusting to new situations is difficult. They are impulsive and so may commit minor crimes, sometimes as part of peer group membership.

Moderate Retardation. These are trainable children with IQs of 49 to 35 with language and motor delays. Many need close supervision and a sheltered workshop.

Severe Retardation. These children with IQs of 34 to 20 are trainable, but to a lesser degree.

Profound Retardation. These children have IQs of 19 or below, usually cannot walk, and have only minimal language skills. The more severely impaired the child, the shorter the life expectancy (Berkow, 1987).

Educable mentally retarded

Trainable mentally retarded

One of the questions that arises is whether to educate mentally retarded children in regular classrooms or in special groups of their own. According to the *Individuals with Disabilities Education Act* (Public Law 94-142, 1975) children with mentally disabling conditions are to be educated in the "least restrictive environment," which means that they should be educated with nondisabled children as much as possible. As a result, many children, especially those with mild retardation, may be found in regular classrooms in the public schools. Sometimes retarded children are taught partially in the regular classroom, and then in groups of their own for varying portions of the day. Teachers with a retarded child in their classroom have to develop special programs to provide the best education to both the retarded child and the rest of the children in the class. A special education category of **educable mentally retarded** refers to those with mild mental retardation (IQs of 70 to 50), whereas special education category **trainable mentally retarded** corresponds with those who are moderately retarded (IQ of 49 to 35). The educable mentally retarded are taught fundamental academic skills needed to function independently as adults. Most trainable mentally retarded children are considered unlikely to progress beyond the second-grade level in school, so their curriculum emphasizes vocational, self-help, and social skills.

The question arises as to whether mentally retarded children should be mainstreamed in regular classes or put in special classes of their own.

School

EARLY CHILDHOOD EDUCATION

The numbers of children in some kind of early childhood education program have grown tremendously. There are several reasons for this trend. In 1993, one-third of all families with children at home were maintained by one parent. The comparable figures for black families were 58 percent (U.S. Bureau of the Census, 1995). Furthermore, in 1988, 60 percent of married women with the youngest child under age 6 were employed outside the home (U.S. Bureau of the Census, 1995). These circumstances necessitated parents' placing their children in some kind of child-care arrangement. In addition, many parents, whether they work or not, have come to recognize the benefits of preschool education for their children. Table 9.2 shows the primary child-care arrangements used by employed mothers for children under 5 (U.S. Bureau of the Census, 1995). Note that 23 percent of these children were cared for in organized child-care facilities: a day-care center, group-care home, nursery school, or other preschool.

TABLE 9.2
PRIMARY CHILD CARE ARRANGEMENTS USED BY EMPLOYED MOTHERS FOR CHILDREN UNDER 5 (1991)

Form of Care	*Percent of Mothers Making Arrangement*
Care in child's home:	35.7
By father	20.0
By grandparent	7.2
By other relative	3.2
By nonrelative	5.4
Care in another home:	31.0
By grandparent	8.6
By other relative	4.5
By nonrelative	17.9
Organized child-care facilities	23.0
Day- or group-care center	15.8
Nursery school or preschool	7.3
Kindergarten or grade school	0.5
Mother cares for child at work	8.7

From U.S. Bureau of the Census, 1995.

Nursery Schools

Nursery schools are usually for children after age 2½ to 3, after they have been toilet trained. They typically operate 3 to 5 half days a week, so do not meet the needs of parents working full time. The best schools offer college-trained teachers, and enriched intellectual and social experiences in informal settings.

Montessori Schools

These schools for children 3 to 7 are named after their founder, Dr. Maria Montessori, an Italian physician. They are expensive private schools featuring a prepared environment and carefully designed, individually paced, self-taught, self-correcting materials. The teacher arranges the environment, but otherwise does not interfere with the learning process.

Group-Care Home

The best of these are licensed by the state to accommodate a small number of children—usually in the home of the teacher. Teachers are not usually as well trained as those in larger day-care centers, but if they are warm, caring persons who love children, the effect on the children may be quite positive.

Day-Care Centers

Day-care centers are licensed by the state, and are open year round, all day, five or more days a week. They are deliberately planned to meet the needs of children of working parents. Day-care centers vary tremendously in quality. The best centers are characterized by the following (American Academy of Pediatrics, 1986; Belsky, 1984; Bredekamp, 1987; Howes & Rubenstein, 1985):

1. Have a low child-to-adult ratio: 3 to 4 infants and toddlers per adult, or 7 to 9 3- to 5-year-olds per adult.
2. Have workers who are trained in early childhood education and who are affectionate, sensitive, and responsive to the needs of children.
3. Have teachers who encourage self-control, set clear limits, reward expected behavior, and redirect troublesome children to more acceptable activities.
4. Provide a safe, clean, and healthy environment both indoors and outdoors that affords optimum physical development.
5. Offer an environment that encourages children to select from a variety of activities, to master cognitive and language skills, to learn to think and to do, and to solve problems.
6. Encourage children's curiosity, creativity, and self-development at their own pace.
7. Foster children's social skills, respect for others, and ability to get along with others.
8. Foster children's self-esteem, emotional development, and security.
9. Promote cooperation and communication with parents and assist them in parenting skills.

A good day-care program helps parents meet the needs of children, helps enrich children's lives, and can strengthen the family rather than simply separate parent and child. The key lies in the quality of service that is provided. A growing number of businesses are offering in-house child care for children of employees.

AMERICAN EDUCATION

We periodically hear outcries that American education is in trouble. In 1983, the National Commission on Excellence in Education (1983) pointed to a "rising tide of mediocrity" in the schools. In 1986, the U.S. Secretary of Education said that education in the first three grades was in "pretty good shape," but that large numbers of schools were failing to teach the more complicated subject matter beginning around the fourth grade (Bennett, 1986). The reports pointed to poor achievement test scores; the long-term decrease in SAT scores for college admission; declining enrollments and achievement in science and math; poor abilities in communication, writing, and thinking skills; and the need for remedial education and training to prepare students for jobs.

SUCCESSFUL SCHOOLS

Before we condemn all U.S. schools as inferior, we need to point out that there are tremendous differences among schools in this country. The American schools in Stevenson's study were from the Minneapolis area, chosen primarily to eliminate ethnicity, because there were few minority children in Minneapolis. These schools were neither the best nor the worst. There are schools that are vastly superior. So our task here is to delineate some of the factors that make schools great.

One of the most important characteristics of successful schools is that *they emphasize academic excellence.* They have high expectations of their students, give regularly assigned and graded homework (Rutter, 1983), and devote a high proportion of classroom time to active teaching. Teachers are expected to plan lessons carefully, and they are adequately supervised to see that this is done. The administration supplies the equipment and materials so teachers can do a good job. Students are encouraged to have pride in their work and their school.

Successful schools *pay attention to the needs of individual students.* Students who have low reading scores, or who are below level in other subjects, are given individual help to bring their achievement up. Staff and teaching personnel are encouraged to build good relations with students, and to be alert to provide assistance with personal problems (Solorzano, Hague, Peterson, Lyons, & Bosc, 1984). Teachers are expected to respect their students and to help them have pride in themselves.

Another characteristic of successful schools is *the emphasis on no-nonsense disci-*

FOCUS

The Importance of the Teacher

Children's relationships with their peers are recognized as important because of their links to later social adjustments. Children involved in child care have multidimensional relationships with their teachers. The ideal child-care teacher not only provides the child with a language-rich, cognitive learning environment, but also, through her or his caregiving and socialization roles, helps a child form trusting relationships with adults and enjoy positive interaction with peers. In one study, three aspects of the teacher–child relationship were examined: emotional security, dependency, and socialization (Howes, Hamilton, & Matheson, 1994).

As might be expected, children who were more emotionally secure with their teachers also were more confident both in their relationship with peers and in general. Toddlers who were secure with their teachers evidenced more prosocial behavior, more complex peer play and gregarious behavior, and less hostile aggression. However, preschoolers who were excessively dependent on their teachers were more socially withdrawn and more hostilely aggressive. Children who clung to their teachers in an immature or fearful way were unable to use her as a base for exploration, and so were less confident with peers because their dependent behavior interfered with developing peer relationships. Children who are high in teacher dependence are also low in social confidence with peers. Toddlers who were positively socialized by teachers were also higher in perceived peer acceptance. This means that teachers who were positive in mediating peer contacts helped children to become socially accepted. A generally sensitive teacher can help the child engage in play with others.

Great teachers are intelligent, well-trained, and have an understanding of the needs, interests, problems, and adjustments of children.

pline. Teachers are not left to their own devices to discipline students. They receive the guidance and support they need from the administration, so it is easier for them to keep order, and they have more time to devote to teaching (Jensen, 1986).

Great teachers are also important in building great schools. Great teachers are well trained, intelligent persons who know the subjects they are teaching. They have superior understanding of instructional knowledge and skills. They keep up to date in their field and are willing to spend time in preparation for class. They are also personable, mature adults who like the students they teach and have a genuine interest in their welfare. The best teachers have a real understanding of children, their developmental needs, interests, problems, and adjustments. They show genuine concern, tolerance, and friendliness, and tremendous respect and love for their pupils.

One study demonstrated the power of a teacher to influence her pupils for the rest of their lives. Miss "A" was a first-grade teacher of disadvantaged children. Her former pupils scored higher on occupational status, type of housing, and personal appearance than did other graduates of the same school (Pederson, Faucher, & Eaton, 1978). There were several reasons for Miss A's success. She believed in her children's ability and encouraged them to work hard. She stayed after school to give extra time to

Dyslexia—a developmental language disorder in which the person reads from right to left, reverses letters and words, omits words or loses his or her place

pupils who needed it. She was affectionate, caring, and unselfish, sometimes sharing her lunch with those who had forgotten theirs. Even twenty years later, she remembered her pupils by name! She succeeded because she cared about her pupils and their success, and worked to help them accomplish their goals.

ACHIEVEMENT

Heredity

Educators have spent a lot of time and energy sorting out the reasons why some pupils achieve in school and others do not. As discussed in Chapter 3, one of the most important factors is heredity. Success is not inherited, but heredity is an important factor in intelligence, and intelligence is an important factor in achievement (Bouchard & McGue, 1981).

Learning Disabilities

Some of the reasons for underachievement are physical: *poor hearing, poor eyesight,* and *various physical illnesses* or *handicaps.* One child did poorly in school for three years before the parents found out that she was seeing images upside down. Another was found to be so *deaf* that he could not hear most of what the teacher was saying. Some children suffer from brain impairments, such as *dyslexia,* which causes reading problems. Others are *hyperkinetic* because of brain injuries. Is the child doing poorly in school because of mental retardation or because of other physical impairments? Parents and teachers need to seek expert advice to see if there are physical causes for problems before they assume that the child is "just lazy" or "not trying."

Learning disabilities—problems with reading, arithmetic, spelling, and written expression even in a person with normal intelligence

Children with **learning disabilities** have average or above average general intelligence but manifest specific problems with reading, arithmetic, spelling, and written expression. Nelson Rockefeller, governor of New York and vice president of the United States, had so much trouble reading that he would ad-lib his speeches. Thomas Edison never learned how to write or spell grammatically. General George Patton read very poorly and depended on his memory to get through West Point (Schulman, 1986).

Each of the above men suffered from **dyslexia,** a developmental language disorder in which the person reads from right to left, reverses letters and words ("saw" becomes "was"; "p" is substituted for "g"), omits words entirely, or loses the place on a page. Children may make up stories when they can't read them; or they may read, but without comprehension. Symptoms of frustration become evident; deficits in learning and school performance may lead to behavioral problems, aggression, delinquency, withdrawal, and alienation from teachers, parents, and other children.

Treatment is multidimensional, by means of corrective, remedial, and compensatory education, since perceptual deficits cannot be corrected. By age 7 or 8, the intelligent child may be able to cope with the problem by developing compensatory techniques. For other children, dyslexia remains a lifelong problem, preventing them from reaching their full potential. Dyslexia is only one of a number of learning disabilities.

Instructional Approaches

Developmental psychologists and educators have, for many years, debated the effects of different instructional approaches on young children's learning and social-motivational development. There is an increasing interest in early childhood education and an apparent trend toward early introduction of basic skills using the teacher-directed approach to instruction. Practices that were previously not usually encountered until first grade or later—such as whole-class, teacher-directed instruction, formal reading instruction, written assignments out of workbooks, frequent grading—are now common in kindergarten.

Many child development experts fear that a proliferation of early childhood programs that focus on basic skills may have more negative than positive effects on children. For example, experts have argued that didactic, teacher-controlled instruction that emphasized performance undermines young children's intrinsic interest in learning, their perceptions of competence, and their willingness to take academic risks. Experts also fear that didactic instruction fosters dependency in young children on adult authority for defining tasks and evaluating outcomes and engenders anxiety about achievement.

One study of 227 poor, minority, and middle-class children between the ages of 4 and 6 sought to evaluate the effects of different instructional approaches in young children's achievement and motivation. Children in didactic programs that stress basic skills had significantly higher scores on letters/reading achievement tests and not on a numbers achievement test. Being enrolled in a didactic early childhood education program was associated with relatively negative outcomes in most of the motivation measures. Compared to children in child-centered programs, children in didactic programs rated their abilities significantly lower, had lower expectations for success on academic tasks, showed more dependency on adults for permission and approval, evidenced less pride in their accomplishments, and claimed they worried more about school. Program effects were the same for economically disadvantaged and middle-class children, and for preschoolers and kindergartners (Stipek, Feiler, Daniels, & Milburn, 1995).

Classroom Behavior

There is considerable evidence to support the generalization that temperament has an important influence on school performance. Some behavior styles are more compatible with school learning than others, and some evoke more favorable responses from teachers than others. As a result, classroom behaviors have consequences for achievement, especially for teachers' evaluations. One study measured the effects of children's classroom behavior on school performance over a four-year period. The study uses teachers' ratings of children's classroom behavior in the first, second, and fourth years of elementary school to predict end-of-year marks and end-of-year performance on achievement tests. The teachers' ratings cluster in three domains: Interest-Participation (IP), Cooperation-Compliance (CC), and Attention Span-Restlessness (AR). Of the three scales, only Interest-Participation and Attention Span-Restlessness proved important. The CC dimension turned out to be completely ineffectual. Simply being a "good citizen"—polite, helpful and so forth—matters little for learning. However, the qualities that pay off are effective use of time and talent, interest in the subject matter, a sufficient attention span, and active participation in the academic routine. Children who are interested and involved in classroom activities and who pay attention spend more time on tasks, and more of this is quality time. These pupils should do better than children who are uninterested or distracted. Such personal qualities lead to superior test scores, especially during the first year. Thus, there appears to be a "window of opportunity" in first grade, before achievement trajectories are fully established, when good classroom adjustment helps establish early learning patterns that place children in favorable trajectories that tend to persist. Test scores matter even more for teachers' marking practices. Marks serve as reinforcement and have an influence upon later learning. Children who apply themselves to the work at hand and who cause fewer problems get more reinforcement in the form of higher marks; this in itself may prompt them to learn more. Classroom behavior thus is an important influence on academic development in the early primary grades, both by enhancing learning and through the dynamics of teacher-pupil relationships (Alexander, Entwistle, & Dauber, 1993).

Achievement Motivation

Another important factor is achievement motivation, or the desire to succeed. Individuals vary in the strength of this desire. Studies of 348 pairs of identical twins at the University of Minnesota showed that heredity accounted for 46 percent of the variance (or differences) in the motivation to work hard to succeed (Goleman, 1986). Some children seem to be born with the desire to succeed; others are more laid back and seem not to care.

One study examined the relationship of family factors to children's intrinsic/extrinsic motivational orientation and academic performance. The study examined three family factors: parental surveillance of homework, parental reactions to grades, and general family style. The subjects were

FOCUS

How American Children Compare with Asian Children

Japanese and Chinese (Taiwanese) students outperform their American counterparts in mathematics and science (Stevenson, Lee, Chen, & Lummis, 1990). These differences begin early. By the first grade, American children's scores in math are significantly below those of both Japanese and Chinese children. By fifth grade, the differences are even greater. According to Stevenson and his colleagues, the average score of fifth-grade children in the highest scoring American classroom was below that of all Japanese classrooms and of all but one Chinese classroom (Stevenson, Lee, & Stigler, 1986). Table 9.3 shows the results.

Several reasons have been given for the discrepancies.

- Asian culture places more emphasis on education and hard work than does American culture. Asian parents have higher educational expectations. Pressure is placed on young children to do well on examinations that are required for admission to upper grades.
- Asian children go to school between 230 and 240 days per year, versus an average of 174 days in the United States. Asians go to school 5½ days per week, and the school day is ½ hour to 2 hours longer.
- Educational policy is centralized in Taiwan and Japan. The Ministry of Education selects the curriculum and textbooks, placing more emphasis on math and science than do boards of education in the United States.

ninety-three fifth-graders and their parents. Results of the study showed that higher parental surveillance of homework, parental reaction to grades that included negative control, uninvolvement, or extrinsic reward, and over- and undercontrolling family styles were found to be related to an extrinsic motivational orientation and to lower academic performance. However, parental encouragement in response to grades children received was associated with an intrinsic motivational orientation, and autonomy-supporting family styles were associated with intrinsic motivation and higher academic performance. In addition, socioeconomic level was a significant predictor of motivational orientation and academic performance (Ginsburg & Bronstein, 1993). It is evident that parental behavior and family styles that control children's independent thinking and behavior and were critical, punitive, or uninvolved were associated with more extrinsic motivational orientation and poorer academic performance. However, it was also evident that parental behavior and styles that were supportive and encouraging of children's autonomous expression and individual development were related to a more intrinsic motivational orientation and better academic performance.

However, part of achievement motivation is instilled in children by parents, teachers, or other influential persons. I was brought up with two brothers and a sister.

- Asian children devote more time to academic activities and to studying arithmetic.
- Asian children receive more instruction from teachers, pay more attention in class, spend less time in irrelevant activities, and less time in transitions from one class to another. American children are frequently left to work alone on material they do not understand, so spend larger amounts of time in irrelevant activities, more time in transition periods, and remarkably little time paying attention to their teachers (Stigler, Lee, & Stevenson, 1987).

TABLE 9.3
MATHEMATIC ACHIEVEMENT IN THE UNITED STATES, JAPAN, AND TAIWAN

	Mean Number of Math Questions Answered Correctly	*Percent of Class Time Spent on Math*	*Percent of Time Spent on Academic Activities*	*Percent of Time Students Paid Attention in Class*
First Grade				
United States	17.1	13.8	69.8	45.3
Japan	20.1	24.5	79.2	66.2
Taiwan	21.2	16.5	85.1	65.0
Fifth Grade				
United States	44.4	17.2	64.5	46.5
Japan	53.8	23.4	87.4	64.6
Taiwan	50.8	28.2	91.5	77.7

Statistics abstracted with permission from "Mathematics Achievement of Chinese, Japanese, and American Children" by H. W. Stevenson, S. Y. Lee, and J. W. Stigler, 1986, *Science, 231*, pp. 693–699. Copyright 1997 by the AAAS.

My parents were both from poor families, were college graduates who worked their way through school, and were successful as professional persons. My parents assumed we would go to college and work hard. We were motivated by these expectations. Three of us earned doctorates and one a master's degree. There is no question that our family background was a primary motivator in our achievement.

In contrast, the parents of some of my students actively discouraged achievement motivation. These parents look very little interest in their children's progress in school during the grade-school years. They could not wait until their children were old enough to leave school and go to work. These parents actively discouraged their children from going to college. Some of the children had to wait until they were on their own to return to school to get their degree. Their motivation came from within, in spite of the negative influence of parents.

Dysfunctional Family Relationships and Divorce

Dysfunctional family relationships have a negative effect on school achievement. Family conflict and tension, physical or emotional abuse, parental rejection and neglect, criticism, or hostility undermine children's sense of security and self-esteem, creating anxieties, tensions, and fears that interfere with school achievement. Divorce

Functional family relationships have a positive influence on school achievement.

itself is perceived as a negative event that can stimulate painful emotions, confusion, and uncertainty in children (Jellinger & Slovik, 1981; Kalter, 1983). Many children regain their psychological equilibrium in a year or so and resume normal intellectual growth and development, but the initial upset may create substantial emotional and social upheaval that affects schoolwork (Wallerstein & Kelly, 1980). The long-term effects on social, emotional, and cognitive growth are not clear and continue to be studied (Kalter, 1983).

One-Parent Families

At the present time, one-third of families with children living at home are maintained by one parent (U.S. Bureau of the Census, 1995). However, this is the proportion of one-parent families at the time of the survey. Projections show that nearly 60 percent of all children born in 1986 may be expected to spend a large part of a year or longer in a one-parent family before reaching the age of 18 (Norton & Glick, 1986). One comparison of 559 youths in the seventh, eighth, and ninth grades showed that children from single-parent homes had the lowest grades and lowest occupational aspirations (Rosenthal & Hansen, 1980). But simple cause-and-effect

FOCUS

Helpless and Mastery-Oriented Children

Research on motivational styles shows that there are important individual differences among children in late elementary school. Two individual behavior patterns among children have emerged. These patterns have been labeled "helpless" and "mastery-oriented." When faced with failure, helpless children experience negative affect, make negative self-attributions of ability, and decrease on-task performance. Following negative experiences, they inaccurately underestimate task performance and expect poor performance in the future. In contrast, mastery-oriented children experience more positive affect during challenging tasks, make self-instructing and self-motivating statements, focus on effort and strategy, and maintain or enhance their on-task performance. Following positive experiences, they accurately recall past performance, they maintain positive self-evaluations of ability, and their expectations for future performance are high. Moreover, these cognition-emotion-performance patterns are unrelated to ability on the particular tasks used (Smiley & Dweck, 1994).

PARENTING ISSUES

Report Cards

Bringing home report cards is one of the most upsetting events in the lives of some children. Children who fear they have done poorly, or those who have not lived up to parental expectations, think up every scheme in the world to keep parents from finding out. They "forget to bring it home"; they "lost it." They are sick, and so they don't go to school that day. They try to erase and change marks. I know one child who didn't come home until midnight because of fear of parental punishment. Another told me that he stole a blank card from the school office, put his own grades on it for each semester (all A's), and brought only that card to his parents. It was the only report card his parents saw for one whole year.

Report cards should be of help to parents and their children, not a major source of family disaster. But how? One, parents should be very cautious about how they react to a poor report. Some parents become violently upset, and resort to severe punishments, physical or verbal thrashings, or threats of disciplinary measures that are excessive or unwise. "Grounding" children every night and weekend for a whole semester, for example—not letting them have any social life at all—may create a lot of resentment and may not accomplish the purpose of stimulating better study habits or grades. No child can study all the time. Nervous, upset children may do far better when they are studying if they have a chance to relax and have fun in between study times. I've known parents to try to force an overactive child to remain inactive and study for long hours at a time. It just doesn't improve grades sometimes. Other parents may try to push a child of average ability to do better than he or she is capable of doing. I know one family where the parents won't let their 10-year-old son watch television until he makes the honor roll. It's been two years and the boy hasn't made it yet—and he may never make it. In fact, such achievement may be beyond his capabilities.

Two, parents should interpret a report card as an evaluation of achievement and progress and as an indication of strengths and weaknesses. They should give praise and recognition for strengths as well as thoughtful consideration for weaknesses. Do parents compliment their children on the good marks and evaluations? Or do they only notice the low ones? Most children need encouragement, morale building, and emotional support in overcoming problems. Poor marks may indicate the need for tutoring, counseling, or remedial attention of some kind.

Three, report cards are more helpful if followed up by parent–teacher conferences to discuss the reasons for the marks and the child's individual needs, and to decide on a course of remedial action, if needed. If children are having trouble, what will help the most? What should the parents' role be? (Author's counseling notes)

relationships have not been established. Many of these children came from minority and low socioeconomic groups. Lower achievement and vocational aspirations are often a result of the financial status of the family. Blechman (1982) has suggested that a number of studies of children's academic performances are based on teacher evaluations and ratings, which reflect prejudices against those from one-parent families: "He comes from a broken home." Teachers' ratings do not always agree with objective evaluations.

Sociocultural Influences

Many of the studies of achievement of minority groups indicate lower achievement levels of blacks, Hispanics, and others (Stevenson, Chen, & Uttal, 1990). Table 9.4 shows the percentage of people age 25 or older with designated years of schooling,

Nearly 60 percent of those born in 1986 may spend a year or longer in a one-parent family.

by race and ethnic origin for 1994 (U.S. Bureau of the Census, 1995). As can be seen, 40 percent of Mexican Americans age 25 or older had only an elementary education. This contrasts with 10.3 percent of blacks and 8.4 percent of whites. However, there are many reasons for this low achievement of Mexican-Americans. There is often a language problem if parents do not speak English at home. Teachers may be poorly trained, may not speak Spanish, or may be prejudiced against Hispanics. The schools they attend are more often poorly funded, and educational programs are inferior (Casas & Ponterotto, 1984). Many parents do not value education or give their children the support they need for academic success. Under these circumstances, it is not surprising that scholastic performance is poor.

TABLE 9.4
PERCENTAGE OF PEOPLE AGE 25 OR OLDER WITH DESIGNATED YEARS OF SCHOOLING, BY RACE AND ETHNIC ORIGIN, 1994

Number of Years of Schooling	*White*	*Black*	*Mexican*
Elementary: 0–8	8.4	10.3	40.0
Four years of high school or more	82.0	72.9	46.2
Four years of more of college	22.9	12.9	5.9

From U.S. Bureau of the Census. (1995). *Statistical Abstract of the United States, 1995* (115th ed.). Washington, DC: U.S. Government Printing Office, 48, 51.

However, many of the studies of minority groups do not take into account socioeconomic status (which is determined by the combination of education, occupation, and income). In many instances, socioeconomic status is a better predictor of achievement than race (Graham, 1986). For example, middle-class blacks have an achievement orientation similar to middle-class whites. Many times, as blacks grow up, their overall achievement is lower than whites, but this is because of prejudices that prevent them from getting ahead, not a lack of motivation to succeed. Middle- and upper-class blacks—like comparable classes of whites—have high expectations of success.

Summary

1. The information-processing approach to cognition describes the way children obtain, remember, retrieve, and utilize information in solving problems.
2. Stimulation is important to the learning process; when infants get used to a particular stimulation, they don't pay any attention to it, a process called habituation. Children are very distractible and attend selectively to stimuli.
3. The ability to remember, which begins in infancy, is basic to all learning.

However, few people can remember events that happened before they were 3 years old.

4. The process of remembering involves three stages: sensory storage, short-term storage, and long-term storage. Short-term memory ability increases during childhood. Long-term memory increases fairly rapidly to young adulthood.
5. Metamemory consists of knowledge of memory strategies people employ to learn and remember information. Mnemonic, or memory-aiding, strategies include: rehearsal, organization, chunking, using memory cues, using the method of loci, and being motivated to learn material because it is interesting and important.
6. Children are better able to remember the spatial locations of things in an organized room than in an unorganized room.
7. The psychometric approach to the study of cognition is concerned with the level of intelligence as measured by test scores.
8. Different psychologists discuss differing views of intelligence. Some of the more important views were those introduced by Binet (mental age versus chronological age), Spearman (two-factor theory of intelligence), Guilford (120 factors), Gardner (seven frames of mind), Sternberg (triarchic theory of intelligence), and Cattell (Crystallized and fluid intelligence).
9. The two most important intelligence tests used with children are the Stanford-Binet and the Wechsler Scales.
10. IQ is correlated with school grades, but still only accounts for 45 percent of the variance in grades. Present school success is a better predictor of future school grades than is IQ.
11. IQ is more predictive of job success in some occupations than in others.
12. By age 10, IQ scores are fairly stable, but there are still wide individual variations in patterns even after this age.
13. There are many personal factors, influencing test results: text anxiety, motivation and interest, and rapport with the test giver.
14. The chief criticism of intelligence tests is that they are culturally biased in favor of white, middle-class families.
15. Differences in IQ between blacks and whites are due to social and environmental influences and not to heredity.
16. SOMPA is a more promising approach in eliminating cultural bias in measuring IQ. The Kaufman Assessment Battery for Children (K-ABC) also was developed to eliminate racial differences.
17. Trying to predict the intelligence of infants by testing before 2 years of age is practically worthless in predicting later IQ. The closer the child is to age 5, the more valid a test becomes. The two principal tests used with the infant are Gesell's Developmental Quotient (DQ) and Bayley's Scales of Infant Development.
18. The Fagan Test of Infant Intelligence utilizes visual recognition memory in appraising intelligence.
19. Parental IQ and educational level and habituation are more reliable predictors of childhood IQ than the developmental tests.
20. High-quality programs for economically deprived children can have lasting and valuable effects.
21. Mental retardation may be genetically or environmentally determined and may be classified as borderline, mild, moderate, severe, or profound.
22. The numbers of children in some kind of early childhood education program continue to rise. The principal programs are nursery schools, Montesorri schools, group-care homes, and day-care centers. Programs differ tremendously in quality.
23. Periodically, reports emphasize that American education is in trouble. When our children are compared to Asians in science and math, our children score considerably lower.
24. Not all American schools are mediocre, however. Successful schools emphasize academic excellence, pay attention to the needs of individual children, emphasize no-nonsense discipline, and have great teachers.
25. Learning disabilities involve problems with reading, arithmetic, spelling, and written expression. One common problem is dyslexia.
26. There are a number of factors that in-

fluence achievement: heredity, physical factors, achievement motivation, family background and relations, and sociocultural influences. However, many of the studies of minority groups don't take into account socioeconomic status.

27. Report cards should be a stimulus to parents to find out how their children are doing, the reasons for their marks, and whether remedial action is needed.

Key Terms

Chronological age (CA) *p. 229*
Chunking *p. 226*
Crystallized intelligence *p. 230*
Developmental quotient (DQ) *p. 234*
Dyslexia *p. 242*
Educable mentally retarded *p. 238*
Fluid intelligence *p. 230*
Habituation *p. 222*
Haptic processing *p. 224*
Infantile amnesia *p. 224*
Intelligence quotient (IQ) *p. 229*
Learning disabilities *p. 242*
Long-term storage *p. 224*
Mental age (MA) *p. 229*
Mental retardation *p. 238*
Metamemory *p. 226*
Method of loci *p. 227*
Mnemonic *p. 226*
Primary Mental Abilities *p. 229*
Recall *p. 224*
Recognition *p. 224*
Sensory storage *p. 224*
Short-term storage *p. 224*
Trainable mentally retarded *p. 238*
Triarchic theory of intelligence *p. 230*
Two-factor theory of intelligence *p. 229*

Discussion Questions

1. What can parents do to stimulate the cognitive development of their children?
2. Why has the influence of Piaget been so felt in the psychological world? What are some of the characteristics of his theories that you like? What are some of your major criticisms of his viewpoints?
3. In what ways is the distractibility of young children a handicap to parents? In what ways is it a help?
4. Can you give examples of the memory ability of children you know?
5. What are the advantages and disadvantages for parents and teachers of knowing the IQ scores of children? In what ways are IQ test results misused?
6. Do you know anyone who is mentally retarded? Tell about that person.
7. Do you know any children who go to nursery school, Montessori school, a group-care home, or a day-care center? What are some of the benefits? What are some of the negative effects or problems?
8. Do you know anyone who has dyslexia? Tell about that person.
9. Describe your experiences as a child when you brought your report card home. What do you think of parents giving the child money for good grades? What should parents do and not do when their child brings home a poor report card?

Suggested Readings

Anastasi, A. (1988). *Psychological testing* (6th ed.) New York: Macmillan. Intelligence tests for children.

Brainerd, C. J., & Pressley, M. (Eds.) (1985). *Basic processes in memory development: Progress in cognitive development research.* New York: Springer-Verlag. Methods and findings. Research and theory.

Clark, B. (1983). *Growing up gifted: Developing the potential of children at home and at school* (2nd ed.). Columbus, OH: Charles E. Merrill. Fostering excellence at home and school.

Eysenck, H. J., & Kamin, L. (1981). *The intelligence controversy.* New York: Wiley.

Garvey, C. (1984). *Children's talk.* Cambridge, MA: Harvard University Press. Research on language of children.

Ginsburg, H., & Opper, S. (1989). *Piaget's theory of intellectual development* (2nd ed.). Englewood Cliffs, NJ: Prentice-Hall. Good explanation.

Gross, T. F. (1985). *Cognitive development.* Monterey, CA: Brooks/Cole. A basic textbook.

Kail, R. (1984). *The development of memory in children.* San Francisco: W. H. Freeman. Changes in children's memory.

McAdoo, H. P., & McAdoo, J. L. (1985). *Black children: Social, educational, and parental environments.* Beverly Hills, CA: Sage. Achievement orientation in blacks.

McDaniel, M. A., & Pressley, M. (1987). *Imagery and related mnemonic processes.* New York: Springer-Verlag. Strategies, especially imagery, for improving memory.

Sattler, J. M. (1981). *Assessment of children's intelligence and special abilities* (2nd ed.). Newton, MA: Allyn and Bacon. Tests and testing.

Siegel, M. G. (1987). *Psychological testing from early childhood through adolescence: A developmental and psychodynamic approach.* Madison, CT: International Universities Press. Common psychological tests.

Wilson, L. C. (1990). *Infants and toddlers: Curriculum and teaching.* Albany, NY: Delman. Designed for teachers and caregivers.

Emotional Development: Attachment, Trust, and Security

Chapter 10

The emotional development of children entails the development of their feelings and the expression of them in relation to themselves, their parents, peers, other people, and, literally, everything in the world. Emotional development is extremely important because emotions play an adaptive function to insure survival (for example, feeling fear may save a child's life). Emotions are also a means of communication, important factors in social relationships, and powerful motivators of behavior. And, as a source of pleasure or pain, they also play an important role in moral development.

The chapter begins with a discussion of the development of attachments or emotional bonds with care givers, and continues with a discussion of the development of trust and security.

Attachment

MEANING AND IMPORTANCE

Attachment—the feeling that binds a child to a parent or care giver

The development of attachment theory is the joint work of John Bowlby and Mary Ainsworth (Ainsworth and Bowlby, 1991; Bretherton, 1992). **Attachment** means the feeling that binds a parent and child together. It is the emotional link between them, the desire to maintain contact through physical closeness, touching, looking, smiling, listening, or talking (Pipp & Harmon, 1987). Young children who have developed a close attachment to their parents run to them when frightened, seek the comfort of their arms when upset, and otherwise derive pleasure and security from just being near them or from being able to see or communicate with them.

All infants need to form a secure emotional attachment to someone: a mother, father, other family member, or a substitute care giver (Bowlby, 1982). To feel emotionally secure, children need warm, loving, stable relationships with a responsive adult on whom they can depend (Kochanska, 1991). If for some reason parents can't be close, the child needs to form a similar attachment to whoever is the primary care giver.

Securely attached infants have affectionate, loving, attentive, and responsive care givers.

The formation of such attachments is vitally important to children's total development (Main & Cassidy, 1988). It gives them security, a developing sense of self, and makes their socialization possible (Cassidy, 1986; Pipp, Easterbrooks, & Harmon, 1992). They are less shy and uninhibited in their relationships with others (Calkins & Fox, 1992). They are better able to get along with other children, both siblings and those outside the family (Jacobson & Willie, 1986; Park & Waters, 1989; Teti & Ablard, 1989). Children begin to identify with, imitate, and learn from the person(s) to whom they feel closest. And it is through these contacts that children learn what society expects of them. Such relationships become the basis for personality and character formation. We know, too, that mental growth is accelerated if children have secure relationships from which to reach out to explore and learn (Bus & van Ijzendoorn, 1988; Frankel & Bates, 1990).

MULTIPLE ATTACHMENTS

Children can develop close attachments to more than one person (Fox, Kimmerly, & Schafer, 1991; Goossens & van Ijzendoorn, 1990). Most studies show that young children can

PARENTING ISSUES

Intergenerational Influences on Attachment

The desire and ability of parents to form close attachments with their children depends partly on the way the parents were brought up. Psychoanalysts have long emphasized that there is an intergenerational concordance in relationship patterns. Parents who were closely attached to their parents in close, affectionate relationships, are more likely to establish such relationships with their own children (Fonagy, Steele, & Steele, 1991). Parents' own emotional experiences, expressive behavior, and personality traits are significant predictors of the level of security of their infant-parent attachment, but these, in turn, are partly the result of the kind of relationships their parents developed with them (Izard, Haynes, Chisholm, & Baak, 1991).

Children can develop multiple attachments.

and often do become equally attached to their mother and father (Dickstein & Parke, 1988; La Rossa, 1988; Ricks, 1985). This represents two significant attachments. Then, if there are other relatives, such as a grandparent or older children in the home, strong attachments may also be developed with these persons. Anthropologists have emphasized that in some societies children are regularly cared for by a number of persons and that these children enjoy healthy interpersonal relations with all the family members. In fact, in such families, the loss of the mother is not completely disastrous because the child has already become closely attached to other adults. The same thing holds true in our own society in extended families. One woman said that when her father deserted the family, she was not very upset because she had her grandmother, grandfather, aunt, mother, and older sisters and brothers in the household, all of whom were very close to her (Author's counseling notes).

Because children can form multiple attachments does not mean that care givers can be constantly changed. Stability of care, whether by a parent, relative, or baby-sitter, is one of the most important elements in the maintenance of emotional security. It *is* upsetting to a child who has formed a close attachment to one person to have that person leave and be replaced by another person and then by another. One of the hardest problems working parents face is to get dependable substitute care that will not be changing continually, yet this is one of the most important keys to the overall effect of substitute care on children. It is also important that the child, before he or she is separated from the primary attachment figure, first has a chance to form a close attachment with the substitute.

The important factor in attachment development is the total dialogue that goes on between parent and child (Isabella & Belsky, 1991). Some parents are supersensitive to their children's needs (Smith & Pederson, 1988). They seem tuned to their children's signals and respond fairly promptly and appropriately to their babies' cries. (Pederson et al., 1990). They are able to interpret behavioral cues to discover what their infants are trying to communicate. They like their babies, are interested in them, spend time interacting with them, and are understanding in their responses to them (Lamb, Frodi, Hwang, & Frodi, 1983). As a result, their babies often smile, bounce, and vocalize in interaction with their parents, and show in other ways that they enjoy the social contacts with them (Lewis & Feiring, 1989).

SPECIFIC ATTACHMENTS

On the average, attachments to specific persons do not develop until about 6 or 7 months of age. Before this age, we find no upset at separa-

Nonattached children—children who have not developed a close emotional relationship with parents or caregivers

tion, whether it is a major one, such as hospitalization, or a minor one, such as the mother leaving the room. It is true that babies left alone in a room may begin to fret, but they may be comforted by anyone. They seek attention in general rather than the attention of a specific person. Consider the following two observations.

> A 10-week-old baby is lying in her crib. Her mother, tidying the blankets, leans over her, talking and smiling, while the baby coos and "talks" back. The mother leaves the room to greet a visitor. The baby cries. The visitor, who has not seen the baby before, comes over, leans down, smiles, and talks to the baby. The baby stops crying and smiles as the visitor picks her up.
>
> An 8-month-old baby is playing on his mother's knee, when his mother puts him down and leaves the room to answer the door. As the visitor enters, the baby cries. When the visitor attempts to comfort him by picking him up, the baby cries more frantically until the mother returns and holds him. Then the baby calms down. From his mother's lap he first stares and later smiles at the visitor (Dunn, 1977, p. 29).

The two situations demonstrate a crucial change. Both the 10-week-old and the 8-month-old babies protested at being left, but the older child protested at his *mother's* departure. The visitor seemed to upset him more. He no longer treats people as interchangeable companions; separation from his mother has taken on new meaning because he is now attached to *her.*

Maturation

Before attachment to parents can take place, three things must occur. *One,* infants must learn to distinguish human beings from inanimate objects in the environment. This ability comes early. By 3 weeks of age, a live human face elicits more excitement from an infant than a drawing of a face. Babies will smile readily at the sight of a human face by 5 or 6 weeks of age. *Two,* infants must learn to distinguish between different human beings so that they can recognize their parents as familiar and strangers as unfamiliar. Some infants are able to recognize their parents by 1 month of age; 81 percent can do so by 3 months; and all normal infants can by 5 months (Fagan, 1977). *Three,* infants must develop a specific attachment to one person. As suggested, infants develop attachments to persons in general before they develop attachments to individuals. Before specific attachments develop, children can accept equally the care of a loving, attentive babysitter or of their parents. Although infants know their parents, they are still content with the attention offered by others.

Decreases in Attachment Behavior

From 12 to 18 months of age is probably the most vulnerable time, when specific attachments are at their maximum (Vaughn & Waters, 1990). Generally, we see a decrease in the attachment behavior of children over the course of the second year, indicating increasing independence and maturity. Also, the need for contact, which is sought primarily through physical closeness and touching at 1 year of age, gradually expands to the social realm. At 3 years, children want contact by looking and talking across a distance. Nursery school children may want to be close to their parents or teachers, but they also seek other forms of comfort, reassurance, and attention. The older children get, the more they seek verbal soothing and reinforcement. Also, as their social contacts expand, so do the number of attachments they form.

NONATTACHED CHILDREN AND INSECURE ATTACHMENT

Some young children whose parents reject them are distant and unemotional, and they don't even seem to notice when their parents come home in the evening or have taken a trip. Of course, sometimes children don't notice because they are preoccupied with their own activities, but if this happens frequently, it may indicate a lack of attachment to the parents. Young children may show marked differences in the degree of attachment. **Nonattached children,** or those whose attachment development is delayed, may make no distinction between their own parents and other members of the household or a caretaker. They accept the attention of any person as readily as they accept that of their own parents. They do not cry when the parents leave the room nor do they attempt to follow them, and they are sometimes precociously independent. This is not normal behavior for children who are old enough to have developed attachments to their parents.

At the other extreme are children who are **insecurely attached,** who are so dependent on their parents that they won't let them out of their sight at all (Lieberman, Weston, & Pawl, 1991). If parents have to leave, the children scream. The clinging, dependent behaviors of these children are symptoms of their insecurities. Insecurely attached infants are fussy babies. They cry not only when they are parted from their parents, but also when they are in close proximity. They cry to be picked up, or they cry when their parents put them down (Belsky & Braungart, 1991). They seek almost continuous physical contact and are unable to tolerate even a little distance from their parents.

P. J. Turner (1991) found some differences in attachment behavior according to gender of insecurely attached children in preschool. Insecure boys showed more aggressive, disruptive, assertive, controlling, and attention-seeking behavior than secure boys. Insecure girls showed more dependent behavior and were less assertive and controlling than secure girls.

Insecurely attached children are overly dependent on parents.

There are various reasons for overdependent behavior (Egeland & Farber, 1984). Children who receive insufficient food and who are chronically hungry may develop these symptoms. Children who are chronically ill may become overly dependent. Children who are rejected and neglected may develop an excessive need for attachment. If parents are highly anxious, nervous, or neurotic persons, this anxiety is felt by their children, who seek reassurance as a result. Also, parents who become depressed, mentally ill (van Ijzendoorn, Goldberg, Kroonenberg, & Frenkel, 1992) or preoccupied with their own personal problems are not able to give their children the attention and assurance they need. Any one or a combination of these conditions may result in children who are overly dependent and insecurely attached (Lyons-Ruth, Connell & Grunebaum, 1990). Parents need to be sensitive, to have a lot of social support, and be secure persons themselves in order to provide their children what they need (Jacobson & Frey, 1991). *One study showed that parent–infant attachment at 12 months of age could be predicted from the qualities of interaction at 3 months and from the amount of time parents spent with their infant* (Cox, Owen, Henderson, & Margand, 1992).

Insecurely attached—children who are overly dependent on parents or care givers because of insufficient attachment

We must be careful, however, in attributing all differences in attachment behavior to the quality of parenting that children receive. Sometimes there seems to be inconsistent and weak associations between parental behavior and attachment security (Rosen & Rothbaum, 1993). This means that hereditary factors and natural differences in temperament also play important roles in attachment behavior. Some children seem to be born needing closeness; others seem more independent from the beginning of life. There does seem to be a relationship between temperament and attachment behavior, but this relationship is often variable and inconsistent, varying from child to child (Vaughn et al., 1992).

SEPARATION ANXIETY

Symptoms

Signs of separation anxiety vary somewhat according to individual children, their ages, and the frequency and length of time they are separated from the attachment figure (Lollis, 1990; Field, 1991b). After infants develop attachments to specific persons, they begin to show signs of distress when these persons leave them (Bridges, Connell, & Belsky, 1988). The simplest manifestations is a baby crying when a parent leaves the room (Vaughn, Lefever, Seifer, & Barglow, 1989). Observers have found that some babies as young as 15 weeks will cry when parents leave. Most babies certainly will by 30 weeks.

The most common separation is a parent leaving a child alone in a room and closing the door. Infants may cry, and their play may cease soon after the parent leaves. If they are old enough to creep or walk, they may try to follow. If the parent leaves the room but the child can observe the parent in the adjacent room, anxiety is minimized. One observer discovered that young children in a park commonly "froze" when their mothers kept in sight while walking away from them, but they did not cry or attempt to follow. However, a group of infants in a laboratory experiment played contentedly for several minutes and then tried to follow their mothers, who had walked out of sight (Corter, 1976).

In the movie *Home Alone*, the parents mistakenly left on vacation without their child.

Effects of Repeated or Long-Term Separation

If separation is repeated or continues for very long, usually over a period of days, symptoms become more serious. The initial phase of protest and searching is followed by a period of despair, during which children become quiet, apathetic, listless, unhappy, and unresponsive to a smile or coo. Finally, if separation continues, the children enter a period of detachment and withdrawal when they seek to sever the emotional ties with the attachment figure. They appear to have lost all interest in the person to whom they were formerly attached. In extreme cases, they seem to lose interest in almost everything going on around them. There is no attempt to contact a stranger and no brightening if strangers contact them. Their activities are retarded. They often sit or lie in a dazed stupor. They lose weight and catch infections easily. There is a sharp decline in general development (Bowlby, 1980).

The trauma of long-term separations without an adequate substitute attachment figure is best illustrated by the following description of a 2-year-old child who had a good relationship with his parents at the time he was hospitalized. He was looked after by the same mother substitute and visited daily by his parents during the first week. However, his behavior deteriorated when the parents reduced their visits to twice a week and then gave up visiting him.

> He became listless, often sat in a corner sucking and dreaming; at other times he was very aggressive. He almost completely stopped talking. . . . He sat in front of his plate eating very little, without pleasure, and started smearing his food over the table. At this time, the nurse who had been looking after him fell ill, and Bobby did not make friends with anyone else, but let himself be handled by everyone without opposition. A few days later he had tonsillitis and went to the sickroom. In the quiet atmosphere there he seemed not quite so unhappy, played quietly but generally gave the impression of a baby. He hardly ever said a word, had entirely lost his bladder and bowel control, sucked a great deal. On his return to

the nursery he looked very pale and tired. He was very unhappy after rejoining the group, always in trouble and in need of help and comfort. He did not seem to recognize the nurse who had looked after him at first (Bowlby, 1973).

The trauma of extensive separation without an adequate substitute can be quite severe.

Age Factors

Generally speaking, distress over separation is greatest after 6 months and until about 3 years of age. It is most evident in young children who have had a close relationship with their parents and who are separated suddenly without an adequate substitute caregiver provided to whom the child has already become attached. Protest over temporary separation begins to decline most sharply around age 3. The decline in anxiety accompanies the increase in the power of recall: Children are able to remember their parents and a promise that they will return; also, increasing autonomy and mobility make them less dependent.

Preschool children from 3 to 5 years of age can still experience a great deal of separation anxiety, however, as every nursery school teacher knows. The older children become, the less they are upset at separation, partially because they are more independent and partially because they will take more readily to mother substitutes. Between the ages of 5 and 8, the risks of upset decrease even further. Contrary to what we find in younger ages, the children of this age who have the happiest relationships with their parents are better able to tolerate separations than those who are only insecurely attached. A happy child, secure in parental love, is not made un-

PARENTING ISSUES

Response to Crying

One mother asked: "If I go in to see what is the matter as soon as the baby cries, isn't he more likely to cry even more the next time? Shouldn't I let him cry it out to show him that he can't get my attention any time he wants?" (Frodi & Senchak, 1990)

Social-learning theorists would agree with this parent: Responding promptly to babies' cries rewards their crying and encourages them to cry more. *Attachment theorists* believe just the opposite. They say that babies whose crying is ignored early in life tend to cry more persistently thereafter. Furthermore, this persistent crying aggravates the parents and discourages response (Bisping, Steingrueber, Oltmann, & Wenk, 1990; Donovan & Leavitt, 1989).

Who is right? Both are. This is not as confusing or impossible as it sounds. Generally speaking, a sensitive and prompt response by the parent to the baby promotes a harmonious relationship with a child who is secure and content. Parents who respond promptly to distress tend to have children who are among the least fretful. This view supports the attachment theorists. However, over-anxious parents who respond unnecessarily when the baby really doesn't need them are encouraging excessive crying and demands. In other words, some of the most fretful babies may have parents who are overly anxious about responding. This view supports the social-learning theorists.

As in many other instances, avoiding extremes in raising children is often the wisest thing. If a parent never responds to the baby's cries of distress, one reaction is for the child to give up crying entirely and become withdrawn, but no one would say such a quiet child is well adjusted. The other extreme is for the parent to respond anxiously to every whimper (Zeskind, Klein, & Marshall, 1992).

bearably anxious. The insecure child, already anxious in his or her attachments, may become even more troubled by forced separation (Ainsworth, 1988).

School-age children or even adolescents are not untouched by separations. Surveys of children between the ages of 5 and 16 who were evacuated from the city of London during World War II confirm the finding that children are not yet emotionally self-supporting. Teachers reported that homesickness was prevalent; that the power of concentration on schoolwork declined; and that bedwetting, nervous symptoms, and delinquency increased. In most cases, there were no serious aftereffects following the children's return home, but in others, the problems persisted for a while afterward (Bowlby, 1982). Young people as old as college age may go through a period of extreme homesickness when first away from home. They get over it, but it's very upsetting for a while.

HOMESICKNESS

The *American Psychiatric Association* includes homesickness as one possible manifestation of separation anxiety disorder, noting that some children with separation anxiety disorder become distressed only after separation. In one longitudinal and clinical investigation of homesickness in children, the moods of 329 boys ages 8–16 were assessed on a daily basis during either a two- or four-week period of separation from primary caregivers. The subjects were all campers at a residential boys' sports camp. The study confirmed four major hypotheses. Homesickness was quite prevalent, varied in intensity, and, for some boys, reached levels associated with severe depression and anxiety. Homesickness was experienced as a combination of depression and anxiety, particularly the former. Younger boys were at greater risk for homesickness than older boys. Home-

PARENTING ISSUES

When a Child Goes to the Hospital

One parent asks: "My 4-year-old may have go to the hospital for a major operation, and he will probably have to stay a week. What should I do to minimize the emotional upset?" It is helpful if one parent can stay with the child, making arrangements to sleep in the same room, if possible. If one parent can't stay all the time, the other parent, older relatives, and/or teenagers can rotate so that a family member is present all the time. Such arrangements can be made in many hospitals and are vitally important to the child's emotional health. Going to the hospital is frightening enough, but having to stay there for a week is far more upsetting than most children, even the best-adjusted ones, can handle. All of the symptoms of separation anxiety are frequently seen after a few days of hospitalization. In addition, children fear being hurt or mutilated or being left alone. Also, they may interpret being sent to the hospital as punishment for wrongdoing. "I will be good, don't make me go" is the way some children feel. One 7½-year-old boy who had been in the hospital three times since the age of 3 recalled: "I thought I was never coming home again because I was only 6 years old. I heard my sister say they were going to dump me and that I'd never come home again" (Bowlby, 1982).

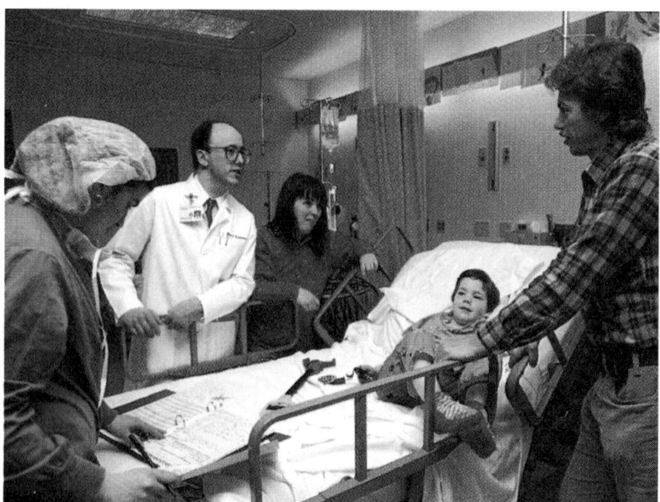

Familial comfort, attention, and support diminish a child's fears of staying in a hospital.

sickness was sometimes detectable to observers who knew the boys most often presented internalizing behavior—such as withdrawal, depression, or somatic complaints—and only occasionally showed externalizing behavior—for example, delinquent behavior. Popular opinion suggests that homesickness in children will gradually disappear over a period of time. But in this study, the most homesick boys became progressively more homesick over the course of their separation, experiencing a significant drop in homesickness just before reuniting with parents (Thurber, 1995).

REUNION BEHAVIOR

Investigators of reunion behavior of children reveal various reactions (Bowlby, 1982). Some children become very dependent and possessive, clinging, whining, crying for attention, and placing great demands on their parents. In such cases, it is helpful if the parents can devote themselves exclusively to their children after they get home; otherwise their attachment behavior may increase.

Some children are quite angry at their parents and resist (at least initially) their efforts to hug them and to pay attention to them. It is evident that they have ambivalent feelings toward their parents. On the one hand, they want their love and attention. On the other hand, they resist it because they are angry and fearful. If a separation has been long and upsetting, any withdrawal behavior of children is their effort to keep from being rejected or deserted again.

Child going to summer camp.

Sometimes, on reunion, children are emotionally cold, unable to speak or express their feelings until tearful sobs finally burst forth, accompanied by accusing questions: "Why did you leave me?" The worse children behave, the more evident it is that they have been upset by the parent's being away.

STRANGERS

Fear of strangers, when it develops, ordinarily begins at about 6 or 7 months of age, and increased to about 2 years, after which it declines (Fagot & Kavanagh, 1990). Usually, this fear begins after the onset of specific attachments. Children who are very frightened may cry or cling to their parents. Less upsetting reactions include general wariness or active turning away and avoidance (refusing to be picked up, refusing to speak, or running away).

Children differ considerably in their reactions to strangers (Thompson, Connell, & Bridges, 1988). Some never seem to show much fear at all. They smile readily, seldom turn away from being approached, and may even approach the strangers after only a few minutes of contact. Individual differences relate to how secure children are and to their background of social experiences. Some children are more accustomed to having pleasant experiences with a variety of persons. However, children who have suffered repeated and upsetting exposures to strangers become even more wary and frightened the next time they are approached.

If children are with their parents at the same time that they are in the presence of strangers, they are less frightened than when they are alone with strangers. Children are less frightened of strangers in familiar surroundings. This means that parents who invite friends over to their own home and let the children stay around during the socializing are helping the children get used to other people in an environment that is not stressful. Or, if parents stay with their children when they go out among strangers, they are getting their children used to other persons at the same time that they are giving them the security of their presence. The most frightening situation is to leave the children with strangers in an unfamiliar setting. Also, it is wise to avoid separations and frightening experiences at a time when the fear of strangers is developing or is at is peak. From 1 to 2 years of age is an especially bad time. Either before fears develop or after children begin to lose their fear of strangers is a better time to expose children to new people.

BABY-SITTERS AND SUBSTITUTE CAREGIVERS

Leaving a child with a stranger can be a very upsetting experience, but it need not affect the child negatively at all if the proper arrangements are made. The arrangement considered the least upsetting is care by the other parent in the child's own home while the one parent is gone, or substitute care by a close, dependable relative in the child's own home (Darling-Fisher & Tiedje, 1990). If neither of these alternatives is possible, the next alternative is a dependable, capable baby-sitter in the child's own home, provided that the child has become acquainted with the sitter over a period of days before the parent has to leave. It is perhaps a good idea to help children become attached to several substitute caregivers in case one cannot show up. It is often worse for the parents to surprise the child with a complete stranger and then leave for several days or longer without warning.

Another alternative is family day care in the home of the day-care provider. Usually, the provider is caring for several children at once. If the home is licensed, the state regulates the number of children per provider. The number of infants permitted is fewer per provider than the number of older children that may be cared for. The effect on children depends greatly on the quality of the care. Home environments that are free of tension and provide the requisite materials and interactions build security and stimulate the cognitive development of children (Goelman, Shapiro, & Pence (1990).

Many children are being cared for in formalized child-care centers. Parents are usually more willing to place older preschool children in such centers than they are to place infants and toddlers. Day-care centers are the most costly type of child-care arrangement, and family resources are limited. These considerations, plus a general parental preference for other child-care arrangements, limits the numbers of children cared for in this manner (Camasso & Roche, 1991; Caruso, 1992). Research comparisons of family day-care homes with child-care centers indicate that children are better off in centers than in homes primarily because of better trained, more intensely involved staff creating higher-quality environments in the child-care setting (Kontos, Hsu, & Dunn, 1994).

The question of the long-term effects of substitute care on children is a very controversial one (Belsky, 1990; Rapp & Lloyd, 1989). Some studies find no association between a mother's work status and the quality of the infant's attachment to her (Chase-Lansdale & Owen, 1987). Belsky and Rovine (1988) have concluded that when infants were from intact families, 12 and 13 months of age, and exposed to twenty or more hours of substitute care per week, they were more likely to be insecurely attached than are infants cared for less than twenty hours per week. However, leaving a child daily in the care of a baby-sitter so that both parents can go to work, even over a period of years, is far different from leaving a child to be cared for by a procession of baby-sitters with whom the child has only superficial attachments. Also, leaving a child in a well-run, well-staffed infant-care center is far different from leaving a child in an overcrowded, understaffed nursery where care is inadequate, where the staff changes frequently

The effect of day care on children depends on the quality of the care.

PARENTING ISSUES

Introduction to Nursery School

If parents are sending a child to nursery school, it is helpful to introduce the child to the school gradually. The best schools allow the parent to first bring the child to the room to play when school is not in session. If the child can become used to the room and become attached to a familiar toy, then he or she will feel more secure the next time. Also, it's important for the child to become acquainted with the teacher, so when school opens the child knows that Ms. Smith is going to be there. Also, having shortened sessions during the opening few days of school can help, as does the practice of allowing the parent to stay for the first few mornings. The parent's presence helps to alleviate the child's anxiety. Gradually, children begin leaving their parents' sides and entering in the play; they forget that they are in a new situation. There is no need for the introduction to nursery school to be a frightening experience. Some parents become so anxious themselves that they transfer this anxiety to their children (Hock, McBride, & Gnezda, 1989). If properly handled, separation anxiety can be kept to a minimum, and the child can very much look forward to going to school.

LIVING ISSUES

The Quality of Teachers

The effect of day care on children depends a lot on the quality of the teachers. The most effective teachers believe in reasonably high standards, are likely to engage in appropriate caregiving, and provide developmentally appropriate activities. Their pupils feel emotionally secure with them and are more competent with peers as a result (Howes, Phillips, & Whitebook, 1992). Teachers who are most sensitive and most involved with the children produce pupils who are most secure. Teacher sensitivity and involvement, in turn, are related to the education and specialized training teachers receive (Howes & Hamilton, 1992a).

(Howes & Hamilton, 1992b), and the personnel cannot give sufficient attention to each child. The biggest problem is finding dependable, high-quality care (Meredith, 1986; Trotter, 1987b).

Evidence is accumulating that the effect of high-quality day care on children is very positive. One study examined the relationship between cognitive and socioemotional competence at ages 8 and 13 to children's earlier day-care experiences (Andersson, 1992). The results indicated long-lasting positive effects of early day-care experiences. At ages 8 and 13, school performance was rated highest among those children who had entered day care before the age of 1. At age 13, school performance was lowest among those without out-of-home care. Similar results were found for some socioemotional variables. School adjustment at age 8 was highest for children who entered day care before age 1, and lowest among those without out-of-home care. The same was true for social competence at age 13. No signs of negative effects of early entry into day care were found.

Another study, this of children 5 and 8 years of age, found that children who had spent time in quality infant day care appeared to be better off socially and emotionally during the early grade school period than those who had not been in day care. According to the parents, children who had experienced quality infant day care were more popular, had more friends, and engaged in more extracurricular activities than those who had had less or lower-quality care. They exhibited greater social skills, assertiveness, and leadership abilities (Field, 1991a). This same researcher found that sixth-graders who had experienced full-time stable infant care in a variety of centers starting at different ages in infancy were more physically affectionate, assertive (not aggressive), more attractive, showed superior emotional well-being, and received higher math grades than those not attending infant-care centers. Time spent in quality infant care was significantly related to being assigned to the gifted program in school (Field, 1991a).

Development of Trust and Security

Symbiosis—a period in which children establish a close dependency on their mothers, to the extent that there is almost a fusing of personalities

Autistic phase—age during which children are aware of their mother only as an agent to meet their basic needs

THEORETICAL PERSPECTIVES

Erik Erikson (1963, 1968) suggested that the "cornerstone of a vital personality" is formed in infancy as the child interacts with parents or other caregivers. This cornerstone is one of basic trust as infants learn that they can depend on the care givers to meet their needs for sustenance, protection, comfort, and affection. If these needs are not met, the infants become mistrustful and insecure.

Margaret Mahler, a clinical psychologist, emphasizes the importance of the mother–child relationship (Mahler, Pine, & Bergman, 1975). From birth to 2 months, infants go through an **autistic phase** during which their only awareness of the mother is as an agent to meet their basic needs. Then from 2 to 5 months, they enter a second phase, **symbiosis,** during which they establish dependency on their mother, building a solid foundation for later growth and independence. Mothers who are sensitive and responsive encourage a symbiotic relationship with their infants. A less sensitive mother can frustrate the infant's need to fuse with her, causing the infant to be insecure. The basic psychosocial task, therefore, is to build trust and security through dependency and need fulfillment.

This Eskimo mother in Canada is sensitive to the needs of her child.

REQUIREMENTS FOR THE DEVELOPMENT OF TRUST AND SECURITY IN INFANTS

There are a number of requirements if trust and security are to be developed. One is for children to receive regular and adequate feedings. The chronically hungry child becomes an anxious child (Valenzuela, 1990).

A second requirement for the development of trust and security is for babies to get sufficient sucking. Most need several hours a day in addition to their nutritional requirements. Since sucking is a source of comfort and emotional security, feeding time needs to be a relaxed, unhurried experience, allowing the baby ample opportunity to suck. Most babies can empty the mother's breast in a short time, but they continue to suck for a period afterward. A pacifier is a helpful way of meeting children's emotional needs.

Another important emotional need of children is for cuddling and physical contact (Anisfeld, Casper, Nozyce, & Cunningham, 1990). Children have an emotional need for fondling, touching, stroking, warmth, the sound of a pleasant voice, and the image of a happy face (Herman & McHale, 1993; MacDonald, 1992).

The most important requirement for the development of trust and security in children is for parents to show them that they love them. Parents need to convey through attitude,

LIVING ISSUES

Learning to Express Affection

A frequent complaint of both men and women is that their partner is not affectionate enough. By affection, they do not always mean sexual intercourse; they mean touching, hugging, cuddling, holding, kissing. In a response to a challenge from one of her readers, Ann Landers (1985) asked women to reply to this question: "Would you be content to be held close and treated tenderly and forget about the act?" Over 100,000 replies poured in. Yes, answered 72 percent of the respondents. Of the total, 40 percent were under 40 years of age. Whatever else the replies indicated, they revealed that these women wanted to feel cared about, that they wanted tender words and loving embraces more than intercourse with an inexpressive partner. The fortunate women were those who received both emotional expressions of affection and complete physical satisfaction as well.

Shere Hite (1981), in her report on male sexuality, discovered that men wanted more than mechanical sex. They wanted physical affection—touching, hugging, kissing, back rubs, and stroking. They also wanted friendship, communication, emotional closeness, warmth, and genuine affection.

Although the need for affection is inborn, learning ways of expressing it are not (Money, 1980). Some children grow up in families in which hugging, kissing, and demonstrations of affection are a part of everyday life. The parents hold children on their laps, cuddle with them, hug and kiss them, tuck them in bed at night, tell them they love them, and show it in word and deed. Other children grow up in families that are not at all demonstrative. If they love one another, they never say or show it in intimate ways. Children from these families may grow up embarrassed to express affection and feelings. When they marry, they may have the same hesitancy in being demonstrative.

word, and deed that they adore their children. It is also important that parents be sensitive and responsive to their children's needs (Bornstein et al., 1992).

SOME CAUSES OF DISTRUST AND INSECURITY

Parental Deprivation

As already discussed, once children have formed close emotional attachments to a parent or parent substitute, any extended separation has negative effects. The longer the deprivation continues, the more pronounced the effects. Such children are typically described as emotionally withdrawn and isolated, with an air of coldness and an inability to show warmth and sincere affection or to make friends in a caring way. One woman, who adopted a 5½-year-old girl who had been shifted from one relative to another, described her daughter as not being able to show affection. The mother complained that she "would kiss you, but it would mean nothing." The adoptive father explained that "you just can't get to her." A year and a half after the adoption, the mother remarked: "I have no more idea today what's going on in that child's mind than I knew the day she came" (Bowlby, 1971, p. 37).

What is significant is that some children can remain with parents and be similarly deprived if their parents are not able to fulfill their needs for affection, for loving care, for understanding and approval, or for protection from harm. Parents who have babies they don't want and who reject them or fail to care for them properly are exposing their children to parental deprivation just as surely as if they went away and left them.

Parents themselves need a lot of social support of their parenting task. This social support can come from family, friends, organizations, or the community at large.

Adequate social support has been associated with parental satisfaction, personal well-being, maternal adjustment, increased verbal and emotional responsiveness on the part of parents, nurturance, mother-child communication, and with the child showing increased compliance with parental requests (Pianta & Ball, 1993). Social support moderates the negative impact of stresses such as poverty, child illness, or disability.

Tension

Another important cause of emotional insecurity is to be cared for by parents who are tense, nervous, anxious, and irritable (Crnic & Greenberg, 1990; Holden & Titchie, 1991; Sternberg et al., 1993). Parents need to be aware that quarreling between family members upsets children, especially if the quarrels are frequent and violent. A husband and wife start to shout at one another; the baby begins to cry. Even the dog hides under the table. Children who are forced to listen to repeated parental fights become more and more anxious themselves. Also, when there is economic stress in the family the children's emotional well-being and behavior are affected. The children often show more depressive symptoms and antisocial and impulsive behavior (Takeuchi, Williams, & Adair, 1991).

Exposure to Frightening Experiences

The effects of isolated exposure to frightening experiences are usually temporary, unless the experience is quite traumatic. Many adults can recall frightening experiences: being locked in a closet, being chased by a dog, getting lost on the way home from school. Sometimes such experiences are traumatic enough or repeated often enough to cause long-term upset. Children who are sexually molested may be deeply affected psychologically, depending on the situation.

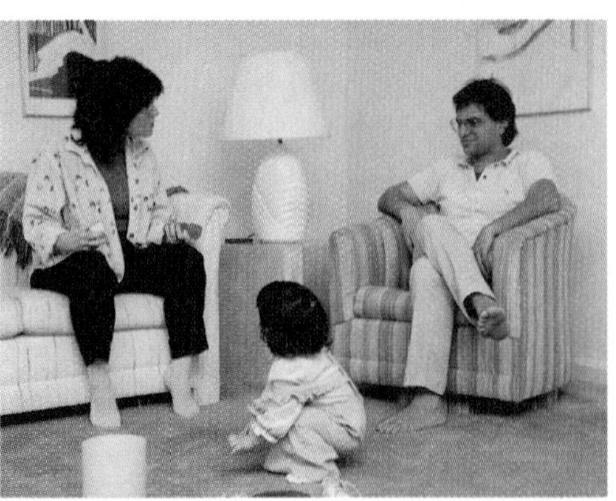

Parents who quarrel openly in front of children stimulate insecurity.

Criticism

Frequent disapproval and criticism may make children unsure of themselves. Actually, some disapproving parents are showing their children that they resent them or even hate them. Two psychiatrists describe the life of a boy whose parents hate him.

> From the time he awakens in the morning until he goes to bed at night he is nagged, scolded, and frequently slapped. His attempts at conversation are received with curt, cold silence or he is told to be quiet. If he attempts to show any demonstration of affection, he is pushed away and told not to bother his parents. He receives no praise for anything he does no matter how well he has done it. If he walks with his parents, and lags a little, his arm is seized and he is yanked forward. If he falls, he is yanked to his feet. . . . At meal times he is either ignored or his table manners and inconsequential food fads are criticized severely. He is made to finish whatever is on his plate. . . . The child soon realizes that he can expect nothing but a hurt body or hurt feelings from his parents, and instead of feeling love for them, he feels fear, loathing, and hatred (English & Pearson, 1945, p. 108).

Frequent criticism can be devastating, resulting in deep-seated insecurities and poor self-esteem.

Overprotection

Parents who are filled with anxieties themselves and who are fearful for the safety and well-being of their children may not permit any activities in which there is an element of danger. One girl remarked: "My parents would never let me go to dances because they were afraid I'd get involved with boys." Overprotected children, whose parents never let them develop autonomy, may become so fearful of making decisions or of doing things on their own that they have difficulty establishing themselves as independent adults.

Overindulgence

One of the chief causes of insecurity in children is poor impulse control on their part, resulting in guilt and anxiety over their own behavior. Children who are permitted every satisfaction and liberty, whether these things are good for them or not, are inadequately prepared to face the frustrations and disappointments of life. Such children are not disciplined or taught to consider others, so they become selfish and demanding. Anxiety results when these persons get into the world and discover that other people resent them or dislike them because of their selfish behavior. They are puzzled that others don't indulge them as their parents have done, and they become more and more anxious that they won't be successful in their social relationships.

PARENTING ISSUES

Child Abuse

Child abuse takes two main forms: neglect and attack (Gelles & Conte, 1990). The effects of parental neglect have been discussed. But the effects caused by parents who physically attack and hurt their children may be devastating—both emotionally and physically. The battered child may suffer burns, lacerations, fractures, hemorrhages, and bruises to the brain or the internal organs. A case in point is that of an 18-month-old infant whose father sat him on the red-hot burner of the stove because he wouldn't stop crying!

Battered children are often unplanned, premature, or sickly children who make extra demands on parents who are not able to cope (Zucavin, 1988). Parents who batter their children expect and demand behavior from them that is far beyond the children's ability. Such parents are immature themselves, with poor impulse control, and in great need of love (Kugler & Hansson, 1988). In some cases they are emotionally ill (Walker, Downey, & Bergman, 1989). Often they were neglected and abused while growing up. One such example is that of Kathy, the mother of a 3-week-old boy, Kenny: "I have never felt loved in all my life. When the baby was born, I thought he would love me, but when he cried all the time, it meant he didn't love me. So I hit him." Not only do battered children suffer the pains of physical abuse, but they are also deeply scarred emotionally by the rage and hatred directed at them. Pathological fear, deep-seated hostility or cold indifference, and an inability to love others are often the results.

The negative effects of child abuse are compounded because abuse has a detrimental effect on children's social relationships. Abused children exhibit a higher proportion of negative behavior, are behaviorally disturbed, are more aggressive and less cooperative, and so are less well liked by their peers (Haskett & Kistner, 1991; Salzinger, Feldman, & Hammer, 1993). Teachers view them as disturbed. The children have more discipline referrals and suspensions and often show poor academic performance (Eckenrode, Laird, & Doris, 1993). One researcher even pointed out that adults who were abused as children show increases use of alcohol and drugs and a higher incidence of HIV infection than adults who were not abused. Evidently they are more willing to engage in self-destructive behavior that reflects very low self-esteem (Allers & Benjack, 1991). Other research indicates that not only is the child who is abused affected, but siblings in the same family are affected as well (Jean-Gillis & Crittenden, 1990). The possibility for success of emotional rehabilitation will depend upon the damage done. There are cases of battered children blossoming into happy persons after being adopted by loving parents.

Some parents who were abused while growing up resolve never to abuse their own children. Unfortunately, other parents who have been abused themselves as children are likely to abuse their own children. This is why it is vitally important to get help, so that the cycle of abuse can be broken. One study found that abused mothers who were able to break the cycle of abuse were likely to have received emotional support from a nonabusive adult during childhood; to have received therapy; and to have married a stable, emotionally supportive mate with whom they had a satisfying relationship (Egeland, Jacobovitz, & Sroufe, 1988).

Adolescents who become parents have a high rate of abuse of their children. One program was designed to lower that rate by teaching pregnant teenagers what they could expect during and after pregnancy and how to properly care for themselves and their children (Rind, 1992c).

Not only is abuse perpetrated by parents, but nongenetic caregivers, such as stepparents, baby-sitters, or child-care workers, especially those in home-based child-care centers, may also be abusive. Small, fussy infants, especially those under the care of adolescents, are particularly subject to abuse (Gelles & Harrop, 1991; Margolin, 1991). Although females are more often accused of abuse, males are frequently guilty of abuse as well (Margolin, 1992).

FOCUS

Play Therapy with Abused Children

Play is recognized as an integral part of children's lives. In the child's development, play is the natural mode of learning and interacting with others. To play, the child attempts to understand the rules and the regulations of the adult world, and transforms reality through developing symbolic representations of that world. The child is also encouraged to master anxiety or guilt by being provided with the repeated opportunity to take an active part in creating previously overwhelming situations to which he or she has been subjected.

In the past decade, there has been increased interest in the use of play therapy (PT) as a clinical approach to early childhood intervention. PT has been used with children manifesting a wide range of emotional and behavioral concerns. PT has been defined as a formal regular relationship between the child exhibiting some maladaptive behavior and a trained provider in which therapeutically derived play activities occupy the central method of treatment. Two basic forms of this therapeutic play relationship are *directive* and *nondirective*. In the directive approaches, the counselor designs the activity, selects the play medium, and creates the rules. In nondirective PT, children select their play medium from a stock of items (e.g., puppets, dolls, paints), set their own rules, and use the play items they choose. Because both forms of PT can be successfully used to facilitate communication with children, many play therapists use combinations of both directive and nondirective play with their young clients.

There are several goals of PT. *First*, as a consequence of their relationship with a caring adult who stimulates play,

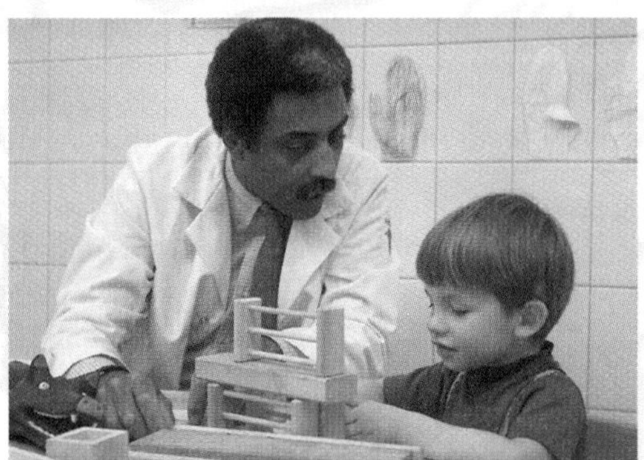

Play therapy helps children to express their feelings.

Summary

1. Attachment is the feeling that binds a parent and child together. The formation of attachment is vitally important to children's total development.
2. Children can develop close attachments to more than one person. Attachments to specific persons do not develop until about 6 or 7 months of age, after infants can distinguish among different human beings. Specific attachments are at their maximum from 12 to 18 months of age.
3. Nonattached children are very unemotional and distant; insecurely attached children are overly dependent.
4. Separation anxiety varies with individual children, depending on their age and the length of the separation. The effects of long-term separation can be serious.
5. Distress over separation is greatest after 6 months of age and until about 3 years of age.
6. If a child has to go to the hospital one parent ought to stay and make arrangements to sleep in the same room.

children are helped to increase feelings of self-worth and self-acceptance. *Second,* children are encouraged to understand their use of play as a way to explore and work through their interpersonal conflicts and issues. *Last,* and most relevant to the abused and aggressive child, young clients are encouraged to understand the purpose of their play, its association with past childhood events, and its connection to feelings and behavior exhibited outside the play room.

In an attempt to facilitate the successful attainment of these goals, authors have begun to examine both specific behaviors and general play themes of the abused and neglected child. Researchers have reported abused and neglected children exhibiting aggressive play behavior. One example of aggressive behavior is the child who pretends the baby doll has been bad, angrily shouts at the doll, and proceeds to pull out the doll's hair. Another type of abused and neglected child is called the "hider." This child has learned to withdraw from novel or stressful situations, using isolation and passivity as a means of self-defense. Physically abused children exhibit avoidant, fearful, withdrawn play behavior while being uncooperative and inattentive with adults. Researchers have reported that neglected and abused children frequently have low self-esteem, and make comments describing themselves as bad or incapable. Abused children have significantly lower self-concepts, are less ambitious, and have fewer friends than do nonabused children. Sexually abused girls frequently describe themselves as being ugly, whereas sexually abused boys often view themselves as weak. These self-deprecating beliefs and self-destructive role models may lead the abused child to use play materials to inflict self-harm.

Inappropriate sexual behavior also may clearly distinguish the group of sexually abused children from other groups examined. Sexually abused children may assume that any relationship with an adult will include sexual contact. They often invite the therapist to be involved with them sexually or they grab the breasts or genitalia of the therapist. Other inappropriate behavior demonstrated by sexually abused children includes excessive sexual curiosity, open masturbation, and exposure of the genitals. Researchers have observed that the play of abused and neglected children is far less creative, elaborate, or imaginative than that of unabused children. These children lack the capacity to play freely, to laugh and enjoy themselves in an uninhibited fashion. Those who have been physically or sexually traumatized may engage in a rigid set of play behaviors repeatedly and unconsciously acting out the trauma they have experienced. One example is the child who stuffs or forces toys into other toys (e.g., attempts to insert baby bottles between teddy's legs). While still in its infancy, PT has become an important clinical technique (White & Allers, 1994).

7. Homesickness is a manifestation of separation anxiety.
8. Children show various forms of reunion behavior. Some children are very dependent; others are angry; others are emotionally cold.
9. Fear of strangers begins at about 6 or 7 months of age and increases until about 2 years, after which it declines.
10. Parents need to let the child develop attachment to baby-sitters or substitute caregivers before leaving the child with them alone. Much depends upon the quality of the substitute care.
11. Family day care and regular child-care centers are another solution to the child-care problem. The effect of high-quality day care on children can be quite positive. The quality of teachers is crucial.
12. Parents need to select nursery schools carefully and to introduce the child to them gradually.
13. Erikson has said that the basic psychosocial task of infancy is the development of trust. Mahler says that infants need to establish a symbiotic relationship with their mother.
14. Development of trust and security is aided by the following: regular and adequate feedings, sufficient sucking, and cuddling and physical contact. Their most important requirement is for parents to show children their love.

15. Children learn to express affection by having affection shown them.
16. There are a number of causes of distrust and insecurity: parental deprivation, tension in the home, exposure to frightening experiences, child abuse, criticism, overprotection, and overindulgence.
17. Play therapy is used with emotionally disturbed children who are too young to be very verbal.
18. Being brought up in an alcoholic family can have a very negative effect on children's proneness to alcoholism, on their mental health and behavior, and on their physical, emotional, and social development. However, there are some COAs who become happy, well-adjusted adults.

Key Terms

Attachment *p. 254*
Autistic phase *p. 264*
Insecurely attached *p. 257*
Nonattached children *p. 256*
Symbiosis *p. 264*

Discussion Questions

1. Describe the attachment behavior of a child you know. Does this child manifest separation anxiety? What suggestions do you have for minimizing separation anxiety?
2. Do you know a child who had to go to the hospital? Describe the experience. How did it affect the child emotionally?
3. Describe the experience of a child you know who went to nursery school or kindergarten for the first time.
4. How can separation anxiety be minimized when employing a baby-sitter?
5. Do you know any parents who placed their child in a day-care center from infancy on? What were some of the effects on the child?
6. Can family arguments cause children to become distrustful and insecure? Explain.
7. Have you ever known a child who had been physically abused? Describe. What were the effects? Would you report parents whom you knew were abusing their child? Why? Why not?
8. Were you a child of an alcoholic? What effect did growing up in an alcoholic family have on you?

Suggested Readings

Bowlby, J. (1982). *Attachment and loss* (Vol. 1). New York: Basic Books. Mother–infant interaction and attachment.

Bowlby, J. A. (1988). *A secure base: Parent–child attachment and healthy human development.* New York: Basic Books. Bowlby's theory.

Collins, W. A. (Ed.). (1984). *Development during middle childhood: The years from 6 to 12.* Washington, DC: National Academy Press. All aspects of development.

Finkelhor, D. et al. (Eds.). (1986). *A sourcebook on child sexual abuse.* Beverly Hills, CA: Sage. A guide for parents and leaders of children.

Helfer, R. E. , & Kempe, R. S. (Eds.). *The battered child* (4th edition). Chicago: University of Chicago Press. Standard work on subject, now revised.

Sroufe, L. A., & Fleeson, J. (1986). Attachment and the construction of relationships. In W. Hartup and Z. Rubin (Eds.), *Relationships and development.* Hillsdale, NJ: Erlbaum. Attachment theory and applications.

White, B. L. (1990). *The first three years of life.* New York: Prentice-Hall. Parent–toddler relationships.

Zigler, E. F., & Lang, M. E. (1991). *Child-care choices: Balancing the needs of children, families, and society.* New York: Free Press. Child-care options in relation to children's needs.

Emotional Development: Emotions, Temperament, and the Self

Chapter 11

DEVELOPMENT OF EMOTIONS

DIFFERENCES IN TEMPERAMENT

DEVELOPMENT OF SELF, AUTONOMY, SELF-CONCEPT, AND SELF-ESTEEM

This chapter begins with a discussion of the development of basic emotions including a developmental timetable and both biological and environmental influences. Attention is then focused on the development of temperament: its components, patterns, and relationship to personality.

The chapter concludes with a discussion of the development of self-awareness, autonomy, separation-individuation, self-definition, self-concept, self-reference, self-efficacy, and self-esteem.

Development of Emotions

COMPONENTS

Psychologists have attempted to explain emotions in various ways. One book quotes over thirty different definitions of emotions (Strongman, 1987). Most of the descriptions include a sequence of four basic components of emotions:

1. Stimuli that provoke a reaction
2. Feelings—positive or negative conscious experiences of which we become aware
3. Physiological arousal produced by the hormonal secretions of the endocrine glands
4. Behavioral response to the emotions

To retrace the sequence, suppose that a child

1. is confronted by a growling dog and interprets this as danger;
2. reacts with fear;
3. experiences physiological arousal from the adrenal hormone secretion **epinephrine,** which produces an increase in heart rate, blood pressure, blood flow, sugar in the blood, respiration, and other changes; and
4. trembles and runs away.

Epinephrine—hormone secreted by the adrenal glands that produces physiological arousal

Psychologists are not in complete agreement as to whether (a) the child trembles and runs because of feeling afraid, or (b) becomes afraid only after experiencing the bodily reactions, or (c) experiences both the fear and the physiological arousal simultaneously. Cognitive theorists would disagree with all these explanations and say that emotional reactions depend upon how the children would interpret the stimuli from the environment (the dog growling), and how they would interpret the internal bodily stimuli. Whatever the explanation, all emotions involve the same four basic components: stimuli (which are interpreted cognitively), feelings, physiological arousal, and behavioral response.

FUNCTIONS

Emotions play a number of important functions in our lives (Barrett & Campos, 1987). They play *an adaptive function* to ensure survival. The fear that children may feel because of a growling dog motivates them to want to get away from the danger. Emotions are also a *means of communication* (Russell, 1990). When children are sad or angry, they are transmitting the message that something is wrong. When they are happy, they are telling others that all is right with their world (Sullivan, Lewis, & Alessandri, 1993). Preschoolers 3–4 years of age are able to recognize their own internal emotional states or those of their younger siblings and to direct comments to their siblings about these feelings (Howe, 1991).

Emotions also are extremely *important in social relationships.* They are operative in forming social bonds and attachments, or in keeping other people at a distance. Emotions *are also powerful motivators* and have a significant influence on behavior. Children tend to act out what they feel, be it love or anger. A boy may become hostile toward all women because he has an abusive, rejecting, cruel mother. His hostility influences his relationships with other women, especially with those who remind him of his mother. Or a girl may become hostile

Emotions are an important means of communication.

toward all men because of an abusive, rejecting, cruel father.

Emotions play an important role in *sociomoral development,* beginning with the awareness of "wrongness" and the feelings of guilt that are experienced when expectations of "rightness" are violated (Cole, Barrett, & Zahn-Waxler, 1992). Emotions are also *a source of pleasure or of pain.* Children who feel joyful and happy are able to enjoy the luxury of these positive feelings. In the same way, negative emotions of anger, disgust, fear, or sadness create disturbing feelings that can be very painful to endure. Yet, without feelings, either positive or negative, life would be colorless and dull. Children who have learned to repress their feelings are emotionally dead. Being able to feel is what adds spice to life. There is considerable evidence that in our culture boys are taught to inhibit their emotions while girls are allowed to express them. This puts considerable burden on the boys to hide their feelings, and makes communication more difficult between the sexes because boys have trouble expressing how they feel (Casey, 1993).

BASIC EMOTIONS

Psychologists have sought to identify and separate different emotions. Ekman (1972) and his colleagues found that people from all over the world were able to distinguish six basic emotions by distinctive facial expressions: *happiness, sadness, anger, surprise, disgust,* and *fear.* Carroll Izard (1977, 1980) has specialized in studying the emotional development of children. Like Ekman, she says that each emotion has its own distinctive facial expression. Four of Izard's basic emotions are shown by the facial expressions in the photos below.

Subsequent research has revealed that identification of infants' emotions from facial expressions is only partly successful. One study revealed that college graduate students were able to identify correctly the emotions of joy, interest, and surprise, but those depicting fear, anger, sadness, and disgust were all labeled distress (Oster, Hegley, & Nagel, 1992). Other research has found some blending of emotional expressions of infants. Some twenty-three facial expressions were classified as interest according to one research study (Matias & Cohn, 1993). Some emotions are easier to recognize than others. Happiness, for example, is easier to recognize than fear and anger (Kestenbaum, 1992). Emotional ex-

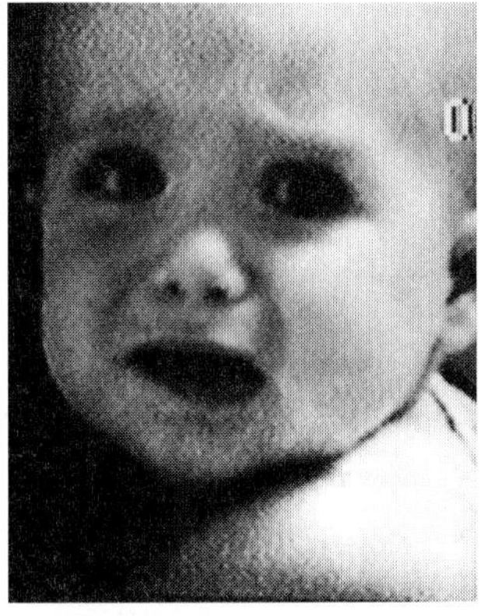
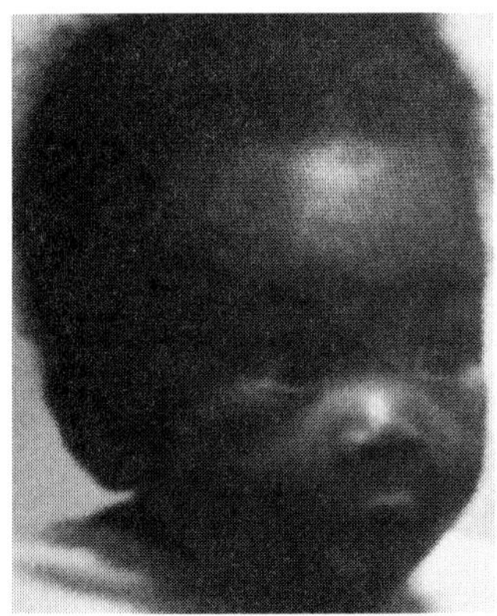

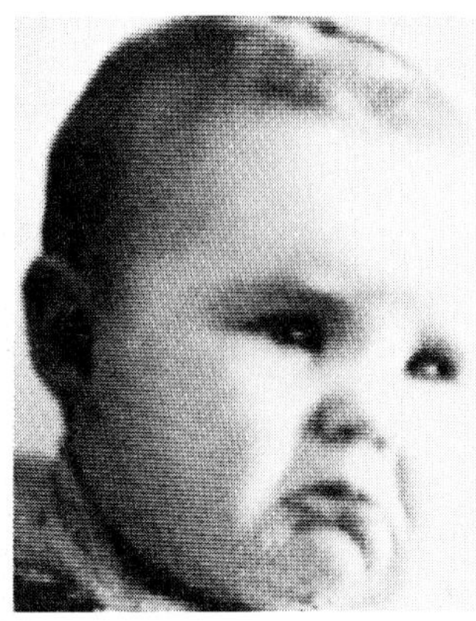

Infants' emotions (left to right): **Fear**—brows level, drawn in and up, eyelids lifted, mouth retracted. **Surprise**—brows raised, eyes widened, mouth rounded in oval shape. **Joy**—mouth forms smile, cheeks lifted, twinkle in eyes. **Sadness**—inner corners of brows raised, mouth corners drawn down.

FOCUS

Children of Alcoholics

In recent years, much attention has been focused on Adult Children of Alcoholics (ACOAs) and the effects of having been brought up in an alcoholic family. In this section we are concerned with the effect on growing children. Approximately seven million children under the age of 18 in the United States have an alcoholic parent (Noll, Zucker, Fitzgerald, & Curtis, 1992). These children are at high risk for a host of emotional and behavioral difficulties during childhood, adolescence, and adulthood.

For one thing, children of alcoholics (COAs) are prone to becoming alcoholics themselves, because the vulnerability to alcoholism is inherited (Perkins & Berkowitz, 1991), especially between fathers and sons (Jacob, 1992). Sons of alcoholics are four times as likely as sons of nonalcoholics to become alcoholics themselves, even if they are adopted at birth, and regardless of whether the adoptive parents are alcoholics (Schuckit, 1987). For another thing, fetal alcohol syndrome is a well-known and disastrous result of mothers drinking heavily during pregnancy.

There are, however, some other possible effects on the children of being raised by one or more alcoholic parents. These children are at high risk for mental health problems (Roosa et al., 1993). Depression, anxiety, and problem behavior are common among children of alcoholic parents (Tubman, 1993). Some findings suggest that parental alcoholism may affect a child's cognitive, fine-motor development (such as drawing and manipulative skills) and personal/social growth (such as ability to play cooperatively). The explanation is that alcoholic parents who manifest antisocial behavior themselves, or who suffer from depression, are not as attentive to their children's needs and are not able to provide the cognitive, social, and emotional experiences and stimulation necessary for their children's development (Noll, Zucker, Fitzgerald, & Curtis, 1992).

Alcoholism affects parents and families in such a way that normal patterns of parent–child interaction and marital relationships are disturbed. In alcoholic families, parental depression, family stress and conflict, and marital discord create problems for the children (Tubman, 1993). Family cohesiveness, positive affect, and pleasant relationships

pressions are easier to recognize when facial features show movement rather than being still-faced (Soken & Pick, 1992).

The ability to correctly interpret the emotions and feelings of others is important in interpersonal relationships. The fact that people are not always able to identify emotions correctly means that what others say, think, and do may be subject to misunderstanding. Studies do indicate that the ability to express and interpret responses correctly improves during childhood so that one would expect that empathy would increase (Strayer, 1993). Both children and adults tend to be overconfident in their ability to interpret how others feel, but there is an increase with age in children's tendency to consider more than one possible emotional reaction of others (Gnepp & Klayman, 1992).

are destroyed, creating stress and antisocial behavior in the children. Family rituals and get-togethers during holidays are disrupted because a parent is drunk, so that even happy times become occasions for stress and conflict (Jacob, 1992). Discipline in the alcoholic family is often inconsistent, and parental guidance and support are lacking (Roosa et al., 1993).

In spite of the negative effects just described, some children reared in alcoholic families become happy, well-adjusted adults (Easley and Epstein, 1991). Some children are remarkable survivors and learn how to cope. In many families where only one parent is an alcoholic, the other parent is able to provide for the children's needs. In one study of families where the fathers were alcoholics, Hispanic mothers particularly were able to exert a strong, positive influence on their children's mental health (Roosa et al., 1993).

Then, too, it often takes many years before negative effects become evident. One study of 3-year-old sons of alcoholics found no difference in development age, IQ or behavior problems when compared with sons of nonalcoholic parents (Fitzgerald et al., 1993). The only apparent difference was that the sons of alcoholics were more impulsive, with less control over their actions than the other children in the study. Just what effect parental alcoholism would have on these sons by adolescence would be interesting to find out.

The whole family is involved in counseling when there is a problem with alcoholism of one family member.

CHILDREN'S FEARS

Children are not born afraid, except for two fears; fear of loud noises and fear of falling. Yet, beginning the first year or so of life, children may begin to develop many types of fears. The baby may become afraid of being bathed after getting soap in her eyes. She may become afraid of the noise made by the water going down the drain. Later, children may become afraid of the toilet flushing, the vacuum cleaner, thunderstorms, the dark, dogs, ghosts and monsters, halloween masks, different-looking people, new situations, or of being left alone. Night terrors in which the preschool child wakes up screaming, sometimes with no clear recollection of the frightening dream, are very upsetting experiences (Hartman et al., 1987).

Children's fears have many different origins. Some fears are learned behavior. They are *conditioned* by actual experiences. One of my clearest recollections of my preschool years was being chased and bitten by a dog that tore my new Easter suit to shreds. My subsequent fear of dogs took several years to overcome, but was based upon real experience. Unwittingly, parents sometimes instill fears in children because of the example they set. I had a sister-in-law who used to hide in the closet during a thunderstorm. Fortunately, she did not do this when children were around.

Children also have *vivid imaginations.* They have trouble separating fact from fantasy, so they become afraid of the monster hiding under the bed. They have *limited experience and understanding,* so if they experience something different, they may scream in terror because they haven't seen anything like that before (Harris et al., 1991). Today, young children are exposed to *scary stories* in books, in the movies, and on television. Even so-called children's stories can be quite scary. Older children may deliberately attend horror movies and then have nightmares that night.

Sometimes, the security of children is threatened by adults who try to scare children into being good. "If you're not good, I'll call the police to come and get you and put you in jail." "If you're not good, I'm going to go away and never come back." One 2-year-old refused to lie down in his crib to fall asleep. Eventually, he fell asleep sitting up. It was found that his mother had punished him severely for wetting the bed while asleep, so he was determined to keep himself awake so he would not wet the bed and be punished. Sometimes older children scare younger ones by saying the bogey man is going to get them.

The best way for parents to help is to accept the fact that children are afraid, offer them reassurance in cheerful, positive ways, and avoid ridiculing or punishing them. Parents who either ignore the fears or make too much fuss over them may make the fears worse (Spock & Rothenberg, 1985).

CHILDREN'S WORRIES

Worry involves thoughts and images that relate to possible negative or threatening outcomes. Worry is difficult to control and is intrusive. Thus, in the same way that fear is viewed as a special state of the biological alarm system preparing the individual for escape, worry is viewed as a special state in the cognitive system, preparing the individual to anticipate possible future danger.

Worry involves rehearsing possible adversive outcomes in advance and, at the same time, searching for ways of avoiding them. At times, worry may serve an adaptive function and resemble problem solving, leading to effective preparation in coping for the future. At other times, however, when worry becomes excessive, it is as if the danger is constantly being rehearsed without a solution of it being found. Irrational or unrealistic threat scenarios predominate that are incompatible with successful problem solving. Indeed, recent research with adults demonstrates that individuals who worry excessively do not engage in adaptive problem solving at the same level as individuals who worry less.

One study examined worry in elementary school–aged children and its relationship to anxiety. The children were from the second through the sixth grade (ages 7–12 years) and they were interviewed using a structured approach and asked to complete several child anxiety measures. The parameters of worry assessed included number of worries, areas of worry, intensity of worry, and perceptions of the frequency of worry events. The findings revealed few age-related differences but found that girls reported more worries than boys and that African-Americans reported more worries than white or Hispanic children.

The three most common areas of worry reported by children in this sample concerned *school, health,* and *personal harm.* Frequent concerns about school are consistent with previous findings. However, personal harm emerged as a central concern of children. In fact, worries about physical harm or attack by others form the single most frequent response reported by the children in the sample as one of their most intense worries. It is interesting that the school that participated in this project was not in a high-crime area. Moreover, children rated these events as low in their frequency of occurrence. Apparently, this finding likely reflects contemporary concerns about high rates of violence and crime in society. Thus,

Some children have to worry about physical attacks from others.

children's worries appear to reflect their current life circumstances.

Health also emerged as a frequent area of worry among children. Specific health concerns were varied and included worries about their parents' health, operations, specific bodily functions (e.g., stomachaches), and contracting AIDS. It's possible that these health-related worries are a reflection of the substantial media attention devoted to health-care problems.

Although the most intense worries pertain to personal safety, the events that children worry about that occur frequently were predominantly social in nature (family, friends, and classmates). This reflects the major roles that family members and peers play in children's everyday lives. Concerns about classmates largely focused on rejection, exclusion from social activities, or being ignored by others, whereas friendship concerns predominantly reflected worries about betrayal (e.g., friends not keeping a secret). Classmates provide children with a sense of acceptance and belonging, whereas close friendships provide intimacy, loyalty, and emotional support. Understandably, then, children may worry about inclusion by and acceptance from classmates and the support and loyalty of their friends.

Rejection by others is a major worry of some children.

Children's frequency of event readings were also very high for worries about their families, and predominantly reflected concerns about family or marital conflict. In light of high rates of divorce and family conflicts, these data also reflect the current circumstances many children confront in their lives. Overall, these findings provide an informative and interesting picture of the kinds of concerns that preoccupy children of elementary school age (Silverman, LaGreca, & Wasserstein, 1995).

TIMETABLE OF DEVELOPMENT

Izard also said that emotions develop according to a biological timetable. Interest, distress, and disgust are present from birth; joy (social smile) develops from 4 to 6 weeks; anger, surprise, and sadness are experienced at 3 to 4 months; and fear at 5 to 7 months. Shame and shyness (Broberg, Lamb, & Hwang, 1990) are experienced after the infant develops self-awareness at 6 to 8 months; contempt and guilt are felt during the second year of life (Lewis,, Alessandri, & Sullivan, 1992). Table 11.1 shows the chronology.

Not all psychologists agree with this timetable. Campos and colleagues (1983)

TABLE 11.1
TIMETABLE OF DEVELOPMENT OF INFANT EMOTIONS

Emotion	*Time of Emergence*
Interest	Present at birth
Distress	Present at birth
Disgust	Present at birth
Joy (social smile)	4–6 weeks
Anger	3–4 months
Surprise	3–4 months
Sadness	3–4 months
Fear	5–7 months
Shame, shyness	6–8 months
Contempt	Second year of life
Guilt	Second year of life

believe that all emotions are experienced at birth, but observers are not always aware that these various feelings are being expressed. Also, the feelings that are being expressed depend a lot on what is experienced and when. Abused children develop fear and sadness earlier than others (Gaensbauer & Hiatt, 1984).

ENVIRONMENTAL AND BIOLOGICAL INFLUENCES IN DEVELOPMENT

Hyson and Izard (1985) agree that emotional responses are partly learned; for example, infants are affected by their mother's moods and emotional expressions. Infants tend to model their mother's emotional expressions. One study found that 3- to 6-month-old infants of depressed mothers also showed depressed behavior and that this behavior carried over in their interactions with other adults who were nondepressed (Field et al., 1988). Another study showed that when 1 1/2-year-old infants smiled, and when their mothers or mother substitutes were attentive and smiled back, the infants' frequency of smiling increased (Jones & Raag, 1989). Thus, open channels of social communication promote the outward expression of internal feelings.

Izard also emphasizes that emotional expressions have a biological component, because they seem to be fairly constant and stable (Trotter, 1987a). Kagan and colleagues found that behavioral inhibition in children may be due to the lower threshold of physical responsivity, so some children don't react as readily to stimuli (Kagan, Reznick, & Snidman, 1987). Kagan and colleagues also found that children who were inhibited or uninhibited at 21 months of age showed the same characteristics of inhibition or lack of inhibition at 4, 5 1/2, and 7 1/2 years of age (Kagan et al., 1988). Thus, *emotional expression and behavior in infancy tell us something about the personality of the child later in life* (Izard, Hembree, & Huebner, 1987). Biology defines the broad outlines and limits of emotional development; environmental influences stimulate and modify that evolution. Part of the task of being a parent or teacher is *socialization:* influencing the feelings and behavior of children so they conform to societal expectations (Malatesta et al., 1986). This would be impossible if feelings and behavior were only biologically determined.

AGGRESSION

Aggression in children takes two forms: verbal aggression and physical aggression. The child who is verbally aggressive may be involved frequently in arguments, name calling, shouting matches, or various attempts to criticize, shame other children, and make them feel guilty or inferior by the way they are talked to. Physical aggression may manifest itself as hitting, wrestling, pushing, shoving, throwing things at someone, getting into fist fights, and doing other things to try to hurt another person.

Naturalistic observations with audiovisual equipment of children playing on a playground revealed that aggression was not a rare event. Aggressive children were observed to be verbally and physically aggressive once every three and eight minutes respectively (Pepler, & Craig, 1995). Teachers and parents worry about overaggressive behavior in children because it has been shown to be an important developmental antecedent to later delinquency, heavy drug use, and other forms of antisocial behavior (Dolan et al., 1993). Aggression puts children at risk for later problem behavior. The consequences of early aggression have been well documented and result in such negative outcomes as low academic achievement, early school dropout, and juvenile delinquency (Graham & Hoehn, 1995).

Overaggression is frequently a cause of poor relationships with peers. Children perceive aggressive peers as responsible for their behavior and deserving of little sympathy, much anger, and relative rejection. Aggressive children are clearly at risk for negative interaction with adults at home and in the school setting. Teachers spend more time in negative interaction with aggressive children than with nonaggressive children, and they rate aggressive behavior as being more disturbing than other classroom problems. Aggressive behavior is also associated with increased school failure. Over time, aggressive children tend to expect more hostility from

PARENTING ISSUES

When Your Child Is Angry

Anger is a basic human emotion. It arises out of frustration, when children find a discrepancy between what they believe ought to happen and what, in fact, is happening (Olthof, Ferguson, & Luiten, 1989). Children with disabilities for example, may show a great deal of anger over their condition and the way others treat them. Anger can be a motivating force in overcoming obstacles, as a means of standing up for oneself or others. In these cases, anger can produce positive results. However, it can also lead to hurting others, to conflict, and to violence. Everyone gets angry sometimes. The real question is: Is it controlled anger and does it produce positive results? A central developmental task for children is learning to control the expression of anger and to direct it in harmless and positive ways.

Parents have several important roles to play in this regard.

1. They can represent positive models for their children; that is, they can show restraint in their own expressions of anger, so that children learn acceptable, helpful means of expression. Children who grow up in a house where there is a lot of anger are more likely to learn negative means of expression themselves (Cummings, 1987).
2. Parents can help children control anger by letting them know that certain expressions of anger such as temper tantrums, hitting, biting, or screaming are not acceptable. Children learn to control their emotions by parents' helping them to exercise control: "I know you're angry, but I can't let you bite your brother. You'll have to sit in the chair for a while."
3. Parents can help children to dissipate anger through physical activity, verbalization, and directed play. "Go out and play in the yard until you're not angry." "Let's talk about why you're mad." "Maybe if we played with the puppets it would help you with your anger." (Then have the child use various puppets that represent both the angry one and the one the child is expressing anger toward.)
4. Parents can tell children that they recognize their being angry, and that feelings of anger are normal, but that children have to learn to control and redirect their reactions to their feelings. Spock and Rothenberg (1985) wrote:

   > It helps children to realize that their parents know they have angry feelings, and that their parents are not enraged at them or alienated from them on account of them. This realization helps them get over their anger and keeps them from feeling too guilty or frightened because of it (p. 402).

5. If anger becomes excessive and persistent, parents need to get at the root causes of the anger and to correct situations that cause it, if possible. If parents don't seem to make progress themselves, it is helpful if they will get counseling for themselves and their children.

Children need to express anger in positive ways.

Parents need to get at the causes of anger and to correct situations that need to be changed.

their teachers, just as they tend to expect more hostility from their peers (Trachtenberg & Biken, 1994).

Prior studies demonstrate that, as a group, boys exhibit significantly higher levels of aggression than do girls, a difference that persists throughout the life span. But this finding may reflect a lack of research on forms of aggression that are relevant to young females rather than an actual gender difference in levels of overall aggressiveness. Boys are more overtly aggressive (i.e., they manifest more physical and verbal aggression), whereas girls show more relational aggression. Relational aggression focuses more on relationships between children. For example, girls might attempt to harm others, showing behavior that intends to significantly damage another child's friendship or increase feelings of exclusion by the peer group. The girl may retaliate against the other child by withdrawing friendship or acceptance in order to hurt or control the child. Spreading rumors about the child so that peers will reject her is another form of relational aggression. In other words, girls seek to harm others through purposeful manipulation and damage of peer relationships, while boys are more likely to harm peers through overt aggression, through physical aggression and verbal threats (Crick & Grotpeter, 1995).

Relationally aggressive children may be at risk for serious adjustment difficulties. For example, they report significantly higher levels of loneliness, depression, and isolation relative to their nonrelationally aggressive peers. These findings provide evidence that the degree of aggressiveness exhibited by girls has been underestimated in prior studies, largely because forms of aggression relevant to girls' peer groups has not been assessed.

Aggressive behavior in children often has its origins in the family situation. Children tend to model their behavior after that of their parents. This is why parents who use severe punishment, especially if it is cruel and abusive, stimulate resentment, rejection, and similar harsh, cruel behavior on the part of children (Rohner et al., 1991; Simons et al., 1993). The more parents use physical discipline, isolation, deprivation of privileges, and the more the children are punished physically at home for aggressive behavior, the more aggressive they become. They learn aggression by modeling the behavior of their punishing parent. One research study found that boys who engage in coercive interactions with their mothers are more likely to exhibit aggressive, antisocial behavior in other contexts (MacKinnon-Lewis et al., 1994). The study showed the relationship between coercive parenting and children's aggression with their peers. The boys' antisocial behavior with parents was associated with rejection by peers.

Aggression in children must also be considered in a social context. Aggression is an interpersonal activity and arises within the context of a group of peers. Therefore, the social characteristics of a group play an influential role in the expression of aggression within a group. When children associate with others who are aggressive, they are stimulated to follow the aggressive patterns themselves. Groups marked by high levels of physical activity, aversive behavior, and competition, appear to provide a setting more conducive to dyadic aggressive interactions. Rough-and-

Some gangs stimulate aggression of members.

FOCUS

Reducing Peer-Directed Aggression among African-American Boys

Childhood aggression is often predictive of low academic achievement, school dropout, juvenile delinquency, and even adult criminality and psychopathology. Therefore, any program that can reduce aggression ought to produce worthwhile, long-term benefits.

Hudley and Graham (1993) conducted an attributional intervention program to reduce peer-directed aggression among 101 elementary school–age African-American boys. Many fights among children are caused by their attributing hostile intent to the actions of others, and then retaliating. However, excessively aggressive children often arrive at inappropriate, incorrect, and therefore maladaptive beliefs about the intent of others. As a result, their aggressive retaliation is unwarranted.

The researchers conducted a twelve-session program to train males to infer nonhostile intent following ambiguous peer provocation, to train them to detect intentionality more accurately, and to practice making attributions and making decisions about how to respond, given attributional uncertainty. Role playing and a variety of training methods were used.

At the end of the four months, the subjects showed a marked reduction in the presumption of hostile intent, a lowering in the preference for aggressive behavior, and a reduction in actual aggressive behavior.

Many fights among children are caused by their attributing hostile intent to others and then retaliating.

tumble play may escalate into overt aggression due to a misinterpretation of another's action (Cole, Zahn-Waxler, & Smith, 1994). Groups that are low on cohesiveness and marked by negative affect have a higher likelihood that members will get into fights. In socially cohesive and friendly atmospheres, children may be less likely to respond with aggression to others' ambiguous behavior. Sometimes older children become members of violent gangs, where aggression is considered norm for the group (DeRosier, Cillessen, Coie, & Dodge, 1994).

Children are also influenced by neighborhood environments. Children living in high-risk neighborhoods have more social and behavioral problems than children living in low-risk neighborhoods. In examining the causes of aggression in children, neighborhood context must be considered as a risk factor. The right kinds of neighborhoods also act as protection against aggressive behavior in children. Neighborhoods may serve a facilitative role in the development of a positive outcome for children who are at risk for social or behavioral problems due to other kinds of risk factors such as family background (Kupersmidt et al., 1995).

EMOTIONAL EXPRESSION AND CONTROL

Ideally, to be an emotionally mature individual means to develop proper balance between emotional expression and control. Mention has already been made of the need of children to learn to express emotions. Emotional expression is one way that children have of communicating desires and feelings, and of relating to other people. When children do not receive something that is desired, they may become angry, which is their way of communicating their disappointment and frustration and their belief that the loss perhaps can be recovered. Or they may become sad if they realize that misfortune cannot be undone. Showing anxiety becomes children's way of expressing their worry over situations. Children learn to display joy, happiness, elation, and pleasure. By expressing their feelings, they are able to communicate their needs, their hopes, and their desires to others. Learning to express positive feelings of love helps children to develop warm bonds with other people (Cole, Zahn-Waxler, & Smith, 1994).

In some families, children are not permitted to express true feelings and emotions. They're not allowed to get angry, they're not allowed to argue with their parents, they're not allowed to express frustration, they're not allowed to be sad or to cry, they're not allowed to be too exuberant, or to show pleasure and joy in living. The parents try to inhibit the emotions of their children, somehow believing that emotions are a sign of weakness. Many men, in particular, grow up never being allowed to express feelings, so it becomes very difficult to communicate with them and to establish what they are really thinking and feeling. It may take hours and hours of therapy to help them unlock their feelings so that they can become genuine persons again.

The author had a woman student in class who was brought up by a very cruel father. The father would line up the children in the family and start to whip them with a belt. He told them if they cried, they were being a sissy, but he continued to beat them until somebody cried and then the person who cried would get beaten even more. Obviously, this was a no-win situation for the children. They learned that to express emotion was to face punishment.

Some parents tell their young sons, "Don't be a crybaby" if the children try to cry. Other parents try to hide their feelings from their children, so the children grow up believing that any expression of true feelings is somehow unacceptable. They learn to repress their feelings, just like their parents had done. The extreme situation is the psychopath, who grows up without any conscience or feelings at all. Such persons have arrived at a completely nonfeeling state, at least as far as outward manifestations are concerned.

At the other extreme are parents who do not try to help their children gain any control over their emotions at all. When their 2-year-old child has a temper tantrum, it frightens the parents, who respond by indulging the child to try to get the tantrum to stop. Children learn that all they have to do is have temper tantrums in order to get their own way. Wise parents know that temper tantrums once in a while are not serious; they are bound to happen because a child's life is full of some frustrations. When the storm breaks, such parents try to take it casually and to help children to cool off by themselves. Sometimes ignoring the tantrum is one of the best ways of accomplishing this. The point is, children learn that they must gain some reasonable control of their feelings. The task of the parent is to help children to gain that control. Young children need external control in the beginning, but as they mature, the goal of discipline is to help the child to experience self-regulation, to move from external authority to internal control.

Children who are exposed to high levels of negative feelings of parents may become distraught and troubled.

Part of the problem parents face is to maintain positive relationships with their children, to communicate positive feelings of love and affection, at the same time that they communicate their displeasure at the children's antisocial or unsocial actions. Parents have to love their children at the same time that they hate what their children are doing. Research studies have found that children who are exposed to high levels of parental positive affect—that is, positive emotions—are the ones who become most socialized and most cooperative human beings. Children who are exposed to high levels of negative parental affect—that is, negative feelings toward children—are more distraught and troubled, manifest more behavioral problems, and are less well accepted by their peers. The relationships with their parents carry over into their relationships with their own friends (Parker, 1995).

Differences in Temperament

PERSONALITY AND TEMPERAMENT

Psychologists make a distinction between personality and temperament. **Personality** is the sum total of the physical, mental, emotional, and social characteristics of an individual. Personality is a global concept and includes all those characteristics that make every person an individual, different from every other person. Personality is not static; it is developed over the years and is always in the process of becoming.

Temperament refers to relatively consistent, basic dispositions inherent in people, which underlie and modulate much of their behavior (McCall, in Goldsmith et al., 1987). Rothbart defines temperament as "relatively stable, primarily biologically based individual differences in reactivity and self-regulation" (Rothbart, in Goldsmith et al., 1987, p. 510). *Reactivity* means excitability or arousability. *Self-regulation* means inhibition (Rothbart, 1988). So temperament involves differences in excitability and inhibition. Goldsmith identifies temperament as "individual differences in the probability of experiencing and expressing the primary emotions and arousal" (Goldsmith et al., 1987, p. 510).

Temperament is comprised primarily of inherited biological factors, so basic dispositions comprising temperament are present early in life (Goldsmith, 1983; Gunnar & Nelson, 1994). However, as development proceeds, the *expression* of temperament becomes increasingly influenced by environmental factors (Goldsmith & Campos, 1990). (Hereditary factors in personality and temperament were discussed in Chapter 3.) A child's activity level, for example, is influenced by heredity, but the environment either permits or inhibits such a level of activity (Saudino & Eaton, 1991). Similarly, an infant's negative emotionality (crying, negative mood, emotional reactions, and social

Personality—the sum total of the physical, mental, social, and emotional characteristics of an individual

Temperament—the relatively consistent, basic dispositions inherent in people that underlie and modulate much of their behavior

demandedness) is associated with less sensitive interaction on the part of the mother, even though basic emotionality is influenced by genetics (Fish, Stifter, & Belsky, 1991). Likewise, studies have concluded that harsh and inconsistent discipline, inadequate supervision, parental rejection, and lack of involvement with the child are important factors. Hence family factors involving discipline practices and the quality of parent–child relationships are at the forefront of results from meta-analyses. From the early school years until adolescence, the stability of aggression in boys is comparable to that of intelligence. Thus, as a result of parenting practices and of children's own contributions to the process, children who were difficult to manage in the early school years were found to show high rates of externalizing behavior problems (Shaw, Keenan, & Vondra, 1994).

COMPONENTS AND PATTERNS OF TEMPERAMENT

Buss and Plomin (1984) specify three traits as constituting temperament. The first is *emotionality,* which is the intensity of emotional reactions. This dimension varies from an almost stoic lack of reaction to very intense, agitated reactions (Mangelsdorf et al., 1990). The second trait is *activity,* which has tempo and vigor as its two major components. Individuals vary from lethargy to almost mania. The third trait is *sociability,* which is the preference for being with others rather than being alone.

In the New York Longitudinal Study of 133 children discussed in Chapter 3, Thomas and Chess (1977) followed their subjects from infancy into early adulthood and identified these nine components of temperament:

1. Rhythmicity—the regularity of biological cycles of eating, sleeping, and toileting
2. Activity level—energy level as expressed by the degree of movement
3. Approach or withdrawal from new stimuli—how a person reacts to new stimuli
4. Adaptability—ability to adjust to change
5. Sensory threshold—sensitivity to sensory stimuli
6. Predominant quality of mood—whether a person is predominantly happy or unhappy
7. Intensity of mood expression—the degree to which a person responds
8. Distractibility—how easily an added stimulus can capture a person's attention
9. Persistency and attention span—how long a person focuses on one activity and pursues it.

The researchers also grouped the children they studied into three categories, or temperament patterns: the *easy child,* the *difficult child,* and the *slow-to-warm-up child* (Chess & Thomas, 1986). Table 11.2 shows the temperament characteristics of each of these categories of children. Some of the components of temperament are not identified with any one cluster. These are indicated by the dashes in some sections of the table.

One study assessed the relationships between early temperament and behavioral problems across twelve years in an unselected sample of over eight hundred children. A battery of medical, psychological, and sociological measures were administered every two years beginning at age 3. They were assessed at ages 3, 5, 7, 9, 11, and 15. Over the years, the sample remained representative of the full range of the general population on important variables such as SES and IQ. Results from the study added to a growing body of research that is beginning to document connections between specific temperamental characteristics in early childhood and specific behavioral problems in later childhood and adolescence. Long-term continuity of individual differences and *lack of control* were apparent for both sexes. Boys and girls who were characterized by lack of control in early childhood were more likely to experience behavioral problems a decade later. Lack of control was significantly associated with later reports of hyperactivity and attention problems. It was also significantly associated with reports of antisocial behavior in late childhood and with conduct disorder in adolescents.

The examiners also rated the children in their degree of caution around the examiner, the quickness of their adjustment to the new situation, their friendliness, self-confidence, and self-reliance when pre-

TABLE 11.2
THREE TEMPERAMENT PATTERNS

Component of Temperament	*Easy Child*	*Difficult Child*	*Slow-to-Warm-Up Child*
Rhythmicity	Regular eating, sleeping, toileting schedules	Irregular schedules	—
Activity level	—	High activity level	Low activity level
Approach or withdrawal	Easily approaches new situations, people	Suspicion of new situations, strangers	Mildly negative initial response to new stimuli
Adaptability	Adjusts easily to new routines, circumstances Accepts most frustrations without fuss	Adjusts slowly Temper tantrums when frustrated	Gradually likes new situations after unpressured repeated exposure
Sensory threshold	—	—	—
Quality of mood	Positive moods	Negative moods	—
Intensity of mood expression	Mild to moderate intensity of mood	High mood intensity. Loud laughter, crying	Low intensity of mood
Distractibility	—	—	—
Persistency, attention span	—	—	—

Adapted from "Genesis and Evolution of Behavioral Disorder: From Infancy to Early Adult Life" by A. Thomas and S. Chess, 1984, *American Journal of Psychiatry, 141*, pp. 1–9. Copyright 1984, American Psychiatric Association. Reprinted by permission.

sented with stimuli. Examiners labeled this factor *approach* where it appears to reflect those tendencies that are characteristic of a child who is willing and eager to explore presented stimuli and new situations. Among the boys, ratings of "approach" in early childhood were consistently and negatively correlated with teacher and parent reports of *anxiety fearfulness* in late childhood. Ratings of boys' approach at age 5 continued to predict the absence of anxiety into midadolescence over a ten-year period. Among the girls, individual differences in approach during early childhood were not consistently associated with later behavior problems.

The third temperamental characteristic that was evaluated was labeled *sluggishness,* which included ratings of *flat affect* (lack of emotions), *passivity*, and extreme *malleability. Shyness* and *fearfulness* were also related to this factor. Sluggishness describes a child who reacts passively to changing situations, withdraws from novelty, and fails to initiate action. This factor is descriptive of a "slow-to-warm-up" child. The analysis revealed long-term continuities of individual differences in sluggishness, which were more apparent for girls than for boys, although as adolescents both groups were described by their parents as having fewer personal strengths.

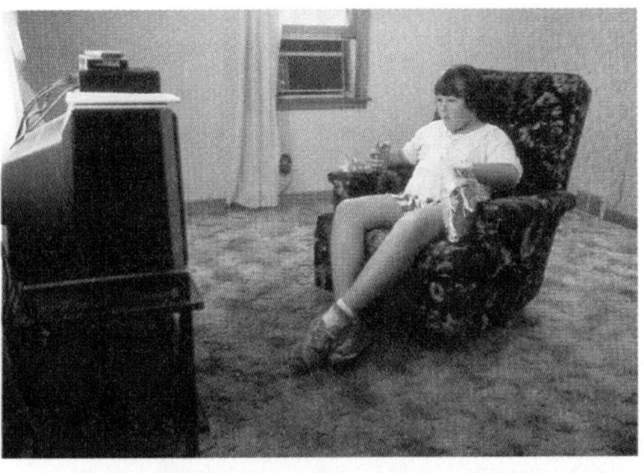
Some children are sluggish and passive by nature.

FOCUS

The Hyperactive Child

Hyperactivity, known as **attention deficit disorder** (ADD), appears in about 3 percent of elementary school children (American Psychiatric Association, 1987). Boys are ten times more likely to have the problem than girls (Moffitt, 1990). Those afflicted have 3 major symptoms: *excessive activity, inattentiveness,* and *impulsivity.* ADD children engage in almost continuous talking, fidgeting, climbing, crawling, or running. They have difficulty remaining seated in the classroom or playing quietly, and often engage in physically dangerous activities. They have difficulty in sustaining attention, do not seem to listen to what is being said, are easily distracted, shift from one uncompleted activity to another, have difficulty following through on instructions, and often lose clothes, school supplies, or notes from school. They have a low frustration tolerance, difficulty in taking turns, and poor peer adjustments; they blurt out answers to questions before they have been completed; and interrupt or intrude on others, butting into conversations and groups (Clark, Cheyne, Cunningham, & Siegel, 1988; Landau & Milich, 1988). Age of onset must be before age 7 to differentiate it from disorders that might arise because of stress. The American Psychiatric Association (1987) stipulates a duration of at least one year to distinguish it from disorders due to stress.

There are many possible causes. *Genetic, neurological, biochemical,* or *environmental factors* are all possibilities. Birth injury, prenatal exposure to teratogens such as alcohol or other drugs, prematurity, infections that affect the brain, lead poisoning, vitamin deficiencies, food allergies, or reactions to food additives and colorings have all been suspected. A delay in maturation of the central nervous system seems likely in some cases because some children outgrow the problem (Connors, 1980; Hadley, 1984; Hartsough & Lambert, 1985; Jacobovitz & Sroufe, 1987; Ross & Ross, 1982; and Streissguth et al., 1984).

Those who were characterized by sluggishness in early childhood were significantly more likely to suffer from anxiety and distress in late childhood, and especially during adolescence. The results of this study suggest that early temperament has predictive value in the development of later psychopathology (Caspi et al., 1995).

Development of Self, Autonomy, Self-Concept, and Self-Esteem

SELF-AWARENESS

The development of self-awareness means that children begin to understand their separateness from others and other things. In the first few months of life, babies discover their arms and hands appearing and disappearing. They see them move and are fascinated by what they see. Imagine coming into the world and never having seen an arm and

It's hard to treat the problem when the cause is not certain. In general, there are various treatment methods.

1. *Ritalin.* This drug is a stimulant that has a reversal effect on hyperactive children. Its results are remarkable for some children (Sprague & Ullman, 1981; Whalen, Henker, Castro, & Granger, 1987). Sometimes, however, the drug produces adverse side effects such as appetite loss, growth retardation, sleeping difficulties, and lethargy in the classroom (Nemeth, 1990). The drug should never be used as a one-step solution; it should always be given in conjunction with other treatment programs.

2. *Diet management.* If nutritional deficiencies, food allergies, food additives, or colorings are suspected, these are eliminated through diet control. Diets free of additives and food colorings help only a small number of hyperactive children (Ross & Ross, 1982).

3. *Psychotherapy* for families and children. This is used to help parents and siblings deal with their resentment and anger. *Behavior-modification techniques* are used as teaching devices to help hyperactive children gain some control over their behavior (Ross & Ross, 1982). Parents need training in how to manage the hyperactive child (Dubey, O'Leary, & Kaufman, 1983). Parents can also receive help from a nationwide support group called Children with Attention Deficit Disorders (C.H.A.D.D.).

4. *Educational planning.* This is needed to offer ADD children the optimum educational environment. Teachers need to be taught how *not* to make the problem worse. The best teachers are flexible in allowing minor disruptions and some physical activity in the classroom, but still provide some structure and guidance. Teachers can help children break up work into small, manageable units (Nemeth, 1990) and to channel excess activity into appropriate instrumental motor and attention responses (Zentall & Meyer, 1987).

hand before! At this time, however, infants are not aware that the hand is part of them. It comes in and out of view by accident. Sometime later, they also discover feet and toes. But they still don't associate them with themselves.

The sense of self emerges gradually. At about 1 year of age, infants become aware that other children are distinct persons they can see, hear, and touch, and who may take a toy. At about 18 months of age, infants are able to recognize their own reflection in a mirror and to develop a sense of *me* and *mine.* As they become aware of themselves, they begin to develop a sense of possessiveness: "my hair," "my chair," "my bed," as distinct from "mama's hair," "mama's chair," or "daddy's bed." Feelings of jealousy, anger, or guilt are possible as a result of increased self-awareness and the need to protect the self from other selves (Campos et al., 1983). This new awareness of others also allows the development of affection toward them and rebellion against them.

AUTONOMY

Erikson (1950, 1959) said that the chief psychosocial task between 1 and 2 years of age is the development of autonomy. This desire for autonomy puts increasing demands on parents (Fagot & Kavanagh, 1993). As the self emerges, children also want some de-

FOCUS

Cross-Cultural Differences and Temperament

Most developmentalists agree that ease and intensity of behavioral arousal from external stimulation is an important temperamental quality of infants. This characteristic has been called *reactivity,* or ease of arousal. An important question is whether infants of different nationalities, different in genetic or cultural backgrounds or both, differ in ease of arousal. Research reports suggest that Asian infants are at a lower level of arousal than Caucasian infants. Newborn Asian-American infants, compared with European Americans, are calmer, less labile, less likely to remove a cloth placed on their face, and more easily consoled when distressed. Chinese-American infants living in Boston were less active, less vocal, and smiled less often to the presentation of visual and auditory events during their first year than did European-American infants. Other studies have shown that Japanese infants are reported to be less easily aroused and are less reactive than European-American infants in the United States. In one study, 4-month-old infants from Boston, Dublin, and Beijing were administered the same battery of visual, auditory, and olfactory stimuli to evaluate differences in levels of reactivity. The Chinese infants were significantly less active, irritable, and vocal than the Boston and Dublin samples, with American infants showing the highest level of reactivity. The data suggests the possibility of temperamental differences between Caucasian infants and Asian infants in reactivity to stimulation (Kagan et al., 1994).

gree of independence: to feed themselves, to explore the world, to do what they want to do without being too restricted by caregivers. If they aren't permitted to do some things (within reasonable limits), they develop a sense of shame and doubt about their abilities. According to Freud, part of the conflict over autonomy centers around toilet training. Parents who are too strict during this anal stage of development create shame and doubt. Children's increasing mobility, however, gets them in trouble, or can endanger lives, so reasonable controls are necessary to keep them safe and to help them manage their actions and emotions. How often parents exercise control is probably not as important in developing autonomy as *how* control is exercised. Control that is fair and reasonable and that shows respect for the child helps the child achieve disciplined autonomy.

Separation-individuation—a period during which the infant gradually develops a self apart from the mother

SEPARATION-INDIVIDUATION

In a previous section, we discussed Margaret Mahler's concept of the period of *symbiosis,* during which infants develop a strong dependency on the mother to such an extent that there is some fusing of personalities. However, at about 5 months of age, lasting until about age 3, Mahler says a new period begins: a period of **separation-individuation,** during which infants gradually develop a self apart from the mother (Mahler, Pine, & Bergman, 1975). Infants are still dependent on their mothers. But as they gradually develop greater physical and psychological separation, they need to achieve a balance in their dependent-independent conflict while developing a sense of self. They want to be independent, yet they are frightened of too great a separation. The development of autonomy is vital to their later

Babies start reaching toward their mirror image at about 4 months of age.

development as an independent adult. However, too much autonomy may produce an inconsiderate, selfish person who has no regard for the rights and needs of others, or an insecure person with excessive fears, anxieties, and doubts about self.

SELF-DEFINITION AND SELF-CONCEPT

As children begin to develop real awareness, they also begin to define themselves, to develop a concept of self, to develop an identity (Spencer & Markstrom-Adams, 1990). For a full discussion of children from minority groups see *Child Development* 61, Number 2 (April 1990). *By 3 years of age, personal characteristics are defined in childlike terms, and are usually positive and exaggerated.* "I'm bigger, strong, the fastest runner; can jump high, can skip, can sing pretty songs." Two researchers found that even when preschool children have just scored low on a game, they predicted they would do very well the next time (Stipek & Hoffman, 1980). Other research indicates that preschool children usually have a very high opinion of their physical and intellectual abilities (Harter & Pike, 1984; Stipek & MacIver, 1989).

By the middle elementary grades, most children begin to develop a more realistic concept of self and admit that they are not as capable in some areas as in others (Butler, 1990). "I'm a good reader, but I don't like arithmetic"; "I'm good in baseball, but I can't run" (Harter, 1983). Markus and Nurius (1984) emphasize that as children enter middle childhood, they begin to develop truer self-understanding; to become aware of their achieved characteristics and their own values, norms, and goals; and to develop standards for their own behavior (Eder, 1990). They begin to be more specific and realistic about themselves and to realize that they do sometimes try to fool themselves (Eder, 1989).

There are, however, children who are highly competent, but who fail to acquire positive perceptions of their abilities. Phillips (1987) found that in these cases, children's self-perceptions of competence are influenced more by their parents' negative appraisals than by objective evidence of their achievements. There are also children with only average abilities who have an inflated perception of themselves because of exaggerated views instilled by parents. One study found that children's perceptions of their academic competence was influenced by the warmth of their relationship with their father (Wagner & Phillips, 1992). The positive father–child relationship gave the children more confidence in their academic abilities.

SELF-REFERENCE AND SELF-EFFICACY

Self-reference has to do with ourselves, our estimates of our abilities, and how capable and effective we are in dealing with others and the world (Ruble & Flett, 1988). Estimates of our effectiveness have been termed **self-efficacy.** Self-efficacy is not so much our actual skill and effectiveness in dealing with situations and with others. Rather, it is our *perceptions* of these things.

Self-reference—estimates of our abilities and of how effectively we deal with others and the world

Self-efficacy—our perceptions of our actual skill and personal effectiveness

Self-efficacy is important because it influences children's relationships, their willingness to undertake difficult tasks, and their feelings about themselves: their self-worth and competence (Schunk, 1984).

Harter (1983) developed a *Perceived Competence Scale for Children.* The scale measures competence in four areas:

- General self-worth—being happy with self the way I am
- Social skills—having friends, being liked
- Cognitive skills—being good at schoolwork, having a good memory
- Physical skills—being able to do well in sports

PARENTING ISSUES

Freedom versus Control

One of the questions that parents face, at all stages of their children's development, is how much autonomy and freedom to allow and still ensure the safety, well-being, and socialization of their children. I once heard a psychiatrist say in a speech to a group that he lived at the top of a steep cliff, but that he wouldn't think of fencing in his yard, because his 2-year-old son had to learn to avoid the danger. Most of us would not be willing to go this far in allowing autonomy and in teaching responsibility. How controlling or permissive to be is one of the difficult dilemmas of parenting (Remley, 1988).

However, the degree of control is not the only important factor to consider. Another one is the attitude of parents toward their children, whether loving or hostile. In our culture, children seem to thrive best in a loving and democratic environment, where there are rules of conduct and social restrictions on behavior, but where the children are also held in high esteem, and are encouraged to explore, to try new things, and to do things themselves (Denham, Renwick, & Holt, 1991). As they get older, they are given opportunities to participate in decision making. Children in this environment tend to be independent, self-confident, assertive, outgoing, and active. Children who are loved in a dominating way tend to be dependent, polite, submissive, and obedient, but lack initiative and self-confidence. Children whose parents are overly permissive and hostile toward them tend to be rebellious, disobedient, angry, aggressive, and delinquent. Children reared by hostile but controlling parents tend to be sullen and socially withdrawn. They are not allowed to express their anger outwardly, so it may erupt sometimes in violence, or turn inward, resulting in self-recrimination (Remley, 1988).

Parents often face the task of how much autonomy and freedom to allow their children.

Note that this scale measures perceived competence and does not represent others' judgments of the child. Some children have very high opinions of their competence, regardless of others' opinions to the contrary. The important consideration is how they perceive themselves.

Bandura (1986) suggests that children's judgment of personal efficacy stems from four main causes:

First, self-efficacy depends upon personal accomplishments and children's judgments about these accomplishments. Children who do well in school or in sports are more likely to feel self-efficacious than those who fail. Bandura calls this sense of self-efficacy *enactive* because it is based on the outcome of actions. Erikson has said that the chief psychosocial task during the 3- to 5-year-old period is *initiative versus guilt.* Children seek to become more assertive and to pursue a variety of activities, yet in ways that bring praise rather than reprimand. If they fail, their efforts result in criticism or self-blame, so they feel guilty. Similarly, the chief psychosocial task during the school years is *industry versus inferiority.* Children strive for competence and proficiency. Failure results in feelings of inferiority.

Second, self-efficacy is derived partly from children's comparison of themselves with others. Ten-year-olds may compare their skill in a game with the skills of others. If they discover they do very well, they feel very good about themselves. Bandura calls this a *vicarious* source of self-efficacy (based on comparison of personal performance with that of others).

Third, self-efficacy is also influenced by persuasion. "You can do it, you're capable." Positive persuasion increases self-efficacy, whereas negative persuasion—"don't try it"—decreases self-efficacy. Bandura calls this the *persuasory* source of self-efficacy.

The fourth source of influence on judgments of self-efficacy is the person's arousal level:

the level of physiological and emotional arousal. High arousal can affect judgments—either positively or negatively. For example, if a child is very aroused and excited before being in a school play, this emotional state may lead to a superior performance if it motivates effort, or to a poor performance if nervousness prevents the child from doing his or her best. Bandura calls this an *emotional* source of self-efficacy.

SELF-ESTEEM

Self-esteem is closely related to self-concept and self-efficacy. When children perceive their worth, their abilities, their accomplishments, do they view themselves positively or negatively? Everyone needs to feel loved, liked, accepted, valued, capable, and competent. How children feel about themselves is their self-esteem (Damon, 1983). It is their liking and respect for themselves.

There are four primary sources of self-esteem: children's emotional relationships with parents, their social competence with peers, their intellectual prowess at school, and the attitudes of society and community toward them. Children who are *loved and wanted,* whose parents are warm, supportive, concerned, interested, and active in their guidance, tend to develop positive self-esteem (Abraham & Christopherson, 1984; Felson & Zielinski, 1989). As children develop, *social competence* becomes an increasing component of self-esteem (Waters & Sroufe, 1983). *School success* is also related to high self-esteem (Entwisle, Alexander, Pallas, & Cadigan 1987). It's hard to feel good about oneself while doing poorly in school (Coopersmith & Gilberts, 1982). And finally, *the attitudes of society* influence self-esteem. Children of some minority groups have trouble in developing a positive self-image if they feel that others look down on them because of their racial or ethnic origin (Rotheram-Borus, 1990a, b). However, society's attitudes are not always enough to produce low self-esteem. Children brought up in families that teach pride in their race or background, where they develop a strong ethnic identity and social pride, are able to maintain high self-esteem despite some of the prejudices they encounter from others.

Parents and teachers both are sometimes inaccurate in judging academic self-esteem abilities of children (Miller & Davis, 1992). A number of self-esteem inventories have been developed to evaluate self-esteem of school-age children (Chiu, 1988). Some of these inventories are self-rating. The *Coopersmith Self-Esteem Inventories* (CSEI) contain short statements such as "I'm a lot of fun to be with" to which children respond positively or negatively (Coopersmith, 1981). The *Culture-Free Self-Esteem Inventories (SEI) for Children and Adults* is a Canadian instrument containing short statements such as "I often feel ashamed of myself." Children are to answer "yes" or "no" (Battle, 1981). The *Piers-Harris Children's Self-Concept Scale (CSCS)* is for children in fourth through twelfth grade and contains statements such as "I can be trusted" to which respondents are to check "yes" or "no" (Piers, 1984).

Self-esteem—our perception of our worth, abilities, and accomplishments; our view of ourselves, negative or positive

Other self-esteem scales are for teachers to rate pupils. The *Behavior Academic Self-Esteem (BASE)* scale is designed to measure the academic self-esteem of children in preschool through the eighth grade. It consists of sixteen statements such as "This child adapts easily to changes in procedures." Teachers respond on a five-point scale from *never* to *always* (Coopersmith & Gilberts, 1982). Similarly, the *Self-Esteem Rating Scale for Children (SERSC)* (Chiu, 1987) is for use with children in kindergarten through ninth grade. It consists of twelve statements such as "Hesitates to speak in class." Teachers evaluate these items for each child on a five-point scale ranging from *never* to *always.*

Together, these instruments can be valuable diagnostic tools when evaluation of self-esteem of children is of major concern.

CONCLUSIONS

Self-definition, self-concept, self-reference, self-efficacy, and self-esteem are all similar concepts. Self-definition and self-concept are our self-perceived identity. Self-reference and self-efficacy are our estimates and perceptions of our self-worth, abilities, and accomplishments. Self-esteem is our overall perception of our self-worth and abilities. How children feel about themselves is crucial to their mental health, and to their later relationships and successes in life.

Summary

1. There are four basic components of emotions: (1) stimuli, (2) feelings, (3) physiological arousal, and (4) behavioral response.
2. Emotions play a number of important functions in our lives: they play an adaptive function, are a means of communication, are important in social relationships, are powerful motivators, and are a source of pleasure or of pain.
3. Ekman and colleagues found six basic emotions: happiness, sadness, anger, surprise, disgust, and fear. Emotions develop according to a biological timetable. Some psychologists say that all motions are present at birth.
4. Children's fears may be conditioned or taught by parents, or they may arise out of children's vivid imaginations and limited experience and understanding, from seeing and hearing scary stories, or out of the actions of other children.
5. The three most common worries reported by children relate to school, health, and personal harm.
6. Emotional responses have a biological basis and are partly learned.
7. Everyone gets angry; the real task for children is learn to express anger and control it in harmless and positive ways.
8. Aggression takes two forms: verbal aggression and physical aggression.
9. Overaggression is frequently a cause of poor relationships with peers. Aggressive children have a lower chance of positive interaction with adults at home and school.
10. Aggression must be considered in social context since peer groups and neighborhood environments have an influence over behavior.
11. Some children have learned to roughhouse—they play too rough and end up hurting other children.
12. Children need to achieve a balance between emotional expression and control.
13. Temperament refers to relatively consistent, basic dispositions inherent in people, which underlie and modulate much of their behavior. Temperament is primarily inherited, so basic dispositions are present early in life; expression of temperament is progressively affected by environment.
14. Different researchers have identified different components of temperament: emotionality, activity level, sociability, rhythmicity, approach or withdrawal from new stimuli, adaptability, sensory threshold, quality of mood, intensity of mood expression, distractibility, and persistency and attention span. Some children are easy to take care of, others difficult, others in between, depending on temperament.
15. Hyperactive children, those with attention deficit disorder (ADD) have 3 major symptoms: excessive activity, inattentiveness, and impulsivity.
16. Children vary in temperament due partly to cross-cultural influences.
17. The development of self-awareness means that children begin to understand their separateness from others and other things. The sense of self emerges gradually.
18. Erikson said that the chief psychosocial task between 1 and 2 years of age is the development of autonomy. One of the parenting tasks is to decide how much freedom to allow and how much control to exercise.
19. Mahler says that after 5 months and until age 3, children go through a period of separation-individuation during which they develop a self apart from the mother.
20. Children also begin to develop real awareness and definition of the self and a self-concept. Preschoolers describe themselves in exaggerated and positive terms. By the middle elementary grades, most children begin to develop a more realistic concept of self. Children's self-perceptions are influenced greatly by their parents' appraisals.
21. Self-reference has to do with our estimates of our abilities; self-efficacy is our perceptions of our effectiveness in dealing with situations and with others.
22. Harter developed a *Perceived Competence Scale for Children* that measures competence in four areas: general self-worth, social skills, cognitive skills, and physical skills.

23. Bandura says that self-efficacy stems from four main causes: Personal accomplishments and perceptions of them; comparison of self with others; persuasion by others; and arousal level.
24. Self-esteem is how children view themselves: positively or negatively. There are four primary sources of children's self-esteem: relationships with parents, social competence, intellectual prowess at school, and the attitudes of society and community toward them.
25. A number of self-esteem inventories have been developed to evaluate self-esteem of school-age children.

Key Terms

Attention deficit disorder (ADD) *p. 288*
Epinephrine *p. 274*
Personality *p. 285*
Self-efficacy *p. 291*
Self-esteem *p. 293*
Self-reference *p. 291*
Separation-individuation *p. 290*
Temperament *p. 285*

Discussion Questions

1. Were you a child of an alcoholic? What effect did growing up in an alcoholic family have on you?
2. Can you experience emotion without physiological arousal? Explain.
3. Are emotions present from birth, or are they developed? Explain.
4. What would you do if your toddler was afraid of water? That is, how would you help the child overcome the fear?
5. What might parents do when their child has temper tantrums?
6. Psychologists feel that temperament is inherited. How do you feel about that statement? Compare your temperament now with your temperament when you were younger.
7. Have you ever known a child who was difficult to care for? Have you ever known a child who was easy to care for? Can two children in the same family be this different?
8. Have you ever known a child who was hyperactive? Describe. What were the causes? What did the parents do?
9. What might happen if children are not allowed to develop autonomy when young? Effects depend not only upon the degree of control but whether parents are loving or hostile. Explain.
10. What are the most important factors in the development of self-esteem?
11. What helps the most in helping children to develop self-efficacy?

Suggested Readings

Izard, C. E. (1982). *Measuring emotion in infants and children.* New York: Cambridge University Press. Classic study on how to assess emotions of infants and children.

Johnson, J. H. (1986). *Life events as stressors in childhood and adolescence.* Beverly Hills, CA: Sage. Effects of major changes in the lives of children and adolescents.

Kellerman, J. (1981). *Helping the fearful child: A parents' guide.* New York: Warner Books.

Lamb, M. E. (1987). *The father's role: Cross-cultural perspectives.* Hillsdale, NJ: Erlbaum. Father's role in English, American, Israeli, Italian, Swedish, Chinese, and AKa pygmy families.

Lewis, M. (1991). *Shame: The exposed self.* New York: Free Press. History, personal development of, reactions to, and how it is handled in the individual.

Social Development: The Family, Society, and Socialization

Chapter 12

SOCIOCULTURAL INFLUENCES

THE FAMILY AND SOCIALIZATION

NONNUCLEAR FAMILIES

Sociocultural Influences

Exosystem—social settings in which the child usually is not an active participant, but that influence the child indirectly through their effects on the microsystem.

Macrosystem—influences of a particular culture

Microsystem—the child's immediate contacts

Mesosystem—social influences involving reciprocal relationships

Children do not develop in a vacuum. They develop in the context of their family, neighborhood, community, country, and world. In this context, children are influenced by parents, siblings, other relatives, friends, and peers; other adults with whom they come in contact; and by the school, the church, and the groups of which they are a part. They are influenced by the media: newspapers, magazines, radio, and TV. They are influenced by community and national leaders, by the culture in which they are growing up, and even by things going on in the world. They are partly a product of social influences.

Bronfenbrenner (1977, 1979, 1987) developed an ecological model for understanding social influences. As can be seen in Figure 12.1, social influences are seen as a series of systems extending beyond the child. The child is at the center of the model. The most immediate influences are within the **microsystem** and include those with which the child has immediate contact. The **mesosystem** involves the reciprocal relationships among microsystem settings. For example, what happens at home influences what happens at school and vice versa. Thus, the child's social development is understood best when the influences from many sources are considered, and in relation to one another.

The **exosystem** includes those settings in which the child usually does not have an active role as a participant, but that influence the child indirectly through their effects on the microsystem. For example, what happens to the parents at work influences them and they in turn influence their child's development. Also, community organizations provide family support that affects child rearing.

The **macrosystem** includes the ideologies, values, attitudes, laws, mores, and customs of a particular culture. Cultures may differ among countries or among racial, ethnic, or socioeconomic groups. There are also differences within each group (Gutierrez, Sameroff, & Carrer, 1988). In Sweden, for example, it is against the law for parents to hit children, yet the practice is condoned by some groups in the United States. Middle-class parents in this country often have goals and philosophies

Numerous sociocultural influences play a part in children's development.

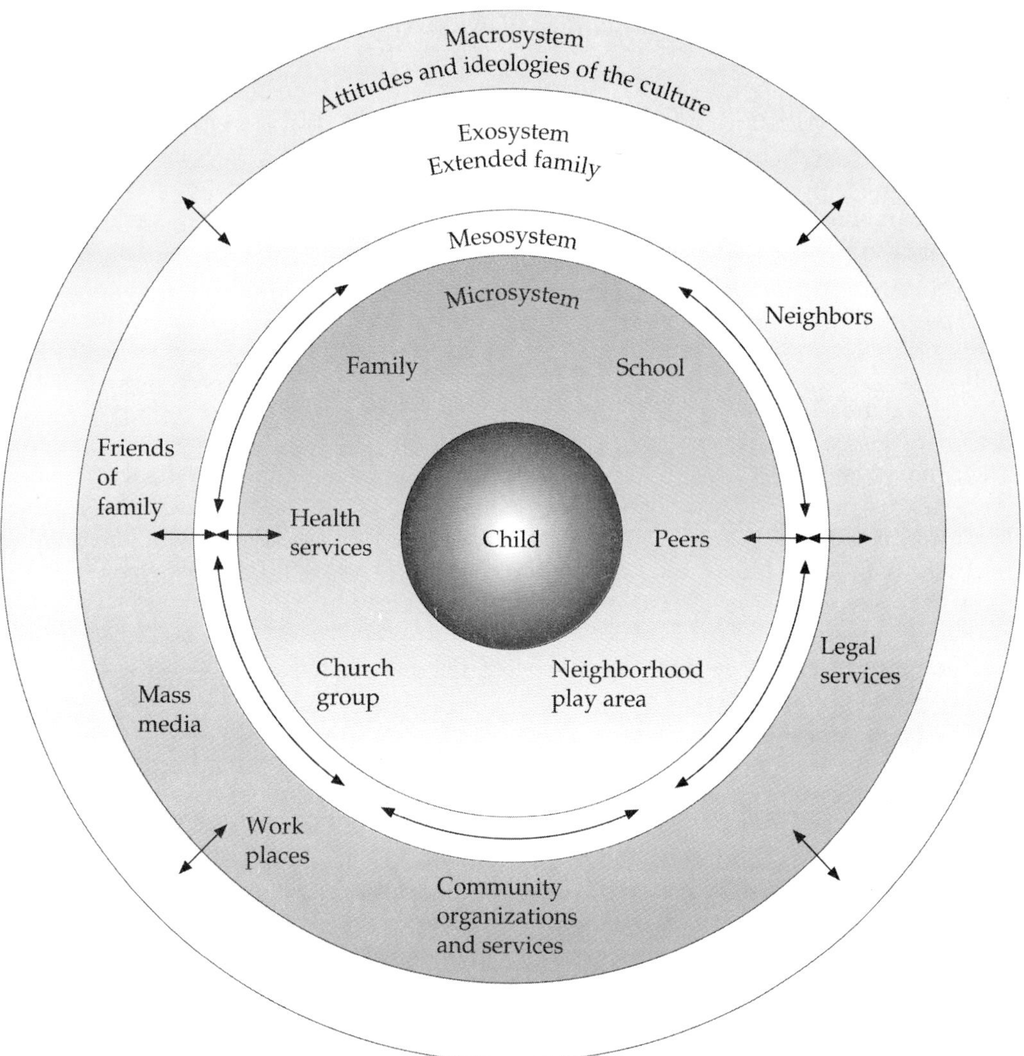

FIGURE 12.1 Bronfenbrenner's ecological model for understanding social influences.

Data from U. Bronfenbrenner (1979), "Contexts of Child Rearing: Problems and Prospects." *American Psychologist 34,* 844–850.

of child rearing different from those in low socioeconomic status groups (Gutierrez & Sameroff, 1990: Harrison, et al., 1990; McLoyd, 1990; Slaughter-Defoe, Nakagawa, Takanishi, & Johnson, 1990). Rural families may have parenting values different from those of urban families (Coleman, Ganong, Clark, & Madsen, 1989). All such value-related and setting-related elements have different effects on children. In talking about social development, therefore, we have to discuss issues and concerns in the contexts in which children are growing up.

The Family and Socialization

THE FAMILY'S ROLE

In the discussion here, a **family** may be defined as "any group of persons united by the ties of marriage, blood, or adoption or any sexually expressive relationship, in which (1) the people are committed to one another in an intimate, interpersonal relationship, (2) the members see their identity as importantly attached to the group, and

(3) the group has an identity of its own" (Rice, 1990b, p. 4).

The following are some of the different types of families.

A **single-parent family** consists of a parent (who may or may not have been married) and one or more children.

A **nuclear family** consists of a father, mother, and their children. This type of family as a proportion of all families has been declining in recent years (White & Tsui, 1986).

The **extended family** consists of one person, a possible mate, any children they might have, and other relatives who live with them in their household. More broadly, the extended family can include relatives living in close proximity to or those who are in frequent contact with a household's members.

The **blended or reconstituted family** is formed when a widowed or divorced person, with or without children, remarries another person who may or may not have been married before and who may or may not have children. If either the remarried husband or wife has children from the former marriage, a **stepfamily** is formed.

A **binuclear family** is an original family divided into two by divorce. It consists of two nuclear families, the maternal nuclear family headed by the mother, and the paternal nuclear family headed by the father. The families include whatever children have been in the original family. Each new family may be headed by a single parent or by two parents if former spouses remarry (Ahrons & Rodgers, 1987).

A **communal family** consists of a group of people who live together and share various aspects of their lives. They can be considered a family if the group falls within the preceding general definition. Some communal groups are not families in this sense.

A **homosexual family** consists of adults of the same sex who live together, with their children, and who share sexual expression and commitment.

A **cohabiting family** consists of two people of the opposite sex who live together, with or without children, and who share sexual expression and commitment to their relationship without formal legal marriage.

When talking about the family, then, we need to specify which type we are referring to. With such a wide variety of family forms, we can no longer assume that the word *family* is synonymous with nuclear family (Cheal, 1993; Wisensale, 1992; Zimmerman, 1992). When families are so different in structure and composition, the influence of different family members is variable. Grandparents or great-grandparents may have considerable influence on children in an extended family, but very little in some nuclear families (Pearson, Hunter, Ensminger, & Kellam, 1990; Tolson & Wilson, 1990). Or, a noncustodial father may have a limited role in socializing his children in a single-parent family where the children are living with the mother. *Total influence varies with family forms* (Stevens, 1988).

Overall, however, the family is the principal transmitter of knowledge, values, attitudes, roles, and habits that one generation passes on to the next (Thornton, Chatters, Taylor, & Allen, 1990). Through word and example the family shapes children's personality and instills modes of thought and ways of acting that become habitual (Kochanska, 1990). Peterson and Rollins (1987) refer to this process as **generational transmission.**

Generational transmission—transmitting of knowledge, values, attitudes, roles, and habits from one generation to the next

Socialization—the process by which persons learn the ways of society or social groups so they can function within them

Socialization is the process by which persons learn the ways of society or social groups so that they can function within it or them (Kalmuss & Seltzer, 1989). A dictionary says it is "to make fit for life in companionship with others." Children are taught the ways and values of their society through contact with already socialized individuals, initially the family (Maccoby, 1992).

The process takes place partly through *formal instruction* that parents provide their children and partly by the efforts of parents to control children through *rewards and punishments.* Learning also takes place through *reciprocal parent–child interaction* as each influences and modifies the behavior of the other in an intense social process (Stryker, 1980). Learning also occurs through *observational modeling*, as children observe, imitate, and model the behavior that they find around them (Bandura, 1986). It is not only what parents say that is important, but it is also what children actually perceive parents to believe and do that most influences them.

Children model their behavior by what they observe in others.

Not all children are influenced to the same degree by their families. The degree of parental influence depends partly on the frequency, duration, intensity, and priority of social contacts that parents have with their children. Parents who are emotionally close to their children, in loving relationships, for long periods of time, exert more influence than do those not so close and who relate to their children less frequently (Russell & Russell, 1987).

Another factor in determining the influence of the family is the difference in individual children (Chess, 1984). Not all children react in the same way to the same family environment, because of differences in heredity, temperament, cognitive perception, developmental characteristics, and maturational levels. Because A happens does not mean that B will inevitably result. When children are brought up in an unhappy, conflicting family, it is more difficult for them to establish happy marriages themselves (Fine & Hovestadt, 1984). However, some do. Not all children are influenced by their families to the same degree, and not all react the same way to the same environment.

PARENTAL COMPETENCE AND FAMILY ENVIRONMENT

Not all parents have a positive influence on their children, nor are all parents able to create a positive and healthy family environment in which children can grow. *The parents' psychological adjustment, parenting style, and the quality of their marriage all have an effect upon the children's emotional maturity, social competence, and cognitive development* (N. B. Miller et al., 1993). This can be illustrated in a number of ways. Let's look first at the psychological adjustment of parents.

Parents' Psychological Adjustment

When parents expose children to high levels of parental anger, the result is heightened emotional and behavioral reactivity on the part of the children. One study showed that if parents suffer from hypertension (high blood pressure), the children show increased cardiovascular reactivity to the stress with consequent high blood pressure and more negative behavior (Ballard, Cummings, & Larkin, 1993). Another study showed the relationship between parent and grandparent drug use and maladjustment among children (Stein, Newcomb, & Bentler, 1993).

Parents who are psychologically healthy are more likely to have a positive effect on their children's development (Hock & Schirtzinger, 1992). For example, mothers who have high self-efficacy, or who believe in their ability to be competent and effective parents, are more likely to have less difficulty in caring for their infants than mothers who do not have confidence (Teti & Gelfand, 1991). Mothers who are satisfied with the quality and quantity of their personal relationships and social networks are more likely to demonstrate optimal maternal behavior (Jennings, Stagg, & Connors, 1991). They praise their children more and are less intrusively controlling. Fathers, too, exert an important influence. Goodman and colleagues found that the father's psychiatric status and the marital status of the couple explain much of the variability in children's social and emotional competence (Goodman, Brogan, Lynch, & Fielding, 1993).

A number of studies have dealt with the relationship between parental depression, especially maternal depression, and the psychological health of children. One study of 6- to 12-year-old children found that maternal depression was associated with lower self-esteem, a reduced sense of personal control, lower cognitive ability, and poorer social-perspective-taking abil-

PARENTING ISSUES

Low Socioeconomic Status and Parenting

The term **low socioeconomic status** (SES) refers to low social class and status, including educational deprivation and low income. In comparison with middle-class families, consider the possible effects of the following conditions under which low SES families bring up their children (Patterson, Kupersmidt, & Vaden, 1990; Wasserman et al., 1990).

Low income means inadequate, crowded housing in poor neighborhoods, where crime rates and social and family problems are greater (Chilman, 1991). Low SES families often have poor medical care, higher mortality rates, and higher rates of physical and mental illnesses. The incidence of accidental death, suicide, and homicide is higher. Expectant mothers are more likely to be young and unmarried (Harris, 1991), to use alcohol and other drugs, and to receive inadequate prenatal care; so they are more likely to deliver premature and difficult babies who are harder to care for and love. One consequence is that child abuse is higher (Young & Gately, 1988). Low SES families are at the mercy of life's unpredictable events: sickness, loss of work, injury, legal problems, and school and family difficulties. Low income means less likelihood of having insurance to cover property, life, disability, or health. Low SES families strive for security to protect themselves, and just to provide themselves with the basic necessities of life (Dill et al., 1980). The families more often are one-parent families, with fathers playing less of an active role in caring for their children (Paasch & Teachman, 1991).

As a result of life circumstances, low SES parents have more stresses, and stress affects the way parents carry out their functions. Low SES parents are less responsive toward their children; they are more irritable, explosive, restrictive, critical, and punitive (Zusman, 1980). They are more authoritarian and issue more imperatives and absolutes, with a tendency to stress obedience, respect for all authority, and staying out of trouble. Discipline tends to be impulsive, harsh, inconsistent, and to emphasize physical punishment rather than verbal explanations and requests (Chilman, 1991).

We should keep in mind that these class-linked differences represent groups averages that do not apply to all low SES families and individuals. One study of low-income, black, urban mothers indicated a rather wide range of disciplinary practices. Mothers varied greatly in their attitude toward physical punishment. In general, the more religious mothers had more child-oriented disciplinary attitudes (Kelley, Power, & Wimbush, 1992).

One study of 585 children from the lowest socioeconomic class found that low socioeconomic status was significantly correlated with eight factors in the child's socialization and social context, including harsh discipline, lack of maternal warmth, exposure to aggressive adult models, maternal aggressive values, family life stressors, mother's lack of social support, peer group instability, and lack of cognitive stimulation (Dodge, Pettit, & Bates, 1994).

Low socioeconomic status families are at the mercy of life's unpredictable events.

ity of boys (Kershner & Cohen, 1992). The boys of depressive mothers received higher ratings of problem behaviors. In another study, depressed mothers less often complied with the requests of their 5-year-olds (Kochanska & Kuczynski, 1991).

Figure 12.2 shows a path model to illustrate the effect of parents' depression on a child's overt behavior. The top path illustrates that the more parents are depressed, the less positive affection they show one another, which in turn affects the warmth they express to their child, which affects the child's external behavior (N. B. Miller et al., 1993). The bottom path shows that the more parents are depressed, the greater the couple's conflict, which in turn affects the child's external behavior. When one or both parents have been diagnosed with a serious disturbance (e.g., psychosis or depression), the children are at risk for cognitive, social, emotional, and school-related difficulties.

Marital Quality

The quality of the marital relationship also affects children's adjustments and development and influences children's behavior problems over a wide age span (Jouriles et al., 1991). Harmonious marriages tend to be associated with sensitive parenting and warm parent–child relationships (Floyd & Zmich, 1991). When husbands and wives are satisfied with their marriage, the children tend to be more secure (Gable, Belsky, & Crnic, 1992). However, when there is marital discord, children tend to be more anxious and/or aggressive, to internalize and externalize behavior problems, and to manifest more insecurities. The simplest way to summarize research findings relating marriage and child development is to say that an association exists between troubled marriages—as measured by the levels of conflict—and child behavior problems (Gable, Belsky, & Crnic 1992).

Not all marital conflict is harmful to children. If discussions are relatively calm, if parents are able to resolve disagreements, and if the emotional atmosphere is pleasant, the net effect is beneficial to the children: They learn how to resolve conflicts by the example set in the home. So it is not conflict itself that creates problems, it is the intensity, the frequency, the content, and the outcome of the conflict that determines the effect on children (Grych & Fineham, 1993). Physical aggression and high levels of verbal abuse result in greater levels of anger, fear, and sadness in children. The subject of the discussion makes a difference also. If the content relates to the children (for example, differences over child rearing), the children are more likely to be upset. Children are more likely to blame themselves and be afraid of becoming involved in the argument. They become very fearful if the argument is likely to escalate and they will be drawn in. How conflicts end also seems to matter. Unresolved conflicts result in the most negative response for the children. The children are left with a great deal of stress, along with bad feelings, **dysphoria**, fear, anger, and a sense of helplessness. After all, what can they do about it (Grych, Seid, & Fineham, 1992)?

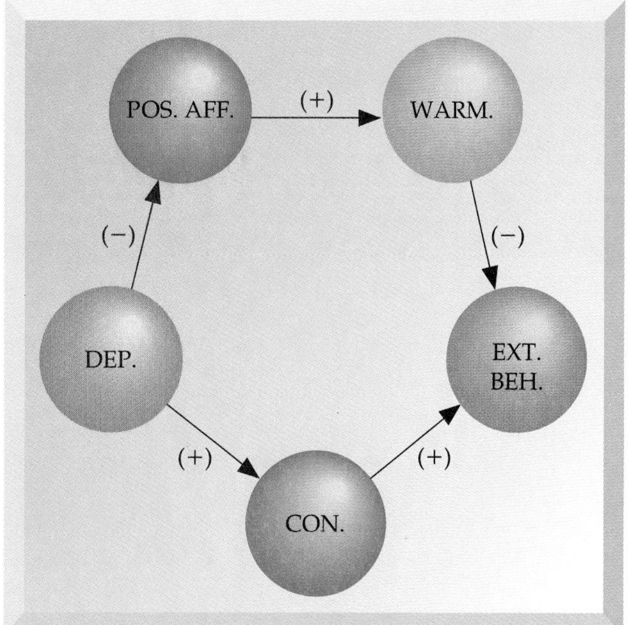

DEP.=Depression; POS. AFF.=Couple's positive affection; WARM.=Parenting warmth; CON.=Couple's conflict; EXT. BEH.=Child's externalized (overt) behavior.

FIGURE 12.2 Parents' depression and child's overt behavior.

PATTERNS OF PARENTING

Just as there are differences in families, there are also various patterns of parenting (McNally, Eisenberg, & Harris, 1991). These patterns partly reflect differences in parental values (Luster, Rhoades, & Haas, 1989; Simons, Beaman, Conger, & Chao, 1993). For example, some parents value conformity in children; others value self-direction (Mills & Rubin, 1990). One study compared the attitudes of Anglo and Puerto Rican mothers in relation to what they considered to be acceptable attachment behavior. The Anglo mothers focused on the degree of individual autonomy. The Puerto Rican mothers placed more emphasis on the child's ability to maintain proper demeanor in public (Harwood, 1992). Another study showed that parents with higher educational and occupational levels used more reasoning in directing their children. In turn, higher levels of reasoning were related to authoritative (not authoritarian) patterns of child rearing, the use of indirect positive control, warmth, acceptance, and support (Dekovic and Gerris, 1992). Still another study showed that increased maternal responsiveness during in-

Dysphoria—generalized unhappiness

FOCUS

Strengths and Weaknesses of Families in the United States

Much has been written about what is right or wrong with the American family. Since the family has always been considered the basic social unit in our society, concern about the quality of family life continues to be a priority. The following summarizes some important trends (Fine, 1992; Wisensale, 1992; Zimmerman, 1992).

STRENGTHS

In spite of the failures of many marriages, marriage continues to be the favorite life-style option, with only about 5 percent of the population never marrying. Americans continue to put their trust in marriage to satisfy their needs and to give life satisfaction. Even when marriage fails, 83 percent of divorced men and 76 percent of divorced women remarry (*Statistical Abstract of the United States,* U.S. Bureau of the Census, 1995). In the face of emotional, social, and political pressure, most families tend to function relatively well. The majority of adults are employed, have good physical and mental health, meaningful social relationships, a high school education, and are not involved in criminal activity. These benefits are due, at least in part, to positive contributions to their development in their families of origin.

Another strength is the increasing acceptance of alternate family forms. The two-parent nuclear family has now been joined by single-parent, stepparent, interethnic, and cohabiting families. The greater acceptance of such families has helped them gain access to social, legal, and financial supports to insure their health and survival. This access is of proven benefit to both adults and children. Couples are also *postponing marriage and parenthood longer*, so that their increased maturity when they reach these milestones of life enables them to cope better with the stresses they encounter. *Improved family planning services* enable them to have fewer children, which has a positive effect upon family members. *Advances in reproduc-*

fancy, particularly verbal responsiveness, was influenced by the mother's cultural background and school attendance (Richman, Miller, & Levine, 1992). Diana Baumrind (1978, 1980) examined the way that parenting styles affected the social characteristics of preschool children from 300 families. Baumrind was particularly concerned with the patterns of control that parents used, and identified three general styles of parenting: authoritarian, permissive, and authoritative.

Authoritarian

Authoritarian parents emphasize obedience, using force to curb children's self-will, keeping children subordinate, restricting

tive technology enable childless couples to have children they would not otherwise be able to have. Greater publicity in the media makes it seem that family violence has increased, but there has actually been a *decrease in spouse and child abuse* over the last decade, thanks to programs of prevention and intervention.

WEAKNESSES

The United States has one of the highest divorce rates in the world. The rate reached an all-time high in 1980 and has remained fairly stable since then. Still, it is predicted that 50 to 60 percent of marriages will end in divorce, exposing the children in those families to the experience of living in a disrupted family and resulting in more women and children living in poverty. *Real family income continues to decline;* greater numbers of families live below the poverty line; increasing numbers of both married and single mothers have to go to work; greater numbers of families live in submarginal housing or deteriorated neighborhoods exposing them to increased crime and violence, substandard educational opportunities, and to a variety of social problems such as drug abuse. Affordable housing has become impossible for an increasing number of families.

There has been a *confusion of family roles.* While there are clearly benefits to increased flexibility of male and female roles, some confusion has resulted from role ambiguity. Women particularly are under stress because they not only are expected to fulfill traditional female functions, but also to become breadwinners. Yet not enough husbands are doing their fair share of the homemaking and child-rearing tasks. There continues to be a *shortage of affordable, high-quality child care* while mothers work, with the result that too many children suffer from inadequate care or are forced to fend for themselves.

There has been a *decline in the socialization functions of the family* due to the increase in the numbers of children living with one parent, decreased parent-child contact, and decreased involvement of parents in child-rearing. Many noncustodial fathers are not only not helping to support their children financially, but are not maintaining regular contact with them. The mass media, the schools, and influences in the community have taken over some of the socialization of children formerly performed by parents. The well-being of U.S. children, primarily in the areas of achievement, socioemotional development, and socioeconomic status has declined in the last decade.

autonomy, and discouraging verbal give and take (Kochanska, Kuczynski, & Radke-Yarrow, 1989). These types of parents tend to use harsh discipline because that is the way they themselves were brought up (Simons, Beaman, Conger, & Chao, 1992). This type of parenting tends to produce withdrawn, fearful children who exhibit little or no independence and are generally irritable, unassertive, and moody, or hostile, angry, and overly aggressive.

Permissive

Permissive parents free children from restraint, and accept their impulses and actions without trying to shape their behavior. Some of these parents are protective

Cultural differences influence parenting practices.

and moderately loving, but others let children do what they want as a way of avoiding responsibility for them. These children tend to be rebellious, self-indulgent, aggressive, impulsive, and socially inept. Lack of discipline in the homes is associated with social aggression which, in turn, is associated with peer rejection (Travillion & Snyder, 1993).

Authoritative

Authoritative parents seek to direct their children's activities in a rational manner, encouraging discussion and also exerting firm control when children disobey, but without being overly restrictive. These parents recognize children's individual needs and interests, but set standards of conduct (Kochanska, Kuczynski, and Radke-Yarrow, 1989). These children are the best adjusted of the three groups; they are the most self-reliant, self-controlled, self-confident, and socially competent (Dekovic & Janssens, 1992).

On the basis of her research, Baumrind concluded that *authoritative parenting, which is firm but reasonable,* and *which is warm, nurturing, and loving, works best in the socialization of children* (Donovan, Leavitt, & Walsh, 1990).

Research by Schaefer (1959) emphasized both the pattern of control—the autonomy versus control dimension—and the degree of affection—the love versus hostility dimension (Amato, 1990). These dimensions interact to form four patterns: *love-autonomy, love-control, hostility-autonomy,* and *hostility-control.* Of course, there are degrees within each pattern. The four dimensions are shown in Figure 12.3. The secret of successful parenting seems to be to show the maximum amount of love (children are never spoiled by love) and the right balance between autonomy and control. Autonomy without any control is permissiveness and overindulgence. Hostility without any control results in a high rate of aggression. Hostility with a high degree of control may produce extreme hostility and anger that sometimes erupt in destructive ways. Of course, children are different and sometimes are affected differently by a specific pattern of parenting. Also, these findings were determined from the study of middle-class populations in the United States. Firm control patterns in some Asian countries are usual, and may produce less reactionary results (Rohner & Rohner, 1981).

Other research has attempted to relate specific child-care practices to children's socialization and personality development. Several studies have shown the relationship between parents' empathy and responsiveness to their children to the children's growing ability to respond empathetically and sympathetically to others (Eisenberg et al., 1991; Eisenberg et al., 1992). In another study in the 1950s, Sears, Maccoby, and Levin (1957) interviewed mothers of 379 kindergarten children, rating each on more than 100 child-rearing practices. They looked at the relationships between these practices, and at the personalities of the children. McClelland and colleagues did a follow-up on 78 of these subjects, who were then 31 years of age (McClelland, Constantian, Regalado, & Stone, 1978). They drew an interesting conclusion:

> Wide variations in the way parents reared their children didn't seem to matter much in the long run. Adult interest and beliefs

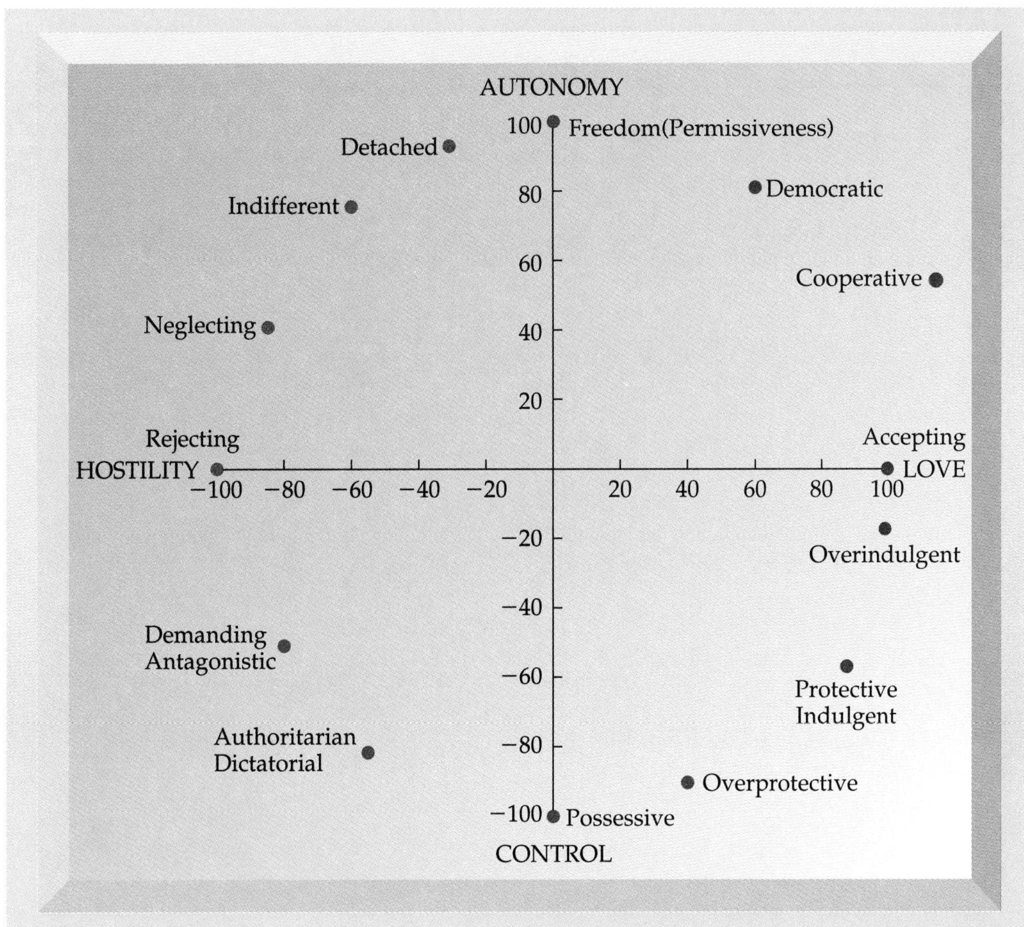

FIGURE 12.3 Dimensions of parenting: autonomy vs. control and love vs. hostility.

From: E. S. Schaefer (1959), "A Circumplex Model for Maternal Behavior." *Journal of Abnormal and Social Psychology 59*, 226–235.

> were by and large not determined by the duration of breast-feeding, the age and severity of toilet training, strictness about bedtimes, or indeed any of these things (p. 46).

This does not mean that parents can do anything they want, without having an effect on children. What McClelland and his associates (1978) did find was that *the one parenting variable that was most related to adjustment was love.* Parents who genuinely loved their children provided them with the most important requirement for successful socialization (Jakab, 1987).

DISCIPLINE

The word **discipline** comes from the same root as does the word *disciple*, which means "a learner." *Discipline, therefore, is a process of learning, of education, a means by which socialization takes place.* Its purpose is to instruct in proper conduct or action rather than to punish (Petersen, Lee, & Ellis, 1982). The ultimate goal of discipline is to sensitize the conscience and to develop self-control, so that individuals live according to the standards of behavior and in accord with the rules and regulations established by the group.

In the beginning, control over the child is established by external authority; but gradually children are encouraged to develop internal controls so that the standards they strive to follow become a part of their own lives, not because they have to, but because they want to. When this happens, these internalized truths become their own standards of conduct.

If discipline is to accomplish its goal of developing inner control, there are a num-

Discipline—a process of learning by which socialization takes place; its purpose is instruction in proper conduct

PARENTING ISSUES

Parental Control Techniques

Smith (1988) has given a helpful summary of seven control techniques that are used by parents.

- *Power-assertive discipline*—physical punishment, deprivation, and threats. Harsh physical punishment especially has been associated with physical aggression in children who model their parent's behavior (Dishion, 1990; Hart, Ladd, & Burleson, 1990; Kandel, 1990; Vuchinich, Bank, & Patterson, 1992).
- *Command*—imperative statements not accompanied by punishment or overt threat of punishment. The success of this technique depends upon the child's acceptance of parental authority. In general, mothers who use negative control in relationships with their children produce children who are aggressive and unsuccessful in their relationships with peers (Kochanska, 1992).
- *Self-oriented induction*—reasoning in pointing out gains or costs children might experience as a result of their behavior. This technique produces positive effects on children. One study found that children of inductive mothers were more popular among their peers and exhibited more prosocial behavior on the playground (Hart, DeWolf, Wozniak, & Burts, 1992).
- *Other-oriented induction*—reasoning in pointing out religious or ethical principles, altruism, or personal obligations and reasons for children to change their behavior. This technique helps in internalizing values and acceptable behavior.
- *Love withdrawal*—temporary coldness or rejection to gain compliance. This method may threaten children's security.
- *Advice*—suggesting how children might accomplish what is desired by the parent. The success of this technique depends on the children's recognition of parents' expert power.
- *Relationship maintenance*—striving to build and maintain a positive relationship with children at the same time that influence is being exerted.

ber of principles that, if followed, enhance this development (Schneider-Rosen & Wenz-Gross, 1990). These are summarized here (Rice, 1990b).

1. Children respond more readily to parents within the context of a *loving, trusting relationship of mutual esteem*. Children who receive nurturance and emotional support from parents show lower levels of aggression than do those who do not receive this support (Zelkowitz, 1987).

2. Discipline is more effective when it is *consistent rather than erratic*. It is helpful if parents agree on discipline (Deal, Halverson, & Wampler, 1989; Vaughn, Block, & Block, 1988).

3. Learning is enhanced if responses involve *rewards and punishments*.

4. Discipline is more effective when applied *as soon after the offense as possible*.

5. *Do not use discipline that inflicts pain.* This means avoiding spanking. Severe punishment, especially if it is cruel and abusive, is counterproductive because it stimulates resentment, feelings of rejection, and similar harsh, cruel behavior on the part of children (Herzberger & Tennen, 1985; Rohner, Kean, & Cournoyer, 1991; Weiss & Dodge, 1992). Sweden has laws making spanking of children a crime.

6. *Discipline becomes less effective if it is too strict or too often applied.* A parent who con-

Talking to children is one of the best methods of discipline.

tinually criticizes a child no matter what the child does is teaching the child that it is impossible to please the parents.

7. All children want and need external controls in the beginning because they are not yet mature enough to exert self-control over their own behavior. Appropriate methods of discipline will vary according to the child's age and level of understanding. However, *extremes of either permissiveness or authoritarianism are counterproductive.* At very young ages, discipline may be accomplished through wise management: providing interesting toys and activities; equipping sections of the residence as a playroom, play yard, or play area; and child-proofing the house by keeping dangerous things out of reach. Young children may be disciplined through distraction and offering substitute activities (Holden & West, 1989). Sometimes the wisest discipline is through environmental manipulation; removing the child from the situation or the situation from the child. Parents can discuss issues with older children and arrive at joint decisions, whereas instruction to preschoolers necessarily involves more imperatives. Even then, explanations and reasons are helpful, depending upon the children's level of understanding.

8. *Discipline needs to take into account children's age.* One study found that discipline among preschoolers peaked between 30 and 36 months of age. That is, there were peaks in negative behavior during these ages. By 48 months, there was a decrease in the discipline problems caused by physical aggression and immaturity of the children (Larzelere, Amberson, & Martin, 1992).

9. *Methods of discipline to be avoided are those that threaten the child's security or development of self-esteem.* In some cases, parents threaten to give children away if they aren't good or to call a policeman to put them in jail. Similarly, threats to withdraw love if children aren't good are harmful means of disciplining, but are often employed by middle-class parents to try to control their children's behavior. They are devastating to children's security if regularly employed (Rice, 1990b).

WORKING MOTHERS

The past two decades have seen a remarkable rise in the number of two-earner and single-parent households in the United States, with corresponding increases in the labor force participation rates of women with young children. Today, fewer than one-third of households fit the definition of the so-called traditional family. Psychologists, economists, sociologists, and other behavioral scientists have stormed into this politically charged arena with dozens of studies evaluating the potential effects of maternal employment and substitute child

Some working mothers take their children to work with them.

FOCUS

China's Patterns of Socialization

David Ho (1989) of the University of Hong Kong has summarized research on China's patterns of socialization in Taiwan and on the China mainland and has found the following distinguishing characteristics (Lin & Fu, 1990):

1. Parents tend to be highly lenient or even indulgent in their attitudes toward the infant and young child, in contrast to the strict discipline they impose on older children.

2. Traditionally, the transition from childhood through adolescence to adulthood takes place gradually and smoothly. A marked departure from this pattern of continuity is evidenced by intergenerational conflicts and increasing rates of juvenile delinquency.

3. Traditionally, sex roles are clearly and sharply differentiated.

4. Traditionally, parental roles between the father and mother are clearly differentiated; the mother is the agent of nurturance; the father assumes the role of disciplinarian when the child grows older.

5. Disciplinary training tends to be more severe for boys than for girls, very likely reflecting the fact that boys present more behavioral problems than girls.

6. The social class and rural–urban patterning of socialization is similar to that observed in other countries. Greater departures from the traditional pattern of parenting are found among younger, better-educated, and urban parents.

7. In traditional Chinese society, the downward social mobility of prominent families resulted in large measure from the progressive degeneracy of the sons and their descendants. Given the wealth and status of their families, the children were not required to be prepared for having to work for a living in adulthood.

8. Despite important variations across geographical boundaries, common features that are distinctively Chinese in character may be discerned; and despite undeniable changes over time, continuity with the traditional pattern of socialization is preserved among the Chinese of today.

Despite some changes, traditional patterns of socialization are preserved in many Asian-American families today.

care on children's well-being. There is a considerable amount of disagreement among researchers. It has been suggested that full-time, nonparental care places infants at considerable risk. Other studies do not reach such a conclusion. Two decades of exhaustive research has failed to document consistent, meaningful negative findings of the effects of maternal employment and substitute child care on children's well-being. While the studies show that maternal employment is not uniformly detrimental to the child's well-being, neither is it likely that it is uniformly beneficial.

Many studies omit the influence of socioeconomic status when considering the

PARENTING ISSUES

Children's Chores

A study of 790 Nebraska homes in which there were children revealed some interesting data on the extent to which children were regularly required to do chores around the house or yard. Apparently, assigning chores was a developmental process. In some households, chores were assigned to very young children (about a third of boys and girls 4 years of age or under were assigned work). The older children became, the more work was assigned, so that by age 9 or 10, well over 90 percent of the children were involved in regular chores. The median number of hours spent on chores was 4 hours per week. Even among the older, hardest workers, only 6 hours per week were required (White & Brinkerhoff, 1981).

In the beginning, children were responsible for themselves, picking up their own toys, making beds, cleaning their rooms. By 10 years of age, children moved beyond self-centered chores and were now required to help the family.

Parents gave five types of reasons for assigning chores:

Developmental—doing chores builds character, develops responsibility, helps children learn.

Reciprocal obligation—it is children's duty to help the family.

Extrinsic—parents need help.

Task learning—children need to learn to do these tasks.

Residual—miscellaneous reasons, including earning an allowance or needing to keep busy (White & Brinkerhoff, 1981).

In many families, children help their parents with household chores.

effects of maternal employment. They also do not take into account the level of emotional support at home as contrasted with the level of emotional support provided by substitute child care. Greenstein (1993) reports on a study of 2,209 children who were between 4 and 6 years of age. The sampling overrepresents children who have been born to younger mothers, less-educated mothers, and minority mothers. A number of the children are black or Hispanic, and economically disadvantaged. The average age of the mothers at the time of their child's birth was approximately 22. The results of the study showed that there was a stronger negative net effect of maternal employment on the child in high SES families. The use of substitute child care resulted in less positive behavioral outcomes for children from high-income households than for children from low-income households. This finding is based on the assumption that when high-income households choose child care, they are not likely to obtain an environment for their children that is significantly better than that which they have at home. However, the additional experiences provided by the formal child-care arrangement to children from low-income households may well significantly expand the developmental opportunities available to such children.

Attention was also given to the level of emotional support in the home and its interaction with the type of substitute child care used during the child's infancy. In homes where children received high levels of emotional support, substitute care (unless it was of extremely high quality) did not adequately substitute for the affective

PARENTING ISSUES

Maternal Responsiveness

Patterns of mother–child interaction from infancy to age 12 were investigated in a longitudinal study of forty-four English-speaking mothers and their preterm children. Maternal responsiveness was evaluated by home observations during infancy and in two structured laboratory situations at age 12. Children of mothers who were consistently more responsive during infancy and early adolescence and those who became more responsive by the time their children were 12 achieved higher IQ and arithmetic scores, had more positive self-esteem, and fewer behavioral and emotional problems as reported by their teachers than children of less responsive mothers (Beckwith, Rodning, & Cohen, 1992).

process lost by the mother's absence from the home. In homes where children received relatively low levels of emotional support, the substitute care arrangement had positive effects on social behavior, because it provided a higher level of emotional support than the child would receive if cared for at home. The findings suggest that among middle- and upper-income families, maternal employment implies a significant loss of resources for the children that are not replaced or compensated for by the child-care setting. However, the additional market goods of services made possible by maternal employment in low-income families may have a far more beneficial effect on child outcomes than negative effect of maternal absence from the home (Greenstein, 1993).

THE FATHER'S ROLE

Traditionally, the father's role has been that of provider and the mother's role has been that of nurturer. But as the mother becomes more involved in providing for the family, there is need for the fathers to be more involved in the role of nurturing children (Atkinson & Blackwelder, 1993).

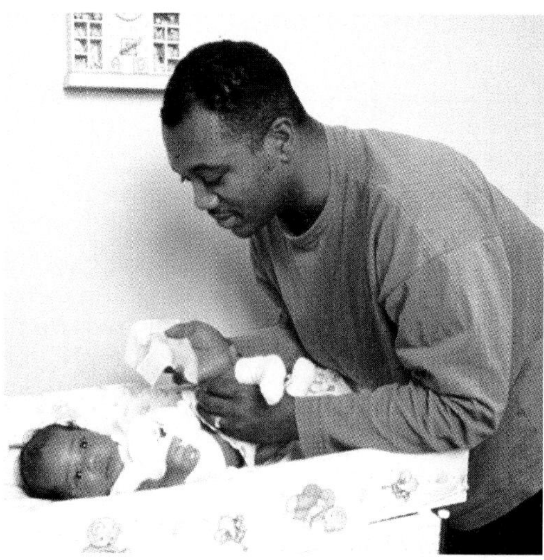

Fathers can play a vital role in the care of their infant children.

With increasing numbers of married women employed outside the home, fairness would seem to demand that husbands take increased responsibility for housework and child care. This has happened to some extent, but *equality of roles has not been fully achieved.* More educated fathers, especially those reared in homes where the father was expected to do housework and care for children, generally participate in these tasks, but study after study shows that in other homes, even those in which the mother works full-time, the mothers still take major responsibility, with the father occasionally "helping" (Coverman & Sheley, 1986; Levant, Slattery, & Loiselle, 1987; Shelton, 1990). When fathers do participate in household tasks and child care, they usually do so in limited ways. They often "help" on tasks of their own choosing (Marsiglio, 1991). Some fathers will spend time with their sons, especially when the sons are old enough to play games, but leave the rearing of their daughters to their wives. Cartoons and other media often picture fathers as too inept to change diapers or otherwise care for infants (LaRossa et al., 1991). Such images further discourage fathers who might otherwise want to take care of the baby.

Not only is paternal involvement fair, but it has other advantages. When both parents share responsibilities, the marital relationship improves, individual well-being of the wife increases, and the children benefit because the quality of parent–child relationships is enhanced (Haas, 1980; Olson, 1981). Kaplan (1990) suggests that combining marriage, work, and motherhood forms an impossible triangle and that, as a result, the whole family suffers.

Research tends to indicate that many fathers have a closer relationship with their sons than with their daughters (Ishii-Kuntz, 1994; Mott, 1994; Smith & Morgan, 1994; Starrels, 1994). In spite of father–son closeness, most mothers are more involved in the day-by-day care of their children than are fathers. Interestingly enough, fathers are less likely to leave home if they have sons (Mott, 1994). If the father does leave home, the mother usually shows greater egalitarianism in child upbringing than if her husband is present.

Siblings exert an important socializing influence on one another.

SIBLING RELATIONSHIPS

Not only are parents an important influence on the social development of children, but siblings also exert considerable influence. Researchers have tried to discover the importance of birth order and number of siblings in the family, the gender of those siblings, whether the siblings are older or younger, and how these factors influence the children themselves. Sibling relationships are unique because they are different from relationships with parents and peers. Siblings are closer although usually not identical in age. Their interests are often different than those of parents and they have a different outlook on life. Sometimes siblings exert important influences on one another well into adulthood and maintain close relationships all their lives. At other times, the relationships are quite troubling from the beginning, and parents have difficulty in knowing how to manage two or more children in the same family. Of these topics, let's look first at birth order.

Birth Order

It does seem to make a difference whether a child is an only child, a first child, a middle child, or a youngest child in the family. *Research tends to indicate that firstborn children have some advantages over other children in the family.* For example, they are statistically overrepresented among students in graduate and professional schools (Goleman, 1985). Fifty-two percent of U.S. presidents are firstborn children.

There are some good reasons for such levels of attainment. Research reveals that parents usually attach greater importance to their first child. The first child is special because he or she is first, and because there are no competing children, parents are able to give their entire attention and energies to raising that child until the next one is born. For this reason, the oldest sibling usually experiences a richer intellectual environment than younger siblings. The research indicates that older, first children are usually more social, affectionate, and achieve more in life than do others in the family.

The youngest in the family are also usually given special attention because they are the youngest. The youngest child gets special attention from older brothers and sisters. Because there are others to socialize with, researchers find that later-born children usually possess better social skills than do the firstborn.

Middle children tend to have lower self-esteem than do firstborn and last born, probably because they have a less well-defined function within the family. The middle children are somewhat overlooked. They are not special because of being the first, nor are they the last. They are there, and accepted as they are, but usually do not receive as much

FOCUS

Everyday Rules of Behavior

One study examined how mothers socialized their young children toward behavior self-regulation. A group of mothers and their children were seen in home and laboratory visits at six-month intervals (i.e., at 13, 18, 24, and 30 months). Only the results at 13 and 30 months of age are reported here. The mothers were asked whether they had communicated particular prohibitions and requests to their children. In reporting this, they were asked to look at a list submitted to them and to check whether or not they had recently asked for each behavior. The list contained everyday rules of behavior divided into eight categories as follows:

Child safety included not touching things that are dangerous, not climbing on the furniture, and not going into the street.

Protection of personal property included keeping away from prohibited objects such as knives or stoves, not tearing up books, not getting into prohibited drawers or rooms, not coloring on walls or furniture.

Respect for others included not taking toys away from other children and not being too rough with other children.

Food and mealtime routines included not playing with food, not leaving the table in the middle of the meal, not spilling drinks or juice.

A delay category included waiting while the mother was on the telephone, not interrupting others' conversations, and being willing to wait for a meal.

Manners included saying "please" and "thank you."

Self-care included dressing self, asking to use the toilet, washing up when requested, brushing teeth when requested, going to bed when requested.

Family routines included helping with chores when requested, putting toys away, and keeping their rooms neat.

As seen in Figure 12.4, when the children were 13 months of age, the mothers were interested in the protection of personal property, respect for others, and child safety. Mothers were least interested in self-care, helping with family routines, and manners. However, when the children were 30 months of age, the mothers were interested in respect for others, manners, child safety, protection of personal property, and in being willing to delay by waiting for the mother while she was on the telephone and not interrupting others' conversations. Mothers were least interested in children helping with family routines, self-care, or mealtime and food routines. It was obvious that the frequency of the mothers' instructions had increased greatly between the time their children were 13 months of age and 30 months of age. (Gralinski & Kopp, 1993).

special attention as the oldest or the youngest child.

Number of Siblings

The total number of children in a family makes a difference also. *In general terms, the greater the number of children, the less they will be able to complete their education.* Usually they have lower levels of schooling, because the parents are not able to offer great educational advantages to all the children in the family. Family size is linked to greater or lesser degrees of achievement (Blake, 1989).

Gender

The sex of a sibling may also be of some significance. Individuals with an older, opposite-sex sibling with whom they have a good relationship usually develop a very positive attitude towards those of the opposite sex. However, if the relationship with the opposite-sex sibling is very troublesome and quarrelsome, the child may develop very negative attitudes toward persons of the opposite sex and have difficulty relating to them later in life (Ickes & Turner, 1985). For example, if girls in the family have brothers within the same family, they

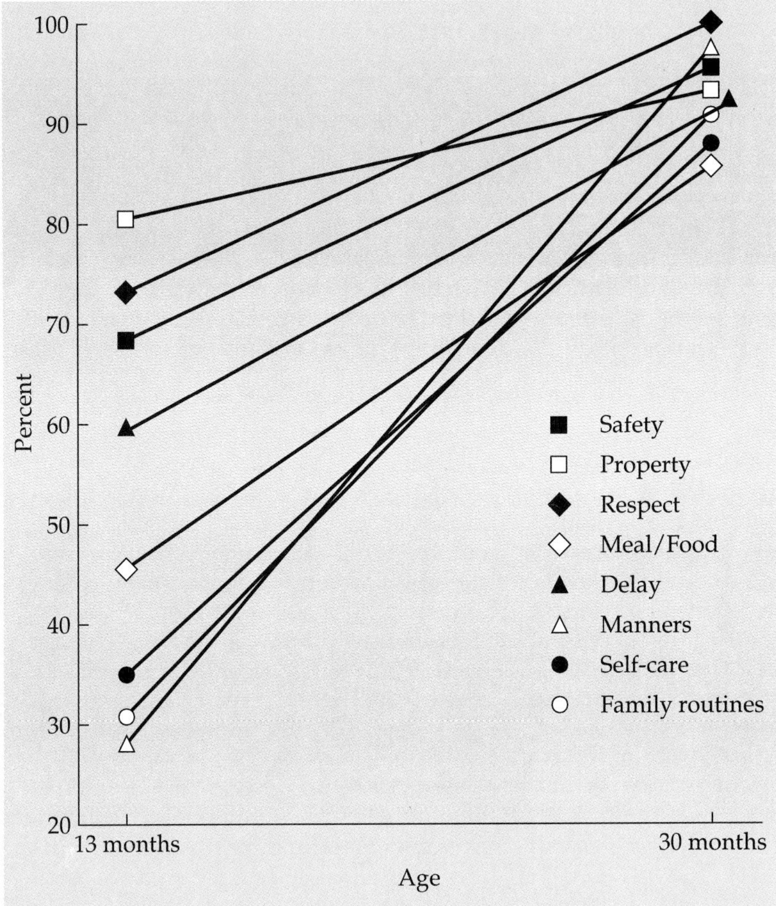

FIGURE 12.4 Developmental trends in proportions of rules requested, by rule category.

Statistics from: J. H. Gralinski & C. B. Kopp (1993). "Everyday Rules for Behavior: Mothers' Requests to Young Children." *Developmental Psychology, 29*, 573–584. Copyright 1997 by the American Psychological Association. Adapted with permission.

get acquainted with men by getting acquainted with their brothers. They feel more comfortable with men and learn how to relate to them if they have good relationships with their own masculine siblings.

Older Brothers and Sisters

Having older brothers and sisters in the same family can have a significant influence on younger children—either positively or negatively. The older siblings can serve as role models for the younger ones. Older siblings generally spend more time with their younger brothers and sisters than their parents do, and have considerable influence in the children's socialization. Some older children are very good with younger brothers and sisters. Others have a very disturbing, negative influence. In the neighborhood in which I grew up, I lived next door to a boy whose older sister was left to care for him. The sister was ten years older than the boy. The boy used to cry almost constantly for hours while his mother was gone, primarily because the sister teased him unmercifully, probably because he was the only son and she was quite jealous of him. This boy grew up really hating girls, especially anyone who reminded him of his sister. My sister grew up in a family where she had three brothers. As a consequence, she became very much of a tomboy for a while because her role models were all masculine.

All we can say is that sometimes brothers or sisters are positive influences, sometimes negative. If mothers or fathers suspect that younger children are not being prop-

PARENTING ISSUES

Me-Generation Parents

I am tired of the pointed finger. We parents blame others for crumbling social values and deteriorating education, when we hold the keys to the solutions. For most of us, finding that solution is going to mean a lifestyle choice we so far refused to make. Parents in the United States used to take the lead in raising children. Some family members were home during the day to direct the children's activities and work with the schools, churches, and other organizations to raise law-abiding, productive, dependable, and honest members of the next generation. This has all changed with a maturing U.S. economy that requires two earners per family to continue a rising trend in material living standards. As a result, children are floundering in malls, movies, fast-food joints, and empty houses across America.

It's not that parents don't care about their children. They do. On weekends, I see children and parents enjoying time together in playgrounds, at pools, eating out, and at school events. But in addition to providing a loving home and secure financial conditions, our responsibility as parents is to guide our children to become self-reliant adults. This comes from example and discipline—neither of which is possible in absentia.

What do we want? For middle-class Americans, the trade-off is between more material goods or more time at home with our offspring. When we insist on a bedroom for every child, drop $25.00 for a quick family meal at McDonalds, join a health club, update our wardrobe, or buy a second VCR or camcorder, we need to ask ourselves, "Is this accumulation of material goods the priority we want to impart to our children? Or should we pare the family budget, cut back on two full-time careers, devote those extra hours to guiding our children?"

Sometimes less is more. Twenty years from now, our children will be grown. Will they remember the extra Reeboks paid for by the second full-time paycheck? Or will they remember the many times Mom or Dad curled up with them on the sofa to talk over a problem, expected good manners and polite behavior, reviewed their homework each and every evening, and pitched in to pull together a scouting or athletic program? Your choice (Symonds, 1995). (Reprinted by permission of Wall St. Journal © 1995, Dow Jones & Company, Inc. All rights reserved worldwide.)

erly cared for, they need to give more guidance and supervision so that older brothers and sisters will not be a negative influence. I have counseled with clients who were given a very poor self-image because they were unmercifully teased and persecuted by older siblings within the same family. On the other hand, many people develop quite positive attitudes toward others by loving relationships with brothers and sisters.

GRANDPARENTS

Research has emphasized the importance of the grandparent–grandchild relationship in the lives of children (Barranti, 1985). Many times grandparents and grandchildren adore one another. Emotional attachments develop and the relationship becomes unique and important in the lives of both the older and the younger people (Cherlin & Furstenberg, 1986). It is an important relationship to children for a number of different reasons (Denham & Smith, 1989). Let's see what some of those reasons are.

Grandparents can help children feel loved and secure. Children can never have too much of the right kind of love. Love that adds security and trust, that accepts and understands, is always needed. The modern role of the grandparent is associated more with warmth and affection and less with authority and power than it used to be

FOCUS

Parenting in Jamaica

The division of child care and household labor and beliefs about the roles of mothers and fathers were examined in eighty-six low-income, dual-earner, and single-earner Jamaican couples in common-law unions. Analysis revealed that there was a markedly gender-differentiated pattern of involvement in child care and household tasks by parents and that they held very traditional conceptions of the roles of mothers and fathers. The researchers found no woman or man who believed that men should be primary caregivers to infants, and the woman chief breadwinners. Jamaican men's participation in child care and household activities was quite similar to what is reported by men in other cultural groups: very minimal. These Jamaican fathers spent between half an hour to an hour each day in cleaning, washing, and feeding the baby. Women did about 94 percent of the diapering. Similarly, the women performed about twice as much housework as the men. Regardless of the mother's employment status, the mean ratings for the degree of involvement in households were lower for men in all areas assessed, compared with the involvement of their partners; men spent slightly less than half the time that their partners spent on household work (Roopnarine et al., 1995).

(Wilcoxon, 1987). Many grandparents continue to play an important role in the lives of their grandchildren even after the parents are divorced (Clingenpeel, Colyar, Brand, & Hetherington, 1992; Gladstone, 1988).

Grandparents can help children to know, trust, and understand other people. Children can learn that other members of the family can be just as comforting as their fathers and mothers. They discover that grandmother's house is a safe and happy home away from home. They learn how to adjust to the way the grandparents think and feel, and learn rules other than the ones that their mothers and fathers find important. This helps children to learn how to be flexible and adjust to the ways others act.

Grandparent–grandchild relationships are important in the lives of children.

Grandparents help children to bridge the gap between the past and the present, to give children a sense of history. Many children enjoy hearing their grandparents tell about life when the grandparents were growing up. Grandchildren will ask to be told about when grandparents were little boys or little girls. This gives children a sense of history, of what has gone before and the way life was back in the old days. It helps them to have a broader foundation on which to base their lives and to build new knowledge (Martin, Hagestad, & Diedrich, 1988). This knowledge about their cultural and family heritage helps children develop an identity based upon their forebears as well as upon the present.

Grandparents can provide children with experiences and supervision that their own par-

PARENTING ISSUES

Sibling Rivalry

Sibling rivalry is a favorite expression in psychological textbooks. *It refers to the competition of brothers and sisters for the attention, approval, and affection of the parents.* The problem arises because of envy or jealousy and the fear that one brother or sister is receiving more physical or emotional care and benefits from parents than another. The problem is actually quite a common one but varies in degree of severity. Sometimes the problem is created by parents who show differential treatment of their children, even when they're well intentioned and try to treat all the children the same. If one child is shown favoritism, the other children develop feelings of jealousy, anger, or inferiority (McHale & Pawletko, 1992). Because each child occupies a special place within the family, the home experiences of each child are quite different. Because children differ in personality, it is impossible for parents to treat them all the same. So no matter what parents do, sometimes their actions result in intensification of feelings of sibling rivalry. Other times, parents are certainly ideal parents and are not at fault. As an example, one child may become very jealous because he has been special for several years before a baby brother or sister has been born.

The effects of differential treatment of siblings were revealed in a study of two different types of family groups. Subjects were forty mothers of toddlers (average age 2 years) and preschoolers (average age 4½ years). Half of these mothers were caring for a younger child with a chronic illness (cystic fibrosis) and half were caring for two healthy children. Both quantitative and qualitative differences in parental treatment were found in cystic fibrosis (CF) versus comparison families. Specifically, mothers spent more individual time with younger chronically ill children in both play- and meal-time activities than they spent with their older, healthy siblings. Further, mothers in the cystic fibrosis group rated time spent with their older children as significantly more negative than time spent with the younger children. One consequence of differences in parental responsiveness, affection, and control was that there was greater conflict between siblings and more negative perceptions of the quality of the sibling relationships. No doubt, differential treatment resulted in jealousy between the siblings. In addition, some evidence suggests that differential treatment within the family may play a role in the psychological well-being of individual siblings (Quittner & Opipari, 1994). Thus study provides a glimpse into the complexity of forces that affect maternal behavior, and maternal behavior, in turn, has a profound influence upon the behavior of children.

Sibling rivalry is common in most families.

ents do not have money or time to provide (Presser, 1989). Most grandparents are called upon to baby-sit and enjoy doing so. Some grandparents now help to take care of the home and children while the parents go to work. In this sense, the grandparent acts as a surrogate parent.

Grandparents—as a result of years of living—can give children a fine sense of values and a philosophy of life. Not everything that is new is good nor everything that is old, bad. Sometimes the old values need to be reaffirmed. In this sense, grandparents play the traditional role of valued elders sharing the wisdom of the ages with their grandchildren (Kivnick, 1982).

Grandparents can give children a wholesome attitude towards old age. In our culture where youth is virtually worshipped, children need to know and learn to respect their elders. Older people can give rich and fruitful meaning to the lives of their children. They provide a role model for the children's future role of grandparents and for family relationships. By getting to know their grandparents, children can learn what the aged are like and can love and respect them as part of the family.

Grandparents' Problems

Some people say that grandparents never discipline children, that they spoil and pamper them, or give them too many gifts. Other people say that grandparents undermine parental authority, try to buy the children's affection, or try to possess children to satisfy their own personal needs. Such is true regarding some grandparents; some grandparents are problems. But others are not; when problems occur, they usually arise over one or more of the following situations.

Grandparents are often puzzled about the roles they're expected to play in relationship to their grandchildren. If they take too much interest and assume too much responsibility, they are accused of taking over the relationship or of meddling. If they do not pay very much attention, they are accused of neglect. One grandmother said, "I don't know what kind of grandmother they really expect me to be." Such a remark points to the need for couples and grandparents to discuss feelings and expectations about the role the grandparents should assume in the family.

Grandparents may have different ideas about raising children. They tend to base their philosophy on the way they were brought up themselves, and the way they raised their own children. Sometimes grandparents have ideas that are sound, but if their ideas conflict with those of parents, disagreements develop. Grandparents do need to be careful not to undermine the authority and discipline of parents. If a grandparent interferes while the parent is disciplining the grandchildren, such interference causes rebellion and resentment and does much harm. Children get mixed up when they don't know what to expect, whether to follow the grandparent's rules or the rules of their parents. It is necessary for grandparents to play a supportive role and not to undermine or contradict the parents (Sistler & Gottfried, 1990).

Grandparents have a tendency to give unsolicited advice to parents and grandchildren and to preach. This tendency may cause rebellion, especially in young parents who need an opportunity to work out their own rules and their own procedures with their own children. It may cause resentment on the part of older grandchildren also, who do not like to be told what to do, or who feel it is their parent's prerogative—not their grandparents—to guide them and direct them (Oyserman, Radin, & Benn, 1993). Certainly, the area of the autocratic grandparent is over. It may take some adjustment on the part of grandparents who were raised in a more authoritarian family, to sit back and realize that their married children have to make their own way and perhaps even to make their own mistakes (Baranowski, 1983).

Sometimes parents become jealous of the affection that the children develop for their grandparents. An insecure parent, in particular, may develop deep-seated resentment at the fact that the children seem to love the grandparent more than they love the parent. Such a mother or father is not emotionally mature or secure in the child's love, and this insecurity poses a problem for the grandparent. This is why grandparents have to realize that the child belongs to the parent, not to the grandparent. The married parent has to realize also that children certainly will usually put their first loyalty with the parent.

Some grandparents become too possessive of their grandchildren. Grandparents who are in need of love and affection and attention, or who are lonely, may use their grandchildren to fill their own empty life. When the grandparents start competing with a child's parents for affection and loyalty, friction and resentment develop. It is necessary for grandparents to accept the fact that the parents have the final responsibility for the children. Grandparents also need to remember that being a grandparent is not a full-time career. They have to continue to live their own lives, not get so wrapped up in the lives of their grandchildren that they have nothing else left.

In the case of disagreements, parents and grandparents need to talk things over. They can learn from one another and learn to respect one another's point of view and feelings. Certainly there is room for compromise, and certainly children need all the love they can get from any member of the family who takes an interest in them.

Nonnuclear Families

ONE-PARENT FAMILIES

Between 1970 and 1994, there was a 200 percent increase in the number of one-parent families in the United States (Demo, 1992; U.S. Bureau of the Census, 1994, 1995). Of this total number, 86 percent were maintained by mothers, but only 14 percent were maintained by fathers. (See Figure 12.5.) High divorce and illegitimacy rates mean that both the number and total percentage of these families will continue to increase. The one-parent family, therefore, represents a major segment of the population, especially among black families and especially among the poor. Among blacks, 59 percent of all children under 18 are currently living with a lone mother, as compared with 18 percent among whites and 29 percent among Hispanics (U.S. Bureau of the Census, 1995). Large numbers of these single mothers have never been married (Campbell, Breitmayer, & Ramey, 1986; Dawson, 1991).

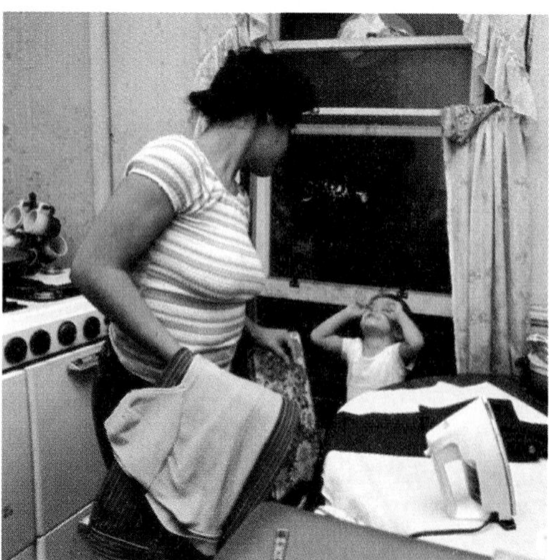

One-parent families with at least one child under 18 years of age represent one-fourth of all families with children.

Children who grow up in single-parent households, especially those whose mothers have never married, are significantly more likely to live below the poverty line. They are also more likely than children who live with both biological parents to perform poorly in school and to have repeated a grade or to have been expelled. And they are also more likely to demonstrate emotional or behavior problems. The most common health problems are accidents, injuries, and poisonings. These conditions hold true after adjusting statistically for social and demographic characteristics (Remez, 1992).

The Female-Headed Family

One of the most important problems of the female-headed family is *limited income* (Pett & Vaughn-Cole, 1986). The median income of families headed by a woman is 50 percent of the income of families with a male head (Duncan & Rodgers, 1987). These women often have to cope with problems such as inadequate child care (Turner & Smith, 1983). Mothers who are left alone to bring up their children themselves may have *difficulty performing all family functions well* (Burden, 1986; Sanik & Mauldin, 1986). There may be little time or energy left to perform household tasks, which means either the house is less clean, less time is available for food preparation, or the physical and emotional care of the children is neglected (Quinn & Allen, 1989). Role strain is common among single mothers (Campbell & Moen, 1992; Goldberg, Greenberger, Hamill, & O'Neil, 1992). Low-income single mothers of young children are especially exposed to high levels of daily stress (Olson & Banyard, 1993).

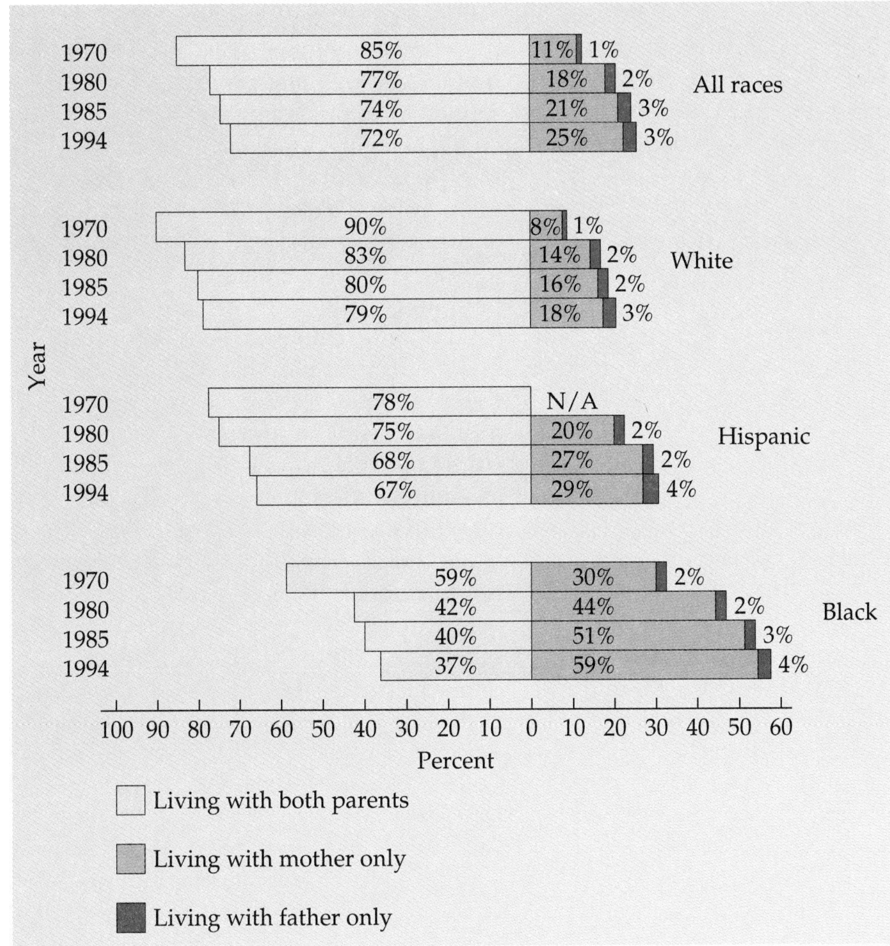

FIGURE 12.5 Percent of children under 18 years old living with parents, 1970–1994.

From U.S. Bureau of the Census (1995). *Statistical Abstract of the United States, 1995.* Washington, DC: U.S. Government Printing Office.

Several studies have shown that, after divorce, many custodial mothers have *more trouble communicating with their children, showing them enough affection, controlling them,* and *spending enough time with them* (Machida & Holloway, 1991). Because of demands on their time, mothers are often too absorbed with their own problems to help their children (Hetherington, Cox, & Cox, 1982; Colletta, 1985; Dornbusch et al., 1985; McLanahan & Booth, 1989). Some of these problems in mother–child relationships improve and stabilize after the first year or two following separation (Wallerstein & Kelly, 1980).

The Male-Headed Family

Solo fathers face many of the same problems as solo mothers do. However, they usually do not suffer poverty to the same extent as do solo mothers (Norton & Glick, 1986), although *financial pressure* is still one of the most common complaints. Also, most single fathers are concerned about not *spending enough time with their children* (Pichitino, 1983; Resman, 1986). If the children are of preschool age, fathers are faced with the same dilemmas as are solo mothers who must work: that of finding adequate child-care services. Part of their stress arises because they are often *forced to change their circle of friends* and to rebuild their social life (Greif, 1988).

Effects of Paternal Absence on Sons

The important question that plagues both parents and professionals is whether children grow up to be maladjusted because of the lack of two parents in the home (Blechman, 1982). The findings reveal that *the earlier a boy is separated from his father and the longer the separation is, the more affected the boy will be in his early years* (Stanley, Weikel, & Wilson, 1986). One study of fifth-grade boys who were father-absent before age 2 found them to be less trusting, less industrious, and to have more feelings of inferiority than did boys who became father-absent between the ages of 3 and 5 (Santrock, 1970a). *Father absence may also affect the development of masculinity.* As boys grow older, however, the earlier effects of father absence decrease (Santrock & Wohlford, 1970). By late childhood, lower-class father-absent boys appear to score as high as their father-present counterparts on certain measures of sex-role preference and sex-role adoption.

There is one fairly certain difference between boys raised in single-parent and dual-parent families. Those in single-parent families have a *lower level of educational attainment and consequent lower income as adults* (Krein & Beller, 1988; Mueller & Cooper, 1986; Nock, 1988).

The effect of father absence is dependent partially on whether boys have surrogate male models (Hawkins & Eggebeen, 1991). Father-absent boys with a father substitute such as an older male sibling are less affected than those without a father substitute (Santrock, 1970b). Young father-absent male children seek the attention of older males and are strongly motivated to imitate and please potential father figures.

Effects of Paternal Absence on Daughters

Some researchers contend that the effect of paternal absence on daughters is not as great as on sons (Stevenson & Black, 1988). The reasoning has been that children make a same-sex identification, and so daughters would be affected less by the father's absence than would sons. Some girls aren't affected as much when they are young, but they may be affected more during adolescence. *Lack of meaningful male–female relationships in childhood can make it more difficult to relate to the opposite sex.* In one study of a group of girls who grew up without fathers, Eberhardt and Schill (1984) found few effects during preadolescence; but during adolescence the girls of divorced parents who had lived with their mothers were inappropriately assertive, seductive, and sometimes sexually promiscuous. Having ambivalent feelings about men because of their negative memories of their fathers, they pursued men in inept and inappropriate ways. They began dating early and were likely to engage in sexual intercourse at an early age. Hepworth, Ryder, and Dreyer (1984) reported two major effects of parental loss on the formation of intimate relationships: avoidance of intimacy and accelerated courtship. In summary, therefore, fathers appear to play a significant role in encouraging their daughters' feminine development (Heilbrun, 1984). The father's acceptance and reinforcement of his daughter's femininity greatly facilitates the development of her self-concept. Interaction with a competent father also provides the girl with basic experiences that help in her relationships with other males.

Nevertheless, *a father-present home is not necessarily always better for the children than a father-absent home.* Some fathers, though home, spend little time in caring for their children or relating to them (Levant, Slattery, & Loiselle, 1987). In such families, father absence would not have as much effect as in homes where the father spent more time with his children. Some fathers are also inappropriate models. If there is a father at home who is rejecting, paternal deprivation may be a significant cause of emotional problems and/or antisocial behavior.

The effect of paternal absence on the mother is crucial in determining the influence on the children. Many father-absence studies have failed to take into account the mother's changed position following a divorce, separation, or the death of her husband. If the mother is quite upset, if her income is severely reduced, if she must be away from home frequently because she has to work, or if she has inadequate care for her children when she is gone, the children are going to be affected—not because of the father's absence, as such, but because of the subsequent effect on their mother and their relationship with her. Furthermore, the presence of surrogate father figures exerts a modifying influence on both boys and girls.

FOCUS

Same-Sex Parent

The belief that children fare better living with the same-sex parent has been widely accepted among certain academic and legal circles. The argument is that the child will have a same-sex parent with whom to identify. Indeed, several social and behavioral scientific frameworks offer convincing reasons to accept the same-sex pattern. Despite the appeal of this argument, the empirical basis for it is limited to scattered, small-scale projects. Downey and Powell (1993) explored a wide array of outcomes by using a nationally representive data set of cases of children living in father-only households. After exhaustive study, they found that they could not find even one case in which either males or females significantly benefited from living with their same-sex parent, as contrasted with their opposite-sex parent.

DIVORCE AND CHILDREN

Parental divorce involves a series of stressful interactions between children and their environment as the family restructures following parental separation. Many of these interactions, such as interparental quarrels, bad-mouthing, and missed visits by the noncustodial parent, present serious adaptation challenges for children. Children's success in coping with these negative interactions has important implications for their mental health. In fact, postdivorce stressors may have a more important impact on chil-

In case of divorce, should children reside with a same-sex parent?

Separation from a parent is a stressful event in the lives of most children.

dren's mental health than does the occurrence of the divorce per se. However, not everyone is affected equally by these stresses (Sandler, Tein, & West, 1994).

A growing number of clinicians emphasize that children perceive divorce as a major, negative event that stimulates painful emotions, confusion, and uncertainty (Jellinger & Slovik, 1981; Kalter, 1983). Some clinicians feel that the majority of children regain psychological equilibrium in a year or so and resume a normal curve of growth and development. Others feel that for a substantial portion of children, the upheaval in their lives will result in interferences in wholesome, social-emotional growth (Amato, 1991; Giudubaldi & Perry, 1985; Wallerstein & Kelly, 1980).

Wallerstein and Blakeslee (1990) found that ten years after divorce, half the women and one-third of the men were still so angry at their former spouses that their anger colored their relationships with their children. The children felt they had been abandoned by the father, that they were denied basic security with which to grow, and that they had been compelled to assume adult responsibilities for their parents' well-being. Half the children entered adulthood as self-deprecating, underachieving young women and men. High levels of alcohol abuse, delinquency, and promiscuity showed up ten to fifteen years after the divorce.

Researchers have found a larger number of variables—individual, family, and environmental—that affect the quality of adjustment to divorce. These variables include the child's gender and age at the time of separation or divorce, the child's temperament, interpersonal knowledge, and level of coping resources, the amount of interparental conflict prior to, during, and following the divorce, the quality of parent–child relationships, the parents' mental and physical health, the type of custody arrangement, parental remarriage, the number of major life experiences following divorce, including the amount of financial decline experienced by the postdivorce family, and the social support available to both the parents and children (Gately & Schwebel, 1991).

However, children are individuals and react differently to the same experience (Hetherington, 1989; Monahan, Buchanan, Maccoby, & Dornbusch, 1993). We do know that children of divorced parents are more likely to marry at an early age, and to get divorced themselves (Amato, 1988b; Amato & Booth, 1991; Glenn & Kramer, 1987). Overall, the long-term impact on social, emotional, and cognitive growth is not clear and continues to be studied and debated (Kalter, 1983).

Short-term reactions have been fairly well described. Children go through a period of *mourning and grief,* and the mood and feeling may be one of sadness, depression, and dejection. One 7-year-old described divorce as "when people go away" (Rice, 1990b, p. 613). Other common reactions are a *heightened sense of insecurity and anxiety* about their future. Children feel that "if you really loved me, you wouldn't go away and leave me." Some become very possessive with the parent (Kalter, 1983). One mother remarked: "Since the divorce, Tommy has been very upset when I go to work or when he goes to school. I think he's afraid that he'll come home and not find me there" (Rice, 1990).

Another common reaction is for children to *blame themselves.* If one major source of couple conflict is over the children, the children feel that the departing parent is abandoning them because they haven't been "good" boys or girls. Another common reaction is *preoccupation with reconciliation,* to try to bring their parents back together. They "wish that everyone could live together and be happy." The longing for a reunited family may go on for a long time, until children fully understand the realities of the situation and the reason for the separation.

After children get over the initial upset of divorce, one common reaction is *anger and resentment,* especially against the parent they blame for the divorce. Sometimes this is directed against the father—especially if they feel he has deserted the family. The child feels: "I hate you because you have gone off and left me." The resentment or hostility may also be directed at the mother, especially if the children blame her for the divorce. One 5-year-old blamed her mother for her father's absence: "I hate you, because you sent my daddy away." (Actually, the mother hadn't wanted the divorce.) An older girl, age 12, asked her

FOCUS

Father Hunger

Psychiatrist Alfred Messer (1989) identifies a new syndrome described by child psychiatrists: **father hunger,** found in boys 18 to 36 months of age, which consists primarily of sleep disturbances that begin one to three months after the father leaves. The syndrome evolves from the abrupt loss of a father during a young boy's critical period for gender development. The absent father deprives the boy of

- A grown male with whom to identify
- A feeling of protection and security
- Emotional support for completion of the separation–individuation phase of development
- A role model for learning how to handle aggressive and erotic impulses and for learning gender-appropriate social behavior

mother, "Why did you leave my father all alone?" It was obvious that the girl did not understand the reason for the divorce (Author's counseling notes).

Children have other adjustments to make. *They have to adjust to the absence of one parent.* Older children may be required to assume more responsibility for homemaking. Money is tight. *Special adjustments are necessary when the parents get emotionally involved with other persons.* Now the children must share their parents with another adult. If the parent remarries, as the majority do, the children are confronted with a total readjustment to a stepparent (Baylar, 1988; Rice, 1990).

Child Custody

The term **custody** refers to both **legal custody** (decision-making rights), and **physical custody** (where the children will live. In sole legal custody, the noncustodial parent forfeits the right to make decisions about the children's education, health, or religious training; the custodial parent is given control over child rearing. In joint legal custody, custody is shared between the two parents, with parental obligations and rights left as they were during the marriage (Ferreiro, Warren, & Konanc, 1986). There are advantages and disadvantages to both arrangements.

Traditionally, sole custody has been given to the mother unless she could be declared unfit. In some cases, the father may be more competent than the mother. The children may be closer to the father and he may be the one who can better afford them and better care for them (Lowery, 1985). Both husbands and wives usually have to work after divorce, so the overriding consideration is what the court considers the best interests of the children. In cases where the two parents are of different races, private prejudices are not permissible considerations if they might inflict injury by removing a child from a competent parent (Myricks & Ferullo, 1986).

Custody

Legal custody

Physical custody

In many states a mediator has to be employed or a child-development expert consulted to investigate the family situation and to recommend custody arrangements to the court. The wishes of older children are often taken into consideration. One study suggested that when parents are divorced, girls who live with their mothers and boys who live with their fathers seem to be warmer, less demanding, more mature, sociable, independent, and to have higher self-esteem than do children living with the parent of the opposite sex. Such children do not become emotional substitutes for a spouse, and they have adult models of the same sex with whom they can identify.

Joint custody

In **joint custody**, both parents are responsible. However, the children usually reside with one parent and visit the other often. In joint custody, children have access to both parents and both are responsible for decisions in relationship to the children. Joint-custody fathers are more likely to be actively involved in parenting than are noncustodial fathers (Bowman & Ahrons, 1985). Some research indicates that joint custody increases parental self-esteem, diminishes anxiety, lessens depression, and eases the fathers' feelings of disruption (Coysh et al., 1989). However, joint custody takes great maturity and a great deal of cooperation on the part of both parents (Lowery & Settle, 1985). If the parents continue to perpetuate all the squabbles of the unhappy marriage, the effect on the children can be very negative. There's general agreement, however, that joint custody, if desired by both parents and if both are able to get along together, is a good solution to a difficult problem (Melli, 1986).

After divorce, children continue to need the love and attention of both parents.

Child Support

Under law, child support is an obligation of both the father and the mother whether the parents are married or not. Since nine out of ten custodial parents are women, child-support awards are the most common mechanism by which noncustodial fathers are required to transfer economic resources to their children. However, about one-fifth of divorced mothers are not awarded child-support payments, either because the father was judged unable to pay or has run away and cannot be found. Hardly any fathers contribute to their children's support without a court agreement (Peterson & Nord, 1990).

There are various systems for determining the amount of child-support awards: (1) a straight percentage of the noncustodial father's income based on the number of dependent children; (2) calculation of support according to the combined income of both parents, with each paying a percentage that is his or her share of the combined income; and (3) taking both parents' incomes into consideration, but allowing for exemptions such as work-related expenses, taxes, or new dependents of the noncustodial father. Investigators suggest that many noncustodial fathers can afford to pay substantially more child support than is awarded under any of these three systems (Klitsch, 1989). Under new laws, child support enforcement amendments require all states to use automatic wage withholdings to collect old or new child support to enter such state income tax refunds, to use legal processes to enforce the court orders, to impose liens against property, or to require security bonds as guarantees of payment. Such support laws appear to reduce delinquency of payments by absent fathers ("Three years after," 1987).

It is important for both parents to make child-support payments. It lets children know that they are loved and cared for by both parents and enables the children to have the necessities of life; to have adequate clothes, food, and education; to live in better neighborhoods and housing; and it prevents the children from being penalized because of the actions of the parents. Children need to know they are loved and nurtured by both parents, regardless of their parents' marital status.

Visitation Rights

Visitation rights are given to the parent who is not given custody. These rights may be unlimited or they may be restrictive, depending upon the situation. Although increased visitation is associated with good noncustodial parent–child relationships, the association is mediated by the quality of the postdivorce parental relationship. The frequency and intensity of parental conflict after the divorce has a marked influence on children's psychological adjustment (Schaeffer, 1989). A vindictive spouse can make life miserable by managing to be away when the children are supposed to visit, by poisoning the children's minds against the other parent, by refusing to allow the children to phone or write, or by using visitation rights as a club to wield over the other parent's head.

COPARENTING

Numerous studies examining the effects of divorce on child development highlight the fundamental importance of conflict between ex-spouses in explaining variations in child functioning. Children's well-being is inversely correlated with the level of postdivorce conflict that exists and persists between parents. The more that separated parents are in conflict regarding parenting practices, the poorer the adjustment their children are able to make (Belsky, Crnic, & Gable, 1995). A new ideal for cooperative postdivorce parenting has been emerging in recent years. It is **coparenting** by divorced parents. Where there are more than two parenting adults after remarriage, the arrangement is called a **parenting coalition.** In coparenting, the two divorced persons cooperate rather than compete in the task of raising their children. In the parenting coalition, the biological parents (now divorced and remarried) plus the stepparents cooperate in raising their own children and the stepchildren. Children have contact with both of their parents and with their stepparents.

There are a number of advantages to these kinds of cooperative parenting. The children's needs as well as those of the parents can be met more adequately than if there is continued antagonism between adults. Children are not caught in the web of hostility; their chances of becoming messengers between two households are greatly reduced; and their fear of losing a parent is minimized. The power struggles between households lessen, and the children's self-esteem is enhanced, so they are easier to live with. Not only that, the parents' responsibilities are lessened since the task of rearing the children is shared.

Sometimes adults are not aware of the pain they are causing their children by their angry behavior. If they decide to control the anger, the children benefit by the new atmosphere of cooperation.

Visitation rights

Coparenting

Parenting coalition

EMOTIONAL SUPPORT

Fathers and mothers are important resources for the developing child; both can serve as sources of emotional support, practical assistance, information, guidance, and supervision. Prolonged absence of either parent from the household may be problematic for children. Following divorce, many children experience a decrease in the quantity and quality of contact with the noncustodial parent—usually the father (King, 1994). One research study is based on the *National Survey of Families and Households* (NSFH). Children involved in this study were all boys between the ages of 5 and 18 and were members of divorced families. When the resident parent reported little conflict with the nonresident parent, boys who had a high-level involvement with the nonresident parent were said to have fewer behavioral problems. But when the resident parent reported conflict with the other parent, boys who had a high level of involvement with the nonresident parent were said to have a larger number of behavioral problems. The findings clearly showed that frequency of contact with nonresident parents is not as important as the quality of the relationship between the divorced parents, which inevitably affects the children in the family (Amato & Rezac, 1994).

The mother is also profoundly affected by what happens. Two factors that result in the greatest impact (including health and mental health) on the mother and child are *payment of child support* and the *frequency and emotional quality of the father's relationship with the child.* Previous impirical literature strongly suggests that divorced, non-

FOCUS

Sequence of Adjustments of Children to Divorce

According to Wallerstein, the sequence of adjustments that children have to make to divorce are the following: 1) acknowledge the marital disruption, 2) regain a sense of direction and freedom to pursue customary activities, 3) deal with loss and feelings of rejection, 4) forgive the parents, 5) accept the permanence of divorce and relinquish longings for the restoration of the predivorced family, and 6) come to feel comfortable and confident in relationships. The successful completion of these tasks, which allows the child to stay on course developmentally, depends on the child's coping resources and the degree of support available to help him deal with the stressors (Gately & Schwebel, 1991).

custodial parents are uninvolved in these respects to a disturbing extent.

First, an alarming instance or nonpayment or underpayment of court-ordered child support has been demonstrated. Only one-half of all noncustodial parents pay the full amount of support they are ordered to pay, with another one-quarter paying nothing at all. There is also a disturbingly low rate of custodial parent–child contact and a decline in the quality of this relationship over time. The low level of contact is detrimental to children, since contact with noncustodial parents has typically been shown to be conducive to better social, academic, and emotional adjustment, provided the relationship between the divorced parents is very harmonious (Braver et al., 1993).

Stepfamily relationships are more complicated than relationships in the nuclear family.

STEPFAMILIES

Approximately 83 percent of divorced men and 76 percent of divorced women remarry (Fine, 1986). Today, 46 percent of marriages involve an adult who has been married before (U.S. Bureau of the Census, 1995). Most of these adults have children. This means that 16 percent of all American children live in stepfamilies (Coleman & Ganong, 1990).

Many couples enter into stepfamily relations expecting relationships similar to those of primary families (Mills, 1984). They are soon disappointed, surprised, and bewildered when they find few similarities (Skeen, Covi, & Robinson, 1985).

One reason for disappointment is that *stepparents have unrealistically high expectations* of themselves and what to expect (Turnbull & Turnbull, 1983). After all, many have been married before and have been parents before. They expect they will be able to fit into the stepparent role very nicely. They are shocked when they discover their stepchildren don't take to them the way they do to biological parents. This creates anxiety, anger, guilt, and low self-esteem. They either blame the children or begin to feel there is something wrong with themselves. They need to realize it may take several years before satisfactory relationships are worked out. Over a period of

FOCUS

Comparisons of African Americans and Whites on Adjustments to Divorce

1. *African Americans, particularly women, are less likely than whites to remarry following marital disruption.* Remarriages are somewhat more stable than first marriages for African Americans, whereas the reverse pattern is evident for whites. Overall, however, remarriage rates for African Americans are lower than for whites because there are fewer African-American men than women of comparable socioeconomic status. Also, single-parent status may be more normal among African Americans than it is among whites. Marriage may be less central to the well-being of African Americans than it is to that of whites, and African-American women, in contrast to white women, are less constrained to marry because of their relative economic independence from men.

2. *Adjustment for African Americans initially, and after four years of separation, is better than for whites.* Divorced African-American females have less depression and fewer adjustment difficulties than do divorced white females. African-American divorced parents, when compared to white divorced respondents on one study, were more satisfied with being parents and were less likely to indicate that someone in the home had a substance abuse problem.

3. *A third way that African-American divorced families differ from their white counterparts is the presence of an extensive kinship support network.* African Americans in both two-parent and single-parent families are more likely than whites to reside in extended-family households. The presence of extended family members could be helpful to parents because they can perform functions and fulfill roles that might otherwise go unfulfilled. Furthermore, by relieving mothers of household tasks, extended-family members may allow them the opportunity to improve their economic situations, primarily through additional employment or education (Fine, McKenry, Donnelly, & Voydanoff, 1992).

time, love, and affection may develop (Marsiglio, 1992).

Parents and stepparents enter into their new family with a great deal of guilt and regret over their failed marriage and divorce. They feel sorry for their children, whom they have put through an upsetting experience. This has several effects. Usually, parents tend to be overindulgent, not as strict as they might otherwise be, and have more trouble guiding and controlling the children's behavior (Amato, 1987). Often they try to buy the children's affection and cooperation.

A stepparent's role is ill-defined (Hobart, 1988). Stepparents are neither parents nor just friends. Their efforts to try to be parents may be rejected by older children.

PARENTING ISSUES

Minimizing the Harmful Effects of Divorce

1. File for no-fault divorce and mediate a settlement including financial, property, child custody, and child-support arrangements. If the divorce is as amicable as possible, the reduced anger and conflict have a positive effect on the parents and their children (Kramer & Washo, 1993).

2. Make it clear to the children that you are divorcing your spouse, not the children, that you will always be their parents, continue to take care of them and see them. One primary goal is to reduce children's anxiety and insecurity.

3. If you are the noncustodial parent, arrange for open access to your children (Depner & Bray, 1990). This means living close to them and seeing them regularly. The primary negative effect of divorce is loss of contact with a parent (Kurdek & Berg, 1983). Predictable and frequent contact with the noncustodial parent is associated with better adjustment unless the father is poorly adjusted or extremely immature (Seltzer, 1990; Warshak, 1986). Adjustment of the children is enhanced if the custodial mother approves of the father's continued contact and rates the relationship positively (Giudubaldi & Perry, 1985).

4. If you are the custodial parent, your psychological adjustment is of great significance in determining the adjustment of your child (Kitson & Morgan, 1990; Umberson, 1989). If you're disturbed, your child is more likely to be disturbed. Get help if you can't make a happy adjustment yourself (Giudubaldi & Perry, 1985; Wallerstein & Kelly, 1980).

5. Keep conflict with your ex-spouse to a minimum (Kline, Johnston, & Tschann, 1991). Reduced conflict after divorce has a major positive effect on children (Demo & Acock, 1988; Tschann, Johnston, Kline, & Wallerstein, 1989). Continued conflict has a negative effect (Amato, 1993; Kelly, 1988).

6. Custody arrangements, whether maternal, paternal, or joint custody, are not as important an issue as the degree of interparental conflict (Leupnitz, 1982). Joint custody is a satisfactory arrangement if ex-spouses get along with one another, but detrimental if it leads to conflict (Donnelly & Finkelhor, 1993; Kolata, 1988; Irving, Benjamin, & Trume, 1984; Maccoby, Depner, & Mnookin, 1988; Schwartz, 1987). One study of the effect of custody arrangements on parent–child relationships found no evidence that children in shared custody had less conflictual or better relationships with their parents. Children in sole-custody households actually gave their parents more support than those in shared custody, but this may be because they feared losing their remaining parent. The study also found that parents who had high levels of disagreement with each other (regardless of the type of custody) also had more disagreements with their children (Donnelly & Finkelhor, 1992).

7. Parents report high levels of satisfaction with shared (joint) physical custody, and the results run positive for children (Steinman, Zemmelman, & Knoblauch, 1985). This requires that parents reside in the same school district if children are of school age.

8. Don't use children to hurt your spouse or get back at him or her. Children become especially upset if they are used as pawns in angry power plays between divorcing spouses. Don't ask children to take sides or try to turn children against the other parent. Children love them both; whose side are they supposed to be on?

9. Share in financial child support as much as you are able. It is one way of assuring that your children have the necessities of life and are not affected by the custodial parent's having to live in poverty (Paasch & Teachman, 1991; Teachman, 1991).

Stepparents are required to assume many of the responsibilities of parents, yet they have none of the privileges and satisfactions of parenthood (Fine & Fine, 1992). In the beginning, being a stepparent seems all give and no receive. It's frustrating.

Fairy tales and folklore have developed the stereotype of the cruel stepmother, a myth that is hard to overcome (Radomski, 1981). Most studies indicate that the stepmother role is more difficult than that of stepfather, primarily because the mother has more responsibilities for direct care of the children (Brand & Clingempeel, 1987; Sauer & Fine, 1988). However, stepfathers are portrayed as being abusive, a stereotype that is also difficult to overcome (Claxton-Oldfield, 1992).

Stepparents confront the necessity of attempting to deal with children who have already been socialized by another set of parents. Stepparents may disagree with the way that their stepchildren are being brought up. But any attempt on their part to suddenly step in and try to change things is deeply resented.

Stepparents expect gratitude and thanks for what they do, but often get rejection and criticism instead. They were expected to support and care for their own biological children, but feel they are being very generous and helpful by offering the same to stepchildren. Yet, stepchildren seem to take help for granted and ask for more, offering little thanks or appreciation for what is done for them.

Stepparents are faced with unresolved emotional issues from the prior marriage and divorce. They need to resolve some of the hostilities that were created through the process of separation and divorce, so that they can make a fresh start.

They must also deal with a network of complex kinship relationships: with their own biological family members, with their former spouse's family members, with their new spouse's family members, plus their own children and stepchildren. This adds a more difficult dimension to their family involvements (Berstein & Collins, 1985).

Stepparents must cope with stepsibling feelings and relationships. Stepchildren are rarely helpful to each other in coping with the strains of the divorce period. Instead, there may be stepsibling rivalry and com-

PARENTING ISSUES

How to Be a Stepparent

1. Give yourself and your own children ample time before marriage to get acquainted with your prospective stepchildren.

2. Don't try to take the place of your stepchildren's parent. Psychologically, children can only accept one father or mother at a time. Children often reject the stepparent as an intruder if the stepparent tries to compete with the child's natural parent for the child's loyalty.

3. Don't expect instant love (Dainton, 1993). Any affection that develops arises only gradually. In many cases, it takes several years to develop a good relationship. The older the stepchildren, the longer it takes (Hobart, 1987).

4. Winning the friendship of your stepchildren is an important first step. If you can be good friends and learn to like one another, you will have come a long way toward developing a close relationship.

5. Recognize that most stepchildren are jealous of the time and attention their parent (your spouse) gives you. Encourage your spouse to spend quality time with them.

6. Let the children's natural parent take the lead in guidance and discipline, then you support the effort. If you as a stepparent try to change the way stepchildren are being taught, they will resent your efforts, especially if they can get their own parent to take their side.

7. Don't try to buy the affection and loyalty of your own children or stepchildren. They will learn to manipulate you to win approval and favors.

8. All stepchildren are different, so you have to deal with them as individuals.

petition for the attention of parents (Amato, 1987).

Family cohesion tends to be lower in stepfamilies than in intact families (Pill, 1990). Life in divorced and reconstituted families tends to be chaotic and stressful during the years following remarriage (Wallerstein & Kelly, 1980). However, as far as the marriages themselves are concerned, in comparison to first-married couples, one study found that if both spouses remarried, stepfather families reported *higher* relationship quality and stronger intrinsic motivations to be in the relationship (Kurdek, 1989; Kurdek & Fine, 1991). One study found that the major strengths for stepfamilies were in the areas of sexual relationships and egalitarian roles. The major stressors were children and parenting (Schultz, Schultz, & Olson, 1991).

FOSTER CARE

The number of children under foster parent care has skyrocketed from 360,000 in 1990 to an estimated 840,000 in 1995. The reason is that child neglect and abuse are prevalent, the number of teenage pregnancies and children born out of wedlock has increased, and the number of parents unable or unfit to care for their children has risen, so that the state has to care for these children by placing them in foster homes. When children are taken from their parents, or when parents voluntarily give them up, *foster care becomes the treatment of last resort*. Even the best foster parents may have difficulty coping. The payment they receive from the state is usually inadequate to cover all expenses. They are asked to take children with severe emotional and behavioral problems who are very difficult to manage. Many children have been moved from home to home and have learned not to trust anyone. Although foster care is certainly preferable to staying in an abusive or neglectful situation, it is still far from ideal. It is supposed to be a temporary arrangement until the child's own parents can care for their child again, but what is supposed to be short-term care often becomes long term in a series of foster homes (Fein, 1981; Wald, Carlsmith, & Leiderman, 1988). Some authorities feel that some children would be better off in group homes (they used to be called orphanages) where they can live with their siblings and peers. Other authorities maintain that these new orphanages are not better than those of yesteryear, which were warehouses for children (Creighton, 1990). There were some 1,000 group homes in the United States in 1990, each caring for 8 to 125 children.

When children are taken from their parents, foster care becomes the treatment of last resort.

ADOPTIVE FAMILIES

Over half of all women who have adopted have also given birth to a child, so adoption is not always because of infertility. It is more likely, in fact, for an adoption to follow the birth of a child within a family rather than the reverse (Bachrach, London, & Maza 1991).

The number of adoptions in the United States increased steadily over the decades and reached a peak of 175,000 in 1970. Since then, however, the number has been declining steadily and is now about 100,000 per year (U.S. Bureau of Census, 1995). There are fewer infants available for adoption today because of more effective contraceptives and legalized abortion and because more unmarried mothers are keeping their babies (Donnely & Voydanoff, 1991). The percentage of African-American mothers relinquishing their children for adoption is low. Relinquishment among Hispanic mothers is virtually nonexistent (Bachrach, Stolley, & London, 1992).

Many adoptive parents seek to adopt foreign-born children.

About half of those who petition for adoption are related to the child they wish to adopt. Among women who never married, nonrelated adoption is more common among whites than among blacks or Hispanics, among those with at least a high school education, and among those in the high income brackets. However, related adoption is more common among those who are black, poor, or poorly educated (Bachrach, London, & Maza, 1991).

In 1991 about 8 percent of adoptions were of orphan children from foreign countries, with Romanian children constituting over 28 percent of the number. Smaller numbers came from Korea, Peru, Colombia, India, the Philippines, and other countries. Orphan children from Russia were first brought to the United States for adoption in 1992 (personal conversation with a client). Interracial adoptions of minority children in the United States have declined due to the influence of social workers and minority group advocates who are concerned about identity problems in the children and their loss to their ethnic communities.

Among petitioners not related to the child, about 40 percent of placements are through public agencies, 30 percent are through private agencies, and another 30 percent are through independent sources (U.S. Bureau of Census, 1992). About three times the number of people seek unrelated adoptions as are able to get them (Bachrach, London, & Maza, 1991). As a result, there are long waiting periods to get a child through established agencies. Some adopting parents turn to private sources, either turning to the mother herself, or an agent who is usually a lawyer specializing in open adoption. In **open adoption**, the natural mother is permitted to meet and play an active role in selecting the new adoptive parents. She usually may continue to have some form of contact with her child and with the adoptive parents after her child has been placed. It depends upon the agreement. Open adoption is usually expensive, including lawyer fees and birth expenses if state laws allow the charges. Some states—such as California and Texas—support private adoptions, but there are six states that forbid them. Many authorities claim that open adoption eases the pain for the birth mother and is in the best interest of the child (Kallen, Griffore, Popovich, & Powell, 1990). Other experts say that it is not in the child's best interest to tell him or her of the adoption unless asked, much less let the child know who the biological mother and father are. Some states have laws allowing adoptees to get copies of their original birth certificates.

Open adoption

One important consideration is how adoptive parents feel about having adoptive children and how adoptees themselves turn out. *The crucial factor here is not whether a child is adopted, but the quality of the family environment in which the child is raised* (Stein & Hoopes, 1986). School and behavior problems are more prevalent in adopted children during the elementary years, but by adolescence most adoptive children do not show any such problems (Brodzinsky, Shechter, Braft, & Singer, 1984). In one study of adoptive parents in their adolescence, parents were able to identify disadvantages of adoption yet felt their lives and those of their children were no different than those of biological families (Kaye & Warren, 1988). The adolescents themselves

PARENTING ISSUES

Women Who Place Their Babies for Adoption

One of the questions that arises is how women feel after they have placed their babies for adoption. Some women say, "I could never give up my baby." Yet a good number of women do. How do they feel about it afterward? One study was of young, unmarried pregnant women under 21 years of age who were interviewed during the final trimester of pregnancy and again at six months postbirth to determine how they felt about relinquishing their babies (Kalmuss, Namerow, & Bauer, 1992). The results of this study indicated that in terms of short-term consequences, young women who placed their babies for adoption (placers) tended to fare as well or better than those who kept and parented their babies. The one exception to this pattern was that at six months after birth, those who placed their babies for adoption were relatively less comfortable with their pregnancy resolution decision than were parenters. Despite this, the absolute level of comfort among placers was quite high. Any discomfort that the women experienced regarding their decision to place the baby did not appear to affect their overall psychological well-being. Placers were indistinguishable from parenters on measures of satisfaction with their social relationships, life satisfaction, and a positive future outlook regarding employment and schooling, finances, and marriage. Finally, placers fared somewhat better than parenters on a set of sociodemographic outcomes assessed at six months postbirth.

acknowledged disadvantages of being adopted even less than their parents.

There is some evidence, however, that adoptees feel that others perceive their adoption as a social stigma. In one study, when adoptees were asked, "Do you think adoptive families are different than biological families?" almost half of the adoptees said no. Even though they personally saw no difference between adoptive and biological families, they felt that others did. Thus, they based their belief on others' reaction to their adoptive status. One adoptee stated:

> It has little to do with my family. Other people outside the family think this way. I can see it in their reactions when they find out that I am adopted. To them, I am different. To my family, I am family. But, I am still not blood. It shouldn't be important, but it is. Not just to me but to everybody (March 1995, page 656).

Another respondent commented:

> I was treated like any child would be treated by their parents. But, outside the family, it's different. They never believe that your adopted parents love you like their parents love them because you aren't biological.

One woman noted:

> When someone is told that you are adopted, they usually start to ask you questions about your birth mother. These questions generally have an underlying implication that she was a loose person. Like, sitting in the back seat of a cab with some guy or something. You carry that image. Because you don't have the information to deny it, it makes you wonder where you come from (page 656).

Partly because of these attitudes, adoptees desire more complete genealogies; they express curiosity over the events surrounding their conception, birth, and relinquishment; they want information that can be passed on to their children, and yearn for more detailed knowledge of their biological family background.

Secrecy about biological kinship ties strengthen their sense of stigma by preventing them from being able to respond to other questions or negative assumptions. The adoptees' search for the birth mother can be seen as an attempt to neutralize the stigma by acquiring information about biological kinship ties and thus gaining the sense that they are "normal" (March, 1995).

ADOLESCENT MOTHERS

There is continuing evidence that adolescent mothers are at greater risk for negative educational and economic outcome and that their children are more likely to experience problem behavior. The negative economic and social factors often associated with teenaged motherhood (e.g., low socioeconomic status, limited education, and family instability) have been implicated in the increased likelihood of behavior problems among these children. One study investigated predictors of behavior problems in preschool children of inner-city African-American and Puerto Rican mothers. One hundred twenty adolescent mothers and their children were followed from between 1 and 28 to 36 months postpartum. The mothers were 13 to 19 years old at delivery. The study found that 13 percent of the children had clinically significant levels of behavioral problems. These figures are similar to incidences of serious behavioral problems (7 to 14 percent) found on large-scale surveys of preschoolers. This is important since a substantial body of research has documented associations between early behavior problems and deviance in later childhood.

The African-American mothers reported the highest levels of problem behaviors in their male children. This may reflect a heightened vigilance in these mothers, given the extreme consequences of problem behavior for adolescent males from inner-city neighborhoods. On the other hand, Puerto Rican mothers reported fewest problem behaviors in male children, perhaps reflecting *machismo* attitudes that may afford more tolerance for aggressive behaviors in Hispanic boys. Previously reported ethnic differences in parenting styles may also have implications for interpreting the findings here. Researchers have observed greater emphasis on obedience and stricter attitudes toward child rearing in Hispanic mothers compared to Caucasian. The pattern of relations found among preschool problem behavior, maternal depressive symptoms, social supports, and stress gives considerable insight into how poverty affects socioemotional development of preschoolers. Maternal psychological distress, assessed as depressive symptoms in the first year postpartum, consistently predicted child problem behaviors at 26 to 36 months. Living with grandmothers or having emotional support from friends might minimize this association (Leadbeater & Bishop, 1994).

Summary

1. Children do not develop in a vacuum. They are influenced by their social relationships in their family, neighborhood, community, country, and the world.
2. Bronfenbrenner developed an ecological model for understanding social influences in the microsystem, mesosystem, exosystem, and macrosystem.
3. There are differences in the way that children are socialized according to socioeconomic status, setting, and ethnic or national background.
4. The modern family in the United States shows both increasing strengths and weaknesses.
5. Socialization is the process by which persons learn the way of society and social groups so they can function within them.
6. The family is the chief socializing influence on children, but there are many family types, each of which may have a somewhat different influence on children.
7. The influence of the family is also variable because of differences in individual children.

8. The parents' psychological adjustment, parenting style, and the quality of their marriage all have an effect upon the child's emotional maturity, social competence, and cognitive development.
9. There are three major styles of parenting in our culture: authoritarian, permissive, and authoritative. Authoritative control seems to work best in our culture.
10. Parental relationships with children can also be divided into four categories according to the degree of control and of affection. These four categories are love-autonomy, love-control, hostility-autonomy, and hostility-control.
11. The one parenting variable that is most related to adjustment is love.
12. Parental control techniques may be divided into seven categories: power-assertive discipline, command, self-oriented induction, other-oriented induction, love withdrawal, advice, and relationship maintenance. Successful parenting seems to depend upon the maximum amount of love and the right balance between autonomy and control.
13. Children of mothers who are more responsive during their children's infancy and through early adolescence have higher arithmetic scores, more positive self-esteem, and fewer behavioral and emotional problems than those of less responsive mothers.
14. The primary purpose of discipline is to teach, not to punish. The ultimate goal is to sensitize the conscience and to develop self-control.
15. The Chinese pattern of parenting seems to follow traditional practices of firm control.
16. With more married women working outside the home, fairness would seem to demand that husbands take more responsibility for housework and child care, but equality of roles has not been fully achieved.
17. Fathers tend to be closer to their sons than to their daughters and are less likely to leave the family if they have sons.
18. Siblings exert considerable influence on the socialization of other children in the family. Birth order, the number of children in the family, the gender, and the relationships with brothers and sisters all influence development.
19. Sibling rivalry refers to the competition of brothers and sisters for the attention, approval, and the affection of parents.
20. Grandparents can help children feel loved and secure; can help children to know, trust, and understand other people; can fill the gap between the past and present; can provide children with experiences and supervision their own parents cannot give; and can teach children a fine sense of values and wholesome attitudes toward old age.
21. Some problems with grandparents are: puzzlement about their roles, having different ideas about raising children, giving unsolicited advice, jealousy, becoming too possessive, and disagreements that need to be discussed.
22. The number of one-parent families is on the increase. The majority are female-headed families. The primary problems of the female family are limited income and pressures to perform all functions well. Like females, single males heading families are concerned about income, not spending enough time with their children, child care, and changes in their social life.
23. Father absence affects boys emotionally, affects their development of masculinity, and affects the level of education they are able to attain. The effect depends partially on the availability of male surrogate models.
24. Father absence affects girls also, especially during adolescence, when girls may develop difficulty with their heterosexual adjustments and with forming a positive and feminine self-concept.
25. Father-absent homes are not always worse for children than father-present homes.
26. One study found no difference in benefits to either males or females in living with a same-sex parent rather than an opposite-sex parent.
27. Divorce is often a major, negative event that stimulates painful emotions, confusion, and uncertainty in children.

Many children are able to regain psychological equilibrium in a year or so.
28. Wallerstein and Blakeslee found a number of long-term negative consequences for children whose parents divorced, but the consequences depend on a number of important variables.
29. The term *custody* refers to legal custody and physical custody. In joint custody both parents are responsible for care and decisions relating to the child.
30. Child support is the obligation of both the mother and father.
31. Ordinarily, visitation rights are given to the parent who does not have physical custody.
32. Children's well-being depends not just on the frequency of visitation but the degree of harmony between the husband and wife after divorce.
33. Coparenting involves the cooperation of both parents in rearing the child.
34. Two factors that affect the mental health of mother and child are payment of child support and the frequency and quality of the father's relationship with the child.
35. There is a sequence to adjustments to divorce that children need to follow.
36. African Americans who are divorced are less likely to marry, and make easier adjustments than whites, partly because of extensive kinship support networks.
37. Parents can do much to minimize the harmful effects of divorce.
38. The problems of children become more complicated when parents remarry and a stepfamily is formed.
39. Stepfamilies have their own unique set of problems, different from those of primary families.
40. There are many things parents can do to learn to be good stepparents.
41. Foster care is a treatment of last resort for children whose parents can't care for them.
42. The number of adoptions has increased steadily; there is a shortage of children to be adopted; about one-half of those who adopt are related to the child they wish to adopt; some adoptions are of children from foreign countries; in open adoption the natural mother is permitted to play an active role in selecting the new adoptive parents; a crucial factor in relation to the adjustment of adopted children is the quality of the family environment in which the child is raised.
43. A study of mothers who placed their babies for adoption found that they were indistinguishable from those who did not as to social relationships, life satisfaction, and in having a positive future outlook regarding employment and schooling, finances, and marriage.

Key Terms

Binuclear family *p. 300*
Blended or reconstituted family *p. 300*
Cohabiting family *p. 300*
Communal family *p. 300*
Coparenting *p. 327*
Custody *p. 325*
Discipline *p. 307*
Dysphoria *p. 303*
Exosystem *p. 298*
Extended family *p. 300*
Family *p. 299*
Father hunger *p. 325*
Generational transmission *p. 300*
Homosexual family *p. 300*
Joint custody *p. 326*
Legal custody *p. 325*
Macrosystem *p. 298*
Mesosystem *p. 298*
Microsystem *p. 298*
Nuclear family *p. 300*
Open adoption *p. 333*
Parenting coalition *p. 327*

Physical custody *p. 325*
Sibling rivalry *p. 318*
Single-parent family *p. 300*
Socialization *p. 300*
Stepfamily *p. 300*
Visitation rights *p. 327*

Discussion Questions

1. In what ways are marriages and families today better for couples and their children, and in what ways are they worse?
2. What are the most important qualities and characteristics of parents in order for them to do the best job of bringing up children?
3. From your own experience, compare authoritarian, permissive, and authoritative patterns of parenting.
4. Did you have to do family chores when you were growing up? What did you think of it? Did it help you? In what ways did it help, and in what ways did it do harm?
5. What methods of discipline do you believe work the best and why? Take children's ages into account.
6. If both the husband and wife work full-time, how should they divide responsibilities for housework, cooking, and child care?
7. In what ways were your siblings a help to you when growing up, and in what ways were they a hindrance?
8. Do you have grandparents with whom you are close? Describe the relationship and the ways grandparents have helped you, and any problems you have encountered with them.
9. Were you brought up in a one-parent family, or do you know someone who was? What were the effects on you or other children?
10. Were your parents divorced while you were growing up, or have you been divorced? What were the effects on you while growing up, or on your children now? What effects have you noticed on friends whose parents were divorced or who are now divorced themselves?
11. Have any of you been divorced? How were you and/or your children affected?
12. What are the major advantages and disadvantages of stepfamilies?
13. Do you know anyone who has been brought up in a foster home? How was that person affected?
14. Are any of you adopted? How has being adopted affected your life? Do you have any desire to know your biological parents? What do you think of open adoption? Would you ever want to adopt a child yourself?

Suggested Readings

Adams, P. L., Milner, J. R., & Schrepf, N. A. (Eds.). (1984). *Fatherless children.* New York: Wiley. Effects of father absence.

Greif, G. L. (1985). *Single fathers.* Lexington, MA: D. C. Heath. Implications of single fatherhood.

Lamb, M. E. (1987). *The father's role: Cross-cultural perspectives.* Hillsdale, NJ: Erlbaum. Fathers' roles in different cultures.

Maccoby, E. E. (1980). *Social development: Psychological growth and the parent-child relationship.* New York: Harcourt Brace. General discussion.

Mitchell, A. (1985). *Children in the middle.* New York: Tavistock. Effects of divorce.

Social Development: Peer Relationships, Television, Gender Roles, and Moral Development

Chapter 13

THE DEVELOPMENT OF PEER RELATIONSHIPS

TELEVISION AS A SOCIALIZING INFLUENCE

THE DEVELOPMENT OF GENDER ROLES

MORAL DEVELOPMENT

The Development of Peer Relationships

PSYCHOSOCIAL DEVELOPMENT

The development of friendships with peers is one of the most important aspects of social development of children. In the process of psychosocial development, all normal children pass through four stages.

Auto-sociality—a stage of psychosocial development during the first year or so of life, during which infants' interests, pleasures, and satisfactions are themselves

1. **Autosociality—**infancy and toddler stage of development, in which children's interests, pleasures, and satisfactions are themselves. Toddlers want to be in the company of others, but they play *alongside* of others, not *with* them. A child who is a loner has not yet progressed beyond this stage of psychosocial development.

Childhood heterosociality—a stage when children seek the companionship of others regardless of sex

Homosociality—a stage during which children prefer to play with others of the same sex

2. **Childhood heterosociality—**ages 2–7, during which children seek the companionship of others regardless of sex.
3. **Homosociality—**ages 8–12, or primary school period of development, during which children prefer to play with others of the same sex (not for sexual purposes, but for friendship and companionship). There is some antagonism between the sexes (Alexander & Himes, 1994).

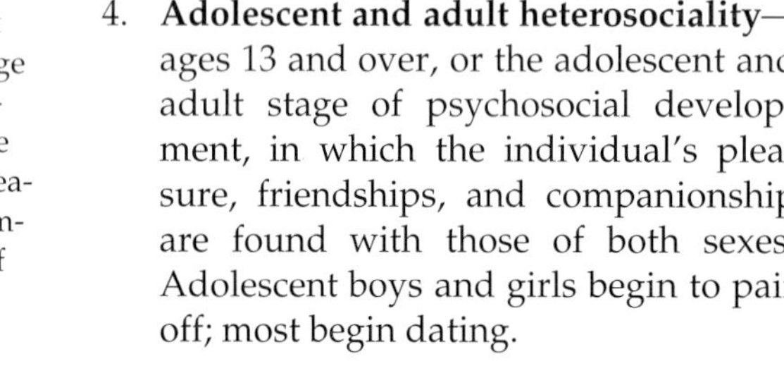

Adolescent and adult heterosociality—a stage of psychosocial development during which those ages 13 and over find pleasure, friendship, and companionship with those of both sexes

4. **Adolescent and adult heterosociality—**ages 13 and over, or the adolescent and adult stage of psychosocial development, in which the individual's pleasure, friendships, and companionship are found with those of both sexes. Adolescent boys and girls begin to pair off; most begin dating.

Satisfactory peer relationships are one of the most important aspects of social relationships.

INFANTS AND TODDLERS

Babies' first social experiences are usually with parents and siblings (Fiese, 1990; Vandell & Wilson, 1987). Observations of babies and toddlers indicate that they interact with one another from about 5 months onward. Their first social response is simply to notice one another and to smile at one another. When they are able to move around, they crawl all over one another. When they can stand up, they occasionally knock one another down. Studies of 6-month-olds reveal little conflict or fussing when infants touch one another's toys, touch one another, or even find themselves trapped beneath a partner (Hay, Nash, & Pedersen, 1983). By 9 months of age, they offer a toy to others and oppose toys being taken away. They also comfort others in distress and pick up the ones who get pushed over. Personal aggression increases with age, but cooperation also increases as children become more experienced in relating to one another. Observation of children in infant centers indicates that helpfulness is more apparent than are efforts to dominate. By the time children are toddlers, they have learned much about fending for themselves in a group and about how to find satisfaction there. They have made a strong beginning in establishing group relations that are a main source of emotional security and orientation.

EARLY CHILDHOOD

Two-Year-Olds

Children of this age enjoy playing alongside one another, rather than with one another, since cooperative play is not very evident, at least in the beginning. However, 2-year-olds begin to show some preferences in playmates. Individuals interact more with familiar play partners (Brownell, 1990). Twins interact more with one another than with unfamiliar peers (Vandell, Owen, Wilson, & Henderson, 1988). Social interchange becomes more frequent; friendly behavior gradually replaces negative behavior (Brownell & Carriger, 1990; Ross & Lollis, 1989). Sex preferences are not yet evident.

Toddlers are not as forbearing as infants when their toys are touched or taken (Shantz, 1987). Two-year-olds do a lot of grabbing, hitting, and pushing, not usually with an intent to hurt, but for the purpose of protecting their own toy or getting a toy someone else has (Caplan, Vespo, Pedersen, & Hay, 1991). Since they are egocentric, they are not aware of the effect that their own actions have upon others, nor of the moods and feelings of others. They think in terms of "my ball" or "my book," and they protest when denied what they want. As a result, they inevitably run into conflict from their social interactions. They need supervision and experience in considering the needs and interests of others.

Three-Year-Olds

As children grow older, they engage in fewer solitary activities, do less passive watching of other children, and become less inclined toward isolated play (Bailey, McWilliam, Ware, & Burchinal, 1993). Friendly contacts occur with increasing frequency, and cooperative behavior also increases (Ladd, Price, & Hart, 1988). Children may select one friend, sometimes two, with whom they identify for short periods of time. Aggressive behavior gradually declines (Cummings, Iannotti, & Zahn-Waxler, 1989).

We see the beginning of group play and activity. The development of language makes communication possible, so that when two children play together they talk about what they are making in the sand, about dressing up their dolls, or about pretending to be a mother or a baby. Group membership, however, is constantly changing, with children moving in and out of a group. (See "Focus" box on p. 344)

Three-years-olds are likely to be victims of aggression by other children in nursery school, so teachers have to provide supervision and be careful to reinforce socially acceptable acts.

Four- and Five-Year-Olds

Children age 4 and 5 gradually develop more socially competent interactions with their peers (Guralnick & Groom, 1987; Park, Lay, & Ramsay, 1993). They begin to depend less on parents and more and more on peers for companionship and social interaction. They now share affection and tangible objects. They offer approval and make demands on one another. They can show empathy when others are distressed, frequently intervening prosocially on behalf of their distressed peers by offering objects, comforting, verbally sympathizing, or making suggestions. However, there are great individual differences. Some children never respond to any peers' distress, whereas others frequently intervene (Farber & Branstetter, 1994).

Best friends in a group will pair off. Groups of three children are quite common. Occasionally, up to five or six children will form a group and spend most of their playtime with one another. Generally speaking, there is some evidence that boys enjoy group interaction more than girls do. Girls enjoy dyadic (one-on-one) relationships more than boys do (Benenson, 1993).

The behavior of children varies. One moment they are aggressive, the next moment cooperative. Conflict occurs more often between friends than with nonfriends, but the conflict with friends is less intense and resolved more quickly, insuring that the children's relationships will continue once the disagreement ends (Hartup, Laursen, Stewart, & Eastenson, 1988). Children's behavior is affected a lot by the attitude of others at home or in school (Cassidy, Parke, Butkovsky, & Broaungart, 1992). If cooperation is stressed, children become less competitive. If competition is encouraged, rivalry becomes a strong motivator of behavior, and jealousy is quite common. For this reason, most experts try to discourage competitive activities for this age group.

Children vary greatly in their social competence and acceptance by peers (Denham, McKinley, Couehoud, & Holt, 1990; Ladd & Price, 1987). Social status and peer interaction depend partly on children's communication skills (Hazen & Black, 1989). Social acceptance among boys depends partially on their physical abilities. (Musun-Miller, 1993). Children develop definite preferences in playmates. Some children in a group become leaders and are quite popular with nearly everyone. Other children are content to be followers.

FOCUS

Preschoolers' Play

Preschoolers' play has been classified in a number of ways. In a classic study, Mildred Parten (1932) observed the play of children in a nursery school setting and established categories of play according to the degree of the children's social involvement. This study is a pertinent today as it was sixty years ago. Parten identified six categories of play involvement.

- *Unoccupied play*—children are not really playing, they are looking around, engaging in random activities.
- *Solitary play*—children play with toys by themselves, making no effort to relate to other children.
- *Onlooker play*—children watch others play, and are talking to them, but do not join the play.
- *Parallel play*—children play alongside of others, not *with* them, but mimic others' behavior.
- *Associative play*—children interact with others, borrowing or lending toys, following or leading one another in similar activities.
- *Cooperative play*—organized groups of children engage in play, such as a game.

Play may also be classified according to the type of activity.

1. *Sensory play*—play that involves sensory experiences such as splashing water, digging in the sand, banging pots and pans, plucking flower petals, or blowing bubbles. Children learn about the world through these sensory experiences (Athey, 1984).
2. *Motor play*—play that involves physical motion such as running, jumping, skipping, or swinging. This type of play helps to develop muscles and motor coordination, and to release pent-up energy.
3. *Rough-and tumble play*—motor play that involves mock-fighting and the controlled release of aggression. Children learn to control their impulses and feelings, and to express them in socially acceptable ways. The development of this type of play is often influenced by the way fathers play with their children at home (Levine, 1988). Sometimes this type of play gets out of hand, gets too rough, and children are hurt.
4. *Cognitive play*—play that involves language, the repetition of sounds and words because they sound funny, or playing word games, or asking riddles. This play gives children a chance to master word sounds and grammar, to think, and to develop cognitive skills (Galda & Pellegrini, 1985; Schwartz, 1981).
5. *Dramatic play or pretend play*—play that involves modeling activities and role-playing, such as playing house, firefighters, nurse or doctor, baby, astronaut, army, or truck driver (Doyle et al, 1992; Howes & Matheson, 1992; Lillard, 1993a, 1993b). This play gives children a chance to recreate experiences and to try out roles (Fein, 1986; Howes, Unger, & Seidner, 1989). It is also called *symbolic play* (Slade, 1987; Wooley & Wellman, 1990). Children of this age also create imaginary companions that become a regular part of their daily routines. Children talk to them, play with them, and treat them as though they were real (Taylor, Cartwright, & Carlson, 1993).
6. *Games and competitive sports*—play that may involve board games such as checkers, games of skill such as darts, or outdoor games and sports such as tag, hide and seek, or baseball. Children learn to follow rules, to take turns, to be able to accept losing or winning, and to cooperate with other children in the group (Kamii & DeVries, 1980).

There is much intermingling between the sexes and races. There is actually conflicting evidence about whether children tend to show same-sex/same-race preferences in playmates. One study of preschoolers evaluated their selection of playmate choices. The results show that white boys preferred playmates who were white boys first; they preferred black boys second; white girls third, and black girls fourth. White girls preferred playmates who were white girls first, black girls second, black boys third, and white boys fourth. Black boys preferred white boys first, black boys second, black girls third, and white girls fourth. Black girls preferred black girls first, black boys second, white girls third, and white boys fourth (Fishbein & Imai, 1993). It is interesting that white boys preferred to play with other boys and preferred to play with black girls least. Black boys also preferred to play with other boys and with white girls least. Both white and black girls preferred to play with white boys least. The reason that girls least preferred playing with white boys is that boys tend to dominate and control other children in their play; girls do not like to be dominated, so they avoid playing with boys. Because white boys have the highest status, on average, in a classroom, they would tend to dominate girls more than the other groups of boys. Hence, girls would avoid them the most. It is probable that young children find that the relationship between physical and social attractiveness is stronger for girls than boys. It is plausible, therefore, that black girls find other black girls most physically attractive, and white girls show parallel preferences. Thus, girls would prefer same-race/same-sex peers as playmates. However, those children, regardless of race or gender, who are friendly, cooperative, less aggressive, and less difficult to get along with are those who are most well liked (Denham & Holt, 1993; Mendelson, Aboud, & Lanthier, 1994).

Preschool children intermingle early with those of other races and genders.

As children get acquainted with one another, they become more selective in their playmate contacts. In early childhood classrooms, during the early weeks of the school year, preschoolers' number of new playmate combinations decline. The similar trend toward selectivity emerges in some year-long sociometric studies. In the spring, children interact with fewer individuals in small groups, especially cross-sex peers, than they did in the fall. Sociometric ratings become more negative over the course of the year, suggesting that children reject certain classmates as they learn to distinguish them from their preferred classmates. This increased selectivity has both advantages and disadvantages for children. Stable peer relationships are the optimal context for the development of social skills, but they may pose hardships for children who are trying to enter the social mainstream (Ramsey, 1995).

As preschool children interact with other children of the same age, they gradually discover that they come from a variety of family situations. Some have siblings, others none. Some have young parents, others old parents, and some only have one parent at home. These initial engagements with peers are broadening experiences that stimulate children to ask numerous questions. "How come I don't have any brothers or sisters?" "Why can't I have a big bike like Mary has?" "Why doesn't Johnny have any daddy?"

Research has revealed that experiences in the family have a definite effect on the development of social competence (Youngblade & Belsky, 1992). One study of economically disadvantaged 4- and 5-year-olds in a Midwestern community revealed the following factors were detrimental to the development of social skills:

- Exposure to aggressive models in the home and parents' endorsement of aggression as a means of solving conflicts
- Restrictive discipline, in which parents used a high degree of constriction

- Parents' hostile reactions to provocation by the child
- Insecure attachment to parents (P. J. Turner, 1991)

In contrast with these negative factors, the study found that parents who used preventive teaching and gave their children opportunity for direct peer experience contributed positively to the development of social skills of their children (Ladd & Hart, 1992; Pettit, Dodge, & Brown, 1988). Research also shows that children's friendships make a significant and unique contribution to their adaptation to becoming a sibling. Those who have the most positive relationships with friends are also able to develop the most positive relationships with siblings at home (Kramer & Gottman, 1992).

MIDDLE CHILDHOOD

Friendships

The older children become, the more important companionship with friends becomes (Buhrmester & Furman, 1987). By the time children start first grade, they are no longer interested in being alone so much of the time. They want to be with friends (Ladd, 1990). They still seek out a special companion, but their circle of friends is widening. During the preschool period, must of their friends were confined to the immediate neighborhood, but now children meet many friends from other areas served by the school. Some of these persons are different from the ones the children are used to playing with. This makes it harder for children to get acquainted and to learn to get along, but it is a broadening experience and helps them to mature.

Parents become concerned about the kinds of friend their children want to bring home or want to visit. They worry, and with justification, about the influence of these friends upon their children. Parents want to know: "What kind of persons are these children?" Parents are wise to be concerned, because peer-group influence over children becomes more and more important. Certainly, parents need to spell out some ground rules about how far away and where children are allowed to play, about what time to come in, and about the types of activities that are permitted. Grade-school children need some supervision, so it is helpful if there are concerned parents nearby.

However, *some parents are overprotective* and won't allow their children to do what others do or allow them to play with other children in the usual way. This is especially likely to happen if children are frail or sickly. The parents try to protect their children from germs, noise, and rough-and-tumble play, but as a result, they keep their children from making friends or from learning how to do what others do.

Others expect too much of their children, try to push them too fast, and are very critical when their children don't measure up. Such attitudes undermine their children's self-confidence. The children become afraid of failure, of rejection, of ridicule, and of criticism, and they react by trying to avoid social groups where they are embarrassed. Thus, in socialization as in other areas, parents need to balance supervision and guidance with freedom and encouragement. Generally speaking, parents who are sociable and agreeable and who have positive feelings toward their children have children who are sociable, agreeable, and have positive attitudes toward others (Putallaz, 1987).

Discerning parents need to be aware when their children are not getting along socially or when their children do not seem to have many friends. Parental action such as arranging play opportunities and supervising peer interaction can facilitate peer friendships and help their children develop social skills (Mize, Pettit, & Brown, 1995).

Popularity

Generally speaking, research points to the fact that children tend to prefer friends who are like themselves. They are similar in play styles and social participation; they may be similar in terms of politeness and sense of humor, and similar in sociability (Rubin et al., 1994).

Peer acceptance during the elementary years is very important to the children themselves and is predictive of later adjustment during adolescence. (Morison & Masten, 1991). Children differ in the degree to which they strive for or achieve popularity. If a group of children are asked individually to name other children whom they most like or with whom they would most like to be associated, it is possible to discover which children are most and least popular (Boulton & Smith, 1990). Usually, such surveys show that even those children who are rated most popular have a few acquaintances who are indifferent to them or dislike them, and those who are least popular are rarely unpopular with everyone. Even low-accepted children have best friends (Parker & Asher, 1993).

Nevertheless, since children place such emphasis on being popular, it is helpful to sort out those qualities of personality and character that make for popularity or unpopularity (Gelb & Jacobson, 1988). What types of children are most popular during middle childhood? Generally speaking, popular children (Chance, 1989; Dekovic & Gerris, 1994):

- Are socially aggressive and outgoing (Dodge, Cole, Pettit, & Price, 1990)
- Have a high energy level that they use in activities approved by the group
- Have positive self-perceptions (Boivin & Begin, 1989)
- Actively participate in social events enthusiastically
- Are friendly and sociable in relation to others (Dozier, 1991)
- Accept others, are sympathetic, protective, and comforting toward them
- Are cheerful, good-natured, have a good sense of humor
- Are above average in intelligence and school performance, but not too high above others
- Are popular with teachers (White & Kistner, 1992)
- Have superior social-cognitive and communication skills (Burleson, Della, & Applegate, 1992)

There are some social and sex differences in the qualities considered important to popularity. Boys need to show physical prowess, athletic ability, and skill in competitive games. In some antisocial groups, the most popular boys show superior fighting ability. In the upper elementary grades, girls are rated most popular who are considered physically attractive and socially sophisticated and mature. Middle-class children put greater emphasis on scholastic achievement than do lower-class children. A lower-class boy who excels in schoolwork risks alienation from his peers. A lower-class girl can be a good student without alienating her friends. In Chinese culture, shyness is associated with leadership and peer acceptance, whereas in Western culture, it is associated with rejection (Chen, Rubin, & Sun, 1992).

Peer Rejection

Peer relationships within the school setting have a great influence on children's concurrent and later academic, behavioral, and emotional adjustment. Rejected children have been found to be at heightened risk for a number of negative outcomes, including delinquency and criminality, dropping out of school, or needing mental health services. Rejected children have few, if any, neighborhood friends. They maintain distinct negative reputations within their peer group; they're seen as nasty, unpleasant children or are actively avoided. Even when rejected children enter new social situations where they are unknown, they rapidly reestablish rejected status. Once a child becomes rejected, there are numerous forces working to maintain negative status. Reputational biases develop within the peer group so that the peers act toward and think about rejected children more negatively than nonrejected children. When rejected children attempt to behave more positively, peers fail to reward their efforts. These group dynamics, in turn, are associated with lower self-esteem and loneliness.

Rejection by peers is a stressful influence on children's total adjustment.

There are fewer opportunities for rejected children to practice and develop appropriate social skills.

Poor peer relationships are a stressful experience for children due to both the experience itself and also the accompanying lack of social support, making children more vulnerable to other life stresses. In fact, children identify peer rejection as a major stressor itself and any changes in peer acceptance are as equally stressful as such other life events as failure of a year of school, death of a close friend, hospitalization of a parent, or serious illness (DeRosier, Kupersmidt, & Patterson, 1994).

What types of children are considered least popular (French, 1990)? Generally speaking, the least popular children (Chance, 1989; Cillessen, van Ijzendoorn, van Lieshout, & Hartup, 1992; Hynel, Bowker, & Woody, 1993; Rogosch & Newcomb, 1989):

- Are self-centered and withdrawn
- Are anxious, fearful, moody, and inhibited (Asendorpf, 1991)
- Are more likely to be emotionally disturbed (Altmann & Gotlieb, 1988; Asarnow, 1988)
- Are impulsive, with poor emotional control (French, 1988)
- Show a lack of sensitivity to others and to social situations
- Behave in inappropriate ways (Gelb & Jacobson, 1988)
- Are hostile and overaggressive (Coie, Dodge, Terry, & Wright, 1991; Parkhurst & Asher, 1992; Rabiner & Gordon, 1992)
- Behave considerably younger or older than their age groups
- Are different looking or unconventional in behavior
- Are more likely to be of low intelligence
- Are more likely to have a poor self-concept (Rabiner, Keane, & MacKinnon-Lewis, 1993)
- Are members of groups that are unpopular (Yee & Brown, 1992)

Conflicts

Conflicts occur more frequently among friends than among nonfriends, and last longer. They occur more frequently between individuals who are socially interdependent and who interact over substantial periods of time. Disagreements between friends become increasingly salient during middle childhood (Bryant, 1992). Children themselves recognize conflicts as major causes of friendship disruption. Effective conflict management is necessary to both friendship formation and maintenance and disagreements are commonly seen in interaction between friends (Hartup et al., 1993).

Social Maladjustment

There is a difference between children who are unliked and those who are disliked. *Unliked children* are socially invisible. They are loners (Coie & Dodge, 1988). *Disliked children* are quite visible and they behave in obnoxious, socially unacceptable ways. Younger and Daniels (1992) classified these types of children in two categories: Those that are characterized by *passive withdrawal* and those characterized by *active isolation*. Passive withdrawal and active isolation comprise very different forms of maladjustment. *A child who is socially withdrawn may be isolated from peers because of social anxiety or perceptions of social inefficacy* (Crick & Ladd, 1993). Other children described the socially withdrawn in the following manner:

> "He wants to play by himself."
>
> "Sometimes in class no one can hear her and when they ask her to speak up, her feelings get hurt."
>
> "She's always afraid when she meets someone for the first time."
>
> "She won't play with other kids because she's shy."
>
> "He keeps to himself. He's shy and doesn't want to bother people."
>
> "Sometimes she cries because she's so nervous."

Behaviors characteristic of passive withdrawal, such as shyness and oversensitivity are relatively common in young children. Consequently, young children who display such behavior are not viewed negatively by their peers. With increase in age, however, such behaviors become more conspicuous to the peer group. At higher grades (i.e., fifth to seventh grades), behaviors characteristic of passive withdrawal tend to be associated with peer rejection (Younger & Daniels, 1992).

Children who fit into the actively isolated category experience social isolation that is brought about by behavior that is obnoxious to others. This is associated with long-term maladjustment, including academic difficulty, delinquency, and possibly psychopathology. Socially aggressive children are disliked at all ages (Younger & Piccinin, 1989). Socially isolated children are described by others in the following manner:

> "No one wants to play with him."
>
> "No one likes her, and when they won't play with her, her feelings get hurt."
>
> "The others don't like him and they won't listen to him."
>
> "He has trouble making friends because he's really mean."
>
> "The other kids don't want to play with her and that makes her sad."

These are the children—hostile, aggressive, and sometimes cruel—whom other children dislike.

Loneliness

Those children who are rejected and actively disliked by their peers in school report significantly more loneliness than average-accepted and popular children (Cassidy & Asher, 1992). Lonely children experience feelings, of sadness, malaise, boredom, and alienation. They demonstrate withdrawn social behavior and experience lower peer acceptance (Renshaw & Brown, 1993). They often feel excluded, which can be damaging to their self-esteem.

There are a number of factors that contribute to loneliness. *The quality of children's attachment to their parents* has been studied extensively (Bullock, 1993). For example, children's early positive attachment to parents is positively correlated with more frequent, sociable, and positive interactions with parents and peers. Conversely, children with insecure attachments are more likely to cling to their parents, show negative interactions with their mothers and peers, show signs of anxiety around them, and are less likely to interact with peers. Children form secure attachments to their parents through positive, reciprocal interaction over time. When attachments with parents are severed by a separation such as divorce, children feel threatened, which can be detrimental to their self-esteem and interpersonal relationships. Children whose parents are going through divorce often report high degrees of sadness and loneliness. Children who are preschool age when their parents split up, report some of the highest feelings of loneliness as adults.

Also, daughters who report of a lack of positive parental involvement (reflected by nurturant, positive parental behaviors and affection) have higher loneliness scores than those who report more positive involvement. Those who report low levels of loneliness describe their parents as being close, warm, and supportive (Bullock, 1993). Thus, parent–child interactions influence loneliness later in life. They also suggest that loneliness is transmitted from generation to generation.

Several other significant losses throughout childhood also contribute to feelings of loneliness. These may include *moving to a new neighborhood or school; losing an object, possession, or pet; losing a friend; conflict within the home or at school; or experiencing the death of a pet or significant person.*

Interestingly enough, a study by Quay (1992) on personal and family effects on loneliness found *that children in one-parent families were not lonelier than children in two-parent families.* However, *children living in both two-parent and single-parent families were less lonely than children in other arrangements, such as with the mother and someone else in the home, with a relative, or in a foster home.* Also, *maternal employment did not affect loneliness.* Children who went home to their mothers after school and children who went to after-school day-care programs did not differ in loneliness, but these two groups were less lonely than latch-key children (Quay, 1992).

Gangs and Clubs

Ages 10 and 11 are when children begin joining clubs and gangs. These groups arise out of children's need to be independent from parents and to be with peers. Children form play clubs, neighborhood gangs, fan clubs,

Youth groups may be helpful or harmful, depending on their nature and purpose. Some youngsters join social clubs, others join gangs.

and secret societies with special rules, observances, passwords, and initiation rites. They make plans to build a fort or clubhouse and to do things in groups. Members are obliged to participate in the group's activities, and outsiders are excluded.

Gangs are usually organized along sex lines. The boys will have their gangs, and the girls their social clubs. Whether groups are helpful or harmful depends upon their nature, purpose, and membership. Gangs of delinquents in tough neighborhoods provide some semblance of protection for individual members, but the members themselves may engage in fighting, stealing, or drinking, or in pushing and using drugs.

The same drive that impels children into gang activities can be channeled into well-organized, supervised clubs where individuals can give acceptable expression to their social needs. This is the age for *Cub Scouts, Brownies, YMCA, YWCA, Police Athletic Leagues,* and many other groups for a variety of general and particular interests. Parents would be wise to encourage their children to join and participate in worthwhile groups.

Competition

One of the problems of some groups is that they place undue emphasis on competition. In our society, individuals are encouraged to compete with one another to see who can be the strongest or the fastest, have the largest collection of baseball cards, or win the game. Some groups encourage this competitiveness by their emphasis on winning, regardless of the effect of this competition on individuals. The American Academy of Pediatrics and many other *authorities feel that it is unwise to push preadolescents into highly competitive sports.* Young school-age children are not ready physically, psychologically, or socially for highly competitive games. The urge to win is so strong that the experience stimulates too much tension and anxiety, and defeat becomes a real blow to self-esteem.

Children ought to be encouraged to compete with themselves. Thus, a Cub Scout or Brownie can be encouraged to work for the next achievement rather than to become involved in stiff competition with other youngsters or groups. Those who are physically inept, unathletic, or unskilled at competitive games suffer terribly if they are excluded from teams or group activities. The purpose of such activities should be enjoyment, recreation, and the enhancement of self-esteem and self-worth, not the destruction of these.

Cruelty and Aggression

Some children of this age can be very cruel (Perry, Williard, & Perry, 1990). They callously exclude one another from their groups, or say things that shame or belittle others. Bullies who pick on those who are younger or weaker are a problem (Roberts, 1988). Their primary motive seems to be to gain control of others as a means of feeling important themselves (Boldizar, Perry, & Perry, 1989). Because of their own angry feelings, they often attribute hostile intentions to the actions of others when none exist (Dodge & Somberg, 1987). Under these circumstances, other children need to learn to stand up for themselves and to protect themselves (Ferguson & Rule, 1988).

There is substantial evidence that a small minority of children are consistently targeted for victimization by their peers. Researchers have suggested that these chronic victims are at high risk for later maladjustment. Accordingly, investigators have devoted considerable effort to identifying the correlates of peer victimization. One study investigated victimization

PARENTING ISSUES

The Bully

I remember counseling with one mother who—because of her religious upbringing—strongly objected to fighting. She had taught her 9-year-old son never to fight; in fact, she had taught him literally to turn the other cheek and never to hit back if someone hit him. Unfortunately, one bully at school found this out and would daily hit, abuse, and taunt this boy each afternoon on the way home from school. The youngster came home battered, bruised, and crying, but he obeyed his mother and would not fight back. Of course, the more he refused to fight, the more the bully called him a "sissie" and picked on him. After several sessions of counseling, the mother became convinced that she could not let her son take any more punishment, so she told him never to start a fight or to hit first, but if the bully hit him, to hit him back. The next day her son came home triumphant: "I really hit him, Mom, I knocked him down and made him cry. He won't pick on me again." And he didn't.

Of course, the best way to deal with bullies is not to have anything to do with them, but if they insist on trouble, children have to be prepared to deal with the situation. However, younger and smaller children can't handle bullies themselves. They need to enlist the aid of teachers, parents, and of older, stronger friends (Author's counseling notes).

Teachers and parents need to protect children from bullies.

among 6- to 8-year-old boys. The results of this investigation provide convincing evidence that there are linkages between children's social behavior and victimization by peers. In particular, there appears to be a strong association between nonassertive behavior and abuse by peers. Victims in the play groups displayed a behavioral pattern that was pervasively nonassertive. These boys initiated poor social overtures at a low rate, and demonstrated a passive, inflexible play style. Victims were also more submissive than other children, particularly in a context in which submission might be considered inappropriate (e.g., rough-and-tumble play). The submissiveness identified the victims as vulnerable targets for the aggressive and coercive overtures of their peers. Once selected for aggression, victims tended to reward their attackers with submission. Victims were selected for aggression at an increasingly high rate over time. Overall, victims were not well liked by their play group peers. The behavior of the group toward the victims became more negative as differences in victimization became extreme. Victims were the object of assertive refusals, aggression, and negative responses from peers at an increasingly high rate over time (Schwartz, Dodge, & Coie, 1993).

SOCIAL COGNITION

Social cognition—the capacity to understand social relationships

Social cognition is the capacity to understand social relationships. In children, it is the ability to understand others: their thoughts, their intentions, their emotions, their social behavior, and their general point of view (Dunn et al., 1991; Zahn-Waxler, Radke-Yarrow, Wagner, & Chapman, 1992). Social cognition is basic to all human interactions. To know what other people think and feel is necessary to understand them and to get along with them (Feldman & Ruble, 1988; Gnepp & Chilamkurti, 1988).

Yet this ability develops very slowly. Robert Selman (1977, 1980) has advanced a theory of social cognition outlining predictable stages in **social role taking.** To Selman, social role taking is the ability to understand the self and others as subjects, to react to others as like the self, and to react to the self's behavior from the other's point of view.

Social role taking—the ability to understand the self and others as subjects and to react to others as like the self

Selman's five stages of development follow.

Stage 0

Egocentric undifferentiated stage—the stage of awareness when another person is seen egocentrically, undifferentiated from the self's own point of view

Egocentric undifferentiated stage (age 0 to 6). Until about age 6, children cannot make a clear distinction between their own interpretation of a social situation and another's point of view, nor can they understand that their own perception may not be correct (Yaniv & Shatz, 1990). When they are asked how someone else feels in a particular situation, their responses reflect how *they* feel, not how *others* feel (Lewis & Osborne, 1990).

Third-person or mutual perspective-taking stage—when children see their own perspective, their partner's, plus a third person's perspective

Stage 1

Differentiated or subjective perspective-taking stage—the stage of awareness when the other is seen as different from the self, but the other person's perception of the self is still undifferentiated

Differentiated or subjective perspective-taking stage (age 6 to 8). Children develop an awareness that others may have a different social perspective, but they have little understanding of the reasons for others' viewpoints (LeMare & Rubin, 1987). Children believe that others would feel the same way if they had the same information. Perspective taking is a one-way street; children cannot accurately judge their own behavior from the perspective of the other person. They do begin to distinguish between intentionality and unintentionality of behavior and to consider causes of actions (P. H. Miller & Aloise, 1989). They are capable of inferring other peoples' intentions, feelings, and thoughts (Arsenio & Kramer, 1992) but base their conclusions on physical observations that may not be correct, not realizing that people may hide their true feelings.

In-depth and societal perspective-taking stage—the stage of social awareness when the self can take a generalized societal perspective of the self–other interaction

Stage 2

Self-reflective thinking or reciprocal perspective-taking stage—the stage of awareness when the self can take the perspective of another person and know that the other person can also take the perspective of the self

Self-reflective thinking or reciprocal perspective-taking stage (age 8 to 10). A child develops reciprocal awareness, realizing that others have a different point of view and that others are aware that he or she has a particular point of view. The principal change from stage 1 to stage 2 is children's ability to take the perspective of others; to reflect about their own behavior and their own motivation as seen from the perspective of another person. This ability includes an awareness of relativity, that no individual's social perspective is necessarily correct or valid in an absolute sense. Another person's point of view may be as correct as one's own. This awareness also means that individuals may take other person's points of view into account (Dizon & Moore, 1990).

Stage 3

Third-person or mutual perspective-taking stage (age 10 to 12). Children can see their own perspective, the perspective of their partner, plus assume the perspective of a neutral third person. As third-person observers, they can see themselves as both actor and object. Thus, they can understand a more generalized perspective that might be taken by an "average" member of the group.

Stage 4

In-depth and societal perspective-taking (adolescence to adulthood). Young people recognize that there is a group perspective, a point of view reflected in a social system. Law and morality depend on some consensual group perspective that the individual must take into account.

Obviously, the more advanced the stage of social cognition, the more capable children become in understanding and getting along with others.

Family Influences

The question arises as to how social competence develops. As in many other instances, the family plays the primary role. Figure 13.2 is a conceptual model that links family characteristics and children's social cognitive knowledge with social competence. Family socialization practices are related to children's knowledge about emotions and social behavior. In turn, children's knowledge is expected to relate directly to their social competence. Family socialization practices include the emotional climate in the family, which is so important to the development of children's peer relationships. Emotion socialization may be negative, including a high level of conflict, maternal anger, and parental discouragement of children's negative emotional expression. Or emotion socialization may be positive, including warm expressions of affection; moderate, manageable levels of conflict; and generally positive feelings between parents and children. Personal distress may result when the child is a direct target of anger or is pressured to suppress negative emotion. Heightened personal distress caused by an emotionally charged event is likely to be particularly disruptive in the child's social relationships. However, when the parental expressions of emotion are generally positive, when there are good feelings existing between children and their parents, children show more positive relationship with other children, and have positive insight as to what friendly relationships should be (Garner, Jones & Miner, 1994).

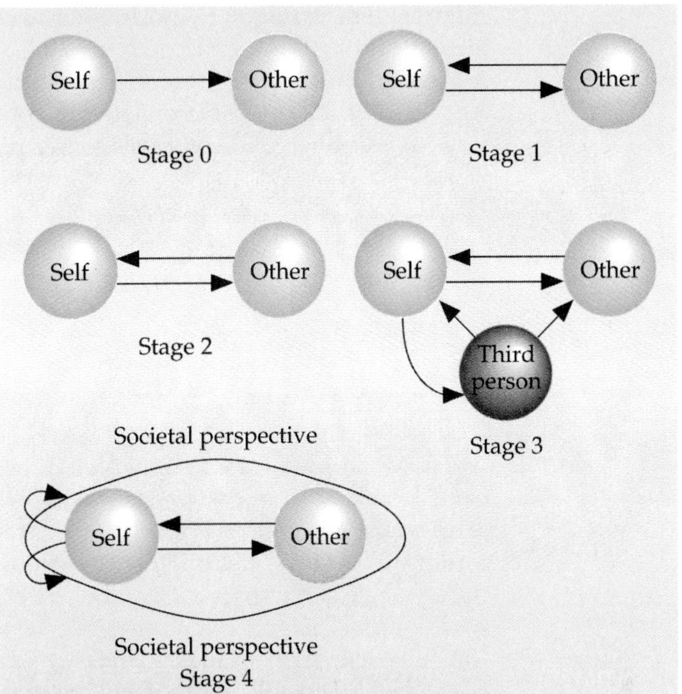

FIGURE 13.1 Selman's five stages of social role taking. *Stage 0.* The other person is seen egocentrically, or undifferentiated from the self's own point of view. *Stage 1.* The other is seen as different from the self, but the other person's perception of the self is still undifferentiated. *Stage 2.* The self can take the perspective of another person and becomes aware that the other person can also take the perspective of the self. *Stage 3.* The self can view the self–other interaction from the perspective of a neutral third person. *Stage 4.* The self can take a generalized societal perspective of the self–other interaction.

From *Theories of Adolescence.* 5th ed. (pp. 249, 251, 254, 256, 258) by R. E. Muuss, 1988. New York: McGraw Hill Publishing Company. Copyright © McGraw Hill Publishing Company. Used by permission.

SOCIAL INFORMATION PROCESSING

According to the social information processing perspective on social competence, behavioral responses to problematic social situations are a function of a series of steps of cognitive processing (Dorsch & Keane, 1994). Competent performance in response to a situation occurs as a function of five sequential processes: *Encoding* of relevant stimulus cues, *accurate interpretation* of those cues, *response generation, response evaluation,* and *behavioral enactment* of a selected response. For example, at the encoding step, socially rejected aggressive children are less attentive to relevant social cues than are less aggressive peers. Attention to relevant cues predicts competent behavioral performance in a peer group entry situation. At the interpretation step, socially rejected aggressive children have been found to be relatively inaccurate at detecting peer intention cues and to be biased toward hostile attributions. Rejected and incompetent children have been found to access fewer competent responses to interpersonal problems or aggressive or inept responses. At the response evaluation step, incompetent, aggressive

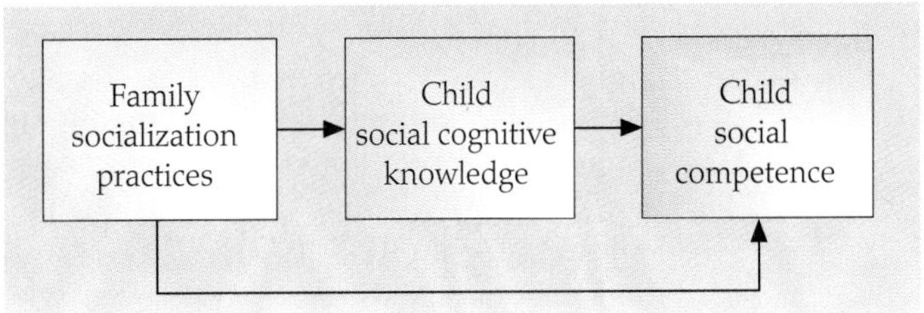

FIGURE 13.2 Conceptual model of the linkages between socialization practices, social cognitive knowledge, and social competence.

From P. W. Garner, D. C. Jones, & J. L. Miner (1994). "Social competence among Low-Income Preschoolers: Emotion Socialization Practices and Social Cognitive Correlates." *Child Development, 65,* 622–637.

children anticipate more positive instrumental and interpersonal outcomes from aggression than do more competent peers. Aggressive children display relatively poor skills at enacting competent behavioral responses. As a result of inadequate social information processing, these children simply do not know how to relate to others, and do not get along as well with them (Dodge & Price, 1994).

Television as a Socializing Influence

VIEWING HABITS

Today, 98 percent of the households in the United States own at least one television set (Christopher, Fabes, & Wilson, 1989). According to a 1985 Nielson report, schoolchildren between the ages of 6 and 11 spend an average of 26 hours, 34 minutes per week watching television (*National Audience Demographics Report,* 1985). Preschool children spend an average of 28 hours, 20 minutes per week. By age 18, children will have watched television approximately 20,000 hours, compared with 11,000 hours in the classroom. Singer and Singer (1983) pointed out that children spend more time watching television than they spend in conversation with adults or siblings. They spend more time watching television than engaging in any other activity (including playing and eating) except sleeping (Institute for Social Research, 1985). These figures are startling, so the real question is: *What effect does watching so much television have on children, on their development and relationships?*

VIOLENCE AND AGGRESSION

A most important concern has been the influence of television as a stimulus of aggressive behavior in children. There is certainly no doubt of the extent of violence on TV. By the time children are in the eighth grade, they will have watched 18,000 human beings killed on television, and violent acts committed against thousands more. Thomas Radicki, a psychiatrist who is head of the National Coalition on Television Violence, reports a deluge of high-action violent cartoon shows (Tooth, 1985). In examining a typical Saturday morning program of the *Bugs Bunny–Roadrunner* cartoon, one analysis revealed an average of fifty violent acts per hour (Zimmerman, 1983). The classic research by Bandura on the relationship between television violence and aggressive behavior in children found that children were less likely to imitate the violent behavior of cartoon models than they were the violence of real-people models (Bandura, Ross, & Ross, 1963a). This is in keeping with other findings that human portrayal exerts more influence than cartoon portrayal. (Hayes & Casey, 1992). Nevertheless, violent cartoons had a negative effect. One study found that television shows with rapid changes of scene and high action, such as cartoons, increase children's aggression, regardless of content, because the sensory excitement stimulates the children to act without reflection (Greer, Potts, Wright, & Huston, 1982).

Real-life models of violence are not hard to find. The National Coalition on Television Violence reports that violent acts on television increased 65 percent from 1981 to 1985. The violent acts to which children are exposed on television include war, assassination, murder, shooting, knifing,

Adults have become concerned with the effects that watching television for long hours has on children.

beating, punching, torture, kicking, choking, burning, rape, cruelty to animals, robbery, violent accidents, and property destruction. While precise cause and effect relationships are hard to establish, extensive research indicates that *television violence is associated with increased aggressive behavior in children who watch it.* After reviewing the research on the subject, the National Institute of Mental Health (NIMH) (1982) concluded that children who see violence on the screen behave more aggressively, regardless of their geographical location or socioeconomic level. This is true of both boys and girls, and of normal children as well as those with emotional problems. The NIMH report concludes that television encourages aggressive behavior in two ways: *Children model and imitate what they see, and they come to accept aggression as appropriate behavior.*

This finding seems to hold true internationally, also. Huesmann and Eron (1986) summarized research from five countries: the United States, Finland, Israel, Poland, and Australia. The conclusion was the same as that reached in other studies: television violence does have an adverse affect on children. Furthermore, *the effect is interdependent. Aggressive children select more violent television programs and view more of them, and those who watch more violent programs tend to be more aggressive.* Other research substantiates that the effect of violence is interactive and cumulative. Children who watch violence on television are more aggressive than children who do not, and children who are aggressive are likely to watch a lot of TV violence (Friedrich-Cofer & Huston, 1986). The effects may be long lasting. One study concluded that the amount of television violence watched by children when they were in elementary school was associated with how aggressive they were at age 19 and at age 30 (Eron, 1987). Of course, this still does not prove cause and effect.

FACTUAL VERSUS FICTIONAL

During the years from about ages 3 to 12, children gradually acquire an understanding of the distinctions between real and fictional television content. By middle childhood, at least two dimensions appear to be discriminated in children's judgment of reality, *factuality* and *social realism.* Although children understand variations in television reality, we know little about how that understanding affects their reaction to content. It is often assumed that content perceived as real will have a greater effect and greater impact on children than content known to be unreal. But, other than a few studies suggesting that real aggression is more likely to be imitated than fictional aggression, there are few data.

In one study, children's emotional and cognitive responses to factual and fictional television programs depicting family conflict were investigated. Ninety-seven third- and fourth-graders saw three fifteen-minute versions of the same content: documentary, drama, or realistic drama. Factuality represents a judgment of whether the events portrayed actually happened in an unrehearsed world. By age 7, children recognize cues for live broadcast for real events versus fictional content. Social realism, the second dimension of reality perception, reflects a judgment about whether the televised people and events are like those in the real world. The judgment for social realism is whether a representation is true to life, even though it may be known to be fictional.

Regardless of whether the experiences depicted are real or fictional, very young children do not have a full understanding of the difference between real and vicarious experience or between appearance and reality, so television can arouse emotion directly. Children are frightened by threatening stimuli (e.g., a swarm of bees approaching) and by physical transformations (e.g., the change from man to monster in "The Incredible Hulk"). Nevertheless, most emotional reactions to television are probably vicarious responses to the situations to people portrayed. A considerable body of literature exists showing that even young children respond emotionally when they observe laboratory films depicting other children in distress. Perceived reality of content may mediate emotional responses. When a television program is perceived as factual rather than fictional, children may be more likely to imagine themselves in the role of the people involved or in similar situations. Children 9 to 12 years old, interviewed shortly after the explosion of the space shuttle *Challenger,* reported higher levels of emotional distress than they felt when they saw comparable fiction events. Emotional effects of fictional content can be reduced by reminding children it is not real, but such reassurance is of little help to children younger than 7 years old.

Sometimes dramatic presentations, because of their deliberate attempt to create excitement, identification with characters, and emotional involvement in the viewer, may elicit more affect than the typically drier, calmer, factual presentation found in news and documentary programs. The small amount of research investigating the effects of perceived reality on emotion is concentrated primarily on frightening television programs and fearful reactions. Studies of empathy, however, demonstrate empathetic concern in response to videotaped physical or psychological distress of another person. Much of television portrays intense human relationships that are often fraught with anger, love, hurt, conflict, and other emotionally charged content. Many educational programs for children deal with emotionally arousing situations and conflict resolution. The effectiveness of such programs may depend in part on their ability to engage the emotions of the audience. Even if a program is fictional, it can elicit emotions and empathy with the people shown, particularly if the viewer judges it to be socially realistic. Thus, it is social realism rather than factuality that appears to be important in emotional arousal. When children consider the people and events as true to life, or similar to their own experiences, they are more apt to share in the emotions of the people they watch (Huston et al., 1995).

FAMILY INTERACTION

Critics argue that television watching has other negative effects on children. One of the effects is felt by the whole family (Fabes, Wilson, & Christopher, 1989). *Extensive viewing has been associated with a decrease in family interaction, social communication, and interpersonal conversation.* Of course, families interact differently depending on the program being watched. Some families talk less but touch more while watching television (Brody & Stoneman, 1983). Interaction is certainly decreased in those families with more than one television set. The parents watch one program, the children another, in separate locations of the house. Experiments with families that decided to give up television viewing for a period of time revealed that the children played together more, family activities increased, mealtimes were longer, the children read more, and bedtimes were earlier (Chira, 1984).

Increased television viewing has also been associated with lower-socioeconomic-status families (Huston, Siegle, & Bremer, 1983), dysfunctional families, and increased parent–child conflict (Price and Feshbach, 1982). However, it is likely that increased television viewing is the result of trouble in the family, not the cause. *Children use television as an escape from the stress of the home environment.* One study found that lack of parental empathy, sensitivity, and adaptive role expectations was related to heavy viewing of violent, fantasy-oriented television content (Tangney, 1988). Another study found that parental viewing preferences, habits, and attitudes towards television influence childrens' viewing habits. The majority of child programs were viewed without parents while the majority of adult programs were watched with parents. Coviewing patterns of adult programs were predicted from parents' individual viewing habits. In other words, the adult programs that children watched depended upon what the parents were watching (St. Peters et al., 1991).

COGNITIVE DEVELOPMENT

Heavy television viewing has also been associated with lower school achievement (Rubenstein, 1983), including lower reading comprehension (Singer & Singer, 1983), poorer language usage, and neglect of homework. Certainly, if their parents will let them, many children will stay up until all hours to watch television rather than do their homework. Interestingly, however, *heavy TV viewing by children of low socioeconomic status has been associated with higher scholastic achievement and reading comprehension* (Morgan & Gross, 1982) *and at the same time with lower abilities among children of high socioeconomic status.* Apparently, television has a leveling effect. The fact remains that any time spent watching television decreases the amount of time that children

PARENTING ISSUES

Nintendo

Nintendo is the video game craze that has swept the nation. By the end of 1989, Nintendo was in 20 million American homes. Forty million of the game devices had been installed around the world. Fifty million of the game cartridges were sold in 1989 alone. There are more than a hundred different Nintendo game cartridges available. The archetypical Nintendo game portrays the adventures of *Mario,* an indomitable, mustached man in a red cap whose goal is to rescue a princess. Mario runs through a stylized landscape while the computer sends hazards toward him. The farther he goes, the more clever his enemies become, until at last he either rescues the princess or dies on the screen with an electronic gurgle. Some players play for weeks or months without ever seeing the princess. In *Super Mario 2,* Mario and his brother Luigi go over hill, dale, and waterfall, through tunnel, and by magic carpet to defeat the evil Wart. In the *Legend of Zelda,* the hero Link searches the mystical labyrinths of the Underworld to find the lost pieces of the golden Triforce of Wisdom. In *Rad Racer,* a Ferrari 328 Twin Turbo competes with Corvettes, Lamborghinis, and Porsches in a 200 km/hr cross-country race. In *Punch Out,* Little Mac, a teenage battler from the Bronx, fights his way up the ranks until he earns a fight against Mike Tyson (Adler, 1989).

Sixty percent of players are males between 8 and 15. For some children and adolescents, Nintendo becomes a compulsion. It seems to speak to primordial and powerful urges. It arouses warrior instincts. As one 14-year-old said:

> You just want to play and play until you beat it. You get so nervous near the end. You perspire. Your heart rate is up. Afterward you just want to drop dead (Adler, 1989, p. 65).

To assist players in mastering the games, the manufacturer has installed hotlines in a room in Redmond, Washington, where a hundred "counselors" answer 50,000 calls a week to offer players hints on how to deal with evil knights or bottomless pits ("Trapped by Mutilator Troy?" 1990).

Nintendo stimulates children to do extreme things. One 14-year-old boy from West Palm Beach, Florida, played continuously for 2 days straight. A female school aide from Hammond, Indiana, played it for 4 months, 4 hours a night, until her doctor gave her a thumb splint for her "Nintendonitis" and told her to lay off video games. She started playing with her palms.

This craze is causing some reactions among adults. One antiviolence group has rated 70 percent of the games "harmful for children." Many parents, seeing their kids play *Super Mario 2* for hours on end, are asking what this nonstop diet of video games is doing to impressionable young minds ("Dr. Nintendo," 1990). Combat on Nintendo is not always conducted according to the Geneva convention. Karate kicks, maces and swords, and bludgeoning are popular. In *Renegade,* the object is to slaughter a gang of muggers before they throw you on the railroad tracks. The body count by the end of the *Double Dragon* is fifty, including the hero's own brother, who has stolen the hero's girlfriend (Adler, 1989). As a result, some parents limit Nintendo to only one hour a night, or to Saturday mornings, or to rainy days. Nintendo has become a principal means of discipline: "No Nintendo until you've done your homework." "Just for that you can't play Nintendo for a whole week."

Peggy Charren, president of Action for Children's Television, considers Nintendo pretty bland compared to such TV programs as "Nightmare on Elm Street." Perhaps to buy some respect, but nevertheless to get more information, Nintendo donated $3 million to MIT's Media Laboratory to study "how children learn while they play." ("Dr. Nintendo," 1990). Since that time dozens of new games have been created to be used on personal computers at home.

Nintendo is the video game craze that swept the nation.

spend on other activities, whether it be playing, engaging in hobbies, reading, or talking with friends or family members. Some authorities feel that television makes children less creative, less verbal, less social, and less independent.

COMMERCIALS

The question also arises regarding the effects of television commercials on children. *There is no question that television advertising is influential.* Part of the effects are positive. Television warns against smoking and the use of drugs, encourages children to brush their teeth to avoid cavities, and encourages them to eat their cereal. However, one study found that a significant portion of commercials advertised food products high in sugar, and the consumption of these products increased because of television advertising (Barcus, 1978). Television is also used to sell every conceivable type of new toy (Dorr, 1986). Children see a toy advertised, want it, and request it from their parents. If parents refuse, parent– child arguments follow. In one study, when children were presented with a hypothetical scenario of a father refusing to purchase a toy his son had requested, less than 40 percent of the children who had been exposed to an advertisement of the toy felt the boy would still want to play with his father, whereas over sixty percent of the children who had not viewed the commercial thought the boy would still want to play with his father (Goldberg & Gorn, 1977). Television is not simply an innocuous form of family entertainment. It is a powerful force.

POSITIVE EFFECTS

Not all effects of television are negative. One of the most watched educational programs is "Sesame Street." Viewing is highest by children between ages 3 and 5, with a peak between 3 1/2 and 4 and a decline between ages 5 and 7 (Pinon, Huston, & Wright, 1989). A series of studies found the following positive benefits: Viewers showed increased abilities to recognize and name letters, to sort different objects, to name body parts, and to recognize and label geometric forms. However, "Sesame Street" has not reduced the difference between the advantaged and disadvantaged in terms of cognitive functioning (Cook et al., 1975). In fact, already advantaged children tend to benefit more. Another children's program, "Mr. Rogers' Neighborhood," was found to increase prosocial behavior in children (Tower, Singer, Singer, & Biggs, 1979). Television can be used to promote good health and nutrition habits among children (Calvert & Cocking, 1992).

There are many other potential benefits of carefully designed children's programs. Children can be taught cooperation, sharing, affection, friendship, control of aggression, coping with frustration, and the necessity of completing tasks. They can be presented models of harmonious family relationships, and of cooperative, sympathetic, and nurturant behavior. As they get older, they can be exposed to greatness; to various ethnic and cultural groups; to world geography and history; to the world of nature; to a wide variety of interpersonal experiences; to literature and the classics; and to science, art, music, and drama. The potentials are unlimited. Unfortunately, television programs have fallen far short of their potential (*Television and Your Children,* 1985).

The Development of Gender Roles

Gender—our biological sex

Gender roles—our outward expressions of masculinity or femininity in social settings

MEANING

One of the negative effects of television is that it sometimes portrays stereotypical gender roles. **Gender** refers to our biological sex, whether male or female. **Gender roles** are outward expressions of masculinity or femininity in social settings. They are how we act and think as males or females. They are our sex roles.

Gender-typed roles are learned through play.

Sex roles are molded by three important influences: *biological, cognitive,* and *environmental.*

INFLUENCES ON GENDER ROLES

Biological

The biological bases for gender have already been discussed in Chapter 3. If an ovum is fertilized by a sperm carrying an X chromosome, a female is conceived. If the ovum is fertilized by a sperm carrying a Y chromosome, a male is conceived. *The chromosomal combination is the initial controlling factor in the development of gender.*

Gender development is also influenced by sex hormones. **Testosterone** is the masculinizing hormone secreted by the testes; **estrogen** is the feminizing hormone secreted by the ovaries. If human females are exposed to excessive *androgenic* (masculinizing) influences prenatally, after birth they become more physically vigorous and more assertive than other females. They prefer boys rather than girls as playmates and choose strenuous activities over relatively docile play. Similarly, boys born to mothers who receive estrogen and progesterone during pregnancy tend to exhibit less assertiveness and physical activity and may be rated lower in general masculine-typed behavior (Ehrhardt & Meyer-Bahlburg, 1981). The studies suggest that *changes in prenatal hormonal levels in humans may have marked effects on gender-role behavior.* After birth, hormonal secretions stimulate the development of masculine or feminine physical characteristics, but have minimal effect on gender-role behavior, usually only accentuating behavior already manifested.

Cognitive

Cognitive theory suggests that *sex-role identity has its beginning in the gender cognitively assigned to the child at birth and subsequently accepted by him or her while growing up.* At the time of birth, gender assignment is made largely on the basis of genital examination. The assignment of gender influences everything that happens thereafter. Kohlberg (1966a), the chief exponent of this view, emphasized that the child's self-categorization (as a boy or girl) is the basic organizer of the sex-role attitudes that develop. A child who recognizes that he is a male begins to value maleness, and a child who recognizes that she is a female begins to value femaleness and to act consistently with gender expectations (Martin & Little, 1990). The child begins to structure experience according to the accepted gender and to act out appropriate sex roles. Sex differentiation takes place gradually as children learn to be male or female according to culturally established sex-role expectations and their interpretations of them. It is important to emphasize that according to this theory *girls do not become girls because they identify with or model themselves after their mothers; they model themselves after their mothers because they have realized that they are girls.* They preferentially value their own sex and are motivated to appropriate sex-role behavior.

Testosterone—the masculinizing hormone

Estrogen—the feminizing hormone

Environmental

Environmentalists reason differently. In their view, *a child learns sex-typed behavior the same way he or she learns any other type of behavior: through a combination of rewards and punishment, indoctrination, observation of others, and modeling.* From the beginning, boys and girls are socialized differently (Fagot & Hagan, 1991). Boys are expected

FOCUS

Androgen and Sex-Typed Behavior

Congenital Adrenal Hyperplasia (CAH) is a condition whereby children experience higher than normal levels of androgen, and in which girls show masculinization of behavior that expresses sex differences. One study examined rough-and-tumble play and sex of preferred playmates in 3 to 8-year-old children with CAH and unaffected 3 to 8-year-old male and female relatives. The expected sex differences in rough-and-tumble play were seen, with unaffected boys showing more rough-and-tumble play then unaffected girls. Unaffected boys also preferred boys and unaffected girls preferred girls as playmates. Girls with CAH showed a preference for male playmates, indicating masculinization of their behavior. Boys with CAH showed playmate preferences similar to those of unaffected boys; that is, they preferred male playmates. In addition, it was predicted in this study that CAH girls would show increased rough-and-tumble play as a result of androgen influences. However, this hypothesis was not confirmed. CAH girls did not differ from unaffected girls in rough-and-tumble play. This result is surprising since prior studies based on interviews with CAH girls and their parents reported a general increase in "tomboyish" behavior and in general role behavior usually associated with males. The results of this study suggested that hormones may not influence all behavior in the same manner or to the same degree. The researchers revealed that boys generally choose other boys rather than girls for partners in rough-and-tumble play. CAH may have enhanced the desire to engagein rough-and-tumble play on the part of the girls, but they were unlikely to show increased rough-and-tumble play because of a lack of male partners. The data from this study and those of other researchers suggest that the prenatal hormone environment contributes to the development of some human behavior that shows sex differences (Hines & Kaufman, 1994).

to be more active and aggressive. When they act according to these expectations, they are praised; when they refuse to fight, they are criticized for being "sissies." Girls are condemned or punished for being too boisterous or aggressive and are rewarded when they are polite and submissive (Williams, 1988). As a consequence, boys and girls grow up manifesting different behaviors.

Traditional sex roles and concepts are taught in many ways as the child grows up (Brody and Steelman, 1985; Roopnarine, 1986). *Giving children gender-specific toys may have considerable influence on vocational choices.* Such toys influence boys to be scientists, astronauts, or football players and girls to be nurses, teachers, or flight attendants. Without realizing it, *many teachers still develop traditional masculine–feminine stereotypical behavior in school.* Studies of teachers' relationships with boys and girls reveal that teachers encourage boys to be more assertive in the classroom (Sadker & Sadker, 1985). When the teacher asks questions, the boys call out comments without raising their hands, literally grabbing the teacher's attention. Most girls sit patiently with their hands raised, but if a girl calls out, the teacher

Gender roles that are outward expressions of masculinity or femininity in social settings are in a state of flux and transition.

reprimands her: "In this class, we don't shout our answers; we raise our hands." The message is subtle but powerful; boys should be academically assertive; girls should be quiet.

Children also find appropriate sex roles through a process of identification, especially with parents of the same sex. Parental identification is the process by which the child adopts and internalizes parental values, attitudes, behavioral traits, and personality characteristics (Weisner & Wilson-Mitchell, 1990). When applied to sex-role development, parental identification theory suggests that children develop sex-role concepts, attitudes, values, characteristics, and behavior by identifying with their parents, especially with the parent of the opposite sex (Hock & Curry, 1983). Identification begins immediately after birth because of the child's early dependency on parents. This dependency in turn normally leads to a close emotional attachment. Sex-role learning takes place almost unconsciously and indirectly in this close parent-child relationship. Through example and through daily contacts and associations (McHale, Bartko, Crouter, & Perry-Jenkins, 1990), children learn what a mother, a wife, a father, a husband, a woman, or a man is.

Peer groups also exert tremendous influence on children in sex-role development. Boys are condemned as "sissies" if they manifest feminine characteristics. Girls are labeled "tomboys" if they are unladylike. Day after day, children are taught to be boys or girls according to the definitions prevalent in their culture (Sroufe, Bennett, Englund, & Urban, 1993).

AGE AND GENDER-ROLE DEVELOPMENT

By *2 years of age* most children are aware that there are boys and girls, mommies and daddies, that daddies have penises and mommies have breasts. They use the pronouns *he* and *she* to refer to brothers and sisters and begin to be aware of what constitutes masculine and feminine dress and behavior. Men wear shirts, trousers, suits, and they shave; women wear slacks, dresses, skirts, and blouses, and they put on makeup. Both wear jeans. Children begin to be aware of sex-typed roles (Fagot, Leinbach, & O'Boyle, 1992). If a person drives a truck and is a firefighter, that person must be a man. If someone washes dishes, cooks, or irons clothes, that person must be a woman. By *3 years of age* children choose gender-typed toys—dolls or cars—and perform sex-typed roles—nurses versus doctors (Weinraub et al., 1984). Yet, at this age, they are unaware that most of the toys they choose are considered appropriate for their gender. There is considerable switching of stereotypical gender-related toys and roles. Three-year-old boys will pretend to be babies, fathers, mothers, or monsters. They will wear mother's high heels or father's cowboy boots. They will play dolls as comfortably as girls do.

By *age 5,* this has usually changed. A boy who wants to dress a doll, or a girl who wants to be a space warrior, is criticized by the family (Roopnarine, 1984). Boys will pretend to be monsters or supermen; girls pretend to be princesses or sisters (Paley, 1984).

Sex differences become evident in play. Boys play outdoors more; use more physical space; engage in more rough-and-tumble, noisy play; more often wrestle, run, push, and tease. Girls more often engage in helping, nurturant play, and more often play house, care for babies, cook, clean, and dress up in hats and other clothes (Pitcher & Schultz, 1983). There is still considerable intermingling of the sexes during play, with some preferences for same-sex companionship becoming evident. By *age 7* children have developed a sense of **gender constancy:** the understanding of which gender they are and the knowledge that their own sex remains constant. Once a girl, always a girl (Frey & Ruble, 1992). However, research with 4- and 8-year-olds and college-age students revealed that gender role flexibility increases over these age spans. Children become more flexible regarding certain social transitions, such as who can play with trucks (Levy, Taylor, & Gelman, 1995).

Gender constancy—the understanding of the gender that one is, and the knowledge that gender is going to remain the same: usually achieved by 7 years of age

Gender stereotypes—widespread, assumed gender characteristics of what boys and girls are like

STEREOTYPES

Children's sex-type beliefs develop early and increase rapidly throughout early childhood. They have been found to affect children's play, memory, attributions, and preferences (Bigler, 1995). **Gender stereotypes** are common concepts and assumed characteristics of what boys and girls, or men and women, are supposed to be like within the context of the culture in which they live. In our society, when we talk about a "real boy" or a "masculine man" we are expressing value judgments based on an assessment of those personal and behavioral characteristics of "maleness" according to the defined standards of our culture (Levant, 1992). Similarly, when we are

TABLE 13.1
STEREOTYPES OF BOYS AND GIRLS

	Boys	*Girls*
Physical characteristics	Bigger stronger, muscular, hard Wear trousers, shirts, suits Short hair	Weaker, softer, littler, delicate Wear dresses, skirts, blouses, makeup, jewelry Long hair, curls, ribbons
Play	Play war, army, fireman, policeman, cowboy, astronaut, build things Play with blocks, cars, trucks, airplanes, boats, soldiers, bulldozers, cranes, tools, space-age toys, video games More physical play, sports: football, soccer, hockey, baseball	Domestic play: play house, wash dishes, cook, iron, sweep, tend babies Play with dollhouses, dolls, kitchen set, pots, stoves, doll carriages, cooking utensils, pots and pans, board games More interest in art, drawing, music
Domestic work	Mow lawn, build and fix things	Domestic chores, housekeeping, care for children, laundry
Behavior	Rough, aggressive, forceful, tough, daring, brave, competitive, like to fight Loud, noisy, naughty Not a sissy, unemotional, not cry, self-confident, independent	Passive, nurturant, helping, caring, compassionate, sympathetic, gentle, kind, scared, like to kiss, don't hit or fight Talk a lot Emotional, high-strung, cry, frivolous, impractical, dependent
Cognitive	Better in math, science, visual–spatial skills, mechanical aptitude	Better in verbal skills, grammar, reading, spelling, languages, history

PARENTING ISSUES

Parental Roles in Androgynous Development

There are many things that parents can do to encourage development of androgyny in their children (Katz & Walsh, 1991).

- Become androgynous role models for children to imitate. If parents can manifest both self-assertive and integrative traits, and exemplify both masculine and feminine roles in the family, children are likely to adopt both traits and roles themselves.
- Eliminate separating "men's work" and "women's work" in the family, with the whole family performing "our work."
- Encourage children to play games and use toys without regard for traditional sex-typed associations.
- Encourage boys to be integrative and girls to be self-assertive. Let boys know it's all right to have tender feelings and to express emotion, and let girls know they can assert their individualism and independence.
- Teach children that both men and women can engage in traditionally male or traditionally female professions. A woman doesn't have to be a secretary; she can have a secretary.

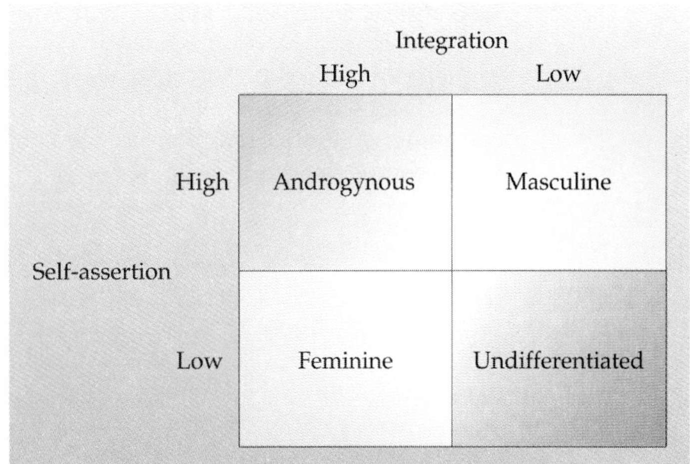

FIGURE 13.3 Classifications of gender-typed roles.

talking about a "feminine woman" we are labeling her according to culturally defined criteria for "femaleness."

Although the standards of maleness and femaleness are undergoing change, *there is still much evidence of traditional stereotypes.* Table 13.1 lists the traditional stereotypes of boys and girls in our culture. These concepts are commonly held by boys and girls themselves (Martin, Wood, & Little, 1990).

There are numerous problems with stereotypes. *One,* they are inaccurate descriptions of those boys and girls who don't fit the stereotypes. To say that all boys are bigger and stronger than girls, or that girls are littler and weaker than boys is simply not true. *Two,* stereotypes define what it means to be a boy or girl within narrowly defined limits, and those who don't match the descriptions are criticized, or even persecuted because they are different. *Three,* stereotypes tend to perpetuate traditional characteristics, many of which may be undesirable. To say that real boys are rough and aggressive and like to fight, that girls are passive, gentle, and don't hit, creates numerous problems. Boys may become too physical and girls too passive. A world full of hostile, aggressive males leads to fighting and wars. A world full of passive females leads to exploitation. Similarly, one of the problems between the sexes is that those very traits of sensitivity and emotionality that women are supposed to exhibit and men are supposed to repress exposes women to the hurts and upsets of intimate living and isolates men from being able to understand why their partners are so upset in the first place. It's difficult for men and women to become real friends and companions.

Four, stereotypes limit the roles that men and women play both at home and work. If women are expected to be breadwinners, as the majority are, then men need to be expected to be homemakers and babytenders (Hilton & Haldeman, 1991). Stereotypes also limit the occupations and professions open to men and women. Men can make good nurses and elementary school teachers (and men elementary school teachers are very much needed) and women can make good scientists and engineers (Jacobs & Eccles, 1992). The important thing is for children to be brought up free to choose their profession.

ANDROGYNY

Androgyny—a mixing of male and female traits in one person

Gender-role concepts are changing slowly. What seems to be developing is a gradual mixing of male and female traits and roles to produce **androgyny** (male and female in one) (Vannoy, 1991). See Figure 13.3. Male traits emphasize *self-assertion:* leadership, dominance, independence, competitiveness, and individualism. Female traits emphasize *integration:* sympathy, affection, and understanding. Children who possess neither masculine nor feminine characteristics are labeled undifferentiated. Androgynous children have a high degree of both self-assertion and integration: of male and female traits (Ford, 1986). Thus, we have four classifications of gender-role types: *masculine, feminine, undifferentiated,* and *androgynous.* Figure 13.3 shows the possible combinations. A person who is high in both self-assertion and integration is androgynous. Similarly, a person who is high in self-assertion and low in integration is masculine; low in self-assertion and high in integration, feminine; and low in both self-assertion and integration, undifferentiated.

Androgynous persons are not sex-typed with respect to roles (although they are distinctly male or female in gender). They match their behavior to the situation rather than being limited by what is culturally defined as male or female. An androgynous male feels comfortable cuddling and caring for a young baby; an androgynous female feels comfortable pumping gas and changing the oil in her car. Androgyny expands the range of human behavior, allowing individuals to cope effectively in a variety of situations.

Moral Development

MORAL JUDGMENT

The process by which children develop moral judgment is extremely interesting (Walker & Taylor, 1991). The most important early research on the development of moral judgment of children is that of Piaget (1948). Piaget emphasized the development of moral judgment as a gradual cognitive process, stimulated by increasing social relationships of children as they get older.

Morality of constraint—conduct coerced by rules or by authority

Piaget's work (1948) is reported in four sections. The *first section* discusses the attitudes of children to the rules of the game when playing marbles. The *second and third* sections report the results of telling children stories that require them to make moral judgments on the basis of the information given. The *last section* reviews his findings in relation to social psychology, particularly to the work of Durkheim (1960), who argues that the sanctions of society are the only source of morality.

In studying children's attitudes to the rules of the game, Piaget concluded that there is, first of all, a **morality of constraint.** In the early stages of moral development, children are constrained by the rules of the game. These rules are coercive because children regard them as inviolable and because they reflect parental authority. Rules constitute a given order of existence and, like parents, must be obeyed without question. (In actual practice, children's attitudes and behavior don't always coincide, however.) Later, according to Piaget, children learn from social interaction a **morality of cooperation,** that rules are not absolute but can be altered by social consensus (Gabennesch, 1990; Helwig, Tisak, & Turiel, 1990). Rules are no longer external laws to be considered sacred because they are laid down by adults, but social creations arrived at through a process of free decision and thus deserving of mutual respect and consent. Children move

Moral development involves learning to make moral judgments, conscience development, and emerging moral behavior.

from *heteronomy* to *autonomy* in making moral judgments (Piaget, 1948).

Piaget also discusses the motives or reasons for judgments. He says there are, first, judgments based solely on the consequences of wrongdoing **(objective judgments)** and, second, judgments that take into account intention or motive **(subjective judgments).** Piaget (1948) claims there is a growing pattern of operational thinking, with children moving from objective to subjective responsibility as they grow older. Piaget would insist that although the two processes overlap, the second gradually supersedes the first. The first stage is superseded when children deem motive or intention more important than consequences.

> The child finds in his brothers and sisters or in his playmates a form of society which develops his desire for cooperation. Then a new type of morality will be created in him, *a morality of reciprocity* and not of *obedience.* This is true morality of intention (p. 133).

Piaget (1948) is careful to note that obedience and cooperation are not always successive stages but nevertheless are formative processes that broadly follow one another: "The first of these processes is the moral constraint of the adult, a constraint which leads to heteronomy and consequently to *moral realism.* The second is cooperation which leads to autonomy" (p. 193). (By moral realism Piaget means submitting meekly to the demands of law.)

Before moral judgment moves from the *heteronomous* to the *autonomous* stage, the self-accepted rules must be internalized. This happens when, in a reciprocal relationship and out of mutual respect, people begin to feel from within the desire to treat others as they themselves would wish to be treated. They pass from *preoperational* to *operational thinking,* from premoral to moral judgment as they internalize the rules they want to follow.

Morality of cooperation—conduct regulated by mutual respect and consent

In the third section of his report, Piaget discusses the child's concept of justice as the child moves from moral restraint to moral cooperation. Two concepts of punishment emerge. The first results from the transgression of an externally imposed regulation; this Piaget calls **expiatory punishment,** which goes hand in hand with constraint and the rules of authority. The second is self-imposed punishment, which comes into operation when the individual, in violation of his or her own conscience, is denied normal social relations and is isolated from the group by his or her own actions. Piaget (1948) calls this the **punishment of reciprocity,** which accompanies cooperation. An ethic of mutual respect, of good as opposed to duty, leads to improved social relationships that are basic to any concept of real equality and reciprocity.

Expiatory punishment—punishment that results from an externally imposed regulation; associated with morality of constraint

Objective judgments—judgments based solely on the consequences of wrongdoing

Subjective judgments—judgments that take into account intention or motive

Punishment of reciprocity—Self-imposed punishment; associated with morality of cooperation

In the last section of his work, Piaget (1948), following Durkheim, asserts that "society is the only source of morality" (p. 326). Morality, to Piaget, consists of a system of rules, but such rules require a sociological context for their development. Thus, "whether the child's moral judgments are heteronomous or autonomous, accepted under pressure or worked out in freedom, this morality is social, and on this point, Durkheim was unquestionably right" (p. 344).

One of the important implications of Piaget's views is that the changes in the moral judgments of children are related to their cognitive growth and to the changes in their social relationships. At first children judge the severity of transgressions by their visible damage or harm. They also develop the concept of **imminent justice:** the child's belief that immoral behavior inevitably brings pain or punishment as a natural consequence of the transgression (Jose, 1990). "If you do wrong, you will certainly be punished." Furthermore, children judge the ap-

Imminent justice—the child's belief that immoral behavior inevitably brings pain or punishment as a natural consequence of the transgression

propriateness of this punishment by its severity rather than by its relevance to the transgression. Only as children get older are they likely to recommend that the transgressor make restitution or that punishment be tailored to fit the wrong done.

As an example, if 6-year-olds are told the story of a little boy who has accidentally dropped a sweet roll in the lake, they are likely to respond: "That's too bad. But it's his own fault for being so clumsy. He shouldn't get another." For them, the punishment implies a crime, and losing a roll in the lake is clearly a punishment in their eyes. They are incapable of taking extenuating circumstances into account. Adolescents, however, make moral judgments on the basis of what Piaget calls **equity,** assigning punishments in accordance with the transgressors' abilities to take responsibility for their crimes.

Equity—assignment of punishments in accordance with transgressors' ability to take responsibility for a crime

Another important implication of Piaget's view is that changes in judgments of children must be related to the changes in their social relationships. As peer-group activity and cooperation increase and as adult constraint decreases, the child becomes more truly an autonomous, cooperative, moral person.

CONSCIENCE DEVELOPMENT

Conscience development has been described as the process of internalization of values. Experts underscore the importance of age 3 as a developmental landmark in the emergence of the "moral self" (Kochanska et al., 1994). The data also indicate that for some signs of early conscience, the important developmental transitions may occur even earlier. Confession and reparation have been described in children as young as 2; for these behaviors, the significant shifts may take place in the second year, paralleling the emergence of self and sensitivity to standards.

The early manifestations of conscience have been divided into two proposed components, *affective discomfort* and *behavioral control.* Affective discomfort appears focused on emotional consequences of wrongdoing and affective response to others; it is expressed in the child's distress, concern, and guilt about the bond with the parent rather than the damage done or the wrongdoing itself; it is also expressed in a wish to be forgiven and reassured of parental love, apology, and emotional empathetic "resonance" with others. The child also shows a capacity for self-regulation prior to wrongdoing and appears "morally vigilant" or concerned about others' moral conduct. This constitutes the development of conscience. Once wrongdoing has occurred, the child confesses and attempts to reverse or repair the damage.

Even in early childhood, the pattern is more pronounced in girls. Even young girls, compared to boys, are more concerned about relationships with others, and they produce more themes of empathy, fear, sadness and concern about relationships in narratives focused on issues of wrongdoing. Girls are more upset after wrongdoing than boys. In addition, girls who are particularly prone to guilt also show highly dependent behaviors, including apology and reassurance seeking. Their mothers report being permissive and rewarding dependency, which is consistent with other findings. (Kochanska et al., 1994).

Efforts have been made to evaluate the effectiveness of discipline in relation to the particular method used. Effectiveness in this case refers to internalization, that is, taking over the values and attitudes of society as one's own so that socially acceptable behavior is motivated, not by anticipation of external consequences, but by intrinsic or internal factors. Both psychoanalytic theory and social learning theory emphasize that internalization develops because of the child's desire to identify with and to imitate positive features of the parent. The child re-creates present experiences by being like the parent. The argument is that parents who rely on love-oriented techniques such as praise, social isolation, and withdrawal of affection will have children with higher levels of conscience development because the children have internalized parental standards and values. Parents who rely on object-oriented techniques such as tangible rewards, deprivation of material objects or privileges, and physical punishment motivate their children to hide, flee, or find other ways of avoiding punishment, reactions that do not foster adoption of parental standards. Parents who rely solely on object-oriented or power-assertive approaches are less likely to be successful in promoting resistance to temptation, guilt over antisocial behavior, reparation after deviation, altruism, and high levels of moral reasoning—all regarded as indexes of the internalization of moral values. Parents who are most successful tend toward a greater use of reasoning or induction. Of particular importance is other-oriented induction, which is reasoning that draws children's attention to the effects of their misdemeanors on others, thereby sensitizing them to events beyond the personal consequences of their actions. Discipline must be authoritive rather than authoritarian or permissive. Authoritive parents set firm controls on the behavior of their children and make strong demands for maturity, but they are willing to listen to the children's point of view and even to adjust to their behavior accordingly. Authoritive parents are most successful in producing children who are socially competent and responsible; that is, children who have accepted parental dictates as their own, without sacrificing curiosity, originality, and spontaneity. Parents who tend to be harshly and arbitrarily authoritarian or power-assertive in their parenting practices are less likely to be successful (Grusec & Goodnow, 1994).

Before internalization can take place, the child must perceive the parents' message, and this perception must be accurate. Secondly, the child must also accept the perceived message. The accuracy of perception will depend upon getting the child's attention and on the clarity or redundancy of the parents' message. Acceptance, in contrast, is seen to depend especially on the warmth of the relationship between parent and child. Warmth affects the occurrence of acceptance, but not necessarily the accuracy of perception. Clarification is necessary if the child's failure to internalize is the result of not having fully heard or understood the parental message.

Figure 13.4 shows those parables that are relevant to an accurate perception of the message and to the acceptance of the message. Accurate perception depends upon clear, redundant, consistent messages, which are fitted to existing schemas that capture the child's attention, require decoding that prompts comprehension, and in which the rules are made clear and their importance to the parent is signaled. Positive intentions are necessary before the child can gain an accurate perception of the message. The child who perceives the good will of the parent and the importance of the message to the parent is more likely to pay attention, promoting the chances of accurate perception.

There are also variables relevant to the acceptance of the parents' message. In Figure 13.4 these variables are grouped according to their impact on (a) the extent to which the child perceives parental behavior to be appropriate, (b) the child's motivation, and (c) the degree to which the child sees the value or standard as self-generated. The first group has to do with a child's evaluation of the acceptability for the parents' intervention. Acceptance is especially likely to be influenced by the child's judgment that the parents' actions are appropriate to the nature of the misdeed, that the parents' intervention has truth and value, that due process has been observed, and that expected procedures have been followed, seen as well intentioned, and fitted to the child's temperament, mood, and developmental status.

The second group deals with the extent to which the child is motivated to accept the parental message. High degrees of empathetic arousal, threats to feelings of security, and the extent to which the value is perceived as important to the parent are important contributors to acceptance here. If the child's desire to identify with a parent is promoted, the desire for reciprocal compliance is promoted, and threats to autonomy minimized, the child is more likely to be willing to accept the message.

The last group of events involve variables that may lead to feelings on the child's part that their value is self-generated with the feeling promoting acceptance. Overall, internalization takes place to the extent that the child has an accurate perception of the message and has accepted that message (Grusec & Goodnow, 1994; Dunn, Brown, & Maguire, 1995).

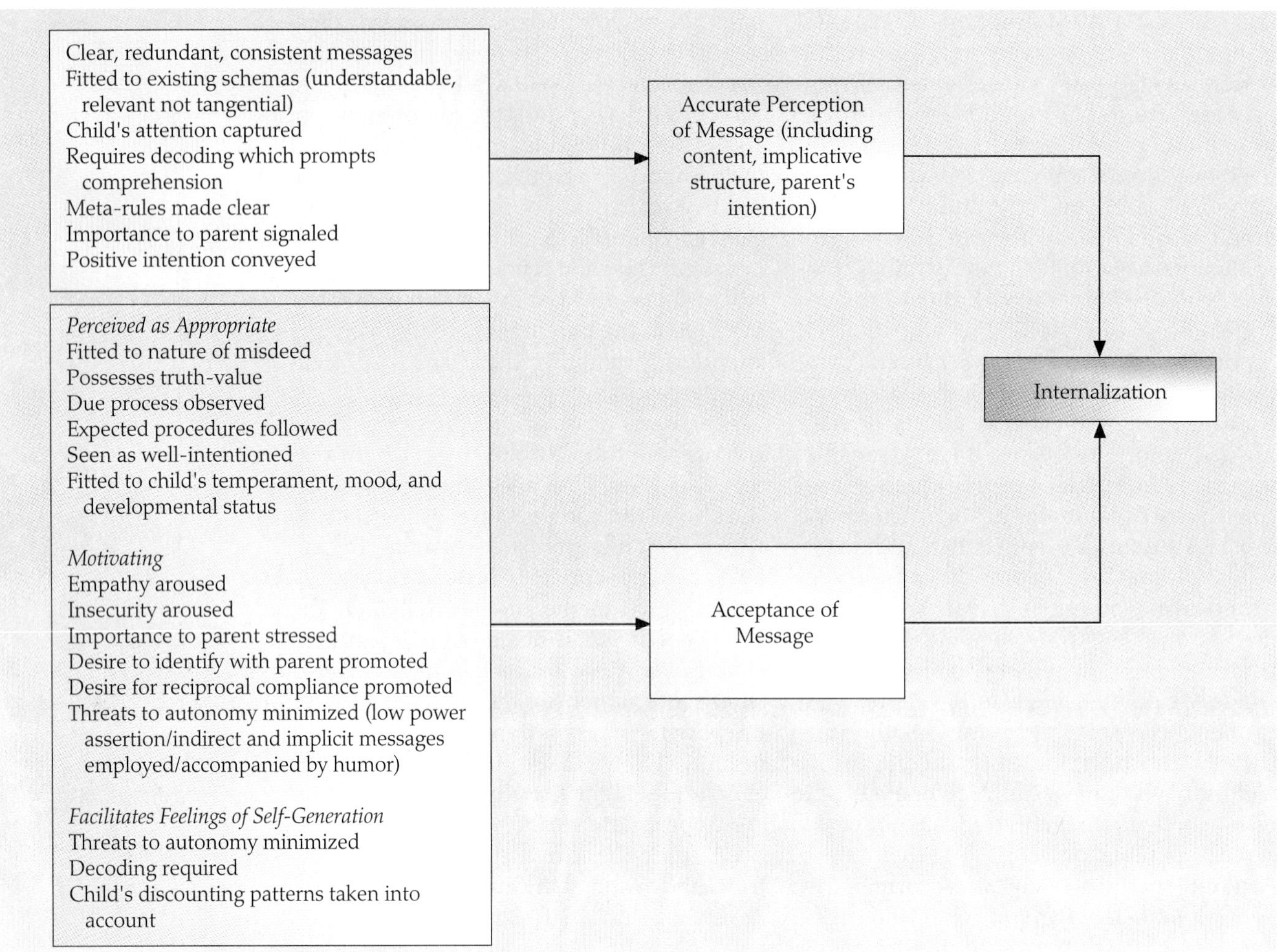

FIGURE 13.4 Features of parental disciplinary actions promoting accurate perception and acceptance (internalization) of a parent's message.

From J. E. Grusec and J. J. Goodnow (1994). "Impact of parental discipline methods on the child's internalization of values: A reconceptualization of current points of view." *Developmental Psychology, 30,* 4–19.

MORAL BEHAVIOR

So far, we have discussed the development of moral judgment and conscience. *Moral judgment is the knowledge of right or wrong.* It is quite evident from experience that knowing the right thing to do and doing it are two different things. The discussion of moral development profits from a clear separation of moral judgment and moral motivation. *Moral motivation is the strength of desire to do right,* the intensity of feelings in relationship to doing right. Another facet, *moral inhibition, as it is manifested in a strong conscience, is the strength of desire or feelings not to do wrong.* Moral behavior depends on both positive moral motivation and the strength of inhibitions against doing wrong. *One study showed that the higher moral motive strength and temperamental inhibitions were, the greater the possibility of moral behavior* (Asendorpf & Nunner-Winkler, 1992). The study showed through group analysis of children low or high in moral motivation and inhibition that cheating or noncheating could be predicted with a rate of about 90 percent accuracy. *Moral behavior in this study was defined as behavior that did not transgress rules that children clearly knew to be valid.* In this study, when the effects of inhibition and moral motive strength were combined, the prediction of immoral behavior became particularly powerful.

Another study investigated children's concepts, standards, and evaluative reactivity to lying or telling the truth about misdeeds (Bussey, 1992). Children in this study were preschool and second- and

PARENTING ISSUES

Taking Small Children to Adult Worship Services

Some parents say: "I'm going to take my children to worship from the time they are young. Then they will get in the habit of going." Other adults say: "I was forced to go when I was growing up and I hated it. I'm never going to do that to my children." Assuming that parents want to give their children a firm foundation of religious teaching, what's the wisest approach?

There are some negative aspects of taking small children to adult worship services. The most important consideration is that children are bored; they don't understand what is going on; they are learning to be inattentive, so they either do something else or fall asleep. They are conditioned not to like going to adult worship services and not to get anything out of them.

Letting children stay home until they are old enough to understand adult services is not the answer either. This teaches them that church, synagogue, mosque, or temple is not important and they miss out on religious instruction during many of their formative years.

One positive approach is to enroll children in religious classes that meet during the adult service. These should be classes that are divided according to age groups with programs appropriate for each age level. If children like to go and they are learning from the experience, they not only are growing in understanding, but they are also developing positive attitudes and feelings toward going that carry over into adulthood. One mother commented: "Every time we go by the church, my two-year-old says: "Horsey, horsey." The child had made an association between the church and riding on the horsey in the nursery, where she was learning one of the most important religious lessons of all: how to get along with other children. She was getting a helpful beginning.

Worship in church has become part of the tradition of this family.

fifth-graders. The study produced clear evidence of the development of moral standards associated with lying and storytelling in all children. Children were more disapproving of lies than of truthfulness about misdeeds. All children evaluated lies about misdeeds significantly more negatively than the misdeeds themselves. Truthful statements were, however, not evaluated by preschoolers more favorably than misdeeds. While young children appreciated the naughtiness of lying, it was more difficult for them to appreciate the value of truthfulness about misdeeds. Older children were able to appreciate the value of truthfulness.

Punishment affected the moral judgment of the preschoolers but not of the older children. Preschoolers placed more value on statements that led to punishment for the misdeed than they did on statements that did not lead to punishment. This agrees with social cognitive theory in *which observable physical consequences are predicted to be major determinants of preschoolers' judgments of lies and truthful statements.*

The study demonstrated two important developmental changes. *First, children react initially with censure for lying but, over time, learn to react with feelings of pride for truthfulness.* As a result, eventually children's reactions to lies are negative, with truthful statements, reactions are positive. *Second, there's a change from children's reliance on punishment as a basis for their moral judgments to a greater reliance on internal evaluative reactions.* This greater reliance on internal rather than external factors, with increasing cognitive maturity and social experience, is consistent with the development of self-regulation. Self-evaluative reactions are expected to promote congruence between moral standards and moral conduct. Ideally, if socialization is successful, there is a transfer from external forms of control to more internal controls, so that there is less reliance on external factors such as punishment.

There are important implications in these ideas. *Young children whose conduct is not regulated to the same extent as older children by internal evaluative reactions, particularly positive evaluative reactions, are helped by adults actively encouraging and rewarding truthfulness.* If children anticipate punishment for admitting to a misdeed, there's little incentive for them to tell the truth. Parents and other caregivers need to encourage children to accept responsibility for misdeeds and simultaneously feel proud of their truthfulness. Furthermore, adults can promote the development of self-evaluative feelings that unite children's thought and action through the use of reasoning techniques. Punishment may teach fear of doing something wrong, but reasoning can help children to want to do right by feeling good about themselves (Bussey, 1992).

Summary

1. The psychosocial development of children and youth can be divided into four stages: autosociality, childhood heterosocialty, homosociality, and adolescent and adult heterosocialty.
2. Children move through progressive stages of social development as they get older. Two-year-olds play alongside one another. Three-year-olds begin group play; four- and five-year-olds gradually develop more socially competent interactions with peers.
3. There is much intermingling of sexes and races, although both boys and girls prefer to play with others of the same sex.
4. The play of preschoolers has been divided into six categories of play involvement: unoccupied play, solitary play, onlooker play, parallel play, associative play, and cooperative play.
5. Play may also be divided into categories according to the type of activity: sensory play, motor play, rough-and-tumble play, cognitive play, dramatic or pretend play, and games and competitive sports.
6. The older children become, the more important companionship with friends becomes. Popularity, gangs and clubs, competition, and cruelty and aggression all become important considerations during middle childhood.
7. Some children are rejected and lonely, which puts a great deal of stress on them.
8. Unliked children are socially invisible; disliked children behave in socially unaccepted ways.
9. Some children can be very cruel to others. A small group is constantly targeted for victimization.
10. Social cognition is the capacity to understand social relationships, an ability that is very important in getting along with others.
11. Robert Selman outlined 5 stages of development of social cognition: the egocentric undifferentiated stage, differentiated or subjective perspective-taking stage, self-reflective thinking or reciprocal perspective-taking stage, third-person or mutual perspective-taking stage, and the in-depth and societal perspective-taking stage.
12. The family plays an important role in the development of social competence.
13. According to the social processing perspective, social competence occurs as a result of five sequential processes: encoding, accurate interpretation of cues, response generation, response evaluation, and behavioral enactment.
14. Television is an important socializing influence. Experts are particularly concerned about its effect on childhood ag-

gression, family interaction, and cognitive development; and about the effects of commercials and video games.

15. Social realism rather than factuality appears to be important in emotional arousal.
16. Television, especially well-designed children's programs, can have a positive effect on children.
17. Gender refers to our biological sex; gender roles are outward expressions of masculinity or feminity.
18. There are three important influences on gender-role development: biological, cognitive, and environmental.
19. Gender-role development begins at birth and continues for many years. Children reach gender-role constancy by age 7.
20. Gender stereotypes are inaccurate descriptions of all boys and girls; boys and girls who don't match the descriptions are criticized; stereotypes tend to perpetuate undesirable characteristics; and they limit the roles that men and women play at home and at work.
21. Androgyny is a gradual mixing of male and female traits. Male characteristics emphasize self-assertion; female emphasize integration. Androgynous persons manifest both sets of traits.
22. According to Piaget, children develop moral judgment in a series of steps. They move from a morality of constraint to a morality of cooperation; from heteronomy to autonomy; from making objective judgments to making subjective judgments; from a morality of obedience to a morality of reciprocity; and from a concept of expiatory punishment to one of punishment of reciprocity. They also move from a concept of imminent justice to a concept of equity.
23. Conscience development involves the internalization of values.
24. Before the child can internalize values, the child must perceive and accept them.
25. Moral behavior depends on moral motivation—the strength of desire to do right—and on moral inhibition—the strength of desire not to do wrong. As children get older, they rely more on internal evaluative reactions and less on the threat of punishment. Adults can encourage the internalization of values by rewarding and encouraging moral behavior.

Key Terms

Adolescent and adult heterosociality *p. 342*
Androgyny *p. 364*
Autosociality *p. 342*
Childhood heterosociality *p. 342*
Differentiated or subjective perspective-taking stage *p. 352*
Egocentric undifferentiated stage *p. 352*
Equity *p. 366*
Estrogen *p. 359*
Expiatory punishment *p. 365*
Gender *p. 357*
Gender constancy *p. 362*
Gender roles *p. 357*
Gender stereotypes *p. 362*
Homosociality *p. 342*
Imminent justice *p. 365*
In-depth and societal perspective-taking stage *p. 352*
Morality of constraint *p. 364*
Morality of cooperation *p. 365*
Objective judgments *p. 365*
Punishment of reciprocity *p. 365*
Self-reflective thinking or reciprocal perspective-taking stage *p. 352*
Social cognition *p. 351*
Social role taking *p. 352*
Subjective judgments *p. 365*
Testosterone *p. 359*
Third-person or mutual perspective-taking stage *p. 352*

Discussion Questions

1. What are the principal problems of social development of preschoolers, and of elementary school-age children?
2. What are your views on the effects of television on children?
3. Whate stereotypes of masculine men or feminine women do you think are helpful; what ones do you object to and why?
4. What do you think of androgynous personalities? Would you want your child to be androgynous in personality development?
5. What can parents do to raise their children as moral persons? How do you feel about enrolling your children in religious school activities from the time they are little? How do you feel about taking young children to adult worship services?

Suggested Readings

Asher, S. R., & Coie, J. D. (Eds.). (1991). *Peer rejection in childhood.* New York: Cambridge University Press. The nature of peer rejection and ways to help.

Askew, W., & Ross, C. (1988). *Boys don't cry: Boys and sexism in education.* Philadelphia: Open University Press. Sexism and how it can be overcome.

Bergen, D. (Ed.). (1988). *Play as a medium for learning and development.* Portsmouth, NH: Heinemann. Various aspects of play.

Damon, W. (1988). *The moral child.* New York: Free Press. The nature of moral development and moral education.

Doyle, J. A., & Paludi, M. A. (1991). *Male and female* (2nd ed.). Dubuque, IA: Wm. C. Brown Publishers. Gender and the female role.

Gilligan, C. (1982). *In a different voice.* Cambridge, MA: Harvard University Press. Pioneering work on women and their moral development.

Gottman, J. M., & Parker, J. G. (Eds.). (1987). *Conversations of friends.* New York: Cambridge University Press. Children's friendships.

Huesmann, L. R., & Eron, L. D. (Eds.). (1986). *Television and the aggressive child: A cross-national comparison.* Hillsdale, NJ: Erlbaum. TV violence and aggression in children.

Liegert, R. M. & Sprakin, J. N. (1988). *The early window: Effects of television on children and youth* (3rd ed.). Elmsford, NY: Pergamon. Updated research on subject.

Paley, V. G. (1984). *Boys and girls: Superheroes in the doll corner.* Chicago: University of Chicago Press. Kindergarten children learn what it means to be a boy or girl.

Reinisch, J. M., Rosenblum, L. A., & Sanders, S. A. (Eds.). (1987). *Masculinity/feminity.* New York: Oxford University Press. A collection of articles.

Rubin, Z. 1980). *Children's friendships.* Cambridge, MA: Harvard University Press. Helpful account.

Schaffer, H. R. (1984). *The child's entry into a social world.* New York: Academic Press. Development in social context, especially that of the family.

Selman, R. L. (1980). *The growth of interpersonal understanding.* New York: Academic Press. Social cognition.

Singer, D. G., & Singer, J. L. (1990). *The house of make-believe: Children's play and the developing imagination.* Cambridge, MA: Harvard University Press. Children's fantasy play.

Stein, S. B. (1983). *Girls and boys: The limits of nonsexist childrearing.* New York: Charles Scribner's Sons. Child-rearing practices and sexism.

Winn, M. (1985). *The plug-in drug* (rev. ed.). New York: Viking. Harmful effects of TV.

Part Four

ADOLESCENT DEVELOPMENT

Perspectives on Adolescent Development: Meaning, Psychic Disequilibrium, Identity, Developmental Tasks, and Anthropologists' Views

Chapter 14

Introduction

In this chapter we are concerned with describing adolescence and a number of terms related to it: maturity, puberty, pubescence, juvenile, and youth. The chapter begins with a discussion of these concepts.

Another way to understand adolescence is to approach it from various points of view: from the studies of the psychobiologist, psychiatrist, psychologist, social psychologist, and anthropologist. This chapter presents the views of theorists from each of these disciplines: psychobiological view—G. Stanley Hall; psychoanalytical view—Anna Freud; sociopsychoanalytical view—Erik Erikson; psychosociological view—Robert Havighurst; and anthropological view—Margaret Mead. By understanding different theories of adolescence, the student can gain a more comprehensive view.

The Meaning of Adolescence

ADOLESCENCE

The word *adolescence* comes from the Latin verb *adolescere,* which means "to grow up" or "to grow to maturity" (Golinko, 1984). Adolescence is a period of growth beginning with puberty and ending at the beginning of adulthood; it is a transitional stage between childhood and adulthood (Matter, 1984). The period has been likened to a bridge between childhood and adulthood over which individuals must pass before they can take their places as grown adults (see Fig. 14.1). In general, the total period of adolescence has been prolonged in industrial societies as the time span of dependency has increased. The transition from childhood to adulthood is complicated (Hammer & Vaglum, 1990), and the amount of time one takes to pass through this stage is variable, but most adolescents eventually complete the passage.

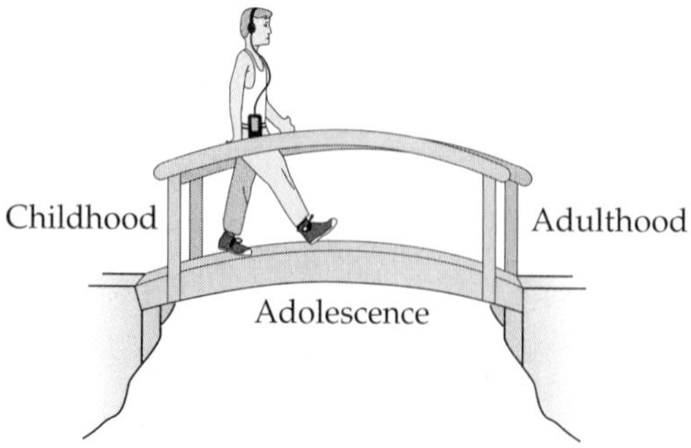

Puberty—the period or age at which a person reaches sexual maturity and becomes capable of reproduction

Pubescence—the whole period during which the physical changes related to sexual maturation take place

Maturity—the time in life when one becomes an adult physically, emotionally, socially, intellectually, and spiritually

Childhood Adolescence Adulthood

FIGURE 14.1 Adolescence as a bridge between childhood and adulthood.

PUBERTY AND PUBESCENCE

Puberty is the period or age at which a person reaches sexual maturity and becomes capable of having children.

Pubescence is used to denote the whole period during which physical changes relative to sexual maturation are taking place. Literally, it means becoming downy or hairy, describing the growth of body hair that accompanies sexual maturation. Puberty is accompanied not only by biological changes, but by psychological and social changes as well (Adams, Day, Dyk, & Frede, 1992; Lerner, 1992). For example, an adolescent who is an early maturer not only changes in physical appearance, but in friendships and social interests as well.

MATURITY

Maturity is that age, state, or time of life at which a person is considered fully developed socially, intellectually, emotionally, physically, and spiritually. Maturity is not reached in all of these characteristics at the same time. Youths who become physically mature at age 12 are usually not mature in other ways. A person may be mature socially, but still be immature emotionally.

JUVENILE PERIOD

The word **juvenile** is a legal term describing an individual who is not accorded adult status in the eyes of the law. In most states, this is a person under 18 years of age. The legal rights of 18-year-olds vary from state to state, however. The Twenty-sixth Amendment gave them the right to vote. They may obtain credit in their own names at some stores or banks, whereas others require cosigners. This depends on the degree to which they have established a good credit rating in their own names. Many landlords will not rent to minors. Youths have to be 21 years of age to purchase alcoholic beverages. In some states, 18-year-olds can marry without parental consent; in other states they have to wait until they are older. In Colorado, adolescents can leave home at age 16, but do not attain full legal rights until age 21. The net result is confusion over their status. When do they fully become adults? Some authorities feel that adolescents have to wait too many years to "get into the club" ("Legal Rights," (1976).

Adolescence is a period of growth beginning with puberty and ending at the beginning of adulthood.

Keniston (1970) suggested the law recognize an intermediate legal status between age 15 and 18 when adolescents are accorded more rights than children but fewer than those of adults. Keniston conceptualized a new stage of life, that of *youth*, which he defined as a developmental period that would follow adolescence. In general, his suggestion was never adopted. In modern terminology, however, youth refers to the younger generation, usually adolescence (Sebald, 1984). It is used in this latter sense in this book.

Juvenile—one who is not yet considered an adult in the eyes of the law

Adolescence and Psychic Disequilibrium

STORM AND STRESS

G. Stanley Hall (1904), the founder of the child-study movement in North America and the first Ph.D. in psychology in the United States, first described adolescence as a period of great "storm and stress," corresponding to the time when the human race was in a turbulent, transitional stage on the way to becoming civilized. Hall said the causes of this storm and stress in adolescents are biological, resulting from changes at puberty. To Hall, puberty represents a time of emotional upset and instability in which the adolescent's moods oscillate between energy and lethargy, joy and depression, or egotism and self-depreciation. The end of adolescence marks a birth of adult traits, corresponding to the beginning of modern civilization. Although Hall was a psychologist, his explanation of the changes at adolescence was biological.

Researchers no longer believe that storm and stress are inevitable consequences of adolescence. Many studies have contributed to debunking this idea. The stereotype of adolescence as a tumultuous period of life still appears in the popular media; but, as a result of recent research, adoles-

FOCUS

Rites of Passage

In some cultures, when a child reaches puberty, ceremonies are conducted to celebrate the passage from childhood to maturity. Once the child successfully passes the prescribed tests, he or she is accepted as a member of adult society.

The ceremonies are often stressful and painful. The most common rite for boys is *circumcision,* usually performed with a sharp stone knife. A tribe in the South Pacific requires that boys leap headfirst from a 100-foot-high platform built in a tree, with nothing but 90-foot-long vines tied to their feet. The vine catches them up short just before their head hits the ground. Sometimes, miscalculations result in permanent injury or death. If the boy is brave enough to go through this experience, he is considered worthy to be an adult. The Mandan Indian tribe, living on the plains of the United States, tested the endurance of their pubertal sons by piercing their pectoral muscles under their breasts with sharp sticks and then suspending the boys from the lodge poles by ropes attached to the sticks. Boys who could endure the longest were considered the bravest.

Initiation rites for girls center around the attainment of reproductive capabilities as marked by the onset of menstruation. The girls are prepared ahead of time by instruction on domestic and parental duties, sexual matters, and modes of dress. Some ceremonies are designed to ensure their fertility.

cence is now considered much more differentiated. The belief that psychological turmoil is normal in adolescence has an unfortunate consequence in that it is often assumed that young people with psychological problems will grow out of them. The evidence is now clear that psychological difficulties in adolescence usually persist and should be treated. They seldom disappear by themselves (Petersen, 1993). One study of fifth- to ninth-graders reported higher rates of negative emotions among adolescents than among preadolescents, but these higher rates of daily distress were partly attributable to the greater number of negative life events encountered by some youths as they got older (Larson & Ham, 1993).

PSYCHIC CONFLICT

Anna Freud (1946), daughter of Sigmund Freud, also characterized adolescence as a period of psychic disequilibrium, emotional conflict, and erratic behavior. On the one hand, adolescents are egotistic and self-centered, and they believe that everyone's attention is focused on them. On the other hand, they are capable of forgetting themselves while they focus on the needs of others and engage in charitable projects. They can become involved in intense infatuations, but can fall out of love just as suddenly. They sometimes want to be with others in their social group, but the next day seek solitude. They oscillate between rebellion and conformity. They are not only selfish and materialistic, but also morally idealistic. They are ascetic, yet hedonistic; inconsiderate and rude, yet loving and tender. They fluctuate between overflowing confidence and fearful self-doubt; between indefatigable enthusiasm and tired indifference (Freud, 1946).

According to Anna Freud, the reason for this conflicting behavior is sexual maturation at puberty, which causes psychic disequilibrium. At puberty, there is a marked increase in the instinctual drives (the *id*), including a greater interest in genitality and sexual impulses. There is also a rise in other instinctual drives at puberty: exhibitionism and rebelliousness increase; physical hunger intensifies; oral and anal interests reappear; and habits of cleanliness give way to dirt and disorder. Instinctual forces that have remained latent since early childhood reappear at puberty (Freud, 1946, p. 159).

The increasing demands of the id during adolescence create conflict with the *superego* that the *ego* tries to resolve. The task of the ego is allow the instinctual drives of the id to be satisfied, within the limits of societal expectations as represented by the superego. The ego is a person's power of reasoning. The superego is the conscience that results from internalizing the social values of one's parents and society, according to Anna Freud. The increase in instinctual drives during adolescence directly challenges the reasoning abilities and the powers of conscience of the individual. Open conflict breaks out between the id and superego, and the ego has trouble keeping the peace. If the ego takes the side of the id, "no trace will be left of the previous character of the individual and the entrance into adult life will be marked by a riot of uninhibited gratification of instinct" (Freud, 1946, p. 163). If the ego sides only with the superego, the id impulses are confined within the narrow limits prescribed for a child. Keeping instinctual forces suppressed requires constant expenditure of psychic energy, because defense mechanisms and other measures are used to hold the id in check. *If this id–ego–superego conflict is not resolved during adolescence, emotional disturbance results.*

Anna Freud described the methods of defense (the *defense mechanisms*) the ego employs to remain in control. The ego denies, rationalizes, or projects the instincts on to others to allow the id to have its way. If conflict over behavior remains, anxiety may result, causing phobias and hysterical symptoms. The appearance of asceticism and intellectualism during adolescence is symptomatic of the mistrust of all instinctual impulses. The rise of neurotic symptoms and excessive inhibitions during adolescence may be a sign of the success of the ego and superego at the expense of the individual.

Anna Freud suggests, however, that *harmony among the id, ego, and superego is possible and does occur finally in most normal adolescents.* The superego needs to be developed during the latency period—but not to the extent that it inhibits the instincts too much, causing extreme guilt and anxiety. The ego needs to be sufficiently strong and wise to mediate the conflict (Freud, 1946).

Adolescence and Identity Achievement

COMPONENTS OF IDENTITY

According to Erikson (1950, 1959) *the chief psychosocial task of adolescence is the achievement of identity* (Archer, 1990a, b; Bilsker & Marcia, 1991; Raskin, 1990; Rotheram-Borus, 1990a; Waterman, 1990). Identity has many components (Rogow, Marcia, & Slugoski, 1983)—*sexual, social, physical, psychological, moral, ideological,* and *vocational characteristics*—that make up the total self. Thus, individuals may be identified by their physical characteristics, looks, and build; by their biological sex and enactment of gender roles; by their skills in social interaction and membership in groups; by their career choice and achievement; by their political alignment, religious affiliations, morals, values, and philosophies; and by their ethnic identity (Phinney & Alipuria, 1990), personality characteristics, psychological adjustment, and mental health. Identity is personal and individual: it is not only the "I," but also, socially and collectively, the "we" within groups and society (Hoare, 1991). Adolescents who are able to accept themselves, who have developed a positive identity, are more likely to

Achieving sexual identity is one of the psychosocial tasks of adolescence.

be mentally healthy than those who have a negative identity or do not like themselves (Goldman, Rosenzweig, & Lutter, 1980).

Some components of identity are established before others (Dellas & Jernigan, 1990). Physical and sexual components of the self seem to be formulated earliest. Early adolescents are concerned with their body image and sexual identity. Later they become concerned about choosing a vocation and about moral values and ideologies. Similarly, they must deal with their social identities fairly early in their development.

Vocational, ideological, and moral identities are formulated gradually (Logan, 1983). After adolescents reach the formal operational stage of cognitive growth and development, they are able to explore alternative ideas and vocations in systematic ways. The exploration of occupational alternatives is the most immediate and concrete task as adolescents select their high school program and decide whether to continue their education after high school (Kroger, 1993). Political and religious ideologies are usually examined during late adolescence, especially during the college years, but may be formulated over a period of many years of adulthood (Blustein & Palladino, 1991).

Identity achievement—that state resulting from having gone through a crisis in the search for identity and having made a commitment

Moratorium—a period of standing back as one continues to search for an identity

Psychosocial moratorium—a socially sanctioned period between childhood and adulthood during which the individual is free to experiment to find a socially acceptable identity and role

PSYCHOSOCIAL MORATORIUM

Erikson invented the term **psychosocial moratorium** to describe a period of adolescence during which the individual may stand back, analyze, and experiment with various roles without assuming any one role. According to Erikson (1968), the length of adolescence and the degree of emotional conflict experienced by adolescents will vary among different societies. However, failure to establish identity during this time causes self-doubt and role confusion that may trigger previously latent psychological disturbances. Some individuals may withdraw or turn to drugs or alcohol to relieve anxiety. Lack of a clear identity and lack of personality integration can also be observed in the chronic delinquent (Muuss, 1988b).

IDENTITY STATUSES

In the mid-1960s, an extensive body of research had emerged and validated Erikson's psychological construct. Among the many studies of Erikson's concepts, those by James Marcia have been particularly influential (Marcia, 1966, 1976, 1989). Marcia built his model upon three assumptions derived from Erikson's theory. *First,* formation of ego identity involves the establishment of firm commitments in such basic identity areas as a vocation or selection of a mate. *Second,* the task of forming identity demands a period of exploration, questioning, and decision making, a period called an identity crisis. *Third,* Western society fosters a period, a psychosocial moratorium, during which the adolescent may experiment with roles and beliefs so as to establish a coherent personal identity (Bilsker, 1992).

From these assumptions, Marcia formulated four identity statuses that are models of dealing with the identity issue characteristic of late adolescence (Marcia, 1980). The statuses are determined by whether there are established commitments and whether there has been a period of exploration and decision making.

The four identity statuses are as follows. **Identity achievement** is the most developmentally advanced status. The individual has gone through a period of exploration of alternatives and has made well-defined commitments. A **moratorium** precedes identity achievement. Here the person is in the exploration period with commitments only vaguely formed. The word *moratorium* means a period of delay granted to someone who is not yet ready to make a decision or assume an obligation. Adolescence is a period of exploration of alternatives before commitments are made. **Foreclosure** refers to the individual who has undergone no, or very little, exploration and remains firmly committed to childhood-based values. Foreclosure subjects have not experienced a crisis, but they have made commitments to occupations and ideologies that are not a result of their own searching, but are ready-made and handed down to them, frequently by parents. Finally, **identity diffusion,** the least developmentally advanced of the statuses, encompasses persons who, whether or not they have explored alternatives, are uncommitted to any definite directions in their lives (Marcia, 1987). Identity-diffused subjects have not experienced a crisis, nor have they made any commitment to a religion, political philosophy, sex role, occupation, or personal standards of behavior (Archer & Waterman, 1990). They have not experienced an identity crisis in relation to any of these issues, nor gone through the period of searching, reevaluating, and considering alternatives. Diffusion is developmentally the most unsophisticated identity status, and is usually a normal characteristic of early adolescence.

Adolescents may try out many roles before occupational identity is achieved.

Foreclosure—establishing an identity without going through a crisis or without searching. Adopting an identity as prescribed by someone else

The identity statuses do not always develop in exact sequence. It was initially believed that a developmental progression would be the norm: most adolescents would enter the identity crisis from the foreclosure status, moving in to a moratorium phase, out of which the achievement status would be attained. Diffusion status during adolescence was seen as an aberration in this natural progression—hopefully, a transient one.

Identity diffusion—the situation of the individual who has not experienced an identity crisis nor explored meaningful alternatives in trying to find an identity

Three important variations from this developmental sequence have been observed. *First,* some individuals seem never to make the transition to the moratorium and identity achievement statuses, remaining firmly entrenched within the foreclosure status. *Secondly, a significant number of individuals enter adolescence in the diffusion status; some remain diffused. Third,* certain individuals who attain an achievement status appeared to have regressed to a lower status upon follow-up, years later (Marcia, 1989). The nature of such a regression to a developmentally prior status is puzzling. Such a regression suggests that *individuals may go through the developmental identity sequence more than once during a lifetime.* A person may have found identity achievement at a certain period of life, then later in life go through another moratorium stage, or a stage of identity diffusion, before identity achievement is again accomplished (Stephen, Fraser, & Marcia, 1992).

ETHNIC IDENTITY

Ethnic identity is the sum total of group members' feelings about those values, symbols, and common histories that identify them as a distinct group. Ethnic identity development is an essential human need. It provides a sense of belonging and a sense of historical continuity for an individual (Smith, 1991). In high school and college students, ethnic identity appears to consist of a single factor, including three intercorrelated compo-

LIVING ISSUES

Women and Identity

As we have seen, Marcia postulated four potential outcomes of the identity development stage: foreclosure, achievement, moratorium, and diffusion. Some researchers have suggested that identity development is essentially the same regardless of gender (Streitmatter, 1993). Some researchers, such as Gilligan, Ward, Taylor, Bardige (1988), suggest that the path of identity development for females may be different than that for males. Gilligan and colleagues argue that Erikson's theory (Erikson, 1959) embodied in the "Eight Stages of Man," is based upon a developmental model that is biased to the point of excluding the developmental process of females. The essence of Gilligan's work is the idea that females tend to define themselves through their relationships with others, while males follow "traditional masculine" lines of self-definition according to their own occupational selves (Streitmatter, 1993). Identity development for females is quite different from that of males. Intimacy is a primacy issue for females.

Still other researchers, especially Josselson (1987), used Marcia's identity research methods to examine how women proceed through Erikson's identity stage and to propose a theoretical model of women's identity development. In so doing, Josselson has sought to integrate opposing viewpoints. She conducted initial interviews with college seniors in the early 1970s and followed their life courses by scheduling second interviews with them in 1980 (Enns, 1991). Approximately one-quarter of Josselson's sample chose a traditional status that was originally identified by Erikson as a universal pattern for women's identity resolution. The pattern was foreclosure in which women often defined their identity in terms of the successful search for a mate. In general, they had high scores on measures of mental health, but showed little evidence of a separate self-definition.

Women with an achievement identity status consciously tested their identities, built self-defined paths, and demonstrated flexibility in integrating needs for connection and self-assertion. For them, personal achievement and occupation often became the medium for expressing values that were formed in the context of supportive relationships.

Moratorium women gave up traditional, safe, relational anchors to try out exploratory identities and atypical roles, but they also had greater difficulty resolving identity issues. When they were in their thirties, moratorium women occasionally adopted a self-chosen achievement status, but they often experienced identity diffusion or opted to go back to a foreclosurelike status. Women who displayed characteristics associated with foreclosure or achievement showed higher levels of mental health than women in moratorium or diffusion statuses. Apparently, women were discouraged by social and family pressures to assume extended exploratory identities: If identity was not achieved by the end of the college years, pressure to return to the safety of childhood experiences was strong. For women, the social expectations, choices, self-reflection, conflict, ambivalence, and isolation associated with choosing nontraditional roles was costly.

Josselson's (1987) observation that significant relationships, rather than work, provided the primary anchor for women's identity is disquieting in light of the occupational changes that have emerged in the wake of the feminist movement.

Many women find identity through marriage and parenthood.

Acculturation—the adjustment of minority groups to the dominant group culture

nents: *positive ethnic attitudes, ethnic identity achievement,* and *ethnic behaviors* (Phinney, 1992). **Acculturation** is the adjustment of minority groups to the culture of the dominant group (Sodowsky, Lai, & Plake, 1991).

The problem for the adolescent from immigrant or ethnic minority families is that the culture into which they were born is not always valued or appreciated by the culture in which they are raised (Feldman, Mont-Reynaud, &

Native Americans, like those from other ethnic groups, are torn by the conflict between cultures.

Rosenthal, 1992). In the early stages of forging an identity, ethnic minorities and immigrants often find conflict between their ethnic culture and the values of the larger society in which they live. The central question is the way in which minority ethnic groups relate to the dominant culture and to one another.

There are four possible ways in which ethnic group members can participate in a culturally diverse society. *Assimilation* is the outcome when ethnic group members choose to identify solely with the culture of the dominant society, and to relinquish all ties to their ethnic culture. *Integration* is characterized by strong identification and involvement with both the dominant society's culture and the traditional ethnic culture. *Separation* involves exclusive focus on the cultural values and practices of the ethnic group and little or no interaction with the dominant society. *Marginality* is defined by the absence or loss of one's culture of origin and the lack of involvement with the dominant society.

Which type of participation contributes most to the positive development of self-esteem and identity in adolescence? One study of high school and college students from a diverse inner-city school sought to answer this question. The students were Asian, black, Hispanic, of mixed background, and white (Phinney, Chavira, & Williamson, 1992). *The results indicate that among the four acculturation options, integration results in better psychological adjustment and higher self-esteem.* The positive relationship between self-esteem and endorsement of integration indicates that a more positive self-concept is associated with identification with both one's own culture and the mainstream culture. In contrast, endorsement of assimilation was found to be related to lower self-esteem, especially among the Asians and the foreign-born subjects. Thus, *giving up one's ethnic culture can have a negative impact on self-concept.* The concept of separation (that ethnic groups should keep to themselves and not mix with mainstream society) was given little support by the students, with no differences among ethnic groups or by socioeconomic status. *Of all four alternatives, marginality—in which one identifies neither with one's own ethnic group, or the dominant culture—is the least satisfactory alternative.*

Black students tend to encounter more barriers to racial identity development than do white students. Moreover, *gifted black students may experience more psychological and emotional problems than do black students not identified as gifted.* The gifted minority children find themselves "between a rock and a hard place." One gifted black student said, "I had to fight to be gifted and then I had to fight because I am gifted." Another student said, "I am not white and I'm not black. I am a freak" (Ford, Harris, & Schuerger, 1993). Essentially, gifted black children confront conflicting values from which they must choose when forming a racial identity. Gifted black students sometimes consciously decide to underachieve academically so as not to be perceived as "acting white," or as selling out. High-achieving black students must assume a "raceless" persona if they wish to succeed academically. This racelessness occurs when they empty themselves of their culture, believing that the door of opportunity will open if they stand raceless before it. Raceless children adopt characteristics of the dominant culture (such as speaking standard English, or straightening their hair). These problems suggest the need for counseling to help gifted black students cope with and appreciate their ability. Group multicultural counseling is especially helpful (Ford, Harris, & Schuerger, 1993).

Adolescence and Developmental Tasks

MEANING

Developmental tasks—the skills, knowledge, functions, and attitudes that individuals have to acquire at certain points in their lives in order to function effectively as mature persons

Robert Havighurst (1972) sought to develop a psychosocial theory of adolescence by combining consideration of societal demands with individuals' needs (Klaczynski, 1990). What society demands and individuals need constitute **developmental tasks.** These tasks are the knowledge, attitudes, functions, and skills that individuals must acquire at certain points in their lives through physical maturation, personal effort, and social expectations. Mastery of the tasks at each stage of development results in adjustment, preparation for the harder tasks ahead, and greater maturity. Failure to master the developmental tasks results in social disapproval, anxiety, and inability to function as a mature person (Gavazzi, Anderson, & Sabatelli, 1993).

EIGHT MAJOR TASKS

Havighurst (1972) outlined eight major psychosocial tasks to be accomplished during adolescence as follows:

1. Accepting one's physique and using the body effectively
2. Achieving emotional independence from parents and other adults
3. Achieving a masculine or feminine social–sex role
4. Achieving new and more mature relations with age-mates of both sexes

One of the psychosocial tasks of adolescence is to achieve mature relations with age-mates of both sexes.

5. Desiring and achieving socially responsible behavior
6. Acquiring a set of values and an ethical system as a guide to behavior
7. Preparing for an economic career
8. Preparing for marriage and family life

These eight developmental tasks need to be interpreted. What did Havighurst say about them?

1. *Accepting one's physique and using the body effectively.* Adolescents become extremely self-conscious about the changes occurring in their bodies at puberty. Adolescents are concerned about body build, image, and appearance (Newell, Hammig, Jurich, & Johnson, 1990). They need to understand the patterns of growth of their own bodies, to accept their own physiques, to care for their health, and to use their bodies effectively in athletics, recreation, work, and everyday tasks (Havighurst, 1972).

2. *Achieving emotional independence from parents and other adults.* Some adolescents are too emotionally dependent on their parents; others are estranged from their parents. Part of the task of growing up is to achieve autonomy from parents and establish adult relationships with them at the same time (Brown & Mann, 1990; Daniels, 1990). Adolescents who are rebellious and in conflict with their parents need help in understanding the situation and learning how to improve it.

3. *Achieving a masculine or feminine social–sex role.* What is a woman? What is a man? What are women and men supposed to look like? How are they supposed to act? What roles are they required to play (Kissman, 1990)? Part of the maturing process for adolescents is to reexamine the changing sex roles of their culture and to decide what roles they can adopt (Havighurst, 1972; Nelson & Keith, 1990).

4. *Achieving new and more mature relations with age-mates of both sexes.* One of the tasks of adolescents is to establish heterosocial

friendships, as opposed to the same-sex friendships that are more prevalent in middle childhood (Verduyn, Lord, & Forrest, 1990). Maturing also means developing the social skills necessary to get along with others and to participate in social groups.

5. *Desiring and achieving socially responsible behavior.* This goal refers to sorting out social values and goals in our pluralistic society, which also includes assuming more responsibility for community and national affairs. Some adolescents are disturbed by the injustices, social inequities, and problems they see around them. Some become radical activists; others work in quieter ways to make a difference; others simply refuse to act. Many adolescents struggle to find their niche in society in a way that gives meaning to their lives (Havighurst, 1972).

6. *Acquiring a set of values and an ethical system as a guide to behavior.* This goal includes the development, adoption, and application of meaningful values, morals, and ideals in one's personal life (Harding & Snyder, 1991; Zern, 1991).

7. *Preparing for an economic career.* Determining life goals, choosing a vocation, and preparing for that career are long-term tasks that begin at adolescence (Berzonsky, Rice, & Neimeyer, 1990; Green, 1990; Harding & Snyder, 1991; Steel, 1991).

8. *Preparing for marriage and family life.* The majority of youths consider a happy marriage and parenthood to be important goals in life. However, they need to develop the social skills, positive attitudes, emotional maturity, objective knowledge, and empathetic understanding to make marriage work. This preparation and development begins in adolescence.

Havighurst feels that many modern youths have not found direction in their lives and therefore suffer from aimlessness and uncertainty. He says that during the first half of the twentieth century, the primary method of identity achievement (especially for boys) was through an occupation. Work was the focus of life. Today, however, many adolescents would say that expressive values have become more important. Identity is established through close, meaningful, and loving relationships with other persons.

Anthropologists' Views of Adolescence

DEVELOPMENTAL CONTINUITY VERSUS DISCONTINUITY

Anthropologists look at adolescence somewhat differently. *They generally reject age and stage theories of development, which say that children go through various stages of development at different ages.* Instead, anthropologists emphasize continuity of development. Margaret Mead said, for example, that Samoan children follow a relatively continuous pattern of growth with relatively little change from one age to the other. Children are not expected to behave one way and adults another. Samoans never have to abruptly change their ways of acting or thinking as they move from childhood to adulthood, so that adolescence as a transition from one pattern of behavior to another is practically nonexistent. This principle of continuity of development may be illustrated with three examples by Mead (1950).

First, the submissive role of children in Western culture is contrasted with the dominant role of children in primitive society. Children in Western culture are taught to be submissive, but as adults they are expected to be dominant. Mead (1950) showed that the Samoan child is not expected to become dominant on reaching adulthood after being taught submission as a child. On the contrary, the Samoan girl dominates her younger siblings and in turn is dominated by the older ones. The older she gets, the more dominating she becomes and the fewer girls who dominate her (the parents never try to dominate her). When she becomes an adult, she does not experience the conflict of dominance and submission that is found among adolescents in Western society.

Second, the nonresponsible roles of children in Western culture are contrasted with the responsible roles of children in primitive societies. Children in Western culture must assume drastically different roles as they grow up; they shift from nonresponsible play to responsible work and must do it rather suddenly. In contrast, children in primitive societies learn responsibility quite early. Work and play often involve the same activity. By "playing" with a bow and arrow, a boy learns to hunt. His youthful hunting "play" is a prelude to his adult hunting "work."

Third, dissimilarity of sex roles of children and adults in Western culture is contrasted with similarity of sex roles of children and adults in primitive cultures. In Western culture, infant sexuality is denied and adolescent sexuality is repressed. When adolescents mature sexually, they must unlearn earlier attitudes and taboos and become sexually responsive adults. Mead indicates that the Samoan girl experiences no real discontinuity of sex roles as she passes from childhood to adulthood. She has the opportunity to experiment and become familiar with sex with almost no taboos (except against incest). Therefore, by the time maturity is reached, she is able to assume a sexual role in marriage very easily.

CULTURAL INFLUENCES

Anthropologists say that storm and stress during adolescence is not inevitable. For example, whether or not menstruation is a disturbing experience depends on its interpretation. One tribe may teach that the menstruating girl may dry up the well or scare the game; another tribe may consider her condition a blessing (a priest could obtain a blessing by touching her, or she could increase the food supply). A girl who is taught that menstruation is a curse will react and act differently from a girl who is taught that it is a positive thing. Therefore, the strains and stresses of pubescent physical changes may be caused by negative teachings of the culture and not by any inherited biological tendencies.

GENERATION GAP

Although anthropologists deny the inevitability of a generation gap (Mead, 1974), they describe the many conditions in Western culture that create such a gap. Those conditions include pluralistic value systems, rapid social change (Dunham & Bengtson, 1992), and modern technology that make the world appear too complex and too unstable to adolescents to provide them with a stable frame of reference. Furthermore, early physiological puberty and the prolongation of adolescence allow many years for the development of a peer-group culture in which adolescent values, customs, and mores may be in conflict with those of the adult world (Finkelstein & Gaier, 1983). Mead (1950) felt that parent–adolescent conflict and tension can be minimized by giving adolescents more freedom to make their own choices and to live their own lives, by requiring less conformity and less dependency, and by tolerating individual differences within the family. Also, Mead felt that youth can be accepted into adult society at younger ages. They should be allowed to have sex and to marry, but parenthood should be postponed. Adolescents should be given greater responsibility for community life. These measures would allow for a smoother, easier transition to adulthood by eliminating discontinuities in development.

Critique

What about the various perspectives on adolescence? Which views are most plausible? Each view adds something to a more complete understanding. Anna Freud made a significant contribution in her emphasis on sexual and psychic drives. Her explanation of the psychic disequilibrium of adolescents helps us understand possible causes of erratic behavior. It is important to remember, however, that not all adolescents go through a period of psychic disequilibrium. Some do, but the majority are not in turmoil, deeply disturbed, at the mercy of their impulses, or rebellious. A survey of 6,000 adolescents from ten nations found few adolescents who were alienated from their parents. Only 7 percent said they thought their parents were ashamed of them or would be disappointed in them in the future (Atkinson, 1988).

Erikson's explanation of the adolescent's need for identity and the process by which identity is formed has had a marked influence on adolescent theory and research for years. Although Erikson discusses identity achievement as the principal psychosocial task of adolescence, he emphasizes that the process neither begins nor ends with adolescence. It is a lifelong process.

Havighurst's outline of the developmental tasks of adolescence can help youth to discover some of the things they need to accomplish to reach adulthood. The outline can also help adults who seek to guide adolescents on their road to maturity.

Anthropologists have emphasized that there are few universal patterns of development of behavior, so that general conclusions about adolescents should be formulated to take into account the cultural differences. By making cultural comparisons, anthropologists enable us to see some of the positive and negative elements in each culture that help or hinder the adolescent. In our culture, it is evident from an anthropological point of view that adolescence is a creation, an increasingly prolonged period of transition from childhood to adulthood, during which the individual is educated and socialized to take his or her adult place in society. In urban, industrialized societies, the process of achieving adulthood is more complicated and takes longer than in primitive cultures. There is fear in the minds of some parents that their adolescents are "never going to grow up." As one father said: "My son is 25 years old and I'm still supporting him." This process does take a long time, especially when years of higher education are involved. Nevertheless, parents can play an important role in the preparatory process as long as they remember that the ultimate goal is mature adulthood.

One perspective of adolescence gives only a partial picture; after all, adolescents are biological creations who are psychologically and sociologically conditioned by the family, community, and society of which they are members. One must stand in many places and look from many points of view to develop the fullest understanding of adolescents (Mead, 1974).

Summary

1. Adolescence means to grow to maturity. Maturity is that age, state, or condition of life in which a person is fully developed physically, emotionally, socially, intellectually, and spiritually. Puberty is the age or period during which a person reaches sexual maturity. Pubescence is the whole period during which sexual maturation takes place. A juvenile is not yet considered an adult in the eyes of the law.
2. Some tribes have specific initiation ceremonies, or rites of passage, to celebrate the transition from childhood to maturity.
3. G. Stanley Hall said that puberty is a time of upset, emotional maladjustment, and instability that corresponds to the transition of mankind from savagery to civilization.
4. Researchers today conclude that storm and stress are not inevitable consequences of adolescence. Psychological turmoil may not be normal and ought to be treated.
5. Anna Freud characterized adolescence as a period of internal conflict, psychic disequilibrium, and erratic behavior. The disequilibrium is caused by the increase of instinctual urges (the id) at

the time that sexual maturation takes place. The increase in the id presents a direct challenge to the ego and superego, which seek to curtail the id's expression. Only when the id–ego–superego conflict is resolved is psychic equilibrium restored. The ego employs defense mechanisms to protect itself, but excessive use of them is detrimental to the individual.

6. According to Erikson, the chief psychosocial task of adolescence is the achievement of identity. Identity has many components: sexual, social, vocational, moral, ideological, and psychological. Some aspects of identity are more easily formed than others.
7. According to Erikson, adolescence is a period of psychosocial moratorium during which the individual can try out various roles. The adolescent who fails in the search for identity will experience self-doubt, role diffusion, and role confusion.
8. Marcia elaborated on Erikson's views of identity by outlining four identity statuses: identity achievement, moratorium, foreclosure, and identity diffusion.
9. These identity statuses do not always occur in exact sequence. Some individuals remain at one status; others go through the process several times; yet others may revert back to an earlier status.
10. Gilligan has suggested that the path of identity development for females may be different than for males. Josselson found that some women at a foreclosure status defined their identity in terms of establishing significant relationships, or in the successful search for a mate.
11. Ethnic identity is the subtotal of group members' feelings about those values, symbols, and common histories that identify them as a single group. Ethnic identity includes three components: positive ethnic attitudes, ethnic identity achievement, and ethnic behaviors.
12. There are four possible ways in which ethnic group members can participate in a culturally diverse society: through assimilation, integration, separation, and marginality.
13. Gifted black students have a special problem finding identity and belonging, both because they are black and because they are gifted.
14. Havighurst outlined eight major psychosocial tasks that need to be accomplished during adolescence: accepting one's physique and using the body effectively, achieving new and more mature relations with age-mates of both sexes, achieving a masculine or feminine social–sex role, achieving emotional independence from parents and other adults, preparing for an economic career, preparing for marriage and family life, desiring and achieving socially responsible behavior, and acquiring a set of values and an ethical system as a guide to behavior.
15. Anthropologists challenge the basic truths of all age and stage theories of child and adolescent development. They say that in some cultures, children follow a relatively continuous growth pattern, with adult roles evolving as a continuation of the roles they learned as children. In our culture, particular roles are learned as children, and other roles as adults. This discontinuous development results in the creation of a period of adolescence during which roles have to be relearned.
16. Anthropologists also challenge the inevitability of the storm and stress of adolescence and of the generation gap.
17. No one view incorporates the total truth about adolescence. To understand adolescence, one must stand in many places and look from many points of view.

Key Terms

Acculturation *p. 382*
Developmental tasks *p. 384*
Foreclosure *p. 381*
Identity achievement *p. 380*
Identity diffusion *p. 381*
Juvenile *p. 377*

Maturity *p. 376*
Moratorium *p. 380*
Psychosocial moratorium *p. 380*
Puberty *p. 376*
Pubescence *p. 376*

Discussion Questions

1. Think back to your adolescence. Was this a period of storm and stress and psychic conflict for you? Why or why not?
2. Name as many rites of passage as you can that mark a transition from childhood into adulthood in our culture. Which one of these was most important to your growing up? Why?
3. Who was the most important person to you in your identity development? In what ways was that person most helpful?
4. Why do some people develop a negative identity? What can they do to form a more positive view of themselves? Which components of identity are most difficult to establish and why?
5. In what identity stage are you now, according to Marcia's classifications? What problems are you experiencing in achieving an identity?
6. Do you feel that some women can find an acceptable identity primarily through marriage and motherhood? Explain.
7. Are you a member of an ethnic minority group? What are your chief problems in finding an identity?
8. Which one of Havighurst's developmental tasks was hardest for you when you were an adolescent? Explain.
9. What do you think of Mead's concepts of continuity and discontinuity of development? Is it possible to eliminate the discontinuity of development experienced by children in our culture? Explain.
10. When you were an adolescent, was there a generation gap between you and your parents? In what respects? Is there a generation gap between you and your parents now? Explain.

Suggested Readings

Bilby, R. W., & Posterski, D. C. (1985). *The emerging generation: An inside look at Canada's teenager.* Toronto: Irwin. A summary of what 3,000 teenagers said.

Erikson, E. H. (1968). *Identity: Youth and crisis.* New York: Norton. A classic.

Feldman, S. S. & Elliott, G. R. (Eds.) (1990). *At the threshold: The developing adolescent.* Cambridge, MA: Harvard University Press. Results of the Carnegie Foundation study of adolescent development in society.

Kaplan, L. J. (1984). *Adolescence: The farewell to childhood.* New York: Simon and Schuster. The conflicts in letting go of childhood in becoming an adult.

Offer, D. O., Ostrov, E., Howard, K., & Atkinson, R. (1988). *The teenage world: Adolescents' self-image in ten countries.* Answers to questions from 6,000 teenagers in 10 countries.

Rice, F. P. (1996). *The adolescent: Development, relationships, and culture* (8th ed.). Boston: Allyn and Bacon. The author's comprehensive textbook.

Physical Development: Endocrine Glands, Sexual Maturation and Education, Physical Growth, Body Image, and Nutrition

Chapter 15

The Endocrine Glands and Hypothalamus

Endocrine glands
Hormones
Gonads
Estrogens
Pituitary gland
Gonadotropic hormones
Human growth hormone (HGH)
Prolactin
Progesterone
Ovum
Corpus luteum

An **endocrine gland,** as shown in Figure 15.1, is a gland that secretes **hormones** internally. Because the hormones are secreting into the bloodstream, they reach every cell of the body. However, each hormone has target organs it influences, telling those organs what to do and when to act.

Only three glands of the endocrine system are discussed here: the *pituitary gland,* the *adrenal glands,* and the *gonads.* The *hypothalamus,* which is a part of the brain, is discussed here as well because it regulates the pituitary secretions.

PITUITARY GLAND

The **pituitary gland** is only about 1/2 inch long, weighs less than 1/2 gram (1/56 oz.), and is located in the base of the brain. Its primary identification is a master gland producing hormones that regulate growth. The best known hormones secreted by the pituitary gland are discussed here along with their functions.

Gonadotropic hormones are secreted by the anterior pituitary gland and influence gonad (or sex gland) functioning. There are two gonadotropic hormones. **Follicle-stimulating hormone** (FSH) and **luteinizing hormone** (LH) stimulate the growth of egg cells in the ovaries and sperm in the testes. In the female, FSH and LH control the production and release of the feminizing hormone estrogen and of the hormone progesterone. Both are produced in the ovaries. In the male, LH controls the production and release of the masculinizing hormone testosterone by the testes (Rice, 1989).

The growth hormone, referred to as **human growth hormone** (HGH) or somatotrophic hormone (SH), affects the overall growth and shaping of the skeleton. A deficiency causes dwarfism; an excess causes giantism.

The pituitary gland also secretes a lactogenic hormone, luteotropic hormone (LTH), that contains the hormone **prolactin,** which influences the secretion of milk by the mammary glands of the breast.

Hypothalamus
Pituitary gland
Parathyroid glands
Thyroid gland
Thymus
Kidney
Adrenal gland
Pancreas
Ovary (in female)
Testis (in male)

FIGURE 15.1 The endocrine glands.

Adapted from David Shier et al., *Holes, Human Anatomy & Physiology,* 7th ed. Copyright © 1996 Times Mirror Higher Education Group, Inc., Dubuque, IA. All rights reserved. Reprinted by permission.

GONADS

The **gonads,** or sex glands, include the ovaries in the female and testes in the male. The ovaries in the female secrete a whole group of hormones known as **estrogens** that stimulate the development of the sexual organs themselves and of female secondary sexual characteristics, such as the growth of pubic hair and breasts, and the distribution of fat on the body.

The ovaries also secrete the female hormone **progesterone.** This hormone is produced following the rupture of the **ovum** from the ovarian follicle. When an egg cell is discharged from a follicle in ovulation, the remaining follicular cells multiply rapidly and fill the cavity. This new cell growth becomes the **corpus luteum** ("yellow body"), and secretes progesterone during the later part of the menstrual cycle. If the ovum has not been fertilized, the corpus luteum disintegrates, and progesterone secretion ceases until the next cycle. Progesterone is of primary importance in preparing the uterus for pregnancy and for maintaining the pregnancy itself.

Under the stimulation of LH from the pituitary, the testes in the male begin the production of the androgenic hormone, testosterone. This male hormone is responsible for the development of the male sex organs: the penis, scrotum, epididymis, prostate gland, and seminal vesicles. Both FSH and LH secretions from the pituitary gland stimulate the production and growth of sperm cells. Testosterone is also responsible for the development and preservation of masculine secondary sexual characteristics, including muscular and skeletal development, voice changes, and facial and body hair.

As the ovaries mature, ovarian estrogenic hormone levels increase dramatically and begin to show the cyclic variation in level during various stages of the menstrual cycle. The level of androgens in girls' bloodstreams increases only slightly. As the testes mature in the male, testosterone production increases dramatically, whereas the level of the estrogens increase only slightly. Figure 15.2 shows the increase in hormones at puberty. The ratio of the levels of the male to the female hormones is partly responsible for the development of male or female characteristics. When ratios are not normal in a growing child, deviations occur in the development of expected masculine or feminine physical traits. A male with an androgen deficiency and an excess of estrogens may evidence decreased potency and sex drive and an enlargement of the breasts. A female with an excess of androgens may grow body and facial hair, develop masculine musculature

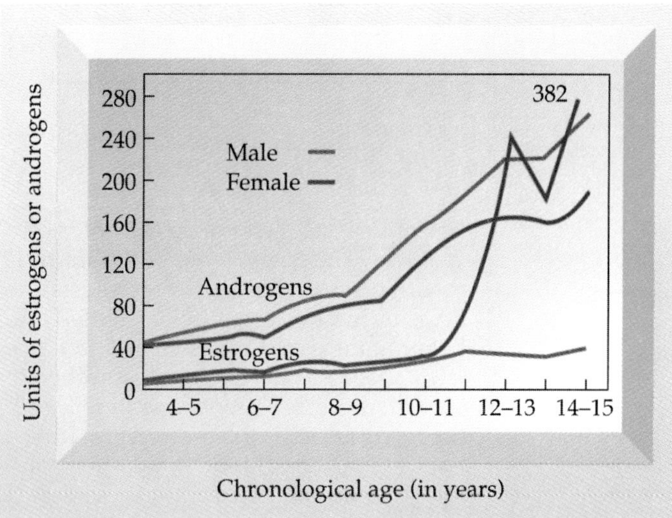

FIGURE 15.2 Hormone secretion with age.

Physical growth and development is an important part of the maturation process during adolescence.

LIVING ISSUES

Use of Steroids by Athletes

Attention has been focused in recent years on the use of **anabolic steroids** by athletes of all ages. A steroid is the male hormone testosterone. Fuller and LaFountain (1987) interviewed fifty athletes, ages 15 to 45 years, who admitted to steroid use. The athletes included both high school and college weight lifters, track stars, body builders, wrestlers, and football players. These athletes said they used the drugs to be competitive.

> We should be allowed to take them because all those other countries take them . . . the women too. You have no choice if you want to compete in the big time (Fuller & LaFountain, 1987, p. 971).

Steroids increase performance, strength, and muscle mass, and reduce fat deposits and fluid retention by the body. They also increase verbal and physical aggression and hostility (Halpern & Udry, 1992). This increase may result in sexual aggression, fights and arguments with others, and beating up girlfriends or boyfriends.

Steroids may cause serious physical harm. Athletes can suffer damage to the stomach, reproductive system, liver, and heart. Liver tumors, stomach ulcers, sterility, and heart attacks are common, in addition to emotional instability. Although the illegal use of steroids has even disqualified some athletes from competition, many continue to use them for the sake of improved performance.

Hypothalamus—small area of the brain controlling motivation, emotion, pleasure, and pain in the body

Adrenal glands—ductless glands that secrete androgens and estrogens, as well as adrenalin, in both men and women

Gonadotropin-releasing hormone (GnRH)—controls the production and release of FSH and LH from the pituitary

and strength, or develop an enlarged clitoris or other masculine characteristics.

ADRENALS AND HYPOTHALAMUS

The **adrenal glands** are located just above the kidneys. In the female, they produce low levels of both androgens (Masculinizing sex hormones) and estrogen (feminizing sex hormone), and they partially replace the loss of ovarian estrogen after menopause. Although the adrenals secrete both androgens and estrogens in the male, androgens are produced in greater amounts.

The **hypothalamus** is a small area of the forebrain about the size of a marble. As the motivational and emotional control center of the brain, it regulates such functions as lactation (milk production), pregnancy, menstrual cycles, hormonal production, drinking, eating, and sexual response and behavior. Since it is the pleasure and pain center of the brain, electrical stimulation of the hypothalamus can produce sexual feelings and thoughts.

The hypothalamus plays an important role in hormonal production and regulation. A chemical called **gonadotropin-releasing hormone (GnRH)** is produced to control the secretion of FSH and LH from the pituitary.

Maturation and Functions of Sex Organs

MALE

The primary male sex organs are the **penis, scrotum, testes, prostate gland, seminal vesicles, epididymis, Cowper's glands, urethra,** and **vas deferens.** They are depicted in Figure 15.3. Important changes occur in these organs during adolescence. The testes and scrotum begin to grow faster at about age 11½, with the growth becoming fairly rapid after age 13½, and slowing thereafter. These ages are aver-

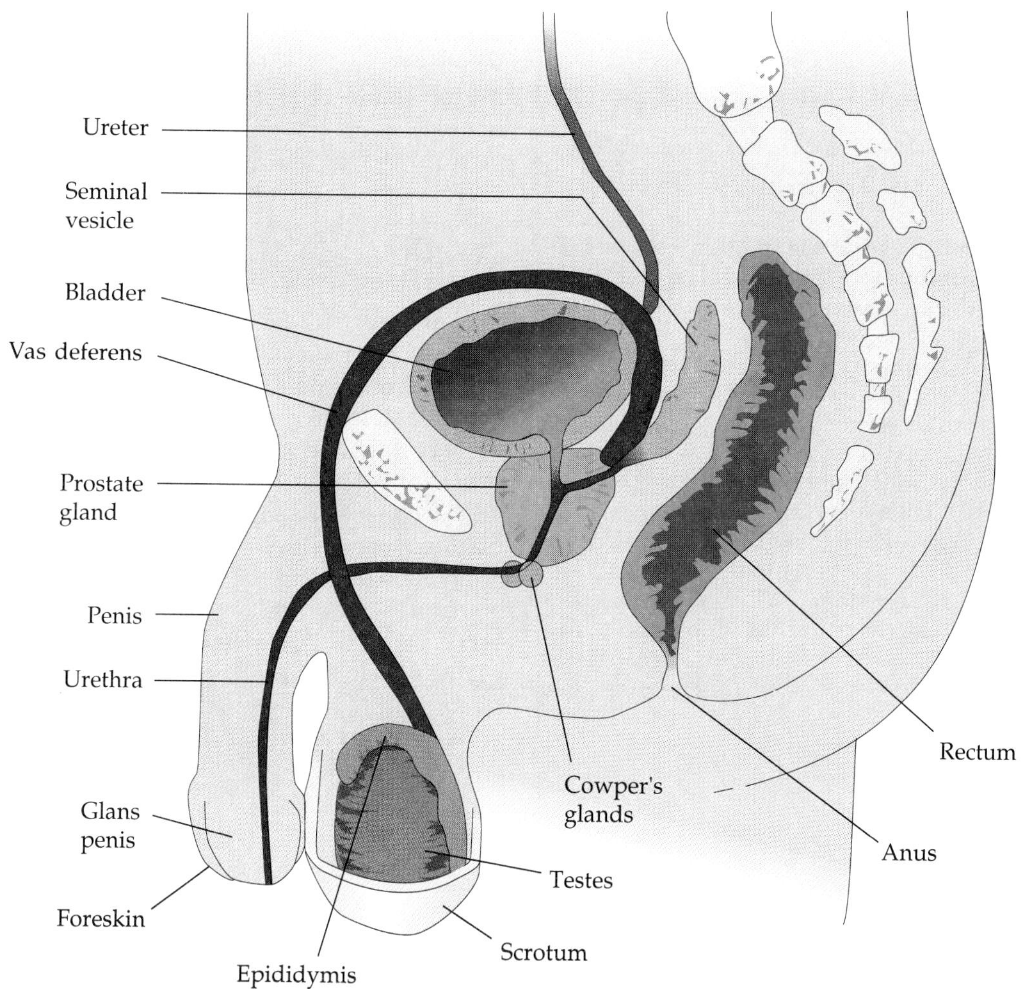

FIGURE 15.3 The male reproductive system.

ages. The testes increase 1½ times in length and about 8½ times in weight during this period. The penis doubles in length and girth during adolescence, with the most rapid growth taking place between ages 14 and 16. Both the prostate gland and the seminal vesicles mature and begin secreting semen. The Cowper's glands mature at this time and begin to secrete the alkaline fluid that neutralizes the acidity of the urethra and lubricates it for safe and easy passage of the sperm. This fluid appears at the opening of the urethra during sexual excitement and before ejaculation. Because this fluid contains sperm in about 25 percent of the cases examined, conception is possible whenever intercourse occurs, even if the male withdraws prior to ejaculation (McCary & McCary, 1982.

The most important change within the testes is the development of mature sperm cells, which occurs when FSH and LH from the pituitary stimulate their production. The total process of spermatogenesis, from the time the primitive spermatogonium is formed until it grows into a mature sperm, is about ten days. After production, the sperm ripen and mature and are stored in the epididymis for as long as six weeks until ejaculated through the vas deferens and urethra or until absorbed into the body.

Adolescent boys may become concerned about **nocturnal emissions,** or so-called wet dreams. Kinsey, Pomeroy, and Martin (1948) reported that almost 100 percent of men have erotic dreams, and about 83 percent of them have dreams that culminate in orgasm. These dreams occur most frequently among males in their teens and twenties, but about half of all adult men continue to have them. Adolescents should be reassured that such experiences are normal, that no harm comes from them, and that they can be accepted as part of their sex-

> **LIVING ISSUES**
>
> *Penis Size and Sexuality*
>
> 
>
> Adolescent boys are often concerned about the size of their penises, for they associate masculinity and sexual capability with penis size. In reality, the size of the erect penis has little to do with sexual capability. The vagina has few internal nerve endings, and female excitation comes primarily from stimulation of the external genitalia (Rowan, 1982). Therefore, the degree of pleasure experienced by both the man and woman has nothing to do with the size of the male organ. Moreover, the size of the flaccid penis has little to do with the size of the erect penis, because a small penis enlarges much more in proportion to its size than does a large penis.

uality. Anxiety may be prevented if adolescents are prepared for nocturnal emissions before they occur (Paddack, 1987).

FEMALE

Menarche—first menstruation

The primary internal female sex organs are **vagina, fallopian tubes, uterus,** and **ovaries.** The external female sex organs are known collectively as the **vulva.** They include the clitoris, the labia majora (major or large outer lips), the labia minora (small inner lips), the mons veneris (mons pubis), and the vestibule (the cleft region enclosed by the labia minora). The **hymen** is a fold of connective tissue that partly closes the vagina in the virginal female. The **Bartholin's glands,** situated on either side of the vaginal orifice, secrete a drop or so of fluid during sexual excitement (see Figure 15.4).

At puberty, the vagina increases in length, and its mucous lining becomes thicker and more elastic, and turns a deeper color. The inner walls of the vagina change their secretion from the alkaline reaction of childhood to an acid reaction in adolescence. The Bartholin's glands begin to secrete their fluids.

The **labia majora,** practically nonexistent in childhood, enlarge greatly, as do the **labia minora** and the **clitoris.** The **mons veneris** becomes more prominent through the development of a fatty pad. The uterus doubles in length, showing a straight-line increase during the period from 10 to 18 years of age. The ovaries increase greatly in size and weight. They show a fairly steady growth from birth to age 8, some acceleration of growth from age 8 to the time of ovulation (age 12 or 13), and a very rapid increase after sexual maturity is reached. This is a result, no doubt, of the maturation of the follicles (the structures that produce the eggs) within the ovaries themselves. Every infant girl is born with about 400,000 follicles in each ovary. By the time she reaches puberty, this number has declined to about 80,000 in each ovary. Ordinarily, one follicle produces a mature ovum about every 28 days for a period of about 38 years, which means that fewer than 500 ripen during the woman's reproductive years (McCary & McCary, 1982).

MENSTRUATION

The adolescent girl begins menstruating at an average age of 12 to 13 years, although she may mature considerably earlier or later (from age 9 to age 18 years is an extreme range). **Menarche** (the onset of menstruation) usually does not occur until maximum growth rates in height and weight have been achieved. Because of superior health care and nutrition, girls start menstruating earlier today than in former generations (Bullough, 1981). The average age has decreased from age 14 in 1905 to about age 12½ today (Gilger, Geary, & Eisele, 1991). An increase in body fat may stimulate menarche, whereas vigorous exercise tends to delay it (Stager, 1988). The menstrual cycle may vary in length from twenty to forty days, with an average of about twenty-eight days. However, there is considerable difference in the length of the cycle when different women are compared, and any one woman may show widespread variations. A regular cycle is quite rare.

The exact time ovulation occurs is an important consideration. *The time of ovulation is ordinarily about fourteen days before the onset of the next menstrual period,* which would be on the twelfth day of a twenty-sixth-day cycle and on the sixteenth day of a thirty-day cycle. There is some evidence

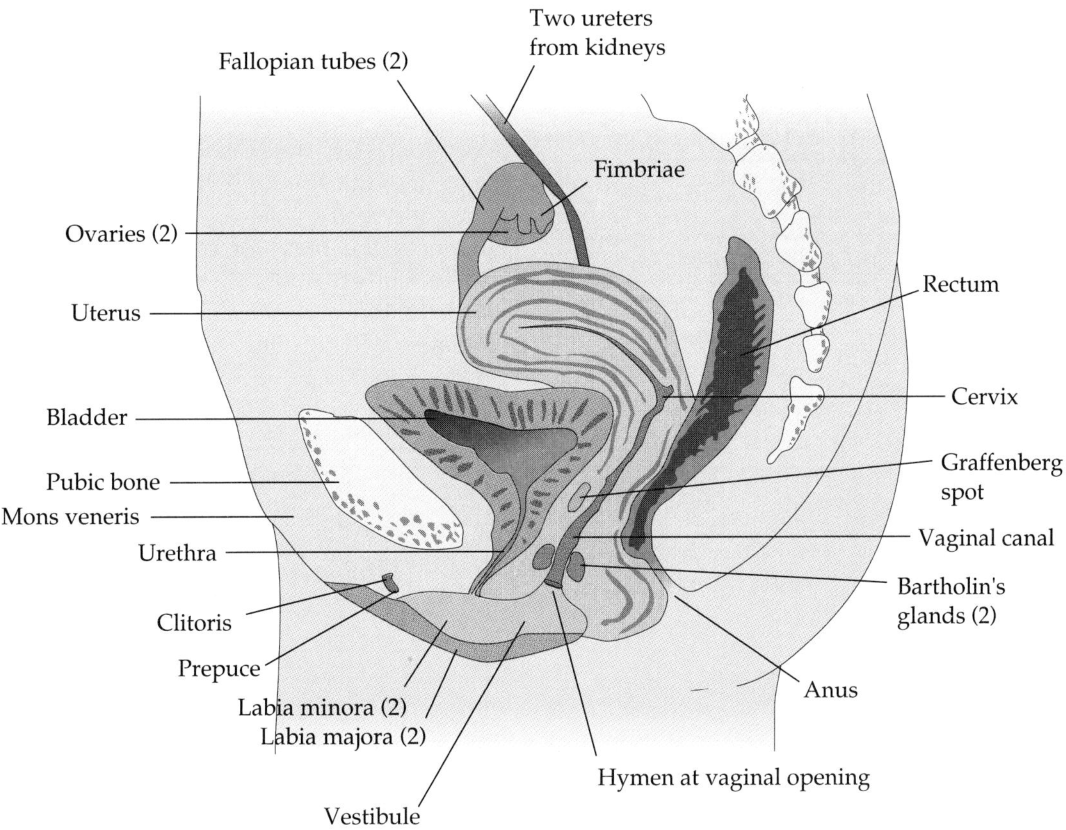

FIGURE 15.4 The female reproductive system.

that women have become pregnant on any one day of the cycle, including during menstruation itself, and that some women may ovulate more than once during a cycle, possibly because of the stimulus of sexual excitement itself.

Menarche can be a traumatic event for some girls who are not prepared ahead of time (Pillemer, Koff, Rhinehart, & Rierdan, 1987). Other girls are able to accept menstruation because they have been taught the basic facts (McGrory, 1990). The young girl's attitudes and feelings about menstruation are very important (Buchanan, 1991). Table 15.1 shows the results of a study of menarche experiences of ninety-five women from 23 countries. The study revealed that negative reactions to first menstruation were very common (Logan, 1980). Many girls from Asian countries had heard little about menstruation, and 50 percent of these females reported embarrassment when it began. Some 50 percent of Japanese women reported being surprised by menarche. Only half of the Asian mothers spoke to their daughters prior to menarche; over one-half of the daughters felt inadequately prepared for their first period. Table 15.1 shows the emotional reactions to menarche of all ninety-five of the foreign women. The more knowledgeable girls are prior to menarche, the more likely they are to report a positive initial experience (Skandhan, Pandya, Skandhan, & Mehta, 1988).

The onset of menstruation may involve a temporary period of disruption and emotional distance in family relationships. One study provides observational evidence that an increase in conflict engagement is associated with menarche, particularly in the mother–daughter dyad (Holmbeck & Hill, 1991). These findings also imply that pubertal maturation increases emotional distance between youngsters and parents.

A further important question is: Why is there increased conflict and emotional distance shortly after the onset of certain pubertal changes? Direct hormonal and genetic factors may be involved. Just as important, the adolescent girl now sees herself as a more mature person and wants to be treated as such. This desire for more autonomy and freedom brings her into di-

TABLE 15.1
Emotional Reactions of Foreign Women to Their Menarche

Reaction	*Percentage Showing Reaction*
Surprised	32
More grown up	24
Embarrassed	23
Sick	15
Frightened	15
Happy	15
More feminine	13
Different	13
Afraid everyone would know	12
Unclean	11
Proud	10
Worried about what to do	10
Sad	8
Closer to mother	5

The number of subjects from each of the 23 countries was as follows: Brazil—6, Burma—1, Chile—1, Colombia—4, El Salvador—2, France—2, Germany—2, Hong Kong—1, India—1, Indonesia—5, Iran—15, Italy—2, Japan—16, Mexico—3, Peru—5, Samoa—1, Spain—1, Switzerland—1, Taiwan—1, Thailand—1, Venezuela—16, Vietnam—1, and Zambia—3.

From "The Menarche Experience in Twenty-Three Foreign Countries" by D. D. Logan, 1980, *Adolescence, 15* (Summer), p. 254.

rect conflict with parents who have trouble accepting her new status.

Factors in Timing

There are many factors that determine the timing of sexual maturation and development (Robertson et al., 1992). Heredity and ethnic factors certainly exert an influence. Also, nutrition and medical care are important. Those children who receive adequate nutrition and medical care are more likely to mature earlier than those whose care and diet are inadequate. Socioeconomic status seems to have an influence, but the factors are mediated through poor nutrition and medical care received by those of low status. Diet and exercise, because they influence body weight and the percentage of body fat, are influential in the timing of pubertal development. Those who tend to be heavier with excess body fat, in general, mature earlier. The latest research indicates that levels of stress in the adolescent's life also have the influence upon the timing of development. The reason is because stress increases the amount of food eaten, which increases body weight, which, in turn, influences the onset of puberty. Therefore, those who are under the most stress tend to mature the earliest (Belsky, Steinberg, & Draper, 1991).

LIVING ISSUES

Menstrual Irregularity in Athletes

Extensive research has established that **amenorrhea,** or irregular menstruation, is common in female athletes; swimmers, distance runners, ballet dancers, and others (Calabrese et al., 1983). The reason is that extensive exercise reduces body fat, which influences the menses. The current evidence, from both anecdotal and investigative sources, suggests that exercise-induced amenorrhea rapidly reverses once training is discontinued (Stager, 1984; Stager, Ritchie, & Robertshaw, 1984). When physical training is reduced or stopped, as a result of either an injury or taking a vacation, amenorrheic athletes report a resumption of normal menstrual periodicity.

In comparing current runners with ex-collegiate distance runners and sedentary controls, a study showed that current runners reported significantly fewer menses than either of the other two groups. The ex-runner and the control group were similar in terms of the number of menses in the previous twelve months. Further, the ex-runners who experienced menstrual irregularity during training reported that they resumed normal menstruation on an average of 1.7 months after training was terminated. No relationship was established between length of amenorrhea and the time of resumption of regular menses (Stager, Ritchie, & Robertshaw, 1984).

Physical Growth and Development

DEVELOPMENT OF SECONDARY SEXUAL CHARACTERISTICS

Sexual maturation at puberty also includes development of **secondary sexual characteristics.** These include the development of mature female and male body contours, voice changes, the appearance of body hair, and other minor changes.

Secondary sexual characteristics—changes in the body at sexual maturation that do not involve the sex organs

The sequence of development for boys and girls is given in Table 15.2. The development of the **primary sexual characteristics** is also included in the table. Primary sexual characteristics are marked with an asterisk. The ages given are averages; actual ages may extend several years before and after these ages (Akinboye, 1984; Westney, Jenkins, Butts, & Williams, 1984). The average girl matures about two years before the average boy, but the time of development is not always consistent. An early-maturing boy may be younger than a late-maturing girl. The mean age for the first ejaculation of semen is 13.7 years. The mean age of menarche is 12.5 years. However, the age of sexual maturity extends over such a wide range (ages 9 to 18 are not unusual) that any age within the range should be considered normal.

Primary sexual characteristics—changes that involve the sex organs at sexual maturation

Sexual maturation at puberty includes the development of secondary sexual characteristics.

GROWTH IN HEIGHT AND WEIGHT

A growth spurt in height begins in early adolescence, accompanied by an increase in weight and changes in body proportions. The combined data from longitudinal studies of individual adolescents provide a composite picture of growth trends in groups of children.

Boys grow fastest in height and weight at approximately 14 years of age; girls grow fastest at approximately 12 years of age, as shown in Figure 15.5 (Tanner, 1962, 1972). Because girls start to mature earlier, between the ages of 12 and 14 they average slightly taller than boys, and between the ages of 10 and 14 girls are heavier than boys. Whereas girls have reached 98 percent of adult height at $16^1/_4$ years, boys do not reach 98 percent of their adult height until $17^3/_4$ years. These rates vary for different individuals.

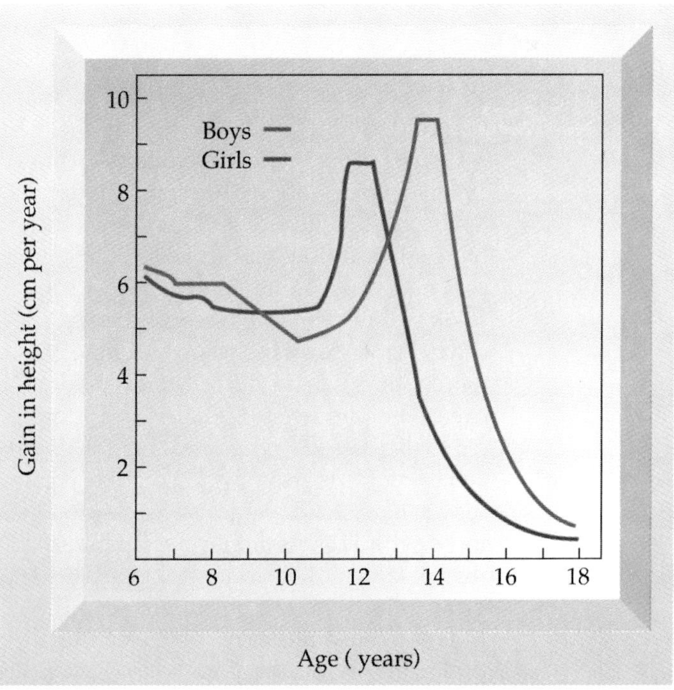

FIGURE 15.5 Increase in height.

From J. M. Tanner (1962), *Growth at Adolescence,* 2d ed. Courtesy of Charles C. Thomas, Publisher, Springfield, IL.

TABLE 15.2
SEQUENCE OF DEVELOPMENT OF PRIMARY AND SECONDARY SEXUAL CHARACTERISTICS

Boys	*Age Span*		*Girls*
Beginning growth of testes, scrotum, pubic hair Some pigmentation, nodulation of breasts (later disappears) Height spurt begins Beginning growth of penis*	11.5–13	10–11	Height spurt begins Slight growth of pubic hair Breasts, nipples elevated to form "bud stage"
Development of straight, pigmented pubic hair Early voice changes Rapid growth of penis, testes, scrotum, prostate, seminal vesicles* First ejaculation of semen* Kinky pubic hair Age of maximum growth Beginning growth of axillary hair	13–16	11–14	Straight, pigmented pubic hair Some deepening of voice Rapid growth of vagina, ovaries, labia, uterus* Kinky pubic hair Age of maximum growth Further enlargement, pigmentation, elevation of nipple, areola to form primary breasts Menarche*
Rapid growth of axillary hair Marked voice change Growth of beard Indentation of frontal hair line	16–18	14–16	Growth of axillary hair Filling out of breasts to form adult conformation, secondary breast stage

Note. Primary sexual characteristics are marked with an asterisk.

One of the most important factors in determining the total mature height of the individual is *heredity* (Eveleth & Tanner, 1976; Gertner, 1986). Short parents tend to have short children; tall parents tend to have tall children. *Nutrition* is the most important environmental factor (Tanner, 1970). Children who receive better diets during the growth years become taller adults than do less well-nourished children. The age when sexual maturation begins also affects the total height finally achieved. Girls and boys who are early maturers tend to be shorter as adults than those who are late maturers. The reason is that a late maturer has a longer time to grow before the sex hormones stop the pituitary from stimulating further growth.

Furthermore, the *growth achieved before puberty is of greater significance to total adult height than is the growth achieved during puberty*. The adolescent growth spurt contributes, in absolute terms, relatively little

LIVING ISSUES

Concern about Breast Size

Many adolescent girls are concerned about the size and shape of their breasts. Some girls who are flat-chested feel self-conscious because they are influenced by society, which emphasizes fullness of breasts as a mark of beauty and sexuality. Some adolescent girls wear padded bras or tight jerseys or sweaters, or even get medical help to enlarge their breasts. Such girls may also be swayed by misleading advertising promises to "put inches on your bosom in only a few days." In contrast, some girls who have large breasts are made to feel self-conscious when they suffer unkind remarks and stares.

to the postadolescent skeletal dimensions and only moderately to strength and weight.

The total process of growth is speeding up. Children and adolescents today experience the growth spurt earlier, grow faster, attain a greater total adult height, and attain this height at an earlier age than did children and adolescents sixty or seventy years ago.

Early and Late Maturation

Figure 15.6 shows the considerable variations in stage of physical development at a given age for each sex. Intensive investigations have been made on the effect of early or late physical maturation on psychological and social adjustments. The results of these studies are important for understanding adolescents who differ from the norm in the timing of their development (Collins & Propert, 1983).

EARLY-MATURING BOYS

Early-maturing boys are large for their age, more muscular, and better coordinated than late-maturing boys, so they enjoy both athletic and social advantages. They are better able to excel in competitive sports. Their superior development and athletic skills enhance their social prestige and position. They participate more frequently in extracurricular activities in high school. They are often chosen for leadership roles; their peers tend to give them greater social recognition by appointing them to positions of leadership in school. They tend to show more interest in girls and to be popular with them because of their adult appearance and sophisticated social interests and skills. Early sexual maturation may thrust them into early heterosexual relationships.

Adults, too, tend to favor early-maturing boys by rating them as more physically attractive, better groomed, and more masculine than late-maturing boys. However, adults tend to be expect more of them in terms of adult behavior and responsibilities, which gives early-maturing boys less time to enjoy the freedom that comes with childhood.

EARLY-MATURING GIRLS

Girls who mature early are at a disadvantage during their elementary school years. They are taller and more physically developed, and they tend to feel self-conscious and awkward. They enjoy less prestige at this age than do prepubertal girls (Alsaker, 1992b).

However, early-maturing girls come into their own socially by the time they reach junior high and high school age. They tend to look grown up and are envied by other girls because of their looks. They also begin to attract the attention of older boys and to start dating earlier than normal (Phinney, Jensen, Olsen, & Cundick, 1990). However, parents may begin to worry because of their daughters' emerging heterosexual interests and strive to curtail their social activities. The girls may find themselves emotionally unequipped to deal with sexual enticement, and with sophisticated social activities (Udry & Cliquet, 1982). Early maturation does lead to increased sexual experience at younger ages (Flannery, Rowe, & Gulley, 1993). Parental restriction and outside pressures may create stress, so for some this is a period of upset and anxiety. Nevertheless, usually by the time early-maturing girls have reached 17 years of age, they score higher on tests of total personal and family adjustments, have more positive self-concepts, and enjoy better personal relations than do later maturers. However, the net positive effect of early maturation does not seem to be as pronounced for girls as for boys.

LATE-MATURING BOYS

Late-maturing boys suffer a number of social disadvantages and may develop feelings of inferiority as a result (Apter, Galatzer, Beth-Halachmi, & Laron, 1981). At age 15 they may be eight inches shorter and thirty pounds lighter than early-maturing males, so they may have less strength and show poorer motor performance, coordination, and reaction time

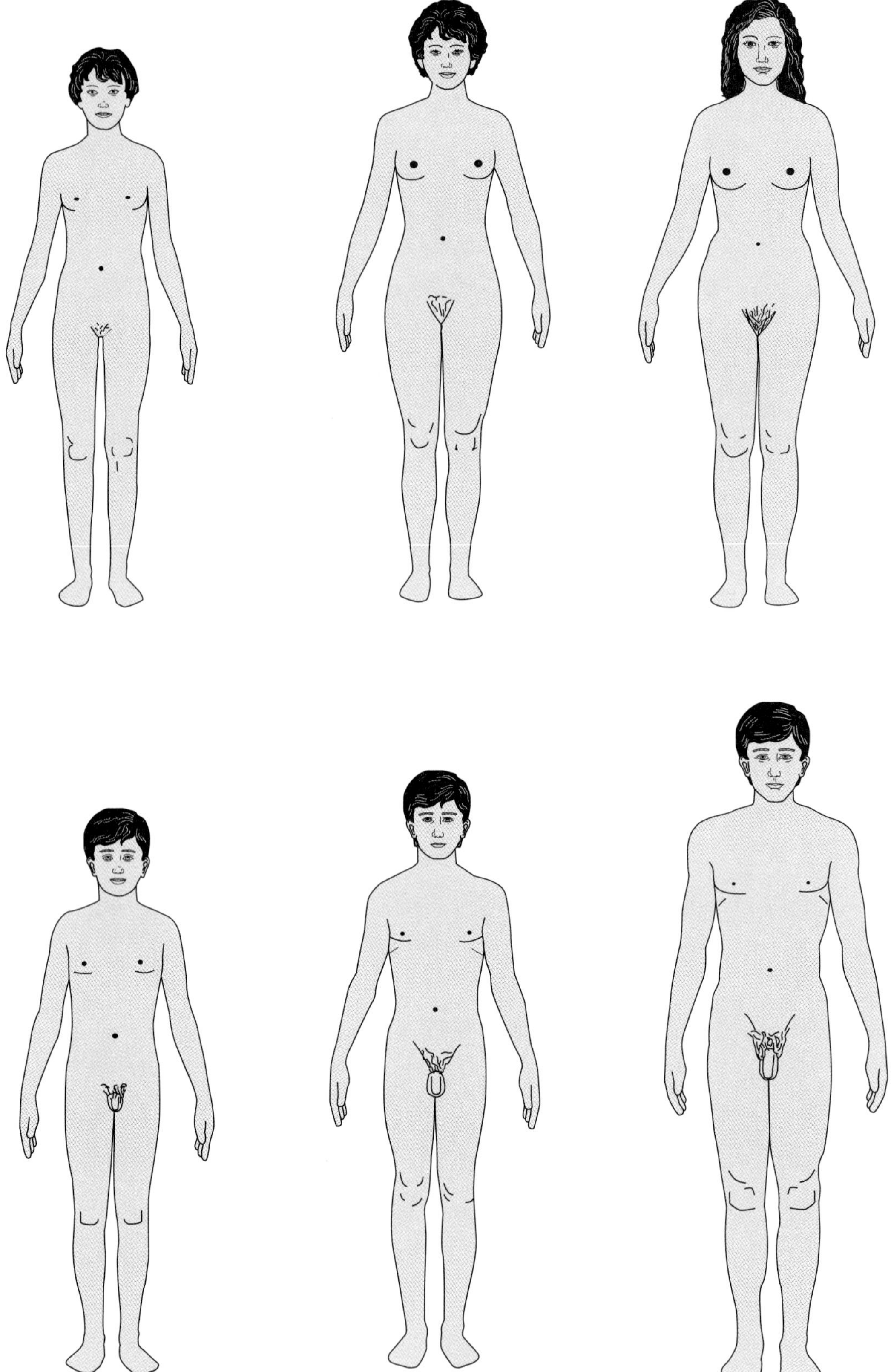

FIGURE 15.6 Variations in pubescent development. All three girls are 12 3/4 years and all three boys are 14 3/4 years of age but in different stages of puberty.

Adapted from J. M. Tanner (1973), "Growing Up." *Scientific American*, September, p. 38.

FOCUS

Early Menarche

One longitudinal study of 16-year-old girls discovered that psychosocial factors have an influence on the onset of menarche (Moffitt, Caspi, Belsky, & Silva, 1992). In summary, this study found that individuals who grow up under conditions of family stress—including paternal absence, family conflict, marital discord, and marital instability—experience behavioral and psychological problems that stimulate earlier pubertal onset and reproductive readiness. In particular, the authors found that family conflict predisposes girls to internalizing disorders that lower metabolism, lead to weight gain, and thus trigger the early onset of menarche.

than those who mature earlier. Physical size and motor coordination play an important role in social acceptance, so later maturers may develop negative self-perceptions. They have been characterized as less popular; less well-groomed; less attractive physically; more restless and affected; bossy and rebellious against their parents; and as being dependent, with feelings of inadequacy and rejection. They often become self-conscious and withdraw because of their social rejection.

LATE-MATURING GIRLS

Late-maturing girls of junior high or senior high school age are often socially handicapped (Apter, Galatzer, Beth-Halachmi, & Laron, 1981). They look and are treated like "little girls." They may not get invited to

FOCUS

Precocious Puberty

Precocious puberty means early sexual maturation. A recent example is that of 9-year-old Maria Eliana Jesus Mascarenhas, who gave birth to a healthy 7-pound daughter in March 1986. She named the girl Diana. The daughter of illiterate Brazilian farmhands, Maria delivered via cesarean section in the rural town of Jequie, 800 miles north of São Paulo. Dr. Fernando Prata Goes, the obstetrician who performed the surgery, explained: "Maria was scared and confused, and so was the father of the baby" ("Mom, Nine, Doing Fine," 1986, p. 15).

Maria suffers from an imbalance of hormones that produce premature puberty. At the time she gave birth, her physical age was estimated to be between 13 and 14. Since making worldwide headlines, Maria has returned to her parents' farm, where she is learning how to be a mother (Rice, 1989, p. 70).

boy–girl parties and social activities. One study in New York City showed that those who first menstruated at ages 14 to 18 tended to be late daters (Presser, 1978). They are often jealous of their friends who are more developed, but have much in common with normal-maturing boys and look on them as friends. However, their activities reflect the interests of those of younger age groups with whom they spend their time. One advantage for late-maturing girls, compared with those who develop early, is that they may not be criticized by parents and other adults. The chief disadvantage for late maturers seems to be the temporary loss of social status because of their relative physical immaturity.

Body Image and Psychological Impact

PHYSICAL ATTRACTIVENESS

Physical attractiveness is important in several ways. It affects the adolescent's positive self-esteem and social acceptance (Koff, Rierdan, & Stubbs, 1990; Thornton & Ryckman, 1991). It affects personality, interpersonal attraction, and social relationships (Shea & Adams, 1984). Attractive adolescents are thought of in positive terms: intelligent, desirable, successful, friendly, and warm (Lerner et al., 1990). Partly as a result of differential treatment, attractive adolescents appear to possess a wider variety of interpersonal skills, to be better adjusted socially, and to have higher self-perceptions and healthy personality attributes (Cash & Janda, 1984).

Anorexia nervosa—an eating disorder characterized by an obsession with food and being thin

Bulimia—an eating disorder characterized by bingeing and purging

As a result, many adolescents develop concern over physical appearance (appearance anxiety), especially if they have had negative social experiences in childhood and early adolescence (Keelan, Dion, & Dion, 1992). One study of sixth-grade male and female adolescents from Pennsylvania revealed that those who differed in physical attractiveness were also expected to differ in peer and parent relations, classroom behaviors, and self-perceptions. Adolescents who were higher in physical attractiveness tended to have more favorable ratings by parents, peers, and teachers than adolescents who were lower in physical attractiveness. This is one of the reasons why adolescents give so much attention to how they look (Lerner et al., 1991).

CONCEPTS OF THE IDEAL

Adolescents' self-appraisals of their physical attractiveness are determined partly by comparing themselves to other persons around them. One study showed that self-appraisals were more favorable after viewing an unattractive same-sex target than after viewing an attractive same-sex target (Brown, Novick, Lord, & Richards, 1992). Adolescents are influenced by the concepts of the ideal build that are accepted by our culture (Cok, 1990). Most adolescents would prefer to be of medium build (Ogundari, 1985). Adolescents who are tall and skinny are unhappy with their builds, as are those who are short and fat. Because Western culture overemphasizes the importance of being slim, the obese adolescent female is especially miserable (Bozzi, 1985; Lundholm & Littrell, 1986). It is partly because of this obsession with slimness that **anorexia nervosa** and **bulimia** develop among adolescents (Grant & Fodor, 1986). If a girl does not have a slim figure, she is less likely to have dates. Social rejection is hard to live with. This means that self-satisfaction and self-esteem are closely related to acceptance of the physical self (Jaquish & Savins-Williams, 1981; Littrell & Littrell, 1990; Padin, Lerner, & Spiro, 1981; Stewart, 1982).

Studies of males provide further proof of the social importance of possessing an average physique and of physical attractiveness. Men with muscular body builds are more socially accepted than those with other types of builds (Tucker, 1982). Tall men with good builds are considered more attractive than short men (Feingold, 1982). College-age men with muscular builds are more likely to feel comfortable and confident in interacting with others than those who are skinny or obese (Tucker, 1983). In another study, adolescents who rated themselves as unattractive were also likely to describe themselves as lonely (Moore & Schultz, 1983).

LIVING ISSUES

The Problem of Acne

At the onset of puberty, because of an increase in the secretion of androgens in the bloodstream, the glands of the skin increase their activity. Three kinds of skin glands cause problems for the adolescent:

1. *Apocrine sweat glands,* located in the armpits and in the mammary, genital, and anal regions
2. *Merocrine sweat glands,* distributed over most of the skin surfaces of the body
3. *Sebaceous glands,* oil-producing glands of the skin

After puberty, the apocrine and merocrine sweat glands secrete a fatty substance causing body odor. The sebaceous glands develop at a greater speed than the skin ducts through which they discharge their skin oils. As a result the ducts may become plugged and turn black as the oil oxidizes and dries upon exposure to the air, creating a blackhead. This in turn may become infected, causing a pimple or **acne** to form. The acne may be fairly mild with spontaneous remission occurring. Deep acne requires medical management to prevent scarring. A variety of treatment options are available.

Sex Education of Adolescents

GOALS

The onset of puberty and the changes that take place in the body, along with developing sexual attitudes and interests, awaken adolescents to the need to begin to understand the subject of human sexuality. There a number of goals in sexual education of adolescents. *The first goal is to develop knowledge and understanding about the bodily changes that are taking place.* Adolescents need to understand that each person matures at his or her own rate, that the development of girls is different from that of boys. Adolescents need to prepare for these changes because—without adequate preparation—the onset of menstruation, or of ejaculation by males, can be upsetting experiences (Adegoke, 1992). By developing adequate knowledge of the changes that take place, adolescents can not only prepare for these changes but welcome them and learn how to adjust to them.

Sex education of adolescents also ought to include basic facts about human reproduction and the process of reproduction and the process of reproduction itself. Actually, the time to give the basic facts about human sexuality is prior to puberty. Adolescents need to know basic facts about conception, pregnancy, and childbirth. They need to know *the process of humans sexual response and expression and the role of human sexual expression in their lives.* Their need to know the *basic facts about contraception and birth control and how to prevent conception,* along with basic *information about sexually transmitted diseases, especially AIDS.*

But sex education involves more than developing objective knowledge and understanding, important as that may be. *A second goal is to develop adolescent sexual health.* This includes not only physical health but emotional and psychological health as well. Adolescent sexual health is based on esteem and respect for oneself and for other people of both sexes, embracing the view that both males and females are essentially equal, though not necessarily the same. Sexually healthy adolescents take pleasure and pride in their own developing bodies. As they mature, they have an increasing ability to communicate honestly and openly to persons of both sexes with whom they have a close relationship. They grow to feel and understand that their sexuality is not a thing apart but an integral part of their total lives. They accept their own sexual desires as natural but to be acted upon with a constraint that takes into account their own values and goals as well as those of significant others. This view of adolescent sexuality includes being sexually responsive and sexually responsible. It does not include the concept that healthy adolescent sexuality involves complete freedom to behave as one wishes so long as contraceptives, including condoms, are used and so long as this behavior is in private with consenting partners. Imposing some constraints on sexual freedom does not necessarily mean unhealthy adolescent sexuality. As a matter of fact, healthy adolescent sexuality is impossible without some constraints (Chilman, 1990).

Another important goal of sex education of adolescents is the prevention of unwanted pregnancy. The incidence of teenage sexual involvement is at an all-time high, producing almost one million pregnancies to United States teenagers each year, most of them unplanned and unwanted. This fact poses a major problem in the lives of adolescents themselves as well as for society. Certainly any responsible program of sex education ought to include adolescent pregnancy prevention, both through the teaching of responsible sex behavior and by teaching basic facts about contraception and birth control. At least, if adolescents are not going to abstain, they can learn to be responsible enough to prevent unwanted pregnancy (Christopher & Roosa, 1990).

The rapid increase in AIDS created a monumental health crisis. Through 1994, 259,000 of the over 427,000 AIDS cases in the United States have resulted in death. *In response to this crisis, sex education programs for adolescents should provide information about AIDS and about changing AIDS-related behavior.* Such education means teaching the basic facts about AIDS and other sexually transmitted diseases, and trying to get adolescents to adopt behavioral changes that will minimize their risk. Sex education is designed to increase the number of adolescents willing to abstain from sexual intercourse until they are ready to settle down with a permanent partner. It also means that they need to learn to spend a longer time getting to know new partners before engaging in sexual activity. It also means decreasing their number of sex partners so that the possibility of AIDS transmission is minimized. And, last, it means that those who are sexually active need to increase their use of condoms as a means of preventing the transmission of AIDS itself (Baldwin, Whiteley, & Baldwin, 1990; Croft & Asmussen, 1992).

THE PARENTS' ROLE

The majority of research studies indicate that adolescents are receiving their information about sexuality primarily from peers (Brock & Jennings, 1993; Moran & Corley, 1991). Although increasing numbers of adolescents are receiving information from sex education programs in the schools, the research does not indicate that increasing numbers of parents are providing information themselves. If sex education belongs in the home, then certainly many parents are not assuming their responsibility. There are a number of reasons for this avoidance. *Some parents are too embarrassed to discuss the subject or they deal with it in negative ways.* They have been brought up to feel uncomfortable whenever this subject of sex comes up. As a result, they are not able to give their children positive attitudes and feelings, or the messages they teach are negative ones that interfere with sexual satisfaction.

Parents also have difficulty overcoming the incest barrier between themselves and their children. The taboo on parent–child sex behavior may be so strong that it is especially difficult for parents to communicate with adolescents about sex. One study showed that parent–daughter communication was more wide-ranging than parent-son communication for each type of sexual discussion. Gender differences were most pronounced for factual and moral discussions—that is, communication that was most likely to transmit sexual information and values directly. Sons were disadvantaged compared to daughters in that they had less communication within the family, less opportunity to discuss sexuality with the same-sex parent, and less discussion of topics likely to teach family values and norms about sexual behavior. Also, sons reported greater discomfort with sexual dis-

Only a minority of parents do a good job of educating their adolescents about sex.

cussions within the family than did daughters (Nolin & Petersen, 1992).

Some parents are uninformed and do not know how to explain to their children. Many parents have not received objective sex information themselves. If they don't understand the basic facts about the human body and about reproduction, how can they transmit these facts to their children?

Many parents are afraid that knowledge will lead to experimentation, so that they do not tell their children because they want to keep the children innocent. However, there is no evidence to show that sexual knowledge, per se, leads to sexual experimentation. There is a lot of evidence to show that it is ignorance—not knowledge—that leads to trouble.

Other parents tell too little too late. The time to begin sex education in the home is during the preschool years. I believe that children ought to have all of the basic facts about human reproduction and human sexuality before they reach puberty. Then, during puberty, parents can concentrate on helping to develop positive attitudes and feelings and in dealing with relationships.

Some parents set a negative example at home. It's not just the words parents use that are important; it is also the lives they lead, the example they set. What parents do speaks louder than what they say (Rice, 1993). One of the most helpful things that parents can do is to back responsible programs of sex education in their schools. Certainly, if parents aren't able to do the task themselves, they need to encourage professionals to help them with it.

THE SCHOOL'S ROLE

Nationwide surveys indicate that about 85 percent of parents favor sex education in the schools (Kenney, Guardaldo, & Brown, 1989). Because so many parents do an inadequate job and adolescents need scientific, reliable sources of information, public schools have a real responsibility. There are several reasons why the public schools need to become involved:

Family life and sex education are natural parts of numerous courses already offered to adolescents. Certainly, sex education ought to be a part of biology classes or health education classes. Home economics classes can deal with parenting relationships, preparation for marriage, and child care. Social studies courses certainly need to focus on the family as the basic social unit and on such problems as sexually transmitted diseases, early marriage, or divorce. Discussions of sex and sexual behavior are hard to avoid in courses in literature. Even the Bible as literature contains a sexual aspect. Therefore, if existing courses are taught properly and honestly, sex education will have a place in many of them.

The school has an important role to play in the sex education of youth.

FOCUS

Education for Abstinence

Recognizing the seriousness and complexity of the teenage pregnancy problem and the problem of increased AIDS transmission, a number of programs have been developed to try to prevent adolescent pregnancy by teaching abstinence. Girls' Clubs of America developed a comprehensive model consisting of two components. The program was designed for 12- to 14-year-old girls. The program's two components were Will Power/Won't Power and a program entitled Growing Together. The Will Power/Won't Power program addresses the social and peer pressures that lead women into early sexual behavior and focuses on building skills that help young teens deal with these issues. This component was offered in cycles of six sessions.

Growing Together is designed to enable parents and daughters to communicate comfortably with each other about human sexuality. This component included five sessions, the first of which was for parents only.

What were the results of the programs? *In the case of Growing Together, nonparticipants were two and a half times as likely as the participants to initiate sexual intercourse during the year being studied.* Factors such as age, religion, race, and having relatives or friends were taken into consideration. The weight of evidence indicated that participation in Growing Together delayed the initiation of sexual intercourse among these young teens.

In the case of Will Power/Won't Power, *those who participated in the program for the longest period of time were less likely to initiate sexual intercourse than those who participated in the program for a lesser period of time.* Those who participated for shorter periods were more than three times as likely to initiate sexual intercourse as those who participated for a longer time (Postrado & Nicholson, 1992).

Preparing youth for happy marriage and responsible parenthood is an important goal. School does not prepare youth for this goal as well as for a vocation. Is it preparing students for living as well as for making a living?

The school, as the professional educational institution, can be equipped to do a fine job. Teachers can be trained, curricula can be developed, and the school can provide necessary resources once the needs are established.

The school is the only social institution that reaches all youth; therefore, it has a unique opportunity to reach the youth who need sex education the most. Parents who are uneducated themselves can't teach their children, but these children, by and large, attend the public schools where they can be exposed to proper programs of sex education. Some community agencies—such as churches and youth organizations—reach only a fraction of youth. All youth attend public school up to a certain age. It's the school alone that can reach these youth.

Increasing numbers of schools are trying to assume a major responsibility in sex education. A national study of sex education at all grade levels in large school districts (cities over 100,000 population) reveals that 75 percent of those districts with junior high schools and 76 percent of those with senior high schools provided some

In another study, the effects of three abstinence-emphasis sex education programs on student attitudes toward sexual activity were evaluated. The programs were administered to seventh- and tenth-grade students in three school districts in the State of Utah. There were three types of programs. The Sex Respect program was presented to students in an urban school district. Teen Aid was taught to suburban students. Values and Choices was presented to students in a rural school district. Socioeconomic statistics showed all districts to be relatively representative of the Utah population. *Findings indicate that all three programs increased abstinence values,* with the Sex Respect producing the most attitude change. The findings indicate that junior high students were more positive than were senior high students in rating the three abstinence programs. This information is important to educators in determining the age at which to initiate a sex education curriculum. Apparently, younger students are influenced more favorably than older students. Also, the females were more positive in rating the programs than males. All the teachers who presented the programs were given favorable ratings.

One finding focused on individual differences and stated that previous sexual behavior (virginity status) and knowledge (informed or naive) would influence student responses to the abstinence program. The findings indicated the virgin–naive students rated the programs most favorably. The researchers concluded that sex education programs that promote abstinence can be effective in producing a positive attitude change towards abstinence, but females have a more positive attitude towards abstinence than do males. Also, although the age of the students must be considered, both high school and junior high students will respond. *The results are interpreted as providing support for the feasibility of introducing abstinence-emphasis sex educational programs into the public school curriculum* (Olsen, Weed, Nielsen, & Jensen, 1992; Olsen, Jensen, & Greaves, 1991).

education to some portion of their students (Sonenstein & Pittman, 1984). Of those secondary districts offering sex education, 73 percent of junior highs and 89 percent of senior highs provided six or more hours of instruction. However, of those offering sex education, only 11 percent of junior high and 16 percent of senior high districts offered separate sex education courses.

Another nationwide study of high schools showed that only about one-third offered separate courses in sex education. Of those four-year schools offering courses, only one-half did so beginning at ninth grade (Orr, 1982). This fact means that a large proportion of adolescents initiates coitis *before* taking a sex education course (Marsiglio & Mott, 1986).

Another nationwide study of sex education in public schools, grades seven through twelve, revealed a gap between what teachers thought should be taught at different grade levels and what was actually being taught (Forrest & Silverman, 1989). Virtually all teachers thought that sex education should cover sexual decision making, abstinence, birth control methods, prevention of pregnancy, and AIDS and other sexually transmitted diseases. Over 82 percent of the schools covered these topics, but generally not until the ninth or tenth grade. Teachers thought that the topic should be covered by grade seven, or eight at the latest. Only about half the schools provided information about sources of birth control. The major problem teachers face in providing sex education is negative pressure from parents, the community, or the school administration (Reis & Seidly, 1989). Teachers of sex education need to be provided with training, support, and agreed-upon guidelines on methodology and procedures (Mellanby, Phelps, & Tripp, 1992).

Nutrition and Weight

CALORIC REQUIREMENTS

During the period of rapid growth, adolescents need greater quantities of food to take care of bodily requirements. As a consequence, they develop voracious appetites. The stomach increases in capacity to be able to digest the increased amounts of food. The caloric requirement for girls may increase on the average by 25 percent from ages 10 to 15. The caloric requirement for boys may increase on the average by 90 percent from ages 10 to 19 (Figure 15.7 shows the increase). As a result, the adolescent boy finds it almost impossible to get enough to eat.

IMPORTANCE OF NUTRITION

Health maintenance depends partly on proper eating habits (Carruth & Goldberg, 1990). Attainment of maximum height, strength, and physical well-being depends on proper nutrition. Nerve, bone, muscle, and other tissue growth requires body-building foods. Nutritional deficiencies are related to emotional instability, premenstrual tension (in females), lower resistance to infection, reduced stamina, and physical and mental retardation. Good nutrition also is extremely important during pregnancy.

DEFICIENCIES

Many adolescents have inadequate diets (U.S. Department of Agriculture and U.S. Department Health and Human Services, 1985). The principal deficiencies are as follows:

1. Insufficient thiamine and riboflavin
2. Insufficient vitamins—especially A and C—caused primarily by lack of fresh vegetables and fruit in the diet
3. Insufficient calcium—caused primarily by an inadequate intake of milk
4. Insufficient iron—especially true in females
5. Insufficient protein—usually true only in females

OVERWEIGHT AND UNDERWEIGHT

Adolescents often worry about being overweight (Cook, Reiley, Stallsmith, & Garretson, 1991). From 10 percent to 15 percent of all adolescents are obese (at least 20 percent overweight or more), girls more than boys. (U.S. Bureau of the Census, 1987b). Being overweight affects the adolescent's emotional adjustment, ego identity development, self-esteem, and social relationships. Being overweight significantly influences adolescents to have negative feelings about their bodies. This is especially true of women's evaluations of themselves (Andersen & LeGrand, 1991). As stated previously, being overweight is also associated with early maturation and affects global, negative self-evaluations of adolescent girls (Alsaker, 1992a). It also is a future health hazard because obesity is related to gynecological disorders, joint disease, hypertension, and cardiovascular disease (Shestowsky, 1983; Stein, 1987).

Underweight adolescents have the opposite condition: They are burning up more calories than they are consuming. Males especially worry about being too skinny or "not having a good build." In one study of 568 adolescent males, over half were dissatisfied with their body, and 71 percent reported eating to gain weight (Fleischer & Read, 1982). Underweight adolescents need to increase the consumption of fattening foods and overcome a poor appetite. They also can conserve energy by spending more hours in bed and omitting strenuous exercise.

ANOREXIA NERVOSA

Anorexia nervosa is a life-threatening emotional disorder characterized by an obsession with being slender (Gilbert & DeBlassie, 1984). About 5 percent to 10 percent of cases are male, and the remainder are females, usually between ages 12 and 18 (Svec, 1987). The major symptoms are a constant preoccupation with dieting; body image disturbance (Mallick, Whipple, & Huerta, 1987) excess weight loss (at least 15 percent below optimal body weight); hyperactivity (excessive exercise) (Warah, 1993); extreme moodiness, loneliness, depression, helplessness, and inadequacy; strong feelings of insecurity; social isolation; and amenorrhea (American Psychiatric Association, 1987). Anorexia is associated with numerous medical conditions: abdominal distress, constipation, metabolic changes, electrolyte abnormalities, hypothermia, dehydration, low blood pressure, sexual dysfunction (Simpson & Ramberg, 1992; Zerbe, 1992), slow heartbeat, and cardiac arrest (which is a frequent cause of death). The anorexic feels cold, even though the body grows fine silky hair to conserve body heat. Kidney malfunction may occur because of a potassium deficiency (Muuss, 1985).

Once the illness had developed, anorexics become thin and emaciated in appearance. Treichel (1982) found that malnutrition causes brain abnormalities, impaired mental performance, and lengthened reaction time and perceptual speed. Medical problems associated with malnutrition cause death in 5 percent to 10 percent of anorexics. Obsession with dieting combined with a compulsion to exercise leads to social isolation and withdrawal from friends and family. Hunger and fatigue are usually denied, and any attempt to interfere with the regime is angrily resisted. Anorexics are very hard to treat (Grant & Fodor, 1984).

BULIMIA

Bulimia is a binge–purge syndrome. It is characterized by a compulsive and rapid consumption of large quantities of high-calorie food followed by efforts to eliminate the food (Stein & Reichert, 1990). According to one study, bulimic clients in an outpatient setting revealed an average of 13.7 hours spent in binge eating each week, with a range of 15 minutes to 8 hours for each episode (Mitchell, Pyle, & Eckert, 1981). Bingeing and purging could occur many times daily. Caloric consumption ranged from 1,200 to 11,500 calories per episode, with carbohydrates as the primary food. Many clients could not perceive a sense of fullness. Episodes took place secretly, usually in the afternoon, evening, or at night. Induced vomiting was the most common purging method. Other times bulimics used amphetamines, enemas, diuretics, laxatives, compulsive exercising, or fasting to offset the huge food intake (LeClair & Berkowitz, 1983).

Bulimics feel a compulsion to eat, but because of concern about their weight, purge

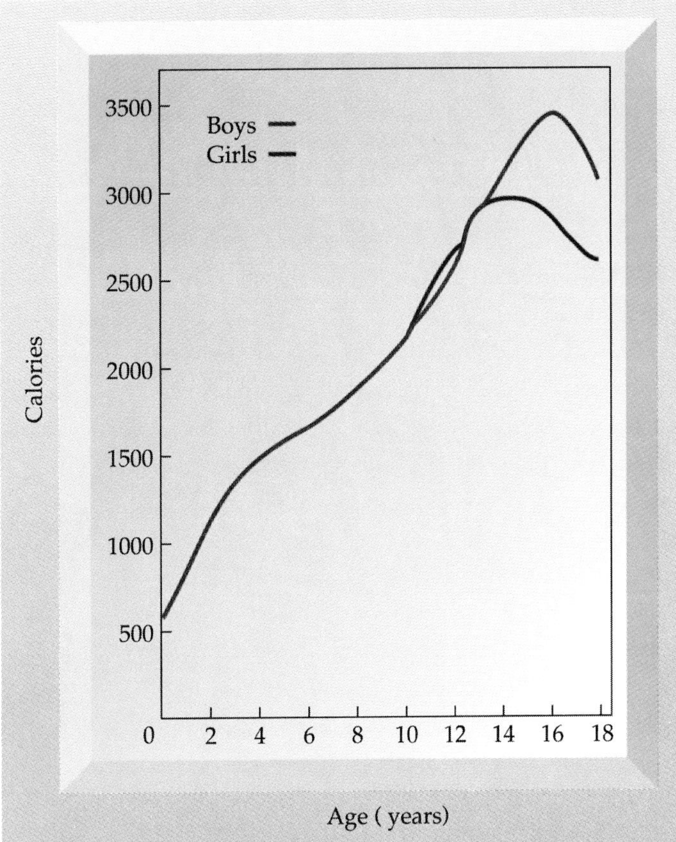

FIGURE 15.7 Daily caloric requirements for both sexes from birth to eighteen years.

Redrawn from "Energy Requirements" by E. L. Holt, Jr., 1972, in H. L. Barnett and A. H. Einhorn (Eds.), *Pediatrics*, 15th ed., p. 131. By permission of Appleton & Lange.

FOCUS

Five Theories about Causes of Anorexia

Biological theory. A disturbance in the hypothalamus causes anorexic behavior.

Psychobiologic regression hypothesis. Once body weight drops below a critical level because of inadequate diet, neuroendocrine functions are impaired, which reverses the developmental changes of puberty. The anorexic regresses to a prepubertal stage of development (Muuss, 1985, pp. 526, 527).

Psychosexual theory. The fact that anorexia appears at puberty after the development of sexual characteristics suggests that sexual conflict is a central issue in the illness (Romeo, 1984). The anorexic is unwilling to accept her role as a woman and her feminine sexuality. She fears sexual intimacy, so she uses the disorder to delay or regress her psychosexual development.

Social theory. Anorexics are brainwashed by a culture that emphasizes being slim, so they become obsessed with food and diet (Hertzler & Grun, 1990).

Family systems theory. Anorexics often have disturbed relationships with their parents (Bailey, 1991; Eisele, Hertsgaard, & Light, 1986). The families are often rigid and overprotective, with a hypochondriacal concern for the child's health (Brone & Fisher, 1988). Often a power struggle develops between the adolescent girl and her parents, particularly with her mother (Goldstein, 1981; Levin, Adelson, Buchalter, & Bilcher, 1983). This desire to guide and control becomes more evident as parental concern grows. The more the parents try to change the pattern, the more intense the power struggle becomes (Russell, Halasz, & Beaumont, 1990).

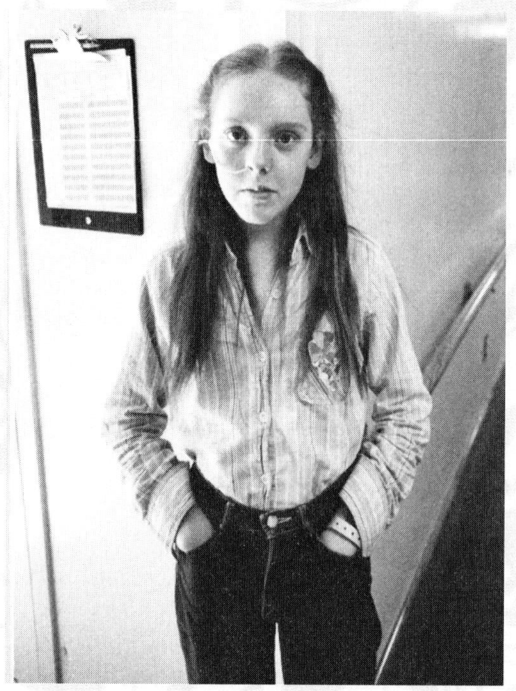

The majority of anorexic victims are female. How would you explain this?

afterward. Binges usually follow periods of stress and are accompanied by anxiety, depressed mood, and self-deprecating thoughts during and after the episode (Ledoux, Choquet, & Manfredi, 1993). The illness is most common in college-age females or those in their early 20s (Lachenmeyer & Muni-Brander, 1988), although frequency of occurrence is increasing among high school females (Johnson et al., 1984). Some female athletes use pathogenic weight-control techniques such as laxatives, vomiting, fasting, and diet aids to control their weight (Taub & Blinde, 1992).

Bulimics have low self-esteem, are anxious and depressed, and have strong moral beliefs (Baird & Sights, 1986; Brouwers, 1988). They wish to be perfect, yet have negative self-worth and a poor self-image, are shy, and lack assertiveness (Holleran, Pascale, & Fraley, 1988). They are often preoccupied with fear of rejection in sexual relationships and with not being attractive enough to please a man (Van Thorre & Vogel, 1985). Because of the drive for perfection, anxiety builds up, which is relieved through lapses of control during bingeing and purging episodes. This is followed by feelings of guilt and shame, which contribute to the sense of low self-esteem and depression. Psychological evaluation of adolescent bulimics indicate they are more depressed, self-punitive, and negativistic than their peers, and that they have more disorganized thoughts, inaccurate perceptions, and impaired judgment (Smith, Hillard, & Roll, 1991). There is an especially high correlation between eating disorders and depression (Nagel & Jones, 1992a). Bulimics are often difficult to treat because they resist seeking help or they sabotage treatment. Both bulimics and anorexics need short-term intervention to restore body weight and to save their life, followed by long-term therapy to ameliorate personality and family problems.

For parents and for professionals in the educational, physical, and mental health-care fields, the need is to be aware of the influence of social pressures on teenagers' perceptions of body image and appearance. Professionals and parents can help adolescents resist societal pressure to conform to unrealistic standards of appearance and provide guidance on nutrition, realistic body ideals, and achievement of self-esteem and self-efficacy (Nagel & Jones, 1992b).

Summary

1. The endocrine glands are ductless glands that secrete hormones directly into the bloodstream. The hormones tell different cells what to do and when to act.
2. The three most important glands related to sexuality are the pituitary gland, the adrenal glands, and the gonads.
3. The pituitary secretes HGH, which regulates growth; gonadotropic hormones (FSH and LH) that stimulate the gonads (ovaries and testes) to function; and LTH, which stimulates milk production.
4. The ovaries secrete estrogen, which is responsible for sexual maturation, and progesterone, which is active in the menstrual cycle.
5. The testes secrete testosterone, which is responsible for sexual maturation in males.
6. Both feminizing and masculinizing hormones (estrogens and androgens) are present in both boys and girls. The ratio of male to female hormones is partly responsible for the development of male or female characteristics.
7. The adrenal glands also secrete both androgens and estrogens in both males and females.
8. The hypothalamus secretes GnRH, which acts on the pituitary to trigger the secretion of the gonadotropic hormones that act on the gonads (the testes and ovaries).
9. The primary sex organs of the male are the testes, scrotum, epididymis, seminal vesicles, prostate gland, Cowper's glands, penis, vas deferens, and urethra, all of which mature at puberty. The most important change within the testes is the production of mature sperm cells. Boys begin ejaculating semen and sperm cells at the mean age of 13.7. Boys need to be prepared for the onset of nocturnal emissions.
10. The primary internal female sex organs that develop during puberty are the ovaries, fallopian tubes, uterus, and vagina. The external female organs are known collectively as the vulva, and include the mons veneris (mons pubis), labia majora, labia minora, clitoris, vestibule, and hymen.
11. On the average, females begin menstruating at 12 to 13 years of age. Girls need to be prepared in a positive way for menarche (first menstruation).
12. There are a number of factors that influence the timing of sexual maturation: heredity and genetics, nutrition, medical care, socioeconomic status as it influences diet, stress as it influences eating habits and body weight, and percentage of body fat.
13. Sexual maturation also includes the development of secondary sexual characteristics.
14. One of the earliest signs of the physical changes of adolescents is the growth spurt that begins early in adolescence.

A number of factors are important in determining the total mature height achieved: heredity, nutrition, age of sexual maturation, and total height achieved before puberty.

15. Some girls and boys are early or late maturers. Early-maturing boys have a physical and social advantage, although parents tend to expect more of them at this age. Some early-maturing girls are at a disadvantage in elementary school, but come into their own in junior high school, enjoying many social advantages.
16. Late-maturing boys tend to suffer social inferiority because of their delayed growth and development. Late-maturing girls also tend to be at a distinct social disadvantage.
17. Precocious puberty means early sexual maturation.
18. Adolescents are very concerned about their body image and physical attractiveness. They have been influenced by images of the ideal build as taught in our culture, which emphasizes medium builds.
19. Acne is a problem for some adolescents.
20. The goals of sex education of adolescents are to develop knowledge and understanding of human sexuality, to improve sexual health, to prevent unwanted pregnancy, and to prevent AIDS and other sexually transmitted diseases.
21. Both the parents and the schools have important roles to play in sex education, but studies indicate that adolescents are still receiving their information primarily from peers.
22. A number of programs have been developed that encourage sexual abstinence before marriage. The research data indicate that some programs increase the likelihood that participants will delay the initiation of sexual intercourse and also increase abstinence values.
23. Good nutrition is very important to good health. Common deficiencies include calcium, iron, and protein; and vitamins A, C, thiamine, and riboflavin.
24. Being either overweight or underweight is a problem.
25. The two most serious eating disorders are anorexia nervosa and bulimia, both of which can be life-threatening diseases, and both of which are hard to treat.

Key Terms

Acne *p. 405*
Adrenal glands *p. 394*
Amenorrhea *p. 398*
Anabolic steroids *p. 394*
Anorexia nervosa *p. 404*
Bartholin's glands *p. 396*
Bulimia *p. 404*
Clitoris *p. 396*
Corpus luteum *p. 392*
Cowper's glands *p. 394*
Endocrine glands *p. 392*
Epididymis *p. 394*
Estrogens *p. 392*
Fallopian tubes *p. 396*
Follicle-stimulating hormone (FSH) *p. 392*
Gonadotropic hormones *p. 392*
Gonadotropin-releasing hormone (GnRH) *p. 394*
Gonads *p. 392*
Hormones *p. 392*
Human growth hormone (HGH) *p. 392*
Hymen *p. 396*
Hypothalamus *p. 394*
Labia majora *p. 396*
Labia minora *p. 396*
Luteinizing hormone (LH) *p. 392*
Menarche *p. 396*
Mons veneris (mons pubis) *p. 396*
Nocturnal emissions *p. 395*
Ovaries *p. 396*
Ovum *p. 392*
Penis *p. 394*
Pituitary gland *p. 392*
Precocious puberty *p. 403*
Primary sexual characteristics *p. 399*
Progesterone *p. 392*
Prolactin *p. 392*
Prostate gland *p. 394*

Scrotum *p. 394*
Secondary sexual characteristics *p. 399*
Seminal vesicles *p. 394*
Testes *p. 394*
Urethra *p. 394*
Uterus *p. 396*
Vagina *p. 396*
Vas deferens *p. 394*
Vulva *p. 396*

Discussion Questions

1. Should athletes be allowed to take steroids to improve their ability? Have you ever known anyone who did? What were the results?
2. To men: When you had your first nocturnal emission, did you understand what was happening? Were you prepared for it? How did you feel?
3. To women: When you first started to menstruate, did you understand what was happening? Were you prepared for it? How did you feel?
4. Comment on the attitudes in American culture toward female breasts and male penis size. What effect do these attitudes have on adolescents?
5. Do you know anyone who matured early? Late? What were the effects?
6. What can be done if a person has acne?
7. What factors prevent some adolescents from getting a balanced diet?
8. What were your principal sources of sex information as you were growing up? Did your parents try to provide sex information for you at home? Describe. What might they have done differently?
9. What is your attitude toward sex education in the schools? What sort of sex education program did you receive in your school? Describe. What did you think of it? How could it have been improved?
10. Do you think a school program in education for abstinence will help prevent early sexual intercourse and pregnancy? Will it change the sex behavior of teenagers?
11. What can be done if a person is overweight? What helps the most? What can be done if a person is underweight? What helps the most?
12. Do you know anyone who suffered from anorexia nervosa? Describe. What were the results? Do you know anyone who was bulimic? Describe. What were the results?

Suggested Readings

Coles, R., & Stokes, G. (1985). *Sex and the American teenager.* New York: Harper & Row, 1985. Interview survey of teen sexual attitudes and behavior.

Colman, W. (1988). *Understanding and preventing AIDS.* Chicago: Children's Press. For teenagers and their parents.

Lerner, R. M., & Foch, T. T. (Eds.). (1987). *Biological-psychological interactions in early adolescence.* Hillsdale, NJ: Erlbaum. Series of articles.

Miller, B. C., Josefina, J. C., Paikoff, R. L., & Peterson, J. L. (Eds.). *Preventing adolescent pregnancy: Model programs and evaluations.* Newbury Park, CA: Sage. Detailed discussions of programs.

Rice, F. P. (1989). *Human sexuality.* Dubuque, IA: Wm. C. Brown. The author's comprehensive college text on human sexuality. Includes all age groups.

Rice, F. P. (1996). *The adolescent: Development, relationships, and culture* (8th ed.). Boston: Allyn and Bacon. The author's comprehensive textbook on adolescence.

Cognitive Development: Formal Operational Thought, Scholastic Aptitude, and School

Chapter 16

FORMAL OPERATIONAL THOUGHT

Characteristics • Effects on Personality and Behavior • FOCUS: *Comparison of Childhood and Adolescent Thought* • Critique of Piaget's Formal Operational Stage • FOCUS: *Formal Operational Thinking and Self-Concept* • Adolescent Education and Formal Operational Thought • Problem-Finding Stage

SCHOLASTIC APTITUDE

Scholastic Aptitude Test (SAT) • Revisions of the SAT • ACT • FOCUS: *Gender Differences in Spatial Abilities and Achievement*

SCHOOL

Trends in American Education • Enrollment in High School • Types of High Schools • LIVING ISSUES: *Tracking* • Dropouts • FOCUS: *Student Alienation* • PARENTING ISSUES: *Middle-Class Parenting and Underachievement* • PARENTING ISSUES: *Changes in Parents' Work Status and Adolescents' Adjustment to School*

Formal Operational Thought

As we have seen in Chapter 8, Piaget outlined four stages of cognitive development: the *sensorimotor stage* (birth 2 years,) the *preoperational stage* (2 to 7 years), the *concrete operational stage* (7 to 11 years), and the *formal operational stage* (11 years and up). The formal operational stage is discussed in this section on the cognitive development of adolescents.

CHARACTERISTICS

During the formal operational stage of development, the thinking of adolescents begins to differ radically from that of children (Piaget, 1972). Children perform concrete operations and arrange things into classes, relations, or numbers, making logical "groupings" and classifications. However, they never integrate their thought into a single, total, logical system. Adolescents, however, are able to use propositional logic. In formal operations, they are able to reason, systematize their ideas, and construct theories. Furthermore, they can test these theories scientifically and logically, considering several variables, and are able to discover truth scientifically (Inhelder & Piaget, 1958). Adolescents are able to assume the role of scientists because they have the capacity to construct and test theories. Elkind (1967) called the formal operational stage *the conquest of thought.*

Piaget conducted an interesting experiment to discover the strategies adolescents use in solving problems. This experiment involved a pendulum suspended by a string (see Figure 16.1). The problem was to find out what would affect the oscillatory speed of the pendulum. The subjects were to investigate four possible effects: starting the pendulum with various degrees of force, releasing the pendulum from various heights, changing its weight, or changing the length of the pendulum. The subjects were free to solve the problem in any way they chose.

The adolescents showed three basic characteristics in their problem-solving behavior. *First,* they planned their investigations systematically. They began to test all possible causes for variation in the pendulum swings: various degrees of force or push, high or low height, light or heavy weight, and long or short string. *Second,* they recorded the results accurately and objectively. *Third,* they formed logical conclusions.

During the formal operational stage of development, the thinking of adolescents begins to differ radically from that of children.

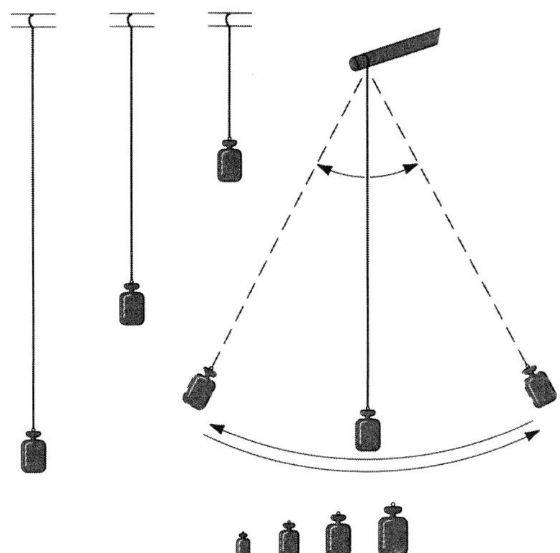

FIGURE 16.1 The Pendulum problem. The pendulum problem utilizes a simple apparatus consisting of a string, which can be shortened or lengthened, and a set of varying weights. The other variables that at first might be considered relevant are the height of the release point and the force of the push given by the subject.

From *The Growth of Logical Thinking: From Childhood to Adolescence* by Jean Piaget and Barbel Inhelder. Copyright © 1958 by Basic Books, Inc. Reprinted by permission of Basic Books, a division of HarperCollins Publishers, Inc., New York.

For example, they first observed that both the force and the height of the drop of the pendulum had no effect on oscillatory speed. They next tried different combinations of weight and found out that the oscillation speed remained the same regardless of the weight. They did discover that changing the string length (the pendulum length) alone determined the speed of oscillation. Other researchers have replicated this experiment many times.

By trial and error, children may come up with the right answer but they fail to use systematic procedures to find the answer and give logical explanations of the solutions. They often form conclusions that are premature and false because they have not considered all of the important facts and are not able to reason logically about them. Children tend to hold tenaciously to their initial opinions even when presented with contrary evidence. They even try to make the circumstances fit their preconceived notions:

> In summary, three interrelated characteristics of adolescent thought have emerged. These are the ability to derive a proposition from two or more variables or a complex relationship; the ability to suggest mentally the possible effect of one or more variables; and the capacity to combine and separate variables in a hypothetical-deductive framework ("if this is so, this will happen") so that a reasonable possibility is recognized before the test is made in reality. The fundamental property of adolescent thought is this reversible maneuvering between reality and possibility (Gallager & Noppe, 1976, p. 202).

To do formal operational thinking, adolescents are able to be *flexible.* They can be quite versatile in their thoughts, and can devise many interpretations of an observed outcome, without relying on preconceived ideas. In contrast, younger children are confused by unexpected results that are inconsistent with their simple preconceptions.

Preoperational children begin to use symbols, but *the formal operational adolescents now begin to use a second symbol system: a set of symbols of symbols.* For example, algebraic signs and metaphorical speech are symbols for numbers and/or words. The capacity to identify symbols makes the adolescent's thought much more flexible than the child's. Words can now carry double or triple meanings. Cartoons can represent a complete story that would otherwise have be explained in words. Junior high school youth have no difficulty understanding religious symbols or political cartoons that younger children cannot comprehend. Algebra may be understood by adolescents but not be elementary school children.

Adolescents are also able to orient themselves toward what is abstract and not immediately present. This facility enables them to distinguish possibility from present reality, to project themselves into the future, and to think about what might be (Bart, 1983). Adolescents have not only the capacity to accept and understand what is given, but also the ability to conceive of what might occur. Because they can construct ideas, they have the ability to elaborate on these ideas and generate new thoughts. They become inventive, imaginative, and original in their thinking, and "possibility dominates reality." "The adolescent is the person who commits himself to possibilities . . . who begins to build 'systems' or 'theo-

Educational experiences can be geared to teaching scientific methods of problem solving.

Sociocentrism—a focus of attention on social problems and the concerns of society

ries' in the largest sense of the term" (Baker, 1982; Inhelder & Piaget, 1958).

In summary, formal thinking, according to Piaget, involves four major aspects: *introspection* (thinking about thought), *abstract thinking* (going beyond the real to what is possible); *logical thinking* (being able to consider all important facts and ideas and to form correct conclusions, such as the ability to determine cause and effect), and *hypothetical reasoning* (formulating hypotheses and examining the evidence for them, considering numerous variables).

EFFECTS ON PERSONALITY AND BEHAVIOR

Idealism

Adolescents' power of reflective thinking enables them to evaluate what they have learned as children (Schmidt & Davison, 1983) and to become more capable of moral reasoning (Steinberg, Greenberger, Jacobi, & Garduque, 1981). Their ability to distinguish the possible from the real enables them to imagine what the adult world might be like under ideal circumstances. They compare the possible with the actual, recognize that the actual is less than ideal, and so become idealistic rebels (White, 1980).

For a while, some adolescents develop the equivalent of a messianic complex, seeing themselves in a major effort to reform the world. Usually the efforts of young adolescents are confined to verbal discussion, but some older adolescents get caught up in group movements that seek the utopian reconstruction of society. By late adolescence, attention shifts from egocentrism to a newfound **sociocentrism.** Adolescents begin to focus on values that have long-term implications rather then those that emphasize immediate gratification and goal satisfaction. They begin to emphasize values that are more noble and altruistic in nature and achievement in the future rather than just in the present. Their attention begins to be focused on others rather than the inner self.

Adolescents also become champions of the underdog. Shapiro (1973) believed that adolescents' own inner conflicts account for their empathetic capacities for the suffering of others. They can easily identify with the oppressed, the victims of selfish society, the poor, and the weak. They perceive that social injustices mirror their own internal, individual struggles. On study focused on the fact that those who score high in formal reasoning tend to give a high ranking to value dimensions associated with self-reliance, competence, and independence (Darmody, 1991).

Discrepancy

Adolescents are sometimes accused of hypocrisy because of the discrepancy between what they say and what they actually do. Elkind (1978) illustrated this tendency with two examples. *First,* his son lamented about his brother's going into his room and taking his things. He berated his father for not punishing the culprit; yet the same boy felt no guilt about going into his father's study, using his calculator and typewriter, and playing his music on his father's stereo without permission. *Second,* a group of young people were involved in a "Walk for Water" drive, in which sponsors were paid for each mile walked. The money was for pollution control. The next day, however, a drive along the route the youths had walked revealed a roadside littered with fast-food wrappers and beverage cans. City workers had be hired to clean up the mess. The question was: Did the cost of cleaning up amount to more money than was collected? And weren't these adolescents hypocritical? They objected to pollution, yet they were among the chief offenders in defacing their environment (Elkind, 1978).

The behavior of these adolescents reveals the discrepancy between idealism and behavior. Early adolescents have the capacity to formulate general principles such as "Thou shalt not pollute" but lack the experience to see the application of these general rules to specific practice. Youths believe that if they can conceive and express high moral principles, they have attained them, and that nothing concrete need be done. This attitude upsets and confuses adults, who insist that ideals cannot be attained instantly and that one must work for them (Elkind, 1978).

Adolescents can manifest hypocrisy in another way. They pretend to be what they are not. They are expected to conform to parental viewpoints and beliefs even when they do not agree with them. They are expected to be open and honest but are chastised when they are. They are expected to like school but rarely do. They are expected not be hurt or angry when they really are. They are expected not to engage in behavior that will hurt or disappoint parents, so they do not talk to them about important things. They are expected to pretend to be what they are not. They are pressured not to be, not to feel, and not to desire. They are expected to deny the self and so behave hypocritically.

Self-Consciousness and Egocentrism

Formal operational thinking also results in the development of a new form of egocentrism (Adams & Jones, 1982; Hudson & Gray, 1986; deRosenroll, 1987). The capacity to think about their own thoughts makes adolescents become acutely aware of themselves. As a result, they become egocentric, self-conscious, and introspective. They become so concerned about themselves that they may conclude that others are equally obsessed with their appearance and behavior (Peterson & Roscoe, 1991). "It is this belief that others are preoccupied with his appearance and behavior that constitutes the egocentrism of the adolescent" (Elkind, 1967, p. 1029). Adolescents feel they are "on stage" much of the time, so that much of their energy is spent "reacting to an imaginary audience." As a result, they become extremely self-conscious. Whether in the lunchroom or on the bus going home, youths feel they are the center of attention (Goossens, Seiffge-Krenke, & Marcoen, 1992).

Elkind (1967) also discusses what he terms **personal fable**—adolescent's belief in the uniqueness of their own experiences. Because of their belief that they are important to so many people, they come to regard themselves as special and unique. This may be why so many adolescents believe that misfortunes such as unwanted pregnancies or accidents happen only to others, never to them.

Personal fable—belief in the uniqueness of one's own experience

Self-consciousness and egocentrism have other manifestations. Adolescents believe everyone is looking at them, but they feel totally alone, unique in a vast, uncaring universe. To always be on stage, scrutinized but rarely understood, imposes a terrific emotional strain. As a result, they employ numerous psychological mechanisms to protect their frail egos. They become critical and sarcastic, partly as a defense against their own feelings of inferiority and as a way of making themselves look good (Elkind, 1975). Those with low self-esteem tend to present a false front to others and to mask their true feelings by fabricating an image (Hauck & Loughead, 1985). The intellectualization and newfound asceticism of college students have been explained as just such a defense mechanism.

Adolescents are often self-centered, and they are frequently self-admiring, too. Their boorishness, loudness, and fadish

Achievement of formal operational thinking is accompanied by increasing egocentrism and self-consciousness.

dress reflect what they feel others admire. The boy who stands in front of the mirror for two hours combing his hair is probably imagining the swooning reactions he will produce from his girlfriend.

Conformity

One would expect that adolescents who are capable of logical reasoning processes would also be creative. But investigations of the relationship of adolescent thinking processes to creative behavior suggest a negative relationship: Adolescents become less creative, not more so (Wolf, 1981). The reason is not because they are less capable of being creative. They have a greater potential than before. But in actuality they are less creative because of the pressures on them to conform—from both their peers and society in general. The price they pay for acceptance is conformity. As a result, they squelch their individuality and begin to dress, think, and act like others in groups to which they want to belong. One study found that adolescents' self-monitoring behavior increased from early to late adolescence. That is, individuals became more conscious of how others wanted them to behave and so they adjusted their behavior accordingly (Pledger, 1992). Another study emphasized that adolescents who rate highest in self-trust (who believe in themselves) are more willing to risk doing things that are imaginative and creative (Earl, 1987).

Decentering and a Life Plan

In the process of becoming adults, adolescents gradually begin to develop more cognitive objectivity and perspective. They begin to cure themselves of their idealistic crises and to return to the reality that is the beginning of adulthood. Piaget and Inhelder (1969) go on to emphasize that "the focal point of the decentering process is the entrance into the occupational world or the beginning of serious professional training. The adolescent becomes an adult when he undertakes a real job. It is then that he is transformed from the idealistic reformer into an achiever" (p. 346).

Piaget refers to the importance of adolescent work in the community as a facilitator of human growth. He states that work helps the adolescent meet the storm and stress of that period. Work experience can also stimulate the development of social understanding and socially competent behavior (Steinberg, Greenberger, Jacobi, & Garduque, 1981). True integration into society comes when the adolescent begins to affirm a life plan and adopt a social role.

CRITIQUE OF PIAGET'S FORMAL OPERATIONAL STAGE

Ages and Percentages

Since Piaget formulated his concept of a formal operational stage of cognitive development, researchers have been examining various components of the formulation. The age at which the formal operational stage replaces the concrete operational stage is one question that has to be raised. Piaget (1972) himself advanced the possibility that in some circumstances, the appearance of formal operations may be delayed to 15 to 20 years of age and "that perhaps in extremely disadvantageous conditions, such a type of thought will never really take shape" (p. 1012). Piaget (1971) acknowledged that social environment can accelerate or delay the onset of formal operations. Research has shown that fewer economically deprived adolescents achieve formal thought than do their more privileged counterparts and that there is a complete absence of formal operations among the mentally retarded (Gaylor-Ross, 1975).

Parents, teachers, and other adults need to realize that not all same-age adolescents are at the same stage of development. Some have not yet achieved formal operations. To ask these youths to make decisions from among numerous alternatives or variables that cannot be grasped simultaneously is to ask the impossible. Very few youths may make the transition to formal operations by age 10 or 11, and only about 40 percent have progressed beyond concrete operations by high school graduation (Bauman, 1978).

Test Level

The measured percentages of people reaching formal operational thinking depend partially on the criteria for formal thinking that are established and the tests

FOCUS

Comparison of Childhood and Adolescent Thought

The way children approach problems and the logical, systematic way adolescents approach problems is described below:

> E. A. Peel . . . asked children what they thought about the following event: "Only brave pilots are allowed to fly over high mountains. A fighter pilot flying over the Alps collided with an aerial cableway and cut a main cable, causing some cars to fall to the glacier below. Several people were killed." A child at the concrete operational level answered: "I think the pilot was not very good at flying." A formal operational child responded: "He was either not informed of the mountain railway on his route or he was flying too low. Also his flying compass may have been affected by something before or after take-off, thus setting him off course causing collision with the cable."

The concrete operational child assumes that if there was a collision the pilot was a bad pilot; the formal operational child considers all the possibilities that might have caused the collision. The concrete operational child adopts the hypothesis that seems most probable or likely to him or her. The formal operational child constructs all possibilities and checks them out one by one (Kohlberg & Gilligan, 1971, pp. 1061, 1062).

employed to evaluate that criteria. Piaget distinguished between an easy level of tests (III-A) and a more advanced level (III-B). Arlin (1975) and Kuhn (1979) observed that only approximately 50 percent of the adult population actually attain the full stage of formal thinking (III-B). Piaget (1980) readily admitted that the subjects of his study were "from the better schools in Geneva" and that his conclusions were based on a "privileged population." However, he still maintained that "all normal individuals are capable of reaching the level of formal operation" (Piaget, 1980, p. 75) as long as the environment provides the necessary cognitive stimulation. Actually, not all adolescents or adults reach the formal level, but there is still a significant increase in the use of formal operational thinking among adolescents between ages 11 and 15.

Maturation and Intelligence

Maturation of the nervous system plays an important role in cognitive development, because the nervous system must be sufficiently developed for any real thought to take place. This is one reason why a greater percentage of older adolescents exhibit formal thought than do younger adolescents. Webb (1974) tested very bright 6- to 11-year-old children (IQs of 160 and above) to determine their levels of thinking. All subjects performed the concrete operational tasks easily, showing that they were cognitively at their developmental age, but only four males, age 10 and older, solved the formal thought problems, indicating that regardless of high intelligence, a degree of maturation was necessary for movement into the next stage of cognitive development. Other research helps explain

Sociocultural and environmental factors influence the development of formal operational thought.

further the relationship among development, intelligence, and cognition. Other things being equal, individuals with high IQs are more likely to develop formal thought sooner than those with low IQs, but *it is the interaction of age and intelligence that contributes to cognitive ability* (Cloutier & Goldschmid, 1976).

Cross-Cultural Studies

Formal thought is, however, more dependent on social experience than is sensorimotor or concrete operational thought (Carlson, 1973). Adolescents from various cultural backgrounds show considerable variability in abstract reasoning abilities. Some cultures offer more opportunities to adolescents to develop abstract thinking than others do, by providing a rich verbal environment and experiences that facilitate growth by exposure to problem-solving situations.

Social institutions such as the family and school accelerate or retard the development of formal operations. Parents who encourage academic excellence, ideational explorations, exchanges of thoughts, and the attainment of ambitious educational and occupational goals are fostering cognitive growth. Schools that encourage students to develop problem-solving skills and to acquire abstract reasoning enhance cognitive development.

ADOLESCENT EDUCATION AND FORMAL OPERATIONAL THOUGHT

Problem-finding stage—a fifth stage of cognitive development characterized by the ability to create, to discover, and to formulate problems

Many students are used to traditional methods of instruction that involve lectures, memorization, and so forth, so they have difficulty adjusting to methods designed to encourage free thinking (Maroufi, 1989). However, development of abstract thinking and formal operations problem solving can be encouraged in a number of ways. Discussion groups, debates, question periods, problem-solving sessions, and science experiments are approaches that encourage the development of formal thinking and problem-solving abilities. Teachers need to be prepared to handle group discussion and stimulate interchange and feedback. Experimental or problematic situations can be presented that allow students opportunities to observe, analyze possibilities, and draw inferences about perceived relationships. Teachers who use authoritarian approaches rather than social interchange stifle real thinking. Some students develop higher cognitive abilities at a relatively slow pace, so teachers must be willing to give explicit help and encouragement and allow the necessary time for reasoning capacities to develop.

Piaget (1972) sets forth two goals of education that incorporate this philosophy.

> *The principal goal of education is to create men who are capable of doing new things,* not simply of repeating what other generations have done—men who are creative, inventive, and discoverers. *The second goal of education is to form minds which can be critical, can verify and not accept everything they are offered. . . .* We need pupils who are active, who learn early to find out by themselves, partly by their own spontaneous activity and partly through material we set up for them, who learn early to tell what is verifiable and what is simply the first idea to come to them (p. 5).

PROBLEM-FINDING STAGE

Progressive changes in thought structure may extend beyond the level of formal operations. The suggestion is that cognitive growth is continuous; there is no end point limiting the possibility for new thought structures to appear. Researchers continue to seek these new structures (Commons, Richards, & Kuhn, 1982).

There is some evidence that a fifth stage of development can be differentiated. It has been labeled a **problem-finding stage.** This new stage represents an ability to discover problems not yet delineated, to describe

FOCUS

Formal Operational Thinking and Self-Concept

The capacity to think about themselves is necessary in adolescents' process of developing self-concept and identity. In doing this, they have to formulate a number of postulates about themselves, such as "I am physically attractive" or "I'm smart in school" or "I'm popular." These postulates are based on a number of specifics, such as "I'm attractive because I have pretty hair, a nice figure, or the boys notice me." Because of formal operational thinking they are able to entertain a number of simultaneous ideas and to test each one by, for example, asking a friend: "What do you think of my hair?" or "Do you think I have ugly hair?" *Gradually they begin to sort out what they feel is truth from error about themselves and to formulate total concepts of self.*

these problems, or to raise general questions from ill-defined problems.

Only some people in the problem-solving stage reach the problem-finding stage. Subjects who score high in problem finding have reached formal operational thinking, but not all subjects who have reached formal thinking score high in problem finding. However, sequencing of development was evident: Formal operations has to be accomplished before persons could move on to the next stage.

Scholastic Aptitude

SCHOLASTIC APTITUDE TEST (SAT)

The **Scholastic Aptitude Test** (SAT) is one of the most widely used tests in the United States. It is a multiple-choice exam with two parts, a verbal section and a math section, which are each scored on a scale of 200–800. The SAT is the predominant college entrance exam in twenty-two states, and 88 percent of all colleges use it (Franco, 1983). Over one million high school seniors took the test in 1990. The combined verbal and math scores often determine eligibility not only for admission but also for financial aid and scholarships. The Education Testing Service (ETS), which produces the test, claims that when combined with high school records, the SAT is a better predictor of students' first-year performance in college than any other measurement. Nevertheless, the complaints over the use or misuse of the test grow louder (Rice, 1979; Robinson, 1983).

Scholastic Aptitude Test (SAT)—the most widely used test for youths to determine their aptitude for college work

The test is supposed to measure basic abilities acquired over a student's lifetime and is thus supposed to be immune to last-minute cramming and "coaching." But a study by the Federal Trade Commission's Bureau of Consumer Protection showed that special coaching can improve SAT scores for each part by an average of 25 points out of the possible 800 (Rice, 1979). In one nationwide chain, more than 80 coaching schools tutored 30,000 students in one year, and improved scored on the average by 25 points. In individual cases, these schools claim they can improve scores up

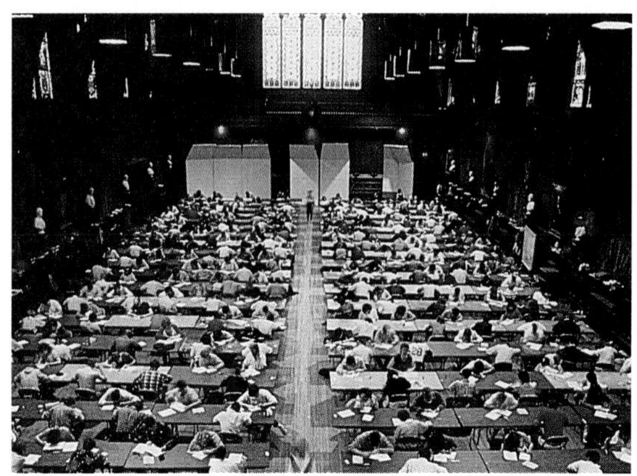

Millions of students are given the SAT as a basis of evaluation of aptitude to do college work.

to 100 points. The author talked to a lawyer who, as a student, wanted to raise his verbal score on the LSAT (Law School Aptitude Test) before applying to law school. He studied a vocabulary list of the 5,000 most-used words and was able to raise his verbal score by 60 points.

The basic question is: If coaching can raise a student's score, should the test be relied on as a basic measure of scholastic aptitude and as a standard for college admission? In all fairness, the College Entrance Examination Board warns against making admission decisions on the basis of the SAT scores alone. The ETS itself has said that an individual's score can vary plus or minus 30 to 35 points, which is a spread of 60 to 70 points. For these reasons, some of the best schools may rely more on class rank, high school grades, interviews, student essays, and other admission procedures (Chance, 1988). Even high marks from high school may be questioned, for standards vary from school to school. Also, grading standards have become more lenient so the number of students with A averages has increased so rapidly that there are now as many A students as there are those with C averages.

Some authorities suggest that achievement tests would be a better way of predicting college success than SATs. (See the following section on the ACT.) Such tests have several advantages. They evaluate a student's mastery of a particular subject area. They encourage high schools to offer more rigorous courses. They also encourage students to work harder in these courses because they would have to pass tests on the subjects to get into college (Chance, 1988).

The verbal SAT score averages of college-bound seniors dropped until 1980, after which they increased until 1986. Since 1986, math scores have declined for males and risen slightly for females, while verbal scores have declined for both males and fe-

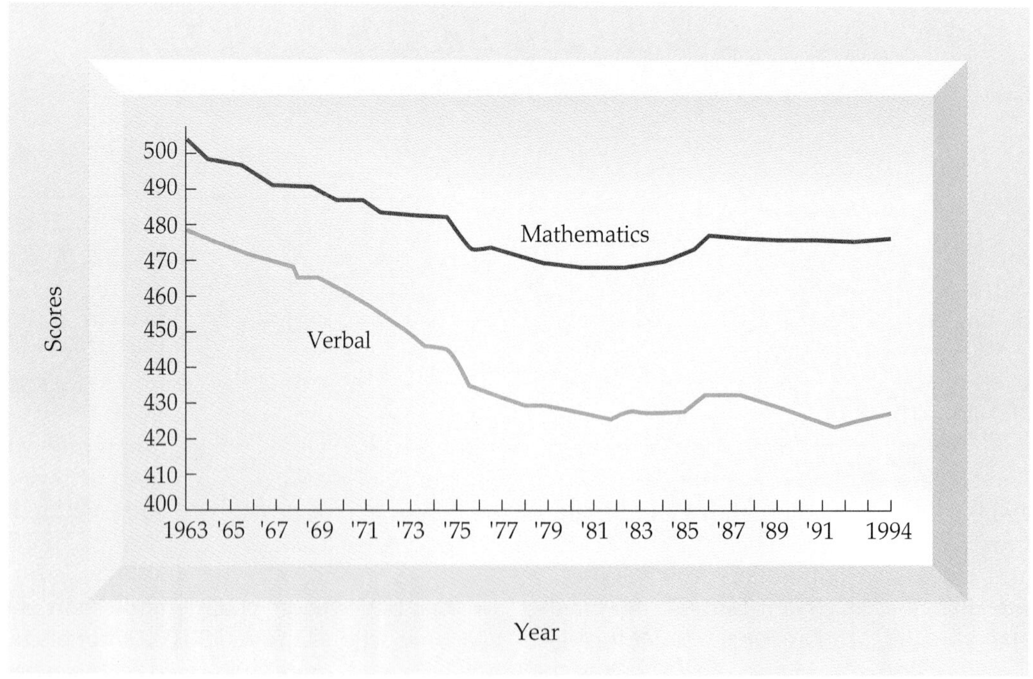

FIGURE 16.2 Scholastic Aptitude Test average scores.

males. Figure 16.2 shows score averages from 1963 through 1994. As can be seen, average scores from the 1993–1994 school year on the verbal section of the SAT fell to 423. Math scores averaged 479.

Declining scores have led to increased criticism of the schools for relaxing teaching standards and not teaching the basics. College Board president Donald M. Stewart commented:

> Students must pay less attention to video games and music videos and begin to read more. The requirement to read through homework has been reduced. Students don't read as much because they don't have to. . . . Reading is in danger of becoming a lost art among too many American students—and that would be a national tragedy (Mitgang, 1980, pp. 1A, 4A).

Part of the blame for the drop was attributed to changes and problems in the family, increased television viewing, and such problems as turbulence in national affairs (Zuckerman, 1985). Males continue to score somewhat higher than females, especially on math scores, probably reflecting differences in cultural conditioning (Denno, 1982; Mills, 1981). On the positive side, in the 1989–1990 school year women's math scores reached their highest levels in sixteen years; scores of Native Americans rose a combined 13 points, and African-American test-takers continued a fifteen-year trend as the most improved ethnic group.

REVISIONS OF THE SAT

The College Board recently approved changes in the SAT that took effect in 1994. The test is known as the Scholastic Assessment Test, with the mandatory section labeled SAT I. Some educators wanted to require a written essay, but others said such a section would discriminate against minorities, so the essay was made optional in a separate part known as the SAT II. Also, scoring millions of essays would require enormous amounts of time and money.

The new SAT I has both a verbal part and a math part. The verbal section in-

FOCUS

Gender Differences in Spatial Abilities and Achievement

For a number of years, a variety of tests have shown gender differences in some specific abilities and achievements. Boys generally score higher in spatial and math tests, and girls score higher in reading and verbal tests. This has been attributed primarily to differences in sex-role socialization. One study predicted that at age 11 those girls who scored high on masculinity would also score high on spatial ability at age 16 (Newcombe & Dubas, 1992). Boys are encouraged to excel in math and spatial skills, but not in reading and verbal skills. Although girls are expected to perform well academically in all subjects, they have not been encouraged to excel in math, or in experiences thought to enhance spatial abilities (e.g., sports). Butcher (1986) reported that girls in grades six through ten ranked "getting good grades" as their primary aspiration at school, well above the choice of "being good at sports." Gender differences may indeed reflect two different sex-role socialization processes (Parson & Ferguson, 1989).

cludes longer critical reading passages about which students must answer questions. The antonyms section has been deleted. But the greatest changes are in the math section. Students may use calculators for solving problems, rather than select answers from multiple-choice slots. There is a new emphasis in the whole test on critical reasoning and "real-life" problem solving. Although the new test is still "coachable," proponents claim it is less coachable than the old test. Maximum scores are still 1600, or 800 for each of the two parts.

ACT

ACT Assessment Program (American College Testing Program)—the second most widely used college admissions test

The **ACT Assessment Program** is the second most widely used college admissions test, administered to more than a million students each year. (High School Profile Report, 1994). The ACT Assessment Program consists of a registration form that includes (1) the Student Profile Section (SPS), (2) the ACT Interest Inventory, and (3) the high school course-grades history. The academic tests include tests in Math, English, Reading, and Science Reasoning.

The ACT Interest Inventory is a survey of students' vocational preferences based on Holland's typology (Kifer, 1985). The Student Profile Section (SPS) is a 190-item inventory of demographics, high school activities and accomplishments, and academic and extracurricular plans for college.

TABLE 16.1
AMERICAN COLLEGE TESTING (ACT) COMPOSITE ACHIEVEMENT SCORES FOR THE ACADEMIC YEAR 1992–1994

Subject	*Score*
English	20.3
M	19.8
F	20.7
Math	20.1
M	20.2
F	20.8
Reading	21.2
M	21.1
F	21.4
Science Reasoning	20.9
M	21.6
F	20.4

Adapted from *High School Profile Report,* Annual Normative Data, 1994. Iowa City, IA: The American College Testing Program.

The ACT Academic Tests yield standard scores of 1 to 36, which are averaged to create the ACT Composite. The mean composite score in 1993 was 20.7. The mean score for males was 21, and for females it was 20.5. Table 16.1 shows the scores.

School

TRENDS IN AMERICAN EDUCATION

Progressives Versus Traditionalists

Progressives—educators emphasizing that education is to prepare pupils for life

Traditionalists—educators who argue that the purpose of education is to teach the basics

The emphasis in American education has shifted from one extreme to the other. **Progressives** have argued that the goal of education is to prepare students for all phases of life: effective personality growth, the effective use of leisure time, physical health, a vocation, home and family living, and citizenship. **Traditionalists** have argued that the goal of education is to teach the basics—foreign languages, history, math, science, and English—to increase student knowledge and intellectual powers.

There are some authorities who insist that education plays an important role in reforming society and addressing social issues. Schools design new programs to deal with social problems as they arise. Driver education was introduced when traffic fatalities rose. Family life and sex education followed a rise in premarital pregnancies, sexually transmitted diseases, and divorce rates. African-American studies and school busing were introduced in response to demands for racial integration. Women's studies were introduced in part as a response to women's demands for equality. New social problems courses were offered when crime rates rose. Because social needs change from time to time, the educational pendulum has been pushed first in one direction and then in another.

Goals of Progressive Education

Traditionalism was the dominant emphasis in American schools until the 1930s. When the Depression came, there were no jobs for adolescents, so many stayed in school instead of seeking employment (Ravitch, 1983). Many of these youths were not bound for college or interested in traditional academic subjects, so they needed special programs. Progressive educators like John Dewey said the schoolroom should be a laboratory of living, preparing students for all of life. As a consequence, many schools introduced vocational and personal service courses, restricting most academic courses to the college preparatory program. These courses included life adjustment education centered around personal concerns, health, leisure activities, vocations, and community problems. Principals boasted that their programs helped students adjust to the demands of real life, freeing them from dry academic studies. Developing an effective personality became as important as improving reading skills (Ravitch, 1983; Wood, Wood, & McDonald, 1988).

Progressive schools include instruction in the use of computers.

After Sputnik

When the Soviet Union launched Sputnik, the first space satellite, in the 1950s, our nation became obsessed with the failure of our schools to keep pace with the technological advances of the Soviet Union. Critics accused the schools of offering a watered-down curriculum that left American youth unprepared to challenge a communist country. Congress passed the *National Defense Education Act* and appropriated nearly $1 billion in federal aid to education, which supported the teaching of science, math, and foreign languages. Schools modernized their laboratories, and courses in math and physical sciences were rewritten by leading scholars to reflect advances in knowledge.

1960s and 1970s

The Cold War had abated by the mid-1960s, but the United States was disturbed by increasing racial tension, social unrest, and antiwar protests. The schools were called on to rescue a society that was in trouble. Major school aid legislation was passed as part of the Johnson administration's "War on Poverty." Once more there was a clamor for educational relevance. Educators demanded that adolescents spend time not only in the classroom, but also in community and work settings. Career and experimental education replaced academic programs so that adolescents could receive "hands-on" experience. Elementary schools knocked down classroom walls, adopted open education, and gave students more choices of what to study. High schools lowered graduation requirements. Enrollments in traditional subjects such as math, science, and foreign language fell and gave way to student-designed courses, independent study, and a flock of electives. By the late 1970s, over 40 percent of all high school students were taking a general rather than a college preparatory or a vocational course of study, and 25 percent of their educational credits came from remedial coursework and courses aimed at personal growth and development (National Commission on Excellence in Education, 1983).

1980s and 1990s

By 1980, many people became alarmed at the steady, slow decline in academic indicators. SAT scores had shown a steady decline from 1963. Verbal scores fell over 50 points and average math scores 35 points. Parental and public outcry grew, resulting in the appointment of the National Commission on Excellence in Education (1983). The commission's findings were as follows:

- The number and proportion of students demonstrating superior achievement on the SATs (those with math or verbal scores of 650 or higher) had declined.
- Scores on achievement tests in such subjects as physics and English had declined.
- There was a steady decline in science achievement scores of 17-year-olds, by national assessments in 1969, 1973, and 1979.
- Average achievement of high school students on most standardized tests was lower than when Sputnik was launched.
- Nearly 40 percent of 17-year-olds could not draw inferences from written material; only one-fifth could write a persuasive essay; and only one-third could solve a mathematics problem requiring several steps.
- About 13 percent of all 17-year-olds were functionally illiterate.

Economic competition from Western Europe and Japan made officials fear that the nation was losing its competitive edge in world markets. Educational reformers demanded more required courses, particularly in math and science; longer school days; more academic rigor in the schools; and tougher standards for graduation. The pendulum began to swing back to a more traditionalist position (Rice, 1990b).

ENROLLMENT IN HIGH SCHOOL

Prior to 1870, free secondary education was not available to all American youths. There were only 800 public high schools in the whole country. Most youths who were preparing for college attended private secondary schools, then called *preparatory schools.* The now-accepted principle that public education need not be restricted to the elementary schools was established by the famous Kalamazoo decision in 1874. Secondary education began to grow. In 1950, only 33 percent of those 25 and over had completed four or more years of high school. By 1994, the number 80.9 percent. Figure 16.3 shows the rise since 1950.

TYPES OF HIGH SCHOOLS

In spite of the rise of public education, there are still a wide variety of high schools in the United States. One study compared four types of secondary schools: *public, Catholic, elite private boarding schools,* and *elite high performance private schools,* in terms of characteristics of the families whose children attend, and the educational and pedagogical characteristics of the schools themselves and their pupils (Persell, Catsambis, & Cookson, 1992). The data comes from a national High School and Beyond (HSB) study that was a national sample of public, Catholic, elite boarding, and other private schools. A national sample of 1980 high school seniors provided a basic data base. There were some 11,500 seniors represented in this study. The data regarding elite boarding schools came from an elite boarding school survey based on a cluster sample drawn from a population of 289 leading secondary boarding schools in the United States listed in the *Handbook of Private Schools* (1981). The schools sampled are representative of the national population of boarding schools. The student sample consisted of 1,383 seniors from nineteen leading private boarding schools surveyed in 1982 and 1983. The results of the survey and comparisons are given in Tables 16.2 and 16.3. A look at the tables indicates considerable differences by high school type.

Let's look first at family background differences. Actually, 60 percent of the fathers whose adolescents were attending the elite boarding schools and graduate or professional degrees. This is in contrast to only 11 percent of the fathers whose adolescents were attending public schools. Similarly, 31 percent of the mothers of adolescents attending elite boarding schools had gradu-

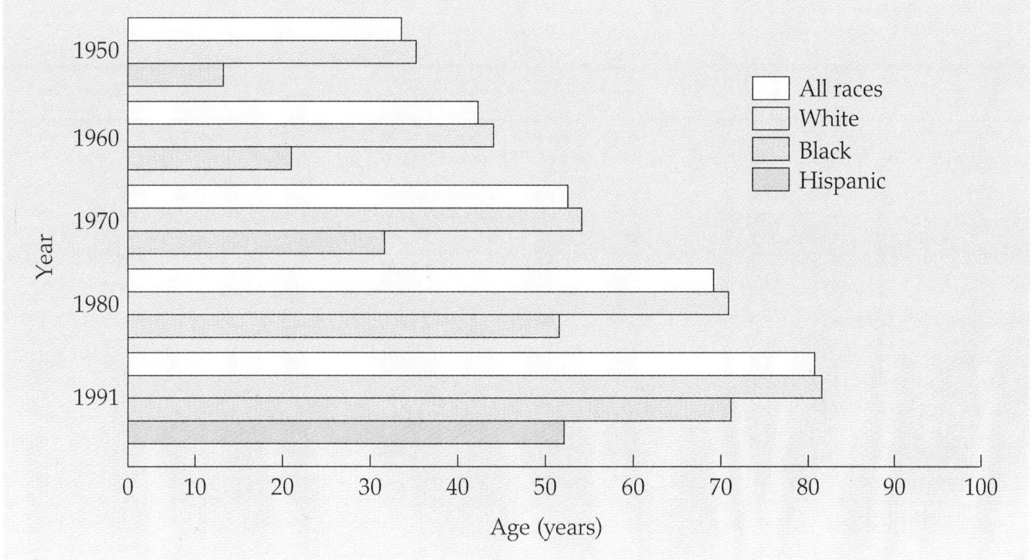

FIGURE 16.3 Percentage of adults who have completed four years of high school or more: 1950–1994.

From *Statistical Abstract of United States, 1995* (p. 157) by U.S. Department of Commerce, Bureau of the Census, 1995, Washington DC: U.S. Government Printing Office.

ate or professional degrees, in contrast to only 5 percent of mothers of adolescents attending public schools. As might be expected, the greatest percentage of families with incomes over $25,000 attended elite boarding schools. The most ethnically diverse were the elite high school (and beyond) students attending private schools—not boarding—schools. Twenty-five percent of the students at these schools were black, as opposed to only 4 percent at the elite boarding schools and 12 percent in public schools. Only 9 percent of the students from the elite private schools were Hispanic in comparison to the 10 percent in the public schools; however, 8 percent were Spanish or Asian as compared to 2 percent in the public schools.

TABLE 16.2
FAMILY BACKGROUND DIFFERENCES BY HIGH SCHOOL TYPE

	Public	*Catholic*	*Elite HSB*	*Elite Boarding*
Father's Education				
College education	35	45	19	32
Graduate or prof. degree	11	15	41	60
Mother's Education				
College education	33	42	53	57
Graduate or prof. degree	5	6	29	31
Family Income over $25,000	29	44	67	85
Racial/Ethnic Background				
Black	12	6	25	4
White	76	82	58	88
Hispanic	10	9	9	0
Asian	2	3	8	8

Note. In percentages—rounded. *Elite HSB* = elite high school and beyond

Adapted from "Family Background, School Type, and College Attendance: A Conjoint System of Cultural Capital Transmission" by C. H. Persell, S. Catsambis, & P. W. Cookson, Jr. (1992). *Journal of Research on Adolescence, 2,* 1–23.

TABLE 16.3
EDUCATIONAL CHARACTERISTICS BY HIGH SCHOOL TYPE

	Public	*Catholic*	*Elite HSB*	*Elite Boarding*
Average School Size	1,415	740	310	391
Average Library Volumes	11,610	12,584	27,968	24,706
Percent of Teachers with MA or Higher Degrees	39	42	59	65
Average Teacher-Student Ratio	.08	.06	.13	.13
Percent of Students in Academic Programs	34	71	100	100
Percent of Schools Offering				
Calculus	47	60	100	100
Trigonometry	77	91	70	95
Economics	63	71	90	88
Psychology	59	56	80	n/a
Art	83	87	100	100
Drama	54	60	50	95
Spanish (3rd Year)	47	86	60	100
German (3rd Year)	20	27	40	68
French (3rd Year)	39	76	100	100
Russian	3	2	30	41
Percent of Students Spending More Than 10 Hrs. Weekly on Homework	6	11	63	86
Percent of Students Watching TV More Than 5 Hrs. Weekly	17	13	3	1
Average Composite SAT Scores	898	878	1160	1129

Adapted from "Family Background, School Type, and College Attendance: A Conjoint System of Cultural Capital Transmission" by C. H. Persell, S. Catsambis, & P. W. Cookson, Jr. (1992). *Journal of Research on Adolescence, 2*, 1–23.

A look at the educational characteristics by high school type indicates some great differences. The average school size of the private schools was smaller; the private schools had more volumes in their library and a greater percentage of teachers with master's degrees or higher. There was a teacher–student ratio of thirteen teachers for each hundred students at both the elite private schools and the elite boarding schools, in contrast to eight per hundred in public schools and six per hundred in Catholic schools. Fully 100 percent of students in both the elite private schools and the elite boarding schools were in academic programs, in contrast to only 34 percent of those in public schools. Private schools also offered superior course programs in terms of academic difficulty. One hundred percent of the private and boarding schools offered calculus. One hundred percent offered French; most of them offered a variety of languages.

It is obvious that the students in the private schools had to work harder than those in the public schools or in the Catholic schools. Fully 86 percent of the students in the elite boarding schools said that they spent ten hours weekly or more on homework. Some 63 percent of the students in the elite private schools spent ten hours or more weekly on homework. The students at both the elite private schools and the elite boarding schools were not able to watch TV very much.

A look at Catholic schools indicated that a greater percentage of Catholic parents had graduate or professional degrees and earned over $25,000 a year than did parents of adolescents attending public schools. Some 71 percent of the students in the Catholic schools surveyed were in the

As a group, elite private schools have higher academic standards than public schools.

academic program as compared to only 34 percent of students in the public schools. A greater percentage of Catholic schools offered advanced courses in math, the social sciences, art, drama, and languages. Interestingly enough, the Catholic schools showed a greater percentage of white students than either the public schools or the elite private schools. There were fewer percentages of blacks than in other schools, especially the public schools.

What do these facts mean in terms of practical implications? It is obvious that *those families than can afford private education are more likely to get superior education there for their adolescents than if they sent the students to the average public school.* But private schools are expensive. In some locations, Catholic schools cost a great deal of money. The average tuition in 1980–1982 of Catholic schools surveyed in this study was over $800 a year. This was in contrast to over $2,700 in the elite private schools and $7,200 a year in the elite boarding schools. Of course, these figures would be much higher today, averaging many thousands of dollars in some Catholic schools, and even more money than that in private schools and elite boarding schools (Persell, Catsambis, & Cookson, 1992).

DROPOUTS

Figure 16.4 shows the percentage of dropouts from school by age and race during 1992. Through age 17, attendance figures are very high, with little difference between whites and blacks. Most dropouts occur during the high school years, especially after age 17, with a greater percentage of Hispanics than blacks or whites leaving school. The total number of dropouts is considerable, though the rate has been decreasing over the years. During 1993, 3.5 million youths were dropouts from school. The overall dropout rate in 1993 was 9.2 percent (U.S. Bureau of the Census, 1995).

Who Drops Out and Why

There are numerous reasons for youths dropping out of school or underachieving (Browne & Rife, 1991; Horowitz, 1992; Zarb, 1984). Lack of interest in school, low marks, school failure, misconduct, reading disability, intellectual difficulties or retardation, health problems, financial problems, social maladjustments (Buhrmester, 1990), personality problems, parental influence and relationships, family background (Sarigiani, Wilson, Petersen, & Viocay, 1990), racial and ethnic prejudice and discrimination, and socioeconomic factors were listed (Kupersmidt & Coie, 1990). Usually problems accumulate over the years until withdrawal occurs, after the legal requirements of the number of years of schooling and age have been met. The actual circumstance or event that results in withdrawal may be minor: a misunderstanding with a teacher, a disciplinary action, a misunderstanding at home, or difficulty with peers. One boy was refused admittance to a class until a late excuse was obtained from his gym teacher in the prior period. The gym teacher would not give an excuse; the boy got angry, walked out of school, and never returned. Another boy withdrew in the last semester of his senior year because his foster parents would not buy him a suit for graduation. In many cases, a whole series of prior events leads to final withdrawal: social maladjustments or isolation, strained family relationships, conduct problems at school, grade retardation, or poor marks. There are a number of factors that correlate with early school withdrawal (Tidwell, 1988).

Family Relationships

The quality of family relationships has a significant impact on school success (Hurrelmann, Engel, Holler, & Nordlohne, 1988; Snodgrass, 1991). Successful students re-

LIVING ISSUES

Tracking

Tracking is *an organizational technique that permits schools to create homogeneous groupings of students within a heterogeneous student population in order to facilitate instruction of all students.* Tracking policies can create unequal opportunities for students to learn, in a number of ways. One obvious way is by restricting access to higher tracks, which many believe to be characterized by a more interesting curriculum and higher-quality instruction. Much theoretical research is critical of tracking, viewing the practice as a means of perpetuating social class and societal values by providing greater learning opportunities for privileged students and fewer opportunities for less privileged ones. From this viewpoint, tracking hinders the attainment of the egalitarian goals associated with American public education.

The problem of how to maximize learning benefits to students when decisions regarding tracking are made is a difficult one. An administrator must make certain trade-offs in an effort to benefit all students. One administrator may believe that high-ability students benefit more from assignment to a small, homogeneous group, whereas low-ability students might be stimulated by the academic diversity of their peers in a more heterogeneous group. Another administrator may feel that low-ability students have a greater need for homogeneous grouping because of their more limited skills and that high achievers learn regardless of their environment, making homogeneous grouping less critical for them. Because the tracking structures and assignment policies that are established in these two schools will reflect these beliefs, they will differ markedly, with different consequences for student placement and subsequent achievement (Hallinan, 1991).

ceive a great deal of social support and encouragement from parents (Cotterell, 1992).

The parents are very involved in school affairs and give their students a lot of encouragement and incentives to do well (Useem, 1991). Bright, high-achieving high school students are more likely to describe their parents as less restrictive or severe in discipline, yet authoritative, encouraging (but not pressuring) with respect to achievement, affectionate, trusting, approving, understanding, and typically sharing recreation and ideas (Rosenthal & Feldman, 1991; Steinberg, Lamborn, Dornbusch, & Darling, 1992). Youth from conflict-oriented family environments are more likely to be underachievers and school dropouts than those who come from cohesive, nonconflicting families (Wood, Chapin, & Hannah, 1988).

Pregnancy and Marriage

Pregnancy and marriage are among the most common reasons for girls dropping out of school (Debolt, Pasley, & Kreutzer, 1990), although it is seldom a reason for boys to drop out (Upchurch & McCarthy, 1989).

Money and Employment

Even high school is expensive. This factor, plus financial pressures at home, forces some adolescents to leave school to go to work. For other students, there is the lure of being financially independent. The desire to have money for social activities, a car, or clothes lures many youths to leave school to accept early employment.

Social Adjustment and Peer Associations

Most adolescents want to do what their friends are doing. A student may be persuaded to leave school if friends are dropping out to get jobs earning "big money" or to get married. Students may also withdraw from school if they don't feel that they fit in with their peers. Those students who suffer social maladjustment are those who most likely do not want to continue their school education (Tierno, 1991). Social competence

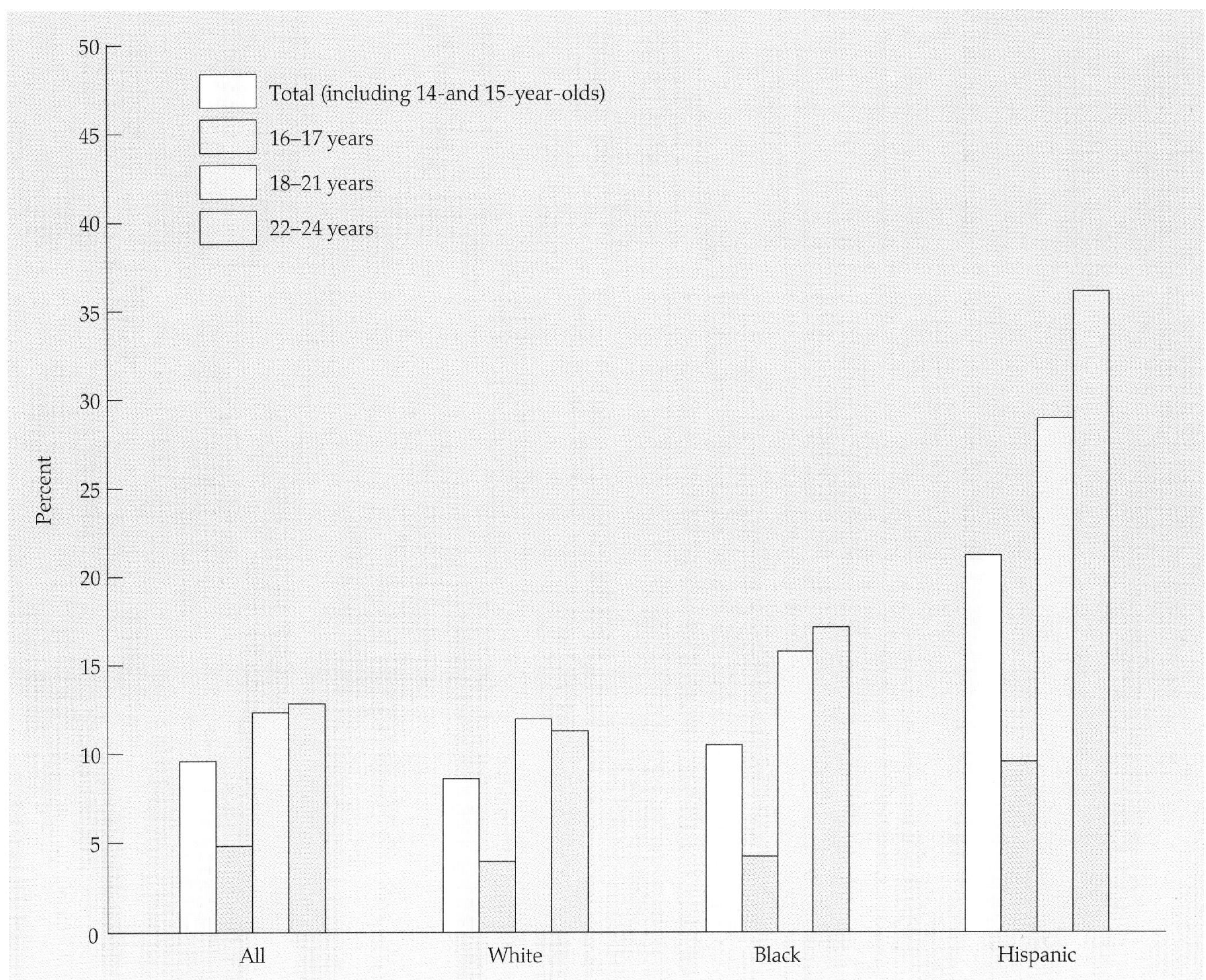

FIGURE 16.4 High school dropouts from 14 to 24 years old, by race and age, 1993.

Statistics from *Statistical Abstract of the United States, 1995* (p. 174) by U.S. Department of Commerce, Bureau of the Census, 1995. Washington DC: U.S. Government Printing Office.

in childhood is often a powerful predictor of academic achievement. Children who are accepted by their peers, or display postsocial and responsible forms of behavior at school, tend to be high achievers, whereas socially rejected and aggressive children appear to be especially at risk for academic failure. These behavioral and interpersonal forms of competence are often more powerful predictors of achievement than intellectual ability (Wentzel, 1991).

School Apathy, Dissatisfaction, and Failure

A number of scholastic factors are correlated with dropping out of school (O'Sullivan, 1990). Among these are low IQ or mental retardation, low or failing marks, misplacement, grade retardation and repetition, poor reading ability, inability to get along with teachers, and misconduct. Many of these students have lost all confidence in their ability to succeed in school (Nunn & Parish, 1992).

Some actually anticipate failure even before it begins. Dropouts' perceptions of their situation is the outcome of cumulative experience in the educational system; that is, their feelings of alienation and failure are already internalized when they enter a new school (Horowitz, 1992).

Some students are not necessarily emotionally or socially maladjusted but are not motivated (Elmen, 1991). They simply lack

FOCUS

Student Alienation

One of the reasons that students drop out of school is that they begin to feel alienated from the total school environment. Mau (1992) outlined four dimensions of alienation that seemed applicable to a school context: *powerlessness, meaninglessness, normlessness,* and *social estrangement.*

People feel powerless when they are controlled and manipulated by authority figures and the rules of social institutions. In school, some students experience powerlessness when they can neither control nor change school policies, tracking, or their marginal academic positions. Such students choose not to compete for rewards such as praise and academic grades, and instead rebel against rules, play truant from classes, or merely attend but do not participate in the classes themselves. Other students, occupying better positions in the academic and tracking hierarchies, experience less powerlessness.

Meaninglessness is a second dimension of student alienation. *Some students may be unclear on the connection between subjects taught in school and their future roles in society.* Students who are in this category of meaninglessness simply do not find school relevant to their own lives.

A third dimension of alienation, *normlessness, occurs when individuals have little sense of the cohesive norms and goals of the social institution.* School norms reward students who achieve academically and who intend to pursue higher education. Official school norms seem less fair to students from low socioeconomic status and minority groups. Alienated students may readily reject official school norms in favor of peer and/or counter-school norms.

Finally, *the fourth dimension of alienation, social estrangement, refers to a lack of involvement and minimal association with others in the school context.* When school work is monotonous, when peers are unfriendly, when school officials are uninspiring, then students become dissatisfied with school. Some manifest their feelings by withdrawing or rebelling (Mau, 1992).

Many students feel alienated from their school environment often because they have lost all confidence in their ability to succeed in school.

interest in schoolwork, feel it is a waste of time, and would rather get married or go to work. Sometimes such students have been placed in the wrong type of program (Knoff, 1983). A switch to a vocational course that students find appealing is helpful to the adolescent wrongly placed in the college prep program. Students who have to repeat grades, causing them to miss friends and feel like social misfits, may develop an intense dislike for school and lose all interest in learning. Similarly, students who have a history of low marks and failure find school to be an unrewarding experience and cannot wait to get out (Deci, 1985).

Many students do not drop out; they are either thrown out or given a temporary suspension and never come back. Teachers and administrators often breathe a sigh of relief when the student does not come back. In the case of expulsion, the student has no choice and is not allowed to return.

Truancy

Those who drop out may have a higher rate of truancy from school. Truants, in turn, are less likely to live with both parents and more likely to have more siblings and to score lower in academic ability and achievement than those who attend school regularly (Sommer & Nagel, 1991). School officials are concerned about truancy because of the relationship between truancy and delinquency. School truants are often characterized by unstable employment and higher levels of antisocial behavior than nontruants. There seems to be a connection therefore, between delinquency, lack of school achievement or school success, and truancy. Delinquents are often students of low ability who give little in school and are truant as well. Another study showed that students who were at risk for dropping out had significantly less positive attitudes toward their school experience, lower self-concepts, more external control orientations, and viewed their parents as less demanding and more casual in their expectations (Browne & Rife, 1991).

Personality

Dropouts are more likely to be emotionally immature and less well adjusted than high school graduates. They manifest symptoms of defective ego functioning: emotional instability; excessive fear and anxiety; feelings of inferiority; low self-esteem; deep-seated feelings of hostility and resentment; and rebellion, negativism, and alienation (Cairns, Cairns, & Neckerman, 1989). What is so often described as lack of willpower or laziness may actually be resentment toward punitive parents, unfair treatment at school, or social rejection, all of which can cause such feelings of rebellion that the adolescent refuses to do anything demanded by authority. Some of these students develop a real phobia about school (Paccione-Dyszlewski & Contessa-Kislus, 1987). Five traits have been identified as common among underachievers: (1) overprotectiveness, (2) boredom, (3) anxiety, (4) inferiority, and (5) negativism (Stevens & Pihl, 1987).

Socioeconomic Factors

Low socioeconomic status correlates positively with early withdrawal from school. There are a number of reasons why this is so. The role models presented by parents may not be conducive to finishing school. Many low socioeconomic parents want their children to have more education than they did, but if parents only finished seventh grade, they may consider graduating from junior high school sufficient. Also, daughters still tend to receive less encouragement to finish school than do sons.

Teachers are sometimes prejudiced against youth from low socioeconomic families, and show preferential treatment to students from high-status families. Students from a low socioeconomic background tend to receive less encouragement to do well and to stay in school than do students from higher-status families. They often do not possess the verbal skills of their middle-class peers. This in itself presents a handicap in learning to read and in almost all other academic work. Peer influences on low so-

PARENTING ISSUES

Middle-Class Parenting and Underachievement

Metcalf and Gaier (1987) studied patterns of parenting among middle-class parents of underachieving eleventh- and twelfth-graders and found four patterns that contributed to academic underachievement.

- Conflicted parents—parents disagree on childrearing.
- Indifferent parents—parents set no consistent limits or standards, and show little interest.
- Overprotective parents—parents are perfectionists, domineering, overdirecting, overrestrictive, and constantly expect their children to do better.
- Upward-striving parents—parents criticize, nag, and pressure adolescents to get good marks.

PARENTING ISSUES

Changes in Parents' Work Status and Adolescents' Adjustment to School

Research has indicated that the transition from elementary to junior high school is a time of stress because the adolescent must adjust to a new school environment and new peer networks. We also know that a decline in work status of family members, which affects family income, has disruptive effects on marital and parent–child relationships, increasing parents' depression, discipline, and conflict with children, and decreasing feelings of nurturance and integration in the family. The loss of a family's income or a parent's job security is associated with children's adjustment problems, such as loneliness, depression, antisocial tendencies, and decreases in academic aspirations and self-esteem.

One study examined the patterns of change or stability in parental work status during a two-year period to determine the effect upon adolescents who were at the same time going from sixth to seventh grade in school. The families of 432 girls and 451 boys were examined. The families were divided into four different groups. One, the *deprived group,* reported permanent layoffs during the two years of the study. Second, the *declining group* experienced a layoff or demotion between the time of the first and the second study. The *stable group* were families who reported no layoffs or demotions at either time of measure. The fourth, the *recovery group,* were families that reported a layoff or demotion at the first study, and reemployment at comparable jobs at the second study. Studies one and two were the times that the data were obtained. These times were about two years apart.

The results show that work status and family income were strongly related to each other both times. The stable group had significantly higher, and the deprived group significantly lower, incomes than any other group. The adolescents in stable families reported significantly less worry than the other three groups. By the time of the second study, the financial boost the recovery families had obtained was obvious in the decline of financial concern to the point where there was no longer a significant difference between the stable and recovery groups. According to the teachers, adolescents in the deprived, and especially in the declining families, exhibited significantly lower social competence than their peers in the stable or recovery families. Moreover, a decline in parental work status that occurred during the same period that the adolescent made the transition to junior high school was associated with an increase in school adjustment problems between the sixth and seventh grades; this was especially true of the students in the deprived or declining families. After the transition to junior high school took place, the adolescents in the declining families had the lowest level of social competence of any group. Although the absolute level of income for this group was not as low as the deprived groups, they now were worse off in terms of both income and security relative to their accustomed standards (Flanagan & Eccles, 1993).

Parental unemployment has a profound effect upon adolescent–parent relationships and adolescent adjustment.

cioeconomic youth are often antischool and delinquency prone. Some low socioeconomic youths reject adult institutions and values, and become involved with groups composed of jobless dropouts.

Ethnic Identity

Students from minority groups, especially those from inner-city schools, have a much higher dropout rate than do white students (U.S. Bureau of the Census, 1995). The value orientation and the familial, social, and economic conditions under which they live tend not to be conducive to continuing education. Youths from poor neighborhoods are frequently truant and tend to drop out as soon as they reach age 16. However, race, per se, is not the important factor in the high dropout rate of minority students. Low economic status is what makes the difference (Nettles, 1989). For example, the dropout rate among black adolescents in poverty is 33 percent, compared with 13 percent for middle-class black adolescents (Children's Defense Fund, 1988).

Intervention

Intervention programs can reduce the dropout rate considerably. This means the conditions that cause the student to drop out need to be corrected. One study of juvenile delinquents and school dropouts revealed four factors that predicted school dropout: poor relationships with parents, negative influence of peers, disliking school, and misbehavior in school (Dunham & Alpert, 1987). Specific interventions are needed to correct these conditions if the likelihood of dropping out is to be reduced (Bloch, 1989; Kammer, Fouad, & Williams, 1988). One approach is to get youths who have dropped out of school to return by offering them some special programs such as those represented by the Job Corps (Johnson & Troppe, 1992).

Summary

1. According to Piaget, the fourth stage of cognitive development is the formal operational stage, achieved by some during adolescence and adulthood.
2. During the formal operational stage, adolescents are capable of introspection (thinking critically about their thoughts); logical thinking (considering all important variables and forming correct conclusions); abstract thinking (going beyond the real to the possible); and hypothetical reasoning (formulating hypotheses, examining the evidence for them, and determining if they are correct). They are able to use symbols of symbols, so that words can carry double or triple meanings, and their thinking is flexible.
3. As a result of formal operational thinking, adolescents' thoughts and behavior are characterized by idealism and sociocentrism, hypocrisy, egocentrism and self-consciousness, and conformity. Gradually adolescents become decentered as they enter into the adult world and begin an occupation.
4. There are several considerations in relation to Piaget's views: The ages and percentages are not precise and not all adolescents or adults achieve formal operations. The test criteria for operational thinking depend partly on the level of the tests employed; environmental influences, as well as maturation, play a role in cognitive development. There is considerable variability in abstract reasoning abilities, depending upon cultural background. Social institutions such as the family and school accelerate or retard the development of formal operations.
5. The development of formal operational thinking can be encouraged in a number of ways by school programs that stimulate students to think.
6. There is some evidence of fifth stage of development known as a problem-finding stage. This stage represents an ability to discover and formulate new problems.
7. One of the most widely used tests in the United States is the SAT—a two-part test consisting of a verbal part and a math part, each scored from 200 to 800. The Educational Testing Service insists that in combination with high school records, the SAT is a better predictor of a student's first-year performance in college than any other measurement. Objections to the test center around the fact that students can be taught through coaching to do better on the test, and it is not fair, therefore, to use it as the sole basis for

college admission. Actually, the test should not be used as the exclusive basis, but in combination with other factors such as high school grades, essays, interviews, class rank, and other admission procedures.

8. SAT score averages of college-bound seniors dropped until 1980 and increased after that until 1985, with the math scores for males declining and for females rising slightly since 1986. The verbal scores for both males and females have declined since that time. A revision of the SAT, to take effect in 1994, will place increased emphasis on critical reasoning and "real-life" problem solving.
9. Some authorities feel that achievement test scores are a more valid measure of scholastic aptitude. The most widely used test of this type is the ACT Assessment Program.
10. Aptitude tests reveal gender differences in abilities. Boys generally score higher in spatial and math abilities, and girls higher in reading and verbal skills. Such differences are due primarily to differences in sex-role socialization.
11. During the past fifty years, the emphasis in American education has shifted from one extreme to another: from traditionalism to progressivism and back again. Until the 1930s, traditionalism was the dominant emphasis in American schools. Then came the Depression and the shift to progressive education. After Sputnik, the call was to return to basics: especially math, science, and foreign languages. In the 1960s and 1970s, the call was to do something about social problems and to achieve relevancy. During the 1980s, the cry was to return to basics again.
12. The percentage of youths attending high school continues to increase.
13. A comparison of public schools with Catholic schools, elite private high schools, and elite boarding schools reveals superior education in all the types of private schools.
14. Tracking is an organizational technique for creating homogeneous groupings of students within a heterogeneous student population in order to facilitate instruction of all students.
15. Over 4 million youths are dropouts from school with the greatest percentage among Hispanics, a lesser percent among blacks, and the lowest percent among whites.
16. Some students drop out because of alienation, which may be described in four dimensions: powerlessness, meaninglessness, normlessness, and social estrangement.
17. There are a number of factors that correlate with early school withdrawal: low socioeconomic status, quality of family relationships, personality, social adjustments and peer associations, financial considerations, school failure, apathy and dissatisfaction, and pregnancy and marriage.
18. Schools that establish intervention programs can reduce the dropout rate considerably.

Key Terms

ACT Assessment Program (American College Testing Program) *p. 428*
Personal fable *p. 421*
Problem-finding stage *p. 424*
Progressives *p. 428*
Scholastic Aptitude Test (SAT) *p. 425*
Sociocentrism *p. 420*
Tracking *p. 434*
Traditionalists *p. 428*

Discussion Questions

1. Give some examples of adolescents you know who are self-conscious and egocentric.
2. Do adolescents think logically? Why or why not? Give some examples.
3. How does the idealism of adolescents compare to that of adults?
4. What evidence is there that adolescents are hypocritical?
5. Comment on the statement: "Adolescents are able to escape the concrete present and think about the abstract and the possible."
6. Why do adolescents tend to be conformists?
7. When you were in high school, did your teachers encourage original thinking? Give example of ways they did and ways they did not.
8. What do you think of the SAT? Should it be used as a basis for admission to college? What criteria would you use for selection?
9. What do you think of requiring certain performance on achievement tests as a basis for college admission?
10. Did any of you attend a private school when you were an adolescent? What did you think of the experience? Would you want your child to attend a private school? Why or why not?
11. Should bright pupils be put in a track along with others like themselves or should they be kept in classes with average students? What about slow learners? Should they be taught in their own sections or placed with others?
12. In your opinion, what are the principal reasons for pupils dropping out of school?
13. What can schools do to reduce the number of dropouts?
14. Should pupils be required by law to stay in school through the twelfth grade? Why or why not?
15. What can and should parents do if their adolescent is not doing well in school?

Suggested Readings

Chipman, S. F., Segal, J. W., & Glaser, R. (Eds.). (1985). *Thinking and learning skills,* Vol. 2: *Research and open questions.* Hillsdale, NJ: Erlbaum. Current approaches to cognition.

Elkind, D. (1981). *Children and adolescents: Interpretive essays on Jean Piaget* (3rd ed.). New York: Oxford University Press. A helpful explanation.

Flavell, J. H. (1977). *Cognitive development.* Englewood Cliffs, NJ: Prentice-Hall. New insights into Piaget's ideas and beyond.

Lipsitz, J. (1984). *Successful schools for young adolescents.* New Brunswick, NJ: Transaction Books. Factors that contribute to effective education of young adolescents and examples of successful schools.

Natriello, G., McDill, E. L., & Pallas, A. M. (1990). *Schooling disadvantaged children: Racing against catastrophe.* New York: Teachers College Press. The current status of disadvantaged children in America.

Emotional Development: Emotions, the Self, and Behavior

Chapter 17

Adolescents' Emotions

THE COMPONENTS OF EMOTIONS

Emotion—a state of consciousness, or a feeling, felt as an integrated reaction of the total organism, accompanied by physiological arousal, and resulting in behavioral responses

Emotions are subjective feelings an individual experiences in response to stimuli. The word *emotion* literally means "the act of being moved out, or stirred up." An **emotion** is a state of consciousness that is felt as an integrated reaction of the total organism. As discussed in Chapter 11, emotions are accompanied by physiological arousal and result in behavioral responses. Emotional growth and development refer to the development of subjective feelings and to the conditioning of physiological and behavioral responses to these feelings.

The kinds of feelings that develop, the intensity with which they are felt, and the period of time they persist are important for several reasons. *One's emotional state affects physical well-being and health.* The entire body participates in and reacts to an emotional experience. The autonomic nervous system, the system that is not under voluntary control, carries stimuli to the adrenal glands, which, in turn, secrete adrenalin that acts on the internal organs—the heart, lungs, stomach, intestines, colon, kidneys, liver, pancreas—and glands such as the tear glands, salivary glands, the gonads, and the genitals. Through this network of connections, emotional stimuli can inhibit or increase the rate of respiration or heartbeat. They can contract the blood vessels, dilate the pupils of the eyes, release blood sugar from the liver, secrete perspiration from the glands of the skin, tense the muscles, cause the skin to blush, result in loss of bladder control, or produce a wide variety of other physical reactions. The more intense the emotional stimulus and the longer it persists, the greater and longer the physical reactions will be. Furthermore, emotional states that persist over long periods of time either enhance or destroy physical well-being and health. For example, intense emotional stimuli that cause the stomach to secrete large amounts of acidic fluids over a long period of time may eventually result in those acids eating away the inner lining of the stomach.

Emotions, such as the joy exhibited by this adolescent boy, are subjective feelings and individual experiences in response to stimuli.

Emotions are also important because they affect behavior in relationships with others (Wintre, Polivy, & Murray, 1990). How people feel partially controls how they act. People who feel loving, consciously or unconsciously, act more kindly toward others. People who feel angry may strike out at others or hurt them. People who feel fearful may try to run away or escape.

The behavior of adolescents can be partly understood by studying and understanding their emotions and feelings. Behavior is caused, in part, by feeling and emotion. In this sense, emotions are a source of motivation; that is, they drive the individual to action. Fear of failure can result in the adolescent's striving for achievement; excessive fear may result in paralysis and prevent action. Emotions, therefore, may have either a positive or negative effect on behavior, depending on the type of emotion and its intensity.

Emotions are important because they can be sources of pleasure, enjoyment, and satisfaction. They can add color and spice to living. A feeling of joy or happy excitement makes an otherwise routine day bearable. The warmth of love and affection, given or received, gives inner satisfaction and genuine pleasure. The individual who can feel may also fully appreciate the beauty and joy that life can offer.

As seen in Chapter 8, emotions are classified into different categories. One helpful classification is to divide them in three categories according to their effect and result:

Joyous states—positive emotions of affection, love, happiness, and pleasure.
Inhibitory states—fear or dread, worry or anxiety, sadness or sorrow, embarrassment, regret or guilt, and disgust.
Hostile states—anger, hatred, contempt, and jealousy.

Each person experiences these three states at some time, but the ones that predominate are going to be the ones that have the most influence over the person's behavior and life. And the choice of which ones predominate depends, in turn, on the events and people to which one is exposed as a child.

JOYOUS STATES

Children are born with an unlimited capacity to love, but the actual development of warm, affectionate, caring, optimistic, and happy feelings comes from a secure environment, pleasurable events, and close interpersonal relationships. According to Maslow (1970), children first need to satisfy physiological needs and the need for physical protection from harm. As these needs are supplied, children experience positive feelings of comfort, satisfaction, and well-being. However, the basic needs of children are not only physical, but also emotional and social. They need love and affection, companionship, approval, acceptance, and respect. If these emotional supports are supplied, their capacity to show positive feelings toward others grows, and they become loving, affectionate, friendly, sociable, approving, accepting, and respecting people. Whether or not children are joyous, happy, and loving will depend on the events taking place around them and on the influence of the people with whom they relate. Certainly, happiness is contagious (Olson, 1992). The continued repetition of pleasant experiences and relationships builds positive emotions, whereas the continued repetition of unpleasant experiences and relationships builds negative emotions.

The important point is that *by the time children reach adolescence they already exhibit well-developed patterns of emotional responses to events and people.* They may already be described as warm, affectionate, and friendly, or as cold, unresponsive, and distant. The pattern of emotional response shown during adolescence is only a continuation of the pattern that has been emerging slowly during childhood.

Adolescents who become warm, affectionate, and friendly people have some distinct advantages (Paul & White, 1990). They not only derive far greater potential satisfaction from human relationships, but they also engage in social relationships that are more harmonious. Love encourages a positive response from others; it minimizes the individual's aggressive behavior; it acts as a therapeutic force in healing hurts; and it is a creative power in individual accomplishment and in social movements. Love stimulates human vitality and longevity; it is the driving force in positive biological and social relationships in marriage. For adolescents, it is necessary as a binding power in their friendships or in relationships with their parents.

INHIBITORY STATES

Fear

Fear is one of the most powerful negative human emotions. The psychologists Watson and Raynor (1920) observed that the infant, by nature, shows fear responses to only two types of situations: when threatened with loss of support or falling, and when startled with a loud noise. They found that children do not naturally fear the dark, fire, snakes, or strangers without either having had frightening exposure to them or having been otherwise conditioned to fear them.

Many of the fears children develop carry over into adolescence. Sometimes, however, the nature and content of fears change as one gets older.

Fears may be divided into four categories:

Fear of material things and natural phenomena—bugs, snakes, dogs, storms, strange noises, fire, water, closed spaces, heights, trains, airplanes, and the like.

Phobia—an anxiety disorder characterized by excessive, uncontrolled fear of objects, situations, or living creatures of some type

LIVING ISSUES

Is It Love or Infatuation?

An adolescent can develop very intense feelings for another person. But there is a difference between infatuation, which is an emotional crush on another person, and a deep love. Some of the differences are the following:

- Infatuation is associated with immaturity, and is more frequent among young adolescents than mature adults (C. Rubenstein, 1983).
- Infatuation may develop toward someone the adolescent doesn't even know. The romance may be entirely fantasized. Mature love is based on knowledge of the other individual.
- Infatuation may be felt toward an unsuitable person; love more likely develops in relation to an appropriate partner.
- Infatuation may cause frustration, insecurity, upset, and anguish; love is more likely to result in fulfillment and happiness (Hatfield and Sprecher, 1986).
- Infatuation is more likely to arise very quickly; love grows slowly. Infatuation can fade as quickly as it arises. Love is more lasting.
- Infatuation centers on intense emotion and strong sexual feelings; love involves the whole personality and includes friendship, admiration, care, and concern as well as sexual attraction.

Fear relating to the self—failure in school, inadequacy in vocational situations, illness, being hurt, death, personal inadequacy, immoral drives or wrongdoings, or temptations.

Fear involving social relationships—parents, meeting people, loneliness, personal appearance, crowds, the opposite sex, adult groups or situations, dates, parties, certain types of people, speaking before a group, or other situations arising when in social groups.

Fear of the unknown—supernatural phenomena, world events, unpredictable future, or tragedies.

Generally, as children grow they lose some of their fears of material things and natural phenomena (although usually not all of them), but develop other fears such as the fear that parents are angry, fear of failure, or fear of particular social situations, persons, or groups. Adolescents become more concerned with the effect they have on others, with what others think of them, and of being disliked or rejected by others. Being ignored by a group, or being put on the spot in front of a class is a terrifying experience for some adolescents.

Phobias

A **phobia** is an irrational fear that exceeds normal proportions and has no basis in reality. The *Diagnostic and Statistical Manual of Mental Disorders III-R* (American Psychiatric Association, 1987) divided phobias into three categories: (1) simple phobias, (2) social phobias, and (3) agoraphobia. *Simple phobias* include *acrophobia,* fear of high places, and *hematophobia,* fear of blood. Other simple phobias are *hydrophobia,* fear of water, and *zoophobia,* fear of animals (usually a specific kind).

Social phobias are characterized by fears of social situations, such as meeting strangers, going to a party, or applying for a job. This kind of phobia limits social relationships, so it can interfere with normal living.

Agoraphobia means literally "fear of open spaces" and involves fear of going outside one's own home. It can include fear of going shopping, to church, to work, or to any kind of public place because of a fear of crowds. For this reason it is a very handicapping phobia. Table 17.1 lists some common phobias.

Worry and Anxiety

Worry and anxiety are closely allied to fear, but they may arise from imagined unpleasant situations as well as from real causes (Moore, Jensen, & Hauck, 1990). The mind imagines what might happen. Many times the worst never happens, so the worry has been unnecessary.

TABLE 17.1
TYPES OF PHOBIAS

Name	*Object or Situation Feared*
Acrophobia	Heights
Agoraphobia	Open places
Algophobia	Pain
Anthophobia	Flowers
Astraphobia	Storms, thunder, lightning
Cardiophobia	Heart attack
Claustrophobia	Enclosed spaces or confinement
Cyberphobia	Computers
Decidophobia	Making decisions
Ergophobia	Work
Gephydrophobia	Crossing bridges
Hematophobia	Blood
Hydrophobia	Water
Iatrophobia	Doctors
Lalophobia	Public speaking
Monophobia	Being alone
Mysophobia	Contamination or germs
Nyctophobia	Darkness
Ochlophobia	Crowds
Ombrophobia	Rain
Pathophobia	Disease
Peccatophobia	Sinning
Phobophobia	Fear
Photophobia	Light
Pyrophobia	Fire
Syphilophobia	Syphilis
Taphophobia	Being buried alive
Thanatophobia	Death
Toxophobia	Being poisoned
Trichophobia	Hair
Xenophobia	Strangers
Zoophobia	Animals (usually a specific kind)

Some worry is directed to a specific person, thing, or situation. Adolescents may worry about what their parents will do because the car battery ran down; they may worry about an examination or about having to give a speech in front of the class. Other causes of adolescent anxiety include not being asked to dance, friends criticizing their dress, or friends making fun of the braces on their teeth. These worries arise out of specific things, but the imagined "happening" has not yet occurred or maybe never takes place. Table 17.2 shows what some young women worry about the most as revealed in one study from the University of Maine (Rice, 1989a). The number one concern was school. Parents, future vocation and employment, and social relationships were also for some concern. It is interesting that few of the young women were worried about marriage or sex.

There are wide variations in the extent to which adolescents worry. Some adolescents are more resistant to worry than others. Some are fairly worry free, not only because of constitutional and hereditary factors, but also because of an environment in which they have had little to worry about as they were growing up. All of their physical needs were supplied; they were loved, accepted, respected, and admired by their parents. They had normal opportunities for companionship, social contacts, and new experiences. They received the necessary guidance and discipline to help them become socialized people. They found successes in school experiences, learned acceptable standards of conduct, and adjusted well to society. They did not have to be anxious.

Some adolescents are reared in conditions that are just the opposite. They learned early they could not depend on their parents to supply their basic needs for food, protection from harm, or physical contact. They were never really loved, accepted, praised, or encouraged. Instead, they were rejected, criticized, belittled, or ignored. These experiences stimulated repeated doubts about their self-worth and their own capabilities and talents. They were denied opportunities for ego building and for fulfilling social experiences and relationships. School was a disaster, and friendships were lacking. Tension, turmoil, and conflict in the family were almost continual and extremely upsetting (Stern & Zevon, 1990).

Under these circumstances, adolescents grow up in an almost constant state of tension and anxiety (Daniels & Moos, 1990). Worry has become a way of life, so much so that they overreact to everyday frustrations or happenings and are anxious about

TABLE 17.2
CAUSES OF WORRY IN 136 COLLEGE FEMALES (SOPHOMORES, JUNIORS, SENIORS) ATTENDING THE UNIVERSITY OF MAINE

Number of Responses	*Worry*
47	School
18	Grades, doing well on exams
16	Meeting deadlines; doing assignments, work on time
9	Schoolwork, studies (general)
2	Getting through school
2	Scholarship, student teaching
23	Family, Parents
6	General, family, parents
3	Stability of parents' marriage; divorce, separation
3	Emotionality of parents; highstrung, upset parents
3	Relationship with parents, independence, obligations
3	Mother
3	Health of parents
2	Future of brothers, sisters
22	Vocation, Employment
17	Getting good job, employment; finding job I enjoy; deciding what to do after graduation
5	Being able to accomplish what I want; realizing potential, doing as well as I want
15	Social Relationships
8	Being accepted, liked; what others think; feeling shy, inferior
3	Boyfriends, meaningful relations with them
2	General or social relations
2	Fear or hurting others; worry about others not arriving
9	Money
6	Money to graduate, pay bills
3	Money in years ahead
9	Future (in general)
6	General
3	Stable, happy, secure future
6	Marriage
3	Getting married; meeting man I can love, can love me
2	Future family happiness; being a good wife
1	Wedding in June
3	Sex
1	Abstaining from premarital sex
1	Mother finding out I'm on pill
1	Sex obligation in future
2	Overweight
136 Total	

From [Causes of worry in college females attending the University of Maine] by F. P. Rice, 1989. Unpublished study.

FOCUS

Generalized Anxiety Disorder

Anxiety is not a mental illness. However, when anxiety becomes so intense and persistent that it interferes with everyday functioning, it is an illness called **generalized anxiety disorder.** Symptoms of generalized anxiety disorder include extreme worry about the smallest mishap, dread that something terrible is going to happen, and anxiety when there is no reason for it to exist. Adolescents suffering from this disorder do not think rationally, so one cannot calm their feelings by presenting all the facts and reasons why they have nothing to worry about. Such intense anxiety may be accompanied by somatic symptoms such as digestive or respiratory disturbances, tearfulness, sweating, shaking and trembling, nervousness, sleep disturbances, feelings of inferiority, or an increase in activity to try to cover up or escape the fear. It may also result in behavior disturbances.

everything that is going to happen. They doubt themselves, other people, and the outcomes of most situations. Whether people or circumstances justify it or not, these adolescents bring anxiety with them to their relationships and to the events they encounter (Frydenberg & Lewis, 1991).

HOSTILE STATES

Anger

Hostile states, which are characterized primarily by feelings of ill will, may be manifested as anger, hatred, contempt, or jealousy (Buss & Perry, 1992). They have been classified as hostile states because there is a natural tendency to express these emotions through various forms of hostility: fighting, swearing, arguing, or temper tantrums. Adolescents may seek to express their hostility in physical activity, such as work or sports. Sometimes they hold in their feelings, but sulk, become withdrawn, or get moody. Many times they express their anger through verbal aggression (Kubany, Richard, Bauer, & Muraoka, 1992). At other times, their anger results in aggressive acts of violence in which damage is inflicted on inanimate objects, the self, or others. In fits of rage, adolescents will vent their anger by attacking family furniture, school property, a teacher, or a helpless victim. Figure 17.1 illustrates some typical responses to anger-producing stimuli during the adolescent years.

Some time ago, newspapers carried headlines of a father and his 12-year-old son who had been shot by a 16-year-old boy. Their bodies were covered over with leaves in the woods. The father had been shot thirty-two times. What prompted such rage and violence? Later investigation revealed that the boy who committed the murders was deeply disturbed emotionally and in desperate need of psychiatric help.

Hartocollis (1972) described the quieter but still destructive expression of anger of a group of four young patients from the mental ward of a hospital.

> One night after bedtime and when nearly everybody had retired . . . four young patients, three boys and a girl, gathered in front of the nurses' central station. They sat down in a circle and, pouring some coke on the carpet, proceeded to deposit the ashes of their cigarettes on the round wet spot as if it were an ashtray. They did this casually, without saying much, as if performing a ritual, smiling in a mocking way at the nurses who were inside the station (p. 483).

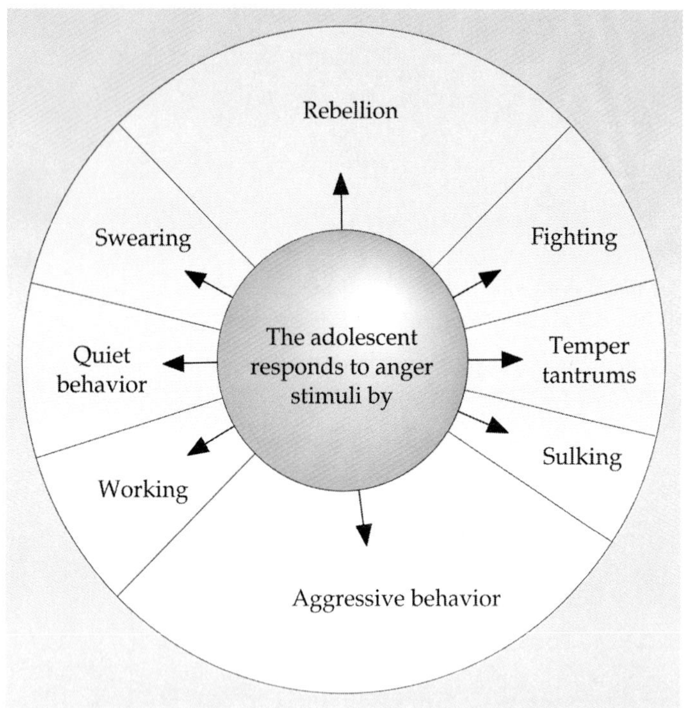

FIGURE 17.1 Responses to anger-producing stimuli during the adolescent years.

Adapted from *Adolescent Development and Adjustment*, 2nd ed. (p. 146) by L. D. Crow and A. Crow, 1965, New York: McGraw-Hill Book Company. Used by permission.

LIVING ISSUES

Relieving Distress

When people are psychologically distressed—that is, when they are anxious, depressed, frightened, or angry—they tend to disclose more than when they are not distressed. That is, they tend to talk out their negative feelings. This is the whole theory of therapy. By talking about what they feel, people are relieved of their tensions and of their upset. This is like draining poison out of a wound so that the wound can heal. The more poison that is drained out, the more healing takes place (Stiles, Shuster, & Harrigan, 1992).

Whenever excessive or uncontrollable anger builds up and is not expressed in socially constructive ways, it takes impulsive, irrational, and destructive forms, and the adolescent becomes a menace (Hart, 1990). This is one explanation for the wanton violence and vandalism found in many communities. Anger that turns into destructive violence usually builds up through a person's repeated and long-standing negative involvement with other people. A father may reject, belittle, and treat his son cruelly for years before the son's anger finally explodes in an act of violence.

Anger in adolescents has many causes. They may get angry when restricted in physical movement or social activity. They become especially resentful when denied opportunities for social life; for example, when they are not allowed to go out on a date or when they are denied the use of the car. They become angry at any attack on their ego, status, or position. Criticism (especially if they feel it is unjust or unfair), shaming, belittling, or rejection arouses their anger, partly because any such negative stimulus is a real threat to an already overly sensitive ego and a precarious social position. Anger stimuli in adolescents are mostly social. People—their personalities and behavior—stimulate anger responses more often than do things. Hypocritical, inconsiderate, intolerant, dishonest, unfair, nosey, selfish, irresponsible people who ridicule, criticize, hurt, snub, boss, gossip about, or take advantage of other people are the major cause of anger.

To a lesser extent, situations as well as things may cause anger. Situations may include such things as injustices in the world, war, and on-the-job frustrations. Petty situations cause anger: A car or lawnmower won't start, a flashlight won't work, the weather turns unfavorable and interrupts a planned picnic, a guitar string breaks, a baked cake falls, or a low door causes a blow to the head. Males are usually more angered by things that don't work than are females. Most females tend to be angered by people and social situations.

Adolescents' anger is sometimes aroused because of their own inability to perform a task or do something they are trying to do. They become angry at their own mistakes, frustrated when they can't paint a picture they imagine or achieve a school grade they desire. They're angry because they receive a low score on a test or because they

LIVING ISSUES

Anger and Gender

Both men and women have a problem with anger. But men and women express anger differently. Women are supposed to be emotionally expressive, with the exception of anger. That is, women are socialized to show their emotions more openly than are men but women's open expressions of anger are viewed as unfeminine. Many women find the idea of anger unthinkable, no matter how much justification there might seem to be. Taught to hide or suppress anger or, at most, to release it indirectly, most women find their anger terrifying.

In contrast to women, men are generally viewed as emotionally inexpressive with the exception of anger. That is, men tend to exhibit a limited array of emotions except anger, which is considered to be the primary male emotion. Men are, quite simply, taught to be emotionally inexpressive except for the emotions of anger and rage. Men tend to transform all negative or painful emotions into anger again and again (Sharkin, 1993).

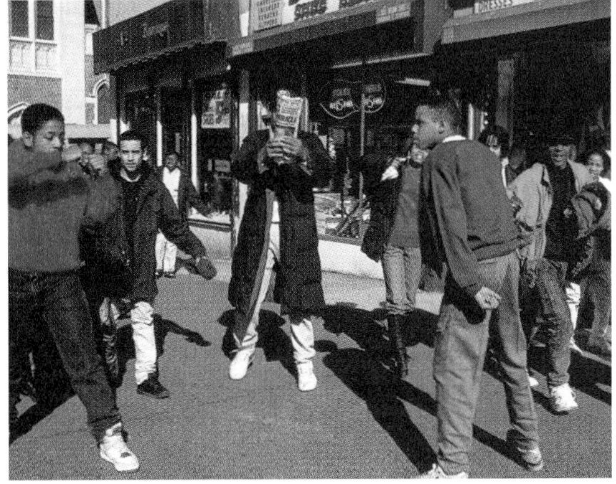
In our culture, males are encouraged to express their anger, females to repress theirs.

are unable to hit a tennis ball the way they feel they should.

There is a wide range of individual differences in the tendency to become angry. Some people are very laid back, seldom getting angry at anything, unless they are given extreme provocation. Other people have almost daily anger reactions and greater tendencies to express verbal and physical aggression when provoked. These high-trait angry people usually describe their family environments as having been less cohesive, having been less tolerant of self-expression, having more conflict, and being more disorganized when they were growing up than the typical family (Lopez & Thurman, 1993).

Hatred

Hatred can be a more serious emotion than anger (at least temporary anger), because it can persist over a longer period of time and can be a result of repeated exposure to a particular person or persons. Adolescents who grow up with parents who do things they detest may develop hatred toward them that is not easy to overcome. Hatred is difficult to hide and almost impossible to suppress over a period of time. The feelings are there, and may be expressed in subtle ways through words or actions, or in violent ways through explosive, aggressive behavior.

Self-Concept and Self-Esteem

DEFINITIONS

Self-Concept

The **self** has been defined as a person's perception of his or her nature, character, and individuality. **Self-concept** is the view or impression people have of themselves; it is their "self-hypothesized identity," which develops over a period of many years. Self-concept is the cognitive perceptions and attitudes people have about themselves. It is the sum total of their self-descriptions or self-appraisals (Chassin & Young, 1981).

Self—overall perception of one's personality, nature, and individuality

Self-concept—an individual's conscious, cognitive perception and evaluation of self; one's thoughts and opinions about oneself

The self is a person's perception of his or her nature, character, and individuality.

Self-concept is multidimensional, with each dimension describing different roles (Griffin, Chassin, & Young, 1981). A person may rate himself or herself as a husband or wife, professional person, community leader, relative, friend, and so forth. These different aspects of the self describe the total person (Niedenthal, Setterlund, & Wherry, 1992).

Individuals may have different self-concepts that change from time to time and that may or may not be accurate portrayals of their real selves. Self-concepts are constantly being formulated depending on the circumstances and relationships confronting the individual (Palazzi, deVito, Luzzati, Guerrini, & Torre, 1990). Research findings reveal that the self becomes increasingly differentiated with age. Contradictions and conflict within the self are lowest in early adolescence, peak in middle adolescence, and then begin to decline in later adolescence. During midadolescence, youth develops the ability to compare—but not to resolve—contradictory self-attributes. In later adolescence, the capacity to coordinate, resolve, and normalize contradictory attributes emerges, reducing the experience of conflict over what type of self the person really wants to be (Harter & Monsour, 1992).

A number of years ago, in *Becoming: Basic Considerations for a Psychology of Personality,* Gordon W. Allport (1950) said that personality has some stability, but it never remains exactly the same; it is always in transition, undergoing revisions. Allport used the word **proprium,** which is defined as "all aspects of personality that make for inward unity." This is one's personal identity, one's self that is developing over a period of time.

Proprium—the self's core of identity that is developing in time

Ruth Strang (1957) said there are four basic dimensions of the self. *First,* there is a general self-concept, which is an adolescent's overall "perceptions of his abilities and his status and roles in the outer world" (p. 68).

Second, there are temporary or changing self-concepts, which are influenced by current experiences. A critical remark from a teacher may produce a temporary feeling of deflated self-worth.

Third, there are adolescents' social selves: their selves in relationships with others, and their selves that others react to (Lackovic-Grgin & Dekovic, 1990). As one adolescent said: "I like the way others respond to me; it makes me feel good about myself." Some adolescents think of themselves only in negative ways because they feel others don't like them. One important influence on self-concept is the way adolescents feel in social groups.

Fourth, adolescents would like to be their conceptualized ideal self. These projected images may or may not be realistic. Imagining themselves to be selves they never can be sometimes leads to frustration and disappointment. At other times, adolescents project an idealized self and then strive to be that person. Those who are in the healthiest emotional state are those whose real selves approximate their projected ideal selves, and who are able to accept the selves they are.

Self-Esteem

Self-esteem is a vital human need (Greenberg et al., 1992). Self-esteem is the value individuals place on the selves they perceive. If their self-appraisal leads to self-acceptance and approval, to a feeling of self-worth, they have high self-esteem. If they view themselves negatively, their self-esteem is low. At various times, adolescents make a thorough assessment of themselves, comparing not only their body parts, but also their motor skills, intellectual abilities, talents, and social skills with those of their peers and their ideals or heroes. If their self-appraisal is negative, it may result in self-conscious, embarrassed

FOCUS

Self-Esteem in Adolescent Girls

In one research study, the *Mooney Problem Check List* and *Rosenberg's Self-Esteem Scale* were administered to 201 adolescents, ages 14 to 16 years (Harper & Marshall, 1991). Sex differences in the number and nature of problems reported, and the relationship to self-esteem were examined. There were no significant differences between girls and boys in the areas of *educational* and *vocational future.* Relative to other areas, *adjustment to school work* was identified as being of considerable concern for both sexes. However, there was a significant relationship between self-esteem and the number of reported problems. And different problem areas were related to self-esteem for girls and boys.

The two problem areas which influenced the self-esteem of girls were *health and physical development* and *home and family.* In both cases, high levels of problems were associated with lower self-esteem. The association between low self-esteem and problematic health and physical development partly reflects the potency of the media in determining the ideal body-image of women and the extreme difficulty adolescent girls have in trying to obtain this image. The association between low self-esteem of girls and having problems with home and family replicates a common finding reflecting the effects on girls of the restrictions posed upon them, as compared to boys, by parents. In contrast with the multiple interaction of the influences of problems on the self-esteem of girls, only one problem area, social and psychological relations, predicted the self-esteem of boys (Harper & Marshall, 1991).

This research study duplicates what other studies have found: that the self-esteem of men and women arise from different sources (Josephs, Markus, & Tafarodi, 1992).

behavior. They become unhappy because they can't measure up to their ideal selves. Hopefully, they learn to accept themselves as they are, to formulate a positive view of themselves, and to integrate their goals into their ideal selves.

CORRELATIONS

Relationships with Others

Those who can accept themselves are more likely to be able to accept others and be accepted by them. There is a positive correlation between self-acceptance, social adjustment, and social support (Blain, Thompson, & Whiffen, 1993). Research indicates that adolescents who are slightly older than their classmates at a particular grade level have more self-esteem than those who tend to be younger than their classmates. Other students tend to look up to the older adolescent (Fenzel, 1992). Adolescents who are more flexible and adaptable in their relationships with others are better liked by others, and these qualities are associated with higher self-esteem (Klein, 1992).

Low self-concept and self-esteem affect social relationships in a number of ways. Adolescents with low self-esteem more often develop feelings of isolation and are more often afflicted with pangs of loneliness. They often feel awkward and tense in social situations, which makes it more difficult for them to communicate with others

(Ishiyama, 1984). Because they want to please others, they are more easily led and influenced by them.

Emotional Well-Being

Self-esteem grows out of human interaction in which the self is considered important to someone. The ego grows through small accomplishments, praise, and success. As a result, high self-esteem is associated with positive psychological adjustment in adolescence (Schweitzer, Seth-Smith, & Callan, 1992). Individuals with low self-esteem often manifest a number of symptoms of emotional ill-health (Ehrenberg, Cox, & Koopman, 1991; Koenig, 1988). They may evidence psychosomatic symptoms of anxiety and stress (Youngs, Rathge, Mullis, & Mullis, 1990). Low self-esteem has also been found to be a factor in drug abuse (Reardon & Griffing, 1983) and in pregnancy among unwed mothers (Black & deBlassie, 1985; Blinn, 1987; Horn & Rudolph, 1987). In fact, pregnancy among unwed mothers may be an effort on the part of young women to enhance their self-esteem (Streetman, 1987).

Sometimes adolescents with low self-esteem try to compensate and overcome the feeling of worthlessness by putting on a false front to convince others that they are worthy. "I try to cover up so that others won't know I'm afraid." But putting on an act is a strain. To act confident, friendly, and cheerful when one feels the opposite is a constant struggle. The anxiety that one might make a false step and let his or her guard slip creates considerable tension.

Adolescents with low self-esteem are vulnerable to criticism, rejection, or any other evidence in their daily lives that testifies to their inadequacy, incompetence, or worthlessness. They may be deeply disturbed when laughed at, scolded, blamed, or when others have a poor opinion of them. The more vulnerable they feel themselves to be, the higher are their anxiety levels. Such adolescents report: "Criticism hurts me terribly" or "I can't stand to have anyone laugh at me or blame me when something goes wrong." As a result, they feel awkward and uneasy in social situations and avoid embarrassment whenever they can.

Achievement

There is a correlation between self-concept and achievement in school (Garzarelli, Everhart, & Lester, 1993). A high self-concept contributes to school success, and scholastic achievement builds a positive self-concept (Liu, Kaplan, & Risser, 1992; Mooney, Sherman & Lopresto, 1991). The relationship is reciprocal (Roberts, Sarigiani, Petersen, & Newman, 1990).

This relationship between school achievement and self-concept begins in the early grades. Those who already have negative self-images before they enter school feel they may not be able to do well, so consequently they do not. Older siblings, close friends, fathers, mothers, grandparents, teachers, and school counselors can have an important influence on students' academic self-concepts. If these people manifest positive attitudes in relation to the academic ability of students, the students are more likely to have confidence in their abilities and do well in school.

Goals

There is a positive correlation between the degree of self-esteem and the level of vocational aspirations (Chiu, 1990). Adolescents with either low or high self-esteem consider it important to get ahead, but those with low self-esteem are less likely to expect they will succeed. They are more likely to say: "I never get any breaks, which is why I don't get ahead, but I really don't care anyhow." Underneath, they are afraid they don't possess those qualities essential to success. Women who aspire to have both marriage and a career tend to have higher self-esteem than those who desire to be homemakers only. Men who have a strong sense of self-worth are more likely to get ahead than those with negative self-perceptions. Not only do they aspire to get ahead, but they have more confidence that they can do so. For these reasons, they are more likely to succeed.

Acting-Out Behavior

Juvenile delinquency and low self-esteem seem to be related. In fact, delinquency is sometimes an attempt to compensate for lower self-esteem. The theory is that those

> **LIVING ISSUES**
>
> ***White Lies and Social Outcasts***
>
> People with negative self-views consistently enact behaviors that alienate the people around them. One reason may be that the social environments that such persons characteristically inhabit may help foster such paradoxical behavior. In particular, although the interaction partners of people with negative self-views become disenchanted with them, they mask their disdain with words of approval. In other words, they really lie to them about how they feel. Although the partners' tone of voice reveals their actual feelings, the targets of their disdain fail to recognize this. The upshot is that people with negative self-views are left with little insight into how badly they are appraised (Swann, Stein-Seroussi, & McNulty, 1992).

who have low self-esteem sometimes adopt deviant patterns of behavior to reduce self-rejecting feelings (Burr & Christensen, 1992). By making their behavior match their low self-concept, they confirm their own rejection of themselves. In these instances, adolescents ally themselves with deviant groups that give them the recognition that society does not give. Those who see themselves as "nondelinquents" or "good people" don't have to prove their own inner worth by becoming delinquent (Krueger & Hansen, 1987).

PARENTAL ROLES IN DEVELOPMENT

Parent–Adolescent Relationships

A number of family variables are related to the development of self-concept and self-esteem (Demo, Small, & Savin-Williams, 1987; Gecas & Schwalbe, 1986; Hoelter & Harper, 1987; Openshaw, Thomas, & Rollins, 1983). Adolescents who identify closely with parents strive to model their personality and behavior after them. Consequently, adolescents whose parents have high self-esteem are more likely to have self-esteem themselves (Brown & Mann, 1991). Erikson (1968) said, however, that too close an identification with parents stifles the ego and retards identity development. However, children with minimal parental identification will also have poor ego development. Overall, the degree of maternal identification is related to self-concept. Thus, ego identity of girls is weak if they have poor maternal identification and weak again if there is overidentification.

Fathers also influence identity development. Girls who have a warm relationship with their fathers are more comfortable with their own femininity and with their relationships with other men. They are able to make more mature heterosocial adjustments. Similarly, if the adolescent boy identifies closely with his father and also has very positive, warm feelings toward his mother, his relationships with other women are more likely to be positive. Adolescents whose parents provide emotional support and who use democratic reasoning methods of control are more likely to have positive self-esteem than those whose parents offer little support or only negative means of control (Barber, Chadwick, & Oerter, 1992). Parents who reject their children contribute to the development of a negative self-concept (Whitbeck et al., 1992).

Divided Families

There are a number of factors that mediate the influence of divorce on a growing child (Sessa & Steinberg, 1991). If the mother has custody of the children, the mother's age at the time of divorce is important. If the mother is young at the time of divorce, the effect on the children will be more negative than if the mother is older because younger mothers are less able to cope with the upset of divorce. The child's age at the time of the marital rupture is also a factor. Young children are more negatively influenced than are older children. Remarriage also influences self-esteem. In one study, children whose parents remarried ("reconstituted families") evaluated themselves more positively than children whose parents had divorced but not remarried (Parish & Dostal, 1980). However, children who did not get along with their stepparents tended to evaluate themselves more negatively than children whose mothers did not remarry. Children from intact families tend to have the most positive self-esteem of all (Parish, 1991).

In one study, no significant differences in self-concept scores were found in third-, sixth-, and eighth-grade children from intact, single-parent, and reconstituted families (Raschke & Raschke, 1979). However, children who reported higher levels of family conflict also had significantly lower self-concept scores regardless of family type. Thus, the quality of interpersonal relationships is more important than the type of family structure. Parish and Parish (1983) also found that whether a child came from an intact, reconstituted, or single-parent family was not as important as whether the existing family was happy or unhappy. Conflicts between parents or between children and parents often result in lower self-esteem in the children (Cooper, Holman, & Braithwaite, 1983). Amato (1986) also found lower self-esteem among adolescents from conflicting families and from those where the parent-adolescent relationship was poor.

One significant finding is that loss of self-esteem when parents divorce may or may not be temporary (Parish & Parish, 1991). Amato (1988a) found little correlation between adult self-esteem and the experience of parental divorce or death during childhood. However, in a longitudinal study of 60 divorced families, Wallerstein (1989) found that more than half of the adolescents entered adulthood as underachieving, self-deprecating, and sometimes angry young men and women. They showed high levels of delinquency, promiscuity, and alcohol abuse both ten and fifteen years after the divorce. Not sur-

Self-concept and self-esteem are influenced partly by identification with parents.

PARENTING ISSUES

Parental Control and Adolescent Self-Esteem

The warmth, concern, and interest parents show adolescents is important in helping youth build a positive ego identity. Parents who show interest and care are more likely to have adolescents who have high self-esteem. Furthermore, parents who are democratic but not permissive are also more likely to have adolescents with high self-esteem. The best parents are strict consistently, demanding high standards, but they are also flexible enough to allow necessary deviations from rules as needed. There seems to be a combination of firmness and emotional warmth. The parent–adolescent relationship is characterized by ties of affection, strong identification, and good communication. Parents who are often inconsistent in expectations and discipline are more likely to have adolescents with low self-esteem.

Some parents are too restrictive or critical of their children. For example, adolescents who are under excessive pressure from their parents to achieve in school are likely to have low self-esteem and feel they are incapable of reaching the goals set for them by their families (Eskilson, Wiley, Muehlbauer, & Dodder, 1986). Certainly adolescents who are physically abused by their parents develop low self-esteem.

prisingly, they had trouble with intimacy in relationships.

Unfortunately, Wallerstein did not study a control group from intact families for a comparison of her findings. The findings were predicated on the assumption that these problems would not occur as often in intact families. Also, her findings were from an affluent sample living in Marin County, California. The findings might not apply to those of other groups. However, Wallerstein's provocative study has shattered the complacent feeling that divorce never has long-term consequences for children.

LIVING ISSUES

Perfectionism

The wish to excel is an admirable attribute. However, there is a difference between normal and neurotic perfectionism. Normal perfectionists derive a real sense of pleasure from painstaking effort, but feel free to be less precise if needed. Neurotic perfectionists pursue excellence to an unhealthy extreme. Their standards are far beyond reach or reason; they strain unremittingly toward impossible goals and measure their own worth in terms of productivity and accomplishment. They are plagued by self-criticism. When faced with "imperfect" actions, their self-worth is lowered. Recurrent and persistent dissatisfaction with themselves leaves perfectionists feeling unrelenting stress. They fear and anticipate rejection when they are judged imperfect; they are overly defensive when criticized. When contradicted, they become angry. Their behavior alienates others who show the very disapproval that the perfectionist fears. Thus, the irrational belief is reinforced that they must be perfect to be accepted.

Perfectionism evolves from interactions with perfectionistic parents. In a desperate pursuit of parental love and acceptance, the children strive to be flawless. When they are less than perfect, they feel terrible, so they are caught up in compulsively striving to avoid failure (Halgin & Leahy, 1989).

SOCIOECONOMIC VARIABLES

Socioeconomic status (SES) has an inconsistent effect on self-esteem. One comparison between college and noncollege youths indicated that college youths had higher self-esteem than noncollege youths (Greene & Reed, 1992). Generally, students with higher SES have higher self-esteem than those with lower SES. However, in their study of eleventh-grade students from three North Carolina high schools, Richman, Clark, and Brown (1985) found that females with higher SES had lower self-esteem than those with middle or low SES. In this instance, females with higher SES felt pressured to excel in social activities, physical attractiveness, academics, and so on. Perceived failure in any one of these areas led to feelings of inadequacy and loss of self-esteem. Females with lower SES were more used to failure, so it was not as traumatic for them as for those with higher SES.

Socioeconomic status of the parents alone does not produce a specific level of self-esteem (Martinez & Dukes, 1991). Families with low SES can raise high self-esteem children if the parents have high self-esteem. Similarly, parents from minority groups can raise high self-esteem children if the parents have high self-esteem. One example is that of Jewish adolescents, who, though they come from a minority religious group in American society, tend to have high self-esteem, probably because of the high self-esteem of the Jewish parents and the generally adequate parent–child relationship, measured by the concern and care Jewish parents show for their children.

RACIAL CONSIDERATIONS

Self-esteem among blacks has risen, partly as civil rights and black consciousness movements have encouraged racial pride. A study of public high school black and white adolescents from Tennessee showed that the black students had significantly higher levels of self-esteem than did the white students (Rust & McCraw, 1984). Richman, Clark, and Brown (1985) found this same thing in North Carolina. However, when blacks are exposed to white prejudices, their self-esteem declines. If

Self-esteem among blacks has risen, partly because of increased opportunities and because of black consciousness movements that have encouraged racial pride.

black adolescents are surrounded by those with similar social class standing, family background, and school performance, they rate themselves much higher in self-esteem than when surrounded by prejudiced white people.

Understandably, some black adolescents have high self-esteem and others have low self-esteem. According to one study, black early adolescents who had established close friendships and achieved some degree of intimacy had high self-concepts and felt good about themselves (Paul & Fischer, 1980). This finding emphasizes an important factor in self-esteem. Social adjustments are important to adolescents' developing high self-concepts. Those who have difficulty maintaining close friendships and gaining group acceptance also show signs of low self-concepts.

SHORT-TERM AND LONGITUDINAL CHANGES

The self-esteem of adolescents is affected by important changes and events in their lives (Balk, 1983). Adolescents who get involved with the wrong crowd and begin to adopt deviant behavior may show less self-respect and an increase in their own self-derogation. One study found that high school juniors had a lower self-concept after they had moved with their families a long distance to another town (Kroger, 1980). Another study showed that self-esteem was lowest at around 12 years of age (Protinsky & Farrier, 1980). By applying careful statistical controls, researchers showed that the onset of puberty itself was not the determining factor. Twelve-year-olds in junior high school had lower self-esteem, higher self-consciousness, and greater instability of self-image than did 12-year-olds in elementary school. When differences in race, socioeconomic class, or marks in school were considered, none of these variables was found to be conclusive. The one factor that was significant was whether the students had entered junior high school. The move from a protected elementary school, where a child had one set of classmates and few teachers, to a more impersonal and larger junior school, where classrooms, classmates, and teachers were constantly shifting, was disturbing to the self-image. Males, particularly, were much more likely to be harassed or beaten up after they entered junior high school. This study clearly illustrates that self-image can be affected, at least temporarily, by disturbing events.

Different schools have a different effect on self-concepts (Tierno, 1983). If pupils aren't doing well in one school, transferring them to another school sometimes changes their behavior, attitudes, and self-concepts. Transferring pupils to different schools is, however, more effective with junior high school pupils than with those in senior high schools.

Self-image and self-esteem can also be improved by helpful events. Positive summer camp experiences can improve the self-concepts of young adolescents (Flynn & Beasley, 1980). Stake, DeVille, and Pennell (1983) and Waksman (1984a, 1984b) offered assertion training to secondary school and college-level students who were timid and withdrawn. Good results were reported by Stake and colleagues (1983) at three-month follow-up, and by Waksman at seven-week follow-up, in helping students to maintain eye contact, talk to others, greet them, ask questions, refuse some requests, and express their feelings when they dealt with other students, teachers, or relatives. Wehr and Kaufman (1987) report improved assertiveness of ninth-grade boys and girls after only four hours of training.

Overall, self-concept gradually stabilizes (Chiam, 1987; Ellis & Davis, 1982). A ten-year longitudinal study of adolescents, beginning in grade five and six and continuing until they were out of high school, showed only a slight increase in positive self-concept. For the majority of youths, those who had a negative self-concept in early adolescence entered adulthood with the same negative feelings (Barnes & Farrier, 1985). This finding is in keeping with another study that indicates no age differences in self-esteem (Mullis, Mullis, & Normandin, 1992).

Emotions and Behavioral Problems

Sometimes negative emotions result in behavioral problems. Three such problems discussed here are drug abuse, delinquency, and running away.

DRUG ABUSE

Commonly Abused Drugs

The drugs most commonly abused may be grouped into a number of categories: alcohol, nicotine, narcotics, stimulants, depressants, hallucinogens, marijuana, and inhalants. Out of these groups, the most frequently used drugs in the United States are alcohol, tobacco, and marijuana, in that order. Table 17.3 shows that the percentage of 12- to 17-year-olds who have ever used and who are current users (past month) of various types of drugs in 1985, 1988, and 1993.

Addiction and Dependency

A distinction must be made between **physical addiction,** or physical dependency, and **psychological dependency.** An addictive drug is one that causes the body to build up a chemical dependency to it, so that withdrawal results in unpleasant physical symptoms (Ralph & Morgan, 1991). Psychological dependency is the development of a powerful psychological need for a drug resulting in a compulsion to take it (Capuzzi & Lecoq, 1983). Drugs become a means of finding relief, comfort, or security. The use of alcohol, for example, becomes self-reinforcing when individuals come to believe that it enhances social and physical pleasure or sexual performance, leads to arousal, or to increased social assertiveness, or reduces tension (Webb et al., 1992).

Physical addiction—the body's chemical dependency on a drug built up through its use

Psychological dependency—an overpowering emotional need for a drug

Some individuals become psychologically dependent on drugs that are also

TABLE 17.3
PERCENTAGE OF YOUTH, AGES 12–17, USING DRUGS

Drug	*Ever Used*			*Past Month*		
	1985	*1988*	*1993*	*1985*	*1988*	*1993*
Marijuana	23.7	17.4	11.7	12.3	6.4	4.9
Inhalants	9.1	8.8	5.9	3.6	2.0	1.4
Hallucinogens	3.2	3.5	2.9	1.1	0.8	0.5
Cocaine	5.2	3.4	1.1	1.8	1.1	0.4
Heroin	<.5	0.6	0.2	<.5	NA	0.2
Stimulants	5.5	4.2	2.1	1.8	1.2	0.5
Sedatives	4.0	2.4	1.4	1.1	0.6	0.2
Tranquilizers	4.8	0.2	1.2	.6	0.2	0.2
Analgesics	5.9	4.2	3.7	1.9	0.9	0.7
Alcohol	55.9	50.2	41.3	31.5	25.2	18.0
Cigarettes	45.3	42.3	34.5	15.6	11.8	9.6

Statistics from U.S. Bureau of the Census (1995). *Statistical Abstract of the United States, 1995.* Washington, DC: U.S. Government Printing Office, p. 142.

Drug abuse education tries to prevent children and youths from starting to use drugs.

physically addicting, such as crack cocaine, barbiturates, alcohol, heroin, and nicotine. Dependence is strongly reinforced by the desire to avoid the pain and distress of physical withdrawal. Sometimes physical dependency is broken, but individuals go back to the drug because of psychological dependency on it. It is a mistake, therefore, to assume that the only dangerous drugs are those that are physically addictive.

Trends in Drug Abuse

Youths are trying drugs at young ages. It is not unusual for children 8 to 10 years old to use drugs. An elementary school official in Washington, D.C., complained that he had not been able to keep one third-grader from smoking marijuana every day at recess. Threats of expulsion did not help because the child insisted he could not break the habit. He did refuse to share his cigarettes with classmates because, he said, "the habit is dangerous" ("Drug Pushers," 1979). One longitudinal study in the San Francisco area showed that socially precocious females were more likely to become involved with drugs earlier than were males, although for both boys and girls, the transition to junior high school played an important role in initiating drug use (Keyes & Block, 1984).

Patterns of Drug Use

Five patterns of drug use may be identified (Pedersen, 1990):

1. *Social-recreational use* occurs among acquaintances or friends as a part of socializing. Usually this use does not include addictive drugs and does not escalate in either frequency or intensity to become uncontrolled use.
2. *Experimental use* is motivated primarily by curiosity or by a desire to experience new feelings on a short-term basis. Users rarely use any drug on a daily basis, and tend not to use drugs to escape the pressures of personal problems. However, if users experiment with physically addictive drugs they may become addicted before they realize it.
3. *Circumstantial–situational use* is indulgence to achieve a known and desired effect. A person may take stimulants to stay awake while driving, or may take sedatives to relieve tension and go to sleep. Some persons use drugs to try to escape problems. The danger is that such use will escalate to intensified use.
4. *Intensified drug use* generally involves using drugs at least once daily over a long period of time to achieve relief from a stressful situation or a persistent problem. Drugs become a customary part of the daily routine. Use may or may not affect functioning depending on the frequency, intensity, and amount of use.
5. *Compulsive drug use* involves both extensive and frequent use for relatively long periods, producing psychological dependence and physiological addiction with discontinuance resulting in psychological stress or physiological discomfort. The threat of psychological and physical discomfort from withdrawal becomes the motivation for continued use. Users in this category include not only the skid-row alcoholic and street "junkie" but also the crack-dependent adolescent, the alcohol-dependent businessman, the barbiturate-dependent housewife, the opiate-dependent physician, and the habitual smoker (Rice, 1990a).

Family Origins

The following family factors correlate closely with excessive drug use by adolescents while growing up (Bettes et al., 1990;

Rees and Wilborn, 1983). In comparison to nonabusers:

- Drug abusers are less likely to have open communication with parents (Kafka & London, 1991).
- Abusers are usually not as close to their parents, are more likely to have negative adolescent-parent relationships, and have a low degree of parental support.
- Abusers are more likely to have parents who drink excessively and/or use other psychotropic drugs (McDermott, 1984; Wodarski, 1990).
- Abusers are more likely to come from broken homes or not to live with both parents (Doherty & Needle, 1991; Johnson, Shontz, & Locke, 1984; Stern, Northman, & Van Slyck, 1984).
- Abusers are more likely to be dissatisfied with parents and experience parental deprivation (Hundleby & Mercer, 1987).
- Abusers' parents less often praise, encourage, and counsel and set limits to adolescents' behavior (Coombs & Landsverk, 1988; Hauser et al., 1991).
- Parental conflict in childbearing practices, inconsistent discipline, restrictive discipline, and maternal rejection are all associated with marijuana and alcohol use in older adolescents (Vicary & Lerner, 1986).
- Abusers are likely to experience parental physical and sexual abuse, which leads to self-derogation (Dembo et al., 1987).
- The family relationships of adolescents who abuse drugs are similar to those of adolescents who are emotionally disturbed.

These types of family situations create personality problems that cause individuals to be more likely to turn to drugs. Numerous other studies associate drug addiction and dependency with disturbed family relationships (Shaver, 1983) and personality problems (Page, 1990).

Other Social and Psychological Correlates

1. Those who abuse drugs are more likely to have peers who use and approve of drug use (Alberts, Hecht, Miller-Rassulo, & Krizek, 1992; van Roosmalen & McDaniel, 1992; Stanton & Silva, 1992; Webb et al., 1991). Abusers spend a lot of time with drug-abusing friends (Shilts, 1991).
2. Abusers are more likely to be involved with deviant peers (Simons & Whitbeck, 1991).
3. Abusers are more likely to suffer psychological distress and feelings of depression (Eisen, Youngman, Grob, & Dill, 1992: Simons & Whitbeck, 1991).
4. Abusers are more likely to show interpersonal distress, lack of self-confidence, self-rejection, and devaluation.
5. Abusers are more likely to have disturbed relationships with others and to be disliked by others (Johnson & Kaplan, 1991).
6. Abusers are more likely to be in rebellion against social sanctions (Kaplan & Fukurai, 1992).
7. Abusers are more likely to be lonely (Page & Cole, 1991).
8. Abusers are more likely to be truant from school (Pritchard, Cotton, & Cox, 1992).
9. Abusers are more likely to have frequent sex, a greater number of coital partners, and show a greater percentage of unprotected sex (Jemmott & Jemmott, 1993).

DELINQUENCY

Incidence

Of all persons arrested in 1993, 17 percent were juveniles—under age 18. Figure 17.2 shows the percentages. As seen in Figure 17.3, the incidence of delinquency among males under 18 is 4 1/4 times that among females of the same age (U.S. Bureau of the Census, 1995). When just serious crimes are considered, 29 percent of these were committed by persons under age 18. This includes 16 percent of all murders, 16 percent of all rapes, 28 percent of all robberies, 45 percent of all automobile thefts, and 49 percent of all arrests for arson.

Psychological Causes

In general, the causes of delinquency may be grouped into three major categories (Farrington, 1990): psychological factors that include emotional and personality fac-

LIVING ISSUES

How Can You Tell If You're an Alcoholic?

A distinction must be made between chronic alcoholism and alcohol abuse. **Chronic alcoholism** is characterized by compulsive drinking, so that the person does not have voluntary control over the amount consumed (McMurran & Whitman, 1990). As a result of chemical and psychological dependence on alcohol, the person drinks too much. Chronic alcoholics may go on binges of heavy drinking followed by a long period of sobriety. Or they may drink heavily only on weekends, or may drink large amounts daily. Drinking patterns vary.

Alcohol abuse is the use of alcohol to a degree that causes physical damage; impairs physical, social, intellectual, or occupational functioning; or results in behavior harmful to others.

Warning Signs. The following are some of the warning signs that a drinking problem is developing:

You drink to relieve feelings of inadequacy, anxiety, depression, or boredom.

You have begun to drink to relieve stress or when problems build up.

You drink before or after others start or are finished with drinking.

You have begun to drink alone.

You drink the "morning after" to counteract the effects of a previous night's drinking.

You get drunk on important occasions.

You indulge in drinking bouts followed by hangovers.

You get drunk when you do not want to, drink more than you plan, and lose control of your drinking.

You want to drink less but cannot.

You feel guilty about your drinking behavior.

You lie about your drinking and deny that you are drinking.

You often regret what you have done or said while you were drinking.

You begin to criticize people who do not drink.

Your drinking is affecting your relationships with family and friends.

You pass out or have memory blackouts while drinking.

You have been absent from school or work because of drinking.

tors and difficulties in interpersonal relationships; sociological factors that include societal and cultural influences; and biological factors that include the effects of organic and physical elements (Caspi, Lynam, Moffitt, & Silva, 1993).

There have been efforts to determine whether certain personality factors predispose the adolescent to delinquency (Holcomb & Kashani, 1991; Weaver & Wooten, 1992). Generally speaking, no one personality type is related to delinquency, but those who become delinquent are more likely to be impulsive, destructive, suspicious, hostile, resentful, ambivalent to authority, defiant, socially assertive, and lack self-control (Ashford & LeCroy, 1990; Thompson and Dodder, 1986). Aggressive conduct is associated with delinquent behavior (Pakiz, Reinherz, & Frost, 1992).

Delinquency is sometimes a manifestation of hostilities, anxieties, fears, or of deeper neuroses. One important cause is love deprivation while growing up (Walsh & Beyer, 1987). In other instances, delinquency occurs in basically healthy adolescents who have been misled by others. In some cases, delinquency is the result of poor socialization that results in adolescents' not developing proper impulse controls (Eisikovits & Sagi, 1982; Stefanko, 1984). The psychodynamics of delinquents' behavior are different, although the results of that behavior are similar (Hoffman, 1984).

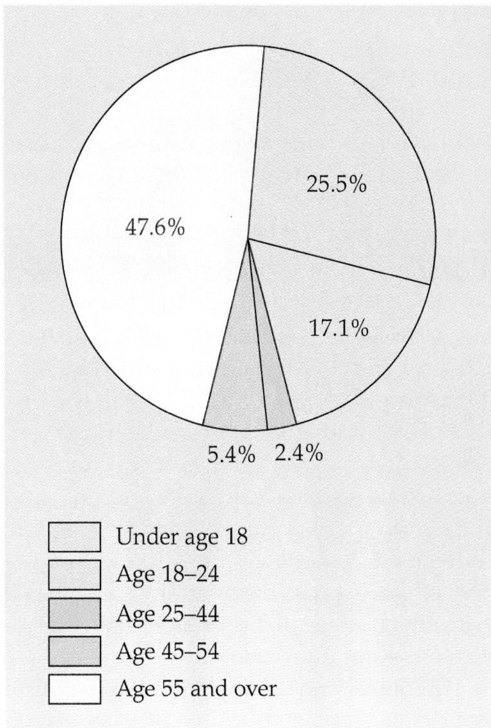

FIGURE 17.2 Age distribution of all people arrested, 1993

From *Statistical Abstract of the United States, 1995* (p. 207) by U.S. Bureau of the Census. Department of Commerce, 1995, Washington, DC: U.S. Government Printing Office.

Sociological Causes

Family factors, such as strained family relationships and lack of family cohesion, are important sources of delinquency (Kroupa, 1988; Mas, Alexander & Turner, 1991; Novy et al., 1992; Tolan, 1988; Tygart, 1991). Broken homes have been associated with delinquency, but are no worse than, and sometimes not as detrimental as, intact but unhappy or disturbed family relationships. Studies of delinquency often compare the rates for adolescents from broken homes with those from intact happy homes. However, if comparisons are made between adolescents from broken homes with adolescents from intact but unhappy homes, the effects on adolescents are similar, indicating that family environment is more important in delinquency than family structure (LeFlore, 1988).

One study demonstrates that *parental controls are significant inhibitors of delinquency*. But this is true more often for males than for females. For males, these controls are more effective in midadolescence, (ages 13 through 16 years); for females, they are better deterrents in later adolescence (ages 15 through 18 years). Attachment varies with age, and parental control decreases as adolescents become older. This means that parental power, in its influence upon delinquency or in its influence in preventing delinquency, becomes less as male adolescents get older (Seydlitz, 1991). However, later study suggests that rebellion against parental control is highest when the adolescent is less attached to the parent. The pattern suggests that adolescents who feel more distant from their parents are less accepting of parental rules and resent parents' controlling actions (Seydlitz, 1993).

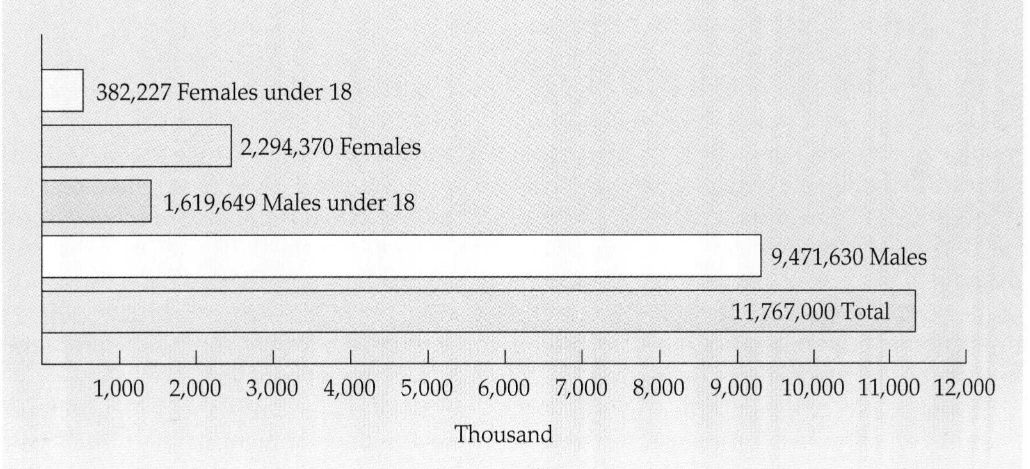

FIGURE 17.3 People arrested, by sex and age, 1993

Statistics from *Statistical Abstract of the United States, 1995* by U.S. Bureau of the Census, Department of Commerce, 1995, Washington, DC: U.S. Government Printing Office.

Sixteen percent of all persons arrested in a recent year were under age 18.

Juvenile delinquency is distributed through all socioeconomic status levels (Lempers & Clark-Lempers, 1990). In fact, as great an incidence of some forms of delinquency among adolescents of middle classes exists as among those of lower classes. Tygart (1988) found, for example, that youths of high socioeconomic status (SES) were more likely to be involved in school vandalism than youths of low SES. One big difference is that middle-class adolescents who commit delinquent offenses are less often arrested and incarcerated than are low-class youths.

Community and neighborhood influences are also important. Most larger communities have areas in which delinquency rates are higher than in other neighborhoods. A larger than average percentage of adolescents growing up in these areas becomes delinquent because of the negative influence of the neighborhood. Adolescents who grow up in these neighborhoods are also more likely to be victims of crimes themselves.

Some adolescents become delinquent because of antisocial influences of peers (Covington, 1982; Pryor & McGarrell, 1993). A high degree of peer orientation is sometimes associated with a high level of delinquency. In fact, association with delinquent peers is the strongest single predictor of delinquency (Pabon, Rodriguez, & Gurin, 1992).

Modern youths are also influenced by affluent and hedonistic values and lifestyles in our culture. Youths may be encouraged to keep late hours, get into mischief, and become involved in vandalism or delinquent acts just for kicks.

Violent youths may have been influenced by the violence they see in our culture and in the media (Snyder, 1991). May (1986) found that youths who behave in a violent manner give more selective attention to violent cues. They tend to choose to attend movies that are more violent, and imitate what they have seen and heard. Today's adolescents are also living in a period of unrest, disorganization, and rapid cultural change, all of which tend to increase delinquency rates.

Dawkins and Dawkins (1983) found that drinking was strongly associated with serious delinquency among both white and black youths, especially when other factors such as drug use, association with drug users, and previous arrests were present (Watts & Wright, 1990). Stuck and Glassner (1985) emphasized the strong correlation between criminal activity and drug use.

The level of school performance is also correlated with delinquency (Grande, 1988). Inability getting along with teachers and administrators, difficulty adjusting to the school program, classroom misconduct, poor grades, and a lack of school success are associated with delinquency.

Biological Causes

Biological causes may play a role in delinquency (Anolik, 1983). Mednick and Christiansen (1977) showed that the autonomic nervous system (ANS) in criminals recovers more slowly from environmental stimulation as compared to that of noncriminals. Slow recovery time reduces the ability to alter their behavior through punishment; thus, it becomes more difficult to unlearn delinquent behavior.

There is a possibility that a maturational lag in the development of the frontal lobe of the brain results in neurophysiological dysfunction and delinquent behavior (Voorhees, 1981). Juveniles are not able to act on the basis of the knowledge they have.

We know also that certain personality characteristics, such as temperament, are partly inherited, so that a child may have a predisposition to behave poorly. If the parents do not know how to cope, the problem is compounded because the child develops a psychological disturbance.

According to Sheppard (1974), at least 25 percent of delinquency can be blamed on organic causes. He cited the case of a 15-year-old girl whose blood sugar level was too low because of an excess of insulin. The girl was fidgety, jumpy, restless, and unable to think or act rationally. Proper diet and medication corrected the difficulty. Sheppard cited other examples of delinquency caused by abnormal brain wave patterns, hyperactivity from hyperthyroidism, and hearing impairment. Other research indicates a definite relationship between delinquency and health problems such as neurological, speech, hearing, and vision abnormalities. Prenatal and perinatal complications may also be the cause of later behavior problems.

Drug-Related Causes

A high percentage of juvenile crime is drug-related. Drugs influence crime in several ways. *First,* youths who cannot otherwise afford drugs commit crimes in order to feed their drug habits. *Second,* youths are more likely to commit crimes when they are under the influence of drugs (McMurran, 1991).

Prevention

Those who work with delinquents are very concerned about prevention. One of the ways to prevent delinquency is to identify

LIVING ISSUES

Teens Who Kill

As indicated earlier, *14 percent of all murders committed in 1990 were committed by teenagers under 18 years of age* (U.S. Bureau of the Census, 1992). A few years ago, a 13-year-old Maine boy was indicted for bludgeoning to death a 3-year-old boy in his neighborhood. This crime is but one of a growing number of senseless murders. In Madison, Indiana, four teenage girls doused 12-year-old Sanda Shrer with gasoline and burned her alive in January 1992 because she was trying to "steal" the friendship of another girl. Henry James, 19, opened fire into a passing car on a Washington-area interstate because he felt like "busting somebody." The somebody turned out to be a 32-year-old woman driving home from work. It seems that in some communities, every teenager has a gun. When everyone has a gun, every argument carries the potential for deadly violence. The FBI reports that, in 1990, nearly three out of four juvenile murderers used guns to commit their crimes. The gun in the hands of a 14-year-old is a very dangerous weapon. A 14-year-old has little investment in life and doesn't really know the meaning of death.

In the inner cities, where weapons are as common as household appliances, the lessons in cruelty usually start at home. Psychologist Charles Patrick Ewing, author of *Kids Who Kill,* has found that many young people committing seemingly motiveless killings were themselves sexually or physically abused. To brutalize another human being, a youngster has to have been brutalized himself. Ewing finds that teenage murderers often don't recall or won't admit that they were once victims. A street tough often would rather go to the gas chamber than admit to having been beaten or sodomized by a male relative (Traver, 1992).

Shannon and Melissa Garrison, and Allen Goul (background) are escorted away from the courthouse in Gulfport, Mississippi, after their preliminary charges of killing the girls' mother.

children (such as hyperactive ones) who may be predisposed to getting into trouble, and then plan intervention programs to help them. Another preventative measure is to focus on dysfunctional family relationships and assist parents in learning more effective parenting skills. Antisocial youths may be placed in groups of prosocial peers, such as at day camps, where their behavior is influenced positively. Young children may be placed in preschool settings before problems arise. Older children need help with learning disabilities before they develop behavior problems. Social skills training may be helpful with some offenders (Cunliffe, 1992). Programs such as *Big Brothers/Big Sisters* have also been found to be beneficial.

Hurley (1985) wrote: "A partial list of the links to crime includes television, poor nutrition, eyesight problems, teenage unemployment or employment, too little punishment, too much punishment, high or low IQ, allergies and fluorescent light" (p. 680). Great commitment is required to sort out the various links to crime and to correct these causes. Certainly incarceration, while it may be necessary, does not really solve the problem of juvenile delinquency (Armistead, Wierson, Forehand, & Frame, 1992).

LIVING ISSUES

Parricide

One form of intrafamilial violence that is attracting more attention is child-to-parent violence. **Parricide,** the killing of one's mother or father, is becoming increasingly publicized, although it remains relatively infrequent. It now accounts for less than 2 percent of all homicides in the United States. **Patricide,** the killing of one's father, accounts for less than 1 percent of all homicides, while **matricide,** the killing of one's mother, accounts for a slightly lower percentage (Young, 1993). Most of the research emphasizes a common theme: Parricide is often a response to a long-standing child abuse problem. Typically, the child who kills the parent is from 16 to 18 years old, from a white, middle-class family. Most have above-average intelligence, although their school work may be below average. They generally are well-adjusted in school and the community, though they tend to be isolated without many friends. They commonly have no prior run-in with the law.

Their target is most often the father—usually a biological or stepparent rather than adoptive or foster parent—and the typical weapon is a gun kept in the home. In most cases of parricide, a bizarre, neurotic relationship exists between the victim and his assassin in which the parent-victim mistreats the child excessively and pushes him to the point of explosive violence. Offenders know they are doing wrong, but they're desperate and helpless, and they don't see alternatives. In fact, dispatching their tormenter can be seen as an act of sanity, a last-resort effort at self-preservation (Toufexis, 1992).

RUNNING AWAY

Incidence

Over 700,000 youths, ages 10 to 17, run away from home for at least one night without adult consent. Almost 60 percent of these youths are females, many of whom are assisted by boyfriends. An analysis of the youths served under the *National Runaway Youth Program* across the United States revealed the following profile (U.S. Dept. of Health and Human Services, 1980).

Race/ethnic origin: White (74 percent)
Age: 16 years (25 percent)
Sex: Female (59 percent)
Living situation past three years: Home with parents or legal guardians (82.4 percent)
Length of stay: Less than fourteen days (84.1 percent)
Juvenile justice system involvement: No involvement (59.4 percent)
Reasons for seeking services: Poor communication with parent figures (51.8 percent)
Parent participation: One or both parents (51.9 percent)
Disposition: Home with parents or legal guardian (30.4 percent)

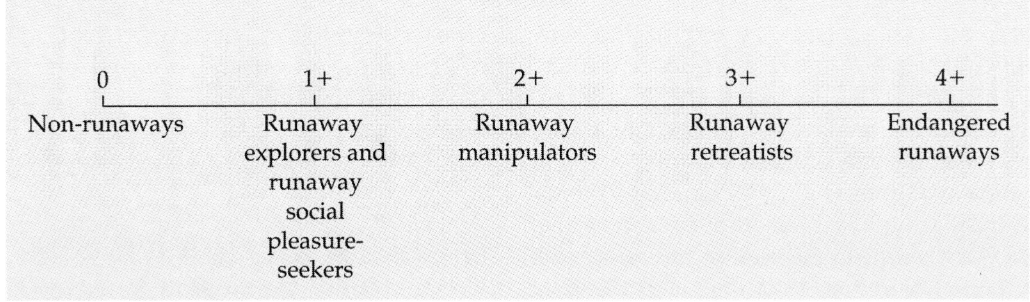

FIGURE 17.4 Formulation of the degree of parent-youth conflict continuum.

From "Adolescent Runaways in Suburbia: A New Typology" by A. R. Roberts, Summer 1982. *Adolescence, 17,* pp. 379–396.

These youths come from a variety of social classes and home backgrounds indicating that the reasons for running away are not a result of any one cause (Adams & Munro, 1979).

Classification

Roberts (1982) made a helpful classification of different types of runaways according to the degree of conflict with parents. Figure 17.4 illustrates the categories. The 0–1 categories include youths who wanted to travel and received permission from parents. Runaway explorers wanted adventure and to assert their independence. They left their parents word about where they had gone, and then left without permission. They generally returned home on their own if they were not picked up by the police. Social pleasure seekers usually had conflict with parents over such issues as dating a certain person, attending an important event, grounding, or an early curfew. They sneaked out to engage in the forbidden activity and then either sneaked back or stopped by a friend's house overnight. They usually telephoned the parents the next morning to ask to come home.

Runaway manipulators tried to manipulate parents by running away to force them to permit return on the runaways' own terms. They had serious conflict with parents over choice of friends, home chores, and other issues.

Runaway retreatists came from families where there was conflict, hitting or throwing objects, frequent yelling, and other manifestations of tension. Some of the homes were broken. In addition, the majority of adolescents had one or more school problems, or problems with alcohol or other types of drugs. They and their families needed counseling help to correct the situations that resulted in running away in the first place.

Endangered runaways left to escape abusive parents or stepparents (Kurtz, Kurtz, & Jarvis, 1991). These youths often used drugs and had drinking problems. A beating or the threat of a beating may have precipitated running away (Roberts, 1982). Physical or sexual abuse of both males and females is often a reason for running away (Janus, Burgess, & McCormack, 1987). Girls often become involved in prostitution, and males in drug dealing. Once on the street, runaways tend to become involved in a social network composed of other runaways and street people who engage in deviant, often illegal, acts of various sorts to support themselves (Simons & Whitbeck, 1991).

Some adolescents who run away from home become street kids.

The simplest classification of runaways is to divide them into two groups: *the running from* and *the running to* (A. T. Miller, Eggertson-Tacon, & Quigg, 1990; Roberts, 1982). The running from adolescents could not tolerate one or both parents, or their home situation. The running to adolescents were pleasure seekers, impulsive, running to places or people providing exciting and different activities. Some enjoyed running away and liked the friends they met on the way. They usually stay away longer and do not return until picked up by the police (Sharlin & Mor-Barak, 1992).

Not all runaways are the same or leave home for similar reasons (Hier, Korboot, & Schweitzer, 1990). However, clusters of personal or situational variables appear repeatedly in their case histories. One study in Hawaii found that children from single-parent families had less chance of becoming chronic runaways than those from intact families (Matthews & Ilon, 1980). This is because there was more quarreling in the two-parent families which the child felt powerless to prevent and from which escape seemed the only solution.

Assistance

The *National Runaway Youth Program,* with the U.S. Youth Development Bureau, has promoted nationwide assistance to youths who are vulnerable to exploitation and to dangerous encounters. The program offers a national toll-free communication system to enable youths to telephone their families and/or centers where they can get help. Most of the individual programs throughout the United States have developed different services to meet various needs. Social service agencies and juvenile justice/law enforcement systems also use their services to assist runaways and their families.

Summary

1. Emotions are subjective feelings and individual experiences in response to stimuli, accompanied by physiological arousal, and which result in behavioral responses.
2. Emotions affect physical well-being and behavior, and are important sources of pleasure and satisfaction.
3. Emotions may be classified into three categories: joyous states including affection, love, happiness, and pleasure; inhibitory states including fear or dread, worry or anxiety, sadness or sorrow, embarrassment, regret or guilt, and disgust; and hostile states including anger, hatred, contempt, and jealousy.
4. By the time children reach adolescence, they already exhibit well-developed patterns of emotional responses to events and people. They may already be described as warm, affectionate, and friendly, or cold, unresponsive, and distant.
5. Fear may be divided into four categories: fear of material things and natural phenomena, fear relating to the self, fear involving social relationships, and fear of the unknown.
6. A phobia is an excessive, uncontrolled fear. Phobias may be divided into three categories: simple phobias, social phobias, and agoraphobia.
7. Worry and anxiety are closely allied with fear but may arise from imagined unpleasant situations as well as from real causes.
8. A study of college females at the University of Maine revealed that the number one worry was school, followed by parents and family, vocation and employment, social relationships, money, the future, marriage, sex, and being overweight, in that order.
9. Some adolescents have grown up in a worry-free environment; others under conditions that cause constant worry and tension.
10. Generalized anxiety disorder occurs when anxiety becomes so pervasive and tenacious that it interferes with normal functioning.

11. One of the ways of relieving emotional distress is by talking out feelings.
12. Hostile states may be manifested as anger, hatred, contempt, or jealousy.
13. Anger in adolescents has many causes: restrictions on social life, attacks on their ego or status, criticism, shaming, rejection, or the actions or treatment of other people. Situations, and the adolescents' own ineptitude, also cause anger.
14. Both men and women have a problem with anger. However, women are taught to inhibit anger; men, to express it.
15. Hatred can be more serious than anger because it persists over a long period of time, is difficult to suppress, and may be expressed through words or actions in violent, aggressive, explosive ways.
16. Self-concept may be defined as a person's perception of his or her nature, character, and individuality.
17. Ruth Strang said there are four basic dimensions of the self: the basic, overall self-concepts; transitory or temporary self-concepts; social selves; and ideal selves.
18. Self-esteem is the value people place on themselves.
19. One study revealed that high levels of problems in the areas of health and physical development and home and family were associated with low self-esteem in adolescent girls.
20. A positive self-esteem is important to interpersonal competence and social adjustments, and to emotional well-being, progress in school, and vocational aspirations. Negative self-esteem is related to delinquency.
21. A number of factors are important to the development of a positive self-concept: the quality of parent-adolescent relationships, the type of parental control, the atmosphere of the home—whether happy or unhappy, the self-esteem of the parents, and the quality of social relationships and friendships.
22. Neurotic perfectionists pursue excellence to an unhealthy extreme, are plagued by self-criticism and low self-worth, and by the stress of having to be perfect.
23. Self-concept gradually stabilizes during adolescence, although adolescents are sensitive to important events and changes in their lives.
24. The most frequently abused drugs are alcohol, tobacco, and marijuana, in that order.
25. A physically addictive drug is one that builds up a chemical craving for it, so that denial results in withdrawal symptoms. Psychological dependence is the development of a persistent, psychological need for a drug. Those who use physically addictive drugs may develop a chemical dependency before they realize it. Those who use nonaddictive drugs to solve emotional problems become psychologically dependent on them.
26. Youths are trying drugs at younger ages.
27. Drug use may be divided into five patterns: social-recreational use, experimental use, circumstantial-situational use, intensified use, and compulsive use.
28. There is a correlation between drug addiction and dependency and disturbed family relationships.
29. Other social and psychological correlates with drug use in adolescents are: peer approval of drug use, involvement with deviant peers, psychological distress and depression, lack of self-confidence, disturbed relationships with others, rebellion against social sanctions, truancy, and frequent, permissive, unprotected sex.
30. Alcoholism is dependence on alcohol: uncontrolled, compulsive, and excessive drinking leading to functional impairment. Alcohol abuse is the use of alcohol to a degree that causes physical damage or impairs functioning.
31. Forty-seven percent of all arrests during 1988 were of people under age 25. Delinquency among males under age 18 is 3½ times that among females of the same age.
32. The causes of delinquency may be grouped into three categories: psychological, sociological, and biological.
33. Psychological causes include emotional and personality factors.
34. Sociological causes include family background influences, socioeconomic status levels, neighborhood and community influences, peer group involve-

ment, affluence and hedonistic values and lifestyles, violence in our culture, cultural change and unrest, drinking and drug use, and school performance.

35. Teens who kill were often themselves sexually or physically abused.
36. Biological or organic factors may also be involved in delinquency.
37. Many crimes are drug related.
38. Parricide is the killing of one's mother or father. Patricide is the killing of one's father; matricide is the killing of one's mother.
39. Any efforts to curb delinquency need to focus on prevention.
40. Adolescents who run away from home have been classified along a continuum as runaway explorers, social pleasure seekers, runaway manipulators, runaway retreatists, and endangered runaways. The simplest classification is to divide them into two groups: the running from and running to. Thus, not all runaways leave home for the same reasons.
41. The National Runaway Youth Program has been developed to provide multiple-service assistance to runaways.

Key Terms

Alcohol abuse *p. 462*
Chronic alcoholism *p. 462*
Emotion *p. 444*
Generalized anxiety disorder *p. 449*
Matricide *p. 466*
Parricide *p. 466*
Patricide *p. 466*
Phobia *p. 446*
Physical addiction *p. 459*
Proprium *p. 452*
Psychological dependency *p. 459*
Self *p. 451*
Self-concept *p. 451*

Discussion Questions

1. What sort of things make you the happiest? most afraid? most worried? most angry?
2. Do you have any phobias? Describe. How did they arise? What do you do about them?
3. Why do some adolescents hate their parents? What can or should they do about these feelings?
4. Do you have a positive or negative self-concept? What factors have been most influential in modeling your ideas about yourself?
5. If you could be any type of person you wanted, what would you be like?
6. Is there any possibility you can become your ideal self? Explain why or why not.
7. Do you have a different self-concept from when you were younger? Explain.
8. What role have your parents played in influencing your self-esteem?
9. Do you accept what your friends say about you? Why or why not?
10. Who have been the most significant others in your life in influencing your self-conception?
11. Does parental divorce or remarriage influence self-esteem? Explain with personal examples.
12. Did you or your friends use drugs when you were in high school? With what effects?
13. What type of drug education programs in high school would help the most?
14. If you were a parent and discovered your adolescent was using alcohol, to-

bacco, marijuana, narcotics, or cocaine, what would you do?

15. To those who have stopped smoking: What helped the most in being able to stop?
16. Why do far fewer females than males become delinquent?
17. If you were a parent, would you forbid your adolescent to run around with a friend who was a convicted delinquent? How would you handle the situation?
18. What factors are most important in causing delinquency?
19. Do you have any firsthand knowledge of gangs in the town where you live, or in which you grew up? Describe.
20. Have you or has a member of your family ever run away from home? Why? What happened?

Suggested Readings

Ammerman, R. T., & Hersen, M. (Eds.). (1991). *Case studies in family violence.* New York: Plenum. Different types of family violence and their treatment.

Davies, J., & Coggans, N. (1991). *The facts about adolescent drug abuse.* London: Cassell. What it is and what can be done about it.

Goldstein, A. P. (1991). *Delinquent gangs: A psychological perspective.* Champaign, IL.: Research Press. The gang phenomenon and how to deal with it.

Johnston, L. L., O'Malley, P. M., & Bachman, J. G. (1987). *National trends in drug use and related factors among American high school students and young adults, 1975–1986.* Ann Arbor: Institute for Social Research, University of Michigan. Trends in adolescent drug use.

Newcomb, M. D., & Bentler, P. M. (1988). *Consequences of adolescent drug use: Impact on the lives of young adults.* Newbury Park, CA: Sage. How does adolescent drug use affect later life?

Offer, D., Ostrov, E., & Howard, K. J. (1981). *The adolescent: A psychological self-portrait.* New York: Basic Books. Descriptive.

Perkins, W. M., & McMurtrie-Perkins, N. (1986). *Raising drug-free kids in a drug-filled world.* Austin, TX: Hazelden. Advice for parents.

Quay, H. C. (Ed.). (1987). *Handbook of juvenile delinquency.* New York: Wiley. Series of articles on description, causes, and prevention of delinquency.

Rothman, J. (1991). *Runaway and homeless youth: strengthening services to families and children.* New York: Longman. Policies and issues in working with runaways.

Stavsky, L., & Mozeson, I. E. (1990). *The place I call home: Voices and faces of homeless teens.* New York: Shapolsky. Monologues of inner-city teenagers.

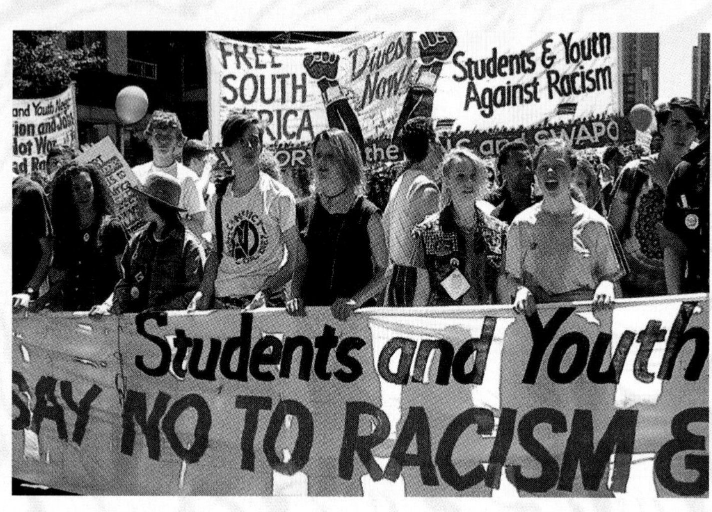

Social Development: Family, Social Relationships, Sexual Behavior, and Morality

Chapter 18

ADOLESCENTS IN THEIR FAMILIES

What Adolescents Expect of Parents • PARENTING ISSUES: *Parental Involvement* • Parent–Adolescent Disagreements • FOCUS: *Parental Functions and Support* • Relationships with Siblings

SOCIAL RELATIONSHIPS

Friendships of Young Adolescents • Heterosocial Development • Group Involvement • FOCUS: *Do Males Value Intimacy?* • Dating • FOCUS: *Sexual Activity, Dating, and Marriage Desirability* • PARENTING ISSUES: *When Parents Object to a Dating Partner*

PREMARITAL SEXUAL BEHAVIOR

Sexual Interests • Masturbation • Premarital Sexual Intercourse • Use of Contraceptives • FOCUS: *Family Relationships and Sexual Behavior among Black Male Adolescents* • Potential Problems • LIVING ISSUES: *Convincing Teens to Use Condoms* • FOCUS: *Sexual Abuse and Adolescent Pregnancy* • FOCUS: *School Birth Control Clinics* • LIVING ISSUES: *Is Sex Becoming Depersonalized?* • Adolescent Marriage • FOCUS: *TV, Sex, and Marriage*

DEVELOPMENT OF MORAL JUDGMENT

Lawrence Kohlberg • FOCUS: *A Theory of Reasoned Action* • FOCUS: *Justice Versus Interpersonal Responsibilities* • Carol Gilligan

WORK

Adolescents in Their Families

The family is the chief socializing influence on adolescents. This means that the family is the principal transmitter of knowledge, values, attitudes, roles, and habits that one generation passes on to the next. Through word and example the family shapes an adolescent's personality and instills modes of thought and ways of acting that become habitual. But what adolescents learn from parents depends partly on the kinds of people the parents are (McKenry, Kotch, & Browne, 1991).

WHAT ADOLESCENTS EXPECT OF PARENTS

The following is a compilation of research findings. These findings indicate that youths want and need parents who

> "Treat us as grown-ups, not like children."
> "Have faith in us to do the right things."
> "Love us and like us the way we are."
> "We can talk to."
> "Listen to us and try to understand us."
> "Are interested in us."
> "Guide us."
> "Are fun and have a sense of humor."
> "We can be proud of."

The family is the chief socializing influence on adolescents.

These characteristics need closer examination (Williamson & Campbell, 1985).

Reasonable Freedom and Privileges

One of the complaints of adolescents is that their parents treat them like kids (Kobak, Cole, Ferenz-Gillies, & Fleming, 1993). Most adolescents push as hard as they can for adult privileges and freedom (Fasick, 1984). They want to feel they can make their own decisions and run their own lives, without their parents always telling them what to do (Pardeck, 1990). However, adolescents need parents who will grant them autonomy in slowly increasing amounts as they learn to use it responsibly (Dornbusch, Ritter, Mont-Reynaud, & Chen, 1990; Gavazzi, Anderson, & Sabatelli, 1993; Gavazzi & Sabatelli, 1990). In his research with adolescent boys, Steinberg (1981) found that assertiveness increases from early puberty to middle adolescence, after which it tapers off as adolescents begin to exert more influence in family decision making (Ellis, 1991; Papini, Roggman, & Anderson, 1990). Too much freedom granted too early may make them think that the parents aren't interested. Youth want freedom—but do not want it all at once. Those who have it suddenly worry about it because they realize they do not know how to use it. Adolescents who have good relationships with their parents still look to them for guidance and advice (Greene & Grimsley, 1990; Papini & Roggman, 1992).

One of the most important ways a parent can assist the adolescent's successful transition into adulthood is to maintain a balance between the adolescent's need for individuality and for remaining emotionally connected to the family (Gavazzi, Anderson, & Sabatelli, 1993). A lack of parental attachment seems to be associated with increased depression in adolescence (Sabatelli & Anderson, 1991). The ideal seems to be to have a moderate degree of emotional attachment to parents (Papini & Roggman, 1992).

Faith

Adolescents say

> "My parents don't trust me. They always seem to expect the worst. I even have trouble getting them to believe me when I tell them where I'm going or what I'm going to do. I might as well not do right; they already accuse me anyhow. If they could expect me to do the right thing, I wouldn't disappoint them."

Some parents seem to have more trouble than others in trusting their adolescents. They tend to project their own guilt, anxieties, and fears onto the adolescent. They worry most about problems that they experienced while growing up.

Approval

All adolescents want their parents to like them, approve of them, and accept them in spite of faults. Adolescents don't want to feel that they have to be perfect before they receive their parents' approval. No adolescent can thrive in an atmosphere of constant criticism and disapproval (Vangelisti, 1992).

Willingness to Communicate

Many of the problems between parents and adolescents can be solved if both are able to communicate with one another (Masselam, Marcus, & Stunkard, 1990; Papini et al., 1990). Parents complain that their adolescents never listen to them. Adolescents say their parents lecture them or preach to them rather than discuss issues with them. One adolescent comments:

> "My parents aren't really willing to listen to what I have to say. They don't understand me. I'm not even allowed to express my point of view. They will tell me to be quiet and not to argue. That's the end of the discussion."

When parents show respect for adolescents' opinions, conflict is minimized and the atmosphere of the home is enhanced. Some parents don't give their adolescents a chance to express their feelings or point of view. This builds up resentment and tension (Rubenstein & Feldman, 1993; Thompson, Acock, & Clark, 1985). The ability to communicate and solve problems keeps tension at a minimum (Openshaw, Mills, Adams, & Durso, 1992).

Parental Concern and Support

Adolescents want their parents to be interested in what they are doing and to give moral and emotional support when necessary (Northman, 1985; Windle & Miller-Tutzauer, 1992). One boy, a baseball player, was angry because his parents never attended a game to see him play ball. Adolescents especially resent parents who are so involved with their own activities that they don't have time for their children or are not around when they are needed (Jensen & Borges, 1986). The term *latch-key children* applies to youth who have to let themselves in the house after school because parents are working outside the home. For a full discussion of parental employment and adolescents see *The Journal of Adolescence* (Volume 10, August 1990).

Guidance

All adolescents need guidance and discipline, but some methods work better than others (Holmbeck, & Hill, 1991; Nurmi & Pulliainen, 1991). Research generally indicates that parental explanations and reasoning (induction) are strongly associated with adolescents' internalizing ethical and moral principles. To talk with adolescents is the most frequent disciplinary measure used and the one considered best for the age group (deTurck & Miller, 1983; T. E. Smith, 1983). The parents and adolescents who are most successful at conflict resolution are those who show mutual respect and exchange and high regard for the needs of one another, and who exchange ideas and information (McCombs, Forehand, & Smith, 1988). Use of physical punishment, deprivation, and threats (power-assertive discipline) is associated with children's aggression, hostility, and delinquency (Feldman & Wentzel, 1990). It impedes the development of emotional, social, and intellectual maturity (Portes, Dunham, & Williams, 1986).

The authoritative but democratic home, where parents encourage individual responsibility, decision making, initiative, and autonomy but still exercise authority and give guidance, has a positive effect upon adolescents (Lamborn, Mounts, Steinberg, & Dornbusch, 1991). The home atmosphere has the character of respect, appreciation, warmth, and acceptance (Kurdek & Fine, 1993). This type of home, where there is warmth, fairness, and consistency of discipline, is associated with conforming, trouble-free, nondelinquent behavior for both boys and girls (Fischer & Crawford, 1992). One study showed that adolescents whose parents are accepting, firm, and democratic earn higher grades in school, are more self-reliant, report less anxiety and depression, and are less likely to engage in delinquent behavior (Steinberg, Mounts, Lamborn, & Dornbusch, 1991).

Inconsistent or sporadic parental control also has a negative effect on adolescents (Parish & McCluskey, 1992). Adolescents become insecure and confused when they lack boundaries and clear guidelines. Such youths may show antisocial, delinquent behavior and rebel against conflicting expectations.

A Happy Home

The most important contribution parents can make to their adolescent children is to create a happy home environment in which to bring them up (Fauber, Forehand, Thomas, & Wierson, 1990; Parish, 1990). One adolescent remarked:

> "I love it at home because we always have such a good time together. Mom and Dad are always laughing and joking. We seldom argue, but when we do, we get over it quickly. No one holds a grudge. We are really happy together."

In contrast to this, some families live in a home climate of anger, unhappiness, and hostility (Barber, 1992; Whittaker & Bry, 1991), all of which has a negative effect on everyone (Forsstrom-Cohen & Rosenbaum, 1985; Parish & Necessary, 1993). The best adjusted adolescents are those who grow up in happy, loving homes where children and parents spend pleasurable time together.

Good Example

Adolescents say they want parents who "make us proud of them," "follow the same principles they try to teach us," "set a good example for us to follow," and "who practice what they preach." They want parents they can admire. As one adolescent expressed it: "It's good to feel our parents are trying to teach us right from wrong and set a good example for us to follow" (Clark-Lempers, Lempers, & Ho, 1991). Research indicates that mothers and fathers convey their parenting beliefs to their adolescent children via their parenting practices. For example, if parents use harsh discipline with their adolescents, these discipline beliefs—for both boys and girls—are likely to

PARENTING ISSUES

Paternal Involvement

Research indicates that fathers are more involved with sons than with daughters. The most advantaged son is the only son. A larger number of sons seems to dilute the attention that one son gets. For the most part, however, all sons receive more paternal attention than daughters within the family. Daughters are not treated equally with sons in the family, but they receive more attention from fathers than they would if they had no brothers. The presence of sons draws the father into more active parenting, and this greater involvement benefits daughters, who in return receive more (but still unequal) attention from their father (Harris & Morgan, 1991).

What about fathers' participation in single-parent versus married-couple families? Children in single-parent families report feeling less close to their fathers than do youths in married-parent families. Noncustodial fathers are perceived as friendlier companions; that is, they play the role of the Disneyland dad more often, but at the cost of emotional intimacy. There is not as much real closeness with the noncustodial dad (Asmussen & Larson, 1991).

be the beliefs that they carry into family living themselves (Simons, Beaman, Conger, & Chao, 1992).

PARENT–ADOLESCENT DISAGREEMENTS

Most parents get along fairly well with their adolescent children (Stefanko, 1984). When disagreement occurs, it usually is in one or more of the following areas (Galambos & Almeida, 1992; Hall, 1987; Leslie, Huston, & Johnson, 1986; Smetana, Braeges, & Yau, 1991).

Moral, Ethical Behavior

Parents are concerned about their adolescents' going to church, synagogue, or temple; obeying the law and staying out of trouble; sexual behavior; honesty; language and speech, drinking, smoking, and use of drugs.

Relationships with Family Members

Disagreements arise over the amount of time adolescents spend with the family (Felson & Gottfredson, 1984; Jurich, Schumm, & Bollman, 1987), relationships with relatives, especially with aged grandparents in the home, quarreling with siblings, the general attitude and level of respect shown to parents (Flint, 1992), and temper tantrums and other manifestations of childish behavior.

Academics

Parents are concerned about adolescents' behavior in school, general attitudes toward school studies and teachers, regularity of attendance, study habits and homework, and grades and level of performance.

Fulfilling Responsibilities

Most parents expect adolescents to show responsibility in the following areas: use of family property or belongings, furnishings, supplies, tools, and equipment; use of the telephone; use of the family automobile; care of personal belongings, clothes, and room; earning and spending money; and performance of family chores (Greif, 1985; Light, Hertsgaard, & Martin, 1985; Sanik & Stafford, 1985).

Social Activities

Adolescents' social activities probably create more conflict with parents than any other areas of concern. The most common sources of friction are the following:

Choice of clothes and hair styles; going steady and age allowed to date, ride in cars, and participate in certain events; curfew hours and where they are allowed to go; how often they are allowed to go out, going out on a school night, or frequency of dating; and choice of friends or dating partners.

Work Outside the Home

Most parents expect adolescents to do some work outside the home to earn money, and most do, but sometimes the amount of work is excessive so that the adolescent neglects the family and school and is away from home too much.

Correlations with Conflict

A number of factors relate to the focus and extent of conflict with parents.

The type of *discipline* that parents use has an effect on conflict (Johnson, Shulman, & Collings, 1991). Authoritarian discipline results in more conflict with parents over home chores, activities outside the home, friends, and spending money than does a democratic approach to guidance.

The *socioeconomic status* of the family influences the focus of conflict. Parents of low socioeconomic status are more often

Adolescent social activities probably create more conflict with parents than any other areas of concern.

FOCUS

Parental Functions and Support

Raising adolescent children in contemporary society is a complex process. This process is influenced by numerous factors that reside both within individuals and families and outside them. These parental functions and social supports are illustrated in Figure 18.1. This figure is in the form of an ecological map (not unlike Bronfenbrenner's, 1979).

In this map, the parenting functions are arranged hierarchically at the center. In the *innermost circle,* we see four parenting functions. The first is the function of *meeting basic needs* of the children. This includes a wide array of resources necessary for survival such as a safe and secure place to live, adequate food and nutrition, clothing, and access to medical services. Basic needs would also include emotional needs.

The second parental function is that of *protection.* Parents are usually responsible for protecting the physical, psychological, spiritual, ethnic, and cultural integrity of their children from threats from the natural environment and other persons, groups, and institutions.

The third function involves *guidance*—guiding and promoting all aspects of the child's development including cognitive, social, physical, emotional, moral, sexual, spiritual, cultural, and educational aspects.

Finally, a fourth function refers to *advocacy,* which is the parents' role as advocates and supporters of their children, and as coordinators and links to experts, individuals, groups, and institutions that help them raise their children.

In the innermost circle surrounding the parenting functions are the most immediate factors that can affect a parent's ability to carry out these functions: *the parent's personal characteristics, characteristics of the adolescent, and the presence and quality of the marital relationship.*

The *second level* in the map involves factors outside of the individual and family, such as the neighborhood, the parent's work situation, and informal networks. These also all impinge upon the parent's ability to function.

The *outer ring* of Figure 18.1 represents broader social influences such as cultural values, formal social programs, and factors related to social class. While these *"macrosystem"* factors seem far removed from the parenting function, they often help to define the entire context in which parenting takes place; for example, social class is known to be related to family size and the division of labor in marriage, and it is also likely to affect which parental functions are deemed most important, how they are performed, and by whom.

It is important to recognize that there is a hierarchy of parenting functions and that not all families will view them as equally important. For example, some parents as a result of economic or other personal circumstances, may have their energies focused more on performing basic parental functions such as providing a safe environment, or adequate food to eat, than on higher-level functions such as improving parent–child communications. Families are different, and the functions that they perform partially reflect these differences (Small & Eastman, 1991).

concerned with respect, politeness, and obedience, whereas middle-income families are more concerned with developing initiative and independence. Parents of low socioeconomic status worry about keeping children out of trouble at school, whereas middle-class parents are more concerned about achievement and grades (McKenry, Kotch, & Browne, 1991).

The *number of children* in the family is a significant factor, at least in middle-class families. The more children in the middle-class family, the more parent–youth conflict and the more parents use physical force to control adolescents (Bell & Avery, 1985).

The *stage of development* of adolescents is another factor. From age 12 on, girls are increasingly in conflict with parents over boyfriends, with the peak years being 14 and 15. The peak age of boys for conflict

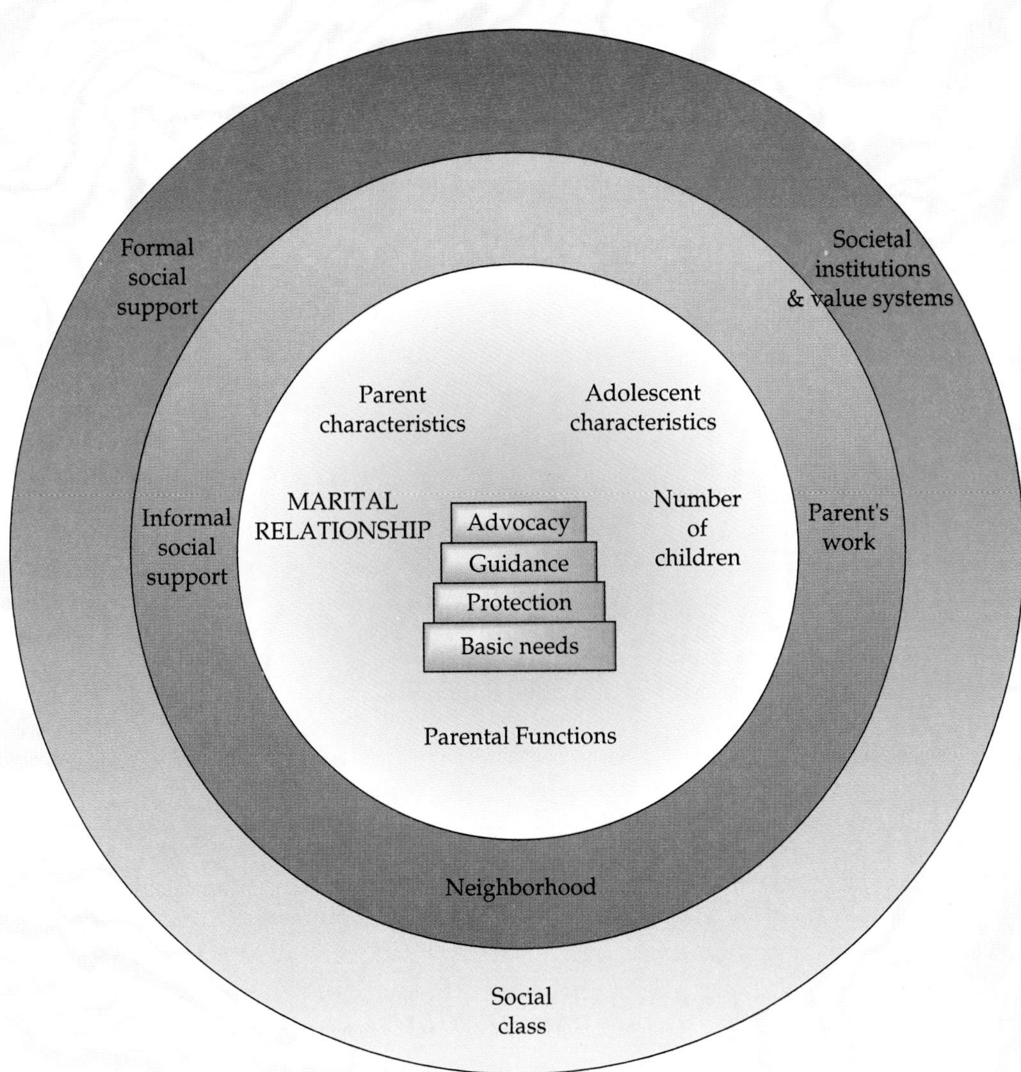

FIGURE 18.1 Parenting functions and social supports.

From "Rearing Adolescents in Contemporary Society: A Conceptual Framework for Understanding the Responsibilities and Needs of Parents" by S. Small and G. Eastman, October 1991, *Family Relations, 40:4*, 455–462.

with parents over girlfriends is around age 16.

The *gender* of the adolescent relates to conflict. Boys report more unresolved conflict with families than do girls, which is an indication of gender differences in communication skills used in conflict resolution (Smetana, Yau, & Hanson, 1991). The gender of the parent also relates to conflict. Adolescents are usually closer to their mothers than to their fathers (Circirelli, 1980; Paulson, Hill, & Holmbeck, 1990). As a result, they usually get along better with their mothers and the mothers exert more influence over them in such areas as educational goals (T. E. Smith, 1981). Most adolescents report more difficulties getting along with their fathers than with their mothers (J. B. Miller & Lane, 1991).

The variables associated with parent–

adolescent conflict are numerous (Flanagan, 1990), but the ones discussed here are representative. Not all parents and adolescents quarrel about the same things or to the same extent.

If conflict between parents and adolescents becomes excessive, parents ought to seek outside help (Raviv, Maddy-Weitzman, & Raviv, 1992). This is particularly true since adolescent adjustment is related to the degree and intensity of family conflict (Nelson et al., 1993).

RELATIONSHIPS WITH SIBLINGS

The relationships between brothers and sisters have a considerable influence on the social development of the adolescent (Buhrmester & Furman, 1990). This development is affected in a number of ways.

Siblings often provide friendship and companionship and meet one another's needs for meaningful relationships and affection. They act as confidants for one another, share many experiences, and are able to help one another when there are problems. However, this is not as true if siblings are six or more years apart in age.

On the negative side, if there is less than six years' difference in their ages, siblings tend to be more jealous of one another than if they are further apart in age. Also, sibling rivalry is greater during early adolescence than later. As adolescents mature, conflicting relationships with siblings tend to subside (Goodwin & Roscoe, 1990).

Older siblings often serve as confidants, playmates, teachers, caretakers, and surrogate parents (Seginer, 1992). Pleasant relationships can contribute to younger children's sense of acceptance, belonging, and security. Rejecting, hostile relationships may create deep-seated feelings of hostility, resentment, insecurity, or anxiety that may be carried into adulthood. Many adolescents learn adult responsibilities and roles by having to care for younger sisters and brothers while growing up. However, some adolescents are given too much responsibility, and provide most of the care that parents ought to be providing. They may grow to resent this responsibility, which prevents them from having any free time of their own. Older siblings represent masculine or feminine personalities and behavior to young siblings. Through appearance, character, and overall behavior, they exemplify a type of person the younger child might become. This can have either a positive or negative effect, depending on the example set.

Social Relationships

Friendship during adolescence has a strategic function. Friendship is a factor in the socialization of adolescents. It is important as a means of learning social skills, and plays a central role in the adolescent's quest for self-knowledge and self-definition. Friendship is important in achieving emancipation from parents, the establishment of heterosexual relationships, and the affirmation of one's identity. Furthermore, the absence of friendships or conflictual relations with friends constitutes predictors of later psychological problems (Claes, 1992). Friends are important sources of companionship and recreation, share advice and valued possessions, serve as trusted confidants and critics, act as loyal allies, and provide stability in times of stress or transition (Lempers & Clark-Lempers, 1993).

FRIENDSHIPS OF YOUNG ADOLESCENTS

Adolescents' need for close friends is different from that of children (Pombeni, Kirchler, & Palmonari, 1990; Yarcheski & Mahon, 1984). Children need playmates of their own age to share common activities and games. However, they do not depend primarily on one another for love and affection. They look to their parents for filling their emotional needs and seek praise, affection, and love from them. Only if they have been rejected and unloved by parents will they have turned to parent substitutes and friends for emotional fulfillment.

Needs change with the advent of puberty. The adolescent desires emotional independence and emancipation from par-

Adolescents turn to their friends for companionship and emotional fulfillment.

ents and emotional fulfillment from friends (Larson & Richards, 1991; Quintana & Lapsley, 1990). Peers now provide part of the emotional support formerly provided by families (Cotterell, 1992; DuBois & Hirsch, 1990; Howes & Wu, 1990; Sebald, 1986).

One study found that mothers and fathers were seen as the most frequent providers of support in the fourth grade. Same-sex friends were perceived to be as supportive as parents in the seventh grade, and were the most frequent providers of support in the tenth grade. Romantic partners moved up in rank with age until college, where they, along with friends and mothers, received the highest ratings for support (Furman & Buhrmester, 1992).

Young adolescents begin to form a small group of friends, and often choose one or several very best friends. Usually these best friends are of the same sex in the beginning (Benenson, 1990). Mutual activities become important in friendships during the early school years (Clark & Ayers, 1993). Adolescents attend school, go to athletic events, and share in recreational activities with these friends (DuBois & Hirsch, 1993; Zarbatany, Hartmann, & Rankin, 1990). Best friends strive to dress alike, look alike, and act alike. They are often similar in personality traits and behavior (Bukowski, Gauze, Hoza, & Newcomb, 1993). After spending all day together, they may come home and talk for additional hours on the telephone.

Early adolescent friendships are sometimes upsetting if expectations are not fulfilled (Yarcheski & Mahon, 1984). The more intense and narcissistic the emotions that drive adolescents to seek companionship, the more likely it is that sustained friendships will be difficult and tenuous. Once disappointed, the frustrated, immature, and unstable adolescent may react with excessive emotions, which may disrupt friendships at least temporarily. Friendships that can be a valuable source of social support sometimes end up as a means of social stress (Moran & Eckenrode, 1991).

Heterosocial Development

Both same-sex and opposite-sex friendships are important in simultaneously providing for many of the social needs of adolescents (Lempers & Clark-Lempers, 1993). Heterosociality means forming friendships with those of both sexes (Goff, 1990). Getting to know and feel comfortable with the opposite sex is a difficult process for some adolescents (K. E. Miller, 1990). Here are typical questions of adolescents who are trying to form heterosocial relationships:

> "Why is it that I'm so shy when I'm around girls?"
>
> "How can you get a girl to like you?"
>
> "How old do you have to be before you can start dating?"
>
> "How can I get boys to think of me as more than a friend?"
>
> "If a girl likes a boy, should she tell him?"
>
> "How can I become more sexy?"
>
> "How can I overcome my fear of asking a girl out?"
>
> "How do you go about talking to a girl?"

Puberty brings on a biological and emotional awareness of the opposite sex, the beginning of sexual attraction, and a decline in negative attitudes. The girl who was looked on before as a giggly kid now becomes strangely alluring. On the one hand, the now-maturing male is attracted and fascinated by this young woman; on the other hand he is perplexed, awed, and terrified. No wonder he ends up asking: "How do you go about talking to a girl?" Girls, who used to feel that boys were too rough and ill-mannered, now feel a strange urge to be near them: "If a girl likes a boy, should she tell him?"

Some boys show their interest through physical contact and teasing: by pulling the girl's hat off, putting snow down her neck, or chasing after her. Girls, too, find ways of attracting attention. Gradually, these initial contacts are replaced by more mature behavior: attempts at conversation, considerate acts to win favor, or other means of expressing interest. The effort is to act more grown up and mannerly in social situations. The group boy–girl relationships change into paired relationships, and these deepen into affectionate friendships and romance as the two sexes discover one another.

GROUP INVOLVEMENT

Need to Belong to a Group

Finding acceptance in social groups also becomes a powerful motivation in the lives of adolescents (Borja-Alvarez, Zarbatany, & Pepper, 1991; Woodward & Kalyan-Masih, 1990). A primary goal of adolescents is to be accepted by members of a group or clique to which they are attracted. At this stage, adolescents are sensitive to criticism or to others' negative reaction to them. They are concerned about what people think because they want to be accepted and admired by them. Also, their degree of self-worth is partly a reflection of the opinions of others.

The following questions are real-life examples of questions asked by adolescents in the seventh, eighth, and ninth grades. The questions reflect adolescents' concern about group involvement.

> "What do you have to do to become a member of a group you like?"
>
> "Why are some kids not friendly? Is there something wrong with me?"
>
> "When other kids ignore you, what do you do?"
>
> "Are kids born popular or do they learn to be that way?"
>
> "If you are too fat, will other kids not accept you?"

Social Acceptance

Considerable evidence shows that personal qualities and social skills such as conversational ability, ability to empathize with others, and poise are the most important factors in social acceptance (Meyers & Nelson, 1986). One study of 204 adolescents in the seventh, ninth, and twelfth grades revealed that personal factors such as social conduct, personality, and character traits were more important in social acceptance than either achievement or physical characteristics. This was true of adolescents at all grade levels (Tedesco & Gaier, 1988). It is especially important to peer group acceptance that adolescents' personality and behavioral characteristics provide a good match with peer group norms. To be accepted by the group, adolescents have to manifest characteristics similar to those of other members of the group (East et al., 1992).

Achievement, which included academic success and athletic prowess, also contributed to popularity. And physical characteristics, including appearance and material things such as money or autos, also affected social acceptance. However, the older they became, the more adolescents emphasized personal factors and deemphasized achievement and physical characteristics in friendship. Other research also emphasizes the importance of personal qualities as a criterion of popularity.

Thus, one of the primary ways adolescents find group acceptance is by developing and exhibiting personal qualities that others admire and by learning social skills that ensure acceptance (D. Miller, 1991; Wise, Bundy, Bundy, & Wise, 1991). In general, popular youths are accepted because of their character, sociability, and personal appearance. They have good reputations and exhibit qualities of moral character that people admire (Gillmore, Hawkins, Day, & Catalano, 1992). They usually possess high self-esteem and positive self-concepts. They are appropriately

FOCUS

Do Males Value Intimacy?

Research indicates that *males continue to have difficulty with intimacy,* and that this gender difference may emerge as early as middle adolescence. The gender differences in intimacy, both expressed and wanted, confirm that females value closeness in relationships more than males, and that males exhibit tendencies toward value and autonomy within relationships (Bakken & Romig, 1992).

These differences between males and females are highlighted by McGill (1985, pp. 157, 158):

> To say that men have no intimate friends seems on the surface too harsh, but the data indicates that it is not far from the truth. Even the most intimate of male friendships (of which there are very few) rarely approached the depth of disclosure a woman commonly has with many other women. One man in ten has a friend with whom he discusses work, money, marriage; only one in more than twenty has friendships in which he discloses feelings about himself, or his sexual feelings. The most common male friendship pattern is for a man to have many friends, each of whom knows something of the man's public self, and therefore little about him, but not one of whom knows more than a small piece of the whole. Most often, they are created in the context of common occupational or recreational interests and pursued very cautiously.
>
> By contrast, women typically have many friends who know everything there is to know about them. Theirs is an open, fully disclosing interaction, not constrained by circumstance or content.

groomed and dressed according to the standards of their group. They are acceptable-looking youths who are friendly, happy, fun-loving, outgoing, and energetic; who have developed a high degree of social skills; and who like to participate in many activities with others (Gifford & Dean, 1990). They may be sexually experienced but are not promiscuous (Newcomer, Udry, & Cameron, 1983).

Deviant Behavior

So far we have been talking about youths who are in the mainstream of group participation. There are other adolescents, however, who find acceptance in deviant groups by conforming to the antisocial standards adopted by their members (Downs & Rose, 1991). Whereas delinquent or antisocial behavior may be unacceptable in society as a whole, it may be required as a condition of membership in a ghetto gang. What might be considered causes of a bad reputation in the local high school (sexual promiscuity, antisocial behavior, being uncooperative, making trouble, or fighting) might be considered causes of a good reputation among a group of delinquents. One study of 12- to 16-year-old boys who were overaggressive and who bullied younger and weaker youths showed that the bullies enjoyed average popularity among other boys (Olweus, 1977); those who were the targets of aggression were far less popular than the bullies. These findings illustrate that standards of group behavior vary with different groups and that popularity depends not so much on a fixed standard as on group conformity.

Sometimes peer groups are formed because of hostility to family authority and a desire to rebel against it. When this happens, the peer groups may become antisocial gangs that are hostile to all established authority, yet supportive of the particular deviancy accepted by the group.

DATING

Dating in American culture is not equivalent to courtship, at least during the early and middle years of adolescence. Traditionally, courtship was for purposes of mate sorting and selection. Today, however, dating has other purposes in the eyes of adolescents (McCabe, 1984; Roscoe, Diana, & Brooks, 1987).

Values

One major purpose of dating is to have *fun.* Dating provides amusement; it is a form of recreation and a source of enjoyment; it can be an end in itself. Wanting the *friendship, acceptance, affection, and love* of the opposite sex is a normal part of growing up. Dating is also used to achieve and *maintain status.* However, adolescents of higher socioeconomic status more often use dating as a symbol of their status than do those of lower socioeconomic status. Membership in certain cliques is associated with the status-seeking aspects of dating. Dating is also a *means of social and personal growth.* It is a way of learning to get along with others and to know and understand many different types of people.

Dating has many purposes, one of which is to provide amusement and recreation.

Dating has become more *sex-oriented* as increasing numbers of adolescents have sexual intercourse. Dating is sometimes used to have sex; at other times sex develops out of dating experiences. Most research indicates that men want sexual involvement in a relationship sooner than women, with the discrepancy a source of potential conflict (Knox & Wilson, 1981).

One of the major purposes of dating is to find *intimacy.* Intimacy is the development of affection, respect, loyalty, mutual trust, sharing, openness, love, and commitment (Roscoe, Kennedy, & Pope, 1987). Some adolescent relationships with friends are superficial. Other relationships are close ones, in which adolescents are sensitive to the innermost thoughts and feelings of their partners and are willing to share personal information, private thoughts, and feelings. Heterosocial relationships vary greatly in intensity of feeling and in depth of communication. Dating can provide the opportunity for intimacy, but whether it develops varies with the individuals and with different pairs. Boys who are socialized to hide feelings may have trouble developing intimate relationships with girls.

As youths get older, dating becomes more a means of *mate sorting and selection,* whether the motive is conscious or not. Those who are similar in personality characteristics are more likely to be compatible than those who are dissimilar in social characteristics, psychological traits, and physical attractiveness. Thus, dating can result in sorting out compatible pairs and can contribute to wise mate selection.

Dating Concerns

A study of 107 men and 227 women, who comprised a random sample of students at East Carolina University, sought to identify dating problems (Knox & Wilson, 1983). Table 18.1 shows the problems experienced by the men. *The most frequently mentioned problems of the men were communication, where to go and what to do on dates, shyness, money, and honesty/openness,* in that order. By honesty and openness the men meant how much to tell about themselves and how soon, and getting their partner to

TABLE 18.1
DATING PROBLEMS EXPERIENCED BY 107 UNIVERSITY MEN

Problem	*Percentage*
Honesty, openness	8
Money	17
Shyness	20
Place to date	23
Communication with date	35

Adapted from "Dating Problems of University Students" by D. Knox and K. Wilson, 1983, *College Student Journal, 17,* 225–228.

TABLE 18.2
DATING PROBLEMS EXPERIENCED BY 227 UNIVERSITY WOMEN

Problem	*Percentage*
Money	9
Sexual misunderstandings	13
Communication with date	20
Places to go	22
Unwanted pressure to engage in sexual behavior	23

Adapted from "Dating Problems of University Students" by D. Knox and K. Wilson, 1983, *College Student Journal, 17,* 225–228.

open up (Knox & Wilson, 1983). *The most frequent problems expressed by the women* (see Table 18.2) *were unwanted pressure to engage in sexual behavior, where to go and what to do on dates, communication, sexual misunderstandings, and money,* in that order. An example of sexual misunderstandings was leading a man on when the woman did not really want to have intercourse. Some of the women complained that the men wanted to move toward a sexual relationship too quickly.

The problem of communication was mentioned frequently by both women and men. Students complained that they didn't know what to talk about and that they ran out of things to say. After they had discussed school, classes, teachers, jobs, or the weather, the conversation lagged and they had trouble filling in long gaps of silence.

Both college women and college men look for honesty and openness in a relationship. Part of the problem is caused by the fact that both the man and woman strive to be on their best behavior. This involves a certain amount of pretense or play acting called **imaging,** to present oneself in the best possible manner.

Imaging—being on one's best behavior to make a good impression

Premarital Sexual Behavior

SEXUAL INTERESTS

Intensified interest in sex accompanies sexual maturation (Weinstein & Rosen, 1991). At first this interest focuses on the adolescent's bodily changes and observable happenings. Most adolescents spend time looking in the mirror and examining body parts in minute detail. Accompanying this self-centered concern is the desire to develop an acceptable body image.

Gradually young adolescents become interested not only in their own development, and that of others of the same gender, but also in the opposite sex (Frydenberg & Lewis, 1991). Curiosity motivates them to try to learn as much as possible about the sexual characteristics of the opposite sex. Adolescents also become fascinated with basic facts about human reproduction. Both boys and girls gradually become aware of their own developing sexual feelings and drives and how these are aroused and expressed. Most adolescents begin some experimentation: touching themselves, playing with their genitals, or exploring various parts of the body. Often by accident they experience orgasm through self-manipulation. From that time on, interest in sex as erotic feeling and expression increases. Adolescents begin to compare their ideas with those of others and spend a lot of time talking about sex, telling jokes, using sex slang, and exchang-

FOCUS

Sexual Activity, Dating, and Marriage Desirability

Over 750 students from three universities were asked to judge the dating and marriage desirability of a person based on information provided about his or her current sexual activity. Overall, the results indicated that a person portrayed as engaging in low sexual activity in a current relationship was perceived to be more desirable as a marriage partner than a person engaging in moderate or high sexual activity, whereas moderate or high sexual activity was preferred more in a dating partner. Evidence was found for a reverse double standard in rating dating desirability: Males were perceived as more desirable as a date when they engaged in moderate sexual activity, whereas females were perceived as more desirable as a date when they engaged in high sexual activity (Sprecher, McKinney, & Orbuch, 1991).

ing sex-oriented literature. Adults are sometimes shocked at the language and jokes. Many parents have been horrified at finding sex-related books hidden under the mattress. But these activities are motivated by a desire to understand human sexuality; they are a means of understanding, expressing, and gaining control over sexual feelings. Wise parents can play a positive role in the sex education of their children (Mueller & Powers, 1990).

MASTURBATION

Masturbation—self-stimulation for purposes of sexual arousal

One of the common practices of adolescents is **masturbation,** which is any type of self-stimulation that produces erotic arousal, whether or not arousal results in orgasm. After adolescents discover that they can sexually arouse themselves through self-manipulation, masturbation may become a regular part of their self-expression. The incidence of masturbation varies somewhat among studies. At the University of Northern Iowa, a study of undergraduate students in a class titled Human Relationships and Sexuality revealed that 64 percent of the females and 90 percent of the males had masturbated (Story, 1982).

Practically all authorities now say that masturbation is a normal part of growing up and does not have any harmful physical and mental effects. Masturbation provides sexual release and serves a useful function in helping the individual to learn about his or her body, to learn how to respond sexually, and to develop sexual identity. The only ill effect that masturbation may stimulate is guilt, fear, or anxiety stemming from the belief that the practice will do harm or create problems (Parcel & Luttman, 1981). Negative emotions concerning masturbation can lead to great anxiety if a youth continues to practice it and feel guilty about it.

PREMARITAL SEXUAL INTERCOURSE

Studies indicated a rapid rise in the percentage of youths engaging in heavy petting and premarital sexual intercourse. The latest survey, conducted in 1992, called the *National Health and Social Life Survey* (NHSLS), is based on 3,432 interviews with people across the United States who were willing to sit down and answer a ninety-minute questionnaire about their sexual behavior and other aspects of their sex lives (Michael, Gagnon, Laumann, and Kolata,

PARENTING ISSUES

When Parents Object to a Dating Partner

Since our system of courtship emphasizes individual freedom, the question arises as to how much influence parents have in the dating process. In a study of 334 university students by Knox and Wilson (1981), women were significantly more likely than men to report that their parents tried to influence their choice of dates. About 60 percent of the women, compared with 40 percent of the men, said parental influence was involved. Daughters also were more likely than sons to say that parents interfered with dating relationships. However, daughters were also more likely than sons to say it was important to them that they dated the kinds of people their parents approved of. About 30 percent of men versus 10 percent of women said they didn't care what their parents thought.

Parental objections are usually based on one or more of the following:

- *The parents don't like the person* because "he's rude; she's impolite; she has a bad reputation; he's not a nice person." These objections are based on dislike of the other's personality.
- *The parents feel the other person has a problem:* "He drinks too much; she has a drug problem; she's too emotional; he has a bad reputation."
- *The other person's family is different from the parents' family.* "His family are rather common people; he's not of our religion; why couldn't he have picked some fine Italian (or Irish, Jewish, or Spanish) girl?"
- *There is a significant age difference.* "He's too old for her."
- *Parents object because they are too possessive of their offspring and are unwilling to let them grow up.* In this case, the parents might object no matter whom their child wanted to go out with.

There are several approaches adolescents can take. They can try to get their parents to like their choice. If objections are based on a lack of knowledge, they can invite the person over to get acquainted. Sometimes parents end up approving. At other times, parents object even more. Parents are not always wrong. The situation needs to be discussed, employing the aid of a counselor if the parents and adolescent are not able to find a solution.

1994). One of the trends revealed by the results was a steadily declining age at first sexual intercourse.

Figure 18.2 shows the cumulative percentages of teenagers and young adults by race and Hispanic origin who have experienced **coitus** at each age from 12 to 25. The graph shows that half of all black men have had intercourse by age 15, half of all Hispanic men by age 16 and a half, and half of all white men by age 17. Half of all black women have had intercourse by about age 17, and half of white women and Hispanic women have had intercourse by age 18. By age 22, about 90 percent of each group has had intercourse.

When asked why they had intercourse the first time, 51 percent of the men attributed it to curiosity and readiness for sex, and 25 percent answered affection for their partner. Among the women, it was the reverse: about half cited affection for their partner, and about 25 percent curiosity and readiness for sex. A very small percentage of both men and women said they had sex because of a desire for physical pleasure. Most of the men said they were not in love with their first sexual partner; most of the women, in contrast, said they were.

Coitus—sexual intercourse

Today, American teenagers are having sex earlier than their parents did, but they do not necessarily have more partners. About half of today's adolescents begin having intercourse with a partner sometime between the ages of 15 and 18, and at least four out of five have had intercourse

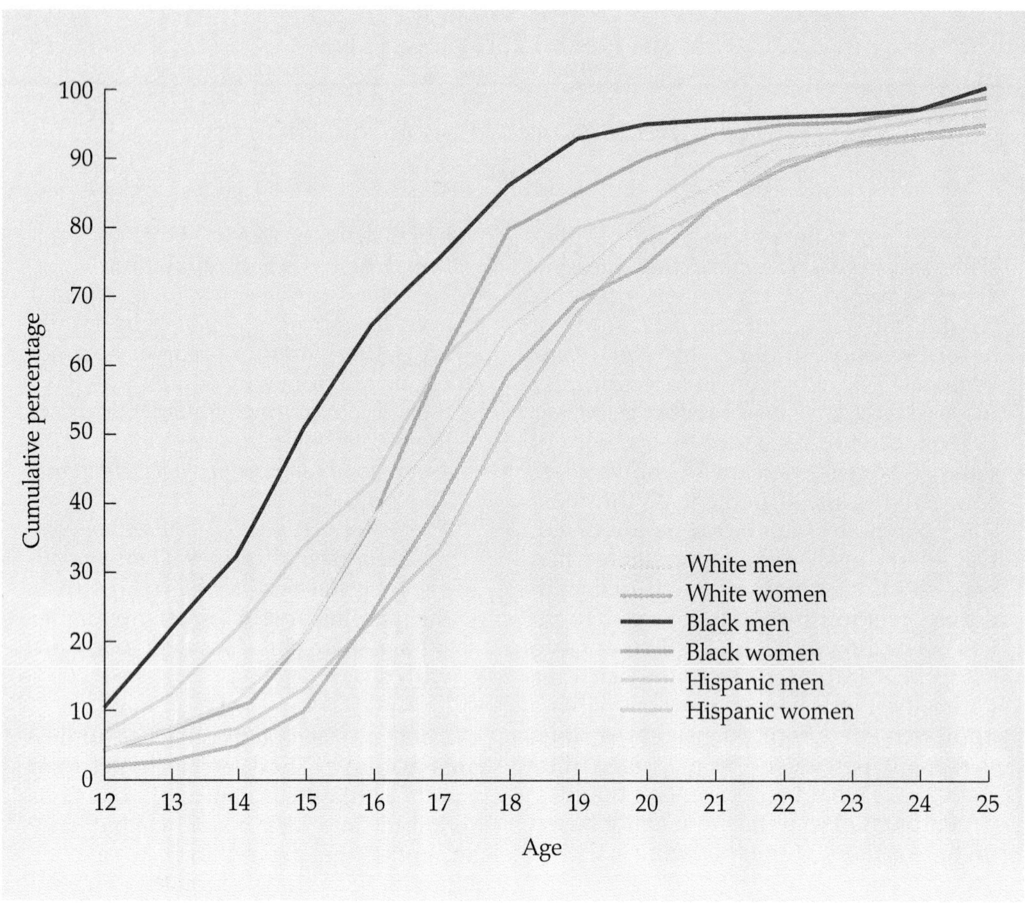

FIGURE 18.2 Cumulative percentage who have had intercourse.

From: *Sex in America*, by R. T. Michael, J. H. Gagnon, E. O. Laumann and G. Kolata, 1994, Boston: Little, Brown.

by the time they are 21. Since the average age of marriage is now in the mid-20s, few Americans are waiting until they marry to have sex, but most sexually active young people show no signs of having large numbers of partners. More than half the men and women between ages 18 and 24 in 1992 had had just one sex partner in the previous year, and 11 percent had had none.

One of the explanations for the increase in early sexual activity is that it is an expression of cultural norms (Slonin-Nevo, 1992). For many youths, particularly boys, sexual activity may be normative and abstinence nonnormative. Sexual socialization of younger adolescents by older youths may be a factor in early initiation into sexual activities. Some youths, especially girls, appear to regard sex as a mechanism for establishing an intimate relationship. Because establishing an intimate relationship is developmentally appropriate for adolescents, some girls feel a sense of urgency about expressing themselves sexually in order that intimacy may be established (Stanton, Black, Kaljee, & Ricardo, 1993). Girls who lack supportive parental relationships try to establish intimate relationships outside of the family (Whitbeck, Hoyt, Miller, & Kao, 1992).

USE OF CONTRACEPTIVES

With large numbers of adolescents having premarital sex (DiBlasio & Benda, 1990), the rate of use of contraceptives becomes important. What percentage of these young people are using some form of protection against pregnancy? The NSFG in 1988 revealed that only 35 percent of 15- to 19-year-olds used any methods of contraception (including withdrawal) at first intercourse (Forrest & Singh, 1990). Only 32 percent of 15- to 19-year-old females or their partners reported they were currently

FOCUS

Family Relationships and Sexual Behavior among Black Male Adolescents

According to one study, black male adolescents who lived with both of their parents reported using condoms more consistently in the past year, and were less likely to report fathering a pregnancy, as compared with adolescents who did not live with both of their parents. Adolescents who perceived that their mothers were more strict than did other adolescents, reported less frequent coitus, and with fewer women. Adolescents who perceived that their fathers were more strict than did other adolescents reported using condoms more consistently in the past year (Jemmott & Jemmott, 1992).

using contraceptives. According to the 1988 *National Survey of Adolescent Males,* of males who were 15 to 19 years old, 23 percent reported that they or their partners used no contraceptive method, or they used an ineffective method (withdrawal, douching, or rhythm) at last intercourse (Sonenstein, Pleck, & Ku, 1991).

These figures indicate large numbers of adolescents are not protected against unwanted pregnancy. As a result, one out of every ten women age 15 to 19 becomes pregnant each year in the United States (Trussell, 1988), and four out of five of these young women are unmarried. Among teenage men and women who use contraceptives, the most popular method is the pill, followed by the condom (Beck & Davies, 1987; Segest et al., 1990). Withdrawal and rhythm, both relatively ineffective methods, are the next most commonly used methods. Only small percentages of adolescents use the diaphragm, sponge, IUD, or foam (U.S. Bureau of the Census, 1995).

POTENTIAL PROBLEMS

Teenage Pregnancy and Parenthood

The net increase in premarital sexual intercourse accompanied by a lack of efficient use of contraceptives has resulted in an increase in the incidence of out-of-wedlock pregnancies, now estimated at one million each year among women less than 20 years of age (Jemmott & Jemmott, 1990; Paikoff, 1990). Of this number, 104,000 are miscarriages or stillbirths, 407,000 (41 percent) are induced abortions, and the remaining 489,000 babies are born alive. About 167,000 expectant mothers marry hastily before their babies are born, leaving 322,000 babies born out of wedlock in 1988 (Trussell, 1988).

Over 90 percent of unwed mothers decide to keep their babies (Alan Guttmacher Institute, 1981). Some let their parents or other relatives adopt their babies, but the remainder want to raise their children themselves, assisted by whatever family or other help they can get (Culp, Culp, Osofsky, & Osofsky, 1991; Hanson, 1990). They have many motives for keeping their babies. One is to have someone to love. One mother said: "I wanted to get pregnant because I always wanted a baby so that I could have someone to care for and to care for me." Other motives are to find identity, a feeling of importance, or to try to be an adult by having a child.

Unmarried motherhood among young teenage girls is a tragedy in most instances (Christmon, 1990; Moore & Stief, 1991). The single mother who decides to keep her baby may become trapped in a self-destructive cycle consisting of dependence on

LIVING ISSUES

Is Sex Becoming Depersonalized?

The question arises regarding the meaning attached to sexual relationships experienced by adolescents: Do adolescents have premarital sexual intercourse as an expression of emotional intimacy and loving feelings accompanied by commitment (Shaughnessy & Shakesby, 1992)?

Past studies have shown that the preferred sexual standard for youth has been permissiveness with affection. However, there are a significant number of adolescents today who engage in coitus without affection or commitment (Roche & Ramsbey, 1993; Wilson & Medora, 1990). Figure 18.3 shows the results of a survey among 237 (male and female) undergraduate students enrolled in 1986 at Illinois State University (Sprecher, McKinney, Walsh, & Anderson, 1988). The students ranged in age from 18 to 47, with a mean age of 20. All four undergraduate classes were represented. About 90 percent of the respondents were white, 8 percent black, and 2 percent other. About 49 percent were Catholic, 22 percent Protestant, 3 percent Jewish, and the remainder either another religion or no religion.

As indicated, 45 percent agreed that heavy petting was acceptable on a first date, 28 percent agreed that sexual intercourse was acceptable on a first date, and 22 percent found oral-genital sex to be acceptable on a first date. For those engaged in casual dating, 61 percent approved of heavy petting, 41 percent approved of intercourse, and 37 percent approved of oral-genital sex. The largest increase in acceptability for various types of sexual behavior occurred between the casual and serious dating stages. Surprisingly, there were no significant differences according to gender, although there were differences according to age. The 18-year-olds were less sexually permissive than those 21 years of age.

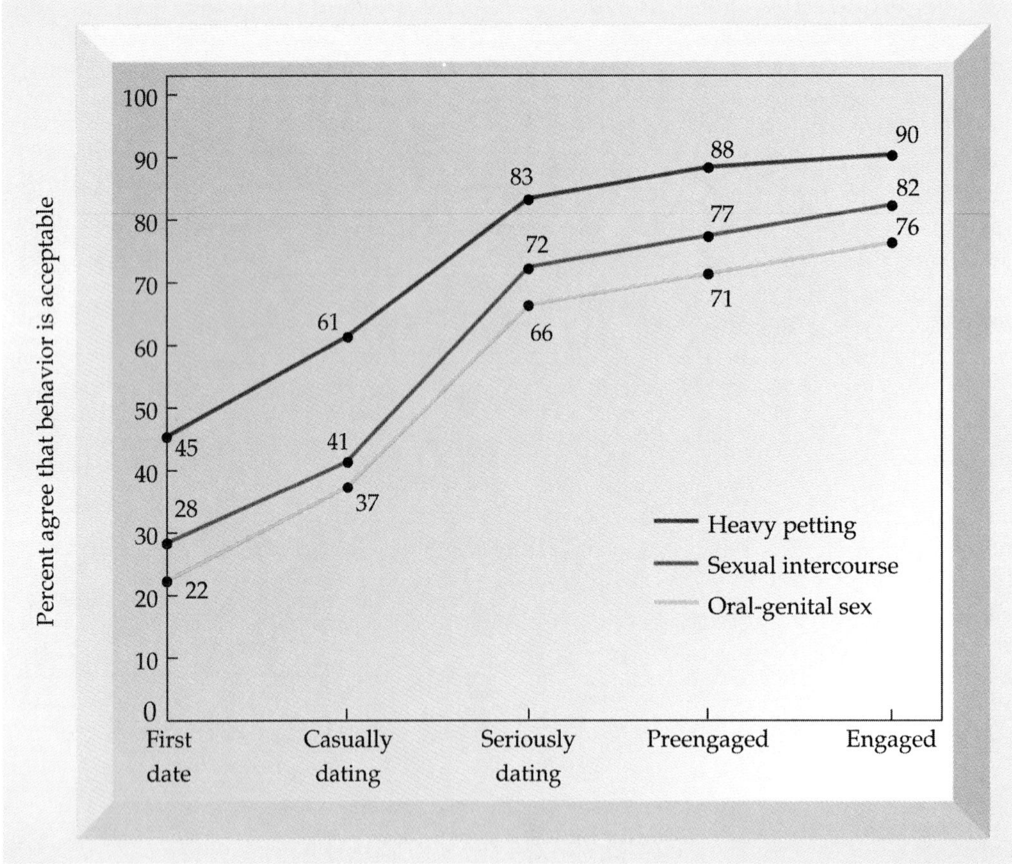

FIGURE 18.3 Acceptance of sexual activity by relationship stage.

From "A Revision of the Reiss Premarital Sexual Permissiveness Scale" by S. Sprecher, K. McKinney, R. Walsh, and C. Anderson, August 1988, *Journal of Marriage and the Family, 50,* 821–828. Copyright 1988 by the National Council on Family Relations, 3989 Central Avenue NE, Suite 550, Minneapolis, MN 55421. Reprinted by permission.

Prenatal education classes are vitally important in preparing pregnant teens for motherhood.

others for support, failure to establish a stable family life, repeated pregnancies, and failure to continue her education (Blinn, 1990; Ohannessian & Crockett, 1993). Marriage is not the answer because only 20 percent of those who marry are still together after five years. Only a minority complete their high school education and are able to get a good job to support themselves and their family, so most are likely to require welfare assistance for years.

LIVING ISSUES

Convincing Teens to Use Condoms

Convincing adolescents to use condoms to lower their risk of contracting HIV and other sexually transmitted diseases has become a major goal for most family planning practitioners. Planned Parenthood of Maryland (PPM) has developed a peer-support program that goes beyond teaching teenagers the basic hows and whys of condom use. It gets them thinking about how they make decisions and what the consequences of those decisions can be. It helps them to understand their own values and the importance of understanding others, and provides them with a supportive atmosphere in which they can talk and ask questions. The project—teen STARS: *Students Taking Responsibility About Sexuality*—is now in its third year (Rind, 1992a).

AIDS and Other Sexually Transmitted Diseases

Adolescents who are sexually active may be exposed to sexually transmitted diseases (STDs) (Holmbeck, Waters, & Brookmen, 1990; Moore & Rosenthal, 1990). *Chlamydial infections* are the most common (Judson, 1985). The incidence of *gonorrhea* exceeds that of chicken pox, measles, mumps, and rubella combined (Silber, 1986). About 1 in 4 cases of gonorrhea involves an adolescent. *Genital herpes* is found in 1 out of every 35 adolescents. *Syphilis* and other STDs are also found among adolescents.

FOCUS

Sexual Abuse and Adolescent Pregnancy

Two-thirds of a sample of 535 young women from the state of Washington who became pregnant as adolescents had been sexually abused. Fifty-five percent had been molested, 42 percent had been victims of attempted rape, and 44 percent had been raped. Sexually victimized teenagers began intercourse a year earlier than the norm, were more likely to abuse drugs and alcohol, and were less likely to practice contraception. Abused adolescents were also more likely to have been hit, slapped, or beaten by a partner, and to have exchanged sex for money, drugs, or a place to stay (Boyer & Fine, 1992).

FOCUS

School Birth Control Clinics

Faced with a desperate situation, some high school administrators offer contraceptive education services in birth control clinics right on the school premises. This idea is shocking to many people. Opponents insist that providing such services condones teenage sex, but advocates say that such programs in high schools are responses to emergency situations. A clinic in DeSable High School in Chicago was established after more than one-third of the 1,000 female students in the school became pregnant each year (Plummer, 1985). A 50 percent dropout rate from school resulted from the high rate of pregnancies. One of the most important services of the clinic was to keep pregnant girls in school to continue their education. Similar programs have been established in other cities across the country. This approach is pragmatic. Its purpose is to protect adolescents against unwanted pregnancy and from sexually transmitted diseases, without necessarily reducing sexual activity.

One study of schoolwide birth rates in St. Paul, Minnesota, both before and after the opening of school-based health clinics, indicated that birth rates were not significantly lower in the years immediately following the opening of the clinic than in the preceding years (Kirby et al., 1993). These results indicate there is no easy way to change adolescent sexual behavior.

Another study analyzed the results of programs of six school-based clinics from around the country. The clinics were in Gary, Indiana; San Francisco, California; Muskeegan, Michigan; Jackson, Mississippi; Quincy, Florida; and Dallas, Texas (Kirby, Waszak, & Ziegler, 1991). Survey data collected both before the clinics opened and two years later indicated that the clinics neither hastened the onset of sexual activity nor increased its frequency. The clinics had varying effects on contraceptive use. The data suggests that the clinics probably prevented small numbers of pregnancies at some schools, but none of the clinics had a statistically significant effect on school-wide pregnancy rates. Condom use did rise sharply at one clinic school that had a strong AIDS education program and was located in a community where AIDS was an important issue.

Those 20 to 24 years old have the highest incidence of STDs, followed by 15- to 19-year-olds (Carroll & Miller, 1982).

Because adolescents are sexually active, there is the possibility that the AIDS epidemic will severely affect this specific age group ("Kids and Contraceptives," 1987). Many adolescents are unrealistic (Roscoe & Kruger, 1990; Slonin-Nevo, Ozaga, & Auslander, 1991). They can't imagine that it will happen to them, so they take unnecessary chances (Andre & Bormann, 1991; Peterson & Murphy, 1990). In one study, one-fifth of an adult female sample and about one-third of an adult male sample reported having had homosexual experience during adolescence (Petersen et al., 1983). Those adolescents who are most heterosexually active, who use alcohol and drugs during sexual activity, who are intravenous drug users, or who engage in homosexual contacts comprise a high-risk group for contracting AIDS (Jemmott & Jemmott, 1993). They can easily become infected and transmit the disease to others, if they do not take necessary precautions. There is a widespread need for education to prevent the spread of AIDS (Hobart, 1992; Maticka-Tyndale, 1991.)

Because the incubation period for AIDS may be from a few years to up to ten years (Wallis, 1987), adolescents can be exposed to the virus and carry it for years without knowing it if blood tests have not been done. During this period they can transmit the disease to others. Because of the long incubation period, few cases of active AIDS are reported during adolescence itself.

Unwanted Sexual Activity

Fifteen percent of a sample of sixth- to twelfth-graders in Los Angeles reported that they had had an unwanted sexual experience, which may or may not have ended in intercourse. Eighteen percent of the females and twelve percent of the males reported unwanted sexual experience. High school students were more likely to report an unwanted sexual experience (17 percent) than were middle school students (11 percent). Of the ethnic groups, Asians were the least likely to report such an experience (7 percent), while Hispanics and non-Hispanic whites were equally likely to do so (16 percent), and blacks were most likely to do so (19 percent) (Turner, 1991).

One study of 507 university men and 486 university women revealed that 97.5 percent of the men and 93.5 percent of the women had experienced unwanted sexual activity (Muehlenhard & Cook, 1988). More men than women experienced unwanted intercourse. More women than men were likely to have engaged in unwanted kissing. The ten most important reasons given for engaging in unwanted sexual activity were verbal coercion, physical coercion, threat to terminate the relationship, sex-role concern (afraid of appearing unmasculine or unfeminine), peer pressure, reluctance (felt obligated, under pressure), intoxication, inexperience (desire to build experience), altruism (desire to please partner), and enticement by partners. Reported incidents of physical coercion were generally of a nonviolent nature.

Another survey of 275 undergraduate single women at Arizona State University revealed that over 50 percent of the participants reported being pressured into oral contact with their partners' genitals, genital and breast manipulation, and kissing (Christopher, 1988). Both the use of physical force and the verbal threat of force were uncommon. However, persistent attempts and verbal pressure were frequent.

ADOLESCENT MARRIAGE

Frequency

Figure 18.4 gives a detailed picture of U.S. statistics on marriage ages between 1890 and 1992. The median age at first marriage stopped declining for males in 1959 and for females in 1956, and has been increasing slowly since. The median age at first marriage in 1993 was 23.9 for females and 26.5 for males (Witwer, 1993). It appears that the steady drop in median age at marriage that was especially noticeable in the 1940s has been arrested. However, there are still numbers of youth, especially females, who are marrying young. Census figures for 1994 shows that 5 percent of females and 1.5 percent of males age 15 to 19 are (or have been) married (U.S. Bureau of the Census, 1995).

Success Rates

To evaluate whether adolescent marriage is desirable or undesirable, one must ask how successful these marriages are. There is no cause for concern if these marriages are strong, happy, and satisfying; but if they are weak, unhappy, and frustrating, causing much personal suffering and numerous social problems, there is ample cause for concern.

Using divorce statistics as the measure of success, adolescent marriages do not work out well (Bishop & Lynn, 1983; Booth & Edwards, 1985). Numerous studies indicate that the younger people are when married, the greater the chance of unhappy marriage and of divorce (Teti, Lamb, & Elster, 1987). The older the couple is at first marriage, the more likely that the marriage will succeed. But this direct correlation between age at first marriage and marital success diminishes for men at about age 27, when the decline in divorce rates with ad-

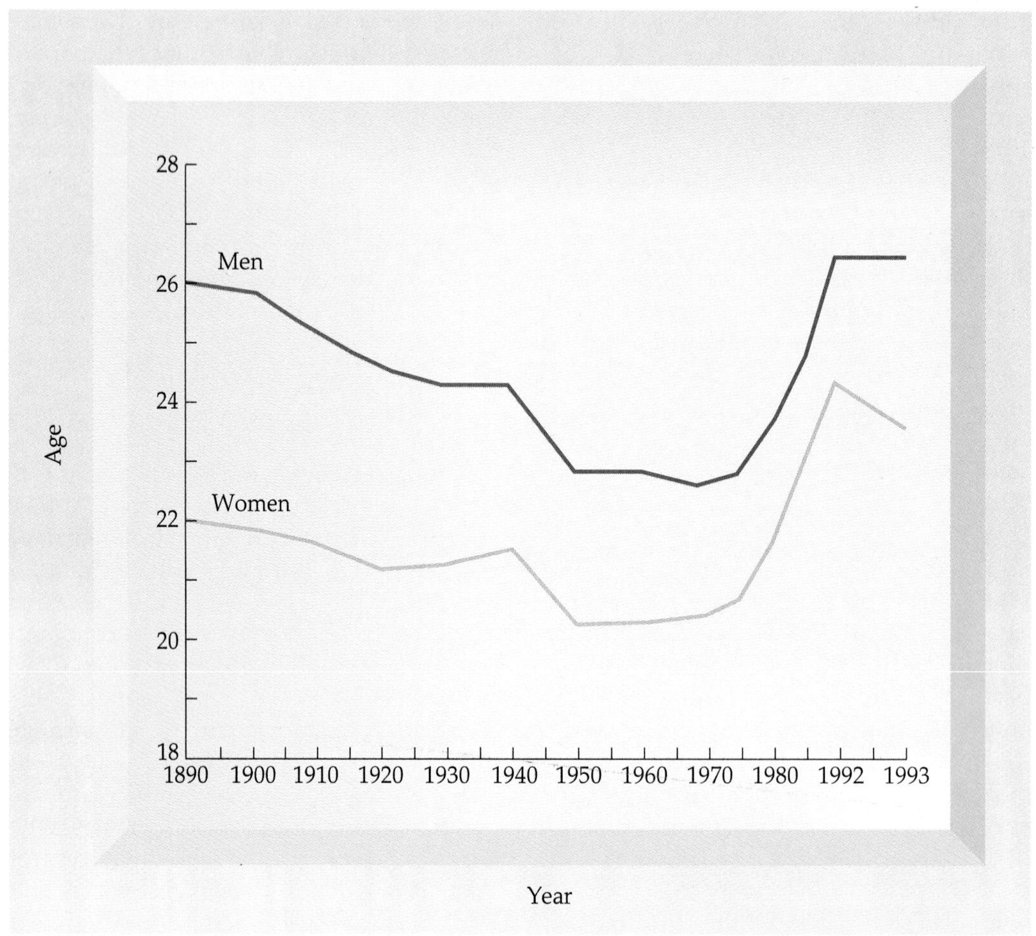

FIGURE 18.4 Median age at first marriage, by sex: 1890–1993.

Data from *Vital Statistics of the United States,* U.S. Department of Health and Human Services, annual, 1890–1993, Washington, DC: U.S. Government Printing Office; and *Statistical Abstract of the United States,* 1994 by U.S. Bureau of the Census, 1994, Washington, DC: U.S. Government Printing Office.

vancing age slows considerably. For women, the divorce rate declines with each year they wait to marry until a gradual leveling off occurs at about age 25. Therefore, strictly from the standpoint of marital stability, men who wait to marry until at least age 27 and women who wait until about age 25 are old enough to maximize their chances of success (Booth & Edwards, 1985).

Motivations

The most influential motivations for adolescents to marry young are

Overly romantic, glamorous views of marriage
Social pressure
Early dating, acceleration of adult sophistication
Sexual stimulation and unwed pregnancy
Escape; attempt to resolve personal or social problems.

The Problem of Immaturity

Many of the adjustments young couples must make become more difficult because of the immaturity of the couple. The less mature are less likely to make a wise choice of mate. The less mature are less likely to evidence the ultimate direction of their personality growth. They change as they get older and so have nothing in common with their partners after awhile. The less mature are less likely to be able to deal with the complex adjustments and problems of marriage. They are immature and insecure, oversensitive, unstable, and rebellious against authority—characteristics that make it harder for them to get along with their

Married teenagers need a variety of support services to help them succeed in their marriages.

mate and to solve problems that arise. Booth and Edwards (1985) found that the principal sources of marital dissatisfaction among couples who married young were lack of faithfulness, presence of jealousy, lack of understanding, disagreement, and lack of communication. Attempts by one partner to dominate or a refusal to talk made communication difficult.

Most youths have not become responsible enough for marriage. One of the major problems of early marriage is financial worry. The primary difficulties are inadequate income and the fact that income has not reached the level expected. Little education, inexperience, and youth do not bring high wages (Grindstaff, 1988). Some couples marry without any income. In many cases, education is interrupted or terminated, so the young person never achieves as much as the person who is able to continue an education.

Another real problem in early marriage is that it often results in *early parenthood.* A majority of teenage brides are pregnant at the time of marriage. In fact, the earlier the age at marriage, the greater is the percentage of brides who are premaritally pregnant, and the sooner they start having children (B. C. Miller & Heaton, 1991). Yet marriage because of pregnancy has a poor prognosis of success (Kahn & London, 1991).

FOCUS

TV, Sex, and Marriage

Sexual content on television has risen steadily, and is now a stable part of many television programs. Sexual activity is most likely to take place between unmarried partners with numerous adulterous liaisons. There is also an obsession with sexual relationships in both the prime-time and daytime serials, with the prime-time serials likely to be steamier and their characters more sexually active. Yet both genres of serial drama are deeply sentimental about marriage. The greatest esteem is awarded to monogamous individuals. Television images thus present an ambivalent picture of marriage and intimate, interpersonal relationships. Numerous programs, especially sitcoms, present happily married husbands and wives in a positive view of marriage. Serial dramas, on the other hand, present a less positive view of marriage and monogamy. They often revolve around characters who may be divorced, who do not express positive notions about marriage, or who may partake in sexual activity outside of marriage. For large segments of the population, television may be the single most important influence in forming concepts of marriage and interpersonal relationships (Signorielli, 1991).

Development of Moral Judgment

An important part of social development is developing the ability to make moral judgments or decisions. The process by which children and youths develop moral judgment is extremely interesting. Two major theories, those of Lawrence Kohlberg and Carol Gilligan, are discussed in this section. Both theories emphasize that the development of moral judgment is a gradual cognitive process, stimulated by increasing, changing social relationships of children as they get older. For a new theory of morality for everyday life, see the discussion by Shelton and McAdams (1990).

LAWRENCE KOHLBERG

Lawrence Kohlberg has made a lasting contribution to the study of the development of moral judgment in children and youth (Kohlberg, 1963, 1966b, 1969, 1970; Kohlberg & Gilligan, 1971; Kohlberg & Kramer, 1969; Kohlberg & Turiel, 1972).

Initially, Kohlberg (1963) studied seventy-two boys aged 10, 13, and 16. Boys in the different age groups were all similar in IQ with half of them from upper middle classes. Ten moral dilemmas were presented to each subject. Each dilemma presented a choice of whether to obey authority figures even though the action violated legal-social rules, or to do what was best for the welfare of others and meet human needs. The choices were taped and the subjects were then questioned about the reasons for their choices. Kohlberg's technique and material were Piagetian in form. In this study, Kohlberg was concerned not with behavior, but with moral judgment and the process of thought by which the individual made a judgment. There were no wrong or right answers expected; the individual was scored according to modes of reasoning, regardless of the direction of the given response.

Kohlberg (1970) identified three major levels of development of moral judgment, each level with two types of motivation. The levels and subtypes are listed in Table 18.3. Kohlberg found that *Level I* of premoral thinking declined sharply from the younger to the older age groups. *Level II* thinking increased until age 13, then stabilized. *Level III* thinking also increased markedly between 10 and 13 years of age, with some additional increase between ages 13 and 16.

Kohlberg cautioned that each type should not be equated with only one age. Individuals of different ages are at different levels of development in their moral thinking: Some are advanced, others are re-

TABLE 18.3
KOHLBERG'S LEVELS OF DEVELOPMENT OF MORAL THOUGHT

Level I. *Premoral level*
- Type 1. *Punishment and obedience orientation*
- (Motivation: to avoid punishment by others)
- Type 2: Naive instrumental hedonism
- (Motivation: to gain rewards from others)

Level II. *Morality of conventional role conformity*
- Type 3. Good-person morality of maintaining good relations with and approval of others
- (Motivation: to avoid disapproval of others)
- Type 4. Authority-maintaining morality
- (Motivation: to maintain law and order and because of concern for the community)

Level III. *Morality of democratically accepted laws*
- Type 5. Morality of democratically accepted laws
- (Motivation: to gain the respect of an individual community)
- Type 6. Morality of individual principles of conduct
- (Motivation: to avoid self-condemnation for lapses)

From Kohlberg, L. (1963). The development of children's orientations toward a moral order. I: Sequence in the development of thought. *Vita humana, 6,* 11–33. Used by permission of S. Karger AG, Basel, Switzerland.

tarded. No person fits neatly into any one of the six types. Kohlberg (1970) indicated that moral thought develops gradually as the individual passes through a sequence of increasingly sophisticated moral stages.

At Level I, the **premoral level,** children respond to the definitions of good and bad provided by parental authority figures. Decisions are made on the basis of self-interest; children interpret acts as good or bad in terms of physical consequences. There are two types under Level I. *Type 1* obeys rules to avoid punishment. *Type 2* conforms to obtain rewards or have favors returned.

Level II, the level of **morality of conventional role conformity,** comprises *type 3* and *type 4* and is less egocentric and more sociocentric in orientation, and is based on a desire to justify, support, and maintain the existing social structure (Muuss, 1988a). *Type 3* under this level is the good boy–nice girl orientation in which the child conforms to avoid disapproval and dislike by others; *type 4* conforms because of a desire to maintain law and order or because of concern for the larger community.

Level III, the level of **morality of self-accepted moral principles,** is made up of individuals who accept democratically recognized principles of universal truths, not because they have to but because they believe in the principles or truths. *Type 5* under this level conforms to maintain mutual respect with another person or group. At this stage, the individual defines moral thinking in terms of general principles such as mutual obligations, contractual agreement, equality, human dignity, and individual rights. Finally, *type 6* conforms to avoid self-condemnation. The motivation is to uphold universal principles of justice that are valid beyond existing laws, peer mores, or social conditions.

Kohlberg's stage concept implies sequence: Each child must go through successive levels of moral judgment. Kohlberg also said that the sequence of development of his stages is universal, even under varying cultural conditions. Developing moral judgment is not merely a matter of learning the rules of a particular culture; it reflects a universal process of development. Kohlberg (1966b) tested and validated his theory with boys aged 10, 13, and 16 in a Taiwanese city, in a Malaysian (Atayal) aboriginal tribal village, and in a Turkish village, as well as in the United States, Canada, and Great Britain.

Kohlberg (1966b) found that the sequence of development was similar in all cultures, but that the last two stages of moral thought did not develop clearly in tribal and preliterate communities. Data from the U.S. showed that the great majority of American adults never reached Level III either, even by age 24. Research has indicated that adolescents can be trained in the process of moral reasoning and in making moral judgments (Santilli & Hudson, 1992).

Kohlberg (1966b) tested his hypothesis with boys and girls of different classes and religions, and with popular and socially isolated children. The same general stages of development were found among all groups, with middle-class children of all ages in advance of the working-class children. Middle-class children moved faster and farther in development compared to working-class children. Working-class children had less understanding of the broader social order and had less participation in it; thus, their development of moral judgment was retarded. This explanation is further substantiated by the fact that children with extensive social participation advance considerably more quickly through the successive stages of development.

In general, researchers have found an increase in the sophistication of moral reasoning through adolescence due in part to an increase in perspective taking, intelligence, and the ability to think abstractly (Carlo, Eisenberg, & Knight, 1992). However, which moral dilemmas adolescents become most concerned about depends partially on their own individual experiences. Research indicates that early adolescents who are the products of divorce, for example, may not advance as soon as other early adolescents from concern about the family to concern about the peer and social culture (Breen & Crosbie-Burnett, 1993).

Moral judgement also correlates highly with IQ indicating that is partly cognitive in nature. Children who participate in social groups lose some of their cognitive naivete and adopt a more sophisticated view of authority and social relationships (Mason & Gibbs, 1993). They acquire a greater capacity for moral thinking, but whether such knowledge leads to better behavior depends on emotional and social in-

Premoral level—the first level of development of moral judgment, based on rewards and punishments, according to Kohlberg

Morality of conventional role conformity—the second level of development of moral thought, based on a desire to conform to social convention, according to Kohlberg

Morality of self-accepted moral principles—the third level of development of moral thought, based on adherence to universal principles, according to Kohlberg

FOCUS

A Theory of Reasoned Action

According to Ajzen and Fishbein (1990), behavior is determined by how one intends to behave. *There are two major factors that determine behavioral intentions: personal attitudes and social norms.* It is suggested that the first component—the person's attitude towards a specific behavior—depends on behavioral beliefs about the perceived consequences of performing the behavior and the person's evaluation of these consequences. The second component—social norms—consists of a person's perceptions of what specific individuals or groups think he or she should do and the motivation to comply with these individuals or norms. The relative importance of the attitudinal and normative components in determining intention is expected to vary according to the behavior, the situation, and the individual differences of the actor (Vallerand et al., 1992).

fluences in their backgrounds and relationships. The point is, the ability to make moral judgments does not always result in more moral behavior.

CAROL GILLIGAN

Kohlberg conducted his research on moral development on male subjects. His scoring method was developed from male responses, with the average adolescent female attaining a rating corresponding to type 3 (the good boy–nice girl orientation). The average adolescent male was rated as type 4 (the law-and-order orientation).

Carol Gilligan (1977), an associate of Kohlberg, found that females approach moral issues from a different perspective (Linn, 1991). Women emphasize sensitivity to others' feelings and rights, and show concern and care for others (Skoe & Gooden, 1993). Women emphasize care of human beings rather than obedience to abstract principles. Men emphasize justice—preserving principles, rules, and rights. Thus, women and men speak with two different voices (Gilligan, 1982). In summarizing six studies, including four longitudinal ones, Gilligan (1984) revealed that women rely on an interpersonal network of care orientation, and men rely more heavily on a justice orientation (Muuss, 1988a).

As a result of the difference in the way women and men think, Gilligan proposed a female alternative to Kohlberg's stages of

Moral development includes developing sensitivity to the needs of others and a willingness to care for them.

FOCUS

Justice Versus Interpersonal Responsibilities

J. G. Miller and Bersoff (1992) give an example to show that *there is sometimes conflict between doing what is just and what it is necessary to fulfill interpersonal responsibilities.* They give the following example:

> Ben was in Los Angeles on business. He planned to travel to San Francisco in order to attend the wedding of his best friend. He needed to catch the very next train if he was going to be on time for the ceremony, as he had to deliver the wedding rings.
>
> However, Ben's wallet was stolen in the train station. He lost all of his money as well as his ticket to San Francisco, and he was not able to borrow any money to make the trip.
>
> While Ben was sitting on a bench trying too decide what to do, a well-dressed man sitting next to him walked away for a minute. Looking over at where the man had been sitting, Ben noticed that the man had left his coat unattended, and sticking out of the man's pocket was a train ticket to San Francisco. Ben knew that he could take the ticket and use it to travel to San Francisco on the next train. He also saw that the man had more than enough money in his coat pocket to buy another train ticket.
>
> Which action should Ben undertake?
>
> 1. Ben should not take the ticket from the man's coat pocket—even though that would mean not getting to San Francisco on time to deliver the wedding rings to his best friend.
> 2. Ben should go to San Francisco to deliver the wedding rings to his best friend, even though it would mean taking the train ticket from the other man's coat pocket.

In this example, the first alternative was scored as a *justice choice,* and the second alternative was scored as an *interpersonal choice* (Smetana, Killen, & Turiel, 1991).

Which alternative would you select?

moral reasoning. Table 18.4 compares Kohlberg and Gilligan.

At *Level I,* women are concerned with survival and self-interest. Gradually, they become aware of the differences between what they want (selfishness) and what they ought to do (responsibility). This leads to *Level II,* in which the need to please others takes precedence over self-interest. Women begin sacrificing their own preferences and become responsible for caring for others. They begin to wonder whether they can remain true to themselves while fulfilling the needs of others. Still, they place others' needs before their own. At *Level III,* which many never attain, women develop a universal perspective, in which they no longer see themselves as powerless and submissive, but as active in decision making. They

Seventy-five percent of today's high school seniors hold a part-time job during the school year.

TABLE 18.4
KOHLBERG'S VERSUS GILLIGAN'S UNDERSTANDING OF MORAL DEVELOPMENT

Kohlberg's Levels and Stages	*Kohlberg's Definition*	*Gilligan's Levels*
Level I. Preconventional morality		*Level I. Preconventional morality*
Stage 1: Punishment orientation	Obey rules to avoid punishment	Concern for the self and survival
Stage 2: Naive reward orientation	Obey rules to get rewards, share in order to get returns	
Level II. Conventional morality		*Level II. Conventional morality*
Stage 3: Good-boy/good-girl orientation	Conform to rules that are defined by others' approval/disapproval	Concern for being responsible, caring for others
Stage 4: Authority orientation	Rigid conformity to society's rules, law-and-order mentality, avoid censure for rule-breaking	
Level III. Postconventional morality		*Level III. Postconventional morality*
Stage 5. Social-contract orientation	More flexible understanding that we obey rules because they are necessary for social order, but the rules could be changed if there were better alternatives	Concern for self and others as interdependent
Stage 6. Morality of individual principles and conscience	Behavior conforms to internal principles (justice, equality) to avoid self-condemnation, and sometimes may violate society's rules conscience	

From *Half the Human Experience* by J. S. Hyde, 12985, Lexington, MA: D. C. Heath. Reprinted with permission.

become concerned about the consequences for all, including themselves, in making decisions.

Obviously, Gilligan's and Kohlberg's stages are parallel. Gilligan does not contend that her theory should replace Kohlberg's. She insists only that her theory is more applicable to the moral reasoning of females and that the highest form of moral reasoning can interpret, use, and combine the female emphasis on responsibility and care with the male emphasis on rights and justice (Muuss, 1988a).

Work

An important part of socialization is to learn to work and hold responsible positions. Of today's high school seniors, 75 percent hold a part-time job during the school year (Bachman, Johnston, & O'Malley, 1987; Johnston, O'Malley, & Bachman, 1987). The proportion of high school students who work has been rising steadily. Generally speaking, teachers, social scientists, and parents have encouraged students to work. The conventional wisdom seems to argue: "Working is good for them" (Otto, 1988).

Among high school seniors, one of four females works at least twenty hours a week, and among males, one of three does the same (Bachman, Johnston, & O'Malley, 1987). These students are working half time while going to school full time.

Some authorities, however, are beginning to say that some adolescents are devoting too much time to jobs and not enough to school. Greenberger and Steinberg (1981) emphasize that when high school students work more than fifteen to twenty hours a week, the disadvantages include diminished involvement with peers, family, and school and increased use of marijuana, alcohol, cigarettes, and other drugs (Steinberg et al., 1982).

Some adolescents today grow up so used to working after school and on weekends that they never have time for fun with peers, healthy recreation, or extracurricular activities. They become adult workaholics who have never learned how to play or relax. Such habits can be detrimental to personal health and marital and family relationships.

Summary

1. Adolescents want parents who will treat them as adults, have faith in them, love and like them the way they are, whom they can communicate with, who are interested in them, who will guide them, who are fun and have a sense of humor, and whom they can be proud of.
2. Research indicates that fathers are more involved with raising sons than daughters and that noncustodial fathers are less close to their children than custodial fathers are.
3. Adolescent–parent conflict usually revolves around six areas: values and morals, family relationships, school, responsibilities, social activities, and work outside the home.
4. A number of variables affect conflict: home environment, discipline, socioeconomic status, family size, and age and sex of the adolescent.
5. Parental functions are fourfold: meeting basic needs of children, protection, guidance, and advocacy.
6. The parents' ability to carry out their functions depends upon personal characteristics of the parents, characteristics of the adolescent, and the quality of the marital relationship.
7. Factors outside the family such as the neighborhood, the parents' work situation, and informal networks also influence the parents' ability to function. Also, broader social values, social programs, social class, and other cultural influences define the context in which parenting takes place.
8. Relationships with brothers and sisters are vitally important because they have a considerable influence on the development of the adolescent. Older siblings provide companionship; serve as surrogate parents, acting as caretakers, teachers, playmates, and confidants; and they can serve as role models.
9. The need for close friendships becomes crucial during adolescence. Young adolescents choose a best friend, a chum or two, usually of the same sex in the beginning. Early adolescent friendships are emotional, intense, sometimes characterized by conflict.
10. One of the most important social goals of mid-adolescence is to achieve heterosociality in which the individual's pleasure and friendships are found with those of both sexes.
11. Males continue to have difficulty establishing intimacy.
12. Adolescents become increasingly aware of their need to belong to a group and to find peer acceptance. Personality and social skills have been found to be very important in gaining social acceptance.
13. Some youths gain social acceptance by joining deviant groups.

14. Dating has many purposes: It provides amusement, enjoyment, friendship, affection; is a means of achieving social status and personal and social growth; provides sexual intimacy and emotional intimacy; and is a means of mate sorting and selection.
15. One study showed that persons ranked low in sexual activity were more desirable as marriage partners than those ranked moderate or high in sexual activity, but those ranked moderate or high in sexual activity were preferred as dating partners. Males were perceived as more desirable dating partners when they engaged in moderate sexual activity, whereas females were perceived as more desirable dates when they engaged in high sexual activity.
16. The most frequent dating problems reported in one study of college women were: unwanted pressure to engage in sex, where to go and what to do on dates, communication, sexual misunderstandings, and money. The most common dating problems reported in one study of college men were: communication, where to go and what to do on dates, shyness, money, and honesty/openness. Both men and women report problems in communication, due partly to imaging—presenting oneself in the best possible manner.
17. Parents sometimes object to their adolescent's selection of a dating partner because they don't like the person, they feel the person has a problem, the other person's family is different from the parents' family, or there is a significant age difference.
18. The onset of puberty is accompanied by an increasing interest in sex.
19. Masturbation is commonly practiced by both adolescent men and women and is a normal part of growing up.
20. Premarital sexual intercourse among white, teenage women has been increasing.
21. Results from the NSAM indicated the following percentages have heterosexual intercourse by the designated birthday: 5 percent by 13th, 11 percent by 14th, 21 percent by 15th, 58 percent by 17th, 79 percent by 19th.
22. Blacks report intercourse at younger ages than whites or Hispanics.
23. Blacks living with both parents use condoms more consistently and report less coitus and with fewer women than those living with one parent.
24. According to the NSFG, only 35 percent of 15- to 19-year-olds used any method of contraception at first intercourse, and only 32 percent reported they were currently using contraceptives. According to the NSAM, only 23 percent of males 15 to 19 years old used no method or an ineffective method of contraception. Convincing sexually active teens to use condoms is important in preventing AIDS.
25. The net result of the increase in premarital sexual intercourse accompanied by a lack of efficient use of contraceptives has been an increase in out-of-wedlock pregnancies, now estimated at over one million per year.
26. Two-thirds of a sample of young women from the state of Washington who became pregnant had been sexually abused.
27. Authorities are also concerned about the increase in sexually transmitted diseases among adolescents: especially chlamydia, gonorrhea, genital herpes, syphilis, and AIDS.
28. Faced with the rising tide of teenage pregnancies and the threat of AIDS, some schools offer birth control clinics on the school premises. The high rate of pregnancies is partly responsible for high dropout rates. One of the goals of the clinic programs is to keep pregnant girls in school.
29. One of the problems faced by both adolescent boys and girls is unwanted sexual activity.
30. There is some evidence that sex among many adolescents is becoming depersonalized, without affection or commitment.
31. The median age at first marriage has been increasing, but there are still large numbers of adolescents who marry. The prognosis for success in most adolescent marriages is poor. Many young marrieds express deep dissatisfaction with their marriage.
32. There are a number of reasons for adolescent marriage: sexual stimulation and pregnancy, early dating and acceleration of adult sophistication, social

pressure, overly romantic views of marriage, desire to escape problems, and affluence and prosperity.

33. Many of the problems of early marriage are due to the immaturity of the couple.
34. Sexual content on TV has risen steadily and often presents sex between unmarried partners or in adulterous liaisons. Ambivalent views of marriage are presented. For large segments of the population, TV is important in forming concepts related to marriage and interpersonal relationships.
35. Lawrence Kohlberg has made a lasting contribution to the study of the development of moral judgment of children and youth.
36. Kohlberg has identified three levels of moral development. Level I is the premoral level; Level II is a morality of conventional role conformity; Level III is a morality of self-accepted moral principles.
37. Although Kohlberg's findings show a similar sequence of development in all cultures, not all persons reach the higher levels of development. This is true in preliterate communities, and among youth from various socioeconomic classes, especially among the working classes of adolescents.
38. The development of moral judgment also correlates highly with IQ.
39. Following rules as the guide to morality is referred to as a *justice choice,* whereas taking into account human situations and needs is labeled an *interpersonal choice.*
40. Carol Gilligan emphasized that women approach moral issues from a different perspective than do men. Men rely more heavily on a justice orientation; women on an interpersonal network or care orientation.
41. Gilligan outlined three levels of development: Level I—self-interest, Level II—caring for the needs of others, and Level III—a universal perspective that takes into account consequences for all people.
42. The theory of reasoned action says that moral behavior is determined by two factors that influence behavioral intentions: personal attitudes and social norms.
43. Most adolescents dislike helping parents around the house but work at jobs outside the home. The proportion of high school students working has been rising steadily.
44. Among high school seniors, one of three males, and one of four females work at least twenty hours a week, leading some authorities to feel that many adolescents are devoting too much time to work and not enough to school.

Key Terms

Coitus *p. 487*
Imaging *p. 485*
Masturbation *p. 486*
Morality of conventional role conformity *p. 497*
Morality of self-accepted moral principles *p. 497*
Premoral level *p. 497*

Discussion Questions

1. When you were growing up how did you get along with your parents? Explain.
2. What did you like about your parents? What did you dislike?
3. When adolescents disobey their parents, what should the parents do?
4. How many brothers and sisters did you have? How did you get along with them?

5. How can an adolescent get over being shy in groups?
6. What qualities are most important in being popular and accepted by others?
7. At what age should adolescents be allowed to start dating?
8. What do you think of going steady in high school?
9. Should seventh-graders be allowed to go to school dances? Explain.
10. Should girls initiate dates? How do boys feel about girls asking them out?
11. Is it all right to date several persons at once?
12. Is it necessary for a girl to be sexually responsive to be popular with boys? Will boys ask a girl out if she is not willing to go all the way?
13. What should a 15-year-old girl do if her parents object to her going out with a boy who is 18?
14. Have sexual attitudes and behavior become more liberal since you were in high school? How or how not?
15. Why don't more sexually active adolescents use contraceptives?
16. What can be done to reduce the number of unwed pregnancies? AIDS?
17. Should adolescents marry because of premarital pregnancy? What are some alternatives? Which would you choose?
18. What sort of sex education did you receive from parents when you were growing up? Describe.
19. Should school teach sex education? Why or why not? Are there any sex subjects that high schools should not teach? Why?
20. What do you think about having birth control clinics in high schools?
21. Explain Kohlberg's three levels of moral development.
22. Do you agree or disagree with Gilligan's idea that the level of moral judgment of women ought to be evaluated differently from that of men?
23. How do you feel about adolescents working twenty or more hours per week when in high school?

Suggested Readings

Berndt, T. J., & Ladd, G. W. (1989). *Peer relationships in child development.* New York: Wiley. Nature of peer relations in childhood and adolescence.

Dekovic, M. (1992). *The role of parents in the development of a child's peer acceptance.* The Netherlands: Van Goreum. Factors that cause or contribute to peer acceptance or rejection. Contributions of parents.

Gibbs, J. C., Bassinger, K. S., & Fuller, D. (1992). *Moral maturity: Measuring the development of sociomoral reflection.* Hillsdale, NJ: Erlbaum. Discussion of the Sociomoral Reflection Measure–Short Form (SRM–SF).

Gilligan, C. (1983). *In a different voice: Psychological theory and women's development.* Cambridge, MA: Harvard University Press. The patterns of moral thought of women as compared to men.

Group for the Advancement of Psychiatry, Committee on Adolescence (1986). *Crises of adolescence: Teenage pregnancy, impact on adolescent development.* New York: Brunner/Mazel.

Greenberger, E., & Steinberg, L. (1986). *When teenagers work.* New York: Basic Books. Impact of working on the teenager.

Gullotta, T. P., Adams, G., & Montemayor, R. (Eds.). (1992). *Adolescent sexuality.* Newbury Park, CA: Sage. Overview.

Noller, P., & Callan, V. (1991). *The adolescent in the family.* New York: Routledge. Thorough coverage of key issues.

Sugar, M. (Ed.). (1984). *Adolescent parenthood.* New York: SP Medical and Scientific Books. Adolescent parenting and programs available.

Youniss, M., & Smollar, J. (1985). *Adolescent relations with mothers, fathers, and friends.* Chicago: University of Chicago Press. Parent–teen relationships.

Glossary

Accommodation according to Piaget, adjusting to new information by creating new structures when the old ones will not do

Acculturation the adjustment of minority groups to the culture of the dominant group

Acne pimples on the skin caused by overactive sebaceous glands

ACT Assessment Program (American College Testing program) the second most widely used college admissions test

Adaptation according to Piaget, the process by which individuals adjust their thinking to new conditions or situations

Adolescence the period of transition from childhood to young adulthood, from about 12 to 19 years of age

Adolescent and adult heterosociality a period of psychosocial development during which those ages 13 and over find pleasure, friendships, and companionship with those of both sexes

Adrenal glands ductless glands located just above the kidneys that secrete androgens and estrogens in both men and women in addition to their secretion of adrenalin

Alcohol abuse excessive use of alcohol so that functioning is impaired

Alcoholism *See* Chronic alcoholism

Alleles genes that govern alternate expressions of a particular characteristic

Amenorrhea absence of menstruation

Amniocentesis removal of cells from the amniotic fluid to test for abnormalities

Amniotic sac (bag of waters) sac containing the liquid in which the fetus is suspended during pregnancy

Anabolic steroids the masculinizing hormone testosterone taken by athletes to build muscle mass

Anal stage Freud's second psychosexual stage of development (2–3 years), in which the child's chief source of pleasure is from anal activity

Androgyny a mixing of male and female traits in one person

Animism ascribing lifelike qualities to inanimate objects

Anorexia nervosa an eating disorder characterized by an obsession with food and being thin

Anoxia oxygen deprivation to the brain, causing neurological damage or death

Apgar score method of evaluating the physical condition of the neonate, developed by Dr. Virginia Apgar

Artificial insemination injection of sperm cells into the vagina or uterus for the purpose of inducing pregnancy

Assimilation according to Piaget, the process of acquiring new information by using already existing structures in response to new stimuli

Associativity the understanding that operations can reach a goal in various ways

Attachment the feeling that binds a child to a parent or care giver

Attachment theory the description of the process by which infants develop close emotional dependence on one or more adult care givers

Attention-deficit disorder a child's hyperactivity, characterized by excessive activity, inattentiveness, and impulsivity

Autistic phase a period between birth and 2 months of age during which children are aware of their mother only as an agent to meet their basic needs

Autonomy vs. shame and doubt Erikson's second stage of psychosocial development (1–2 years), in which toddlers learn that they are capable of some independent actions, or they develop the fear that they are not capable

Autosociality a stage of psychosocial development during the first year or so of life, during which infants' interests, pleasures, and satisfactions are themselves, when they play alongside of others, not with them

Autosomes twenty-two pairs of chromosomes that are responsible for most aspects of the individual's development

Babbling one-syllable utterances containing vowels and consonants in combination

Bartholin's glands glands on either side of the vaginal opening that secrete fluid during sexual arousal

Behaviorism the school of psychology emphasizing that behavior is modified through conditioning

Binuclear family an original family divided into two by divorce

Blastocyst inner layer of the blastula that develops into the embryo

Blastula zygote after the cells have divided into 100–150 cells

Blended or reconstituted family a family formed by any widowed or divorced person remarrying another person who may or may not have children

Bonding the formation of a close relationship between a person and a child through early and frequent association

Brazelton Neonatal Behavior Assessment Scale method of evaluating the neurological condition and behavior of the neonate, developed by Dr. T. Berry Brazelton

Bulimia an eating disorder characterized by binging and purging

Canalization tendency for inherited characteristics to persist along a certain path regardless of environmental conditions

Case studies a research method involving in-depth, longitudinal investigations and records of individuals

Centration focusing attention on one aspect of a situation, or one detail, and being unable to take into account other details

Cephalocaudal principle physical growth, which occurs first in the head and proceeds, by stages, down the body to the feet

Cerebral cortex two large hemispheres of the forebrain, which control intellectual, motor, and sensory functions

Cesarean section removal of the fetus through a surgical incision of the abdominal and uterine walls

Child development all aspects of human growth from birth to adolescence; the study of this growth

Childhood heterosociality a period of psychosocial development between ages 2 and 7, during which children seek the companionship of others regardless of sex

Chorionic villi sampling (CVS) removal of a sample of chorionic villi from the membrane enclosing the fetus, to be analyzed for possible birth defects

Chromosomes rodlike structures in each cell, occurring in pairs, that carry the hereditary material

Chronic alcoholism chemical dependency on alcohol accompanied by compulsive and excessive drinking

Chronological age (CA) age in years

Chunking dividing material into meaningful parts to remember it

Circumcision surgical removal of the foreskin of the penis

Classical conditioning a form of learning through association, in which a previously neutral stimulus is paired with an unconditioned stimulus to stimulate a conditioned response that is similar to the unconditioned response

Classification arranging objects into categories or classes

Class inclusion relationships the inclusion of objects in different levels of hierarchy at the same time

Client-centered therapy Rogers' approach to humanistic therapy, in which the discussion focuses on the client's thoughts and feelings and the therapist creates an atmosphere of acceptance so that the client can gain insight and grow toward his or her full potential

Clitoris the small shaft containing erectile tissue located above the vaginal and urethral openings and that is highly responsive to sexual stimulation

Cognition the act of knowing

Cognitive development all the changes in the intellectual processes of thinking, learning, remembering, judging, problem solving, and communicating

Cohabiting family a family formed by two people of the opposite sex who live together, with or without children; who are committed to the relationship, without formal legal marriage, within the general definition in this book

Cohort a group of subjects born during the same time period

Cohort-sequential study the best sequential design for separating the effects of age and cohorts

Coitus sexual intercourse

Colostrum high-protein liquid secreted by the mother's breasts prior to her milk coming in; contains antibodies to protect the nursing infant from diseases

Combinativity ability to combine two or more classes into one larger, more comprehensive class

Communal family a group of people who live together and who qualify as a family according to the general definition in this book

Concrete operational stage Piaget's third stage of cognitive development (7–11 years), during which the child gains some mastery over classes, relations, and quantities

Conditional positive regard giving love, praise, and acceptance only if the individual conforms to parental or social standards

Conditioning a simple process of learning

Congenital deformity defect present at birth, which may be the result of hereditary factors, conditions during pregnancy, or damage occurring at the time of birth

Conservation the idea that an object stays the same quantity regardless of how the shape changes

Cooing the initial squeals, gurgles, or vowel-like sound utterances by young infants

Coparenting cooperation of two parents in rearing their children

Corpus luteum yellow body that grows from the ruptured ovarian follicle and becomes a mass of progesterone-secreting endocrine tissue

Correlation the extent to which two factors are associated or related to one another

Cowper's glands small twin glands in the male that secrete a fluid to neutralize the acid environment of the urethra

Cross-modal perception the ability to perceive objects with more than one sense

Cross-sectional study comparing one age group with others at one time of testing

Custody refers to legal custody (who has decision-making rights over the child) and physical custody (where the children live)

Crystallized intelligence knowledge and skills arising out of acculturation and education. Concept developed by Cattell

Deductive reasoning beginning with a hypothesis or premise and breaking it down to see if it is true

Defense mechanisms according to Freud, unconscious strategies used by the ego to protect itself from disturbance and to discharge tension

Deferred imitation imitating someone or something no longer present

Denial a Freudian defense mechanism in which the individual refuses to admit that something exists

Dependent variable in an experiment, a factor that is influenced by the independent or manipulated variable

Developmental pediatrics a new field of study that integrates medical knowledge, psychological understanding, health care, and parental guidance in relation to children

Developmental quotient (DQ) a score developed by Gesell to evaluate an infant's behavioral level in four categories: motor, language, adaptive, and personal-social

Developmental tasks the skills, knowledge, functions, and attitudes that individuals have to acquire at certain points in their lives in order to function effectively as mature persons

Dick-Read method a natural childbirth method emphasizing childbirth without fear, developed by Dr. Dick-Read of England

Differentiated or subjective perspective-taking stage the stage of awareness when the other is seen as different from the self, but the other person's perception of the self is still undifferentiated—stage 1 in Selman's theory

Discipline a process of learning by which socialization takes place, whose purpose is instruction in proper conduct

Displacement a Freudian defense mechanism in which an individual diverts aggressive, sexual, or disturbed feelings away from a primary object to something useful

Dizygotic (fraternal) twins two-egg, or fraternal, twins

DNA complex molecules in genes that form the basis for the genetic structure, deoxyribonucleic acid

Dominant gene gene that exerts its full characteristic regardless of its gene pair

Duos two-word utterances

Dyslexia a developmental language disorder in which the person reads from right to left, reverses letters and words, omits words entirely, or loses the place on a page

Dysphoria generalized unhappiness

Early childhood the preschool period of development from ages 3 to 5

Ectopic pregnancy attachment and growth of the embryo in any location other than inside the uterus

Educable mentally retarded those with mild retardation with IQs of 70 to 50

Ego according to Freud, the rational part of the mind, which uses the reality principle to satisfy the id

Egocentricism the inability to take the perspective of another, to imagine the other person's point of view

Egocentric undifferentiated stage the stage of awareness when the other person is seen egocentrically, undifferentiated from the self's own point of view—stage 0 in Selman's theory of development of social cognition

Electra complex according to Freud, the unconscious love and sexual desire of female children for their father, after they blame the mother for the fact that they have no penis

Embryo growing baby from the end of the second week to the end of the eighth week after conception

Embryonic period period from 2 weeks to 8 weeks after conception

Embryo transplant insemination of a volunteer female with the sperm of an infertile woman's partner, with the resulting zygote being transferred, about 5 days later, from the volunteer into the uterus of the mother-to-be, who carries the child during pregnancy

Emotion a state of consciousness, or a feeling, felt as an integrated reaction of the total organism, accompanied by physiological arousal, and resulting in behavioral responses

Emotional development the development of attachment, trust, love, feelings, temperament, concept of self, autonomy, and emotional disturbances

Endocrine glands ductless glands that secrete hormones

Epididymis a system of ducts, running from the testes to the vas deferens, in which sperm ripen, mature, and are stored

Epinephrine hormone secreted by the adrenal glands that produces physiological arousal

Episiotomy a surgical incision of the perineum to allow room for passage of the baby from the birth canal without tearing the mother's tissue

Equilibriation a Piagetian concept meaning a balance between schemas and accommodation, a state in which children feel comfortable because what they find in their environment is compatible with what they have been taught to believe

Equity assignment of punishments in accordance with transgressors' ability to take responsibility for a crime

Estrogen a group of feminizing hormones produced by the ovaries and to some extent by the adrenal glands in both males and females

Ethology the view that behavior is a product of evolution and biology

Exosystem social settings in which the child usually is not an active participant, but that influence the child indirectly through their effects on the microsystem

Experimental methods methods of gathering scientific data, in which procedures are closely controlled and the experimenter manipulates variables to determine how one affects the other

Expiatory punishment punishment that results from an externally imposed regulation; associated with morality of constraint

Extended family a family consisting of one person, a possible mate, their children, and other relatives who live with them in the household; more broadly, can include relatives living in close proximity or who are in regular or frequent contact with a household's members

Fallopian tubes tubes that transport the ova from the ovaries to the uterus

Family any group of persons united by the ties of marriage, blood, adoption, or any sexually expressive relationship, in which (1) people are committed to one another in an intimate, interpersonal relationship, (2) the members see their identity as importantly attached to the group, and (3) the group has an identity of its own

Father hunger an emotional disturbance, most common in boys from 18 to 36 months of age, brought about by the abrupt loss of a father, characterized by sleep disturbances

Fertilization or conception union of sperm and ovum

Fetal period period of prenatal development from the beginning of the third month through the remainder of the pregnancy

Fetoscope scope passed through a narrow tube inserted into the uterus to observe the fetus and placenta directly

Fetus growing baby from the beginning of the third month of development to birth

Fixated according to Freud, remaining at a particular psychosexual stage because of too much or too little gratification

Fluid intelligence a person's inherited ability to think and reason abstractly; concept developed by Cattell

Follicle the structure in the ovary that nurtures the ripened ovum and releases it

Follicle-stimulating hormone (FSH) a pituitary hormone that stimulates the maturation of the follicles and ova in the ovaries and of sperm in the testes

Foreclosure establishing an identity without going through a crisis or without searching; adopting an identity as prescribed by someone else

Formal operational stage Piaget's highest stage of cognitive development (11 years and up), during which individuals are able to use logic and abstract concepts

Free association a method of treatment of Freud in which the patient is encouraged to say anything that comes to mind, allowing unconscious thoughts to slip out

Full-term infant an infant who is born with a gestational age between 37 and 42 weeks

Gamete intrafallopian transfer (GIFT) inserting sperm cells and an egg cell directly into the fallopian tube, where fertilization is expected to occur

Gametes sex cells

Gap threshold the minimum detectable gap between sounds

Gender our biological sex

Gender constancy the understanding of the gender that one is, and that it is going to remain the same; usually achieved by 7 years of age

Gender roles our outward expressions of masculinity or femininity in social settings; how we act and think as males or females, our sex roles

Gender stereotypes widespread, assumed gender characteristics of what boys and girls are like

General anesthesia a drug acting on the central nervous system and used to suppress pain during childbirth; affects the fetus also

Generalized anxiety disorder a mental illness involving fixated perceptions of catastrophe in the smallest mishap or in imagined events, an overexaggeration of anxiety out of proportion to the situation

Generational transmission transmitting of knowledge, values, attitudes, roles, and habits from one generation to the next

Generativity vs. stagnation Erikson's seventh psychosocial stage of development (middle adulthood), during which adults assume responsible, adult roles in their community and in caring for the younger generation, or they lead impoverished, self-centered lives

Genes the hereditary material of the chromosomes

Genital stage Freud's fifth psychosexual stage of development (puberty through adulthood), in which sexual urges are directed toward one's peers in a desire to relieve sexual tension

Genotype underlying genetic pattern of an individual

Germinal period the period from conception to 14 days later

Gonadotropic hormones sex hormones secreted by the gonads

Gonadotropin-releasing hormone (GnRH) a hormone secreted by the hypothalamus that controls the production and release of FSH and LH from the pituitary

Gonads the sex glands: testes and ovaries

Grammar the formal description of structure and rules that a language uses in order to communicate meaning

Habituation the tendency to get used to a repeated stimulus and to lose interest in it

Handedness preference for using one hand rather than the other

Haptic processing involves the use of touch to convey information about objects and identify them

Heterologous insemination ALD artificial insemination using donor's sperm

Heterozygous having paired alleles that are different

Hierarchical classification arranging objects into categories according to level

Holistic view emphasizes the functioning of the total individual to try to grow, improve, and reach his or her full potential

Holophrases single words that infants use to convey different meanings, depending on the context in which they are used

Homologous insemination (AIH) artificial insemination with the husband's sperm

Homosexual family a family formed by adults of the same sex who live together, with their children, and who share sexual expression and commitment according to the general definition in this book

Homosociality a period of psychosocial development during which children prefer to play with others of the same sex

Homozygous having paired alleles that are alike

Hormones biochemical substances secreted into the bloodstream by the endocrine glands that act as an internal communication system telling the different cells what to do

Hospice an institution committed to making the end of life free from pain and as comfortable and supportive as possible in a homelike environment with family members present

Human growth hormone (HGH) a pituitary hormone that regulates overall body growth

Humanistic theory psychological theory that emphasizes the ability of individuals to make the right choices and to reach their full potential

Hymen tissue partly covering the vaginal opening

Hypothalamus a small area of the brain controlling motivation, emotion, pleasure, and pain in the body; that is, controls eating, drinking, hormonal production, menstruation, pregnancy, lactation, and sexual response and behavior

Id according to Freud, the inborn instinctual urges that a person seeks to satisfy

Identity achievement that state resulting from the individual having gone through a crisis in the search for identity and having made a commitment

Identity diffusion the situation of the individual who has not experienced an identity crisis, nor explored meaningful alternatives in trying to find an identity

Identity or nullifiability the understanding that an operation that is combined with its opposite becomes nullified, and the element remains unchanged

Identity vs. role confusion Erikson's fifth psychosocial stage of development (12–19 years), during which the adolescent develops a strong sense of self or becomes confused about identity and roles in life

Imaging being on one's best behavior to make a good impression

Imitation copying the behavior of another

Imminent justice the child's belief that immoral behavior inevitably brings pain or punishment as a natural consequence of the transgression

Implantation attachment of the blastocyst to the uterine wall

Imprinting a biological ability to establish an attachment on first exposure to an object or person

Inanition starvation

Incomplete dominance when one paired allele is not completely dominant over the other

Independent variable in an experiment, a factor that is manipulated or controlled by the experimenter to determine its effect on the subjects' behavior

In-depth and societal perspective-taking stage the stage of social awareness during which the self can take a generalized society perspective of the self–other interaction—stage 4 in Selman's theory

Inductive reasoning gathering individual items of information and putting them together to form a hypothesis or conclusions

Industry vs. inferiority Erikson's fourth psychosocial stage of development (6–11 years), during which children develop feelings of adequacy and self-worth for accomplishments or begin to feel inadequate

Infancy the first two years of life

Infantile amnesia the essential lack of memory of events experienced before 3 years of age

Infertile unable to conceive or to effect pregnancy

Information-processing approach an approach to cognition that emphasizes the steps, actions, and operations by which persons receive, perceive, remember, think about, and utilize information

Initiative vs. guilt Erikson's third psychosocial stage of development (3–5 years), during which children are encouraged to assume responsibility for planning and carrying out actions, or are criticized and made to feel guilty for such actions

Insecurely attached overly dependent on parents or care givers because of insufficient attachment

Integrity vs. despair Erikson's eighth psychosocial stage of development (late adulthood), in which adults evaluate their lives and either accept them for what they are, or despair because they have not found meaning in life

Intelligence quotient (IQ) MA divided by CA × 100

Interviews a research method conducted face-to-face between an interviewer and subject where information is obtained through recorded responses to questions

Intimacy vs. isolation Erikson's sixth psychosocial stage of development (young adulthood), during which the young adult develops close relationships with others, or is unable to, resulting in feelings of isolation

In vitro fertilization removal of the ovum from the mother and fertilizing it in the laboratory, then implanting the zygote within the uterine wall

Irreversibility failure to recognize that an operation can go both ways

Joint custody both parents share in decisions regarding the welfare of the child

Juvenile one who is not yet considered an adult in the eyes of the law

Kwashiorkor protein deficiency

Labia majora the major or large lips of tissue on either side of the vaginal opening

Labia minora the smaller lips of tissue on either side of the vagina

Labor rhythmic muscular contractions of the uterus that expel the baby through the birth canal

Lamaze method a natural childbirth method emphasizing education, physical condition, controlled breathing, and emotional support, developed by the French obstetrician Fernand Lamaze

Language acquisition device the inherited characteristics that enable children to listen to and imitate speech sounds and patterns

Latency stage Freud's fourth psychosexual stage of development (6 years to puberty), during which sexual interests are sublimated and concentrated on social and education activities

Lateralization the preference for using one side of the body more than the other in performing special tasks, depending on which hemisphere is dominant for the task

Law of dominant inheritance Mendel's law that says that when an organism inherits competing traits, only one trait will be expressed

Learning disabilities problems with reading, arithmetic, spelling, and written expression even though the person has normal intelligence

Leboyer method ideas for gentle birth procedure developed by the French obstetrician Frederick Leboyer

Legal custody right to make decisions regarding the welfare of the child

Local or regional anesthesia a drug injected into localized areas or regions to block pain during childbirth; some types may have little effect on the fetus

Longitudinal research the repeated measurement of a group of subjects over a period of years

Long-term storage long-term memory: the process by which information is perceived and processed deeply so it passes into the layers of memory below the conscious level—the third stage in a three-stage memory model

Low socioeconomic status low social class, including cultural deprivation and low income

Luteinizing hormone (LH) a pituitary hormone that stimulates the development of the ovum and estrogen and progesterone in females and of sperm and testosterone in males

Macrosystem influences of a particular culture

Marasmus starvation in young children

Masturbation self-stimulation for purposes of sexual arousal

Matricide the killing of one's mother

Maturation the unfolding of the genetically determined patterns of growth and development

Maturity the time in life when one becomes an adult physically, emotionally, socially, intellectually, and spiritually

Mechanistic or deterministic as applied to behaviorism, a criticism that behavior is a result of mindless reactions to stimuli

Meiosis process of cell division by which gametes reproduce

Menarche first menstruation

Mental age (MA) term used by Binet to describe the intellectual level of a person

Mental retardation below normal intelligence

Mesosystem social influences involving reciprocal relationships among the child's microsystem settings; for example, reciprocal influences of the home and school

Metamemory knowledge of memory strategies people employ to learn and remember information

Method of loci remembering by visualizing the position of something

Microsystem social influences with whom the child has immediate contact

Middle childhood the elementary school years, from 6 to 11 years

Mnemonic memory-aiding

Modeling learning through observing and imitating the behavior of others

Monozygotic (identical) twins one-egg, or identical, twins

Mons veneris (mons pubis) the mound of flesh (mound of Venus) located above the vagina in the female, over which pubic hair grows

Morality of constraint conduct coerced by rules or by authority

Morality of conventional role conformity the second level of development of moral thought, based on a desire to conform to social convention, according to Kohlberg

Morality of cooperation conduct regulated by mutual respect and consent

Morality of self-accepted moral principles the third level of development of moral thought, based on adherence to universal principles, according to Kohlberg

Moratorium a period of standing back as one continues to search for an identity

Morpheme the smallest unit of meaning in a language

Morula zygote after a number of cell divisions have taken place, resembling a mulberry

Motherese baby talk that adults use in speaking to infants

Myelinization the process by which neurons become coated with an insulating, fatty substance called myelin

Nativist view biological theory of language development

Naturalistic observation research conducted in a natural setting by watching and recording behavior

Natural selection Charles Darwin's concept that certain species have been selected to survive because of characteristics that help them adapt to their environment; part of the process implying that the human species has evolved from lower forms of life

Nature biological and genetic factors that influence development

Neurons nerve cells

Nightmares frightening dreams during REM (rapid eye movement) sleep

Night terrors upsetting nocturnal experiences during sleep that often cause children to wake up terrified and screaming

Noble savages beings endowed with a sense of right and wrong, term used by Jean-Jacques Rousseau to describe his view of children

Nocturnal emissions male ejaculations during sleep

Nonattached children children who have not developed a close emotional relationship with parents or care givers

Nuclear family a family consisting of a mother, father, and their children

Nurture the influence of environment and experience on development

Objective judgments judgments based solely upon the consequences of wrongdoing

Object permanence the concept that an object continues to exist independent of our perceiving it

Oedipal complex according to Freud, the unconscious love and sexual desire of male children for their mother, and jealousy, hostility, and fear of the father

Oogenesis process by which ova mature

Open adoption adoption system in which the natural mother is permitted to meet and play an active role in selecting the new adoptive parents

Operant conditioning learning from the consequences of behavior so that the consequences change the probability of the behavior's recurrence

Oral stage Freud's first psychosexual stage of development (0–1 year), in which the child's chief source of pleasure is from oral activity

Original sin the Christian doctrine that, because of Adam's sin, a sinful nature has been passed on to succeeding generations

Otitis media middle-ear disease in children often causing partial hearing loss

Ova female egg cells

Ovaries female gonads, or sex glands, which secrete estrogen and progesterone and produce mature egg cells

Ovulation process by which the mature ovum separates from the ovarian wall and is released from the ovary

Ovum egg cell

Parenting coalition cooperation of biological and stepparents in the rearing of children

Parricide the killing of one's mother or father

Patricide the killing of one's father

Penis the male sexual organ for coitus and urination

Perception the act of apprehending or understanding by means of the senses

Perineum area of skin between the vagina and anus

Personal fable beliefs in the uniqueness of one's own experience

Personality the sum total of the physical, mental, social, and emotional characteristics of an individual

Phallic stage Freud's third psychosexual stage of development (4–5 years), in which the child's chief source of pleasure is through exploration and self-manipulation of the genitals

Phenotype observed characteristics of an individual

Phobia an anxiety disorder characterized by excessive, uncontrolled fear of objects, situations, or living creatures of some type

Phoneme the smallest unit of sound in a language

Phonics approach method of teaching reading by teaching the child to sound out the various phonemes of the word

Physical addiction the physical need for a drug; the

body's chemical dependency on it built up through its use

Physical custody legal residence of parent child lives with

Physical development the genetic foundations of development, the physical growth of all of the components of the body, their functioning and care

Piagetian approach the approach to the study of cognitive development emphasizing the qualitative changes in the ways children think, created by Jean Piaget

Pituitary gland master gland of the body, located at the base of the brain, that produces hormones

Pleasure principle the motivation of the id to seek pleasure and avoid pain, regardless of the consequences

Polygenic system of inheritance a number of interacting genes that produce a phenotype

Positive reinforcement a consequence of behavior that leads to an increase in the probability of its occurrence

Postmature infant an infant who is born with a gestational age over 42 weeks

Postpartal depression feelings of sadness, crying, depression, insomnia, irritability, and fatigue commonly experienced by the mother several days after her baby is born

Pragmatics the practical use of language to communicate with others in a variety of social contexts

Precocious puberty very early pubertal changes

Premature infant an infant who is born with a gestational age less than 37 weeks

Premoral level the first level of development of moral judgment, based on rewards and punishments, according to Kohlberg

Prenatal period the period from conception to birth

Preoperational stage Piaget's second stage of cognitive development (2–7 years), during which the child gains some conquest over symbols

Prepared childbirth the physical, social, intellectual, and emotional preparation for the birth of a baby

Primary mental abilities seven basic abilities described by Thurstone

Primary sexual characteristics changes that involve the sex organs at the time of sexual maturation

Problem-finding stage a fifth stage of cognitive development characterized by the ability to create, to discover, and to formulate problems

Progesterone female sex hormone produced by the corpus luteum of the ovary

Progressives educators who emphasize that the purpose of education is to prepare pupils for all of life

Prolactin pituitary hormone found in LTH that stimulates the secretion of milk by the mammary glands of the breast

Prolapsed umbilical cord squeezing of the umbilical cord between the baby's body and the wall of the birth canal during childbirth, causing oxygen deprivation to the fetus

Proprium the self's core of identity that is developing in time

Prostate gland a gland that secretes a portion of the seminal fluid

Proximodistal principle outward distribution of physical growth, which starts at the center of the body and proceeds outward to the extremities

Psychoanalytical theory Freud's theory that the structure of personality is composed of the id, ego, and superego, and that mental health depends on keeping the balance among them

Psychological dependency an overpowering emotional need for a drug

Psychometric approach the approach to the study of cognitive development that measures the quantitative changes in children's intelligence

Psychosexual theory a theory developed by Freud in which development occurs in stages as the center of sensual sensitivity shifts from one body zone to another as children mature

Psychosocial moratorium a socially sanctioned period between childhood and adulthood during which the individual is free to experiment to find a socially acceptable identity and role

Psychosocial theory the term used to describe Erikson's stage theory of development in which there are psychosocial tasks to master at each level of development

Puberty the period or age at which a person reaches sexual maturity and becomes capable of reproduction

Pubescence the whole period during which the physical changes related to sexual maturation take place

Punishment of reciprocity self-imposed punishment; associated with morality of cooperation

Questionnaires a research method whereby the subject writes out answers to written questions

Random sample research subjects selected at random

Rationalization a Freudian defense mechanism in which excuses are given for one's behavior

Reaction formation a Freudian defense mechanism in which an individual deals with an unacceptable impulse by overemphasizing the exact opposite in thought and behavior

Reaction range range of possible phenotypes given a particular genotype and environmental influences

Recall remembering without use of any cues

Recessive gene gene whose characteristic is masked by a dominant gene, and is expressed only when paired with a matching recessive gene

Recognition remembering after cues have been given

Reflexes unlearned behavioral responses to particular stimuli in the environment

Regression a Freudian defense mechanism in which there is a reverting to an earlier, childish form of behavior in response to anxiety

Reliability the extent to which a test reveals the same

scores with repeated administration and when given by two or more examiners

Representative sample a population sample that includes the same percentage of people with specific personal or background characteristics as contained in the population studied

Repression a Freudian defense mechanism in which unpleasant thoughts are pushed down into the unconscious

Reversibility the concept that every operation has an opposite operation that reverses it

Sample the group of subjects chosen for research

Schema Piagetian term referring to mental structures, the original patterns of thinking that people use for dealing with the specific situations in their environment

Scholastic Aptitude Test (SAT) the most widely used test for youths to determine their aptitude to do college work

Scientific method a series of steps used to obtain accurate data; these include formulating the problem, developing a hypothesis, testing the hypothesis, and drawing conclusions that are stated in the form of a theory

Scrotum the pouch of skin containing the testes

Secondary sexual characteristics changes in the body at the time of sexual maturation that do not involve the sex organs themselves

Self the overall perception of one's personality, nature, and individuality of which one is aware

Self-actualization according to Buhler, the drive of individuals to try to grow, improve, and reach their full potential

Self-concept an individual's conscious, cognitive perception and evaluation of self; one's thoughts and opinions about oneself

Self-efficacy our perceptions of our actual skill and personal effectiveness in dealing with situations and others

Self-esteem our perception of our worth, abilities, and accomplishments; our view of ourselves: negative or positive

Self-reference our estimate of our abilities and of how capable and effective we are in dealing with others and the world

Self-reflective thinking or reciprocal perspective-taking stage the stage of awareness during which the self can take the perspective of another person and know that the other person can also take the perspective of the self—stage 2 in Selman's theory

Semantics the meaning of words and sentences

Seminal vesicles twin glands that secrete fluid into the vas deferens to enhance sperm viability

Sensitive period a period during which a given effect can be produced more readily than at other times

Sensorimotor stage Piaget's first stage of cognitive development (birth–2 years), during which the child coordinates motor actions with sensory experiences

Sensory storage sensory memory: the process by which information is received and transduced by the senses, usually in a fraction of a second—the first stage in a three-stage model of memory

Separation anxiety anxiety experienced by children when they are separated from care givers to whom they are emotionally attached

Separation-individuation a period during which the infant gradually develops a self apart from the mother, a concept of Mahler

Sequential study a combination of cross-sectional and longitudinal research designs that attempts to sort out age, cohort, and time effects. Age changes are not measured

Serialization arranging objects into a hierarchy of classes

Sex chromosomes twenty-third pair of chromosomes that determine the gender of the offspring

Sex-linked disorders disorders carried only by the mother, through defective, recessive genes on the X chromosome

Short-term storage short-term memory: the process by which information is still in the conscious mind and being rehearsed and focused on—the second stage in a three-stage memory model

Show blood-tinged mucus expelled from the cervix, usually when labor and contractions begin

Siamese twins monozygotic twins where complete separation did not occur during development

Sibling rivalry the competition of brothers and sisters for the attention, approval, and affection of the parents

Single-parent family a family consisting of one parent and one or more children

Skills approach method of teaching reading that involves either a phonics approach or a word recognition approach

Sleepwalking walking and carrying on various activities during deep sleep

Social cognition the capacity to understand social relationships

Social development the socialization process, moral development, and relationships with peers, family, and at work

Socialization the process by which persons learn the ways of society or social groups so they can function within them

Social learning theory a view of learning that emphasizes that behavior is learned through social interaction with other persons

Social role taking the ability to understand the self and others as subjects, to react to them as like the self, and to react to the self's behavior from the other's point of view

Sociocentrism a focus of attention on social problems and the concerns of society

Sonogram visual image of fetus, produced from sound waves, used to detect fetal abnormalities

Spermatogenesis process by which sperm are produced

Stepfamily a family formed when a remarried husband or wife brings children from a former marriage

Subjective judgments judgments that take into account intention or motives

Sublimation a Freudian defense mechanism in which a socially acceptable goal or action is substituted for an unacceptable, socially harmful one

Superego according to Freud, the socially induced moral restrictions that strive to keep the id in check and help the individual attain perfection

Surrogate mother a woman whose services are obtained by a couple, who is to be inseminated with the man's sperm, to carry the resulting baby until birth, and then to give the baby and all rights to it to the couple

Survival of the fittest Darwin's concept that only the fittest live to pass on their superior traits to future generations, thereby evolving into higher and higher forms of life

Symbiosis a child's close dependency on the mother, to the extent that there is almost a fusing of personalities

Symbolic play using one object to represent another in play

Syncretism trying to link ideas together that are not always related

Syntax the grammatical rules of a language

Tabula rasa literally, a blank slate; refers to John Locke's view that children are born morally neutral

Telegraphic speech several-word utterances that convey meaning

Temperament the relatively consistent, basic dispositions inherent in people that underlie and modulate much of their behavior

Teratogen harmful substance that crosses the placenta barrier and harms the embryo or fetus and causes birth defects

Testes the male gonads that produce sperm and male sex hormones

Testosterone the masculinizing hormone secreted by the testes

Tests research instruments used to measure specific characteristics such as intelligence, aptitude, achievement, vocational interests, personality traits, and so forth

Theory a tentative explanation of facts and data that have been observed

Third person or mutual perspective-taking stage the stage of social awareness during which the self can view the self–other interaction from the perspective of a neutral third person—stage 3 in Selman's theory

Tracking an organizational technique that permits schools to create homogeneous groupings of students within a heterogeneous student population in order to facilitate instruction of all students

Traditionalists educators who argue that the purpose of education is to teach the basics

Trainable mentally retarded those who are moderately retarded with IQs of 49 to 35

Transductive reasoning proceeding from particular to particular in thought, without making generalizations

Triarchic theory of intelligence three components of intelligence described by Sternberg

Trimester one-third of the gestation period, or about 12.7 weeks

Trust vs. distrust Erikson's first stage of psychosocial development (0–1 year) in which the infant learns that needs will be met or becomes anxious that needs will be frustrated

Two-factor theory of intelligence concept developed by Spearman that intelligence consists of a general factor "g" and a number of specific abilities—"s" factors

Unconditional positive regard giving acceptance and appreciation of the individual regardless of socially unacceptable behavior

Urethra the tube that carries urine from the bladder to the outside; in males it also carries the semen to the outside

Uterus womb, in which the baby grows and develops

Vagina canal from the cervix to the vulva that receives the penis during intercourse and acts as the birth canal through which the baby passes to the outside

Validity the extent to which a test measures what it claims to measure

Vas deferens the tubes running from the epididymis to the urethra that carry semen and sperm to the ejaculatory duct

Vernix caseosa waxy substance covering the skin of the neonate

Viable capable of living on its own

Vicarious punishment observing the punishment of the behavior of another that decreases the probability of the same behavior in the observer

Vicarious reinforcement observing the positive consequences of the behavior of another that increases the probability of the behavior in the observer

Visitation rights right to visit the child given by law

Vulva a collective term for the external genitalia of the female

Whole-language approach method of teaching reading that presents reading materials as a whole so the child learns the meaning of the passage before learning individual words

Word recognition approach method of teaching reading by teaching the child to recognize the whole word

Zone of proximal development the distance between a child's actual development level reached through individual problem solving and a higher level of potential development

Zygote a fertilized ovum

Bibliography

Abbey, A., Andrews, F. M., & Halman, L. J. (1992). Infertility and subjective well-being: The mediating roles of self-esteem, internal control, and interpersonal conflict. *Journal of Marriage and the Family, 54,* 408–417.

Abraham, K. G., & Christopherson, V. A. (1984). Perceived competence among rural middle school children: Parental antecedents and relations to locus of control. *Journal of Early Adolescence, 4,* 343–351.

Abramovitch, R., Freedman, J. L., Thoden, K., & Nikolich, C. (1991). Children's capacity to consent to participation in psychological research: Empirical findings. *Child Development 62,* 1100–1109.

Achenbach, T. M., Phares, V., & Howell, C. T. (1990). Seven-year outcome of the Vermont intervention program for low-birthweight infants. *Child Development, 61,* 1672–1681.

Acredolo, L. P., & Hake, J. L. (1982). Infant perception. In B. B. Wolman (Ed.), *Handbook of developmental psychology.* Englewood Cliffs, NJ: Prentice-Hall.

Adams, G. R., Day, T., Dyk, P. H., & Frede, E. (1992). On the dialectics of pubescence and psychosocial development. *Journal of Early Adolescence, 12,* 348–365.

Adams, G. R., & Jones, R. M. (1982, February). Adolescent egocentrism: Exploration into possible contributions of parent-child relations. *Journal of Youth and Adolescence, 11,* 25–31.

Adams, G. R., & Munro, G. (1979, September). Portrait of the North American runaway: A critical review. *Journal of Youth and Adolescence, 8,* 359–373.

Adams, M., Oakley, G., & Marks, J. (1982). Maternal age and births in the 1980s. *JAMA, Journal of the American Medical Association, 247,* 493–494.

Adegoke, A. (1992). Relationship between parental socioeconomic status, sex, and initial pubertal problems among school-going adolescents in Nigeria. *Journal of Adolescence, 15,* 323–326.

Adler, J. (1989, March). The Nintendo kid. *Newsweek, 113,* 64–68.

Affleck, G., Tennen, H., Rowe, J., Roscher, B., & Walker, L. (1989). Effects of formal support on mother's adaptation to the hospital-to-home transition of high-risk infants: The benefits and costs of helping. *Child Development, 60,* 488–501.

Ahrons, C., & Rodgers, R. (1987). *Divorced families: A multidisciplinary view.* New York: W. W. Norton.

Ainsworth, M. D. S. (1988, August). *Attachment beyond infancy.* Paper presented at the meeting of the American Psychological Association.

Ainsworth, M. D. S., & Bowlby, J. (1991). An ethological approach to personality development. *American Psychologist, 46,* 331–341.

Ajzen, I., & Fishbein, M. (1980). *Understanding attitudes and predicting social behavior.* Englewood Cliffs, NJ: Prentice-Hall.

Akinboye, J. O. (1984, Summer). Secondary sexual characteristics and normal puberty in Nigerian and Zimbabwian adolescents. *Adolescence, 19,* 483–492.

Alan Guttmacher Institute. (1981). *Teenage pregnancy.* New York: Alan Guttmacher Institute.

Alberts, J. K., Hecht, M. L., Miller-Rassulo, M., & Krizek, R. L. (1992). The communicative process of drug resistance among high school students. *Adolescence, 27,* 203–226.

Albright, A. (1993). Postpartum depression: An overview. *Journal of counseling and development, 71,* 316–320.

Alexander, G. M., & Himes, M. (1994). Gender labels and play styles: Their relative contribution to children's selection of playmates. *Child Development, 65,* 869–879.

Alexander, K. L., Entwistle, D. R., & Dauber, S. L. (1993). First-grade classroom behavior: Its short- and long-term consequences for school performance. *Child Development, 64,* 801–814.

Allen, K. E., Hart, R. M., Buell, J. S., Harris, F. R., & Wolf, M. M. (1964). Effects of social reinforcement on isolate behavior of a nursery school child. *Child Development, 35,* 511–518.

Allers, C. T., & Benjack, K. J. (1991). Connections between childhood abuse and HIV infection. *Journal of Counseling and Development, 70,* 309–313.

Allport, G. W. (1950). *Becoming: Basic considerations for a psychology of personality.* New Haven, CT: Yale University Press.

Alsaker, F. D. (1992a). Being overweight and psychological adjustment. *Journal of Early Adolescence, 12,* 396–419.

Alsaker, F. D. (1992b). Pubertal timing, overweight, and psychological adjustment. *Journal of Early Adolescence, 12,* 396–419.

Althaus, F. (March/April, 1991a). Expansion of Medicaid alone may not result in healthier newborns. *Family Planning Perspectives, 23,* 91–92.

Althaus, F. (November/December 1991b). A woman's risk of ectopic pregnancy varies according to the contraceptive she chooses. *Family Planning Perspectives, 23,* 291–292.

Altmann, E. O., & Gottlieb, I. H. (1988). The social behavior of depressed children: An observational study. *Journal of Abnormal Child Psychology, 16,* 29–44.

Amabile, T. A., & Rovee-Collier, C. (1991). Contextual variation and memory retrieval at six months. *Child Development, 62,* 1155–1166.

Amato, P. R. (1986). Marital conflict, the parent-child relationship, and self-esteem. *Family Relations, 35,* 403–410.

Amato, P. R. (1987). Family process in one-parent, stepparent, and intact families: The child's point of view. *Journal of Marriage and the Family, 49,* 327–337.

Amato, P. R. (1988a). Long-term implications of parental divorce for adult self-concept. *Journal of Family Issues, 9,* 201–213.

Amato, P. R. (1988b). Parental divorce and attitudes toward marriage and family life. *Journal of Marriage and the Family, 50,* 453–461.

Amato, P. R. (1990). Dimensions of the family environment as perceived by children: A multidimensional scaling analysis. *Journal of Marriage and the Family, 52,* 613–620.

Amato, P. R. (1991). The "child of divorce" as a person prototype: Bias in the recall of information about children in divorced families. *Journal of Marriage and the Family, 53,* 59–69.

Amato, P. R. (1991). Psychological distress and the recall of childhood family characteristics. *Journal of Marriage and the Family, 53,* 1011–1019.

Amato, P. R. (1993). Children's adjustment to divorce: Theories, hypothesis, & empirical support. *Journal of Marriage and the Family, 55,* 23–38.

Amato, P. R., & Booth, A. (1991). The consequences of divorce for attitudes towards divorce and gender roles. *Journal of Family Issues, 12,* 306–322.

Amato, P. R., & Rezac, S. J. (1994). Contact with nonresident parents, interparental conflict, and children's behavior. *Journal of Family Issues, 15,* 191–207.

American Academy of Pediatrics. (1982, March). Guidelines for health supervision. *News and Comment.*

American Academy of Pediatrics. (1986). *Positive approaches to daycare dilemmas: How to make it work.* Elk Grove Village, IL: American Academy of Pediatrics.

American Academy of Pediatrics, Committee on Nutrition. (1986). Prudent life-style for children: Dietary fat and cholesterol. *Pediatrics, 78,* 521–525.

American Academy of Pediatrics, Committee on Pediatric Aspects of Physical Fitness, Recreation, and Sports. (1981). Competitive athletics for children of elementary school age. *Pediatrics, 67.*

American Psychiatric Association. (1987). *Diagnostic and statistical manual of mental disorders* (3rd ed., rev.). Washington, DC: American Psychiatric Association.

American Psychological Association (APA). (1982). *Ethical principles in the conduct of research with human participants.* Washington, DC: American Psychological Association.

Ames, L. B., Gillespie, C., Haines, J., & Ilg, F. L. (1978). *The Gesell Institute's child from one to six.* New York: Harper & Row.

Andersen, B. L., & LeGrand, J. (1991). Body image for women: Conceptualization, assessment, and a test of its importance to sexual dysfunction and to mental illness. *The Journal of Sex Research, 28,* 457–477.

Anderson, D. R., Choi, H. P., & Lorch, E. P. (1987). Attentional inertia reduces distractibility during young children's TV viewing. *Child Development, 58,* 798–806.

Andersson, B. E. (1992). Effects of day-care on cognitive and socioemotional competence of thirteen-year-old Swedish schoolchildren. *Child Development, 63,* 20–36.

Andersson, L., & Stevens, N. (1993). Associations between early experiences with parents and well-being in old age. *Journal of Gerontology, 48,* P109–P116.

Andre, T., & Bormann, L. (1991). Knowledge of acquired immune deficiency syndrome and sexual responsibility among high school students. *Youth and Society, 22,* 339–361.

Andrews, S. R., Blumenthal, J. B., Johnson, D. L, Kahn, A. J., Ferguson, C. J., Lasater, T. M., Malone, P. E., & Wallace, D. B. (1982). The skills of mothering—a study of parent-child development centers. *Monographs of the Society for Research in Child Development, 47*(6, Serial No. 198).

Anisfeld, E., Casper, V., Nozyce, M., & Cunningham, N. (1990). Does infant carrying promote attachment? An experimental study of the effects of increased physical contact on the development of attachment. *Child Development, 61,* 1617–1627.

Anolik, S. A. (1983, Fall). Family influences upon delinquency: Biosocial and psychosocial perspectives. *Adolescence, 18,* 489–498.

Ansbacher, R., & Adler, J. P. (1988). Infertility workup and sexual stress. *Medical Aspects of Human Sexuality, 22,* 55–63.

Apgar, V. A. (1953). A proposal for a new method of evaluation of a newborn infant. *Anesthesia and Analgesia, 32,* 260–267.

Apter, A., Galatzer, A., Beth-Halachmi, N., & Laron, Z. (1981, December). Self-image in adolescents with delayed puberty and growth retardation. *Journal of Youth and Adolescence, 10,* 501–505.

Aptitude test scores. Grumbling gets louder. (1979, May 14). *U.S. News and World Report,* pp. 76ff.

Archer, S. L. (1990a). Adolescent identity: An appraisal of health and intervention. *Journal of Adolescence, 13,* 341–344.

Archer, S. L. (1990b). The status of identity: Reflections on the need for intervention. *Journal of Adolescence, 13,* 345–360.

Archer, S. L., & Waterman, A. S. (1990). Varieties of identity diffusions and foreclosures: An exploration of subcategories of the identity statuses. *Journal of Adolescent Research, 5,* 96–111.

Aries, P. (1962). *Centuries of childhood: A social history of family life.* New York: Vintage Books.

Arkin, E. B. (1989, July). *Infant care.* U.S. Department of HHS, Public Health Service, Health Resources and Services Administration, Bureau of Maternal and Child Health and Resources Development. Washington, DC: U.S. Government Printing Office.

Arlin, P. K. (1975). cognitive development in adulthood: A fifth stage? *Developmental Psychology, 11,* 602–606.

Armistead, L., Wierson, M., Forehand, R., & Frame, C. (1992). Psychopathology in incarcerated juvenile delinquents: Does it extend beyond externalizing problems? *Adolescence, 27,* 309–314.

Arsenio, W. F., & Kramer, R. (1992) Victimizers and their victims: Children's conceptions of the mixed emotional consequences of moral transgressions. *Child Development, 63,* 915–927.

Asarnow, J. R. (1988). Peers status and social competence in child psychiatric inpatients: A comparison of children with depressive, externalizing, and concurrent depressive and externalizing disorders. *Journal of Abnormal Child Psychology, 16,* 151–162.

Asendorpf, J. B. (1991). Development of inhibited children's coping with unfamiliarity. *Child Development, 62,* 1460–1474.

Asendorpf, J. B., & Nunner-Winkler, G. (1992). Children's moral motive strength and temperamental inhibition reduce their immoral behavior in real moral conflicts. *Child Development, 63,* 1223–1235.

Ashford, J., & LeCroy, C. W. (1990). Juvenile recidivism: A comparison of three prediction instruments. *Adolescence, 25,* 441–450.

Ashmead, D. H., Davis, D. L., Whalen, T., & Odom, R. D. (1991). Sound localization and sensitivity to interaural time differences in human infants. *Child Development, 62,* 1211–1226.

Ashmead, D. H., & Perlmutter, M. (1979, August). *Infant memory in everyday life.* Paper presented at the meeting of the American Psychological Association, New York City.

Aslin, R. N., Pisoni, D. P., & Jusczyk, P. W. (1983). Auditory development and speech perception in infancy. In P. H. Mussen, M. H. Haith, & J. J. Campos (Eds.), *Handbook of child psychology: Vol. 2. Infancy and developmental psychology.* New York: Wiley.

Aslin, R. N., & Smith, L. B. (1988). Perceptual development. *Annual Review of Psychology, 39,* 435–473.

Asmussen, L., & Larson, R. (1991). The quality of family time among young adolescents in single-family and married-parent families. *Journal of Marriage and the Family, 53,* 1021–1030.

Athey, I. J. (1984). Contributions of play to development. In T. D. Yawkey & A. D. Pellegrini (Eds.), *Child's play.* Hillsdale, NJ: Erlbaum.

Atkinson, M. B., & Blackwelder, S. B. (1993). Fathering in the 20th century. *Journal of Marriage and the Family, 55,* 975–986.

Atkinson, R. (1988). *Teenage world: Adolescent self-image in ten countries.* New York: Plenum.

Bachman, J. G., Johnston, L. D., & O'Malley, P. M. (1987). *Monitoring the future: Questionnaire responses from the nation's high school seniors, 1986.* Ann Arbor, MI: Institute for Social Research.

Bachrach, C. A., London, R. A., & Maza, P. L. (1991). On the path to adoption: Adoption seeking in the United States, 1988. *Journal of Marriage and the Family, 53,* 705–718.

Bachrach, C. A., Stolley, K. S., & London, K. A. (1992, January/February). Relinquishment of premarital births: Evidence from national survey data. *Family Planning Perspectives, 24,* 27–32.

Backscheider, A. D., Shatz, M., & Gelman, S. A. (1993). Preschoolers' ability to distinguish living kinds as a function of regrowth. *Child Development, 64,* 1242–1257.

Bahr, S. J., Hawks, R. D., & Wang, G. (1993). Family and religious influences on adolescent substance abuse. *Youth and Society, 24,* 443–465.

Bai, D. O., & Bertenthal, B. I. (1992). Locomotor status and the development of spatial search skills. *Child Development, 63,* 215–226.

Baillargeon, R. (1987). Object permanence in $3\frac{1}{2}$–$4\frac{1}{2}$-month-old infants. *Developmental Psychology, 23,* 655–664.

Baillargeon, R., & DeVos, J. (1991). Object permanence in young infants: Further evidence. *Child Development, 62,* 1227–1246.

Bailey, C. A. (1991). Family structure and eating disorders: The family environment scale and bulimic-like symptoms. *Youth and Society, 23,* 251–272.

Bailey, D. B., Jr., McWilliam, R. A., Ware, W. B., & Burchinal, M. A. (1993). Social interactions with toddlers and preschoolers in same-age and mixed-age play groups. *Journal of Applied Developmental Psychology, 14,* 261–276.

Baird, P., & Sights, J. R. (1986). Low self-esteem as a treatment issue in the psychotherapy of anorexia and bulimia. *Journal of Counseling and Development, 64,* 449–451.

Baker, C. C. (1982, June). The adolescent as theorist: An interpretative view. *Journal of Youth and Adolescence, 11,* 167–181.

Bakken, L., & Romig, C. (1992). Interpersonal needs in middle adolescents: Companionship, leadership, and intimacy. *Journal of Adolescence, 15,* 301–316.

Baldwin, D. A. (1991). Infants' contribution to the achievement of joint references. *Child Development, 62,* 875–890.

Baldwin, D. A. (1993). Early referential understanding: Infants' ability to recognize referential acts for what they are. *Developmental Psychology, 29,* 832–843.

Baldwin, J. I., Whiteley, S., & Baldwin, J. D. (1990). Changing AIDS- and fertility-related behavior: The effectiveness of sexual education. *The Journal of Sex Research, 27,* 245–262.

Balk, D. (1983, April). Adolescents' grief reactions and self-concept perceptions following sibling death: A study of 33 teenagers. *Journal of Youth and Adolescence, 12,* 137–161.

Ballard, M. E., Cummings, E. M., & Larkin, K. (1993). Emotional and cardiovascular responses to adults' angry behavior and to challenging tasks in children of hypertensive and normotensive parents. *Child Development, 64,* 500–515.

Baltes, P. B. (1987). Theoretical propositions of life-span developmental psychology: On the dynamics between growth and decline. *Developmental Psychology, 23,* 611–626.

Bandura, A. (1977). *Social learning theory.* Englewood Cliffs, NJ: Prentice-Hall.

Bandura, A. (1986). *Social foundations of thought and action: A social cognitive theory.* Englewood Cliffs, NJ: Prentice-Hall.

Bandura, A., Ross, D., & Ross, S. A. (1963a). Imitation of film-mediated aggressive models. *Journal of Abnormal and Social Psychology, 66,* 3–11.

Bandura, A., Ross, D., & Ross, S. A. (1963b). Imitation of film-mediated aggressive males. *Journal of Abnormal and Social Psychology, 67,* 601–607.

Banks, M. S., & Salapatek, P. (1983). Infant visual perception. In P. H. Mussen (Ed)., *Handbook of child psychology* (4th ed., Vol. 2). New York: Wiley.

Baranowski, M. D. (1983). Strengthening the grandparent-grandchild relationship. *Medical Aspects of Human Sexuality, 17,* 106–126.

Barber, B. K. (1992). Family, personality, and adolescent problem behaviors. *Journal of Marriage and the Family, 54,* 69–79.

Barber, B. K., Chadwick, B. A., & Oerter, R. (1992). Parental behaviors and adolescent self-esteem in the United States and Germany. *Journal of Marriage and the Family, 54,* 128–141.

Barcus, F. E. (1978). *Commercial children's television on weekends and weekday afternoons.* Newtonville, MA: Action for Children's Television.

Barnes, M. E., & Farrier, S. C. (1985, Spring). A longitudinal study of the self-concept of low-income youth. *Adolescence, 20,* 199–205.

Barranti, C. C. R. (1985). The grandparent-grandchild relationship: Family resource in an era of voluntary bonds. *Family Relations, 34,* 343–352.

Barrett, K. C., & Campos, J. J. (1987). A functionalist approach to emotions. In J. D. Osofsky (Ed.), *Handbook of infant development.* New York: Wiley.

Barrett, M. D. (1986). Early semantic representations and early word-usage. In S. A. Kuczaj & M. C. Barett (Eds.), *The development of word meaning: Progress in cognitive developmental research.* New York: Springer-Verlag.

Bart, W. M. (1983, Winter). Adolescent thinking and the quality of life. *Adolescence, 18,* 875–888.

Barton, M. C., & Tomasello, M. (1991). Joint attention and conversation in mother-infant-sibling triads. *Child Development, 62,* 517–529.

Battle, J. (1981). *Culture-free self-esteem inventories for children and adults.* Seattle, WA: Special Child Publications.

Bauer, P. J., & Hertsgaard, L. A. (1993). Increasing steps in recall of events: Factors facilitating immediate and long-term memory in 13.5- and 16.5-month-old children. *Child Development, 64,* 1204–1223.

Bauer, P. J., & Mandler, J. M. (1992). Putting the horse before the cart: The use of temporal order in recall of events by one-year-old children. *Developmental Psychology, 28,* 441–452.

Bauman, R. P. (1978, Spring). Teaching for cognitive development. *Andover Review, 5,* 83–98.

Baumrind, D. (1978). Parental disciplinary patterns and social competence in children. *Youth and Society, 9,* 239–276.

Baumrind, D. (1980). New directions in socialization research. *American Psychologist, 35, 639–652.*

Baydar, N., Brooks-Gunn, J., & Furstenberg, F. F. (1993). Early warning signs of functional illiteracy: Predictors in childhood and adolescence. *Child Development, 64,* 815–829.

Baylar, N. (1988). Effects of parental separation and re-entry into union on the emotional well-being of children. *Journal of Marriage and the Family, 50,* 967–981.

Bayley, N. (1956). Individual patterns of development. *Child Development, 27,* 45–74.

Bayley, N. (1969). *Manual for the Bayley Scales of infant development.* New York: The Psychological Corporation.

Bean, C. (1974). *Methods of childbirth.* New York: Dolphin.

Beauchamp, G., & Cowart, B. (1985). Congenital and experiential factors in the development of human flavor preferences. *Appetite, 6,* 357–372.

Beck, J. G., & Davies, D. K. (1987). Teen contraception: A review of perspectives on compliance. *Archives of Sexual Behavior, 16,* 337–368.

Beckwith, L., Rodning, C., & Cohen, S. (1992). Preterm children at early adolescence and continuity and discontinuity in maternal responsiveness from infancy. *Child Development, 63,* 1198–1208.

Bee, H. L., Barnard, K. E., Eyres, S. J., Gray, C. A., Hammond, M. A., Spietz, A. L., Snyder, C., & Clark, B. (1982). Predictor of IQ and language skill from perinatal status, child performance, family characteristics, and mother-infant interaction. *Child Development, 53,* 1134–1156.

Behrman, R. E., & Vaughn, B. E. (Eds.). (1983). *Nelson textbook of pediatrics* (12th ed.). Philadelphia, PA: Saunders.

Beilin, H. (1992). Piaget's enduring contribution to developmental psychology. *Developmental Psychology, 28,* 191–204.

Bell, M. A., & Fox, N. A. (1992). The relations between frontal brain electrical activity and cognitive development during infancy. *Child Development, 63,* 1142–1163.

Bell, N. J., & Avery, A. W. (1985). Family structure and parent-adolescent relationships: Does family structure really make a difference? *Journal of Marriage and Family Therapy, 47,* 503–508.

Bellinger, D., Leviton, A. A., Watermaux, C., Needleman, H., & Rabinowitz, M. (1987). Longitudinal analyses of prenatal and postnatal lead exposure and early cognitive development. *New England Journal of Medicine, 316,* 1037–1043.

Belsky, J. (1984). Two waves of day care research: Developmental effects and condition of quality. In R. Ainslie (Ed.), *The child and the day care setting.* New York: Praeger.

Belsky, J. (1990). Parental and nonparental child care and children's socioemotional development: A decade in review. *Journal of Marriage and the Family, 52,* 885–903.

Belsky, J., & Braungart, J. M. (1991). Are insecure-avoidant infants with extensive day-care experience less stressed by and more independent in the strange situation? *Child Development, 62,* 567–571.

Belsky, J., Crnic, K., & Gable, S. (1995). The determinants of coparenting in families with toddler boys: Spousal differences and daily hassles. *Child Development, 66,* 629–642.

Belsky, J., & Rovine, M. J. (1988). Nonmaternal care in the first year of life and the security of infant-parent attachment. *Child Development, 59,* 157–167.

Belsky, J., Steinberg, L., & Draper, P. (1991). Further reflections on an evolutionary theory of socialization. *Child Development, 62,* 682–685.

Benasich, A. A., & Bejar, I. I. (1992). The Fagan Test of Infant Intelligence: A critical review. *Journal of Applied Developmental Psychology, 13,* 153–171.

Benazon, N., Wright, J., and Sabourin, S. (1992). Stress, sexual satisfaction, and marital adjustment in infertile couples. *Journal of Sex and Marital Therapy, 18,* 273–284.

Benenson, J. F. (1990). Gender differences in social networks. *Journal of Early Adolescence, 10,* 472–495.

Benenson, J. F. (1993). Greater preference among females and males for dyadic interaction in early childhood. *Child Development, 64,* 544–555.

Benin, M. H., & Nienstedt, B. C. (1985). Happiness in single- and dual-earner families: The effect of marital happiness, job satisfaction, and the life cycle. *Journal of Marriage and the Family, 47,* 975–984.

Bennett, W. J. (1986). *First lessons: A report on elementary education in America.* Washington, DC: U.S. Government Printing Office.

Berch, D. B., & Bender, B. G. (1987). Margins of sexuality. *Psychology Today, 21,* 54–57.

Berkow, R. (1987). Postpartum Care. *The Merck Manual* (15th ed.) Rahway, N.J.: Merck & Company, Inc.

Berman, P. W., O'Nan, B. A., & Floyd, W. (1981). The double standard of aging and the social situation: Judgments of attractiveness of the middle-aged woman. *Sex Roles, 7,* 87–96.

Berstein, B. E., & Collins, S. K. (1985). Remarriage counseling: Lawyer and therapists' help with the second time around. *Family Relations, 34,* 387–391.

Bertenthal, B. I., & Bradbury, A. (1992). Infants' detection of shearing motion in random-dot displays. *Developmental Psychology, 28,* 1056–1066.

Berzonsky, M. D., Rice, K. G., & Neimeyer, G. J. (1990). Identity status and self-construct systems: Process × structure interactions. *Journal of Adolescence, 13,* 251–264.

Best, D. L. (1993). Inducing children to generate mnemonic organizational strategies: An examination of long-term retention and materials. *Developmental Psychology, 29,* 324–336.

Bettes, B. A., Dusenbury, L., Kerner, J., James-Ortiz, S., & Botvin, G. J. (1990). Ethnicity and psychosocial factors in alcohol and tobacco use in adolescence. *Child Development, 61,* 557–565.

Bialystok, E. (1992). Attentional control in children's metalinguistic performance and measures of field independence. *Developmental Psychology, 28,* 654–664.

Bigler, R. S. (1995). The role of classification skill in moderating environmental influences on children's gender stereotyping: A study of the functional use of gender in the classroom. *Child Development, 66,* 1072–1087.

Bilsker, D. (1992). An existentialist account of identity formation. *Journal of Adolescence, 15,* 177–192.

Bilsker, D., & Marcia, J. E. (1991). Adaptive regression and ego identity. *Journal of Adolescence, 14,* 75–84.

Binet, A., & Simon, T. (1916). *The development of intelligence in children.* Baltimore, MD: William & Wilkins.

Bingol, N., Fuchs, M., Diaz, V., Stone, R. K., & Gromisch, D. S. (1987). Teratogenicity of cocaine in humans. *Journal of Pediatrics, 110,* 93–96.

Biringen, Z., Emde, R. N., Campos, J. J., & Applebaum, M. I. (1995). Affective reorganization in the infant, the mother, and the dyad: The role of upright locomotion and its timing. *Child Development, 66,* 499–514.

Birnholz, J. C., & Benacerraf, B. R. (1983). The development of human fetal hearing. *Science, 222,* 516–518.

Bisher, E. B., & Bisher, J. S. (1989). Parenting coalition after remarriage: Dynamics and therapeutic guidelines. *Family Relations, 38,* 65–70.

Bishop, S. M., & Lynn, A. G. (1983). Multi-level vulnerability of adolescent marriages: An eco-system model for clinical assessment and intervention. *Journal of Marital and Family Therapy, 9,* 271–282.

Bisping, R., Steingrueber, H. J., Oltmann, M., & Wenk, C. (1990). Adults' tolerance of cries: An experimental investigation of acoustic features. *Child Development, 61,* 1218–1229.

Bjorklund, D. F., Schneider, W., Cassel, W. S., & Ashley, E. (1994). Training an extension of a memory strategy: Evidence for utilization deficiencies in the acquisition of an organizational strategy in high- and low-IQ children. *Child Development, 65,* 951–965.

Black, C., & deBlassie, R. R. (1985). Adolescent pregnancy: Contributing factors, consequences, treatment, and plausible solutions. *Adolescence, 20,* 281–290.

Blain, M. D., Thompson, J. M., & Whiffen, V. E. (1993). Attachment and perceived social support in late adolescence: The interaction between working models of self and others. *Journal of Adolescent Research, 8,* 226–241.

Blake, J. (1989). *Family size and achievement.* Berkeley: University of California Press.

Blake, J. (1991). Number of siblings and personality. *Family Planning Perspectives, 23,* 273–274.

Blass, E. M., & Smith, B. A. (1992). Differential effects of sucrose, fructose, glucose, and lactose on crying in 1- to 3-day old human infants: Qualitative and quantitative considerations. *Developmental Psychology, 28,* 804–810.

Blechman, E. A. (1982, February). Are children with one parent at psychological risk? A methodological review. *Journal of Marriage and the Family, 44,* 179–195.

Blecke, J. (1990). Exploration of children's health and self-care behavior within a family context through qualitative research. *Family Relations, 39,* 284–291.

Blewitt, P. (1994). Understanding categorical hierarchies: The earliest levels of skill. *Child Development, 65,* 1259–1298.

Blinn, L. M. (1987). Phototherapeutic intervention to improve self-concept and prevent repeat pregnancies among adolescents. *Family Relations, 36,* 252–257.

Blinn, L. M. (1990). Adolescent mothers' preceptions of their work lives in the future: Are they stable? *Journal of Adolescent Research, 5,* 206–221.

Bloch, D. P. (1989). Using career information with drop-outs and at-risk youth. *Career Development Quarterly, 38,* 160–171.

Block, C. R., Norr, K. L., Meyering, S., Norr, J., & Charles, A. G. (1981, April). Husband gatekeeping in childbirth. *Family Relations, 30,* 197–204.

Block, J., Block, J. H., & Keyes, S. (1988). Longitudinally foretelling drug usage in adolescence: Early childhood personality and environmental precursors. *Child Development, 59,* 336–355.

Bloom, L., Merkin, S., & Wooten, J. (1982). Wh-Questions: Linguistic factors that contribute to the sequence of acquisition. *Child Development, 53,* 1084–1092.

Blustein, D. L., & Palladino, D. E. (1991). Self and identity in late adolescence: A theoretical and empirical integration. *Journal of Adolescent Research, 6,* 437–453.

Boivin, M., & Begin, G. (1989). Peer status and self-perceptions among early elementary school children: The case of the rejected children. *Child Development, 60,* 571–579.

Boldizar, J. P., Perry, D. G., & Perry, L. C. (1989). Outcomes, values and aggression. *Child Development, 60,* 591–596.

Booth, A., & Edwards, J. N. (1985). Age at marriage and marital instability. *Journal of Marriage and the Family, 47,* 67–75.

Borja-Alvarez, T., Zarbatany, L., & Pepper, S. (1991). Contributions of male and female guests and hosts to peer group entry. *Child Development, 62,* 1079–1090.

Bornstein, M. H. (1985a). How infant and mother jointly contribute to developing cognitive competence in the child. *Proceedings of the National Academy of Sciences of the U.S.A., 82,* 7470–7473.

Bornstein, M. H. (1985b). Human infant color vision and color perception. *Infant Behavior and Development, 8,* 109–113.

Bornstein, M. H. (1987). *Sensitive periods of development.* Hillsdale, NJ: Erlbaum.

Bornstein, M. H., & Sigman, M. D. (1986). Continuity in mental development from infancy. *Child Development, 57,* 251–274.

Bornstein, M. H. Tal, J., Rahn, Galperin, C. Z., Pecheux, M., Lamour, M., Toda, S., Azuma, H., Ogino, M., & Tamis-LeMonda, C. S. (1992). Functional analysis of the contents of maternal speech to infants of 5 and 13 months in four cultures: Argentina, France, Japan, & the United States. *Developmental Psychology, 28,* 593–603.

Bornstein, M. H., Tamis-LeMonda, C. S., Tal, J., Ludemann, P., Toda, S., Rahn, C. W., Pecheux, M., & Azuma, H. (1992). Maternal responsiveness to infants in three societies: The United States, France, and Japan. *Child Development, 63,* 808–821.

Borovsky, D., & Rovee-Collier, C. (1990). Contextual constraints on memory retrieval at six months. *Child Development, 61,* 1569–1583.

Borstelmann, L. J. (1983). Children before psychology: Ideas about children from antiquity to the late 1800s. In P. H. Mussen (Ed.), *Handbook of child psychology* (4th ed., Vol. 1). New York: Wiley.

Boston Women's Health Book Collective. (1984). *The new our bodies, ourselves.* New York: Simon & Schuster.

Bouchard, T. J., Jr. (1984). Twins reared together and apart: What they tell us about human diversity. In S. W. Fox (Ed.), *Individuality and determinism: Chemical and biological bases* (pp. 147–184). New York: Plenum.

Bouchard, T. J., Jr., & McGue, M. (1981). Familial studies of intelligence: A review. *Science, 212,* 1055–1059.

Boulton, M. J., & Smith, P. K. (1990). Affective bias in children's perceptions of dominance relationships. *Child Development, 61,* 221–229.

Bowlby, J. (1969). *Attachment and loss: Vol. 1. Attachment.* London: Hogarth.

Bowlby, J. (1971). *Child care and the growth of love.* Baltimore, MD: Pelican Books.

Bowlby, J. (1973). *Attachment and loss: Vol. 2. Separation.* London: Hogarth.

Bowlby, J. (1980). *Attachment and loss: Vol. 3. Loss, sadness, and depression.* London: Hogarth.

Bowlby, J. (1982). *Attachment and loss: Vol. 1. Attachment* (2nd ed.). London: Hogarth.

Bowman, M. E., & Ahrons, C. R. (1985). Impact of legal custody status on fathers' parenting post divorce. *Journal of Marriage and the Family, 47,* 481–488.

Boyer, D., & Fine, D. (1992). Sexual abuse as a factor in adolescent pregnancy and child maltreatment. *Family Planning Perspectives, 24,* 4–11.

Bozzi, V. (1985). Body talk. *Psychology Today, 19,* 20.

Braine, L. G., Schauble, L., Kugelmass, S., & Winter, A. (1993). Representation of depth by children: Spatial strategies and lateral biases. *Developmental Psychology, 29,* 466–479.

Brainerd, C. J., & Reyna, V. F., (1995). Learning rate, learning opportunities, and the development of forgetting. *Developmental Psychology, 31,* 251–262.

Branch, C. W., & Newcombe, N. (1986). Racial attitude development among young black children as a function of parental attitudes: A longitudinal and cross-sectional study. *Child Development, 57,* 712–721.

Brand, E., & Clingenpeel, W. G. (1987). Interdependence of marital and stepparent-stepchild relationships and children's psychological adjustments: Research findings and clinical implications. *Family Relations, 36,* 140–145.

Braun, J. (1975, November 23). The struggle for acceptance of a new birth technique. *Parade.*

Braungart, J. M., Plomin, R., DeFries, J. C., & Fulker, D. W. (1992). Genetic influence on tester-rated infant temperament as assessed by Bayley's infant behavior record: Nonadoptive and adoptive siblings and twins. *Developmental Psychology, 28,* 40–47.

Braver, S. L., Wolchik, S. A., Sandler, I. M., Sheets, V. L., Fogas, B., & Bay, R. C. (1992). A longitudinal study of noncustodial parents: Parents without children. *Journal of Family Psychology, 7,* 9–23.

Brazelton, T. B. (1974). *Toddlers and parents.* New York: Delacorte Press.

Brazelton, T. B. (1983). *Infants and mothers.* New York: Delacorte Press.

Brazelton, T. B. (1984). *Neonatal behavior assessment scale.* Philadelphia, PA: Lippincott.

Brazelton, T. B. (1990). Saving the bathwater. *Child Development, 61,* 1661–1671.

Bready, J. W. (1926). *Lord Shaftesbury and social industrial progress.* London: Allen & Unwin.

Breault, K. D., & Kposowa, A. J. (1987). Explaining divorce in the United States: A study of 3,111 counties, 1980. *Journal of Marriage and the Family, 49,* 549–558.

Bredekamp, S. (Ed.). (1987). *Developmentally appropriate practice* (pp. 50, 51). Washington, DC: National Association for the Education of Young Children.

Breen, D. T., & Crosbie-Burnett, M. (1993). Moral dilemmas of early adolescents of divorced and intact families: A qualitative and quantitative analysis. *Journal of Early Adolescence, 13,* 168–182.

Bretherton, I. (1992). The origins of attachment theory. *Developmental Psychology, 28,* 759–775.

Bretherton, I. (1992). The origins of attachment theory: John Bowlby and Mary Ainsworth. *Developmental Psychology, 28,* 759–775.

Bridges, L. H., Connell, J. P., & Belsky, J. (1988). Similarities and differences in infant-mother and infant-father interaction in the strange situation: A composite process analysis. *Developmental Psychology, 24,* 92–100.

Britton, S., Chir, B., Fitzhardinge, P., & Ashby, S. (1981). Is intensive care justified for infants weighing less than 801 grams at birth? *Journal of Pediatrics, 99,* 939–943.

Broberg, A., Lamb, M. E., & Hwang, P. (1990). Inhibition: Its stability and correlates in sixteen- to forty-month-old children. *Child Development, 61,* 1153–1163.

Brock, L. J., & Jennings, G. H. (1993). Sexuality education: What daughters in their thirties wish their mothers had told them. *Family Relations, 42,* 61–65.

Brody, C. J., & Steelman, L. C. (1985, May). Sibling structure and parental sex-typing of children's household tasks. *Journal of Marriage and the Family, 47,* 265–273.

Brody, G. G., & Stoneman, Z. (1983). The influence of television viewing on family interaction. *Journal of Family Issues, 4,* 329–348.

Brody J. (1981, March 10). Sperm count found especially vulnerable to environment. *New York Times,* p. C1.

Brody, L., Zelago, P. R., & Chaike, M. (1984). Habituation-dishabituation to speech in the neonate. *Developmental Psychology, 20,* 114–119.

Brodzinsky, D., Schechter, D., Braff, A., & Singer, L. (1984). Psychological and academic adjustment in adopted children. *Journal of Consulting and Clinical Psychology, 52,* 582–590.

Brone, R. J., & Fisher, C. B. (1988). Determinants of adolescent obesity: A comparison with anorexia nervosa. *Adolescence, 23,* 155–169.

Bronfenbrenner, U. (1977). Toward an experimental ecology of human development. *American Psychologist, 32,* 513–521.

Bronfenbrenner, U. (1979). *The ecology of human development.* Cambridge, MA: Harvard University Press.

Bronfenbrenner, U. (1987, August). *Recent advances in theory and design.* Paper presented at the meeting of the American Psychological Association, New York.

Bronson, G. (1977, March 1). Long exposure to waste anesthetic gas in peril to workers, United States safety unit says. *Wall St. Journal,* p. 10.

Bronson, G. W. (1991). Infant differences in rate of visual encoding. *Child Development, 62,* 44–54.

Brouwers, M. (1988). Depressive thought content among female college students with bulimia. *Journal of Counseling and Development, 66,* 425–428.

Brown, A. L., Bransford, J. D., Ferrara, R. A., & Champione, J. C. (1983). Learning, remembering, and understanding. In P. H. Mussen (Ed.), *Handbook of child psychology* (4th ed., Vol. 3). New York: Wiley.

Brown, J. D., Novick, N. J., Lord, K. A., & Richards, J. M. (1992). When Gulliver travels: Social context, psychological closeness, and self appraisals. *Journal of Personality and Social Psychology, 62,* 717–727.

Brown, J. E., & Mann, L. (1990). The relationship between family structure and process variables and adolescent decision making. *Journal of Adolescence, 13,* 25–38.

Brown, J. E., & Mann, L. (1991). Decision-making competence and self-esteem: A comparison of parents and adolescents. *Journal of Adolescence, 14,* 363–371.

Brown, J. R., & Dunn, J. (1992). Talking with your mother or your sibling. Developmental changes in early family conversations about feelings. *Child Development, 63,* 336–349.

Brown, R. (1975). *First language.* Cambridge, MA: Harvard University Press.

Browne, C. S., & Rife, J. C. (1991). Social, personality, and gender differences in at-risk and not-at-risk sixth-grade students. *Journal of Early Adolescence, 11,* 482–495.

Brownell, C. A. (1990). Peer social skills in toddlers: Competencies and constraints illustrated by same-age and mixed-age interaction. *Child Development, 61,* 838–848.

Brownell, C. A., & Carriger, M. S. (1990). Changes in cooperation and self-other differentiation during the second year. *Child Development, 61,* 1164–1174.

Brownell, K. D. (1982). Obesity: Understanding and treating a serious, prevalent and refractory disorder. *Journal of Consulting and Clinical Psychology, 50,* 820–840.

Bruck, M. (1992). Persistence of dyslexics' phonological awareness deficits. *Developmental Psychology, 28,* 874–888.

Bryant, B. K. (1992). Conflict resolution strategies in relation to children's peer relations. *Journal of Applied Developmental Psychology, 13,* 35–50.

Buchanan, C. M. (1991). Pubertal status in early-adolescent girls: Relations to moods, energy, and restlessness. *Journal of Early Adolescence, 11,* 185–200.

Bugental, D. B., Blue, J., Cortez, V., Fleck, K., & Rodrigues, A. (1992). Influences of witnessed affect on information processing in children. *Child Development, 63,* 774–786.

Buhler, C. (1935). The curve of life as studied in biographies. *Journal of Applied Psychology, 19,* 405–409.

Buhler, C., & Massarik, F. (1968). *The course of human life: A study of goals in the humanistic perspective.* New York: Springer.

Buhrmester, D. (1990). Intimacy of friendships, interpersonal competence, and adjustment during preadolescence and adolescence. *Child Development, 61,* 1101–1111.

Buhrmester, D., & Furman, W. (1987). The development of companionship and intimacy. *Child Development, 58,* 1101–1113.

Buhrmester, D., & Furman, W. (1990). Perceptions of sibling relationships during middle childhood and adolescence. *Child Development, 61,* 1387–1398.

Bukowski, W. M., Gauze, C., Hoza, B., & Newcomb. A. F. (1993). Differences and consistency between same-sex and other-sex peer relationships during early adolescence. *Developmental Psychology, 29,* 255–263.

Bullock, J. R. (1993). Children's loneliness and their relationships with family and peers. *Family Relations, 42,* 46–49.

Bullock, M. (1985). Animism in childhood thinking: A new look at an old question. *Developmental Psychology, 21,* 217–225.

Bullough, V. L. (1981). Age at menarche: A misunderstanding. *Science, 213,* 365–366.

Burden, D. S. (1986). Single parents and the work setting: The impact of multiple job and homelife responsibilities. *Family Relations, 35,* 37–43.

Burleson, B. R., Della, J. G., & Applegate, J. L. (1992). Effects of maternal communication and children's social-cognitive and communication skills on children's acceptance by the peer group. *Family Relations, 41,* 264–272.

Burr, W. R., & Christensen, C. (1992). Undesirable side effects of enhancing self-esteem. *Family Relations, 41,* 460–464.

Bus, A. B., & van Ijzendoorn, M. H. (1988). Mother-child interaction, attachment, and emergent literacy: A cross-sectional study. *Child Development, 59,* 1262–1272.

Bushnell, E. W., McKenzie, B. E., Lawrence, D. A., & Connell, S. (1995). The special coding strategies of 1-year-old infants in a locomotor search task. *Child Development, 66,* 937–958.

Bushnell, H. (1888). *Christian nurture.* New Haven, CT: Yale University Press.

Buss, A. H., & Perry, M. (1992). The aggression questionnaire. *Journal of Personality and Social Psychology, 63,* 452–459.

Buss, A. H., & Plomin, R. (1984). *Temperament: Early developing personality traits.* Hillsdale, NJ: Erlbaum.

Bussey, K. (1992). Lying and truthfulness: Children's definitions, standards, and evaluative reactions. *Child Development, 63,* 129–137.

Butcher, J. (1986). Longitudinal analysis of adolescent girls' aspirations at school and perceptions of popularity. *Adolescence, 21,* 133–143.

Butler, R. N. (1990). The effects of mastery and competitive conditions on self-assessment at different ages. *Child Development, 61,* 201–210.

Cadkin, A., Ginsberg, N., Pergament, E., & Verlinski, Y. (1984). Chorionic villi sampling: A new technique for detection of genetic abnormalities in the first trimester. *Radiology, 151,* 159–162.

Cadman, D., Gafni, A., & McNamee, J. (1984). Newborn circumcision: An economic perspective. *Canadian Medical Association Journal, 131,* 1353–1355.

Caggiula, A. R., & Hoebel, B. G. (1966). Copulation-record site in the posterior hypothalamus. *Science, 153,* 1284–1285.

Cahan, E. D. (1992). John Dewey and Human Development. *Developmental Psychology, 28,* 205–214.

Cairns, R. B., Cairns, B. D., & Neckerman, H. J. (1989). Early school dropout: Configuration and determinants. *Child Development, 60,* 1436–1452.

Calabrese, L. H., Kirkendall, D. T., Floyd, M. et al. (1983). Menstrual abnormalities, nutritional patterns and body composition in female classic ballet dancers. *Physicians' Sports Medicine, 11,* 86.

Calderone, M. S. (1983). Fetal erection and its message to us. *SIECUS Report, II*(5/6), 9–16.

Calkins, S. D., & Fox, N. A. (1992). The relations among infant temperament, security of attachment, and behavioral inhibition at twenty-four months. *Child Development, 63,* 1456–1472.

Calvert, S. L., & Cocking, R. R. (1992). Health promotion through mass media. *Journal of Applied Developmental Psychology, 13,* 143–149.

Camasso, M. J., & Roche, S. E. (1991). The willingness to change to formalized child care arrangements: Parental considerations of cost and quality. *Journal of Marriage and the Family, 53,* 1071–1082.

Campbell, F. A., Breitmayer, B., & Ramey, C. T. (1986). Disadvantaged single teenage mothers and their children: Consequences of free educational day care. *Family Relations, 35,* 63–68.

Campbell, F. A., & Ramey, C. P. (1994). Effects of early intervention on intellectual and academic achievement: A follow-up study of children from low-income families. *Child Development, 65,* 684–698.

Campbell, M. L., & Moen, P. (1992). Job-family role strain among employed, single mothers of preschoolers. *Family relations, 41,* 205–211.

Campos, J., Barrett, K. C., Lamb, M. E., Goldsmith, H., & Stenberg, C. (1983). Socioemotional development. In P. H. Mussen, M. M. Haith, & J. J. Campos (Eds.), *Handbook of child psychology:* Vol. 2. *Infancy and developmental psychobiology.* New York: Wiley.

Capelli, C. A., Nakagawa, N., & Madden, C. M. (1990). How children understand sarcasm: The role of context and intonation. *Child Development, 61,* 1824–1841.

Caplan, F. (1973). *The first twelve months of life.* New York: Grosset & Dunlap.

Caplan, M., Vespo, J., Pedersen, J., & Hay, D. F. (1991). Conflict and its resolution in small groups of one- and two-year-olds. *Child Development, 62,* 1513–1524.

Capuzzi, D., & Lecoq, L. L. (1983, December). Social and personal determinants of adolescent use and abuse of alcohol and marijuana. *Personnel and Guidance Journal, 62,* 199–205.

Cardon, L. R., Fulker, D. W., DeFries, J. C., & Plomin, R. (1992). Continuity and change in general cognitive ability from 1 to 7 years of age. *Developmental Psychology, 28,* 64–73.

Carey, S. (1977). The child as word learner. In M. Halle, J. Bresman, & G. A. Miller (Eds.), *Linguistic theory and psychological reality.* Cambridge, MA: MIT Press.

Carlo, G., Eisenberg, N., & Knight, G. P. (1992). An objective measure of adolescents' prosocial moral reasoning. *Journal of Research on Adolescence, 2,* 331–349.

Carlson, J. S. (1973). *Cross-cultural Piagetian studies: What can they tell us?* Paper presented at the biennial meeting of the International Society for the Study of Behavioral Development, Ann Arbor, MI.

Carmines, E. G., & Baxter, D. J. (1986). Race, intelligence, and political efficacy among school children. *Adolescence, 22,* 437–442.

Carroll, C., & Miller, D. (1982). *Health: The science of human adaptation* (3rd ed.). Dubuque, IA: Wm. C. Brown.

Carruth, B. R., & Goldberg, D. L. (1990). Nutritional issues of adolescents: Athletics and the body image mania. *Journal of Early Adolescence, 10,* 122–140.

Caruso, G-A. L. (1992). Patterns of maternal employment and child care for a sample of two-year-olds. *Journal of Family Issues, 13,* 297–311.

Casas, J. M., & Ponterotto, J. G. (1984, February). Profiling an invisible minority in higher education: The Chicano. *Personnel and Guidance Journal, 62,* 349–353.

Casey, R. (1993). Children's emotional experience: Relations among expression, self-report, and understanding. *Developmental Psychology, 29,* 119–129.

Cash, T. F., & Janda, L. H. (1984, December). The eye of the beholder. *Psychology Today, 18,* 46–52.

Caspi, A., Henry, B., McGee, R. O., Moffitt, T. E., & Silva, P. N. (1995). Temperamental origins of child and adolescent behavior problems: From age three to age fifteen. *Child Development, 66,* 55–68.

Caspi, A., Lynam, D., Moffitt, T. E., & Silva, P. A. (1993). Unraveling girls' delinquency: Biological, dispositional, and contextual contributions to adolescent misbehavior. *Developmental Psychology, 29,* 19–30.

Cassidy, J. (1986). The ability to negotiate the environment: An aspect of infant competence as related to quality of attachment. *Child Development, 57,* 331–337.

Cassidy, J., & Asher, S. R. (1992). Loneliness and peer relations in young children. *Child Development, 63,* 350–365.

Cassidy, J., Parke, R. D., Butkovsky, L., & Braungart, J. M. (1992). Family-peer connections: The roles of emotional expressiveness within the family and children's understanding of emotions. *Child Development, 63,* 603–618.

Casto, G., & Mastropieri, M. A. (1986). The efficacy of early intervention programs: A meta-analysis. *Exceptional Children, 52,* 417–424.

Cates, W., Jr., & Stone, K. M. (March/April 1992a). Family planning, sexually transmitted diseases and contraceptive choice: A literature update—Part I. *Family Planning Perspectives, 24,* 75–84.

Cates, W., Jr., & Stone, K. M. (May/June 1992b). Family planning, sexually transmitted diseases and contraceptive choice: A literature update—Part II. *Family Planning Perspectives, 24,* 122–128.

Catherwood, D. (1993). The robustness of infant haptic memory: Testing its capacity to withstand delay and haptic interference. *Child Development, 64,* 702–710.

Cattell, R. B. (1963). Theory of fluid and crystallized intelligence: A critical experiment. *Journal of Educational Psychology, 54,* 1–22.

Center for Science in the Public Interest. (1990). *CSPI's fast food eating guide.* Washington, DC: CSPI.

Cernoch, J. M., & Porter, R. H. (1985). Recognition of maternal axillary odors by infants. *Child Development, 56,* 1593–1598.

Chance, P. (1988). Testing education. *Psychology Today, 22,* 20–21.

Chance, P. (1989). Kids without friends. *Psychology Today, 23,* 29–31.

Charlesworth, W. R. (1992). Darwin and developmental psychology: Past and present. *Developmental Psychology, 28,* 5–16.

Chase-Lansdale, P. L., & Owen, M. T. (1987). Maternal employment in a family context: Effects on infant-mother and infant-father attachments. *Child Development, 58,* 1505–1512.

Chasnoff, I. J., Burns, W. J., Schnoll, S. H., & Burns, K. A. (1985). Cocaine use in pregnancy. *New England Journal of Medicine, 313,* 666–669.

Chassin, L. C., & Young, R. D. (1981, Fall). Salient self-conceptions in normal and deviant adolescents. *Adolescence, 16,* 613–620.

Cheal, D. (1993). Unity and difference in postmodern families. *Journal of Family Issues, 14,* 5–19.

Chen, X., Rubin, K. H., & Sun, Y. (1992). Social reputation and peer relationships in Chinese and Canadian children: A cross cultural study. *Child Development, 63,* 1336–1343.

Cherlin, A., & Furstenberg, F. F., Jr. (1986). *The new American grandparent.* New York: Basic Books.

Chess, S., & Thomas, A. (1986). *Temperament in clinical practice.* New York: Guilford.

Chess, T. A. (1984). The genesis and evolution of behavioral disorders: From infancy to early adult life. *American Journal of Psychiatry, 141,* 1.

Chiam, H. (1987). Changes in self-concept during adolescence. *Adolescence, 16,* 613–620.

Childers, J. S., Durham, R. W., Bolen, L. M., & Taylor, L. H. (1985). A predictive validity study of the Kaufman Assessment Battery for children taking the California Achievement Test. *Psychology in the Schools, 22,* 29–33.

Children's Defense Fund (1988). *A children's defense budget.* Washington, DC: Children's Defense Fund.

Chilman, C. S. (1990). Promoting healthy adolescent sexuality. *Family Relations, 39,* 123–131.

Chilman, C. S. (1991). Working poor families: Trends, causes, effects, & suggested policies. *Family Relations, 40,* 191–198.

Chipuer, H. M., Plomin, R., Persensen, N. L., McClearn, G. E., & Nesselroade, J. R. (1993). Genetic influence on family environment: The role of personality. *Developmental Psychology, 29,* 110–118.

Chira, S. (1984, February 11). Town experiment cuts TV. *New York Times.*

Chiu, L. H. (1987). Development of the Self-esteem Rating Scale for Children (revised). *Measurement and Evaluation in Counseling and Development, 20,* 36–41.

Chiu, L. H. (1988). Measures of self-esteem of school-age children. *Journal of Counseling and Development, 66,* 298–301.

Chiu, L. H. (1990). The relationship of career goal and self-esteem among adolescents. *Adolescence, 25,* 593–598.

Chollar, S. (1988a, April). Food for thought. *Psychology Today, 22,* 30–34.

Chollar, S. (1988b, December). Stuttering: The parental influence. *Psychology Today, 22,* 12–16.

Chomsky, N. (1968). *Language and mind.* New York: Harcourt, Brace, World.

Chomsky, N. (1980). *Rules and representations.* New York: Columbia University Press.

Christmon, K. (1990). Parental responsibility of African-American unwed adolescent fathers. *Adolescence, 25,* 645–654.

Christopher, F. S. (1988). An initial investigation into a continuum of premartial sexual pressure. *Journal of Sex Research, 25,* 255–266.

Christopher, F. S., Fabes, R. A., & Wilson, P. M. (1989). Family television viewing and implications for family life education. *Family Relations, 38,* 210–214.

Christopher, F. S., & Roosa, M. W. (1990). An evaluation of an adolescent pregnancy prevention program: Is "Just say no" enough? *Family Relations, 39,* 73–80.

Chugani, H. T., & Phelps, M. E. (1986). Maturational changes in cerebral function in infants determined by FFG positron emission tomography. *Science, 231,* 840–843.

Cillessen, A. H. N., van Izendoorn, H. W., van Lieshout, C. F. M., & Hartup, W. W. (1992). Heterogeneity among peer-rejected boys: Subtypes and stabilities. *Child Development, 63,* 893–905.

Circirelli, V. G. (1980). A comparison of college women's feelings toward their siblings and parents. *Journal of Marriage and the Family, 78,* 111–118.

Claes, M. E. (1992). Friendship and personal adjustment during adolescence. *Journal of Adolescence, 15,* 39–55.

Clark, A. J. (1991). The identification and modification of defense mechanisms in counseling. *Journal of Counseling and Development, 69,* 231–235.

Clark, E. V. (1983). Meaning and concepts. In P. H. Mussen (Ed.), *Handbook of child psychology* (4th ed., Vol. 4). New York: Wiley.

Clark, E. V., Gelman, S. A., & Lane, N. M. (1985). Compound nouns and category structure in young children. *Child Development, 56,* 84–94.

Clark, M. L., & Ayers, M. (1993). Friendship expectations and friendship evaluations. Reciprocity and gender effects. *Youth and Society, 24,* 299–313.

Clark, M. L., Cheyne, J. A., Cunningham, C. E., & Siegel, L. S. (1988). *Journal of Abnormal Child Psychology, 16,* 1–15.

Clark-Lempers, D. S., Lempers, J. D., & Ho, C. (1991). Early, middle, and late adolescents' perceptions of their relationships with significant others. *Journal of Adolescent Research, 6,* 296–315.

Claxton-Oldfield, S. (1992). Perceptions of stepfathers. *Journal of Family Issues, 13,* 378–389.

Clingenpeel, W. G., Colyar, J. Y., Brand, E., & Hetherington, E. M. (1992). Children's relationships with maternal grandparents: A longitudinal study of family structure and pubertal status effects. *Child Development, 63,* 1404–1422.

Cloutier, R., & Goldschmid, M. L. (1976, December). Individual differences in the development of formal reasoning. *Child Development, 47,* 1097–1102.

Coates, D. L., & Lewis, M. (1984). Early mother-infant interaction and infant cognitive status as predictors of school performance and cognitive behavior in six-year-olds. *Child Development, 55,* 1219–1230.

Coffman, S., Levitt, M. J., Deets, C., & Quigley, K. L. (1991). Close relationships in mothers of distressed and normal newborns: Support, expectancy, confirmation, and maternal well-being. *Journal of Family Psychology, 5,* 93–107.

Coie, J. D., & Dodge, K. A. (1988). Multiple sources of data on social behavior and social status in the school: A cross-age comparison. *Child Development, 59,* 815–829.

Coie, J. D., & Dodge, K. A., Terry, R., & Wright, B. (1991). The role of aggression in peer relations: An analysis of aggression episodes in boys' playgroups. *Child Development, 62,* 812–826.

Cok, F. (1990). Body image satisfaction in Turkish adolescents. *Adolescence, 25,* 409–414.

Cole, P. M., Barrett, K. C., & Zahn-Waxler, C. (1992). Emotion displays in two-year-olds during mishaps. *Child Development, 63,* 314–324.

Cole, P. M., Zahn-Waxler, C., & Smith, K. D., (1994). Expressive control during a disappointment: Variations related to preschoolers' behavior problems. *Developmental Psychology, 30,* 835–846.

Coleman, M., & Ganong, L. H. (1990). Remarriage and step-family research in the 1980s: Increased interest in an old family form. *Journal of Marriage and the Family, 52,* 925–940.

Coleman, M., Ganong, L. H., Clark, J. M., & Madsen, R. (1989). Parenting perceptions in rural and urban families. *Journal of Marriage and the Family, 51,* 329–335.

Coll, C. T. G. (1990). Developmental outcome of minority infants: A process-oriented look into our beginnings. *Child Development, 61,* 270–289.

Colletta, N. D. (1985). Stressful lives: The situation of divorced mothers and their children. *Journal of Divorce, 6,* 19–31.

Collins, J. A., Wrixon, W., Janes, L. B., & Wilson, E. H. (1983). Treatment-independent pregnancy among infertile couples. *New England Journal of Medicine, 309,* 1201–1209.

Collins, J. D., & Propert, D. S. (1983, Winter). A developmental study of body recognition in adolescent girls. *Adolescence, 18,* 767–774.

Colombo, J. Mitchell, D. W., Coldren, J. T., & Freeseman, L. J. (1991). Individual differences in infant visual attention: Are short lookers faster processors or feature processors? *Child Development, 62,* 1247–1257.

Commons, M. L., Richards, F. A., & Kuhn, D. (1982). Systematic and metasystematic reasoning: A case for level of reasoning beyond Piaget's stage of formal operations. *Child Development, 53,* 1058–1069.

Connors, C. K. (1980). *Food additives and hyperactive children.* New York: Plenum.

Conway, J. (1978). *Men in mid-life crisis.* Elgin, IL: David C. Cook.

Cook, K. V., Reiley, K. L., Stallsmith, R., & Garretson, H. B. (1991). Eating concerns on two Christian and two nonsectarian college campuses: A measure of sex and campus differences in attitudes toward eating. *Adolescence, 26,* 273–286.

Cook, T. D., Appleton, H., Conner, R. F., Shaffer, A., Tamkin, G., & Weber, S. J. (1975). *Sesame Street revisited.* New York: Russell Sage Foundation.

Cooke, R. A. (1982). The ethics and regulation of research involving children. In B. B. Wolman (Ed.), *Handbook of developmental psychology.* Englewood Cliffs, NJ: Prentice-Hall.

Coombs, R. H., & Landsverk, J. (1988). Parenting styles and substance use during childhood and adolescence. *Journal of Marriage and the Family, 50,* 473–482.

Cooper, J. E., Holman, J., & Braithwaite, V. A. (1983, February). Self-esteem and family cohesion: The child's perspective and adjustment, *Journal of Marriage and the Family, 45,* 153–159.

Cooper, R. P., & Aslin, R. N. (1990). Preference for infant-directed

speech in the first month after birth. *Child Development, 61,* 1584–1595.
Cooper, R. P., & Aslin, R. N. (1994). Developmental differences in infant attention to the spectral properties of infant-directed speech. *Child Development, 65,* 1663–1677.
Coopersmith, S. (1981). *Self-esteem inventories.* Palo Alto, CA: Consulting Psychologists Press.
Coopersmith, S., & Gilberts, R. (1982). *BASE: Behavioral Academic Self-Esteem.* Palo Alto, CA: Consulting Psychologists Press.
Coren, S., & Halpern, D. F. (1991). Left-handedness: A marker for decreased survival fitness. *Psychological Bulletin, 109,* 90–106.
Corrigan, R. L. (1983). The development of representational skills. In K. W. Fischer (Ed.), *Levels and transitions of childhood development. New directions for child development* (No. 21). San Francisco, CA: Jossey-Bass.
Corter, C. M. (1976, September). The nature of the mother's absence and the infant's response to brief separations. *Developmental Psychology, 12,* 428–434.
Cotterell, J. L. (1992). The relation of attachments and supports to adolescent well-being and school adjustment. *Journal of Adolescent Research, 7,* 28–42.
The court edges away from Roe v. Wade. (1989). *Family Planning Perspectives, 21,* 184–187.
Coverman, S., & Sheley, J. F. (1986). Change in men's housework and child-care time, 1965–1975. *Journal of Marriage and the Family, 48,* 413–422.
Covington, J. (1982, August). Adolescent deviation and age. *Journal of Youth and Adolescence, 11,* 329–344.
Cowan, M., Hellman, D., Chudwin, D., Wara, D., Chang, R., & Ammann, A. (1984). Maternal transmission of acquired immune deficiency syndrome. *Pediatrics, 73,* 382–386.
Cox, M. J., Owen, M. T., Henderson, V. K., & Margand, N. A. (1992). Prediction of infant-father and infant-mother attachment. *Developmental Psychology, 28,* 474–483.
Coysh, W. S., Johnston, J. R., Tschann, J. M., Wallerstein, J. S., & Kline, M. (1989). Parental postdivorce adjustment in joint and sole physical custody families. *Journal of Family Issues, 10,* 52–71.
Crain-Thoreson, C., & Dale, P. S. (1992). Do early talkers become early readers? Linguistic precocity, preschool language, and emergent literacy. *Developmental Psychology, 28,* 421–439.
Creighton, L. L. (1990, October 8). The new orphanages: *U.S. News and World Report,* 37–41.
Crick, N. R., & Grotpeter, J. K. (1995). Relational aggression, gender, and social-psychological adjustment. *Child Development, 66,* 710–722.
Crick, N. R., & Ladd, G. W. (1993). Children's perceptions of their peer experiences: Attributions, loneliness, social anxiety, and social avoidance. *Developmental Psychology, 29,* 244–254.
Crnic, K. A., & Greenberg, M. T. (1990). Minor parenting stresses with young children. *Child Development, 61,* 1628–1637.
Croft, C. A., & Asmussen, L. (1992). Perception of mothers, youth, and educators: A path towards detente regarding sexuality education. *Family Relations, 41,* 452–459.
Crow, L. D., & Crow, H. (1965). *Adolescent development and adjustment* (2nd ed.). New York: McGraw-Hill.
Crum, C., & Ellner, P. (1985). Chlamydial infections: Making the diagnosis. *Contemporary Obstetrics and Gynecology, 25,* 153–159, 163, 165, 168.
Culp, R. E., Culp, A. M., Osofsky, J. D., & Osofsky, H. J. (1991). Adolescent and older mothers' interaction patterns with their six-month-old infants. *Journal of Adolescence, 14,* 195–200.
Cummings, E. M. (1987). Coping with background anger in early childhood. *Child Development, 58,* 976–984.
Cummings, E. M., Iannotti, R. J., & Zahn-Waxler, C. (1989). Aggression between peers in early childhood: Individual continuity and developmental change. *Child Development, 60,* 887–895.
Cummins, J. (1986). Empowering minority students: A framework for intervention. *Harvard Educational Review, 56,* 18–36.
Cummins, J., & Swain, M. (1986). *Bilingualism in education: Aspects of theory, research, and practice.* London: Taylor & Fry.
Cunliffe, T. (1992). Arresting youth crime: A review of social skills training with young offenders. *Adolescence, 27,* 891–900.
Curtis, S. (1977). *Genie: A psychological study of a modern-day "wild child."* New York: Academic Press.
Cushner, I. M. (1986). Reproductive technologies: New choices, new hopes, new dilemmas. *Family Planning Perspectives, 18,* 129–132.
Dainton, M. (1993). The myth and misconceptions of the stepmother identity. Descriptions and prescriptions for identity management. *Family Relations, 42,* 93–98.
Dalterio, S. L. (1984, November). Marijuana and the unborn. *Listen,* pp. 8–11.
Damon, W. (1983). *Social and personality development.* New York: W. W. Norton.
Daniels, J. A. (1990). Adolescent separation-individuation and family transitions. *Adolescence, 25,* 105–116.
Daniels, D., & Moos, R. H. (1990). Assessing life stressors and social resources among adolescents: Applications to depressed youth. *Journal of Adolescent Research, 5,* 268–289.
Daniluk, J. C. (1991). Strategies for counseling infertile couples. *Journal of Counseling and Development, 69,* 317–320.
Darling-Fisher, C. S., & Tiedje, L. B. (1990). The impact of maternal employment characteristics on fathers' participation in child care. *Family Relations, 39,* 20–26.
Darmody, J. P. (1991). The adolescent personality, formal reasoning, and values. *Adolescence, 26,* 731–742.
Darwin, C. A. (1877). A biographical sketch of an infant. *Mind, 2,* 285–294.
Darwin, C. A. (1936). *The origin of species.* New York: Modern Library. (Original work published in 1859.)
Davis, B. (1986, April 25). Survival odds are improving for even smallest "preemies." *Wall Street Journal,* p. 19.
Davis, M., & Emory, E. (1995). Sex differences in neonatal stress reactivity. *Child Development, 66,* 14–27.
Dawkins, R. L., & Dawkins, M. P. (1983, Winter). Alcohol use and delinquency among black, white, and Hispanic adolescent offenders. *Adolescence, 18,* 799–809.
Dawson, D. A. (1991). Family structure and childrens' health and well-being: Data from the 1988 National Health Interview Survey on child health. *Journal of Marriage and the Family, 53,* 573–584.
Deal, J. E., Halverson, C. F., & Wampler, K. S. (1989). Parental agreement on child-rearing orientations: Relations to parental, marital, family, and child characteristics. *Child Development, 60,* 1025–1034.
Debolt, M. E., Pasley, B. K., & Kreutzer, J. (1990). Factors affecting the probability of school dropout: A study of pregnant and parenting adolescent females. *Journal of Adolescent Research, 5,* 190–205.
Deci, E. L. (1985, March). The well-tempered classroom. *Psychology Today, 19,* 52–53.
Deković, M., & Gerris, J. R. M. (1992). Parental reasoning complexity, social class, and child-rearing behaviors. *Journal of Marriage and the Family, 54,* 675–685.
Deković, M., & Gerris, J. R. M. (1994). Developmental analysis of social cognitive and behavioral differences between popular and rejected children. *Journal of Applied Developmental Psychology, 15,* 367–386.
Deković, M., & Janssens, J. M. A. M. (1992). Parents' child-rearing style and child's sociometric status. *Developmental Psychology, 28,* 925–932.
Dellas, M., & Jernigan, L. P. (1990). Affective personality characteristics associated with undergraduate ego identity formation. *Journal of Adolescent Research, 5,* 306–324.
DeLoache, J. S. (1991). Symbolic functioning in very young children: Understanding of pictures and models. *Child Development, 62,* 736–752.
DeMarie-Dreblow, D. (1991). Relation between knowledge and memory: A reminder that correlation does not imply causality. *Child Development, 62,* 484–498.
DeMarie-Dreblow, D., & Miller, P. H. (1988). The development of children's strategies for selective attention: Evidence for a transitional period. *Child Development, 59,* 1504–1513.
Dembo, R., Dertke, M., LaVoie, L., Borders, S., Washburn, M., & Schmeidler, J. (1987). Physical abuse, sexual victimization and illicit drug use: A structural analysis among high risk adolescents. *Journal of Adolescence, 10,* 13–33.
Demo, D. H. (1992). Parent-child relations: Assessing recent changes. *Journal of Marriage and the Family, 54,* 104–117.
Demo, D. H., & Acock, A. C. (1988). The impact of divorce on children. *Journal of Marriage and the Family, 50,* 619–648.
Demo, D. H., Small, S. A., & Savin-Williams, R. C. (1987). Family relations and the self-esteem of adolescents and their parents. *Journal of Marriage and the Family, 49,* 705–715.

Dempster, F. N. (1981). Memory span: Sources of individual and developmental differences. *Psychological Bulletin, 80,* 63–100.
Denham, S. A., & Holt, R. W. (1993). Preschoolers likeability as cause or consequence of their social behavior. *Developmental Psychology, 29,* 271–275.
Denham, S. A., McKinley, M., Couehoud, E. Z., & Holt, R. (1990). Emotional and behavioral predictors of preschool peer ratings. *Child Development, 61,* 1145–1152.
Denham, S. A., Renwick, S. M., & Holt, R. W. (1991). Working and playing together: Prediction of preschool social-emotional competence from mother-child interaction. *Child Development, 62,* 242–249.
Denham, T. E., & Smith, C. W. (1989). The influence of grandparents and grandchildren: A review of the literature and resources. *Family Relations, 38,* 345–350.
Denno, D. (1982, Winter). Sex differences in cognition: A review and critique of the longitudinal evidence. *Adolescence, 17,* 779–788.
Depner, C. E., & Bray, J. H., (1990). Modes of participation for non-custodial parents: The challenge for research, policy, practice and education. *Family Relations, 39,* 379–381.
deRosenroll, D. A. (1987). Creativity and self-trust: A field of study. *Adolescence, 22,* 419–432.
DeRosier, M. E., Cillessen, A. H. M., Coie, J. D., & Dodge, K. A. (1994). Group social context in children's aggressive behavior. *Child Development, 65,* 1068–1079.
DeRosier, M. E., Kupersmidt, J. B., & Patterson, C. J. (1994). Children's academics and behavioral adjustment as a function of the chronicity and proximity of peer rejection. *Child Development, 65,* 1799–1813.
deTurck, M. A., & Miller, G. R. (1983). Adolescent perceptions of parental persuasive message strategies. *Journal of Marriage and the Family, 34,* 533–542.
DiBlasio, F. A., & Benda, B. B. (1990). Adolescent sexual behavior: Multivariate analysis of a social learning model. *Journal of Adolescent Research, 5,* 449–466.
Dick-Read, G. D. (1973). *Childbirth without fear.* New York: Harper & Row.
Dickstein, S., & Parke, R. D. (1988). Social referencing in infancy: A glance at fathers and marriage. *Child Development, 59,* 506–511.
Dietz, W. H., & Gortmacher, S. L. (1985). Do we fatten our children at the television set? Obesity and television watching in children and adolescents. *Pediatrics, 75,* 807–812.
Dill, D., Feld, E., Martin, J., Beukema, S., & Belle, D. (1980). The impact of the environment on the coping effects of low-income mothers. *Family Relations, 29,* 503–509.
DiPietro, J. A., & Allen, M. C. (1991). Estimation of gestational age: Implications for developmental research. *Child Development, 62,* 1200–1208.
DiPietro, J. A., Porges, S. W., & Uhly, B. (1992). Reactivity and developmental competence in preterm and full-term infants. *Developmental Psychology, 28,* 831–841.
DiPetro, J. B. (1981). Rough and tumble play: A function of gender. *Developmental Psychology, 17,* 50–58.
Dishion, T. J. (1990). The family ecology of boys' peer relations in middle childhood. *Child Development, 61,* 874–892.
Dizon, J. A., & Moore, C. F. (1990). The development of perspective taking: Understanding differences in information and weighting. *Child Development, 61,* 1502–1513.
Dr. Nintendo. (1990, May 28). *Time, 135,* 72.
Dodge, K. A., Cole, J. D., Pettit, G. S., & Price, J. M. (1990). Peer status and aggression in boys' groups: Developmental and contextual analyses. *Child Development, 61,* 1289–1309.
Dodge, K. A., Pettit, G. S., & Bates, J. E. (1994). Socialization mediators or the relation between socioeconomic status and child conduct problems. *Child Development, 65,* 649–665.
Dodge, K. A., & Price, J. M. (1994). On the relation between social information processing and socially competent behavior in early school-aged children. *Child Development, 65,* 1385–1397.
Dodge, K. A., & Somberg, D. R. (1987). Hostile attributional biases among aggressive boys are exacerbated under conditions of threats to self. *Child Development, 58,* 215–224.
D'Odorico, L., & Franco, F. (1985). The determinants of baby talk: Relationships and context. *Journal of Child Language, 12,* 567–586.
Dodwell, P., Humphrey, G. K., & Muir, D. (1987). Shape and pattern perception. In P. Salapatek & L. Cohen (Eds.). *Handbook of Infant Perception.* New York: Academic Press.
Doherty, W. J., & Needle, R. H. (1991). Psychological adjustment and substance use among adolescents before and after a parental divorce. *Child Development, 62,* 328–337.
Dolan, L. J., et al. (1993). The short-term impact of two classroom-based preventive interventions on aggressive and shy behavior and poor achievement. *Journal of Applied Developmental Psychology, 14,* 317–345.
Dolgin, K. B., & Behrend, D. A. (1984). Children's knowledge about animates and inanimates. *Child Development, 55,* 1646–1650.
Donnely, B. W., & Voydanoff, P. (1991). Factors associated with releasing for adoption among adolescent mothers. *Family Relations, 39,* 311–316.
Donnelly, D., & Finkelhor, D. (1992). Does equality and custody arrangements improve the parent-child relationship? *Journal of Marriage and the Family, 54,* 837–845.
Donnelly, D., & Finkelhor, D. (1993). Who has joint custody? Class differences in the determination of custody arrangements. *Family Relations, 42,* 57–60.
Donovan, P. (1994). Experimental prenatal care program reduced preterm deliveries by 20%, saves $1,800 per high-risk woman. *Family Planning Perspectives, 26,* 280–281.
Donovan, W. L., & Leavitt, L. A. (1989). Maternal self-efficacy and infant attachment: Integrating physiology, perceptions, and behavior. *Child Development, 60,* 460–472.
Donovan, W. L., Leavitt, L. A., & Walsh, R. O. (1990). Maternal self-efficacy: Illusory control and its effect on susceptibility to learned helplessness. *Child Development, 61,* 1638–1647.
Dornbusch, S. M., Ritter, P. L., Mont-Reynaud, R., & Chen, Z. (1990). Family decision making and academic performance in a diverse high school population. *Journal of Adolescent Research, 5,* 143–160.
Dornbusch, S. M., Carlsmith, J. M., Bushwall, S. J., Ritter, P. L., Leidman, H., Historff, A. H., & Gross, R. T. (1985). Single parents, extended households, and the control of adolescents. *Child Development, 56,* 326–341.
Dorr, A. (1986). *Television and children.* Beverly Hills, CA: Sage.
Dorsch, A., & Keane, S. B. (1994). Contextual factors in children's social information processing. *Developmental Psychology, 30,* 611–616.
Dorval, B., & Eckerman, C. O. (1984). Developmental trends in the quality of conversation achieved by small groups of acquainted peers. *Monographs of the Society for Research in Child Development, 49*(2, Serial No. 206).
Downey, D. B., & Powell, B. (1993). Do children in single-parent households fare better living with the same-sex parents? *Journal of Marriage and the Family, 55,* 55–71.
Downs, W. W., & Rose, S. R. (1991). The relationship of adolescent peer groups to the incidence of psychosocial problems. *Adolescence, 26,* 473–492.
Doyle, A. B., Doehring, P., Tessier, O., deLorimier, S., & Shapiro, S. (1992). Transitions in children's play: A sequential analysis of states preceding and following social pretense. *Developmental Psychology, 28,* 137–144.
Dozier, M. (1991). Functional measurement assessment of young children's ability to predict future behavior. *Child Development, 62,* 1091–1099.
Drug pushers go for even younger prey. (1979, August 13). *U.S. News and World Report,* p. 31.
Dubey, D. R., O'Leary, S. G., & Kaufman, K. F. (1983). Training parents of hyperactive children in child management: A comparative outcome study. *Journal of Abnormal Child Psychology, 11,* 229–246.
DuBois, D. L., & Hirsch, B. J. (1990). School and neighborhood friendship patterns of blacks and whites in early adolescence. *Child Development, 61,* 524–536.
Dubois, D. L., & Hirsch, B. J. (1993). School/nonschool friendship patterns in early adolescence. *Journal of Adolescence, 13,* 102–122.
Dubow, E. F., Huesmann, L. R., & Eron, L. D. (1987). Childhood correlates of adult ego development. *Child Development, 58,* 859–869.
Duffy, F. H., Als, H., & McAnulty, G. B. (1990). Behavioral and electrophysiological evidence for gestational age effects in healthy preterm and full-term infants; studies two weeks after expected due date. *Child Development, 61,* 1271–1286.
Duncan, G. J., & Rodgers, W. (1987). Single-parent families: Are their economic problems transitory or persistent? *Family Planning Perspectives, 19,* 171–178.
Dunham, C. C., & Bengston, V. L. (1992). The long-term effects of polit-

ical activism on intergenerational relations. *Youth and Society, 24,* 31–51.

Dunham, P., Dunham, F., Hurshman, A., & Alexander, T. (1989). Social contingency effects on subsequent perceptual-cognitive tasks in young infants. *Child Development, 60,* 1486–1696.

Dunham, R. G., & Alpert, G. P. (1987). Keeping juvenile delinquents in school: A prediction model. *Adolescence, 23,* 45–57.

Dunn, J. (1977). *Distress and comfort.* Cambridge, MA: Harvard University Press.

Dunn, J., Brown, J. R., & Maguire, M. (1995). The development of children's moral sensibility: Individual differences and emotion understanding. *Developmental Psychology, 4,* 649–659.

Dunn, J., Brown, J., Slomkowski, C., Desla, C., & Youngblade, L. (1991). Young children's understanding of other peoples feelings and beliefs: Individual differences and their antecedents. *Child Development, 62,* 1352–1366.

Dunn, P. C., Ryan, I. J., & O'Brien, K. (1988). College students' acceptance of adoption and five alternative fertilization techniques. *Journal of Sex Research, 24,* 282–287.

Durkheim, E. (1960). *Moral education.* New York: Free Press.

Eakins, P. S. (Ed.). (1986). *The American way of birth.* Philadelphia, PA: Temple University Press.

Earl, W. L. (1987). Creativity and self-thrust: A field of study. *Adolescence, 22,* 419–432.

Easley, M. J., & Epstein, N. (1991). Coping with stress in a family with an alcoholic parent. *Family Relations, 40,* 218–224.

East, P. L., Lerner, R. M., Lerner, J. B., Soni, R. T., Ohannessian, C. M., & Jacobson, L. P. (1992). Early adolescent-peer group fit, peer relations, and psychosocial competence: A short-term longitudinal study. *Journal of Early Adolescence, 12,* 132–152.

Easterbrooks, M. A. (1989). Quality of attachment to mother and to father: Effects of perinatal risk status. *Child Development, 60,* 825–830.

Eaton, W. O., & Yu, A. P. (1989). Are sex differences in child motor activity level a function of sex differences in maturational status? *Child Development, 60,* 1005–1011.

Ebeling, K. S., & Gelman, S. A. (1994). Children's use of context in interpreting "big" and "little." *Child Development, 65,* 1178–1192.

Eberhardt, C. A., & Schill, T. (1984). Differences in sexual attitudes and likeliness of sexual behavior of black lower-socioeconomic father-present versus father-absent female adolescents. *Adolescence, 19,* 99–105.

Eckenrode, J., Laird, M., & Doris, J. (1993). School performance and disciplinary problems among abused and neglected children. *Developmental Psychology, 29,* 53–62.

Eder, R. A. (1989). The emergent personologist: The structure and content of 3½, 5½, and 7½-year-olds' concepts of themselves and other persons. *Child Development, 60,* 1218–1228.

Eder, R. A. (1990). Uncovering young children's psychological selves: Individual and developmental differences. *Child Development, 61,* 849–863.

Edwards, S. (1992). Use of coffee, alcohol, cigarettes raises risk of poor birth outcomes. *Family Planning Perspectives, 24,* 188–189.

Egeland, B., & Farber, E. A. (1984). Infant-mother attachment: Factors related to its development and changes over time. *Child Development, 55,* 753–771.

Egeland, B., Jacobvitz, D., & Sroufe, L. A. (1988). Breaking the cycle of abuse. *Child Development, 55,* 1080–1088.

Egeland, B., & Vaughn, B. (1981). Failure of "bond formation" as a cause of abuse, neglect, and maltreatment. *American Journal of Orthopsychiatry, 51,* 78–84.

Ehrenberg, M. F., Cox, D. N., & Koopman, R. F. (1991). The relationships between self-efficacy and depression in adolescents. *Adolescence, 26,* 361–374.

Ehrhardt, A., & Meyer-Bahlburg, H. (1981). Effects of prenatal sex hormones on gender-related behavior. *Science, 211,* 312–318.

Eichorn, D. M., Hunt, J. V., & Honzik, M. P. (1981). Experience, personality, and IQ: Adolescence to middle age. In D. Eichorn, J. Clausen, N. Haan, M. Honzik, & P. H. Mussen (Eds.), *Present and past in middle life.* New York: Academic Press.

Eiger, M. S. (1987). The feeding of infants and children. In R. A. Hoekelman, S. Blotman, S. B. Friedman, N. M. Nelson, & H. M. Siedel (Eds.), *Primary pediatric care.* St. Louis, MO: Mosby.

Eiger, M. S., & Olds, S. W. (1987). *The complete book of breastfeeding.* New York: Workman.

Eimas, P. D., & Quinn, P. C. (1994). Studies on the formation of perceptually basic-level category in young infants. *Child Development, 65,* 903–917.

Eisele, J., Hertsgaard, D., & Light, H. K. (1986). Factors related to eating disorders in young adolescent girls. *Adolescence, 82,* 283–290.

Eisen, S. B., Youngman, D. J., Grob, M. C., & Dill, D. L. (1992). Alcohol, drugs, and psychiatric disorders: A current view of hospitalized adolescents. *Journal of Adolescent Research, 7,* 250–265.

Eisenberg, N., Fabes, R. A., Carlo, G., Troyer, D., Speer, A. L., Karbon, M., & Switzer, G. (1992). The relations of maternal practices and characteristics to children's vicarious emotional responsiveness. *Child Development, 63,* 583–602.

Eisenberg, N., Fabes, R. A., Schaller, M., Carlo, G., & Miller, P. A. (1991). The relations of parental characteristics and practices to children's vicarious emotional responding. *Child Development, 62,* 1393–1408.

Eisikovits, Z., & Sagi, A. (1982, June). Moral development and discipline encounter in delinquent and nondelinquent adolescents. *Journal of Youth and Adolescence, 11,* 217–230.

Ekman, P. (1972). Universals in cultural differences in facial expressions of emotions. In J. K. Cole (Ed.), *Nebraska symposium on motivation* (Vol. 19). Lincoln: University of Nebraska Press.

Elkind, D. (1967). Egocentrism in adolescence. *Child Development, 38,* 1025–1034.

Elkind, D. (1970). *Children and adolescents: Interpretive essays on Jean Piaget.* New York: Oxford University Press.

Elkind, D. (1975). Recent research on cognitive development in adolescence. In S. E. Dragastin & G. H. Elder, Jr. (Eds.), *Adolescence in the life cycle.* New York: Wiley.

Elkind, D. (1978, Spring). Understanding the young adolescent. *Adolescence, 13,* 127–134.

Ellis, D. W., & Davis, L. T. (1982, Fall). The development of self-concept boundaries across the adolescent years. *Adolescence, 17,* 695–710.

Ellis, N. B. (1991). An extension of the Steinberg accelerating hypothesis. *Journal of Early Adolescence, 11,* 221–235.

Elmen, J. (1991). Achievement orientation in early adolescence: Developmental patterns and social correlates. *Journal of Early Adolescence, 11,* 125–151.

Emde, R. N. (1992). Individual meaning and increasing complexity: Contributions of Sigmund Freud and Rene Spitz to developmental psychology. *Developmental Psychology, 28,* 347–359.

Emde, R. N., Plomin, R., Robinson, J., Corley, R., DeFries, J., Fulker, D. W., Reznick, J. S., Campos, J., Kagan, J., & Zahn-Waxler, C. (1992). Temperament, emotion, and cognition at fourteen months: The MacArthur Longitudinal Twin Study. *Child Development, 63,* 1437–1455.

English, O. S., & Pearson, G. H. J. (1945). *Emotional problems of living.* New York: W. W. Norton.

Enns, C. Z. (1991). The "new" relationship models of women's identity: A review and critique for counselors. *Journal of Counseling and Development, 69,* 209–217.

Entwisle, D. R., Alexander, K. L., Pallas, A. M., & Cadigan, W. (1987). The emergent academic self-image of first graders: Its response to social structure. *Child Development, 58,* 1190–1206.

Ephron, N. (1975). *Crazy salad.* New York: Alfred A. Knopf.

Erikson, E. (1950). *Childhood and society.* New York: W. W. Norton.

Erikson, E. (1959). *Identity and the life cycle.* New York: International Universities Press.

Erikson, E. (1963). *Childhood and society* (2nd ed.). New York: W. W. Norton.

Erikson, E. (1968). *Identity: Youth and crisis.* New York: W. W. Norton.

Erikson, E. (1982). *The life cycle completed.* New York: W. W. Norton.

Eron, L. D. (1987). The development of aggression from the perspective of a developing behaviorism. *American Psychologist, 42,* 435–442.

Eskilson, A., Wiley, M. G., Muehlbauer, G., & Dodder, L. (1986). Parental pressure, self-esteem, and adolescent reported deviance: Bending the twig too far. *Adolescence, 21,* 501–515.

Eveleth, P., & Tanner, J. (1976). *Worldwide variations in human growth.* New York: Cambridge University Press.

Fabes, R. A., Wilson, P., & Christopher, F. S. (1989). A time to reexamine the role of television in family life. *Family Relations, 38,* 337–341.

Fabricius, W. V., & Wellman, H. M. (1993). Two roads diverged: Young children's ability to judge distance. *Child Development, 64,* 399–414.

Fagan, J. F. III. (1977, March). Infant recognition memory: Studies in forgetting. *Child Development, 48,* 68–78.

Fagot, B. I., & Hagan, R. (1991). Observations of parent reactions to sex-stereotype behaviors: age and sex effects. *Child Development, 62,* 617–628.

Fagot, B. I., & Kavanagh, K. (1990). The prediction of antisocial behavior from avoidant attachment classifications. *Child Development, 61,* 864–873.

Fagot, B. I., & Kavanagh, K. (1993). Parenting during the second year. Effects of children's age, sex, and attachment classification. *Child Development, 64,* 258–271.

Fagot, B. I., Leinbach, M. D., & O'Boyle, C. (1992). Gender labeling, gender stereotyping, and parenting behaviors. *Developmental Psychology, 28,* 255–260.

Farber, J. A. M. & Branstetter, W. H. (1994). Preschoolers' prosocial responses to their peers' distress. *Developmental Psychology, 30,* 334–341.

Farmer, A. E., McGuffin, P., & Gottesman, I. I. (1987). Twin concordance for DSM-III schizophrenia. Scrutinizing the validity of the definition. *Archives of General Psychiatry, 44,* 634–641.

Faro, S. (1985). Chlamydia trachomatic infection in women. *Journal of Reproductive Medicine, 30*(Suppl.), 273–278.

Farrar, M. J. (1992). Negative evidence and grammatical morpheme acquisition. *Developmental Psychology, 28,* 90–98.

Farrar, M. J., & Goodman, G. S. (1992). Developmental changes in event memory. *Child Development, 63,* 173–187.

Farrar, W. J., Raney, G. E., & Boyer, M. E. (1992). Knowledge, concepts, and inferences in childhood. *Child Development, 63,* 673–691.

Farrington, D. P. (1990). Implications of criminal career research for the prevention of offending. *Journal of Adolescence, 13,* 93–114.

Farver, J. M., Kim, Y. K., & Lee, Y. (1995). Cultural differences in Korean- and Anglo-American preschoolers' social interaction and play behaviors. *Child Development, 66,* 1088–1099.

Fasick, F. A. (1984). Parents, peers, youth culture and autonomy in adolescence. *Adolescence, 19,* 143–157.

Fauber, R., Forehand, R., Thomas, A. M., & Wierson, M. (1990). A mediational model of the impact of marital conflict on adolescent adjustment in intact and divorced families: The role of disrupted parenting. *Child Development, 61,* 1112–1123.

Feagans, L. B., Kipp, E., & Blood, I. (1994). The effects of otitis media on the attention skills of day-care-attending toddlers. *Developmental Psychology, 30,* 701–708.

Fein, E. (1981). Issues in foster family care: Where do we stand? *American Journal of Orthopsychiatry, 61,* 578–583.

Fein, G. G. (1986). Pretend play. In D. Gorletz & J. F. Wohlwill (Eds.), *Curiosity, imagination, and play.* Hillsdale, NJ: Erlbaum.

Feingold, A. (1982). Do taller men have prettier girlfriends? *Psychological Reports, 50,* 810.

Feldman, N. A., & Ruble, D. N. (1988). The effect of personal relevance on psychological inference: A developmental analysis. *Child Development, 59,* 1339–1352.

Feldman, S. S., Mont-Reynaud, R., & Rosenthal, D. A. (1992). When East moves West: The acculturation of values of Chinese adolescence in the United States and Australia. *Journal of Research on Adolescence, 2,* 147–173.

Feldman, S. S., & Wentzel, K. R. (1990). The relationship between parenting styles, sons' self-restraint, and peer relations in early adolescence. *Journal of Early Adolescence, 10,* 439–454.

Felson, M., & Gottfredson, M. (1984). Social indicators of adolescent activities near peers and parents. *Journal of Marriage and Family, 46,* 709–714.

Felson, R. B., & Zielinski, M. A. (1989). Children's self-esteem and parental support. *Journal of Marriage and the Family, 51,* 727–735.

Fenzel, L. M. (1992). The effect of relative age on self-esteem, role strain, GPA, and anxiety. *Journal of Early Adolescence, 12,* 253–266.

Ferguson, T. J., & Rule, B. G. (1988). Children's evaluations of retaliatory aggression. *Child Development, 59,* 961–968.

Fernald, A., & Morikawa, H. (1993). Common themes and cultural variations in Japanese and American mothers' speech to infants. *Child Development, 64,* 637–656.

Ferreira, F., & Morrison, F. J. (1994). Children's meta-linguistic knowledge of syntactic constituents: Effects of age and schooling. *Developmental Psychology, 30,* 663–678.

Ferreiro, B W., Warren, N. J., & Konanc, J. T. (1986). ADAP: A divorce assessment proposal. *Family Relations, 35,* 439–449.

Ferriss, L. (1989, October 30). *Women's life crisis deepens says author.* Portland, ME: Portland Press Herald.

Field, T., Healy, B., Goldstein, S., Perry, S., & Bendell, D. (1988). Infants of depressed mothers show "depressed" behavior even with nondepressed adults. *Child Development, 59,* 1569–1579.

Field, T., Woodson, R., Greenberg, R., & Cohen, D. (1982). Discrimination and imitation of facial expressions by neonates. *Science, 218,* 179–181.

Field, T. M. (1991a). Quality infant day-care and grade school behavior and performance. *Child Development, 62,* 863–870.

Field, T. M. (1991b). Young children's adaptations to repeated separations from their mothers. *Child Development, 62,* 539–547.

Fiese, B. H. (1990). Playful relationships: A contextual analysis of mother–toddler interaction and symbolic play. *Child Development, 61,* 1648–1656.

Fincham, F. D., Hokoda, A., & Sanders, R., Jr. (1989). Learned helplessness, test anxiety, and academic achievement: A longitudinal analysis. *Child Development, 60,* 138–145.

Fincher, J. (1982). Before their time. *Science, 82.*

Fine, M. A. (1986). Perceptions of stepparents: Variation in stereotypes as a function of current family structure. *Journal of Marriage and Family, 48,* 537–543.

Fine, M. A. (1992). Families in the United States: Their current status and future prospects. *Family Relations, 41,* 430–435.

Fine, M. A., & Fine, D. R. (1992). Recent changes in laws effecting stepfamilies: Suggestions for legal reform. *Family Relations, 41,* 334–340.

Fine, M. A., & Hovestadt, A. J. (1984, April). Perceptions of marriage rationality by levels of perceived health in the family of origin. *Journal of Marital and Family Therapy, 10,* 193–195.

Fine, M. A., McKenry, P. C., Donnelly, B. W., & Voydanoff, P. (1992). Received adjustment of parents and children: Variations by family structure, race, and gender. *Journal of Marriage and the Family, 54,* 118–127.

Finkelstein, M. J., & Gaier, E. L. (1983, Spring). The impact of prolonged student status on late adolescent development. *Adolescence, 18,* 115–129.

Fischer, J. L., & Crawford, D. W. (1992). Codependency and parenting styles. *Journal of Adolescent Research 7,* 352–363.

Fischer, K. W., & Silvern, L. (1985). Stages and individual differences in cognitive development. *Annual Review of Psychology, 36,* 613–648.

Fischman, J. (1988, September). Type A situations. *Psychology Today, 22,* 22.

Fish, M., Stifler, C. A., & Belsky, J. (1991). Conditions of continuity and discontinuity in infant negative emotionality: Newborn to five months. *Child Development, 62,* 1525–1537.

Fishbein, H. D., & Imai, S. (1993). Preschoolers select playmates on the basis of gender and race. *Journal of Applied Developmental Psychology, 14,* 303–316.

Fisher, T. D., & Hall, R. G. (1988). A scale for the comparison of the sexual attitudes of adolescents and their parents. *Journal of Sex Research, 24,* 90–100.

Fitness Finders. (1984). *Feelin' good.* Spring Arbor, MI: Fitness Finders.

Fitzgerald, H. E., Sullivan, L. A., Ham, H. P., Zucker, R. A., Bruckel, S., & Schneider, A. M. (1993). Predictors of behavior problems in three-year-old sons of alcoholics: Early evidence for the onset of risk. *Child Development, 64,* 110–123.

Fivush, R., Kuebli, J., & Clubb, P. A. (1992). The structure of events and event representations: A developmental analysis. *Child Development, 63,* 188–201.

Flanagan, C. A. (1990). Change in family work status: Effects on parent–adolescent decision making. *Child Development, 61,* 163–177.

Flanagan, C. A., & Eccles, J. S. (1993). Change in parents' work status in adolescents' adjustment at school. *Child Development, 64,* 246–257.

Flannery, D. J., Rowe, D. C., & Gulley, B. L. (1993). Impact of pubertal status, timing, and age on adolescent sexual experience and delinquency. *Journal of Adolescent Research, 8,* 21–40.

Flavell, J. H., Mumme, D. L., Green, F. L., & Flavell, E. R. (1992). Young children's understanding of different types of beliefs. *Child Development, 63,* 960–977.

Fleischer, B., & Read, M. (1982, Winter). Food supplement usage by adolescent males. *Adolescence, 17,* 831–845.

Flint, L. (1992). Adolescent parental affinity-seeking: Age- and gender-mediated strategy use. *Adolescence, 27,* 417–444.

Floyd, F. J., & Zmich, D. E. (1991). Marriage and the parenting partnership: Perceptions and interactions of parents with mentally retarded and typically developing children. *Child Development, 62,* 1434–1448.

Flynn, T. M., & Beasley, J. (1980, Winter). An experimental study of the effects of competition on the self-concept. *Adolescence, 15,* 799–806.

Fonagy, P., Steele, H., & Steele, M. (1991). Maternal representations of attachment during pregnancy predict the organization of infant-mother attachment at one year of age. *Child Development, 62,* 891–905.

Ford, D. Y., Harris, J., & Schuerger, J. N. (1993). Racial identity development among gifted black students: Counseling issues and concerns. *Journal of Counseling and Development, 71,* 409–416.

Ford, M. E. (1986). *Androgyny as self-assertion and integration: Implications for psychological and social competence.* Unpublished manuscript, Stanford University School of Education, Stanford, CA.

Forrest, J. D., & Silverman, J. (1989). What public school teachers teach about preventing pregnancy, AIDS, and sexually transmitted diseases. *Family Planning Perspectives, 21,* 65–72.

Forrest, J. D., & Singh, S. (1990). The sexual and reproductive behavior of American women, 1982–1988 *Family Planning Perspectives, 22,* 206–214.

Forsstrom-Cohen, B., & Rosenbaum, A. (1985). The effects of parental marital violence on young adults: An exploratory investigation. *Journal of Marriage and the Family, 47,* 467–472.

Fox, N. A., Kimmerly, N. L., & Schafer, W. D. (1991). Attachment of mother/attachment to father: A meta-analysis. *Child Development, 62,* 210–225.

Franco, J. N. (1983, January). Aptitude tests: Can we predict their future? *Personnel and Guidance Journal, 61,* 263, 264.

François, G. R. (1990). *The lifespan* (3rd ed.). Belmont, CA: Wadsworth.

Frankel, K. A., & Bates, J. E. (1990). Mother–toddler problem solving: Antecedents in attachment, home behavior, and temperament. *Child Development, 61,* 810–819.

Frankenburg, W. K., Frandal, A., Sciarillo, W., & Burgess, D. (1981). The newly abbreviated and revised Denver Developmental Screening Test. *Journal of Pediatrics, 99,* 995–999.

French, D. C. (1988). Heterogeneity of peer-rejected boys: Aggressive and nonaggressive subtypes. *Child Development, 59,* 976–985.

French, D. C. (1990). Heterogeneity of peer-rejected girls. *Child Development, 61,* 2028–2031.

Freud, A. (1946). *The ego and the mechanism of defense.* New York: International Universities Press.

Freud, S. (1917). *A general introduction to psychoanalysis.* New York: Washington Square Press.

Frey, K. S., & Ruble, D. N. (1992). Gender constancy and the "cost" of sex-typed behavior: a test of the conflict hypothesis. *Developmental Psychology, 28,* 714–721.

Fried, P. A., Watkinson, B., & Willan, A. (1984). Marijuana use during pregnancy and decreased length of gestation. *American Journal of Obstetrics and Gynecology, 150,* 23–27.

Friedrich-Cofer, L., & Huston, A. C. (1986) Television violence and aggression: The debate continues. *Psychological Bulletin, 100,* 364–371.

Frodi, A., & Senchak, M. (1990). Verbal and behavioral responsiveness to the cries of atypical infants. *Child Development, 61,* 76–84.

Frydenberg, E., & Lewis, R. (1991). Adolescent coping: The different ways in which boys and girls cope. *Journal of Adolescence, 14,* 119–134.

Fuller, J. R., & LaFountain, M. J. (1987). Performance-enhancing drugs in sport: A different form of drug abuse. *Adolescence, 22,* 969–976.

Furman, W., & Buhrmester, D. (1992). Age and sex differences in perceptions of networks of personal relationships. *Child Development, 63,* 103–115.

Gabennesch, H. (1990). The perception of social conventionality by children and adults. *Child Development, 61,* 2047–2059.

Gable, S., Belsky, J., & Crnic, K. (1992). Marriage, parenting, and child development: Progress and prospects. *Journal of Family Psychology, 5,* 276–294.

Gaensbauer, T., & Hiatt, S. (1984). *The psychobiology of affective development.* Hillsdale, NJ: Erlbaum.

Galambos, N. L., & Almeida, D. N. (1992). Does parent-adolescent conflict increase in early adolescence? *Journal of Marriage and the Family, 54,* 737–747.

Galda, L., & Pellegrini, A. D. (Eds.). (1985). *Play, language, and stories: The development of children's literate behavior.* Norwood, NJ: Ablex.

Gallagher, J. M., & Noppe, J. C. (1976). Cognitive development and learning. In J. F. Adams (Ed.), *Understanding adolescence* (3rd ed.). Boston, MA: Allyn & Bacon.

Gardner, H. (1983). *Frames of mind.* New York: Basic Books.

Gardner, J. M., Zarmel, B. Z., & Magnano, C. L. (1992). Arousal/visual preference interactions in high-risk neoantes. *Developmental Psychology, 28,* 821–830.

Gardner, L. I. (1972). Deprivation dwarfism. *Scientific American, 227,* 76–82.

Garelik, G. (1985, October). Are the progeny prodigies? *Discover Magazine, 6,* 45–47, 78–84.

Garner, P. W., Jones, D. C., & Miner, J. L. (1994). Social competence among low-income preschoolers: Emotion socialization practices and social cognitive correlates. *Child Development, 65,* 622–637.

Garzarelli, P., Everhart, B., & Lester, D. (1993). Self-concept and academic performance in gifted and academically weak students. *Adolescence, 28,* 233–237.

Gately, D. W., & Schwebel, A. I. (1991). The challenge model of children's adjustment to parental divorce: Explaining favorable post-divorce outcomes in children. *Journal of Family Psychology, 5,* 60–81.

Gathercole, S. E., Willis, C. S., Emslie, H., & Baddelep, A. D. (1992). Phonological memory and vocabulary development during the early school years: A longitudinal study. *Development Psychology, 28,* 887–898.

Gavazzi, S. M., Anderson, S. A., & Sabatelli, R. M. (1993). Family differentiation, peer differentiation, and adolescence adjustment in a clinical sample. *Journal of Adolescent Research, 8,* 205–225.

Gavazzi, S. M., & Sabatelli, R. M. (1990). Family system dynamics, the individuation process, and psychosocial development. *Journal of Adolescent Research, 5,* 500–519.

Gaylor-Ross, R. J. (1975). Paired associate learning and formal thinking in adolescence. *Journal of Youth and Adolescence, 4,* 375–382.

Geasler, M. J., Dannison, L. L., & Edlund, C. J. (1995). Sexuality education of young children. Parental concerns. *Family Relations, 44,* 184–188.

Gecas, V., & Schwalbe, M. L. (1986). Parental behavior and adolescent self-esteem. *Journal of Marriage and the Family, 48,* 37–46.

Gelb, R., & Jacobson, J. L. (1988). Popular and unpopular children's interaction during cooperative and competitive peer group activities. *Journal of Abnormal Child Psychology, 16,* 247–261.

Gelles, R. J., & Conte, J. R. (1990). Domestic violence and sexual abuse of children: A review of research in the eighties. *Journal of Marriage and the Family, 52,* 1045–1058.

Gelles, R. J., & Harrop, J. W. (1991). The risk of abusive violence among children with nongenetic caretakers. *Family Relations, 40,* 78–83.

Gellman, E., et al. (1983). Vaginal delivery after Cesarean section. *JAMA, Journal of American Medical Association, 249,* 2935–2937.

Genesee, F. (1985). Second language learning through immersion: A review of U.S. programs. *Review of Educational Research, 55,* 541–546.

Gerken, L., & McIntosh, B. J. (1993). Interplay of function morphemes and prosody in early language. *Developmental Psychology, 29,* 448–457.

Gershenson, H. P. (1983). Redefining fatherhood in families with white adolescent mothers. *Journal of Marriage and the Family, 45,* 591–599.

Gertner, M. (1986). Short stature in children. *Medical Aspects of Human Sexuality, 20,* 36–42.

Gesell, A. (1934). *An atlas of infant behavior.* New Haven, CT: Yale University Press.

Gesell, A., & Ames, L. B. (1956). *Youth: The years from ten to sixteen.* New York: Harper & Row.

Gesell, A., & Ilg, F. L. (1943). *Infant and child in the culture of today.* New York: Harper.

Gesell, A., & Ilg, F. L. (1946). *The child from five to ten.* New York: Harper.

Gifford, V. D., & Dean, M. M. (1990). Differences in extracurricular activity participation, achievement, and attitudes toward school between ninth-grade students attending junior high school and those attending senior high school. *Adolescence, 25,* 799–802.

Gilbert, E. H., & DeBlassie, R. R. (1984, Winter). Anorexia nervosa: Adolescent starvation by choice. *Adolescence, 19,* 839–846.

Gilger, J. W., Geary, D. C., & Eisele, L. M. (1991). Reliability and validity of retrospective self-reports of the age of pubertal onset using twin, sibling, and college student data. *Adolescence, 26,* 41–54.

Gilligan, C. (1977). In a different voice: Women's conceptions of self and of morality. *Harvard Educational Review, 47,* 481–517.

Gilligan, C. (1982). *In a different voice: Psychological theory and women's development.* Cambridge, MA: Harvard University Press.

Gilligan, C. (1984). *Remapping the moral domain in personality research and assessment.* Invited address presented to the American Psychological Association Convention, Toronto.

Gilligan, C., Ward, J. V., Taylor, J. M., & Bardige, B. (1988). *Mapping the moral domain.* Cambridge, MA: Harvard University Press.

Gillmore, M. R., Hawkins, J. D., Day, L. E., & Catalano, R. F. (1992). Friendship and deviance: New evidence on an old controversy. *Journal of Early Adolescence, 12,* 80–95.

Ginsburg, G. S., & Bronstein, P. (1993). Family factors related to children's intrinsic/extrinsic motivational orientation and academic performance. *Child Development, 64,* 1461–1474.

Giudubaldi, J., & Perry, J. D. (1985). Divorce and mental health sequelae for children. A two-year follow up of a nation-wide sample. *Journal of the American Academy of Child Psychiatry, 24,* 531–537.

Gladstone, J. W. (1988). Perceived changes in grandmother-grandchild relations following a child's separation or divorce. *The Gerontologist, 28,* 66–72.

Glass, R., & Ericsson, R. (1982). *Getting pregnant in the 1980s.* Berkeley: University of California Press.

Glenn, N. D., & Kramer, K. B. (1987). The marriages and divorces of children of divorce. *Journal of Marriage and the Family, 49,* 811–825.

Glovinsky-Fahsholtz, D. (1992). The effect of free or reduced-price lunches on the self-esteem of middle school students. *Adolescence, 27,* 633–638.

Gnepp, J., & Chilamkurti, C. (1988). Children's use of personality attributions to predict other people's emotional and behavioral reactions. *Child Development, 59,* 743–754.

Gnepp, J., & Klayman, J. K. (1992). Recognition of uncertainty in emotional inferences: Reasoning about emotionally equivocal situations. *Developmental Psychology, 28,* 145–158.

Goelman, H., Shapiro, E., & Pence, A. R. (1990). Family environment and family day care. *Family Relations, 39,* 14–19.

Goff, J. L. (1990). Sexual confusion among certain college males. *Adolescence, 25,* 599–614.

Golbeck, S. L. (1992). Young children's memory for spatial locations in organized and unorganized rooms. *Journal of Applied Developmental Psychology, 13,* 75–96.

Goldberg, M. E., & Gorn, G. J. (1977, March). *Material vs. social preferences, parent-child relations, and the child's emotional responses.* Paper presented at the Telecommunications Policy Research Conference, Raleigh House, VA.

Goldberg, S. (1983). Parent-infant bonding: Another look. *Child Development, 54,* 331–355.

Goldberg, W. A., Greenberger, E., Hamill, S., & O'Neil, R. (1992). Role demands in the lives of employed single mothers with preschoolers. *Journal of Family Issues, 13,* 312–333.

Goldman, J. A., Lerman, R. H., Contois, J. H., & Udall, J. N. (1986). Behavioral effects of sucrose on preschool children. *Journal of Abnormal Child Psychology, 14,* 565–577.

Goldman, J. A., Rosenzweig, C. M., & Lutter, A. D. (1980, April). Effect of similarity of ego identity status on interpersonal attraction. *Journal of Youth and Adolescence, 9,* 153–162.

Goldsmith, H. H. (1983). Genetic influences on personality from infancy to adulthood. *Child Development, 54,* 331–355.

Goldsmith, H. H., Buss, A. H., Plomin, R., Rothbart, M. K., Thomas, A., Chess, S., Hinde, R. A., & McCall, R. B. (1987). Roundtable: What is temperament? Four approaches. *Child Development, 58,* 505–529.

Goldsmith, H. H., & Campos, J. J. (1990). The structure of temperamental fear and pleasure in infants: A psychometric perspective. *Child Development, 61,* 1944–1964.

Goldsmith, H. H., & Gottesman, I. I. (1981). Origins of variation in behavioral style: A longitudinal study of temperament in young twins. *Child Development, 52,* 91–103.

Goldstein, M. J. (1981, October). Family factors associated with schizophrenia and anorexia nervosa. *Journal of Youth and Adolescence, 10,* 385–405.

Goleman, D. (1980, February). 1,528 little geniuses and how they grew. *Psychology Today, 13,* 28–143.

Goleman, D. (1985). Spacing of siblings strongly link to success in life. *New York Times* (May 28th), 17, 18.

Goleman, D. (1986, December 2). Major personality study finds that traits are mostly inherited. *New York Times,* pp. 17–18.

Goleman, D. (1989, October 22). Pushing preschoolers may not be a good idea. *Maine Sunday Telegram,* p. 20.

Golinko, B. E. (1984, Fall). Adolescence: Common pathways through life. *Adolescence, 19,* 749–751.

Golinkoff, R. M., Hirsh-Pasek, K., Bailey, L. M., & Wenger, N. R. (1992). Young children and adults use lexical principles to learn new nouns. *Developmental Psychology, 28,* 99–108.

Goodman, G. A., & Haith, M. M. (1987). Memory development and neurophysiology: Accomplishments and limitations. *Child Development, 58,* 713–717.

Goodman, S. H., Brogan, D., Lynch, M. E., & Fielding, B. (1993). Social and emotional competence in children of depressed mothers. *Child Development, 64,* 516–531.

Goodwin, M. P., & Roscoe, B. (1990). Sibling violence and agonistic interactions among middle adolescents. *Adolescence, 25,* 451–468.

Goodwyn, S. W., & Acredolo, L. P. (1993). Symbolic gesture versus word: Is there a modality advantage for onset of symbol use? *Child Development, 64,* 688–701.

Goossens, F. A., & van Ijzendoorn, M. H. (1990). Quality of infant's attachments to professional caregivers: Relation to infant–parent attachment and day-care characteristics. *Child Development, 61,* 832–837.

Goossens, L., Seiffge-Krenke, I., & Marcoen, A. (1992). The many faces of adolescent egocentrisim: Two European replications. *Journal of Adolescent Research, 7,* 43–58.

Gopnik, A., & Meltzoff, A. N. (1992). Categorization and naming: Basic-level sorting in eighteen-month-olds and its relation to language. *Child Development, 63,* 1091–1102.

Gordon, J. S., & Haire, D. (1981). Alternatives in childbirth. In P. Ahmed (Ed.), *Pregnancy, childbirth, and parenthood.* New York: Elsevier.

Goswami, U. (1991a). Analogical reasoning: What develops? A review of research and theory. *Child Development, 62,* 1–22.

Goswami, U. (1991b). Learning about spelling sequences: The role of onsets and rimes in analogies to reading. *Child Development, 62,* 1119–1123.

Graham, S. (1986, August). *Can attribution theory tell us something about motivation in blacks?* Paper presented at the meeting of the American Psychological Association, Washington, DC.

Graham, S., & Hoehn, S. (1995). Children's understanding of aggression and withdrawal as social stigmas: An attributional analysis. *Child Development, 66,* 1143–1161.

Gralinski, J. H., & Kopp, C. B. (1993). Everyday rules for behavior: Mothers' requests to young children. *Developmental Psychology, 29,* 573–584.

Grande, C. G. (1988). Delinquency: The learning disabled students' reaction to academic school failure. *Adolescence, 23,* 209–219.

Grant, C. L., & Fodor, J. G. (1984, April). *Body image and eating disorders: A new role for school psychologist in screening and prevention.* Mimeographed paper, New York University, School of Education, Health, Nursing, and Arts Profession.

Grant, C. L., & Fodor, J. G. (1986). Adolescent attitudes toward body image and anorexic behavior. *Adolescence, 21,* 269–281.

Grattan, M. P., DeVos, E., Levy, J., & McClintock, M. K. (1992). Asymmetric action in the human newborn: Sex differences in patterns of organization. *Child Development, 63,* 273–289.

Green, D. L. (1990). High school student employment in social context: Adolescents' perceptions of the role of part-time work. *Adolescence, 25,* 425–434.

Green, J. A. (1992). Testing whether correlation matrices are different from each other. *Developmental Psychology, 28,* 215–224.

Greenberg, J., Pyszczynski, T., Burling, J., Simon, L., Solomon, S., Rosenblatt, A., Lyon, D., & Pinel, E. (1992). Why do people need self-esteem? Converging evidence that self-esteem serves an anxiety-buffering function. *Journal of Personality and Social Psychology, 63,* 913–922.

Greenberg, J. S., Bruess, C. E., & Sands, D. W. (1986). *Sexuality. Insights and issues.* Dubuque, IA: Wm. C. Brown.

Greenberg, M. T., & Crnic, K. A. (1988). Longitudinal predictors of developmental status and social interactions in premature and full-term infants at age two. *Child Development, 59,* 554–570.

Greenberger, E., & Steinberg, L. (1981). The work-place as a context for the socialization of youth. *Journal of Youth and Adolescence, 10,* 185–210.

Greene, A. L., & Grimsley, M. D. (1990). Age and gender differences in adolescents' preferences for parental advice: Mum's the word. *Journal of Adolescent Research, 5,* 396–413.

Greene, A. L., & Reed, E. (1992). Social context differences in the relation between self-esteem and self-concept during late adolescence. *Journal of Adolescent Research, 7,* 266–282.

Greenough, W. T., Black, J. R., & Wallace, C. S. (1987). Experience and brain development. *Child Development, 58,* 539–559.

Greenstein, T. N. (1993). Maternal employment and child behavioral outcomes. *Journal of Family Issues, 3,* 323–354.

Greer, D., Potts, R., Wright, J. C., & Huston, A. (1982). The effects of television commercial form and commercial placement on children's social behavior and attention. *Child Development, 53,* 611–619.

Greif, G. L. (1985). Children and housework in the single father family. *Family Relations, 34,* 353–357.

Greif, G. L. (1988). Single fathers: Helping them cope with day-to-day problems. *Medical Aspects of Human Sexuality, 22,* 18–25.

Griffin, N., Chassin, L., & Young, R. D. (1981, Spring). Measurement of global self-concept versus multiple role-specific self-concepts in adolescents. *Adolescence, 16,* 49–56.

Grindstaff, C. F. (1988). Adolescent marriage and childbearing: The long-term economic outcome: Canada in the 1980s. *Adolescence, 23,* 45–58.

Grobstein, C. (1989). When does life begin? *Psychology Today, 23,* 42–46.

Grossman, J. H. (1986). Congenital syphilis. In J. L. Sever & R. L. Brent (Eds.), *Teratogen update: Environmentally induced birth defect risks.* New York: Liss.

Grusec, J. E. (1992). Social learning theory and developmental psychology: The legacies of Robert Sears and Albert Bandura. *Developmental Psychology, 28,* 776–786.

Grusec, J. E., & Goodnow, J. J. (1994). Impact of parental discipline methods on the child's internalization of values: A reconceptualization of current points of view. *Developmental Psychology, 30,* 4–19.

Grych, J. H., and Fineham, F. D. (1993). Children's appraisal of marital conflict: Initial investigations of the cognitive-contextual framework. *Child Development, 64,* 215–230.

Grych, J. H., Seid, M., and Fineham, F. D. (1992). Assessing marital conflict from the child's perspective: The children's perception of interparental conflict scale. *Child Development, 63,* 558–572.

Guilford, J. P. (1967). *The nature of human intelligence.* New York: McGraw-Hill.

Gunnar, M. R., & Nelson, C. A. (1994). Event-related potentials in year-old infants: Relations with emotionality and cortisol. *Child Development, 65,* 80–94.

Guralnick, M. J., & Groom, J. M. (1987). The peer relations of mildly delayed and non-handicapped preschool children in mainstream playgroups. *Child Development, 58,* 1556–1572.

Guthrie, D. M. (1980). *Neuroethology.* New York: Halsted Press.

Gutierrez, J., & Sameroff, A. (1990). Determinants of complexity in Mexican-American and Anglo-American mothers' conceptions of child development. *Child Development, 61,* 384–394.

Gutierrez, J., Sameroff, A. J., & Carrer, B. M. (1988). Acculturation and SES effects on Mexican American parents' concepts of development. *Child Development, 59,* 250–255.

Guttentag, R. E., & Hunt, R. R. (1988). Adult age differences in memory for imagined and performed actions. *Journal of Gerontology, 43,* P107–P108.

Guttmacher, A. F. (1983). *Pregnancy, birth and family planning* (rev. ed.). New York: New American Library.

Haas, L. (1980). Role-sharing couples: A study of egalitarian marriages. *Family Relations, 29,* 289–296.

Hadley, J. (1984, July/August). Facts about childhood hyperactivity. *Children Today,* pp. 8–13.

Hagan, P. (1983, May). Does 180 mean supergenius? *Psychology Today, 17,* 18.

Haith, M. M. (1986). Sensory and perceptual processes in early infancy. *Journal of Pediatrics, 109,* 158–171.

Hakuta, K., & Garcia, E. E. (1989). Bilingualism and education. *American Psychologist, 44,* 374–379.

Halgin, R. P., & Leahy, P. M. (1989). Understanding and treating perfectionistic college students. *Journal of Counseling and Development, 68,* 222–225.

Hall, D. G. (1991). Acquiring proper nouns for familiar and unfamiliar animate objects: Two-year-olds' word-learning biases. *Child Development, 62,* 1142–1154.

Hall, D. G. (1994). Semantic constraints on word learning: Proper names and adjectives. *Child Development, 65,* 1299–1317.

Hall, D. G., & Waxman, S. R. (1993). Assumptions about word meaning: Individuation and basic-level kinds. *Child Development, 64,* 1550–1570.

Hall, E. G., & Lee, A. M. (1984). Sex differences in motor performances of young children: Fact or fiction? *Sex Roles, 10,* 217–230.

Hall, G. S. (1891). The contents of childrens' minds on entering school. *Pedagogical Seminary, 1,* 139–173.

Hall, G. S. (1904). *Adolescence: Its psychology and its relation to physiology, anthropology, sociology, sex, crime, religion, and education* (2 vols.). New York: Appleton.

Hall, J. A. (1987). Parent-adolescent conflict: An empirical review. *Adolescence, 22,* 767–789.

Hallinan, M. T. (1991). School differences in tracking structures and track assignments. *Journal of Research on Adolescence, 1,* 251–275.

Hallinan, M. T., & Teixeira, R. A. (1987). Students' interracial friendships: Individual characteristics, structural effects, and racial differences. *American Journal of Education, 95,* 563–583.

Halpern, C. T., & Udry, J. R. (1992). Variation in adolescent hormone measures and implications for behavioral research. *Journal of Research on Adolescence, 2,* 103–122.

Halverson, H. (1940). Genital and sphincter behavior of the male infant. *Journal of Genetic Psychology, 56,* 95–136.

Hamachek, D. E. (1988). Evaluating self-concept and ego development with Erikson's psychosocial framework: A formulation. *Journal of Counseling and Development, 66* 354–360.

Hammer, T., & Vaglum, P. (1990). Use of alcohol and drugs in the transitional phase from adolescence to young adulthood. *Journal of Adolescence, 13,* 129–142.

Hansen, J., & Bowey, J. A. (1994). Phonological analysis skills, verbal working memory, and reading ability in second-grade children. *Child Development, 65,* 938–950.

Hanson, R. A. (1990). Initial parent attitudes of pregnant adolescents and a comparison with the decision about adoption. *Adolescence, 25,* 629–645.

Harding, G., & Snyder, K. (1991). Tom, Huck, and Oliver Stone as advocates in Kohlberg's just community: Theory-based strategies for moral education. *Adolescence, 26,* 319–330.

Harkness, S. (1992). Cross-cultural research in child development: A sample of the state of the art. *Developmental Psychology, 28,* 622–625.

Harper, J. F., & Marshall, E. (1991). Adolescents' problems and their relationship to self-esteem. *Adolescence, 26,* 799–808.

Harris, K. M. (1991). Teenage mothers and welfare dependency: working off welfare. *Journal of Family Issues, 12,* 492–519.

Harris, K. M., & Morgan, S. P. (1991). Fathers, sons, and daughters: Differential paternal involvement in parenting. *Journal of Marriage and the Family, 53,* 531–544.

Harris, P. L. (1983). Infant cognition. In P. H. Mussen, M. Haith, & J. J. Campos (Eds.), *Handbook of child psychology* (4th ed., Vol. 2). New York: Wiley.

Harris, P. L., Brown, E., Marriot, C., Whittal, S., & Harmer, S. (1991). Monsters, ghosts, and witches: Testing the limits of the fantasy-reality distinction in young children. *British Journal of Developmental Psychology, 9,* 105–123.

Harris, P. L., Kadanaugh, R. D., & Meredith, M. C. (1994). Young children's comprehension of pretend episodes: The integration of successive actions. *Child Development, 65,* 16–30.

Harrison, A. O., Wilson, M. N., Pine, C. J., Chan, S. Q., & Buriel, R. (1990). Family ecologies of ethnic minority children. *Child Development, 61,* 347–362.

Hart, B., & Risley, T. R. (1992). American parenting of language-learning children: Persisting differences in family-child interactions observed in natural home environments. *Developmental Psychology, 28,* 1096–1105.

Hart, C. H., DeWolf, M., Wozniak, P., & Burts, D. C. (1992). Maternal and paternal disciplinary styles: Relations with preschoolers, playground behavioral orientations and peer status. *Child Development, 63,* 79–892.

Hart, C. H., Ladd, G. W., & Burleson, B. R. (1990). Children's expectations of the outcomes of social strategies: Relations with sociometric status and maternal disciplinary styles. *Child Development, 61,* 127–137.

Hart, K. E. (1990). Coping with anger-provoking situations: Adolescent coping in relation to anger reactivity. *Journal of Adolescent Research, 6,* 357–370.

Harter, S. (1983). Developmental perspectives on the self system. In P. H. Mussen (Ed.), *Handbook of child psychology* (4th ed., vol. 4). New York: Wiley.

Harter, S., & Monsour, A. (1992). Developmental analysis of conflict caused by opposing attributes in the adolescent self-portrait. *Developmental Psychology, 28,* 251–260.

Harter, S., & Pike, R. (1984). The pictorial scale of perceived competence and social acceptance for young children. *Child Development, 55,* 1969–1982.

Hartman, E., Russ, D., Oldfield, M., Sivian, I., & Cooper, S. (1987). Who has nightmares? The personality of the lifelong nightmare sufferer. *Archives of General Psychiatry, 44,* 49–56.

Hartocollis, P. (1972). Aggressive behavior and the fear of violence. *Adolescence, 7,* 479–490.

Hartsough, C. S., Lambert, N. M. (1985). Medical factors in hyperactive and normal children: Prenatal developmental and health history findings. *American Journal of Orthopsychiatry, 55,* 190–201.

Hartup, W. W. (1983). Peer relations. In P. H. Mussen (Ed.), *Handbook of child psychology* (4th ed., Vol. 4). New York: Wiley.

Hartup, W. W., French, D. C., Lursen, B., Johnston, M. K., & Ogawa, J. R. (1993). Conflict and friendship relations in middle childhood: Behavior in a closed-field situation. *Child Development, 64,* 445–454.

Hartup, W. W., Laursen, B., Stewart, M. I., & Eastenson, A. (1988). Conflict and the friendship relations of young children. *Child Development, 59,* 1590–1600.

Harvey, M. A. S., McRorie, M. M., & Smith, D. W. (1981). Suggested limits to the use of the hot tubs and sauna by pregnant women. *Canadian Medical Association Journal, 125,* 50–53.

Harvey, S. M., & Faber, K. S. (Jan./Feb. 1993). Obstacles to prenatal care following implementation of a community-based program to reduce financial barriers. *Family Planning Perspectives, 25,* 32–36.

Harwood, R. L. (1992). The influence of culturally derived values on Anglo and Puerto Rican mothers' perceptions of attachment behavior. *Child Development, 63,* 822–839.

Haskett, M. E., & Kistner, J. A. (1991). Social interactions and peer perceptions of young physically abused children. *Child Development, 62,* 979–990.

Hasselhorn, M. (1992). Task dependency and the role of category typicality and metamory in the development of an organizational strategy. *Child Development, 63,* 202–214.

Hatcher, P. J., Hulme, C., & Ellis, A. W. (1994). Ameliorating early reading failure by integrating the teaching of reading and phonological skills: The phonological linkage hypothesis. *Child Development, 65,* 41–57.

Hatfield, E., & Sprecher, S. (1986). Measuring passionate love in intimate relationships. *Journal of Adolescence, 9,* 383–410.

Hauck, W. E., & Loughead, M. (1985). Adolescent self-monitoring. *Adolescence, 20,* 567–574.

Hauser, S. T., Borman, E. H., Jacobson, A. M., Powers, S. I., & Noam, G. G. (1991). Understanding family contexts of adolescent coping: A study of parental ego development and adolescent coping strategies. *Journal of Early Adolescence, 11,* 96–124.

Havighurst, R. J. (1972). *Developmental tasks and education* (3rd ed.). New York: David McKay.

Hawkins, A. J., Eggebeen, D. J. (1991). Are fathers fungible? Patterns of co-resident adult men in maritally disruptive families and young children's well-being. *Journal of Marriage and the Family, 53,* 958–972.

Hay, D. F., Nash, A., & Pedersen, J. (1983). Interaction between six-month-old peers. *Child Development, 54,* 557–562.

Hayes, D. S., & Casey, D. M. (1992). Young children and television: The retention of emotional reactions. *Child Development, 63,* 1423–1436.

Hayne, H., & Rovee-Collier, C. (1995). The organization of reactivated memory in infancy. *Child Development, 66,* 893–906.

Hayne, H., Rovee-Collier, C., & Perris, E. E. (1987). Categorization and memory retrieval by three-month-olds. *Child Development, 58,* 750–767.

Hazen, N. L., & Black, B. (1989). Preschool peer communication skills: The role of social status and interaction context. *Child Development, 60,* 867–876.

Heath, A. C., Kessler, R. C., Neale, M. C., Eaves, L. J., & Kendler, K. S. (1992). Evidence for genetic influences on personality from self-reports and informant ratings. *Journal of Personality and Social Psychology, 63,* 85–96.

Heatherington, L., Friedlander, M. L., & Johnson, W. F. (1989). Informed consent in family therapy research: Ethical dilemmas and practical problems. *Journal of Family Psychology, 2,* 373–385.

Heckhausen, J., & Krueger, J. (1993). Developmental expectations for the self and most other people: Age grading in three functions of social comparison. *Developmental Psychology, 29,* 539–548.

Heilbrun, A. B. (1984). Identification with the father and peer intimacy of the daughter. *Family Relations, 33,* 597–605.

Helwig, C. C., Tisak, M. S., & Turiel, E. (1990). Children's social reasoning in context: Reply to Gabennesch. *Child Development, 61,* 2068–2078.

Hepworth, J., Ryder, R. G., & Dreyer, A. S. (1984). The effects of parental loss on the formation of intimate relationships. *Journal of Marital and Family Therapy, 10,* 73–82.

Herman, M. A., & McHale, S. M. (1993). Coping with parental negativity: Links with parental warmth and child adjustment. *Journal of Applied Developmental Psychology, 14,* 121–136.

Herrera, A., & Macaraeg, A. (1984). Physicians' attitudes toward circumcision. *American Journal of Obstetrics and Gynecology, 148,* 825.

Herzberger, S. D., & Tennen, H. (1985). The effect of self-relevance on judgments of moderate and severe disciplinary encounters. *Journal of Marriage and the Family, 47,* 311–318.

Hertzler, A. A., & Grun, I. (1990). Potential nutrition message in magazines read by college students. *Adolescence, 25,* 717–724.

Hetherington, E. M. (1989). Coping with family transitions: Winners, losers, and survivors. *Child Development, 60,* 1–14.

Hetherington, E. M., Cox, M., & Cox, R. (1982). Effects of divorce and children. In M. Lamb (Ed.), *Nontraditional families: Parenting and child development.* Hillsdale, NJ: Erlbaum.

Hickling, A. K., & Gelman, S. A. (1995). How does your garden grow? Early conceptualization of seeds and their place in the plant growth cycle. *Child Development, 66,* 856–876.

Hicks, M. W., & Williams, J. W. (1981, October). Current challenges in educating for parenthood. *Family Relations, 30,* 579–584.

Hier, S. J., Korboot, P. J., & Schweitzer, R. D. (1990). Social adjustment and symptomatology in two types of homeless adolescents: Runaways and throwaways. *Adolescence, 25,* 761–772.

Higgins, B. S. (1990). Couple infertility: From the perspective of the close-relationship model. *Family Relations, 39,* 81–86.

High school profile report. (1992). Annual. Iowa City, IA: American College Testing Program.

Hill, L. M., Breckle, R., & Gehrking, W. C. (1983). The prenatal detection of cogenital malformations by ultrasonography. *Mayo Clinic Proceedings, 58,* 805–826.

Hilton, J. N., & Haldeman, V. A. (1991). Gender differences in the performance of household tasks by adults and children in single-parent and two-parent, two-earner families. *Journal of Family Issues, 12,* 114–130.

Himelstein, S., Graham, S., & Weinter, B. (1991). An attributional analysis of maternal beliefs about the importance of child-rearing practices. *Child Development, 62,* 301–310.

Hinde, R. (1983). Ethology and child development. In P. H. Mussen (Ed.), *Handbook of child psychology* (4th ed., Vol. 2). New York: Wiley.

Hinde, R. A. (1991). When is an evolutionary approach useful? *Child Development, 62,* 671–675.

Hinde, R. A. (1992). Developmental psychology in the context of other behavioral sciences. *Developmental Psychology, 28,* 1018–1029.

Hinds, M. D. (1982, May 2). Countries acting on baby formula. *New York Times,* p. 10.

Hines, M., & Kaufman, F. R. (1994). Androgen and the development of human sex-typical behavior: Rough-and-tumble play and sex of preferred playmates in children with congenital adrenal hyperplasia (CAH). *Child Development, 65,* 1042–1053.

Hite, S. L. (1981). *The Hite report: A nation-wide study of female sexuality.* New York: Dell.

Ho, D. Y. F. (1989). Continuity and variation in Chinese patterns of socialization. *Journal of Marriage and the Family, 51,* 149–163.

Hoare, C. H. (1991). Psychosocial identity development and cultural others. *Journal of Counseling and Development, 70,* 45–53.

Hobart, C. (1987). Parent-child relations in remarried families. *Journal of Family Issues, 8,* 259–277.
Hobart, C. (1988). The family system in remarriages: An exploratory study. *Journal of Marriage and the Family, 50,* 649–661.
Hobart, C. (1992). How they handle it: Young Canadians, sex, and AIDS. *Youth and Society, 23,* 411–433.
Hock, E., McBride, S., & Gnezda, M. T. (1989). Maternal separation anxiety: Mother-infant separation from the maternal perspective. *Child Development, 60,* 793–802.
Hock, E., & Schirtzinger, M. B. (1992). Maternal separation anxiety: Its developmental course and relation to maternal mental health. *Child Development, 63,* 93–102.
Hock, R. A., & Curry, J. F. (1983, December). Sex-role identification of normal adolescent males and females as related to school achievement. *Journal of Youth and Adolescence, 12,* 461–470.
Hoelter, J., & Harper, L. (1987). Structural and interpersonal family influences on adolescent self-conception. *Journal of Marriage and the Family, 49,* 129–139.
Hofer, M. A. (1981). *The roots of human behavior: An introduction to the psychology of early development.* San Francisco, CA: Freeman.
Hoff-Ginsberg, E. (1991). Mother-child conversation in different social classes and communicative settings. *Child Development, 62,* 782–796.
Hofferth, S., Kahn, J. R., & Baldwin, W. (1987). Premarital sexual activity among U.S. teenage women over the past three decades. *Family Planning Perspectives, 19,* 46–53.
Hoffman, V. J. (1984, Spring). The relationship of psychology to delinquency: A comprehensive approach. *Adolescence, 19,* 55–61.
Holcomb, W. R., & Kashani, J. H. (1991). Personality characteristics of a community sample of adolescents with conduct disorders. *Adolescence, 26,* 579–586.
Holden, G. W., & Titchie, K. L. (1991). Linking extreme marital discord, child rearing, and child behavior problems: Evidence from battered women. *Child Development, 62,* 311–327.
Holden, G. W., & West, M. J. (1989). Proximate regulation by mothers: A demonstration of how differing styles affect young children's behavior. *Child Development, 60,* 64–69.
Hole, J. W. (1987). *Human anatomy and physiology* (4th ed.). Dubuque, IA: Wm. C. Brown.
Holleran, P. R., Pascale, J., & Fraley, J. (1988). Personality correlates of college-age bulimics. *Journal of Counseling and Development, 66,* 378–381.
Holmbeck, G. N., & Hill, J. P. (1991). Conflictive engagement, positive affect, and menarche in families with seventh-grade girls. *Child Development, 62,* 1030–1048.
Holmbeck, G. N., & Hill, J. P. (1991). Rules, rule behaviors, and biological maturation in families with seventh-grade boys and girls. *Journal of Early Adolescence, 11,* 236–257.
Holmbeck, G. N., Waters, K. A., & Brookmen, R. R. (1990). Psychosocial correlates of sexually transmitted diseases and sexual activity in black adolescent females. *Journal of Adolescent Research, 5,* 431–448.
Holt, E. L. (1972). Energy requirements. In H. L. Barnett & A. H. Einhorn (Eds.), *Pediatrics* (15th ed.). New York: Appleton-Century-Crofts.
Hopkins, J., Marcues, M., & Campbell, S. B. (1984). Postpartum depression: A critical review. *Psychological Bulletin, 95,* 498–515.
Horn, J. M. (1983). The Texas Adoption Project. *Child Development, 54,* 268–275.
Horn, M. E., & Rudolph, L. B. (1987). An investigation of verbal interaction knowledge of sexual behavior and self-concept in adolescent mothers. *Adolescence, 87,* 591–598.
Horowitz, F. D. (1992). John B. Watson's legacy: Learning and environment. *Developmental Psychology, 28,* 360–367.
Horowitz, T. R. (1992). Dropout—Mertonian or reproduction scheme? *Adolescence, 27,* 451–459.
Howe, N. (1991). Sibling-directed internal state language, perspective taking, and affective behavior: *Child Development, 62,* 1503–1512.
Howes, C., & Hamilton, C. E. (1992a). Children's relationships with caregivers: Mothers and child care teachers. *Child Development, 63,* 859–866.
Howes, C., & Hamilton, C. E. (1992b). Children's relationships with child care teachers: Stability and concordance with parental attachments. *Child Development, 63,* 867–878.
Howes, C., Hamilton, C. E., & Matheson, C. C. (1994). Children's relationships with peers: Differential associations with aspects of the teacher-child relationship. *Child Development, 65,* 253–263.
Howes, C., & Matheson, C. C. (1992). Sequences in the development of competent play with peers: Social and social pretend play. *Developmental Psychology, 28,* 961–974.
Howes, C., Phillips, D. A., & Whitebook, M. (1992). Thresholds of quality: Implications for the social development of children in center-based child care. *Child Development, 63,* 449–460.
Howes, C., & Rubenstein, J. (1985). Determinants of toddler experiences in day care: Age of entry and quality of setting. *Child Care Quarterly, 14,* 140–151.
Howes, C., Unger, O., & Seidner, L. B. (1989). Social pretend play in toddlers: Parallels with social play and solitary pretend. *Child Development, 66,* 77–84.
Howes, C., & Wu, F. (1990). Peer interactions and friendships in an ethnically diverse school setting. *Child Development, 61,* 537–541.
Howes, C., and Wu, F. (1990). Peer interactions and friendships in an ethnically diverse school setting. *Child Development, 61,* 531–541.
Hudley, C., & Graham, S. (1983). An attributional intervention to reduce peer-directed aggression among African-American boys. *Child Development, 64,* 124–138.
Hudson, L. M., & Gray, W. M. (1986). Formal operations, the imaginary audience and the personal fable. *Adolescence, 84,* 751–765.
Huesmann, L. R., & Eron, L. D. (Eds.). (1986). *Television and the aggressive child: A cross national comparison.* Hillsdale, NJ: Erlbaum.
Hundleby, J. D., & Mercer, G. W. (1987). Family and friends as social environments and their relationship to youth adolescents' use of alcohol and marijuana. *Journal of Marriage and the Family, 49,* 151–164.
Hurley, D. (1985, March). Arresting delinquency. *Psychology Today, 19,* 62–68.
Hurrelmann, K., Engel, U., Holler, B., & Nordlohne, E. (1988). Failure in school, family conflicts, and psychosomatic disorders in adolescence. *Journal of Adolescence, 11,* 237–249.
Huston, A. C., Siegle, J., & Bremer, M. (1983, April). *Family environment and television use by preschool children.* Paper presented at the biennial meeting of the Society for Research in Child Development, Detroit, MI.
Huston, A. C., Wright, J. C., Albarez, M., Truglio, R., Fitch, M., & Piemyat, S. (1995). Perceived television reality in children's emotional and cognitive responses to its social content. *Journal of Applied Developmental Psychology, 16,* 231–251.
Hutchins, E. (1991). The social organization of distributed cognition. In J. M. Levine and S. D. Teasley (Eds.). *Perspectives on Socially Shared Cognition.* Washington, DC: American Psychological Association.
Hyde, J. S. (1985). *Half the human experience.* Lexington, MA: D.C. Heath.
Hynel, S., Bowker, A., & Woody, E. (1993). Aggressive versus withdrawn, unpopular children. Variations in peer and self-perceptions in multiple domains. *Child Development, 64,* 879–896.
Hyson, M. C., & Izard, C. E. (1985). Continuities and changes in emotional expressions during brief separations at 13 and 18 months. *Developmental Psychology, 21,* 1065–1170.
Ickes, W., & Turner, M. (1985). On the social advantages of having an older, opposite-sex sibling. *Journal of Personality and Social Psychology, 55,* 210–222.
Inagaki, K., & Hatano, G. (1993). Young children's understanding of the mind-body distinction. *Child Development, 64,* 1534–1549.
Increasing rates of ectopic pregnancies. (1984, December). *Medical Aspects of Human Sexuality, 18,* 14.
Inhelder, B., & Piaget, J. (1958). *The growth of logical thinking from childhood to adolescence.* New York: Basic Books.
Institute for Social Research. (1985). How children use time. In *Time, goals, and well-being.* Ann Arbor: University of Michigan.
Iosub, S., Bamji, H., Stone, R. K., Gromisch, D. S., & Waserman, E. (1987). More on human immune deficiency virus embryopathy. *Pediatrics, 80,* 512–516.
Irving, H., Benjamin, M., & Tracme, N. (1984). Shared parenting: An empirical analysis utilizing a large Canadian data base. *Family Process, 23,* 561–569.
Isabella, R. A., & Belsky, J. (1991). Interactional synchrony and the origins of infant–mother attachment: A replication study. *Child Development, 62,* 373–384.
Ishii-Kuntz, M., (1994). Parental involvement and perception toward

fathers' roles: A comparison between Japan and the United States. *Journal of Family Issues, 15,* 30–48.

Ishiyama, F. I. (1984, Winter). Shyness: Anxious social sensitivity and self-isolating tendency. *Adolescence, 19,* 903–911.

Istvan, J. (1986). Stress, anxiety, and birth outcomes: A critical review of the evidence. *Psychological Bulletin, 100,* 331–348.

Izard, C. E. (1977). *Human emotions.* New York: Plenum.

Izard, C. E. (1980). The young infant's ability to produce discreet emotion expression. *Developmental Psychology, 16,* 132–140.

Izard, C. E., Hembree, E. A., & Huebner, R. R. (1987). Infants' emotion expressions to acute pain: Developmental change and stability of individual differences. *Developmental Psychology, 23,* 105–113.

Izard, C. E., Haynes, O. M., Chisholm, G., & Baak, K. (1991). Emotional determinants of infant-mother attachment. *Child Development, 62,* 906–917.

Jacob, T. (1992). Family studies of alcoholism. *Journal of Family Psychology, 5,* 319–338.

Jacobovitz, D., & Sroufe, L. A. (1987). The early caregiver-child relationship and attention-deficit disorder with hyperactivity in kindergarten: A prospective study. *Child Development, 58,* 1496–1504.

Jacobs, J. E., & Eccles, J. S. (1992). The impact of mothers gender-role stereotypic beliefs on mothers and childrens' ability perceptions. *Journal of Personality and Social Psychology, 63,* 932–944.

Jacobs, J. E., & Potenza, M. (1991). The use of judgment heuristics to make social and object decisions: A developmental perspective. *Child Development, 62,* 166–178.

Jacobson, J. E., & Willie, D. E. (1986). The influence of attachment pattern on developmental changes in peer interaction from the toddler to the preschool period. *Child Development, 57,* 338–347.

Jacobson, J. L., Jacobson, S. W., Fein, G. G., Schwartz, P. M., & Dowler, J. K. (1984). Prenatal exposure to an environmental toxin: A test of multiple effects. *Developmental Psychology, 20,* 523–532.

Jacobson, S. W., & Frye, K. F. (1991). Effects of maternal support on attachment: Experimental evidence. *Child Development, 62,* 572–582.

Jakab, I. (1987). Growing up in the 80s: Prescriptions for raising a happy and successful child. *Medical Aspects of Human Sexuality, 21,* 53–63.

Jamieson, D. J., & Buescher, P. A. (Sept./Oct., 1992). The effect of family planning participation on prenatal care use and low birth weight. *Family Planning Perspectives, 24,* 214–218.

Janus, M., Burgess, A. W., & McCormack, A. (1987). Histories of sexual abuse in adolescent male runaways. *Adolescence, 22,* 405–417.

Jaquish, G. A., & Savins-Williams, R. C. (1981, December). Biological and ecological factors in the expression of adolescent self-esteem. *Journal of Youth and Adolescence, 10,* 473–485.

Jean-Gillis, M., & Crittenden, P. M. (1990). Maltreating families: A look at siblings. *Family Relations, 39,* 323–329.

Jellinger, M. S., & Ślovik, L. S. (1981). Current concepts in psychiatry: Divorce-input on children. *New England Journal of Medicine, 305,* 552.

Jemmott, J. B., III., & Jemmott, L. S. (1993). Alcohol and drug use during sexual activity. Predicting the HIV-risk-related behaviors of inner-city black male adolescents. *Journal of Adolescent Research, 8,* 41–57.

Jemmott, L. S., & Jemmott, J. B., III (1990). Sexual knowledge, attitudes, and risky sexual behavior among inner-city black male adolescents. *Journal of Adolescent Research, 5,* 346–369.

Jemmott, L. S., & Jemmott, J. B., III (1992). Family structure, parental strictness, and sexual behavior among inner-city black male adolescents. *Journal of Adolescent Research, 7,* 192–207.

Jennings, K. D., Stagg, V., & Connors, R. E. (1991). Social networks and mothers' interactions with their preschool children. *Child Development, 62,* 966–978.

Jennings, K. D., Stagg, V., Connors, R. E., & Ross, S. (1995). Social networks of mothers of physically handicapped preschoolers: Group differences and relations to mother–child interaction. *Journal of Applied Developmental Psychology, 16,* 193–209.

Jensen, G. F. (1986). Explaining differences in academic behavior between public-school and Catholic-school students. A quantitative case study. *Sociology of Education, 59,* 32–41.

Jensen, L., & Borges, M. (1986). The effect of maternal employment on adolescent daughters. *Adolescence, 21,* 659–666.

Joesch, J. M. (1994). Children and the timing of women's paid work after childbirth: A further specification of the relationship. *Journal of Marriage and the Family, 56,* 429–440.

Johnson, B. M., Shulman, S., & Collings, W. A. (1991). Systemic patterns of parenting as reported by adolescents: Developmental differences and implications for psychosocial outcomes. *Journal of Adolescent Research, 6,* 235–252.

Johnson, C., Lewis, C., Love, S., Lewis, L., & Stuckey, M. (1984, February). Incidence and correlates of bulimic behavior in a female high school population. *Journal of Youth and Adolescence, 13,* 15–26.

Johnson, G. M., Shontz, F. C., & Locke, T. P. (1984, Summer). Relationships between adolescent drug use and parental drug behavior. *Adolescence, 19,* 295–299.

Johnson, R. J., & Kaplan, H. B. (1991). Developmental processes leading to marijuana use. Comparing civilians and the military. *Youth and Society, 23,* 3–30.

Johnson, T. R., & Troppe, N. (1992). Improving literacy and employability among disadvantaged youths. The Job Corps model. *Youth and Society, 23,* 335–355.

Johnston, L. D., O'Malley, P. M., & Bachman, J. G. (1987). *National trends in drug use and related factors among American high school students and young adults, 1975–1986.* Washington, DC: U.S. Government Printing Office.

Jones, E. F., & Forrest, J. D. (Jan./Feb. 1992). Contraceptive failure rates based on the 1988 NSFG. *Family Planning Perspectives, 24,* 12–19.

Jones, R. E. (1984). *Human reproduction and sexual behavior.* Englewood Cliffs, NJ: Prentice-Hall.

Jones, S. S., & Raag, T. (1989). Smile production in older infants. The importance of a social recipient for the facial signal. *Child Development, 60,* 811–818.

Jones, S. S., Smith, L. B., & Landau, B. (1991). Object properties and knowledge in early lexical learning. *Child Development, 62,* 499–516.

Jose, P. E. (1990). Just-world reasoning in children's immanent justice judgments. *Child Development, 61,* 1024–1033.

Josephs, R A., Markus, H. R., & Tafarodi, R. W. (1992). Gender and self-esteem. *Journal of Personality and Social Psychology, 63,* 391–402.

Josselson, R. (1987). *Finding herself: Pathways to identity development in women.* San Francisco: Jossey-Bass.

Jouriles, E. N., Murphy, C. M., Farris, A. M., Smith, D. A., Richters, J. E., & Waters, E. (1991). Marital adjustment, parental disagreements about child rearing, and behavior problems in boys: Increasing the specificity of the marital assessment. *Child Development, 62,* 1424–1433.

Judson, F. (1985). Assessing the number of genital chlamydial infections in the United States. *Journal of Reproductive Medicine, 30*(Suppl.), 269–272.

Julian, T. W., McKenry, P. C., & McKelvey, M. W. (1994). Cultural variations in parenting: Perceptions of Caucasian, African-American, Hispanic, and Asian-American parents. *Family Relations, 43,* 30–37.

Jurich, A. P., Polson, C. J., Jurich, J. A., & Bates, R. A. (1985). Family factors in the lives of drug users and abusers. *Adolescence, 20,* 143–159.

Jurich, A. P., Schumm, W. R., & Bollman, S. R. (1987). The degree of family orientation perceived by mothers, fathers, and adolescents. *Adolescence, 22,* 119–238.

Jusczyk, P. W., Cutler, A., & Redanz, N. J. (1993). Infants' preference for the predominant stress patterns of English words. *Child Development, 64,* 675–687.

Kafka, R. R., & London, B. (1991). Communication and relationships in adolescent substance use: The influence of parents and friends. *Adolescence, 26,* 587–598.

Kagan, J. (1984). *The nature of the child.* New York: Basic Books.

Kagan, J., Arcus, D., Snidman, N., YuFeng, W., Hendler, J., & Greene, S. (1994). Reactivity in infants: A cross-national comparison. *Developmental Psychology, 30,* 342–345.

Kagan, J., Reznick, J. S., Clarke, C., Snidman, N., & Garcia-Cole, C. (1984). Behavioral inhibitors to the unfamiliar. *Child Development, 55,* 2212–2225.

Kagan, J., Reznick, J. S., & Snidman, N. (1987). The physiology and psychology of behavioral inhibition in children. *Child Development, 58,* 1459–1473.

Kagan, J., Reznick, J. S., Snidman, N., Gibbons, J., & Johnson, M. (1988). Childhood derivatives of inhibition and lack of inhibition to the familiar. *Child Development, 59,* 1580–1589.

Kahn, J. R., & London, K. A. (1991). Premarital sex and the risk of divorce. *Journal of Marriage and the Family, 53,* 845–855.

Kail, R. (1979). *Memory development in children.* San Francisco, CA: Freeman.

Kail, R., & Bisanz, J. (1982). Information processing and cognitive development. In H. Reese (Ed.), *Advances in child development and behavior* (Vol. 17). New York: Academic Press.

Kail, R. (1992). Processing speed, speech rate, and memory. *Developmental Psychology, 28,* 899–904.

Kaitz, M., Meschulach-Sarfaty, O., Auerbach, J., & Eidelman, A. (1988). A reexamination of newborn ability to imitate facial expressions. *Developmental Psychology, 24,* 3–7.

Kaitz, M., Lapidot, P., Bronner, R., & Eidelman, A. I. (1992). Parturient women can recognize their infants by touch. *Developmental Psychology, 28,* 35–39.

Kalish, C. W., & Gelman, S. A. (1992). On wooden pillows: Multiple classifications and children's category-based inductions. *Child Development, 63,* 1536–1557.

Kallen, D. J., Griffore, R., J., Popovich, S., & Powell, V. (1990). Adolescent mothers and their mothers view adoption. *Family Relations, 39,* 311–316.

Kalmuss, D., Namerow, P. B., & Bauer, U. (1992). Short-term consequences of parenting versus adoption among young, unmarried women. *Journal of Marriage and the Family, 54,* 80–90.

Kalmuss, D., & Seltzer, J. A. (1989). A framework for studying family socialization over the life cycle. *Journal of Family Issues, 10,* 339–358.

Kalter, N. (1983). How children perceive divorce. *Medical Aspects of Human Sexuality, 17,* 18–45.

Kamii, C., & deVries, R. (1980). *Group games in early education.* Washington, DC: National Association for Education of Young Children.

Kammer, P. P., Fouad, N., & Williams, R. (1988). Follow-up of a precollege program for minority and disadvantaged students. *Career Development Quarterly, 37,* 40–45.

Kandel, D. B. (1990). Parenting styles, drug use, and children's adjustment in families of young adults. *Journal of Marriage and the Family, 52,* 183–196.

Kaplan, E. A. (1990). Sex, work, and motherhood: The impossible triangle. *The Journal of Sex Research, 27,* 409–425.

Kaplan, H. B., & Fukurai, H. (1992). Negative social sanctions, self-rejection, and drug use. *Youth and Society, 23,* 275–298.

Kasari, C., Sigman, M., Mundy, P., & Yirmiya, N. (1988). Caregiver interactions with autistic children. *Journal of Abnormal Child Psychology, 16,* 45–56.

Katz, P. H., & Walsh, P. V. (1991). Modification of children's gender-stereotypes behavior. *Child Development, 62,* 338–351.

Kaye, K., & Warren, S. (1988). Discord about adoption in adoptive families. *Journal of Family Psychology, 1,* 406–433.

Kee, D. W., Gottfried, A. W., Bathurst, K., & Brown, K. (1987). Left-hemisphere language specialization and consistency in hand preference and sex differences. *Child Development, 58,* 718–724.

Keelan, J. P. R., Dion, K. K., & Dion, K. L. (1992). Correlates of appearance anxiety in late adolescents and early adulthood among young women. *Journal of Adolescence, 15,* 193–205.

Keesey, R. E., & Pawley, T. L. (1986). The regulation of body weight. *Annual Review of Psychology, 37,* 109–133.

Kelley, M. L., Power, T. G., & Winbush, D. D. (1992). Determinants of disciplinary practices in low income black mothers. *Child Development, 63,* 573–582.

Kelly, J. B. (1988). Longer-term adjustment in children of divorce: Converging findings and implications for practice. *Journal of Family Planning, 2,* 119–140.

Kendall, P. C., & Brophy, C. (1981). Activity and attentional correlates of teacher ratings of hyperactivity. *Journal of Pediatric Psychology, 6,* 451–458.

Keniston, K. (1970). Youth: A new stage of life. *American Scholar, 39,* 4.

Kenney, A. M., Guardaldo, S., & Brown, L. (1989). Sex education and AIDS education in the schools: What states and large school districts are doing. *Family Planning Perspectives, 21,* 56–64.

Kershner, J. G., & Cohen, N. J. (1992). Maternal depressive symptoms and child functioning. *Journal of Applied Developmental Psychology, 13,* 51–63.

Kestenbaum, R. (1992). Feeling happy versus feeling good: The processing of discrete and global categories of emotional expressions by children and adults. *Developmental Psychology, 28,* 1132–1142.

Ketterlinus, R. D., Henderson, S., & Lamb, M. E. (1991). The effects of maternal age-at-birth on children's cognitive development. *Journal of Research on Adolescence, 1,* 173–188.

Keyes, S., & Block, J. (1984, February). Prevalence and patterns of substance use among early adolescents. *Journal of Youth and Adolescence, 13,* 1–13.

Kids and contraceptives. (1987, February 16). *Newsweek,* pp. 54–65.

Kifer, E. (1985). Review of the ACT Assessment Program. In J. V. Mitchell (Ed.), *Ninth mental measurement yearbook* (pp. 31–45). Lincoln: University of Nebraska Press, Buros Mental Measurement Institute.

Kii, T. (1982). A new index for measuring demographic aging. *Gerontologist, 22,* 438–442.

King, B. (1994). Nonresident father involvement and child well-being: Can dads make a difference? *Journal of Family Issues, 15,* 78–96.

Kinney, D. K., & Matthysse, S. (1978). Genetic transmission of schizophrenia. *Annual Review of Medicine, 29,* 459–473.

Kinsey, A. C., Pomeroy, W., and Martin, C. (1948). *Sexual behavior in the human male.* Philadelphia, PA: Saunders.

Kirby, D., Resnick, M. D., Downes, B., Kocher, T., Gunderson, P., Potthoff, S., Zelterman, D., Blum, R. W. (1993). The effects of school-based health clinics in St. Paul on school-wide birth rates. *Family Planning Perspectives 25,* 12–16.

Kirby, D., Waszak, C., & Ziegler, J. (1991). Six school-based clinics: The reproductive health services and impact on sexual behavior. *Family Planning Perspectives, 23,* 6–16.

Kirkendall, L. (1981, May). The case against circumcision. *Sexology Today,* pp. 56–59.

Kisilevsky, B. S., Muir, D. W., & Low, J. A. (1992). Maturation of human fetal responses to vibroacoustic stimulation. *Child Development, 63,* 1497–1508.

Kissman, K. (1990). Social support and gender role attitude among teenage mothers. *Adolescence, 25,* 709–716.

Kit-fong Au, T., Sidle, A. L., & Rollins, K. B. (1993). Developing an intuitive understanding of conservation and contamination: Invisible particles as a plausible mechanism. *Developmental Psychology, 29,* 286–299.

Kitson, G. C., & Morgan, L. A. (1990). The multiple consequences of divorce: A decade review. *Journal of Marriage and the Family, 52,* 913–924.

Kivnick, H. Q. (1982). Grandparenthood: An overview of meaning and mental health. *The Gerontologist, 22,* 59–66.

Klaczynski, P. A. (1990). Cultural-developmental tasks and adolescent development: Theoretical and methodological considerations. *Adolescence, 25,* 811–824.

Klaus, M., & Kennel, J. (1982). *Parent-infant bonding* (2nd ed.). St. Louis, MO: Mosby.

Klein, H. A. (1992). Treatment and self-esteem in late adolescence. *Adolescence, 27,* 689–694.

Kleinman, J. C., Cooke, M., Machlin, S., & Kessel, S. S. (1983). *Variations in use of obstetric technology* (DHHS Publication No. PHS84-1232). Washington, DC: U.S. Government Printing Office.

Kline, M., Johnston, J. R., & Tschann, J. M. (1991). The long shadow of marital conflict: A model of children's postdivorce adjustment. *Journal of Marriage and the Family, 53,* 297–309.

Klitsch, M. (1989). Noncustodial fathers can probably afford to pay far more for child support than they now provide. *Family Planning Perspectives, 21,* 278–279.

Klitsch, M. (1991). Hispanic ethnic groups face variety of serious health, social problems. *Family Planning Perspectives, 23,* 186–188.

Klitsch, M. (March/April 1992). Maternal cocaine use raises delivery costs, need for neonatal care. *Family Planning Perspectives, 24,* 93–95.

Klitsch, M. (1993). Close to half of women aged 13–44 are at risk of unintended pregnancy. *Family Planning Perspectives, 25,* 44–45.

Klitsch, M. (1994). Prenatal exposure to tobacco, alcohol, and other drugs found in more than one in ten California newborns. *Family Planning Perspectives, 26,* 95–96.

Knoff, H. M. (1983, Fall). Learning disabilities in the junior high school: Creating the six-hour emotionally disturbed adolescent. *Adolescence, 18,* 541–550.

Knox, D., & Wilson, K. (1981). Dating behavior of university students. *Family Relations, 30,* 255–258.

Knox, D., & Wilson, K. (1983). Dating problems of university students. *College Student Journal, 17,* 225–228.

Kobak, R. R., Cole, H. E., Ferenz-Gillis, R., & Fleming, W. S. (1993). Attachment and emotional regulation during mother-teen problem solving: A controlled theory analysis. *Child Development, 64,* 231–245.

Kochanska, G. (1990). Maternal beliefs as long-term predictors of mother–child interaction and rapport. *Child Development, 61,* 1934–1943.

Kochanska, G. (1991). Patterns of inhibition to the unfamiliar in children of normal and affectively ill mothers. *Child Development, 62,* 250–263.

Kochanska, G. (1992). Children's interpersonal influence with mothers and peers. *Developmental Psychology, 28,* 491–499.

Kochanska, G., DeVet, K., Goldman, M., Murray, K., & Putnam, S. P. (1994). Maternal reports of conscience development and temperament in young children. *Child Development, 65,* 852–868.

Kochanska, G., & Kuczynski, L. (1991). Maternal autonomy granting: Predictors of normal and depressed mothers' compliance and noncompliance with the requests of five-year-olds. *Child Development, 62,* 1449–1459.

Kochanska, G., Kuczynski, L., & Radke-Yarrow, M. (1989). Correspondence between mothers' self-reported and observed child-rearing practices. *Child Development, 60,* 56–63.

Koenig, L. J. (1988). Self-image of emotionally disturbed adolescents. *Journal of Abnormal Child Psychology, 16,* 111–126.

Koff, E., Rierdan, J., & Stubbs, M. L. (1990). Gender, body image, and self-concept in early adolescence. *Journal of Early Adolescence, 10,* 56–68.

Kohlberg, L. (1963). The development of children's orientation toward a moral order. *Vita Humana, 6,* 11–33.

Kohlberg, L. (1966a). A cognitive-developmental analysis of children's sex role concepts and attitudes. In E. Maccoby (Ed.), *The development of sex differences.* Palo Alto, CA: Stanford University Press.

Kohlberg, L (1966b). Moral education in the schools: A developmental view. *School Review, 74,* 1–30.

Kohlberg, L. (1969). *Stages in the development of moral thought and action.* New York: Holt, Rinehart, & Winston.

Kohlberg, L. (1970). Moral development and the education of adolescents. In R. F. Purnell (Ed.), *Adolescents and the American high school.* New York: Holt, Rinehart, & Winston.

Kohlberg, L., & Gilligan, C. (1971, Fall). The adolescent as a philosopher: The discovery of the self in a postconventional world. *Daedalus,* 1051–1086.

Kohlberg, L., & Kramer, M. S. (1969). Continuities and discontinuities in childhood and adult development. *Human Development, 12,* 93–120.

Kohlberg, L., & Turiel, E. (Eds.). (1972). *Recent research in moral development.* New York: Holt, Rinehart, & Winston.

Kohn, A. (1988). Make love, not war. *Psychology Today, 22,* 34–38.

Kohn, A. S. (1993). Preschoolers' reasoning about density: Will it float? *Child Development, 64,* 1637–1650.

Kolata, G. (1986). Obese children: A growing problem. *Science, 232,* 20–21.

Kolata, G. (1988). Child splitting. *Psychology Today, 22,* 34–36.

Kolodny, R. C. (1980, November). *Adolescent sexuality.* Paper presented at the annual convention of the Michigan Personnel and Guidance Association, Detroit.

Kontos, S., Hsu, H., & Dunn, L. (1994). Children's cognitive and social competence in child-care centers and family day-care homes. *Journal of Applied Developmental Psychology, 15,* 387–411.

Koop, C. E. (1986). *Surgeon general's reports on acquired immune deficiency syndrome.* Washington, DC: U.S. Department of Health and Human Services.

Kopp, C. B. (1983). Risk factors in development. In P. H. Mussen, M. Haith, & J. J. Campos (Eds.). *Handbook of child psychology* (4th ed., Vol. 2, pp. 1081–1088). New York: Wiley.

Kopp, C. B., & Kaler, S. R. (1989). Risk in infancy: Origins and implications. *American Psychologist, 44,* 224–230.

Kopp, C. B., & McCall, R. B. (1982). Predicting later mental performance for normal, at risk, and handicapped infants. In P. B. Baltes & O. G. Brim (Eds.), *Life-span development and behavior* (Vol. 4). New York: Academic Press.

Korner, A. F., Constantinou, J., Dimiceli, S., & Brown, B. W., Jr. (1991). Establishing the reliability and developmental validity of a neurobehavioral assessment for preterm infants: A methodological process. *Child Development, 62,* 1200–1208.

Kramer, L., & Gottman, J. M. (1992). Becoming a sibling: "With a little help from my friends." *Developmental Psychology, 28,* 685–699.

Kramer, L., & Washo, C. A. (1993). Evaluation of a court-mandated prevention program for divorcing parents. The children first program. *Family Relations, 42,* 179–186.

Kramer, M. S. (1981). Do breast feeding and delayed introduction of solid foods protect against subsequent obesity? *Journal of Pediatrics, 98,* 883–887.

Krause, C. M., & Saarnio, D. A. (1993). Deciding what is safe to eat: Young children's understanding of a parent's reality, and edibleness. *Journal of Applied Developmental Psychology, 14,* 231–244.

Krein, S. F., & Beller, A. H. (1988). Educational attainment of children from single-parent families: Differences by exposure, gender, and race. *Demography, 25,* 221–224.

Krieshock, S. I., & Karpowitz, D. H. (1988). A review of selected literature on obesity and guidelines for treatment. *Journal of Consulting and Development, 66,* 326–330.

Kroger, J. (1993). The role of historical context in the identity formation process of late adolescence. *Youth and Society, 24,* 363–376.

Kroger, J. A. (1980, Winter). Residential mobility and self-concept in adolescence. *Adolescence, 15,* 967–977.

Kroupa, S. E. (1988). Perceived parental acceptance and female juvenile delinquency. *Adolescence, 23,* 171–185.

Krueger, R., & Hansen, J. C. (1987). Self-concept changes during youth-home placement of adolescents. *Adolescence, 86,* 385–392.

Kubany, E. S., Richard, D. C., Bauer, G. B., & Muraoka, M. Y. (1992). Verbalized anger and accusatory "you" messages as cues for anger and antagonism among adolescents. *Adolescence, 27,* 505–516.

Kuczaj, S. A. (1986). Thoughts on the intentional basis of early object word extension. Evidence from comprehension and production. In S. A. Kuczaj & M. D. Barrett (Eds.), *The development of word meaning. Progress in cognitive developmental research.* New York: Springer-Verlag.

Kugler, D. E., & Hansson, R. O. (1988). Relational competence and social support among parents at risk of child abuse. *Family Relations, 37,* 328–332.

Kuhn, D. (1979). The significance of Piaget's formal operations stage in education. *Journal of Education, 161,* 34–50.

Kupersmidt, J. B., & Coie, J. D. (1990). Preadolescent peer status, aggression, and school adjustment as predictors of externalizing problems in adolescence. *Child Development, 61,* 1350–1362.

Kupersmidt, J. B., Griesler, P. C., DeRosier, M. E., Patterson, C. J., & Davis, P W. (1995). Childhood aggression and peer relations in the context of family and neighborhood factors. *Child Development, 66,* 360–375.

Kurdek, L. A. (1989). Relationship quality for newly married husbands and wives: Marital history, stepchildren, and individual-difference predictors. *Journal of Marriage and the Family, 51,* 1053–1064.

Kurdek, L. A., & Berg, B. (1983). Correlates of children's adjustment to their parents' divorce. In L. A. Kurdek (Ed.), *Children and divorce.* San Francisco, CA: Jossey-Bass.

Kurdek, L. A., & Fine, M. A. (1991). Cognitive correlates of satisfaction for mothers and stepfathers in stepfather families. *Journal of Marriage and the Family, 53,* 565–572.

Kurdek, L. A., & Fine, M. A. (1993). The relation between family structure and the young adolescent's appraisals of family climate and parenting behavior. *Journal of Family Issues, 14,* 279–290.

Kurtz, P. D., Kurtz, G. L., & Jarvis, S. B. (1991). Problems of maltreated runaway youths. *Adolescence, 26,* 543–555.

Lachenmeyer, J. R., & Muni-Brander, P. (1988). Eating disorders in a nonclinical adolescent population: Implications for treatment. *Adolescence, 23,* 303–312.

Lackovic-Grgin, K., & Dekovic, M. (1990). The contribution of significant others to adolescents' self-esteem. *Adolescence, 25,* 839–846.

Ladd, G. W. (1990). Having friends, keeping friends, making friends, and being liked by peers in the classroom: Predictors of children's early school adjustment. *Child Development, 61,* 1081–1100.

Ladd, G. W., & Hart, C. H. (1992). Creating informal play opportunities: Are parents' and preschoolers' initiations related to children's confidence with peers? *Developmental Psychology, 28,* 1179–1187.

Ladd, G. W., & Price, J. M. (1987). Predicting children's social and school adjustment following the transition from preschool to kindergarten. *Child Development, 58,* 1168–1189.

Ladd, G. W., Price, J. M., & Hart, C. H. (1988). Predicting preschoolers' peer status from their playground behaviors. *Child Development, 59,* 986–992.

Lagercrantz, H., & Slotkin, T. A. (1968). The "stress" of being born. *Scientific American, 254,* 100–107.

Lamaze, F. (1970). *Painless childbirth.* Chicago, IL: Regency.

Lamb, M. E., Frodi, M., Hwang, C., & Frodi, A. M. (1983). Effects of paternal involvement on infant preference for mothers and fathers. *Child Development, 54,* 450–458.

Lamborn, S. D., Mounts, N. S., Steinberg, L., & Dornbusch, S. M. (1991). Patterns of competence and adjustment among adolescents from authoritative, authoritarian, indulgent, and neglectful families. *Child Development, 62,* 1049–1065.

Landau, S., & Milich, R. (1988). Social communication patterns of attention-deficit-disordered boys. *Journal of Abnormal Child Psychology, 16,* 69–81.

Landers, A. (1985, June 11). Is affection more important than sex? *Family Circle.*

Landry, R. (1987). Additive bilingualism, schooling, and special education: A minority group perspective. *Canadian Journal for Exceptional Children, 3,* 109–114.

Lange, G., & Pierce, S. H. (1992). Memory-strategy learning and maintenance in preschool children. *Developmental Psychology, 28,* 453–462.

Langfeldt, T. (1981). Sexual development in children. In H. Cook & H. Howells (Eds.), *Adult sexual interest in children.* London: Academic Press.

LaRossa, R. (1988). Fatherhood and social change. *Family Relations, 37,* 451–457.

LaRossa, R., Gordon, B. A., Wilson, R. J., Bairan, A., & Jaret, C. (1991). The fluctuating image of the 20th-century American father. *Journal of Marriage and the Family, 53,* 987–997.

Larsen, J. W. (1986). Congenital toxoplasmas. In J. L. Sever & R. L. Brent (Eds.), *Teratogen update: Environmentally induced birth defect risks.* New York: Liss.

Larson, R., & Ham, M. (1993). Stress and "storm and stress" in early adolescence: Relationship of negative events with dysphoric effect. *Developmental Psychology, 29,* 130–140.

Larson, R., & Richards, M. H. (1991). Daily companionship in later childhood and early adolescence: Changing developmental contexts *Child Development, 62,* 284–300.

Larzelere, R. E., Amberson, T. G., & Martin, J. A. (1992). Age differences in perceived and discipline problems from nine to 48 months. *Family Relations, 41,* 192–199.

Lasley, J. R. (1992). Age, social context, and street gang membership: Are youth gangs becoming adult gangs? *Youth and Society, 23,* 435–451.

Latham, M. C. (1977). Infant feeding in national and international perspective: An examination of the decline in human lactation, and the modern crisis in infant and young child feeding practices. *Annals of the New York Academy of Sciences, 300,* 197–209.

Lavin, J., Stephens, R., Miodovnik, M., & Barden, T. (1982). Vaginal delivery in patients with a prior cesarean section. *Obstetrics and Gynecology, 59,* 135–148.

Leadbeater, B. J., & Bishop, S. J., (1994). Predictors of behavior problems in preschool children of inner-city Afro-American and Puerto Rican adolescent mothers. *Child Development, 65,* 638–648.

Leaper, C. (1991). Influence and involvement in children's discourse: Age, gender, and partner effects. *Child Development, 62,* 797–811.

Leboyer, F. (1975). *Birth without violence.* New York: Alfred A. Knopf.

LeBreck, D. B., & Baron, A. (1987). Age and practice effects in continuous recognition memory. *Journal of Gerontology, 42,* 89–91.

LeClair, N., & Berkowitz, B. (1983, February). Counseling concerns for the individual with bulimia. *Personnel and Guidance Journal, 61,* 352–355.

Lederberg, A. J. (1982). A framework for research on preschool children's speech modification. In S. A. Kuczaj, II (Ed.), *Language development: Vol. 2. Language, thought, and culture.* Hillsdale, NJ: Erlbaum.

Ledoux, S., Choquet, M., & Manfredi, R. (1993). Associated factors for self-reported binge eating among male and female adolescents. *Journal of Adolescence, 16,* 75–91.

Lee, V. E., Brooks-Gunn, J., Schnur, E., & Liaw, F. (1990). Are Head Start effects sustained: A longitudinal follow-up comparison of disadvantaged children attending Head Start, no preschool, and other preschool programs. *Child Development, 61,* 495–507.

LeFlore, L. (1988). Delinquent youths and family. *Adolescence, 23,* 629–642.

Legal rights still cloudy for 18-year-olds. (1976, March 8). *U.S. News and World Report,* pp. 27–28.

Leifer, M. (1980). *Psychological effects of motherhood: Study of first pregnancy.* New York: Praeger.

LeMare, L. J., & Rubin, K. H. (1987). Perspective taking and peer interaction: Structural and developmental analysis. *Child Development, 58,* 306–315.

Lempers, J. D., & Clark-Lempers, D. (1990). Family economic stress, maternal and paternal support and adolescent distress. *Journal of Adolescence, 13,* 217–230.

Lempers, J. D., & Clark-Lempers, D. S. (1993). A functional comparison of same-sex and opposite-sex friendships during adolescence. *Journal of Adolescent Research, 8,* 89–108.

Leo, J. (1987, January 12). Exploring the traits of twins. *Time,* p. 63.

Lerner, J. V., Hertzog, C., Hooker, K., Hassibi, M., & Thomas, A. (1988). Longitudinal study of negative emotional states and adjustment from early childhood through adolescence. *Child Development, 59,* 356–366.

Lerner, R. M. (1992). Dialectics, developmental contextualism, and the further enhancement of theory about puberty and psychosocial development. *Journal of Early Adolescence, 12,* 366–388.

Lerner, R. M., Delaney, M., Hess, L. E., Jovanovic, J., & von Eye, A. (1990). Early adolescent physical attractiveness and academic competence. *Journal of Early Adolescence, 10,* 4–20.

Lerner, R. M., Lerner, J. V., Hess, L. E., Schwab, J., Jovanovic, J., Talwar, R., & Kucher, J. S. (1991). Physical attractiveness and psychosocial functioning among early adolescents. *Journal of Early Adolescence, 11,* 300–320.

Leslie, L. A., Huston, T. L., & Johnson, M. P. (1986). Parental reactions to dating relationships: Do they make a difference? *Journal of Marriage and the Family, 48,* 57–66.

Lester, B. M. (1987). Prediction of developmental outcome from accoustical cry analysis in term and preterm infants. *Pediatrics, 80,* 529–534.

Lester, B. M., & Dreher, M. (1989). Effects of marijuana use during pregnancy on newborn cry. *Child Development, 60,* 765–771.

Lester, B. M., Corwin, M. J., Sepkoski, C., Seifer, R., Peucker, M., McLaughlin, S., & Golub, H. L. (1991). Neurobehavioral syndromes in cocaine-exposed newborn infants. *Child Development, 62,* 694–705.

Leupnitz, D. A. (1982). *Child custody: A study of families after divorce.* Lexington, MA: Lexington Books.

Levant, R. F. (1992). Toward the reconstruction of masculinity. *Journal of Family Psychology, 5,* 379–402.

Levant, R. F., Slattery, S. C., & Loiselle, J. E. (1987). Fathers' involvement in housework and child care with school-age daughters. *Family Relations, 36,* 152–157.

Levin, E., Adelson, S., Buchalter, G., & Bilcher, L. (1983, February). Karen Carpenter, *People.*

Levine, J. B. (1988). Play in the context of the family. *Journal of Family Psychology, 2,* 164–187.

Levy, J. (1985, May). Right brain, left brain. Fact and fiction. *Psychology Today, 19,* 28–44.

Levy, T. B., & Taylor, M. G., & Gelman, S. A. (1995). Traditional and evaluative aspects of flexibility in gender roles, social conventions, moral rules, and physical laws. *Child Development, 66,* 515–531.

Levy-Schiff, R., Sharir, H., & Mogilner, M. B. (1989). Mother- and father-preterm infant relationships in the hospital preterm nursery. *Child Development, 60,* 93–102.

Lew, A. R., & Butterworth, G. (1995). The effects of hunger on hand-mouth coordination in newborn infants. *Developmental Psychology, 31,* 456–463.

Lewis, C., & Osborne, A. (1990). Three-year-olds' problems with false belief: Conceptual deficit or linguistic artifact? *Child Development, 61,* 1514–1519.

Lewis, M., Alessandri, S. M., & Sullivan, M. W. (1992). Differences in shame and pride as a function of children's gender and task difficulty. *Child Development, 63,* 630–638.

Lewis, M., & Feiring, C. (1989). Infant, mother, and mother-infant interaction behavior and subsequent attachment. *Child Development, 60,* 831–837.

Licht, B. G., & Dweck, C. S. (1984). Determinants of academic achievement: The interaction of children's achievement orientations and skill areas. *Developmental Psychology, 20,* 628–638.

Lieberman, A. F., Weston, D. R., & Pawl, J. H. (1991). Preventive intervention and outcome with anxiously attached dyads. *Child Development, 62,* 199–209.

Light, H. K., Hertsgaard, D., & Martin, R. E. (1985). Farm children's work in the family. *Adolescence, 20,* 425–432.

Lillard, A. S. (1993a). Pretend play skills and the child's theory of mind. *Child Development, 64*, 348–371.

Lillard, A. S. (1993b). Young children's conceptualization of pretense: action or mental representational state? *Child Development, 64*, 372–386.

Lillard, A. S., & Flavell, J. H. (1992). Young children's understanding of different mental states. *Developmental Psychology, 28*, 626–634.

Lin, C. C., & Fu, V. R. (1990). A comparison of child-rearing practices among Chinese, immigrant Chinese, and Caucasian-American parents. *Child Development, 61*, 429–433.

Linn, R. (1991). Sexual and moral development of Israeli female adolescents for city and kibbutz: Perspectives of Kohlberg and Gilligan. *Adolescence, 26*, 59–72.

Linde, E. V., Morrongiello, B. A., & Rovee-Collier, C. (1985). Determinants of retention in 8-week-old infants. *Developmental Psychology, 21*, 601–613.

Lips, H. M. (1991). *Women, men, and power*. Mountain View, CA: Mayfield.

Lipsitt, L. (1986). Learning in infancy: Cognitive development in babies. *Journal of Pediatrics, 109*, 172–182.

Littrell, M. L. D., & Littrell, J. M. (1990). Clothing interests, body satisfaction, and eating behavior of adolescent females: Related or independent dimensions? *Adolescence, 25*, 77–96.

Liu, X., Kaplan, H. B., & Risser, W. W. (1992). Decomposing the reciprocal relationships between academic achievement and general self-esteem. *Youth and Society, 24*, 123–148.

Locke, J. (1982). Some thoughts concerning education. In P. H. Quick (Ed.), *Locke on education* (pp. 1–236). Cambridge, England: Cambridge University Press.

Loehlin, J. C. (1985). Fitting heredity-environment models jointly to twin and adoption data from the California Psychological inventory. *Behavior Genetics, 15*, 199–221.

Logan, D. D. (1980). The menarche experience in twenty-three foreign countries. *Adolescence, 58*, 247–256.

Logan, R. D. (1983, Winter). A re-conceptualization of Erikson's identity stage. *Adolescence, 18*, 943–946.

Lollis, S. P. (1990). Effects of maternal behavior on toddler behavior during separation. *Child Development, 61*, 99–103.

Lopez, A., Gelman, S. A., Gutheil, G., & Smith, E. E. (1992). The development of category-based induction. *Child Development, 63*, 1070–1090.

Lopez, F. G., & Thurman, C. W. (1993). High-trait and low-trait angry college students: A comparison of family environments. *Journal of Counseling and Development, 71*, 524–527.

Lorch, E. P., Bellack, D. R., & Augsbach, L. H. (1987). Young children's memory for televised stories: Effects of importance. *Child Development, 58*, 453–463.

Lorenz, K. Z. (1965). *Evolution and the modification of behavior*. Chicago, IL: University of Chicago Press.

Lovell, J. (1984, October 21). Why sexual abusers often get away with it. *Maine Sunday Telegram*, Portland, ME.

Lowery, C. R. (1985). Child custody in divorce: Parents' decisions and perceptions. *Family Relations, 34*, 241–249.

Lowery, C. R., & Settle, S. A. (1985). Effects of divorce on children: Differential impact on custody and visitation patterns. *Family Relations, 34*, 455–463.

Ludemann, P. M. (1991). Generalized discrimination of positive facial expression by seven- and ten-month-old infants. *Child Development, 62*, 55–67.

Lundholm, J. K., & Littrell, J. M. (1986). Desire for thinness among high school cheerleaders. Relationship to disordered eating and weight control behavior. *Adolescence, 21*, 573–579.

Luster, T., Rhoades, K., & Haas, B. (1989). The relation between parental values and parenting behavior: A test of the Kohn hypothesis. *Journal of Marriage and the Family, 51*, 139–147.

Lyons-Ruth, K., Connell, D. B., & Grunebaum, H. U. (1990). Infants at special risk: Maternal depression and family support services as mediators of infant development and security of attachment. *Child Development, 61*, 85–98.

Maccoby, E. E. (1992). The role of parents in the socialization of children: An historical overview. *Developmental Psychology, 28*, 1006–1017.

Maccoby, E. E., Depner, C., & Mnookin, R. (1988). *Family functioning in three forms of residence: Maternal, paternal, and joint*. Paper presented at the annual meeting of the American Orthopsychiatry Association, San Francisco, CA.

MacDonald, K. (1992). Warmth as a developmental construct: An evolutionary analysis. *Child Development, 63*, 753–773.

Machida, S., & Holloway, S. D. (1991). The relationship between divorced mothers' perceived control over child rearing and children's post-divorce development. *Family Relations, 40*, 272–278.

MacKenzie, B. (1984). Explaining race differences in IQ: The logic, the methodology, and the evidence. *American Psychologist, 39*, 1214–1233.

MacKinnon-Lewis, C., Volling, B. L., Lamb, M. E., Dechman, K., Rabiner, D., & Curtner, M. E. (1994). A cross-contextual analysis of boys' social competence: From family to school. *Developmental Psychology, 30*, 325–333.

MacWhinney, B. (1982). Basic syntactic processes. In S. Kuczaj, II (Ed.), *Language development: Vol. 1. Syntax and semantics*. Hillsdale, NJ: Erlbaum.

Madison, L. S., Madison, J. K., & Adubato, S. A. (1986). Infant behavior and development in relation to fetal movement and habituation. *Child Development, 57*, 1475–1482.

Mahler, M. S., Pine, F., & Bergman, A. (1975). *The psychological birth of the human infant: Symbiosis and individuation*. New York: Basic Books.

Main, M., & Cassidy, J. (1988). Categories of response in reunion with the parent at age 6: Predictable from infant attachment classifications and stable over a 1-month period. *Developmental Psychology, 24*, 415–426.

Makin, J. W., & Porter, R. H. (1989). Attractiveness of lactating females breast odors to neonates. *Child Development, 60*, 803–810.

Malatesta, C. Z., Grigoryev, P., Lamb, C., Albin, M., & Culver, C. (1986). Emotion socialization and expressive development in preterm and full-term infants. *Child Development, 57*, 316–330.

Malinak, R., & Wheeler, J. (1985). Endometriosis. *Female Patient, 6*, 35–36.

Mallick, M. J., Whipple, T. W., & Huerta, E. (1987). Behavioral and psychological traits of weight-conscious teenagers: A comparison of eating-disordered patients and high- and low-risk groups. *Adolescence, 85*, 157–168.

Mandler, J. M. (1983). Representation. In J. H. Flavell & E. M. Marman (Eds.), *Handbook of child psychology* (4th ed., Vol. 3, pp. 420–494). New York: Wiley.

Mangelsdorf, S., Gunnar, M., Kestenbaum, R., Lang, S., & Andreas, D. (1990). Infant proneness-to-distress temperament, maternal personality, and mother-infant attachment: Associations and goodness of fit. *Child Development, 61*, 820–831.

March, T. (1995). Perception of adoption as social stigma: Motivation for search and reunion. *Journal of Marriage and the Family, 57*, 653–660.

Marcia, J. E. (1966). Development and validation of ego identity status. *Journal of Personality and Social Psychology, 3*, 551–558.

Marcia, J. E. (1976). Identity six years after: A follow-up study. *Journal of Youth and Adolescence, 5*, 145–160.

Marcia, J. E. (1980). Identity in adolescence. In J. Adelson (Ed.). *Handbook of Adolescence*. New York: John Wiley & Sons.

Marcia, J. E. (1987). The identity status approach to the study of ego development. In T. Honess, & K. Yardley (Eds.). *Self and identity: Perspectives across the life span*. London & New York: Routledge & Kegan Paul.

Marcia, J. E. (1989). Identity and intervention. *Journal of Adolescence, 12*, 401–410.

Marean, G. C., Werner, L. A., & Kuhl, P. K. (1992). Vowel categorization by very young infants. *Developmental Psychology, 28*, 396–405.

Margolin, L. (1991). Abuse and neglect in nonparental child care: A risk assessment. *Journal of Marriage and the Family, 53*, 694–704.

Margolin, L. (1992). Beyond maternal blame. *Journal of Family Issues, 13*, 419–423.

Marion, R. W., Wiznia, A. A., Hutcheon, G., & Rubinstein, A. (1986). Human T-cell lymphotropic virus type III (HTLV-III) embryopathy. *American Journal of Diseases of Children, 140*, 638–640.

Markus, H. J., & Nurius, P. S. (1984). Self-understanding and self-regulation in middle childhood. In W. A. Collins (Ed.), *Development during middle childhood: The years from six to twelve* (pp. 147–183). Washington, DC: National Academy Press.

Maroufi, C. (1989). A study of student attitude toward traditional and generative models of instruction. *Adolescence, 24*, 65–72.

Marsiglio, W. (1991). Male procreative consciousness and responsibility: A conceptual analysis and research agenda. *Journal of Family Issues, 12,* 268–290.

Marsiglio, W. (1991). Paternal engagement activities with minor children. *Journal of Marriage and the Family, 53,* 973–986.

Marsiglio, W., (1992). Stepfathers with minor children living at home. *Journal of Family Issues, 13,* 195–214.

Marsiglio, W., & Mott, F. L. (1986). The impact of sex education on sexual activity, contraceptive use, and premarital pregnancy among American teenagers. *Family Planning Perspectives, 18,* 151–162.

Martens, R. (1988). Helping children become independent, responsible adults through sports. In E. W. Brown & C. T. Branta (Eds.), *Competitive sports for children and youth: An overview of research and issues* (pp. 297–307). Champaign, IL: Human Kinetics.

Martin, C. L., & Little, J. K. (1990). The relation of gender understanding to children's sex-typed preferences and gender stereotypes. *Child Development, 61,* 1427–1439.

Martin, C. L., Wood, C. H., & Little, J. K. (1990). The development of gender stereotype components. *Child Development, 61,* 1861–1904.

Martin, P., Hagestad, G. O., Diedrich, P. (1988). Family stories: Events (temporarily) remembered. *Journal of Marriage and the Family, 40,* 533–541.

Martinez, G. A., Dodd, D. A., & Samaltgedes, J. (1981). Milk-feeding patterns in the United States during the first twelve months of life. *Pediatrics, 68,* 863–868.

Martinez, R., & Dukes, R. L. (1991). Ethnic and gender differences in self-esteem. *Youth and Society, 22,* 318–338.

Mas, C. H., Alexander, J. F., & Turner, C. W. (1991). Dispositional attributions and defensive behavior in high- and low-conflict families. *Journal of Family Psychology, 5,* 176–191.

Masataka, N. (1992). Early ontogeny of vocal behavior of Japanese infants in response to maternal speech. *Child Development, 63,* 1177–1185.

Maslin, J. (1991, July 17). A false goddess: Thinness for women: Review of "The famine within." *New York Times,* p. C13.

Maslow, A. H. (1968). *Toward a psychology of being* (2nd ed.). Princeton, NJ: Van Nostrand.

Maslow, A. H. (1970). *Motivation and personality* (2nd ed.). New York: Harper.

Maslow, A. H. (1971). *The farther reaches of human nature.* New York: Viking.

Mason, G., & Gibbs, J. C. (1993). Social perspective taking and moral judgment among college students. *Journal of Adolescent Research, 8,* 109–123.

Masselam, V. S., Marcus, R. F., & Stunkard, C. L. (1990). Parent–adolescent communication, family functioning, and school performance. *Adolescence, 25,* 725–738.

Masson, J. M. (1984). *The assault on truth: Freud's suppression of the seduction theory.* New York: Farrar, Straus, & Giroux.

Masters, W. H., & Johnson, V. E. (1966). *Human sexual response.* Boston, MA: Little, Brown.

Mathew, A., & Cook, M. (1990). The control of reaching movements by young infants. *Child Development, 61,* 1238–1257.

Matias, R., & Cohn, J. F. (1993). Are Max-specified infant facial expressions during face-to-face interaction consistent with differential emotions theory? *Developmental Psychology, 29,* 524–531.

Maticka-Tyndale, E. (1991). Modification of sexual activities in the era of AIDS: A trained analysis of adolescent sexual activities. *Youth and Society, 23,* 31–49.

Matlin, M. (1983). *Cognition.* New York: Holt, Rinehart, & Winston.

Matter, R. M. (1984, Spring). The historical emergence of adolescence: Perspectives from developmental psychology and adolescent literature. *Adolescence, 19,* 131–142.

Matthews, L. J., & Ilon, L. (1980, July). Becoming a chronic runaway: The effects of race and family in Hawaii. *Family Relations, 29,* 404–409.

Mau, R. Y. (1992). The validity and devolution of a concept: Student alienation. *Adolescence, 27,* 731–741.

May, J. M. (1986). Cognitive processes and violent behavior in young people. *Journal of Adolescence, 9,* 17–27.

Maziade, M., Boudréault, M., Cote, R., & Thivierge, J. (1986). Influence of gentle birth delivery procedures and other perinatal circumstances on infant temperament and developmental and social implications. *Journal of Pediatrics, 108,* 134–136.

McAdams, D. P., & de St. Aubin, E. (1992). A theory of generativity and its assessment through self-report, behavioral acts, and narrative themes in autobiography. *Journal of Personality and Social Psychology, 62,* 1003–1015.

McCabe, M. P. (1984). Toward a theory of adolescent dating. *Adolescence, 19,* 159–170.

McCall, R. B., & Carriger, M. S. (1993). A meta-analysis of infant habituation and recognition memory performance as predictors of later IQ. *Child Development, 64,* 57–79.

McCary, J. L., & McCary, S. P. (1982). *McCary's human sexuality* (4th ed.). Belmont, CA: Wadsworth Publishing Co.

McCauley, E., Kay, T., Ito, J., & Treder, R. (1987). The Turner syndrome: Cognitive deficits, affective discrimination, and behavior problems. *Child Development, 58,* 464–473.

McClelland, D., Constantian, C. S., Regalado, D., & Stone, C. (1978, June). Making it to maturity. *Psychology Today, 11,* 42–53, 114.

McCombs, A., Forehand, A., & Smith, K. (1988). The relationship between maternal problem-solving style and adolescent social adjustment. *Journal of Family Psychology, 2,* 57–66.

McCormick, C. M., & Maurer, D. M. (1988). Unimanual hand preferences in 6-month-olds: Consistency and relation to familial handedness. *Infant Behavior and Development, 11,* 21–29.

McCullers, J. C., & Love, J. M. (1976). The scientific study of the child. In B. J. Taylor & T. J. White (Eds.), *Issues and ideas in America.* Norman: Oklahoma University Press.

McDermott, D. (1984, Spring). The relationship of parental drug use and parents' attitude concerning adolescent drug use to adolescent drug use. *Adolescence, 19,* 89–97.

McGill, M. (1985). *The McGill report on male intimacy.* New York: Harper and Row.

McGraw, M. B. (1940). Neural maturation as exemplified in achievement of bladder control. *Journal of Pediatrics, 16,* 580–590.

McGrory, A. (1990). Menarche: Response of early adolescent females. *Adolescence, 25,* 265–270.

McHale, S. M., Bartko, W. T., Crouter, A. C., & Perry-Jenkins, M. (1990). Children's housework and psychosocial functioning: The mediating effects of parents' sex-role behaviors and attitudes. *Child Development, 61,* 1413–1426.

McHale, S. M., & Pawletko, T. M. (1992). Differential treatment of siblings in two family contexts. *Child Development, 63,* 68–91.

McKenry, P. C., Kotch, J. B., & Browne, D. H. (1991). Correlates of dysfunctional parenting attitudes among low-income adolescent mothers. *Journal of Adolescent Research, 6,* 212–234.

McKenzie, B. E., Skouteris, H., Day, R. H., Hartman, B., & Yonas, A. (1993). Effective action by infants to contact objects by reaching and learning. *Child Development, 64,* 415–429.

McKusick, V. A. (1986). *Mendelian inheritance in man* (7th ed.). Baltimore, MD: Johns Hopkins University Press.

McLanahan, S., & Booth, K. (1989). Mothers-only families: Problems, prospects, and politics. *Journal of Marriage and the Family, 51,* 557–580.

McLaren, N. M., & Nieburg, P. (1988, August). Fetal tobacco syndrome and other problems caused by smoking during pregnancy. *Medical Aspects of Human Sexuality, 22,* 69–75.

McLaughlin, B. (1985). *Second language acquisition in childhood: Vol. 2. School-age children* (2nd ed.). Hillsdale, NJ: Erlbaum.

McLoyd, V. C. (1990). The impact of economic hardship on black families and children: Psychological distress, parenting, and socioemotional development. *Child Development, 61,* 311–346.

McMurran, M. (1991). Young offenders and alcohol-related crime: What interventions will address the issues? *Journal of Adolescence, 14,* 245–253.

McMurran, M., & Whitman, J. (1990). Strategies of self-control in male young offenders who have reduced their alcohol consumption without formal intervention. *Journal of Adolescence, 13,* 115–128.

McNally, S., Eisenberg, N., & Harris, J. E. (1991). Consistency and change in maternal child-rearing practices and values: A longitudinal study. *Child Development, 62,* 190–198.

McNeill, D. (1970). Language development in children. In P. H. Mussen (Ed.), *Handbook of child psychology* (3rd ed.). New York: Wiley.

McWhirter, E. H. (1991). Empowerment in counseling. *Journal of Counseling and Development, 69,* 222–227.

Mead, M. (1950). *Coming of age in Samoa.* New York: New American Library.

Mead, M. (1974). Adolescence. In H. V. Kraemer (Ed.), *Youth and culture: A human development approach.* Monterey, CA: Brooks/Cole.

Mednick, S. S., & Christiansen, K. O. (1977). *Biosocial bases of criminal behavior.* New York: Gardner Press.

Mehl, L. E., & Peterson, G. (1981). Home birth versus hospital birth: Comparisons of outcomes of matched populations. In P. Ahmed (Ed.), *Pregnancy, childbirth, and parenthood.* New York: Elsevier.

Meier, B. (1987, February 5). Companies wrestle with threats to workers' reproductive health. *Wall Street Journal,* p. 21.

Mellanby, A., Phelps, F., & Tripp, J. (1992). Sex education: More is not enough. *Journal of Adolescence, 15,* 449–466.

Melli, M. S. (1986). The changing legal status of the single parent. *Family Relations, 35,* 31–35.

Meltzoff, A. N. (1988). Infant imitation after a 1-week delay: Long-term memory for novel acts and multiple stimuli. *Developmental Psychology, 24,* 470–476.

Meltzoff, A. N., & Moore, M. K. (1977). Imitation of facial and manual gestures by human neonates. *Science, 198,* 75–78.

Meltzoff, A. N., & Moore, M. K. (1979). Interpreting "imitative" responses in early infancy. *Science, 205,* 217–219.

Mendelson, M. J., Aboud, F. E., & Lanthier, R. P. (1994). Personality predictors of friendship and popularity in kindergarten. *Journal of Applied Developmental Psychology, 15,* 413–435.

Meredith, D. (1986). Day care: The nine-to-five dilemma. *Psychology Today, 20,* 36–44.

Mervis, C. B., & Bertrand, J. (1994). Acquisition of the novel name–nameless category (N3C) principle. *Child Development, 65,* 1646–1662.

Messer, A. A. (1989). Boys' father hunger: The missing father syndrome. *Medical Aspects of Human Sexuality, 23,* 44–50.

Metcalf, K., & Gaier, E. L. (1987). Patterns of middle-class parent and adolescent underachievement. *Adolescence, 23,* 919–928.

Meyers, J. E., & Nelson, W. M. III (1986). Cognitive strategies and expectations as components of social competence in young adolescents. *Adolescence, 21,* 291–303.

Mezynski, K. (1983). Issues concerning the acquisition of knowledge: Effects of vocabulary training on reading comprehension. *Review of Educational Research, 53,* 253–279.

Michael, R. T., Gagnon, J. H., Laumann, E. O., and Kolata, G. (1994). *Sex in America.* Boston: Little, Brown.

Michel, G. F., Harkins, D. A., & Ovrut, M. R. (1986, April). Assessing infant (6–13 months old) handedness status. Paper presented at the 5th International Conference on Infant Studies. Los Angeles, CA.

Micheli, L. J. (1988). The incidence of injuries in children's sports: A medical perspective. In E. W. Brown & C. F. Branta (Eds.), *Competitive sports for children and youth: An overview of research and issues* (pp. 280–284). Champaign, IL: Human Kinetics.

Middleton, D. (1987). Collective memory and remembering: Some issues and approaches. *Quarterly Newsletter of the Laboratory of Comparative Human Cognition, 9,* 2–5.

Miller, A. T., Eggertson-Tacon, C., & Quigg, B. (1990). Patterns of runaway behavior within a larger systems context: The road to empowerment. *Adolescence, 25,* 271–290.

Miller, B. C., & Bowen, S. L. (1982, January). Father-to-newborn attachment behavior in relation to prenatal classes and presence at delivery. *Family Relations, 31,* 71–78.

Miller, B. C., & Heaton, T. B. (1991). Age at first sexual intercourse and the timing of marriage and childbirth. *Journal of Marriage and the Family, 53,* 719–732.

Miller, D. (1991). Do adolescents help and share? *Adolescence, 26,* 449–456.

Miller, E., Cradock-Watson, J. E., & Pollack, T. M. (1982, October). Consequences of confirmed maternal rubella and successive stages of pregnancy. *Lancet,* pp. 781–784.

Miller, J. B., & Lane, M. (1991). Relations between young adults and their parents. *Journal of Adolescence, 14,* 179–194.

Miller, J. E. (1991). Birth intervals and perinatal health: An investigation of three hypotheses. *Family Planning Perspectives, 23,* 63–70.

Miller, J. G., & Bersoff, B. M. (1992). Culture and moral judgment: How are conflicts between justice and interpersonal responsibilities resolved? *Journal of Personality and Social Psychology, 62,* 541–544.

Miller, K. E. (1990). Adolescents' same-sex and opposite-sex peer relations: Sex differences in popularity, perceived social competence, and social cognitive skills. *Journal of Adolescent Research, 5,* 222–241.

Miller, L. (1988). The emotional brain. *Psychology Today, 22,* 34–42.

Miller, M. (1978, October). Geriatric suicide: The Arizona study. *Gerontologist, 18,* 488–495.

Miller, M. W. (1985, January 17). Study says birth defects more frequent in areas polluted by technology firms. *Wall Street Journal,* p. 6.

Miller, N. B., Cowan, P. A., Cowan, C. P., Hetherington, E. M., & Clingempeel, W. G. (1993). Externalizing in preschoolers and early adolescents. A cross-study replication of a family model. *Developmental Psychology, 29,* 3–18.

Miller, P. H., & Aloise, P. A. (1989). Young children's understanding of the psychological causes of behavior: A review. *Child Development, 60,* 257–285.

Miller, S. A., & Davis, T. L. (1992). Beliefs about children: A comparative study of mothers, teachers, peers, and self. *Child Development, 63,* 1251–1265.

Mills, C. J. (1981, April). Sex roles, personality, and intellectual abilities in adolescents. *Journal of Youth and Adolescence, 10,* 85–112.

Mills, D. M. (1984). A model for stepfamily development. *Family Relations, 33,* 365–372.

Mills, J. L., Graubard, B. I., Harley, E. E., Rhoads, G. G., & Berendes, H. W. (1984). Maternal alcohol consumption and birth weight: How much drinking is safe during pregnancy? *JAMA, Journal of the American Medical Association, 252,* 1875–1879.

Mills, R. S. L., & Rubin, K. H. (1990). Parents' beliefs about problematic social behaviors in early childhood. *Child Development, 61,* 138–151.

Mistry, J. J., & Lange, G. W. (1985). Children's organization and recall of information in scripted narratives. *Child Development, 56,* 953–961.

Mitchell, J. E., Pyle, R. L., & Eckert, E. D. (1981). Frequency and duration of binge-eating episodes in patients with bulimia. *American Journal of Psychiatry, 138,* 835, 836.

Mitgang, L. (1980, April 28). *Student SAT scores decline for third year.* Portland, ME: Portland Press Herald.

Mize, J., Pettit, G. S., & Brown, E. G. (1995). Mothers' supervision of their children's peer play: Relations with beliefs, perceptions, and knowledge. *Developmental Psychology, 31,* 311–321.

Moely, B. E., Hart, S. S., Leal, L., Santulli, K. A., Rao, N., Johnson, T., & Hamilton, L. B. (1992). The teacher's role in facilitating memory and study strategy development in the elementary school classroom. *Child Development, 63,* 653–672.

Moffitt, T. E. (1990). Juvenile delinquency and attention deficit disorder: Boys' developmental trajectories from age 3 to 15. *Child Development, 61,* 893–910.

Moffitt, T. E., Caspi, A., Belsky, J., & Silva, P. A. (1992). Childhood experience and the onset of menarche: A test of sociobiological model. *Child Development, 63,* 47–58.

Mom, nine, doing fine. (1986, June 15). *Parade,* p. 15.

Monahan, S. C., Buchanan, C. N., Maccoby, E. E., & Dornbusch, S. M. (1993). Sibling differences in divorced families. *Child Development, 64,* 152–168.

Money, J. (1980). *Love and love sickness.* Baltimore, MD: Johns Hopkins University Press.

Montgomery, D. E. (1993). Young children's understanding of interpretive diversity between different-age listeners. *Developmental Psychology, 29,* 337–345.

Mooney, S. P., Sherman, M. F., & Lopresto, C. T. (1991). Academic locus of control, self-esteem, and perceived distance from home as predictors of college adjustment. *Journal of Counseling and Development, 69,* 445–448.

Moore, D., & Schultz, N. R. (1983). Loneliness at adolescence: Correlates, attributions, and coping. *Journal of Youth and Adolescence, 12,* 95–100.

Moore, J. W., Jensen, B., & Hauck, W. E. (1990). Decision-making processes of youth. *Adolescence, 25,* 583–592.

Moore, K. A., & Stief, T. M. (1991). Changes in marriage and fertility behavior: Behavior versus attitudes of young adults. *Youth and Society, 22,* 362–386.

Moore, L. M., Nielsen, C. R., & Mistretta, C. M. (1982). Sucrose taste thresholds: Age-related differences. *Journal of Gerontology, 37,* 64–69.

Moore, S., & Rosenthal, D. (1990). Adolescent invulnerability and perceptions of AIDS risk. *Journal of Adolescent Research, 6,* 164–180.

Moran, G. F., & Vinovskis, M. A. (1986). The great care of godly parents: Early childhood in Puritan New England. *Monographs of the Society for Research in Child Development, 50* (4–5, Serial No. 211).

Moran, J. R., & Corley, M. D. (1991). Sources of sexual information and sexual attitudes and behaviors of Anglo and Hispanic adolescent males. *Adolescence, 26,* 857–864.

Moran, P. B., & Eckenrode, J. (1991). Gender differences in the costs and benefits of peer relations during adolescence. *Journal of Adolescent Research, 6,* 396–409.

Morell, P., & Norton, W. T. (1980). Myelin. *Scientific American, 24,* 88–118.

Morelli, G. A., Oppenheim, D., Rogoff, B., & Goldsmith, D. (1992). Cultural variation in infants' sleeping arrangements: Questions of independence. *Developmental Psychology, 28,* 604–613.

Morgan, M., & Gross, L. (1982). Television and educational achievement. In D. Pearl, L. Bouthilet & J. Lazer (Eds.), *Television and behavior: Ten years of scientific progress and implications for the eighties* (Vol. 2). Washington, DC: U.S. Government Printing Office.

Morison, P., & Masten, A. S. (1991). Peer reputation in middle childhood as a predictor of adaptation in adolescence: A seven-year follow up. *Child Development, 62,* 991–1007.

Mott, F. L. (1994). Sons, daughters, and fathers' absence: Differentials in father-leaving probabilities and in home environments. *Journal of Family Issues, 15,* 97–128.

Muehlenhard, C. L., & Cook S. W. (1988). Men's self-reports of unwanted sexual activity. *The Journal of Sex Research, 24,* 58–72.

Mueller, D. P., & Cooper, P. W. (1986). Children of single parent families: How they fare as young adults. *Family Relations, 35,* 169–172.

Mueller, K. E., & Powers, W. G. (1990). Parent–child sexual discussion: Perceived communicator style and subsequent behavior. *Adolescence, 25,* 469–482.

Mullis, A. K., Mullis, R. L., & Normandin, D. (1992). Cross-sectional and longitudinal comparisons of adolescent self-esteem. *Adolescence, 27,* 51–61.

Murray, A. D. (1988). Newborn auditory brainstem evoked responses (ABRs): Prenatal and contemporary correlates. *Child Development, 59,* 571–588.

Murry, D. M. (1992). Sexual career paths of black adolescent females: A study of socioeconomic status and other life experiences. *Journal of Adolescent Research, 7,* 4–27.

Musun-Miller, L. (1993). Social acceptance and social problem-solving in preschool children. *Journal of Applied Developmental Psychology, 14,* 59–70.

Muuss, R. E. (1985). Adolescent eating disorder: Anorexia nervosa. *Adolescence, 20,* 525–536.

Muuss, R. E. (1988a). Carol Gilligan's theory of sex differences in the development of moral reasoning during adolescence. *Adolescence, 23,* 229–243.

Muuss, R. E. (1988b). *Theories of adolescence* (5th ed.). New York: McGraw-Hill.

Myers, D. A. (1991). Work after cessation of career job. *Journal of Gerontology, 46,* S93–S102.

Myricks, N., & Ferullo, D. L. (1986). Race and child custody disputes. *Family Relations, 35,* 325–328.

Nadi, N. S., Nurnberger, J. L., & Gershon, E. S. (1984). Muscarinic cholinergic receptors on skin fibroblasts in familial affective disorder. *New England Journal of Medicine, 311,* 225–230.

Nagel, K. L., & Jones, K. H. (1992a). Predisposition factors in anorexia nervosa. *Adolescence, 27,* 381–386.

Nagel, K. L., & Jones, K. H. (1992b). Sociological factors in the development of eating disorders. *Adolescence, 27,* 107–113.

Nagy, W., & Anderson, R. C. (1984). The number of words in printed school English. *Reading Research Quarterly, 19,* 304–330.

Nagy, W., Herman, P. A., & Anderson, R. C. (1985). Learning words from context. *Reading Research Quarterly, 20,* 233–253.

Nathanson, M., Baird, A., & Jemail, J. (1986). Family functioning and the adolescent mother: A systems approach. *Adolescence, 21,* 827–841.

National audience demographics. Report 1985. (1985). Northrock, IL: A. C. Nielsen Co.

National Children and Youth Fitness Study. (1984). Washington, DC: U.S. Public Health Service, Office for Disease Prevention and Health Promotion.

National Commission for the Protection of Human Subjects of Biomedical and Behavioral Research. (1978). Institutional review boards: Report and recommendations. *Federal Register, 43,* 56174–56198.

National Commission on Excellence in Education. (1983). *A nation at risk: The imperative for educational reform.* Washington, DC: Department of Education.

National Foundation for the March of Dimes. (1977). *Birth defects: Tragedy and hope.*

National Institute on Alcohol Abuse and Alcoholism (NIAA). (1986). *Media alert: FAS awareness campaign: My baby . . . strong and healthy.* Rockville, MD: National Clearinghouse for Alcohol Information.

National Institute on Mental Health (NIMH). (1982). *Television and behavior: Ten years of scientific progress and implications for the eighties:* Vol. 1. *Summary Report* (DHHS Publication No. ADM 82-1195). Washington, DC: U.S. Government Printing Office.

Nelson, C., & Keith, J. (1990). Comparison of female and male early adolescent sex role attitude and behavior development. *Adolescence, 25,* 183–204.

Nelson, C. A., & Dolgin, K. G. (1985). The generalized discrimination of facial expressions by seven-month-old infants. *Child Development, 56,* 58–61.

Nelson, K. (1981). Individual differences in language development: Implications for development and language. *Developmental Psychology, 17,* 170–189.

Nelson, W. L., Hughes, H. M., Handal, P., Katz, B., & Searight, H. R. (1993). The relationship of family structure and family conflict to adjustment in young adult college students. *Adolescence, 28,* 29–40.

Nemeth, P. (1990, April). Kids on ritalin: Are they better off? *On campus.* Washington, DC: American Federation of Teachers.

Nettles, S. M. (1989). The role of community involvement in fostering investment behavior in low-income black adolescents: A theoretical perspective. *Journal of Adolescent Research, 4,* 190–201.

Neugarten, B. L., & Neugarten, D. A. (1987). The changing meanings of age. *Psychology Today, 21,* 29–33.

Newcombe, N., & Dubas, J. S. (1992). A longitudinal study of predictors of spatial ability in adolescent females. *Child Development, 63,* 37–46.

Newcombe, N., & Fox, N. A. (1994). Infantile amnesia: Through a glass darkly. *Child Development, 65,* 31–40.

Newcombe, N., & Huttenlocher, J. (1992). Children's early ability to solve perspective-taking problems. *Developmental Psychology, 28,* 635–641.

Newcomer, S. F., Udry, J. R., & Cameron, F. (1983). Adolescent sexual behavior and popularity. *Adolescence, 18,* 515–522.

Newell, G. K., Hammig, C. L., Jurich, A. P., & Johnson, D. E. (1990). Self-concept as a factor in the quality of diets of adolescent girls. *Adolescence, 25,* 117–130.

Nieburg, P., Marks, J. S., McLaren, N. M., & Remington, P. L. (1985). The fetal tobacco syndrome. *JAMA, Journal of the American Medical Association, 253,* 2998–2999.

Niedenthal, P. M., Setterlund, M. B., & Wherry, M. B. (1992). Possible self-complexity and affective reactions to goal-relevant evaluation. *Journal of Personality and Social Psychology, 63,* 5–16.

Nock, S. L. (1988). The family and hierarchy. *Journal of Marriage and the Family, 50,* 957–966.

Nolin, M. J., & Petersen, K. K. (1992). Gender differences in parent-child communication about sexuality. *Journal of Adolescent Research, 7,* 59–71.

Noll, R. B., Zucker, R. A., Fitzgerald, H. E., & Curtis, W. J. (1992). Cognitive and motor functioning of sons of alcoholic fathers and controls: The early childhood years. *Developmental Psychology, 28,* 665–675.

Northman, J. E. (1985). The emergence of an appreciation for help during childhood and adolescence. *Adolescence, 20,* 775–781.

Norton, A. J., & Glick, P. B. (1986). One-parent families: A social and economic profile. *Family Relations, 35,* 9–13.

Novy, D. M., Gaa, J. P., Frankiewicz, R. G., Liberman, D., & Amerikaner, M. (1992). The association between patterns of family functioning and ego development of the juvenile offender. *Adolescence, 27,* 25–35.

Nunn, G. D., & Parish, T. S. (1992). The psychosocial characteristics of at-risk high school students. *Adolescence, 27,* 435–440.

Nurmi, J. A., & Pulliainen, H. (1991). The changing parent–child relationships, self-esteem, and intelligence as determinants of orientation to the future during early adolescence. *Journal of Adolescence, 14,* 17–34.

Ogundari, J. T. (1985, Spring). Somatic deviations in adolescence: Reactions and adjustments. *Adolescence, 20,* 179–183.

Ohannessian, C. M., & Crockett, L. J. (1993). A longitudinal investigation of the relationship between educational investment and adolescent sexual activity. *Journal of Adolescent Research, 8,* 167–182.

Olsen, J., Weed, S., Nielsen, A., & Jensen, L. (1992). Student evaluation of sex education programs advocating abstinence. *Adolescence, 27,* 369–380.

Olsen, J. A., Weed, S. E., Ritz, G. M., & Jensen, L. C. (1991). The effects of three abstinence sex education programs on student attitudes towards sexual activity. *Adolescence, 26,* 631–641.

Olson, J. M. (1992). Self-perception of humor: Evidence for discounting and augmentation effects. *Journal of Personality and Social Psychology, 62,* 369–377.

Olson, J. T. (1981). The impact of housework on child care in the home. *Family Relations, 31,* 75–81.

Olson, S. L., & Banyard, V. (1993). Sources of daily stress in the lives of low-income single mothers of young children. *Family Relations, 42,* 50–56.

Olson, S. L., Bates, J. E., & Bayles, K. (1984). Mother-infant interaction and the development of individual differences in children's cognitive competence. *Developmental Psychology, 20,* 166–179.

Olthof, T., Ferguson, T. J., & Luiten, A. (1989). Personal responsibility antecedents of anger and blame reactions on children. *Child Development, 60,* 1328–1336.

Olvera-Ezzell, N., Power, T. G., & Cousins, J. H. (1990). Maternal socialization of children's eating habits: Strategies used by obese Mexican-American mothers. *Child Development, 61,* 395–400.

Olweus, D. (1977). Aggression and peer acceptance in adolescent boys: Two short-term longitudinal studies of ratings. *Child Development, 48,* 1301–1313.

Openshaw, D. K., Mills, P. A., Adams, G. R., & Durso, D. D. (1992). Conflict resolution in parent-adolescent dyads: The influence of social skills training. *Journal of Adolescent Research, 7,* 457–468.

Openshaw, D. K., Thomas, D. L., & Rollins, B. C. (1983, Summer). Socialization and adolescent self-esteem: Symbolic interaction and social learning explanations. *Adolescence, 18,* 317–329.

Orr, M. T. (1982). Sex education and contraceptive education in U.S. public high schools. *Family Planning Perspectives, 14,* 304–313.

Oster, H., Hegley, D., & Nagel, L. (1992). Adult judgments and fine-grained analysis of infant facial expressions: Testing the validity of a priori coding formulas. *Developmental Psychology, 28,* 1115–1131.

O'Sullivan, R. G. (1990). Validating a method to identify at-risk middle school students for participation in a dropout prevention program. *Journal of Early Adolescence, 10,* 209–220.

Otto, L. B. (1988). America's youth: A changing profile. *Family Relations, 37,* 385–391.

Overpeck, M. D., et al. (1989). A comparison of the childhood health status of normal birth weight and low birth weight infants. *Public Health Reports, 104,* 58.

Oyserman, D., Radin, N., & Benn, R. (1993). Dynamics in a three-generational family: Teens, grandparents and babies. *Developmental Psychology, 29,* 564–572.

Paasch, K. M., & Teachman, J. D. (1991). Gender, of children and receipt of assistance from absent fathers. *Journal of Family Issues, 12,* 450–466.

Pabon, E., Rodriguez, O., & Gurin, G. (1992). Clarifying peer relations and delinquency. *Youth and Society, 24,* 149–165.

Paccione-Dyszlewski, M. R., & Contessa-Kislus, M. A. (1987). School phobia: Identification of subtypes as a prerequisite to treatment intervention. *Adolescence, 22,* 277–384.

Paddack, C. (1987). Preparing a boy for nocturnal emissions. *Medical Aspects of Human Sexuality, 21,* 15, 16.

Padin, M. A., Lerner, R. M., & Spiro, A. III. (1981, Summer). Stability of body attitudes and self-esteem in late adolescents. *Adolescence, 16,* 371–384.

Page, R. M. (1990). Shyness and sociability: A dangerous combination for illicit substance use in adolescent males? *Adolescence, 25,* 803–806.

Page, R. M., & Cole, G. E. (1991). Loneliness and alcoholism risk in late adolescence: A comparison study of adults and adolescents. *Adolescence, 26,* 924–930.

Paikoff, R. B. (1990). Attitudes toward consequences of pregnancy in young women attending a family planning clinic. *Journal of Adolescence Research, 5,* 467–484.

Pakiz, B., Reinherz, H. Z., & Frost, A. K. (1992). Antisocial behavior in adolescence: A community study. *Journal of Early Adolescence, 12,* 300–313.

Palazzi, S., deVito, E., Luzzati, G., Guerrini, A., & Torre, I. (1990). A study of the relationships between life events and disturbed self-image in adolescents. *Journal of Adolescence, 13,* 53–64.

Paley, V. G. (1984). *Boys and girls: Superheroes in the doll corner.* Chicago, IL: University of Chicago Press.

Palti, H., Mansbach, I., Pridan, H., Adler, B., & Palti, Z. (1984). Episodes of illness in breast-fed and bottle-fed infants in Jerusalem. *Journal of Medical Sciences, 20,* 395–399.

Papini, D. R., Farmer, F. F., Clark, S. M., Micka, J. C., & Barnett, J. W. (1990). *Adolescence, 25,* 958–976.

Papini, D. R., & Roggman, L. A. (1992). Adolescent perceived attachments to parents in relation to competence, depression, and anxiety: A longitudinal study. *Journal of Early Adolescence, 12,* 420–440.

Papini, D. R., Roggman, L. A., & Anderson, J. (1990). Early-adolescent perceptions of attachment to mother and father: A test of the emotional-distancing and buffering hypotheses. *Journal of Early Adolescence, 11,* 258–275.

Parachini, A. (1987, August 19). Condoms fail government tests. *Portland Press Herald,* Portland, ME.

Parcel, G. S., & Luttman, D. (1981). Evaluation of a sex education course of young adolescents. *Family Relations, 30,* 55–60.

Pardeck, J. T. (1990). Family factors related to adolescent autonomy. *Adolescence, 25,* 311–320.

Parfitt, R. R. (1977). *The birth primer.* Philadelphia, PA: Reunion Press.

Parish, J. G., & Parish, T. S. (1983, Fall). Children's self-concepts as related to family structure and family concept. *Adolescence, 18,* 649–658.

Parish, T. S. (1990). Evaluations of family by youth: Do they vary as a function of family structure, gender, and birth order? *Adolescence, 25,* 353–356.

Parish, T. S. (1991). Ratings of self and parents by youth: Are they affected by family status, gender, and birth order? *Adolescence, 26,* 105–112.

Parish, T. S., & Dostal, J. W. (1980, August). Evaluations of self and parent figures by children from intact, divorced and reconstituted families. *Journal of Youth and Adolescence, 9,* 347–351.

Parish, T. S., & McCluskey, J. J. (1992). The relationship between parenting styles and young adults' self-concepts and evaluations of parents. *Adolescence, 27,* 915–918.

Parish, T. S., & Necessary, J. R. (1993). Received actions of parents and attitudes of youth. *Adolescence, 28,* 185–198.

Parish, T. S., & Parish, J. G. (1991). The effects of family configuration and support system failures during childhood and adolescence on college students' self-concepts and social skills. *Adolescence, 26,* 441–448.

Park, K. A., Lay, K., & Ramsay, L. (1993). Individual differences and developmental changes in preschoolers' friendships. *Developmental Psychology, 29,* 264–270.

Park, K. A., & Waters, E. (1989). Security of attachment and preschool friendships. *Child Development, 60,* 1076–1081.

Parker, J. G., & Asher, S. R. (1993). Friendship and friendship quality in middle childhood: Links with peer group acceptance and feelings of loneliness and social dissatisfaction. *Developmental Psychology, 29,* 611–621.

Parker, R. D. (1995). The role of family emotional expressiveness in the development of children's social competence. *Journal of Marriage and the Family, 57,* 593–608.

Parkhurst, J. T., & Asher, S. R. (1992). Peer rejection in middle school: Subgroup differences in behavior, loneliness, and interpersonal concerns. *Developmental Psychology, 28,* 231–241.

Parten, M. B. (1932). Social participation among preschool children. *Journal of Abnormal and Social Psychology, 27,* 243–269.

Patterson, C. J., Kupersmidt, J. B., & Vaden, N. A. (1990). Income level, gender, ethnicity, and household composition as predictors of children's school-based competence. *Child Development, 61,* 485–494.

Paul, E. L., & White, K. M. (1990). The development of intimate relationships in late adolescence. *Adolescence, 25,* 375–400.

Paul, M. J., & Fischer, J. L. (1980, April). Correlates of self-concept among black early adolescents. *Journal of Youth and Adolescence, 9,* 163–173.

Paulson, S. E., Hill, J. P., & Holmbeck, G. N. (1990). Distinguishing between perceived closeness and parental warmth in families with seventh-grade boys and girls. *Journal of Early Adolescence, 11,* 276–293.

Pearson, J. L., & Ferguson, L. R. (1989). Gender differences in patterns of spatial ability, environmental cognition, and math and English achievement in late adolescence. *Adolescence, 24,* 421–431.

Pearson, J. L., Hunter, A. G., Ensminger, M. E., & Kellam, S. G. (1990). Black grandmothers in multigenerational households: Diversity in family structure and parenting involvement in the Woodlawn community. *Child Development, 61,* 434–442.

Pedersen, W. (1990). Adolescents initiating cannabis use: Cultural opposition or poor mental health? *Journal of Adolescence, 13,* 327–340.

Pederson, D. R., Moran, G., Sitko, C., Campbell, K., Ghesquire, & Acton, H. (1990). Maternal sensitivity and the security of infant–mother attachment: A Q-sort study. *Child Development, 61,* 1974–1983.

Pederson, E., Faucher, A., & Eaton, W. W. (1978). A new perspective of the effects of first-grade teacher on children's subsequent adult status. *Harvard Educational Review, 48,* 1–31.

Pellegrini, A. D., Perlmutter, J. C., Galda, L., & Brody, G. H. (1990). Joint reading between black Head Start children and their mothers. *Child Development, 61,* 443–453.

Pepe, M. V., & Byrne, T. J. (1991). Women's perceptions of immediate and long-term effects of failed infertility treatment on marital and sexual satisfaction. *Family Relations, 40,* 303–309.

Pepler, D. J., & Craig, W. N. (1995). I peeked behind the fence: Naturalistic observation of aggressive children with remote audio-visual recording. *Developmental Psychology, 31,* 548–553.

Perkins, H. W., & Berkowitz, A. D. (1991). Collegiate COAs and alcohol abuse: Problem drinking in relation to assessments of parent and grandparent alcoholism. *Journal of Counseling and Development, 69,* 237–240.

Perris, E. E., Myers, N. A., & Clifton, R. K. (1990). Long-term memory for a single infancy experience. *Child Development, 61,* 1796–1807.

Perry, D. G., Williard, J. C., & Perry, L. C. (1990). Peers' perceptions of the consequences that victimized children provide aggressors. *Child Development, 61,* 1310–1325.

Persell, C. H., Catsambis, S., & Cookson, P. W., Jr. (1992). Family background, school type, and college attendance: A conjoint system of cultural capital transmission. *Journal of Research on Adolescence, 2,* 1–23.

Pestrak, V. A., & Martin, D. (1985). Cognitive development and aspects of adolescent sexuality. *Adolescence, 22,* 981–987.

Pete, J. M., & DeSantis, L. (1990). Sexual decision making in young black adolescent females. *Adolescence, 25,* 145–154.

Petersen, A. C. (1993). Presidential address: Creating adolescence: The role of context and process in developmental trajectories. *Journal of Research on Adolescence, 3,* 1–18.

Petersen, J. R., Kretchner, A., Nellis, B., Lever, J., & Hertz, R. (1983). The playboy readers sex survey. Part 2. *Playboy,* p. 90.

Petersen, L. R., Lee, G. R., & Ellis, G. J. (1982). Social structure, socialization values, and disciplinary techniques: A cross-cultural analysis. *Journal of Marriage and the Family, 44,* 131–142.

Peterson, G. W., & Rollins, B. C. (1987). Parent-child socialization. In M. B. Sussman & S. K. Steinmetz (Eds.), *Handbook of marriage and the family* (pp. 471–507). New York: Plenum.

Peterson, C., & McCabe, A. (1994). A social interactionist's account of developing decontextualized narrative skill. *Developmental Psychology, 30,* 937–948.

Peterson, C. C., & Murphy, L. (1990). Adolescents' thoughts and feelings about AIDS in relation to cognitive maturity. *Journal of Adolescence, 13,* 185–188.

Peterson, J. L., & Nord, C. W. (1990). The regular receipt of child support: A multistep process. *Journal of Marriage and the Family, 52,* 539–551.

Peterson, K. L., & Roscoe, B. (1991). Imaginary audience behavior in older adolescent females. *Adolescence, 26,* 195–200.

Pett, M. B., & Vaughan-Cole, B. (1986). The impact of income issues and social status in post-divorce adjustment of custodial parents. *Family Relations, 35,* 103–111.

Pettit, G. S., Doge, K. H., & Brown, M. M. (1988). Early family experience, social problem solving patterns, and children's social competence. *Child Development, 59,* 107–120.

Pezdek, K. (1987). Memory of pictures: A life-span study of the role of visual detail. *Child Development, 58,* 807–815.

Phillips, D. A. (1987). Socialization of perceived academic competence among highly competitive children. *Child Development, 58,* 1308–1320.

Phinney, J. S. (1992). The multigroup ethnic identity measure. A new scale for youths with diverse groups. *Journal of Adolescent Research, 7,* 156–176.

Phinney, J. S., Chavira, V., & Williamson, L. (1992). The acculturation attitudes and self-esteem among high-school and college students. *Youth and Society, 23,* 299–312.

Phinney, J. S., & Alipuria, L. L. (1990). Ethnic identity in college students from four ethnic groups. *Journal of Adolescence, 13,* 171–184.

Phinney, V. G., Jensen, L. C., Olsen, J. A., & Cundick, B. (1990). The relationship between early development and psychosexual behaviors in adolescent females. *Adolescence, 25,* 321–332.

Piaget, J. (1926). *The language of the child* (M. Warden, Trans.). New York: Harcourt.

Piaget, J. (1948). *The moral judgment of the child* (1932 reprint). Glencoe, IL: Free Press.

Piaget, J. (1950). *The psychology of intelligence.* London: Routledge and Kegan Paul.

Piaget, J. (1954). *The construction of reality in the child.* New York: Basic Books.

Piaget, J. (1962). *Play, dream, and imitation in childhood.* New York: W. W. Norton.

Piaget, J. (1963). *The origins of intelligence in children.* New York: W. W. Norton.

Piaget, J. (1967a). *The child's construction of the world.* Totowa, NJ: Littlefield, Adams.

Piaget, J. (1967). *Six psychological studies* (A. Tenzer, & D. Elkind, Trans.). New York: Random House.

Piaget, J. (1971). The theory of stages in cognitive development. In D. R. Green (Ed.), *Measurement and Piaget.* New York: McGraw-Hill.

Piaget, J. (1972). Intellectual evolution from adolescence to adulthood. *Human Development, 15,* 1012.

Piaget, J. (1980). Intellectual evolution from adolescence to adulthood. In R. E. Muuss (Ed.), *Adolescent behavior and society: A body of readings* (3rd ed.). New York: Random House.

Piaget, J., & Inhelder, B. (1969). *The psychology of the child.* (H. Weaver, Trans.). New York: Basic Books.

Pianta, R. C., & Ball, R. M. (1993). Maternal support as a predictor of child adjustment in kindergarten. *Journal of Applied Developmental Psychology, 14,* 107–120.

Pichitino, J. P. (1983). Profile of the single father: A thematic integration of the literature. *Personnel and Guidance Journal, 5,* 295–299.

Pienciak, R. T. (1984, September 17). Abuse cases found in record numbers. *Portland Press Herald,* Portland, ME.

Piers, E. V. (1984). *Revised manual for the Piers-Harris children's self-concept scale.* Los Angeles, CA: Western Psychological Services.

Piers, M. W. (1978). *Infanticide: Past and present.* New York: W. W. Norton.

Pierson, E. C., & D'Antonio, W. V. (1974). *Female and male: dimensions of human sexuality.* Philadelphia, PA: Lippincott.

Pill, C. J. (1990). Stepfamilies: Redefining the family. *Family Relations, 39,* 186–193.

Pillemer, D. B., Koff, E., Rhinehart, E. D., & Rierdan, J. (1987). Flashbulb memories of menarche and adult menstrual distress. *Journal of Adolescence, 10,* 187–199.

Pillow, B. H. (1988). Young children's understanding of attentional limits. *Child Development, 58,* 38–46.

Pines, M. (1981, September). The civilizing of Genie. *Psychology Today, 14,* 28–34.

Pines, M. (1984). In the shadow of Huntington's. *Science, 84, 5,* 32–39.

Pinneau, S. R. (1961). *Changes in intelligent quotient.* Boston, MA: Houghton Mifflin.

Pinon, M. F., Huston, A. C., & Wright, J. C. (1989). Family ecology and child characteristics that predict young children's educational television viewing. *Child Development, 60,* 846–856.

Pipp, S., Easterbrooks, M. A., & Harmon, R. J. (1992). The relation between attachment and knowledge of self and mother in one- to three-year old infants. *Child Development, 63,* 738–750.

Pipp, S., & Harmon, R. J. (1987). Attachment as regulation: A commentary. *Child Development, 58,* 648–652.
Pitcher, E. G., & Schultz, L. H. (1983). *Boys and girls at play: The development of sex roles.* New York: Holt, Rinehart, & Winston.
Pledger, L. M. (1992). Development of self-monitoring behavior from early to late adolescence. *Adolescence, 27,* 329–338.
Plumert, J. N., Ewert, J., & Spear, S. J. (1995). The early development of children's communication about nested spatial relations. *Child Development, 66,* 959–969.
Plumert, J. N., Pick, H. L., Jr., Marks, R. A., Kintsch, A. S., & Wegesin, D. (1994). Locating objects and communicating about locations: Organizational differences in children's searching and direction-giving. *Developmental Psychology, 30,* 443–453.
Plummer, W. (1985, October 28). A school's Rx for sex. *People,* pp. 39–41.
Pombeni, J. L., Kirchler, E., & Palmonari, A. (1990). Identification with peers as a strategy to muddle through the troubles of the adolescent years. *Journal of Adolescence, 13,* 351–370.
Porjesz, B., & Begleitner, H. (1985). Human brain electrophysiology and alcoholism. In R. Tarter & D. Thiel (Eds.), *Alcohol and the brain.* New York: Plenum.
Porreco, R., & Meier, P. (1983). Trials of labor in patients with multiple previous cesarean sections. *Journal of Reproductive Medicine, 28,* 770–772.
Porter, F. L., Porges, S. W., & Marshall, R. E. (1988). Newborn pain cries and vagal tone: Parallel changes in response to circumcision. *Child Development, 59,* 495–505.
Porter, N. L., & Christopher, F. S. (1984). Infertility: Toward an awareness of a need among family life practitioners. *Family Relations, 33,* 309–315.
Portes, P. R., Dunham, R. M., & Williams, S. (1986). Assessing child-rearing style in ecological settings: Its relation to culture, social class, early age intervention, and scholastic achievement. *Adolescence, 21,* 723–735.
Postrado, L. T., & Nicholson, H. J. (1992). Effectiveness in delaying the initiation of sexual intercourse in girls aged 12–14. *Youth in Society, 23,* 356–379.
Powell, D. A., Milligan, W. L., and Furchtgott, E. (1980). Peripheral autonomic changes accompanying learning and reaction time performance in older people. *Journal of Gerontology, 35,* 57–65.
Powers, P. S. (1980). *Obesity: The regulation of weight.* Baltimore, MD: Williams & Wilkins.
Presser, H. B. (1978, Summer). Age, at menarche, socio-sexual behavior, and fertility. *Social Biology, 25,* 94–101.
Presser, H. D. (1989). Some economic complexities of child care provided by grandmothers. *Journal of Marriage and the Family, 51,* 581–591.
Price, D. W. W., & Goodman, G. S. (1990). Visiting the wizard: Children's memory for a recurring event. *Child Development, 61,* 664–680.
Price, J., & Feshbach, S. (1982, August). *Emotional adjustment correlates of televising viewing in children.* Paper presented at the meeting of the American Psychological Association, Washington, DC.
Pritchard, C., Cotton, A., & Cox, M. (1992). Truancy and illegal drug use, and knowledge of HIV infection in 932 14–16-year-old adolescents. *Journal of Adolescence, 15,* 1–17.
Pritchard, J., MacDonald, D., & Grant, N. (1985). *Williams obstetrics* (17th ed.). New York: Appleton-Century-Crofts.
Protinsky, H., & Farrier, S. (1980, Winter). Self-image changes in pre-adolescence and adolescents. *Adolescence, 15,* 887–893.
Pryor, D. W., & McGarrell, E. F. (1993). Public perceptions of youth gang crime: An exploratory analysis. *Youth and Society, 24,* 399–418.
Putallaz, M. (1987). Maternal behavior and children's sociometric status. *Child Development, 58,* 324–340.
Quay, L. C. (1992). Personal and family effects on loneliness. *Journal of Applied Developmental Psychology, 13,* 97–110.
Quinn, P., & Allen, K. R. (1989). Facing challenges and making compromises: How single mothers endure. *Family Relations, 38,* 390–395.
Quintana, S. M., & Lapsley, D. K. (1990). Rapprochement in late adolescent separation-individuation: A structural equations approach. *Journal of Adolescence, 13,* 371–386.
Quittner, A. L., & Opipari, L. C., (1994). Differential treatment of siblings: Interview and diary analyses comparing two family contexts. *Child Development, 65,* 800–814.
Rabiner, D. L., & Gordon, L. B. (1992). The coordination of conflicting social goals: Differences between rejected and nonrejected boys. *Child Development, 63,* 1344–1350.
Rabiner, D. L., Keane, S. P., & MacKinnon-Lewis, C. (1993). Children's beliefs about familiar and unfamiliar peers in relation to their sociometric status. *Developmental Psychology, 29,* 236–243.
Radomski, M. (1981). Stereotypes, stepmothers, and splitting. *American Journal of Psychoanalysis, 41,* 121–127.
Raine, A., Hulme, Ch., Chadderton, H., & Bailey, P. (1991). Verbal short-term memory span in speech disordered children: Implications for articulatory coding in short-term memory. *Child Development, 62,* 415–423.
Raloff, J. (1986). Even low levels in mom affect baby. *Science News, 130,* 164.
Ralph, N., & Morgan, K. A. (1991). Assessing differences in chemically dependent adolescent males using the child behavior checklist. *Adolescence, 26,* 183–194.
Ramsey, B. G. (1995). Changing social dynamics in early childhood classrooms. *Child Development, 66,* 764–773.
Ramsey, D. S. (1985). Fluctuations in unimanual hand preference in infants following the onset of duplicated syllable babbling. *Developmental Psychology, 21,* 318–324.
Ramsey, D. S., & Weber, S. L. (1986). Infants' hand preference in a task involving complementary roles for the two hands. *Child Development, 57,* 300–307.
Rapp, G. S., & Lloyd, S. A. (1989). The role of "home as haven" ideology in child care use. *Family Relations, 38,* 426–430.
Raschke, H. J., & Raschke, V. J. (1979, May). Family conflict and children's self-concepts: A comparison of intact and single-parent families. *Journal of Marriage and the Family, 41,* 367–374.
Raskin, P. M. (1990). Identity status research: Implications for career counseling. *Journal of Adolescence, 13,* 375–388.
Rauh, V. A., Achenbach, T. M., Nurcombe, B., Howell, C. T., & Teti, D. M. (1988). Minimizing adverse effects of low birthweight: Four-year results of an early intervention program. *Child Development, 59,* 544–553.
Ravitch, B. (1983, October). The educational pendulum. *Psychology Today, 17,* 62–71.
Raviv, A., Maddy-Weitzman, E., & Raviv, A. (1992). Parents of adolescents: Help-seeking intentions as a function of health sources and parenting issues. *Journal of Adolescence, 15,* 115–135.
Reardon, B., & Griffing, P. (1983, Spring). Factors related to the self-concept of institutionalized, white, male, adolescent drug abusers. *Adolescence, 18,* 29–41.
Reaves, J., & Roberts, A. (1983). The effects of the type of information on children's attraction to peers. *Child Development, 54,* 1024–1031.
Reed, E. S. (1988). *James J. Gibson and the Psychology of Perception.* New Haven, CT: Yale University Press.
Rees, D. D., & Wilborn, B. L. (1983, February). Correlates of drug abuse in adolescents: A comparison of families of drug abusers with families of nondrug abusers. *Journal of Youth and Adolescence, 6,* 1–9.
Reich, P. A. (1986). *Language development.* Englewood Cliffs, NJ: Prentice-Hall.
Reis, J., & Seidly, A. (1989). School administrators, parents, and sex education: A resolvable paradox? *Adolescence, 24,* 639–645.
Reissland, N. (1988). Neonatal imitation in the first hour of life: Observations in rural Nepal. *Developmental Psychology, 24,* 464–469.
Relman, A. S. (1982). *Marijuana and health.* Washington, DC: National Academy Press.
Remez, L. (July/August 1991). Decision on Cesarean can often be influenced by nonclinical factors. *Family Planning Perspectives, 23,* 191–193.
Remez, L. (1992, January/February). Children who don't live with both parents face more behavior problems. *Family Planning Prospectives, 24,* 41–43.
Remez, L. (May/June 1992). Infant mortality on Oregon Indian reservation is almost three times higher than the overall U.S. rate. *Family Planning Perspectives, 24,* 138–139.
Remley, A. (1988). From obedience to independence. *Psychology Today, 22,* 56–59.
Renshaw, P. D., & Brown, P. J. (1993). Loneliness in middle childhood: Concurrent longitudinal predictors. *Child Development, 64,* 1271–1284.
Resman, B. (1986). Can men "mother"? Life as a single father. *Family Relations, 35,* 95–102.
Resnick, L. A., Levine, R., & Behrend, A. (1991). *Perspectives On Socially*

Shared Cognition. Washington, DC: American Psychological Association.

Reznick, J. S., & Goldfield, B. A. (1992). Rapid change in lexical development in comprehension and production. *Developmental Psychology, 28,* 406–413.

Reznick, J. S., Kagan, J., Snidman, N., Gersten, M., Baak, K., & Rosenberg, A. (1986). Inhibited and uninhibited children: A follow-up study. *Child Development, 57,* 660–680.

Rice, B. (1979a, September). Brave new world of intelligent testing. *Psychology Today, 12,* 27ff.

Rice, B. (1979b, September). The SAT controversy: When an aptitude is coachable. *Psychology Today, 13,* 30ff.

Rice, F. P. (1979). *The working mother's guide to child development.* Englewood Cliffs, NJ: Prentice-Hall.

Rice, F. P. (1989a). *Causes of worry in college females attending the University of Maine.* Unpublished study.

Rice, F. P. (1989b). *Human sexuality.* Dubuque, IA: Wm. C. Brown.

Rice, F. P. (1990a). *The adolescent: Development, relationships, and culture* (6th ed.). Boston, MA: Allyn & Bacon.

Rice, F. P. (1990b). *Intimate relationships, marriages, and families.* Mountain View, CA: Mayfield Publishing Co.

Rice, F. P. (1993). *The adolescent: Development, relationships, and culture.* (7th ed.) Boston: Allyn and Bacon.

Rice, M. (1980). *Cognition to Language Categories: Word, Meaning and Training.* Baltimore: University Park Press.

Richman, A. L., Miller, P. M., & Levine, R. A. (1992). Cultural and educational variations in maternal responsiveness. *Developmental Psychology, 28,* 614–621.

Richman, C. L., Clark, M. L., & Brown, K. P. (1985). General and specific self-esteem in late adolescent students: Race and gender × SES effects. *Adolescence, 20,* 555–566.

Ricks, S. S. (1985). Father-infant interactions: A review of empirical research. *Family Relations, 34,* 505–511.

Riese, M. L. (1990). Neonatal temperament in monozygotic and dizygotic twin pairs. *Child Development, 61,* 1230–1237.

Rind, P. (1992a). Peer support to keep teenagers alive and well. *Family Planning Perspectives, 24,* 36–37.

Rind, P. (1992b). Smoking in pregnancy nearly triples women's risk of placenta praevia. *Family Planning Perspectives, 24,* 47–48.

Rind, P. (January/February 1992c). Program Spotlight: 'Teens and toddlers' aims to reduce child abuse among adolescent parents. *Family Planning Perspectives, 24,* 37, 40.

Ritter, J. M., Casey, R. J., & Longlois, J. H. (1991). Adults' responses to infants varying in appearance of age and attractiveness. *Child Development, 62,* 68–82.

Ritvo, E. R., Freeman, B. J., Mason-Brothers, A., Mo, A., & Ritvo, A. M. (1985). Concordance for the syndrome of autism in 40 pairs of afflicted twins. *American Journal of Psychiatry, 142,* 74–77.

Roberts, A. R. (Summer, 1982). "Adolescent Runaways in Suburbia: A New Typology." *Adolescence, 17,* 379–396.

Roberts, E., & DeBlossie, R. R. (1983, Winter). Test bias and the culturally different early adolescent. *Adolescence, 18,* 837–843.

Roberts, L. R., Sarigiani, P. A., Petersen, A. C., & Newman, J. L. (1990). Gender differences in the relationship between achievement and self-image during early adolescence. *Journal of Early Adolescence, 10,* 159–175.

Roberts, M. (1988). School yard menace. *Psychology Today, 22,* 52–56.

Robertson, E. B., Skinner, M. L., Love, M. M., Elder, G. H., Conger, R. D., Dubas, J. S., & Petersen. A. C. (1992). The pubertal development scale: A rural and suburban comparison. *Journal of Early Adolescence, 12,* 174–186.

Robinson, J. L., Reznick, J. S., Kagan, J., & Corley, R. (1992). The heritability of inhibited and uninhibited behavior: A twin study. *Developmental Psychology, 28,* 1030–1037.

Robinson, S. I. (1983, January). Nader versus ETS: Who should we believe? *Personnel and Guidance Journal, 61,* 260–262.

Roche, J. P., & Ramsbey, T. W. (1993). Premarital sexuality: A five-year follow-up study of attitudes and behavior by dating stage. *Adolescence, 28,* 67–80.

Rodgers, J. (1988). Pains of complaint. *Psychology Today, 22,* 26, 27.

Rodin, J. (1982). Obesity: Why the losing battle. In B. B. Wolman (Ed.), *Psychological aspects of obesity: A handbook* (pp. 30–87). New York: Van Nostrand.

Roe v. Wade, 410 U.S. 113 (1973).

Rogers, C. R. (1951). *Client-centered therapy: Its current practice, implications, and theory.* Boston, MA: Houghton Mifflin.

Rogers, C. R. (1961). *On becoming a person.* Boston, MA: Houghton Mifflin.

Rogers, C. R. (1980). *A way of being.* Boston, MA: Houghton Mifflin.

Rogers, M. F. (1985). AIDS in children: A review of the clinical, epidemiological and public health aspects. *Pediatric Infectious Disease, 4,* 230–236.

Rogosch, F. A., & Newcomb, A. F. (1989). Children's perceptions of peer reputation and their social reputations among peers. *Child Development, 60,* 597–610.

Rogow, A. M., Marcia, J. E., & Slugoski, B. R. (1983, October). The relative importance of identity status interview components. *Journal of Youth and Adolescence, 12,* 387–400.

Rohner, R. P., Kean, K. J., & Cournoyer, D. E. (1991). Effects of corporal punishment, perceived caretaker warmth, and cultural beliefs on the psychological adjustment of children in St. Kitts, West Indies. *Journal of Marriage and the Family, 53,* 681–693.

Rohner, R. P., & Rohner, E. C. (1981). Parental acceptance-rejection and parental control: Cross cultural codes. *Ethnology, 20,* 245–260.

Romaine, S. (1984). *The language of children and adolescents. The acquisition of communication competence.* Oxford: Blackwell.

Romeo, F. F. (1984, Fall). Adolescence, sexual conflict, and anorexia nervosa. *Adolescence, 19,* 551–555.

Roopnarine, J. L. (1984). Sex-typed socialization in mixed age preschool classrooms. *Child Development, 55,* 1078–1084.

Roopnarine, J. L. (1986, January). Mothers' and fathers' behavior toward the toy play of their infant sons and daughters. *Sex Roles: A Journal of Research, 14,* 59.

Roopnarine, J. L., Brown, J., Snell-White, P., Riegraf, M. B., Crossley, D., Sossain, Z., & Webb, B. (1995). Father involvement in child-care and household work in common-law, dual-earner, and single-earner Jamaican families. *Journal of Applied Developmental Psychology, 16,* 35–52.

Roosa, M. W., Tein, J., Croppenbacher, N., Michaels, M., & Dumea, L. (1993). Mothers' parenting behavior and child mental health in families with a problem drinking parent. *Journal of Marriage and the Family, 55,* 107–118.

Roscoe, B., Diana, M. S., & Brooks, R. H. II. (1987). Early, middle, and later adolescents' views on dating and factors influencing partner selection. *Adolescence, 87,* 511–516.

Roscoe, B., Kennedy, D., & Pope, H. (1987). Distinguishing intimacy from nonintimate relationships. *Adolescence, 87,* 511–516.

Roscoe, B., & Kruger, T. L. (1990). AIDS: Late adolescents' knowledge and its influence on sexual behavior. *Adolescence, 25,* 39–48.

Rose, S. A. (1984). Developmental changes in hemispheric specialization for tactual processing in very young children. Evidence from cross-modal transfer. *Developmental Psychology, 20,* 568–574.

Rose, S. A. (1994). Relation between physical growth and information processing in infants born in India. *Child Development, 65,* 889–902.

Rose, S. A., & Feldman, J. S. (1995). Prediction of IQ and specific cognitive abilities at 11 years of infancy measures. *Developmental Psychology, 31,* 685–696.

Rose, S. A., Feldman, J. F., McCarton, C. M., & Wolfson, J. (1988). Information processing in seven-month old infants as a function of risk status. *Child Development, 59,* 589–603.

Rose, S. A., Feldman, J. F., & Wallace, I. F. (1992). Infant information processing in relation to six-year cognitive outcomes. *Child Development, 63,* 1126–1141.

Rose, S. A., & Orlian, E. K. (1991). Asymmetries in infant cross-modal transfer. *Child Development, 62,* 706–718.

Rosen, A. B., & Rozin, P. (1993). Now you see it, now you don't: The preschool child's conception of invisible particles in the context of dissolving. *Child Development, 29,* 300–311.

Rosen, K. S., & Rothbaum, F. (1993). Quality of parental caregiving and security of attachment. *Developmental Psychology, 29,* 358–367.

Rosenblith, J. F., & Sims-Knight, J. E. (1985). *In the beginning: Development in the first two years.* Monterey, CA: Brooks/Cole.

Rosenfeld, A., & Stark, E. (1987). The prime of our lives. *Psychology Today, 21,* 62–70.

Rosengren, K. S., Gelman, S. A., Kalish, C. W., & McCormick, M. (1991). As time goes by: Children's early understanding of growth in animals. *Child Development, 62,* 1302–1320.

Rosengren, K. S., & Hickling, A. K. (1994). Seeing is believing: Children's explanations of commonplace, magical, and extraordinary transformations. *Child Development, 65,* 1605–1626.

Rosenstein, D., & Oster, H. (1988). Differential facial responses to four basic tastes in newborns. *Child Development, 59,* 1555–1568.

Rosenthal, D., & Hansen, J. (1980, October). Comparison of adolescents. Perception and behavior in single- and two-parent families. *Journal of Youth and Adolescence, 9,* 407–414.

Rosenthal, D. A., & Feldman, S. S. (1991). The influence of perceived family and personal factors on self-reported school performance of Chinese and Western high school students. *Journal of Research on Adolescence, 1,* 135–154.

Rosoff, J. I. (1989, July/August). The Webster decision: A giant step backwards. *Family Planning Perspectives, 21,* 148–149.

Ross, D. M., & Ross, S. A. (1982). *Hyperactivity: Current issues, research, and theory* (2nd ed.). New York: Wiley.

Ross, G., Tesman, J., Auld, P. A. M., & Nass, R. (1992). Effects of subependymal and mild intraventricular lesions on visual attention and memory in premature infants. *Developmental Psychology, 28,* 1067–1074.

Ross, H. S., & Lollis, S. P. (1989). A social relations analysis of toddler peer relationships. *Child Development, 60,* 1082–1091.

Rothbart, M. K. (1988). Temperament and the development of inhibited approach. *Child Development, 59,* 1249–1250.

Rotheram-Borus, M. J. (1990a). Ethnic differences in adolescents' identity status and associated behavior problems. *Journal of Adolescence, 13,* 361–374.

Rotheram-Borus, M. J. (1990b). Patterns of social expectations among black and Mexican-American children. *Child Development, 61,* 542–556.

Rousseau, J. J. (1955). *Emile.* New York: Dutton. (Original work published 1762)

Rovee-Collier, C., Schecter, A., Shyi, G. C. W., & Shields, P. (1992). Perceptual identification of contextual attributes and infant memory retrieval. *Developmental Psychology, 28,* 307–318.

Rovee-Collier, C. K. (1987a). Learning and memory in infancy. In J. D. Osofsky (Ed.), *Handbook of infant development* (2nd ed.). New York: Wiley.

Rovee-Collier, C. K. (1987b). Learning and memory in children. In J. D. Osofsky (Ed.), *Handbook of infant development* (2nd ed.). New York: Wiley.

Rowan, R. L. (1982, July). Irrelevance of penis size. *Medical Aspects of Human Sexuality, 16,* 153, 156.

Rubenstein, C. (1983, July). The modern art of courtly love. *Psychology Today, 14,* 40–49.

Rubenstein, E. A. (1983). Television and behavior: Research conclusions of the 1982 NIMH report and their policy implications. *American Psychologist, 38,* 820–825.

Rubenstein, J. L., & Feldman, S. S. (1993). Conflict-resolution behavior in adolescent boys: Antecedente and adaptational correlates. *Journal of Research on Adolescence, 3,* 41–66.

Rubin, D. H., Craskilnikoff, P. A., Leventhal, J. M., Weile, B., & Berget, A. (1986, August 23). Effect of passive smoking on birth weight. *Lancet,* pp. 415–417.

Rubin, K. E., Lynch, D., Coplan, R., Rose-Krasnor, L., & Booth, C. L. (1994). "Birds of a feather . . . ": Behavioral concordances and preferential personal attraction in children. *Child Development, 65,* 1778–1785.

Rubin, K. H., Fein, G. G., & Vanderberg, B. (1983). Play. In P. H. Mussen (Ed.), *Handbook of child psychology* (4th ed., Vol. 4). New York: Wiley.

Ruble, D. N., & Flett, G. L. (1988). Conflicting goals in self-evaluative information seeking: Developmental and ability level analysis, *Child Development, 59,* 97–106.

Ruff, H. A., Lawson, K. R., Parrinello, R., & Weissberg, R. (1990). Long-term stability of individual differences in sustained attention in the early years. *Child Development, 61,* 60–75.

Ruff, H. A., Saltarelli, L. M., Capozzoli, M., & Dubiner, K. (1992). The differentiation of activity in infants' exploration of objects. *Developmental Psychology, 28,* 851–861.

Ruffman, T., Perner, J., Olson, D. R., & Doherty, N. (1993). Reflecting on scientific thinking: Children's understanding of hypothesis-evidence relation. *Child Development, 64,* 1617–1636.

Russell, B., & Russell, A. (1987). Mother-child and father-child relationships in middle childhood. *Child Development, 58,* 1573–1585.

Russell, J., Halasz, G., & Beaumont, P. J. V. (1990). Death related themes in anorexia nervosa: A practical exploration. *Journal of Adolescence, 13,* 311–326.

Russell, J. A. (1990). The preschooler's understanding of the causes and consequences of emotion. *Child Development, 61,* 1872–1881.

Rust, J. O., & McCraw, A. (1984, Summer). Influence of masculinity-femininity on adolescent self-esteem and peer acceptance. *Adolescence, 19,* 357–366.

Rutter, M. (1983). School effects on pupil progress: Research findings and policy implications. *Child Development, 54,* 1–29.

Rutter, M., & Schopher, E. (1987). Autism and persuasive developmental disorders: Concepts and diagnostic issues. *Journal of Autism and Developmental Disorders, 17,* 159–186.

Sabatelli, R. M., & Anderson, S. A. (1991). Family system dynamics, peer relationships, and adolescents' psychological adjustment. *Family Relations, 40,* 363–369.

Sadker, M., & Sadker, M. (1985, March). Sexism in the schoolroom of the 80s. *Psychology Today, 19,* 54–57.

St. Peters, M., Fitch, M., Huston, A. C., Wright, J. C., & Eakins, D. J. (1991). Television and families: What do young children watch with their parents? *Child Development, 62,* 1409–1423.

Salk, L. (1974). *Preparing for parenthood.* New York: David McKay Co.

Salzinger, S., Feldman, R. S., & Hammer, M. (1993). The effects of physical abuse on children's social relationships. *Child Development, 64,* 169–187.

Sameroff, A. J., Seifer, R., Baldwin, A., & Baldwin, C. (1993). Stability of intelligence from preschool to adolescence: The influence of social and family risk factors. *Child Development, 64,* 80–97.

Sandler, D. P., Everson, R. B., Wilcox, A. J., & Browder, J. P. (1985). Cancer risk in adulthood from early life exposure to parents smoking. *American Journal of Public Health, 75,* 487–492.

Sandler, I. N., Tein, J., & West, S. G. (1994). Coping, stress, and the psychological symptoms of children of divorce: A cross-sectional and longitudinal study. *Child Development, 65,* 1744–1763.

Sanik, M. M., & Mauldin, T. (1986). Single versus two-parent families: A comparison of mothers' time. *Family Relations, 35,* 53–56.

Sanik, M. M., & Stafford, D. (1985). Adolescents' contributions to household production: Male and female differences. *Adolescence, 20,* 207–215.

Santee, B., & Henshaw, S. K. (July/August 1992). The abortion debate: Measuring gestational age. *Family Planning Perspectives, 24,* 172–173.

Santilli, M. R., & Hudson, L. N. (1992). Enhancing moral growth: Is communication the key? *Adolescence, 27,* 145–160.

Santrock, J. W. (1970a). Paternal absence, sex-typing, and identification. *Developmental Psychology, 6,* 264–272.

Santrock, J. W. (1970b). Influence of onset and type of paternal absence on the first four Eriksonian developmental crises. *Developmental Psychology, 6,* 273–274.

Santrock, J. W., & Wohlford, P. (1970). *Effects of father absence: Influences of, reasons for, and onset of absence.* Proceedings of the 78th annual convention of the American Sociological Association (Vol. 5, pp. 265–266).

Sarigiani, P. A., Wilson, J. L., Petersen, A. C., & Viocay, J. R. (1990). Self-image and educational plans of adolescents from two contrasting communities. *Journal of Early Adolescence, 10,* 37–55.

Saudino, K. J., & Eaton, W. O. (1991). Infant temperament and genetics: An objective twin study of motor activity level. *Child Development, 62,* 1167–1174.

Sauer, L. E., & Fine, M. A. (1988). Parent-child relationships in stepparent families. *Journal of Family Psychology, 1,* 434–451.

Scafidi, F. A. (1986). Effects of tactile/kinesthetic stimulation on the clinical course and sleep/wake behavior of preterm neonates. *Infant Behavior and Development, 9,* 91–105.

Scarr, S. (1984, May). What's a parent to do? *Psychology Today, 18,* 58–63.

Scarr, S., & Weinberg, R. A. (1983). The Minnesota adoptions studies: Genetic differences and malleability. *Child Development, 54,* 260–267.

Scarr, S. (1992). Developmental theories for the 1990's: Development and individual differences. *Child Development, 63,* 1–19.

Schaefer, E. S. (1959). A circumplex model for maternal behavior. *Journal of Abnormal and Social Psychology, 59,* 226–235.

Schaffer, H. R. (1984). *The child's entry into the social world.* Orlando, FL: Academic Press.

Schaeffer, N. C. (1989). The frequency and intensity of parental conflict:

Choosing response dimensions. *Journal of Marriage and the Family, 51,* 759–766.

Schallenberger, M. E. (1894). A study of children's rights as seen by themselves. *Pedagogical Seminary, 3,* 87–96.

Schatten, G., & Schatten, H. (1983). The energetic egg. *Science, 23,* 28–34.

Schmidt, J. A., & Davison, M. L. (1983, May). Helping students think. *Personnel and Guidance Journal, 61,* 563–569.

Schneider, W., & Bjorklund, D. F. (1992). Expertise, aptitude, and strategic remembering. *Child Development, 63,* 461–473.

Schneider-Rosen, K., & Wenz-Gross, M. (1990). Patterns of compliance from eighteen to thirty months of age. *Child Development, 61,* 104–112.

Schuckit, M. A. (1985). Genetics and the risk for alcoholism. *JAMA, Journal of the American Medical Association, 254,* 2614–2617.

Schuckit, M. A. (1987). Biological vulnerability to alcoholism. *Journal of Consulting and Clinical Psychology, 55,* 301–309.

Schulman, S. (1986). Facing the invisible handicap. *Psychology Today, 20,* 58–64.

Schultz, N. C., Schultz, C. L., & Olson, D. H. (1991). Couple strengths and stressors in complex and simple stepfamilies in Australia. *Journal of Marriage and the Family, 53,* 555–564.

Schunk, D. H. (1984). Self-efficacy perspective on achievement behavior. *Educational Psychologist, 19,* 48–58.

Schwartz, D., Dodge, K. A., & Coie, J. D. (1993). The emergence of chronic peer victimization in boys' play groups. *Child Development, 64,* 1755–1772.

Schwartz, J. I. (1981). Children's experiments with language. *Young Children, 36,* 16–26.

Schwartz, L. L. (1987). Joint custody: Is it all right for all children? *Journal of Family Psychology, 1,* 120–134.

Schweinhart, L. J., & Weikert, D. P. (1985). Evidence that good early childhood programs work. *Phi Delta Kappan, 66,* 545–551.

Schweitzer, R. D., Seth-Smith, M., & Callan, V. (1992). The relationship between self-esteem and psychological adjustment in young adolescents. *Journal of Adolescence, 15,* 83–97.

Searleman, A., Porac, C., & Coran, S. (1989). Relationship between birth order, birth stress, and lateral preferences: A critical review. *Psychological Bulletin, 105,* 397–408.

Sears, R. R., Maccoby, G. P., & Levin, H. (1957). *Patterns of child rearing.* New York: Harper & Row.

Sebald, H. (1984). *Adolescence: A social psychological analysis* (3rd ed.). Englewood Cliffs, NJ: Prentice-Hall.

Sebald, H. (1986). Adolescents' shifting orientation toward parents and peers: A curvilinear trend over recent decades. *Journal of Marriage and Family, 48,* 5–13.

Seefeldt, V. (1982). The changing image of youth sports in the 1980s. In R. A. Magill, M. J. Ash, & F. L. Smoll (Eds.), *Children in sport* (pp. 16–26). Champaign, IL: Human Kinetics.

Segest, E., Mygind, O., Jergensen, W., Bechgaard, M., & Fallov, J. (1990). Free condoms in youth clubs in Copenhagen. *Journal of Adolescence, 13,* 17–24.

Seginer, R. (1992). Sibling relationships in early adolescence: A study of Israeli-Arab sisters. *Journal of Early Adolescence, 12,* 96–110.

Seitz, V., & Apfel, N. H. (1994). Parent-focused intervention: Diffusion effects on siblings. *Child Development, 65,* 677–683.

Selman, R. L. (1977). A structural-developmental model of social cognition: Implications for intervention research. *Counseling Psychologists, 6,* 3–6.

Selman, R. L. (1980). *The growth of interpersonal understanding: Development and clinical analysis.* New York: Academic Press.

Seltzer, J. A. (1990). Relationships between fathers and children who live apart: The father's role after separation. *Journal of Marriage and the Family, 53,* 79–101.

Sessa, F. M., & Steinberg, L. (1991). Family structure and the development of autonomy during adolescence. *Journal of Early Adolescence, 11,* 38–55.

Seydlitz, R. (1991). The effects of age and gender on parental control and delinquency. *Youth and Society, 23,* 175–201.

Seydlitz, R. (1993). Complexity in the relationships among direct and indirect parental controls and delinquency, *Youth and Society, 24,* 243–275.

Shantz, C. U. (1987). Conflicts between children. *Child Development, 58,* 283–305.

Shapiro, S. H. (1973). Vicissitudes of adolescence. In S. L. Copel (Ed.), *Behavior pathology of childhood and adolescence.* New York: Basic Books.

Sharkin, B. S. (1993). Age and gender: Theory, research, and implications. *Journal of Counseling and Development, 71,* 386–389.

Sharlin, S. A., & Mor-Barak, M. (1992). Runaway girls in distress: Motivation, background, and personality. *Adolescence, 27,* 387–405.

Shaughnessy, M. F., & Shakesby, P. (1992). Adolescent sexual and emotional intimacy. *Adolescence, 27,* 475–480.

Shaver, P. (1983, May). Down at college. *Psychology Today, 17,* 16.

Shaw, D. S., Keenan, K., & Vondra, J. I. (1994). Developmental precursors of externalizing behavior: Ages one to three. *Developmental Psychology, 30,* 355–364.

Shea, J. A., & Adams, G. R. (1984). Correlates of romantic attachment: A path analysis study. *Journal of Youth and Adolescence, 13,* 27–44.

Sheingold, D. K., & Tenney, Y. J. (1982). Memory for a salient childhood event. In U. Neisser (Ed.), *Memory observed.* San Francisco, CA: Freeman.

Shelton, B. A. (1990). The distribution of household tasks. *Journal of Family Issues, 11,* 115–135.

Shelton, C. M., & McAdams, D. P. (1990). In search of everyday morality: The development of a measure. *Adolescence, 25,* 923–944.

Sheppard, B. J. (1974). Making the case for behavior as an expression of physiological condition. In B. L. Kratonile (Ed.), *Youth in trouble.* San Rafael, CA: Academic Therapy Publications.

Shestowsky, B. J. (1983, Fall). Ego identity development and obesity in adolescent girls. *Adolescence, 18,* 551–559.

Shields, P. J., & Rovee-Collier, C. (1992). Long-term memory for context-specific category information at six months. *Child Development, 63,* 245–259.

Shilts, L. (1991). The relationship of early adolescent substance use to extracurricular activities, peer influence, and personal attitudes. *Adolescence, 26,* 613–617.

Shinn, M. W. (1900). *The biography of a baby.* Boston, MA: Houghton Mifflin.

Short, R. V. (1984). Breast feeding. *Scientific American, 250,* 35–41.

Siegel, A., & White, S. H. (1982). The child study movement: Early growth and development of the symbolized child. In H. W. Reese (Ed.), *Advances in child development and behavior* (Vol. 17). New York: Academic Press.

Siegler, R. S. (1989). Mechanisms of cognitive development. *Annual Review of Psychology, 40,* 353–379.

Siegler, R. S. (1992). The other Alfred Binet. *Developmental Psychology, 28,* 179–190.

Signorielli, N. (1991). Adolescents and ambivalence towards marriage: A cultivation analysis. *Youth and Society, 23,* 121–149.

Silber, S. J. (1980). *How to get pregnant.* New York: Scribner.

Silber, T. J. (1986). Gonorrhea in children and adolescents. *Medical Aspects of Human Sexuality, 16,* 92H–92X.

Silverman, W. K., LaGreca, A. M., & Wasserstein, S. (1995). What do children worry about? Worries and their relation to anxiety. *Child Development, 66,* 671–686.

Simcock, B. (1985). Sons and daughters—a sex preselection study. *Medical Journal of Australia, 142,* 541–542.

Simon, L. (1988). Freud, in his time and ours. *Psychology Today, 22,* 68, 69.

Simons, R. L., Beaman, J., Conger, R. D., & Chao, W. (1992). Gender differences in the intergenerational transmission of parenting beliefs. *Journal of Marriage and the Family, 54,* 823–836.

Simons, R. L., Beaman, J., Conger, R. D., Chao, W. (1993). Childhood experience, conceptions of parenting, and attitudes of spouse as determinants of parental behavior. *Journal of Marriage and the Family, 55,* 91–106.

Simons, R. L., & Whitbeck, L. B. (1991). Sexual abuse as a precursor to prostitution and victimization among adolescent and adult homeless women. *Journal of Family Issues, 12,* 361–379.

Simpson, W. S., & Ramberg, J. A. (1992). Sexual dysfunction in married female patients with anorexia and bulimia nervosa. *Journal of Sex and Marital Therapy, 18,* 44–54.

Singer, J. L. (1984). *The human personality.* San Diego, CA: Harcourt Brace Jovanovich.

Singer, J. L., & Singer, D. G. (1983). Implications of childhood television viewing for cognition, imagination, and emotion. In J. Bryant & Dr.

R. Anderson (Eds.), *Children's understanding of television: Research on attention and comprehension* (pp. 265–297). New York: Academic Press.

Singer, J. M., & Fagan, J. W. (1992). Negative affect, emotional expression, and forgetting in young infants. *Developmental Psychology, 28,* 48–57.

Sistler, A. K., & Gottfried, N. W. (1990). Shared child development knowledge between grandmother and mother. *Family Relations, 39,* 92–96.

Skandhan, K. P., Pandya, A. K., Skandhan, S., & Mehta, Y. B. (1988). Menarche: Prior knowledge and experience. *Adolescence, 89,* 149–154.

Skeen, P., Covi, R. B., & Robinson, B. E. (1985). Stepfamilies: A review of the literature with suggestions for practitioners. *Journal of Counseling and Development, 64,* 121–125.

Skinner, B. F. (1953). *Science and human behavior.* New York: Macmillan.

Skinner, B. F. (1957). *Verbal behavior.* New York: Appleton-Century-Crofts.

Skinner, B. F. (1983). *A matter of consequences. Part 3 of an autobiography.* New York: Alfred A. Knopf.

Skoe, E. E., & Gooden, A. (1993). Ethic of care and real-life moral dilemma content in male and female early adolescents. *Journal of Early Adolescence, 13,* 154–167.

Slade, A. (1987). A longitudinal study of maternal involvement and symbolic play during the toddler period. *Child Development, 58,* 367–375.

Slater, A., Morison, V., & Rose, D. (1983). Perception of shape by the newborn baby. *British Journal of Developmental Psychology, 1,* 135–142.

Slaughter-Defoe, D. T., Nakagawa, K., Takanishi, R., & Johnson, D. J. (1990). Toward cultural/ecological perspectives on schooling and achievement in African- and Asian-American children. *Child Development, 61,* 363–383.

Slomkowski, C. L., Nelson, K., Dunn, J., & Plomin, R. (1992). Temperament and language: Relations from toddlerhood to middle childhood. *Development Psychology, 28,* 1090–1095.

Slonin-Nevo, B. (1992). First premarital intercourse among Mexican-American and Anglo-American adolescent women. Interpreting ethnic differences. *Journal of Adolescent Research, 7,* 332–351.

Slonin-Nevo, V., Ozaga, M. N., & Auslander, W. F. (1991). Knowledge, attitudes and behaviors related to AIDS among youths in residential centers: Results from an exploratory study. *Journal of Adolescence, 14,* 1–16.

Small, S. A., & Eastman, G. (1991). Rearing adolescents in contemporary society: A conceptual framework for understanding the responsibilities and needs of parents. *Family Relations, 40,* 455–462.

Smetana, J. G., Braeges, J. L., & Yau, J. (1991). Doing what you say and saying what you do: Reasoning about adolescent–parent conflict in interviews and interactions. *Journal of Adolescent Research, 6,* 276–295.

Smetana, J. G., Killen, M., & Turiel, E. (1991). Children's reasoning about interpersonal and moral conflicts. *Child Development, 62,* 629–644.

Smetana, J. G., Yau, J., & Hanson, S. (1991). Conflict resolution in families with adolescents. *Journal of Research on Adolescence, 1,* 189–206.

Smiley, T. A., & Dweck, C. S. (1994). Individual differences in achievement goals among young children. *Child Development, 65,* 1723–1743.

Smith, B. A., Stevens, K., Torgerson, W. S., & Kim, J. H. (1992). Diminished reactivity of postmature human infants to sucrose compared with term infants. *Developmental Psychology, 28,* 811–820.

Smith, E. J. (1991). Ethnic identity development: Toward the development of a theory within the context of majority/minority status. *Journal of Counseling and Development, 770,* 181–188.

Smith, J. E., Hillard, M. C., & Roll, S. (1991). Rorschach evaluation of adolescent bulimics. *Adolescence, 26,* 687–696.

Smith, H. L., & Morgan, S. P. (1994). Children's closeness to father as reported by mothers, sons, and daughters: Evaluated subjected assessments with the Rasch model. *Journal of Family Issues, 15,* 3–29.

Smith, L. B., Jones, S., & Landau, B. (1992). Count nouns, adjectives, and perceptual properties in children's novel word interpretations. *Developmental Psychology, 28,* 273–286.

Smith, P. B., & Pederson, D. R. (1988). Maternal sensitivity and patterns of infant-mother attachment. *Child Development, 59,* 1097–1101.

Smith, P. B., Weinman, M., & Malinak, L. R. (1984). Adolescent mothers and fetal loss, what is learned from experience? *Psychological Reports, 55,* 775–778.

Smith, T. E. (1981). Adolescent agreement with perceived maternal and paternal educational goals. *Journal of Marriage and the Family, 43,* 85–93.

Smith, T. E. (1983). Adolescent reactions to attempted parental control and influence techniques. *Journal of Marriage and the Family, 45,* 533–542.

Smith, T. E. (1988). Parental control techniques. *Journal of Family Issues, 9,* 155–176.

Snodgrass, D. M. (1991). The parent connection. *Adolescence, 26,* 83–88.

Snyder, S. (1991). Movies and juvenile delinquency. *Adolescence, 26,* 121–132.

Sobel, D. (1981, June 29). Surrogate mothers: Why women volunteer. *New York Times,* p. B-5.

Social factors not age are found to affect risk of low birth weight (1984, May/June). *Family Planning Perspectives, 16,* 142–143.

Sodian, B., Taylor, C., Harris, P. L., & Perner, J. (1991). Early deception and the child's theory of mind: False trails and genuine markers. *Child Development, 62,* 468–483.

Sodian, B., Zaitchik, D., & Carey, S. (1991). Young children's differentiation of hypothetical beliefs from evidence. *Child Development, 62,* 753–766.

Sodowsky, G. R., Lai, E. W. M., & Plake, B. S. (1991). Moderating effects of sociocultural variables on acculturation attitudes of Hispanics and Asian Americans. *Journal of Counseling and Development, 70,* 195–204.

Soja, N. N. (1994). Young children's concept of color and its relation to the acquisition of color words. *Child Development, 65,* 918–937.

Soken, N. H., & Pick, A. D. (1992). Intermodal perception of happy and angry expressive behaviors by seven-month-old infants. *Child Development, 63,* 787–795.

Solorzano, L., Hague, J. R., Peterson, S., Lyons, D. C., & Bosc, M. (1984, August 27). What makes great schools great. *U.S. News and World Report,* pp. 46–49.

Sommer, B., & Nagel, S. (1991). Ecological and typological characteristics in early adolescent truancy. *Journal of Early Adolescence, 11,* 379–392.

Sonenstein, F. L., & Pittman, K. J. (1984). Availability of sex education in large school districts. *Family Planning Perspectives, 16,* 19–25.

Sonenstein, F. L., Pleck, J. H., & Ku, L. C. (1989). Sexual activity, condom use and AIDS awareness among adolescent males. *Family Planning Perspectives, 21,* 152–158.

Sonenstein, F. L., Pleck, J. H., & Ku, L. C. (1991). Levels of sexual activity among adolescent males in the United States. *Family Planning Perspectives, 23,* 162–167.

Sostek, A. M., Smith, Y. F., Katz, K. S., & Grant, E. G. (1987). Developmental outcome of preterm infants with intraventricular hemorrhage at one and two years of age. *Child Development, 58,* 779–786.

Southard, B. (1985). Interlimb movement control and coordination in children. In J. E. Clark & J. H. Humphrey (Eds.), *Motor development: Current selected research.* Princeton, NJ: Princeton Book Co.

Spearman, C. (1927). *The abilities of man: Their nature and measurement.* New York: Macmillan.

Spencer, M. B., & Markstrom-Adams, C. (1990). Identity processes among racial and ethnic minority children in America. *Child Development, 61,* 290–310.

Spetner, N. B. & Olsho, L. W. (1990). Auditory frequency resolution in human infancy. *Child Development, 61,* 632–652.

Spiker, D., Kraemer, H. C., Constantine, N. A., & Bryant, D. (1992). Reliability and validity of behavior problem checklists as measures of stable traits in low birth weight, premature preschoolers. *Child Development, 63,* 1481–1496.

Spinillo, A. G., & Bryant, P. (1991). Children's proportional judgments: The importance of "half." *Child Development, 62,* 427–440.

Spock, B. (1946). *Commonsense book of baby and child care.* New York: Duell, Sloan & Pearce.

Spock, B. (1990, May 30). *Spock would abolish Little League.* Portland, ME: Portland Press Herald.

Spock, B., & Rothenberg, M. B. (1985). *Dr. Spock's baby and child care.* New York: Pocket Books.

Spock, B. & Rothenberg, M. B. (1985). *Baby and child care.* New York: Pocket Books.

Sporns, O., & Edelman, G. M. (1993). Solving Bernstein's problem: A proposal for the development of coordinated movement by selection. *Child Development, 64,* 960–981.

Sprague, R. L., & Ullman, R. K. (1981). Psychoactive drugs and child management. In J. M. Kaufman & D. P. Hallahan (Eds.), *Handbook of special education.* New York: Prentice-Hall.

Sprecher, S., McKinney, K., & Orbuch, T. L. (1991). The effect of current sexual behavior on friendship, dating, and marriage desirability. *The Journal of Sex Research, 28,* 387–408.

Sprecher, S., McKinney, K., Walsh, R., & Anderson, C. (1988). A revision of the Reiss premarital sexual permissiveness scale. *Journal of Marriage and the Family, 50,* 821–828.

Spreen, O., Tupper, D., Risser, A., Tuokko, H., & Edgell, D. (1984). *Human developmental neuropsychology.* New York: Oxford University Press.

Springer, K. (1992). Children's awareness of the biological implications of kinship. *Child Development, 63,* 950–959.

Springer, S. P., & Deutsch, G. (1985). *Left brain, right brain.* New York: Freeman.

Sroufe, L. A., Bennett, C., Englund, M., & Urban, J. (1993). The significance of gender boundaries in preadolescents: The contemporary correlates and antecedents of boundary violations and maintenance. *Child Development, 64,* 455–466.

Sroufe, L. A., Egeland, B., & Kreutzer, T. (1990). The fate of early experience following developmental change: Longitudinal approaches to individual adaptation in childhood. *Child Development, 61,* 1363–1373.

Stager, J. M. (1984). Reversibility of amenorrhea in athletes: A review. *Sports Medicine, 1,* 337.

Stager, J. M. (1988). Menarche and exercise. *Medical Aspects of Human Sexuality, 22,* 118, 133.

Stager, J. M., Ritchie, B. A., & Robertshaw, D. (1984). Reversal of aligo/amenorrhea in collegiate distance runners. *New England Journal of Medicine, 310,* 51.

Stake, J. E., DeVille, C. J., & Pennell, C. L. (1983, October). The effects of assertive training on the performance self-esteem of adolescent girls. *Journal of Youth and Adolescence, 12,* 435–442.

Stanley, B. K., Weikel, W. J., & Wilson, J. (1986). The effects of father absence on interpersonal problem-solving skills of nursery school children. *Journal of Counseling and Development, 64,* 383–385.

Stanton, B. F., Black, M., Kaljee, L., & Ricardo, I. (1993). Perceptions of sexual behavior among urban early adolescents: Translating theory through focus groups. *Journal of Early Adolescence, 13,* 44–66.

Stanton, W. R., & Silva, P. A. (1992). A longitudinal study of the influence of parents and friends on children's initiation of smoking. *Journal of Applied Developmental Psychology, 13,* 423–434.

Starrels, M. E. (1994). Gender differences in parent-child relations. *Journal of Family Issues, 15,* 148–165.

Steel, L. (1991). Early work experience among white and nonwhite youths: Implications for subsequent enrollment and employment. *Youth and Society, 22,* 419–447.

Stefanko, M. (1984, Spring). Trends in adolescent research: A review of articles published in adolescence, 1976–1981. *Adolescence, 19,* 1–14.

Stein, D. M., & Reichert, P. (1990). Extreme dieting behaviors in early adolescence. *Journal of Early Adolescence, 10,* 108–121.

Stein, L., & Hoopes, J. (1986). *Identity formation in the adopted child.* New York: Child Welfare League of America.

Stein, J. A., Newcomb, M. D., & Bentler, P. M. (1993). Differential effects of parent and grandparent drug use on behavior problems of male and female children. *Developmental Psychology, 29,* 31–43.

Stein, R. F. (1987). Comparison of self-concept of non-obese and obese university junior female nursing students. *Adolescence, 22,* 77–90.

Steinberg, L., Lamborn, S. D., Dornbusch, S. M., & Darling, M. (1992). Impact of parenting practices on adolescent achievement: Authoritative parenting, school involvement, and encouragement to succeed. *Child Development, 63,* 1266–1281.

Steinberg, L., Mounts, N. S., Lamborn, S. D., & Dornbusch, S. M. (1991). Authoritative parenting and adolescent adjustment across varied ecological niches. *Journal of Research on Adolescence, 1,* 19–36.

Steinberg, L. D. (1981). Transformations in family relations at puberty. *Developmental Psychology, 17,* 833–840.

Steinberg, L. D., Greenberger, E., Garduque, L., Ruggiero, M., & Vaux, A. (1982). Effects of early work experience on adolescent development. *Developmental Psychology, 18,* 385–395.

Steinberg, L. D., Greenberger, E., Jacobi, M., & Garduque, L. (1981, April). Early work experience: A partial antidote for adolescent egocentrism. *Journal of Youth and Adolescence, 10,* 141–157.

Steinman, S., Zemmelman, S., & Knoblauch, T. (1985). A study of parents who sought joint custody and who returns to court. *Journal of the American Academy of Child Psychiatry, 24,* 554–562.

Stephen, J., Fraser, E., & Marcia, J. E. (1992). Moratorium achievement (Mama) cycles in lifespan identity development: Value orientations and reasoning systems correlates. *Journal of Adolescence, 15,* 283–300.

Stern, J. A., Oster, P. J., & Newport, K. (1980). Reaction time measure, hemisphere specialization, and age. In L. W. Poon (Ed.), *Aging in the 80's: Psychological issues.* Washington, DC: American Psychological Association.

Stern, M., Northman, J. E., & Van Slyck, M. R. (1984, Summer). Father absence and adolescent "problem behaviors": Alcohol consumption, drug use, and sexual activity. *Adolescence, 17,* 847–853.

Stern, M., & Zevon, M. A. (1990). Stress, coping, and family environment: The adolescent's response to naturally occurring stressors. *Journal of Adolescent Research, 5,* 290–305.

Sternberg, K. J., Lamb, M. E., Greenbaum, C., Cicchetti, D., Dawud, S., Cortes, R. M., Krispin, O., & Lorey, F. (1993). Effects of domestic violence on children's behavior problems and depression. *Developmental Psychology, 29,* 44–52.

Sternberg, R. J. (1985). *Beyond IQ.* Cambridge, England: Cambridge University Press.

Sternberg, R. J., & Wagner, R. K. (Eds.). (1986). *Practical intelligence: Nature and origins of competence in the everyday world.* Cambridge, England: Cambridge University Press.

Stevens, J. H., Jr. (1988). Social support, locus of control, and parenting in three low-income groups of mothers: Black teenagers, black adults, and white adults. *Child Development, 59,* 635–642.

Stevens, R., & Pihl, R. O. (1987). Seventh-grade students at risk for school failure. *Adolescence, 22,* 333–345.

Stevenson, H. W., Chen, C., & Uttal, D. H. (1990). Beliefs and achievement: A study of black, white, and Hispanic children. *Child Development, 61,* 508–523.

Stevenson, H. W., Hale, G. A., Klein, R. E., & Miller, L. K. (1968). Interrelations and correlates in children's learning and problem solving. *Monographs of the Society for Research in Child Development, 33*(Serial No. 123).

Stevenson, H. W., Lee, S., Chen, C., & Lummis, M. (1990). Mathematics achievement of children in China and the United States. *Child Development, 61,* 1053–1066.

Stevenson, H. W., Lee, S. Y., & Stigler, J. W. (1986). Mathematics achievement in Chinese, Japanese, and American children. *Science, 231,* 693–699.

Stevenson, M. R., & Black, K. N. (1988). Paternal absence and sex-role developments: A meta-analysis. *Child Development, 59,* 793–814.

Stewart, H. S. (1982, Fall). Body type, personality, temperament, and psychotherapeutic treatment of female adolescents. *Adolescence, 22,* 77–90.

Stigler, J. W., Lee, S., & Stevenson, H. W. (1987). Mathematics classrooms in Japan, Taiwan, and the United States. *Child Development, 58,* 1272–1285.

Stiles, W. B., Shuster, P. L., & Harrigan, J. A. (1992). Disclosure and anxiety: A test of the fever model. *Journal of Personality and Social Psychology, 63,* 980–988.

Stipek, D., Feiler, R., Daniels, D., & Milburn, S. (1995). Effects of different instructional approaches on young children's achievement and motivation. *Child Development, 66,* 209–223.

Stipek, D. J., & Hoffman, J. (1980). Development of children's performance-related judgments. *Child Development, 51,* 912–914.

Stipek, D., & MacIver, D. (1989). Developmental change in children's assessment of intellectual competence. *Child Development, 60,* 521–538.

Stjernfeldt, M., Berglund, K., Lindsten, J., & Ludvigsson, J. (1986). Maternal smoking during pregnancy and risk of childhood cancer. *Lancet,* pp. 1350–1352.

Stockman, I. J., & Cooke-Vaughn, F. (1992). Lexical elaboration in children's locative action expressions. *Child Development, 63,* 1104–1125.

Stokols, D. (1992). Environmental quality, human development, and health: An ecological view. *Journal of Applied Developmental Psychology, 13,* 121–124.

Story, M. D. (1982). A comparison of university student experience with various sexual outlets in 1974 and 1980. *Adolescence, 17,* 737–747.

Strang, R. (1957). *The adolescent views himself.* New York: McGraw-Hill.

Strayer, J. (1993). Children's concordant emotions and cognitions in response to observed emotions. *Child Development, 64,* 188–201.

Streetman, L. G. (1987). Contrasts in self-esteem of unwed teenage mothers. *Adolescence, 23,* 459–464.

Streissguth, A. P., Martin, D. C., Barr, H. M., Sandman, B. M., Kirshner, G. L., & Darby, B. L. (1984). Intrauterine alcohol and nicotine exposure: Attention and reaction time in 4-year-old children. *Development Psychology, 20,* 533–541.

Streitmatter, J. (1993). Gender differences in identity development: An examination of longitudinal data. *Adolescence, 28,* 55–66.

Strongman, K. T. (1987). *The psychology of emotion* (3rd ed.), New York: Wiley.

Stroufe, L. A. (1985). Attachment classification from the perspective of infant-caregiver relationships and infant temperament. *Child Development, 56,* 1–14.

Stryker, S. (1980). *Symbolic interactionism.* Menlo Park, CA: Benjamin/Cummings.

Stuck, M. F., & Glassner, B. (1985). The transition from drug use and crime to noninvolvement: A case study. *Adolescence, 20,* 669–679.

Stunkard, A. J., Foch, T. T., & Hrubec, Z. (1986). A twin study of human obesity. *JAMA, Journal of the American Medical Association, 256,* 51–54.

Subak-Sharpe, G. J. (Ed.). (1984). Genital herpes. *The physicians manual for patients* (pp. 370–372). New York: Times Books.

Sullivan, M. W., Lewis, M., & Alessandri, S. M. (1993). Cross-age stability in emotional expressions during learning and extinction. *Developmental Psychology, 28,* 58–63.

Svec, H. (1987). Anorexia nervosa: A misdiagnosis of the adolescent male. *Adolescence, 87,* 617–623.

Swain, I. U., Zelazo, P. R., & Clifton, R. K. (1993). Newborn infants' memory for speech sounds retained over 24 hours. *Developmental Psychology, 29,* 312–323.

Swann, W. B., Stein-Seroussi, A., & McNulty, S. E. (1992). Outcasts in a white-tie society: The enigmatic worlds of people with negative self-conceptions. *Journal of Personality and Social Psychology, 62,* 618–624.

Sweet, A. Y. (1979). Classification of the low-birth-weight infant. In M. H. & A. A. Fanaroff (Eds.), *Care of the high-risk infant* (2nd ed.). New York: Saunders.

Symonds, A. (1995, October 31). "Me generation" parents should grow up. *Wall Street Journal,* A-18.

Takeuchi, D. T., Williams, D. R., & Adair, R. K. (1991). Economic stress in the family and children's emotional and behavior problems. *Journal of Marriage and the Family, 53,* 1031–1041.

Tamis-LeMonda, C. S., & Bornstein, M. H. (1986). Habituation and maternal encouragement of attention in infancy as predictors of toddler language, play and representational competence. *Child Development, 60,* 738–751.

Tan, L. (1985). Laterality and motor skills in 4-year-olds. *Child Development, 56,* 119–124.

Tangney, J. P. (1988). Aspects of the family and children's television viewing control preferences. *Child Development, 59,* 1070–1079.

Tanner, J. M. (1962). *Growth of adolescence.* Springfield, IL: Charles C. Thomas.

Tanner, J. M. (1970). Physical growth. In P. H. Mussen (Ed.), *Carmichael's manual of child psychology* (3rd ed., Vol. 1). New York: Wiley.

Tanner, J. M. (1972). Sequence, tempo, and individual variation in growth and development of boys and girls aged twelve to sixteen. In J. Kegan & R. Coles (Eds.), *Twelve to sixteen: Early adolescence.* New York: W. W. Norton.

Tanner, J. M. (1973, September), Growing Up, *Scientific American.*

Taub, D. E., & Blinde, E. M. (1992). Eating disorders among adolescent female athletes: Influence of athletic participation and sport team membership. *Adolescence, 27,* 833–848.

Taylor, M., Cartwright, B. S., & Carlson, S. M. (1993). A developmental investigation of children's imaginary companions. *Developmental Psychology, 29,* 276–285.

Teachman, J. D. (1991). Who pays? Receipt of child support in the United States. *Journal of Marriage and the Family, 53,* 759–772.

Teasley, S. D., (1995). The role of talk in children's peer collaborations. *Developmental Psychology, 31,* 207–220.

Tedesco, L. A., & Gaier, E. L. (1988). Friendship bonds in adolescence. *Adolescence, 89,* 127–136.

Television and your children. (1985). Ontario, Canada: TV Ontario, Ontario Educational Communications Authority.

Tennstedt, S. L., Dettling, U., & McKinley, J. B. (1992). Refusal rates in a longitudinal study of older people: Implications for field methods. *Journal of Gerontology, 47,* S313–S318.

Terman, L. (1925). *Genetic studies of genius: Vol. 1. Mental and physical traits of a thousand gifted children.* Stanford, CA: Stanford University Press.

Terman, L., & Oden, M. H. (1959). *Genetic studies of genius: Vol. 4. The gifted group at midlife.* Stanford, CA: Stanford University Press.

Teti, D. M., & Ablard, K. E. (1989). Security of attachment and infant-sibling relationships: A laboratory study. *Child Development, 60,* 1519–1528.

Teti, D. M., & Gelfand, D. M. (1991). Behavioral competence among mothers of infants in the first year. The mediational role of maternal self-efficacy. *Child Development, 62,* 918–929.

Teti, D. M., Lamb, M. E., & Elster, A. B. (1987). Long-range economic and marital consequences of adolescent marriage in three cohorts of adult males. *Journal of Marriage and the Family, 49,* 499–506.

Teyler, T. J., & Fountain, S. B. (1987). Neuronal plasticity in the mammalian brain: Relevance to behavioral learning and memory. *Child Development, 58,* 698–712.

Thelen, E. (1981). Rhythmical behavior in infancy: An ethological perspective. *Developmental Psychology, 17,* 237–257.

Thomas, A., & Chess, S. (1977). *Temperament and development,* New York: Brunner/Mazel.

Thomas, A., & Chess, S. (1984). Genesis and evaluation of behavioral disorders: From infancy to early adulthood. *American Journal of Orthopsychiatry, 14,* 1–9.

Thomas, A. & Chess, S. (1987). Roundtable: What is temperament? *Child Development, 58,* 505–529.

Thomas, H. (1995). Modeling class inclusion strategies. *Developmental Psychology, 31,* 170–179.

Thomas, K. R. (1991). Oedipal issues in counseling psychology. *Journal of Counseling and Development, 69,* 203–205.

Thompson, L., Acock, A. C., & Clark, K. (1985). Do parents know their children? The ability of mothers and fathers to gauge the attitudes of their young adult children. *Family Relations, 34,* 315–320.

Thompson, R. A., Connell, J. P., & Bridges, L. J. (1988). Temperament, emotion, and social interactive behavior in the strange situation: A component process analysis of attachment system functioning. *Child Development, 59,* 1102–1110.

Thompson, W. E., & Dodder, R. A. (1986). Containment theory and juvenile delinquency: A reevaluation through fact analysis. *Adolescence, 21,* 365–376.

Thompson, W. R., & Grusec, J. E. (1970). Studies of early experience. In P. H. Mussen (Ed.), *Carmichael's manual of child psychology* (Vol. 1). New York: Wiley.

Thorndike, R. L., Hagen, E. P., & Sattler, J. M. (1985). *Stanford-Binet* (4th ed.). Chicago, IL: Riverside Publishing.

Thornton, B., & Ryckman, R. M. (1991). Relationships between physical attractiveness, physical effectiveness, and self-esteem: A cross-sectional analysis among adolescents. *Journal of Adolescence, 14,* 85–98.

Thornton, M. C., Chatters, L. M., Taylor, R. J., & Allen, W. R. (1990). Sociodemographic and environmental correlates of racial socialization by black parents. *Child Development, 61,* 401–409.

Three years after enactment, child support laws appear to increase payments by absent fathers (1987). *Family Planning Perspectives, 19,* 272–273.

Thurber, C. A. (1995). The experience and expression of homesickness in preadolescent and adolescent boys. *Child Development, 66,* 1162–1178.

Thurstone, L. L. (1938). *Primary mental abilities. Psychometric monographs.* No. 1. Chicago, IL: University of Chicago Press.

Thurstone, L. L., & Thurstone, T. B. (1953). *Examiner manual for the Primary Mental Abilities for Ages 5 to 7* (3rd ed.). Chicago, IL: Science Research Associates.

Tidwell, R. (1988). Dropouts speak out: Qualitative data on early school departures. *Adolescence, 92,* 939–954.

Tierno, M. J. (1983, Fall). Responding to self-concept disturbance among early adolescents: A psychosocial view for educators. *Adolescence, 18,* 577–584.

Tierno, M. J. (1991). Responding to the socially motivated behaviors of early adolescence: Recommendations from classroom management. *Adolescence, 26,* 567–577.

Tinsley, B. J. (1992). Multiple influences on the acquisition and socialization of children's health attitudes and behavior: An integrative review. *Child Development, 63,* 1043–1069.

Tolan, P. (1988). Socioeconomic, family, and social stress correlates of adolescent antisocial and delinquent behavior. *Journal of Abnormal Child Psychology, 16,* 317–331.

Tolson, T. F. J., & Wilson, M. N. (1990). The impact of two- and three-generational black family structure on perceived family climate. *Child Development, 61,* 416–428.

Tooth, G. (1985, February 18). Why children's TV turns off so many parents. *U.S. News and World Report,* p. 65.

Toufexis, A. (1992). When kids kill abusive parents. *Time, 140,* 60–61.

Tower, R. B., Singer, D. G., Singer, L. J., & Biggs, A. (1979). Differential effects of television programming on preschooler's cognition, imagination, and social play. *American Journal of Orthopsychiatry, 49,* 265–281.

Trachtenberg, S., & Biken, R. J. (1994). Aggressive boys in the classroom: Biased attributions or shared perceptions? *Child Development, 65,* 829–835.

Trapped by mutilator troy? Need help finding dracula's heart? Just call the Nintendo hotline (1990, January 8). *People, 33,* 82.

Traver, N. (1992, October 26). Children without pity. *Time, 140,* 46–51.

Travillion, K., & Snyder, J. (1993). The role of maternal discipline and involvement in peer rejection and neglect. *Journal of Applied Developmental Psychology, 14,* 37–55.

Treichel, J. (1982). Anorexia nervosa: A brain shrinker? *Science News, 122,* 122–123.

Tribich, D., & Klein, M. (1981). On Freud's blindness. *Colloquium, 4,* 52–59.

Troster, H., & Brambring, M. (1993). Early motor development in blind infants. *Journal of Applied Developmental Psychology, 14,* 83–106.

Trotter, R. J. (1986). Three heads are better than one. *Psychology Today, 20,* 56–62.

Trotter, R. J. (1987a). Project day-care. *Psychology Today, 21,* 32–38.

Trotter, R. J. (1987b, May). You've come a long way, baby. *Psychology Today, 21,* 34–45.

Trussell, J. (1988). Teenage pregnancy in the United States. *Family Planning Perspectives, 20,* 262–272.

Trussell, J., Warner, D. L., & Hatcher, R. A. (1992). Condom slippage and breakage rates. *Family Planning Perspectives, 24,* 21–23.

Tschann, J. M., Johnston, J. R., Kline, M., & Wallerstein, J. S. (1989). Family process and children's functioning during divorce. *Journal of Marriage and the Family, 51,* 431–444.

Tubman, J. G. (1993). Family risk factors, parental alcohol use, and problem behaviors among school-age children. *Family Relations, 42,* 81–86.

Tucker, L. A. (1982). Relationship between perceived conatotype of body cathexis of college males. *Psychology Reports, 50,* 983–989.

Tucker, L. A. (1983). Muscular strength and mental health. *Journal of Personality and Social Psychology, 45,* 1355–1360.

Tudor, C. G., Petersen, D. M., & Elifson, K. W. (1980, Winter). An examination of the relationship between peer and parental influences and adolescent drug use. *Adolescence, 15,* 783–795.

Turnbull, S. K., & Turnbull, J. M. (1983). To dream the impossible dream: An agenda for discussion with stepparents. *Family Relations, 32,* 227–230.

Turner, P. H., & Smith, R. M. (1983). Single parents and day care. *Family Relations, 32,* 227–230.

Turner, P. J. (1991). Relations between attachment, gender, and behavior with peers in preschool. *Child Development, 62,* 1475–1488.

Turner, R. (1991). One in seven 6th–12th graders had an unwanted sexual encounter, including one in five females. *Family Planning Perspectives, 23,* 286–287.

Turner, R. (1992a). First-trimester chorionic villus sampling may raise risk of spontaneous abortion and limb abnormality. *Family Planning Perspectives, 24,* 45–46.

Turner, R. (March/April 1992b). Births to women in their middle and late 30s have risen among both blacks and whites since 1980. *Family Planning Perspectives, 24,* 91–92.

Turner, R. (March/April 1992c). Underweight births are equally likely among poor blacks and whites. *Family Planning Perspectives, 24,* 95–96.

Turner, R. (November/December 1992d). Low birth weight linked to physical, behavioral problems at school age. *Family Planning Perspectives, 24,* 279–280.

Turner, R. (1994). Receiving recommended prenatal health advice can increase birth weight. *Family Planning Perspectives, 26,* 187–189.

Tygart, C. (1988). Public school vandalism: Toward a synthesis of theories and transition to paradigm analysis. *Adolescence, 15,* 783–795.

Tygart, C. E. (1991). Juvenile delinquency and number of children in a family: Some empirical and theoretical updates. *Youth and Society, 22,* 525–536.

Ubell, E. (1990, January 14). You don't have to be childless. *Parade Magazine,* pp. 14, 15.

Udry, J. R., & Cliquet, R. L. (1982). A cross-cultural examination of the relationship between ages at menarche, marriage, and first birth. *Demography, 19,* 53–63.

Uhr, S., Stahl, S. M., & Berger, P. A. (1984). Unmasking schizophrenia. *VA Practitioner,* 42–53.

Ulbrich, P. M., Coyle, A. T., & Llabre, M. M. (1990). Involuntary childlessness and marital adjustment: His and hers. *Journal of Sex and Marital Therapy, 16,* 147–158.

Umbel, V. M., Pearson, B. Z., Fernandes, M. C., & Oiler, D. K. (1992). Measuring bilingual children's receptive vocabularies. *Child Development, 63,* 1012–1020.

Umberson, D. (1989). Relationships with children: Explaining parents' psychological well-being. *Journal of Marriage and the Family, 51,* 499–1012.

Upchurch, D. M., & McCarthy, J. (1989). Adolescent childbearing and high school completion in the 1980s: Have things changed? *Family Planning Perspectives, 21,* 199–202.

U.S. Bureau of the Census. (1988). *Statistical abstract of the U.S., 1988* (108th ed.). Washington, DC: U.S. Government Printing Office.

U.S. Bureau of the Census. (1995). *Statistical abstract of the United States,* 1995 (115th ed.). Washington, DC: U.S. Government Printing Office.

U.S. Bureau of the Census. (1992). *Statistical abstract of the United States, 1992* (112th ed.). Washington, DC: U.S. Government Printing Office.

U.S. Department of Agriculture and U.S. Department of Health and Human Services. (1985). *Dietary guidelines for Americans* (Home and Garden Bulletin, No. 232). Washington, DC: U.S. Government Printing Office.

U.S. Department of Health and Human Services. (1979). *The Belmont Report: Ethical Principles and Guidelines for the Protection of Human Subjects of Research* (Publication No. 1983, pp. 81–132, 1305). Department of Health, Education, and Welfare, Washington, DC: U.S. Government Printing Office.

U.S. Department of Health and Human Services. (1980, June). *Marijuana research findings: 1980.* Rockville, MD: National Institute on Drug Abuse.

U.S. Department of Health and Human Services. (1981). *Statistics on incidence of depression.* Washington, DC: U.S. Government Printing Office.

U.S. Department of Health and Human Services: Office of Human Development (1980, August). *Status of children, youth, and families, 1979* (DHHS Publication No. [OHDS] 80-30274). Washington, DC: U.S. Government Printing Office.

Useem, E. L. (1991). Student selection into course sequences, in mathematics: The impact of parental involvement and school policies. *Journal of Research on Adolescence, 1,* 231–250.

Uttl, D., & Graf, P. (1993). Episodic spatial memory in adulthood. *Psychology & Aging, 8,* 257–273.

Vaillant, G. E. (1977a). *Adaptation to Life.* Boston, MA: Little, Brown.

Vaillant, G. E. (1977b). The climb to maturity: How the best and brightest come of age. *Psychology Today, 11,* 34ff.

Valdez-Menchaca, M. C., & Whitehurst, G. J. (1992). Accelerating language development through picture book reading: A systematic extension to Mexican day care. *Developmental Psychology, 28,* 1106–1114.

Valencia, R. R. (1985). Predicting academics achievement in Mexican-American children using the Kaufman Assessment Battery for Children. *Education and Psychological Research, 5,* 11–17.

Valenzuela, M. (1990). Attachment in chronically underweight young children. *Child Development, 61,* 1984–1996.

Vallerand, R. J., Deshaies, P., Cuerrier, J., Pelletier, L. G., & Mongeau, C. (1992). Ajzen and Fishbein's theory of reasoned action as applied to moral behavior: A confirmatory analysis. *Journal of Personality and Social Psychology, 62,* 98–109.

van Ijzendoorn, M. H., Goldberg, S., Kroonenberg, P. M., & Frenkel, O. J. (1992). The relative effects of maternal and child problems on the quality of attachment: A meta-analysis of attachment in clinical samples. *Child Development, 63,* 840–858.

Vandell, D. L., Owen, M. T., Wilson, K. S., & Henderson, V. K. (1988). Social development in infant twins: Peer and mother-child relationships. *Child Development,* 168–177.

Vandell, D. L., & Wilson, K. S. (1987). Infants' interactions with mother, sibling, peers: Contrasts and relations between interaction systems. *Child Development, 58,* 176–186.

Vangelisti, A. L. (1992). Older adolescents' perceptions of communication problems with their parents. *Journal of Adolescent Research, 7,* 382–402.

Vannoy, D. (1991). Social differentiation, contemporary marriage, and human development. *Journal of Family Issues, 12,* 251–267.

van Roosmalen, E. H., & McDaniel, S. A. (1992). Adolescent smoking intentions: Gender differences in peer context. *Adolescence, 27,* 87–105.

Van Thorre, M. D., & Vogel, F. X. (1985, Spring). The presence of bulimia in high school females. *Adolescence, 20,* 45–51.

Vaughn, B. E., Block, J. H., & Block, J. (1988). Parents' agreement on child rearing during early childhood and the psychological characteristics of adolescents. *Child Development, 59,* 1020–1033.

Vaughn, B. E., Lefever, G. B., Seifer, R., & Barglow, P. (1989). Attachment behavior, attachment security, and temperament during infancy. *Child Development, 60,* 728–737.

Vaughn, B. E., Stevenson-Hinde, J., Waters, E., Kotsaftis, A., Lefever, G. B., Shouldice, A., Trudel, M., & Belsky, J. (1992). Attachment security and temperament in infancy and early childhood: Some conceptual clarifications. *Developmental Psychology, 28,* 463–473.

Vaughn, B. E., & Waters, E. (1990). Attachment behavior at home and in the laboratory: Q-short observations and strange situation classifications of one-year olds. *Child Development, 61,* 1965–1973.

Vaughn, V. C., III. (1983). Developmental pediatrics. In R. E. Behrman & V. C. Vaughn III. (Eds.), *Pediatrics.* Philadelphia, PA: Saunders.

Verduyn, C. M., Lord, W., & Forrest, G. C. (1990). Social skills training in schools: An evaluation study. *Journal of Adolescence, 13,* 3–16.

Vicary, J. R., & Lerner, J. V. (1986). Parental attributes and adolescent drug use. *Journal of Adolescence, 9,* 115–122.

Voorhees, J. (1981, Spring). Neuropsychological differences between juvenile delinquents and functional adolescents: A preliminary study. *Adolescence, 16,* 57–66.

Vuchinich, S., Bank, L., & Patterson, G. R. (1992). Parenting, peers and the stability of antisocial behavior in pre-adolescent boys. *Developmental Psychology, 28,* 510–521.

Vygotsky, L. S. (1978). *Mind in society: The development of higher psychological processes.* Cambridge, MA: Harvard University Press.

Wagner, B. M., & Phillips, D. A. (1992). Beyond beliefs: Parent and child behaviors and children's perceived academic competence. *Child Development, 63,* 1380–1391.

Wagner, R. K., Torgesen, J. K., & Rashotte, C. A. (1994). Development of reading-related phonological processing abilities: New evidence of bidirectional causality from a latent variable longitudinal study. *Developmental Psychology, 30,* 73–87.

Waksman, S. A. (1984a, Spring). Assertion training with adolescents. *Adolescence, 19,* 123–130.

Waksman, S. A. (1984b, Summer). A controlled evaluation of assertion training on performance in highly anxious adolescents. *Adolescence, 19,* 277–282.

Wald, M. S., Carlsmith, J. M., & Leiderman, P. H. (1988). *Protecting abused and neglected children.* Stanford, CA: Stanford University Press.

Waletzky, L. (1981). Emotional illness in the postpartum period. In P. Ahmed (Ed.), *Pregnancy, childbirth, and parenthood.* New York: Elsevier.

Walker, E., Downey, G., & Bergman, A. (1989). The effects of parental psychopathology and maltreatment on child behavior: A test of the diathesis-stress model. *Child Development, 60,* 15–24.

Walker, L. J., & Taylor, J. H. (1991). Family interactions and the development of moral reasoning. *Child Development, 62,* 264–284.

Wallerstein, E. (1980). *Circumcision.* New York: Springer.

Wallerstein, J., & Blakeslee, S. (1990). *Second chances: Men, women, and children a decade after divorce.* London: Grant McIntyre.

Wallerstein, J. S. (1989, January 23). Children after divorce: Wounds that don't heal. *New York Times Magazine,* pp. 19–21, 41–44.

Wallerstein, J. S., & Kelly, J. B. (1980). *Surviving the breakup: How children and parents cope with divorce.* London: Grant McIntyre.

Wallinga, C., Paguio, L, & Skeen, P. (1987, August). When a brother or sister is ill. *Psychology Today, 21,* 42–43.

Wallis, C. (1984, March 26). Hold the eggs and butter. *Time, 123,* 56–63.

Wallis, C. (1987, February). You haven't heard anything yet. *Time.*

Walsh, A., & Beyer, J. A. (1987). Violent crime, sociopathy, and love deprivation among adolescent delinquents. *Adolescence, 22,* 705–717.

Warah, A. (1993). Overactive and boundary setting in anorexia nervosa: An existential perspective. *Journal of Adolescence, 16,* 93–100.

Warshak, R. A. (1986). Father-custody and child development: A review of analysis of psychological research. *Behavioral Science and the Law, 4,* 185–202.

Wasik, B. H., Ramey, C. T., Bryant, D. M., & Sparling, J. J. (1990). A longitudinal study of two early intervention strategies: Project CARE. *Child Development, 61,* 1682–1696.

Wasserman, G. A., Raugh, V. A., Brunelli, S. A., Garcia-Castro, M., & Necos, B. (1990). Psychosocial attributes and life experiences of disadvantaged minority mothers: Age and ethnic variations. *Child Development, 61,* 566–580.

Waterman, A. S. (1990). Curricula interventions for identity change: Substantive and ethical considerations. *Journal of Adolescence, 13,* 389–400.

Waters, E., & Sroufe, L. A. (1983). Social competence as a developmental construct. *Developmental Review, 3,* 79–97.

Watson, J. B., & Raynor, R. R. (1920). Conditional emotional reactions. *Journal of Experimental Psychology, 3,* 1–4.

Watts, W. D., & Wright, L. S. (1990). The relationship of alcohol, tobacco, marijuana, and other illegal drug use to delinquency among Mexican-American, black, and white adolescent males. *Adolescence, 25,* 171–182.

Waxman, S. R., & Hall, D. G. (1993). The development of a linkage between count nouns and object categories: Evidence from fifteen-to-twenty-one-month-old infants. *Child Development, 64,* 1224–1241.

Waxman, S. R., & Kosowski, T. D. (1990). Nouns mark category relations: Toddlers' and preschoolers' word-learning biases. *Child Development, 61,* 1461–1473.

Waxman, S. R., & Senghas, A. (1992). Relations among word meanings in early lexical development. *Developmental Psychology, 28,* 862–873.

Waxman, S. R., Shipley, E. F., & Shepperson, B. (1991). Establishing new subcategories: The role of category labels and existing knowledge. *Child Development, 62,* 127–138.

Weaver, G. M., & Wooton, R. R. (1992). The use of the MMPI special scales in the assessment of delinquent personality. *Adolescence, 27,* 545–554.

Webb, J. A., Baer, P. E., Caid, C. D., McKelvey, R. S., & Converse, R. E. (1992). Development of an abbreviated form of the alcoholic expectancy questionnaire for adolescents. *Journal of Adolescence, 12,* 441–456.

Webb, J. A., Baer, P. E., Caid, C. D., McLaughlin, R. J., & McKelvey, R. S. (1991). Concurrent and longitudinal assessment of risk for alcohol use among seventh graders. *Journal of Early Adolescence, 11,* 450–465.

Webb, R. A. (1974). Concrete and formal operations in very bright 6- to 11-year-olds. *Human Development, 17,* 292–300.

Webster v. Reproductive Health Services, Inc., 951 F. 2d., at 1079 (1988).

Wechsler, D. (1967). *Wechsler preschool and primary scale for intelligence.* New York: Psychological Corporation.

Wechsler, D. (1974). *Wechsler intelligence scale for children.* New York: Psychological Corporation.

Wechsler, D. (1981). *Wechsler adult intelligence scale—revised.* New York: Psychological Corporation.

Wechsler, D. (1989). *Wechsler preschool and primary scale of intelligence—Revised.* San Antonio, TX: The Psychological Corporation.

Wehr, S. H., & Kaufman, M. E. (1987). The effects of assertive training on performance in highly anxious adolescents. *Adolescence, 85,* 195–205.

Weinraub, M., Clemens, L. P., Sockloff, A., Ethridge, T., Gracely, E., & Myers, B. (1984). The development of sex role stereotypes in the third year: Relationships to gender labeling, gender identity, sex-typed toy preferences, and family characteristics. *Child Development, 55,* 1493–1503.

Weinstein, E., & Rosen, E. (1991). The development of adolescent sexual intimacy: Implications for counseling. *Adolescence, 26,* 331–340.

Weisner, T. S., & Wilson-Mitchell, J. E. (1990). Nonconventional family life-styles and sex typing in six-year-olds. *Child Development, 61,* 1915–1933.

Weiss, B., & Dodge, K. A. (1992). Some consequences of early harsh discipline: Child aggression and a maladaptive social information processing style. *Child Development, 63,* 1321–1335.

Weiss, M. J., Zelazo, P. R., & Swain, I. U. (1988). Newborn response to auditory stimulus discrepancy. *Child Development, 59,* 1530–1541.

Welsh, M. C., Pennington, B. F., Ozonoff, S., Rouse, B., & McCabe, E. R. B. (1990). Neuropsychology of early-treated phenylketonuria: Specific executive function deficits. *Child Development, 61,* 1697–1713.

Wentzel, K. R. (1991). Relations between social competence and academic achievement in early adolescence. *Child Development, 62,* 1066–1078.

Werner, E. E., & Smith, R. R. (1982). *Vulnerable but invincible: A longitudinal study of resilient children and youth.* New York: McGraw-Hill.

Werner, L. A., Marean, G. C., Halpin, C. F., Spetner, N. B., & Gillenwater, J. M. (1992). Infant auditory temporal acuity. Gap detection. *Child Development, 63,* 260–272.

Wertsch, J. V., & Tulviste, P. (1992). L. S. Vygotsky and contemporary developmental psychology. *Developmental Psychology, 28,* 548–557.

West Berlin Human Genetics Institute. (1987). *Studies on effect of nuclear radiation at Chernobyl on fetal development.* West Berlin: Human Genetics Institute.

Westney, O. J., Jenkins, R. R., Butts, J. D., & Williams, I. (1984, Fall). Sexual development and behavior in black preadolescents. *Adolescence, 19,* 557–568.

Wetherby, A., & Prutting, C. (1984). Profiles of communicative and cognitive-social abilities in autistic children. *Journal of Speech and Hearing Research, 27,* 364–377.

Whalen, C. K., Henker, B., Castro, J., & Granger, D. (1987). Peer perceptions of hyperactivity and medication effects. *Child Development, 58,* 816–828.

Whitbeck, L. B., Hoyt, D. R., Miller, M., & Kao, M. (1992). Parental support, depressed affect, and sexual experience among adolescents. *Youth and Society, 24,* 166–177.

Whitbeck, L. B., Hoyt, D. R., Simons, R. L., Conger, R. D., Elder, G. H., Jr., Lorenz, F. O., & Huck, S. (1992). Integenerational continuity of parental rejection and depressed affect. *Journal of Personality and Social Psychology, 63,* 1036–1049.

White, J., & Allers, C. T. (1994). Play therapy with abused children: A review of the literature. *Journal of Counseling and Development, 72,* 390–394.

White, K. J., & Kistner, J. (1992). The influence of teacher feedback on young children's peer preferences and perceptions. *Developmental Psychology, 28,* 933–940.

White, K. M. (1980, Spring). Problems and characteristics of college students. *Adolescence, 15,* 23–41.

White, L. K., & Brinkerhoff, D. B. (1981). Children's work in the family: Its significance and meaning. *Journal of Marriage and the Family, 43,* 789–798.

White, M. J., & Tsui, A. O. (1986). A panel study of family-level structural change. *Journal of Marriage and the Family, 48,* 435–446.

Whittaker, S., & Bry, B. H. (1991). Overt and covert parental conflict in adolescent problems: Observed marital interaction in clinic and nonclinic families. *Adolescence, 26,* 865–876.

Widmayer, S. M., Peterson, L. M., Larner, M., Carnahan, S., Calderon, A., Wingerd, J., & Marshall, R. (1990). Predictors of Haitian-American infant development at twelve months. *Child Development, 61,* 410–415.

Wilcoxon, S. A. (1987). Grandparents and grandchildren. *Journal of Counseling and Development, 65,* 289–290.

Williams, K. (1988). Parents reinforce feminine role in girls. *Medical Aspects of Human Sexuality, 22,* 106–107.

Williams, L. B. (1991). Determinants of unintended childbearing among never-married women in the United States: 1973–1988. *Family Planning Perspectives, 23,* 213–215.

Williams, L. S. (1992). Adoption actions and attitudes of couples seeking in vitro fertilization. *Journal of Family Issues, 13,* 19–113.

Williamson, J. A., & Campbell, L. P. (1985). Parents and their children comment on adolescence. *Adolescence, 20,* 745–748.

Wilson, J., Carrington, E., & Ledger, W. (1983). *Obstetrics and Gynecology.* St. Louis, MO: Mosby.

Wilson, P. T. (1985). *Amount of reading, reading instruction, and reading achievement.* Paper presented at the annual meeting of the National Reading Conference.

Wilson, R., & Matheny, A. (1983). Assessment of temperament in infant twins. *Developmental Psychology, 19,* 172–183.

Wilson, S. M., & Medora, N. P. (1990). Gender comparisons of college students' attitudes toward sexual behavior. *Adolescence, 25,* 615–628.

Wiltse, S. E. (1984). A preliminary sketch of the history of child study in America. *Pedagogical Seminary, 3,* 189–212.

Windle, M., & Miller-Tutzauer, C. (1992). Confirmatory factor analysis and concurrent validity of the perceived social support-family measure among adolescents. *Journal of Marriage and the Family, 54,* 777–787.

Wintre, M. G., Polivy, J., & Murray, M. A. (1990). Self-predictions of emotional response patterns: Age, sex, and situational determinants. *Child Development, 61,* 1124–1133.

Wise, K. L., Bundy, K. A., Bundy, E. A., & Wise, L. A. (1991). Social skills training for young adolescents. *Adolescence, 26,* 233–242.

Wisensale, S. K. (1992). Toward the 21st century: Family change and public policy. *Family Relations, 41,* 417–422.

Witelson, S. F. (1987). Neurobiological aspects of language in children. *Child Development, 58,* 653–688.

Witters, W. L., & Jones-Witters, P. (1980). *Human sexuality: A biological perspective.* New York: Van Nostrand.

Witwer, M. (1993). U.S. men and women now have highest mean age at marriage in this century, Census Bureau finds. *Family Planning Perspectives, 25,* 190–191.

Wodarski, J. S. (1990). Adolescent substance abuse: Practical implications. *Adolescence, 25,* 667–688.

Wolf, F. M. (1981, Summer). On why adolescent formal operators may not be critical thinkers. *Adolescence, 16,* 345–348.

Wood, B. S. (1981). *Children and communication: Verbal and nonverbal language development* (2nd ed.). Englewood Cliffs, NJ: Prentice-Hall.

Wood, J., Chapin, K., & Hannah, M. E. (1988). Family environment and its relationship to underachievement. *Adolescence, 23,* 283–290.

Wood, N. L., Wood, R. A., & McDonald, T. D. (1988). Integration of student development theory into the academic classroom. *Adolescence, 23,* 349–356.

Woodward, J. C., & Kalyan-Masih, V. (1990). Loneliness, coping strategies and cognitive styles of the gifted rural adolescent. *Adolescence, 25,* 977–988.

Woody-Ramsey, J., & Miller, P. H. (1988). The facilitation of selective attention in preschoolers. *Child Development, 59,* 1497–1503.

Wooley, J. D., & Wellman, H. M. (1990). Young children's understanding of realities, nonrealities, and appearances. *Child Development, 61,* 946–961.

Yaniv, I., & Shatz, M. (1990). Heuristics of reasoning and analogy in children's visual perspective taking. *Child Development, 61,* 1491–1501.

Yarcheski, A., & Mahon, N. E. (1984). Chumship relationships, altruistic behavior, and loneliness in early adolescents. *Adolescence, 19,* 913–924.

Yee, M. D., & Brown, R. (1992). Self-evaluations and intergroup attitudes in children aged three to nine. *Child Development, 63,* 619–629.

Yonas, A. & Hartman, B. (1993). Perceiving the affordance of contact in four- and five-month-old infants. *Child Development, 64,* 298–308.

Young, G., & Gately, T. (1988, June). Neighborhood impoverishment and child maltreatment. *Journal of Family Issues, 9,* 240–254.

Young, K. T. (1990). American conceptions of infant development from 1955 to 1984: What the experts are telling parents. *Child Development, 61,* 17–28.

Young, T. J. (1993). Parricide rates and criminal street violence in the United States: Is there a correlation? *Adolescence, 28,* 171–172.

Youngblade, L. M., & Belsky, J. (1992). Parent-child antecedents of five-year-olds' close friendships: A longitudinal analysis. *Development Psychology, 28,* 700–713.

Younger, A. J., & Daniels, T. N. (1992). Children's reasons for nominating their peers as withdrawn: passive withdrawal versus active isolation. *Developmental Psychology, 28,* 955–960.

Younger, A. J., & Piccinin, A. M. (1989). Children's recall of aggressive and withdrawn behavior: Recognition memory and likability judgments. *Child Development, 60,* 580–590.

Younger, B. (1992). Developmental change in infant categorization: The perception of correlations among facial features. *Child Development, 63,* 1526–1535.

Youngs, G. A., Jr., Rathge, R., Mullis, R., & Mullis, A. (1990). Adolescent stress and self-esteem. *Adolescence, 25,* 333–342.

Zahn-Waxler, C., Radke-Yarrow, M., Wagner, E., & Chapman, M. (1992). Development of concern for others. *Developmental Psychology, 28,* 126–136.

Zahn-Waxler, C., Robinson, J. L., & Emde, R. N. (1992). The development of empathy in twins. *Developmental Psychology, 28,* 1038–1047.

Zarb, J. M. (1984, Summer). A comparison of remedial failure and successful secondary students across self-perception and past and present school performance variables. *Adolescence, 19,* 335–348.

Zarbatany, L., Hartmann, D. P., & Rankin, D. B. (1990). The psychological functions of preadolescent peer activities. *Child Development, 61,* 1067–1080.

Zarling, C. L., Hirsch, B. J., & Landry, S. (1988). Maternal social networks and mother-infant interactions in full-term and very low birthweight, preterm infants. *Child Development, 59,* 178–185.

Zebrowitz, L. A., & Montepare, J. M. (1992). Impressions of babyfaced individuals across the life span. *Developmental Psychology, 28,* 1143–1152.

Zelazo, N. A., Zelazo, P. R., Cohen, K. M., & Zelazo, P. D. (1993). Specificity of practice effects on elementary neuromotor patterns. *Developmental Psychology, 29,* 686–691.

Zelkowitz, P. (1987). Social support and aggressive behavior in young children. *Family Relations, 36,* 129–134.

Zelnik, M., & Kantner, J. P. (1980). Sexual activity, contraceptive use and pregnancy among metropolitan-area teenagers, 1971–1979. *Family Planning Perspectives, 12,* 230ff.

Zentall, S. A., & Meyer, M. J. (1987). Self-regulation of stimulation from ADD-H children during reading and vigilance task performance. *Journal of Abnormal Child Psychology, 15,* 519–536.

Zerbe, K. J. (1992). Why eating-disordered patients resist sex therapy: A response to Simpson and Ramberg. *Journal of Sex and Marital Therapy, 18,* 55–64.

Zern, D. S. (1991). Stability and change in adolescents' positive attitudes toward guidance in moral development. *Adolescence, 26,* 261–272.

Zeskind, P. S., & Iacino, R. (1984). Effects of maternal visitation to preterm infants in the neonatal intensive care unit. *Child Development, 55,* 1887–1893.

Zeskind, P. S., Klein, L., & Marshall, T. R. (1992). Adults' perceptions of experimental modifications of durations of pauses and expiratory sounds in infant crying. *Developmental Psychology, 28,* 1153–1162.

Zimmerman, D. (1983, December 22). Where are you Captain Kangaroo? *U.S.A. Today,* p. 1D.

Zimmerman, S. L. (1982, April). Alternative in human reproduction for involuntary childless couples. *Family Relations, 31,* 233–241.

Zimmerman, S. L. (1992). Family trends: What implications for family policy? *Family Relations, 41,* 423–429.

Zucavin, S. J. (1988). Fertility patterns: Their relationships to child physical abuse and child neglect. *Journal of Marriage and the Family, 50,* 983–993.

Zucavin, S. J. (1991). Unplanned childbearing and family size: Their relationship to child neglect and abuse. *Family Planning Perspectives, 23,* 155–161.

Zucker, R. A., & Gomberg, E. S. L. (1986). Etiology of alcoholism reconsidered: The case for a biopsychosocial process. *American Psychologist, 41,* 783–793.

Zuckerman, D. (1985, January). Too many sibs put our nation at risk? *Psychology Today, 19,* 5, 10.

Zusman, J. U. (1980). Situational determinants of parental behavior: Effects of competing activity. *Child Development, 51,* 792–800.

Photo Credits

The photos on the following pages are used courtesy of the photographer and © Lawrence Migdale: pp. 4, 5, 8, 9, 28, 75, 83, 97, 98, 110 (top left), 112, 114, 124, 133, 142, 144, 149, 154 (top left), 156, 162, 168, 188, 192 (top), 195, 206, 211, 234 (bottom right), 237, 241, 248, 254, 291, 292, 298, 310, 354, 361, 377, 393, 399, 418, 420, 424, 444, 452, 456, 499.

Other photos: p. 2, Walter Hodges/Woodfin Camp & Associates; p. 10, Frank White, Inc./Gamma-Liaison, Inc.; p. 13 (top left), Mimi Forsyth/Monkmeyer Press Photo Service; p. 13 (top right), Liebhardt Photography; p. 13 (bottom left), Victor Englebert/Photo Researchers, Inc.; p. 16, Michal Heron/Monkmeyer Press Photo Service; p. 21 (middle right), Susan McCartney/Photo Researchers, Inc.; p. 21 (bottom right), Bill Aron/Photo Researchers, Inc.; p. 26, Christine Cardone; p. 29, Archiv/Photo Researchers, Inc.; p. 31, UPI/The Bettmann Archive; p. 34, Sovfoto; p. 35, The Bettmann Archive; p. 36, courtesy of Chuck Pant/Stanford University; pp. 39 and 41, The Bettmann Archive; p. 42, Bill Anderson/Monkmeyer Press Photo Service; p. 45, Thomas McEvoy/LIFE © 1955 Time Inc.; p. 54, Barbara Campbell/Gamma-Liaison, Inc.; pp. 56 (bottom left and bottom right), 57 (top left and top right), and 61 (top left and bottom left), Lennart Nilsson/Bonnier Fakta; p. 67, Hank Morgan/Science Source/Photo Researchers, Inc.; p. 70 (top left), John Ficara/Woodfin Camp & Associates; p. 70 (bottom left), Grant Heilman Photography; p. 72, Barbara Campbell/Gamma-Liaison Inc.; p. 76, Suzanne Szasz/Photo Researchers, Inc.; p. 82, Stock Boston; p. 94, Pete Saloutos/The Stock Market; p. 100, Margaret Miller/Photo Researchers, Inc.; p. 102 (top left), J. T. Miller/The Stock Market; p. 102 (bottom right), Craig Hammell/The Stock Market; p. 110 (bottom right), Hyman/Stock Boston; p. 111, Susan Leavines/Photo Researchers, Inc.; p. 122, Paul Avis/Gamma-Liaison, Inc.; p. 125, Scala/EPA/Art Resource, N.Y.; p. 126 (top), Culver Pictures, Inc., p. 126 (bottom left and bottom right), The Bettmann Archive; p. 127, Culver Pictures, Inc.; p. 128, Suzanne Arms/The Image Works; p. 129, Culver Pictures, Inc.; p. 131 (top left), The Bettmann Archive; p. 131 (top right), Louise Bates Ames/Gesell Institute; p. 131 (bottom right), News Service/Stanford University; p. 135 (top left), The Bettmann Archive; p. 135 (bottom right), courtesy of Simon & Schuster, Inc.; p. 140, Lisa Law/The Image Works; p. 154 (bottom left), Bob Daemmrich/The Image Works; p. 157, Byron/ Monkmeyer Press Photo Service; p. 158, Dollarhide/Monkmeyer Press Photo Service; p. 164 (bottom left), Elizabeth Crews/The Image Works; p. 164 (bottom right), W. Hill, Jr./The Image Works; p. 167, Brady/ Monkmeyer Press Photo Service; p. 171, Alexis Duclos/Gamma-Liaison, Inc.; p. 172, Lori Adamski Peek/Tony Stone Images; p. 177, Crews/The Image Works; p. 179, Frank Pedrick/The Image Works; p. 184, The Stock Market; p. 189, David H. Wells/The Image Works; p. 190, Paul Liebhardt/Liebhardt Photography; p. 192 (bottom right), Christine Cardone; p. 197, Robert Burke/Gamma-Liaison, Inc.; p. 198, Joseph Schuyler/Stock Boston; p. 200, Billy E. Barnes/Stock Boston; p. 201, John Eastcott/Yva Momatiuk/The Image Works; p. 203, Robert Burke/Gamma-Liaison, Inc.; p. 204, MENKE/ Monkmeyer Press Photo Service; p. 209 (top left), Markwise/Stock Boston; p. 209 (bottom left), Bob Daemmrich/The Image Works; p. 220, Bob Daemmrich/The Image Works; p. 222, Shahn Kermani/Gamma-Liaison, Inc.; p. 223, Dr. Rovee-Collier/Izard; p. 228, Kopstein/Monkmeyer Press Photo Service; p. 229, Merrim/Monkmeyer Press Photo Service; p. 230, Jeffry W. Myers/Stock Boston; p. 232, Hugh Rogers/Monkmeyer Press Photo Service; p. 234 (bottom left), Bob Daemmrich/Stock Boston; p. 238, Paul Conklin/Monkmeyer Press Photo Service; p. 246, J. Carini/The Image Works; p. 252, Susan Johns/Photo Researchers, Inc.; p. 255, Crandall/The Image Works; p. 257, Shackman/Monkmeyer Press Photo Service; p. 258, Photofest; p. 260, Dorothy Littell Greco/The Image Works; p. 261, Bob Daemmrich/The Image Works; p. 262, Rameshwar Das/Monkmeyer Press Photo Service; p. 264, John Eastcott/Yva Momatiuk/The Image Works; p. 266, Shackman/Monkmeyer Press Photo Service; p. 268, Michal Heron/Monkmeyer Press Photo Service; p. 272, James P. Dwyer/Stock Boston; p. 275 (top left), Brownie Harris/The Stock Market; p. 275 (bottom), Dr. Caroll Izard; p. 277, Pedrick/The Image Works; p. 279 (top left), Siteman/Monkmeyer Press Photo Service; p. 279 (bottom left), Collins/Monkmeyer Press Photo Service; p. 281, M. Greenlar/The Image Works; p. 282 (top left), Shackman/Monkmeyer Press Photo Service; p. 282 (bottom right), Robery Yager/Tony Stone Images; p. 283, Catherine Ursillo/Photo Researchers, Inc.; p. 285, Markwise/Stock Boston; p. 287, M. Siluk/The Image Works; p. 296, Frank Siteman/Monkmeyer Press Photo Service; p. 301, Tony English; p. 302, Christopher Brown/Stock Boston; p. 306, Charles Gupton/Stock Boston; p. 309 (top left), Jim Whitmer/Stock Boston; p. 309 (bottom right), Alan Carey/The Image Works; p. 311, Spencer Grant/Monkmeyer Press Photo Service; p. 312, James Marshall/The Stock Market; p. 313, Dorothy Littell/Stock Boston; p. 317, E. Greenland/Photo Researchers, Inc.; p. 318, Goodwin/Monkmeyer Press Photo Service; p. 320, K. McGlynn/The Image Works; p. 323 (bottom left), Richard Shock/Gamma-Liaison, Inc.; p. 323 (bottom right), M. Siluk/The Image Works; p. 326, Frank Siteman/Stock Boston; p. 328, Michael Newman/PhotoEdit; p. 332, Jim Pickerell/Stock Boston; p. 333, Esbin-Anderson/The Image Works; p. 340, Grantpix/Monkmeyer Press Photo Service; p. 342, Bruce Plotkin/Gamma-Liaison, Inc.; p. 345, Bob Daemmrich/Stock Boston; p. 347, Bob Daemmrich/Stock Boston; p. 350, Douglas Burrows/Gamma-Liaison, Inc.; p. 351, Yale/Monkmeyer Press Photo Service; p. 357, Peter Freed/Peter Freed; p. 359, Gish/Monkmeyer Press Photo Service; p. 365, John Griffin/The Image Works; p. 369, Richard Shock/Stock Photography/Gamma-Liaison, Inc.; p. 374, Bob Schatz/Gamma-Liaison, Inc.; p. 380, Richard Hutchings/Photo Researchers, Inc.; p. 381, Bob Daemmrich/The Image Works; p. 382, Joe Polillio/Gamma-Liaison, Inc.; p. 383, Farrell Grehan/Photo Researchers, Inc.; p. 384, Richard Shock/Stock Photography/Gamma-Liaison, Inc.; p. 390, Bob Daemmrich/The Image Works; p. 407 (top left), Frank Siteman/Stock Boston, p. 407 (bottom right), James Schnepf/Gamma-Liaison, Inc.; p. 412, Paul Fusco/Magnum Photos; p. 416, Robert McElroy/Woodfin Camp & Associates; p. 421, Bob Daemmrich/The Image Works; p. 426, Jim Harrison/Stock Boston; p. 429, Kay Chernush/The Image Bank; p. 433, Jim Bourg/Monkmeyer Press Photo Service; p. 436, Rashid/Monkmeyer Press Photo Service; p. 438, Paul S. Howell/Gamma-Liaison, Inc.; p. 442, Richard Pasley/Stock Boston; p. 451, Barbara Alper/Stock Boston; p. 458, Paul Barton/The Stock Market; p. 460, Grant LeDuc/Monkmeyer Press Photo Service; p. 464, Smith/Monkmeyer Press Photo Service; p. 465, Kevin Cooper/AP-Wide World Photos; p. 467, Tom McKillerick/Impact Visuals Photo & Graphics, Inc.; p. 472, Laima Druskis/Photo Researchers, Inc.; p. 474, Dunn/Monkmeyer Press Photo Service; p. 477, PBJ Pictures/Gamma-Liaison, Inc.; p. 481, Paul Avis/Gamma-Liaison, Inc.; p. 484, Gabe Palmer/The Stock Market; p. 491, C. John Griffin/The Image Works; p. 495, Bob Daemmrich/Stock Boston; p. 498, Jeff Isaac Greenberg/Photo Researchers, Inc.

Name Index

G

L

N

Subject Index